Co

LON

Contents

Key to map pages 2-3
Key to central London map symbols 4
Key to street map symbols 5
Central London maps 6-89
Street maps 90-187
West End theatres & cinemas 188-189
West End shopping 190-191
London Congestion Charging Zone.......... 192-193
London Low Emission Zone..................... 194-195
Index 196-317
London Underground map 318-319
London websites 320

Published by Collins
An imprint of HarperCollins Publishers
77-85 Fulham Palace Road, Hammersmith,
London W6 8JB

www.harpercollins.co.uk

Mapping generated from Collins Bartholomew digital databases

London Underground Map by permission of Transport Trading Limited
Registered User No. 08/1077/LS

The grid on this map is the National Grid taken from the Ordnance Survey map with the permission of the Controller of Her Majesty's Stationery Office.

Printed in China

ISBN 978 0 00 730356 4 Imp 001
WM12423 / CDDA

e-mail: roadcheck@harpercollins.co.uk

Key to map pages

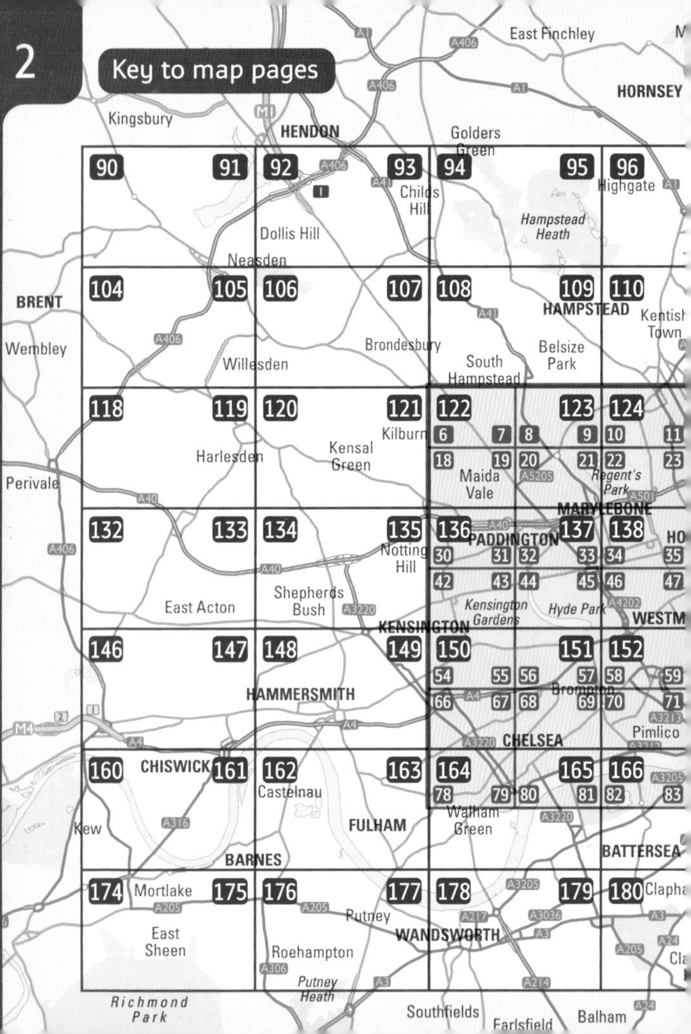

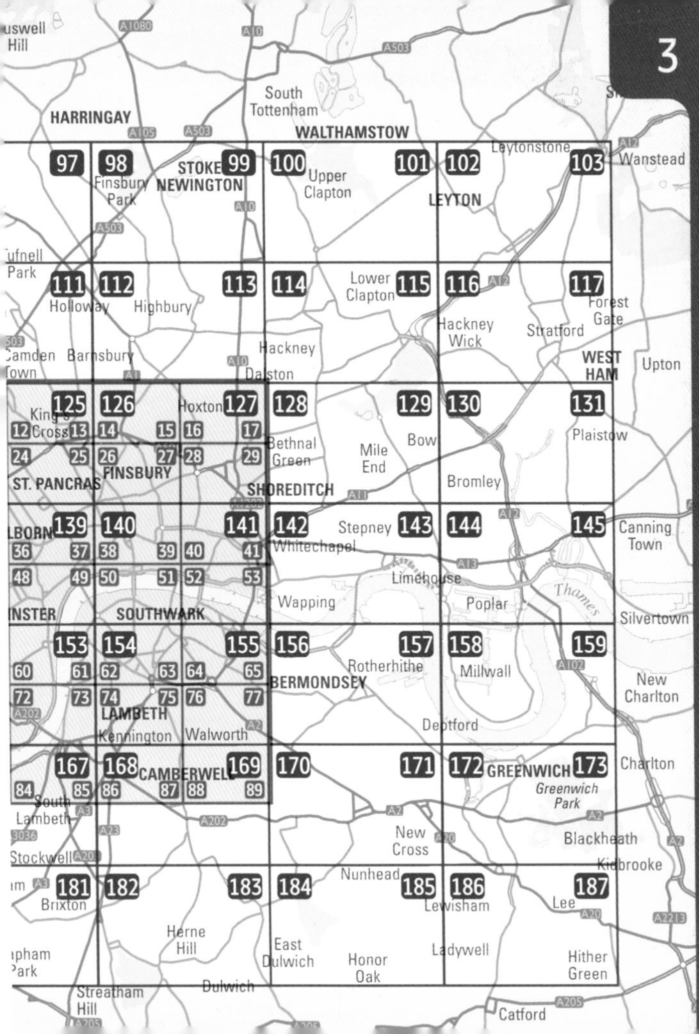

HARRINGAY
South Tottenham
WALTHAMSTOW
Leytonstone
Wanstead
97
98
STOKE NEWINGTON
99
100
101
102
103
Finsbury Park
Upper Clapton
LEYTON
Tufnell Park
111
112
113
114
115
116
117
Holloway
Highbury
Lower Clapton
Forest Gate
Hackney
Hackney Wick
Stratford
Camden Town
Barnsbury
Dalston
WEST HAM
Upton
125
126
127
128
129
130
131
King's Cross
Hoxton
Bethnal Green
Mile End
Bow
Plaistow
ST. PANCRAS
FINSBURY
SHOREDITCH
Bromley
139
140
141
142
143
144
145
Stepney
Whitechapel
Canning Town
Limehouse
Wapping
Poplar
Thames
SOUTHWARK
Silvertown
153
154
155
156
157
158
159
Rotherhithe
BERMONDSEY
Millwall
New Charlton
LAMBETH
Kennington
Walworth
Deptford
167
168
CAMBERWELL
169
170
171
172
GREENWICH
173
Charlton
Greenwich Park
South Lambeth
New Cross
Blackheath
Stockwell
Kidbrooke
Nunhead
181
182
183
184
185
186
187
Brixton
Lewisham
Lee
Herne Hill
East Dulwich
Honor Oak
Ladywell
Hither Green
Streatham Hill
Dulwich
Catford
A1080
A10
A503
A105
A12
A1
A11
A13
A102
A2
A202
A3
A23
A20
A205
A2213

Key to symbols on map pages 6-89

Dual A4	Primary route
Dual A40	'A' road
B504	'B' road
43	Address number ('A' & 'B' roads only)
	Other road/One way street
	Street market
	Pedestrian street
	Access restriction
	Long distance footpath
	Track/Footpath
CITY	Borough boundary
NW1	Postal district boundary
	Main national rail station
	Other national rail station
	London Overground station
	Docklands Light Railway station
	London Underground station
	Pedestrian ferry with landing stage
	Bus/Coach station
P	Car park
i	Information centre for visitors
i	Other information centre
	Theatre
	Major hotel
	Electric car recharging site
24	24 hour petrol station

	Youth hostel
m	Historic site
Pol TPol	Police station/ Transport Police station
PO PO	Post office/ Postal delivery office
Lib	Library
	Cinema
USA	Embassy
	Church
	Mosque
	Synagogue
Mormon	Other place of worship
	Community centre/Hall
Amb Sta	Ambulance station
	Monument/Statue
	Public toilet
	Leisure & tourism
	Shopping
	Market
	Administration & law
	Health & welfare
	Education
	Industry & commerce
	Major office
	Other landmark building/ Tower block
	Public open space
	Woodland
	Park/Garden/Sports ground
	Cemetery

SCALE

0 — 1/4 mile

0 — 0.25 — 0.5 kilometre

Key to symbols on map pages 90-187

M4	Motorway
Dual A4	Primary route
Dual A40	'A' road
B504	'B' road
	Other road/One way street
	Toll
	Street market
	Restricted access road
	Pedestrian street
	Cycle path
	Track/Footpath
THAMES PATH	Long distance footpath
LC	Level crossing
V P	Vehicle/Pedestrian ferry
	County/Borough boundary
	Postal district boundary
	Main national rail station
	Other national rail station
	London Overground station
	Docklands Light Railway station
	London Underground station
	Tramlink station
	Pedestrian ferry landing stage
	Bus/Coach station
	Electric car recharging site
24	24 hour petrol station
	Extent of London congestion charging zone

	Leisure & tourism
	Shopping
	Market
	Administration & law
	Health & welfare
	Education
	Industry & commerce
	Major office
	Other landmark building/ Tower block
	Cemetery
	Golf course
	Public open space/Allotments
	Park/Garden/Sports ground
	Wood/Forest
USA	Embassy
Pol	Police station
Fire Sta	Fire station
PO/Lib	Post Office/Library
	Youth hostel
i	Information centre for visitors
i	Other information centre
m	Historic site
P	Car park
	Toilets
H	Heliport
+	Church
	Mosque
	Synagogue

SCALE

0 — 1/4 — 1/2 mile

0 — 0.25 — 0.5 — 0.75 — 1 kilometre

A
B
C
1
2
3
4
KILBURN
NW6
KILBURN HIGH ROAD
KILBURN PARK
BELSIZE ROAD
HIGH
ROAD
VICTORIA
VICTORIA MS
CHARTERIS
ELMERE
ALGERNON RD
Charteris Comm Sports Cen
KILBURN SQ
Clinic
QUEX MS
BIRCH
COLAS MS
WEST END LANE
WEST KILBURN PL
PRIORY
108
HERMIT PL
KILB. VALE
KILBURN
ABB
LANGTRY RD
SPRINGFIELD WK
GOLDSMITH'S PL
MORTIMER PL
MORTIMER ESTATE
SPRINGFIELD LA
GREVILLE MS
GREVILLE
KILBURN PRIORY
Lib
Marriott
KILBURN GATE
KILBURN BRI
MALLARD CL
VILLAS
ROAD
COVENTRY CL
MANOR MS
CAMBRIDGE AV
TOLLGATE HO
TOLLGATE GDNS
MAPLE MS
VIVIAN CT
MAIDA
ALPHA PL
St. Mary's RC Prim Sch
Salvation Army
St. Augustine's Prim Sch
GOREFIELD PL
121
CANTERBURY TER
CANTERBURY RD
CHICHESTER ROAD
CAMBRIDGE GDNS
OXFORD RD
RUDOLPH RD
St. Augustine's HighSch
ANDOVER PLACE
DIBDIN HOUSE
RANDOLPH GARDENS
TORRIDON HO
WOODVILLE RD
DENMARK
NEVILLE RD
PRINCESS ROAD
PRIN. RD
St. Mary's RC Inf & Jun Sch (Annexe)
PEEL PREC
GRANVILLE RD
CAMBRIDGE RD
Granville Youth & Comm Cen
Iranian Sch
HEREFORD HO
GLOUCESTER HO
THURSO HO
St. Augustine
St. Cath
PARK
CARLTON VALE
B413
CARLTON
Kilburn Pk Jun Sch
MALVERN
CARLTON VALE
PENTLAND RD
NELSON CL
STAFFORD RD
Carlton Vale Inf Sch
Comm Cen
Immaculate Heart of Mary (RC)
BRONTE HO
FIELDING HO
DICKENS HO
AUSTEN HO
MACROOM RD
CITY OF WESTMINSTER COLL (Queen's Pk Cen)
HAMPTON
BRENT
WESTMINSTER
PADDINGTON RECREATION GROUND
ATHLETICS TRACK
CRICKET GROUND
Pav
Pav
Tennis Court
18
MORSHEAD
ROXLEY
Methodist
FORDINGLEY ROAD
0 250 yds
0 250 m

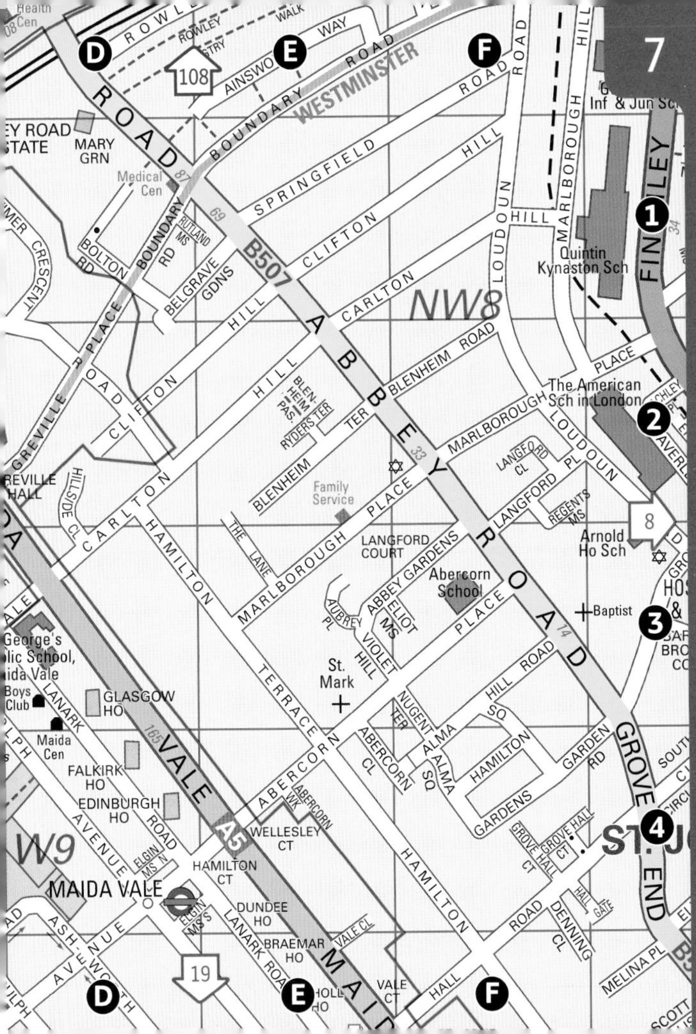
D
E
F
ROWLEY WALK
ROWLEY
AINSWORTH WAY
108
WESTMINSTER
BOUNDARY ROAD
ROAD
MARY GRN
Medical Cen
SPRINGFIELD ROAD
HILL
CLIFTON HILL
CARLTON HILL
NW8
LOUDOUN ROAD
HILL
MARLBOROUGH HILL
Quintin Kynaston Sch
FINCHLEY
1
34
BOLTON RD
RUTLAND MS
BOUNDARY RD
BELGRAVE GDNS
B507
ABBEY ROAD
GREVILLE PLACE
GREVILLE ROAD
CLIFTON
CARLTON
HILLSIDE CL
BLENHEIM ROAD
BLENHEIM PAS.
RYDERS TER
BLENHEIM TER
MARLBOROUGH PLACE
PLACE
The American Sch in London
2
LOUDOUN
LANGFORD CL
LANGFORD RD
LANGFORD PL
REGENTS MS
8
Arnold Ho Sch
Family Service
THE LANE
HAMILTON TERRACE
LANGFORD COURT
ABBEY GARDENS
Abercorn School
AUBREY PL
ELIOT MS
VIOLET HILL
PLACE
Baptist
3
St. Mark
George's
Maida Vale
Boys Club
GLASGOW HO
LANARK ROAD
Maida Cen
FALKIRK HO
EDINBURGH HO
VALE
A5
ABERCORN PLACE
ABERCORN WK
ABERCORN CL
NUGENT TER
ALMA SQ
HILL ROAD
HAMILTON GARDENS
GARDEN RD
GROVE END ROAD
4
GROVE HALL CT
HALL GATE
DENNING CL
W9
AVENUE
ELGIN MS N
MAIDA VALE
WELLESLEY CT
HAMILTON CT
ELGIN MS S
DUNDEE HO
BRAEMAR HO
VALE CL
ASHWORTH
19
VALE CT
HAMILTON
HALL ROAD
MELINA PL
MAIDA
ST. J

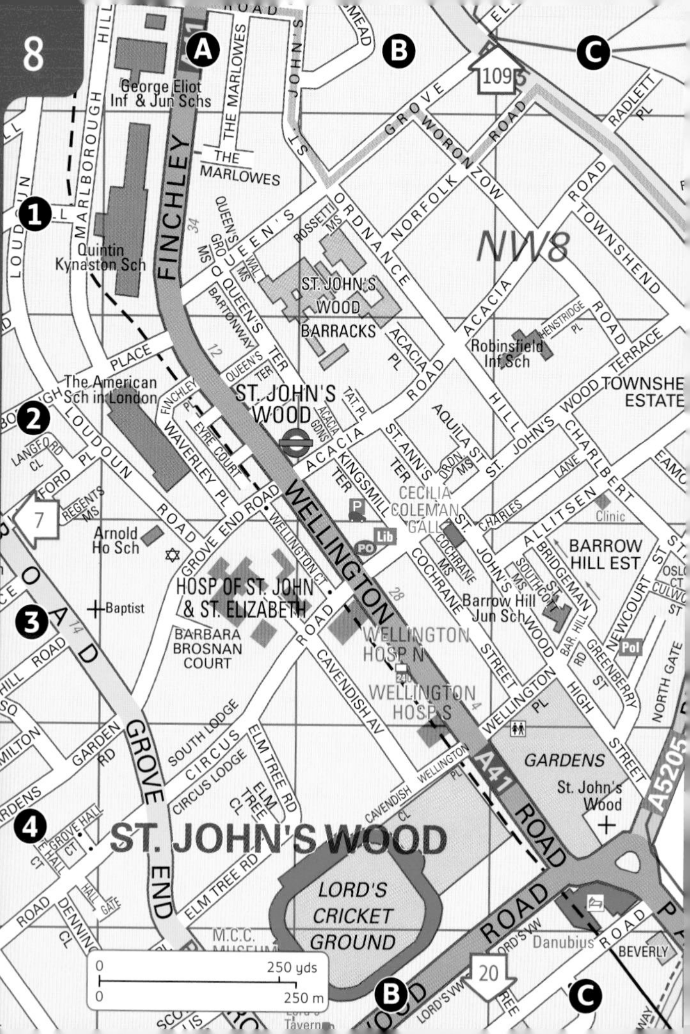
A
B
C
1
2
3
4
109
7
20
NW8
ST. JOHN'S WOOD
St. John's Wood
George Eliot Inf & Jun Schs
THE MARLOWES
Quintin Kynaston Sch
ST. JOHN'S WOOD BARRACKS
Robinsfield Inf Sch
The American Sch in London
TOWNSHEND ESTATE
BARROW HILL EST
Barrow Hill Jun Sch
Arnold Ho Sch
Baptist
HOSP OF ST. JOHN & ST. ELIZABETH
BARBARA BROSNAN COURT
CECILIA COLEMAN GALL
WELLINGTON HOSP N
WELLINGTON HOSP S
Clinic
Lib
PO
Pol
GARDENS
LORD'S CRICKET GROUND
M.C.C. MUSEUM
Danubius
BEVERLY
FINCHLEY
WELLINGTON
ROAD
A41
A5205
GROVE END ROAD
ST. JOHN'S WOOD ROAD
ST. JOHN'S WOOD TERRACE
ST. JOHN'S WOOD HIGH STREET
ST. JOHN'S WOOD PARK
GROVE END
WORONZOW ROAD
NORFOLK ROAD
ORDNANCE HILL
ACACIA ROAD
ACACIA PL
ACACIA GDNS
TOWNSHEND ROAD
RADLETT PL
HENSTRIDGE PL
QUEEN'S GROVE
QUEEN'S GRO MS
QUEEN'S TER
ROSSETTI MS
WAL MS
BARTONWAY
MARLBOROUGH HILL
MARLBOROUGH PL
LOUDOUN ROAD
PLACE
FINCHLEY PL
EYRE COURT
WAVERLEY PL
LANGFORD CL
LANGFORD PL
REGENTS MS
WELLINGTON CT
KINGSMILL TER
ST. ANN'S TER
AQUILA ST
ORDNANCE MS
TAT. PL
CHARLBERT ST
CHARLES LANE
ALLITSEN ROAD
BRIDGEMAN ST
SOUTHCOTT MS
COCHRANE MS
COCHRANE ST
BAR. HILL RD
GREENBERRY ST
NEWCOURT ST
NORTH GATE
OSLO CT
CULWORTH ST
WELLINGTON PL
WELLINGTON RD
CAVENDISH AV
CAVENDISH CL
SOUTH LODGE
CIRCUS LODGE
CIRCUS RD
ELM TREE RD
ELM TREE CL
GARDEN RD
HILL ROAD
GROVE HALL CT
HALL GATE
DENNING CL
LORD'S VW
Lord's Tavern
0 250 yds
0 250 m

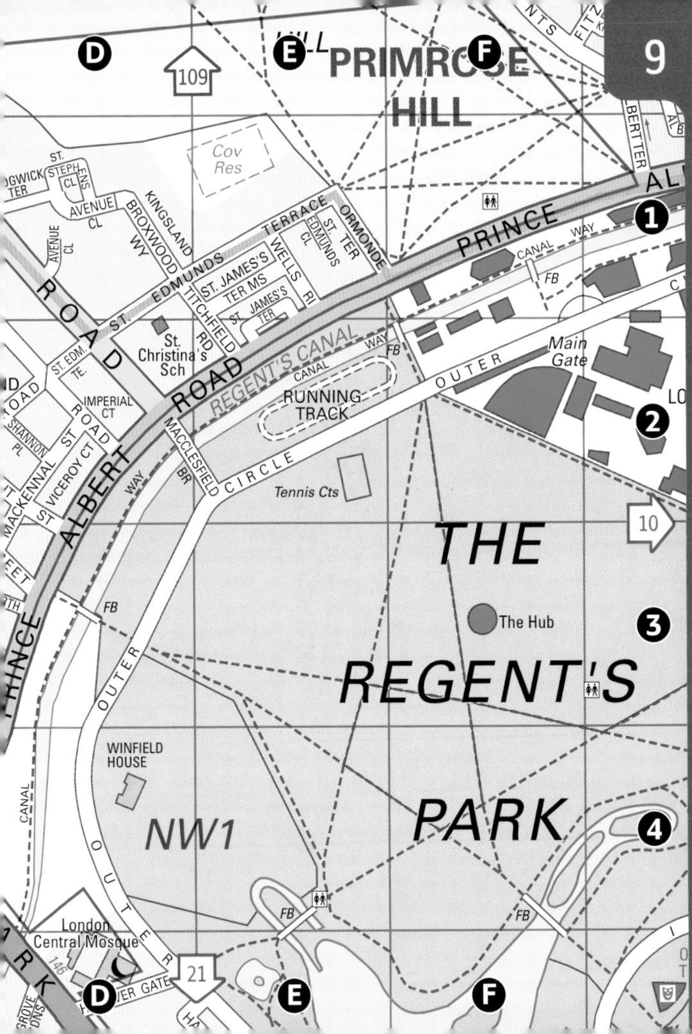
D
E
F
109
PRIMROSE
HILL
Cov
Res
ST. STEPHENS CL
AVENUE CL
AVENUE CL
BROXWOOD WY
KINGSLAND
ST. EDMUNDS TERRACE
ORMONDE TER
ST. EDMUNDS CL
WELLS RI
ST. JAMES'S TER MS
ST. JAMES'S TER
TITCHFIELD RD
St. Christina's Sch
PRINCE ALBERT ROAD
CANAL WAY
FB
REGENT'S CANAL
RUNNING TRACK
Main Gate
OUTER CIRCLE
ST. EDM. TE.
IMPERIAL CT
SHANNON PL
VICEROY CT
MACKENNAL ST
MACCLESFIELD BR
Tennis Cts
10
THE REGENT'S PARK
The Hub
1
2
3
4
WINFIELD HOUSE
NW1
CANAL
London Central Mosque
21
E
F

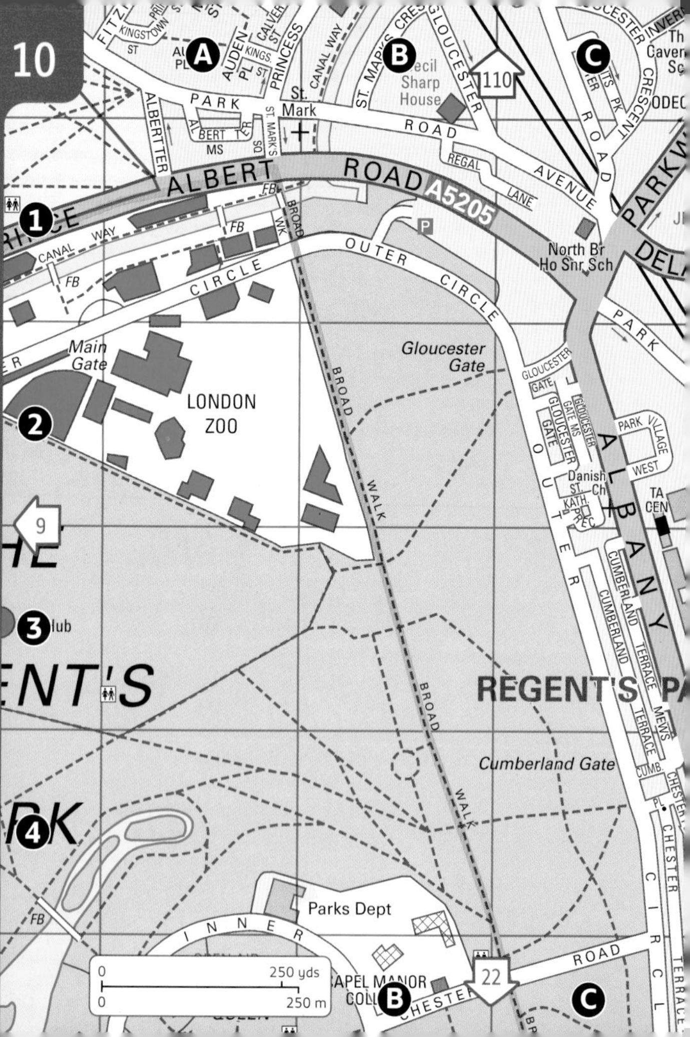
A
B
C
PARK
ROAD
ALBERT ROAD
A5205
ST. MARK'S CRES
GLOUCESTER
AVENUE
REGAL LANE
PARKWAY
DELANCEY
Cecil Sharp House
110
St. Mark
PRINCESS
CANAL WAY
AUDEN PL
KINGS. ST
KINGSTOWN ST
ALBERT TER
ALBERT TER MS
ST. MARK'S SQ.
FB
BROAD WK.
OUTER CIRCLE
North Br Ho Snr Sch
The Cavendish Sq
ODEON
GLOUCESTER CRESCENT
INVERNESS
PRINCE
CANAL WAY
Main Gate
LONDON ZOO
BROAD WALK
Gloucester Gate
GLOUCESTER GATE
GLOUCESTER GATE MS
GLOUCESTER GATE
OUTER CIRCLE
ALBANY
PARK VILLAGE WEST
Danish Ch
ST. KATH. PREC.
TA CEN
CUMBERLAND TERRACE
CUMBERLAND TERRACE MEWS
1
2
3
Hub
4
9
REGENT'S PARK
Cumberland Gate
CUMB. PL.
CHESTER TERRACE
CHESTER CIRCLE
Parks Dept
INNER CIRCLE
CAPEL MANOR COLL
CHESTER ROAD
22
0
250 yds
0
250 m

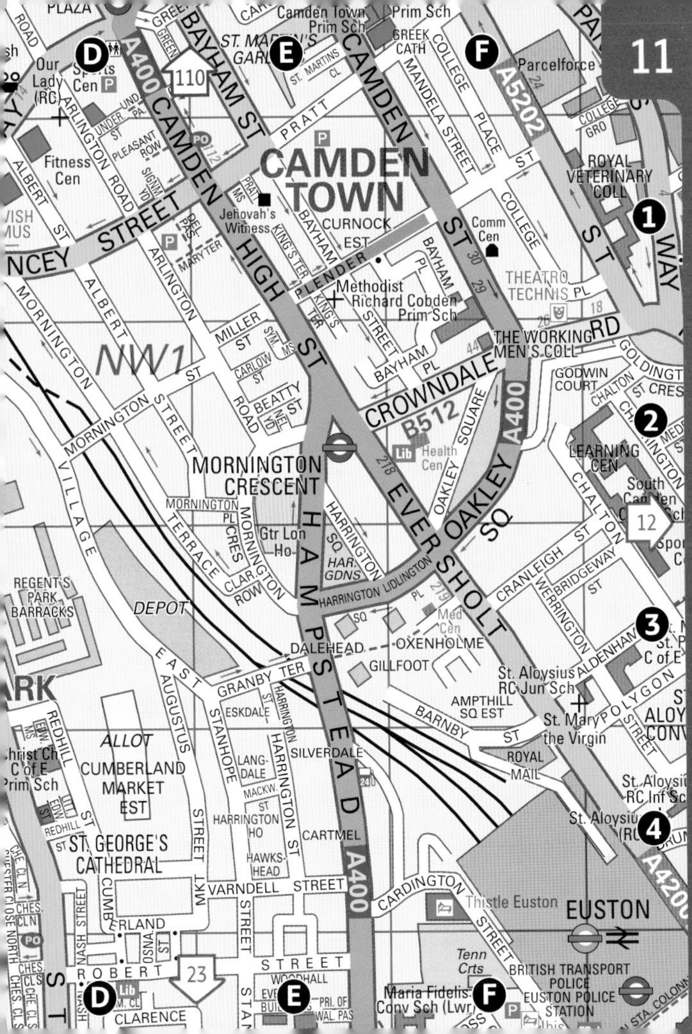

CAMDEN TOWN
NW1
A400
CAMDEN HIGH ST
HAMPSTEAD RD
EVERSHOLT ST
CAMDEN ST
BAYHAM ST
PRATT ST
PLENDER ST
CROWNDALE RD
B512
OAKLEY SQ
A5202
ROYAL COLLEGE ST
COLLEGE PL
MANDELA STREET
PANCRAS WAY
ROYAL VETERINARY COLL
Parcelforce
COLLEGE GRO
Camden Town Prim Sch
GREEK CATH
ST. MARTIN'S GARDENS
ST. MARTINS CL
Our Lady (RC)
Sports Cen
Fitness Cen
ARLINGTON ROAD
ALBERT ST
PLEASANT ROW
UNDER. ST
DELANCEY STREET
MARY TER
Jehovah's Witness
CURNOCK EST
KING'S TER
Methodist
Richard Cobden Prim Sch
BAYHAM PL
THEATRO TECHNIS
Comm Cen
THE WORKING MEN'S COLL
GODWIN COURT
CHALTON ST
GOLDINGTON CRES
LEARNING CEN
South Camden
MILLER ST
CARLOW ST
BEATTY ST
MORNINGTON ST
MORNINGTON CRESCENT
MORNINGTON PL
MORNINGTON TERRACE
MORNINGTON CRES
Gtr Lon Ho
HARRINGTON SQ
HAR. GDNS
LIDLINGTON PL
Lib
Health Cen
Med Cen
CRANLEIGH ST
WERRINGTON ST
BRIDGEWAY ST
ALDENHAM ST
POLYGON RD
St. Aloysius RC Jun Sch
St. Mary the Virgin
St. Aloysius RC Inf Sch
St. Aloysius (RC)
REGENT'S PARK BARRACKS
DEPOT
PARK
GRANBY TER
DALEHEAD
OXENHOLME
GILLFOOT
AMPTHILL SQ EST
BARNBY ST
ROYAL MAIL
EAST ST
AUGUSTUS ST
STANHOPE ST
ESKDALE
LANGDALE
SILVERDALE
HARRINGTON ST
MACKW. ST
HARRINGTON HO
HAWKSHEAD
CARTMEL
ALLOT
CUMBERLAND MARKET EST
Christ Ch C of E Prim Sch
REDHILL ST
ST. GEORGE'S CATHEDRAL
CUMBERLAND MKT
VARNDELL STREET
CARDINGTON STREET
Thistle Euston
EUSTON
Tenn Crts
BRITISH TRANSPORT POLICE EUSTON POLICE STATION
Maria Fidelis Conv Sch (Lwr)
ROBERT ST
CLARENCE
WOODHALL
NASH STREET
OSNABURGH ST
CHESTER CLOSE NORTH
A4200
110
12
23

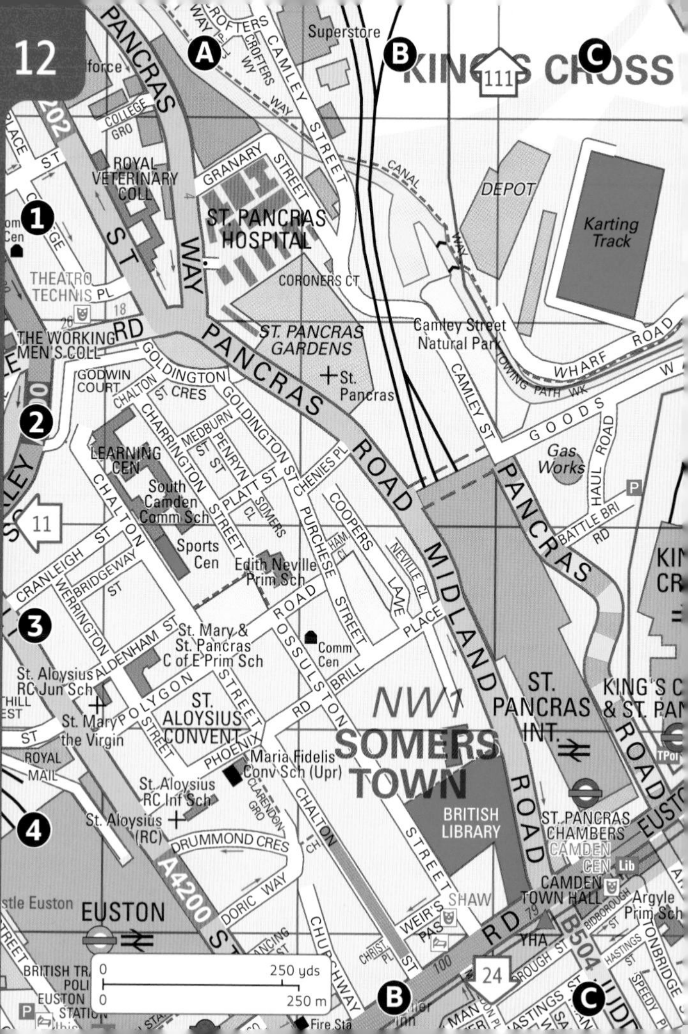
A
B
C
KINGS CROSS
111
Superstore
CROFTERS WAY
CAMLEY STREET
PANCRAS WAY
COLLEGE GRO
ROYAL VETERINARY COLL
GRANARY STREET
CANAL
DEPOT
Karting Track
ST. PANCRAS HOSPITAL
CORONERS CT
THEATRO TECHNIS PL
THE WORKING MEN'S COLL
ST. PANCRAS GARDENS
St. Pancras
Camley Street Natural Park
WHARF ROAD
TOWING PATH WK
GODWIN COURT
GOLDINGTON ST
CHALTON ST
MEDBURN ST
PENRYN ST
LEARNING CEN
CHARRINGTON STREET
PLATT ST
SOMERS CL
CHENIES PL
PANCRAS ROAD
GOODS WAY
Gas Works
HAUL ROAD
BATTLE BRI RD
South Camden Comm Sch
Sports Cen
11
COOPERS LANE
HAMPDEN CL
NEVILLE CL
PURCHESE STREET
Edith Neville Prim Sch
MIDLAND ROAD
CRANLEIGH ST
BRIDGEWAY ST
WERRINGTON ST
ALDENHAM ST
St. Mary & St. Pancras C of E Prim Sch
OSSULSTON STREET
Comm Cen
BRILL PLACE
NW1
SOMERS TOWN
ST. PANCRAS INT.
KING'S CROSS & ST. PANCRAS
St. Aloysius RC Jun Sch
POLYGON RD
ST. ALOYSIUS CONVENT
St. Mary the Virgin
ROYAL MAIL
PHOENIX RD
Maria Fidelis Conv Sch (Upr)
CLARENDON GRO
St. Aloysius RC Inf Sch
St. Aloysius (RC)
DRUMMOND CRES
CHALTON ST
BRITISH LIBRARY
ST. PANCRAS CHAMBERS
CAMDEN CEN
Lib
CAMDEN TOWN HALL
Argyle Prim Sch
EUSTON RD
A4200
DORIC WAY
EUSTON
CHURCHWAY
WEIR'S PAS
SHAW
CHRIST PL
YHA
B504
BIDBOROUGH ST
HASTINGS ST
TONBRIDGE ST
SPEEDY PL
24
BRITISH TRANSPORT POLICE
EUSTON STATION
Fire Sta
0 250 yds
0 250 m

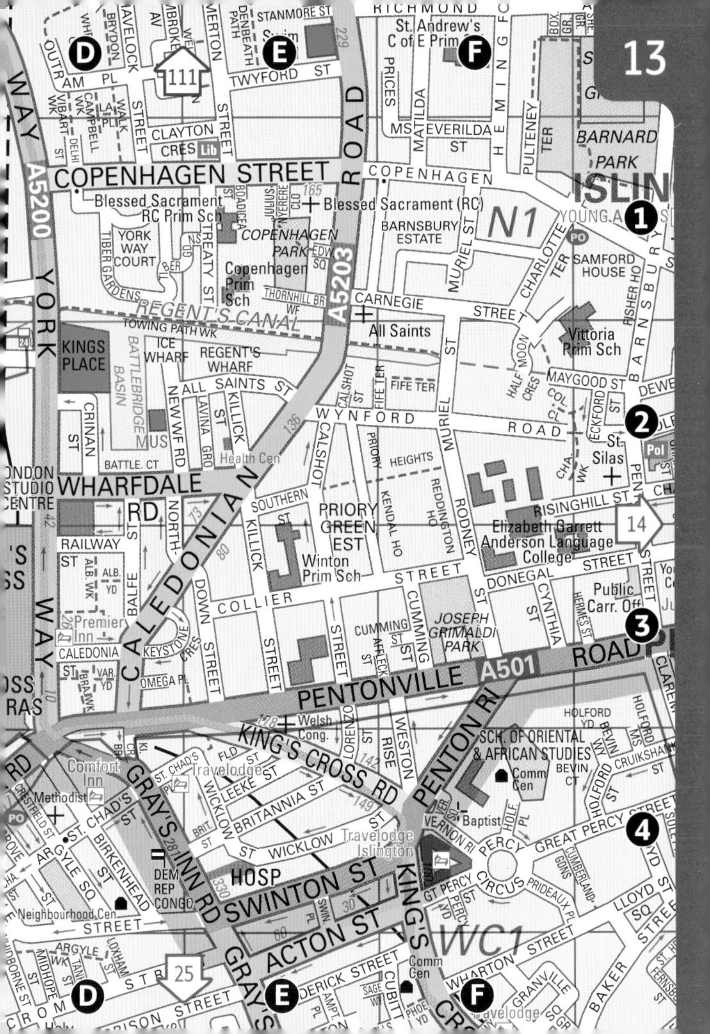
D
E
F
111
25
14
COPENHAGEN STREET
COPENHAGEN
YORK WAY
A5200
CALEDONIAN ROAD
A5203
PENTONVILLE ROAD
A501
KING'S CROSS RD
GRAY'S INN RD
SWINTON ST
ACTON ST
WHARFDALE RD
REGENT'S CANAL
N1
WC1
ISLIN
BARNARD PARK
TWYFORD ST
CLAYTON CRES
Lib
Blessed Sacrament RC Prim Sch
Blessed Sacrament (RC)
COPENHAGEN PARK
Copenhagen Prim Sch
BARNSBURY ESTATE
CARNEGIE STREET
All Saints
KINGS PLACE
ICE WHARF
REGENT'S WHARF
BATTLEBRIDGE BASIN
ALL SAINTS ST
WYNFORD ROAD
PRIORY GREEN EST
Winton Prim Sch
COLLIER STREET
JOSEPH GRIMALDI PARK
Elizabeth Garrett Anderson Language College
DONEGAL STREET
RISINGHILL ST
Vittoria Prim Sch
SAMFORD HOUSE
MAYGOOD ST
St. Silas
Public Carr. Off
SCH. OF ORIENTAL & AFRICAN STUDIES
Comm Cen
Baptist
PERCY CIRCUS
GREAT PERCY STREET
LLOYD SQ
WHARTON STREET
HOSP
Travelodge
Travelodge Islington
Comfort Inn
Methodist
Neighbourhood Cen
DEM REP CONGO
Premier Inn
CALEDONIA ST
KEYSTONE CRES
RAILWAY ST
LONDON STUDIO CENTRE
Health Cen
MUS
St. Andrew's C of E Prim
Welsh Cong.
1
2
3
4

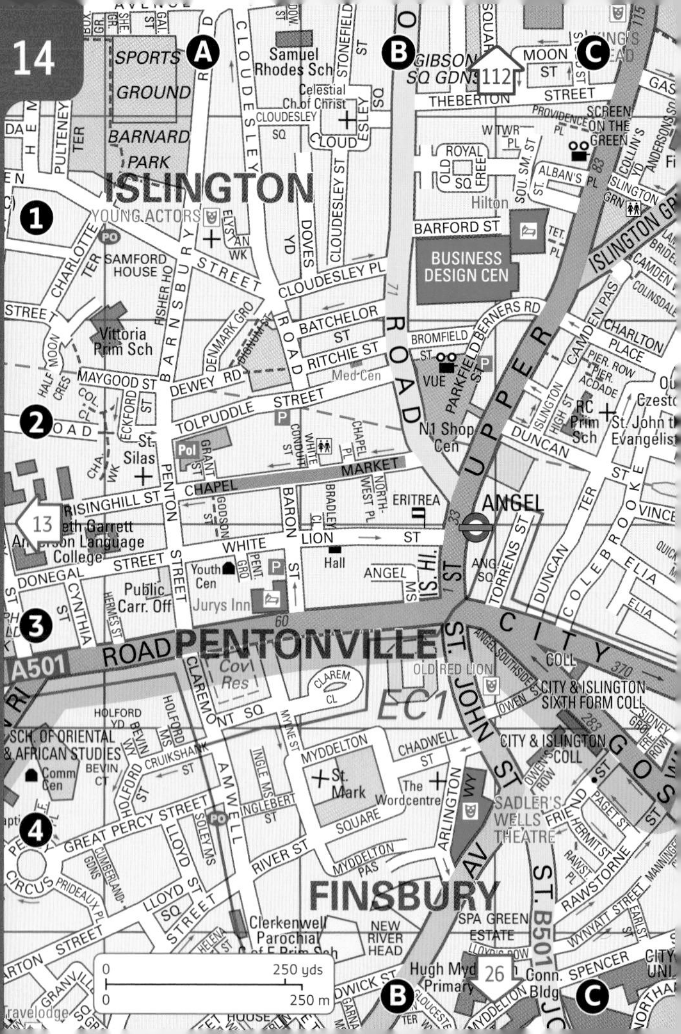
A
B
C
1
2
3
4
SPORTS GROUND
BARNARD PARK
ISLINGTON
YOUNG ACTORS
Samuel Rhodes Sch
Celestial Ch. of Christ
CLOUDESLEY SQ
CLOUDESLEY ST
STONEFIELD ST
GIBSON SQ GDNS
112
MOON ST
KING'S HEAD
THEBERTON STREET
PROVIDENCE PL
SCREEN ON THE GREEN
ROYAL FREE SQ
OLD ROYAL FREE SQ
ST. ALBAN'S PL
ISLINGTON GRN
ISLINGTON GREEN
COLLIN'S YD
ANDERSONS
Hilton
BARFORD ST
BUSINESS DESIGN CEN
TET. PL
CAMDEN PAS
CHARLTON PLACE
PIER. ROW
PIER. ACDADE
COLINSDALE
CAMDEN
CHARLOTTE TER
SAMFORD HOUSE
BARNSBURY STREET
FISHER HO
CLOUDESLEY PL
BATCHELOR ST
RITCHIE ST
Med-Cen
BROMFIELD ST
BERNERS RD
PARKFIELD ST
VUE
N1 Shop Cen
UPPER ST
ISLINGTON HIGH ST
RC Prim Sch
St. John the Evangelist
DUNCAN ST
DUNCAN TER
STREET
Vittoria Prim Sch
HALF MOON CRES
DENMARK GRO
DIGNUM ST
DEWEY RD
MAYGOOD ST
COL. CL
ECKFORD ST
TOLPUDDLE STREET
CONDUIT ST
WHITE CONDUIT ST
CHAPEL PL
ROAD
St. Silas
Pol
GRANT ST
CHAPEL MARKET
NORTH-WEST PL
BRADLEY CL
ERITREA
ANGEL
RISINGHILL ST
PENTON STREET
BARON ST
GODSON ST
WHITE LION ST
13
Elizabeth Garrett Anderson Language College
DONEGAL STREET
CYNTHIA ST
Youth Cen
PENT. GRO
Hall
ANGEL MS
ANG. SQ
TORRENS ST
COLEBROOKE
VINCENT
ELIA ST
Public Carr. Off
HERMES ST
Jurys Inn
ST. JOHN ST
CITY ROAD
A501
ROAD
PENTONVILLE
CLAREMONT SQ
Cov. Res
CLAREM. CL
OLD RED LION
ANGEL SOUTHSIDE
COLL
CITY & ISLINGTON SIXTH FORM COLL
OWEN ST
SIDNEY GRO
EC1
HOLFORD YD
HOLFORD MS
BEVIN WY
SCH. OF ORIENTAL & AFRICAN STUDIES
CRUIKSHANK ST
BEVIN CT
Comm Cen
HOLFORD ST
AMWELL ST
MYDDELTON SQUARE
St. Mark
CHADWELL ST
The Wordcentre
ARLINGTON WY
CITY & ISLINGTON COLL
OWEN'S ROW
GOSWELL
PAGET ST
SADLER'S WELLS THEATRE
FRIEND ST
HERMIT ST
RAWST. PL
RAWSTORNE ST
INGLE MS
INGLEBERT ST
GREAT PERCY STREET
SOLEY MS
LLOYD ST
CUMBERLAND GDNS
PERCY CIRCUS
PRIDEAUX PL
LLOYD SQ
RIVER ST
MYDDELTON PAS
FINSBURY
MANNINGFORD
WYNYATT STREET
EARLSTOKE ST
SPA GREEN ESTATE
LLOYD'S ROW
ST. JOHN ST. B501
HELENA ST
Clerkenwell Parochial C of E Prim Sch
NEW RIVER HEAD
Hugh Myddelton Primary
26
Conn. Bldg
SPENCER ST
CITY UNI.
NORTHAMPTON
0 250 yds
0 250 m
Travelodge
GRANVILLE SQ
MYDDELTON
GLOUCESTER

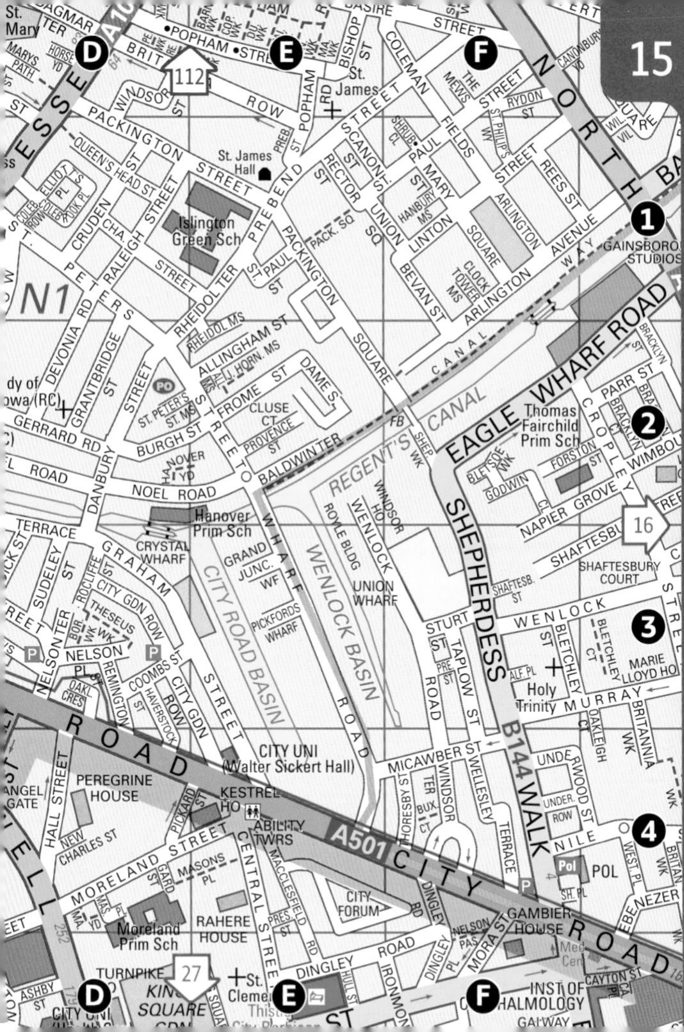
112
POPHAM STREET
BRIT
WINDSOR ST
ROW
PACKINGTON STREET
QUEEN'S HEAD ST
ESSEX
St. James
St. James Hall
BISHOP ST
POPHAM RD
COLEMAN STREET
THE MEWS
FIELDS
STREET
RYDON ST
CANONBURY YD
NORTH
WIL. VIL
CANON ST
RECTOR ST
UNION SQ
PAUL ST
MARY ST
SHRUB CL
ST. PHILIP'S WY
REES ST
ARLINGTON SQUARE
ARLINGTON AVENUE
WAY
GAINSBOROUGH STUDIOS
HANBURY MS
LINTON
BEVAN ST
CLOCK TOWER MS
PREBEND
PACK. SQ
Islington Green Sch
ELLIOTT'S PL
CRUDEN
CHA.
RALEIGH STREET
ST. PETERS ST
N1
DEVONIA RD
GRANTBRIDGE ST
RHEIDOL TER
RHEIDOL MS
ALLINGHAM ST
J. HORN. MS
PACKINGTON SQUARE
CANAL
EAGLE WHARF ROAD
BRACKLYN ST
PARR ST
CROPLEY
Thomas Fairchild Prim Sch
FORSTON ST
STREET
PO
ST. PETER'S ST. MS
FROME ST
DAMES
CLUSE CT
PROVENCE ST
BURGH ST
GERRARD RD
NOEL ROAD
DANBURY
BALDWINTER
FB
REGENT'S CANAL
SHEP. WK
WINDSOR HO
WENLOCK HO
ROYLE BLDG
BLETSOE WK
GODWIN CL
NAPIER GROVE
WIMBOU
16
SHAFTESBURY
SHAFTESBURY COURT
SHEPHERDESS
HANOVER YD
Hanover Prim Sch
TERRACE
CRYSTAL WHARF
GRAHAM
CITY ROAD BASIN
GRAND JUNC. WF
WHARF
WENLOCK BASIN
UNION WHARF
PICKFORDS WHARF
SUDELEY ST
ROCLIFFE ST
CITY GDN ROW
THESEUS WK
NELSON PL
NELSON TER
OAKL CRES
REMINGTON ST
COOMBS ST
HAVERSTOCK ST
CITY GDN ROW
STREET
ROAD
STURT ST
TAPLOW ST
PRE. ST
SHAFTESB. ST
WENLOCK STREET
BLETCHLEY ST
BLETCHLEY CT
ALF. PL
Holy Trinity
MURRAY
MARIE LLOYD HO
OAKLEIGH CT
BRITANNIA WK
ROAD
B144
WALK
MICAWBER ST
WELLESLEY TERRACE
UNDERWOOD ST
UNDER. ROW
NILE
CITY UNI (Walter Sickert Hall)
KESTREL HO
ABILITY TWRS
PEREGRINE HOUSE
ANGEL GATE
HALL STREET
NEW CHARLES ST
PICKARD ST
MORELAND STREET
MASONS PL
CENTRAL STREET
MACCLESFIELD RD
A501 CITY ROAD
THORESBY ST
BUX. CT
WINDSOR TER
DINGLEY RD
CITY FORUM
Pol
POL
SH. PL
WEST. PL
EBENEZER
GAMBIER HOUSE
Moreland Prim Sch
RAHERE HOUSE
PRES. ST
NELSON PAS
MORA ST
DINGLEY PL
DINGLEY ROAD
IRONMONGER
HULL ST
TURNPIKE HO
27
KING SQUARE
ASHBY ST
CITY UNI
St. Clement
INST OF OPHTHALMOLOGY
CAYTON ST
GALWAY
D
E
F
1
2
3
4

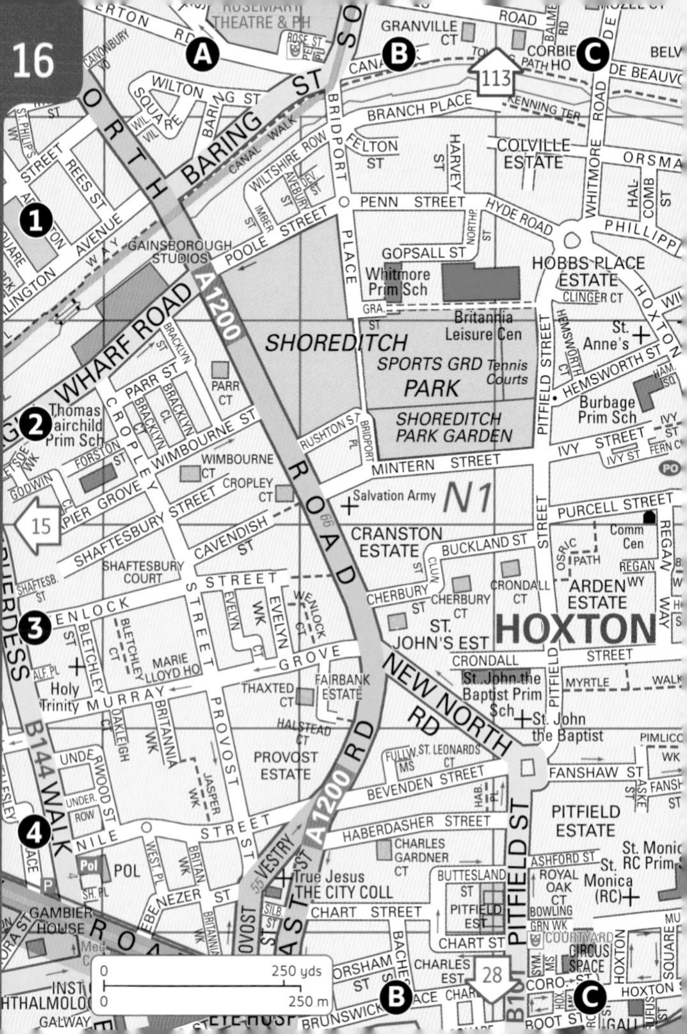
A
B
C
1
2
3
4
113
15
28
ROSEMARY THEATRE & PH
ROSE ST
GRANVILLE CT
ROAD
CANONBURY YD
WILTON SQUARE
BARING ST
BARING ST
CANAL WALK
BRIDPORT PLACE
BRANCH PLACE
KENNING TER
CORBIERE HO
DE BEAUVOIR
BELV
WHITMORE ROAD
COLVILLE ESTATE
ORSMAN
FELTON ST
HARVEY ST
WILTSHIRE ROW
AVEBURY ST
DEV. ST
IMBER ST
PENN STREET
HYDE ROAD
HALCOMB ST
PHILLIPP
NORTHP. ST
ST. PHILIP'S WY
STREET
REES ST
AVENUE
ISLINGTON
GAINSBOROUGH STUDIOS
POOLE STREET
WHARF ROAD
A1200
GOPSALL ST
Whitmore Prim Sch
HOBBS PLACE ESTATE
CLINGER CT
HOXTON
Britannia Leisure Cen
SHOREDITCH
SPORTS GRD
PARK
Tennis Courts
SHOREDITCH PARK GARDEN
St. Anne's
HEMSWORTH ST
HEMSWORTH CT
PITFIELD STREET
Burbage Prim Sch
BRACKLYN ST
PARR ST
PARR CT
BRACKLYN CT
BRACKLYN CL
Thomas Fairchild Prim Sch
CROPLEY
WIMBOURNE ST
RUSHTON ST
BRIDPORT PL
FORSTON ST
WIMBOURNE CT
GODWIN
NAPIER GROVE
CROPLEY CT
MINTERN STREET
IVY STREET
IVY ST
FERN CL
PO
SHAFTESBURY STREET
ROAD
Salvation Army
N1
PURCELL STREET
CAVENDISH ST
CRANSTON ESTATE
BUCKLAND ST
Comm Cen
REGAN WAY
SHAFTESBURY COURT
CLUN ST
OSRIC PATH
REGAN WY
SHAFTESB. ST
STREET
CHERBURY ST
CHERBURY CT
CRONDALL CT
ARDEN ESTATE
WENLOCK
EVELYN WK
EVELYN ST
WENLOCK CT
ST. JOHN'S EST
HOXTON
BLETCHLEY ST
BLETCHLEY CT
MARIE LLOYD HO
GROVE
CRONDALL STREET
NEW NORTH RD
ALF. PL
Holy Trinity
MURRAY
BRITANNIA WK
PROVOST
THAXTED CT
FAIRBANK ESTATE
St. John the Baptist Prim Sch
MYRTLE WALK
St. John the Baptist
HALSTEAD CT
PIMLICO WK
B144
UNDERWOOD ST
OAKLEIGH CT
JASPER WK
PROVOST ESTATE
RD
FULLW. MS
ST. LEONARDS CT
FANSHAW ST
WALK
UNDER. ROW
BEVENDEN STREET
HAB. PL
ASKE ST
PITFIELD ESTATE
NILE STREET
HABERDASHER STREET
PITFIELD ST
VESTRY ST
A1200
CHARLES GARDNER CT
ASHFORD ST
St. Monica RC Prim
Pol
POL
WEST PL
BRITAN. WK
True Jesus
THE CITY COLL
BUTTESLAND ST
ROYAL OAK CT
St. Monica (RC)
SH. PL
EBENEZER ST
SILB. ST
CHART STREET
PITFIELD EST
BOWLING GRN WK
GAMBIER HOUSE
ROAD
BRITANNIA
PROVOST ST
EAST RD
BACHES ST
CHART ST
COURTYARD
CIRCUS SPACE
HOXTON SQUARE
CHARLES SQ. EST
SYM. MS
CORONET ST
Med C
INST
OPHTHALMOLOGY
0
250 yds
250 m
ORSHAM ST
BRUNSWICK PLACE
B101
HOXTON
HOX. ST
BOOT ST
GALWAY
EYE HOSP

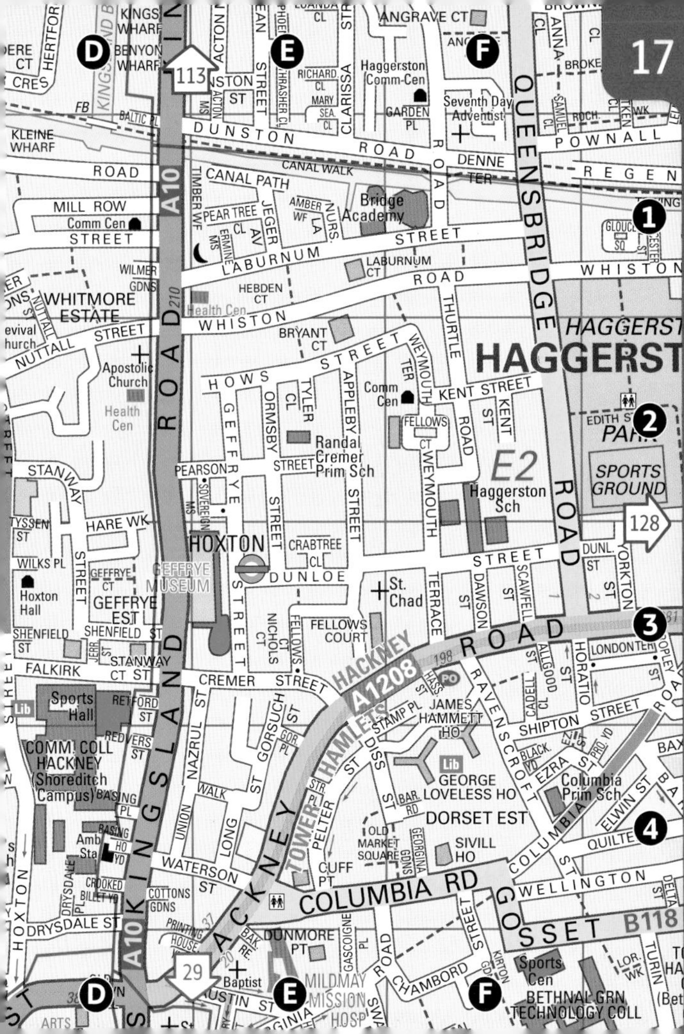
KINGS WHARF
BENYON WHARF
HERTFORD
CRES
113
KLEINE WHARF
BALTIC PL
DUNSTON ROAD
ANGRAVE CT
Haggerston Comm-Cen
Seventh Day Adventist
GARDEN PL
RICHARD CL
MARY
SEA CL
CLARISSA
QUEENSBRIDGE ROAD
POWNALL
REGENT
DENNE TER
ROAD
MILL ROW
Comm Cen
STREET
A10
CANAL WALK
CANAL PATH
TIMBER WF
PEAR TREE CL
JEGER AV
ERMINE MS
AMBER WF
NURS. LA
Bridge Academy
LABURNUM STREET
LABURNUM CT
WHISTON ROAD
WILMER GDNS
WHITMORE ESTATE
NUTTALL STREET
HEBDEN CT
Health Cen
BRYANT CT
THURTLE
HAGGERSTON
HAGGERST
Apostolic Church
Health Cen
HOWS STREET
WEYMOUTH TER
Comm Cen
KENT STREET
KENT ST
EDITH ST
PARK
SPORTS GROUND
KINGSLAND ROAD
GEFFRYE STREET
ORMSBY STREET
TYLER CL
APPLEBY STREET
FELLOWS CT
WEYMOUTH ROAD
Randal Cremer Prim Sch
E2
Haggerston Sch
STANWAY
PEARSON STREET
SOVEREIGN MS
128
TYSSEN ST
HARE WK
HOXTON
CRABTREE CL
DUNLOE STREET
DUNL. ST
YORKTON ST
WILKS PL
Hoxton Hall
GEFFRYE CT
GEFFRYE EST
GEFFRYE MUSEUM
NICHOLS CT
FELLOWS COURT
St. Chad
TERRACE
DAWSON ST
SCAWFELL ST
SHENFIELD ST
STANWAY CT
FALKIRK ST
CREMER STREET
HACKNEY ROAD
A1208
198
PO
RAVENSCROFT ST
CADELL CL
ALLGOOD ST
HORATIO ST
LONDON TER
COPLEY
Sports Hall
Lib
RETFORD ST
REDVERS ST
COMM. COLL HACKNEY (Shoreditch Campus)
BASING PL
NAZRUL ST
GORSUCH ST
GOR. PL
TOWER HAMLETS
STAMP PL
JAMES HAMMETT HO
SHIPTON STREET
BLACK YD
EZRA ST
Columbia Prim Sch
Lib
GEORGE LOVELESS HO
DISS ST
BAR. RD
DORSET EST
WALK
UNION
LONG ST
ELWIN ST
QUILTER
Amb Sta
BASING HO YD
DRYSDALE PL
CROOKED BILLET YD
WATERSON ST
HACKNEY ROAD
PELTER ST
OLD MARKET SQUARE
GEORGINA GDNS
SIVILL HO
CUFF PT
COLUMBIA RD
COLUMBIA ROAD
WELLINGTON
GOSSET ST
B118
DELTA ST
HOXTON ST
DRYSDALE ST
COTTONS GDNS
PRINTING HOUSE
29
BAK. RE.
DUNMORE PT
GASCOIGNE PL
Baptist
AUSTIN ST
MILDMAY MISSION HOSP
CHAMBORD ST
KIRTON GDNS
Sports Cen
BETHNAL GRN TECHNOLOGY COLL
LOR. WK
TURIN
ARTS
D
E
F
1
2
3
4

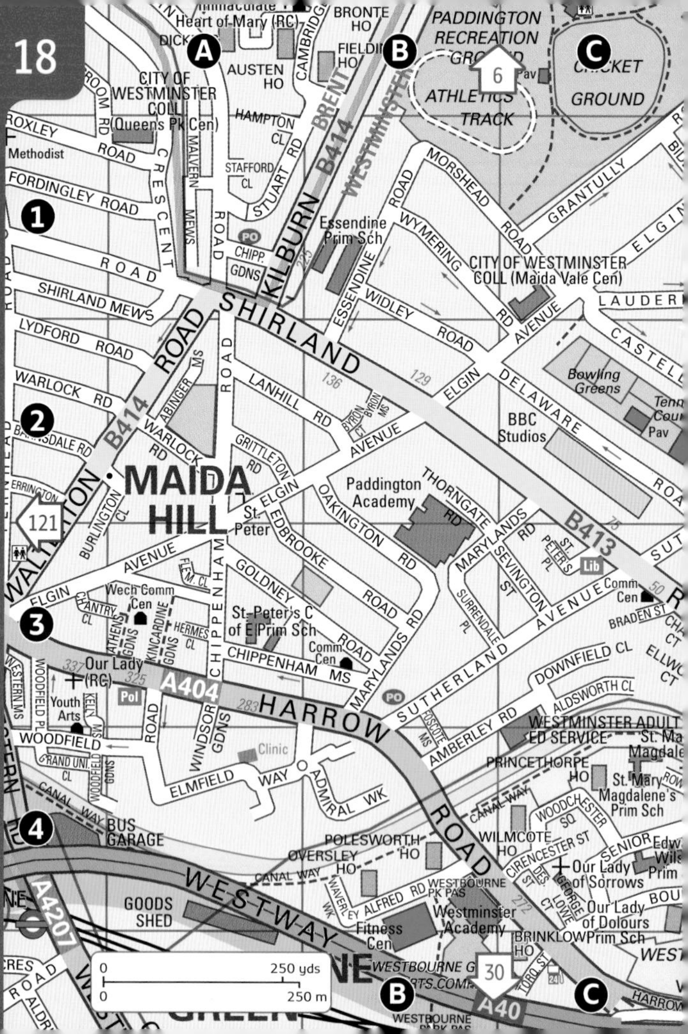

Heart of Mary (RC)
BRONTE HO
FIELDING HO
AUSTEN HO
CAMBRIDGE
PADDINGTON RECREATION GROUND
ATHLETICS TRACK
6
Pav
CRICKET GROUND
A
B
C
CITY OF WESTMINSTER COLL (Queens Pk Cen)
ROXLEY ROAD
Methodist
FORDINGLEY ROAD
CRESCENT
MALVERN MEWS
ROAD
HAMPTON CL
STAFFORD CL
STUART RD
BRENT
B414
WESTMINSTER
KILBURN
PO
CHIPP. GDNS
Essendine Prim Sch
MORSHEAD ROAD
GRANTULLY
ROAD
WYMERING ROAD
ELGIN
CITY OF WESTMINSTER COLL (Maida Vale Cen)
1
ROAD
SHIRLAND MEWS
SHIRLAND
ESSENDINE
WIDLEY ROAD
AVENUE
LAUDER
CASTELL
LYDFORD ROAD
ROAD
ABINGER MS
LANHILL RD
136
129
ELGIN
DELAWARE
Bowling Greens
WARLOCK RD
BYRON CT
BYRON MS
BBC Studios
Pav
2
WARLOCK RD
B414
GRITTLETON RD
AVENUE
MAIDA HILL
ELGIN
Paddington Academy
THORNGATE RD
OAKINGTON RD
121
BURLINGTON CL
St. Peter
EDBROOKE
MARYLANDS RD
B413
ST. PETER'S PL
SEVINGTON ST
Lib
AVENUE
GOLDNEY ROAD
WALTERTON
ELGIN
FLEM. CL
Wech Comm Cen
CHANTRY CL
ATHENS GDNS
KINCARDINE GDNS
HERMES CL
CHIPPENHAM
St. Peter's C of E Prim Sch
ROAD
MARYLANDS RD
SURRENDALE PL
SUTHERLAND AVENUE
Comm Cen
BRADEN ST
ELLWOOD CT
3
Our Lady (RC)
337
325
CHIPPENHAM MS
Comm Cen
DOWNFIELD CL
ALDSWORTH CL
WESTERN MS
WOODFIELD PL
Youth Arts
Pol
A404
283
HARROW
PO
KELLY MS
ROAD
WINDSOR GDNS
SUTHERLAND
FOSCOTE MS
AMBERLEY RD
WESTMINSTER ADULT ED SERVICE
WOODFIELD
GRAND UNI. CL
WOODFIELD GDNS
Clinic
ELMFIELD WAY
ADMIRAL WK
PRINCETHORPE HO
St. Mary Magdalene's Prim Sch
CANAL WAY
BUS GARAGE
4
ROAD
CANAL WAY
WOODCHESTER SQ
POLESWORTH HO
OVERSLEY HO
WILMCOTE HO
CIRENCESTER ST
SENIOR
Our Lady of Sorrows
CANAL WAY
WESTWAY
WAVERLEY WK
ALFRED RD
WESTBOURNE PK PAS
DES. CT
GEORGE LOWE CT
Our Lady of Dolours Prim Sch
A4207
GOODS SHED
Westminster Academy
Fitness Cen
BRINKLOW HO
0 250 yds
0 250 m
B
30
TORO ST
C
A40
HARROW
WESTBOURNE PARK PAS

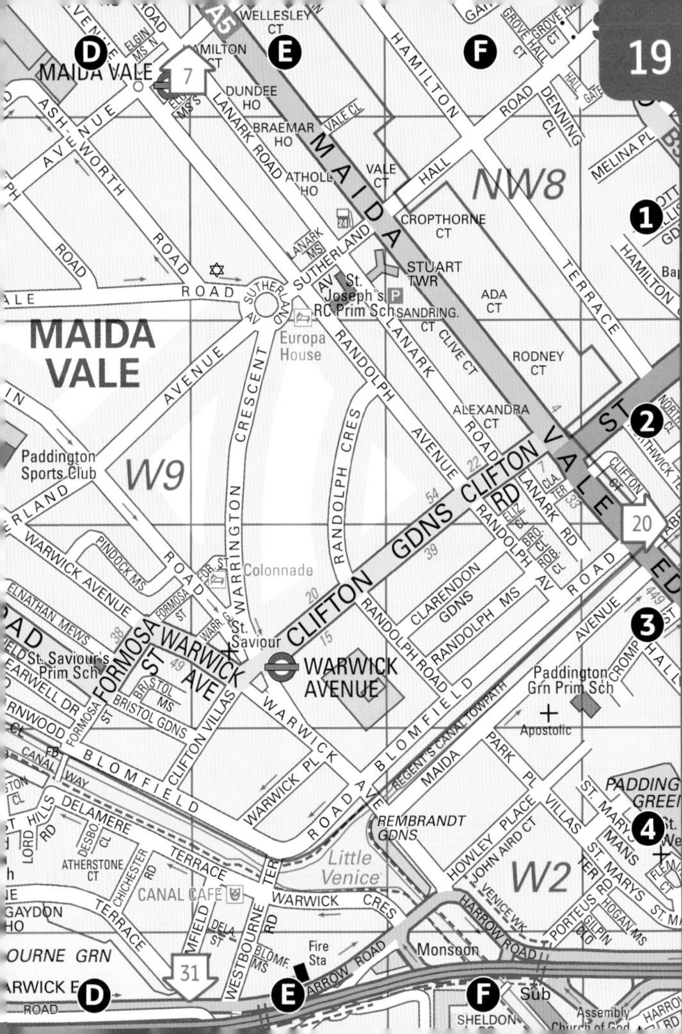
D
E
F
MAIDA VALE
ELGIN MS N
HAMILTON CT
WELLESLEY CT
A5
7
DUNDEE HO
BRAEMAR HO
VALE CL
LANARK ROAD
ATHOLL HO
VALE CT
HAMILTON
GROVE HALL CT
ROAD
DENNING CL
HALL
NW8
MELINA PL
1
ASHWORTH
AVENUE
ROAD
CROPTHORNE CT
STUART TWR
ADA CT
HAMILTON
TERRACE
LANARK MS
SUTHERLAND
AV
St. Joseph's RC Prim Sch
SANDRING. CT
SUTHERLAND AV
ROAD
MAIDA VALE
Europa House
RANDOLPH
LANARK
CLIVE CT
RODNEY CT
AVENUE
CRESCENT
ALEXANDRA CT
ROAD
ST
2
Paddington Sports Club
W9
RANDOLPH CRES
AVENUE
CLIFTON
RD
LANARK RD
CLA. TER
VALE
CLIFTON CT
20
WARWICK AVENUE
PINDOCK MS
WARRINGTON
RANDOLPH
GDNS
CLIFTON
ELIZ. CL
RANDOLPH
BRO. CL
ROB. CL
ROAD
Colonnade
CLARENDON GDNS
AV
ELNATHAN MEWS
FORMOSA ST
FOR. ST
WARR. G
St. Saviour
CLIFTON
RANDOLPH MS
AVENUE
3
St. Saviour's Prim Sch
FORMOSA ST
WARWICK AVE
BRISTOL MS
WARWICK AVENUE
RANDOLPH ROAD
Paddington Grn Prim Sch
BRISTOL GDNS
CLIFTON VILLAS
BLOMFIELD
REGENT'S CANAL TOWPATH
Apostolic
FORMOSA ST
WARWICK
MAIDA
PARK PL
CANAL WAY
BLOMFIELD
WARWICK PL
AVE
VILLAS
PADDING GREEN
DELAMERE
ROAD
REMBRANDT GDNS
HOWLEY PLACE
ST. MARYS MANS
4
LORD HILLS RD
DESBO. CL
TERRACE
TER
Little Venice
JOHN AIRD CT
W2
ST. MARYS TER
ATHERSTONE CT
CHICHESTER RD
CANAL CAFE
WARWICK
CRES
VENICE WK
PORTEUS RD
HOGAN MS
GAYDON HO
TERRACE
DELA. ST
WESTBOURNE RD
HARROW ROAD
GILPIN CL
BOURNE GRN
31
BLOMF. MS
Fire Sta
ROAD
Monsoon
HARROW
Sub
WARWICK E
ROAD
SHELDON
Assembly Church of God

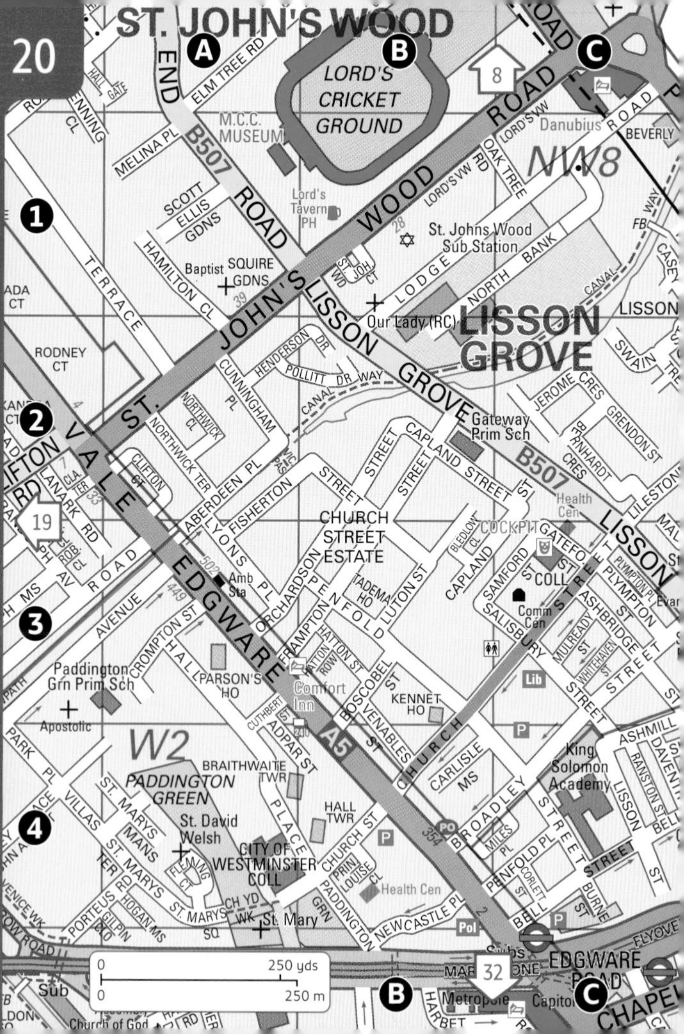
ST. JOHN'S WOOD
A
B
C
LORD'S CRICKET GROUND
8
M.C.C. MUSEUM
ELM TREE RD
END
B507
ROAD
MELINA PL
HALL GATE
SCOTT ELLIS GDNS
HAMILTON CL
Lord's Tavern PH
WOOD
ROAD
Danubius
ROAD
BEVERLY
LORD'S VW
OAK TREE RD
LORD'S VW
NW8
St. Johns Wood Sub Station
NORTH BANK
LODGE
Baptist
SQUIRE GDNS
TERRACE
1
ADA CT
RODNEY CT
JOHN'S
ST.
LISSON
Our Lady (RC)
LISSON GROVE
CANAL
LISSON
SWAIN
HENDERSON DR
POLLITT DR
WAY
CUNNINGHAM PL
GROVE
Gateway Prim Sch
JEROME CRES
GRENDON ST
BERNHARDT CRES
2
CLIFTON
VALE
NORTHWICK CL
NORTHWICK TER
ABERDEEN PL
FISHERTON
STREET
CAPLAND STREET
B507
Health Cen
LILESTONE
CLIFTON CT
19
LANARK RD
CLA. TER
ROAD
CHURCH STREET ESTATE
COCKPIT
GATEFORTH ST
LISSON
BLEDLOW CL
CAPLAND
SAMFORD ST
COLL
PLYMPTON PL
PLYMPTON ST
Comm Cen
SALISBURY
ASHBRIDGE ST
ROB. CL
EDGWARE
LYONS PL
Amb Sta
ORCHARDSON
PENFOLD
TADEMA HO
LUTON ST
3
AVENUE
CROMPTON ST
HALL
FRAMPTON
HATTON ROW
HATTON ST
BOSCOBEL ST
MULREADY ST
WHITEHAVEN ST
STREET
Lib
Paddington Grn Prim Sch
PARSON'S HO
Comfort Inn
KENNET HO
Apostolic
CUTHBERT ST
ADPAR ST
A5
VENABLES
ST
CHURCH
P
ASHMILL
PARK PL
W2
BRAITHWAITE TWR
CARLISLE MS
King Solomon Academy
PADDINGTON GREEN
HALL TWR
PLACE
BROADLEY
STREET
LISSON
RANSTON ST
4
VILLAS
ST. MARYS MANS
St. David Welsh
CITY OF WESTMINSTER COLL
CHURCH ST
PO
MILES PL
PENFOLD PL
CORLETT ST
STREET
ST. MARYS TER
FLEMING CT
PRIN. LOUISE CL
Health Cen
BURNE ST
PORTEUS RD
HOGAN MS
ST. MARYS SQ
CH YD WK
St. Mary
PADDINGTON GRN
NEWCASTLE PL
Pol
BELL
P
GILPIN
VENICE WK
ROAD
FLYOVER
0
250 yds
0
250 m
Sub
MARYLEBONE
32
EDGWARE ROAD
B
C
Metropole
Capitol
CHAPEL
Church of God

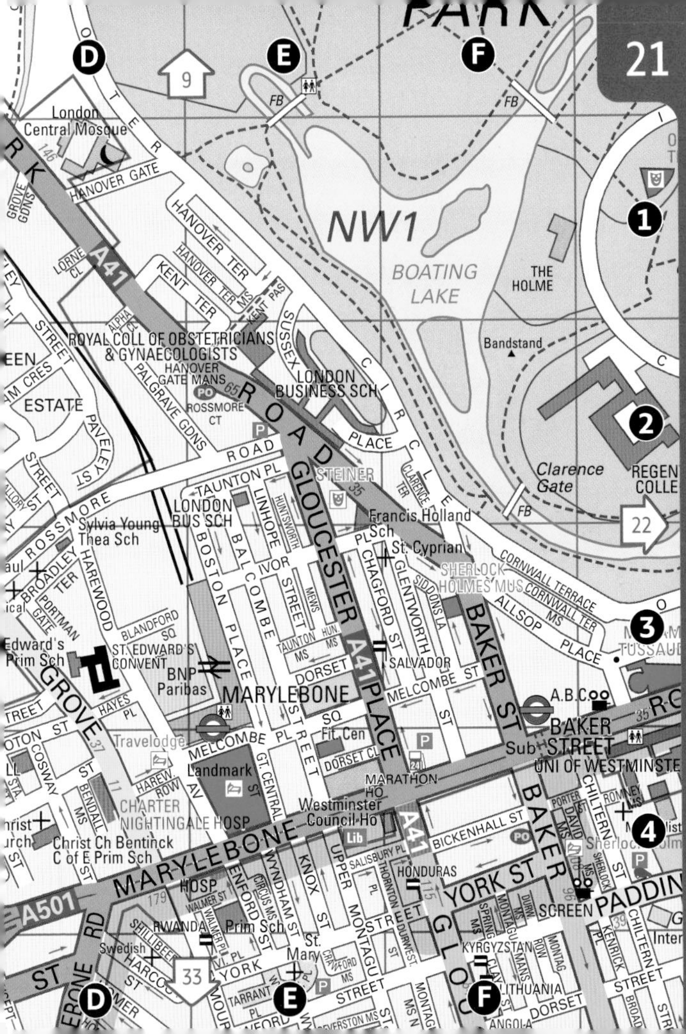
PARK
D
E
F
9
FB
London Central Mosque
HANOVER GATE
GROVE GDNS
OUTER CIRCLE
NW1
BOATING LAKE
THE HOLME
HANOVER TER
HANOVER TER MS
KENT TER
KENT PAS
LORNE CL
A41
ALPHA CL
SUSSEX PLACE
ROYAL COLL OF OBSTETRICIANS & GYNAECOLOGISTS
HANOVER GATE MANS
ROSSMORE CT
PALGRAVE GDNS
LONDON BUSINESS SCH
Bandstand
1
2
Clarence Gate
REGENT'S COLLEGE
22
ESTATE
PAVELEY ST
ROSSMORE ROAD
TAUNTON PL
STEINER
CLARENCE TER
LONDON BUS SCH
LINHOPE ST
HUNTSWORTH MS
GLOUCESTER PLACE
Francis Holland Sch
St. Cyprian
Sylvia Young Thea Sch
BROADLEY TER
HAREWOOD AV
BOSTON PLACE
BALCOMBE ST
IVOR PL
CHAGFORD ST
GLENTWORTH ST
SHERLOCK HOLMES MUS
CORNWALL TERRACE
CORNWALL TER MS
SIDDONS LA
BAKER ST
ALLSOP PLACE
3
TUSSAUDS
PORTMAN GATE
BLANDFORD SQ
ST. EDWARD'S CONVENT
Edward's Prim Sch
GROVE
TAUNTON MS
HUN MS
DORSET SQ
SALVADOR
MELCOMBE ST
BNP Paribas
MARYLEBONE
HAYES PL
A.B.C.
BAKER STREET
Sub
UNI OF WESTMINSTER
Travelodge
MELCOMBE PL
Fit Cen
COSWAY ST
BENDALL MS
HAREW. ROW
Landmark
GT. CENTRAL ST
DORSET CL
MARATHON HO
CHARTER NIGHTINGALE HOSP
Westminster Council Ho
BICKENHALL ST
PORTER ST
DAVID MS
CHILTERN ST
ROMNEY MS
4
Christ Ch Bentinck C of E Prim Sch
MARYLEBONE ROAD
Lib
SALISBURY PL
HONDURAS
YORK ST
A501
HOSP
WALMER ST
ENFORD ST
CIRCUS MS
WYNDHAM ST
KNOX ST
UPPER MONTAGU STREET
THORNTON PL
DURWEST
SPRING MS
MONTAGU ROW
SHERLOCK MS
SCREEN
PADDINGTON
KENRICK PL
CHILTERN STREET
RWANDA
Prim Sch
SHILLIBEER PL
Swedish
HARCOURT ST
33
YORK
St. Mary
CRAWFORD MS
KYRGYZSTAN
MONTAGU MANS
LITHUANIA
DORSET
TARRANT PL
MONTAGU STREET
ANGOLA
BROADLEY ST

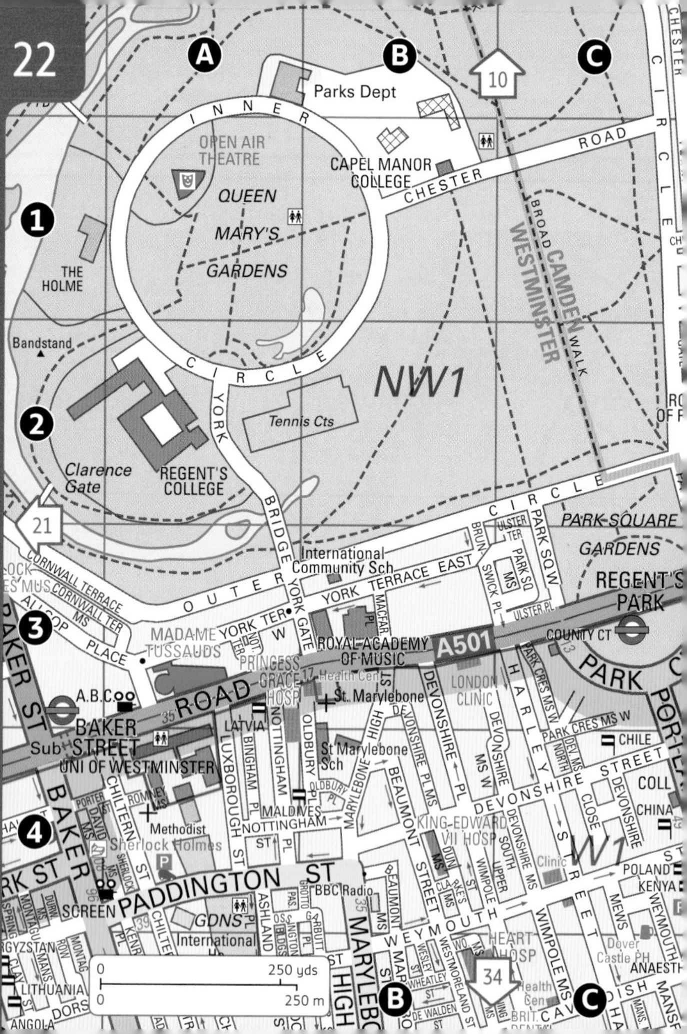
A
B
C
1
2
3
4
10
21
34
Parks Dept
INNER CIRCLE
OPEN AIR THEATRE
QUEEN MARY'S GARDENS
CAPEL MANOR COLLEGE
CHESTER ROAD
THE HOLME
Bandstand
BROAD WALK
CAMDEN
WESTMINSTER
NW1
Tennis Cts
YORK BRIDGE
Clarence Gate
REGENT'S COLLEGE
OUTER CIRCLE
PARK SQUARE GARDENS
International Community Sch
YORK TERRACE EAST
ULSTER TER
PARK SQ MS
PARK SQ W
BRUNSWICK PL
ULSTER PL
REGENT'S PARK
CORNWALL TERRACE
CORNWALL TER MS
ALLSOP PLACE
YORK TER W
YORK GATE
MADAME TUSSAUDS
ROYAL ACADEMY OF MUSIC
A501
COUNTY CT
PARK CRES MS W
PARK CRES MS E
PRINCESS GRACE HOSP
Health Cen
St. Marylebone
LONDON CLINIC
DEVONSHIRE PL
HARLEY ST
BAKER ST
A.B.C.
BAKER STREET
ROAD
LATVIA
NOTTINGHAM ST
OLDBURY PL
MARYLEBONE HIGH ST
St Marylebone Sch
DEVONSHIRE PL MS
BEAUMONT ST
DEVONSHIRE MS W
CHILE
DEVONSHIRE STREET
Sub
UNI OF WESTMINSTER
LUXBOROUGH ST
BINGHAM PL
CHILTERN ST
ROMNEY MS
PORTER ST
DAVID MS
Methodist
MALDIVES
NOTTINGHAM PL
KING EDWARD VII HOSP
DEVONSHIRE MS SOUTH
UPPER WIMPOLE ST
DEVONSHIRE CLOSE
COLL
CHINA
W1
Clinic
Sherlock Holmes
PADDINGTON ST
GDNS
BBC Radio
DUNSTABLE MS
CLARKE'S MS
WIMPOLE MS
POLAND
KENYA
MEWS
WEYMOUTH
WEYMOUTH ST
SCREEN
KYRGYZSTAN
MONTAGU MANS
MONTAGU ROW
International
ASHLAND PL
GARBUTT PL
MARYLEBONE HIGH
WESLEY ST
WHEATLEY ST
WESTMORELAND ST
HEART HOSP
Dover Castle PH
ANAESTH
Health Cen
DE WALDEN ST
BRIT. DENTAL
LITHUANIA
ANGOLA
DORSET
0 250 yds
0 250 m

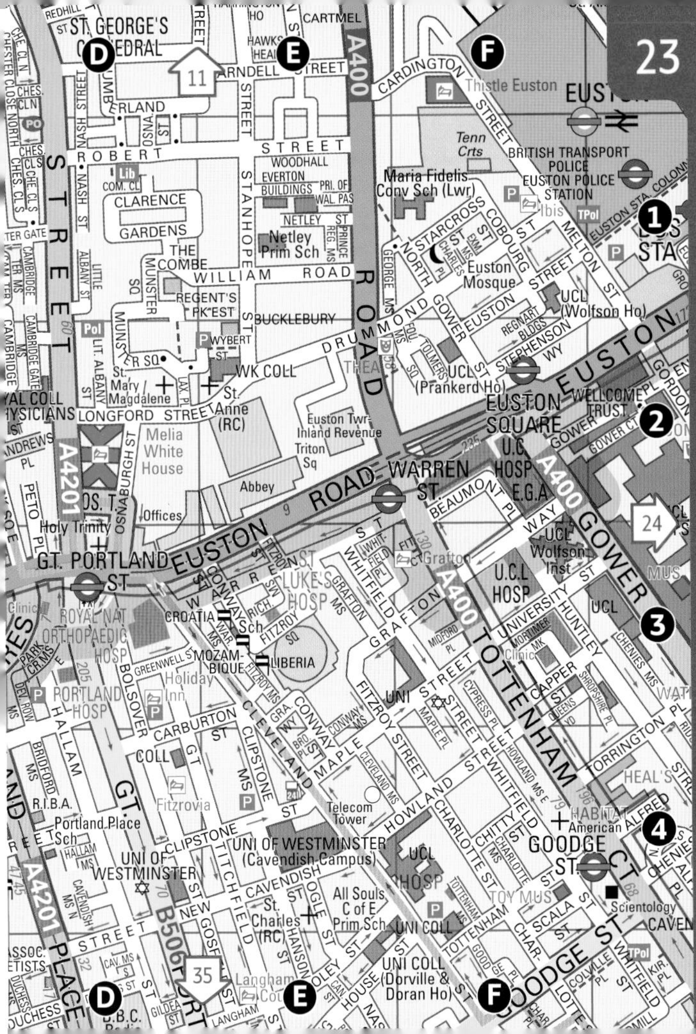

REDHILL ST
ST. GEORGE'S CATHEDRAL
CARTMEL
HAWKSHEAD
ARNDELL STREET
A400
CARDINGTON STREET
Thistle Euston
EUSTON
11
D
E
F
CUMBERLAND
NASH STREET
OSNABURGH
ROBERT STREET
Lib
COM. CL
CLARENCE GARDENS
WOODHALL
EVERTON BUILDINGS
PRI. OF WAL. PAS
NETLEY ST
Netley Prim Sch
PRINCE REGENT MS
STANHOPE STREET
Tenn Crts
BRITISH TRANSPORT POLICE
EUSTON POLICE STATION
Maria Fidelis Conv Sch (Lwr)
Ibis
TPol
EUSTON STA. COLONNADE
BUS STA
STARCROSS ST
COBOURG ST
MELTON ST
CHARLES PL
Euston Mosque
NORTH GOWER ST
GEORGE MS
THE COMBE
WILLIAM ROAD
REGENT'S PK EST
MUNSTER SQ
BUCKLEBURY
ROAD
DRUMMOND
EUSTON STREET
UCL (Wolfson Ho)
REGNART BLDGS
STEPHENSON WY
TOLMERS SQ
UCL (Prankerd Ho)
THEA
WYBERT ST
WK COLL
St. Mary Magdalene
St. Anne (RC)
LONGFORD STREET
Pol
LIT. ALBANY ST
ALBANY ST
LITTLE ALBANY ST
CAMBRIDGE GATE
CAMBRIDGE TER MS
CHESTER CLOSE NORTH
CHES. CLN
PO
ROYAL COLL PHYSICIANS
ANDREWS PL
PETO PL
A4201
Melia White House
OSNABURGH ST
Euston Twr Inland Revenue
Triton Sq
Abbey
Offices
Holy Trinity
EUSTON ROAD
EUSTON SQUARE
WELLCOME TRUST
GORDON ST
GOWER PL
GOWER CT
WARREN ST
BEAUMONT PL
U.C. HOSP E.G.A.
WAY
UCL Wolfson Inst
U.C.L HOSP
GOWER ST
24
MUS
UCL
GT. PORTLAND ST
Clinic
ROYAL NAT ORTHOPAEDIC HOSP
PARK CRMS
DEV. ROW
PORTLAND HOSP
WARREN ST
CONWAY ST
CROATIA
MOZAMBIQUE
LIBERIA
Sch
RICH. ST
FITZROY SQ
ST. LUKE'S HOSP
WHITFIELD PL
GRAFTON MS
WHITFIELD ST
Grafton
GRAFTON WAY
A400
TOTTENHAM
UNIVERSITY ST
HUNTLEY ST
MORTIMER MK
Clinic
MIDFORD PL
CHENIES MS
CAPPER ST
SHROPSHIRE PL
QUEENS YD
GREENWELL ST
Holiday Inn
BOLSOVER
CARBURTON ST
HALLAM ST
BRIDFORD MS
R.I.B.A.
Portland Place Sch
COLL
GT.
Fitzrovia
CLEVELAND
CLIPSTONE MS
FITZROY MS
CONWAY MS
MAPLE PL
FITZROY STREET
UNI
STREET
CYPRESS PL
MAPLE ST
BRO. PL
CLEVELAND MS
Telecom Tower
HOWLAND STREET
CHARLOTTE ST
WHITFIELD
HOWLAND MS E
TORRINGTON PL
HEAL'S
HABITAT
American
ALFRED PL
GOODGE ST
CHITTY ST
CHARLOTTE MS
CLIPSTONE ST
UNI OF WESTMINSTER (Cavendish Campus)
UCL HOSP
TOY MUS
Scientology
CAVENDISH
UNI OF WESTMINSTER
HALLAM MS
CAVENDISH MS N
B506
NEW CAVENDISH STREET
TITCHFIELD
OGLE ST
St. Charles (RC)
All Souls C of E Prim Sch
UNI COLL
TOTTENHAM MS
SCALA ST
GOODGE ST
TPol
COLVILLE PL
WHITFIELD ST
KIRK. PL
ASSOC. ANAESTHETISTS
DUCHESS
PLACE
35
CAV. MS
Langham
HANSON ST
FOLEY ST
HOUSE
UNI COLL (Dorville & Doran Ho)
GOODGE PL
CHARLOTTE PL
B.B.C.
GILDEA ST
LANGHAM

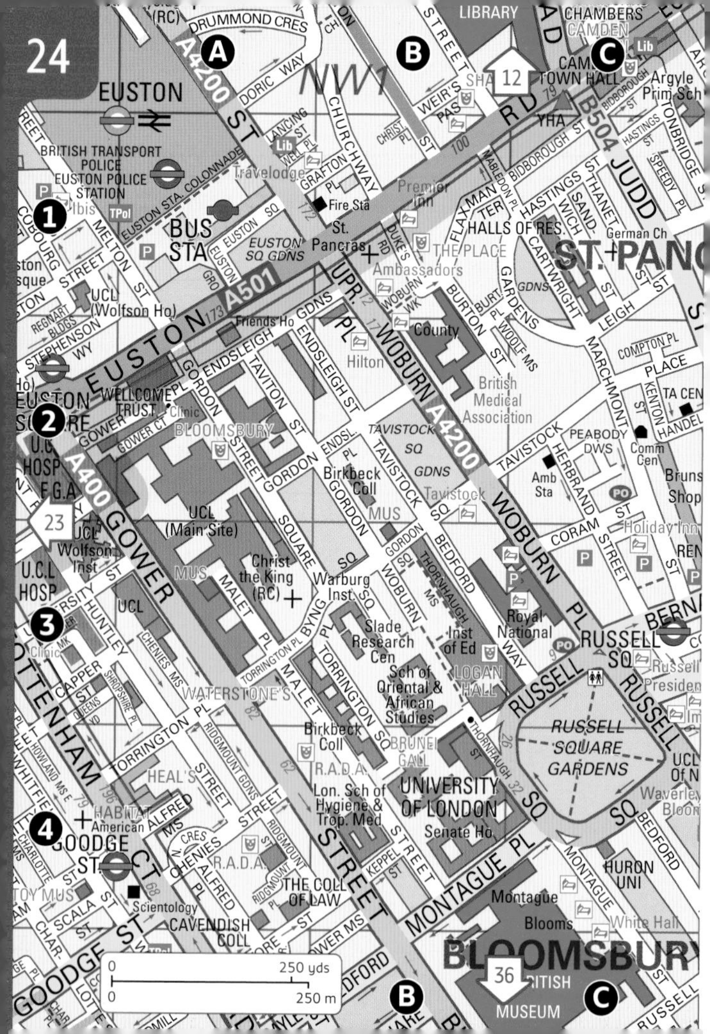
A
B
C
1
2
3
4
NW1
EUSTON
BRITISH TRANSPORT POLICE
EUSTON POLICE STATION
Ibis
TPol
BUS STA
EUSTON STA. COLONNADE
EUSTON SQ
EUSTON SQ GDNS
DRUMMOND CRES
DORIC WAY
A4200
ST
LANCING ST
Lib
WELL PL
GRAFTON PL
Travelodge
Fire Sta
St. Pancras
CHURCHWAY
CHRIST PL
ST
WEIR'S PAS
LIBRARY
CHAMBERS
CAMDEN
CAMDEN TOWN HALL
12
RD
YHA
B504
BIDBOROUGH ST
Argyle Prim Sch
HASTINGS ST
TONBRIDGE ST
SPEEDY PL
JUDD
MABLEDON PL
Premier Inn
FLAXMAN TER
HALLS OF RES.
THANET
SANDWICH
CARTWRIGHT GDNS
German Ch
ST. PANC
DUKE'S RD
THE PLACE
Ambassadors
WOBURN WK
BURTON ST
BURTON PL
WOOLF MS
LEIGH ST
MARCHMONT
COMPTON PL
PLACE
KENTON ST
TA CEN
HANDEL
A501
EUSTON
173
Friends Ho
ENDSLEIGH GDNS
UPR. WOBURN PL
County
Hilton
British Medical Association
COBOURG
MELTON ST
STREET
UCL (Wolfson Ho)
REGNART BLDGS
STEPHENSON WY
EUSTON SQUARE
WELLCOME TRUST
Clinic
GORDON ST
ENDSLEIGH PL
TAVITON ST
ENDSLEIGH ST
GOWER PL
GOWER CT
BLOOMSBURY
TAVISTOCK SQ GDNS
TAVISTOCK PL
PEABODY DWS
HERBRAND ST
Comm Cen
Amb Sta
Bruns Shop
PO
A400
U.C.L HOSP
F.G.A
23
UCL Wolfson Inst
GOWER
UCL (Main Site)
GORDON SQ
ENDSL. PL
Birkbeck Coll
MUS
Tavistock
CORAM ST
Holiday Inn
A4200
WOBURN PL
SQUARE
Christ the King (RC)
Warburg Inst.
GORDON SQ
BEDFORD WAY
THORNHAUGH MS
UNIVERSITY ST
HUNTLEY ST
UCL
MALET PL
BYNG PL
WOBURN SQ
Slade Research Cen
Inst of Ed
Royal National
RUSSELL SQ
BERNARD
CHENIES MS
TORRINGTON PL
Sch of Oriental & African Studies
LOGAN HALL
RUSSELL SQUARE GARDENS
Russell
CAPPER ST
SHROPSHIRE PL
QUEENS YD
WATERSTONE'S
MALET ST
TORRINGTON SQ
TOTTENHAM
HOWLAND MS E
WHITFIELD
TORRINGTON PL
RIDGMOUNT GDNS
HEAL'S
STREET
Birkbeck Coll
BRUNEI GALL
THORNHAUGH ST
R.A.D.A.
UNIVERSITY OF LONDON
Senate Ho
HABITAT
American
ALFRED MS
Lon. Sch of Hygiene & Trop. Med
UCL Of N
Waverley
Bloom
GOODGE ST.
N. CRES
CHENIES ST
ALFRED PL
R.A.D.A.
RIDGMOUNT ST
RIDGMOUNT PL
STORE STREET
KEPPEL ST
MONTAGUE PL
MONTAGUE ST
HURON UNI
BEDFORD
CHARLOTTE ST
TOY MUS
SCALA ST
Scientology
THE COLL OF LAW
Montague
Blooms
White Hall
CAVENDISH COLL
GOODGE ST
CHAR. ST
BLOOMSBURY
36
BRITISH MUSEUM
RUSSELL
0 250 yds
0 250 m

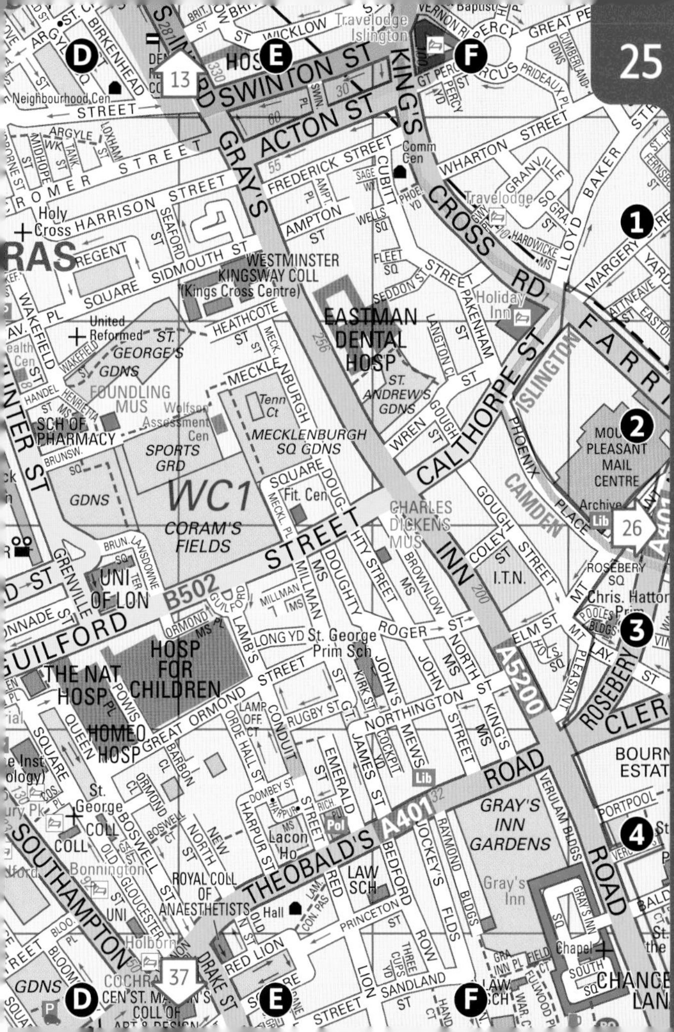
D
E
F
13
SWINTON ST
ACTON ST
KING'S
WICKLOW
Travelodge Islington
GREAT PERCY
PERCY CIRCUS
PRIDEAUX PL
CUMBERLAND GDNS
BIRKENHEAD
ARGYLE
Neighbourhood Cen
STREET
ARGYLE WK
LOXHAM ST
TANK.
MIDHOPE ST
CROMER STREET
GRAY'S
FREDERICK STREET
SAGE WY
CUBITT
Comm Cen
WHARTON STREET
GRANVILLE SQ
LLOYD BAKER
Travelodge
HARDWICKE MS
CROSS
AMPTON ST
WELLS SQ
PHOE. YD
Holy Cross
HARRISON STREET
SEAFORD ST
REGENT SQUARE
SIDMOUTH ST
WESTMINSTER KINGSWAY COLL
(Kings Cross Centre)
FLEET SQ
SEDDON ST
STREET
RD
1
MARGERY
YARD
FARR
ATTNEAVE ST
EASTON
WAKEFIELD
United Reformed
ST. GEORGE'S GDNS
HEATHCOTE ST
EASTMAN DENTAL HOSP
ST. ANDREW'S GDNS
Holiday Inn
PAKENHAM ST
LANGTON CL
ISLINGTON
CALTHORPE ST
FOUNDLING MUS
Wolfson Assessment Cen
MECKLENBURGH
Tenn Ct
MECKLENBURGH SQ GDNS
WREN ST
GOUGH ST
PHOENIX PL
CAMDEN
2
MOUNT PLEASANT MAIL CENTRE
Archive
Lib
26
A401
SCH OF PHARMACY
HANDEL ST
HENRIETTA MS
SPORTS GRD
GDNS
BRUNSW. SQ
WC1
CORAM'S FIELDS
SQUARE
DOUGHTY
Fit. Cen
MECKL. PL
CHARLES DICKENS MUS
INN
COLEY ST
GOUGH STREET
I.T.N.
ROSEBERY SQ
Chris. Hatton Prim
3
STREET
BRUN. SQ
LANSDOWNE TER
UNI OF LON
GRENVILLE ST
B502
GUILFORD ST
GUILFORD
MILLMAN MS
MILLMAN
DOUGHTY STREET
BROWNLOW MS
ROGER ST
NORTH MS
JOHN ST
ELM ST
HOLSWORTHY SQ
MT PLEASANT
POOLES BLDGS
LAY.
ROSEBERY AV
CLER
A5200
ORMOND MS
LAMB'S
LONG YD
St. George Prim Sch
JOHN'S MS
KIRK ST
NORTHINGTON ST
KING'S MS
HOSP FOR CHILDREN
THE NAT HOSP
POWIS PL
HOMEO HOSP
QUEEN SQUARE
GREAT ORMOND
STREET
ORDE HALL ST
LAMP OFF. CT
CONDUIT
RUGBY ST
GT. JAMES ST
COCKPIT YD
MEWS
STREET
EMERALD ST
Lib
ROAD
BOURNE ESTATE
PORTPOOL
4
GRAY'S INN GARDENS
VERULAM BLDGS
Gray's Inn
ROAD
St. George
COLL
COLL
BARBON CL
ORMOND CL
BOSWELL CT
BOSWELL
NORTH ST
NEW NORTH
DOMBEY ST
HARPUR MS
HARPUR ST
RICH.
Pol
Lacon Ho
THEOBALD'S
A401
JOCKEY'S
RAYMOND BLDGS
SOUTHAMPTON
Bonnington
GLOUCESTER
UNI
ROYAL COLL OF ANAESTHETISTS
Hall
LAW SCH
RED
BEDFORD ROW
PRINCETON ST
FLDS
GRAY'S INN SQ
Chapel
SOUTH SQ
CHANCERY LANE
Holborn
37
DRAKE ST
RED LION
LION
THREE CUPS YD
SANDLAND ST
GRA. INN PL
FIELD CT
FULWOOD PL
WAR. C.
LAW SCH
GDNS
COCHRANE
CEN ST. MARTIN'S COLL OF ART & DESIGN
STREET
HAND CT
E
F

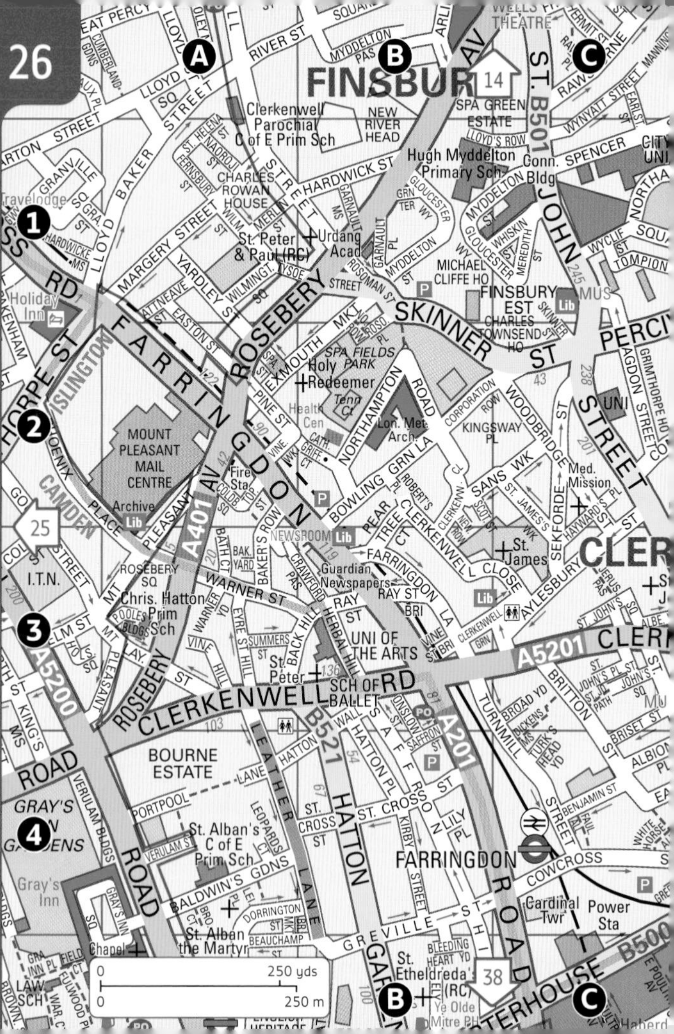
A
B
C
FINSBURY
14
WELLS THEATRE
RIVER ST
MYDDELTON PAS
LLOYD SQ
LLOYD BAKER STREET
GRANVILLE SQ
Travelodge
Clerkenwell Parochial C of E Prim Sch
NEW RIVER HEAD
SPA GREEN ESTATE
LLOYD'S ROW
ST. JOHN STREET
B501
Hugh Myddelton Primary Sch
Conn. Bldg
SPENCER
CITY UNI
HARDWICK ST
CHARLES ROWAN HOUSE
MARGERY STREET
St. Peter & Paul (RC)
Urdang Acad
ROSEBERY AV
FARRINGDON RD
SKINNER ST
MICHAEL CLIFFE HO
FINSBURY EST
CHARLES TOWNSEND HO
Lib
MUS
PERCIVAL
Holiday Inn
WYCLIF ST
TOMPION
WYNYATT STREET
EXMOUTH MKT
SPA FIELDS PARK
Holy Redeemer
Health Cen
Tenn Ct
NORTHAMPTON ROAD
Lon. Met. Arch.
CORPORATION ROW
KINGSWAY PL
WOODBRIDGE ST
UNI
MOUNT PLEASANT MAIL CENTRE
ISLINGTON
CAMDEN
PHOENIX PLACE
Archive
A401
Fire Sta.
BOWLING GRN LA
SANS WK
Med. Mission
25
NEWSROOM
Guardian Newspapers
FARRINGDON LA
CLERKENWELL CLOSE
St. James
AYLESBURY
CLERKENWELL
I.T.N.
ROSEBERY SQ
Chris. Hatton Prim Sch
WARNER ST
RAY ST
BRI
UNI OF THE ARTS
A5201
ELM ST
A5200
VINE HILL
St. Peter
SCH OF BALLET
CLERKENWELL RD
BRITTON
TURNMILL
ROAD
BOURNE ESTATE
B521
LEATHER LANE
HATTON
SAFFRON
A201
GRAY'S INN GARDENS
PORTPOOL
ST. CROSS ST
Gray's Inn
St. Alban's C of E Prim Sch
BALDWIN'S GDNS
FARRINGDON
COWCROSS
DORRINGTON ST
Cardinal Twr
Power Sta
St. Alban the Martyr
GREVILLE ST
Chapel
St. Etheldreda's (RC)
38
CHARTERHOUSE
B500
Ye Olde Mitre PH
LAW SCH
1
2
3
4
0 250 yds
0 250 m

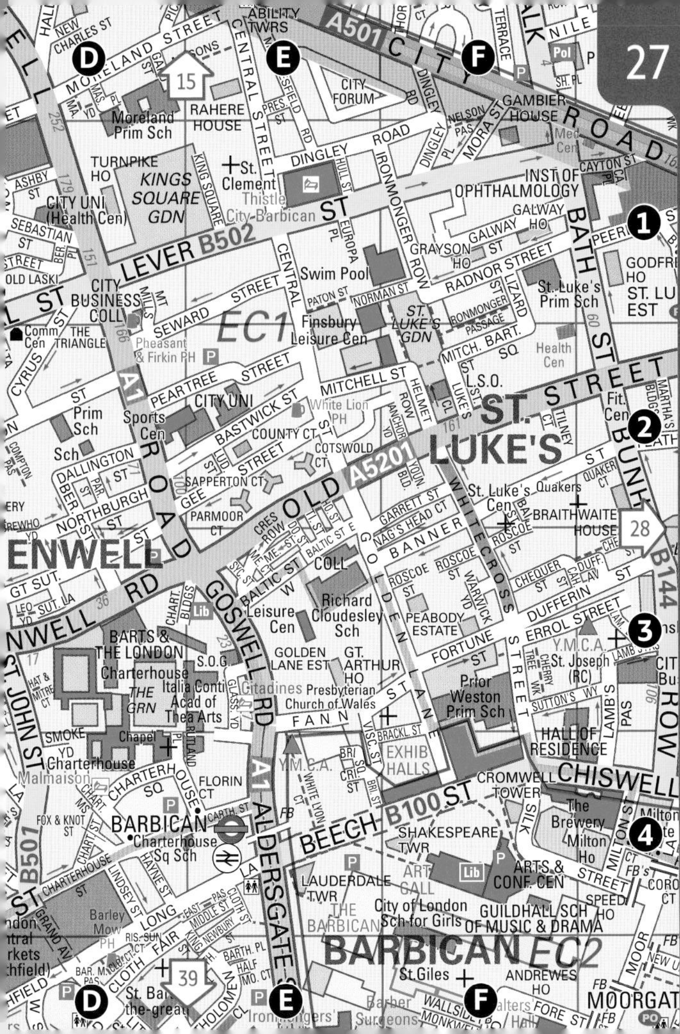
D
E
F
15
NEW CHARLES ST
MORELAND STREET
CENTRAL STREET
ABILITY TWRS
A501 CITY ROAD
CITY FORUM
DINGLEY RD
GAMBIER HOUSE
NILE
TERRACE
Pol
SH. PL
Moreland Prim Sch
RAHERE HOUSE
PRES. ST
DINGLEY ROAD
NELSON PAS
MORA ST
DINGLEY PL
Med Cen
TURNPIKE HO
KINGS SQUARE GDN
KING SQUARE
St. Clement
Thistle City Barbican
HULL ST
IRONMONGER ROW
CAYTON ST
INST OF OPHTHALMOLOGY
ASHBY ST
CITY UNI (Health Cen)
SEBASTIAN ST
LEVER B502 ST
EUROPA PL
GALWAY HO
GALWAY ST
GRAYSON HO
BATH ST
PEERLESS
1
GODFREY HO
ST. LUKE'S EST
OLD LASKI
CITY BUSINESS COLL
MT MILLS
SEWARD STREET
Swim Pool
PATON ST
NORMAN ST
RADNOR STREET
LIZARD ST
St. Luke's Prim Sch
EC1
Finsbury Leisure Cen
ST. LUKE'S GDN
IRONMONGER PASSAGE
MITCH. BART. SQ
Health Cen
Comm Cen
THE TRIANGLE
Pheasant & Firkin PH
CYRUS ST
A1
PEARTREE STREET
MITCHELL ST
HELMET ROW
L.S.O. ST.
LUKE'S CL
ST. LUKE'S
ST STREET
Fit. Cen
MARTHA'S BLDGS
2
Prim Sch
Sch
Sports Cen
CITY UNI
BASTWICK ST
White Lion PH
ANCHOR YD
COUNTY CT
COTSWOLD CT
TILNEY CT
BUNHILL
COMPTON PAS
DALLINGTON ST
GOSWELL ROAD
SAPPERTON CT
GEE STREET
A5201 OLD
YOUN. BLD.
WHITECROSS
St. Luke's Cen
Quakers
QUAKER CT
BRAITHWAITE HOUSE
28
NORTHBURGH ST
BER. ST
PAR. ST
PARMOOR CT
CRES ROW
DO. ST
LT. ST
HO. ST
GARRETT ST
NAG'S HEAD CT
BANNER
ROSCOE ST
CHEQUER ST
DUFF. ST
CAH. LAV
CLERKENWELL
BALTIC ST E
BALTIC ST W
ME. ST
COLL
GOLDEN LANE
ROSCOE ST
WARWICK YD
DUFFERIN ST
B144
GT SUT. ST
SUT. LA
LEO. YD
CLERKENWELL RD
CHART. BLDGS
Lib
Leisure Cen
Richard Cloudesley Sch
PEABODY ESTATE
ERROL STREET
3
Y.M.C.A.
BARTS & THE LONDON
Charterhouse
S.O.G.
GOLDEN LANE EST
GT. ARTHUR HO
FORTUNE ST
St. Joseph (RC)
LAMB'S BLDGS
CITY ROW
ST JOHN ST
HAT & MITRE CT
THE GRN
Italia Conti Acad of Thea Arts
GLASS. YD
Citadines
Presbyterian Church of Wales
CHERRY TREE WK
SUTTON'S WY
LAMB'S PAS
Prior Weston Prim Sch
FANN ST
SMOKE YD
Chapel
RUTLAND PL
BRACKL. ST
HALL OF RESIDENCE
Charterhouse
Malmaison
CHARTERHOUSE SQ
FLORIN CT
Y.M.C.A.
WHITE LYON CT
BRI. SQ
CRIO. ST
VISC. ST
BRI. ST
EXHIB HALLS
CHISWELL
CROMWELL TOWER
CHART. MS
CARTH. ST
A1 ALDERSGATE ST
B100 ST
The Brewery
Milton Ho
MILTON ST
4
FOX & KNOT ST
BARBICAN
Charterhouse Sq Sch
CHART. ST
BEECH
SHAKESPEARE TWR
SILK ST
ARTS & CONF. CEN
B501
CHARTERHOUSE ST
LINDSEY ST
HAYNE ST
LAUDERDALE TWR
ART GALL
STREET
FB's
CORO CT
SPEED HO
Barley Mow PH
GRAND AV
EAST PAS
MIDDLE ST
CLOTH ST
THE BARBICAN
City of London Sch for Girls
GUILDHALL SCH OF MUSIC & DRAMA
London Central Markets (Smithfield)
RIS. SUN CT
LONG LA
CLOTH FAIR
NEWBURY ST
KING ST
BARTH. PL
HALF MO. CT
BARBICAN EC2
MOOR LA
NEW UN
BAR. M. PAS
39
St. Giles
ANDREWES HO
St. Bartholomew-the-great
BARTHOLOMEW CL
Ironmongers'
Barber Surgeons'
WALLSIDE
MONKWELL
Salters' Hall
FORE ST
FB
MOORGATE
PO

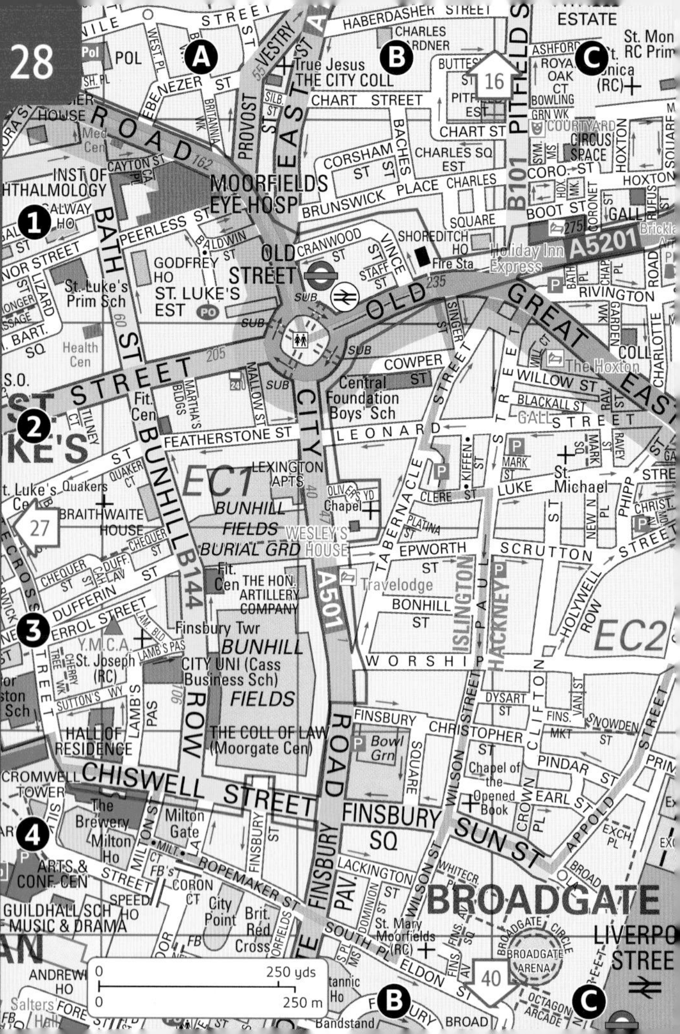
A
B
C
1
2
3
4
16
27
40
ROAD
MOORFIELDS EYE HOSP
INST OF
HTHALMOLOGY
OLD STREET
CITY ROAD
BATH ST
BUNHILL ROW
B144
A501
A5201
B101
EC1
EC2
BUNHILL FIELDS BURIAL GRD
BUNHILL FIELDS
WESLEY'S HOUSE
Chapel
LEXINGTON APTS
THE HON. ARTILLERY COMPANY
Finsbury Twr
CITY UNI (Cass Business Sch)
THE COLL OF LAW (Moorgate Cen)
CHISWELL STREET
FINSBURY SQ
FINSBURY SQUARE
FINSBURY PAV.
FINSBURY ST
BROADGATE
BROADGATE ARENA
BROADGATE CIRCLE
LIVERPO
STREE
SUN ST
WILSON ST
APPOLD ST
CHRISTOPHER ST
WORSHIP
SCRUTTON STREET
HOLYWELL ROW
TABERNACLE STREET
PAUL ST
LEONARD STREET
GREAT EASTERN
RIVINGTON
CHARLOTTE ROAD
The Hoxton
Holiday Inn Express
SHOREDITCH HO
Fire Sta
CRANWOOD ST
VINCE ST
STAFF ST
BRUNSWICK PLACE
CHARLES SQUARE
CHARLES SQ EST
CORSHAM ST
BACHES ST
CHART STREET
CHART ST
PITFIELD ST
PITFIELD EST
HABERDASHER STREET
CHARLES GARDNER
True Jesus
THE CITY COLL
EAST ROAD
VESTRY ST
PROVOST ST
BRITANNIA WK
EBENEZER ST
WEST PL
POL
Pol
CAYTON ST
PEERLESS ST
BALDWIN ST
GALWAY HO
GODFREY HO
ST. LUKE'S EST
St. Luke's Prim Sch
LIZARD ST
BART. SQ
Health Cen
PO
SUB
COWPER ST
Central Foundation Boys' Sch
FEATHERSTONE ST
MARTHA'S BLDGS
MALLOW ST
Fit. Cen
TILNEY CT
QUAKER CT
Quakers
BRAITHWAITE HOUSE
CHEQUER ST
DUFFERIN ST
ERROL STREET
Y.M.C.A.
St. Joseph (RC)
LAMB'S PAS
SUTTON'S WY
HALL OF RESIDENCE
CROMWELL TOWER
The Brewery
Milton Ho
Milton Gate
MILTON ST
ARTS & CONF. CEN
GUILDHALL SCH MUSIC & DRAMA
ROPEMAKER ST
CORON CT
City Point
Brit. Red Cross
SOUTH PL
ELDON ST
St. Mary Moorfields (RC)
LACKINGTON ST
DOMINION ST
Travelodge
EPWORTH ST
BONHILL ST
CLERE ST
KIFFEN ST
PLATINA ST
LUKE ST
St. Michael
MARK ST
GALL STREET
BLACKALL ST
WILLOW ST
HOXTON SQUARE
COURTYARD
CIRCUS SPACE
CORONET ST
BOOT ST
ASHFORD
ROYAL OAK CT
BOWLING GRN WK
ESTATE
DYSART ST
CLIFTON ST
PINDAR ST
EARL ST
SNOWDEN ST
Chapel of the Opened Book
CROWN PL
FINS. MKT
Bowl Grn
OCTAGON ARCADE
Bandstand
ANDREWE HO
Salters
FORE ST
0 250 yds
0 250 m

D
E
F
17
41
128
COLUMBIA RD
GOSSET
HACKNEY
KINGSLAND
A10
HOXTON
DRYSDALE ST
BASING
CROOKED BILLET YD
CUFF PT
OLD MARKET SQUARE
SIVILL HO
DUNMORE PT
PRINTING HOUSE YD
Baptist
MILDMAY MISSION HOSP
AUSTIN ST
VIRGINIA RD
SWANFIELD ST
CHAMBORD ST
E2
Sports Cen
BETHNAL GRN TECHNOLOGY COLL
OLD TOWN HALL
ARTS CEN
St. Leonard
Virginia Prim Sch
CALVERT AV
ARNOLD CIRCUS
Crowne Plaza
RIVINGTON ST
DEREHAM PL
BATEMAN'S ROW
NEW INN YARD
SHOREDITCH HIGH STREET
BOUNDARY ST
NAVARRE ST
CAMLET ST
CLUB ROW
Comm Cen
OLD NICHOL ST
REDCHURCH ST
St. Matthias Prim Sch
BACON STREET
BRICK LANE
CHESHIRE
SCLATER ST
BETHNAL GREEN RD
SHOREDITCH
SHOREDITCH HIGH STREET
CURTAIN RD
GREAT EASTERN ST
HOLYWELL LA
HEWETT ST
PLOUGH YARD
Sports Centre
GRIMSBY ST
PEDLEY STREET
ALLEN GDNS
BUXTON STREET
QUAKER STREET
WHELER ST
CALVIN STREET
GREY EAGLE ST
E1
COMMERCIAL STREET
NORTON FOLGATE
FOLGATE STREET
FLEUR DE LIS ST
ELDER ST
BLOSSOM ST
B134
WOODSEER ST
SPITAL STREET
St. Anne
HANBURY ST
Comm Cen
PRINCELET STREET
Pride Of Spitalfield
HUGUENOT PL
SPELMAN ST
HENEAGE ST
FOURNIER ST
Christ Church
Christ Ch C of E Sch
FASHION STREET
LAMB ST
OLD SPITALFIELDS MARKET
A1202
BRUSHFIELD STREET
E.B.R.D EXCH. ARCADE
ABN AMRO
BISHOPSGATE
ARTILLERY LANE
CRISPIN ST
CHICKSAND ST

BUS GARAGE
GOODS SHED
WESTWAY
POLESWORTH HO
OVERSLEY HO
CANAL WAY
WAVERLEY WK
ALFRED RD
WESTBOURNE PK PAS
Fitness Cen
Westminster Academy
WILMCOTE HO
CIRENCESTER ST
DES. ST
GEORGE LOWE CT
SENIOR ST
Our Lady of Sorrows
Our Lady of Dolours Prim Sch
BRINKLOW HO
TORO ST
18
272
WESTBOURNE GREEN
WESTBOURNE GREEN SPORTS COMPLEX
A40
HARROW
WESTBOURNE PARK PAS
BRUNEL ESTATE
St. Stephen's C of E Prim Sch
KEYHAM HO
WESTBOURNE PARK VILLAS
Baptist
GT WESTERN RD
ALDRIDGE ROAD VILLAS
ROAD
CRES
ST. STEPHENS MS
ST. STEPHENS GDNS
SHREWSBURY MS
REWS.
SHREWSBURY RD
ST. STEPHENS GDNS
St. Mary of the Angels RC Prim Sch
DARTMOUTH CL
CHEPSTOW A4207 ROAD
BELARUS
ST. STEP.
CR.
St. Stephen & St. Luke
WESTBOURNE PARK ROAD
TALBOT ROAD
DURHAM TER
ALEXANDER MS
ALEXANDER ST
SUNDERLAND TER
WESTBOURNE TER
WESTBOURNE GARDENS
WESTB. PK MS
BURDETT MS
HATHERLEY GRO
WESTBOURNE GRO TER
219
LEDBURY MS
LEDBURY RD
ST. STEPHENS GDN EST
CARADOC CL
TALBOT ROAD
POWIS SQUARE
135
COURTNELL ST
MOORHOUSE RD
SUTHERLAND PL
NORTHUMBERLAND PL
BRIDSTOW PLACE
HEREFORD ROAD
KILDARE TER
KILD. GDNS
Medical Cen
NEWTON RD
MONMOUTH PL
MONM. RD
HEREF. MS
BO. PAS
BOTTS MS
St. Mary of the Angels (RC)
TERRACE
ARTESIAN RD
NEEDHAM RD
HEAD'S MS
WELLINGTON CL
ST. JOHN'S MS
COLVILLE MS
LONSDALE MS
ROAD
Westbourne Grove Ch
GROVE
WESTBOURNE GROVE
WESTBOURNE GRO MS
ROSEHART MS
PO
Hall
LAMBTON PL
LEDBURY MS N
LEDBURY MS W
PENCOMBE MS
DENBIGH RD
VILLAS
PEMBRIDGE VILLAS
New Church
REDE PL
CHEPSTOW PLACE
HEREFORD RD
MONMOUTH RD
College Pk Sch
GARWAY ROAD
Westminster
LEINSTER SQ
PRINCES SQ
PRINCES
KENSINGTON GDNS SQ
ILCHESTER GDNS
PRINCES SQ
QUEEN'S MS
MOSCOW PL
Fit. Cen
W11
CHEPSTOW CRES
PEMBRIDGE MS
CHEPSTOW MS
PEMBRIDGE PL
Spiritual
DAWSON PL
Premier Inn
SQ Bayswater
PRINCES MS
GREEK CATH
MOSCOW RD
St. Matthew
ST. PETERSBURGH MS
ST. PETERSBURGH PL
BARK PLACE
ORME
PEMBRIDGE CRES
PEMBRIDGE SQUARE
PEMBRIDGE SQ
Pembridge Hall Sch
PALACE
CHAPEL SIDE
Spanish Chapel (RC)
42
SIMON CL
CHEPSTOW
PARK
PORTOBELLO
0 250 yds
0 250 m
A
B
C
1
2
3
4

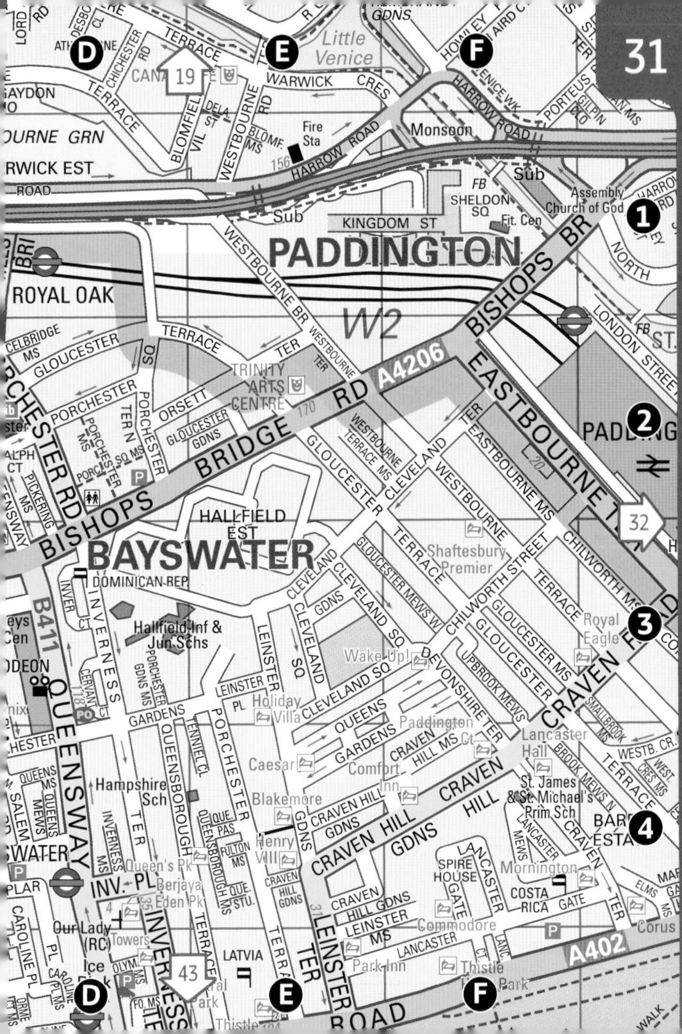
D
E
F
Little Venice
19
43
32
WARWICK CRES
HARROW ROAD
Monsoon
Fire Sta
156
Sub
FB
SHELDON SQ
Fit. Cen
Assembly Church of God
KINGDOM ST
PADDINGTON
W2
ROYAL OAK
BISHOPS BR
NORTH
LONDON STREET
ST.
A4206
EASTBOURNE TER
TRINITY ARTS CENTRE
170
GLOUCESTER TERRACE
WESTBOURNE TER
PORCHESTER RD
PADDINGTON
20
BISHOPS BRIDGE RD
HALLFIELD EST
BAYSWATER
DOMINICAN REP
Hallfield Inf & Jun Schs
Shaftesbury Premier
CHILWORTH STREET
CHILWORTH MS
Royal Eagle
CRAVEN RD
CLEVELAND SQ
CLEVELAND GDNS
GLOUCESTER MEWS W
DEVONSHIRE TER
UPBROOK MEWS
Wake Up!
LEINSTER SQ
LEINSTER GARDENS
QUEENS GARDENS
Holiday Villa
Paddington Ct
Lancaster Hall
Caesar
Comfort Inn
CRAVEN HILL
CRAVEN HILL GDNS
Blakemore
St. James & St. Michael's Prim Sch
Henry VIII
Mornington
SPIRE HOUSE
LANCASTER GATE
COSTA RICA
Commodore
Corus
A402
LANCASTER TERRACE
Park Inn
Thistle
ROAD
WALK
B411
QUEENSWAY
ODEON
Hampshire Sch
INVERNESS TER
QUEENSBOROUGH TER
PORCHESTER TERRACE
Queen's Pk
Berjaya Eden Pk
INV. PL
Our Lady (RC)
Towers
LATVIA
LEINSTER TER
CAROLINE PL
BAYSWATER
BARRIE ESTATE

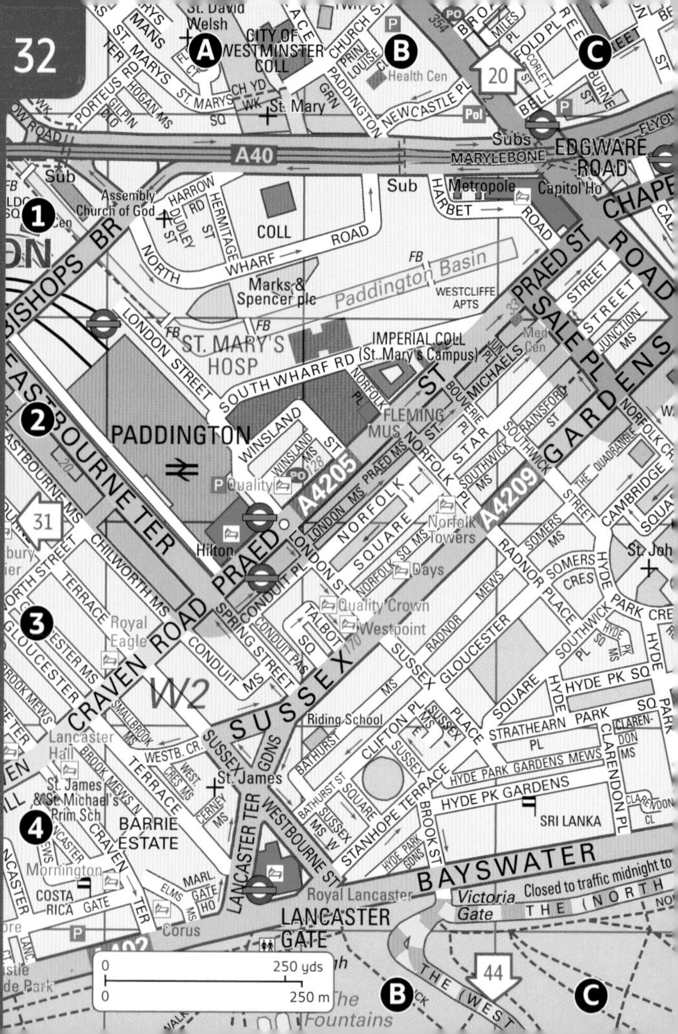
A
B
C
1
2
3
4
St. David Welsh
CITY OF WESTMINSTER COLL
ST. MARYS MANS
ST. MARYS TER
PORTEUS RD
HOGAN MS
GILPIN CLO
ST. MARYS SQ
CH YD WK
St. Mary
PADDINGTON GRN
CHURCH ST
PRIN LOUISE CL
Health Cen
NEWCASTLE PL
Pol
BROADLEY ST
MILES PL
FOLD PL
CORLETT ST
BELL ST
BURNE ST
20
354
Subs
MARYLEBONE
EDGWARE ROAD
FLYOVER
A40
Sub
Metropole
Capitol Ho
HARBET ROAD
CHAPEL
Assembly Church of God
HARROW RD
DUDLEY ST
HERMITAGE ST
COLL
NORTH WHARF ROAD
Marks & Spencer plc
Paddington Basin
FB
WESTCLIFFE APTS
BISHOPS BR
LONDON STREET
ST. MARY'S HOSP
IMPERIAL COLL (St. Mary's Campus)
SOUTH WHARF RD
NORFOLK PL
PRAED ST
SALE PL
STREET
JUNCTION MS
GARDENS
Med Cen
ST MICHAELS ST
BOUVERIE PL
RAINSFORD ST
FLEMING MUS
NORFOLK CRES
EASTBOURNE TER
EASTBOURNE MS
PADDINGTON
WINSLAND ST
WINSLAND MS
Quality
A4205
A4209
PRAED MS
LONDON MS
NORFOLK SQUARE
NORFOLK SQ MS
Norfolk Towers
Days
STAR ST
SOUTHWICK ST
SOUTHWICK MS
THE QUADRANGLE
CAMBRIDGE SQUARE
31
CHILWORTH MS
CHILWORTH STREET
Hilton
PRAED ST
LONDON ST
CONDUIT PL
SOMERS MS
SOMERS CRES
RADNOR PLACE
RADNOR MEWS
St. John
HYDE PARK CRES
TALBOT SQ
Quality Crown
Westpoint
SPRING STREET
CONDUIT PAS
CONDUIT MS
CRAVEN ROAD
CRAVEN TER
Royal Eagle
W2
SUSSEX GDNS
SUSSEX PLACE
GLOUCESTER SQUARE
SOUTHWICK PL
HYDE PK SQ
HYDE PK SQ MS
HYDE PARK SQ
STRATHEARN PL
CLARENDON PL
CLARENDON MS
GLOUCESTER MS
GLOUCESTER TER
BROOK MEWS
SMALLBROOK MS
WESTB. CR.
WEST. CRES MS
Riding School
BATHURST ST
CLIFTON PL
SUSSEX SQUARE
HYDE PARK GARDENS MEWS
HYDE PK GARDENS
SRI LANKA
Lancaster Hall
BROOK MEWS N
WESTBOURNE TERRACE
St. James
St. James & St. Michael's Prim Sch
CERNEY MS
LANCASTER TER
WESTBOURNE ST
SUSSEX MS W
STANHOPE TERRACE
BROOK ST
HYDE PARK GDNS
BARRIE ESTATE
CRAVEN TER
Mornington
COSTA RICA
GATE
ELMS MS
MARL. GATE HO
Royal Lancaster
BAYSWATER
Victoria Gate
Closed to traffic midnight to
THE (NORTH
LANCASTER GATE
Corus
44
THE (WEST
The Fountains
0
250 yds
250 m

Christ Ch Bentinck
MARYLEBONE
UPPER
Lib
SALISBURY PL
BICKENHALL
PO
D
E
F
KNOX ST
HONDURAS
YORK ST
SCREEN
21
179
A501
RD
RWANDA
Prim Sch
SHILLIBEER PL
St. Mary
MONTAGU STREET
THORNTON PL
DURWESTON ST
GLOUCESTER PL
SPRING MS
MONTAGU MANS
KENRICK PL
CHILTERN STREET
Swedish
HARCOURT ST
SEYMOUR PL
YORK ST
CRAWFORD MS
KYRGYZSTAN
MONTAGU ROW
ST
MARYLEBONE
HOMER ST
TARRANT PL
WYNDHAM PL
P
STREET
LITHUANIA
DORSET
STREET
CRAWFORD
WYNDHAM ST
BEVERSTON MS
MONTAGU MS N
ANGOLA
RODMARTON ST
1
BELIZE
Our Lady (RC)
WYNDHAM MS
SWEDEN
WATSONS MS
Seymour Leisure Cen
WYNDHAM YD
MONTAGU
St. Mark
SHOULDHAM ST
SWITZERLAND
BRYANSTON
BRYANSTON SQUARE
MONTAGU SQUARE
GLOUCESTER PL MEWS
N.M.R.
MOLYNEUX ST
TONGA
BRYANSTON PL
SEYMOUR PL
BRYANSTON MS W
BRYANSTON MS E
BLANDFORD
CRAWFORD PL
CATO STREET
WALLACE C
BRENDON ST
STREET
MONTAGU MS W
CARTON ST
EDGWARE
HARROWBY ST
CASTLEREAGH ST
BROWN
Christian Science
GEORGE
A41
DNS
Prim Sch
Jazz FM
NUTFORD PL
MARYLEBONE
PORTMAN CL
2
PORTMAN
P
BURWOOD PL
STREET
MONT. MS S
Portman
NORFOLK
PARK WEST PLACE
Marriott
GEORGE ST
W1
GREAT CUMBERLAND PL
BRUNSWICK MS
PORTMAN
FORSET ST
CLENSTON MS
BERKELEY ST
22
WEST GDN
WYTHBURN PL
Montcalm
34
A5
STOURCLIFFE
UPPER BERKELEY
QUEBEC MS
NEW QUEBEC ST
BERKELEY MS
30
Churchill
PORCHESTER PL
STREET
PORTSEA PL
PORT MS
GT CUMB. MS
P
SQUARE
KENDAL ST
HAMPDEN GUR ST
Mostyn
CONNAUGHT
STREET
SEYMOUR
ST
Pol
PORTMAN ST
3
GRANVILLE
ARCHERY CL
CONNAUGHT SQ
ROAD
Annun.
OLD QUEBEC ST
STREET
M & S
ALBION
ST. GEORGES FLDS
143
BRYANSTON
The Cumberland
P
Thistle Marble Arch
OXF
SEYMOUR ST
Connaught Ho Sch
ODEON
STANHOPE PL
FREDERICK CL
CONNAUGHT PL
Subs
MARBLE ARCH
MARBLE ARCH
Marriott
ALBION STREET
ALBION MS
PREM. & FOOTBALL LEAGUE
TYBURN WY
Marble Arch
Subs
139
NORTH
BRAZIL
HYDE PK PL
RD
CUMBERLAND GATE
GREEN
4
A402
CYPRUS
CARRIAGE DRIVE
RING
Speaker's Corner
P
Sub
Sub
RIDE
PARK
PARK
WOODS MEWS
UPPER
BROOK
45
D
E
F
CULROSS
GROSVENOR

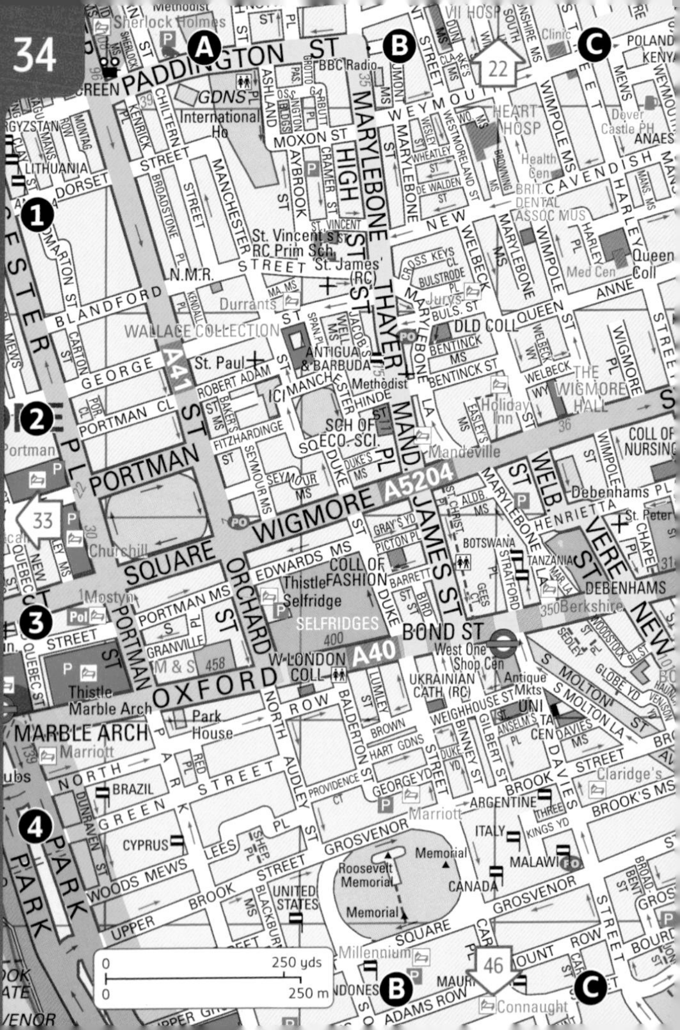
A
B
C
1
2
3
4
PADDINGTON ST
Sherlock Holmes
BBC Radio
22
33
46
Clinic
POLAND
KENYA
GDNS
International Ho
MOXON ST
HIGH
MARYLEBONE
WEYMOUTH
HEART HOSP
Health Cen
BRIT. DENTAL ASSOC MUS
CAVENDISH
WIMPOLE MS
HARLEY
Med Cen
Queen Coll
Dover Castle PH
LITHUANIA
DORSET
KYRGYZSTAN
MONTAG
BLANDFORD
N.M.R.
Durrants
St. Vincent's RC Prim Sch
St. James' (RC)
WALLACE COLLECTION
CHILTERN
MANCHESTER
BROADSTONE
STREET
GEORGE
A41
St. Paul
ROBERT ADAM
ANTIGUA & BARBUDA
Methodist
THAYER
BENTINCK
DLD COLL
QUEEN ANNE
Jurys
CROSS KEYS CL
BULSTRODE
WELBECK
WIGMORE
THE WIGMORE HALL
Holiday Inn
COLL OF NURSING
PORTMAN CL
FITZHARDINGE
SCH OF ECO. SCI.
HINDE
DUKE
SEYMOUR MS
Portman
Mandeville
A5204
WIGMORE
PORTMAN
SQUARE
Churchill
Mostyn
ORCHARD
EDWARDS MS
COLL OF FASHION
Thistle Selfridge
SELFRIDGES
A40
BOND ST
West One Shop Cen
JAMES ST
BOTSWANA
TANZANIA
STRATFORD
Debenhams
DEBENHAMS
HENRIETTA
VERE
St. Peter
Berkshire
NEW BOND
PORTMAN MS
GRANVILLE
M & S
Thistle Marble Arch
OXFORD
MARBLE ARCH
W LONDON COLL
Park House
UKRAINIAN CATH (RC)
Antique Mkts
WEIGHHOUSE ST
S MOLTON
GLOBE YD
Marriott
NORTH
BRAZIL
GREEN
CYPRUS
NORTH AUDLEY
PROVIDENCE CT
BROWN HART GDNS
GEORGE YD
BROOK
ARGENTINE
Claridge's
BROOK'S MS
ITALY
MALAWI
CANADA
GROSVENOR
Roosevelt Memorial
Memorial
SQUARE
UNITED STATES
WOODS MEWS
PARK
UPPER BROOK
Millennium
MOUNT ROW
ADAMS ROW
Connaught
0
250 yds
0
250 m

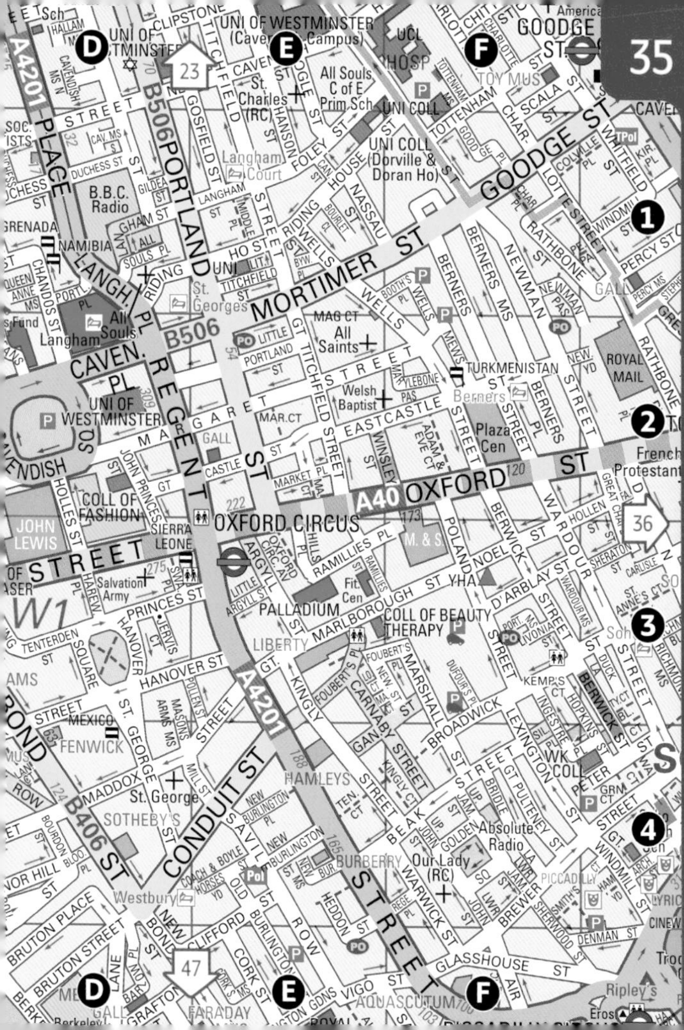
D
E
F
23
UNI OF WESTMINSTER (Cavendish Campus)
UCL HOSP
GOODGE ST
CLIPSTONE
TITCHFIELD
GOSFIELD ST
B506 PORTLAND
A4201
PLACE
STREET
B.B.C. Radio
DUCHESS ST
CAV. MS
GRENADA
NAMIBIA
Langham Court
LANGHAM ST
St. Charles (RC)
HANSON ST
FOLEY ST
All Souls C of E Prim Sch
UNI COLL
UNI COLL (Dorville & Doran Ho)
TOY MUS
TOTTENHAM
SCALA ST
CHARLOTTE
WHITFIELD ST
GOODGE ST
COLVILLE PL
TPol
1
RATHBONE
PERCY ST
WINDMILL ST
NEWMAN ST
BERNERS MS
BERNERS
MORTIMER ST
NASSAU
HOUSE
RIDING HO ST
ALL SOULS PL
CHANDOS ST
QUEEN ANNE MS
PORTL. PL
Langham
All Souls
CAVEN. PL
St. George's
B506
LITTLE PORTLAND ST
All Saints
MAG CT
WELLS
BOOTH'S PL
NEWMAN PAS
PO
ROYAL MAIL
NEW. YD
TURKMENISTAN
Berners
Plaza Cen
2
French Protestant
UNI OF WESTMINSTER
CAVENDISH SQ
MARGARET
REGENT ST
Welsh Baptist
EASTCASTLE
MAR.CT
GALL
CASTLE
MARKET PL
A40 OXFORD ST
120
173
222
OXFORD CIRCUS
JOHN LEWIS
COLL OF FASHION
HOLLES ST
JOHN PRINCES ST
SIERRA LEONE
36
M. & S.
POLAND
BERWICK
WARDOUR
HOLLEN ST
NOEL ST
D'ARBLAY ST
YHA
RAMILLIES PL
ARGYLL
LITTLE ARGYLL ST
Fit. Cen
PALLADIUM
MARLBOROUGH
COLL OF BEAUTY THERAPY
STREET
275
Salvation Army
PRINCES ST
W1
TENTERDEN ST
HANOVER SQUARE
HANOVER ST
LIBERTY
KINGLY
FOUBERT'S PL
CARNABY
MARSHALL
BROADWICK
ST. ANNE'S CT
3
KEMP'S CT
BERWICK ST
MEXICO
FENWICK
ST. GEORGE
MADDOX
St. George
SOTHEBY'S
CONDUIT ST
A4201
HAMLEYS
NEW BURLINGTON
SAVILE
188
165
BEAK
GOLDEN
Absolute Radio
LEXINGTON
WK COLL
PETER
GRN CT
4
B406 ST
BRUTON PLACE
BRUTON STREET
Westbury
NEW BOND ST
47
CLIFFORD
CORK ST
BURLINGTON
ROW
Poi
BURBERRY
Our Lady (RC)
WARWICK ST
PICCADILLY
BREWER
DENMAN ST
GLASSHOUSE ST
HEDDON ST
VIGO
AQUASCUTUM
Ripley's
Eros
FARADAY
GRAFTON
BERKELEY
D
E
F

A
B
C
1
2
3
4
24
35
48
BLOOMSBURY
THE BRITISH MUSEUM
WC1
W1
SOHO
COVENT GARDEN
GOODGE ST
TOTTENHAM COURT RD
LEICESTER SQ
NEW OXFORD ST
ST. GILES HIGH ST
CHARING CROSS RD
SHAFTESBURY AV
OXFORD ST
BLOOMSBURY ST
BEDFORD SQUARE
SOHO SQUARE
GREEK ST
DEAN ST
FRITH ST
WARDOUR ST
OLD COMPTON ST
BERWICK ST
RATHBONE PL
NEWMAN ST
BERNERS ST
WHITFIELD ST
GOWER ST
MONTAGUE PL
GREAT RUSSELL ST
ENDELL ST
MONMOUTH ST
NEAL ST
SHORTS GDNS
LONG ACRE
GARRICK ST
ST. MARTIN'S LA
CRANBOURN ST
LISLE ST
GERRARD ST
RUPERT ST
BREWER ST
GT. PULTENEY ST
LEXINGTON ST
BROADWICK ST
D'ARBLAY ST
NOEL ST
PERCY ST
CHARLOTTE ST
HANWAY ST
SUTTON ROW
DENMARK ST
FLITCROFT ST
EARLHAM ST
STACEY ST
NEW COMPTON ST
A401
ROYAL MAIL
CENTREPOINT
DOMINION
PHOENIX
PALACE
PRINCE EDWARD
FOYLES
CURZON
ODEON
GIELGUD
APOLLO
LYRIC
QUEEN'S
PRINCE CHARLES
HIPPODROME
VUE
EMPIRE
WYNDHAM'S
NOEL COWARD
CINEWORLD
DONMAR WAREHO
CARTOON MUS.
THE COLL OF LAW
CAVENDISH COLL
SCH OF ARCHIT
St. Patrick (RC)
St. Anne
St. Giles
Soho Parish Sch
Fire Sta
Senate Ho
Myhotel
Kenilworth
Marlborough
Jurys
Travelodge
Scientology
French Protestant
Baptist
Swiss
Quakers
Sports Cen
Comm Cen
Mountbatten
Orion Ho
PHOTO GALL
AFRICA CEN
0 — 250 yds
0 — 250 m

D
E
F
25
38
49
1
2
3
4
SOUTHAMPTON
THEOBALD'S
GARDENS
Gray's Inn
LAW SCH
BEDFORD
PRINCETON ST
RED LION
SQUARE
EAGLE STREET
LION
SANDLAND ST
THREE CUPS YD
HAND CT
BROWN ST
LAW SCH
FULWOOD PL
WAR. CT
GRAY'S INN SQ
SOUTH SQ
Chapel
CHANCERY LANE
PO
Cittie Of York PH
London Silver Vaults
SOUTHAMPTON BLDGS
STONE BLDGS
B400
CHANCERY
NAT ARCH
QUALITY CT
COCHRANE
CEN ST. MARTIN'S COLL OF ART & DESIGN
DRAKE ST
PROCTER ST
FISHER ST
CATTON ST
SICILIAN AV
SOUTH. PL
BLOOMSBURY SQUARE
GDNS
BLOOMSBURY WAY
Holborn
HOLBORN
Citadines
94
268
Lib
BT Archive
Renaissance
NEW TURNSTILE
LITTLE TURNSTILE
WHETSTONE PK
LINCOLN'S
GATE ST
HIGH HOLBORN
BARTER ST
NEWTON ST
ARIA HO
Parker Twr
(RC)
REMNANT ST
MUS
HOLBORN
LINCOLN'S INN FIELDS
CAMDEN
Chapel
Hall
Lincoln's Inn
NEW SQUARE
SERLE ST
STAR YD
BISHOP'S CT
CHI. RE.
KENSINGTON BUS COLL
Tenn Ct
OLD CURIOSITY SHOP
INN FIELDS
H.M. LAND REGISTRY
ROYAL COLL OF SURGEONS OF ENGLAND
CAREY ST
COMP. COMM.
ROYAL COURTS OF JUSTICE
YARD
STUKELEY ST
CITY LIT
Stukeley St
St. Joseph's RC Prim Sch
MACKLIN ST
PARKER MS
PARKER ST
DRURY
QUEEN ST
KINGSWAY
Kingsway Hall
WILD CT
KEELEY ST
Freemasons' Hall
CITY LIT
C.A.A.
WILD ST
NEW LON
GT
LANE
SARDINIA ST
PORTSMOUTH ST
SHEFF ST
PORTUGAL ST
CLEM. LA
CLARE MKT
CLEM. INN PAS
GRANGE CT
WC2
B402
PEACOCK
KEMBLE ST
KEAN ST
LON SCH OF ECO & POL SCI.
CLEMENT'S INN
NEW INN PAS
HOUGH. ST
PO
St. Clement Danes Prim Sch
DRURY
BROAD CT
MARTLETT CT
CROWN CT
ENDELL
BOW ST
BALLET SCH
ROYAL OPERA HO
FORTUNE THEATRE
ROYAL
RUSSELL
CATH.
WELLINGTON ST
TAVISTOCK ST
ALDWYCH
Waldorf
NOVELLO
ALDWYCH
St. Clement Danes
George PH
STRAND
AUSTRALIA
MELB. PL
B.B.C.
INDIA
INDIA PL
STRAND
St. Mary-le-Strand
NEW THEA
ARUNDEL ST
ARUNDEL GREAT CT
SURREY ST
MILFORD LA
ESSEX ST
DEV. CT
NEW CT
MALTR. ST
WAT. ST
TW. ALL
COVENT GDN
The Market
TRANSPORT MUS
St. Paul
Jubilee Hall
Rec Cen
DUCHESS
One Aldwych
COURTAULD GALL & MUS
KING'S COLL (Strand Campus)
Chapel
STRAND LA
Howard
TEMPLE PL
TEMPLE
HENRIETTA ST
SOUTHAMPTON ST
TAVIST.
EXETER ST
BURLEIGH ST
LYCEUM
LANCASTER PL
SOMERSET HOUSE
VICTORIA
EMB
STRAND
Strand Palace
A4
SAVOY ST
Chapel
MAIDEN LA
BULL INN CT
ADEL
ZIMBABWE
VAUDEVILLE
404
Temple Pier
ST. KATHERINE
WESTMINSTER
WELL MASTER

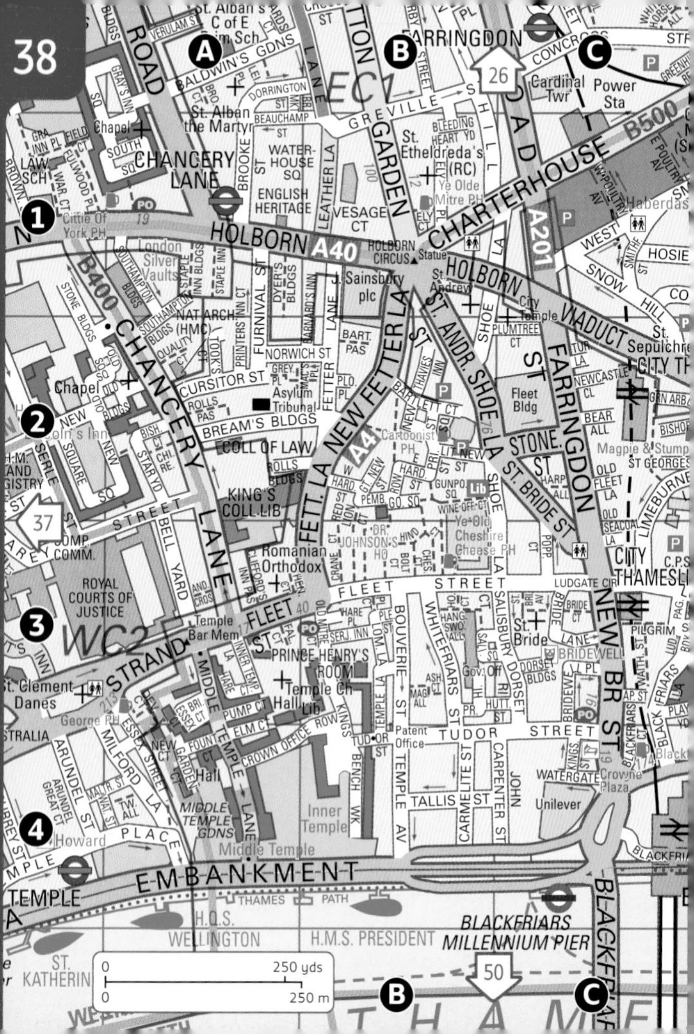
A
B
C
1
2
3
4
FARRINGDON
EC1
WC2
26
37
50
St. Alban's C of E Prim Sch
BALDWIN'S GDNS
DORRINGTON ST
St. Alban the Martyr
BEAUCHAMP ST
GREVILLE ST
BLEEDING HEART YD
St. Etheldreda's (RC)
Ye Olde Mitre PH
COWCROSS ST
Cardinal Twr
Power Sta
B500
CHARTERHOUSE
A201
Haberdas
WEST
HOSIER
SNOW HILL
GRAY'S INN SQ
Chapel
SOUTH SQ
CHANCERY LANE
LAW SCH
FULWOOD PL
WAR. CT
BROOKE ST
WATER-HOUSE SQ
ENGLISH HERITAGE
LEATHER LA
VESAGE CT
HATTON GARDEN
ELY PL
ELY CT
PO
Cittie Of York PH
HOLBORN A40
HOLBORN CIRCUS
Statue
London Silver Vaults
SOUTHAMPTON BLDGS
STAPLE INN BLDGS
STAPLE INN
FURNIVAL ST
DYER'S BLDGS
BARNARD'S INN
FETTER LANE
J. Sainsbury plc
St. Andrew
HOLBORN VIADUCT
City Temple
SHOE LA
PLUMTREE CT
St. Sepulchre
CITY TH
B400
STONE BLDGS
CHANCERY LANE
NAT. ARCH. (HMC)
QUALITY CT
TOOK'S CT
PRINTERS INN CT
NORWICH ST
BART. PAS
NEW FETTER LA
ST. ANDR. SHOE LA
THAVIES INN
FLEET BLDG
FARRINGDON ST
NEWCASTLE CL
BEAR ALL
Magpie & Stump
ST GEORGES
CURSITOR ST
Asylum Tribunal
ROLLS PAS
BREAM'S BLDGS
COLL OF LAW
ROLLS BLDGS
KING'S COLL LIB
Chapel
NEW SQUARE
Lincoln's Inn
SERLE ST
BISH. CT
CHI. RE.
STAR YD
A4
Cartoonist PH
BARTLETT CT
HARD
PEMB.
GUNPO. SQ
WINE OFF. CT
Lib
Ye Olde Cheshire Cheese PH
STONE. CUTTER ST
ST. BRIDE ST
OLD FLEET LA
OLD SEACOAL LA
LIMEBURNER
CITY THAMESLINK
C.P.S.
H.M. LAND REGISTRY
CAREY ST
COMP. COMM.
STREET
BELL YARD
Romanian Orthodox
DR. JOHNSON'S HO
CRANE CT
BOLT CT
FLEET STREET
LUDGATE CIR
ROYAL COURTS OF JUSTICE
Temple Bar Mem
FLEET ST
OLD MITRE CT
HARE PL
SERJ. INN
PRINCE HENRY'S ROOM
Temple Ch
Hall
Lib
BOUVERIE ST
WHITEFRIARS ST
SALISBURY CT
DORSET RI
St. Bride
BRIDE LANE
BRIDEWELL
NEW BR ST
PILGRIM ST
St. Clement Danes
STRAND
George PH
AUSTRALIA
ARUNDEL ST
MILFORD LA
ESSEX ST
MIDDLE TEMPLE LANE
PUMP CT
ELM CT
CROWN OFFICE ROW
KINGS BENCH WK
TUDOR ST
Patent Office
TEMPLE AV
TUDOR STREET
CARMELITE ST
CARPENTER ST
JOHN CARPENTER ST
TALLIS ST
Gov. Off
DORSET BLDGS
WATERGATE
Crowne Plaza
Unilever
BLACKFRIARS LA
PLAYHOUSE YD
NEW CT
Hall
MIDDLE TEMPLE GDNS
Inner Temple
Middle Temple
Howard
TEMPLE PLACE
TEMPLE
EMBANKMENT
THAMES PATH
H.Q.S. WELLINGTON
H.M.S. PRESIDENT
BLACKFRIARS MILLENNIUM PIER
BLACKFRIARS
ST. KATHERINE
0
250 yds
0
250 m

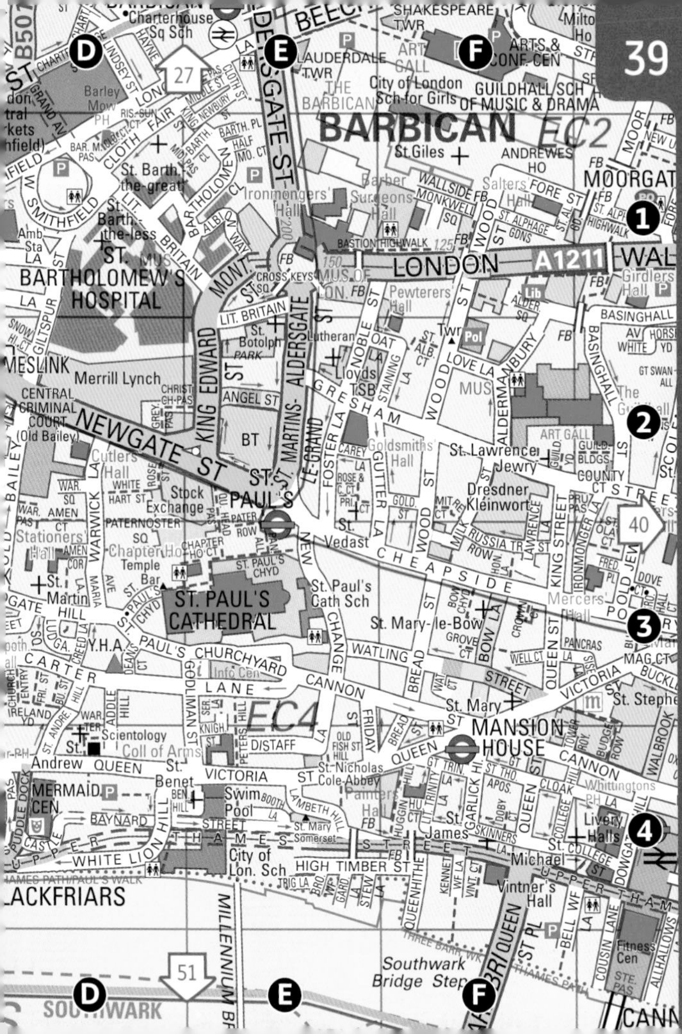
D
E
F
Charterhouse Sq Sch
27
SHAKESPEARE TWR
ARTS & CONF. CEN
LAUDERDALE TWR
ART GALL
THE BARBICAN
City of London Sch for Girls
GUILDHALL SCH OF MUSIC & DRAMA
BARBICAN
EC2
St. Giles
ANDREWES HO
MOORGATE
Barley Mow PH
CLOTH FAIR
St. Barth.-the-great
St. Barth.-the-less
W. SMITHFIELD
LIT. BRITAIN
BARTHOLOMEW CL
Ironmongers' Hall
Barber Surgeons' Hall
WALLSIDE
MONKWELL SQ
FORE ST
Salters' Hall
ST. ALPHAGE GDNS
HIGHWALK
1
BASTION HIGHWALK
LONDON WALL
A1211
MUS. OF LON.
Pewterers' Hall
Girdlers' Hall
ALDER. SQ
BASINGHALL AV
ST. BARTHOLOMEW'S HOSPITAL
MONT. ST
CROSS KEYS SQ
St. Botolph PARK
Lutheran
ALDERSGATE
KING EDWARD ST
ANGEL ST
BT
ST. MARTINS-LE-GRAND
Lloyds TSB
NOBLE ST
OAT LA
STAINING LA
WOOD ST
LOVE LA
ALDERMANBURY
BASINGHALL ST
MUS
The Guildhall
2
ART GALL
Merrill Lynch
CENTRAL CRIMINAL COURT (Old Bailey)
NEWGATE ST
GRESHAM ST
FOSTER LA
Goldsmiths' Hall
St. Lawrence Jewry
GUTTER LA
Dresdner Kleinwort
KING STREET
IRONMONGER LA
COUNTY
40
Cutlers' Hall
WARWICK LA
Stock Exchange
ST. PAUL'S
PATERNOSTER SQ
PATERNOSTER ROW
St. Vedast
MILK ST
RUSSIA ROW
CHEAPSIDE
OLD JEWRY
Mercers' Hall
POULTRY
3
Stationers' Hall
AMEN CT
Chapter Ho
Temple Bar
ST. PAUL'S CHYD
ST. PAUL'S CATHEDRAL
St. Paul's Cath Sch
St. Martin
LUDGATE HILL
St. Mary-le-Bow
BOW LA
GROVE CT
Y.H.A.
PAUL'S CHURCHYARD
NEW CHANGE
WATLING ST
BREAD ST
QUEEN ST
MAG. CT
CARTER LANE
Info Cen
CANNON ST
VICTORIA ST
St. Stephen
St. Mary
MANSION HOUSE
EC4
Scientology
St. Andrew
Coll of Arms
DISTAFF LA
OLD FISH ST HILL
FRIDAY ST
QUEEN VICTORIA ST
St. Benet
St. Nicholas Cole Abbey
Painters' Hall
GARLICK HILL
CANNON ST
Whittingtons PH
MERMAID CEN
BAYNARD
Swim Pool
LAMBETH HILL
St. Mary Somerset
St. James
St. Michael
Livery Halls
4
COLLEGE ST
UPPER THAMES STREET
WHITE LION HILL
City of Lon. Sch
HIGH TIMBER ST
QUEENHITHE
Vintner's Hall
DOWGATE HILL
THAMES PATH/PAUL'S WALK
BLACKFRIARS
MILLENNIUM BR
THREE BARR. WK
THAMES PATH
Southwark Bridge Steps
SOUTHWARK BRIDGE
QUEEN ST PL
BELL WF LA
COUSIN LANE
ALLHALLOWS LA
Fitness Cen
51
SOUTHWARK
CANNON

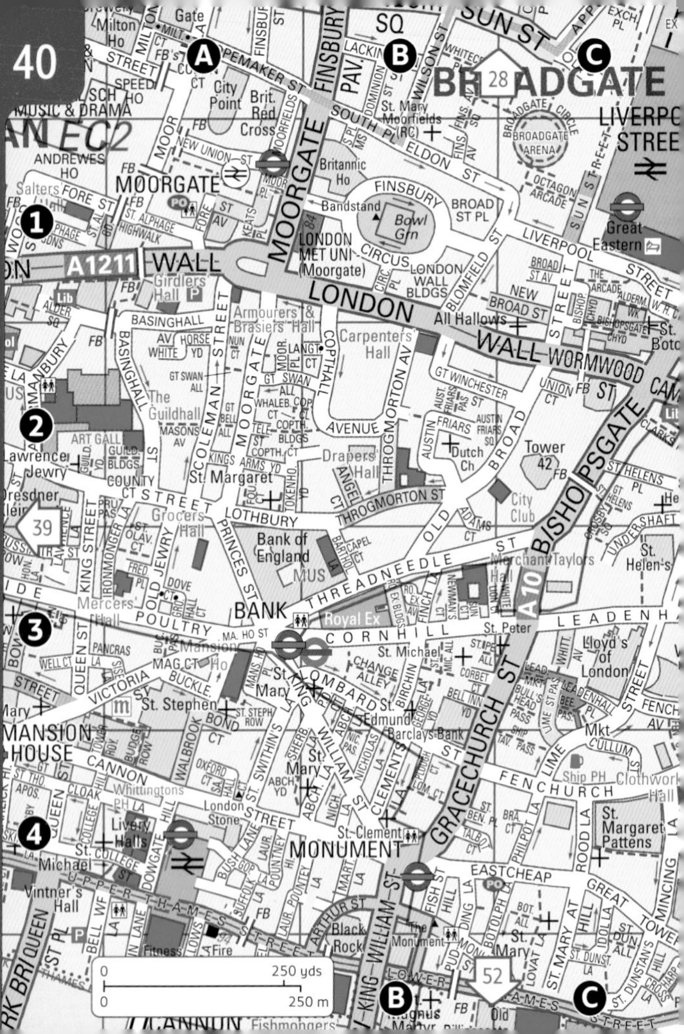
A
B
C
BROADGATE
28
LIVERPOOL STREET
EC2
MOORGATE
FINSBURY CIRCUS
Bowl Grn
Bandstand
Britannic Ho
City Point
Brit. Red Cross
ROPEMAKER ST
FINSBURY PAV.
SOUTH PL
ELDON ST
St. Mary Moorfields (RC)
BROADGATE ARENA
BROADGATE CIRCLE
OCTAGON ARCADE
Great Eastern
ANDREWES HO
Salters Hall
FORE ST
ST. ALPHAGE HIGHWALK
A1211
LONDON WALL
LONDON MET UNI (Moorgate)
LONDON WALL BLDGS
BLOMFIELD ST
BROAD ST PL
NEW BROAD ST
All Hallows
WORMWOOD ST
Girdlers' Hall
Armourers' & Brasiers' Hall
Carpenters' Hall
BASINGHALL ST
BASINGHALL AV
ALDERMANBURY
COLEMAN STREET
MOORGATE
COPTHALL AV
THROGMORTON AV
AUSTIN FRIARS
Dutch Ch
Tower 42
The Guildhall
ART GALL
Drapers' Hall
THROGMORTON ST
St. Margaret
St. Lawrence Jewry
GRESHAM STREET
39
LOTHBURY
Grocers' Hall
Bank of England
MUS
City Club
OLD BROAD ST
BISHOPSGATE
A10
Merchant Taylors' Hall
St. Helen's
THREADNEEDLE ST
BANK
Royal Ex
CORNHILL
St. Peter
St. Michael
LEADENHALL ST
Lloyd's of London
POULTRY
Mercers' Hall
Mansion Ho
KING STREET
QUEEN ST
VICTORIA ST
St. Stephen
St. Mary
LOMBARD ST
St. Edmund
Barclays Bank
GRACECHURCH ST
FENCHURCH ST
Clothworkers' Hall
Ship PH
MANSION HOUSE
CANNON ST
Whittingtons
London Stone
St. Mary
St. Clement
MONUMENT
St. Margaret Pattens
EASTCHEAP
GREAT TOWER ST
Livery Halls
St. Michael
Vintner's Hall
UPPER THAMES ST
Fire
Fitness
Black Rock
KING WILLIAM ST
The Monument
St. Mary
52
LOWER THAMES STREET
St. Magnus Martyr
Fishmongers
CANNON
SOUTHWARK BRIDGE
0 250 yds
0 250 m

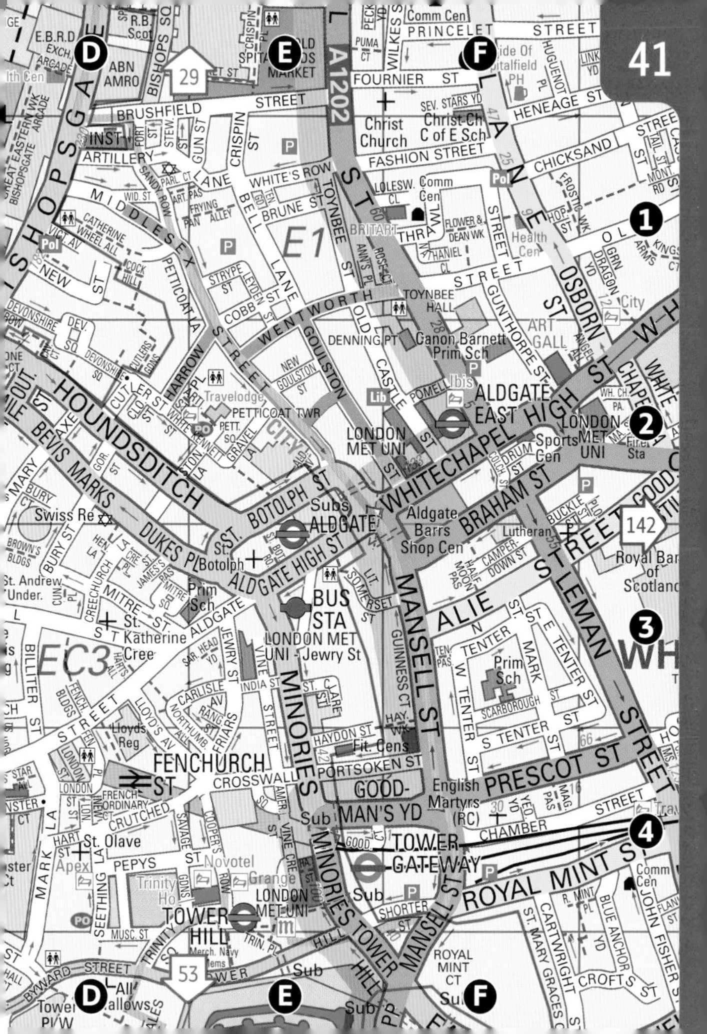
D
E
F
1
2
3
4
29
142
53
A1202
E1
EC3
E.B.R.D
EXCH. ARCADE
ABN AMRO
R.B. Scot
BISHOPS SQ
BISHOPSGATE
OLD SPITALFIELDS MARKET
PRINCELET STREET
FOURNIER ST
HENEAGE ST
BRUSHFIELD STREET
Christ Church
Christ Ch C of E Sch
FASHION STREET
CHICKSAND STREET
ARTILLERY LANE
GUN ST
CRISPIN ST
WHITE'S ROW
TOYNBEE ST
BRICK LANE
MIDDLESEX STREET
CATHERINE WHEEL ALL
FRYING PAN ALLEY
BELL LANE
BRUNE ST
THRAWL ST
FLOWER & DEAN WK
Health Cen
OSBORN ST
OLD MONTAGUE ST
NEW ST
COCK HILL
PETTICOAT LA
STRYPE ST
COBB ST
WENTWORTH STREET
TOYNBEE HALL
GUNTHORPE ST
City
DEVONSHIRE SQ
CUTLERS GDNS
GOULSTON ST
OLD CASTLE ST
DENNING PT
Canon Barnett Prim Sch
ART GALL.
WHITECHAPEL HIGH ST
HARROW PL
Travelodge
PETTICOAT TWR
NEW GOULSTON ST
Ibis
ALDGATE EAST
LONDON MET UNI
Sports Cen
Fire Sta
HOUNDSDITCH
CUTLER ST
WHITE KENNETT ST
GRAVEL LA
CITY
BEVIS MARKS
BRAHAM ST
DRUM ST
ST. BOTOLPH ST
Subs
ALDGATE
Aldgate Barrs Shop Cen
BUCKLE ST
Lutheran
Swiss Re
DUKES PL
St. Botolph
ALDGATE HIGH ST
CAMPERDOWN ST
HALF MOON PAS
LEMAN STREET
Royal Bank of Scotland
BURY ST
St. Andrew Under.
CREECHURCH LA
MITRE ST
Prim Sch
BUS STA
LIT. SOMERSET ST
MANSELL ST
ALIE ST
St. Katherine Cree
ALDGATE
JEWRY ST
LONDON MET UNI - Jewry St
GUINNESS CT
TENTER GROUND
MARK ST
E TENTER ST
W TENTER ST
S TENTER ST
SCARBOROUGH ST
BILLITER ST
LEADENHALL STREET
Lloyds Reg
LLOYD'S AV
CARLISLE AV
INDIA ST
VINE STREET
MINORIES
ST. CLARE ST
HAYDON ST
Fit. Cens
PORTSOKEN ST
PRESCOT ST
FENCHURCH ST
CROSSWALL
GOODMAN'S YD
English Martyrs (RC)
CHAMBER STREET
MARK LA
HART ST
St. Olave
CRUTCHED FRIARS
COOPER'S ROW
Sub
TOWER GATEWAY
ROYAL MINT ST
Comm Cen
PEPYS ST
Novotel
Grange
Apex
Trinity Ho
LONDON MET UNI
SEETHING LA
MUSC. ST
TOWER HILL
TRIN. PL
SHORTER ST
ST. MARY GRACES CT
CARTWRIGHT ST
BLUE ANCHOR YD
JOHN FISHER ST
CROFTS ST
ROYAL MINT CT
Merch. Navy Mems
BYWARD STREET
All Hallows
Tower Pl W
TOWER HILL
TRINITY SQ

A
B
C
1
2
3
4
30
135
54
PEMBRIDGE CRES
PEMBRIDGE
PEMBRIDGE RD
PEMBRIDGE SQUARE
PEMBRIDGE SQ
PEMBRIDGE PL
DAWSON PL
Spiritual
Premier
Bayswater Inn
PRINCES MS
GREEK CATH
Fit. Cen
MOSCOW RD
MOSCOW PL
BARK PLACE
ST. PETERSBURGH PL
ST. PETERSBURGH MS
St. Matthew
ORME LA
ORME SQ
Ormonde Square
Spanish Chapel (RC)
Ramada
GUYANA
Pembridge Hall Sch
Pembridge Hall School
GARDEN MS
LINDEN GARDENS
LINDEN GDNS
THE LIMES
CLANRICARDE GDNS
VICTORIA GRO MS
OSSINGTON STREET
OSSINGTON CL
PALACE CT
CHAPEL SIDE
BAYSWATER
PARK
B415
PORTOBELLO MS
Southbank Int Sch
LADBROKE SQUARE
LADBROKE TERRACE
LADBROKE WALK
HORBURY CR.
HORBURY MS
Temple
Lib
NOTTING HILL GATE
Comfort
LIN. MS.
GATE
HILL GATE
CZECH REP
SLOVAK REP
Unitarian
BROADWALK CT
WEST MALL
RAP. ROW
PO
KENS. MA.
KENSINGTON PALACE GDNS
KENSINGTON PALACE
Christian Science
LEBANON
NEPAL
RUSSIA
ROMANIA
ISRA
PALACE GARDENS TER
PALACE GARDENS MS
VICTORIA GDNS
CAMPDEN HILL TWRS
BULMER MS
BULMER PL
CORONET
Sub
UXBRIDGE STREET
FARM PL
FARMER ST
CALL. ST.
HILLGATE ST
HILLGATE PLACE
JAMESON ST
NEWCOMBE ST
KENSINGTON PLACE
EDGE ST
AVENUE
CAMPDEN HILL
CAMPDEN HILL SQ
CAMPDEN HILL RD
HILLSLEIGH RD
CAM. HILL GDNS
CAMPDEN HILL GDNS
St. George
WALK
WYCOMBE SQ
WY. SQ
Pav
Tenn Cts
PALMERSTON HOUSE
Fox Prim Sch
FOX STREET
PEEL STREET
PEEL PAS
CAMPDEN STREET
BEDFORD GARDENS
SHEFFIELD TERRACE
AIRLIE GDNS
STRATHM. GDNS
LUC. MS
BRUNSWICK GARDENS
BERK. GD.
INVER. GDNS
W8
KENSINGTON CHURCH STREET
St Mary Abbots Church Hall
VICARAGE GATE
VIC. GDNS
MELON PL
NICARAGUA
KENSINGTON
HOLLAND PARK
Holland Park Sch
CAMPDEN HILL
THORNWOOD GDNS
TOR GDNS
CAMPDEN HO CL
HORNTON STREET
GLOUCESTER WK
CAMPDEN GRO
GORDON PL
OBSER.V. GDNS
Our Lady (R.C.)
CHURCH CL
HOUSE PL
YORK HOUSE PL
DUKES LA
CARM. CT
HOLL. PL
PITT ST
GORDON PL
LANCER SQ
Fire Sta
OLD CT
SHELDRAKE PLACE
ACADEMY GARDENS
CAMPDEN HILL GATE
CAMPDEN HILL COURT
DUCHESS OF BEDFORD'S WK
HOLLAND STREET
DRAYSON MS
KEN. CH WK.
GREGORY PL
St. Mary Abbots
St. Mary Abbots C of E Prim Sch
YHA
0 250 yds
0 250 m
CAMPDEN
KENSINGTON
JORDAN
Northcliffe

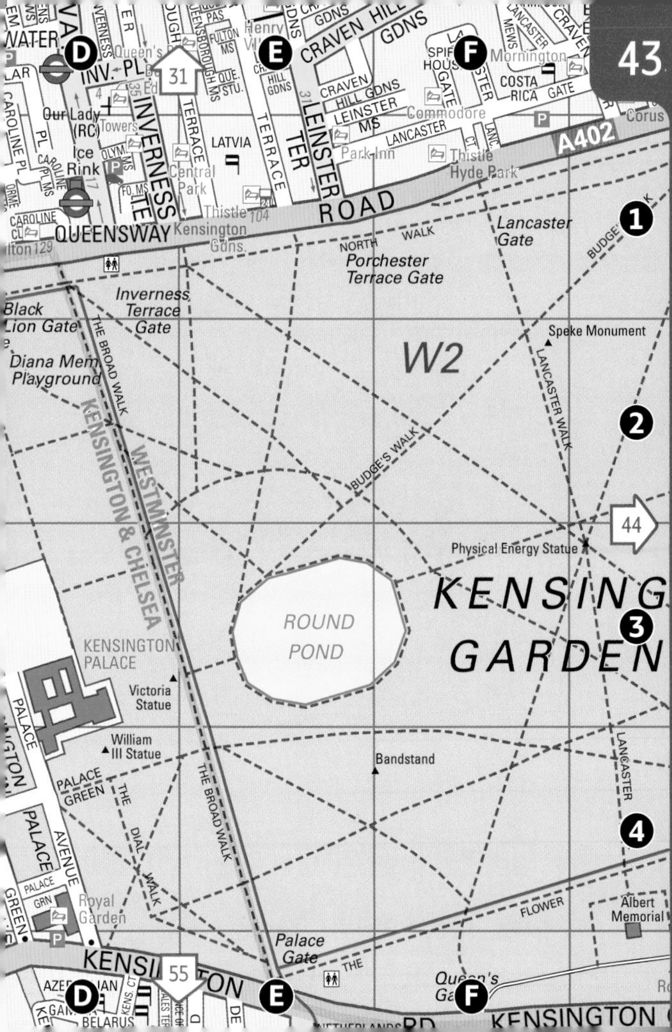
CRAVEN HILL GDNS
CRAVEN HILL GDNS
LEINSTER MS
LEINSTER TER
LANCASTER
COSTA RICA GATE
Mornington
Commodore
Corus
A402
Park Inn
Thistle Hyde Park
LATVIA
Central Park
Thistle
INVERNESS TER
TERRACE
Our Lady (RC)
Towers
Ice Rink
QUEENSWAY
Kensington Gdns.
ROAD
31
Lancaster Gate
NORTH WALK
Porchester Terrace Gate
Inverness Terrace Gate
Black Lion Gate
Diana Mem. Playground
THE BROAD WALK
BUDGE'S WALK
Speke Monument
W2
LANCASTER WALK
KENSINGTON & CHELSEA
WESTMINSTER
44
Physical Energy Statue
ROUND POND
KENSINGTON GARDEN
KENSINGTON PALACE
Victoria Statue
William III Statue
Bandstand
PALACE GREEN
THE DIAL WALK
THE BROAD WALK
PALACE AVENUE
Royal Garden
FLOWER
Albert Memorial
Palace Gate
55
KENSINGTON RD
BELARUS
D
E
F
1
2
3
4

BARRIE ESTATE
CRAVEN
LANCASTER
STANHOPE
BAYSWATER
Closed to traffic midnight to
Royal Lancaster
LANCASTER GATE
Vic Gate
THE (NORTH
A402
Corus
Marlborough Gate
The Fountains
THE (WEST CARRIAGE DRIVE) RING
BUCK HILL WALK
Closed to traffic midnight to 5 am
NORTH RIDE
Lancaster Gate
BUDGE'S WALK
Speke Monument
LANCASTER WALK
Peter Pan
THE LONG WATER
W2
43
Physical Energy Statue
Queens Temple
KENSINGTON GARDENS
SERPENTINE GALLERY
THE (WEST CARRIAGE DRIVE) RING
Lido
Diana Princess of Wales Memorial
ROAD
NEW RIDE
WALK
FLOWER WALK
Tenn Cts
PUTTING GREEN
Pav
Bowl Grn
SW7
Prince of Wales Gate
Albert Memorial
Coalbrookdale Gate
EXHIBITION
SOUTH CARRIAGE
St. Nicholas
KENSINGTON RD
56
UAE
PRINCES GATE
IRAN
KENSINGTON GORE
0 250 yds
0 250 m
A
B
C
1
2
3
4

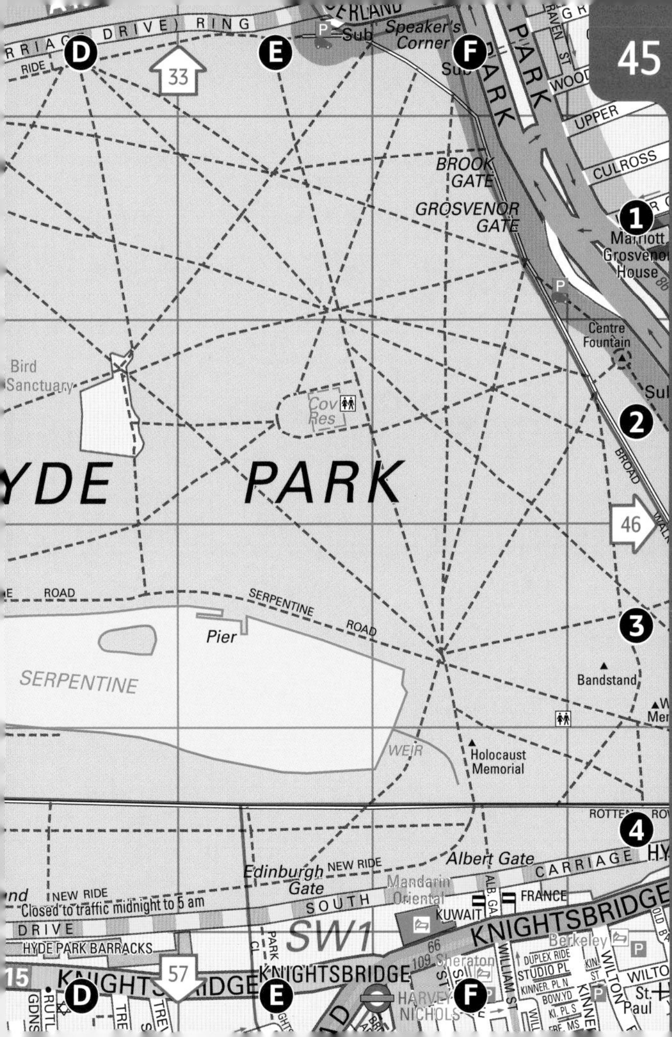
(DRIVE) RING
RIDE
D
E
F
33
Sub
Speaker's Corner
Sub
PARK
PARK
RAVEN ST
WOOD
UPPER
CULROSS
BROOK GATE
GROSVENOR GATE
1
Marriott Grosvenor House
P
Centre Fountain
Sub
2
BROAD WALK
46
Bird Sanctuary
Cov Res
HYDE PARK
ROAD
SERPENTINE ROAD
Pier
SERPENTINE
3
Bandstand
WEIR
Holocaust Memorial
ROTTEN ROW
4
Albert Gate
CARRIAGE
Edinburgh Gate
NEW RIDE
NEW RIDE
Closed to traffic midnight to 5 am
Mandarin Oriental
ALB. GA
FRANCE
KUWAIT
SOUTH
DRIVE
SW1
KNIGHTSBRIDGE
HYDE PARK BARRACKS
PARK CL
Berkeley
P
66
109
Sheraton
WILLIAM ST
DUPLEX RIDE
STUDIO PL
KINNER. PL N
BOW.YD
KI. PL S
KIN.
ST.
KINNE
WILTON
WILTO
St. Paul
15
KNIGHTSBRIDGE
57
KNIGHTSBRIDGE
D
E
F
HARVEY NICHOLS
GDNS
RUTL
TRE
TREV
P

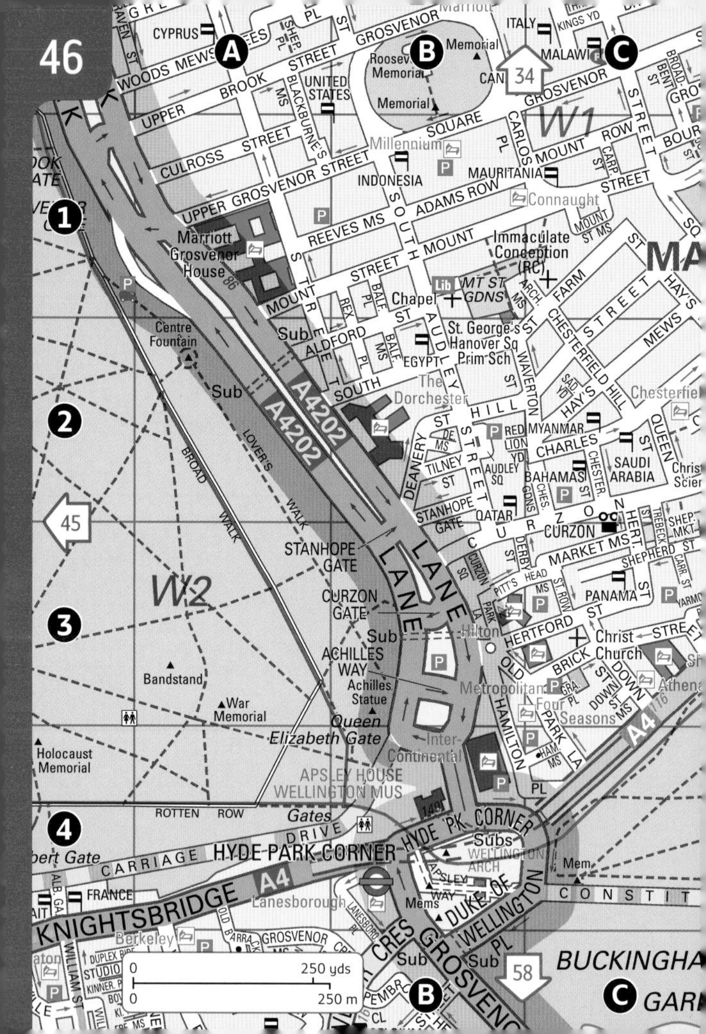
A
B
C
1
2
3
4
34
45
58
W1
W2
CYPRUS
WOODS MEWS
UPPER BROOK STREET
GROSVENOR
SHEP. PL
BLACKBURNE'S MS
UNITED STATES
Roosevelt Memorial
Memorial
ITALY
KINGS YD
MALAWI
CAN
CULROSS STREET
UPPER GROSVENOR STREET
GROSVENOR SQUARE
Millennium
INDONESIA
CARLOS PL
MOUNT ROW
CARP. ST
MAURITANIA
Connaught
UPPER GROSVENOR STREET
REEVES MS
ADAMS ROW
SOUTH
MOUNT ST MS
Immaculate Conception (RC)
Marriott Grosvenor House
MOUNT STREET
STREET
Lib
MT ST GDNS
ARCH.
FARM
STREET
HAY'S MEWS
Chapel
BALF. PL
REX
Centre Fountain
Sub
ALDFORD ST
St. George's Hanover Sq Prim Sch
AUDLEY
CHESTERFIELD HILL
BALF. MS
EGYPT
WAVERTON ST
SOUTH
The Dorchester
HAY'S
Chesterfield
A4202
LOVER'S WALK
BROAD WALK
DEANERY ST
DE. MS
HILL
RED LION YD
MYANMAR
CHARLES
QUEEN ST
SAUDI ARABIA
TILNEY ST
AUDLEY SQ
STREET
BAHAMAS
CHESTER. ST
STANHOPE GATE
QATAR
CURZON
CURZON
HERT. ST
TREBECK ST
SHEP. MKT
STANHOPE GATE
LANE
LANE
DERBY ST
MARKET MS
SHEPHERD ST
CURZON SQ
PITT'S HEAD MS
ST. ROW
PANAMA
CURZON GATE
HERTFORD ST
Hilton
Christ Church
Sub
PARK LA
OLD PARK LA
BRICK ST
DOWN ST
ACHILLES WAY
Achilles Statue
Bandstand
War Memorial
Metropolitan
Four Seasons
HAMILTON
PARK LA
HAM. MS
A4
Queen Elizabeth Gate
Inter-Continental
Holocaust Memorial
APSLEY HOUSE WELLINGTON MUS
PL
ROTTEN ROW
Gates
HYDE PK CORNER
CARRIAGE DRIVE
HYDE PARK CORNER
Subs
WELLINGTON ARCH
Mem
CONSTIT
bert Gate
A4
APSLEY WAY
FRANCE
KNIGHTSBRIDGE
Lanesborough
DUKE OF WELLINGTON PL
Mems
Berkeley
GROSVENOR CRES
LANESBORO. PL
CRES
GROSVENOR
Sub
WILLIAM ST
DUPLEX RIDE
STUDIO
0 250 yds
0 250 m
BUCKINGHAM
GAR

D
E
F
35
48
59
1
2
3
4
SOTHEBY'S
BOURDON ST
HILL ST
BRUTON PLACE
BRUTON STREET
BERKELEY
MEDICI GALL
Berkeley Sq Ho
FAIR
BRUTON
HAY HILL
Lansdowne Ho
LANSDOWNE ROW
FITZM. PL
Radisson Edwardian
Washington
CLARGES
BOLTON ST
STRATTON ST
Flemings
HALF MOON ST
Hilton
HORSE
Westbury
NEW BOND ST
CLIFFORD
GRAFTON ST
ALBEMARLE
FARADAY MUS
DOVER
Brown's
STAFFORD ST
DOVER ST
MAYFAIR PL
Holiday Inn
BURLINGTON GDNS
CORK ST
OLD BURLINGTON ST
SAVILE ROW
VIGO ST
AQUASCUTUM
ROYAL ACAD. OF ARTS
BURLINGTON ARCADE
Burlington Ho
OLD BOND ST
FORTNUM & MASON
WATERSTONE'S
ALBANY
SACKVILLE
BURBERRY
HEDDON ST
REGENT STREET
WARWICK ST
Our Lady (RC)
GOLDEN
Absolute Radio
BREWER
GLASSHOUSE ST
AIR
PICCADILLY
DENMAN ST
SHERWOOD ST
Ripley's
Eros
PICCADILLY CIRCUS
LILLYWHITES
CRITERION
JERMYN ST.
APOLLO
Le Meridien
MALTA
St. James
Mkt
REGENT ST
BRITAIN VISITOR CEN
B.P.
CHARLES
JERMYN STREET
DUNHILL
Cavendish
WHITE CUBE
MASON'S YD
DUKE OF YORK ST
ORMOND YD
APPLE TREE YD
ST. JAMES'S
ST. JAMES SQ
SQUARE
RYDER ST
DUKE ST
BURY ST
WATER. WEDGW.
ARLINGTON ST
The Ritz
A4
PICCADILLY
GREEN PARK
ST. JAMES'S ST
PARK PL
BLUE BALL YD
Stafford
ST. JAMES'S PL
LITTLE ST. JAMES'S ST
KING ST
CHRISTIE'S
PRINCES
CROWN PAS
ANGEL CT
ROSE & CROWN YD
CLEVELAND PL
PALL MALL
ST. JAMES'S
PRIVY COUNCIL
Queen's Chapel
MARLBOROUGH HOUSE
COMMONWEALTH SECRETARIAT
SUDAN
RUSSELL CT
CATHERINE WHEEL YD
Spencer House
QUEEN'S WALK
CLEVELAND ROW
STABLE YARD
AMBASS. CT
FRIARY CT
MARLBOROUGH RD
STABLE YD
St. James's Palace
Clarence House
LANCASTER HOUSE
STABLE YARD RD
THE MALL
HORSE
Closed to Traffic on
ST.
Bandstand
THE GREEN PARK
Canadian War Mem
SW1
MEMORIAL
CONSTITUTION HILL
Closed to Traffic on Sundays
Queen Victoria Memorial
PALACE
GDNS
SPUR RD
BUCKINGHAM
FB

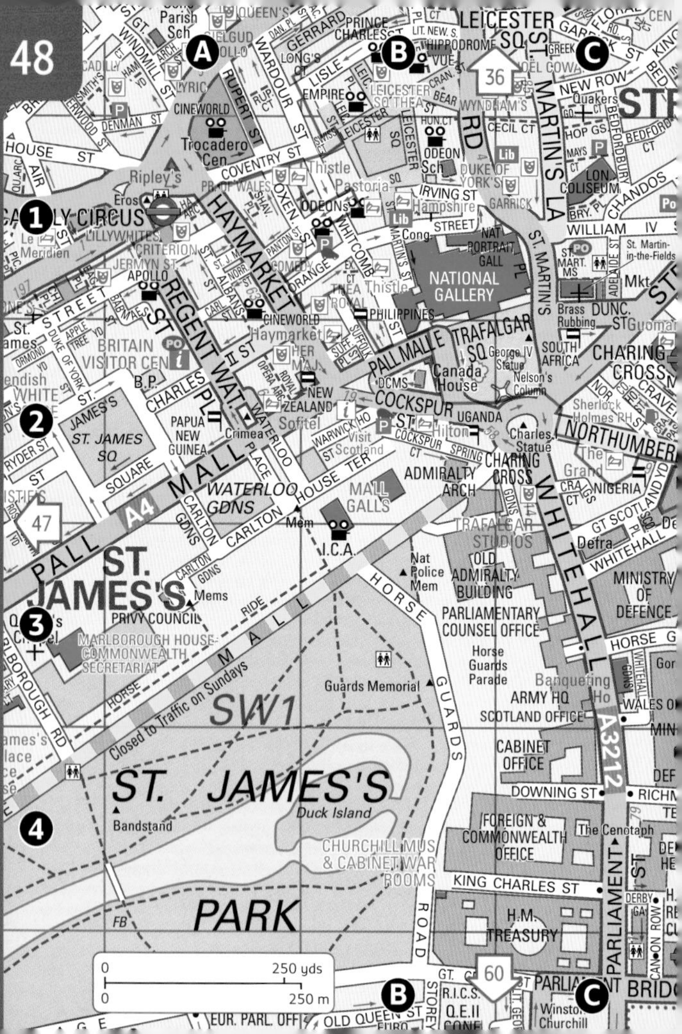
A
B
C
1
2
3
4
36
47
60
Parish Sch
QUEEN'S
GIELGUD
LYRIC
WINDMILL ST
GERRARD
PRINCE CHARLES
LEICESTER SQ
HIPPODROME
VUE
GARRICK ST
WARDOUR ST
LISLE
EMPIRE
LEICESTER SQ THEA
WYNDHAM'S
NEW ROW
Quakers
CINEWORLD
Trocadero Cen
RUPERT ST
DENMAN ST
HOUSE ST
AIR
COVENTRY ST
CECIL CT
HOP GS.
BEDFORD CT
BEDFORDBURY
ODEON
Sch
DUKE OF YORK'S
Lib
LON. COLISEUM
CHANDOS
Ripley's
Thistle
Pastoria
GARRICK
Eros
PICCADILLY CIRCUS
HAYMARKET
OXEN. ST
ODEONs
IRVING ST
Hampshire
ST. MARTIN'S LA
WILLIAM IV
Le Meridien
LILLYWHITES
CRITERION
JERMYN ST
APOLLO
COMEDY
ORANGE
WHITCOMB
Cong
STREET
NAT PORTRAIT GALL
ST. MARTIN'S PL
ST. MART. MS
St. Martin-in-the-Fields
ADELAIDE ST
Mkt
NATIONAL GALLERY
THEA ROYAL
Thistle
REGENT ST
ST. ALBANS
CINEWORLD
Haymarket
PHILIPPINES
Brass Rubbing
DUNC. ST
Guoman
St. James
DUKE OF YORK ST
APPLE TREE YD
BRITAIN VISITOR CEN
PO
HER MAJ.
SUFFOLK
PALL MALL E
TRAFALGAR SQ
George IV Statue
SOUTH AFRICA
CHARING CROSS
CRAVEN
WHITE
CHARLES II ST
B.P.
REGENT WAT. PL
NEW ZEALAND
DCMS
Canada House
Nelson's Column
ST. JAMES'S
ST. JAMES SQ
PAPUA NEW GUINEA
Crimea
WATERLOO PLACE
Sofitel
COCKSPUR ST
UGANDA
Charles I Statue
Sherlock Holmes PH
NORTHUMBERLAND
RYDER ST
WARWICK HO ST
Visit Scotland
Hilton
COCKSPUR CT
SPRING
CHARING CROSS
The Grand
SQUARE
MALL
WATERLOO GDNS
HOUSE TER
MALL GALLS
ADMIRALTY ARCH
NIGERIA
CRA. CT
A4
CARLTON GDNS
CARLTON
Mem
I.C.A.
TRAFALGAR STUDIOS
GT SCOTLAND YD
Defra
WHITEHALL
PALL
ST. JAMES'S
CARLTON GDNS
Mems
Nat Police Mem
OLD ADMIRALTY BUILDING
MINISTRY OF DEFENCE
PRIVY COUNCIL
RIDE
HORSE
Queen's Chapel
MARLBOROUGH HOUSE COMMONWEALTH SECRETARIAT
MALL
PARLIAMENTARY COUNSEL OFFICE
Horse Guards Parade
HORSE GUARDS
MARLBOROUGH RD
HORSE
Closed to Traffic on Sundays
Guards Memorial
Banqueting Ho
ARMY HQ
WALES OFFICE
SW1
SCOTLAND OFFICE
A3212
St. James's Palace
CABINET OFFICE
GUARDS
DOWNING ST
RICHMOND
ST. JAMES'S
Duck Island
Bandstand
FOREIGN & COMMONWEALTH OFFICE
The Cenotaph
CHURCHILL MUS & CABINET WAR ROOMS
KING CHARLES ST
PARLIAMENT ST
DERBY GA
CANNON ROW
PARK
FB
ROAD
H.M. TREASURY
0
250 yds
250 m
GT. GEORGE ST
R.I.C.S.
STOREY
Q.E.II CONF
PARLIAMENT
BRIDGE
Winston Churchill
EUR. PARL. OFF
OLD QUEEN ST

One Aldwych
Rec Cen
Jubilee Hall
Chapel
KING'S COLL (Strand Campus)
Howard
COURTAULD & MUS
LYCEUM
SOMERSET HOUSE
TEMPLE
D
E
F
37
A4
Strand Palace
SAVOY
VAUDEVILLE
ADELPHI
ZIMBABWE
Chapel
SAVOY WAY
The Savoy
Shell Mex Ho
LANCASTER PL
VICTORIA
Temple Pier
ST. KATHERINE
WELLINGTON
MASTER
WC2
WESTMINSTER
LAMBETH
1
A3211
T.S. QUEEN MARY
SAVOY PIER
WATERLOO BRI
RIVER
GDNS
Cleopatra's Needle
Charing Cross Pier
EMBANKMENT PIER
EMBANKMENT
Bandstand
NEW PLAYERS
PLAYHOUSE
THE ARCHES
Adelphi
THAMES PATH/THE QUEEN'S WK
BFI SOUTHBANK
IBM
2
QUEEN ELIZABETH HALL & PURCELL ROOM
NATIONAL THEATRE
A301
UPPER GROUND
Golden Jubilee Bri
Festival Pier
B308
Thistle
Savoy Pier
HUNGERFORD BRI
HISPANIOLA
ROYAL FESTIVAL HALL
HAYWARD GALLERY
50
KING'S COLL
SCHILLER INT UNI
Royal Horseguards Thistle
PS TATTERSHALL CASTLE
Golden Jubilee Bri
WHITEHOUSE APARTMENTS
CONCERT HALL APP
TENISON WAY
BFI IMAX
3
St. John the Evang
SE1
Shell Centre
SUTTON WK
MEPHAM ST
STATION
RAF Mem
JUBILEE GDNS
BELVEDERE
ROAD
WATERLOO MILLENNIUM PIER
A3200
WATERLOO
4
Battle of Britain Mem
LONDON EYE
CHICHELEY ST
County Hall
MOVIEUM
Premier Inn
LEAKE
Park Plaza
London Aquarium
YORK
WESTMINSTER MILLENNIUM PIER
WESTMINSTER
FORUM MAGNUM SQ
ADDINGTON ST
Boudicca
61
WESTMINSTER BRI
A302
Marriott
St. Stephen's Tower
LOWER
STATION
Lib

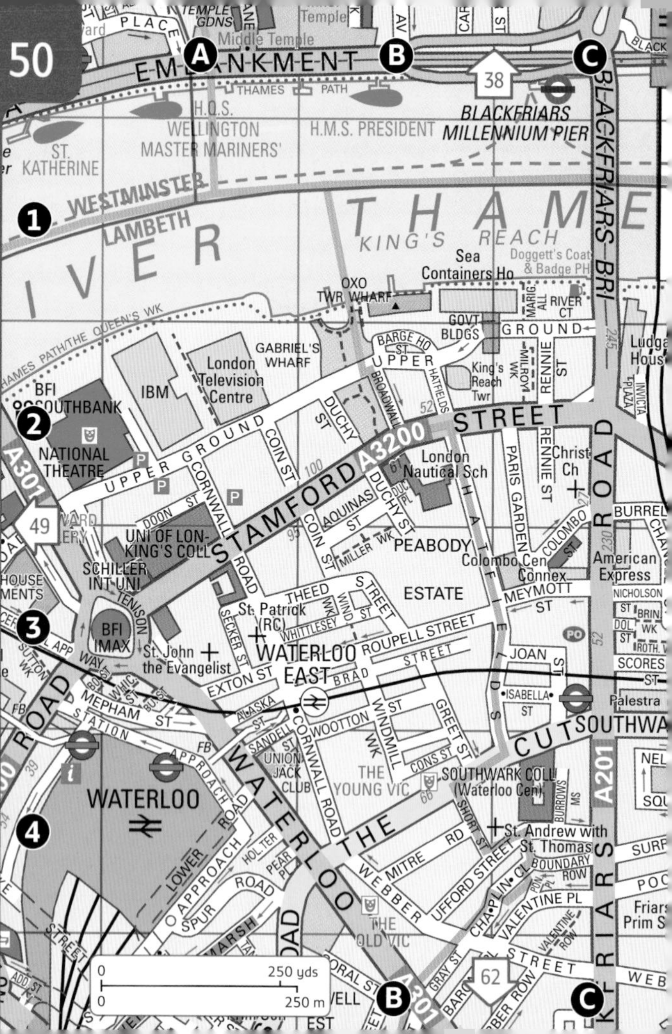
A
B
C
1
2
3
4
EMBANKMENT
TEMPLE GDNS
PLACE
Temple
Middle Temple
THAMES PATH
H.Q.S. WELLINGTON MASTER MARINERS'
H.M.S. PRESIDENT
38
BLACKFRIARS MILLENNIUM PIER
BLACKFRIARS BRI
ST. KATHERINE
WESTMINSTER
LAMBETH
RIVER THAMES
KING'S REACH
Sea Containers Ho
Doggett's Coat & Badge PH
OXO TWR WHARF
RIVER CT
GOVT BLDGS
GROUND
THAMES PATH/THE QUEEN'S WK
GABRIEL'S WHARF
London Television Centre
IBM
BARGE HO ST
UPPER
HATFIELDS
King's Reach Twr
MILROY WK
RENNIE ST
Ludgate House
INVICTA PLAZA
BFI SOUTHBANK
NATIONAL THEATRE
A301
UPPER GROUND
COIN ST
DUCHY ST
BROADWALL
STAMFORD STREET
A3200
London Nautical Sch
PARIS GARDEN
RENNIE ST
Christ Ch
ROAD
BURRELL
49
CORNWALL ROAD
DOON ST
AQUINAS ST
DUCHY ST
MILLER WK
PEABODY ESTATE
COLOMBO ST
Colombo Cen
Connex
American Express
UNI OF LONDON KING'S COLL
SCHILLER INT UNI
TENISON
THEED STREET
WIND WK
MEYMOTT ST
NICHOLSON
BRIN WK
BFI IMAX
St. Patrick (RC)
WHITTLESEY
ROUPELL STREET
HATFIELDS
St. John the Evangelist
WATERLOO EAST
SECKER ST
EXTON ST
BRAD STREET
JOAN ST
ISABELLA ST
SCORESBY ST
Palestra
SUTTON WK
MEPHAM ST
STATION
ALASKA ST
SANDELL ST
WOOTTON ST
WINDMILL WK
GREET ST
THE CUT
SOUTHWARK
A201
APPROACH
UNION JACK CLUB
CORNWALL ROAD
THE YOUNG VIC
CONS ST
SOUTHWARK COLL (Waterloo Cen)
BURROWS MS
WATERLOO
WATERLOO ROAD
SHORT ST
St. Andrew with St. Thomas
HOL. TER
PEAR PL
LOWER
ROAD
MITRE RD
BOUNDARY ROW
WEBBER
UFFORD STREET
CHAPLIN CL
VALENTINE PL
VALENTINE ROW
Friars Prim Sch
SPUR ROAD
APPROACH ROAD
MARSH
THE OLD VIC
GRAY ST
62
STREET
WEBBER
BLACKFRIARS ROAD
0 250 yds
0 250 m

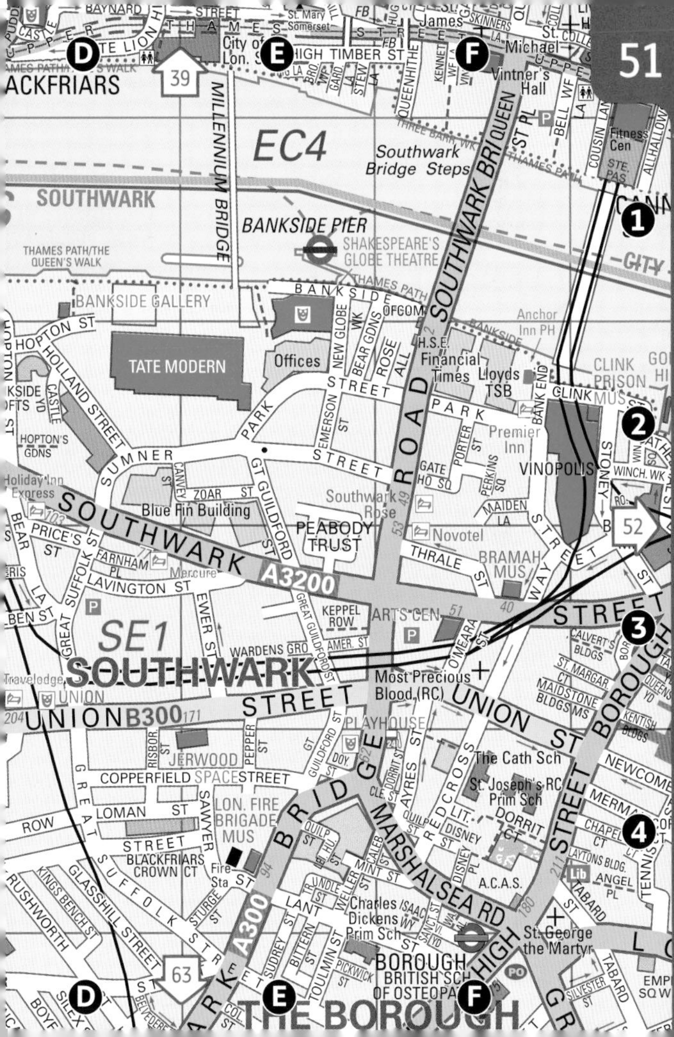
BAYNARD
STREET
THAMES
St. Mary Somerset
FB
James
SKINNERS
St. Michael
D
E
F
City of Lon.
HIGH TIMBER ST
BLACKFRIARS
39
MILLENNIUM BRIDGE
QUEENHITHE
Vintner's Hall
EC4
Southwark Bridge Steps
SOUTHWARK BRIDGE
QUEEN ST PL
BELL WF LA
COUSIN LANE
Fitness Cen
ALLHALLOWS
SOUTHWARK
BANKSIDE PIER
SHAKESPEARE'S GLOBE THEATRE
THAMES PATH/THE QUEEN'S WALK
THAMES PATH
CITY
1
BANKSIDE
BANKSIDE GALLERY
OFCOM
NEW GLOBE WK
BEAR GDNS
ROSE ALL
Anchor Inn PH
HOPTON ST
HOLLAND STREET
TATE MODERN
Offices
H.S.E.
Financial Times
Lloyds TSB
BANK END
CLINK PRISON MUS
CLINK ST
2
PARK STREET
EMERSON ST
HOPTON'S GDNS
SUMNER STREET
PORTER ST
Premier Inn
VINOPOLIS
STONEY STREET
WINCH. WK
ROAD
GATE HO SQ
PERKINS SQ
MAIDEN LA
Holiday Inn Express
SOUTHWARK STREET
CANVEY ST
ZOAR ST
GT GUILDFORD ST
Blue Fin Building
Southwark Rose
PEABODY TRUST
Novotel
52
BEAR
PRICE'S ST
SUFFOLK ST
FARNHAM PL
Mercure
THRALE ST
BRAMAH MUS
WAY
A3200
LAVINGTON ST
KEPPEL ROW
ARTS CEN
GREAT GUILDFORD ST
AMER. ST
SE1
GREAT SUFFOLK
EWER ST
WARDENS GRO
O'MEARA ST
STREET
3
CALVERT'S BLDGS
ST. MARGAR. CT
MAIDSTONE BLDGS MS
QUEENS YD
SOUTHWARK
Travelodge
UNION
Most Precious Blood (RC)
UNION ST
BOROUGH
KENTISH BLDGS
UNION B300 STREET
PLAYHOUSE
RISBOR. ST
JERWOOD SPACE
PEPPER ST
GT GUILDFORD ST
DOY.
DORRIT ST
AYRES ST
REDCROSS WAY
The Cath Sch
St. Joseph's RC Prim Sch
NEWCOMEN
COPPERFIELD STREET
BRIDGE
CLE. ST
MERMAID
ROW
LOMAN ST
SAWYER
LON. FIRE BRIGADE MUS
QUILP ST
LIT. DORRIT CT
DISNEY ST
CHAPEL CT
4
STREET
MARSHALSEA RD
DISNEY PL
STREET
LAYTONS BLDG.
ANGEL PL
BLACKFRIARS CROWN CT
Fire Sta
MINT ST
CALEB ST
A.C.A.S.
Lib
TABARD ST
TENNIS
RUSHWORTH
KINGS BENCH ST
GLASSHILL STREET
SUFFOLK ST
STURGE ST
A300
LANT ST
WELLER ST
Charles Dickens Prim Sch
ISAAC WY
SANCT. ST
St. George the Martyr
HIGH
BOROUGH
BRITISH SCH OF OSTEOPATHY
PO
EMPIRE SQ W
63
SUDREY ST
BITTERN ST
TOULMIN ST
PICKWICK ST
SILVESTER ST
TABARD
BOYFIELD
SILEX
BELVEDERE
COL.
THE BOROUGH

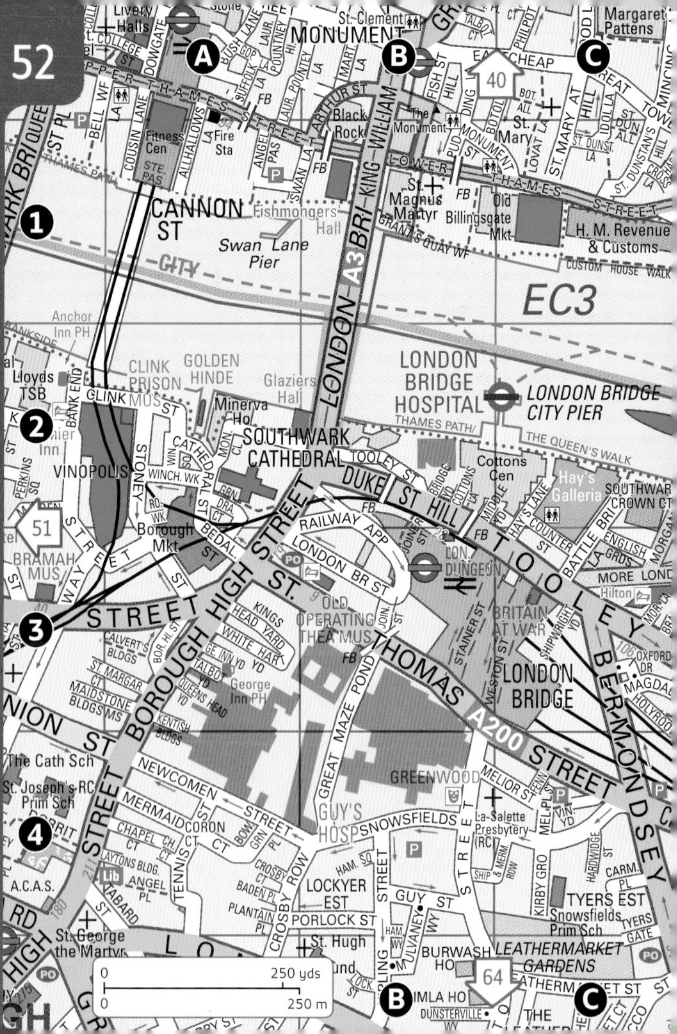

A
B
C
1
2
3
4
MONUMENT
St. Clement
Margaret Pattens
Livery Halls
COLLEGE ST
DOWGATE
BUSH LANE
SUFFOLK LA
LAUR. POUNTNEY HI.
LAUR. POUNTNEY LA
MART. LA
ARTHUR ST
KING WILLIAM
FISH ST HILL
EASTCHEAP
40
BOT. ALL
St. Mary
LOVAT LA
ST. MARY AT HILL
IDOL LA
ST. DUNST. LA
ST. DUNSTAN'S HILL
GREAT TOWER
MINCING
UPPER THAMES STREET
BELL WF LA
COUSIN LANE
ALLHALLOWS LA
Fitness Cen
STE. PAS
Fire Sta
ANGEL PAS
SWAN LA
FB
Black Rock
The Monument
PUD. LA
MONUMENT ST
BOTOLPH
LOWER THAMES STREET
St. Magnus Martyr
Old Billingsgate Mkt
GRANT'S QUAY WF
H. M. Revenue & Customs
CUSTOM HOUSE WALK
ST PL
SOUTHWARK BRIDGE
THAMES PATH
CANNON ST
Fishmongers' Hall
Swan Lane Pier
CITY
LONDON BRI A3
EC3
Anchor Inn PH
BANKSIDE
Lloyds TSB
BANK END
CLINK ST
CLINK PRISON MUS
GOLDEN HINDE
Glaziers' Hall
Minerva Ho
LONDON BRIDGE HOSPITAL
LONDON BRIDGE CITY PIER
THAMES PATH
THE QUEEN'S WALK
Inn
PERKINS SQ
VINOPOLIS
STONEY ST
WIN. SQ
CATHEDRAL ST
WINCH. WK
MON. CL
SOUTHWARK CATHEDRAL
TOOLEY ST
DUKE ST HILL
BRIDGE YD
COTTONS LA
Cottons Cen
MIDDLE YD
HAY'S LANE
Hay's Galleria
SOUTHWARK CROWN CT
51
RO. WK
GRN. DRA. CT
Borough Mkt
BEDALE ST
RAILWAY APP
LONDON BR ST
JOINER ST
LON. DUNGEON
COUNTER ST
BATTLE BRI LA
ENGLISH GRDS
MORGAN
MORE LOND
Hilton
TOOLEY
BRAMAH MUS
SOUTHWARK STREET
BOROUGH HIGH STREET
ST.
PO
OLD OPERATING THEA MUS
JOIN. ST
STAINER ST
BRITAIN AT WAR
WESTON ST
SHIPWRIGHT YD
LONDON BRIDGE
BERMONDSEY
OXFORD DR
MAGDALEN
HOLYROOD
KINGS HEAD YARD
WHITE HART YD
GE. INN YD
TALBOT YD
QUEENS HEAD YD
George Inn PH
CALVERT'S BLDGS
BOR. HI. ST
ST. MARGAR. CT
MAIDSTONE BLDGS MS
KENTISH BLDGS
ST THOMAS ST
GREAT MAZE POND
A200
UNION ST
The Cath Sch
St. Joseph's RC Prim Sch
NEWCOMEN STREET
MERMAID CT
CORON ST
BOW. GRN. PL
GREENWOOD
GUY'S HOSP
SNOWSFIELDS
MELIOR ST
FENN. ST
MEL. PL
VIN. YD
La-Salette Presbytery (RC)
WESTON STREET
SHIP & MERM. ROW
KIRBY GRO
HARDWIDGE ST
CARM. PL
TYERS EST
Snowsfields Prim Sch
TYERS GATE
CORRIT
CHAPEL CT
CH. CT
TENNIS
A.C.A.S.
LAYTONS BLDG.
Lib
ANGEL PL
TABARD ST
CROSBY CT
BADEN PL
PLANTAIN PL
CROSBY ROW
HAM. SQ
LOCKYER EST
PORLOCK ST
STREET
GUY ST
HAM. WY
MULVANEY WY
St. Hugh
LEATHERMARKET GARDENS
BURWASH HO
SIMLA HO
DUNSTERVILLE WY
64
THE
LEATHERMARKET ST
St. George the Martyr
RD
HIGH
0 250 yds
0 250 m

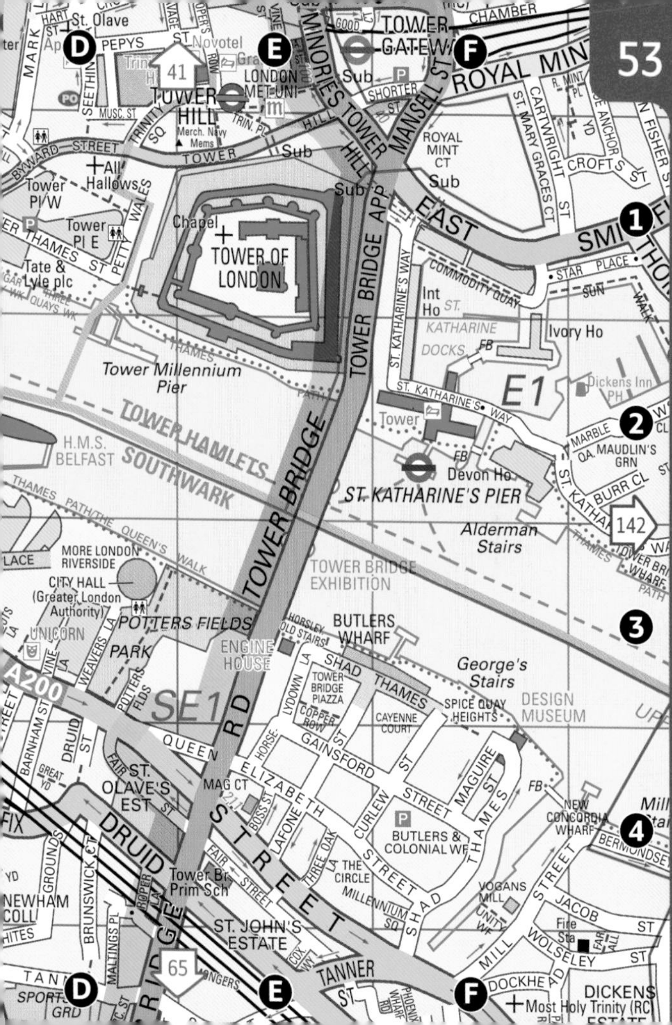
D
E
F
1
2
3
4
St. Olave
PEPYS
Novotel
41
LONDON MET UNI
MINORIES
TOWER GATEWAY
CHAMBER
ROYAL MINT
MANSELL ST
SHORTER ST
TOWER HILL
TRINITY SQ
Merch. Navy Mems
MUSC. ST
SEETHING
MARK
BYWARD STREET
TOWER HILL
TOWER
All Hallows
Tower Pl W
Tower Pl E
WALES
THAMES ST
PETTY
Tate & Lyle plc
THREE QUAYS WK
ROYAL MINT CT
Sub
ST. MARY GRACES CT
CARTWRIGHT
CROFTS ST
FISHER ST
EAST SMITHFIELD
Chapel
TOWER OF LONDON
TOWER BRIDGE APP
ST. KATHARINE'S WAY
COMMODITY QUAY
STAR PLACE
SUN WALK
THOMAS MORE
Int Ho
ST. KATHARINE DOCKS
FB
Ivory Ho
E1
Dickens Inn PH
THAMES PATH
Tower Millennium Pier
Tower
MARBLE QA.
MAUDLIN'S GRN
BURR CL
Devon Ho
TOWER HAMLETS
SOUTHWARK
H.M.S. BELFAST
ST. KATHARINE'S PIER
TOWER BRIDGE
142
Alderman Stairs
THAMES PATH/THE QUEEN'S WALK
MORE LONDON RIVERSIDE
CITY HALL (Greater London Authority)
TOWER BRIDGE EXHIBITION
TOWER BRIDGE WHARF
THAMES PATH
POTTERS FIELDS PARK
UNICORN
WEAVERS LA
VINE LA
ENGINE HOUSE
HORSLEY OLD STAIRS
BUTLERS WHARF
George's Stairs
A200
SE1
SHAD THAMES
TOWER BRIDGE PIAZZA
LYDOWN LA
COPPER ROW
SPICE QUAY HEIGHTS
DESIGN MUSEUM
CAYENNE COURT
POTTERS FLDS
QUEEN ELIZABETH ST
GAINSFORD ST
MAGUIRE ST
BARNHAM ST
DRUID ST
GREAT YD
FAIR ST
ST. OLAVE'S EST
MAG CT
BOSS ST
LAFONE ST
CURLEW STREET
THAMES
FB
NEW CONCORDIA WHARF
BERMONDSEY
TOWER BRIDGE RD
DRUID
TOOLEY STREET
BUTLERS & COLONIAL WF
THREE OAK LA
THE CIRCLE
MILLENNIUM SQ
SHAD
VOGANS MILL
UNITY WF
MILL STREET
JACOB ST
Fire Sta
NEWHAM COLL
GROUNDS
BRUNSWICK CT
ROPER LA
Tower Br Prim Sch
FAIR STREET
ST. JOHN'S ESTATE
COX WY
WOLSELEY ST
MALTINGS PL
65
TANNER ST
DOCKHEAD
DICKENS ESTATE
Most Holy Trinity (RC)
PHOENIX WHARF RD
SPORTS GRD

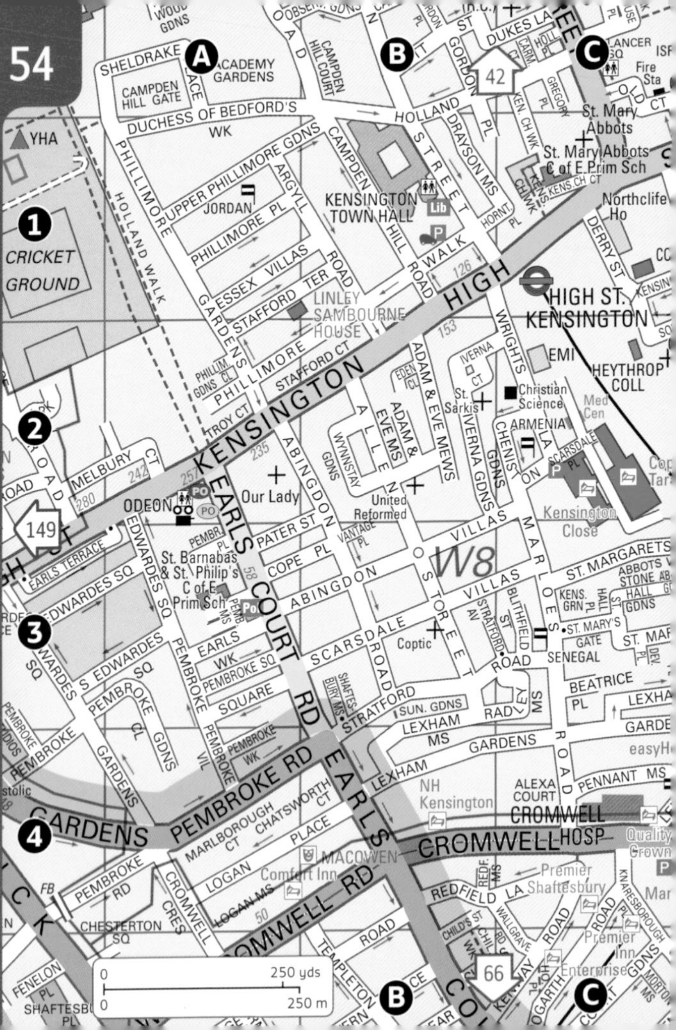

A
B
C
1
2
3
4
42
149
66
SHELDRAKE PLACE
ACADEMY GARDENS
CAMPDEN HILL GATE
CAMPDEN HILL COURT
DUCHESS OF BEDFORD'S WK
HOLLAND ST
DUKES LA
GORDON PL
DRAYSON MS
CARM.
HOLL PL
GREGORY PL
KEN. CH WK
LANCER SQ
Fire Sta
OLD CT
St. Mary Abbots
St. Mary Abbots C of E Prim Sch
KENS. CH CT
YHA
CRICKET GROUND
PHILLIMORE GARDENS
HOLLAND WALK
UPPER PHILLIMORE GDNS
JORDAN
PHILLIMORE PL
ARGYLL ROAD
CAMPDEN HILL ROAD
KENSINGTON TOWN HALL
Lib
STREET
HORNT. PL
WALK
126
Northclife Ho
DERRY ST
HIGH ST. KENSINGTON
ESSEX VILLAS
STAFFORD TER
LINLEY SAMBOURNE HOUSE
PHILLIMORE
STAFFORD CT
PHILLIM GDNS CL
TROY CT
KENSINGTON HIGH
153
ADAM & EVE MEWS
IVERNA CT
WRIGHTS LA
EMI
HEYTHROP COLL
EDEN CL
St. Sarkis
Christian Science
Med Cen
ARMENIA
ALLEN
ADAM & EVE MS
WYNNSTAY GDNS
IVERNA GDNS
CHENISTON GDNS
SCARSDALE PL
MELBURY CT
242
280
ROAD
257
235
ABINGDON
Our Lady
United Reformed
ODEON
PO
EARLS COURT RD
PEMBR. PL
PATER ST
VANTAGE PL
COPE PL
VILLAS
Kensington Close
MARLOES ROAD
EARLS TERRACE
EDWARDES SQ
St. Barnabas & St. Philip's C of E Prim Sch
58
ABINGDON VILLAS
W8
ST. MARGARETS
ABBOTS STONE
KENS. GRN
HALL GDNS
PEMB. MS
EARLS WK
SCARSDALE
STRATFORD AV
BLITHFIELD ST
ST. MARY'S GATE
Coptic
STRATFORD ROAD
SENEGAL
S EDWARDES SQ
PEMBROKE SQ
SQUARE
SHAFTESBURY MS
SUN. GDNS
RADLEY MS
BEATRICE PL
LEXHAM
PEMBROKE CL
PEMBROKE GDNS
PEMBROKE STUDIOS
PEMBROKE GARDENS
PEMBROKE VIL
PEMBROKE WK
LEXHAM MS
LEXHAM GARDENS
easyH
PEMBROKE RD
NH Kensington
ALEXA COURT
PENNANT MS
CROMWELL HOSP
Quality Crown
GARDENS
MARLBOROUGH CT
CHATSWORTH CT
PLACE
CROMWELL
MACOWEN
Comfort Inn
LOGAN
LOGAN MS
PEMBROKE RD
CROMWELL CRES
FB
REDE. MS
Premier Shaftesbury
REDFIELD LA
KNARESBOROUGH PL
CHESTERTON SQ
CROMWELL RD
50
ROAD
CHILD'S ST
WALLGRAVE RD
Premier Inn
TEMPLETON PL
Enterprise
HOGARTH ROAD
KENWAY
FENELON PL
SHAFTESBURY PL
MORTON MS
0 250 yds
0 250 m

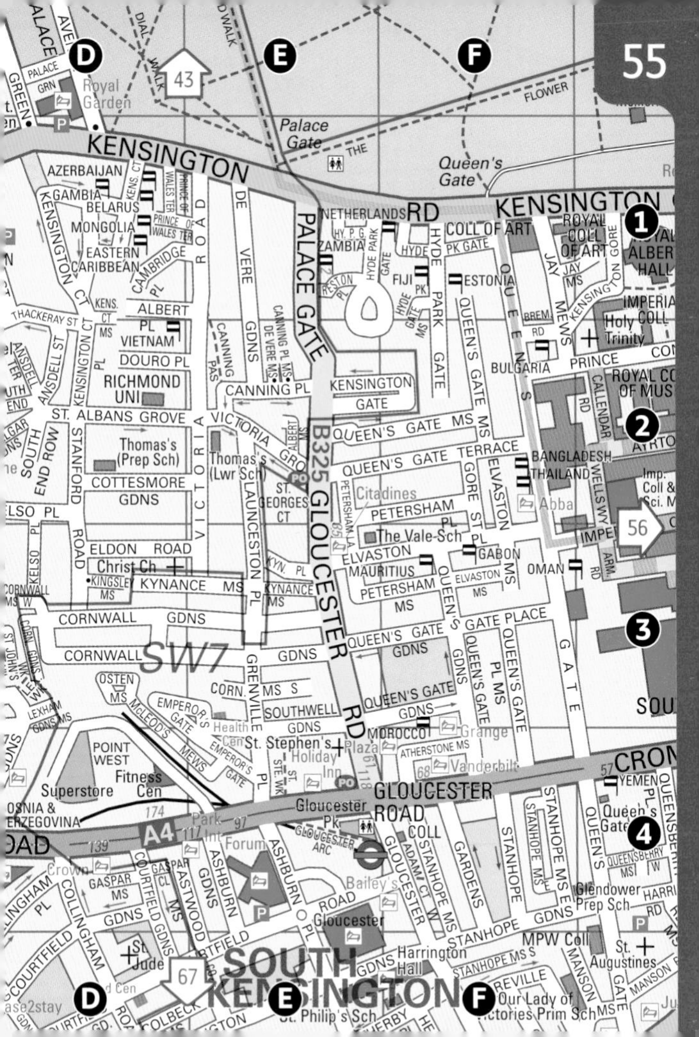
D
E
F
43
Royal Garden
KENSINGTON
Palace Gate
THE
FLOWER
Queen's Gate
KENSINGTON RD
AZERBAIJAN
GAMBIA
BELARUS
MONGOLIA
EASTERN CARIBBEAN
KENSINGTON CT
CAMBRIDGE PL
PRINCE OF WALES TER
VICTORIA ROAD
DE VERE GDNS
PALACE GATE
NETHERLANDS
ZAMBIA
HYDE PARK GATE
COLL OF ART
PK GATE
ROYAL COLL OF ART
ROYAL ALBERT HALL
FIJI
ESTONIA
QUEEN'S GATE
JAY MEWS
KENSINGTON GORE
IMPERIAL COLL
Holy Trinity
THACKERAY ST
KENS. CT MS
ALBERT PL
VIETNAM
DOURO PL
RICHMOND UNI
CANNING PAS
CANNING PL
KENSINGTON GATE
BULGARIA
PRINCE CONSORT
ROYAL COLL OF MUSIC
CALLENDAR RD
ST. ALBANS GROVE
VICTORIA GRO
QUEEN'S GATE MS
QUEEN'S GATE TERRACE
BANGLADESH
THAILAND
Thomas's (Prep Sch)
Thomas's (Lwr Sch)
ST. GEORGES CT
B325 GLOUCESTER RD
COTTESMORE GDNS
Citadines
PETERSHAM PL
Abba
56
ELSO PL
ELDON ROAD
The Vale Sch
ELVASTON PL
GABON
OMAN
Christ Ch
MAURITIUS
KYNANCE MS
PETERSHAM MS
ELVASTON MS
CORNWALL GDNS
QUEEN'S GATE PLACE
QUEEN'S GATE GDNS
SW7
GRENVILLE PL
CORN. MS S
SOUTHWELL GDNS
QUEEN'S GATE GDNS
MOROCCO
Grange
EMPEROR'S GATE
McLEOD'S MEWS
POINT WEST
Fitness Cen
Superstore
Health Cen
St. Stephen's
Holiday Inn
Plaza
ATHERSTONE MS
Vanderbilt
CROMWELL
YEMEN
GLOUCESTER ROAD
BOSNIA & HERZEGOVINA
A4
Park Int
Forum
Gloucester Pk
GLOUCESTER ARC
COLL
STANHOPE GARDENS
Queen's Gate
QUEENSBERRY MS W
Glendower Prep Sch
HARRINGTON RD
COURTFIELD GDNS
GASPAR MS
ASHBURN GDNS
Bailey's
Gloucester
COLLINGHAM PL
St. Jude
67
SOUTH KENSINGTON
Harrington Hall
STANHOPE GDNS
MPW Coll
St. Augustines
MANSON MS
REVILLE
Our Lady of Victories Prim Sch
St. Philip's Sch

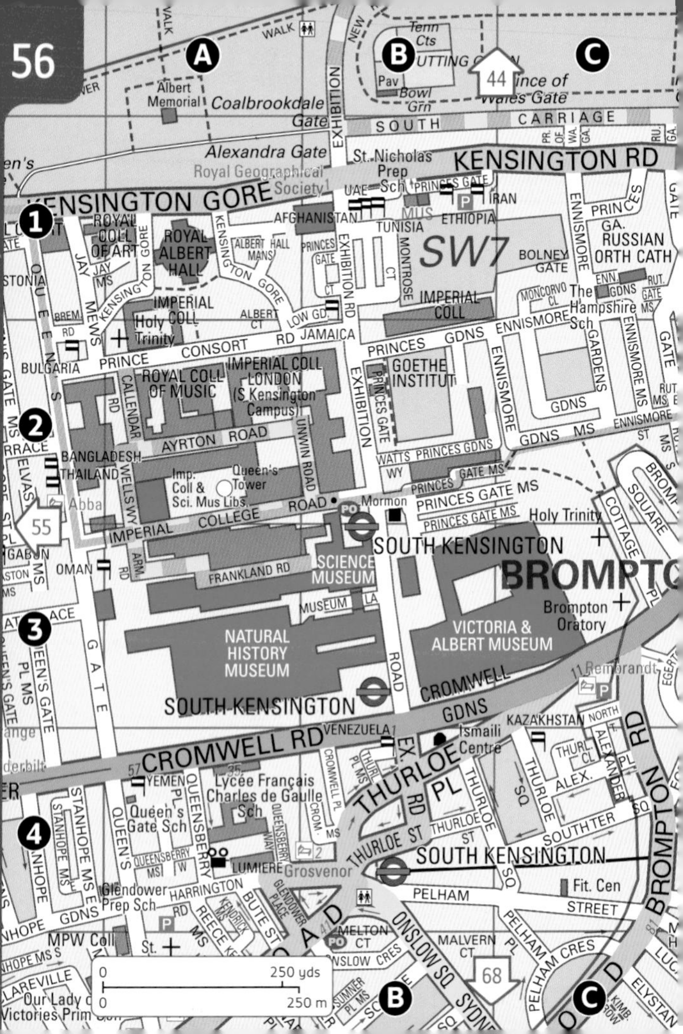
A
B
C
1
2
3
4
44
55
68
Albert Memorial
Coalbrookdale Gate
Alexandra Gate
Tenn Cts
Pav
Bowl Grn
Prince of Wales Gate
SOUTH CARRIAGE
KENSINGTON RD
KENSINGTON GORE
Royal Geographical Society
St. Nicholas Prep Sch
UAE
PRINCES GATE
IRAN
MUS
ETHIOPIA
AFGHANISTAN
TUNISIA
SW7
ROYAL COLL OF ART
ROYAL ALBERT HALL
ALBERT HALL MANS
JAY MS
KENSINGTON GORE
IMPERIAL COLL
Holy Trinity
ALBERT CT
LOW GD.
JAMAICA RD
EXHIBITION RD
MONTROSE CT
IMPERIAL COLL
BOLNEY GATE
ENNISMORE GDNS
PRINCES GA.
RUSSIAN ORTH CATH
The Hampshire Sch
MONCORVO CL
ENNISMORE GARDENS
ENNISMORE MS
QUEEN'S GATE
ESTONIA
BULGARIA
PRINCE CONSORT RD
ROYAL COLL OF MUSIC
IMPERIAL COLL LONDON (S Kensington Campus)
CALLENDAR RD
AYRTON ROAD
UNWIN ROAD
PRINCES GDNS
GOETHE INSTITUT
PRINCES GATE
WATTS WY
BANGLADESH
THAILAND
WELLS WY
Imp. Coll & Sci. Mus Libs.
Queen's Tower
Abba
IMPERIAL COLLEGE ROAD
Mormon
PRINCES GATE MS
Holy Trinity
SOUTH KENSINGTON
BROMPTON
COTTAGE PL
BROMPTON SQUARE
GABON
OMAN
ARM. RD
FRANKLAND RD
SCIENCE MUSEUM
MUSEUM LA
Brompton Oratory
NATURAL HISTORY MUSEUM
VICTORIA & ALBERT MUSEUM
SOUTH KENSINGTON
CROMWELL GDNS
Rembrandt
VENEZUELA
KAZAKHSTAN
NORTH
CROMWELL RD
Ismaili Centre
THURLOE PL
THURLOE SQ
ALEXANDER PL
YEMEN
Lycée Français Charles de Gaulle Sch
Queen's Gate Sch
QUEENSBERRY PL
QUEENSBERRY MS W
QUEENSBERRY WAY
STANHOPE MS E
HARRINGTON RD
LUMIERE
Grosvenor
THURLOE ST
SOUTH KENSINGTON
PELHAM STREET
Fit. Cen
BROMPTON RD
Glendower Prep Sch
STANHOPE GDNS
MPW Coll
REECE MS
KENDRICK MS
BUTE ST
GLENDOWER PLACE
MELTON CT
ONSLOW SQ
ONSLOW CRES
MALVERN CT
PELHAM PL
PELHAM CRES
ELYSTAN
SUMNER PL MS
Our Lady of Victories Prim
0 250 yds
0 250 m

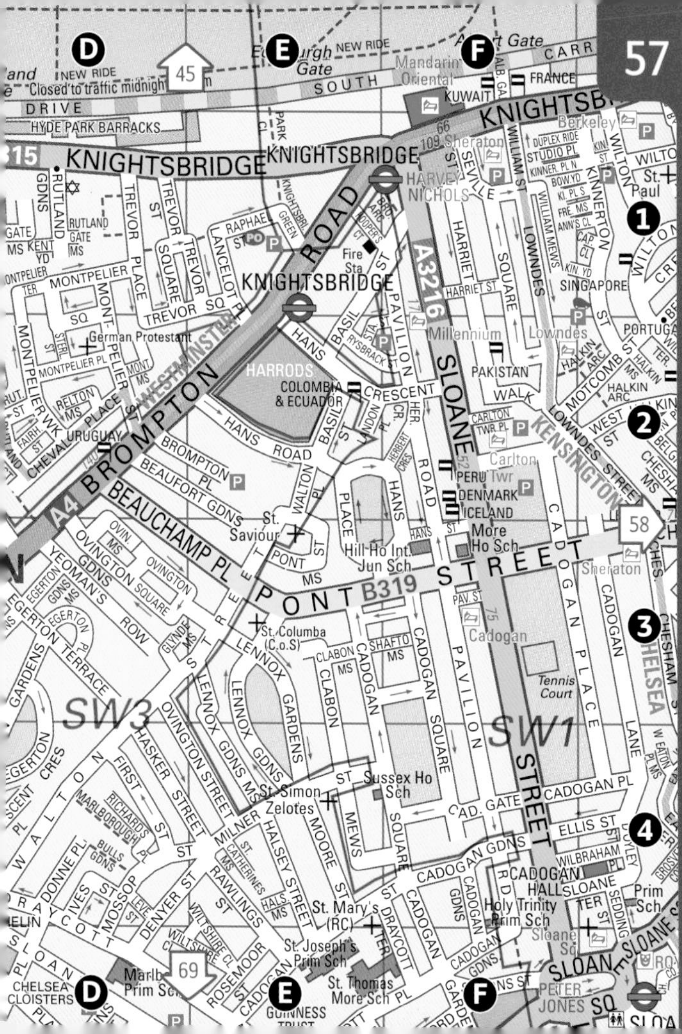
D
E
F
45
NEW RIDE
Closed to traffic midnight
Edinburgh Gate
SOUTH
CARR
Albert Gate
Mandarin Oriental
KUWAIT
FRANCE
DRIVE
HYDE PARK BARRACKS
KNIGHTSBRIDGE
315
KNIGHTSBRIDGE
Berkeley
WILTON
St. Paul
HARVEY NICHOLS
Sheraton
109
66
SEVILLE
WILLIAM ST
DUPLEX RIDE
STUDIO PL
KINNER. PL N
BOW YD
KL. PL S
FRE. MS
ANN'S CL
CAP CL
KIN. YD
KINNERTON
WILLIAM MEWS
LOWNDES
RUTLAND GDNS
RUTLAND GATE MS
GATE MS
KENT YD
TREVOR PLACE
TREVOR ST
TREVOR SQUARE
TREVOR
LANCELOT
RAPHAEL ST
PO
PARK CL
KNIGHTSBRIDGE GREEN
ROAD
BRO. ARC
COOPER'S CT
Fire Sta
KNIGHTSBRIDGE
A3216
HARRIET
HARRIET ST
SQUARE
SINGAPORE
1
MONTPELIER
MONTPELIER TER
SQ
MONT. PELIER
TREVOR SQ
LANCELOT PL
BASIL
STA. ST
RYSBRACK ST
PAVILION
Millennium
Lowndes
PORTUGAL
HALKIN ARC
MOTCOMB
HALKIN MS
HALKIN ARC
German Protestant
MONTPELIER PL
WESTMINSTER
HANS
HARRODS
SLOANE
PAKISTAN
WALK
COLOMBIA & ECUADOR
CRESCENT
CARLTON TWR PL
KENSINGTON
LOWNDES STREET
WEST HALKIN
2
CHESHAM MS
RELTON MS
MONTPELIER WK
FAIRH. ST
CHEVAL PLACE
URUGUAY
BROMPTON
HANS ROAD
BASIL ST
LANDON PL
HERBERT CRES
CR.
HER.
ROAD
Carlton Twr
PERU
DENMARK
ICELAND
A4
BROMPTON PL
BEAUFORT GDNS
WALTON PL
PLACE
HANS
St. Saviour
PONT ST
HANS
More Ho Sch
CADOGAN PLACE
58
BEAUCHAMP PL
OVIN. MS
OVINGTON
OVINGTON SQUARE
YEOMAN'S ROW
Hill Ho Int. Jun Sch
MS
PONT B319 STREET
Sheraton
PAV. ST
Cadogan
EGERTON GDNS MS
EGERTON TERRACE
EGERTON PL
GLYNDE MS
St. Columba (C.o.S)
LENNOX
CLABON MS
CLABON
SHAFTO MS
CADOGAN
CADOGAN SQUARE
PAVILION
Tennis Court
CADOGAN
3
CHESHAM
CHELSEA
SW3
GARDENS
LENNOX GDNS
LENNOX GDNS MS
GARDENS
SW1
STREET
LANE
W EATON PL MS
EGERTON CRES
HASKER STREET
OVINGTON STREET
FIRST ST
RICHARDS PL
MARLBOROUGH
WALTON
St. Simon Zelotes
MILNER ST
MOORE
MEWS
SQUARE
Sussex Ho Sch
CAD. GATE
CADOGAN PL
ELLIS ST
4
D'OYLEY
BULLS GDNS
DONNE PL
IVES ST
MOSSOP ST
LEVE ST
DENYER ST
ST. CATHERINES MS
HALSEY STREET
RAWLINGS ST
HALS. MS
CADOGAN GDNS
WILBRAHAM PL
CADOGAN HALL
SLOANE TER
SEDDING ST
Prim Sch
St. Mary's (RC)
DRAYCOTT
CADOGAN
Holy Trinity Prim Sch
Sloane Sq
WILTSHIRE CL
WILTSHIRE CL
69
St. Joseph's Prim Sch
CADOGAN GDNS
SLOANE
SLOANE SQ
CHELSEA CLOISTERS
Marlb Prim Sch
ROSEMOOR ST
GUINNESS TRUST
St. Thomas More Sch
PETER JONES
SLOA

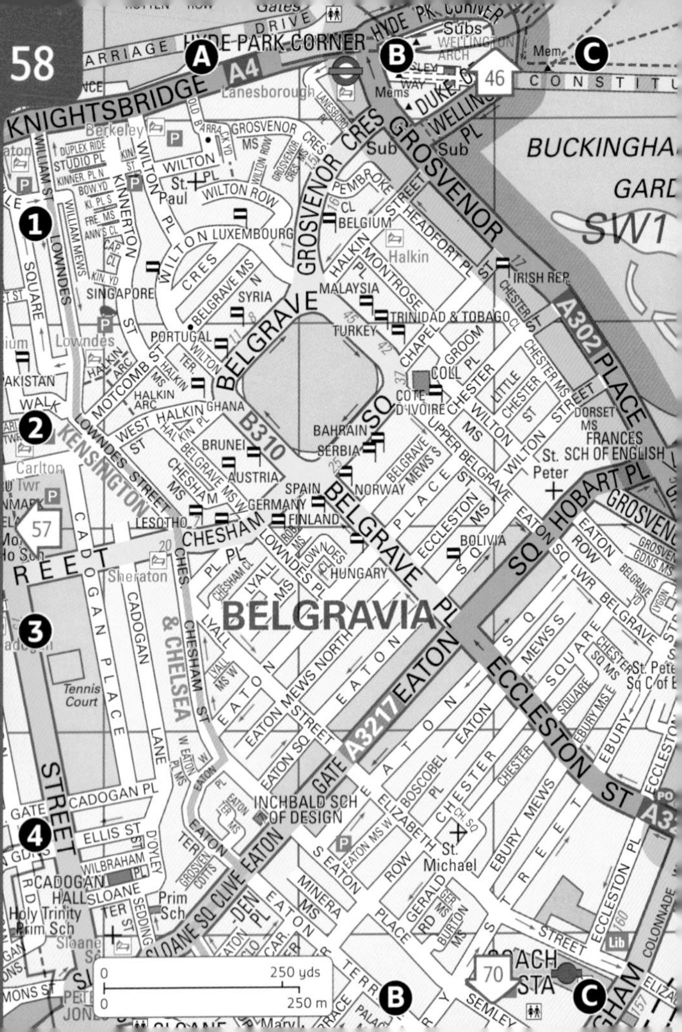
A
B
C
1
2
3
4
HYDE PARK CORNER
CARRIAGE DRIVE
A4
KNIGHTSBRIDGE
Lanesborough
Berkeley
Subs
WELLINGTON ARCH
Mem
Mems
APSLEY WAY
DUKE OF WELLINGTON PL
46
CONSTITUTION
BUCKINGHAM GARDENS
SW1
DUPLEX RIDE
STUDIO PL
KINNERTON PL N
BOW YD
KI. PL S
FRE. MS
ANN'S CL
CAP. CL
KIN. YD
WILLIAM ST
WILLIAM MEWS
LOWNDES SQUARE
KINNERTON ST
WILTON PL
OLD BARRACK YD
GROSVENOR CRES MS
WILTON ROW
WILTON PL
St. Paul
WILTON CRES
LUXEMBOURG
GROSVENOR CRES
GROSVENOR PL
PEMBROKE CL
BELGIUM
HALKIN ST
HEADFORT PL
Halkin
MONTROSE PL
IRISH REP.
CHESTER CL
A302
GROSVENOR PLACE
SINGAPORE
BELGRAVE MS N
SYRIA
MALAYSIA
TRINIDAD & TOBAGO
TURKEY
BELGRAVE SQ
PORTUGAL
WILTON TER.
CHAPEL ST
GROOM PL
COLL
COTE D'IVOIRE
CHESTER ST
LITTLE CHESTER ST
CHESTER MS
WILTON ST
DORSET MS
FRANCES
SCH OF ENGLISH
Lowndes
HALKIN ARC
PAKISTAN
WALK
MOTCOMB ST
HALKIN MS
HALKIN ARC
WEST HALKIN ST
GHANA
B310
BAHRAIN
SERBIA
BRUNEI
AUSTRIA
KENSINGTON
LOWNDES STREET
BELGRAVE MS W
CHESHAM MS
UPPER BELGRAVE ST
BELGRAVE MEWS S
WILTON MS
St. Peter
HOBART PL
GROSVENOR GDNS
GROSVENOR GDNS MS
Carlton Twr
57
SPAIN
NORWAY
GERMANY
FINLAND
LESOTHO
CHESHAM ST
BELGRAVE PL
ECCLESTON MS
BOLIVIA
EATON SQ
EATON ROW
LWR BELGRAVE ST
BELGRAVE YD
LYGON PL
Sheraton
CADOGAN PLACE
CADOGAN LANE
CHESHAM PL
CHESHAM CL
LYALL MS
LOWNDES PL
LOWNDES CL
HUNGARY
BELGRAVIA
LYALL ST
LYALL MS W
EATON MEWS NORTH
EATON SQ
A3217
EATON SQ MEWS S
CHESTER SQ MS
SQUARE
EBURY MS E
St. Peter's Sq C of E
ECCLESTON ST
Tennis Court
& CHELSEA
W EATON PL MS
EATON PL
EATON SQ
EATON GATE
ECCLESTON
EBURY ST
SLOANE STREET
CADOGAN PL
ELLIS ST
D'OYLEY ST
WILBRAHAM PL
CADOGAN HALL
SLOANE TER
SEDDING ST
Prim Sch
Holy Trinity Prim Sch
INCHBALD SCH OF DESIGN
EATON TER MS
EATON TER
GROSVENOR COTTS
CLIVE
SLOANE SQ.
ELIZABETH ST
BOSCOBEL PL
EATON MS W
S EATON PL
MINERA MS
St. Michael
CHESTER SQ
CHESTER ROW
GERALD RD
GERALD MS
BURTON MS
EBURY MEWS
ECCLESTON PL
COLONNADE
Lib
COACH STA
70
SEMLEY
PALACE
TERRACE
0 250 yds
0 250 m

D
E
F
47
Closed to Traffic on Sundays
Queen Victoria Memorial
PALACE
BUCKINGHAM PALACE
THE QUEEN'S GALLERY
THE ROYAL MEWS
BUCKINGHAM GATE
SPUR ROAD
BIRDCAGE
WELLINGTON BARRACKS
GUARDS MUS
Guards Chapel
GOVT. OFF.
B323
BUCKINGHAM GATE
SWAZILAND
ALBANIA
MACEDONIA
PETTY FRANCE
ST. JAMES PARK
DFID
STAFFORD PL
CATHERINE PL
WILFRED ST
CASTLE LA
Crowne Plaza
VAND. ST
CAXTON
PALACE ST
ROAD
PALACE PL
PALACE
W.K.COLL
COMM. & LOCAL GOV.
WESTMINSTER
Westminster City Sch
S KOREA
SPENSER ST
MofJ
BUTLER PL
CHRIST GDNS
GROSVENOR PL
Rubens
BRESSENDEN PL
Goring
Thistle
Cardinal Pl
WESTMINSTER CITY HALL
HOUSE OF FRASER
60
BEESTON PL
VICTORIA SQ
ALLINGTON ST
EATON LA
Fit. Cen
Portland Ho
VICTORIA
WILCOX PL
DfT
ARTILLERY PL
ARTILLERY ROW
VICTORIA PALACE
VICTORIA ST
WESTMINSTER CATH(RC)
CATH. PIAZZA
HOWICK PLACE
ASHLEY GDNS
THIRLEBY RD
TERMINUS PL
Victoria Visitor Info Cen
BUS STA
WILTON RD
APOLLO VICTORIA
A202
ASHLEY PL
CARLISLE PL
St. Vincent de Paul RC Prim Sch
AMBROSDEN AV
STREET
GREENC. ROW
EMERY HILL ST
ROW
GREYCOAT
ROCH. ST
Prim Sch
W.K. COLL
Eaton Sq Sch
Thistle Victoria
VICTORIA
KING'S SCHOLARS PAS
MORPETH TER
Westminster Cath Choir Sch
WINDSOR PL
COBURG CL
B324
Grange
ROY. HORT. SOC. LINDLEY HALL
PALACE
Victoria Place
NEATHO. PL
PLACE
FRANCIS ST
WILLOW PL
STILLINGTON ST
GREENCOAT PL
ROCHESTER ROW
VINCENT ST
PLAYING FIELDS
ECCLESTON BR
BRIDGE PL
Plaza
Hesperia
PASSPORT OFFICE
PEABODY EST
Queen Mother Sports Cen
VAUXHALL
GILLINGHAM ST
WILTON ROAD
HINDON CT
GUILDHOUSE ST
TACHBR. MS
UPPER TACHB. ST
GORDON HOSP
Comfort Inn
Quality Westminster
71
LONGMOORE ST
Med Cen
WAY
SQUARE
UDALL ST
BLOOMBURG ST
NAT SCH GOVT
WARWICK
CHURTON
Westminster Under Sch
PO
1
2
3
4

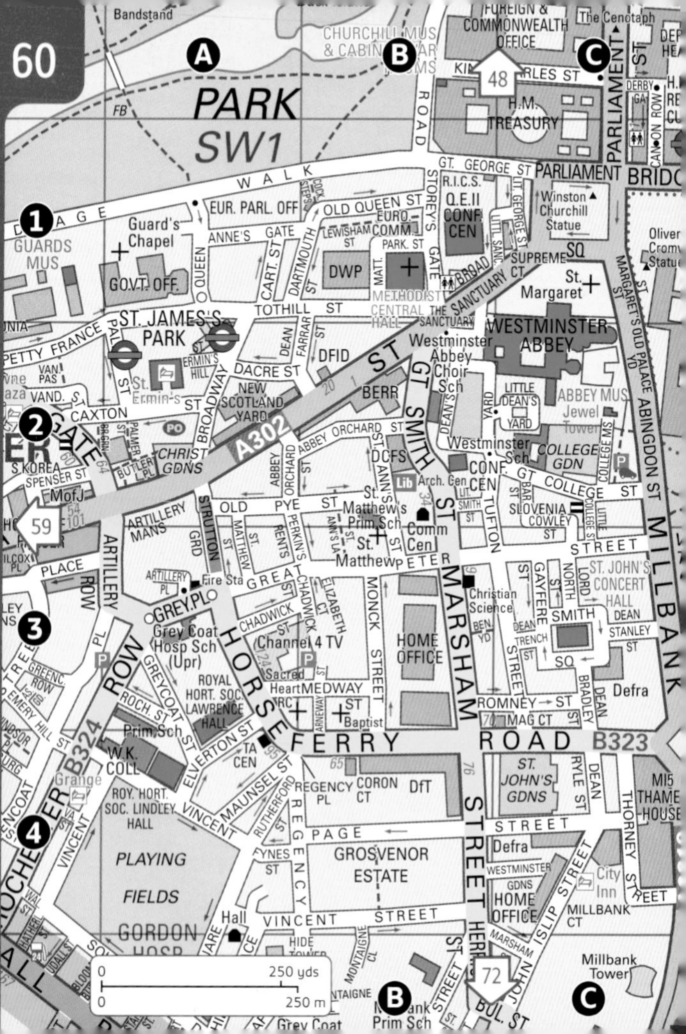

Bandstand
A
B
C
CHURCHILL MUS & CABINET WAR ROOMS
FOREIGN & COMMONWEALTH OFFICE
The Cenotaph
48
KING CHARLES ST
PARK
SW1
FB
H.M. TREASURY
PARLIAMENT ST
DERBY GA
CANON ROW
PARLIAMENT SQ
BRIDGE
BIRDCAGE WALK
1
GUARDS MUS
Guard's Chapel
EUR. PARL. OFF
COCK. STEPS
OLD QUEEN ST
STOREY'S GATE
GT. GEORGE ST
R.I.C.S.
Q.E.II CONF CEN
LIT. GEORGE ST
LITTLE SANC.
Winston Churchill Statue
Oliver Cromwell Statue
QUEEN ANNE'S GATE
LEWISHAM ST
EURO. COMM.
PARK. ST
GOVT. OFF.
CART. ST
DARTMOUTH ST
DWP
MATT. PARL.
METHODIST CENTRAL HALL
BROAD SANCTUARY
SUPREME CT
St. Margaret
MARGARET'S ST
OLD PALACE YD
TOTHILL ST
THE SANCTUARY
WESTMINSTER ABBEY
PETTY FRANCE
ST. JAMES'S PARK
PALMER ST
DEAN FARRAR ST
DFID
VAN. PAS
VAND. ST
St. Ermin's
ERMIN'S HILL
BROADWAY
DACRE ST
NEW SCOTLAND YARD
VICTORIA ST
BERR
GT SMITH ST
Westminster Abbey Choir Sch
DEAN'S YARD
LITTLE DEAN'S YARD
ABBEY MUS
Jewel Tower
2
CAXTON ST
PO
BUTLER PL
CHRIST GDNS
A302
ABBEY ORCHARD ST
ST. ANN'S ST
DCFS
Westminster Sch
COLLEGE GDN
COLLEGE MS
ABINGDON ST
S KOREA
SPENSER ST
MofJ
59
ARTILLERY MANS
STRUTTON GRD
OLD PYE ST
Lib
Arch. Gen
CONF. CEN
LIT. SMITH ST
GT COLLEGE ST
BARTON ST
SLOVENIA
COWLEY ST
LITTLE COLLEGE ST
MILLBANK
ARTILLERY ROW
MATTHEW ST
ST. MATTHEW ST
RENTS
PERKIN'S
ANN'S LA
St. Matthew's Prim Sch
Comm Cen
St. Matthew
TUFTON ST
STREET
ARTILLERY PL
Fire Sta
GREAT PETER ST
MARSHAM ST
Christian Science
ST. JOHN'S CONCERT HALL
GAYFERE ST
NORTH ST
LORD NORTH ST
GREY.PL
CHADWICK ST
ELIZABETH CT
MONCK STREET
SMITH SQ
DEAN STANLEY ST
3
Grey Coat Hosp Sch (Upr)
HORSEFERRY ROAD
Channel 4 TV
HOME OFFICE
BEN. YD
DEAN TRENCH ST
GREENC. ROW
GREYCOAT ST
ROYAL HORT. SOC. LAWRENCE HALL
Sacred Heart
MEDWAY ST
ROMNEY ST
BRADLEY
DEAN
Defra
ROCH. ST
Prim.Sch
ARNEWAY ST
Baptist
MAG CT
B324
B323
W.K. COLL
ELVERTON ST
TA CEN
MAUNSEL ST
REGENCY PL
CORON CT
DfT
ST. JOHN'S GDNS
RYLE ST
DEAN
THORNEY STREET
MI5 THAMES HOUSE
Grange
ROY. HORT. SOC. LINDLEY HALL
VINCENT SQ
RUTHERFORD ST
REGENCY ST
PAGE STREET
4
ROCHESTER ROW
VINCENT ST
PLAYING FIELDS
TYNES ST
GROSVENOR ESTATE
Defra
WESTMINSTER GDNS
HOME OFFICE
City Inn
JOHN ISLIP STREET
MILLBANK CT
GORDON HOSP
Hall
VINCENT STREET
HIDE TOWER
MONTAIGNE CL
MARSHAM ST
HERRICK ST
72
Millbank Tower
Millbank Prim Sch
Grey Coat
BUL. ST
0 250 yds
0 250 m

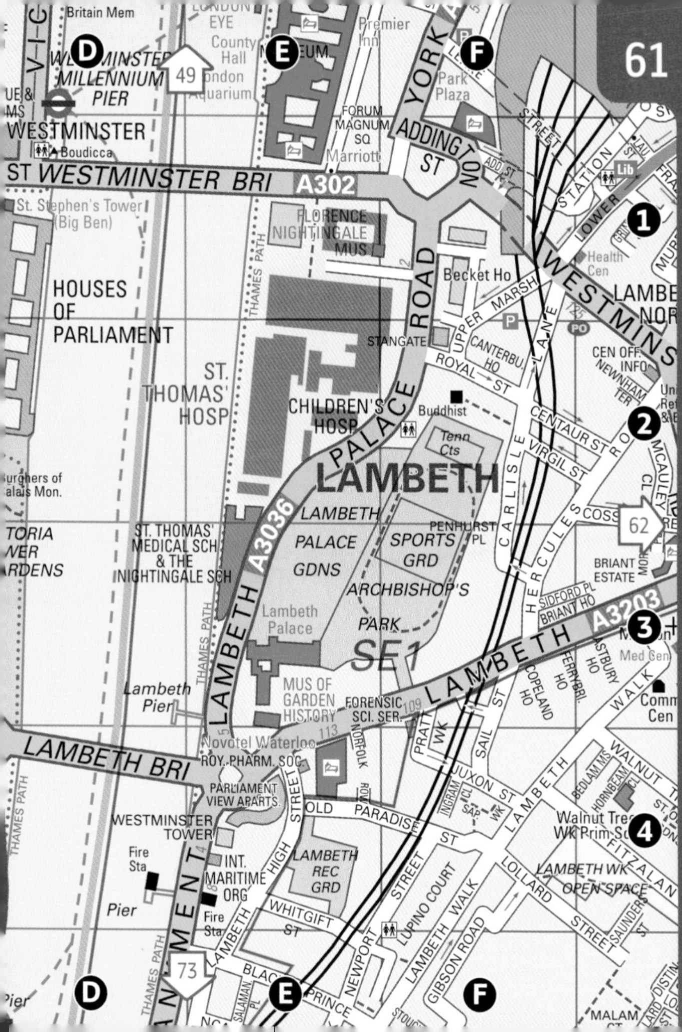
Britain Mem
LONDON EYE
County Hall
London Aquarium
MUSEUM
Premier Inn
YORK
LEAKE
Park Plaza
49
D
E
F
WESTMINSTER MILLENNIUM PIER
WESTMINSTER
Boudicca
FORUM MAGNUM SQ
Marriott
ADDINGTON
ST
ADD. ST
STREET
STATION
LOWER
Lib
ST WESTMINSTER BRI
A302
St. Stephen's Tower (Big Ben)
FLORENCE NIGHTINGALE MUS
Health Cen
WESTMINS
LAMBE
NOR
HOUSES OF PARLIAMENT
THAMES PATH
ROAD
Becket Ho
UPPER MARSH
LANE
PO
STANGATE
CANTERBU. HO
CEN OFF. INFO
NEWNHAM TER
ROYAL ST
ST. THOMAS' HOSP
CHILDREN'S HOSP
PALACE
Buddhist
Tenn Cts
CENTAUR ST
VIRGIL ST
MCAULEY CL
LAMBETH
Burghers of Calais Mon.
COSSER
62
A3036
LAMBETH PALACE GDNS
SPORTS GRD
PENHURST PL
CARLISLE
HERCULES
VICTORIA TOWER GARDENS
ST. THOMAS' MEDICAL SCH & THE NIGHTINGALE SCH
ARCHBISHOP'S PARK
BRIANT ESTATE
SIDFORD PL
BRIANT HO
A3203
Lambeth Palace
SE1
Med Cen
LAMBETH
MUS OF GARDEN HISTORY
FORENSIC SCI. SER.
COPELAND HO
FERRYBRI. HO
ASTBURY HO
WALK
Comm Cen
Lambeth Pier
Novotel Waterloo
NORFOLK ROW
PRATT WK
SAIL ST
LAMBETH BRI
ROY. PHARM. SOC.
PARLIAMENT VIEW APARTS.
STREET
OLD PARADISE
JUXON ST
INGRAM CL
SAP. WK
LAMBETH
BEDLAM MS.
HORNBEAM CL
WALNUT TREE
Walnut Tree Wk Prim Sch
WESTMINSTER TOWER
HIGH
ST
FITZALAN
Fire Sta
INT. MARITIME ORG
LAMBETH REC GRD
LOLLARD STREET
LAMBETH WK OPEN SPACE
Pier
WHITGIFT ST
STREET
LUPINO COURT
LAMBETH WALK
GIBSON ROAD
SAUNDERS
EMBANKMENT
73
BLACK PRINCE
NEWPORT
SALAMAN PL
MALAM

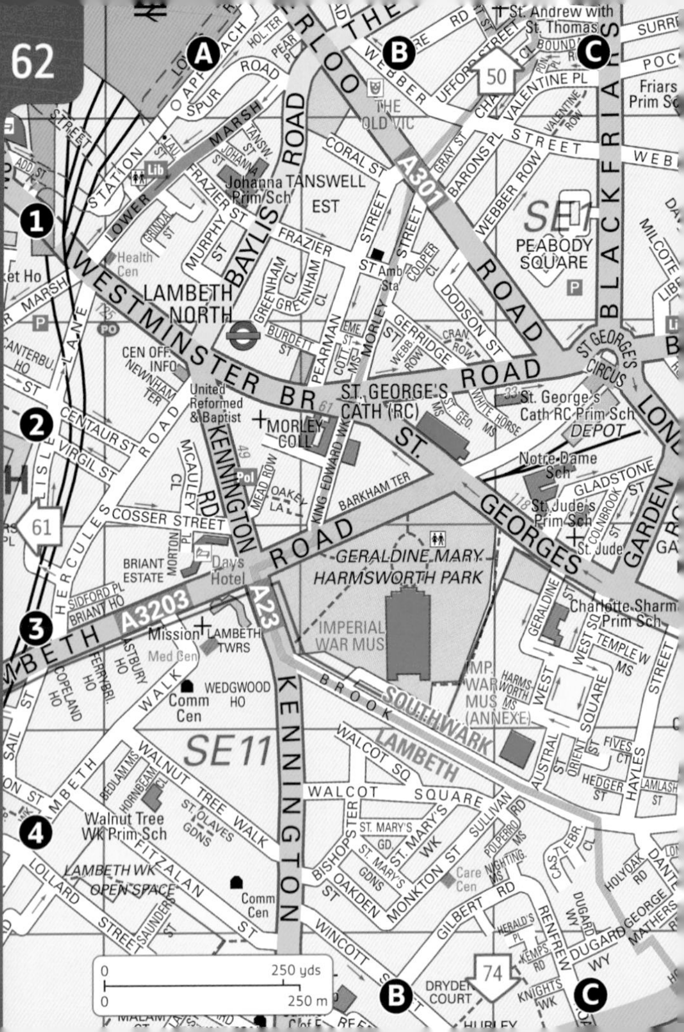
A
B
C
1
2
3
4
50
61
74
St. Andrew with St. Thomas
SURR
POC
Friars Prim Sc
WEB
LOWER MARSH
STATION
SPUR ROAD
HOL. TER
PEAR PL
WEBBER
UFFORD STREET
BOUNDARY
VALENTINE PL
VALENTINE ROW
THE OLD VIC
CORAL ST
A301
GRAY ST
BARONS PL
STREET
WEBBER ROW
BLACKFRIARS
SE1
PEABODY SQUARE
MILCOTE
LIB
ADD ST
Lib
TANSW.
JOHANNA ST
Johanna Prim Sch
TANSWELL EST
FRAZIER ST
BAYLIS ROAD
MURPHY ST
GRINDAL ST
FRAZIER
STREET
ST Amb Sta
COOPER CL
DODSON ST
ROAD
Health Cen
MARSH
WESTMINSTER BR ROAD
LAMBETH NORTH
GREENHAM CL
BURDETT ST
PEARMAN
EME.
COTT. MS
MORLEY
ST
WEBB ROW
GERRIDGE
CRAN. ROW
ST GEORGE'S CIRCUS
CANTERBU. HO
LANE
PO
CEN OFF. INFO
NEWNHAM TER
United Reformed & Baptist
MORLEY COLL
ST. GEORGE'S CATH (RC)
ST. GEO. MS
WHITE HORSE MS
St. George's Cath RC Prim Sch
DEPOT
LOND
CENTAUR ST
VIRGIL ST
LISLE
MCAULEY CL
KENNINGTON RD
Pol
MEAD ROW
OAKEY LA
KING EDWARD WK
BARKHAM TER
ST.
GEORGES
Notre Dame Sch
GLADSTONE ST
St. Jude's Prim Sch
COLNBROOK ST
St. Jude
GARDEN
GA
COSSER STREET
HERCULES
BRIANT ESTATE
MORTON PL
Days Hotel
ROAD
GERALDINE MARY HARMSWORTH PARK
SIDFORD PL
BRIANT HO
A3203
A23
LAMBETH
Mission
Med Cen
LAMBETH TWRS
IMPERIAL WAR MUS
GERALDINE ST
Charlotte Sharman Prim Sch
WEST SQ
TEMPLE W MS
STREET
COPELAND HO
FERRYBRI. HO
ASTBURY HO
WALK
Comm Cen
WEDGWOOD HO
KENNINGTON
BROOK
SOUTHWARK
LAMBETH
IMP. WAR MUS (ANNEXE)
HARMSWORTH MS
WEST
SQUARE
SE11
WALCOT SQ
AUSTRAL ST
ORIENT ST
FIVES CT
HAYLES
HEDGER ST
LAMLASH ST
SAIL ST
BEDLAM MS
HORNBEAM CL
WALNUT TREE WALK
ST. OLAVES GDNS
WALCOT SQUARE
SULLIVAN RD
POLPERRO MS
Walnut Tree Wk Prim Sch
ST. MARY'S GD.
ST. MARY'S WK
BISHOPSTER
ST. MARY'S GDNS
MONKTON ST
NIGHTING. MS
CASTLEBR. CL
HOLYOAK RD
DANTE
FITZALAN
LAMBETH WK OPEN SPACE
Comm Cen
OAKDEN ST
Care Cen
GILBERT RD
HERALD'S PL
RENFREW
DUGARD WY
GEORGE MATHERS
LOLLARD STREET
SAUNDERS ST
ST
WINCOTT ST
KEMPS. RD
DUGARD WY
0 250 yds
0 250 m
DRYDEN COURT
KNIGHTS WK
HURLEY

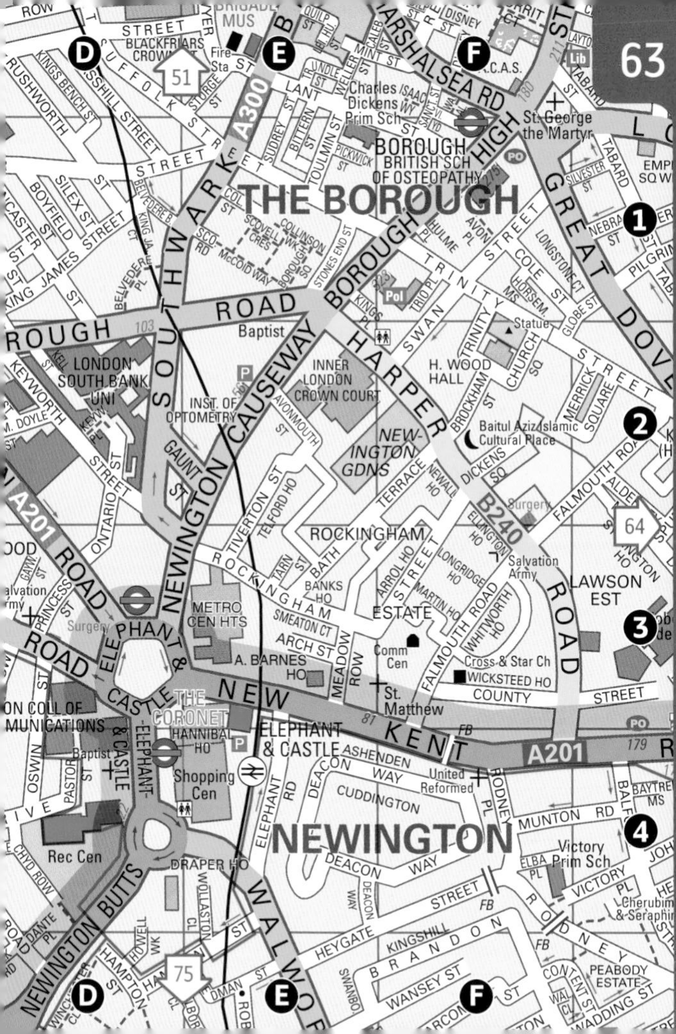
D
E
F
51
64
75
1
2
3
4
THE BOROUGH
NEWINGTON
BLACKFRIARS CROWN
Fire Sta
BRIGADE MUS
SUFFOLK ST
RUSHWORTH
KINGS BENCH ST
GLASSHILL STREET
STREET
SILEX ST
BOYFIELD ST
KING JAMES STREET
BELVEDERE PL
BELVEDERE B
KING JA CT
SOUTHWARK
A300
LANT
SUDREY ST
BITTERN ST
TOULMIN ST
PICKWICK ST
Charles Dickens Prim Sch
BOROUGH
BRITISH SCH OF OSTEOPATHY
MARSHALSEA RD
MINT ST
WELLER
TRUNDLE ST
DISNEY ST
St. George the Martyr
HIGH
GREAT DOVE
TABARD
SILVESTER ST
NEBRASKA ST
PILGRIM
EMPIRE SQ
COL ST
SCO. RD
SCOVELL CRES
COLLINSON WK
McCOID WAY
BOROUGH SQ
STONES END ST
HULME PL
AVON PL
TRINITY STREET
COLE ST
LONGSTONE CT
HORSEM. MS
GLOBE ST
KINGS PL
Pol
TRIO PL
SWAN
Statue
TRINITY CHURCH SQ
H. WOOD HALL
BROCKHAM ST
MERRICK SQUARE
STREET
BOROUGH ROAD
103
Baptist
LONDON SOUTH BANK UNI
KEYWORTH ST
M. DOYLE
CAUSEWAY
HARPER
INNER LONDON CROWN COURT
INST. OF OPTOMETRY
AVONMOUTH ST
NEW-INGTON GDNS
Baitul Aziz Islamic Cultural Place
DICKENS SQ
FALMOUTH ROAD
ALDERNEY
GAUNT ST
TIVERTON ST
TELFORD HO
TERRACE
NEWALL HO
Surgery
B240
A201
ROAD
ONTARIO ST
ROCKINGHAM
BATH
TARN ST
BANKS HO
ROCKINGHAM
ELLINGTON HO
LONGRIDGE HO
Salvation Army
LAWSON EST
ARROL HO
STREET
MARTIN HO
ESTATE
WHITWORTH HO
PRINCESS ST
Salvation Army
ELEPHANT & CASTLE
METRO CEN HTS
SMEATON CT
ARCH ST
A. BARNES HO
MEADOW ROW
Comm Cen
Cross & Star Ch
WICKSTEED HO
COUNTY STREET
St. Matthew
NEW KENT
81
FB
A201
179
THE CORONET
HANNIBAL HO
ELEPHANT & CASTLE
Shopping Cen
ASHENDEN
DEACON WAY
CUDDINGTON
United Reformed
RODNEY PL
MUNTON RD
BAYTREE MS
BALFOUR
Victory Prim Sch
ELBA PL
VICTORY PL
Cherubim & Seraphim
Baptist
PASTOR ST
OSWIN
Rec Cen
DRAPER HO
WOLLASTON CL
WALWORTH
ELEPHANT RD
DEACON WAY
STREET
HEYGATE
KINGSHILL
BRANDON
RODNEY
WANSEY ST
PEABODY ESTATE
CONTENT ST
WADDING ST
NEWINGTON BUTTS
DANTE PL
HAMPTON ST
HOWELL WK
ST

A
B
C
1
2
3
4
52
63
76
CHAPEL CT
LAYTONS BLDG.
ANGEL PL
TENNIS ST
TABARD ST
HOSP
LOCKYER EST
CROSBY ROW
CROSBY CT
BADEN PL
PLANTAIN PL
PORLOCK ST
HAM. SQ
GUY ST
Presbytery (RC)
KIRBY GRO
TYERS EST
Snowsfields Prim Sch
TYERS GATE
CARM. PL
St. George the Martyr
HIGH
LONG LANE
St. Hugh
Beormund Sch
EMPIRE SQ WEST
SILVESTER ST
TABARD
SOL. PL
LOCK. ST
KIPLING ST
ULVANEY WY
BURWASH HO
LEATHERMARKET GARDENS
LEATHERMARKET ST
SIMLA HO
DUNSTERVILLE WY
KIPLING EST
THE LEATHER MKT
LEATHER-MARKET CT
MOROCCO
LAMB
NEBRAS. ST
STERRY ST
PILGRIMAGE ST
GREAT DOVER STREET
LONGSTONE CT
COLE ST
HORSEM. MS
TRINITY
GLOBE ST
Statue
CHURCH SQ
MANCIPLE ST
HANKEY PL
STAPLE ST
TABARD GARDENS
TABARD GARDENS ESTATE
A2198
WESTON ST
ANTONINE HTS
CITY WK
ROYAL OA
BLUE LION PL
ELIM ST
ELIM ESTATE
PARD. ST
MERRICK SQUARE
STREET
BECK ST
165
SPORTS GROUND
PARDONER ST
WILD'S RENTS
DECIMA STREET
CLUNY EST
CLUNY PL
Missio
Bait-ul-Aziz Islamic Cultural Place
DICKENS SQ
KING'S COLLEGE (Hall Of Residence)
SE1
LAW STREET
ROTHSAY STREET
MEAKIN EST
SOUTHWARK COL
Surgery
FALMOUTH ROAD
ALDERNEY MS
SPURGEON ST
CHETTLE CL
A2
SIDNEY WEBB HO
BLACK HORSE CT
TABARD STREET
LANSDOWNE PL
POTIER ST
Salvation Army
SYMINGTON HO
BURBAGE CL
DEVERELL STREET
LAWSON EST
ROAD
WHITWORTH
CARD. BOURNE ST
BURGE ST
HUNTER CL
PRIORESS ST
REPHIDIM ST
GREEN WK
ALICE ST
TOWER BRIDGE
WEBB
BUSH CL
SWAN MEAD
Globe Academy
Tenn Cts
BARTHOLOMEW ST
Cross & Star Ch
WICKSTEED HO
COUNTY STREET
THEOBALD ST
St. Saviour's & St. Olave's Sch
OLD KENT RD
Baptist
CREASY EST
PO
240
A201
179
ROAD
BRICKLAYER'S ARMS ROUNDABOUT
ABERDOUR ST
LEROY ST
QUADRANGLE CL
172
PARAGON MS
SEARLES ROAD
RODNEY PL
BAYTREE MS
MUNTON RD
BALFOUR
WOOSTER PL
JOHN MAURICE CL
STREET
HENSHAW STREET
Victory Prim Sch
ELBA PL
VICTORY PL
SE17
Townsend Prim Sch
Sub
PRESTON CL
AUGUSTUS CT
KINGS FLATS
OLD
FB
RODNEY
Cherubim & Seraphim
CHATHAM
SALISBURY CL
HEMP WK
DARWIN STREET
GAVEL ST
MASON STREET
CROSS ST
TOWNSEND ST
THORNTON HO
CONGREVE
BARLOW ST
DARWIN CT
CRAIL ROW
MASSINGER ST
STANFORD PL
0 250 yds
0 250 m

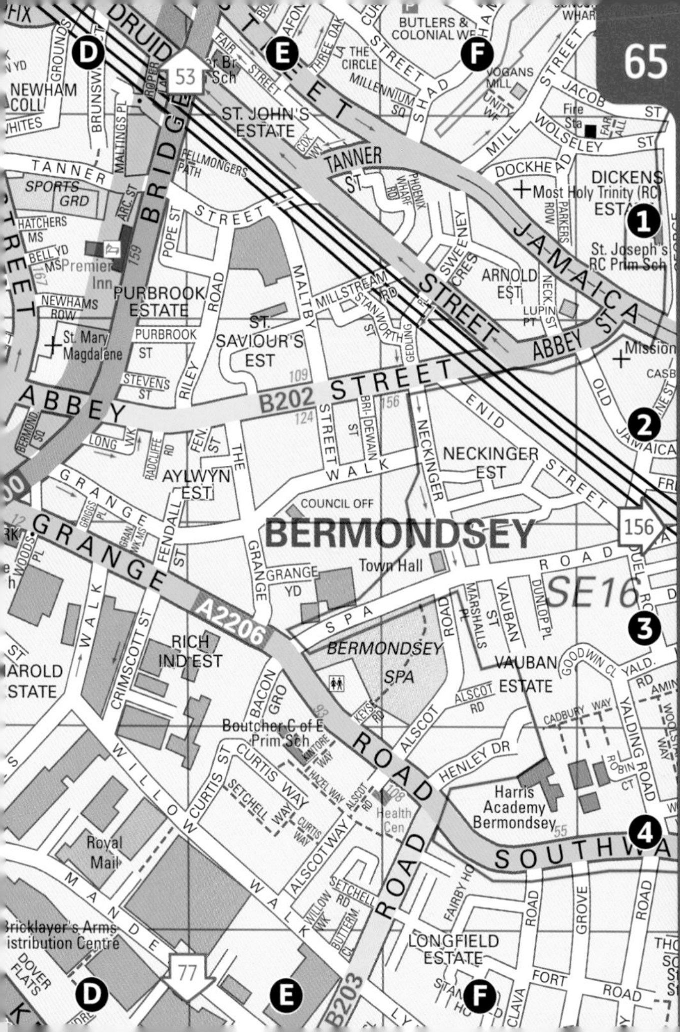
D
E
F
1
2
3
4
53
156
77
DRUID
BRIDGE
BUTLERS & COLONIAL WF
THREE OAK
THE CIRCLE
MILLENNIUM SQ
SHAD
VOGANS MILL
UNITY WF
JACOB
Fire Sta
ST
WOLSELEY ST
MILL
NEWHAM COLL
GROUNDS
BRUNSWICK
WHITES
MALTINGS PL
ROPER
FAIR STREET
ST. JOHN'S ESTATE
COX WAY
TANNER ST
TANNER
FELLMONGERS PATH
PHOENIX WHARF RD
DOCKHEAD
Most Holy Trinity (RC)
DICKENS ESTATE
PARKERS ROW
JAMAICA
St. Joseph's RC Prim Sch
SPORTS GRD
ARC. ST
HATCHERS MS
BELL YD
Premier Inn
159
POPE ST
STREET
SWEENEY CRES
ARNOLD EST
NECK ST
LUPIN PT
MALTBY
MILLSTREAM RD
STANWORTH ST
PURBROOK ESTATE
NEWHAMS ROW
ROAD
ST. SAVIOUR'S EST
GEDLING PL
STREET
ABBEY ST
Mission
PURBROOK ST
St. Mary Magdalene
STEVENS ST
RILEY
109
B202
STREET
OLD JAMAICA
ABBEY
BERMOND SQ
LONG WK
RADCLIFFE RD
FEN ST
THE
124
STREET
BRI-DEWAIN ST
156
WALK
NECKINGER
NECKINGER EST
ENID STREET
AYLWYN EST
GRANGE
GRIGGS PL
GRAN WK MS
FENDALL ST
COUNCIL OFF
BERMONDSEY
Town Hall
ROAD
GRANGE
WOODS PL
GRANGE
GRANGE YD
SPA
A2206
MARSHALLS PL
VAUBAN ST
DUNLOP PL
SE16
WALK
CRIMSCOTT ST
RICH IND EST
BERMONDSEY SPA
GOODWIN CL
YALDING RD
HAROLD ESTATE
BACON GRO
ROAD
VAUBAN ESTATE
ALSCOT RD
KEYSE RD
ALSCOT
CADBURY WAY
YALDING ROAD
93
Boutcher C of E Prim Sch
HENLEY DR
ROBIN CT
WILLOW
CURTIS ST
CURTIS WAY
KINTORE WAY
HAZEL WAY
ALSCOT RD
108
Health Cen
Harris Academy Bermondsey
55
SETCHELL WAY
CURTIS WAY
ALSCOT WAY
ROAD
SOUTHWA
Royal Mail
MANDE
WALK
WILLOW WK
SETCHELL RD
BUTTERM. CL
FAIRBY HO
ROAD
GROVE
ROAD
Bricklayer's Arms Distribution Centre
DOVER FLATS
B203
LONGFIELD ESTATE
FORT
ROAD
CLAVA

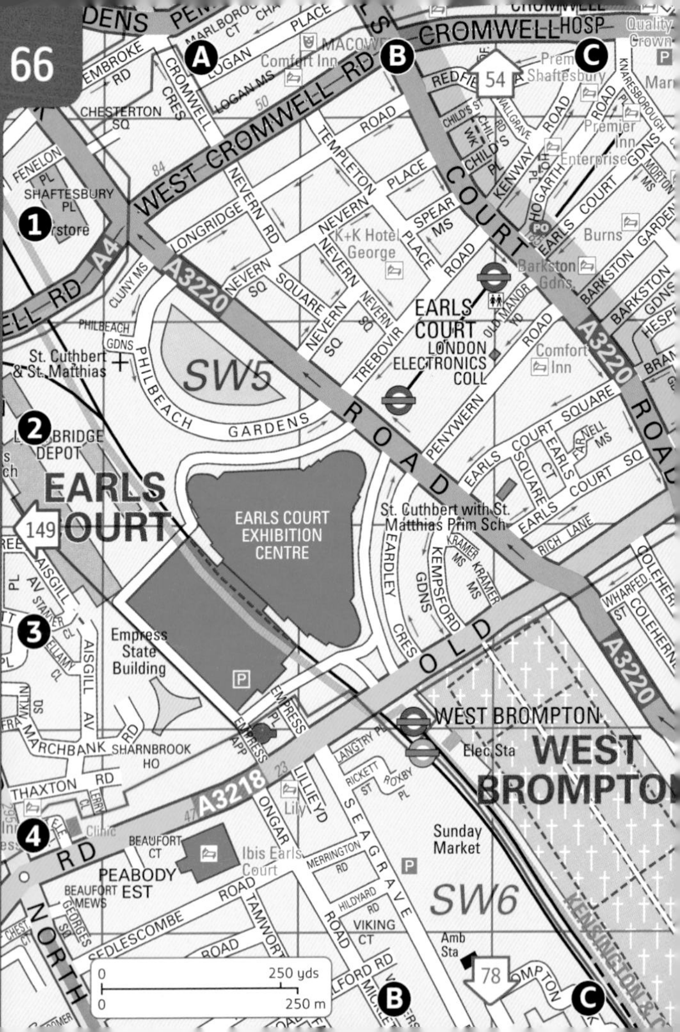
A
B
C
1
2
3
4
54
149
78
WEST CROMWELL RD
CROMWELL
HOSP
MARLBOROUGH CT
LOGAN PLACE
LOGAN MS
PEMBROKE RD
CROMWELL CRES
CHESTERTON SQ
FENELON PL
SHAFTESBURY PL
A4
A3220
A3218
LONGRIDGE
NEVERN RD
NEVERN SQ
NEVERN SQUARE
NEVERN PLACE
TEMPLETON PLACE
ROAD
SPEAR MS
K+K Hotel George
Comfort Inn
Quality Crown
Premier Inn
Enterprise
Shaftesbury
Burns
Barkston Gdns.
REDFIELD
CHILD'S ST
CHILD'S WK
CHILD'S PL
WALLGRAVE RD
KENWAY ROAD
HOGARTH RD
HOGARTH PL
KNARESBOROUGH PL
MORTON MS
EARLS COURT GDNS
BARKSTON GDNS
BARKSTON GARDENS
EARLS COURT ROAD
CLUNY MS
PHILBEACH GDNS
PHILBEACH GARDENS
SW5
TREBOVIR ROAD
EARLS COURT
LONDON ELECTRONICS COLL
OLD MANOR YD
PENYWERN ROAD
EARLS COURT SQUARE
EARLS COURT SQ
FARNELL MS
EARLS CT SQUARE
RICH LANE
St. Cuthbert & St. Matthias
LILLIE BRIDGE DEPOT
EARLS COURT
EARLS COURT EXHIBITION CENTRE
St. Cuthbert with St. Matthias Prim Sch
EARDLEY CRES
KEMPSFORD GDNS
KRAMER MS
COLEHERNE
WHARFEDALE ST
AISGILL AV
STANIER CL
BELLAMY CL
FRANKLIN MS
MARCHBANK RD
SHARNBROOK HO
THAXTON RD
Empress State Building
EMPRESS PL
EMPRESS APP
OLD BROMPTON ROAD
WEST BROMPTON
Elec Sta
WEST BROMPTON
LANGTRY PL
RICKETT ST
ROXBY PL
LILLIE RD
ONGAR RD
SEAGRAVE ROAD
Lily
Clinic
BEAUFORT CT
Ibis Earls Court
PEABODY EST
BEAUFORT MEWS
MERRINGTON RD
HILDYARD RD
VIKING CT
Sunday Market
SW6
Amb Sta
TAMWORTH
SEDLESCOMBE ROAD
NORTH
GEORGES SQ
CHESTON CT
0 250 yds
0 250 m
KENSINGTON & C

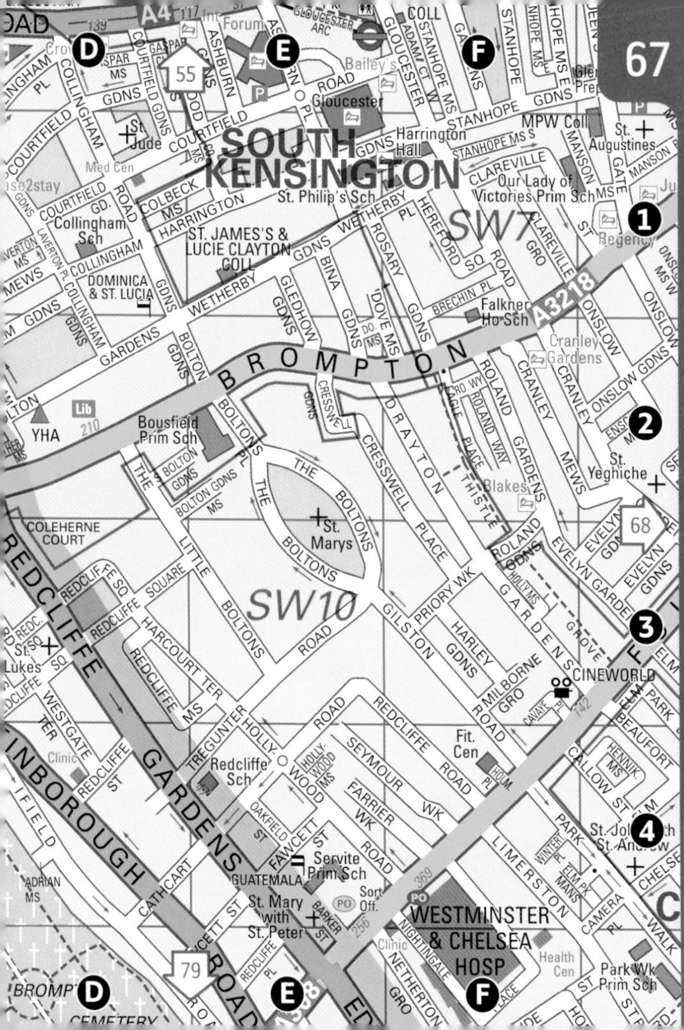
SOUTH KENSINGTON
SW7
SW10
BROMPTON
A3218
A4
55
68
79
D
E
F
1
2
3
4
Gloucester
Harrington Hall
St. Jude
Med Cen
Collingham Sch
ST. JAMES'S & LUCIE CLAYTON COLL
DOMINICA & ST. LUCIA
St. Philip's Sch
Our Lady of Victories Prim Sch
MPW Coll
St. Augustines
Regency
Falkner Ho Sch
Cranley Gardens
Bousfield Prim Sch
YHA
Lib
COLEHERNE COURT
St. Marys
Blakes
St. Yeghiche
CINEWORLD
St. Lukes
Clinic
Redcliffe Sch
Servite Prim Sch
St. Mary with St. Peter
Sort Off.
Fit. Cen
WESTMINSTER & CHELSEA HOSP
Health Cen
Park Wk Prim Sch
St. John with St. Andrew
BROMPTON CEMETERY
COLLINGHAM PL
COURTFIELD GDNS
COURTFIELD RD
COLBECK MS
HARRINGTON GDNS
HARRINGTON RD
WETHERBY GDNS
WETHERBY PL
GLEDHOW GDNS
BINA GDNS
ROSARY GDNS
DOVE MS
HEREFORD SQ
BRECHIN PL
STANHOPE GDNS
STANHOPE MS
CLAREVILLE ST
CLAREVILLE GRO
ONSLOW GDNS
CRANLEY GDNS
CRANLEY MEWS
DRAYTON GDNS
ROLAND GDNS
ROLAND WAY
THISTLE GRO
CRESSWELL PL
THE BOLTONS
BOLTON GDNS
LITTLE BOLTONS
REDCLIFFE SQUARE
REDCLIFFE GARDENS
REDCLIFFE RD
HARCOURT TER
TREGUNTER RD
GILSTON ROAD
PRIORY WK
HARLEY GDNS
MILBORNE GRO
EVELYN GDNS
ELM PARK GARDENS
BEAUFORT ST
CALLOW ST
LIMERSTON ST
SEYMOUR WK
FARRIER WK
HOLLYWOOD RD
FAWCETT ST
CATHCART RD
FINBOROUGH ROAD
NETHERTON GRO
NIGHTINGALE PLACE
CAMERA PL
PARK WALK
FULHAM ROAD

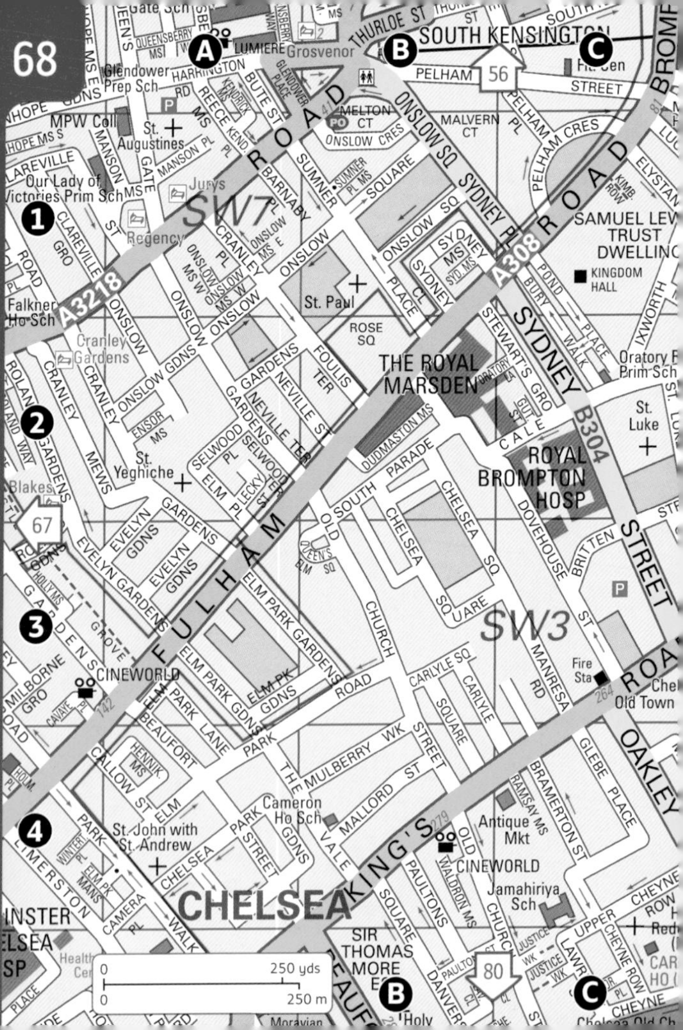
SOUTH KENSINGTON
THURLOE ST
LUMIERE
Grosvenor
Glendower Prep Sch
HARRINGTON RD
QUEENSBERRY MS
BUTE ST
GLENDOWER PLACE
KENDRICK MS
REECE MS
PELHAM STREET
Fr. Cen
56
MELTON CT
PO
ONSLOW CRES
ONSLOW SQ
MALVERN CT
PELHAM CRES
PELHAM PL
MPW Coll
St. Augustines
MANSON PL
MANSON MS
GATE
CLAREVILLE
Our Lady of Victories Prim Sch
Jurys
Regency
SW7
CRANLEY PL
BARNABY PL
SUMNER PL
SUMNER PL MS
SQUARE
SYDNEY PL
ROAD
ELYSTAN
KIMB. ROW
SAMUEL LEWIS TRUST DWELLINGS
KINGDOM HALL
ONSLOW MS E
ONSLOW MS W
ONSLOW
SYDNEY MS
SYD. MS
SYDNEY CL
PLACE
A308
POND PL
BURY WALK
SYDNEY STREET
IXWORTH
CLAREVILLE GRO
ROAD
Falkner Ho Sch
A3218
ONSLOW GDNS
St. Paul
ROSE SQ
THE ROYAL MARSDEN
ORATORY LA
STEWART'S GRO
Oratory Prim Sch
Cranley Gardens
CRANLEY GARDENS
CRANLEY MEWS
ROLAND GARDENS
ROLAND WAY
GARDENS
NEVILLE TER
FOULIS TER
NEVILLE ST
GUTTER ST
CALE
B304
St. Luke
ENSOR MS
St. Yeghiche
SELWOOD PL
SELWOOD TER
ELM PL
LECKY ST
DUDMASTON MS
PARADE
SOUTH
ROYAL BROMPTON HOSP
Blakes
67
EVELYN GDNS
EVELYN GARDENS
FULHAM
OLD
QUEEN'S ELM SQ
CHELSEA SQUARE
DOVEHOUSE
BRITTEN ST
STREET
P
HOLLY MS
GARDENS
GROVE
ELM PARK GARDENS
ELM PARK GDNS
ELM PK GDNS
CHURCH
SW3
MANRESA RD
CINEWORLD
MILBORNE GRO
CAVAYE PL
142
ELM PARK LANE
BEAUFORT
ROAD
CARLYLE SQ
CARLYLE SQUARE
Fire Sta
264
Chelsea Old Town
OAKLEY
HENNIKER MS
CALLOW ST
ELM
PARK
THE VALE
MULBERRY WK
MALLORD ST
STREET
RAMSAY MS
BRAMERTON ST
GLEBE PLACE
PARK WALK
WINTERTON PL
ELM PK MANS
LIMERSTON
St. John with St. Andrew
CHELSEA
CAMERA PL
Cameron Ho Sch
PARK STREET
GDNS
KING'S
279
CINEWORLD
WALDRON MS
Antique Mkt
OLD CHURCH
Jamahiriya Sch
UPPER CHEYNE ROW
CHEYNE ROW
CHELSEA
PAULTONS SQUARE
PAULTONS
SIR THOMAS MORE EST
DANVERS
PAULTON ST
JUSTICE WK
LAWRENCE
80
BEAUFORT
CHEYNE
CARLYLE HO
Health Cen
WESTMINSTER
CHELSEA HOSP
PLACE
Moravian
Holy
Chelsea Old Ch
0
250 yds
0
250 m

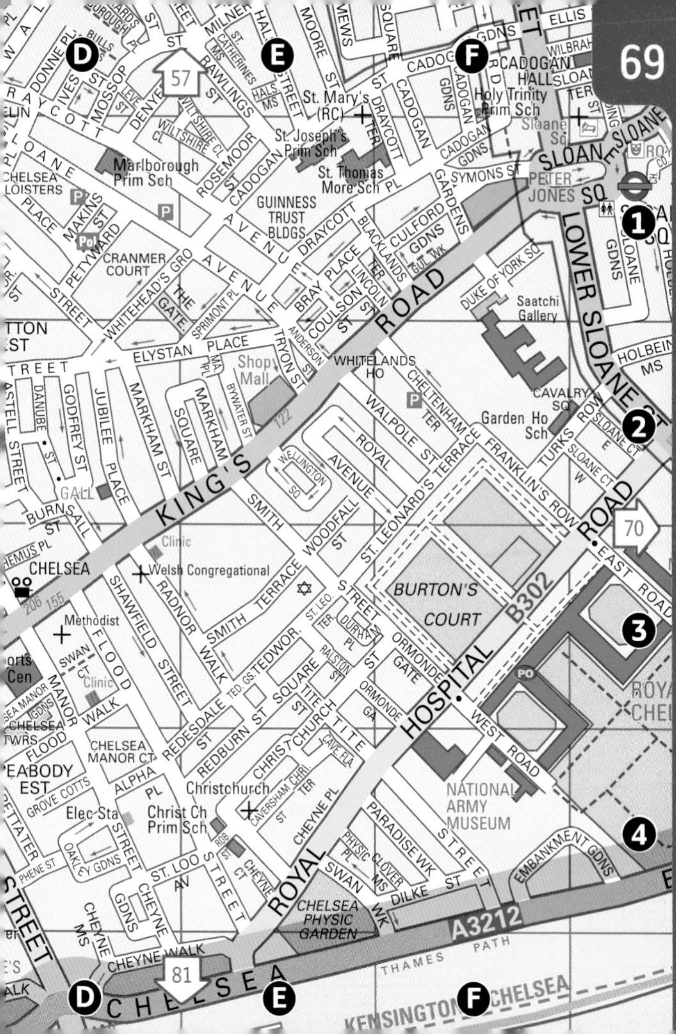
D
E
F
57
70
81
1
2
3
4
KING'S ROAD
122
SLOANE SQ
LOWER SLOANE ST
SLOANE GDNS
HOLBEIN MS
CADOGAN HALL
Holy Trinity Prim Sch
Sloane Sq
PETER JONES
SYMONS ST
CADOGAN GDNS
CADOGAN GARDENS
CADOGAN ST
DRAYCOTT AVENUE
DRAYCOTT PL
St. Mary's (RC)
St. Joseph's Prim Sch
St. Thomas More Sch
GUINNESS TRUST BLDGS
BLACKLANDS TER
CULFORD GDNS
CUL WK
LINCOLN ST
BRAY PLACE
COULSON ST
ANDERSON ST
TRYON ST
DUKE OF YORK SQ
Saatchi Gallery
CAVALRY SQ
Garden Ho Sch
TURKS ROW
SLOANE CT E
SLOANE CT W
WHITELANDS HO
CHELTENHAM TER
WALPOLE ST
ROYAL AVENUE
WELLINGTON SQ
SMITH ST
WOODFALL ST
ST. LEONARD'S TERRACE
FRANKLIN'S ROW
BURTON'S COURT
B302
ROYAL HOSPITAL ROAD
EAST ROAD
WEST ROAD
PO
NATIONAL ARMY MUSEUM
ROYAL HOSPITAL CHELSEA
EMBANKMENT GDNS
A3212
CHELSEA EMBANKMENT
THAMES PATH
KENSINGTON CHELSEA
CHELSEA PHYSIC GARDEN
SWAN WK
DILKE ST
PARADISE WK
CLOVER MS
PHYSIC PL
CHEYNE PL
TITE ST
CHRISTCHURCH ST
CAVE FLA
CHRISTCHURCH TER
CAVERSHAM ST
Christchurch
Christ Ch Prim Sch
ROB ST
CHEYNE CT
ROYAL AV
ST. LOO AV
FLOOD STREET
CHEYNE GDNS
CHEYNE MS
CHEYNE WALK
OAKLEY GDNS
PHENE ST
OAKLEY STREET
Elec Sta
GROVE COTTS
ALPHA PL
CHELSEA MANOR CT
PEABODY EST
CHELSEA MANOR GDNS
CHELSEA TWRS
FLOOD WALK
Clinic
SWAN CT
MANOR ST
Methodist
CHELSEA
SHAWFIELD STREET
RADNOR WALK
Welsh Congregational
SMITH TERRACE
REDESDALE ST
REDBURN ST
TEDWORTH SQUARE
TED. GS.
ST. LEO. TER
DURHAM PL
RALSTON ST
ORMONDE GATE
ORMONDE GA
BURNSALL ST
GALL
JUBILEE PLACE
MARKHAM ST
MARKHAM SQUARE
BYWATER ST
Shop Mall
ELYSTAN PLACE
MARKHAM PL
GODFREY ST
DANUBE ST
ASTELL STREET
SPRIMONT PL
THE GATE
WHITEHEAD'S GRO
CRANMER COURT
PETYWARD
MAKINS ST
Pol
P
CHELSEA CLOISTERS
SLOANE AVENUE
Marlborough Prim Sch
ROSEMOOR ST
CADOGAN ST
WILTSHIRE CL
DENYER ST
LEVER ST
MOSSOP ST
IVES ST
DONNE PL
BULLS GDNS
RAWLINGS ST
MILNER ST
ST. CATHERINES MS
HALSEY ST
HALS. MS
MOORE ST
MEWS
SQUARE
ELLIS ST
WILBRAHAM PL
SLOANE TER
HOLBEIN PL

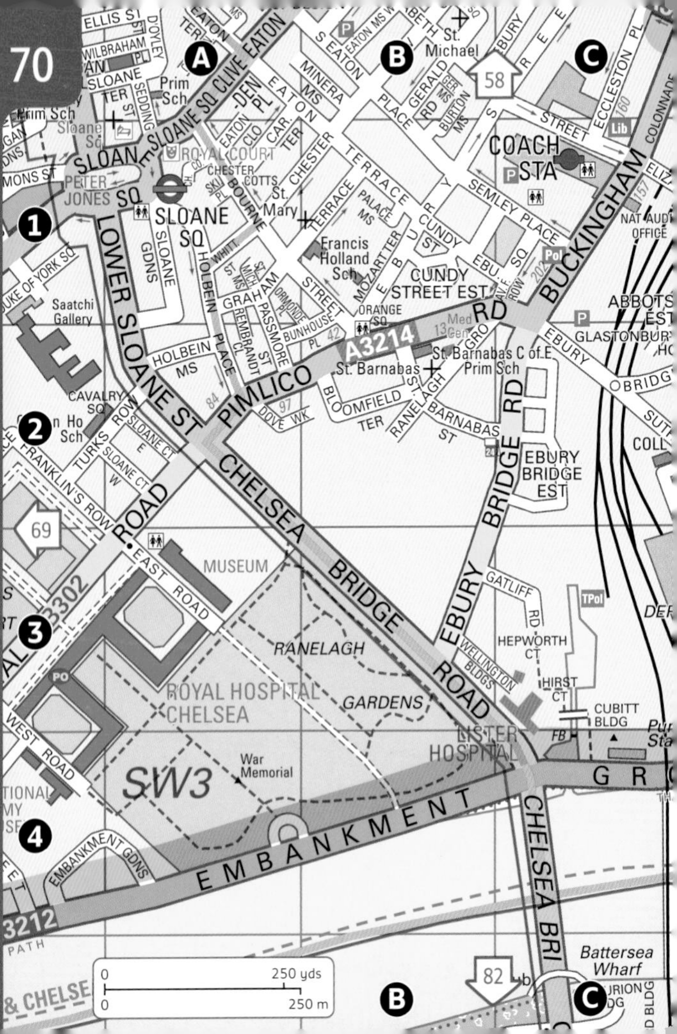
A
B
C
B
C
1
2
3
4
58
69
82
ELLIS ST
WILBRAHAM PL
D'OYLEY
SLOANE TER
SEDDING ST
Prim Sch
Sloane Sq
SLOANE SQ
CLIVE
EATON
EATON TER
S EATON
EATON MS W
MINERA MS
EATON PL
-DEN PL
EATON CLO
CAR. TER
ROYAL COURT
CHESTER COTTS
SKI PL
BOURNE
ST. CHESTER
St. Mary
TERRACE
PALACE MS
PLACE
GERALD RD
GER MS
BURTON MS
St. Michael
STREET
ECCLESTON PL
COLONNADE
Lib
COACH STA
SEMLEY PLACE
CUNDY ST
EBURY SQ
Pol
BUCKINGHAM
NAT AUDIT OFFICE
PETER JONES
SLOANE SQ
LOWER SLOANE ST
SLOANE GDNS
HOLBEIN
WHITT.
Francis Holland Sch
MOZART TER
CUNDY STREET EST
DUKE OF YORK SQ
Saatchi Gallery
GRAHAM
PASSMORE ST
ORMONDE PL
BUNHOUSE PL
ORANGE SQ
Med Cen
RD
ABBOTS
GLASTONBURY
EBURY
BRIDGE
HOLBEIN MS
PLACE
REMBRANDT CL
PIMLICO
A3214
St. Barnabas C of E Prim Sch
St. Barnabas
BLOOMFIELD TER
RANELAGH GRO
ST. BARNABAS ST
EBURY BRIDGE RD
CAVALRY SQ
TURKS ROW
SLOANE CT E
SLOANE CT W
DOVE WK
ROAD
FRANKLIN'S ROW
CHELSEA
EBURY BRIDGE EST
COLL
MUSEUM
EAST ROAD
BRIDGE
A3302
GATLIFF RD
TPol
HEPWORTH CT
RANELAGH
EBURY BRIDGE
WELLINGTON BLDGS
HIRST CT
CUBITT BLDG
ROAD
ROYAL HOSPITAL CHELSEA
GARDENS
PO
LISTER HOSPITAL
FB
WEST ROAD
War Memorial
SW3
G R
EMBANKMENT
EMBANKMENT GDNS
CHELSEA BRI
A3212
PATH
& CHELSEA
0
250 yds
0
250 m
Battersea Wharf

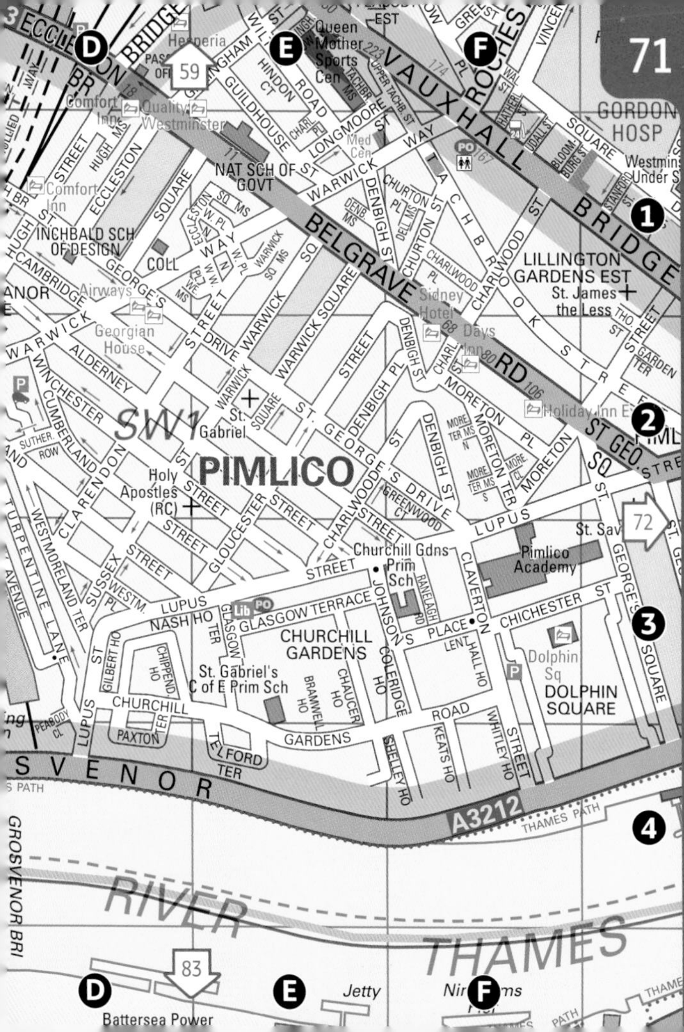
D
E
F
59
72
83
1
2
3
4
ECCLESTON BR
BRIDGE
Hesperia
Queen Mother Sports Cen
VAUXHALL BRIDGE RD
ROCHESTER
GORDON HOSP
Westminster Under S
Comfort Inn
Quality Westminster
GUILDHOUSE ST
HINDON CT
LONGMOORE ST
Med Cen
WARWICK WAY
NAT SCH OF GOVT
BELGRAVE RD
ECCLESTON SQUARE
ECCLESTON SQ MS
INCHBALD SCH OF DESIGN
COLL
CAMBRIDGE ST
Airways
GEORGE'S DRIVE
ST GEORGE'S DRIVE
WARWICK SQUARE
WARWICK SQ MS
Georgian House
ALDERNEY STREET
WINCHESTER STREET
DENBIGH ST
DENBIGH PL
CHURTON PL
CHURTON ST
CHARLWOOD PL
CHARLWOOD ST
Sidney Hotel
Days Inn
TACHBROOK STREET
LILLINGTON GARDENS EST
St. James the Less
Holiday Inn
MORETON PL
MORETON TER
MORETON ST
MORETON TER MS N
MORETON TER MS S
MORETON CL
ST GEO. SQ
SW1
PIMLICO
St. Gabriel
Holy Apostles (RC)
CUMBERLAND ST
SUTHERLAND ROW
CLARENDON ST
GLOUCESTER STREET
GREENWOOD CT
LUPUS ST
Churchill Gdns Prim Sch
Pimlico Academy
St. Sav
CLAVERTON ST
CHICHESTER ST
ST GEORGE'S SQUARE
RANELAGH RD
JOHNSON'S PLACE
GLASGOW TERRACE
Lib
PO
NASH HO
GLASGOW TER
CHURCHILL GARDENS
St. Gabriel's C of E Prim Sch
CHAUCER HO
BRAMWELL HO
COLERIDGE HO
LENTHALL HO
Dolphin Sq
DOLPHIN SQUARE
TURPENTINE LANE
WESTMORELAND TER
SUSSEX STREET
WESTM. PL
GILBERT HO
CHIPPEND. HO
CHURCHILL GARDENS ROAD
PAXTON TER
PEABODY CL
TELFORD TER
SHELLEY HO
KEATS HO
WHITLEY HO
GROSVENOR RD
A3212
THAMES PATH
GROSVENOR BRI
RIVER THAMES
Jetty
Battersea Power

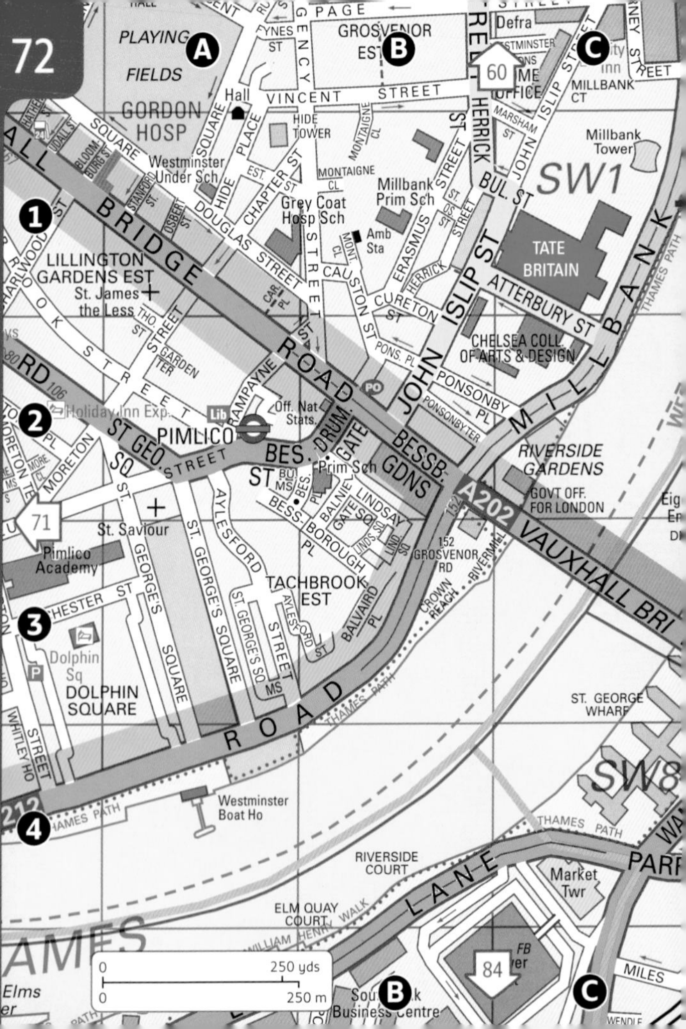
A
B
C
1
2
3
4
PLAYING FIELDS
GORDON HOSP
GROSVENOR EST
PAGE
FYNES ST
VINCENT STREET
Defra
60
MILLBANK CT
Millbank Tower
SW1
HIDE TOWER
MONTAIGNE CL
Westminster Under Sch
Hall
VINCENT SQUARE
HIDE PLACE
CHAPTER ST
MARSHAM ST
JOHN ISLIP STREET
HERRICK ST
BUL. ST
Millbank Prim Sch
Grey Coat Hosp Sch
Amb Sta
DOUGLAS STREET
BRIDGE
TATE BRITAIN
ATTERBURY ST
ERASMUS ST
CURETON ST
CAUSTON ST
JOHN ISLIP ST
LILLINGTON GARDENS EST
St. James the Less
ROOK STREET
THO ST
GARDEN TER
CHELSEA COLL. OF ARTS & DESIGN
PONS. PL
PONSONBY PL
PONSONBY TER
RAMPAYNE ST
ROAD
PO
MILLBANK
THAMES PATH
Holiday Inn Exp.
Lib
Off. Nat Stats.
PIMLICO
ST GEO. STREET
BES. ST
DRUM. GATE
BESSB. GDNS
Prim Sch
RIVERSIDE GARDENS
A202
GOVT OFF. FOR LONDON
VAUXHALL BRI
MORETON PL
MORETON TER
71
St. Saviour
Pimlico Academy
ST. GEORGE'S SQUARE
AYLESFORD STREET
BALNIE GATE
LINDSAY SQ
BESSBOROUGH PL
152 GROSVENOR RD
CROWN REACH
RIVERMILL
TACHBROOK EST
BALVAIRD PL
CHESTER ST
Dolphin Sq
DOLPHIN SQUARE
WHITLEY HO
ROAD
ST. GEORGE WHARF
SW8
Westminster Boat Ho
THAMES PATH
A212
RIVERSIDE COURT
LANE
Market Twr
PARRY
ELM QUAY COURT
WILLIAM HENRY WALK
THAMES
Elms
84
MILES
South Bank Business Centre
0 250 yds
0 250 m

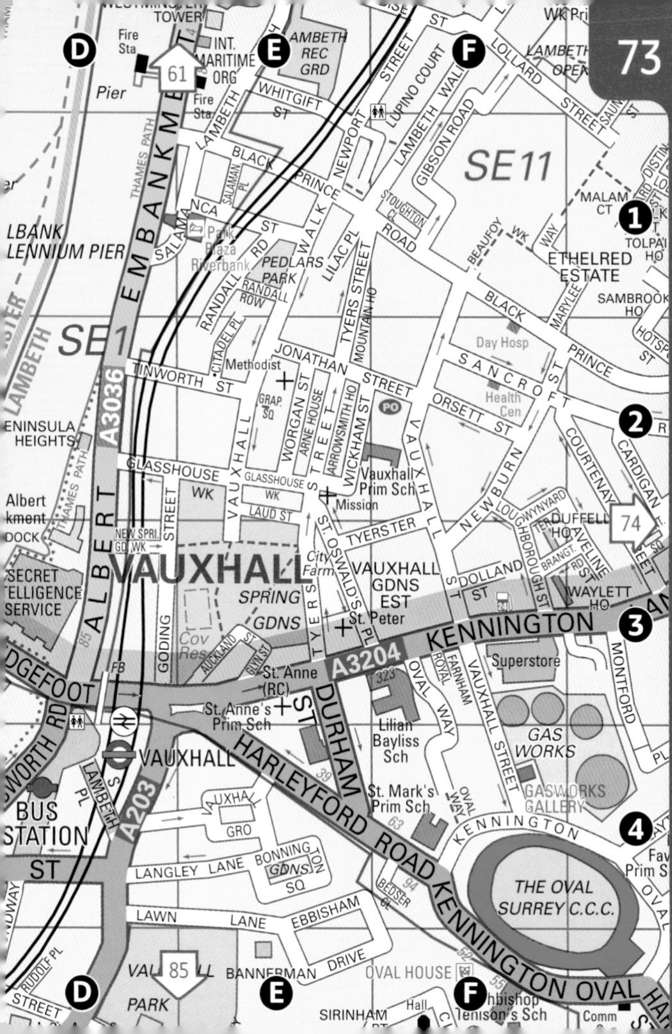

D
E
F
61
Fire Sta
INT. MARITIME ORG
Pier
LAMBETH REC GRD
WHITGIFT ST
LOLLARD STREET
LAMBETH OPEN
SE11
LUPINO COURT
NEWPORT STREET
LAMBETH WALK
GIBSON ROAD
BLACK PRINCE ROAD
STOUGHTON CL
MALAM CT
1
ETHELRED ESTATE
SAMBROOK HO
BEAUFOY WK
MARYLEE WAY
SALAMANCA ST
Park Plaza Riverbank
PEDLARS PARK
RANDALL RD
RANDALL ROW
LILAC PL
TYERS STREET
MOUNTAIN HO
ALBERT EMBANKMENT
THAMES PATH
LENNIUM PIER
SE1
A3036
TINWORTH ST
CITADEL PL
Methodist
JONATHAN STREET
GRAP. SQ
WORGAN ST
ARNE HOUSE
ARROWSMITH HO
WICKHAM ST
PO
Day Hosp
SANCROFT ST
Health Cen
ORSETT ST
2
COURTENAY
CARDIGAN
PENINSULA HEIGHTS
GLASSHOUSE WK
VAUXHALL STREET
LAUD ST
Vauxhall Prim Sch
Mission
NEWBURN
LOUGHBOROUGH ST
WYNYARD TER
DUFFELL HO
AVELINE ST
BRANGT. RD
74
Albert Embankment
NEW SPRI. GD WK
SECRET INTELLIGENCE SERVICE
VAUXHALL
City Farm
SPRING GDNS
TYERS ST
ST. OSWALD'S PL
VAUXHALL GDNS EST
St. Peter
TYERS TER
DOLLAND ST
WAYLETT HO
KENNINGTON LANE
3
GODING STREET
AUCKLAND ST
GLYN ST
A3204
Superstore
FARNHAM ROYAL
VAUXHALL STREET
MONTFORD PL
BRIDGEFOOT
FB
St. Anne (RC)
St. Anne's Prim Sch
DURHAM ST
OVAL WAY
Lilian Bayliss Sch
GAS WORKS
WANDSWORTH RD
VAUXHALL
BUS STATION
LAMBETH PL
A203
HARLEYFORD ROAD
St. Mark's Prim Sch
GASWORKS GALLERY
KENNINGTON
4
VAUXHALL GRO
BONNINGTON SQ
LANGLEY LANE
BEDSER CL
THE OVAL SURREY C.C.C.
LAWN LANE
EBBISHAM DRIVE
KENNINGTON OVAL
85
VAUXHALL PARK
BANNERMAN
OVAL HOUSE
RUDOLF PL
STREET
SIRINHAM
Hall
Archbishop Tenison's Sch
Comm

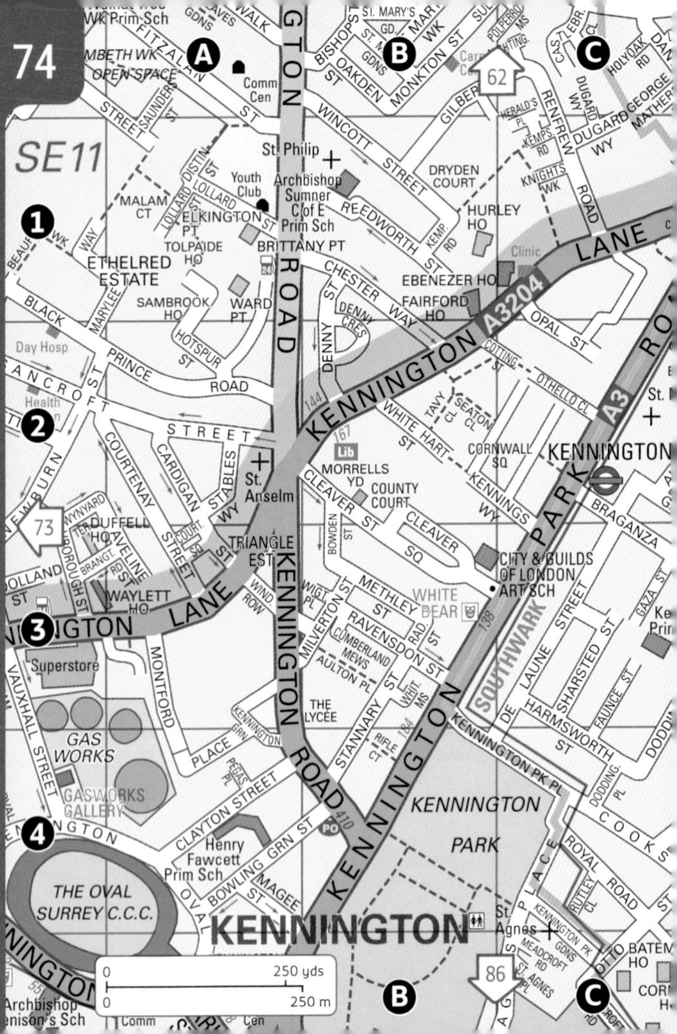
A
B
C
1
2
3
4
SE11
Wk Prim Sch
LAMBETH WK OPEN SPACE
FITZALAN ST
SAUNDERS ST
STREET
Comm Cen
KENNINGTON ROAD
BISHOPS TER
ST. MARY'S GD.
ST. MARY'S GDNS
OAKDEN ST
MONKTON ST
POLPERRO MS
LIGHTING
WINCOTT STREET
GILBERT RD
62
HERALD'S PL
KEMPS. RD
RENFREW ROAD
KNIGHTS WK
CASTLEBR. CL
HOLYOAK RD
DUGARD WY
GEORGE MATHERS
St. Philip
Archbishop Sumner C of E Prim Sch
Youth Club
DISTIN ST
LOLLARD ST
MALAM CT
ELKINGTON PT
TOLPAIDE HO
BRITTANY PT
REEDWORTH ST
DRYDEN COURT
HURLEY HO
KEMP. RD
Clinic
BEAUFOY WK
WAY
ETHELRED ESTATE
MARYLEE WAY
SAMBROOK HO
WARD PT
HOTSPUR ST
BLACK PRINCE ROAD
Day Hosp
CHESTER WAY
DENNY ST
DENNY CRES
EBENEZER HO
FAIRFORD HO
LANE
A3204
OPAL ST
COTTING. ST
OTHELLO CL
A3
KENNINGTON LANE
TAVY CL
SEATON CL
WHITE HART ST
St. M
144
167
Lib
MORRELLS YD
COUNTY COURT
CORNWALL SQ
KENNINGTON
KENNINGS WY
BRAGANZA
TYERS ST
BANCROFT ST
Health Cen
STREET
COURTENAY ST
CARDIGAN ST
STABLES WY
St. Anselm
CLEAVER ST
BOWDEN ST
CLEAVER SQ
KENNINGTON PARK ROAD
SOUTHWARK
NEWBURN
73
WYNYARD TER
DUFFELL HO
AVELINE ST
COURT SQ
STREET
TRIANGLE EST
CITY & GUILDS OF LONDON ART SCH
DOLLAND ST
BRANGT. RD
BOROUGH ST
WAYLETT HO
WIND. ROW
WIGT PL
METHLEY ST
WHITE BEAR
GAZA ST
Ke Prim
KENNINGTON LANE
MILVERTON ST
RAVENSDON ST
RAD. ST
138
LAUNE STREET
SHARSTED ST
Superstore
MONTFORD PLACE
CUMBERLAND MEWS
AULTON PL
STANNARY ST
WHIT. MS
DE LAUNE
HARMSWORTH ST
FAUNCE ST
DODDING.
VAUXHALL STREET
GAS WORKS
KENNINGTON GRN
THE LYCÉE
RIFLE CT
184
KENNINGTON PK PL
DODDING. PL
GASWORKS GALLERY
PEGAS PL
CLAYTON STREET
410
PO
KENNINGTON PARK
COOKS
KENNINGTON OVAL
Henry Fawcett Prim Sch
BOWLING GRN ST
MAGEE ST
ROYAL ROAD
RUTLEY CL
THE OVAL SURREY C.C.C.
OVAL
KENNINGTON
St. Agnes
KENNINGTON PK GDNS
MEADCROFT RD
ST. AGNES PL
ST. AGNES PL
OTTO ST
BATEM HO
CORN
0 250 yds
0 250 m
86
Archbishop Tenison's Sch
Comm Cen
55

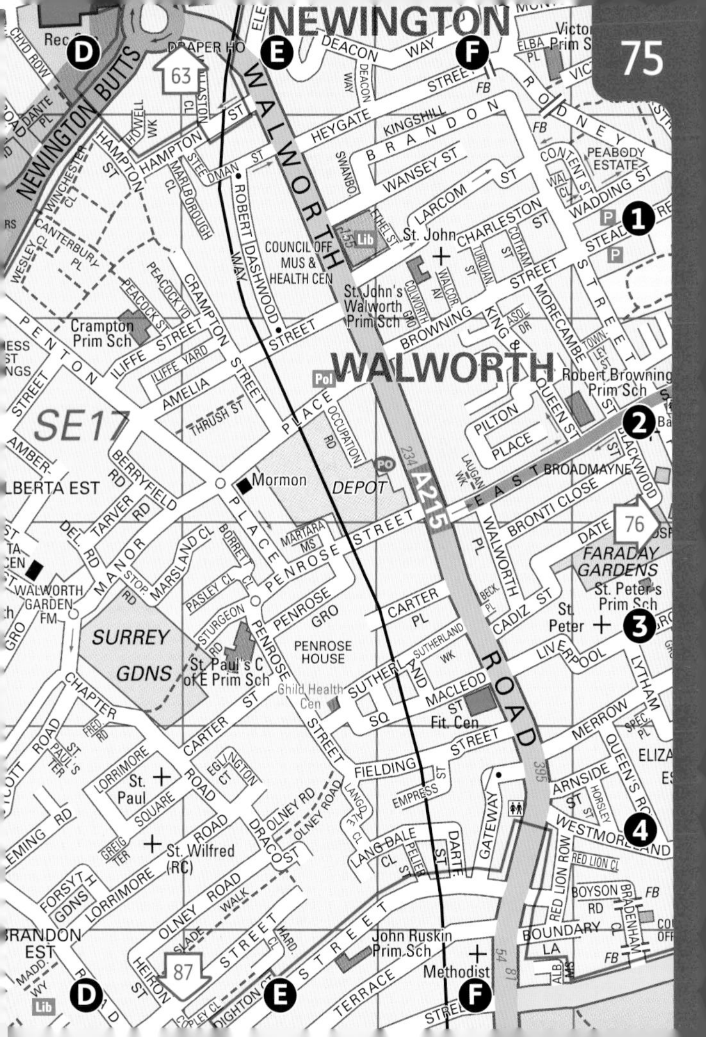
NEWINGTON
WALWORTH
SE17
D
E
F
1
2
3
4
63
76
87
NEWINGTON BUTTS
WALWORTH ROAD
A215
DEACON WAY
HEYGATE STREET
BRANDON ST
WANSEY ST
LARCOM ST
CHARLESTON ST
RODNEY RD
PEABODY ESTATE
WADDING ST
STEAD STREET
COUNCIL OFF
MUS & HEALTH CEN
St. John
St. John's Walworth Prim Sch
BROWNING STREET
ROBERT DASHWOOD WAY
HAMPTON ST
CRAMPTON STREET
Crampton Prim Sch
PENTON PLACE
ILIFFE STREET
ILIFFE YARD
AMELIA STREET
THRUSH ST
OCCUPATION RD
DEPOT
Mormon
BERRYFIELD RD
TARVER RD
MANOR PL
MARSLAND CL
PENROSE STREET
PENROSE GRO
PENROSE HOUSE
EAST STREET
BROADMAYNE
BRONTI CLOSE
FARADAY GARDENS
St. Peter's Prim Sch
St. Peter
Robert Browning Prim Sch
PILTON PLACE
MORECAMBE ST
KING & QUEEN ST
CARTER PL
SUTHERLAND SQ
SUTHERLAND WK
MACLEOD ST
Fit. Cen
CADIZ ST
LIVERPOOL
LYTHAM
MERROW
SURREY GDNS
St. Paul's C of E Prim Sch
Child Health Cen
CHAPTER RD
CARTER ST
FIELDING STREET
EMPRESS ST
St. Paul
LORRIMORE SQUARE
LORRIMORE RD
St. Wilfred (RC)
OLNEY ROAD
DRACO ST
LANGDALE CL
GATEWAY
ARNSIDE ST
WESTMORELAND
RED LION ROW
RED LION CL
BOYSON RD
BOUNDARY LA
John Ruskin Prim Sch
Methodist
BRANDON EST
WALWORTH GARDEN FM
ALBERTA EST
HEIRON ST
TERRACE
STREET

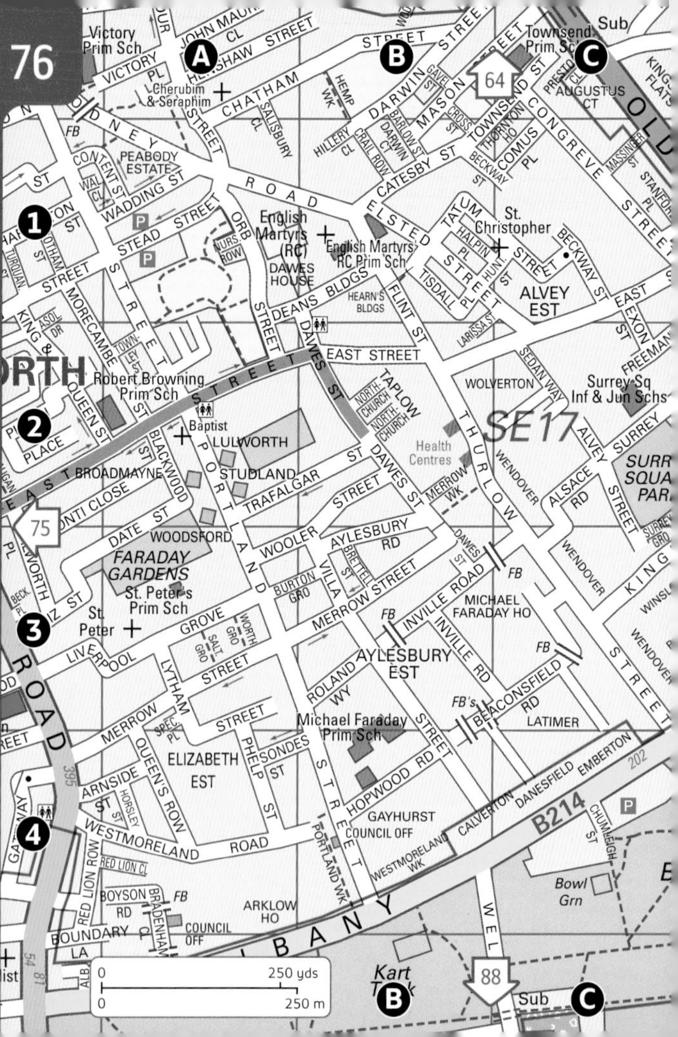
A
B
C
1
2
3
4
64
75
88
Victory Prim Sch
VICTORY PL
JOHN MAURICE CL
HENSHAW STREET
Cherubim & Seraphim
CHATHAM STREET
SALISBURY CL
HEMP WK
STREET
DARWIN ST
GAVEL ST
MASON STREET
Townsend Prim Sch
Sub
PRESTO CL
AUGUSTUS CT
KINGS FLATS
OLD
CONGREVE STREET
TOWNSEND ST
THORNTON HO
COMUS PL
CROSS ST
BARLOW ST
DARWIN CT
CRAIL ROW
HILLERY CL
CATESBY ST
BECKWAY ST
MASSINGER ST
STANFORD PL
FB
CONTENT ST
PEABODY ESTATE
WAL CL
WADDING ST
ST
SIDNEY ROAD
ORB ST
NURS. ROW
English Martyrs (RC)
English Martyrs' RC Prim Sch
ELSTED ST
TATUM ST
HALPIN PL
St. Christopher
STREET
BECKWAY ST
ALVEY EST
EAST ST
EXON ST
FREEMAN
STEAD STREET
OTHAM ST
TURQUAND ST
STREET
KING & QUEEN ST
ASOLANDO DR
MORECAMBE ST
STREET
TOWNLEY ST
DAWES HOUSE
DEANS BLDGS
HEARN'S BLDGS
FLINT ST
TISDALL PL
HUNT. ST
LARISSA ST
EAST STREET
DAWES ST
ORTH
Robert Browning Prim Sch
QUEEN ST
PLACE
NORTHCHURCH
TAPLOW
WOLVERTON
SEDAN WAY
Surrey Sq Inf & Jun Schs
SE17
Baptist
LULWORTH
STUDLAND
BROADMAYNE
BLACKWOOD ST
PORTLAND
TRAFALGAR ST
DAWES ST
Health Centres
MERROW WK
THURLOW
WENDOVER
ALVEY ST
SURREY SQUARE PARK
ALSACE RD
STREET
EAST STREET
BONTI CLOSE
DATE ST
WOODSFORD
WOOLER STREET
AYLESBURY RD
BRETTELL ST
DAWES ST
FARADAY GARDENS
St. Peter's Prim Sch
BURTON GRO
VILLA
MERROW STREET
INVILLE ROAD
FB
MICHAEL FARADAY HO
WENDOVER
KING
WINSLOW
BECK. PL
LIZ ST
St. Peter
GROVE
SALT. GRO
WORTH GRO
LIVERPOOL
STREET
FB
AYLESBURY EST
INVILLE RD
BEACONSFIELD RD
FB's
LATIMER
ROAD
ROLAND WY
LYTHAM
MERROW
SPEC. PL
STREET
Michael Faraday Prim Sch
STREET
ELIZABETH EST
PHELP ST
SONDES ST
QUEEN'S ROW
HOPWOOD RD
395
ARNSIDE ST
HORSLEY ST
GATEWAY
WESTMORELAND ROAD
GAYHURST
COUNCIL OFF
CALVERTON
DANESFIELD
EMBERTON
202
B214
CHUMLEIGH ST
PORTLAND WK
WESTMORELAND WK
RED LION ROW
RED LION CL
BOYSON RD
BRADENHAM CL
FB
ARKLOW HO
ALBANY
COUNCIL OFF
BOUNDARY LA
Bowl Grn
WELLS
Kart Track
Sub
ALB
0 250 yds
0 250 m

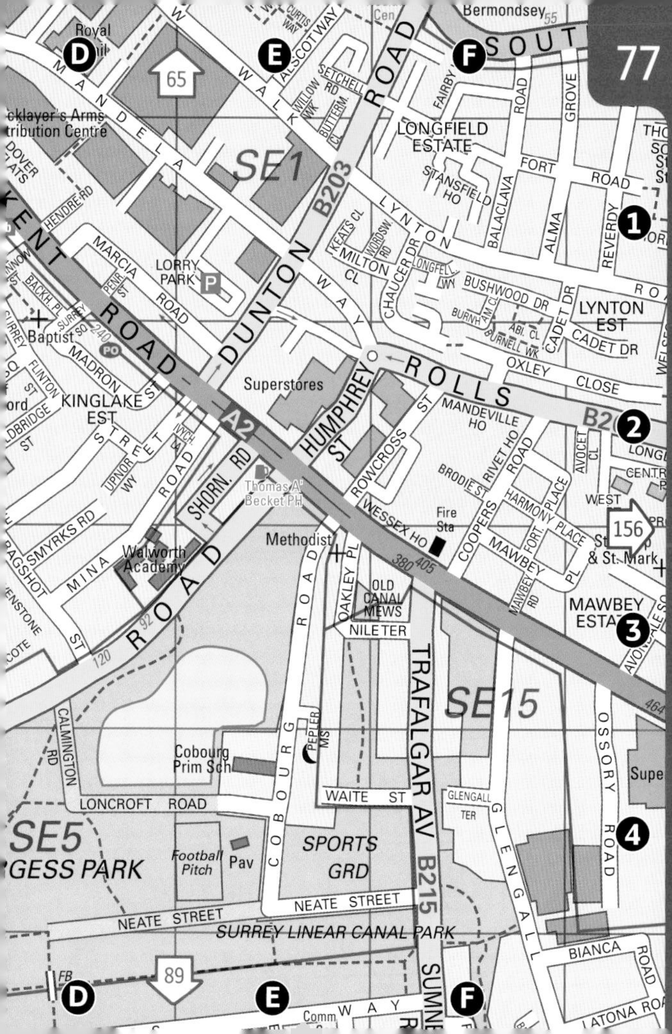
SE1
SE15
SE5
MANDELA WAY
KENT ROAD
DUNTON ROAD
B203
ROLLS ROAD
A2
TRAFALGAR AV
B215
COBOURG ROAD
LYNTON ROAD
HUMPHREY ST
MARCIA ROAD
MADRON ST
MINA ROAD
SMYRKS RD
CALMINGTON RD
LONCROFT ROAD
NEATE STREET
SURREY LINEAR CANAL PARK
OSSORY ROAD
GLENGALL ROAD
BIANCA ROAD
LATONA ROAD
LONGFIELD ESTATE
LYNTON EST
KINGLAKE EST
MAWBEY ESTATE
Superstores
LORRY PARK
Bricklayer's Arms Distribution Centre
Walworth Academy
Cobourg Prim Sch
Football Pitch
Pav
SPORTS GRD
Methodist
Thomas A' Becket PH
Fire Sta
Baptist
Bermondsey
ROWCROSS ST
WESSEX HO
OLD CANAL MEWS
NILE TER
WAITE ST
PEPLER MS
OAKLEY PL
SHORN. RD
MANDEVILLE HO
BRODIE ST
RIVET HO
COOPERS ROAD
HARMONY PLACE
MAWBEY PL
MAWBEY RD
AVOCET CL
OXLEY CLOSE
CADET DR
BUSHWOOD DR
CHAUCER DR
MILTON CL
KEATS CL
STANSFIELD HO
BALACLAVA ROAD
ALMA GROVE
FORT ROAD
REVERDY ROAD
FAIRBY
ASCOT WAY
SETCHELL RD
WILLOW WK
BUTTERM. CL
HENDRE RD
DOVER FLATS
BACKH. PL
SURREY SQ
FLINTON ST
UPNOR WY
GLENGALL TER
AVONDALE SQ
St Philip & St Mark
WEST
65
156
89
D
E
F
1
2
3
4

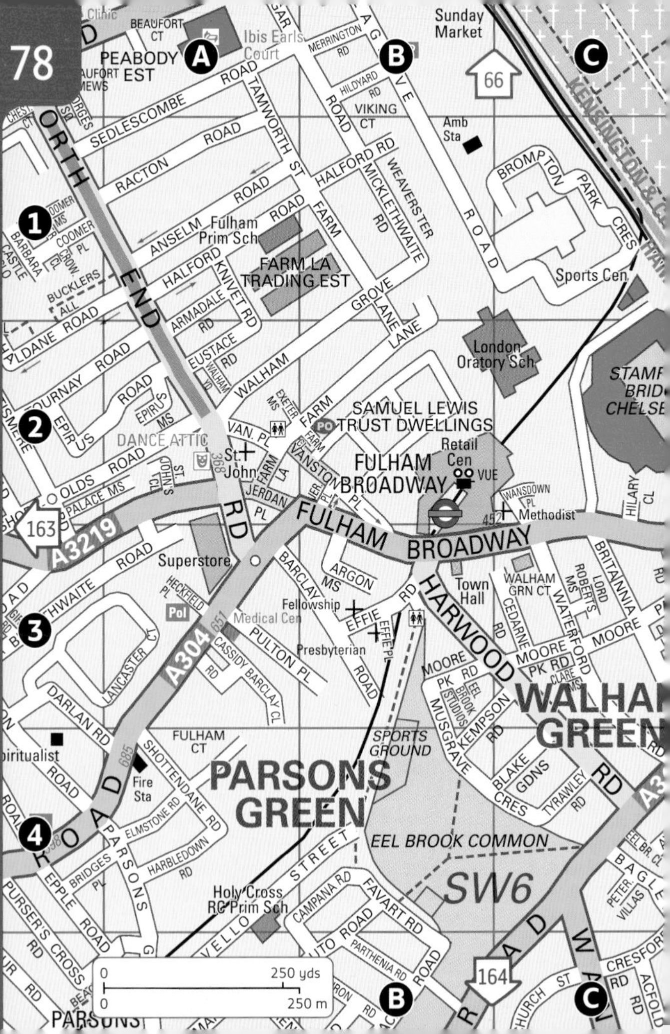
A
B
C
1
2
3
4
Clinic
BEAUFORT CT
PEABODY EST
Ibis Earls Court
MERRINGTON RD
Sunday Market
66
KENSINGTON & C
SEDLESCOMBE ROAD
RACTON ROAD
ANSELM ROAD
TAMWORTH ST
HILDYARD RD
VIKING CT
Amb Sta
HALFORD RD
MICKLETHWAITE RD
WEAVERSTER
BROMPTON PARK CRES
NORTH END RD
COOMER MS
COOMER PL
BARBARA CASTLE CL
CROW. CL
Fulham Prim Sch
FARM LA TRADING EST
FARM LA
HALFORD RD
KNIVET RD
ARMADALE RD
BUCKLERS ALL
HALDANE ROAD
GROVE LANE
Sports Cen
London Oratory Sch
EUSTACE RD
WALHAM YD
WALHAM GROVE
STAMFORD BRIDGE CHELSEA
TOURNAY ROAD
EPIRUS ROAD
EPIRUS MS
EXETER MS
FARM LANE
SAMUEL LEWIS TRUST DWELLINGS
Retail Cen
VAN. PL
VANSTON PL
DANCE ATTIC
St. John
368
ST. JOHN'S CL
FULHAM BROADWAY
VUE
OLDS ROAD
PALACE MS
JERDAN PL
WANSDOWN PL
Methodist
452
HILARY CL
163
A3219
FULHAM BROADWAY
BRITANNIA RD
THWAITE ROAD
Superstore
BARCLAY RD
ARGON MS
LORD ROBERTS MS
HECKFIELD PL
Pol
Fellowship
Town Hall
WALHAM GRN CT
Medical Cen
651
EFFIE RD
EFFIE PL
HARWOOD RD
CEDARNE RD
WATERFORD RD
MOORE PK RD
LANCASTER CT
A304
CASSIDY RD
PULTON PL
Presbyterian
BARCLAY CL
MOORE PK RD
CLARE MS
DARLAN RD
EEL BROOK STUDIOS
MUSGRAVE CRES
KEMPSON RD
WALHAM GREEN
FULHAM CT
SPORTS GROUND
Spiritualist
685
Fire Sta
SHOTTENDANE RD
PARSONS GREEN
BLAKE GDNS
TYRAWLEY RD
ELMSTONE RD
PARSONS GREEN
HARBLEDOWN RD
EEL BROOK COMMON
EEL BR. CL
BAGLEYS LA
PETER. VILLAS
BRIDGES PL
EPPLE ROAD
SW6
STREET
Holy Cross RC Prim Sch
CAMPANA RD
FAVART RD
PURSER'S CROSS RD
ROAD
PARTHENIA RD
NEW KINGS RD
164
CRESFORD RD
ACFOLD RD
CHURCH ST
0 250 yds
0 250 m
PARSONS

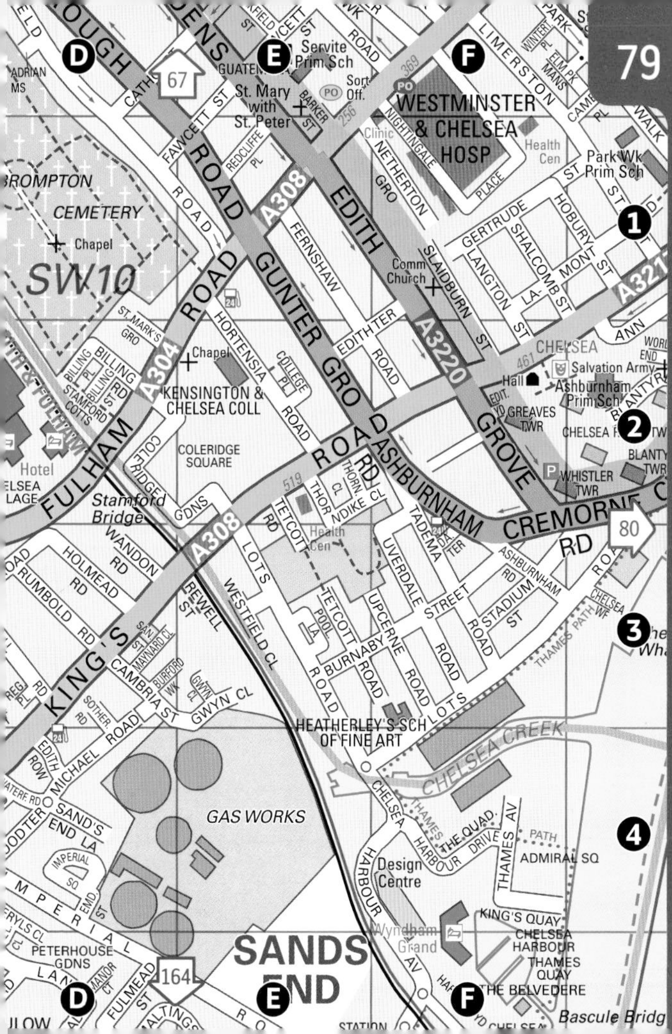
WESTMINSTER & CHELSEA HOSP
BROMPTON CEMETERY
SW10
KENSINGTON & CHELSEA COLL
COLERIDGE SQUARE
Stamford Bridge
GAS WORKS
SANDS END
HEATHERLEY'S SCH OF FINE ART
CHELSEA CREEK
Design Centre
Wyndham Grand
CHELSEA HARBOUR
Bascule Bridg

CHELSEA
SW10
St. John with St. Andrew
A
B
C
1
2
3
4
68
79
165
KING'S
CHEYNE WALK
CREMORNE RD
A3217
A3320
A3220
B305
BEAUFORT ST
BATTERSEA BRI
SIR THOMAS MORE EST
Holy Sacrament (RC)
Crosby Hall
ROPERS ORCHARD
Chelsea Old
Moravian
MORAVIAN PL
MILMAN'S STREET
MUNRO TER
RILEY ST
CREMORNE EST
WORLD'S END PASS
APOLLO PL
Salvation Army
Hall
Ashburnham Prim Sch
BLANTYRE
BERENGER TWR
CHELSEA REACH TWR
BLANTYRE TWR
WHISTLER TWR
GREAVES TWR
EDIT.
Health Cen
Park Wk Prim Sch
CAMERA PL
PARK WALK
HOBURY ST
STREET
MONT
LAMONT RD
SHALCOMB ST
LANGTON ST
ANN LANE
CHELSEA
PLACE
ELM PK
CINEWORLD
Antique Mkt
PAULTONS SQUARE
PAULTONS ST
WALDRON MS
OLD CHURCH STREET
JUSTICE WK
LAWRENCE ST
UPPER CHEYNE ROW
DANVERS ST
PETYT PL
OLD CHE. MS
Ho Sch
VALE
GDNS
STREET
Chelsea Wharf
CHELSEA WF
THAMES PATH
ASHBURNHAM RD
STADIUM ST
ROAD
CHELSEA CREEK
ADMIRAL SQ
KING'S QUAY
CHELSEA HARBOUR
THE BELVED
Bascule Bridge
MONTEVETRO
St. Mary
Wharves
HESTER
ROYAL COLL OF ART
HOWIE
THORNEY CRES
PAV. DR
WHISTLERS AV
CHURCH ROAD
CONDRAY PL
BOLINGBROKE WALK
Westbridge Prim Sch
SELWORTHY HO
SOMERSET EST
SPARKFORD HO
SUNBURY LA
BATTERSEA
RANDALL RD
RANDALL CL
SURREY LANE EST
WESTBRIDGE
BLOMFIELD CT
GRANFIELD ST
THORPE
Salesian Coll
0 250 yds
0 250 m

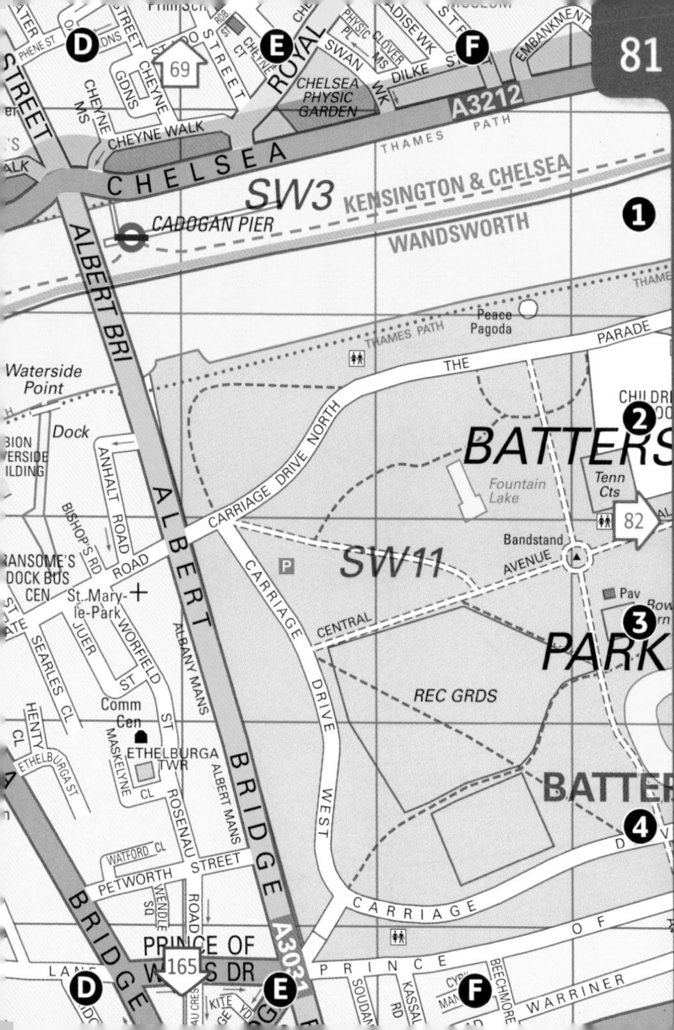
D
E
F
PHENE ST
69
CHEYNE GDNS
CHEYNE MS
CHEYNE WALK
ROYAL
SWAN WK
PHYSIC PL
CLOVER MS
PARADISE WK
DILKE ST
EMBANKMENT
CHELSEA PHYSIC GARDEN
A3212
THAMES PATH
CHELSEA
SW3
KENSINGTON & CHELSEA
WANDSWORTH
CADOGAN PIER
1
ALBERT BRI
Peace Pagoda
THAMES PATH
THE PARADE
Waterside Point
Dock
ANHALT ROAD
BISHOP'S RD
CARRIAGE DRIVE NORTH
BATTERS
2
Fountain Lake
Tenn Cts
82
Bandstand
AVENUE
CENTRAL
SW11
ALBERT
ROAD
RANSOME'S DOCK BUS CEN
St. Mary-le-Park
JUER
WORFIELD ST
SEARLES CL
HENTY CL
ETHELBURGA ST
Comm Cen
MASKELYNE CL
ETHELBURGA TWR
ALBANY MANS
ALBERT MANS
ROSENAU ROAD
CARRIAGE DRIVE WEST
Pav
3
PARK
REC GRDS
BATTER
4
BRIDGE
WATFORD CL
PETWORTH STREET
WENDLE SQ
PRINCE OF WALES DR
165
A3031
CARRIAGE
PRINCE OF
LANE
SOUDAN
KASSALA RD
BEECHMORE
WARRINER
KITE YD

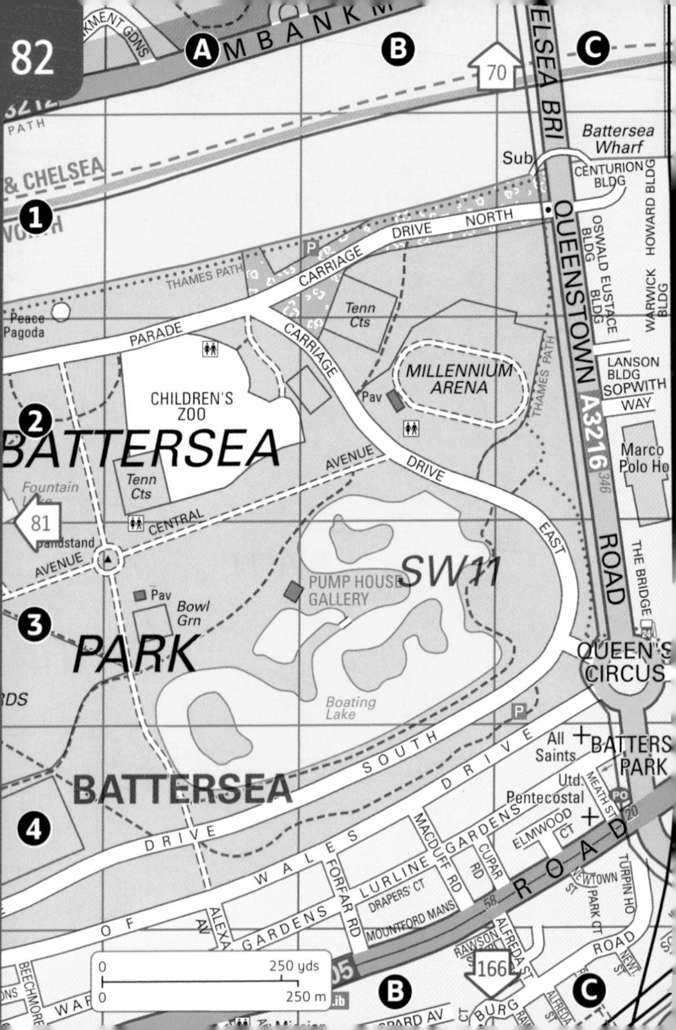
EMBANKMENT GDNS
EMBANKMENT
A
B
C
70
CHELSEA BRI
PATH
& CHELSEA
1
Battersea Wharf
Sub
CENTURION BLDG
HOWARD BLDG
OSWALD EUSTACE BLDG
WARWICK BLDG
QUEENSTOWN
A3216
ROAD
346
CARRIAGE DRIVE NORTH
THAMES PATH
P
Tenn Cts
Peace Pagoda
PARADE
CARRIAGE
MILLENNIUM ARENA
THAMES PATH
LANSON BLDG
SOPWITH WAY
Marco Polo Ho
CHILDREN'S ZOO
Pav
2
BATTERSEA
AVENUE
DRIVE
Tenn Cts
Fountain Lake
81
Bandstand
CENTRAL
AVENUE
EAST
SW11
PUMP HOUSE GALLERY
THE BRIDGE
Pav
Bowl Grn
3
PARK
QUEEN'S CIRCUS
Boating Lake
P
All Saints
BATTERSEA PARK
BATTERSEA
SOUTH
DRIVE
Utd. Pentecostal
MEATH ST
PO
4
DRIVE
WALES
OF
MACDUFF RD
GARDENS
ELMWOOD CT
ROAD
FORFAR RD
LURLINE
CUPAR RD
NEWTOWN ST
TURPIN HO
DRAPERS' CT
PARK CT
ALEXANDRA AV
GARDENS
MOUNTFORD MANS
58
ALFREDA ST
RAWSON ST
ROAD
BEECHMORE
0
250 yds
250 m
166
B
C
BURG
LEOPARD AV

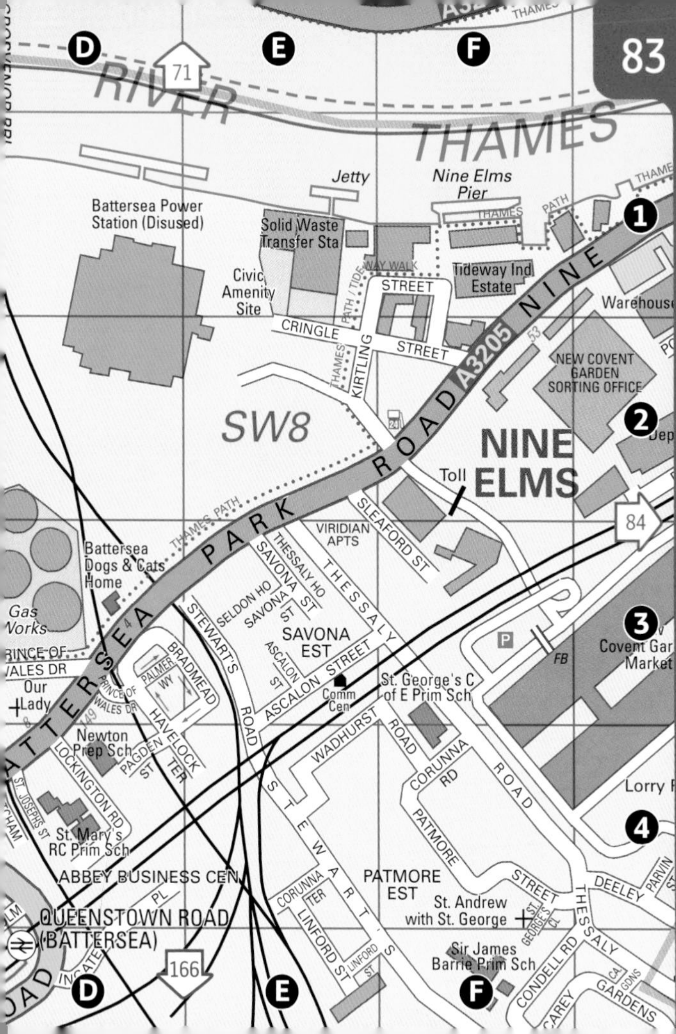
D
E
F
71
RIVER
THAMES
Jetty
Nine Elms Pier
Battersea Power Station (Disused)
Solid Waste Transfer Sta
THAMES PATH
Civic Amenity Site
Tideway Ind Estate
STREET
CRINGLE
STREET
KIRTLING
Warehouse
A3205
NINE
ELMS
NEW COVENT GARDEN SORTING OFFICE
SW8
NINE ELMS
Toll
84
Battersea Dogs & Cats Home
Gas Works
PARK
ROAD
BATTERSEA
VIRIDIAN APTS
SLEAFORD ST
THESSALY HO
SAVONA ST
SELDON HO
THESSALY
SAVONA EST
ASCALON STREET
ASCALON ST
STEWART'S ROAD
BRADMEAD
PALMER WY
PRINCE OF WALES DR
Our Lady
Comm Cen
St. George's C of E Prim Sch
FB
Covent Garden Market
WADHURST ROAD
CORUNNA RD
HAVELOCK TER
PAGDEN ST
Newton Prep Sch
LOCKINGTON RD
ST. JOSEPHS ST
St. Mary's RC Prim Sch
PATMORE
Lorry
ABBEY BUSINESS CEN
PATMORE EST
PATMORE STREET
DEELEY
PARVIN ST
St. Andrew with St. George
ST. GEORGE'S CL
CORUNNA TER
LINFORD ST
QUEENSTOWN ROAD (BATTERSEA)
166
Sir James Barrie Prim Sch
CONDELL RD
CAREY GARDENS
CA. GDNS
STEWART'S
INGATE
ROAD

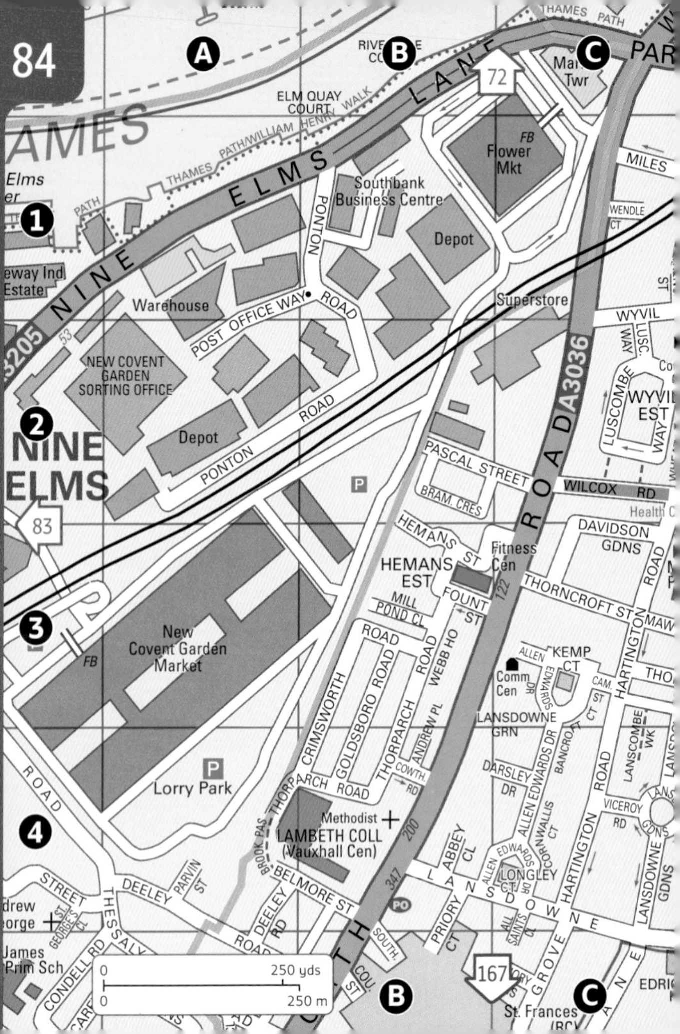
A
B
C
THAMES PATH
Mkt Twr
72
ELM QUAY COURT
THAMES PATH/WILLIAM HENRY WALK
NINE ELMS LANE
1
FB
Flower Mkt
MILES
Southbank Business Centre
WENDLE CT
PONTON ROAD
Depot
Warehouse
POST OFFICE WAY
Superstore
WYVIL
A3205
53
NEW COVENT GARDEN SORTING OFFICE
A3036
LUSCOMBE WAY
WYVIL EST
2
NINE ELMS
Depot
PONTON ROAD
P
PASCAL STREET
WILCOX RD
BRAM. CRES
83
HEMANS ST
DAVIDSON GDNS
Fitness Cen
HEMANS EST
THORNCROFT ST
MILL POND CL
FOUNT ST
122
3
FB
New Covent Garden Market
ROAD
CRIMSWORTH ROAD
GOLDSBORO ROAD
THORPARCH ROAD
WEBB HO
ANDREW PL
ALLEN EDWARDS DR
KEMP CT
Comm Cen
CAM. ST
HARTINGTON ROAD
LANSDOWNE GRN
BANCROFT CT
LANSCOMBE WK
DARSLEY DR
COWTH. RD
P
Lorry Park
ROAD
THORPARCH ROAD
4
BROOK PAS
Methodist
LAMBETH COLL (Vauxhall Cen)
200
VICEROY RD
LANSDOWNE GDNS
ABBEY CL
CORNWALLIS CT
LONGLEY CT
ALLEN EDWARDS DR
BELMORE ST
347
LANSDOWNE
STREET
DEELEY
PARVIN ST
ST. GEORGE'S CL
THESSALY
PRIORY CT
ALL SAINTS CT
DEELEY RD
PO
SOUTH.
GROVE
CONDELL RD
0
250 yds
0
250 m
COU. ST
B
167
C
St. Frances

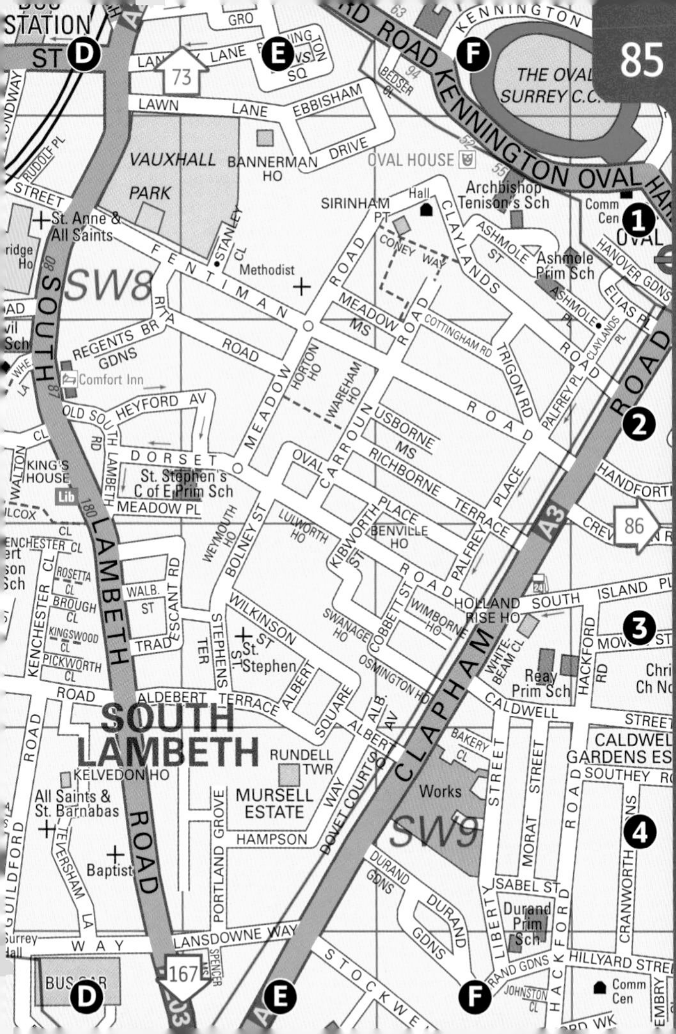
BUS STATION
ST
D
E
F
GRO
LANE
73
SQ
LAWN LANE
EBBISHAM
KENNINGTON
RD ROAD
THE OVAL
SURREY C.C.
BEDSER CL
KENNINGTON OVAL
OVAL HOUSE
VAUXHALL PARK
BANNERMAN HO
DRIVE
Hall
Archbishop Tenison's Sch
Comm Cen
OVAL
SIRINHAM PT
RUDOLF PL
STREET
St. Anne & All Saints
FENTIMAN
STANLEY CL
Methodist
ROAD
CONEY WAY
CLAYLANDS
ASHMOLE ST
Ashmole Prim Sch
HANOVER GDNS
ELIAS PL
ASHMOLE PL
SW8
SOUTH
RITA ROAD
REGENTS BR GDNS
MEADOW MS
ROAD
COTTINGHAM RD
TRIGON RD
CLAYLANDS PL
ROAD
ROAD
Comfort Inn
HORTON HO
WAREHAM HO
PALFREY PL
HEYFORD AV
OLD SOUTH LAMBETH RD
MEADOW
USBORNE MS
RICHBORNE TERRACE
HANDFORTH
DORSET
St. Stephen's C of E Prim Sch
KING'S HOUSE
WALTON
Lib
OVAL
CARROUN
PLACE
MEADOW PL
LAMBETH
BOLNEY ST
LULWORTH HO
KIBWORTH ST
PLACE
BENVILLE HO
PALFREY
A3
CREW
86
WEYMOUTH HO
ROAD
ENCHESTER CL
KENCHESTER CL
ROSETTA CL
BROUGH CL
KINGSWOOD CL
PICKWORTH CL
WALB. ST
TRAD
ESCANT RD
TER
STEPHENS
WILKINSON ST
St. Stephen
SWANAGE HO
COBBETT ST
WIMBORNE HO
HOLLAND RISE HO
SOUTH ISLAND PL
CLAPHAM
WHITEBEAM CL
Reay Prim Sch
HACKFORD RD
MOWLL ST
OSMINGTON HO
ROAD
ALDEBERT TERRACE
ALBERT SQUARE
ALB. AV
ALBERT SQ
CALDWELL STREET
CALDWELL GARDENS EST
SOUTH LAMBETH
RUNDELL TWR
KELVEDON HO
All Saints & St. Barnabas
MURSELL ESTATE
WAY
DOVET COURT
BAKERY CL
Works
STREET
STREET
SOUTHEY RD
ROAD
SW9
MORAT
CRANWORTH
HAMPSON
GUILDFORD
TEVERSHAM LA
Baptist
ROAD
PORTLAND GROVE
DURAND GDNS
DURAND GDNS
ISABEL ST
LIBERTY
Durand Prim Sch
HACKFORD
Surrey Hall
WAY
LANSDOWNE WAY
SPENCER
167
STOCKWELL
HILLYARD STREET
RAND GDNS
JOHNSTON CL
Comm Cen
BUS CAR
A
ORD WK

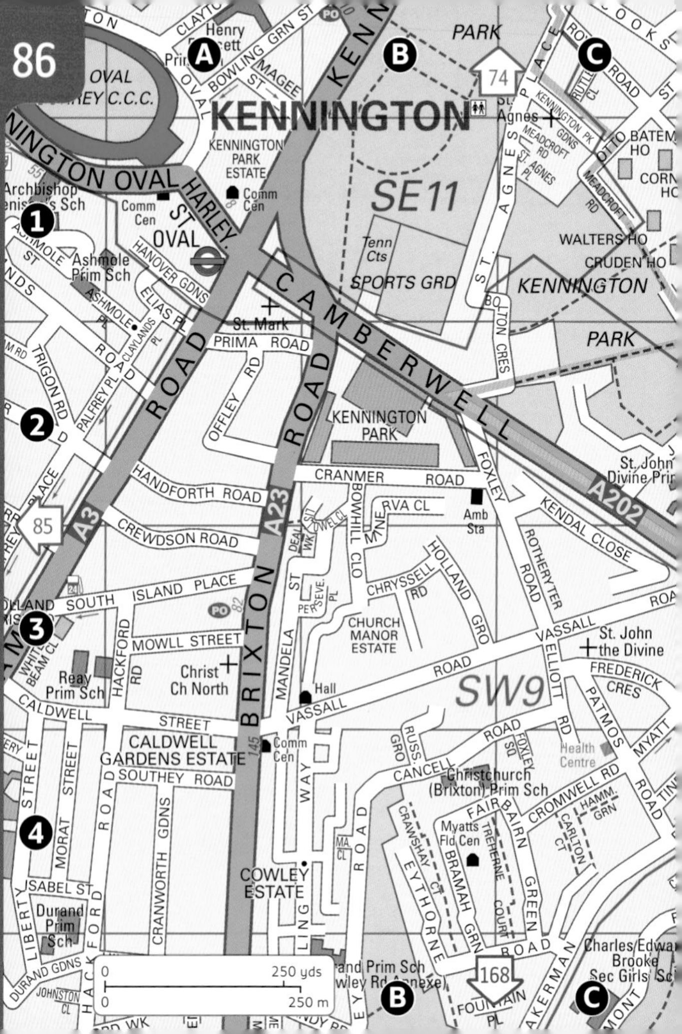
A
B
C
1
2
3
4
KENNINGTON
SE11
SW9
OVAL
SURREY C.C.C.
KENNINGTON OVAL
Henry Fawcett Prim Sch
BOWLING GRN ST
MAGEE ST
KENNINGTON PARK ESTATE
Comm Cen
Archbishop Tenison's Sch
HARLEY ST
OVAL
HANOVER GDNS
ASHMOLE ST
Ashmole Prim Sch
ASHMOLE PL
ELIAS PL
CLAYLANDS PL
ROAD
TRIGON RD
PALFREY PL
CAMBERWELL
St. Mark
PRIMA ROAD
OFFLEY RD
ROAD
A3
A23
A202
Tenn Cts
SPORTS GRD
KENNINGTON PARK
PARK
74
85
168
St. Agnes
KENNINGTON PK GDNS
MEADCROFT RD
ST. AGNES PL
ST. AGNES PL
RUTLEY CL
ROAD
OTTO ST
BATEMAN HO
CORNELL HO
WALTERS HO
CRUDEN HO
KENNINGTON PARK
BOLTON CRES
St. John Divine Prim
KENDAL CLOSE
HANDFORTH ROAD
CRANMER ROAD
BOWHILL CLO
MINERVA CL
Amb Sta
FOXLEY
CREWDSON ROAD
DEAL WK
SEVE PL
ROTHERY TER
ROAD
HOLLAND GRO
CHRYSSELL RD
SOUTH ISLAND PLACE
PO
MOWLL STREET
HACKFORD RD
Christ Ch North
BRIXTON ROAD
MANDELA ST
CHURCH MANOR ESTATE
VASSALL ROAD
St. John the Divine
FREDERICK CRES
ELLIOTT RD
PATMOS ROAD
MYATT
Reay Prim Sch
WHITEBEAM CL
CALDWELL STREET
CALDWELL GARDENS ESTATE
Hall
Comm Cen
WAY
RUSSELL GRO
CANCELL ROAD
FOXLEY SQ
Health Centre
Christchurch (Brixton) Prim Sch
CROMWELL RD
HAMM. GRN
SOUTHEY ROAD
MORAT STREET
STREET
ROAD
CRANWORTH GDNS
FAIRBAIRN GREEN
Myatts Fld Cen
CRAWSHAY CT
EYTHORNE CT
BRAMAH GRN
TREHERNE COURT
CARLTON CT
MA. CL
COWLEY ESTATE
ISABEL ST
LIBERTY
Durand Prim Sch
HACKFORD
DURAND GDNS
JOHNSTON CL
0 250 yds
0 250 m
Durand Prim Sch (Cowley Rd Annexe)
ROAD
AKERMAN
FOUNTAIN PL
Charles Edward Brooke Sec Girls' Sch

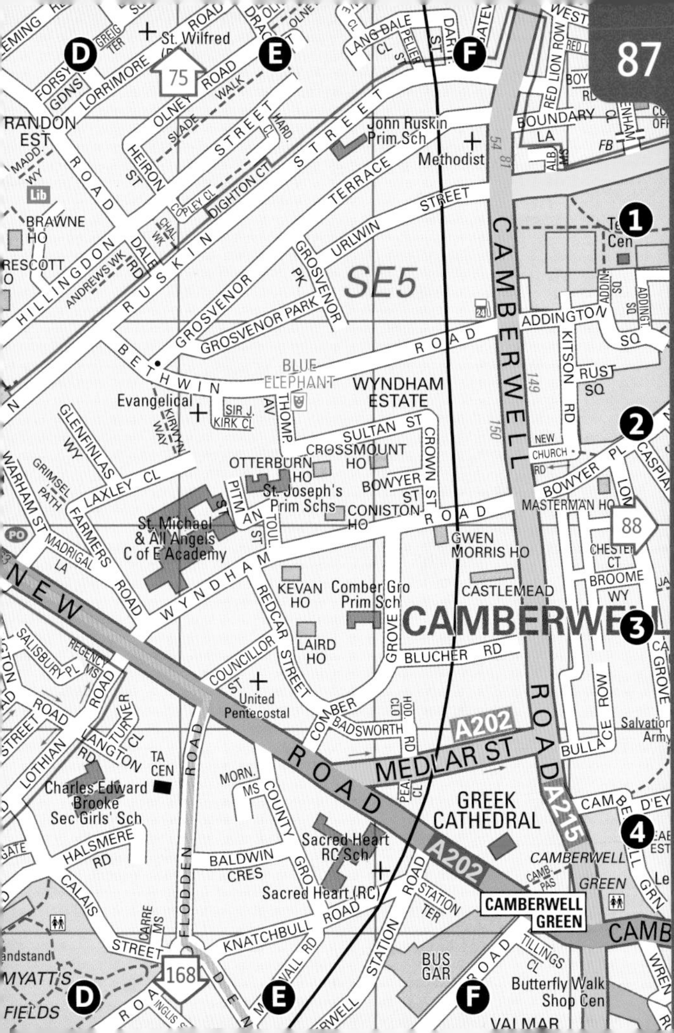
D
E
F
1
2
3
4
75
88
168
St. Wilfred
LORRIMORE ROAD
OLNEY ROAD
SLADE WALK
FORSYTH GDNS
GREIG TER
RANDON EST
MADD. WY
Lib
BRAWNE HO
PRESCOTT HO
HILLINGDON ST
ANDREWS WK
DALE RD
RUSKIN
HEIRON ST
COPLEY CL
CHAL. WK
DIGHTON CT
HARD. CL
STREET
John Ruskin Prim Sch
Methodist
LANG DALE CL
PELIER ST
DARTREY
WEST
RED LION ROW
BOYSON RD
BOUNDARY LA
ALB. MS
FB
TERRACE
URLWIN STREET
GROSVENOR PK
GROSVENOR
GROSVENOR PARK
SE5
CAMBERWELL ROAD
Tech Cen
ADDINGTON SQ
ADDINGT.
KITSON RD
RUST SQ
BETHWIN ROAD
BLUE ELEPHANT
WYNDHAM ESTATE
Evangelical
KIRWYN WAY
SIR J. KIRK CL
THOMP. AV
SULTAN ST
CROWN ST
CROSSMOUNT HO
OTTERBURN HO
St. Joseph's Prim Schs
BOWYER ST
CONISTON HO
NEW CHURCH RD
BOWYER PL
CASPIAN
MASTERMAN HO
GLENFINLAS WY
GRIMSEL PATH
LAXLEY CL
WARHAM ST
FARMERS ROAD
PITMAN ST
TOUL. ST
St. Michael & All Angels C of E Academy
MADRIGAL LA
PO
WYNDHAM ROAD
GWEN MORRIS HO
CHESTER CT
BROOME WY
CASTLEMEAD
KEVAN HO
Comber Gro Prim Sch
REDCAR STREET
CAMBERWELL
LAIRD HO
GROVE
BLUCHER RD
NEW ROAD
SALISBURY PL
REGENCY MS
COUNCILLOR ST
United Pentecostal
COMBER
BADSWORTH RD
HOD. CLO.
A202
BOW ROW
BULLACE ROW
Salvation Army
LOTHIAN ROAD
LANGTON RD
TURNER CL
TA CEN
Charles Edward Brooke Sec Girls' Sch
MORN. MS
COUNTY GRO
MEDLAR ST
PEA. CL
GREEK CATHEDRAL
A215
CAMBERWELL GREEN
CAMB. PAS
CAMBERWELL GRN
HALSMERE RD
BALDWIN CRES
Sacred Heart RC Sch
Sacred Heart (RC)
FLODDEN ROAD
CALAIS STREET
CARRE MS
KNATCHBULL ROAD
STATION ROAD
STATION TER
BUS GAR
TILLINGS CL
Butterfly Walk Shop Cen
VALMAR
CAMB
WREN
Bandstand
MYATT'S FIELDS
DENMARK
INGLIS ST
RD

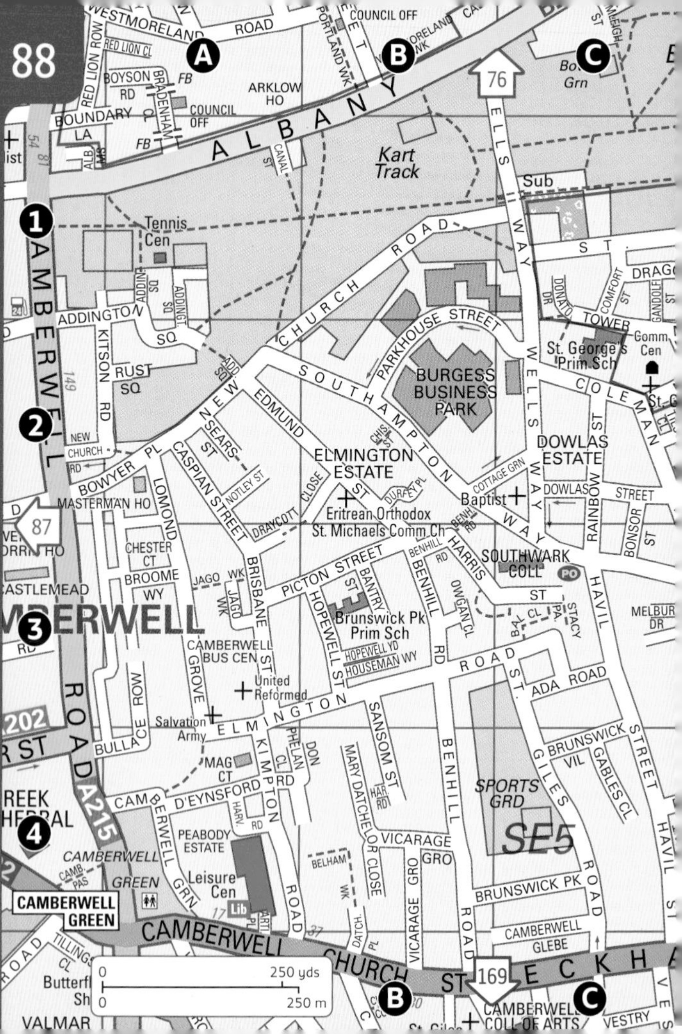

A
B
C
1
2
3
4
76
87
169
WESTMORELAND ROAD
RED LION CL
RED LION ROW
BOYSON RD
BRADENHAM CL
FB
ARKLOW HO
COUNCIL OFF
BOUNDARY LA
ALBANY
CANAL ST
Kart Track
Sub
WELLS WAY
Tennis Cen
ADDINGTON SQ
ADDINGTON
KITSON RD
RUST SQ
CHURCH ROAD
PARKHOUSE STREET
BURGESS BUSINESS PARK
SOUTHAMPTON WAY
EDMUND ST
NEW CHURCH RD
BOWYER PL
SEARS ST
NOTLEY ST
CASPIAN STREET
LOMOND GRO
CLOSE
DRAYCOTT
ELMINGTON ESTATE
Eritrean Orthodox St. Michaels Comm Ch
DURFEY PL
COTTAGE GRN
Baptist
DONATO DR
COMFORT ST
GANDOLFI ST
TOWER
St. George's Prim Sch
Comm. Cen
COLEMAN
DOWLAS ESTATE
DOWLAS STREET
RAINBOW ST
BONSOR ST
MASTERMAN HO
CHESTER CT
BROOME WY
JAGO WK
CASTLEMEAD
CAMBERWELL
CAMBERWELL ROAD
BRISBANE ST
PICTON STREET
BANTRY ST
HOPEWELL ST
BENHILL RD
HARRIS ST
OWGAN CL
SOUTHWARK COLL
PO
BAY CL
STACY PA.
HAVIL ST
MELBURNE DR
Brunswick Pk Prim Sch
HOPEWELL YD
HOUSEMAN WY
CAMBERWELL BUS CEN
GROVE
United Reformed
Salvation Army
ELMINGTON ROAD
BULLACE ROW
A202
A215
MAG CT
KIMPTON RD
PHELAN CL
DON
SANSOM ST
MARY DATCHELOR CLOSE
HAR. RD
SPORTS GRD
SE5
GILES ST
ADA ROAD
BRUNSWICK VIL
GABLES CL
BRUNSWICK STREET
D'EYNSFORD RD
CAMBERWELL GRN
HARV. RD
PEABODY ESTATE
Leisure Cen
Lib
VICARAGE GRO
BELHAM WK
BRUNSWICK PK
CAMBERWELL GLEBE
CAMBERWELL GREEN
CAMB. PAS
CAMBERWELL CHURCH ST
PECKHAM
DATCH. PL
TILLINGS CL
Butterfl Sh
VALMAR
CAMBERWELL COLL OF ARTS
VESTRY
0 250 yds
0 250 m

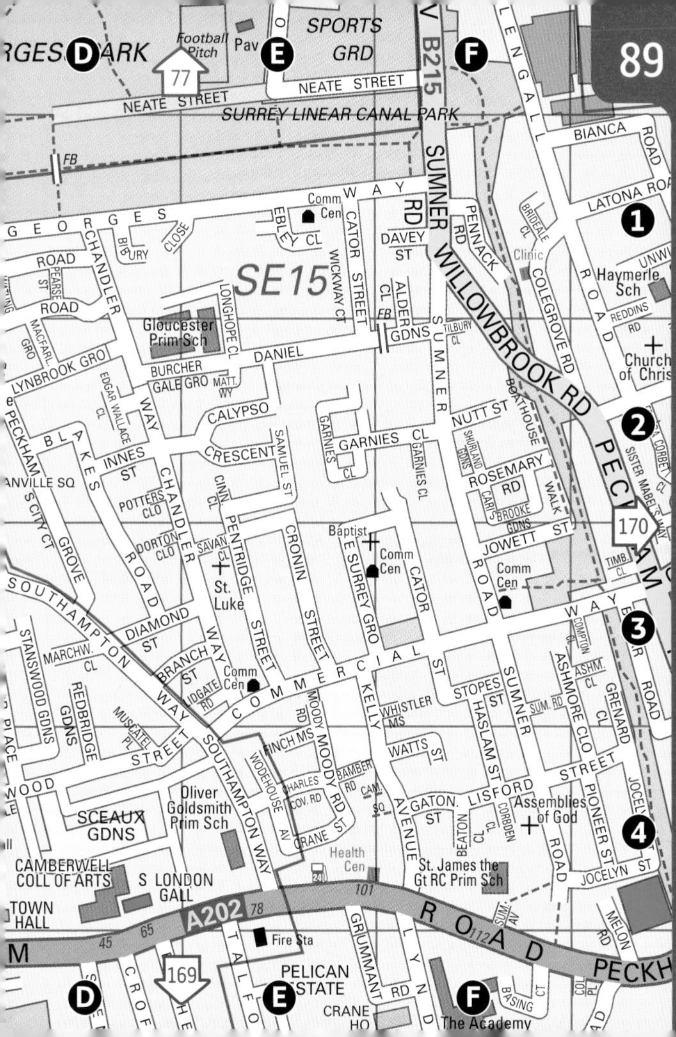
RGES PARK
D
E
F
Football Pitch
Pav
77
SPORTS GRD
NEATE STREET
NEATE STREET
B215
SURREY LINEAR CANAL PARK
FB
LENGALL
BIANCA ROAD
LATONA ROA
1
GEORGES WAY
Comm Cen
EBLEY CL
CATOR STREET
RD
SUMNER
WILLOWBROOK RD
PENNACK RD
BRIDEALE CL
Clinic
COLEGROVE RD
ROAD
UNWI
Haymerle Sch
REDDINS RD
CHANDLER
BIBURY
CLOSE
DAVEY ST
ROAD
PEARSE ST
ROAD
SE15
WICKWAY CT
ALDER CL
FB
GDNS
TILBURY CL
SUMNER
Church of Christ
MACFARL. GRO
LONGHOPE CL
Gloucester Prim Sch
LYNBROOK GRO
BURCHER
DANIEL
GALE GRO
MATT. WY
EDGAR WALLACE CL
WAY
CALYPSO
GARNIES
GARNIES CL
NUTT ST
BOATHOUSE
2
PECKHAM
BLAKES
INNES ST
CRESCENT
SAMUEL ST
SHURLAND GDNS
GARNIES CL
ROSEMARY RD
WALK
SISTER MABEL'S WAY
CORBET CL
ANVILLE SQ
PECKHAM'S CITY CT
GROVE
CHANDLER
POTTERS CLO
CINN. CL
PENTRIDGE
CRONIN
CARLS
BROOKE GDNS
170
DORTON CLO
ROAD
SAVAN. CL
Baptist
Comm Cen
JOWETT ST
TIMB. CL
St. Luke
STREET
STREET
E SURREY GRO
CATOR
ROAD
Comm Cen
WAY
3
SOUTHAMPTON
DIAMOND ST
STANSWOOD GDNS
MARCHW. CL
BRANCH ST
WAY
COMMERCIAL ST
COMPTON CL
ASHM. CL
GRENARD
ROAD
Comm Cen
LIDGATE RD
STOPES ST
SUMNER
ASHMORE CLO
SUM. RD
REDBRIDGE GDNS
MUSCATEL PL
WAY
MOODY RD
KELLY
WHISTLER MS
HASLAM ST
PLACE
STREET
SOUTHAMPTON WAY
FINCH MS
MOODY RD
WATTS ST
STREET
WOOD
WODEHOUSE AV
CHARLES COV. RD
BAMBER RD
CAM. SQ
AVENUE
GATON. ST
LISFORD
CORBDEN CL
PIONEER ST
JOCELYN
Oliver Goldsmith Prim Sch
SCEAUX GDNS
CRANE ST
BEATON CL
Assemblies of God
ROAD
4
CAMBERWELL COLL OF ARTS
S LONDON GALL
Health Cen
St. James the Gt RC Prim Sch
JOCELYN ST
TOWN HALL
A202
78
101
SUM. AV
ROAD
112
MELON RD
M
45
65
Fire Sta
GRUMMANT RD
LYND
PECKH
CROF
169
TALFO
PELICAN ESTATE
CRANE HO
The Academy
BASING CT
COL. PL

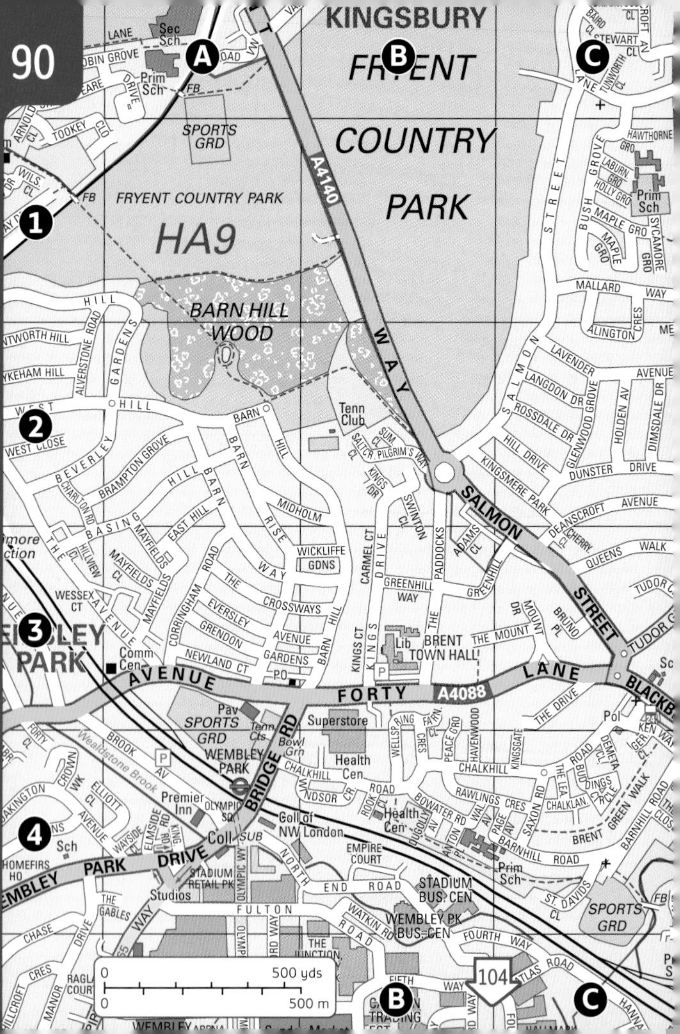
KINGSBURY
FRYENT COUNTRY PARK
FRYENT COUNTRY PARK
HA9
SPORTS GRD
BARN HILL WOOD
A4140
WAY
SALMON STREET
A4088
FORTY AVENUE
FORTY LANE
BLACKBIRD
TOOKEY CLO
ARNOLD CL
WILS. CL
ROBIN GROVE
PRIM SCH
SEC SCH
FB
HAWTHORNE GRO
LABURN. GRO
HOLLY GRO
MAPLE GRO
SYCAMORE GRO
BUSH GROVE
STREET
MALLARD WAY
ALINGTON CRES
LAVENDER AVENUE
LANGDON DR
ROSSDALE DR
GLENWOOD GROVE
HOLDEN AV
DIMSDALE DR
HILL DRIVE
DUNSTER DRIVE
KINGSMERE PARK
DEANSCROFT AVENUE
CHERRY CL
QUEENS WALK
TUDOR CL
TUDOR GDNS
BRUNO PL
MOUNT DR
THE MOUNT
BRENT TOWN HALL
Lib
WENTWORTH HILL
WYKEHAM HILL
ALVERSTONE ROAD
GARDENS
WEST HILL
WEST CLOSE
BEVERLEY GARDENS
BRAMPTON GROVE
BARN HILL
BARN RISE
MIDHOLM
WICKLIFFE GDNS
THE CROSSWAYS
EVERSLEY AVENUE
GRENDON GARDENS
NEWLAND CT
CORRINGHAM ROAD
EAST HILL
MAYFIELDS
MAYFIELDS CL
BASING HILL
CHARLTON RD
HILLVIEW CL
WESSEX CT
THE AVENUE
Comm Cen
Tenn Club
SUM. CL
SALTCR. CL
PILGRIM'S WAY
KINGS DR
SWINTON CL
PADDOCKS
ADAMS CL
CARMEL CT
KINGS DRIVE
GREENHILL WAY
GREENHILL
KINGS CT
THE PADDOCKS
PO
P
PARK
Pav
SPORTS GRD
Tenn Cts
Bowl Grn
WEMBLEY PARK
BRIDGE RD
Superstore
Health Cen
CHALKHILL RD
WINDSOR CR.
ROOK CL
BOWATER RD
DUGOLLY AV
WELLSPRING CRES
FARM CL
PEACE GRO
HAVENWOOD
KINGSGATE
CHALKHILL
RAWLINGS CRES
SAXON RD
THE LEA
CHALKLAN.
BUDDINGS CIRCLE
DEMETA CL
GREEN WALK
BARNHILL ROAD
THE CLOSE
BRENT
THE DRIVE
Pol
GER. CL.
KEN WAY
Health Cen
Prim Sch
ST. DAVIDS CL
SPORTS GRD
FB
FORTY CL
BROOK AV
Wealdstone Brook
CROWN WK
ELLIOTT CL
PAKINGTON
Sch
HOMEFIRS HO
WEMBLEY PARK DRIVE
WAYSIDE CT
ELMSIDE RD
KING. RD
Premier Inn
OLYMPIC SQ
Coll
Coll of NW London
SUB
NORTH END ROAD
EMPIRE COURT
STADIUM RETAIL PK
OLYMPIC WY
Studios
STADIUM BUS CEN
WEMBLEY PK BUS CEN
THE GABLES
WAY
FULTON
WATKIN RD
FOURTH WAY
ATLAS ROAD
CHASE
DRIVE
CRES
MANOR
RAGLAN COURT
THE JUNCTION
FIFTH WAY
TRADING
WEMBLEY ARENA
104
0 500 yds
0 500 m
A
B
C
1
2
3
4

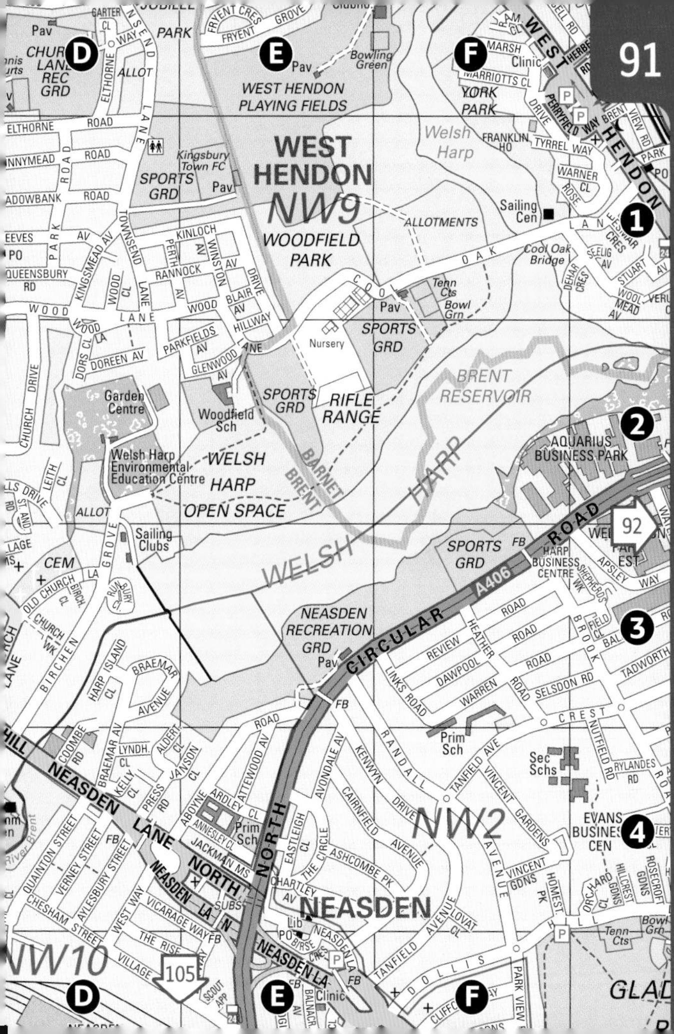

D
E
F
1
2
3
4
WEST HENDON
NW9
WOODFIELD PARK
WEST HENDON PLAYING FIELDS
CHURCH LANE REC GRD
Pav
PARK
ALLOT
GARTER CL
WAY
ELTHORNE
ELTHORNE ROAD
TOWNSEND LANE
FRYENT CRES
FRYENT GROVE
Bowling Green
MARSH
Clinic
MARRIOTTS CL
YORK PARK
WEST HENDON
PERRYFIELD WAY
DRIVE
BRENT VIEW RD
Welsh Harp
FRANKLIN HO
TYRREL WAY
WARNER CL
ROSE
Sailing Cen
Kingsbury Town FC
SPORTS GRD
ROAD
ROAD
ROAD
PARK
KINLOCH
PERTH AV
WINSTON AV
DRIVE
RANNOCK
BLAIR AV
HILLWAY
KINGSMEAD AV
QUEENSBURY RD
WOOD CL
WOOD LANE
WOOD
WOOD LA
PARKFIELDS AV
GLENWOOD AV
DORS CL
DOREEN AV
ALLOTMENTS
OAK LANE
COOL OAK LANE
Cool Oak Bridge
DEHAR CRES
SELIG AV
STUART AV
WOOLMEAD AV
ESMAR CRES
Tenn Cts
Bowl Grn
Nursery
SPORTS GRD
RIFLE RANGE
BRENT RESERVOIR
AQUARIUS BUSINESS PARK
Garden Centre
Woodfield Sch
Welsh Harp Environmental Education Centre
WELSH HARP OPEN SPACE
BARNET
BRENT
WELSH HARP
CHURCH DRIVE
LEITH CL
ALLOT
Sailing Clubs
GROVE
CEM
OLD CHURCH LA
BIRCH CL
RUNBURY CL
CHURCH WK
BIRCHEN
SPORTS GRD
FB
ROAD
A406
HARP BUSINESS CENTRE
SHEPHERDS WK
APSLEY WAY
92
NEASDEN RECREATION GRD
CIRCULAR
REVIEW ROAD
HEATHER
DAWPOOL ROAD
WARREN
ROAD
LINKS ROAD
SELSDON RD
BROOK
FIELD CL
TADWORTH
CREST
NUTFIELD RD
RYLANDES RD
Prim Sch
Sec Schs
EVANS BUSINESS CEN
TANFIELD AVE
VINCENT GARDENS
RANDALL
KENWYN DRIVE
CAIRNFIELD AVENUE
NW2
AVENUE
VINCENT GDNS
HOMESTEAD PK
ORCHARD CL
HILLCREST GDNS
ROSECROFT GDNS
Bowl Grn
Tenn Cts
GLAD
HARP ISLAND CL
BRAEMAR AVENUE
BRAEMAR AV
COOMBE RD
LYNDH. CL
KELLY CL
ALDERTON CL
JANSON CL
PRESS RD
ABOYNE
ARDLEY CL
ATTEWOOD AV
ANNESLEY CL
Prim Sch
JACKMAN MS
AVONDALE AV
EASTLEIGH CL
THE CIRCLE
ASHCOMBE PK
CHARTLEY AV
NORTH
NEASDEN LANE NORTH
HILL
NEASDEN LANE
QUAINTON STREET
VERNEY STREET
AYLESBURY STREET
CHESHAM STREET
WEST WAY
VICARAGE WAY
THE RISE
VILLAGE
NEASDEN LA
SUBS
NEASDEN
Lib
PO
NEASDEN LA
Clinic
TANFIELD AVENUE
LOVAT CL
DOLLIS
PARK VIEW
NW10
105
SCOUT APP
River Brent

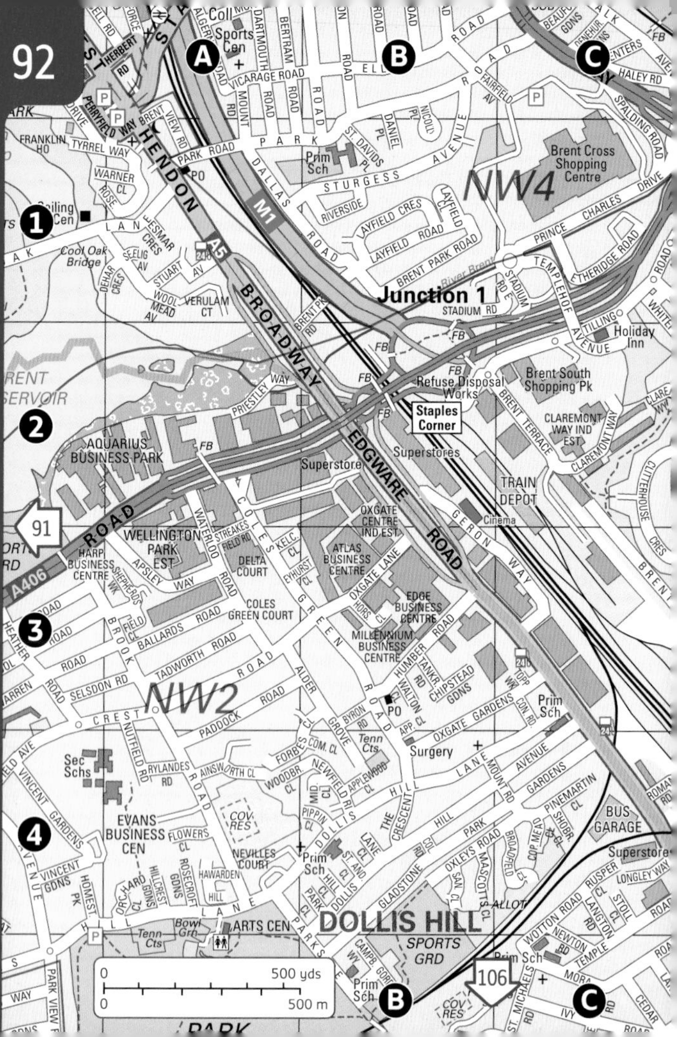
A
B
C
1
2
3
4
NW4
NW2
Brent Cross Shopping Centre
Junction 1
Staples Corner
Brent South Shopping Pk
Holiday Inn
Refuse Disposal Works
AQUARIUS BUSINESS PARK
WELLINGTON PARK EST
HARP BUSINESS CENTRE
DELTA COURT
COLES GREEN COURT
ATLAS BUSINESS CENTRE
OXGATE CENTRE IND EST
EDGE BUSINESS CENTRE
MILLENNIUM BUSINESS CENTRE
CLAREMONT WAY IND EST
TRAIN DEPOT
Cinema
Superstore
Superstores
BRENT RESERVOIR
EVANS BUSINESS CEN
DOLLIS HILL
SPORTS GRD
BUS GARAGE
ARTS CEN
Sec Schs
Prim Sch
Surgery
Sports Cen
Sailing Cen
Cool Oak Bridge
River Brent
HENDON
BROADWAY
EDGWARE ROAD
A5
M1
A406
ROAD
PARK ROAD
VICARAGE ROAD
STURGESS AVENUE
BRENT PARK ROAD
LAYFIELD CRES
LAYFIELD ROAD
PRINCE CHARLES DRIVE
TEMPLEHOF AVENUE
GERON WAY
OXGATE LANE
OXGATE GARDENS
COLES GREEN
BALLARDS ROAD
TADWORTH ROAD
SELSDON RD
PADDOCK ROAD
CREST ROAD
DOLLIS HILL LANE
GLADSTONE PARK GARDENS
OXLEYS ROAD
WOTTON ROAD
VINCENT GARDENS
HUMBER ROAD
CHIPSTEAD GDNS
PRIESTLEY WAY
STADIUM RD
CLAREMONT WAY
CLITTERHOUSE CRES
SPALDING ROAD
HALEY RD
91
106
0 500 yds
0 500 m

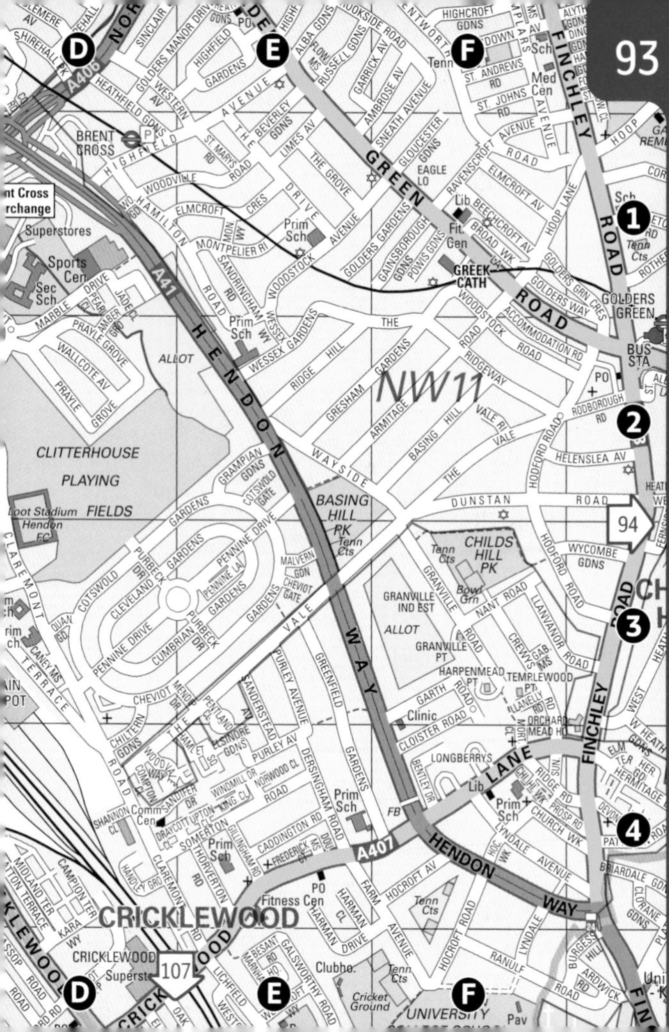
D
E
F
NW11
CRICKLEWOOD
CLITTERHOUSE
PLAYING
FIELDS
HENDON WAY
A41
A406
A407
GREEN
ROAD
FINCHLEY
ROAD
BRENT
CROSS
Superstores
Sports
Cen
Sec
Sch
Prim
Sch
ALLOT
BASING
HILL
PK
Tenn
Cts
CHILDS
HILL
PK
Bowl
Grn
GRANVILLE
IND EST
GRANVILLE
PT
HARPENMEAD
PT
Clinic
Lib
Fit
Cen
GREEK
CATH
EAGLE
LO
GOLDERS
GREEN
BUS
STA
PO
Med
Cen
Fitness Cen
Clubhse.
Cricket
Ground
UNIVERSITY
Pav
Comm
Cen
CRICKLEWOOD
Superst
Loot Stadium
Hendon
FC
HIGHFIELD
WOODVILLE
HAMILTON
ELMCROFT
MONTPELIER RI
SANDRINGHAM
WOODSTOCK
AVENUE
THE
DRIVE
GOLDERS GARDENS
GAINSBOROUGH
GDNS
POWIS GDNS
WESSEX GARDENS
RIDGE
HILL
GRESHAM
GARDENS
ARMITAGE
BASING
HILL
WAYSIDE
DUNSTAN
ROAD
THE
VALE
RIDGEWAY
HODFORD ROAD
RODBOROUGH
RD
HELENSLEA AV
WYCOMBE
GDNS
NANT ROAD
LLANVANOR
ROAD
CREWYS
GRANVILLE
ROAD
GARTH
ROAD
CLOISTER ROAD
LONGBERRYS
LANE
CHURCH WK
LYNDALE
AVENUE
HENDON
WAY
HOCROFT AV
HOCROFT ROAD
RANULF
ROAD
BURGESS
HILL
ARDWICK
RD
BRIARDALE
CLORANE
GDNS
MARBLE
DRIVE
PRAYLE GROVE
WALLCOTE AV
PRAYLE
GROVE
GRAMPIAN
GDNS
COTSWOLD
GATE
GARDENS
PURBECK
DR
CLEVELAND
GARDENS
PENNINE DRIVE
CUMBRIAN
GARDENS
CHEVIOT
GATE
MALVERN
CHEVIOT
CHILTERN
GDNS
CLAREMONT
TERRACE
ROAD
PURLEY AVENUE
PURLEY AV
SANDERSTEAD
GREENFIELD
GARDENS
DERSINGHAM ROAD
ELSINORE
GDNS
WINDMILL DR
NORWOOD CL
CADDINGTON RD
SOMERTON
THORVERTON
HARMAN
DRIVE
FARM
AVENUE
GALSWORTHY ROAD
LICHFIELD
CAMPION TER
MIDLAND TER
KARA
WY
HIGHCROFT
GDNS
ST. ANDREWS
RD
ST. JOHNS
RD
RAVENSCROFT AVENUE
ELMCROFT AV
BEECHCROFT AV
HOOP LANE
GOLDERS WAY
ACCOMMODATION RD
ALBA GDNS
RUSSELL GDNS
GARRICK AV
AMBROSE AV
SNEATH AVENUE
GLOUCESTER
GDNS
LIMES AV
THE GROVE
BEVERLEY
GDNS
ST. MARYS
RD
SINCLAIR
GOLDERS MANOR DR
HEATHFIELD GDNS
94
107
1
2
3
4

A
B
C
1
2
3
4
HOOP LANE CEMETERY (JEWISH)
Crem
GARDEN OF REMEMBRANCE
GOLDERS GREEN
HAMPSTEAD HEATH EXTENSION
NW11
HAMPSTEAD GOLF COURSE
Bunkers Hill
TURNERS WOOD
Pav
Ponds
SANDY HEATH
FINCHLEY ROAD
HOOP LANE
CORRINGHAM ROAD
MIDDLETON RD
ROTHERWICK ROAD
Tenn Cts
Sch
DEPOT
GOLDERS GREEN
Tennis Courts
Clubho.
BUS STA
NORTH END ROAD
A598
A502
ELMCROFT AV
BROAD WK
GOLDERS GRN CRES
GOLDERS WAY
ACCOMMODATION RD
RIDGEWAY
RODBOROUGH RD
HODFORD ROAD
HELENSLEA AV
PO
ST. ALBANS LA
WEST HEATH DRIVE
ST. ALBANS CL
WEST HEATH AVENUE
GOLDERS PK CL
PARK DR
PARK AV
THE PARK
HEATHSIDE
WEST HEATH AVE
HAMPSTEAD WAY
REYNOLDS CL
CHANDOS WY
HEATHCROFT
WELLGARTH RD
WILDWOOD ROAD
INGRAM
FAIRWAY CL
TURNERS WOOD
MOUNT VIEW CL
ROMNEY CL
WILDWOOD TER
Comm Cen
The Old Bull & Bush PH
NORTH END
NORTH END AV
LILY POND
SWAN POND
Tenn Cts
GOLDERS HILL PARK
Bandstand
Deer Enclosure
CHILDS HILL
HILL GARDEN
The Hill
WEST HEATH
CYCLE PATH
LEG OF MUTTON POND
HEATHLANDS
NORTH END WAY
SPANIARDS
WYCOMBE GDNS
HODFORD ROAD
CHILDS HILL PK
NANT ROAD
LLANVANOR ROAD
TEMPLEWOOD PT.
FERNSIDE
CARLTON CL
EDEN CL
WESTOVER HILL
ELM WALK
BEECHWORTH CL
SANDY ROAD
WEST HEATH ROAD
W HEATH GDNS
BEAUM. GDNS
CENACLE CL
W HEATH CL
HERMITAGE LANE
PLATT'S LANE
TELEG. HILL
HEATH
REDINGTON ROAD
TEMPLEWOOD AVENUE
MANSION GDNS
FIRECREST DRI
BIRCHWOOD DR
GRANGE GDNS
WHITESTONE POND
WHITESTONE LA
ROAD
Radio Mast
LOWER TER
UPPER TER
BRANCH HILL
HEYSHAM LA
SPEDAN CL
ADMIR. WALK
FENTON HO
HAMPSTEAD HIGH
HEATH STREET
HOLFORD RD
ELM ROW
Holly Bush PH
HAMPSTEAD
LANE
Lib
Prim Sch
CHURCH WK
PROSP. RD
PATTISON ROAD
DEVONSHIRE PL
BRIARDALE GDNS
CLORANE GDNS
HOLLYCROFT AVENUE
ROSECROFT AVENUE
FERNCROFT AVENUE
PLATT'S LANE
REDINGTON GDNS
TEMPLE GDNS
OAK HILL WY
FROGNAL
MT VERNON
HOLLY HILL
WAY
LYNDALE
RANULF
Pav
500 yds
500 m
0
93
108

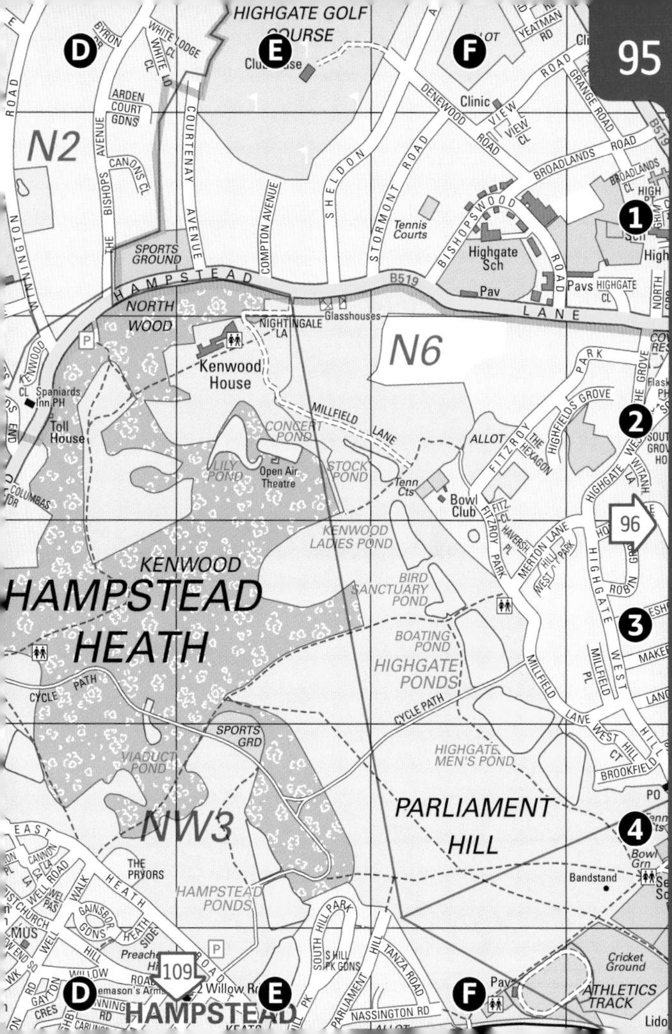
HIGHGATE GOLF COURSE
Club House
D
E
F
N2
N6
NW3
HAMPSTEAD LANE
B519
NORTH WOOD
Kenwood House
NIGHTINGALE LA
Glasshouses
MILLFIELD LANE
CONCERT POND
LILY POND
Open Air Theatre
STOCK POND
Tenn Cts
Bowl Club
ALLOT
KENWOOD LADIES POND
KENWOOD
HAMPSTEAD HEATH
BIRD SANCTUARY POND
BOATING POND
HIGHGATE PONDS
CYCLE PATH
SPORTS GRD
VIADUCT POND
HIGHGATE MEN'S POND
PARLIAMENT HILL
HAMPSTEAD PONDS
THE PRYORS
Spaniards Inn PH
Toll House
SPORTS GROUND
Highgate Sch
Pav
Pavs
Tennis Courts
Clinic
BROADLANDS ROAD
BISHOPSWOOD ROAD
DENEWOOD ROAD
VIEW ROAD
VIEW CL
GRANGE ROAD
YEATMAN RD
SHELDON AVENUE
STORMONT ROAD
COMPTON AVENUE
COURTENAY AVENUE
THE BISHOPS AVENUE
CANONS CL
ARDEN COURT GDNS
WHITE LODGE CL
BYRON DR
WINNINGTON ROAD
KENWOOD CL
FITZROY PARK
THE HEXAGON
HIGHFIELDS GROVE
PARK
THE GROVE
HIGHGATE WEST HILL
WITANHURST LA
MERTON LANE
MILLFIELD PL
WEST HILL CT
BROOKFIELD
Bandstand
Bowl Grn
Cricket Ground
ATHLETICS TRACK
Lido
PO
96
109
HAMPSTEAD
EAST HEATH ROAD
WELL WALK
WILLOW ROAD
GAYTON RD
SOUTH HILL PARK
S HILL PK GDNS
TANZA ROAD
PARLIAMENT HILL
NASSINGTON RD
2 Willow Rd
1
2
3
4

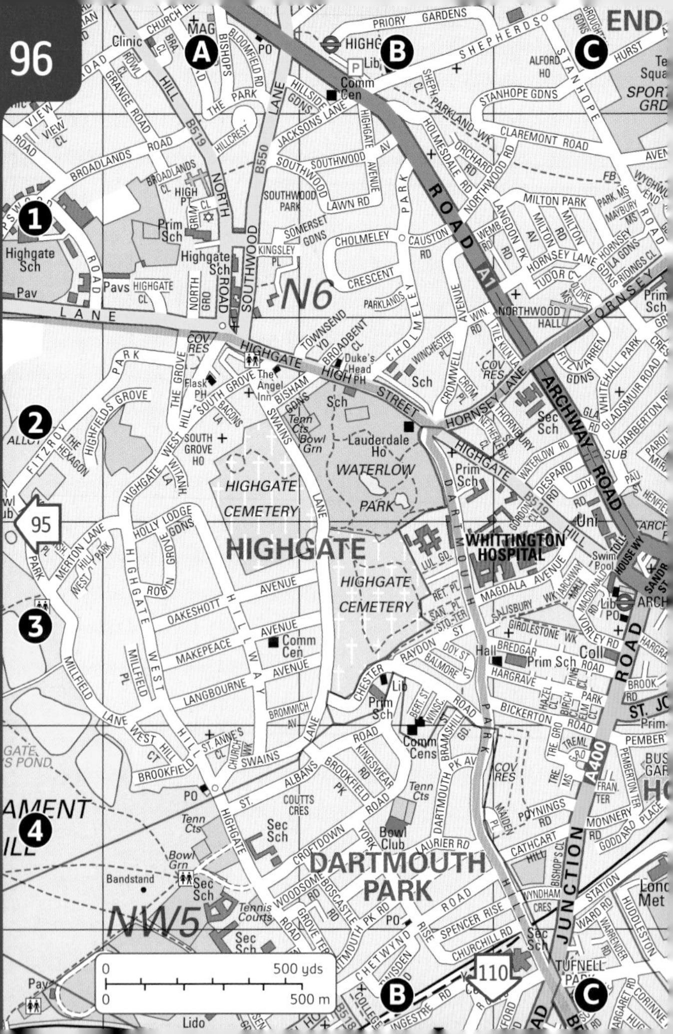
A
B
C
1
2
3
4
N6
NW5
HIGHGATE
DARTMOUTH PARK
HIGHGATE CEMETERY
WATERLOW PARK
WHITTINGTON HOSPITAL
Highgate Sch
Lauderdale Ho
Flask PH
The Angel Inn
Duke's Head PH
SOUTH GROVE HO
NORTHWOOD HALL
SOUTHWOOD PARK
NORTH HILL
SOUTHWOOD LANE
HIGHGATE HIGH STREET
HIGHGATE WEST HILL
SWAINS LANE
DARTMOUTH PARK HILL
ARCHWAY ROAD
JUNCTION ROAD
HORNSEY LANE
CHOLMELEY CRESCENT
SHEPHERDS HILL
PRIORY GARDENS
BROADLANDS ROAD
MILLFIELD LANE
MERTON LANE
FITZROY PARK
HOLLY LODGE GDNS
OAKESHOTT AVENUE
MAKEPEACE AVENUE
LANGBOURNE AVENUE
ST. ALBANS ROAD
YORK RISE
CHETWYND RD
SPENCER RISE
MAGDALA AVENUE
HARGRAVE PARK
BICKERTON ROAD
CATHCART HILL
TUFNELL PARK
Bandstand
Lido
95
110
0 500 yds
0 500 m

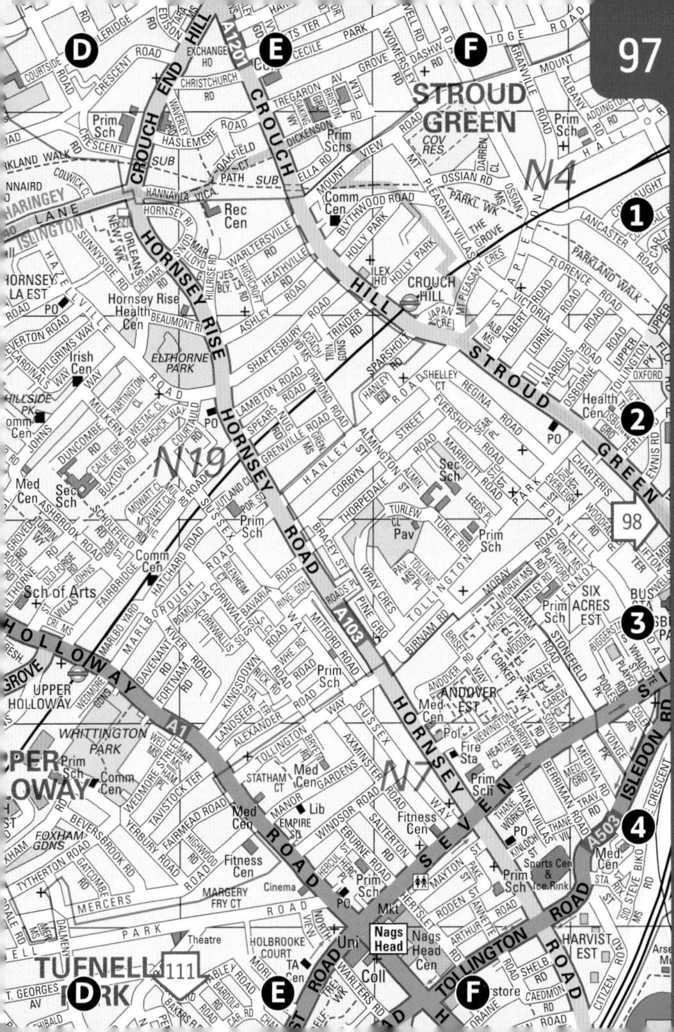
STROUD GREEN
N4
N19
N7
CROUCH END HILL
CROUCH HILL
HORNSEY RISE
HORNSEY ROAD
HOLLOWAY ROAD
SEVEN SISTERS ROAD
STROUD GREEN ROAD
TOLLINGTON ROAD
ISLEDON RD
HORNSEY LANE
HARINGEY
ISLINGTON
Crouch Hill
Upper Holloway
Whittington Park
Elthorne Park
Hornsey Rise Health Cen
Six Acres Est
Andover Est
Harvist Est
Nags Head
Tufnell Park
A1201
A103
A1
A503
98
111

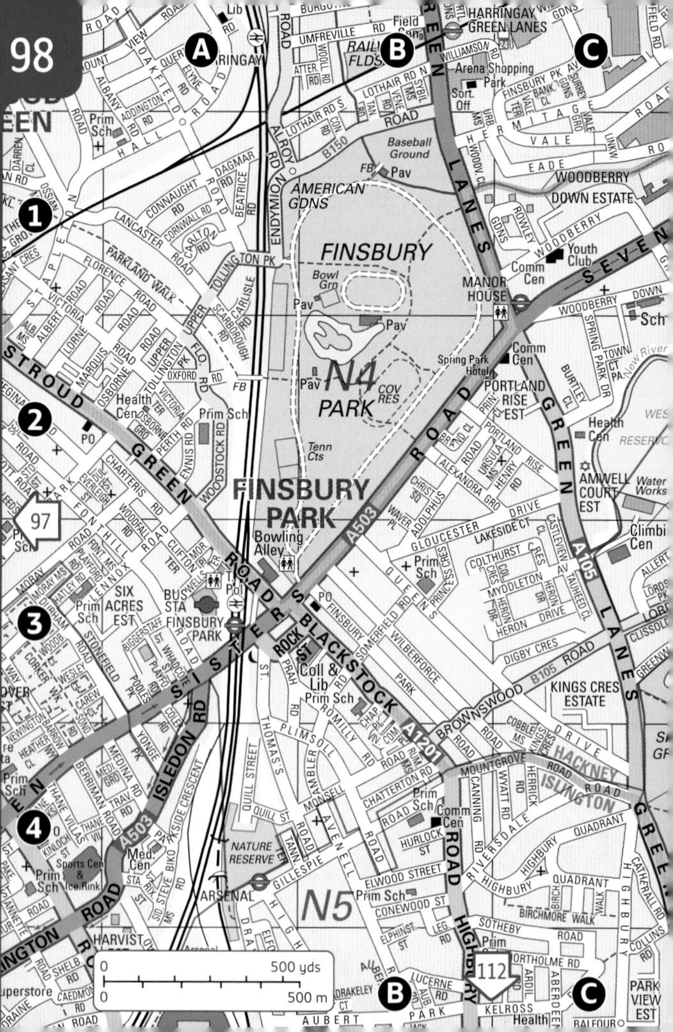
A
B
C
1
2
3
4
HARRINGAY GREEN LANES
RAILW. FLDS
Arena Shopping Park
FINSBURY PK AV
HERMITAGE ROAD
VALE
EADE
WOODBERRY DOWN ESTATE
Baseball Ground
AMERICAN GDNS
FINSBURY
N4
PARK
Bowl Grn
Pav
COV RES
Tenn Cts
FINSBURY PARK
Bowling Alley
MANOR HOUSE
Youth Club
Comm Cen
Spring Park Hotel
PORTLAND RISE EST
AMWELL COURT EST
Water Works
Climbi Cen
New River
STROUD GREEN ROAD
SEVEN SISTERS ROAD
GREEN LANES
BLACKSTOCK ROAD
A503
A1201
A105
B105
B150
LANCASTER ROAD
PARKLAND WALK
TOLLINGTON PK
ENDYMION RD
CONNAUGHT RD
DAGMAR ROAD
WOODSTOCK RD
GLOUCESTER DRIVE
BROWNSWOOD ROAD
KINGS CRES ESTATE
HACKNEY ISLINGTON
MOUNTGROVE ROAD
SIX ACRES EST
BUS STA
FINSBURY PARK
ROCK ST
Coll & Lib
ISLEDON RD
PARKSIDE CRESCENT
QUILL STREET
ST. THOMAS'S RD
NATURE RESERVE
ARSENAL
N5
Sports Cen & Ice Rink
Med. Cen
HOLLOWAY
HIGHBURY ROAD
HIGHBURY QUADRANT
BIRCHMORE WALK
SOTHEBY ROAD
ELWOOD STREET
CONEWOOD ST
HARVIST
Superstore
PARK VIEW EST
97
112
0 500 yds
0 500 m

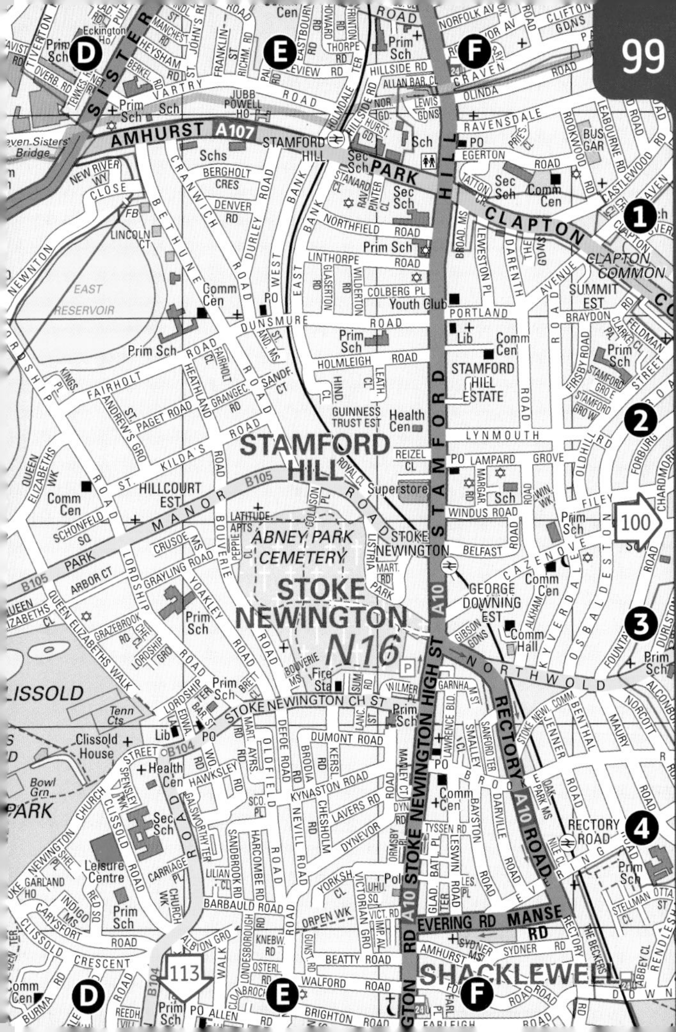
STAMFORD HILL
STOKE NEWINGTON
N16
ABNEY PARK CEMETERY
SHACKLEWELL
EAST RESERVOIR
CLISSOLD PARK
CLAPTON COMMON
AMHURST A107
PARK
CLAPTON
STAMFORD HILL
STOKE NEWINGTON HIGH ST
A10
RECTORY A10 ROAD
NORTHWOLD
MANOR B105
PARK
B104
STOKE NEWINGTON CH ST
STOKE NEWINGTON CHURCH STREET
EVERING RD
MANSE RD
SEVEN SISTERS
VARTRY ROAD
RAVENSDALE
EGERTON ROAD
NORTHFIELD ROAD
LINTHORPE ROAD
PORTLAND
DUNSMURE ROAD
HOLMLEIGH ROAD
LYNMOUTH
LAMPARD GROVE
WINDUS ROAD
BELFAST
CAZENOVE
KYVERDALE
OSBALDESTON
FAIRHOLT
ST. KILDA'S ROAD
PAGET ROAD
BETHUNE ROAD
CRANWICH
DURLEY ROAD
WEST BANK
EAST BANK
GRAYLING ROAD
LORDSHIP
YOAKLEY ROAD
BOUVERIE ROAD
DUMONT ROAD
KYNASTON ROAD
BARBAULD ROAD
WALFORD ROAD
BEATTY ROAD
BRIGHTON ROAD
CLISSOLD CRESCENT
SYDNER RD
AMHURST
HILLCOURT EST
STAMFORD HILL ESTATE
GEORGE DOWNING EST
GUINNESS TRUST EST
SUMMIT EST
Superstore
Youth Club
Health Cen
Leisure Centre
Clissold House
STAMFORD HILL
STOKE NEWINGTON
RECTORY ROAD
100
113
D
E
F
1
2
3
4

A
B
C
1
2
3
4
RESERVOIR
WEST
Filter Beds
COPPERMILL PLAYING FIELD
E17
LEE VALLEY REGIONAL
Coppermill Stream
Coppermill Bridge
Horse Shoe Point
Walthamstow Marsh
Horse Shoe Bridge
Nature Reserve
Anchor & Hope PH
Hall
Walthamstow Marsh Reserve
MAPLE CL
FAIRW.
WATERMINT QUAY
WALK
MOUNDFIELD RD
LEABOURNE RD
ROOKWOOD RD
BUS GAR
CASTLEWOOD RD
LINGWOOD
ASHTEAD ROAD
CRAVEN
OVERLEA ROAD
SPRING HILL
Pav
SPRINGHILL SPORTS GRD
Rowing Club
Clubho.
FB
Springfield Marina
SPRINGFIELD PARK
Tenn Cts
WEBB EST
Comm Hall
FAWCETT EST
White Lodge
RAVENSDALE
Sec Sch
Comm Cen
CLAPTON COMMON
SUMMIT EST
BRAYDON RD
FELDMAN CL
CLARKE PA.
Prim Sch
STAMFORD GRO E
STAMFORD GRO W
FIRSBY ROAD
STREET
LEWESTON PL
DARENTH RD
THE GDNS
AVENUE
STAMFORD HILL ESTATE
LYNMOUTH
LAMPARD GROVE
OLDHILL RD
FORBURG RD
CHARDMORE RD
SPRINGFIELD
HAWKW. MT
HOLMB. VW
BIG HILL
HILL HO
HARRINGT. HILL
BAKERS HILL
LEASIDE RD
SPRING LA
UPPER CLAPTON
JESSAM AV
MORESBY RD
GILDA CRES
Sec Sch
Prim Sch
WIGAN HO
WARWICK GROVE
CEDRA CT
FILEY
ROAD
HALBERD MS
KNIGHTLAND RD
MORETON CL
GROSVENOR WAY
CHILTERN RD
PLEASANT
RIVERSIDE CLOSE
WOODMILL RD
BAMBOO CT
ASTER CT
PLEASANT HILL
MOUNT
SACH RD
NORTHWOLD ESTATE
Health Cen
UPPER CLAPTON A107 ROAD
WEALD SQ
CAZENOVE
KYVERDALE
OSBALDESTON
FOUNTAYNE
Comm Cen
GEORGE DOWNING EST
Comm Hall
ALKHAM
DURLSTON
HOGAN WAY
GELDESTON
BRIGGEFORD CL
ROSSINGTON ST
ROSSEND. ST
CHARN. ST
CYPRESS CL
Lib
THE MT PO
ALCEST.
COMBERT. RD
THE MOUNT
BRA. CL
DETMOLD ROAD
THEYDON RD
MUND. RD
DUDLIN
Prim Sch
NORTHWOLD ROAD
B111
SOUTHWOLD ROAD
CLAPTON
GUNTON ROAD
CLEVELEYS ROAD
NORTH MILLFIELDS RECREATION GROUND
E5
RECTORY ROAD
A10
STOKE NEWI. COMM.
BENTHAL
JENNER
MAURY
NORCOTT
ALCONBURY
NARFORD ROAD
REIGHTON ROAD
ICKBURGH EST
ICKBURGH RD
Sch
N16
CASIMIR
PROUT RD
BROOKE ROAD
OAK PARK MS
NIGHTINGALE RD
LAUNDRESS LA
WALSINGHAM RD
Coll
BEECHOLME EST
LEA
SOUTH
WATTISFIELD RD
COTESBACH RD
THORNBY RD
CORNTHWAITE
THISTLEWAITE RD
FLETCHING
CHALLEY
NEWICK RD
MILDENHALL
MILLFIELDS
SARAT
COLENSO RD
RECTORY ROAD
Prim Sch
Med Cen
KENNINGHALL ROAD
GOOCH HO
MONTEAGLE WAY
MUIR RD
DELLA PATH
FERRON RD
NAPOLEON RD
POWELL RD
NIGHTINGALE EST
Prim Sch
STELLMAN CL
OTTA ST
CHARNOC.
HEYWORTH RD
Comm Cen
NOLAN WY
GLIDDON DR
SEATON PT
MANSE RD
SYDNER RD
DOLEHAM
LOWER CLAPTON
Prim Sch
HILSEA ST
RUSHMORE
YOLA ROAD
LAWLEY
0 500 yds
0 500 m
99
114

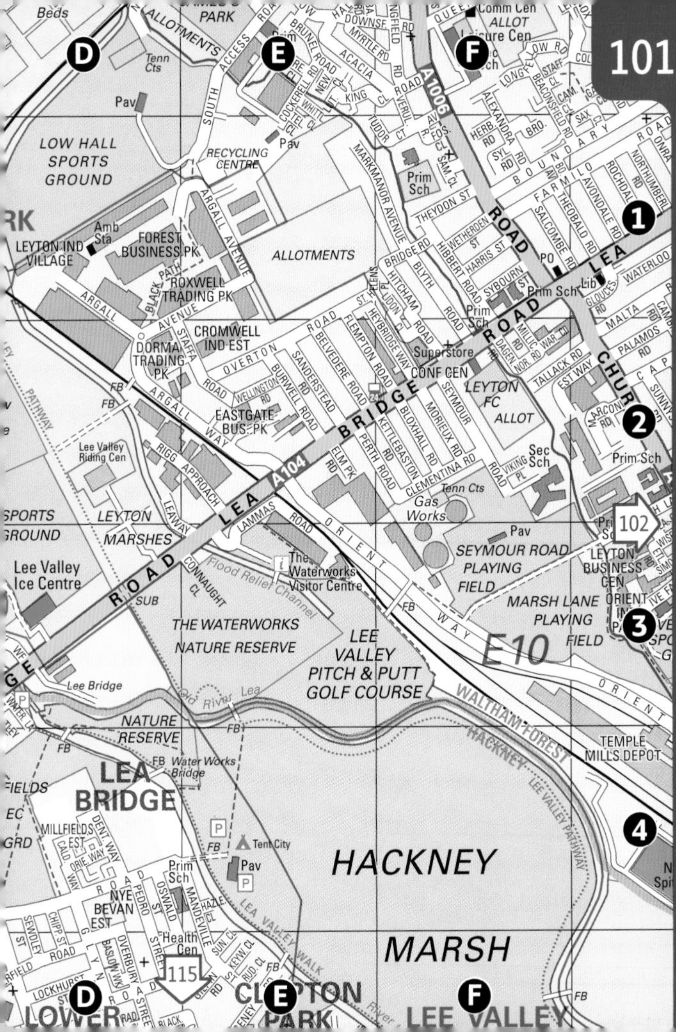
D
E
F
1
2
3
4
LOW HALL SPORTS GROUND
RECYCLING CENTRE
ALLOTMENTS
LEYTON IND VILLAGE
Amb Sta
FOREST BUSINESS PK
ROXWELL TRADING PK
CROMWELL IND EST
DORMA TRADING PK
EASTGATE BUS. PK
Lee Valley Riding Cen
LEYTON MARSHES
SPORTS GROUND
Lee Valley Ice Centre
THE WATERWORKS NATURE RESERVE
The Waterworks Visitor Centre
Flood Relief Channel
LEE VALLEY PITCH & PUTT GOLF COURSE
LEA BRIDGE ROAD
A104
A1006
LEA BRIDGE
Lee Bridge
NATURE RESERVE
Water Works Bridge
Old River Lea
MILLFIELDS EST
NYE BEVAN EST
Health Cen
Tent City
HACKNEY
MARSH
CLAPTON PARK
LOWER
LEE VALLEY
LEA VALLEY WALK
LEE VALLEY PATHWAY
WALTHAM FOREST
HACKNEY
E10
ORIENT WAY
SEYMOUR ROAD PLAYING FIELD
MARSH LANE PLAYING FIELD
Gas Works
LEYTON FC
ALLOT
Superstore
CONF CEN
LEYTON BUSINESS CEN
TEMPLE MILLS DEPOT
BOUNDARY ROAD
CHURCH ROAD
FARMILO
Prim Sch
Sec Sch
PO
Lib
Pav
Tenn Cts
Comm Cen
Leisure Cen
102
115

A
B
C
1
2
3
4
LEA BRIDGE ROAD
CHURCH ROAD
A1006
HIGH ROAD
LEYTON
A112
E10
LEYTON
Comm Cen
Prim Sch
Sec Sch
Superstores
Swim Pool
ALL SAINTS TWR
BUS GAR
Heath Cen
ABBOTS PK
Brooks Farm
LEYTON MIDLAND RD
Cricket Ground
Youth Cen
Med Cen
Pol
Clinic
Fire Sta
LEYTON FC
LEYTON BUSINESS CEN
ORIENT IND PARK
IVE FM SPORTS GRD
MARSH LANE PLAYING FIELD
TEMPLE MILLS DEPOT
ALLOT
SIDMOUTH PARK
LEYTON ORIENT FC
Sports Cen
COUNCIL OFF
Lib
PO
New Spitalfields Market
ORIENT WAY
WARREN RD
A106
A12
B161
LEE VALLEY PATHWAY
WALTHAM FOREST
HACKNEY
VALLEY
101
116
0
500 yds
0
500 m

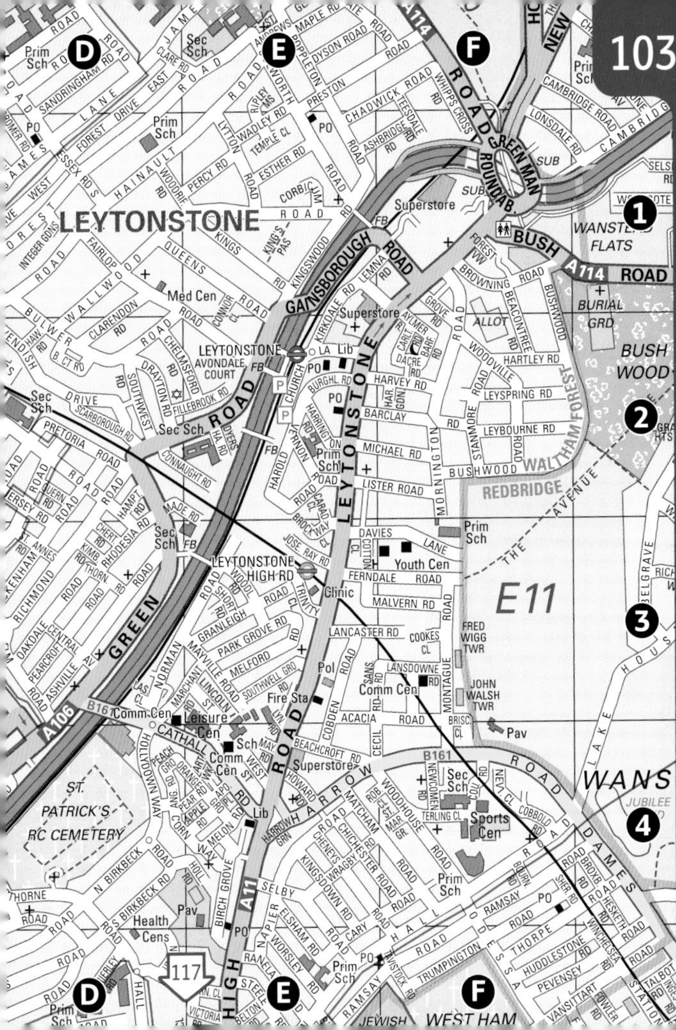
D
E
F
1
2
3
4
LEYTONSTONE
E11
WANSTEAD FLATS
BUSH WOOD
BURIAL GRD
ALLOT
REDBRIDGE
THE AVENUE
GREEN MAN ROUNDAB.
BUSH ROAD
A114
A11
A106
B161
LEYTONSTONE HIGH ROAD
GREEN MAN ROAD
WHIPPS CROSS ROAD
GAINSBOROUGH ROAD
LEYTONSTONE
LEYTONSTONE HIGH RD
LEYTONSTONE AVONDALE COURT
HARROW ROAD
CATHALL RD
ST. PATRICK'S RC CEMETERY
WEST HAM
JEWISH
WANS
JUBILEE
Superstore
Med Cen
Youth Cen
Clinic
Comm Cen
Leisure Cen
Sports Cen
Fire Sta
Pol
Lib
Pav
Health Cens
Prim Sch
Sec Sch
PO
FRED WIGG TWR
JOHN WALSH TWR
117

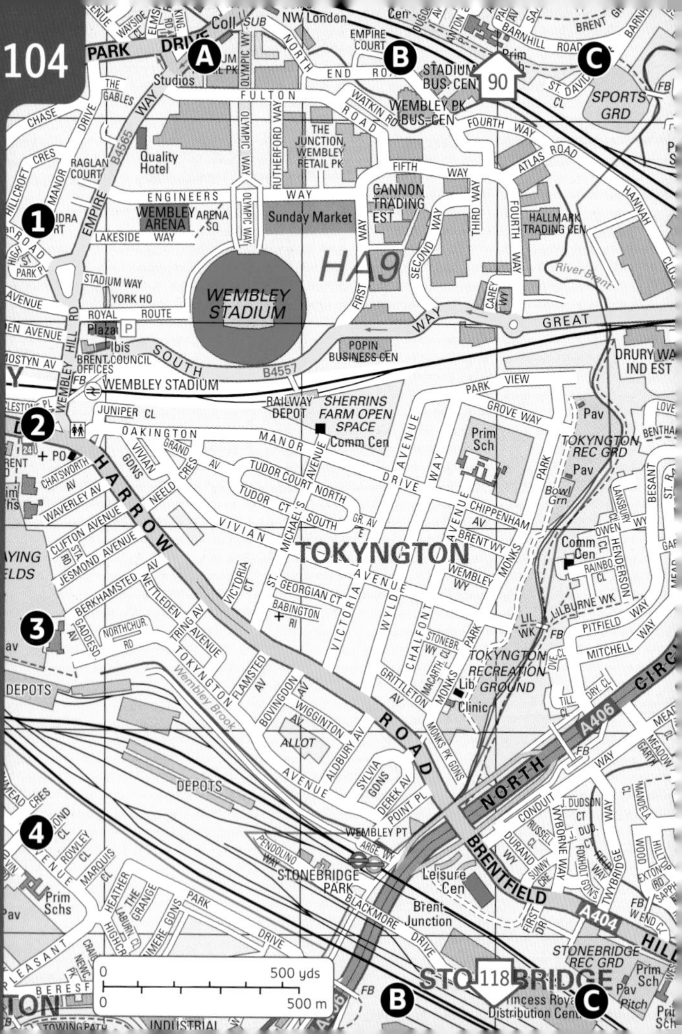
A
B
C
1
2
3
4
90
118
PARK DRIVE
NW London Coll
EMPIRE COURT
NORTH END ROAD
Studios
THE GABLES
FULTON
OLYMPIC WAY
STADIUM BUS CEN
WEMBLEY PK BUS CEN
WATKIN RD
BARNHILL ROAD
BRENT
ST. DAVIDS CL
SPORTS GRD
FOURTH WAY
ATLAS ROAD
CHASE
DRIVE
CRES
MANOR
HILLCROFT
RAGLAN COURT
B4565
Quality Hotel
RUTHERFORD WAY
THE JUNCTION, WEMBLEY RETAIL PK
FIFTH WAY
ENGINEERS WAY
WEMBLEY ARENA
ARENA SQ
Sunday Market
CANNON TRADING EST
THIRD WAY
HALLMARK TRADING CEN
HANNAH
EMPIRE WAY
LAKESIDE WAY
HA9
SECOND WAY
FIRST WAY
CAREY WY
River Brent
HIGH ST
PARK PL
STADIUM WAY
YORK HO
WEMBLEY STADIUM
ROYAL ROUTE
Plaza
Ibis
GREAT WAY
SOUTH WAY
POPIN BUSINESS CEN
DRURY WAY IND EST
MOSTYN AV
BRENT COUNCIL OFFICES
B4557
WEMBLEY HILL RD
FB
WEMBLEY STADIUM
PARK VIEW
JUNIPER CL
RAILWAY DEPOT
SHERRINS FARM OPEN SPACE
GROVE WAY
Pav
OAKINGTON MANOR DRIVE
Comm Cen
Prim Sch
TOKYNGTON REC GRD
+ PO
CHATSWORTH AV
HARROW ROAD
VIVIAN GDNS
GRAND AV
TUDOR COURT NORTH
TUDOR CT SOUTH
ST. MICHAEL'S AVENUE
GR. AV
WAY
PARK
Bowl Grn
WAVERLEY AV
NEELD CRES
CHIPPENHAM AV
CLIFTON AVENUE
VIVIAN AVENUE
BRENT WY
OWEN CL
HENDERSON
JESMOND AVENUE
STA RD
TOKYNGTON
Comm Cen
MONKS PARK
RAINBOW CL
BERKHAMSTED AV
NETTLEDEN AV
VICTORIA CT
GEORGIAN CT
WEMBLEY WY
LILBURNE WK
BABINGTON RI
VICTORIA AVENUE
WYLDE
CHALFONT
PITFIELD WAY
GADDESDEN AV
NORTHCHURCH RD
TRING AVENUE
STONEBR. WY
MACARTH. CL
TOKYNGTON RECREATION GROUND
MITCHELL WAY
DEPOTS
TOKYNGTON AVENUE
FLAMSTED AV
GRITTLETON AV
Lib
Clinic
CIRCULAR
Wembley Brook
BOVINGDON AV
WIGGINTON AV
ALDBURY AV
ROAD
MONKS PK GDNS
A406
ALLOT
NORTH
WAY
DEPOTS
SYLVIA GDNS
DEREK AV
POINT PL
CONDUIT WAY
J. DUDSON CT
MEAD CRES
WEMBLEY PT
BRENTFIELD
RUSSELL CL
DURAND WY
WYBORNE WAY
FOXHOLT GDNS
TWYBRIDGE WAY
ROWLEY CL
MARQUIS CL
PENDOLINO WAY
STONEBRIDGE PARK
Leisure Cen
Prim Schs
HEATHER
THE GRANGE
PARK
BLACKMORE DRIVE
Brent Junction
FIRST DR
A404
Pav
DRIVE
HILL
PLEASANT
STONEBRIDGE REC GRD
STONEBRIDGE
Princess Royal Distribution Cen
Prim Sch
Pav
Pitch
BERESF
INDUSTRIAL
TOWING PATH
0 500 yds
0 500 m

NEASDEN
91
106
119
D
E
F
1
2
3
4
NEASDEN RAIL DEPOT
NEASDEN LA
DUDDEN HILL
A4088
MULGRAVE ROAD
PROUT GROVE
FALCON PK IND EST
Prim Sch
Clinic
Superstore
BRENT PARK
PO
DRURY WAY
NEASDEN
B453
B4557
Coll of North West London
CHURCH END
ALLOT
GIBBONS REC GRD
The Swaminarayan Sch
Power Station
CEM
CHAPMAN PK IND EST
SAPCOTE TRD CEN
CYGNUS BUS. CEN
HIGH ROAD
WILLESDEN
Synagogue
WILLESDEN NEW CEMETERY
NW10
WILLESDEN CEMETERY (JEWISH)
CHURCH ROAD
A407
ROUNDWOOD PARK
Bowling Green
The Hilltop Club
Health Cen
CRAVEN PARK
COBBOLD EST
BUS GAR
GLAD

A
B
C
1
2
3
4
92
105
120
DOLLIS HILL
GLADSTONE PARK
SPORTS GRD
BUSINESS CEN
FLOWERS CL
NEVILLES COURT
ARTS CEN
Tenn Cts
Bowl Grn
Tennis Courts
FB
Prim Sch
Pumping Sta
COV RES
Lib
Pav
Comm Cen
Health Clinic
KENDAL ROAD
MULGRAVE ROAD
NORMANBY RD
LENNOX GDNS
PARK VIEW ROAD
CORNMOW DR
LANCASTER RD
GEARY RD
FLEETWOOD
ELLESMERE
DEWSBURY ROAD
BURNLEY ROAD
HAMILTON
ABERDEEN RD
HELENA ROAD
CULLINGWORTH ROAD
SHERRICK GREEN ROAD
DOLLIS HILL
PARK AVENUE NORTH
MELROSE AVENUE
ANSON ROAD
OLIVE ROAD
OXLEYS ROAD
WOTTON ROAD
NEWTON RD
TEMPLE
MORA
IVY ROAD
CEDAR
ST. MICHAELS RD
BRIAR RD
AGAVE RD
OMAN AV
DICEY AVENUE
SNEYD ROAD
WREN AVENUE
DAWSON ROAD
TRACEY AV
HENSON AV
GARDINER AV
JAMES AV
MEREDITH AV
IMPERIAL CL
GAY CL
KENNETH CRES
RIFFEL
CHANDOS ROAD
CRANHURST ROAD
BLENHEIM
JEYMER AV
LENNON ROAD
ELVIS ROAD
STATION PAR
ST. PAUL'S AVENUE
GROVE
DEAN ROAD
WALM
A4088
A407
HILL LANE
COOPER ROAD
CHAPTER ROAD
DEACON ROAD
VILLIERS
CHAPLIN ROAD
BELTON ROAD
PRESTON PL
WATERWAY
GRIFFIN CLOSE
GRIF CL
SUB
CHAPMAN PK IND EST
COLIN RD
MEYRICK RD
PO
ROAD
Superstore
COBBOLD EST
GLEBE ROAD
BEACONSFIELD
WILLESDEN
Synagogue
WILLESDEN NEW CEMETERY
WILLESDEN CEMETERY (JEWISH)
NW10
ROUNDWOOD PARK
ALLOT
LONGSTONE
FRY ROAD
Bowling
SANDRINGHAM ROAD
CHURCHILL ROAD
WINDSOR RD
OSBORNE RD
BUXTON RD
BALMORAL ROAD
HUDDLESTONE RD
LECHMERE
LINACRE RD
ACLAND RD
Prim Schs
Pol
HIGH ROAD
BUS GAR
BERTIE RD
POUND
UNITY CL
STRODE RD
EURO CL
LITCHFIELD GDNS
CLARE RD
STERLING CL
TOWER RD
Fire Sta
HAWTHORN
PARKFIELD RD
HARLESDEN RD
MAYBURY GDNS
GOWAN RD
KINGS ROAD
Coll
ST. ANDR RD
CORNW. GD.
GRANGE
MUS
BRONDESBURY PARK
STAVERTON
ALVERSTONE RD
CHAMBERS LANE
BRYAN
ROWDON AV
WILLESDEN GREEN
DOBREE AV
ALEXANDER AV
PETER AVENUE
DONNINGTON CT
DONNINGTON ROAD
Health Cen
COV RES
LIBERAL JEWISH CEM
ROBSON AVENUE
CROSS WY
HARLESDEN RD
SIDMOUTH ROAD
HANOVER
MOUNT PLEASANT
HENLEY RD
S. Ham C.
Pav
WILLESDEN SPORT STADIUM
Sports Centre
Capital City
MAPESHILL PL
HEATHFIELD PK
RUTLAND
Superstore
LONGLEY WAY
GARAGE
0 500 yds
0 500 m

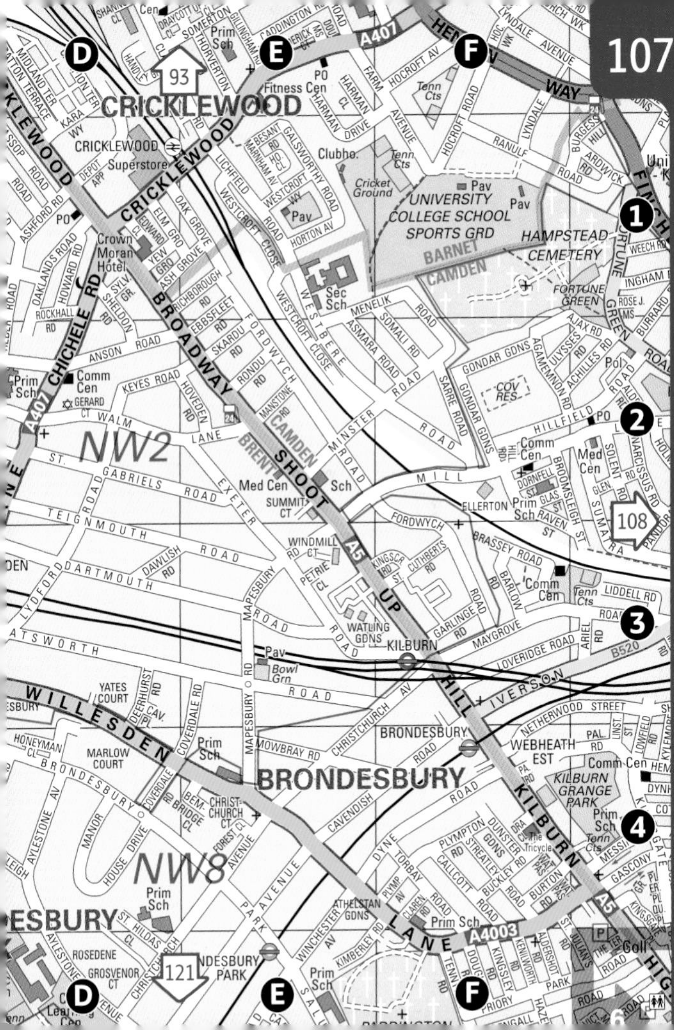
CRICKLEWOOD
CRICKLEWOOD
Superstore
BROADWAY
SHOOT
UP
HILL
KILBURN
NW2
NW8
BRONDESBURY
BRONDESBURY
KILBURN
UNIVERSITY
COLLEGE SCHOOL
SPORTS GRD
HAMPSTEAD
CEMETERY
FORTUNE
GREEN
BARNET
CAMDEN
BRENT
Cricket
Ground
KILBURN
GRANGE
PARK
WEBHEATH
EST
A407
A5
A4003
B520
93
108
121
D
E
F
1
2
3
4
WILLESDEN
LANE
CHICHELE RD
MILL
LANE
HILLFIELD
MINSTER
ROAD
MAPESBURY
ROAD
TEIGNMOUTH
ROAD
DARTMOUTH
ROAD
GABRIELS
ROAD
WALM
LANE
ANSON
ROAD
BRONDESBURY
PARK
NDESBURY
PARK
CHRISTCHURCH
AV
BRASSEY
ROAD
LOVERIDGE ROAD
MAYGROVE
IVERSON
NETHERWOOD STREET
GONDAR GDNS
MENELIK
ROAD
WESTBERE
ROAD
ASMARA ROAD
SOMALI RD
FORDWYCH
ROAD
EXETER
ROAD
GARLINGE
RD
KILBURN
Med Cen
Prim Sch
Comm Cen
Sec Sch
Tenn Cts
Bowl Grn
Pav
PO

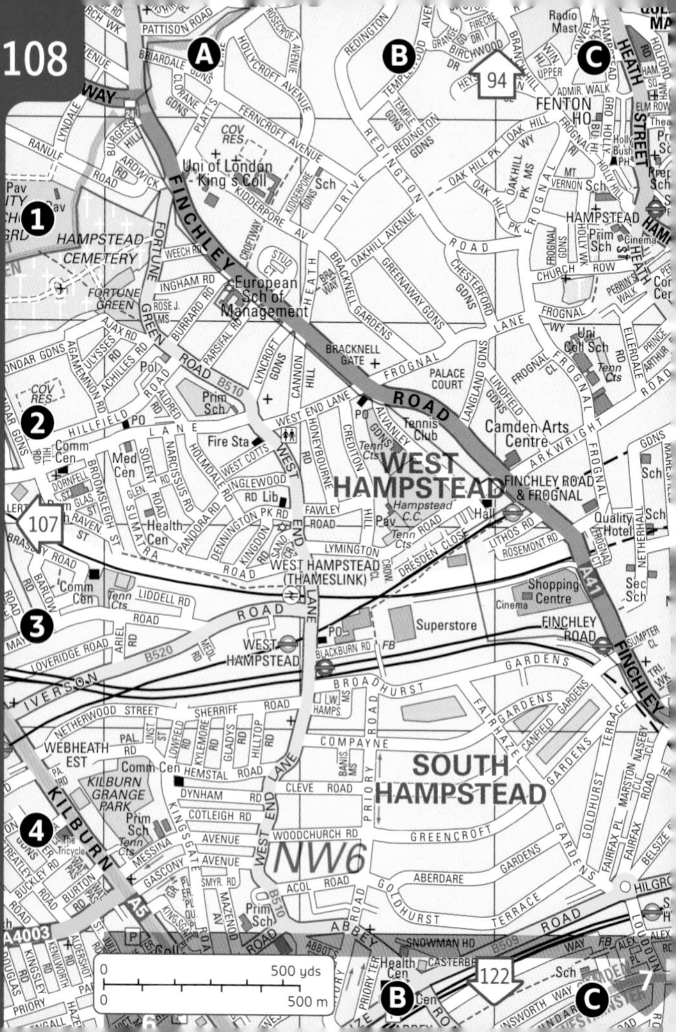
A
B
C
1
2
3
4
94
107
122
PATTISON ROAD
BRIARDALE GDNS
CLORANE GDNS
PLATT'S LANE
HOLLYCROFT AVENUE
ROSECROFT AVENUE
FERNCROFT AVENUE
REDINGTON ROAD
TEMPLEWOOD AVE
TEMPLE GDNS
REDINGTON GDNS
BIRCHWOOD DR
HEYSHAM LA
BRANCH HILL
UPPER
Radio Mast
HEATH STREET
HOLFORD RD
FENTON HO
ADMIR. WALK
FROGNAL RI
OAK HILL PK
OAK HILL WY
OAKHILL PK MS
MT VERNON
Sch
HAMPSTEAD
Prim Sch
Cinema
Holly Bush PH
HOLLY HILL
Prep Sch
CHURCH ROW
PERRIN'S WALK
LYNDALE
BURGESS HILL
RANULF ROAD
ARDWICK RD
FINCHLEY
Uni of London King's Coll
COV RES
KIDDERPORE AV
KIDDERPORE GDNS
CROFTWAY
DRIVE
OAKHILL AVENUE
GREENAWAY GDNS
CHESTERFORD GDNS
FROGNAL LANE
FROGNAL
FROGNAL GDNS
HOLLY WK
ELLERDALE RD
PRINCE ARTHUR RD
Uni Coll Sch
Tenn Cts
HAMPSTEAD CEMETERY
FORTUNE GREEN
FORTUNE GREEN ROAD
WEECH RD
INGHAM RD
ROSE J. MS
BURRARD RD
PARSIFAL RD
European Sch of Management
STUD CT
HEATH
BRACKNELL WAY
BRACKNELL GARDENS
BRACKNELL GATE
FROGNAL
PALACE COURT
LANGLAND GDNS
LINDFIELD GDNS
FROGNAL CL
AJAX RD
ULYSSES RD
ACHILLES RD
AGAMEMNON RD
Pol
ALDRED RD
B510
Prim Sch
LYNCROFT GDNS
CANNON HILL
ROAD
Camden Arts Centre
ARKWRIGHT ROAD
COV RES
HILLFIELD PO LANE
Comm Cen
Fire Sta
WEST END LANE
HONEYBOURNE RD
CREDITON HILL
ALVANLEY GDNS
Tennis Club
Tenn Cts
WEST HAMPSTEAD
FINCHLEY ROAD & FROGNAL
Hall
Quality Hotel
NETHERHALL
Sch
DORNFELL ST
GLAS. ST
BROOMSLEIGH ST
Med Cen
SOLENT RD
NARCISSUS RD
HOLMDALE RD
WEST COTTS
INGLEWOOD RD Lib
FAWLEY ROAD
Hampstead C.C.
Pav
Tenn Cts
ROAD
LITHOS RD
ROSEMONT RD
RAVEN. ST
GLEN.
SUMATRA ROAD
Health Cen
PANDORA RD
DENNINGTON PK RD
KINGDON RD
SAND. CR.
LYMINGTON ROAD
DRESDEN CLOSE
CROW. CL
WEST HAMPSTEAD (THAMESLINK)
A41
Shopping Centre
Sec Sch
Cinema
BRASSEY ROAD
BARLOW RD
Comm Cen
Tenn Cts
LIDDELL RD
ROAD
Superstore
FINCHLEY ROAD
SUMPTER CL
PO
WEST HAMPSTEAD
BLACKBURN RD
FB
LOVERIDGE ROAD
ARIEL RD
B520
MEDLEY RD
GARDENS
TRI. WK
IVERSON
BROADHURST
LW. HAMPS.
FAIRHAZEL GARDENS
CANFIELD GARDENS
NETHERWOOD STREET
SHERRIFF ROAD
PRIORY ROAD
COMPAYNE
TERRACE
NASEBY CL
WEBHEATH EST
PAL. RD
LINST. ST
LOWFIELD RD
KYLEMORE RD
GLADYS RD
HILLTOP RD
Comm Cen
HEMSTAL ROAD
BANIS. MS
SOUTH HAMPSTEAD
GARDENS
GOLDHURST
MARSTON CL
ROAD
KILBURN GRANGE PARK
DYNHAM RD
CLEVE ROAD
KILBURN
Prim Sch
Tenn Cts
KINGSGATE
COTLEIGH RD
AVENUE
WOODCHURCH RD
GREENCROFT
FAIRFAX PL
FAIRFAX
BELSIZE
The Tricycle
MESSINA AVENUE
WEST END LANE
NW6
GARDENS
ABERDARE GARDENS
HILGROVE
STREATLEY
BUCKLEY RD
BURTON RD
GASCONY AVENUE
SMYR. RD
ACOL ROAD
GOLDHURST TERRACE
A5
MAZENOD AV
Prim Sch
B510
ABBEY ROAD
A4003
KENILWORTH RD
ALDERSHOT RD
KINGSLEY RD
DOUGLAS RD
PRIORY
ABBOTS
SNOWMAN HO
CASTERBRIDGE
B509
FB
ALEX. PL
Health Cen
Cen
Sch
WAY
LOUDOUN RD
0 500 yds
0 500 m

D
E
F
D
E
F
1
2
3
4
95
110
123
9
HILL
HAMPSTEAD PONDS
NW3
HAMPSTEAD
BELSIZE PARK
PRIMROSE HILL
PRIMROSE
Cricket Ground
ATHLETICS TRACK
Pav
LISMORE CIRCUS
MAITLAND PARK ESTATE
ST. DOMINIC'S PRIORY
ST. SILAS ST EST
ROYAL FREE HOSP
KEATS HOUSE
HAMPSTEAD HEATH
BELSIZE PK
CHALK FARM
SWISS COTTAGE
TAVISTOCK CEN
Preacher's Hill
Freemason's Arms PH
2 Willow Rd
THE PRYORS
HEATH SIDE
GAINSBOR GDNS
WILLOW ROAD
DENNING RD
GAYTON CRES
CARLINGFORD RD
KEMPLAY RD
WILLOUGHBY RD
PILGRIM'S LA
DOWNSHIRE HILL
KEATS GRO
HEATH HURST RD
SOUTH END ROAD
ST CRISPINS CL
S END CL
SOUTH HILL PK
SOUTH HILL PARK
S HILL PK GDNS
PARLIAMENT HILL
TANZA ROAD
NASSINGTON RD
ALLOT
FB
SAVERNAKE ROAD
ROAD
COURTHOPE RD
SHIRLOCK ROAD
RODERICK ROAD
LISBURNE RD
MACKESON RD
ESTELLE RD
RONA RD
CONSTANTINE ROAD
AGINCOURT ROAD
B518
MANSFIELD ROAD
CRESSY RD
BYRON MS
FLEET RD
PALGRAVE HO
WAXHAM
LAMBLE ST
ELAINE GRO
OAK VILL
GRAFTON
BAR. CL
HIGH ST
ROSSLYN HILL
POND ST
HAMPSTEAD HILL GDNS
THURLOW ROAD
ELDON GRO
LYNDHURST ROAD
LYNDHURST GDNS
LYNDHURST TER
SHEPHERDS WK
VANE CL
Fitness Cen
Amb Sta
Prim Sch
Sports Cen
Comm Cen
LAWN ROAD
GARNETT RD
ROWLAND HILL ST
CAYFORD HO
ASPERN GRO
UPPER PARK ROAD
PARKHILL RD
DUN. RD
KINGS. ST
SOUTHAMPTON RD
ST WENDLING
HAVERSTOCK RD
WELLESLEY RD
WELLESL. RD
VICARS RD
WEEDINGTON RD
BACTON
Clinic
Lib
PO
MALDEN RD
QUADRANT GRO
GRAFTON TER
HERBERT ST
Prep. Sch
WEDDERBURN RD
Hospice
AKENSIDE ROAD
LYNDHURST GDNS
BELSIZE LANE
ORNAN
Premier Inn
T.H. CEN
Cinema
Ten Cts
DOWNSIDE CRES
TASKER RD
HILLFIELD CT
TUDOR CL
GLENLOCH ROAD
GLENMORE RD
HOWITT RD
HOLMEFIELD CT
BELSIZE GROVE
HAVERSTOCK HILL
A502
FOUNTAIN MS
ANTRIM GRO
ANTRIM RD
ANTRIM MAN
MAITLAND PARK VILLAS
MAITLAND PARK RD
QUEEN'S CRES
TERRACE
DALEHAM GARDENS
DAL. MS
BELSIZE CRES
BELSIZE PARK GARDENS
GLENILLA ROAD
GILLING COURT
PRIMROSE GARDENS
ELIZABETH MS
ENGLANDS LANE
CHALCOT GDNS
STEELES RD
ETON VIL
ETON ROAD
ETON COLLEGE RD
PROVOST RD
BEAUMONT WALK
PRINCE OF WALES RD
Sec Sch
CROGSLAND RD
B511 AVENUE
Health Clinic
BELSIZE SQUARE
GABRIELLE CT
LAMBOLLE RD
LAMBOLLE PL
LANCASTER DR
LANCASTER GROVE
Fire Sta
BUCKLAND CRES
ADAMSON RD
CROSSFIELD RD
STRATH. GD.
ETON AVENUE
MERTON RISE
PRIMROSE HILL ROAD
KINGS. C.
DORNEY
TOBIN CL
BRAY
FELLOWS ROAD
HUS. CL
BURNHAM
B509
Med Cen
BLASHFORD
REGENTS PK RD
COLLEGE CR
Mkt
Thea
Comm Cen
Leisure Cen
HORNBY CL
TAPLOW
HAWTREY RD
ELLIOTT SQ
HENRY'S
ELSWORTHY RI
LWR MERTON RI
Marriott Regents Park
KING HENRY'S ROAD
PRIMROSE HILL CT
OPPIDANS RD
MEADOWBANK
AINGER RD
ERSKINE RD
BERKLEY RD
SHARPLESS ST
CHALCOT SQ
GLOUCESTER AVENUE
ADELAIDE ROAD
AVENUE RD
Odeon
Lib
HARLEY RD
WADHAM GARDENS
ELSWORTHY TER
ELSWORTHY ROAD
MIDDLE FLD
WOOD PARK
QUEEN'S MEAD
REGENTS PARK ROAD
CHALCOT CRES
FITZROY RD
KING. ST
AUDEN PL
MANLEY ST
PRINCESS

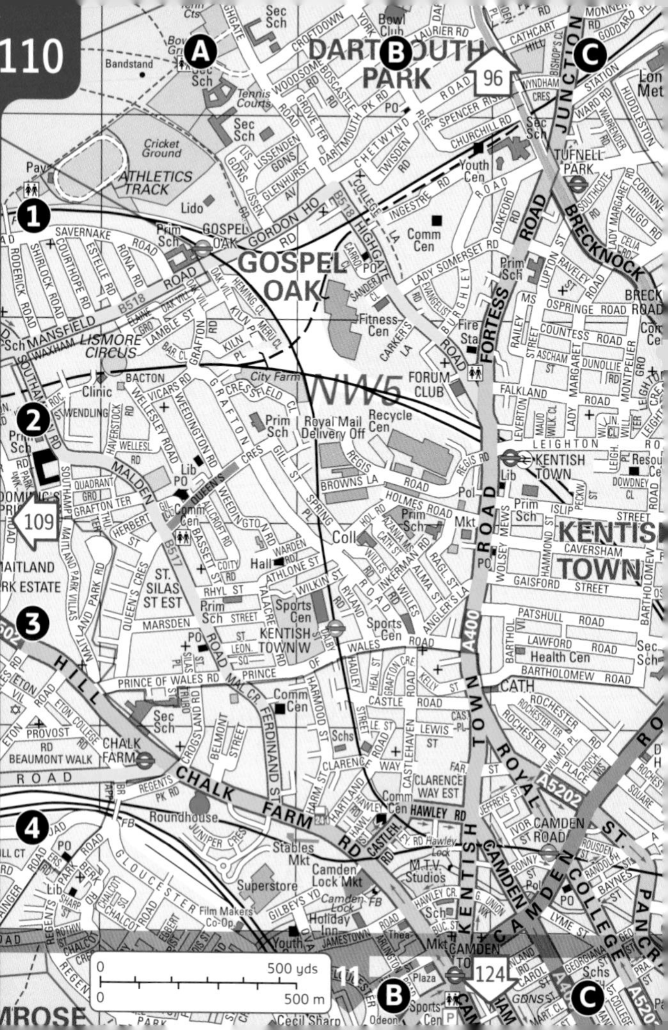
A
B
C
DARTMOUTH PARK
96
Bandstand
Sec Sch
Tennis Courts
Bowl Club
Cricket Ground
ATHLETICS TRACK
Lido
Pav
1
2
3
4
SAVERNAKE ROAD
GOSPEL OAK
GORDON HO RD
Prim Sch
MANSFIELD RD
LISMORE CIRCUS
WAXHAM
LAMBLE ST
GRAFTON RD
KILN PL
City Farm
NW5
Fitness Cen
Comm Cen
HIGHGATE RD
COLLEGE LA
INGESTRE RD
LADY SOMERSET RD
FORTESS ROAD
FORUM CLUB
Fire Sta
Youth Cen
TUFNELL PARK
BRECKNOCK RD
JUNCTION RD
CHURCHILL RD
SPENCER RISE
DARTMOUTH PK RD
CHETWYND RD
Royal Mail Delivery Off
Recycle Cen
Prim Sch
Clinic
BACTON
MALDEN RD
WELLESLEY RD
WEEDINGTON RD
QUEEN'S CRES
HAVERSTOCK
109
MAITLAND PARK ESTATE
ST. SILAS ST EST
MARSDEN
PRINCE OF WALES RD
KENTISH TOWN W
Sports Cen
KENTISH TOWN
KENTISH TOWN ROAD
LEIGHTON RD
ISLIP STREET
CAVERSHAM
GAISFORD STREET
PATSHULL ROAD
LAWFORD ROAD
Health Cen
BARTHOLOMEW ROAD
A400
WALES ROAD
CASTLE ROAD
ROCHESTER
ROYAL COLLEGE ST
CAMDEN RD
A5202
HAVERSTOCK HILL
CHALK FARM
CHALK FARM RD
Roundhouse
Stables Mkt
Camden Lock Mkt
M.T.V. Studios
Superstore
Holiday Inn
Film Makers Co-Op
GLOUCESTER AVE
REGENTS PK RD
CLARENCE WAY
CLARENCE WAY EST
HAWLEY RD
CAMDEN TOWN
124
Plaza
Odeon
Cecil Sharp
0 500 yds
0 500 m

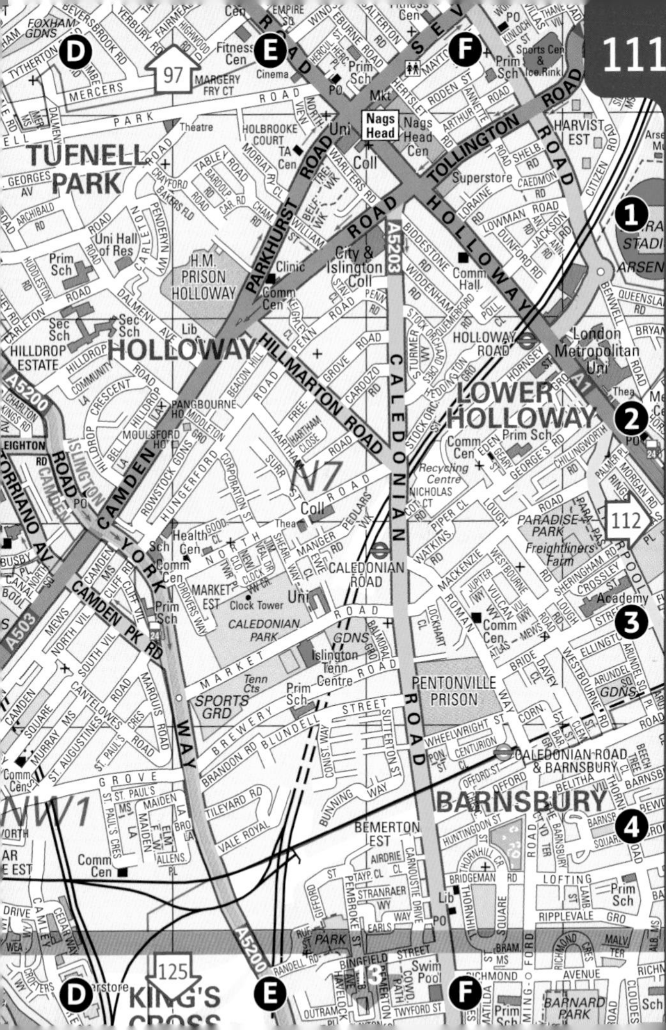
D
E
F
97
112
125
13
1
2
3
4
TUFNELL PARK
HOLLOWAY
LOWER HOLLOWAY
BARNSBURY
KING'S CROSS
N7
NW1
FOXHAM GDNS
BEVERSBROOK RD
YERBURY RD
FAIRMEAD
HIGHWOOD RD
TYTHERTON RD
MERCERS RD
MARGERY FRY CT
PARK RD
DALMENY RD
Theatre
HOLBROOKE COURT
Fitness Cen
Cinema
EMPIRE SQ
SEVEN SISTERS ROAD
PARKHURST ROAD
Nags Head
Nags Head Cen
Mkt
Uni
Coll
TOLLINGTON ROAD
HOLLOWAY ROAD
HARVIST EST
CITIZEN RD
Sports Cen & Ice Rink
Prim Sch
PO
Superstore
CAEDMON RD
LORAINE RD
LOWMAN ROAD
DUNFORD RD
JACKSON RD
ARSENAL STADIUM
QUEENSLAND RD
BENWELL RD
BRYANT
GEORGES AV
ARCHIBALD RD
CRAYFORD ROAD
TABLEY ROAD
BARDOLPH RD
MORIATRY CL
TA Cen
Uni Hall of Res
CARLETON RD
PENDERYN WY
H.M. PRISON HOLLOWAY
Clinic
Comm Cen
City & Islington Coll
A5203
BIDDESTONE RD
WIDDENHAM RD
Comm Hall
HUDDLESTON RD
Sec Sch
DALMENY AVE
Lib
HILLDROP ESTATE
HILLMARTON ROAD
PENN ROAD
GROVE ROAD
CARDOZO RD
CALEDONIAN ROAD
TURMER MS
STOCK ORCHARD CRES
HOLLOWAY ROAD
HORNSEY ST
London Metropolitan Uni
Thea
A1
A5200
COMMUNITY RD
CRESCENT RD
HILLDROP RD
PANGBOURNE HO
MIDDLETON GRO
MOULSFORD HO
BEACON HILL
FREELING ST
HARTHAM CLOSE
HARTHAM RD
SURR ST
CORPORATION ST
ROWSTOCK GDNS
HUNGERFORD RD
CAMDEN ROAD
CAMDEN RD
ISLINGTON
LEIGHTON RD
TORRIANO AV
Comm Cen
EDEN GRO
GEARY ST
GEORGE'S RD
CHILLINGWORTH RD
Recycling Centre
NICHOLAS CT
PIPER CL
Coll
Thea
PEDLARS WK
Health Cen
GOODINGE CL
NORTH RD
MANGER RD
CALEDONIAN ROAD
PARADISE PARK
Freightliners Farm
PALMER PL
MORGAN RD
LIVERPOOL RD
SHERINGHAM RD
CROSSLEY ST
Academy
YORK WAY
MARKET EST
Clock Tower
CALEDONIAN PARK
Uni
MARKET ROAD
WATKINS RD
MACKENZIE RD
WESTBOURNE RD
ROMAN WAY
JUPITER WY
VULCAN WY
Comm Cen
ATLAS MEWS
ELLINGTON ST
ARUNDEL SQ
ARUNDEL GDNS
BUSBY PL
CANAL BOUL
CAMDEN PK RD
CAMDEN MEWS
NORTH VIL
SOUTH VIL
CLIFF RD
CLIFF VIL
DROVERS WAY
Prim Sch
GDNS
BALMORAL GRO
LOCKHART CL
Islington Tenn Centre
Tenn Cts
SPORTS GRD
PENTONVILLE PRISON
BRIDE ST
DAVEY CL
A503
CAMDEN SQUARE
MURRAY MS
ST. AUGUSTINES RD
CANTELOWES RD
MARQUIS ROAD
ST. PAUL'S CRES
BREWERY RD
BLUNDELL STREET
SUTTERTON ST
WHEELWRIGHT ST
CENTURION CL
PONSONBY
CALEDONIAN ROAD & BARNSBURY
BRANDON RD
CONISTON WAY
BUNNING WAY
OFFORD ST
OFFORD RD
BELITHA VIL
THORNHILL RD
BARNSBURY
GROVE
ST. PAUL'S MS
MAIDEN LA
TILEYARD RD
VALE ROYAL
BEMERTON EST
AIRDRIE CL
CARNOUSTIE DRIVE
HUNTINGDON ST
THORNHILL CR.
BARNSBURY SQUARE
Comm Cen
ELM
ALLENS.
STRANRAER WY
PEMBROKE ST
GIFFORD ST
BRIDGEMAN RD
Lib
PO
LOFTING RD
RIPPLEVALE GRO
Prim Sch
CAMLEY ST
CEDAR WAY
PARK
RANDELL RD
BINGFIELD ST
EARLS
HAVELOCK
PEMBERTON
COWDRY PATH
Swim Pool
TWYFORD ST
THORNHILL SQUARE
BRAM. MS
RICHMOND AVENUE
RICHMOND CRES
MALVERN TER
BARNARD PARK
CLOUDESLEY RD
Superstore
OUTRAM

A
B
C
1
2
3
4
98
111
126
EMIRATES STADIUM
ARSENAL FC
Arsenal Mus
ARSENAL
NATURE RESERVE
GILLESPIE
HURLOCK ST
ELWOOD STREET
Prim Sch
CONEWOOD ST
HIGHBURY QUADRANT
BIRCHMORE WALK
SOTHEBY ROAD
NORTHOLME RD
HIGHBURY PARK
N5
HIGHBURY
HIGHBURY GROVE
HIGHBURY GRANGE
KELROSS
Health Cen
BALFOUR RD
PARK VIEW EST
ABERDEEN PARK
ABERDEEN PK MS
ATHENAEUM CT
KELVIN
Uni-Met. Lon.
Clock Twr
A1201
LEIGH ROAD
HAMILTON PK
HAMILTON PARK WEST
JACK WALKER CT
AUBERT PARK
AUBERT CT
LUCERNE RD
DRAKELEY CT
DRAYTON PARK
STAVORDALE RD
QUEENSLAND RD
BENWELL ROAD
BRYANTWOOD RD
London Metropolitan Uni
HOLLOWAY ROAD
HOLLOWAY ROAD
LOWER HOLLOWAY
A1
HORNSEY ST
HARVIST EST
CITIZEN ROAD
CAEDMON RD
JACKSON RD
SHELB. RD
Superstore
Comm Hall
POLL CL
ROAD
A503
Med. Cen
HIGHBURY FIELDS
CHURCH PATH
Tenn Cts
Sec Sch
ABERDEEN LA
SEAFORTH CRES
HIGHBURY NEW PARK
HIGHBURY EST
Coll
GROSVENOR ROAD
CANONBURY
BAALBEC RD
HIGHBURY PLACE
CALABRIA
LIBERIA RD
CORSICA
Airshaft
PAUL'S ST.
A1199
CANONBURY PK N
CANONBURY PK SOUTH
MARQUESS EST
ALWYNE SQ
CANONBURY
NEW RIVER WK
ESTORICK GALL
CANONBURY SQUARE
ALWYNE VILLAS
CANONBURY ROAD
A104
ESSEX ROAD
Comm Cen
Health Cen
RIVER PL
NEW NORTH
GREENMAN ST
BASIRE ST
HIGHBURY & ISLINGTON
HIGHBURY COR.
HIGHBURY STA RD
UPPER STREET
COMPTON TER
COMPTON AV
THE SUTTON EST
TOWN HALL
HALTON
SEBBON ST
HAWES ST
Fire Sta
Almeida
Little Angel
CROSS ST
Lib
DAGMAR TER
BRITANNIA ROW
Thea
PO
Hall
ISLINGTON PK ST
LAYCOCK ST
Prim Sch
EDWARDS MS
BARNSBURY ST
BARNSBURY
CALEDONIAN ROAD & BARNSBURY
BARNSBURY PK
BEWDLEY ST
BROOKSBY ST
BARNSBURY SQUARE
LOFTING RD
RIPPLEVALE GRO
THORNHILL SQUARE
THORNHILL ROAD
OFFORD RD
RICHMOND
LIVERPOOL ROAD
N7
Freightliners Farm
PARADISE PARK
SHERINGHAM RD
CROSSLEY ST
Academy
ELLINGTON ST
ARUNDEL SQ
ARUNDEL GDNS
WESTBOURNE RD
FURLONG RD
ORLESTON RD
MAG CT
Swim Pool
War Mem
RONALDS RD
MELGUND RD
FIELDWAY CRES
WITHERINGTON RD
DRAYTON PK
Med Cen
Prim Sch
Comm Cen
FRAMFIELD RD
HIGHBURY TER
HIGHBURY CRES
HIGHBURY TER MS
CHILLINGWORTH RD
GEORGE'S RD
MORGAN RD
RINGCROFT ST
MADRAS PL
B515
0 500 yds
0 500 m

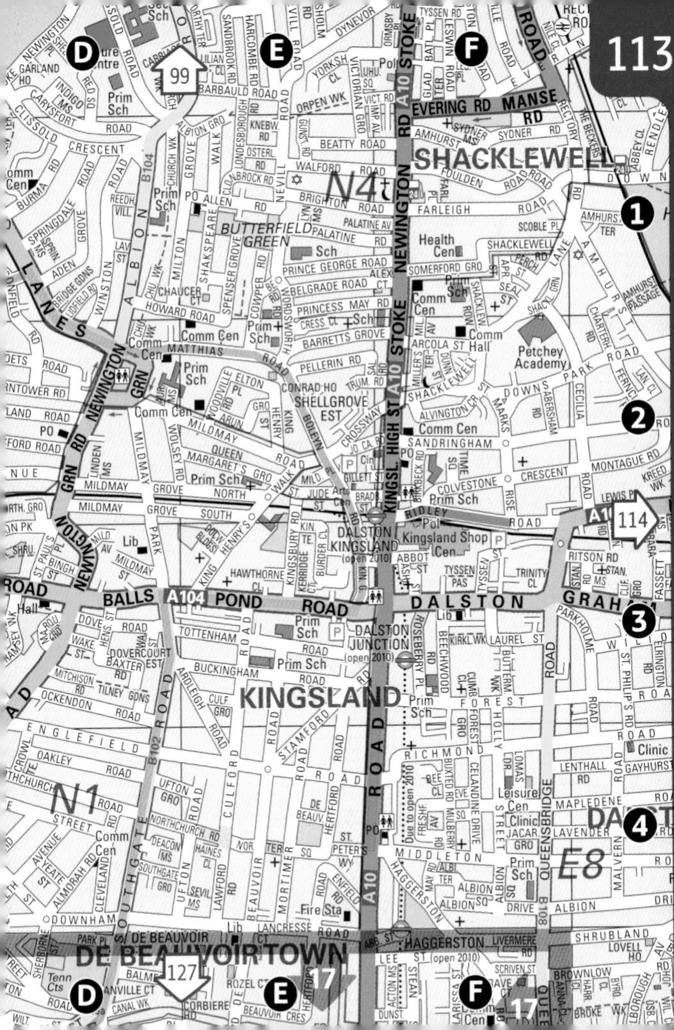
D
E
F
99
114
127
17
1
2
3
4
N4
N1
E8
SHACKLEWELL
KINGSLAND
DE BEAUVOIR TOWN
DALSTON KINGSLAND (open 2010)
DALSTON JUNCTION (open 2010)
HAGGERSTON (open 2010)
BUTTERFIELD GREEN
SHELLGROVE EST
Petchey Academy
Kingsland Shop Cen
STOKE NEWINGTON RD
A10
KINGSL. HIGH ST
KINGSLAND ROAD
BALLS POND ROAD
A104
DALSTON LANE
GRAHAM ROAD
RIDLEY ROAD
EVERING RD
MANSE RD
NEWINGTON GRN
GRN RD
ALBION ROAD
B104
SOUTHGATE ROAD
B102
QUEENSBRIDGE ROAD
B108
BARBAULD ROAD
BEATTY ROAD
WALFORD ROAD
BRIGHTON ROAD
FARLEIGH ROAD
FOULDEN ROAD
AMHURST RD
SHACKLEWELL LANE
SHACKLEWELL RD
PALATINE RD
PRINCE GEORGE ROAD
BELGRADE ROAD
PRINCESS MAY RD
BARRETTS GROVE
PELLERIN RD
HOWARD ROAD
MATTHIAS ROAD
MILDMAY PARK
MILDMAY GROVE NORTH
MILDMAY GROVE SOUTH
QUEEN MARGARET'S GRO
DOWNS PARK ROAD
SANDRINGHAM ROAD
COLVESTONE CRESCENT
MONTAGUE RD
TOTTENHAM ROAD
BUCKINGHAM ROAD
OCKENDON ROAD
ENGLEFIELD ROAD
NORTHCHURCH ROAD
FOREST ROAD
RICHMOND ROAD
MIDDLETON ROAD
ALBION DRIVE
LENTHALL RD
MAPLEDENE ROAD
LAVENDER GRO
DOWNHAM ROAD
LANCRESSE CT
HAGGERSTON ROAD
SHRUBLAND ROAD
BROWNLOW RD
CLISSOLD CRESCENT
CARYSFORT ROAD
Comm Cen
Prim Sch
Lib
PO
Health Cen
Comm Hall
Clinic
Leisure Cen
Fire Sta
Tenn Cts
Due to open 2010

A
B
C
1
2
3
4
RECTORY ROAD
WALSINGHAM RD
Med-Cen
KENNINGHALL ROAD
BEECHOLME EST
COTESBACH RD
THORNBY RD
FLETCHING RD
CHALFORD
100
MANSE RD
SYDNER RD
SHACKLEWELL
NIGHTINGALE EST
Prim Sch
STELLMAN CL
OTTAWAY ST
RENDLESHAM RD
CLAPTON WY
SEATON PT
NOLAN WY
GLIDDON DR
NAPOLEON RD
FERRON RD
POWELL RD
CHARNOCK RD
HEYWORTH RD
TIGER WY
MUIR RD
DELLA PATH
MONTEAGLE WAY
Comm Cen
NEWICK RD
MILDENHALL RD
MILLFIELDS RD
COLENSO RD
MAYOLA ROAD
DOWNS ROAD
HACKNEY DOWNS
E5
AMHURST TER
SCOBLE PL
SHACKLEWELL LANE
PERCH ST
SEAL ST
Comm Hall
Petchey Academy
AMHURST PASSAGE
CHARTERHOUSE RD
DOWNS PARK ROAD
ANDRE STREET
ANTON ST
Sec Sch
BODNEY ROAD
MARDEN HO
PEMBURY ROAD
CRICKETFIELD RD
QUEENSDOWN ROAD
CLARENCE ROAD
LOWER CLAPTON RD
ROWHILL RD
GOULTON RD
POWERSCROFT
GLENARM
MEDIAN RD
Leisure Cen
Health Cen
A102
URSWICK RD
SHELLNESS RD
HINDREY RD
TOLSFORD RD
ORCHARD PL
LOWER CLAPTON RD
DALSTON LA
AMHURST RD
FERNCLIFF RD
CECILIA RD
ABERSHAM RD
MONTAGUE RD
SIGDON RD
WAYLAND AV
CRESCENT
LEWIS PL
LANE
A104
113
SUTTON HO (NT)
BUS GAR
MEHETABEL RD
Superstore
HACKNEY DOWNS
RITSON RD
TRINITY CL
GRAHAM ROAD
A1207
NAVARINO
GREENWOOD RD
Airshaft
HACKNEY CENTRAL
SYLVESTER RD
MORNING LA
TRELAWNEY EST
TOWN HALL
Ocean
PARAGON RD
Sec Sch
WILTON WAY
PARKHOLME RD
ST. PHILIP'S RD
ELRINGTON RD
LANSDOWNE
ELEANOR RD
HORTON RD
READING LA
Mus & Lib
Amb Sta
HACKNEY
DARNLEY ROAD
BRENTHOUSE ROAD
FRAMPTON PK EST
Clinic
RICHMOND ROAD
Comm Hall
Lido
Tenn Cts
LONDON FIELDS
ELLINGFORT RD
A107
MARE ST
LODDIGES
LENTHALL RD
GAYHURST RD
Leisure Cen
MAPLEDENE ROAD
DALSTON
E8
LAVENDER GROVE
Prim Sch
MARTELLO TER
LONDON FLDS
LONDON LA
Coll
Superstore
WELL ST
Surgery
BLACKSTONE EST
FIELDS EST
ALBION DRIVE
QUEENSBRIDGE ROAD
B108
SPORTS GRD
SOUTH HACKNEY
SHRUBLAND RD
LIVERMERE RD
SCRIVEN ST
0 500 yds
0 500 m
TUDOR RD
128
ST. JOSEPH'S
VICTORIA
17

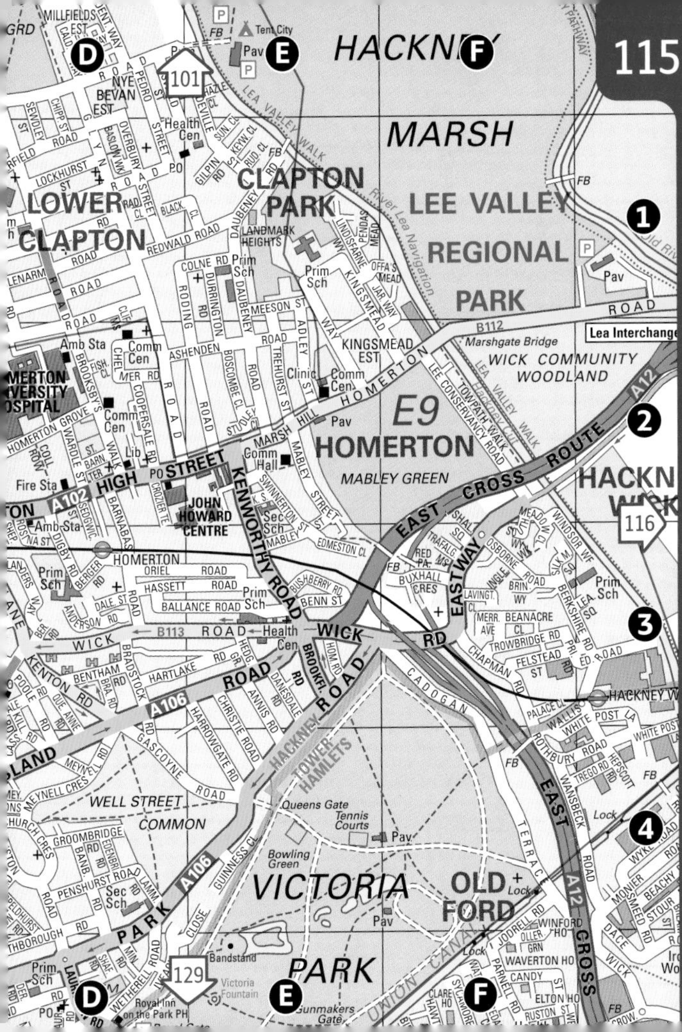
HACKNEY
MARSH
LEE VALLEY
REGIONAL
PARK
CLAPTON
PARK
LOWER
CLAPTON
E9
HOMERTON
MABLEY GREEN
HACKNEY WICK
WICK COMMUNITY
WOODLAND
Lea Interchange
Marshgate Bridge
KINGSMEAD EST
JOHN HOWARD CENTRE
HOMERTON UNIVERSITY HOSPITAL
LANDMARK HEIGHTS
NYE BEVAN EST
MILLFIELDS EST
Tent City
Pav
FB
Prim Sch
Sec Sch
Comm Cen
Comm Hall
Health Cen
Amb Sta
Fire Sta
Lib
Clinic
PO
WELL STREET
COMMON
VICTORIA
PARK
OLD
FORD
TOWER HAMLETS
HACKNEY
Queens Gate
Tennis Courts
Bowling Green
Bandstand
Victoria Fountain
Royal Inn on the Park PH
Gunmakers Gate
UNION CANAL
Lock
River Lea Navigation
LEA VALLEY WALK
EAST CROSS ROUTE
A12
A102
A106
B112
B113
HIGH STREET
HOMERTON HIGH STREET
WICK ROAD
HACKNEY ROAD
KENWORTHY ROAD
EASTWAY
HOMERTON ROAD
MARSH HILL
LEE CONSERVANCY ROAD
TOWPATH WALK
CADOGAN TERRACE
EAST CROSS ROUTE
WANSBECK ROAD
MABLEY STREET
SWINNERTON ST
EDMESTON CL
ORIEL ROAD
HASSETT ROAD
BALLANCE ROAD
BENN ST
BUSHBERRY RD
HARTLAKE RD
BENTHAM RD
KENTON RD
GASCOYNE ROAD
HARROWGATE RD
CHRISTIE ROAD
ANNIS RD
DANESDALE RD
BRADSTOCK RD
MEYNELL CRES
GROOMBRIDGE RD
PENSHURST ROAD
GUINNESS CL
WETHERELL ROAD
PARK RD
CLOSE
REDWALD ROAD
LOCKHURST ST
DAUBENEY RD
RODING RD
DURRINGTON RD
MEESON ST
ADLEY ST
KINGSMEAD WAY
ASHENDEN RD
BOSCOMBE CL
TREHURST ST
COOPERSALE RD
BROOKSBY'S WALK
HOMERTON GROVE
WARDLE ST
DIGBY RD
BERGER RD
HOMERTON
BUXHALL CRES
OSBORNE RD
TROWBRIDGE RD
BEANACRE CL
FELSTEAD ST
CHAPMAN RD
BERKSHIRE RD
WINDSOR WF
WHITE POST LA
ROTHBURY ROAD
TREGO RD
HEPSCOTT RD
HACKNEY WICK
WYKE ROAD
MONIER RD
SMEED RD
STOUR RD
DACE RD
WICK
WAVERTON HO
CANDY ST
ELTON HO
RUSTON ST
PARNELL RD
JODRELL RD
WINFORD HO
SYCAMORE
CLARE HO
101
116
129
D
E
F
1
2
3
4

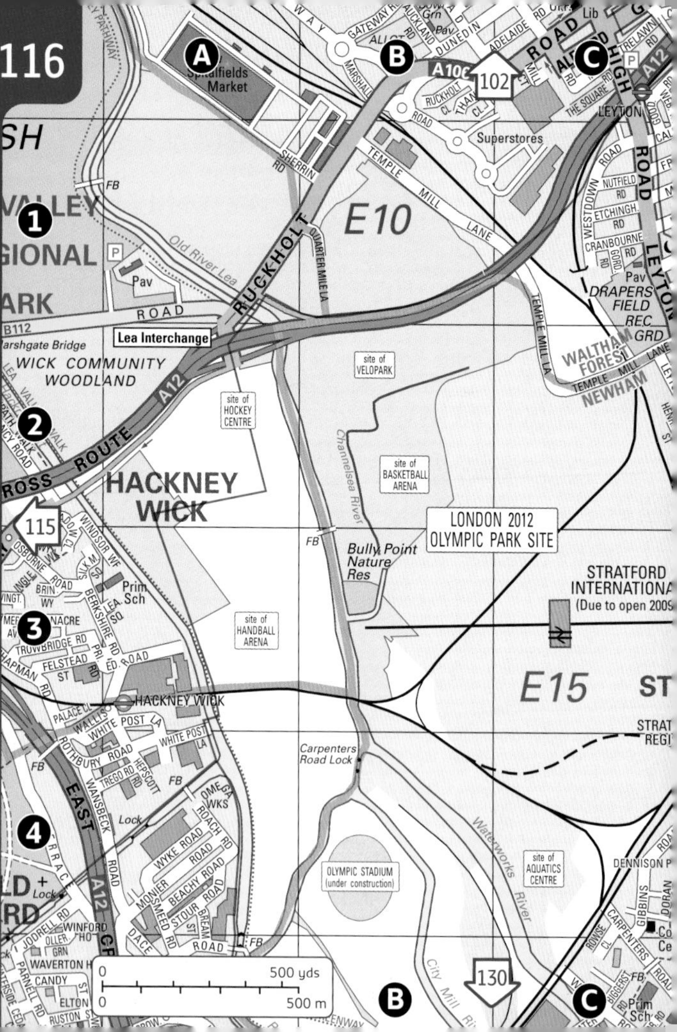
A
B
C
Spitalfields Market
GATEWAY RD
AUCKLAND RD
DUNEDIN
ADELAIDE RD
MARSHALL
ALLOTS
A106
102
RUCKHOLT CL
THANE CL
RUCKHOLT ROAD
MILL CT
ALFRED RD
HIGH
THE SQUARE
TRELAWN RD
A12
LEYTON
Lib
Superstores
SHERRIN RD
TEMPLE MILL LANE
E10
SH
VALLEY
1
GIONAL
ARK
FB
Old River Lea
Pav
RUCKHOLT
QUARTER MILE LA
ROAD
B112
Lea Interchange
Marshgate Bridge
WICK COMMUNITY WOODLAND
site of VELOPARK
site of HOCKEY CENTRE
2
CROSS ROUTE
HACKNEY WICK
115
WESTDOWN ROAD
NUTFIELD RD
ETCHINGH. RD
CRANBOURNE RD
GORD. RD
DRAPERS FIELD REC GRD
LEYTON
WALTHAM FOREST
NEWHAM
TEMPLE MILL LA
TEMPLE MILL LANE
Channelsea River
site of BASKETBALL ARENA
LONDON 2012 OLYMPIC PARK SITE
Bully Point Nature Res
STRATFORD INTERNATIONAL
(Due to open 2009)
site of HANDBALL ARENA
E15
OSBORNE ROAD
WINDSOR WF
SILK M. SQ
BERKSHIRE RD
LEA SQ
Prim Sch
NACRE
3
TROWBRIDGE RD
FELSTEAD ST
CHAPMAN RD
ED. ROAD
HACKNEY WICK
PALACE CL
WALLIS RD
WHITE POST LA
ROTHBURY ROAD
TREGO RD
HEPSCOTT
WANSBECK ROAD
EAST
A12
OMEGA WKS
ROACH RD
WYKE ROAD
MONIER
SMEED RD
BEACHY ROAD
STOUR ROAD
BREAM ST
DACE
ROAD
Lock
4
Carpenters Road Lock
OLYMPIC STADIUM (under construction)
Waterworks River
site of AQUATICS CENTRE
City Mill River
STRAT
DENNISON P
GIBBINS
ROWSE CL
CARPENTERS ROAD
BIGGERST.
Prim Sch
JODRELL RD
WINFORD HO
WAVERTON H
PARNELL RD
CANDY ST
ELTON
RUSTON ST
0 500 yds
0 500 m
130

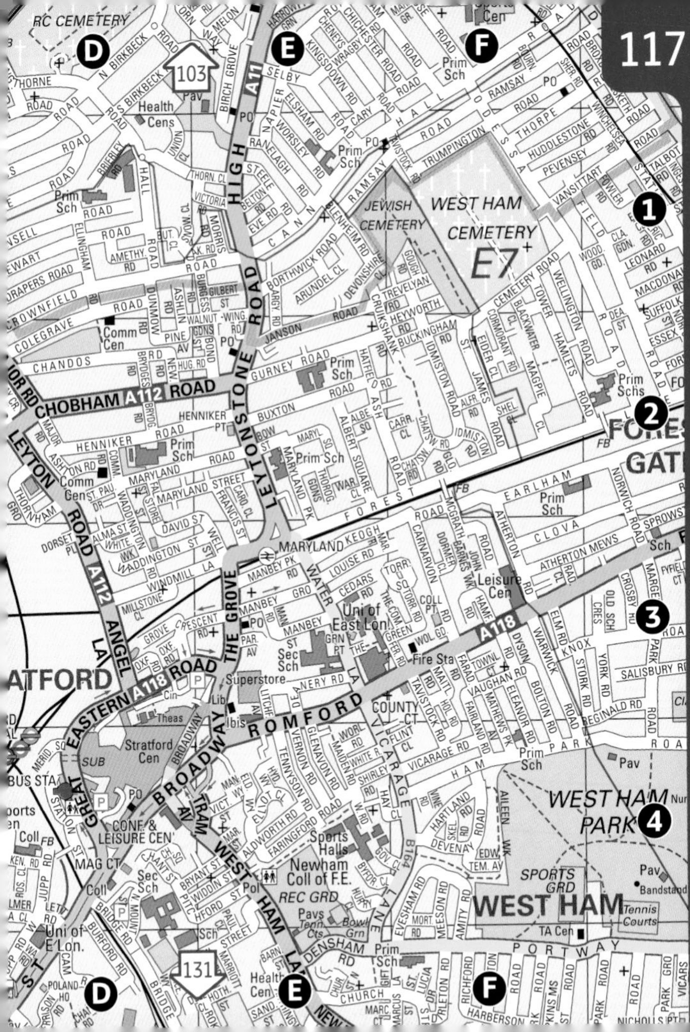
RC CEMETERY
D
E
F
103
N BIRKBECK ROAD
S BIRKBECK ROAD
Health Cens
BIRCH GROVE
A11
HIGH ROAD
LEYTONSTONE
SELBY
KINGSDOWN RD
CHICHESTER ROAD
WRAGBY RD
CHENEYS RD
NAPIER RD
ELSHAM RD
WORSLEY RD
RANELAGH RD
STEELE RD
BELTON RD
EVE RD
CANN HALL ROAD
CARY RD
RAMSAY RD
TAVISTOCK RD
TRUMPINGTON ROAD
ODESSA ROAD
THORPE ROAD
HUDDLESTONE RD
PEVENSEY RD
VANSITTART RD
FOWLER RD
WINCHELSEA RD
TALBOT RD
JEWISH CEMETERY
WEST HAM CEMETERY
E7
1
2
3
4
Prim Sch
PO
UNION CL
THORN. CL
VICTORIA RD
MORRIS RD
HALL RD
BRIERLEY RD
ELLINGHAM RD
AMETHY. RD
DRAPERS ROAD
CROWNFIELD RD
COLEGRAVE ROAD
CHANDOS RD
Comm Cen
DUNMOW RD
ASHLIN RD
BURGESS RD
GILBERT ST
WALNUT GDNS
WING RD
PINE AV
BOND ST
BRYDGES RD
HUG. RD
BORTHWICK ROAD
ARUNDEL CL
DEVONSHIRE CL
BLENHEIM RD
JANSON ROAD
TREVELYAN RD
HEYWORTH RD
BUCKINGHAM RD
CRUIKSHANK RD
GOUGH RD
CEMETERY ROAD
WELLINGTON RD
TOWER HAMLETS ROAD
CORMORANT RD
BLACKWATER CL
EIDER CL
MAGPIE CL
ST. JAMES ROAD
IDMISTON ROAD
LEONARD RD
MACDONALD RD
SUFFOLK RD
ESSEX RD
WOOD. GD.
CLA. GDN.
DEA. ST
Prim Schs
CHOBHAM A112 ROAD
HENNIKER PT
HENNIKER ROAD
BUXTON ROAD
GURNEY ROAD
HATFIELD RD
ASH RD
ALBERT SQUARE
CARR. CL
CHATSW. RD
ALFR. RD
SHEL. CL
FOREST GATE
FB
EARLHAM GRO
NORWICH ROAD
SPROWSTON
LEYTON ROAD
A112
MARYLAND ROAD
MARYLAND STREET
FRANCIS ST
MARYLAND SQ
THOROLD
GDNS
WAR. CL
FOREST ROAD
CARNARVON RD
DORMER CL
McGRATH
BARNES WK
JOHN ROAD
ATHERTON ROAD
CLOVA RD
ATHERTON MEWS
THORNHAM GRO
DORSET PL
ALMA ST
DAVID ST
WADDINGTON ST
WADDINGTON RD
WELL ST
WINDMILL LA
MILLSTONE CL
MARYLAND
KEOGH RD
LOUISE RD
MANBEY PK RD
MANBEY GRO
MANBEY ST
WATER LA
CEDARS RD
TORR. SQ
TORR RD
COLL PT.
Leisure Cen
CROSBY RD
MARGERY
OLD SCH CRES
ELM RD
KNOX
STORK RD
YORK RD
SALISBURY RD
REGINALD RD
THE GROVE
GROVE CRESCENT RD
ANGEL LA
STRATFORD
GREAT EASTERN A118 ROAD
Uni of East Lon
Sec Sch
Superstore
DEANERY RD
Fire Sta
A118
DYSON RD
WARWICK ROAD
BOLTON RD
ELEANOR RD
VAUGHAN RD
MATHEWS PK AV
TOWNL. CT
FAIRLAND RD
TAVISTOCK RD
Lib
Ibis
ROMFORD
COUNTY CT
VICARAGE LANE
VICARAGE RD
FLINT CL
HAM PARK ROAD
Prim Sch
WEST HAM PARK
Pav
Cin
Theas
Stratford Cen
SUB
BROADWAY
BUS STA.
MERID. SQ
STATION ST
CONF. & LEISURE CEN
TRAM WAY
WEST HAM LA
TENNYSON RD
GLENAVON RD
VERNON RD
ELLIOT CL
ALDWORTH RD
FARINGFORD ROAD
Sports Halls
Newham Coll of F.E.
REC GRD
Bowl Grn
Pavs
Tenn Cts
B164
HARTLAND RD
DEVENAY RD
EDW. TEM. AV
AILEEN WK
SPORTS GRD
WEST HAM
Tennis Courts
Bandstand
TA Cen
PORTWAY
Coll
MAG CT
Sec Sch
Uni of E Lon.
BURFORD RD
131
BRIDGE RD
Health Cen
DENSHAM RD
CHURCH ST
Prim Sch
RICHFORD ROAD
HARBERSON
PARK GRO
VICARS
EVESHAM RD
MEESON RD
AMITY RD
MORT. RD
POLAND HO
NEW

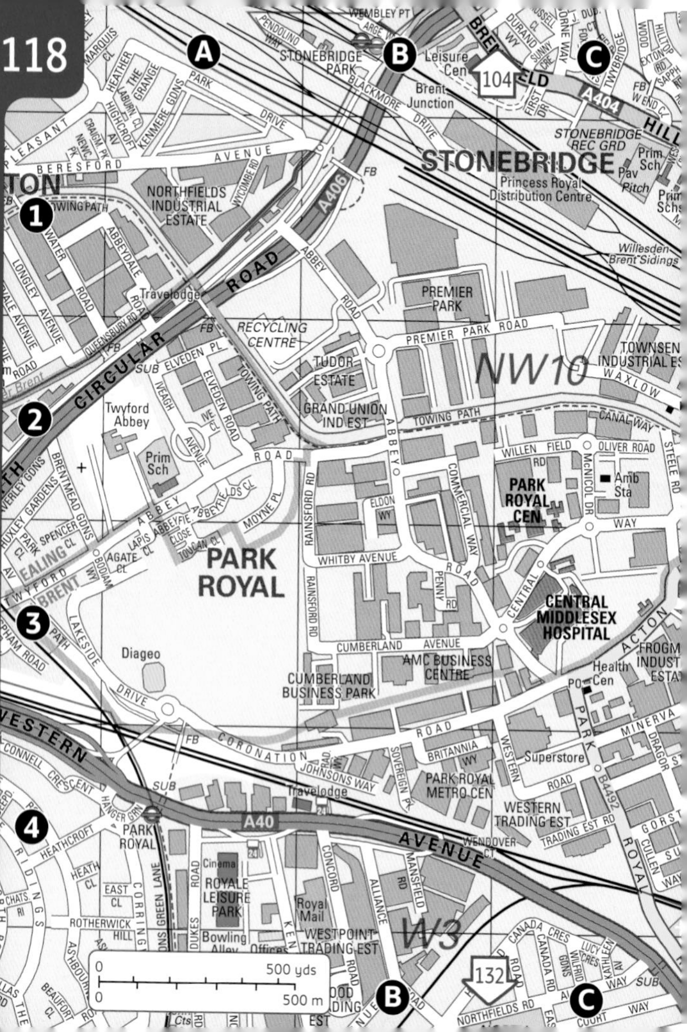
A
B
C
WEMBLEY PT
STONEBRIDGE PARK
Leisure Cen
104
Brent Junction
A404
STONEBRIDGE REC GRD
STONEBRIDGE
Princess Royal Distribution Centre
Willesden Brent Sidings
BERESFORD AVENUE
NORTHFIELDS INDUSTRIAL ESTATE
TOWING PATH
A406
NORTH CIRCULAR ROAD
Travelodge
PREMIER PARK
PREMIER PARK ROAD
RECYCLING CENTRE
TUDOR ESTATE
GRAND UNION IND EST
NW10
TOWNSEND INDUSTRIAL ES
WAXLOW
CANAL WAY
Twyford Abbey
Prim Sch
ABBEY ROAD
PARK ROYAL CEN
Amb Sta
PARK ROYAL
WHITBY AVENUE
CUMBERLAND AVENUE
CENTRAL MIDDLESEX HOSPITAL
Diageo
AMC BUSINESS CENTRE
CUMBERLAND BUSINESS PARK
Health Cen
FROGM INDUST ESTAT
CORONATION ROAD
WESTERN AVENUE
Superstore
PARK ROYAL METRO CEN
WESTERN TRADING EST
Travelodge
A40
PARK ROYAL
Cinema
ROYALE LEISURE PARK
Royal Mail
Bowling Alley
WESTPOINT TRADING EST
W3
132
0 500 yds
0 500 m
1
2
3
4

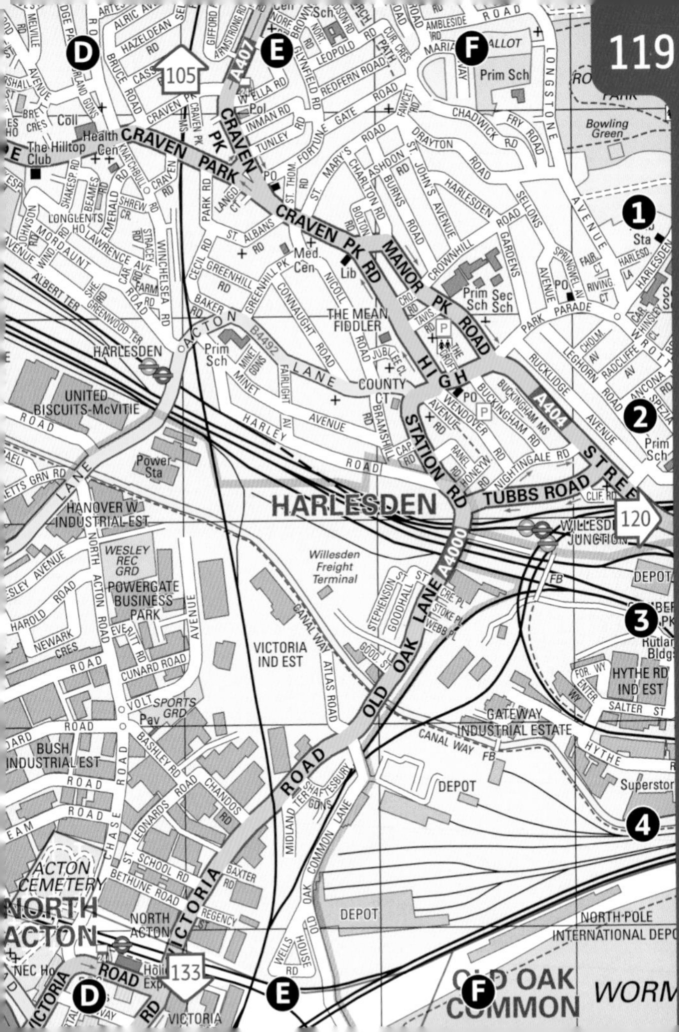
105
120
133
D
E
F
1
2
3
4
HARLESDEN
NORTH ACTON
OLD OAK COMMON
WORM
CRAVEN PARK
CRAVEN PK RD
CRAVEN PK
A407
MANOR PK ROAD
HIGH STREET
A404
STATION RD
TUBBS ROAD
A4000
OLD OAK LANE
VICTORIA ROAD
ACTON LANE
B4492
NORTH ACTON ROAD
The Hilltop Club
Health Cen
Coll
LONGLENTS HO
UNITED BISCUITS-McVITIE
Power Sta
HANOVER W. INDUSTRIAL EST
WESLEY REC GRD
POWERGATE BUSINESS PARK
VICTORIA IND EST
Willesden Freight Terminal
THE MEAN FIDDLER
COUNTY CT
Med. Cen
Lib
Prim Sch
Sec Sch
WILLESDEN JUNCTION
DEPOT
HYTHE RD IND EST
GATEWAY INDUSTRIAL ESTATE
BUSH INDUSTRIAL EST
ACTON CEMETERY
SPORTS GRD
Pav
NORTH POLE INTERNATIONAL DEPOT
Superstore
Rutland Bldgs
Bowling Green
Sta
CANAL WAY
HARLEY ROAD
HARLESDEN ROAD
PARK PARADE
LONGSTONE AVENUE
CHADWICK RD
FORTUNE GATE ROAD
CUNARD ROAD
BASHLEY RD
CHANDOS RD
ST. LEONARDS ROAD
BETHUNE ROAD
SCHOOL RD
ATLAS ROAD
OLD OAK COMMON LANE
SHAFTESBURY GDNS
MIDLAND TER
WELLS HOUSE RD
BAXTER RD
REGENCY ST
NIGHTINGALE RD
BUCKINGHAM RD
WENDOVER RD
RUCKLIDGE AVENUE
LEGHORN ROAD
SALTER ST
HYTHE RD

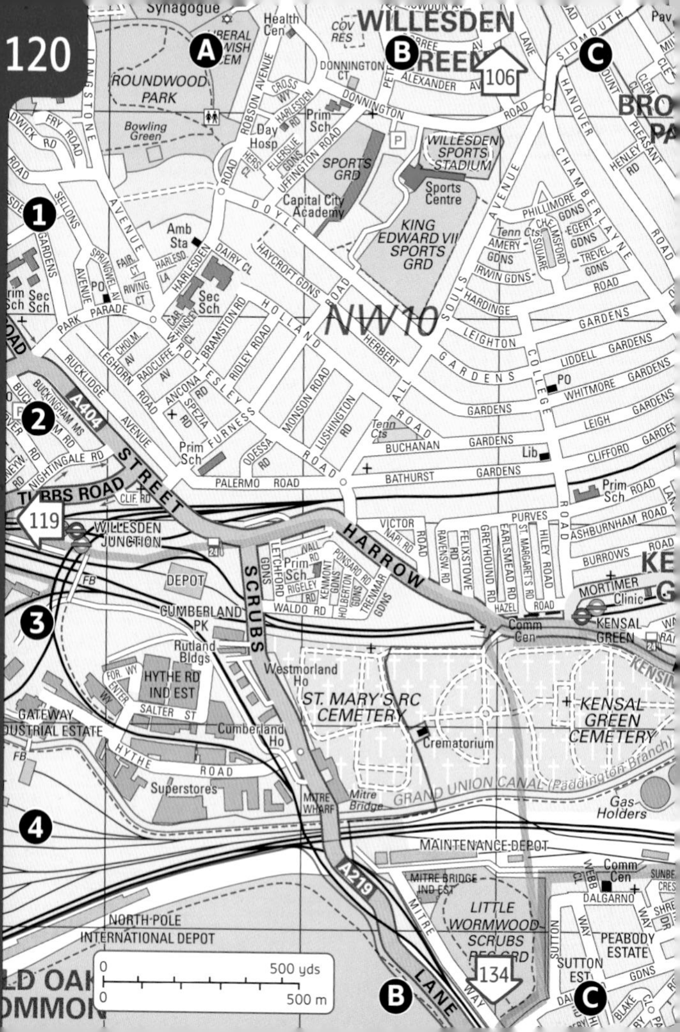
WILLESDEN GREEN
106
119
134
NW10
A
B
C
1
2
3
4
Synagogue
Health Cen
COV RES
ROUNDWOOD PARK
Bowling Green
DONNINGTON CT
ALEXANDER AV
DONNINGTON ROAD
ROBSON AVENUE
CROSS WY
HARLESDEN RD
Day Hosp
Prim Sch
UFFINGTON ROAD
SPORTS GRD
WILLESDEN SPORTS STADIUM
Sports Centre
Capital City Academy
KING EDWARD VII SPORTS GRD
DOYLE
HAYCROFT GDNS
HERBERT
HOLLAND ROAD
DAIRY CL
Amb Sta
Sec Sch
SELLONS AVENUE
SPRINGWELL AV
FAIR CT
RIVING CT
HARLESD LA
PO
PARK PARADE
FRY ROAD
LONGSTONE AVENUE
Sec Sch
BRAMSTON RD
RIDLEY ROAD
WROTTESLEY
CHOLM AV
RADCLIFFE AV
LEGHORN ROAD
RUCKLIDGE AVENUE
ANCONA RD
SPEZIA RD
FURNESS ROAD
MONSON ROAD
LUSHINGTON RD
ODESSA RD
Prim Sch
PALERMO ROAD
A404
HARROW ROAD
NIGHTINGALE RD
BUCKINGHAM MS
TUBBS ROAD
CLIF RD
WILLESDEN JUNCTION
DEPOT
CUMBERLAND PK
SCRUBS LANE
Rutland Bldgs
HYTHE RD IND EST
SALTER ST
GATEWAY INDUSTRIAL ESTATE
HYTHE ROAD
Superstores
Cumberland Ho
Westmorland Ho
LETCHFORD GDNS
WALDO RD
RIGELEY RD
KEMPONT GDNS
HOLBERTON GDNS
PONSARD RD
TRENMAR GDNS
ST. MARY'S RC CEMETERY
Crematorium
KENSAL GREEN CEMETERY
GRAND UNION CANAL (Paddington Branch)
Gas Holders
MITRE WHARF
Mitre Bridge
MAINTENANCE DEPOT
MITRE BRIDGE IND EST
A219
LITTLE WORMWOOD SCRUBS REC GRD
NORTH POLE INTERNATIONAL DEPOT
MITRE WAY
0 500 yds
0 500 m
VICTOR ROAD
RAVENSW RD
FELIXSTOWE
GREYHOUND RD
EARLSMEAD RD
ST. MARGARET'S RD
HILEY ROAD
HAZEL ROAD
PURVES ROAD
Comm Cen
KENSAL GREEN
MORTIMER
Clinic
ASHBURNHAM ROAD
BURROWS ROAD
Prim Sch
BATHURST GARDENS
BUCHANAN GARDENS
Lib
CLIFFORD GARDENS
LEIGH GARDENS
WHITMORE GARDENS
LIDDELL GARDENS
LEIGHTON GARDENS
HARDINGE ROAD
ALL SOULS AVENUE
COLLEGE ROAD
IRWIN GDNS
AMERY GDNS
Tenn Cts
CHELMSFORD SQUARE
PHILLIMORE GDNS
EGERT GDNS
TREVEL GDNS
CHAMBERLAYNE ROAD
HANOVER
SIDMOUTH
HENLEY RD
PLEASANT
Tenn Cts
DALGARNO WAY
WEBB CL
Comm Cen
PEABODY ESTATE
SUTTON EST
SUTTON WAY
GDNS

D
E
F
107
ESBURY
BRONDESBURY PARK
NW6
PADDINGTON OLD CEMETERY
KENSAL RISE
QUEEN'S PARK
Pitch'n'Putt
Tennis Courts
QUEEN'S PARK
KILBURN
1
2
3
4
6
18
122
WEST KILBURN
MAIDA HILL
KENSAL TOWN
W10
135
ST. CHARLES
LANE
A4003
B451
B413
A404
A40
HARROW ROAD
KILBURN LANE
HARVIST ROAD
CHAMBERLAYNE RD
SALUSBURY ROAD
BRONDESBURY ROAD
CARLTON
MALVERN
SHIRLAND ROAD
KILBURN PARK
KENSAL ROAD
LADBROKE GROVE
SOUTHERN ROW
CANAL WAY
BARLBY ROAD
WORNINGTON
ELKSTONE
GREAT WESTERN ROAD
WESTBOURNE
MEANWHILE GARDENS
TRELLICK TWR
City Learning Cen
SPORTS GRD
ROSEDENE
GROSVENOR CT
CHEVENING
KESLAKE
KEMPE
CREIGHTON RD
PEPLOE
MILMAN
TIVERTON
DUNDONALD RD
WRENTHAM AVENUE
ALLINGTON RD
HERRIES
SELBY
DOWLAND
BRAVINGTON RD
ST. LUKE'S YD
PORTNALL
ASHMORE
FERNHEAD
MARBAN RD
SALTRAM
DENMARK
ALBERT
WILLIAM DUNBAR HO
WILLIAM SAVILLE HO
PRINCESS
DICKENS HO
AUSTEN
City of Westminster Coll
FORDINGLEY RD
LYDFORD RD
WARLOCK RD
CROXLEY
ELGIN
CHIPPENHAM
FERMOY
HORMEA RD
WOODFIELD RD
Youth Arts
Clinic
BUS GARAGE
NUTBOURNE ST
MARNE STREET
LOTHROP STREET
KILRAVOCK STREET
OLIPHANT
PEACH ROAD
QUEENS PARK COURT
SIXTH
HUXLEY ST
FIFTH
GALTON ST
FOURTH AV
ENBROOK ST
DROOP STREET
CAIRD ST
SECOND AV
BARFETT ST
FIRST AV
PARRY RD
BRUCKNER ST
LANCEFIELD ST
BEETHOVEN ST
THIRD
DART
ILBERT
PEMBER RD
BRENT
& CHELSEA
Activity Cen
Superstore
Coll
Lib
Sports Cen
Health Cen
Comm Cen
Prim Sch
Muslim Cen
Fire Sta
Med Cen
Jubilee Sch
ATHLONE GDNS
BOSWORTH RD
HAZLEWOOD CRES
ADAIR RD
MANCHESTER DR
APPLE
ST ERVANS RD
ACKLAM RD
GOLBORNE
MIDDLE ROW
CONLAN ST
EAST ROW
SALTERS RD
MATTHEW CL
EXMOOR
HEWER ST
VICTORIA
BRONDESBURY
KINGSWOOD AVENUE
WINDERMERE AV
HOPEFIELD AV
MONTROSE AV
SUMMERFIELD AV
DUDLEY RD
LONSDALE
HARTLAND
HONITON
LYNTON RD
DONALDSON RD
TENNYSON RD
DOUGLAS RD
KINGSLEY RD
KENILWORTH RD
PRIORY
GLENGALL
ESMOND RD
HAZELMERE RD
CHARTERIS
WINCHESTER AV
KIMBERLEY RD
ATHELSTAN GDNS
TORBAY ROAD
DYNE
PLYMPTON
DUNSTER GDNS
CALLCOTT RD
BUCKLEY RD
BURTON RD
The Tricycle
Corrib Rest PH
Fitness Cen
CARLISLE RD
BROOKSVILLE AV
RADNOR RD
AYLESTONE AVENUE
CHRISTCHURCH AVENUE
MANOR HOUSE DRIVE
FOREST CL
ST. HILDAS CL
MOSTYN GDNS
BOLTON GDNS
KILBURN

A
B
C
108
121
136
6
7
18
1
2
3
4
NW6
NW8
W9
KILBURN
MAIDA VALE
MAIDA HILL
KILBURN HIGH ROAD
KILBURN PARK
MAIDA VALE
WARWICK AVENUE
HIGH ROAD
MAIDA VALE
A5
A4003
B509
B507
B510
B413
B414
B451
WOODCHURCH RD
GREENCROFT GARDENS
ACOL ROAD
ABERDARE GARDENS
GOLDHURST TERRACE
ABBEY ROAD
MESSINA AVENUE
GASCONY AVENUE
MAZENOD AV
QUEX ROAD
MUTRIX RD
BELSIZE ROAD
WEST END LANE
PRIORY TER
KILBURN PRIORY
ROWLEY WAY
AINSWORTH WAY
BOUNDARY ROAD
SPRINGFIELD ROAD
HILL ROAD
LOUDOUN ROAD
ABBEY ROAD EST
MORTIMER EST
GREVILLE PL
CLIFTON HILL
CARLTON HILL
HAMILTON TER
BLENHEIM TER
MARLBOROUGH PL
ABERCORN PL
VIOLET HILL
KILBURN SQ
ALGERNON RD
CHARTERIS RD
ESMUND RD
VICTORIA RD
DONALDSON RD
BRONDESBURY RD
CHICHESTER RD
PRINCESS ROAD
CAMBRIDGE RD
OXFORD ROAD
RANDOLPH GDNS
ANDOVER PL
CARLTON VALE
MALVERN RD
DICKENS HO
AUSTEN HO
BRONTE HO
FIELDING HO
PADDINGTON RECREATION GROUND
Athletics Track
Cricket Ground
City of Westminster Coll
City of Westminster Coll (Maida Vale)
MORSHEAD RD
ASHWORTH RD
ELGIN AV
LAUDERDALE ROAD
CASTELLAIN ROAD
SHIRLAND ROAD
FORDINGLEY RD
ESSENDINE RD
WYMERING RD
WIDLEY RD
LANHILL RD
DELAWARE RD
B.B.C. Studios
Sports Club
WARWICK AVENUE
WARRINGTON CRESCENT
RANDOLPH AVENUE
CLIFTON GDNS
ELGIN AVENUE
HARROW ROAD
GREAT WESTERN ROAD
SUTHERLAND AVENUE
FORMOSA ST
BLOMFIELD RD
DELAMERE TER
CHIPPENHAM RD
EDBROOKE RD
OAKINGTON RD
MARYLANDS RD
Health Centre
Marriott
GREVILLE HALL
GLASGOW HO
FALKIRK HO
EDINBURGH HO
WELLESLEY CT
VALE CT
CROPTHORNE CT
STUART TWR
SNOWMAN HO
CASTERBRIDGE
ST. J
Portobello Junction
WESTBOURNE
0 500 yds
0 500 m

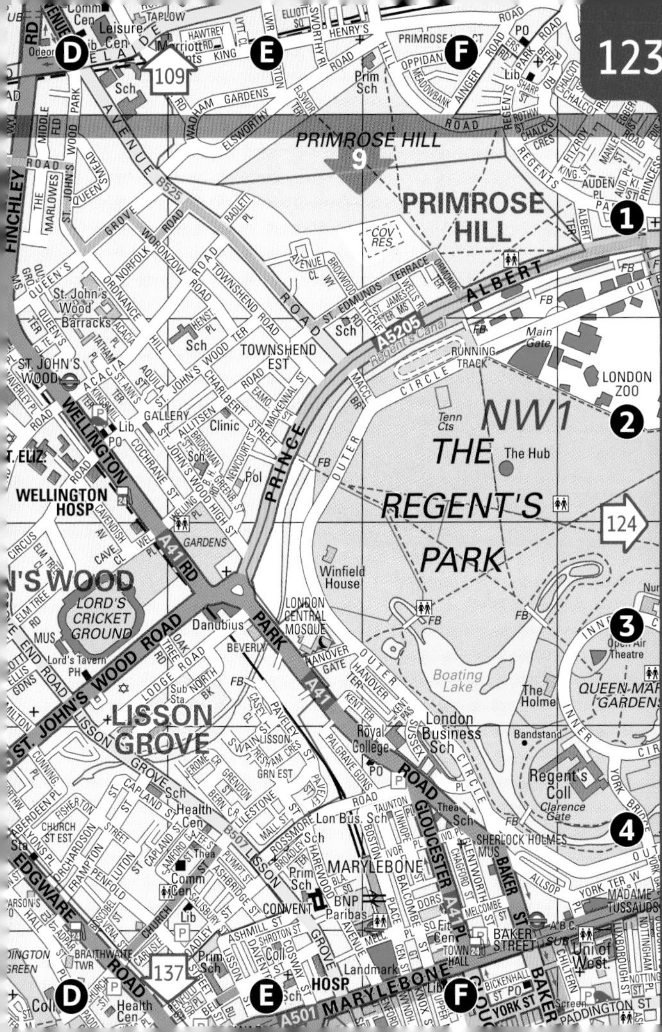
D
E
F
109
PRIMROSE HILL
9
PRIMROSE
HILL
COV RES.
ALBERT ROAD
PRINCE ALBERT ROAD
A5205
Regent's Canal
RUNNING TRACK
Main Gate
LONDON ZOO
OUTER CIRCLE
NW1
THE
REGENT'S
PARK
The Hub
Tenn Cts
Winfield House
LONDON CENTRAL MOSQUE
Boating Lake
The Holme
Open Air Theatre
QUEEN MARY'S GARDENS
INNER CIRCLE
Bandstand
Regent's Coll
Clarence Gate
London Business Sch
Royal College
124
1
2
3
4
ST. JOHN'S WOOD
St. John's Wood Barracks
WELLINGTON ROAD
WELLINGTON HOSP
A41
LORD'S CRICKET GROUND
Lord's Tavern PH
ST. JOHN'S WOOD ROAD
Danubius
PARK ROAD
TOWNSHEND EST
FINCHLEY ROAD
AVENUE ROAD
B525
LISSON GROVE
EDGWARE ROAD
MARYLEBONE
MARYLEBONE ROAD
A501
BAKER ST
BAKER STREET
GLOUCESTER PL
SHERLOCK HOLMES MUS
MADAME TUSSAUDS
Uni of West.
Landmark
BNP Paribas
CONVENT
Lon Bus. Sch
Prim Sch
HOSP
Coll
Health Cen
Comm Cen
137
D
E
F

A
B
C
1
2
3
4
110
123
138
NW1
CAMDEN TOWN
REGENT'S PARK
LONDON ZOO
QUEEN MARY'S GARDENS
Open Air Theatre
The Hub
Stables Mkt
Camden Lock Mkt
Superstore
M.T.V. Studios
Film Makers Co-Op
Holiday Inn
Youth Cen
Cecil Sharp Ho
Prim Sch
Sports Cen
Fit. Cen
Plaza
Odeon
CAMDEN TOWN
MORNINGTON CRESCENT
TA Cen
Regent's Park Barracks
DEPOT
ST. GEORGE'S CATHEDRAL
Gloucester Gate
Cumberland Gate
Main Gate
Clarence Gate
Nursery
The Holme
Bandstand
Regent's Coll
Tenn Cts
PARK SQUARE GARDENS
Royal Acad. of Music
MADAME TUSSAUDS
LONDON CLINIC
BAKER STREET
REGENT'S PARK
GT. PORTLAND ST.
WARREN STREET
EUSTON SQUARE
Melia White House
Abbey
Euston Twr
Telecom Tower
UCL
Euston
ALBERT ROAD
PRINCE ALBERT ROAD
PARKWAY
DELANCEY ST
CAMDEN HIGH ST
HAMPSTEAD ROAD
EUSTON ROAD
MARYLEBONE RD
ALBANY STREET
PARK CRES
OUTER CIRCLE
INNER CIRCLE
CHESTER RD
BROAD WALK
CAMDEN WESTMINSTER
A400
A4201
A5202
0 500 yds
0 500 m

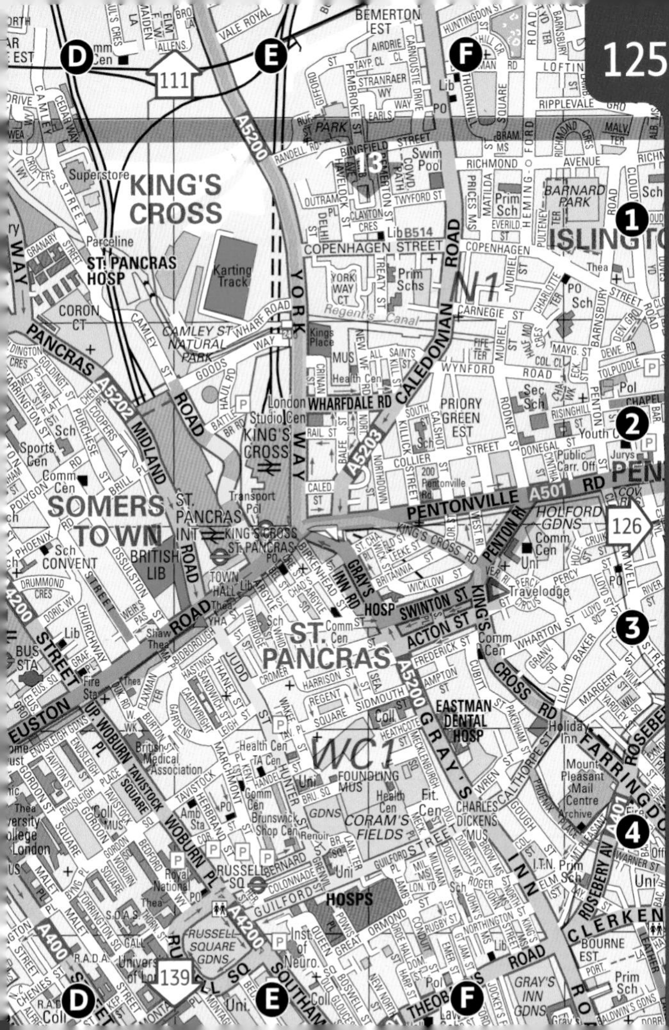
D
E
F
111
KING'S CROSS
ISLINGTON
N1
SOMERS TOWN
ST. PANCRAS
WC1
CLERKENWELL
BEMERTON EST
BARNARD PARK
Superstore
Parceline
ST. PANCRAS HOSP
Karting Track
CAMLEY ST NATURAL PARK
Regent's Canal
Kings Place
London Studio Cen
KING'S CROSS
ST. PANCRAS INT
KING'S CROSS ST. PANCRAS
Transport Pol
BRITISH LIB
TOWN HALL
PRIORY GREEN EST
HOLFORD GDNS
Travelodge
Holiday Inn
EASTMAN DENTAL HOSP
Mount Pleasant Mail Centre Archive
CORAM'S FIELDS
FOUNDLING MUS
CHARLES DICKENS MUS
British Medical Association
Royal National
RUSSELL SQ
RUSSELL SQUARE GDNS
HOSPS
Inst of Neuro.
GRAY'S INN GDNS
R.A.D.A.
S.O.A.S.
University College London
YORK WAY
CALEDONIAN ROAD
PENTONVILLE RD
A501
A5200
A5202
A5203
A4200
A400
MIDLAND ROAD
EUSTON ROAD
GRAY'S INN ROAD
KING'S CROSS RD
FARRINGDON
ROSEBERY AV
COPENHAGEN STREET
RICHMOND AVENUE
WHARFDALE RD
SWINTON ST
ACTON ST
WOBURN PL
SOUTHAMPTON
THEOBALDS ROAD
GUILFORD STREET
1
2
3
4
126
139

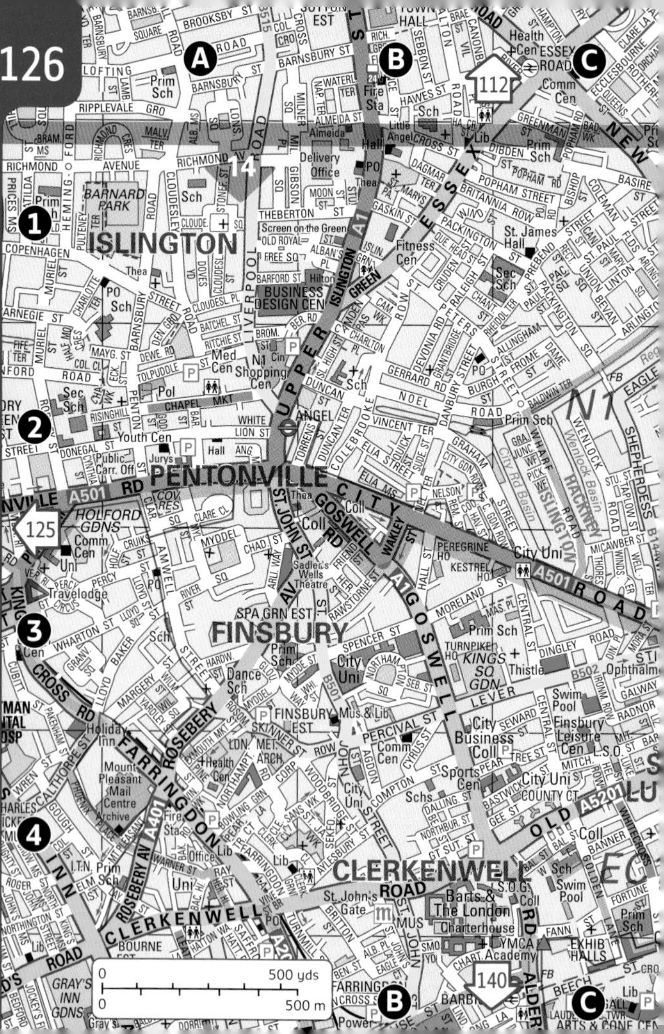
A
B
C
1
2
3
4
ISLINGTON
PENTONVILLE
FINSBURY
CLERKENWELL
112
125
140
14
BARNARD PARK
UPPER STREET
ISLINGTON GREEN
ESSEX ROAD
PENTONVILLE RD
A501
CITY ROAD
GOSWELL RD
ST. JOHN ST
FARRINGDON RD
ROSEBERY AV
KINGS CROSS RD
CLERKENWELL ROAD
OLD ST
A5201
A1
A401
B502
B501
LIVERPOOL ROAD
RICHMOND AVENUE
COPENHAGEN ST
CALEDONIAN RD
BARNSBURY ST
BARNSBURY ROAD
CLOUDESLEY ROAD
CHAPEL MKT
WHITE LION ST
BUSINESS DESIGN CEN
N1 Shopping Cen
ANGEL
NOEL ROAD
VINCENT TER
DUNCAN TER
COLEBROOKE ROW
CITY GDN ROW
City Rd Basin
Wenlock Basin
SHEPHERDESS WALK
WHARF ROAD
DANBURY STREET
CROSS ST
ALMEIDA ST
Almeida
Little Angel
Screen on the Green
Fitness Cen
Sadler's Wells Theatre
SPA GRN EST
FINSBURY EST
City Uni
City Business Coll
Holiday Inn
Travelodge
Mount Pleasant Mail Centre
Archive
Mus & Lib
St. John's Gate
Barts & The London
Charterhouse
YMCA
Academy
Finsbury Leisure Cen
Swim Pool
Prim Sch
Sec Sch
Youth Cen
Jurys
Public Carr. Off
HOLFORD GDNS
MYDDELTON SQ
AMWELL ST
LLOYD BAKER
WHARTON ST
GOSWELL ROAD
KINGS SQ GDN
BASTWICK ST
GREEN MAN ST
ROSEBERY AV
GRAY'S INN GDNS
0
500 yds
0
500 m

DE BEAUVOIR TOWN
HOXTON
SHOREDITCH
HAGGERST
SHOREDITCH PARK
HAGGERSTON PK
KINGSLAND
QUEENSBRIDGE ROAD
HACKNEY ROAD
OLD ST
GREAT EASTERN ST
SHOREDITCH HIGH ST
COMMERCIAL
BETHNAL GRN
CITY ROAD
EAST RD
A10
A1200
A1208
A1209
A501
B108
B134
E2
EC2
113
141
128
17
29
D
E
F
1
2
3
4
MILDMAY MISS. HOSP
Britannia Leisure Cen
Community Coll Hackney
BUNHILL FIELDS
BURIAL GRD
Spitalfields Mkt
Spitalfields City Fm
BROADGATE
Bethnal Grn Tech Coll
HOXTON (open 2010)
HAGGERSTON (open 2010)
GEFFRYE MUS
DORSET EST
ARDEN EST
COLVILLE EST
WHITMORE EST
PROVOST EST
CRANSTON EST
ST. JOHN'S EST
WESLEY'S HO
ARNOLD CIRCUS
REGENT'S

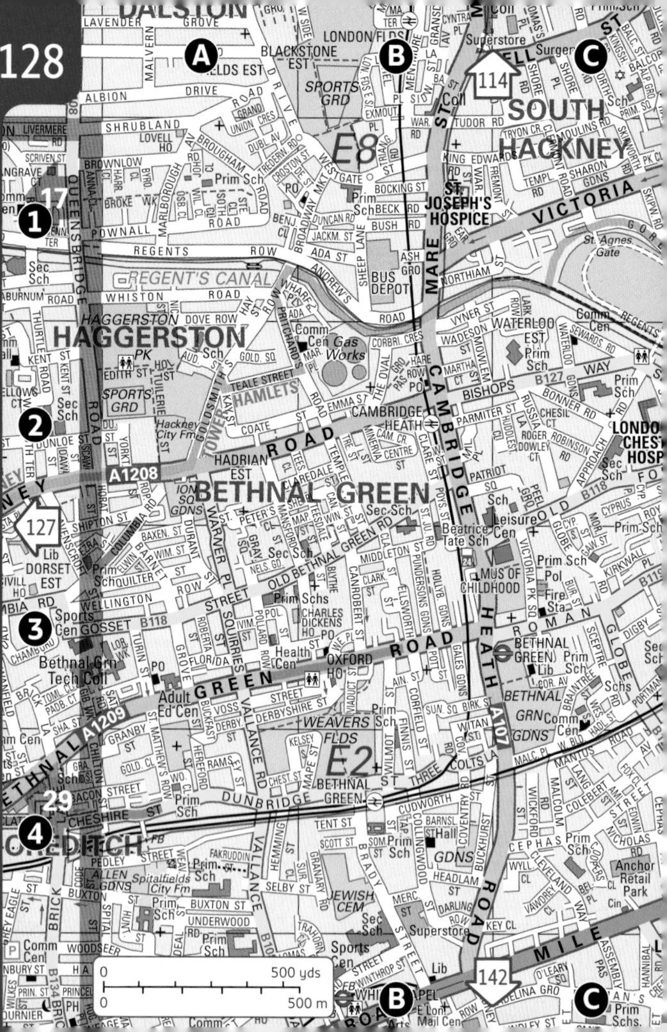
A
B
C
1
2
3
4
17
29
114
127
142
DALSTON
SOUTH HACKNEY
HAGGERSTON
BETHNAL GREEN
E8
E2
LAVENDER GROVE
MALVERN
BLACKSTONE EST
LONDON FLDS
SPORTS GRD
ALBION DRIVE
SHRUBLAND
LIVERMERE RD
LOVELL HO
BROUGHAM
DUBL. AV
WESTGATE ST
BROADWAY MKT
PRIM SCH
BROWNLOW
BROKE WK
MARLBOROUGH
QUEENSBRIDGE ROAD
POWNALL
REGENTS ROW
REGENT'S CANAL
WHISTON ROAD
LABURNUM
DOVE ROW
HAGGERSTON PK
GOLD. SQ
TEALE STREET
KENT ST
THURTLE
SPORTS GRD
Hackney City Fm
GOLDSMITHS ROW
TOWER HAMLETS
COATE ST
HADRIAN EST
A1208
ROAD
CLAREDALE ST
CAMBRIDGE HEATH
MARE ST
CAMBRIDGE HEATH ROAD
VICTORIA PK RD
ST. JOSEPH'S HOSPICE
BOCKING ST
BECK RD
BUSH RD
ASH GRO
BUS DEPOT
NORTHIAM ST
VYNER ST
WATERLOO EST
Gas Works
Comm Cen
THE OVAL
EMMA ST
BISHOPS WAY
B127
BONNER RD
Leisure Cen
Beatrice Tate Sch
OLD FORD ROAD
B118
MUS OF CHILDHOOD
ROMAN ROAD
BETHNAL GREEN Lib
BETHNAL GRN GDNS
A107
LONDON CHEST HOSP
GLOBE ROAD
Prim Sch
Sec Sch
Fire Sta
Pol
TUDOR RD
KING EDWARDS RD
VICTORIA PARK
SHARON GDNS
St. Agnes Gate
Superstore
Surgery
Coll
SHIPTON ST
COLUMBIA RD
DORSET EST
WELLINGTON ROW
OLD BETHNAL GREEN RD
WARNER PL
CANROBERT ST
MIDDLETON ST
CHARLES DICKENS HO
OXFORD HO
Health Cen
GOSSET
Sports Cen
Bethnal Grn Tech Coll
A1209
BETHNAL GREEN ROAD
Adult Ed Cen
DERBYSHIRE ST
WEAVERS FLDS
VALLANCE RD
DUNBRIDGE ST
BETHNAL GREEN
THREE COLTS LA
CHESHIRE ST
SHOREDITCH
CUDWORTH ST
COLLINGWOOD
BUCKHURST
GDNS
HEADLAM ST
CEPHAS ST
Anchor Retail Park
MILE END
BRADY ST
JEWISH CEM
Spitalfields City Fm
ALLEN GDNS
BUXTON ST
PEDLEY ST
BRICK LA
UNDERWOOD RD
Superstore
Sec Sch
Sports Cen
WHITECHAPEL
Lib
Comm Cen
WOODSEER
500 yds
500 m

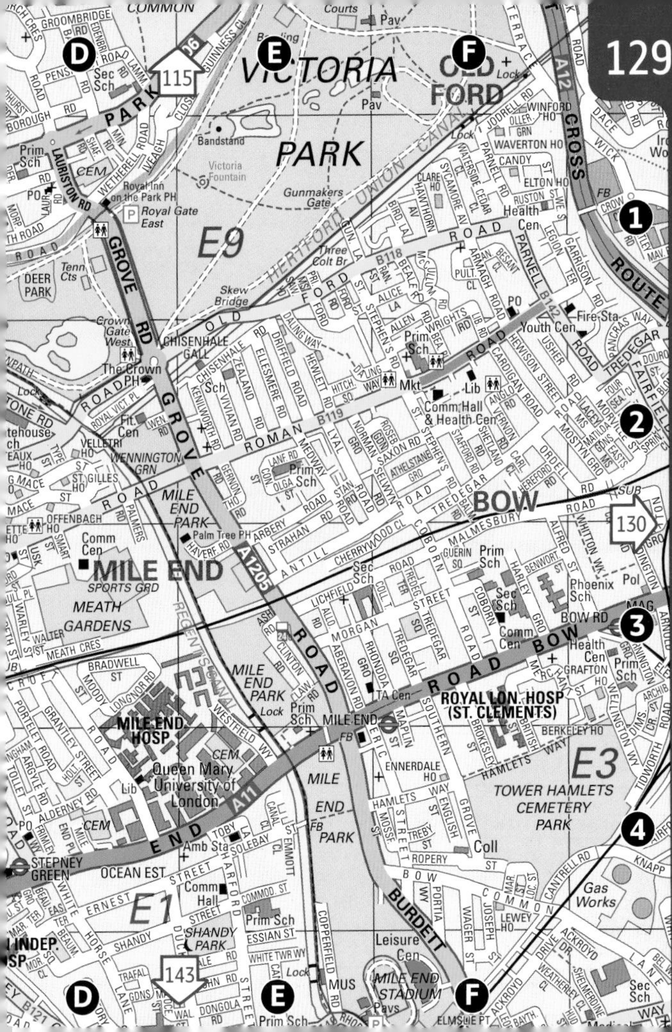
D
E
F
115
VICTORIA
PARK
OLD FORD
Bandstand
Victoria Fountain
Royal Inn on the Park PH
Royal Gate East
Gunmakers Gate
E9
HERTFORD UNION CANAL
Three Colt Br
Skew Bridge
Crown Gate West
The Crown PH
CHISENHALE GALL
GROVE RD
GROVE ROAD
LAURISTON RD
WETHERELL ROAD
OLD FORD ROAD
ROMAN ROAD
TREDEGAR ROAD
PARNELL ROAD
CROSS ROUTE
A12
B118
B119
B142
Health Cen
Fire Sta
Youth Cen
Mkt
Lib
Comm Hall & Health Cen
Prim Sch
BOW
130
MILE END
SPORTS GRD
MEATH GARDENS
MILE END PARK
Palm Tree PH
A1205
REGENT'S CANAL
MILE END HOSP
Queen Mary University of London
A11
MILE END ROAD
BOW ROAD
ROYAL LON. HOSP (ST. CLEMENTS)
TA Cen
E3
TOWER HAMLETS CEMETERY PARK
Gas Works
Coll
STEPNEY GREEN
OCEAN EST
E1
SHANDY PARK
BURDETT ROAD
Leisure Cen
MILE END STADIUM
Pavs
MUS
Amb Sta
Phoenix Sch
143
1
2
3
4

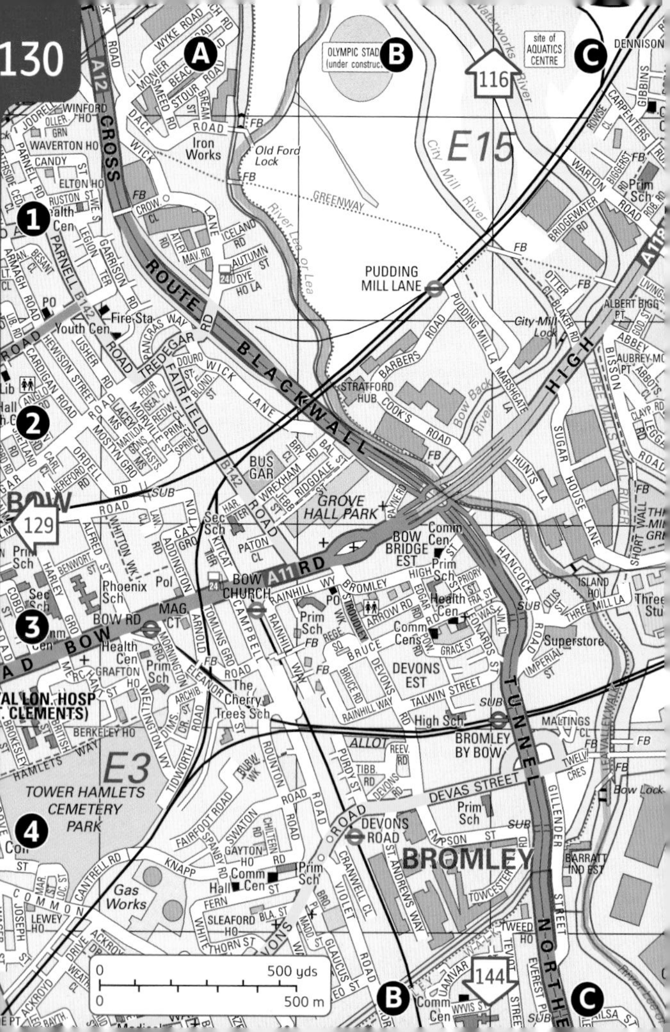
A
B
C
1
2
3
4
OLYMPIC STAD
(under construc
site of
AQUATICS
CENTRE
DENNISON
116
129
144
E15
E3
WYKE ROAD
MONIER
BEACH
SMEED RD
STOUR
BREAM
DACE
ROAD
WICK
Iron
Works
Old Ford
Lock
FB
GREENWAY
City Mill River
River Lee or Lea
Waterworks River
A12
CROSS
ROUTE
BLACKWALL
TUNNEL
NORTHE
WINFORD
HO
JODREL
WAVERTON HO
CANDY ST
ELTON HO
RUSTON ST
Health Cen
PARNELL RD
LEGION
GARRISON
CROW CL
ICELAND RD
ATLEY
MAV. RD
AUTUMN ST
DYE HO LA
PUDDING
MILL LANE
PUDDING MILL LA
MARSHGATE LA
BARBERS
City Mill
Lock
PO
Fire Sta
Youth Cen
ROAD
HEWISON STREET
USHER
CARDIGAN ROAD
PANCRAS WAY
TREDEGAR
DOURO
WICK LANE
FAIRFIELD
Lib
Hall
MORVILLE
MOSTYN GRO
STRATFORD
HUB
COOK'S ROAD
Bow Back River
BOW
ORDELL RD
HEREFORD
CARL
B142
BUS
GAR
WREXHAM
RIDGDALE ST
GROVE
HALL PARK
HIGH
SUGAR HOUSE LANE
HUNTS LA
THREE MILLS WALL RIVER
ROAD
SUB
ALFRED ST
WHITTON WK
ADDINGTON
Sec
Sch
KITCAT TER
PATON CL
A11
RD
BOW
BRIDGE
EST
Comm
Cen
Prim
Sch
HANCOCK
ISLAND HO
THREE MILL LA
Three
Stu
BOW
CHURCH
RAINHILL WY
BROMLEY HIGH ST
PRIORY ST
Health
Cen
Phoenix
Sch
Pol
BOW RD
MAG. CT
ARNOLD
TOMLINS GRO
CAMPBELL
ARROW RD
STROUDLEY WK
BRUCE
Comm
Cens
GRACE ST
Superstore
IMPERIAL ST
Health
Cen
GRAFTON HO
MORNINGTON GRO
ELEANOR
The
Cherry
Trees Sch
DEVONS
EST
TALWIN STREET
RAINHILL WAY
BRUCE RD
High Sch
BROMLEY
BY BOW
MALTINGS CL
LEA VALLEY WALK
AL LON. HOSP
T. CLEMENTS)
BERKELEY HO
WAY
HAMLETS
WELLINGTON WY
TIDWORTH
ROUNTON
ALLOT
REEV. RD
TIBB. RD
PURDY ST
DEVAS STREET
TWELV. CRES
Bow Lock
GILLENDER
TOWER HAMLETS
CEMETERY
PARK
FAIRFOOT ROAD
SWATON
CHILTERN RD
ROAD
DEVONS
ROAD
Prim
Sch
EMPSON ST
BROMLEY
Coll
CANTRELL RD
KNAPP
GAYTON HO
Comm
Cen
Hall
Gas
Works
CRANWELL CL
VIOLET
ST. ANDREWS WAY
TOWCESTER
BARRATT
IND EST
STREET
COMMON
LEWEY HO
FERN
SLEAFORD HO
BLA. ST
THORN ST
WHITE
JOSEPH ST
ACKROYD
DRIVE
GLAUCUS
ROAD
TWEED HO
TEVIOT
EVEREST PL
WYVIS ST
Comm
Cen
0
500 yds
0
500 m

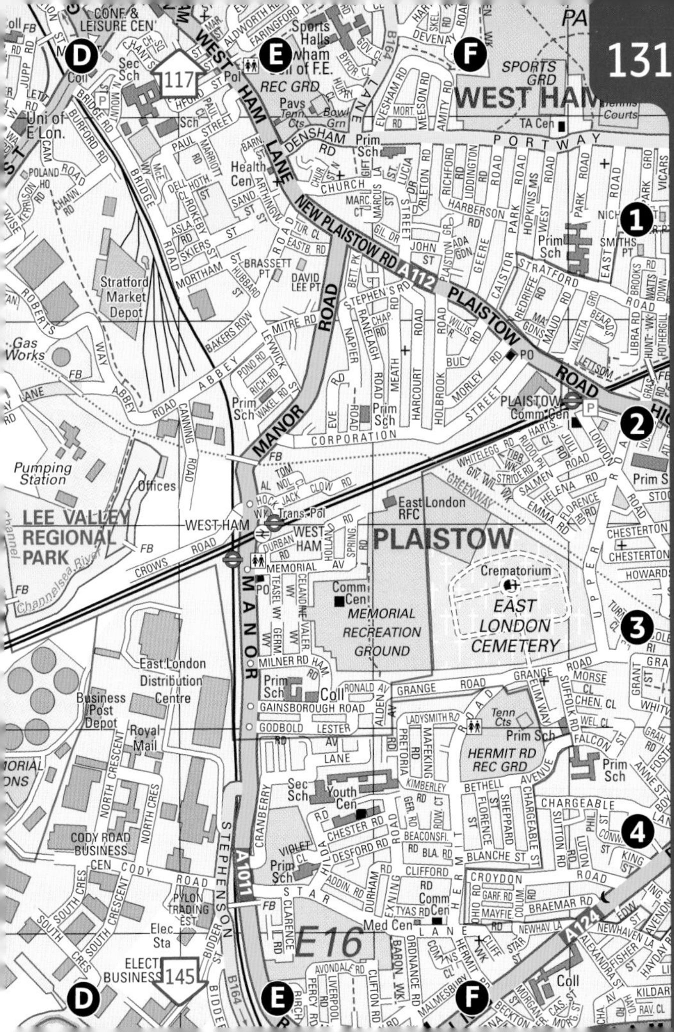
D
E
F
117
145
1
2
3
4
WEST HAM
PLAISTOW
E16
LEE VALLEY REGIONAL PARK
Channelsea River
CONF & LEISURE CEN'
Uni of E Lon.
Sec Sch
Sports Halls
Newham Coll of F.E.
REC GRD
Pavs
Tenn Cts
Bowl Grn
SPORTS GRD
Tennis Courts
TA Cen
Prim Sch
Health Cen
Stratford Market Depot
Gas Works
Pumping Station
Offices
East London RFC
Trans. Pol
MEMORIAL RECREATION GROUND
Comm Cen
Crematorium
EAST LONDON CEMETERY
PLAISTOW
Comm Cen
PO
East London Distribution Centre
Business Post Depot
Royal Mail
Coll
Tenn Cts
HERMIT RD REC GRD
Youth Cen
CODY ROAD BUSINESS CEN
PYLON TRADING EST
Elec Sta
ELECT BUSINESS
Med Cen
WEST HAM LANE
NEW PLAISTOW RD
A112
PLAISTOW ROAD
PORTWAY
MANOR ROAD
A1011
A124
B164
STEPHENSON
ABBEY ROAD
CROWS ROAD
CORPORATION
MEMORIAL AV
GRANGE ROAD
GAINSBOROUGH ROAD
GODBOLD
LESTER AV
STAR LANE
CODY ROAD
CROYDON ROAD
BRAEMAR RD
NEWHAVEN LA
CHARGEABLE
CHURCH
DENSHAM RD
PAUL STREET
BURFORD RD
BRIDGE RD
ROBERTS
POLAND HO
MORTHAM ST
MITRE RD
BAKERS ROW
NAPIER
RANELAGH
MEATH
HARCOURT
HOLBROOK
MORLEY
STRATFORD ROAD
UPPER ROAD
LONDON
HERMIT
GREENWAY
NORTH CRESCENT
SOUTH CRESCENT
CRANBERRY
CLARENCE
BARON WK
ORDNANCE RD
CLIFTON RD
LIVERPOOL RD
MALMESBURY
CLIFFORD
BLANCHE ST
SUTTON RD
LUTON RD
AVENUE

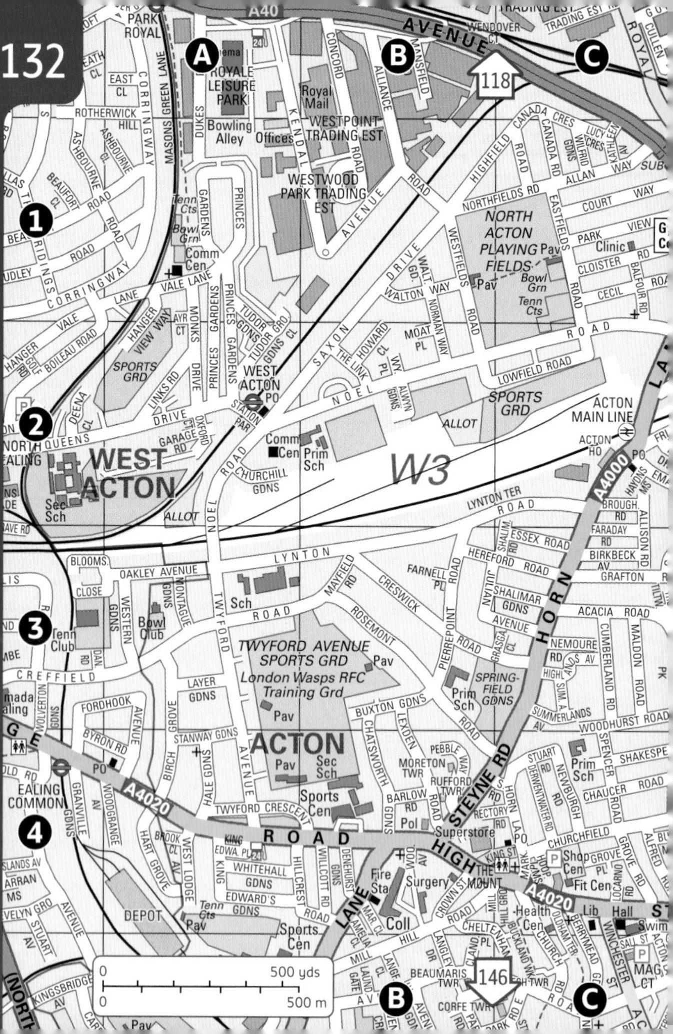
A40
PARK ROYAL
A
B
C
AVENUE
WENDOVER CT
TRADING EST
ROYAL
CULLEN
118
ROYALE LEISURE PARK
Bowling Alley
Offices
Royal Mail
WESTPOINT TRADING EST
WESTWOOD PARK TRADING EST
CONCORD
MANSFIELD
ALLIANCE
KENDAL ROAD
EAST CL
ROTHERWICK HILL
CORRINGWAY
MASONS GREEN LANE
DUKES
ASHBOURNE
BEAUFORT CL
ROAD
RIDINGS
CORRINGWAY
Tenn Cts
Bowl Grn
Comm Cen
GARDENS
PRINCES
1
CANADA CRES
CANADA RD
HIGHFIELD ROAD
LUCY CRES
WILFRID GDNS
KATHLEEN AV
ALLAN WAY
NORTHFIELDS RD
COURT WAY
PARK VIEW
Clinic
CLOISTER RD
CECIL
BALFOUR RD
EASTFIELDS ROAD
NORTH ACTON PLAYING FIELDS
Pav
Bowl Grn
Tenn Cts
WESTFIELDS ROAD
WALTON WAY
NORMAN WAY
MOAT PL
HOWARD
THE LINK
SAXON DRIVE
VALE LANE
HANGER VALE
BOILEAU ROAD
HANGER VIEW WAY
AYR CT
MONKS DRIVE
PRINCES GARDENS
TUDOR GDNS
TUDOR GRO
GDNS CL
SPORTS GRD
LINKS RD
WEST ACTON
PO
NOEL
LOWFIELD ROAD
ROAD
SPORTS GRD
ALLOT
ACTON MAIN LINE
ACTON HO
2
DEENA CL
DRIVE
QUEENS
NORTH EALING
GARAGE RD
OXFORD
STATION PAR
Comm Cen
Prim Sch
CHURCHILL GDNS
WEST ACTON
Sec Sch
ALLOT
W3
LYNTON TER
ROAD
A4000
BROUGH. RD
FARADAY RD
ESSEX ROAD
HEREFORD ROAD
BIRKBECK AV
GRAFTON
ALLISON RD
BLOOMS.
OAKLEY AVENUE
CLOSE
LYNTON
MAYFIELD RD
CRESWICK
FARNELL PL
PIERREPOINT ROAD
JULIAN
SHALIMAR GDNS
AVENUE
ACACIA ROAD
HORN
3
Tenn Club
WESTERN GDNS
MONTAGUE GDNS
Bowl Club
Sch
ROAD
TWYFORD
ROSEMONT
NEMOURE RD
CUMBERLAND RD
MALDON ROAD
CREFFIELD
TWYFORD AVENUE SPORTS GRD
Pav
London Wasps RFC Training Grd
SPRING-FIELD GDNS
Prim Sch
SUMMERLANDS AV
WOODHURST ROAD
SPENCER
LAYER GDNS
FORDHOOK AVENUE
GROVE
Pav
BUXTON GDNS
LEXDEN
WOLVERTON GDNS
BYRON RD
STANWAY GDNS
ACTON
PEBBLE WAY
MORETON TWR
RUFFORD TWR
STEYNE RD
STUART RD
DERWENTWATER RD
NEWBURGH
Prim Sch
SHAKESPE
CHAUCER ROAD
EALING COMMON
PO
A4020
BIRCH
HALE GDNS
Pav
Sec Sch
Sports Cen
CHATSWORTH GDNS
BARLOW RD
ROAD
RECTORY RD
GRANVILLE GDNS
WOODGRANGE AV
TWYFORD CRESCENT
Pol
Superstore
PO
4
BROOK CL
WEST LODGE AV
HART GROVE
KING EDWA. PL
ROAD
HIGH
KING ST
THE MOUNT
CHURCHFIELD
Shop Cen
GROVE PL
Fit Cen
GROVE RD
ALFRED
ARRAN MS
EVELYN GRO
STUART AV
AVENUE
WHITEHALL GDNS
EDWARD'S GDNS
HILLCREST ROAD
WILLCOTT RD
DENEHURST GDNS
Fire Sta
Surgery
CROWN ST
A4020
Health Cen
Lib
Hall
Swim
DEPOT
Tenn Cts
Pav
Sports Cen
LANE
Coll
HILL
ROAD
CHELTENHAM PL
HILL GRO
BUCKLAND WK
OLDHAM TER
CHURCH
BERRYMEAD
WINCHESTER
MAG CT
0
500 yds
500 m
KINGSBRIDGE AV
MILL
LAUND GATE
BEAUMARIS TWR
146
CORFE TWR
B
C
Pav

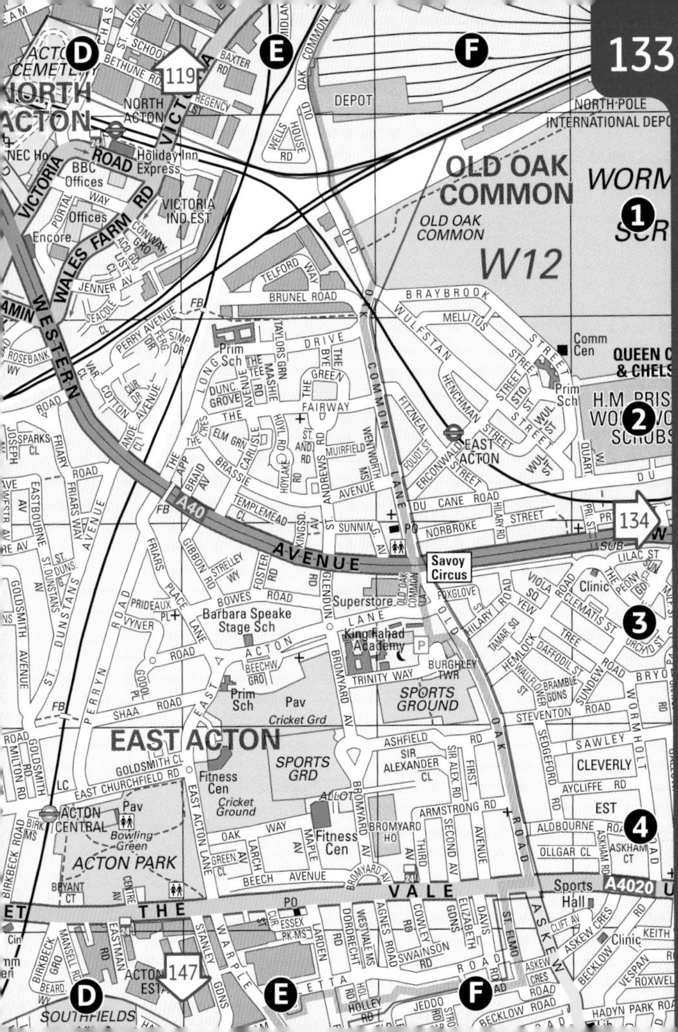

D
E
F
119
ACTON CEMETERY
NORTH ACTON
NORTH ACTON
ST. LEONARDS
SCHOOL
BETHUNE RD
BAXTER RD
REGENCY ST
VICTORIA
MIDLAND
OAK COMMON
DEPOT
NORTH POLE INTERNATIONAL DEPOT
WELLS HOUSE RD
OLD
Holiday Inn Express
NEC Ho
BBC Offices
Offices
Encore
VICTORIA ROAD
PORTAL WAY
WALES FARM RD
VICTORIA IND EST
CONWAY GRO
JENNER AV
SEACOLE CL
OLD OAK COMMON
OLD OAK COMMON
WORM
W12
TELFORD WAY
BRUNEL ROAD
BRAYBROOK
WULFSTAN
MELLITUS
STREET
Comm Cen
QUEEN C & CHELS
Prim Sch
H.M. PRIS WORMWO SCRUBS
HENCHMAN
FITZNEAL
EAST ACTON
ERCONWALD STREET
FOLIOT ST
WESTERN
PERRY AVENUE
ROSEBANK WY
FB
Prim Sch
TAYLORS GRN
LONG DRIVE
THE MASHIE
THE TEE
DUNC. GROVE
THE FAIRWAY
THE GREEN
THE BYE
ELM GRN
CARLISLE
HOYLAKE RD
ST. ANDREWS RD
MUIRFIELD
WENTWORTH MS
BRASSIE
AVENUE
COTTON AVENUE
JOSEPH
SPARKS CL
FRIARY ROAD
EASTBOURNE AV
FRIARS WAY
BRAID AV
THE APP
TEMPLEMEAD CL
A40
AVENUE
SUNNING AV
PO
DU CANE ROAD
NORBROKE STREET
HILARY RD
134
Savoy Circus
GIBBON RD
STRELLEY WY
FOSTER RD
KINGSD. AV
GLENDUN
Superstore
LILAC ST
VIOLA SQ
CLEMATIS ST
Clinic
3
ST. DUNSTANS AVENUE
GOLDSMITH AVENUE
FRIARS PLACE LANE
PRIDEAUX PL
VYNER ROAD
BOWES ROAD
Barbara Speake Stage Sch
ACTON LANE
King Fahad Academy
FOXGLOVE ST
HILARY ROAD
YEW TREE
TAMAR SQ
HEMLOCK
DAFFODIL ST
BRAMBLE GDNS
SUNDEW
WALLFLOWER ST
PERRYN ROAD
ROAD
GODOL PL
BEECHW GRO
Prim Sch
Pav
Cricket Grd
BROMYARD AV
TRINITY WAY
BURGHLEY TWR
SPORTS GROUND
STEVENTON ROAD
WORMHOLT RD
SHAA ROAD
EAST ACTON
SPORTS GRD
ASHFIELD RD
SIR ALEXANDER CL
FIRST
SAWLEY
CLEVERLY EST
SEDGEFORD RD
AYCLIFFE RD
ALDBOURNE ROAD
ASKHAM CT
4
OLLGAR CL
GOLDSMITH CL
EAST CHURCHFIELD RD
Fitness Cen
Cricket Ground
ALLOT
ARMSTRONG RD
ACTON CENTRAL
Pav
Bowling Green
ACTON PARK
OAK WAY
MAPLE AV
Fitness Cen
BROMYARD HO
SECOND AV
THIRD AV
AVENUE
OAK ROAD
LARCH AV
GREEN CL
BEECH AVENUE
EAST ACTON LANE
BIRKBECK ROAD
BRYANT CT
CENTRE AV
THE VALE
Sports Hall
A4020
PO
ESSEX PK MS
LARDEN RD
DORDRECHT RD
WESTVALE MS
AGNES ROAD
COWLEY RD
GDNS
ELIZABETH
DAVIS
ST. ELMO RD
ASKEW ROAD
CLIFT AV
ASKEW CRES
Clinic
KEITH
BECKLOW
VESPAN
ROXWELL
Cin
BIRKBECK GRO
MANSELL RD
EASTMAN RD
ACTON EST
147
STANLEY GDNS
WARPLE
BEARD. WY
SOUTHFIELDS
SWAINSON RD
ASKEW CRES
HOLLEY RD
JEDDO RD
BECKLOW ROAD
HADYN PARK ROAD

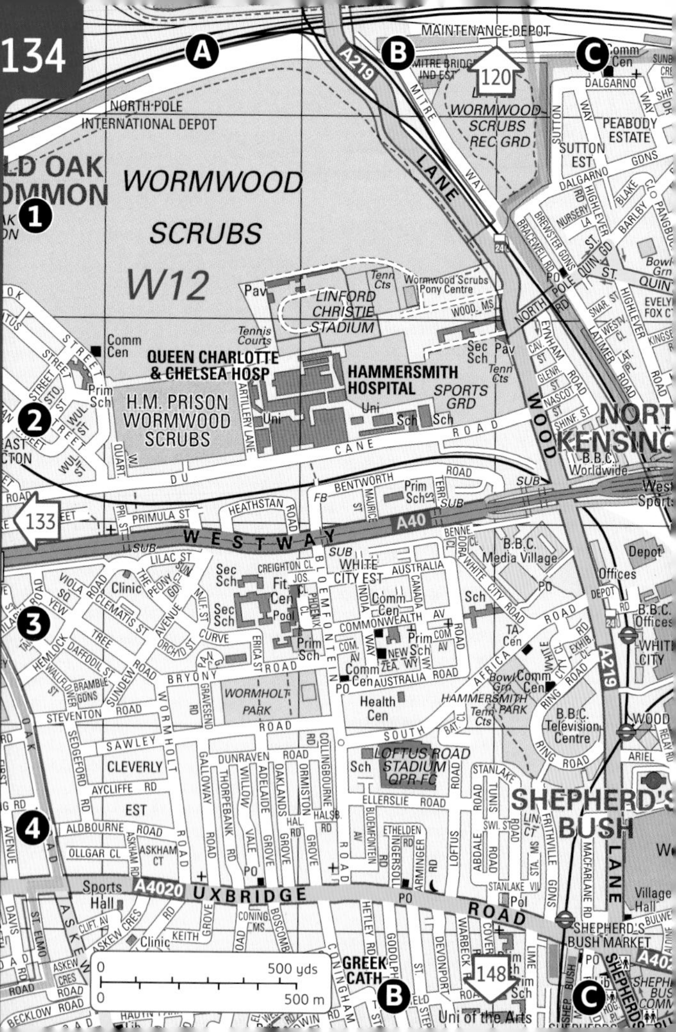
A
B
C
1
2
3
4
MAINTENANCE DEPOT
A219
MITRE BRIDGE IND EST
120
WORMWOOD SCRUBS REC GRD
MITRE WAY
DALGARNO WAY
PEABODY ESTATE
SUTTON EST
SUTTON WAY
DALGARNO GDNS
NORTH POLE INTERNATIONAL DEPOT
WORMWOOD SCRUBS
W12
LANE
LINFORD CHRISTIE STADIUM
Wormwood Scrubs Pony Centre
Tennis Courts
Pav
Tenn Cts
WOOD MS
NORTH POLE RD
Comm Cen
QUEEN CHARLOTTE & CHELSEA HOSP
HAMMERSMITH HOSPITAL
H.M. PRISON WORMWOOD SCRUBS
SPORTS GRD
Sec Sch
Prim Sch
Uni
ARTILLERY LANE
DU CANE ROAD
WOOD LANE
NORTH KENSING
B.B.C. Worldwide
BENTWORTH ROAD
HEATHSTAN ROAD
PRIMULA ST
MAURICE ST
TERR. ST
FB
SUB
133
A40
WESTWAY
WEST SPORTS
B.B.C. Media Village
Depot
Offices
B.B.C. Offices
WHITE CITY
WHITE CITY EST
AUSTRALIA ROAD
COMMONWEALTH AV
INDIA WAY
CANADA WAY
BLOEMFONTEIN ROAD
WHITE CITY ROAD
SOUTH AFRICA ROAD
Fit. Cen
Pool
Clinic
VIOLA SQ
YEW TREE ROAD
CLEMATIS ST
PEONY GDNS
LILAC ST
CREIGHTON CL
HEMLOCK ROAD
DAFFODIL ST
BRAMBLE GDNS
WALLFLOWER ST
SUNDEW ROAD
ORCHID ST
BRYONY ROAD
ERICA ST
WORMHOLT PARK
WORMHOLT ROAD
GRAVESEND RD
Health Cen
HAMMERSMITH PARK
B.B.C. Television Centre
RING ROAD
WOOD LANE
ARIEL WAY
STEVENTON ROAD
SAWLEY ROAD
CLEVERLY EST
AYCLIFFE RD
SEDGEFORD RD
ALDBOURNE ROAD
OLLGAR CL
ASKHAM CT
ASKHAM RD
GALLOWAY ROAD
DUNRAVEN ROAD
THORPEBANK RD
WILLOW VALE
ADELAIDE GROVE
OAKLANDS GROVE
ORMISTON GROVE
COLLINGBOURNE RD
LOFTUS ROAD STADIUM QPR-FC
ELLERSLIE ROAD
ETHELDEN RD
INGERSOLL RD
ARMINGER RD
LOFTUS ROAD
ABDALE ROAD
TUNIS ROAD
STANLAKE ROAD
FRITHVILLE GDNS
SHEPHERD'S BUSH
MACFARLANE RD
Village Hall
Sports Hall
A4020 UXBRIDGE ROAD
CONINGHAM MS
BOSCOMBE RD
CONINGHAM RD
HETLEY RD
GODOLPHIN RD
DEVONPORT RD
WARBECK RD
Pol
PO
SHEPHERD'S BUSH MARKET
SHEPHERD'S BUSH GREEN
A402
ASKEW ROAD
ASKEW CRES
CLIFT. AV
KEITH GROVE
Clinic
DAVIS RD
ST. ELMO RD
BECKLOW ROAD
GREEK CATH
148
Uni of the Arts
0 500 yds
0 500 m

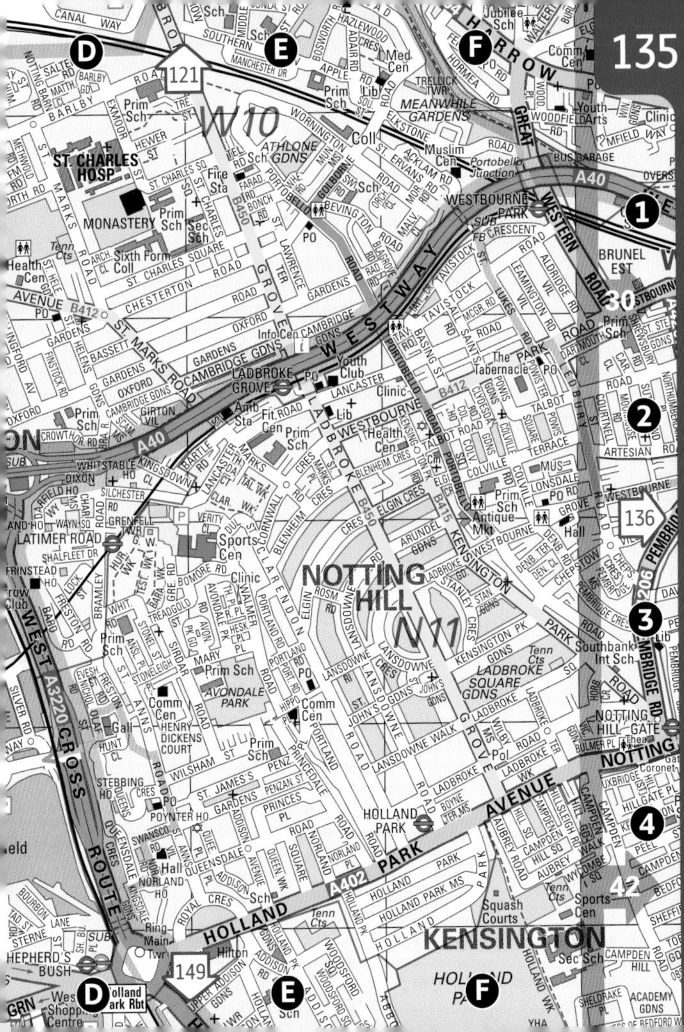
121
136
149
30
42
W10
W11
NOTTING HILL
KENSINGTON
HOLLAND PARK
ST. CHARLES HOSP
MONASTERY
WESTWAY
A40
A402
A3220
B450
B412
B415
WESTBOURNE PARK
LADBROKE GROVE
LATIMER ROAD
NOTTING HILL GATE
HOLLAND PARK
SHEPHERD'S BUSH
Holland Park Rbt
CANAL WAY
SOUTHERN ROW
MANCHESTER DR
GREAT WESTERN ROAD
HARROW ROAD
MEANWHILE GARDENS
Portobello Junction
ATHLONE GDNS
BRUNEL EST
ST. CHARLES SQUARE
CHESTERTON ROAD
OXFORD GARDENS
CAMBRIDGE GDNS
ST. MARKS ROAD
BASSETT ROAD
LADBROKE GROVE
PORTOBELLO ROAD
WESTBOURNE PARK ROAD
TALBOT ROAD
COLVILLE TERRACE
ELGIN CRES
LANSDOWNE CRES
LADBROKE SQUARE GDNS
KENSINGTON PARK GDNS
PEMBRIDGE RD
CLARENDON ROAD
PORTLAND RD
AVONDALE PARK
WEST CROSS ROUTE
HOLLAND PARK AVENUE
HOLLAND PARK MS
QUEENSDALE CRES
ROYAL CRES
CAMPDEN HILL
Squash Courts
Sports Cen
Antique Mkt
The Tabernacle
Southbank Int Sch
Westfield Shopping Centre

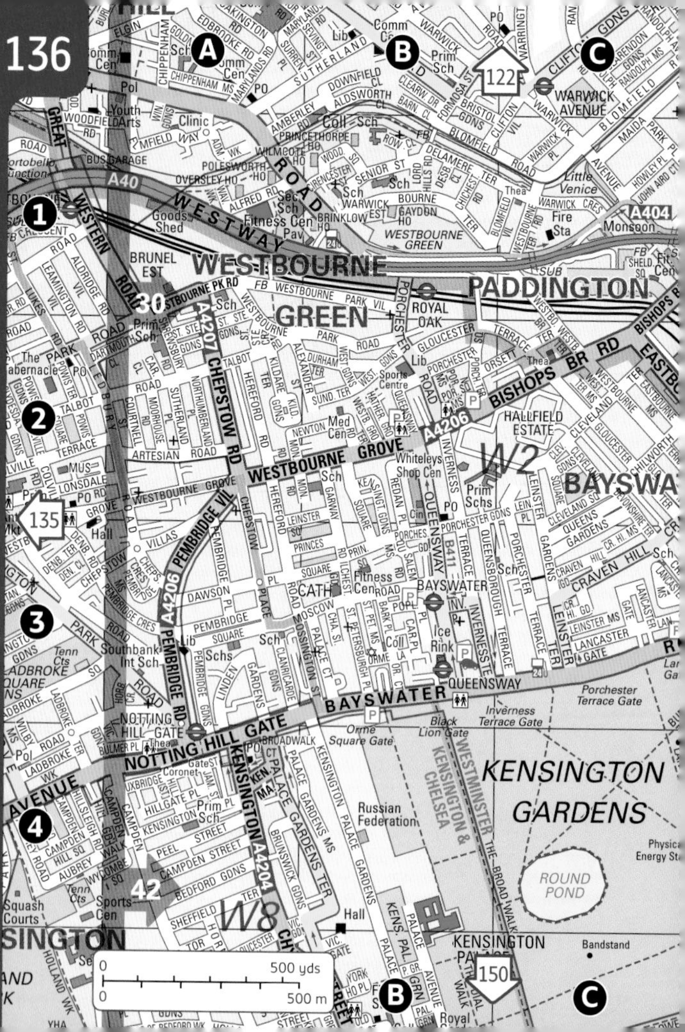
A
B
C
1
2
3
4
122
135
150
30
42
WESTBOURNE
GREEN
PADDINGTON
BAYSWA
W2
W8
KENSINGTON
GARDENS
ROUND
POND
WESTWAY
A40
A404
A4206
A4207
A4204
B411
WESTBOURNE GROVE
CHEPSTOW RD
BISHOPS BR RD
BAYSWATER
NOTTING HILL GATE
QUEENSWAY
PEMBRIDGE RD
PEMBRIDGE VIL
KENSINGTON
HARROW ROAD
GREAT WESTERN ROAD
LEDBURY ROAD
WESTBOURNE PARK VIL
WESTBOURNE PK RD
PORCHESTER
ROYAL OAK
GLOUCESTER TERRACE
WARWICK AVENUE
BLOMFIELD ROAD
Little Venice
DELAMERE TER
WESTBOURNE TER
CLIFTON GDNS
SUTHERLAND AVENUE
ELGIN
CHIPPENHAM
EDBROOKE RD
FORMOSA ST
WARWICK CRES
Monsoon
Fire Sta
Goods Shed
BRUNEL EST
HALLFIELD ESTATE
Whiteleys Shop Cen
ARTESIAN ROAD
TALBOT RD
LONSDALE RD
HEREFORD RD
LEINSTER SQ
PRINCES SQUARE
MOSCOW ROAD
PORCHESTER TERRACE
INVERNESS TERRACE
QUEENSBOROUGH TERRACE
LEINSTER TER
CRAVEN HILL
LANCASTER GATE
CLEVELAND SQ
QUEENS GARDENS
Ice Rink
Porchester Terrace Gate
Inverness Terrace Gate
Black Lion Gate
Orme Square Gate
KENSINGTON & CHELSEA
WESTMINSTER
THE BROAD WALK
Russian Federation
KENSINGTON PALACE GARDENS
KENSINGTON PALACE
Bandstand
Physical Energy St
PALACE GARDENS TER
BRUNSWICK GDNS
CAMPDEN HILL
CAMPDEN STREET
PEEL STREET
BEDFORD GDNS
SHEFFIELD TER
HILLGATE PL
Coronet
LADBROKE SQUARE
LADBROKE ROAD
HOLLAND PARK AVENUE
Southbank Int Sch
Squash Courts
Sports Cen
Tenn Cts
Portobello Junction
BUS GARAGE
Youth Arts
Clinic
Coll Sch
Fitness Cen
Med Cen
Prim Schs
Hall
Lib
0 500 yds
0 500 m

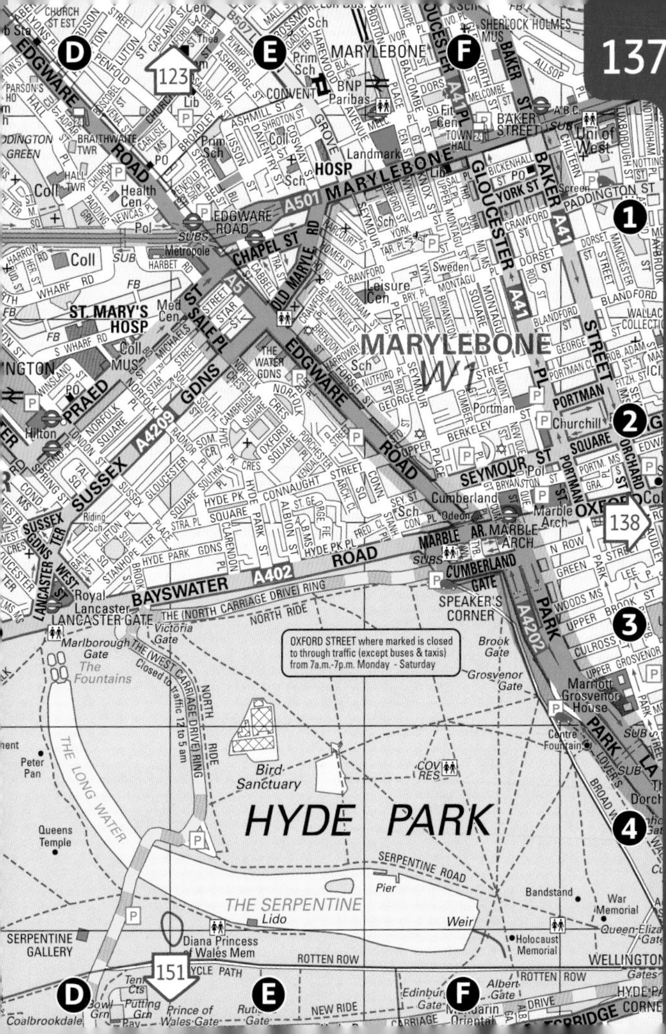
D
E
F
123
138
151
1
2
3
4
EDGWARE ROAD
MARYLEBONE
SHERLOCK HOLMES MUS
BAKER ST
BAKER STREET
Uni of West.
A.B.C.
BNP Paribas
CONVENT
Prim Sch
Landmark
HOSP
MARYLEBONE
A501
GLOUCESTER PL
A41
YORK ST
PADDINGTON ST
CRAWFORD ST
DORSET ST
BLANDFORD ST
GEORGE ST
MARYLEBONE W1
Sweden
Leisure Cen
OLD MARYLEBONE RD
CHAPEL ST
EDGWARE ROAD
Metropole
ST. MARY'S HOSP
PRAED ST
SUSSEX GDNS
A4209
Hilton
Coll
PORTMAN SQUARE
Churchill
SEYMOUR ST
Cumberland
Odeon
MARBLE ARCH
OXFORD
NORFOLK CRES
CONNAUGHT SQ
HYDE PK SQUARE
HYDE PARK GDNS
BAYSWATER ROAD
A402
CUMBERLAND GATE
SPEAKER'S CORNER
PARK LANE
A4202
Marriott Grosvenor House
UPPER BROOK ST
UPPER GROSVENOR
Royal Lancaster
LANCASTER GATE
Victoria Gate
Marlborough Gate
The Fountains
THE (NORTH CARRIAGE DRIVE) RING
NORTH RIDE
OXFORD STREET where marked is closed to through traffic (except buses & taxis) from 7a.m.-7p.m. Monday - Saturday
Brook Gate
Grosvenor Gate
THE (WEST CARRIAGE DRIVE) RING
Closed to traffic 12 to 5 am
Bird Sanctuary
HYDE PARK
THE LONG WATER
Peter Pan
Queens Temple
COV RES
Centre Fountain
SERPENTINE ROAD
Pier
THE SERPENTINE
Lido
Weir
Bandstand
War Memorial
Holocaust Memorial
SERPENTINE GALLERY
Diana Princess of Wales Mem
ROTTEN ROW
WELLINGTON
CYCLE PATH
NEW RIDE
Prince of Wales Gate
Rutland Gate
Edinburgh Gate
Albert Gate
Mandarin Oriental
Coalbrookdale
Queen Elizabeth Gate

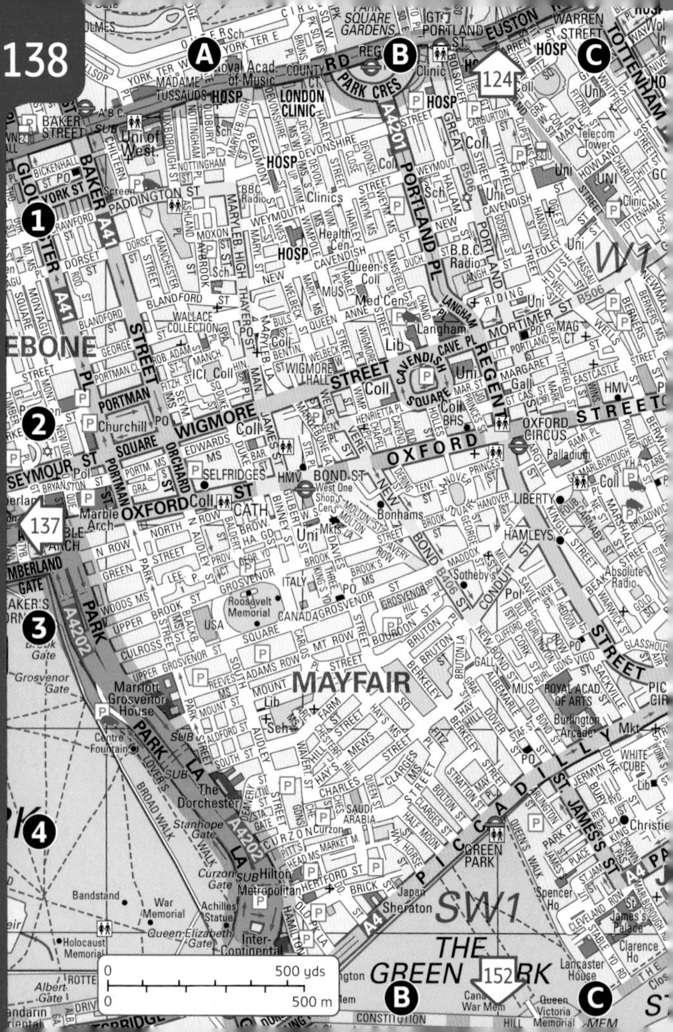
A
B
C
1
2
3
4
124
137
152
MAYFAIR
W1
SW1
EBONE
THE GREEN PARK
BAKER STREET
YORK TER E
Royal Acad. of Music
MADAME TUSSAUDS
HOSP
LONDON CLINIC
PARK CRES
PORTLAND PL
EUSTON RD
WARREN STREET
TOTTENHAM
Telecom Tower
Uni of West.
PADDINGTON ST
BBC Radio
Clinics
Health Cen
WEYMOUTH
Queen's Coll
Med Cen
Langham
CAVENDISH SQUARE
RIDING HOUSE ST
MORTIMER ST
MARGARET
WALLACE COLLECTION
BLANDFORD
MANCHESTER SQ
WIGMORE HALL
WIGMORE STREET
PORTMAN SQUARE
Churchill
SEYMOUR ST
SELFRIDGES
OXFORD STREET
BOND ST
West One Shop Cen
OXFORD CIRCUS
Palladium
LIBERTY
HAMLEYS
Absolute Radio
Marble Arch
CUMBERLAND GATE
PARK LANE
A4202
A41
A4201
A4
Roosevelt Memorial
USA
GROSVENOR SQUARE
Bonhams
Sotheby's
CONDUIT ST
NEW BOND ST
OLD BOND ST
ROYAL ACAD. OF ARTS
Burlington Arcade
PICCADILLY
Marriott Grosvenor House
Centre Fountain
The Dorchester
Stanhope Gate
Grosvenor Gate
Brook Gate
Curzon Gate
Hilton Metropolitan
Achilles Statue
Inter-Continental
War Memorial
Queen Elizabeth Gate
Holocaust Memorial
Bandstand
Albert Gate
CURZON ST
SAUDI ARABIA
GREEN PARK
Japan
Sheraton
ST JAMES'S ST
Spencer Ho
St James's Palace
Clarence Ho
Lancaster House
WHITE CUBE
Christie's
Canada War Mem
Queen Victoria Memorial
CONSTITUTION HILL
0 500 yds
0 500 m

BLOOMSBURY
BRITISH MUSEUM
HOLBORN
WC2
STRAND
SE1
University of London
RUSSELL SQUARE GDNS
RUSSELL SQ
SOUTHAMPTON ROW
KINGSWAY
HIGH HOLBORN
NEW OXFORD ST
ST GILES HIGH ST
CHARING CROSS RD
SHAFTESBURY AV
TOTTENHAM COURT RD
THEOBALD'S ROAD
GRAY'S INN GDNS
CHANCERY LANE
LINCOLN'S INN FIELDS
ROYAL COURTS OF JUSTICE
Lon. Sch. of Econ.
ALDWYCH
COVENT GARDEN
ROYAL OPERA HO
LEICESTER SQ
TRAFALGAR
Nelson's Column
PALL MALL
THE MALL
HAYMARKET
NAT. PORT. GALL
NAT. GALL
CHARING CROSS
EMBANKMENT
VICTORIA EMBANKMENT
SOMERSET HOUSE
TEMPLE
WATERLOO BR
WHITEHALL
SCOTLAND OFFICE
CABINET OFFICE
Horse Guards Parade
DUCK ISLAND
London Eye
JUBILEE GARDENS
ROYAL FESTIVAL HALL
QUEEN ELIZABETH HALL
HAYWARD GALLERY
National Theatre
London Television Centre
WATERLOO
County Hall
TATTERSHALL CASTLE
Cleopatra's Needle
SAVOY PIER
EMBANKMENT PIER
WATERLOO MILLENNIUM PIER
WESTMINSTER MILLENNIUM
HUNGERFORD BR
GOLDEN JUBILEE BRI
125
140
153
D
E
F
1
2
3
4

A
B
C
1
2
3
4
CLERKENWELL
CLERKENWELL ROAD
ROSEBERY AV
GRAY'S INN GDNS
Gray's Inn
Law Sch
CHANCERY LANE
HOLBORN
HOLBORN VIADUCT
FARRINGDON
FARRINGDON ROAD
A201
CHARTERHOUSE ST
Charterhouse
BARBICAN
ALDERSGATE ST
EC1
Cen Mkts (Smithfield)
ST BART'S HOSP
Merrill Lynch
Mus of Lon
LONDON WALL
NEWGATE ST
ST. PAUL'S
ST. PAUL'S CATH
CHEAPSIDE
Stock Exchange
CENT. CRIM CT (Old Bailey)
CITY THAMESLINK
FLEET ST
FLEET STREET
NEW FETTER LA
FETTER LA
DR JOHNSON'S HO
ROYAL COURTS OF JUSTICE
LINCOLN'S INN FIELDS
Lincoln's Inn
STRAND
Prince Henry's Room
The Temple
TEMPLE
VICTORIA EMBANKMENT
H.Q.S. WELLINGTON
H.M.S. PRESIDENT
BLACKFRIARS MILLENNIUM PIER
BLACKFRIARS
NEW BR ST
BLACKFRIARS BR
RIVER
EC4
QUEEN VICTORIA ST
UPPER THAMES ST
Southwark Bridge Steps
MILLENNIUM BRIDGE
SHAKESPEARE GLOBE THEATRE
BANKSIDE PIER
BANKSIDE GALL
TATE MODERN
SOUTHWARK BR
SOUTHWARK ROAD
Oxo Tower Wharf
THAMES PATH
THE QUEEN'S WALK
London Television Centre
IBM
BFI Southbank
National Theatre
QUEEN ELIZABETH HALL
HAYWARD GALLERY
WATERLOO BR
STAMFORD ST
UPPER GROUND
London Nautical Sch
Colombo Cen
BFI IMAX
WATERLOO EAST
BLACKFRIARS RD
SOUTHWARK ST
A3200
SE1
SOUTHWARK
Blue Fin Building
PEABODY TRUST
SUMNER STREET
Shell Cen
YORK RD
126
139
154
0 500 yds
0 500 m

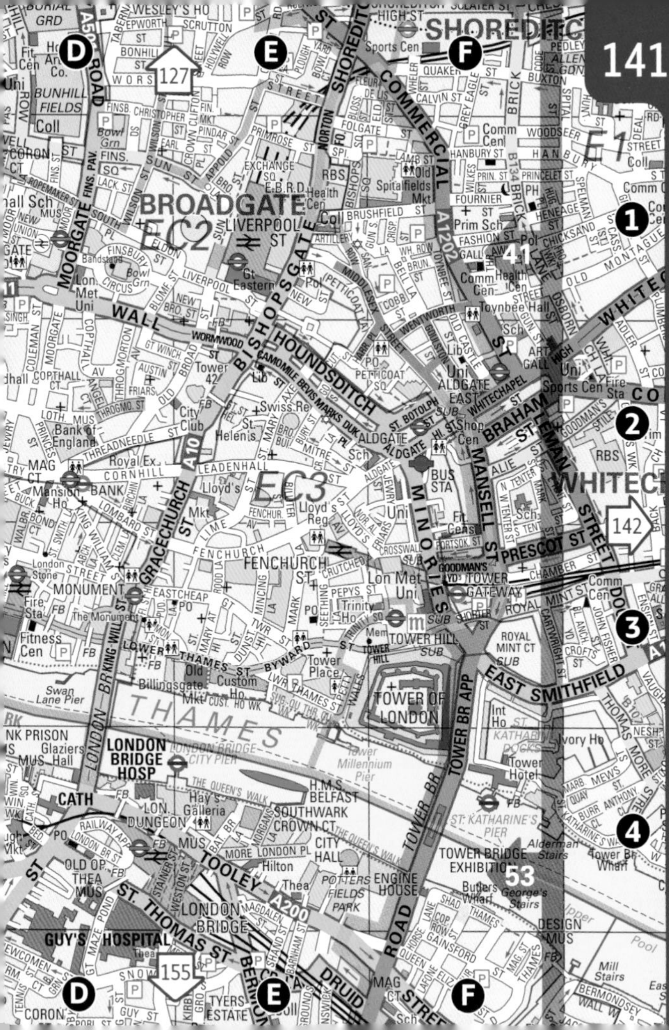
D
E
F
127
SHOREDITCH
HIGH ST
Sports Cen
BUNHILL FIELDS
Coll
EPWORTH
SCRUTTON
BONHILL
WORSHIP
COMMERCIAL
QUAKER
CALVIN ST
FOLGATE
BRICK
BUXTON
PEDLEY
WOODSEER
HANBURY ST
E1
Coll
FINSB. CHRISTOPHER
PRIMROSE ST
NORTON FOLGATE
EXCHANGE SQ
E.B.R.D.
Health Cen
RBS
BISHOPS SQ
Spitalfields Mkt
FOURNIER
PRINCELET ST
Comm Cen
MOORGATE
FINS. PAV.
ROPEMAKER ST
BROADGATE
EC2
LIVERPOOL ST
BRUSHFIELD ST
A1202
Prim Sch
FASHION ST
41
HENEAGE
CHICKSAND ST
MONTAGUE
1
Bandstand
FINSBURY CIRCUS
Lon. Met Uni
LIVERPOOL ST
Gt Eastern
BISHOPSGATE
ARTILLERY
MIDDLESEX
PETTICOAT LA
NEW ST
Comm Cen
Health Cen
Toynbee Hall
OLD
WHITECHAPEL
WALL
WORMWOOD ST
HOUNDSDITCH
CAMOMILE ST
WENTWORTH
OLD CASTLE ST
Lib
Sch
ART GALL
HIGH
Uni
Sports Cen
Fire Sta
COPTHALL AV
COLEMAN ST
Tower 42
AUSTIN FRIARS
Swiss Re
BEVIS MARKS
DUKE'S PL
PO
PETTICOAT SQ
ALDGATE EAST
ST. BOTOLPH ST
BRAHAM ST
LEMAN
2
Bank of England
THREADNEEDLE ST
LOTH.
City Club
St. Helen's
ST. MARY AXE
BURY ST
MITRE ST
ALDGATE
Sch
Shop Cen
MANSELL ST
GOODMAN'S STILE
RBS
Royal Ex.
CORNHILL
LEADENHALL
EC3
BUS STA
MINORIES
ALIE ST
WHITECHAPEL
142
Mansion Ho
BANK
LOMBARD ST
GRACECHURCH ST
A10
Lloyd's
Mkt
LIME ST
FENCHURCH AV
Lloyd's Reg.
Uni
Fit. Cens
PORTSOKEN ST
PRESCOT ST
STREET
KING WILLIAM ST
London Stone
FENCHURCH ST
CRUTCHED FRIARS
CROSSWALL
GOODMAN'S YD
CHAMBER ST
MONUMENT
The Monument
EASTCHEAP
MINCING LA
MARK LA
PEPYS ST
Lon Met Uni
TOWER GATEWAY
ROYAL MINT ST
Comm Cen
Fire Sta
PO
SEETHING LA
Trinity Sq
Trinity Ho
Mem
TOWER HILL
SHORTER ST
3
Fitness Cen
LOWER THAMES ST
BYWARD ST
Tower Place
SUB
ROYAL MINT CT
CROFTS ST
EAST SMITHFIELD
Swan Lane Pier
Old Custom Ho
Billingsgate Mkt
LONDON BR
THAMES
TOWER OF LONDON
TOWER BR APP
Int Ho
ST. KATHARINE DOCKS
Ivory Ho
NK PRISON MUS
Glaziers Hall
LONDON BRIDGE HOSP
LONDON BRIDGE CITY PIER
Tower Millennium Pier
Tower Hotel
THOMAS MORE ST
CATH
THE QUEEN'S WALK
Hay's Galleria
H.M.S. BELFAST
TOWER BR
ST. KATHARINE'S PIER
LON. DUNGEON
SOUTHWARK CROWN CT
CITY HALL
MORE LONDON PL
4
PO
MUS
TOOLEY ST
Hilton
TOWER BRIDGE EXHIBITION
53
Alderman Stairs
Tower Br Wharf
OLD OP. THEA MUS
ST. THOMAS ST
A200
Thea
POTTERS FIELDS PARK
ENGINE HOUSE
Butlers Wharf
George's Stairs
LONDON BRIDGE
ROAD
DESIGN MUS
Pool
GUY'S HOSPITAL
GAINSFORD
SHAD THAMES
155
DRUID
MAG CT
Mill Stairs
TYERS ESTATE
BERMONDSEY WALL W
CORON

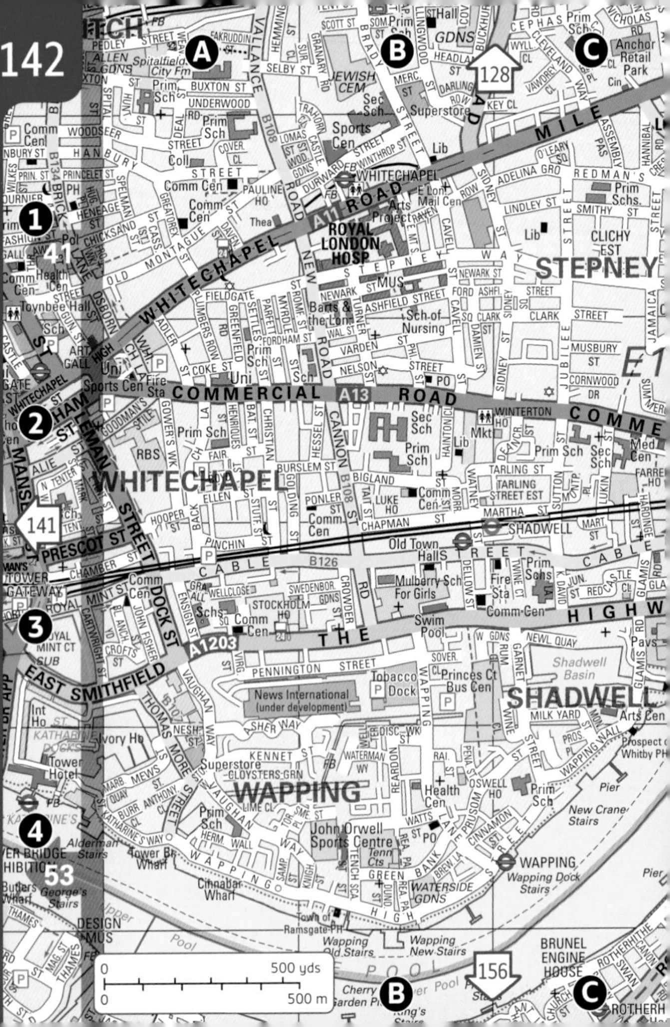
A
B
C
1
2
3
4
128
141
156
41
53
WHITECHAPEL
STEPNEY
SHADWELL
WAPPING
E1
WHITECHAPEL ROAD
A11
MILE
COMMERCIAL ROAD
A13
THE HIGHWAY
A1203
CABLE STREET
B126
EAST SMITHFIELD
PRESCOT ST
LEMAN STREET
MANSELL
ROYAL MINT ST
DOCK ST
THOMAS MORE STREET
VAUGHAN WAY
WAPPING LANE
WAPPING HIGH
WAPPING WALL
PENNINGTON STREET
NEW ROAD
CANNON ST RD
B108
HANBURY STREET
OLD MONTAGUE STREET
FASHION ST
BRICK LANE
B134
COMMERCIAL STREET
VALLANCE ROAD
SIDNEY STREET
JUBILEE STREET
STEPNEY WAY
ASHFIELD STREET
NEWARK ST
VARDEN ST
NELSON STREET
FIELDGATE
TURNER ST
BURSLEM ST
BIGLAND
CHAPMAN ST
PINCHIN ST
HOOPER ST
ELLEN ST
CHRISTIAN ST
HESSEL ST
FORDHAM ST
COKE ST
MARTHA ST
TARLING ST
WATNEY
SUTTON
GARNET
GLAMIS RD
NEWL QUAY
MILK YARD
KENNET ST
ASHER WAY
GREEN BANK
CINNAMON STREET
ROYAL LONDON HOSP
Barts & the Lon.
Sch of Nursing
Whitechapel
Shadwell
Wapping
Tower Gateway
Royal Mint Ct
St Katharine Docks
Ivory Ho
Tower Hotel
Int Ho
Tower Br Wharf
Cinnabar Wharf
Design Mus
Butlers Wharf
Toynbee Hall
Spitalfields City Fm
Jewish Cem
Sports Cen
Superstore
Anchor Retail Park
Clichy Est
Tarling Street Est
Mulberry Sch For Girls
Swim Pool
News International (under development)
Tobacco Dock
Princes Ct Bus Cen
Shadwell Basin
John Orwell Sports Centre
Waterside Gdns
Town of Ramsgate PH
Prospect of Whitby PH
Brunel Engine House
New Crane Stairs
Wapping Dock Stairs
Wapping Old Stairs
Wapping New Stairs
Cherry Garden Pier
King's Stairs
Aldermans Stairs
George's Stairs
Upper Pool
Pool
Old Town Halls
Lib
Mkt
Arts Project
E Lon Mail Cen
0 500 yds
0 500 m

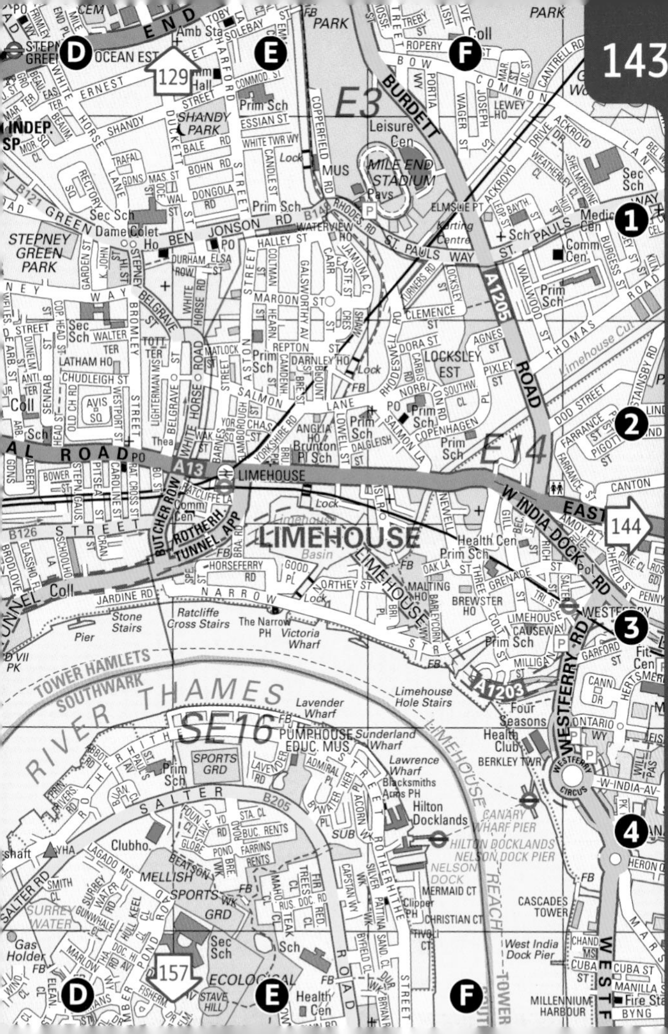
D
E
F
129
144
157
1
2
3
4
E3
E14
SE16
LIMEHOUSE
Limehouse Basin
RIVER THAMES
TOWER HAMLETS
SOUTHWARK
LIMEHOUSE REACH
MILE END STADIUM
Leisure Cen
Pavs
Karting Centre
STEPNEY GREEN PARK
SHANDY PARK
LOCKSLEY EST
Limehouse Cut
BURDETT ROAD
A1205
A13
A1203
B126
B121
B148
B205
COMMERCIAL ROAD
EAST INDIA DOCK RD
W INDIA DOCK RD
BEN JONSON RD
ST PAULS WAY
BOW COMMON LA
SALMON LANE
NARROW STREET
LIMEHOUSE CAUSEWAY
WESTFERRY RD
WESTFERRY CIRCUS
ROTHERHITHE STREET
SALTER RD
ROTHERHITHE TUNNEL APP
BUTCHER ROW
WHITE HORSE ROAD
THOMAS ROAD
DOD STREET
CANTON ST
Stone Stairs
Ratcliffe Cross Stairs
The Narrow PH
Victoria Wharf
Lavender Wharf
Sunderland Wharf
Lawrence Wharf
Blacksmiths Arms PH
Hilton Docklands
Limehouse Hole Stairs
CANARY WHARF PIER
HILTON DOCKLANDS NELSON DOCK PIER
NELSON DOCK
MERMAID CT
CASCADES TOWER
West India Dock Pier
MILLENNIUM HARBOUR
Four Seasons Health Club
BERKLEY TWR
PUMPHOUSE EDUC. MUS
SPORTS GRD
ECOLOGICAL
STAVE HILL
SURREY WATER
Gas Holder
Clubho.
MELLISH
Health Cen
Prim Sch
Sec Sch
LIMEHOUSE

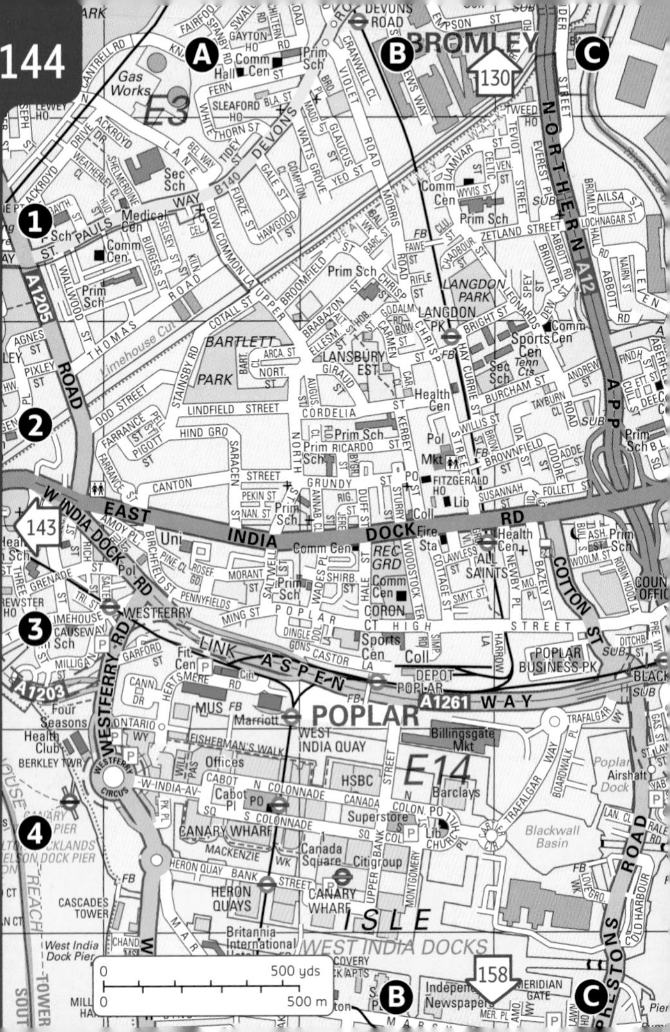
A
B
C
1
2
3
4
BROMLEY
130
143
158
E3
E14
POPLAR
Gas Works
DEVONS ROAD
EMPSON ST
FAIRFOOT
GAYTON HO
Comm Hall
Comm Cen
Prim Sch
CRANWELL CL
VIOLET
FERN
SLEAFORD HO
WHITETHORN ST
DEVONS
WATTS GROVE
GLAUCUS ST
ROAD
LEWEY HO
ACKROYD DR
DRIVE
LANE
Sec Sch
BEL WAY
TIDEY ST
B140
FURZE ST
GALE ST
COMPTON CL
YEO ST
WEATHERLEY CL
SHELMERDINE CL
ST PAULS WAY
Medical Cen
BOW COMMON LA
HAWGOOD ST
MORRIS ROAD
VALLEY
UAMVAR ST
Comm Cen
WYVIS ST
CELTIC ST
TEVIOT ST
EVEREST PL
NORTHERN APP
A12
BROMLEY HALL RD
AILSA ST
LOCHNAGAR ST
ZETLAND STREET
ABBOTT RD
BRION PL
NAIRN ST
LEVEN RD
Prim Sch
TWEED HO
SUB
F Sch
Comm Cen
BURGESS ST
SELSEY ST
WALLWOOD ST
Prim Sch
A1205
ROAD
THOMAS ROAD
Limehouse Cut
COTALL ST
UPPER
BROOMFIELD ST
BRABAZON ST
Prim Sch
CHRISP ST
FB
RIFLE ST
FAWE ST
LANGDON PARK
LANGDON PK
BRIGHT ST
LEONARDS
SPEY ST
DEWBERRY
Comm Cen
Sports Cen
Tenn Cts
Sec Sch
BARTLETT PARK
ARCA ST
NORT ST
LANSBURY EST
GIRAUD ST
CARMEN ST
HAY CURRIE ST
BURCHAM ST
TAYBURN CL
ANDREW ST
AGNES ST
PIXLEY ST
DOD STREET
STAINSBY RD
LINDFIELD STREET
CORDELIA ST
Health Cen
Pol
Mkt
WILLIS ST
BROWNFIELD ST
IDA ST
LODORE ST
ADDEY ST
Prim Sch
FARRANCE ST
PIGOTT ST
HIND GRO
SARACEN
NORTH
Prim Sch
RICARDO ST
KERBEY ST
FITZGERALD HO
SUSANNAH ST
FOLLETT ST
CANTON ST
STREET
GRUNDY ST
PEKIN ST
NAN. ST
Prim Sch
DUFF ST
STURRY ST
PO
Lib
Coll
EAST INDIA DOCK RD
W INDIA DOCK RD
AMOY PL
BIRCHFIELD ST
PINE CL
Uni
Comm Cen
REC GRD
Fire Sta
Health Cen
ALL SAINTS
NEWBY PL
BAZELY ST
COTTON ST
ASH. Prim Sch
WOOLM. ST
ROBIN HOOD LA
COUN OFFIC
MORANT ST
SALTWELL ST
Prim Sch
WADES PL
SHIRB. ST
HALE ST
Comm Cen
WOODSTOCK TER
COTTAGE ST
LAWLESS ST
SMYT. ST
MO. PL
Pol
GRENADE ST
THREE
BREWSTER HO
LIMEHOUSE CAUSEWAY
WESTFERRY
PENNYFIELDS
MING ST
POPLAR HIGH STREET
CORON CT
DINGLE GDNS
CASTOR LA
Sports Cen
Coll
HARROW LA
POPLAR BUSINESS PK
DITCHB. ST
Fit Cen
LINK
ASPEN WAY
A1261
DEPOT
POPLAR
BLACKWALL
SUB
GARFORD ST
MILLIGAN ST
A1203
CANN DR
HERTSMERE RD
Cin
MUS
Marriott
WEST INDIA QUAY
Billingsgate Mkt
TRAFALGAR WY
Four Seasons
Health Club
WESTFERRY RD
ONTARIO WY
FISHERMAN'S WALK
Offices
HSBC
BERKLEY TWR
WESTFERRY CIRCUS
W INDIA AV
CABOT SQ
N COLONNADE
Cabot Pl
PO
CANADA SQ
Barclays
N COLON.
S COLONNADE
Superstore
Lib
CHURCH PL
CARTIER CIR
TRAFALGAR WAY
BOARDWALK PL
Poplar Dock
Airshaft
Blackwall Basin
CANARY PIER
DOCKLANDS
NELSON DOCK PIER
CANARY WHARF
MACKENZIE WK
Canada Square
Citigroup
UPPER BANK ST
MONTGOMERY ST
HERON QUAY
BANK STREET
HERON QUAYS
CANARY WHARF
ISLE
PRESTONS ROAD
COLD HARBOUR
LOVEGROVE WK
CASCADES TOWER
REACH
West India Dock Pier
CHANDLERS MS
Britannia International Hotel
WEST INDIA DOCKS
DISCOVERY DOCK APTS
Independent Newspapers
MERIDIAN GATE
MER. PL
Pier
TOWER
0
500 yds
0
500 m

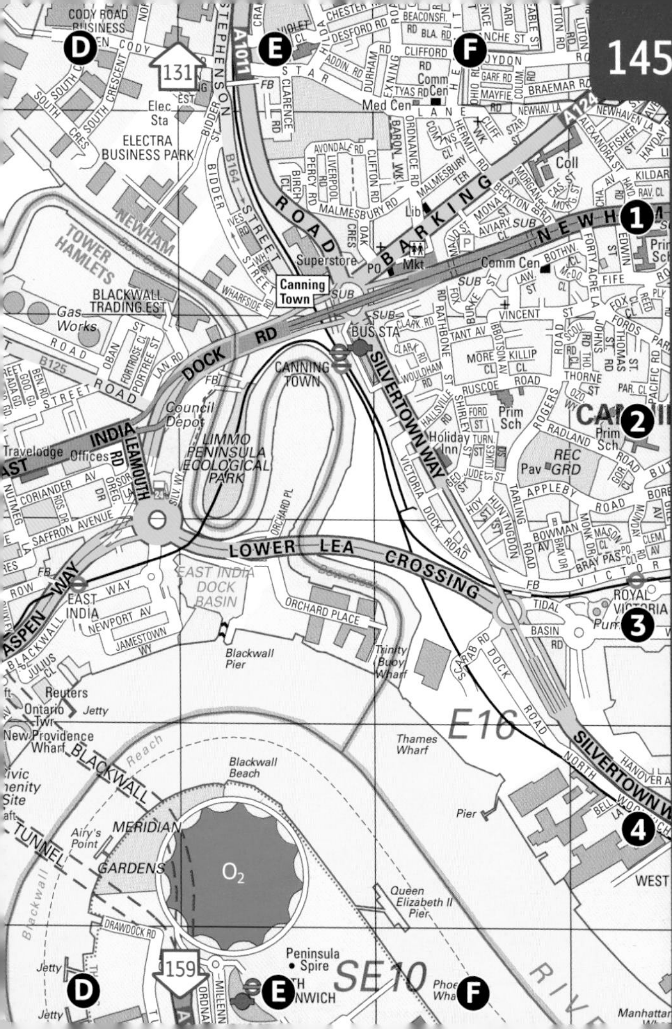
D
E
F
131
CODY ROAD BUSINESS CEN
CODY
SOUTH CRESCENT
SOUTH CRES
Elec Sta
ELECTRA BUSINESS PARK
NEWHAM
TOWER HAMLETS
Bow Creek
BLACKWALL TRADING EST
Gas Works
STEPHENSON
A1011
BIDDER ST
B164
STREET
WHARFSIDE RD
ROAD
STAR
CLARENCE RD
CHESTER
DESFORD RD
VIOLET CL
HILDA
FB
BEACONSFI.
BLA. RD
CLIFFORD RD
DURHAM
EXNING RD
TYAS RD
Comm Cen
Med Cen
LANE
BARON WK
ORDNANCE RD
HERMIT RD
CLIFF WK
STAR LA
NEWHAV. LA
BRAEMAR RD
MAYFIE.
GARF. RD
CROYDON
A124
NEWHAVEN LA
ALEXANDRA ST
FISHER ST
HAYDAY RD
KILDARE
RAV. CL
AVONDALE RD
PERCY RD
LIVERPOOL RD
CLIFTON RD
BIRCH CL
MALMESBURY RD
MALMESBURY TER
OAK CRES
Lib
Mkt
BARKING
MONA ST
BECKTON RD
MORGAN ST
CAS. ST
Coll
AVIARY CL
MAUD ST
Superstore
PO
Canning Town
SUB
NEWHAM
FORTY ACRE LA
EDWIN ST
Prim Sch
Comm Cen
BOTHW. CL
FIFE RD
McDO. CL
LAW. ST
FOX CL
REED CL
FORDS PARK
BURKE ST
VINCENT ST
RATHBONE ST
BUS STA
CLARK RD
TANT AV
IBBOTSON AV
KILLIP CL
MORE CL
ROAD
JOHNS ST
THOMAS ST
PACIFIC RD
PAR. CL
THORNE ST
ROGERS
RADLAND ROAD
CAN
Prim Sch
REC GRD
Pav
CANNING TOWN
SILVERTOWN WAY
WOULDHAM RD
HALLSVILLE RD
SHIRLEY ST
RUSCOE ROAD
FORD ST
Prim Sch
Holiday Inn
TURN. ST
ST LUKES SQ
JUDE ST
APPLEBY ROAD
TARLING ROAD
HUNTINGDON
HOY ST
VICTORIA DOCK ROAD
BOWMAN AV
MONK DR
MASON CL
BRAY DR
BRAY PAS
CLEM AV
MUNDAY RD
DOCK RD
ROAD
B125
OBAN ST
FORTROSE CL
PORTREE ST
LAN. RD
STREET
ROAD
INDIA
EAST
LEAMOUTH RD
Council Depot
Travelodge
Offices
FB
LIMMO PENINSULA ECOLOGICAL PARK
ORCHARD PL
CORIANDER AV
NUTMEG LA
SAFFRON AVENUE
ROS. DR
OREG. DR
SILV. WY
LOWER LEA CROSSING
FB
ASPEN WAY
EAST INDIA
EAST INDIA DOCK BASIN
NEWPORT AV
JAMESTOWN WY
BLACKWALL WAY
JULIUS CL
Bow Creek
ORCHARD PLACE
Trinity Buoy Wharf
Blackwall Pier
TIDAL BASIN RD
ROYAL VICTORIA
SCARAB RD
DOCK ROAD
Reuters
Ontario Twr
Jetty
New Providence Wharf
E16
Thames Wharf
NORTH WOOLWICH
SILVERTOWN WAY
HANOVER AV
BELL LA
Blackwall Beach
Reach
BLACKWALL TUNNEL
MERIDIAN GARDENS
Airy's Point
Pier
WEST
O2
Queen Elizabeth II Pier
Peninsula Spire
DRAWDOCK RD
159
Jetty
SE10
RIVER
Manhattan
1
2
3
4

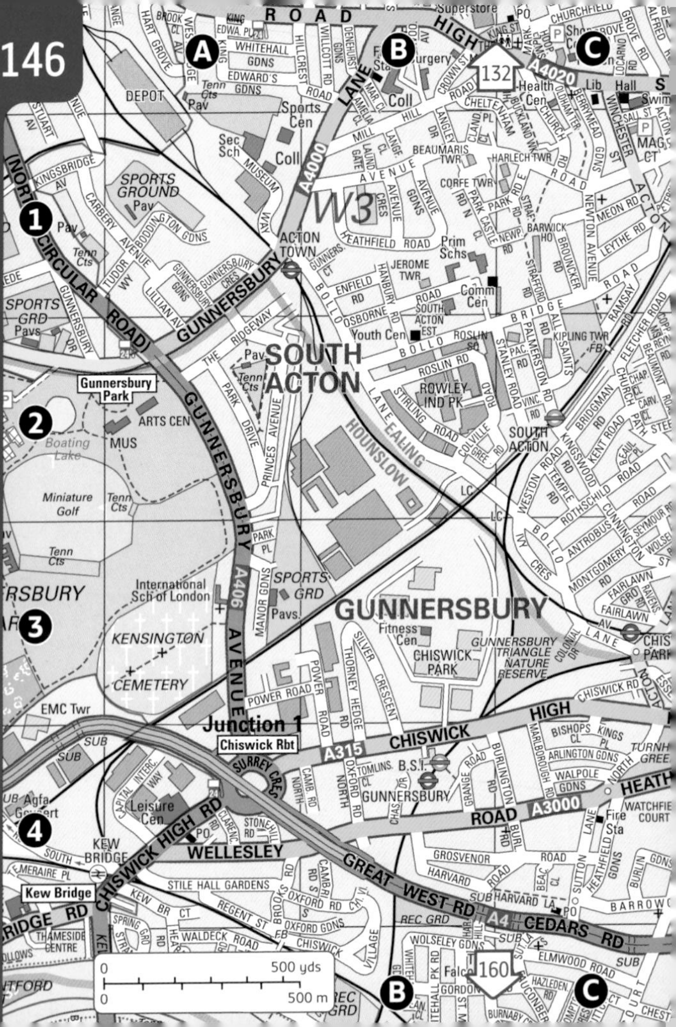
A
B
C
1
2
3
4
132
160
W3
SOUTH ACTON
GUNNERSBURY
ACTON TOWN
SOUTH ACTON
CHISWICK PARK
GUNNERSBURY
KEW BRIDGE
Kew Bridge
Gunnersbury Park
Junction 1
Chiswick Rbt
A4000
A4020
A406
A315
A3000
A4
NORTH CIRCULAR ROAD
GUNNERSBURY LANE
GUNNERSBURY AVENUE
CHISWICK HIGH ROAD
GREAT WEST RD
CEDARS RD
BOLLO LANE
BOLLO BRIDGE ROAD
BOLLO LANE
EALING
HOUNSLOW
HIGH ROAD
MILL HILL ROAD
AVENUE ROAD
DEPOT
SPORTS GROUND
SPORTS GRD
Pavs
Pav
Tenn Cts
Sports Cen
Sec Sch
Coll
MUSEUM
ARTS CEN
MUS
Boating Lake
Miniature Golf
International Sch of London
KENSINGTON CEMETERY
EMC Twr
Leisure Cen
Agfa Gevaert
ROWLEY IND PK
Youth Cen
Comm Cen
Prim Schs
JEROME TWR
BEAUMARIS TWR
HARLECH TWR
CORFE TWR
KIPLING TWR
Fitness Cen
CHISWICK PARK
GUNNERSBURY TRIANGLE NATURE RESERVE
Health Cen
Lib
Hall
Swim
MAG CT
Superstore
Surgery
THAMESIDE CENTRE
WATCHFIELD COURT
Fire Sta
B.S.I.
REC GRD
WHITEHALL GDNS
EDWARD'S GDNS
HILLCREST RD
WILLCOTT RD
DENEHURST GDNS
HART GROVE
STUART AV
KINGSBRIDGE AV
CARBERY AVENUE
BODDINGTON GDNS
TUDOR WY
LILLIAN AV
GUNNERSBURY CRES
GUNNERSBURY GDNS
GUNNERSBURY DR
THE RIDGEWAY
PARK DRIVE
PRINCES AVENUE
PARK PL
MANOR GDNS
ENFIELD RD
OSBORNE RD
HANBURY RD
SOUTH ACTON EST
HEATHFIELD ROAD
ROSLIN RD
ROSLIN SQ
STIRLING ROAD
COLVILLE RD
STANLEY ROAD
PALMERSTON RD
ALL SAINTS
STRAFFORD RD
BROUNCKER RD
NEWTON AVENUE
MEON RD
LEYTHE RD
RAMSAY ROAD
FLETCHER ROAD
CHURCH PATH
BRIDGMAN RD
KENT ROAD
KINGSWOOD RD
WESTON ROAD
TEMPLE RD
ROTHSCHILD ROAD
CUNNINGTON ST
ANTROBUS RD
MONTGOMERY RD
FAIRLAWN AV
COLONIAL DR
CHISWICK RD
POWER ROAD
THORNEY HEDGE RD
SILVER CRESCENT
BISHOPS CL
KINGS
ARLINGTON GDNS
WALPOLE GDNS
MARLBOROUGH RD
BURLINGTON RD
GRANGE ROAD
OXFORD RD NORTH
CAMB. RD NORTH
SURREY CRES
CAPITAL INTERC. WAY
STONEHILL RD
WELLESLEY
STILE HALL GARDENS
KEW BR CT
REGENT ST
OXFORD RD S
OXFORD GDNS
WALDECK ROAD
GROSVENOR
HARVARD ROAD
HARVARD LA
HEATHFIELD GDNS
SUTTON LANE
BARROWGATE
WOLSELEY GDNS
ELMWOOD ROAD
HAZLEDEN RD
CHISWICK VILLAGE
BRIDGE RD
MERAIRE PL
SOUTH
CHELTENHAM PL
BUCKLAND WK
CHURCH RD
OLDHAM TER
BERRYMEAD GDNS
WINCHESTER ST
ACTON LANE
TURNHAM GREEN
HEATHFIELD
SALISBURY ST
0
500 yds
0
500 m

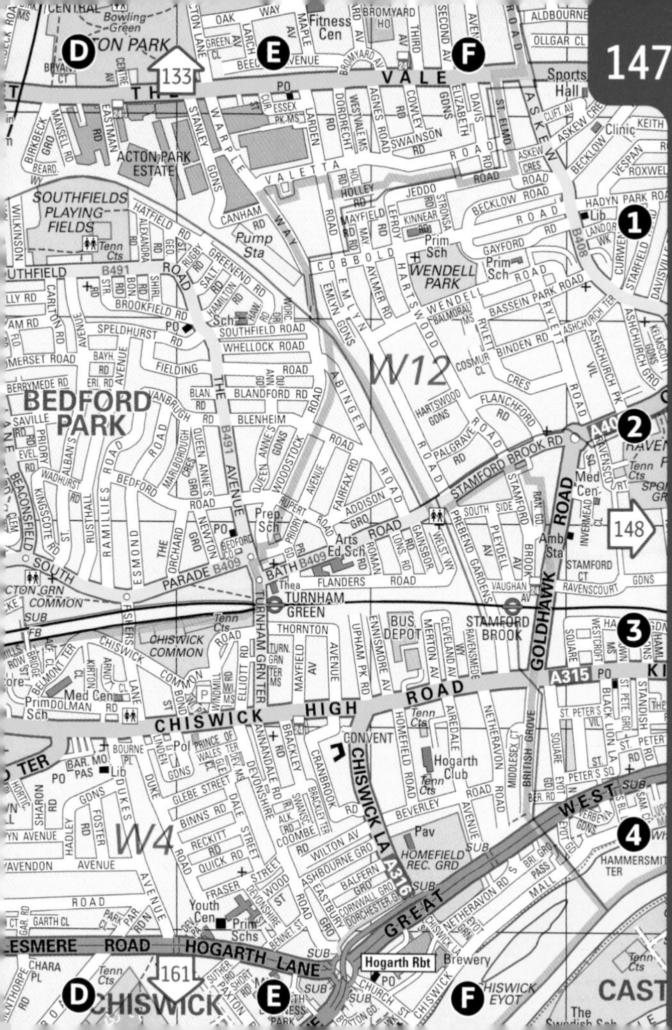
ACTON PARK
Bowling Green
Fitness Cen
BROMYARD HO
ALDBOURNE
OLLGAR CL
133
THE VALE
Sports Hall
ACTON PARK ESTATE
SOUTHFIELDS PLAYING FIELDS
Tenn Cts
Pump Sta
WENDELL PARK
Prim Sch
Clinic
Lib
W12
BEDFORD PARK
SOUTHFIELD ROAD
WHELLOCK ROAD
BLANDFORD RD
STAMFORD BROOK RD
GOLDHAWK ROAD
Med Cen
Amb Sta
148
TURNHAM GREEN
STAMFORD BROOK
BUS DEPOT
CHISWICK COMMON
CHISWICK HIGH ROAD
Hogarth Club
CONVENT
W4
HOMEFIELD REC. GRD
GREAT WEST RD
Youth Cen
Prim Schs
HOGARTH LANE
Hogarth Rbt
Brewery
CHISWICK EYOT
161
CHISWICK
ELLESMERE ROAD
HAMMERSMITH TER
CAST
The Swedish Sch
D
E
F
1
2
3
4

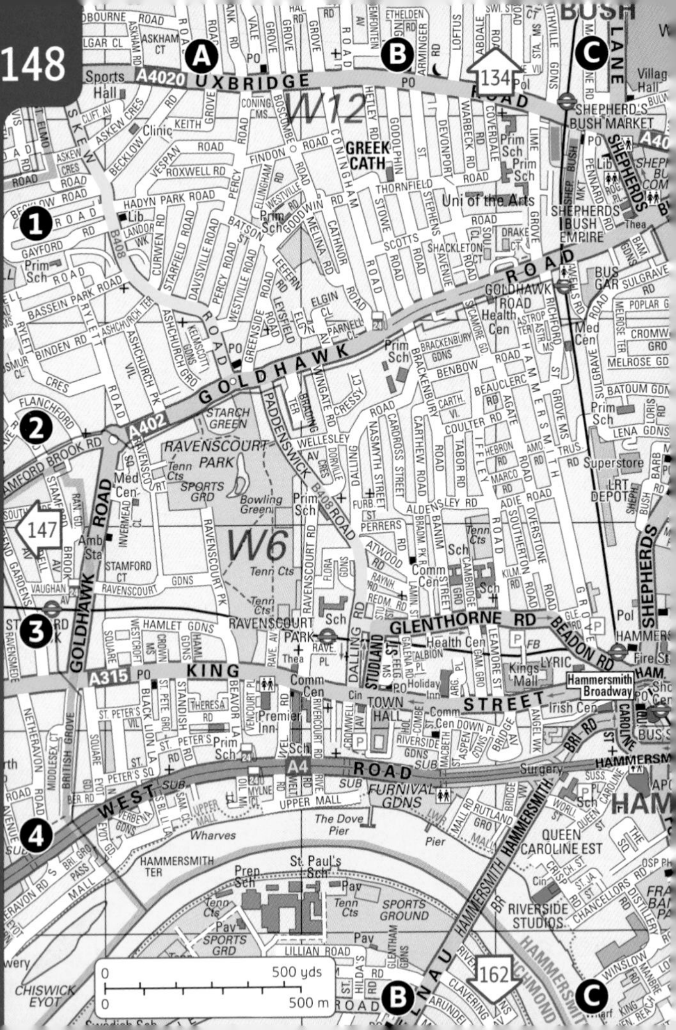
A
B
C
1
2
3
4
W12
W6
134
147
162
UXBRIDGE ROAD
A4020
SHEPHERD'S BUSH MARKET
SHEPHERDS BUSH EMPIRE
SHEPHERDS BUSH
GOLDHAWK ROAD
A402
GREEK CATH
Uni of the Arts
RAVENSCOURT PARK
STARCH GREEN
SPORTS GRD
Bowling Green
Tenn Cts
PADDENSWICK ROAD
B408
HAMMERSMITH GROVE
GLENTHORNE RD
BEADON RD
KING STREET
A315
TOWN HALL
Kings Mall
LYRIC
Hammersmith Broadway
Premier Inn
GREAT WEST ROAD
A4
FURNIVAL GDNS
UPPER MALL
The Dove Pier
Wharves
HAMMERSMITH TER
St. Paul's Sch
Prep Sch
SPORTS GROUND
LILLIAN ROAD
HAMMERSMITH BR
QUEEN CAROLINE EST
RIVERSIDE STUDIOS
CHISWICK EYOT
LRT DEPOT
Superstore
Health Cen
Comm Cen
0 500 yds
0 500 m

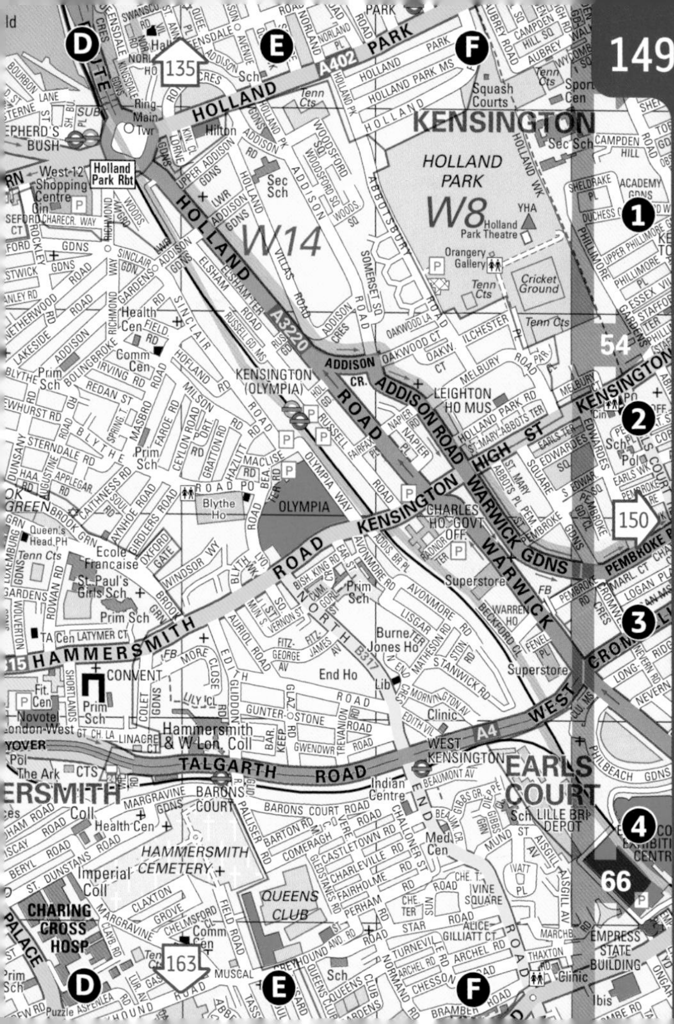
D
E
F
135
HOLLAND PARK
A402
HOLLAND PARK MS
HOLLAND
KENSINGTON
HOLLAND PARK
W8
YHA
Holland Park Theatre
Orangery Gallery
Cricket Ground
Tenn Cts
Squash Courts
Sport Cen
Sec Sch
CAMPDEN HILL ROAD
ACADEMY GDNS
DUCHESS OF BEDFORD WK
PHILLIMORE GDNS
UPPER PHILLIMORE GDNS
ESSEX VILLAS
STAFFORD TER
1
54
SHEPHERD'S BUSH
West 12 Shopping Centre
Holland Park Rbt
Ring Main Twr
Hilton
UPPER ADDISON GDNS
LWR ADDISON GDNS
ADDISON RD
ADDISON GDNS
WOODSFORD SQ
ABBOTSBURY ROAD
SOMERSET SQ
HOLLAND ROAD
A3220
W14
ELSHAM ROAD
RUSSELL RD
ADDISON CRES
OAKWOOD CT
ILCHESTER PL
MELBURY ROAD
LEIGHTON HO MUS
HOLLAND PARK RD
ST MARY ABBOTS TER
KENSINGTON HIGH ST
2
EDWARDES SQ
EARLS TER
ADDISON ROAD
ADDISON CR.
KENSINGTON (OLYMPIA)
RICHMOND WAY
SINCLAIR ROAD
Health Cen
Comm Cen
Prim Sch
MILSON RD
BLYTHE RD
MASBRO RD
FAROE RD
CEYLON ROAD
GRATTON RD
HAZLITT RD
MACLISE RD
OLYMPIA WAY
OLYMPIA
Blythe Ho
KENSINGTON ROAD
CHARLES HO GOVT OFF.
WARWICK GDNS
WARWICK ROAD
PEMBROKE RD
150
LOGAN PL
Superstore
WARREN HO
BECKFORD CL
FENELON PL
3
CROMWELL RD
Queen's Head PH
Ecole Francaise
St. Paul's Girls Sch
BROOK GRN
OXFORD GATE
WINDSOR WY
AVONMORE RD
LISGAR TER
MATHESON RD
STANWICK RD
NORTH END ROAD
B317
Burne Jones Ho
End Ho
Lib
HAMMERSMITH ROAD
CONVENT
Prim Sch
Fit. Cen
Novotel London West
LINACRE CT
Hammersmith & W Lon. Coll
GUNTERSTONE ROAD
GWENDWR ROAD
TREVANION RD
EDITH VIL
Clinic
A4
WEST CROMWELL ROAD
WEST KENSINGTON
TALGARTH ROAD
EARLS COURT
PHILBEACH GDNS
4
66
HAMMERSMITH
MARGRAVINE GDNS
BARONS COURT
BARONS COURT ROAD
Indian Centre
BEAUMONT AV
Health Cen
HAMMERSMITH CEMETERY
Imperial Coll
CHARING CROSS HOSP
QUEENS CLUB
COMERAGH RD
CASTLETOWN RD
CHARLEVILLE RD
FAIRHOLME RD
PERHAM RD
Med. Cen
LILLE BRIDGE DEPOT
IVATT PL
VINE SQUARE
AISGILL AV
EMPRESS STATE BUILDING
MARGRAVINE
CLAXTON GROVE
Comm Cen
163
TURNEVILLE RD
ARCHEL RD
CHESSON RD
NORMAND RD
QUEENS CLUB GARDENS
Sch
Clinic
Ibis
MUSCAL

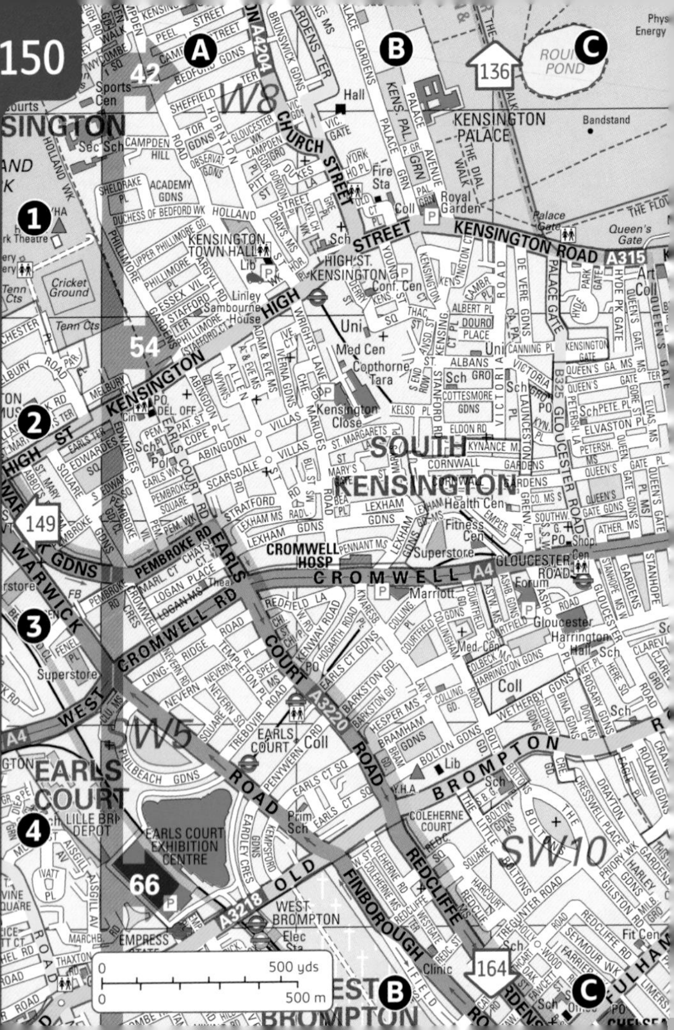
A
B
C
1
2
3
4
42
136
149
54
66
164
W8
SW5
SW10
KENSINGTON
KENSINGTON PALACE
ROUND POND
Bandstand
Physical Energy
Hall
Royal Garden
Fire Sta
Coll
Palace Gate
Queen's Gate
KENSINGTON ROAD
A315
Art Coll
KENSINGTON TOWN HALL
Lib
HIGH ST. KENSINGTON
Conf. Cen
Uni
Med Cen
Copthorne Tara
Linley Sambourne House
Sports Cen
Sec Sch
YHA
Cricket Ground
Tenn Cts
CHURCH STREET
HIGH STREET
KENSINGTON HIGH ST
Kensington Close
SOUTH KENSINGTON
Health Cen
Fitness Cen
Superstore
CROMWELL HOSP
CROMWELL
CROMWELL ROAD
A4
GLOUCESTER ROAD
Forum
Marriott
Gloucester
Harrington Hall
Med. Cen
WARWICK GDNS
WARWICK
PEMBROKE RD
EARLS COURT ROAD
A3220
WEST CROMWELL RD
EARLS COURT
Coll
LILLE BRI DEPOT
EARLS COURT EXHIBITION CENTRE
BROMPTON ROAD
OLD BROMPTON ROAD
A3218
WEST BROMPTON
Elec Sta
REDCLIFFE
FINBOROUGH ROAD
COLEHERNE COURT
Y.H.A.
Prim Sch
Clinic
Fit Cen
FULHAM
WEST BROMPTON
0
500 yds
0
500 m

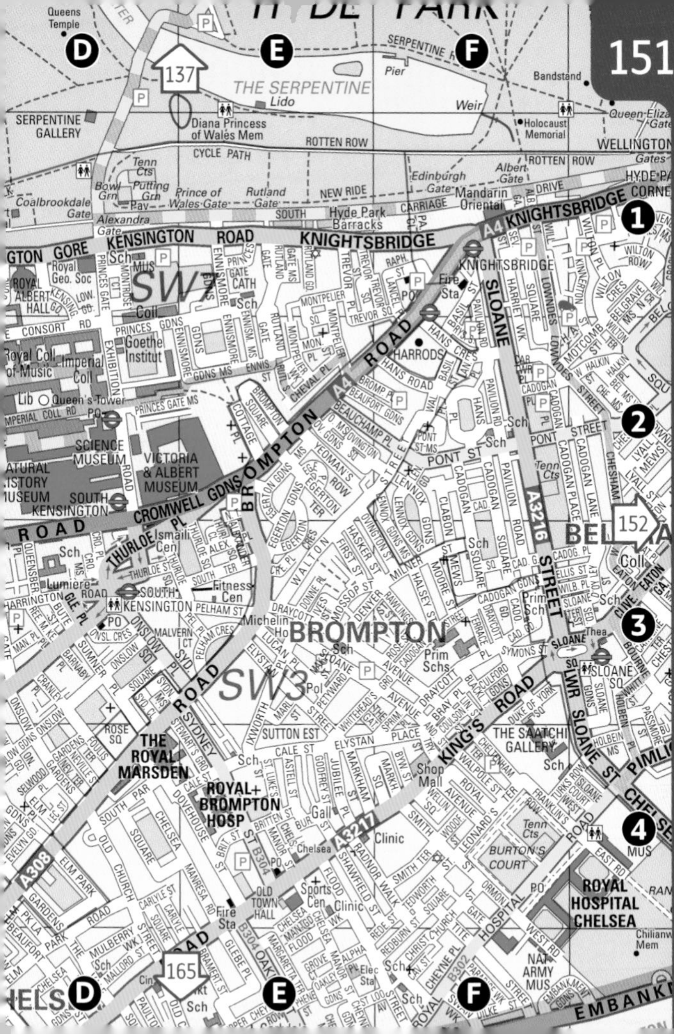
HYDE PARK
Queens Temple
D
E
F
137
SERPENTINE RD
Pier
THE SERPENTINE
Lido
Weir
Bandstand
Queen Eliza Gate
SERPENTINE GALLERY
Diana Princess of Wales Mem
Holocaust Memorial
ROTTEN ROW
CYCLE PATH
WELLINGTON
ROTTEN ROW
Gates
Tenn Cts
Putting Grn
Bowl Grn
Pav
Prince of Wales Gate
Rutland Gate
NEW RIDE
Edinburgh Gate
Albert Gate
Mandarin Oriental
DRIVE
HYDE PA CORNE
Coalbrookdale Gate
Alexandra Gate
SOUTH CARRIAGE
Hyde Park Barracks
KENSINGTON ROAD
KNIGHTSBRIDGE
A4 KNIGHTSBRIDGE
1
Royal Geo. Soc
ROYAL ALBERT HALL
SW7
PRINCES GATE
ENNISMORE GDNS
CATH
Sch
MUS
Coll
CONSORT RD
PRINCES GDNS
Goethe Institut
Royal Coll of Music
Imperial Coll
EXHIBITION RD
KNIGHTSBRIDGE
Fire Sta
SLOANE
HARRODS
HANS CRES
HANS ROAD
MONTPELIER SQ
TREVOR SQ
CHEVAL PL
BROMPTON ROAD
A4
BEAUFORT GDNS
BEAUCHAMP PL
LOWNDES SQUARE
WILTON CRES
BELGRAVE MS N
MOTCOMB ST
W. HALKIN ST
CADOGAN PL
LOWNDES STREET
2
CHESHAM
LYALL MEWS
Lib
Queen's Tower
IMPERIAL COLL RD
PRINCES GATE MS
SCIENCE MUSEUM
VICTORIA & ALBERT MUSEUM
NATURAL HISTORY MUSEUM
SOUTH KENSINGTON
CROMWELL GDNS
CROMWELL ROAD
EGERTON GDNS
YEOMAN'S ROW
PONT ST
STREET
CADOGAN PLACE
CADOGAN LANE
Tenn Cts
A3216
152
BEL
Sch
PONT ST MS
LENNOX GDNS
CLABON MS
CADOGAN SQUARE
PAVILION ROAD
THURLOE PL
Ismaili Cen
THURLOE SQ
SOUTH TER
PELHAM ST
Fitness Cen
Lumiere
SOUTH KENSINGTON
WALTON ST
HASKER ST
FIRST ST
MILNER ST
MOORE ST
CADOGAN GDNS
STREET
Coll
EATON
CLIVE
3
SW3
Michelin Ho
BROMPTON
Sch
Prim Schs
Pol
SLOANE AVENUE
DRAYCOTT AVENUE
SYMONS ST
SLOANE SQ
SLOANE SQUARE
Thea
LWR SLOANE ST
ONSLOW SQUARE
PELHAM CRES
ROAD
SYDNEY
IXWORTH PL
SUTTON EST
CALE ST
ELYSTAN PLACE
THE SAATCHI GALLERY
KING'S ROAD
HOLBEIN MS
PIMLIC
ROSE SQ
THE ROYAL MARSDEN
ROYAL BROMPTON HOSP
Sch
JUBILEE PL
MARKHAM ST
Shop Mall
Sch
TURKS ROW
FRANKLIN'S ROW
CHELSE
4
MUS
EAST RD
SOUTH PARADE
CHELSEA SQUARE
Gall
Chelsea
A3217
Clinic
Tenn Cts
BURTON'S COURT
ROYAL HOSPITAL CHELSEA
ELM PARK GARDENS
A308
OLD CHURCH ST
PO
Sports Cen
Clinic
ROYAL HOSPITAL ROAD
OLD TOWN HALL
Fire Sta
RAN
Chilianwala Mem
MULBERRY WK
GLEBE PL
B304
OAKLEY ST
FLOOD ST
CHRIST CHURCH ST
TITE ST
NAT ARMY MUS
WEST RD
165
Sch
Elec Sta
B302
CHEYNE PL
EMBANKMENT GDNS
EMBANK
Sch
ELSEA
D
E
F

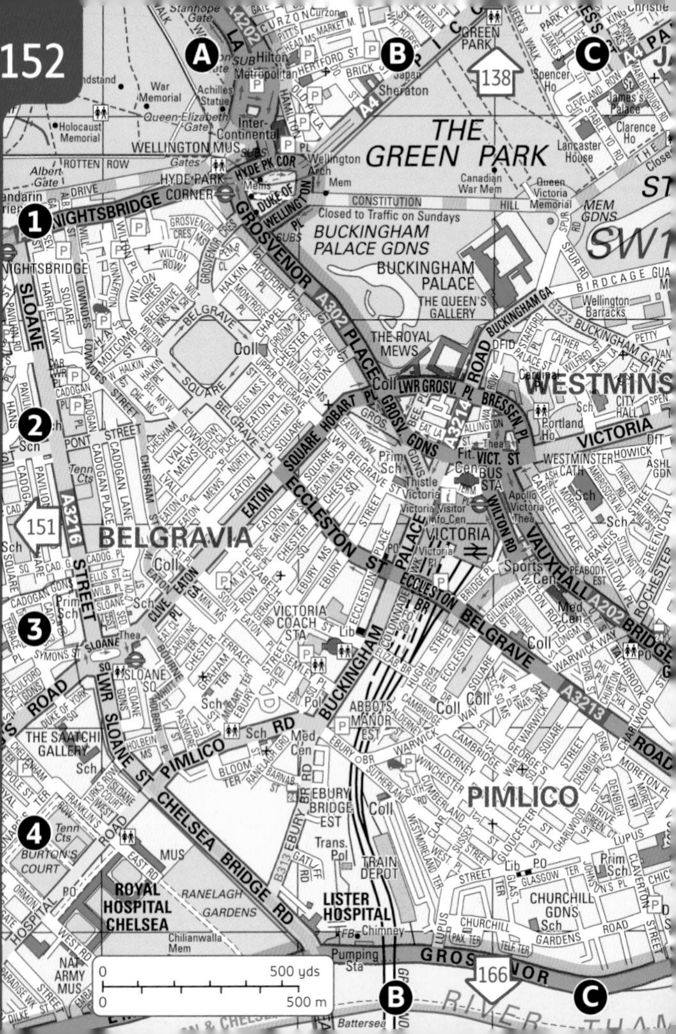
A
B
C
1
2
3
4
138
151
166
THE GREEN PARK
BUCKINGHAM PALACE GDNS
BUCKINGHAM PALACE
THE QUEEN'S GALLERY
THE ROYAL MEWS
Closed to Traffic on Sundays
CONSTITUTION HILL
HYDE PARK CORNER
WELLINGTON MUS
Wellington Arch
Hilton Metropolitan
Inter-Continental
Sheraton
Japan
Achilles Statue
War Memorial
Holocaust Memorial
Queen Elizabeth Gate
Stanhope Gate
Albert Gate
ROTTEN ROW
KNIGHTSBRIDGE
GROSVENOR PLACE
A302
A4
A4202
Canadian War Mem
Queen Victoria Memorial
Spencer Ho
St James's Palace
Clarence Ho
Lancaster House
MEM GDNS
SW1
BIRDCAGE
Wellington Barracks
BUCKINGHAM GATE
WESTMINS
VICTORIA
WESTMINSTER CATH
Portland Ho
BELGRAVIA
BELGRAVE SQUARE
EATON SQUARE
ECCLESTON ST
ECCLESTON BRIDGE
BELGRAVE RD
VICTORIA
Victoria Visitor Info Cen
VICT. BUS STA
Apollo Victoria Thea
VICTORIA COACH STA
BUCKINGHAM PALACE RD
VAUXHALL BRIDGE RD
A202
A3213
A3214
A3216
SLOANE STREET
SLOANE SQ
LWR SLOANE ST
PIMLICO RD
CHELSEA BRIDGE RD
THE SAATCHI GALLERY
BURTON'S COURT
ROYAL HOSPITAL CHELSEA
RANELAGH GARDENS
Chilianwalla Mem
NAT ARMY MUS
LISTER HOSPITAL
Chimney
Pumping Sta
TRAIN DEPOT
EBURY BRIDGE EST
ABBOTS MANOR EST
PIMLICO
CHURCHILL GDNS
GROSVENOR RD
RIVER THAMES
Battersea
0 500 yds
0 500 m

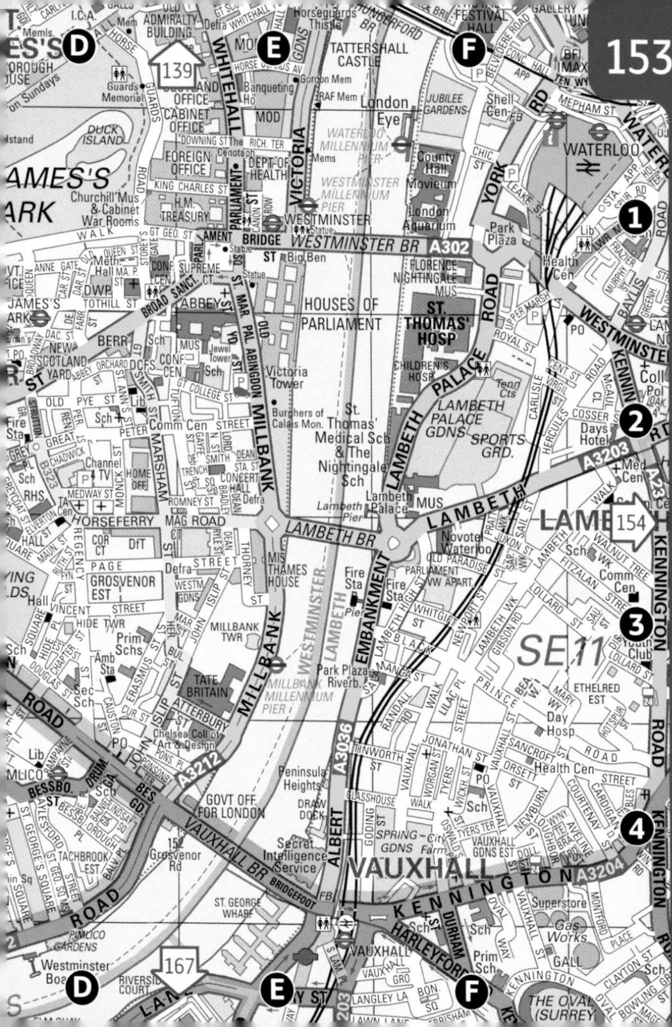
139
154
167
D
E
F
1
2
3
4
I.C.A.
ADMIRALTY BUILDING
Horseguards Thistle
TATTERSHALL CASTLE
FESTIVAL HALL
BFI IMAX
Guards Memorial
Banqueting Ho
Gordon Mem
RAF Mem
London Eye
JUBILEE GARDENS
Shell Cen
MEPHAM ST
WATERLOO
CABINET OFFICE
MOD
DUCK ISLAND
DOWNING ST
RICH. TER
WATERLOO MILLENNIUM PIER
County Hall
Movieum
FOREIGN OFFICE
Cenotaph
DEPT OF HEALTH
VICTORIA
WESTMINSTER MILLENNIUM PIER
London Aquarium
YORK
LEAKE ST
ST. JAMES'S PARK
Churchill Mus & Cabinet War Rooms
KING CHARLES ST
H.M. TREASURY
PARLIAMENT
WESTMINSTER
Park Plaza
BIRDCAGE WALK
BRIDGE ST
WESTMINSTER BR
A302
Big Ben
Health Cen
ANNE GATE
QUEEN ST
Meth. Hall
SUPREME CT.
FLORENCE NIGHTINGALE MUS
DWP
TOTHILL ST
BROAD SANCT.
ABBEY
HOUSES OF PARLIAMENT
ST. THOMAS' HOSP
ROAD
UPPER MARSH
WESTMINSTER
BAYLIS
NEW SCOTLAND YARD
BERR
Jewel Tower
PALACE
ROYAL ST
PO
CHILDREN'S HOSP
Victoria Tower
LAMBETH PALACE GDNS
SPORTS GRD.
Tenn Cts
CARLISLE
COSSER
Days Hotel
OLD PYE ST
GT COLLEGE ST
MILLBANK
Burghers of Calais Mon.
St. Thomas' Medical Sch & The Nightingale Sch
LAMBETH
HERCULES
A3203
Med Cen
A23
Comm Cen
MARSHAM
GREAT PETER STREET
Channel 4 TV
HOME OFF.
CONCERT HALL
Lambeth Palace
MUS
Lambeth Pier
LAMBETH
MEDWAY ST
ROMNEY ST
HORSEFERRY
MAG ROAD
LAMBETH BR
Novotel Waterloo
KENNINGTON
WALNUT TREE WK
DfT
PAGE STREET
MI5 THAMES HOUSE
OLD PARADISE ST
PARLIAMENT VW APART.
FITZALAN
Fire Sta
GROSVENOR EST
Defra
EMBANKMENT
WHITGIFT ST
LOLLARD
VINCENT STREET
HIDE TWR
MILLBANK TWR
BLACK PRINCE
SE11
Youth Club
Prim Schs
ERASMUS ST
WESTMINSTER
Park Plaza Riverb.
MANCA ST
ETHELRED EST
TATE BRITAIN
MILLBANK MILLENNIUM PIER
Day Hosp
ROAD
ATTERBURY ST
Chelsea Coll of Art & Design
A3212
A3036
JONATHAN ST
SANCROFT ST
TINWORTH ST
Health Cen
ORSETT ST
Lib
PIMLICO
BESSBO. ST
Peninsula Heights
GOVT OFF. FOR LONDON
DRAW DOCK
GLASSHOUSE WALK
SPRING GDNS
City Farm
TYERS TER
VAUXHALL GDNS EST
COURTENAY
CARDIGAN
VAUXHALL BR
Secret Intelligence Service
ALBERT
VAUXHALL
KENNINGTON
A3204
152 Grosvenor Rd
ST. GEORGE'S SQUARE
ROAD
BRIDGEFOOT
ST. GEORGE WHARF
HARLEYFORD
DURHAM ST
Superstore
Gas Works
PIMLICO GARDENS
Westminster Boat
RIVERSIDE COURT
VAUXHALL GRO
BON. SQ
Prim Sch
GALL
KENNINGTON OVAL
THE OVAL (SURREY)
CLAYTON ST
LANGLEY LA
LAWN LANE

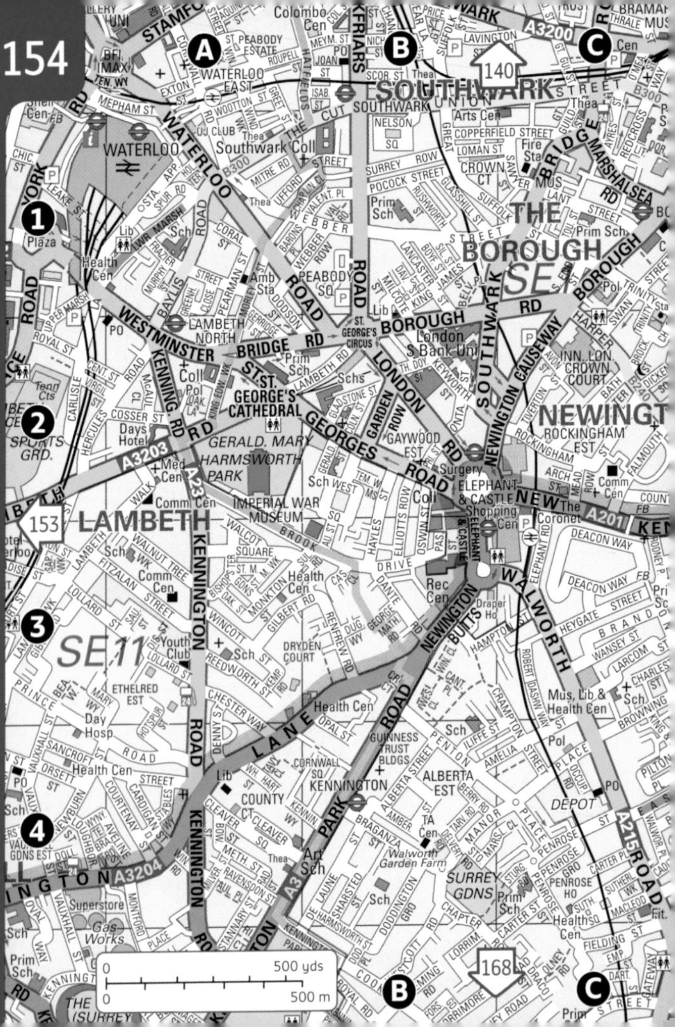
A
B
C
140
SOUTHWARK
WATERLOO
WATERLOO EAST
Southwark Coll
WATERLOO ROAD
STAMFORD ST
BLACKFRIARS ROAD
THE CUT
UNION STREET
ST. PEABODY ESTATE
Colombo Cen
NELSON SQ
COPPERFIELD STREET
LOMAN ST
CROWN CT
MARSHALSEA RD
THE BOROUGH
SE1
BOROUGH HIGH STREET
SOUTHWARK BRIDGE RD
LAMBETH NORTH
WESTMINSTER BRIDGE RD
ST. GEORGE'S CIRCUS
BOROUGH RD
London S Bank Uni
LONDON RD
ST. GEORGE'S CATHEDRAL
ST. GEORGES ROAD
GERALD. MARY HARMSWORTH PARK
IMPERIAL WAR MUSEUM
ELEPHANT & CASTLE
Shopping Cen
NEWINGTON CAUSEWAY
NEW KENT RD
A201
NEWINGTON
ROCKINGHAM EST
INN. LON. CROWN COURT
The Coronet
DEACON WAY
HEYGATE STREET
WALWORTH ROAD
NEWINGTON BUTTS
LAMBETH
153
SE11
KENNINGTON ROAD
KENNINGTON LANE
A3204
A3203
A23
A3
A215
KENNINGTON PARK ROAD
KENNINGTON
CORNWALL SQ
GUINNESS TRUST BLDGS
ALBERTA EST
ALBERTA STREET
PENTON PLACE
Walworth Garden Farm
SURREY GDNS
MANOR PLACE
DEPOT
ETHELRED EST
WALCOT SQUARE
DRYDEN COURT
CHESTER WAY
COUNTY CT
Superstore
Gas Works
VAUXHALL ST
LAMBETH SPORTS GRD.
Days Hotel
168
0 500 yds
0 500 m

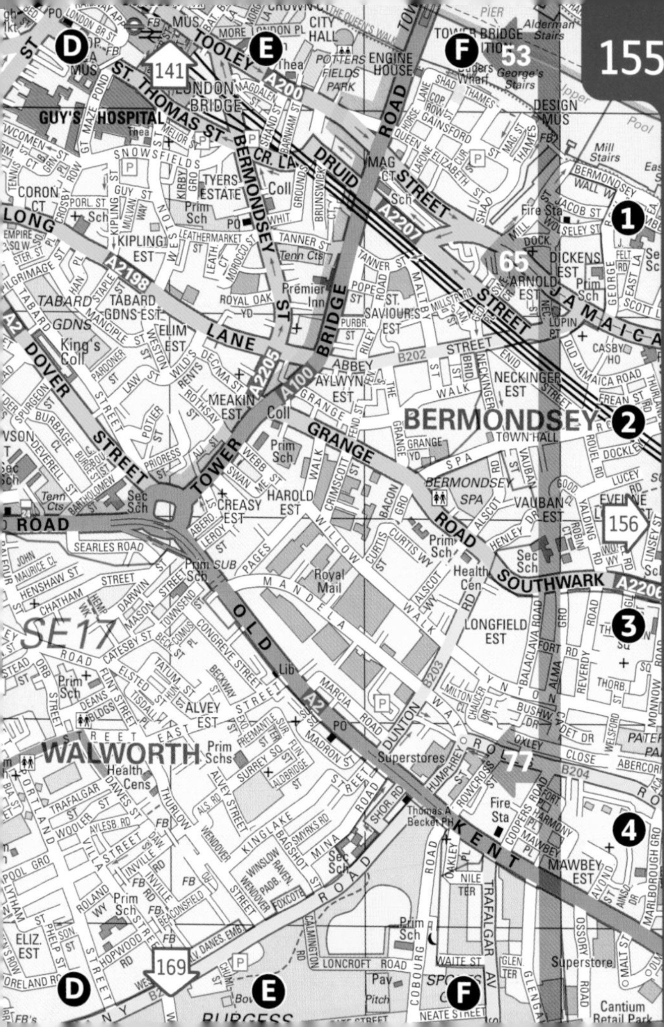
D
E
F
53
141
TOOLEY
CITY HALL
POTTERS FIELDS PARK
ENGINE HOUSE
TOWER BRIDGE
George's Stairs
Alderman Stairs
DESIGN MUS
Mill Stairs
GUY'S HOSPITAL
ST. THOMAS ST
LONDON BRIDGE
A200
ROAD
BERMONDSEY ST
DRUID
STREET
SNOWSFIELDS
TYERS ESTATE
CORON CT
LONG
KIPLING EST
A2198
TABARD GDNS
TABARD GDNS EST
King's Coll
LANE
ELIM EST
A2205
A100
BRIDGE
TOWER
A2207
Tenn Cts
Premier Inn
ROYAL OAK YD
ST. SAVIOUR'S EST
JACOB ST
1
DICKENS EST
65
ARNOLD EST
JAMAICA
OLD JAMAICA ROAD
CASBY HO
ABBEY
B202
STREET
NECKINGER EST
BERMONDSEY
TOWN HALL
2
AYLWYN EST
GRANGE
MEAKIN EST
DOVER
STREET
ROAD
Sec Sch
CREASY EST
HAROLD EST
BERMONDSEY SPA
ROAD
VAUBAN EST
156
SEARLES ROAD
Royal Mail
MANDELA
SOUTHWARK
A2206
3
LONGFIELD EST
SE17
OLD
KENT
A2
B203
ALVEY EST
WALWORTH
Superstores
77
B204
Fire Sta
4
MAWBEY EST
Thomas A Becket PH
NILE TER
TRAFALGAR AV
ELIZ. EST
169
LONCROFT ROAD
WAITE ST
NEATE STREET
Superstore
Cantium Retail Park
BURGESS

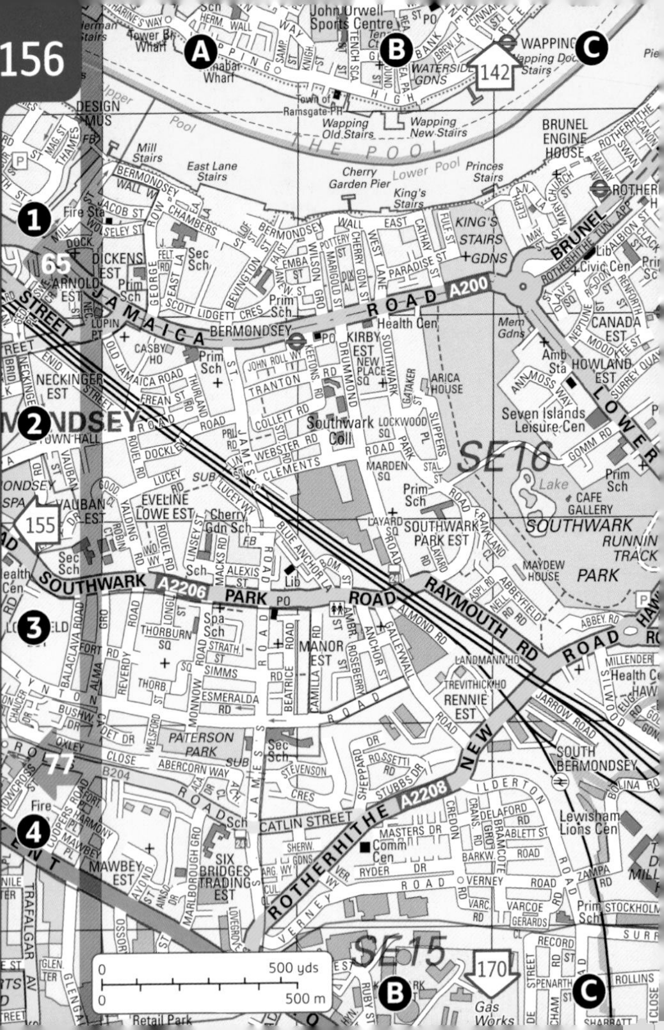
A
B
C
1
2
3
4
142
155
170
65
77
John Urwell Sports Centre
WAPPING
Wapping Dock Stairs
Tower Br. Wharf
Cinnabar Wharf
WATERSIDE GDNS
Town of Ramsgate PH
Wapping Old Stairs
Wapping New Stairs
THE POOL
Upper Pool
Lower Pool
DESIGN MUS
Mill Stairs
East Lane Stairs
Cherry Garden Pier
King's Stairs
Princes Stairs
BRUNEL ENGINE HOUSE
ROTHERHITHE
BERMONDSEY WALL W
BERMONDSEY WALL EAST
JACOB ST
Fire Sta
DICKENS EST
ARNOLD EST
CHAMBERS ST
Sec Sch
Prim Sch
KING'S STAIRS GDNS
PARADISE ST
BRUNEL RD
Civic Cen
Lib
JAMAICA ROAD
A200
BERMONDSEY
Health Cen
KIRBY EST
CANADA EST
Mem Gdns
Amb Sta
HOWLAND EST
NECKINGER EST
BERMONDSEY
TOWN HALL
OLD JAMAICA ROAD
TRANTON RD
ARICA HOUSE
Seven Islands Leisure Cen
LOWER RD
Southwark Coll
SE16
EVELINE LOWE EST
VAUBAN EST
Cherry Gdn Sch
SOUTHWARK PARK EST
Lake
CAFE GALLERY
SOUTHWARK PARK
RUNNING TRACK
MAYDEW HOUSE
SOUTHWARK PARK ROAD
A2206
RAYMOUTH RD
ABBEY RD
Lib
Spa Sch
THORBURN SQ
MANOR EST
LANDMANN HO
TREVITHICK HO
RENNIE EST
SIMMS RD
ESMERALDA RD
PATERSON PARK
ABERCORN WAY
B204
NEW ROAD
SOUTH BERMONDSEY
ROTHERHITHE NEW ROAD
A2208
CATLIN STREET
ILDERTON ROAD
Lewisham Lions Cen
Comm Cen
SIX BRIDGES TRADING EST
MAWBEY EST
VERNEY ROAD
SE15
Gas Works
Retail Park
TRAFALGAR AV
0
500 yds
0
500 m

D
E
F
1
2
3
4
143
158
171
ROTHERHITHE
Surrey Docks Farm
ECOLOGICAL PARK
STAVE HILL
RUSSIA DOCK WOODLAND
Associated Newspapers Print Works
Bowling Alley
Cinema
MAST LEISURE PK
Surrey Quays Shopping Cen
SURREY QUAYS
GREENLAND DOCK
SOUTH DOCK
Surrey Docks Water Sports Cen
NORWAY DOCK
REDRIFF EST
CUSTOM HOUSE REACH
NEW CALEDONIAN WF
KING FREDERIK IX TWR
QUEEN OF DENMARK CT
PRINCES CT
GREENLAND PIER
South Lock
St. George's Stairs
Lock
RAINBOW QUAY
CALYPSO WAY
PLOUGH WAY
B206
A2202
REDRIFF ROAD
EVELYN STREET
A200
LOWER ROAD
GROVE STREET
CANNON WHARF BUSINESS CEN
DEPTFORD PARK
DEPTFORD TRADING EST
PEPYS PARK
SAYES COURT PARK
DEPTFORD
SE8
E14
SOUTHWARK
TOWER HAMLETS
LEWISHAM
West India Dock Pier
HILTON DOCKLANDS
NELSON DOCK PIER
WHARF PIER
CASCADES TOWER
MILLENNIUM HARBOUR
SEACON TOWER
OCEAN WHARF
WESTFERRY ROAD
A1206
Landing Stage
Palmer's Wharf
ARAGON TWR
DEPTFORD STRAND
THAMES PATH
Power Station
Chimney
Recycling Cen
Med Cen
Health Cen
Comm Cen
Youth Club
Prim Sch
Sec Sch
Fire Sta
PO
Pump. Sta
Pav
THE NEW RD
BUSH RD
TRUNDLEYS ROAD
SCAWEN ROAD
GRINSTEAD
CANAL
BLACKHORSE ROAD
PRINCE STREET
DACCA ST
SUBS

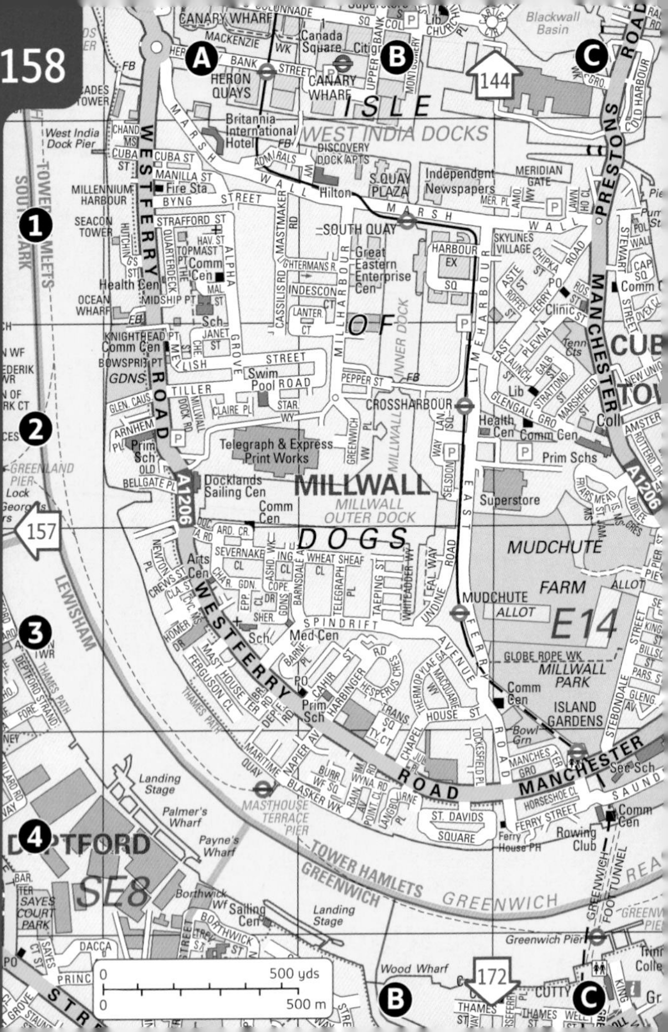
A
B
C
1
2
3
4
144
157
172
CANARY WHARF
COLUNNADE
MACKENZIE WK
Canada Square
Citigroup
UPPER BANK
COL
SQ
Lib
CHURCH PL
CARTIER CIR
Blackwall Basin
HERON QUAYS
BANK STREET
CANARY WHARF
ISLE
Britannia International Hotel
WEST INDIA DOCKS
DISCOVERY DOCK APTS
ADMIRALS WY
S.QUAY PLAZA
Independent Newspapers
MERIDIAN GATE
Hilton
MARSH WALL
SOUTH QUAY
HARBOUR EX SQ
SKYLINES VILLAGE
West India Dock Pier
TOWER HAMLETS
SOUTHWARK
CHAND MS
CUBA ST
MANILLA ST
Fire Sta
MILLENNIUM HARBOUR
BYNG STREET
SEACON TOWER
STRAFFORD ST
HAV. ST
TOPMAST PT
QUARTERDECK
Comm Cen
Health Cen
ALPHA GROVE
MASTMAKER RD
LIGHTERMANS R.
Great Eastern Enterprise Cen
INDESCON CT
LANTERN CT
CASSILIS RD
MILLHARBOUR
OF
INNER DOCK
LIMEHARBOUR
OCEAN WHARF
MIDSHIP PT
MAL.
Sch
JANET ST
KNIGHTHEAD PT
Comm Cen
MELLISH STREET
BOWSPRIT PT
GDNS.
WESTFERRY ROAD
Swim Pool
ROAD
PEPPER ST
FB
CROSSHARBOUR
TILLER
GLEN. CAUS.
DOCK RD
MILLWALL
CLAIRE PL
STAR. WY
GREENWICH VW PL
ARNHEM PL
Prim Sch
OLD BELLGATE PL
Telegraph & Express Print Works
MILLWALL
MILLWALL OUTER DOCK
Docklands Sailing Cen
Comm Cen
A1206
GREENLAND PIER
Lock
ARD. CR.
DOGS
NEWTON PL
CREWS ST
Arts Cen
SEVERNAKE CL
ING. CL
WHEAT SHEAF CL
TELEGRAPH PL
TAEPING ST
WHITEADDER WY
UNDINE RD
FAL WAY
MUDCHUTE
MUDCHUTE
FARM
ALLOT
E14
SPINDRIFT AV
Sch
Med Cen
HOMER DR
MAST HOUSE TER
FERGUSON CL
DEPTFORD STRAND
THAMES PATH
LEWISHAM
PO
CAHIR ST
HARBINGER RD
HESPERUS CRES
THERMOPYLAE GA
MACQUARIE WY
AVENUE
FERRY
GLOBE ROPE WK
MILLWALL PARK
Comm Cen
ISLAND GARDENS
Prim Sch
TRANS SQ
HOUSE ST
CHAPEL
LOCKESFIELD PL
ROAD
Bowl Grn
MANCHESTER GRO
MANCHESTER ROAD
Sec Sch
HORSESHOE CL
FERRY STREET
Ferry House PH
ST. DAVIDS SQUARE
Rowing Club
Comm Cen
MARITIME QUAY
NAPIER AV
BLASKER WK
BURR. WF SQ.
MASTHOUSE TERRACE PIER
Landing Stage
Palmer's Wharf
Payne's Wharf
DEPTFORD
SE8
Borthwick Wf
Sailing Cen
BORTHWICK ST
TOWER HAMLETS
GREENWICH
GREENWICH
Landing Stage
SAYES COURT PARK
DACCA
PRINC
Wood Wharf
GREENWICH FOOT TUNNEL
Greenwich Pier
CUTTY
THAMES ST
KING
0 500 yds
0 500 m
PRESTONS ROAD
COLD HARBOUR
MANCHESTER ROAD
CUBITT TOWN
Comm Cen
Clinic
Tenn Cts
Lib
Health Cen
Comm Cen
Prim Schs
Superstore
EAST FERRY ROAD
SELSDON WAY
GLENGALL GRO
LAUNCH ST
PLEVNA ST
CHIPKA ST
ASTE ST
ROFFEY ST
MARSHFIELD ST
FRIARS MEAD
JUBILEE CRES
A1206
STEBONDALE ST
GLENG. AV
PARS. SQ
SAUNDERS

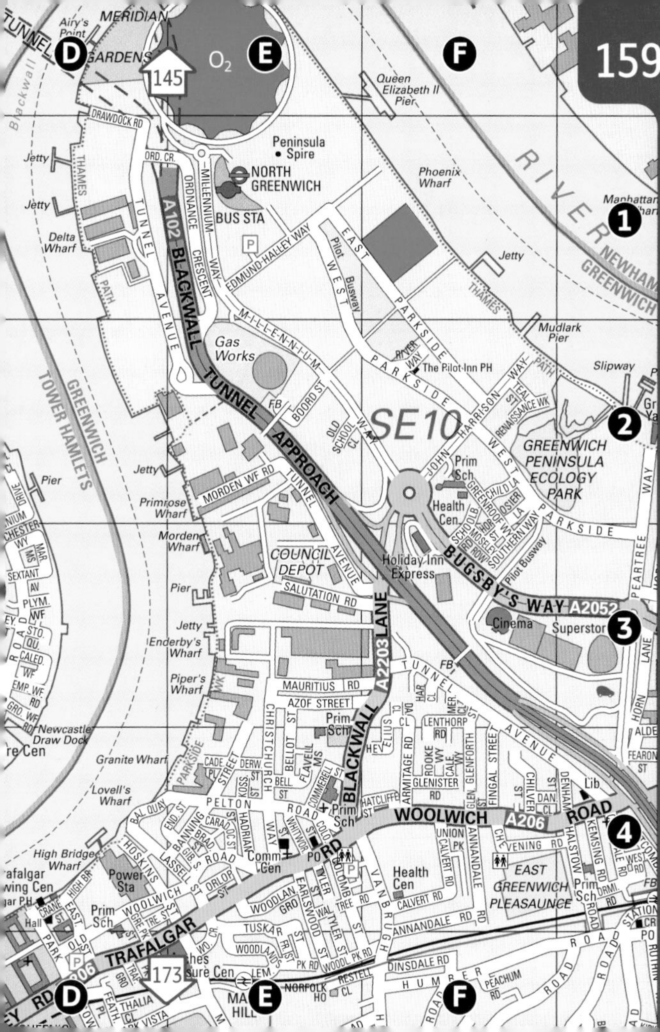

MERIDIAN
Airy's Point
GARDENS
TUNNEL
Blackwall
145
O2
D
E
F
Queen Elizabeth II Pier
DRAWDOCK RD
Peninsula Spire
ORD. CR.
NORTH GREENWICH
BUS STA
Jetty
THAMES
Delta Wharf
A102 BLACKWALL TUNNEL APPROACH
ORDNANCE CRESCENT
MILLENNIUM WAY
EDMUND HALLEY WAY
TUNNEL AVENUE
PATH
WEST Pilot Busway
EAST PARKSIDE
Phoenix Wharf
RIVER
Manhattan Wharf
NEWHAM
GREENWICH
Mudlark Pier
Slipway
Gas Works
RIVER WAY
The Pilot Inn PH
PARKSIDE
JOHN HARRISON WAY
WEST PARKSIDE
TEAL ST
RENAISSANCE WK
BOORD ST
FB
OLD SCHOOL CL
SE10
GREENWICH PENINSULA ECOLOGY PARK
Prim Sch
Health Cen.
GREENROOF WY
CHILD LA
OSIER LA
SOUTHERN WAY
SCHOOLBANK RD
MOSELEY ROW
HOP ST
PARKSIDE
WAY
PEARTREE
Pilot Busway
TOWER HAMLETS
GREENWICH
Pier
Primrose Wharf
MORDEN WF RD
Morden Wharf
COUNCIL DEPOT
AVENUE
Holiday Inn Express
BUGSBY'S WAY A2052
SALUTATION RD
A2203 BLACKWALL LANE
Cinema
Superstore
Enderby's Wharf
Piper's Wharf
MAURITIUS RD
AZOF STREET
TUNNEL AVENUE
HAR. CL
MER. CL
LENTHORP RD
Prim Sch
CHRISTCHURCH WAY
BELLOT ST
FLAVELL MS
Newcastle Draw Dock
Granite Wharf
PARKSIDE
CADE PL
STREET
DERW. ST
BELL ST
KOSS. ST
COMMERELL ST
ARMITAGE RD
ROOKE WY
CALE WY
GLENISTER RD
GLENFORTH ST
FINGAL STREET
CHILVER ST
DANIEL CL
DENHAM ST
Lib.
HORN LANE
FEARON ST
Lovell's Wharf
BAL. QUAY
PELTON ROAD
HATCLIFFE ST
WOOLWICH A206 ROAD
Prim Sch
Comm Cen
UNION PK
CALVERT RD
ANNANDALE RD
CHEVENING RD
EAST GREENWICH PLEASAUNCE
HALSTOW RD
KEMSING RD
High Bridge Wharf
Trafalgar
Power Sta
HOSKINS ST
LASSELL ST
ORLOP ST
WOOLWICH RD
Health Cen
VANBRUGH HILL
WOODLANDS GRO
EARLSWOOD ST
TYLER ST
TREE RD
CALVERT RD
ANNANDALE RD
Prim Sch
TRAFALGAR RD
HIGH BR
CRANE ST
EAST ST
OLD WOOLWICH
Hall
PARK
TUSKAR ST
WOODLANDS PK RD
DINSDALE RD
173
A206
THALIA
NORFOLK HO
MAZE HILL
RESTELL CL
HUMBER ROAD
PEACHUM RD
ROAD
STATION

A
B
C
1
2
3
4
146
174
KEW
GROVE PARK
NORTH SHEEN
TW9
KEW GREEN
KEW BRIDGE
CHISWICK HIGH
WELLESLEY
STILE HALL GARDENS
REGENT ST
GREAT WEST RD
A4
CEDARS RD
GROSVENOR ROAD
STRAND ON THE GRN
THAMESIDE CENTRE
KEW ROAD
MORTLAKE ROAD
A205
(SOUTH CIRCULAR ROAD)
RIVER THAMES
OLIVER'S ISLAND
Kew Pier
THE NATIONAL ARCHIVES
Sewage Works
Kew Retail Park
Recycling Cen
Crematorium
HAMMERSMITH CEMETERY
NORTH SHEEN CEMETERY
CLIFFORD AVENUE
CHISWICK BR
Boathouses
The Mortlake Brewery
The Ship PH
KEW GARDENS
Kew Green
KEW GARDENS GALLERY
Alpine House
Sch of Horticulture
Chalkers Corner
A316
A307
B353
GROVE PARK ROAD
HARTINGTON ROAD
STRAND DRIVE
BURLINGTON AVENUE
WEST PARK RD
HIGH PARK ROAD
LICHFIELD ROAD
BROOMFIELD RD
CLARENCE ROAD
ALEXANDRA RD
WINDSOR ROAD
ATWOOD AVENUE
0 500 yds
0 500 m

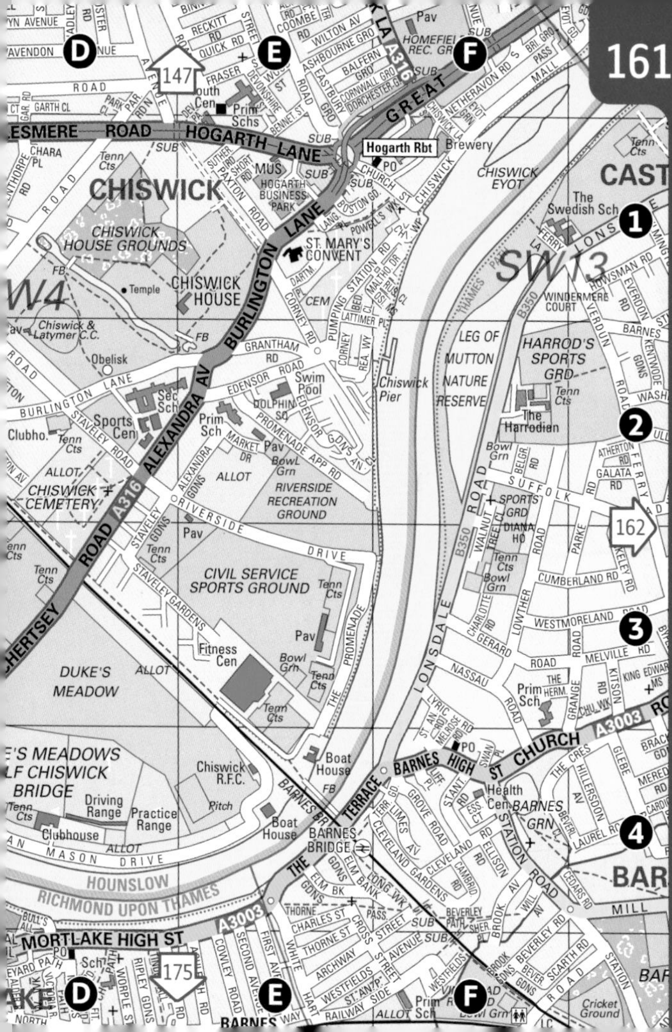
D
E
F
147
CHISWICK
CHISWICK HOUSE GROUNDS
CHISWICK HOUSE
Temple
Obelisk
Chiswick & Latymer C.C.
W4
ESMERE ROAD
HOGARTH LANE
GREAT
Hogarth Rbt
Brewery
MUS
HOGARTH BUSINESS PARK
ST. MARY'S CONVENT
CEM
BURLINGTON LANE
ALEXANDRA AV
GRANTHAM RD
EDENSOR ROAD
Swim Pool
DOLPHIN SQ
PROMENADE APP RD
Sec Sch
Sports Cen
Prim Sch
Clubho.
STAVELEY ROAD
CHISWICK CEMETERY
ALLOT
RIVERSIDE RECREATION GROUND
RIVERSIDE DRIVE
CIVIL SERVICE SPORTS GROUND
Fitness Cen
DUKE'S MEADOW
CHERTSEY ROAD
A316
Chiswick Pier
CHISWICK EYOT
LEG OF MUTTON NATURE RESERVE
THAMES
SW13
The Swedish Sch
CAST
HARROD'S SPORTS GRD
The Harrodian
WINDERMERE COURT
LONSDALE ROAD
B350
SUFFOLK RD
CUMBERLAND RD
WESTMORELAND ROAD
MELVILLE RD
162
NASSAU ROAD
GERARD ROAD
Prim Sch
BARNES HIGH ST
CHURCH ROAD
A3003
Health Cen
BARNES GRN
THE TERRACE
Boat House
Chiswick R.F.C.
Pitch
Driving Range
Practice Range
Clubhouse
MASON DRIVE
HOUNSLOW
RICHMOND UPON THAMES
BARNES BRIDGE
MORTLAKE HIGH ST
175
STATION ROAD
CLEVELAND GARDENS
GROVE ROAD
WESTFIELDS
RAILWAY SIDE
Cricket Ground
1
2
3
4
BAR
MILL

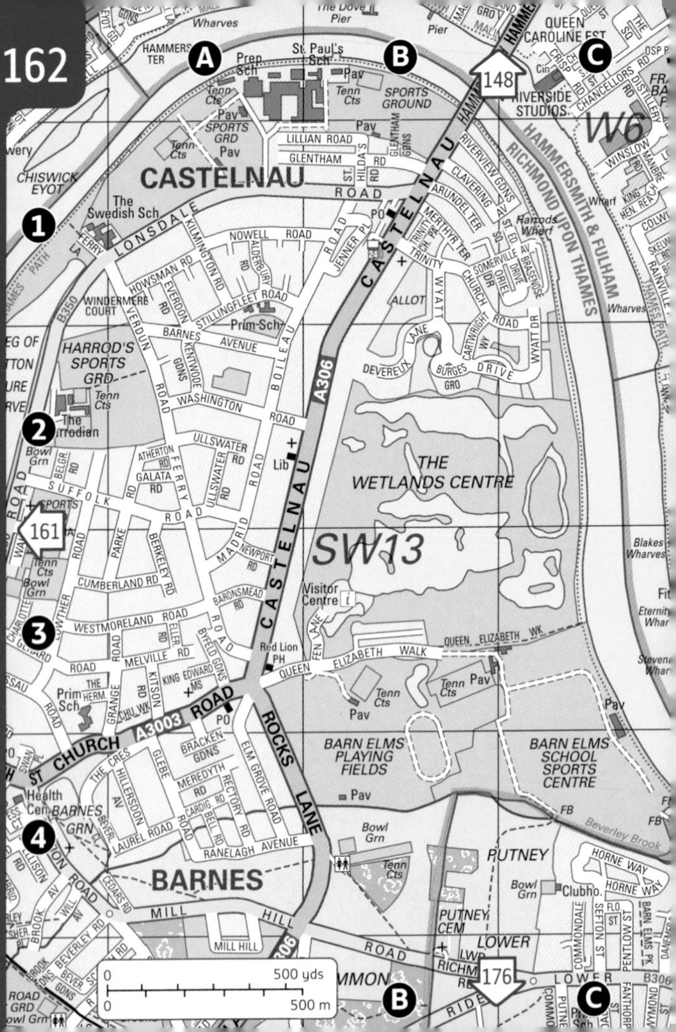
A
B
C
1
2
3
4
148
161
176
CASTELNAU
BARNES
PUTNEY
SW13
W6
THE WETLANDS CENTRE
Visitor Centre
HARROD'S SPORTS GRD
BARN ELMS PLAYING FIELDS
BARN ELMS SCHOOL SPORTS CENTRE
SPORTS GROUND
SPORTS GRD
CHISWICK EYOT
QUEEN CAROLINE EST
RIVERSIDE STUDIOS
HAMMERSMITH & FULHAM
RICHMOND UPON THAMES
St. Paul's Sch
Prep. Sch
The Swedish Sch
The Harrodian
WINDERMERE COURT
LONSDALE ROAD
CASTELNAU ROAD
LILLIAN ROAD
GLENTHAM RD
NOWELL ROAD
STILLINGFLEET ROAD
BARNES AVENUE
WASHINGTON ROAD
ULLSWATER RD
SUFFOLK ROAD
CUMBERLAND RD
WESTMORELAND ROAD
MELVILLE RD
CHURCH ROAD
A3003
A306
B350
B306
ROCKS LANE
QUEEN ELIZABETH WALK
RANELAGH AVENUE
LAUREL ROAD
MILL HILL
LOWER RICHMOND ROAD
PUTNEY CEM
Beverley Brook
HORNE WAY
Prim Sch
Lib
Red Lion PH
Harrods Wharf
Wharves
Blakes Wharves
0 500 yds
0 500 m

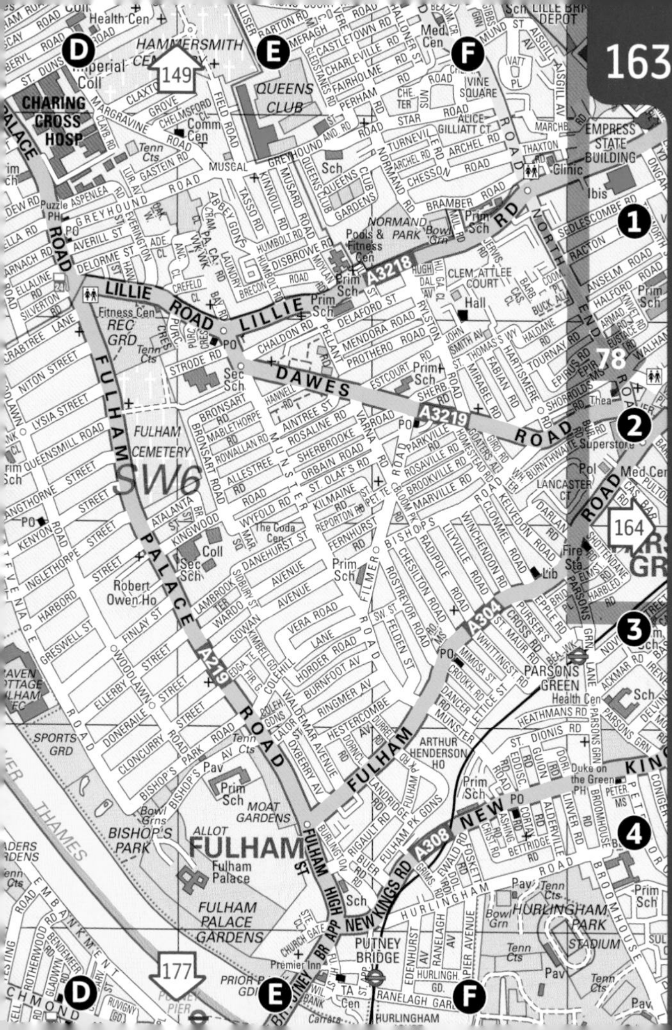
D
E
F
D
E
F
1
2
3
4
149
164
177
78
HAMMERSMITH CEMETERY
Imperial Coll
Health Cen
CHARING CROSS HOSP
QUEENS CLUB
EMPRESS STATE BUILDING
Ibis
Clinic
LILLIE ROAD
A3218
DAWES ROAD
A3219
FULHAM PALACE ROAD
A219
FULHAM ROAD
A304
NEW KINGS RD
A308
NORTH END ROAD
FULHAM CEMETERY
SW6
Fitness Cen
REC GRD
Pools & Fitness Cen
NORMAND PARK
CLEM ATTLEE COURT
Hall
Superstore
LANCASTER CT
Fire Sta
Lib
PARSONS GREEN
Health Cen
ARTHUR HENDERSON HO
Duke on the Green PH
Robert Owen Ho
The Coda Cen
Coll
Sec Sch
Prim Sch
SPORTS GRD
BISHOP'S PARK
MOAT GARDENS
ALLOT
FULHAM
Fulham Palace
FULHAM PALACE GARDENS
HURLINGHAM PARK
STADIUM
PUTNEY BRIDGE
Premier Inn
HURLINGHAM
THAMES
EMBANKMENT
FULHAM HIGH ST
NEW KINGS RD
GREYHOUND ROAD
MARGRAVINE ROAD
MUNSTER ROAD
BISHOP'S ROAD
HURLINGHAM ROAD
PARSONS GRN LANE
VARNA ROAD
ROSTREVOR ROAD
HESTERCOMBE AV
WALDEMAR AVENUE
STEVENAGE ROAD
INGLETHORPE STREET
QUEENSMILL ROAD
LYSIA STREET
NITON STREET
CRABTREE LANE
HARBORD STREET
GRESWELL ST
WOODLAWN STREET
ELLERBY STREET
DONERAILE STREET
CLONCURRY STREET

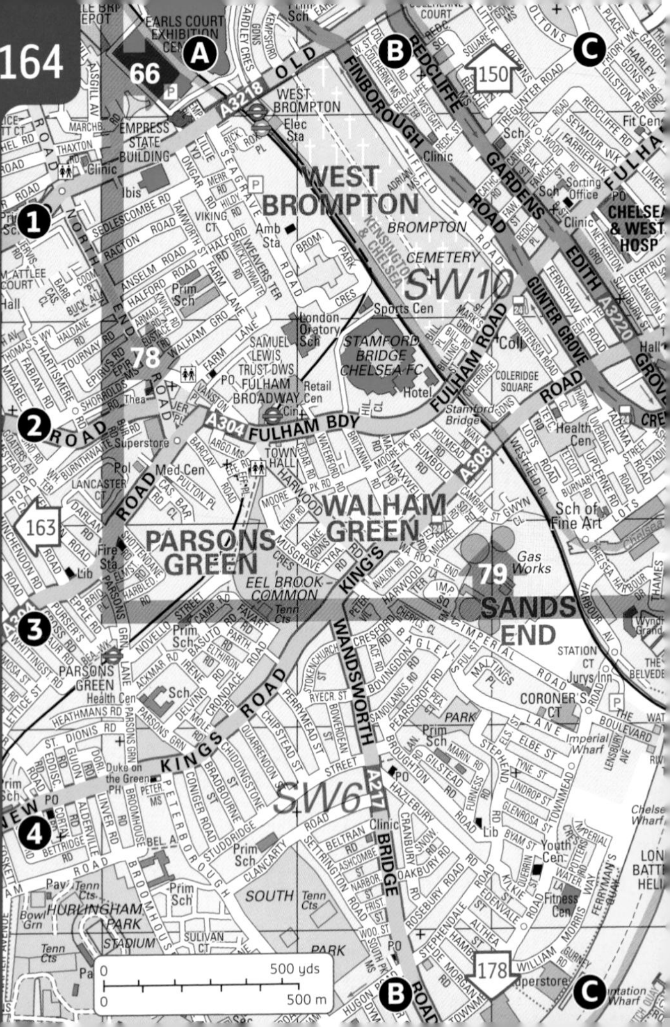
A
B
C
1
2
3
4
66
78
79
150
163
178
EARLS COURT EXHIBITION CEN
EMPRESS STATE BUILDING
WEST BROMPTON
WEST BROMPTON
BROMPTON CEMETERY
KENSINGTON & CHELSEA
SW10
STAMFORD BRIDGE CHELSEA FC
FULHAM BROADWAY
WALHAM GREEN
PARSONS GREEN
EEL BROOK COMMON
SANDS END
Gas Works
SW6
SOUTH PARK
HURLINGHAM PARK
CHELSEA & WEST HOSP
CORONER'S CT
Imperial Wharf
Chelsea Wharf
A3218
A304
A308
A3220
A217
OLD BROMPTON ROAD
FINBOROUGH ROAD
REDCLIFFE GARDENS
FULHAM ROAD
FULHAM BDY
NORTH END ROAD
KINGS ROAD
NEW KINGS ROAD
WANDSWORTH BRIDGE ROAD
GUNTER GROVE
EDITH GROVE
IMPERIAL ROAD
TOWNMEAD ROAD
0 500 yds
0 500 m

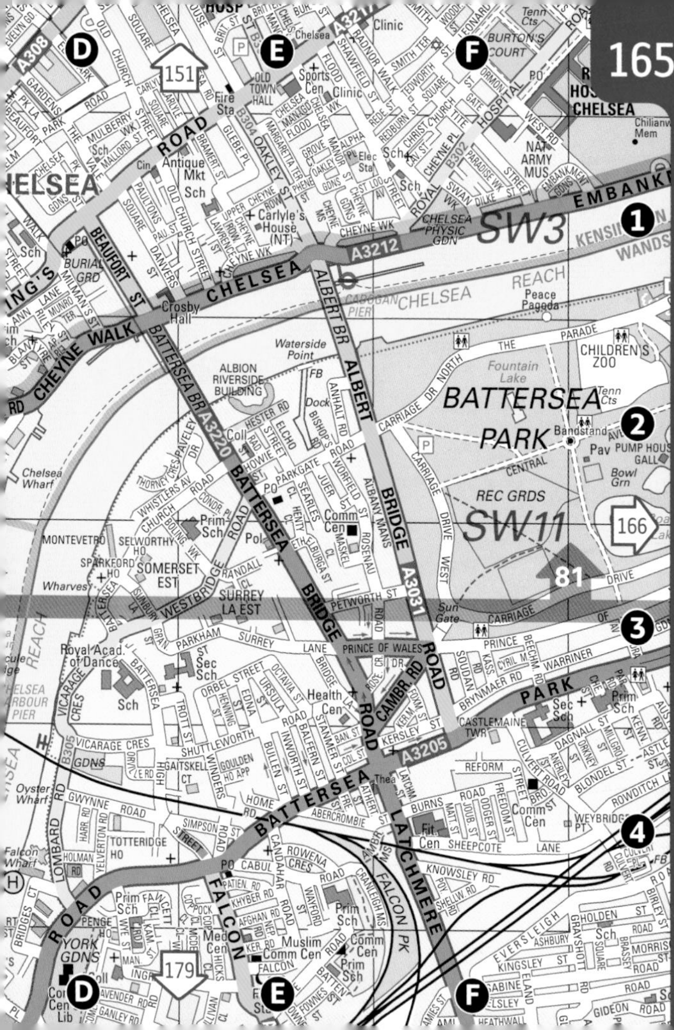
D
E
F
151
HOSP
Clinic
Chelsea
Sports Cen
Clinic
OLD TOWN HALL
Fire Sta
BURTON'S COURT
Tenn Cts
ROYAL HOSPITAL CHELSEA
Chilianwala Mem
NAT ARMY MUS
CHELSEA
Antique Mkt
Sch
Cin
Elec Sta
Carlyle's House (NT)
CHELSEA PHYSIC GDN
SW3
EMBANKMENT
KENSINGTON
WANDSWORTH
1
KING'S ROAD
ROAD
OAKLEY ST
BEAUFORT ST
OLD CHURCH STREET
CHEYNE WK
CHEYNE WALK
CHELSEA
A3212
A308
B304
B302
BURIAL GRD
PO
Crosby Hall
CADOGAN PIER
CHELSEA REACH
Peace Pagoda
Waterside Point
FB
Dock
ALBION RIVERSIDE BUILDING
ALBERT BR
ALBERT BRIDGE ROAD
BATTERSEA BR
A3220
THE PARADE
CHILDREN'S ZOO
Fountain Lake
BATTERSEA PARK
Tenn Cts
Bandstand
2
Pav
PUMP HOUSE GALL
Bowl Grn
CARRIAGE DR NORTH
CENTRAL
REC GRDS
SW11
166
81
CARRIAGE DRIVE WEST
Sun Gate
CARRIAGE DRIVE
3
Chelsea Wharf
Coll
Prim Sch
Pol
Comm Cen
PO
MONTEVETRO
SELWORTHY HO
SPARKFORD HO
SOMERSET EST
Wharves
SURREY LA EST
WESTBRIDGE RD
BATTERSEA BRIDGE ROAD
A3031
PETWORTH ST
PRINCE OF WALES DR
SURREY LANE
PARKHAM ST
Royal Acad. of Dance
St Sec Sch
Sch
CHELSEA HARBOUR PIER
VICARAGE CRES
Health Cen
CAMBR. RD
PRINCE OF WALES DRIVE
WARRINER GDNS
PARK
Sec Sch
Prim Sch
CASTLEMAINE TWR
KERSLEY ST
A3205
REFORM ST
CULVERT ROAD
DAGNALL ST
BLONDEL ST
ROWDITCH LA
SHUTTLEWORTH RD
GAITSKELL CT
B305
Oyster Wharf
GWYNNE ROAD
LOMBARD RD
TOTTERIDGE HO
BATTERSEA HIGH ST
BATTERSEA
Thea
LATCHMERE ROAD
BURNS RD
Fit. Cen
SHEEPCOTE LANE
Comm Cen
WEYBRIDGE PT
4
Falcon Wharf
HOLMAN RD
ROWENA CRES
CABUL RD
KNOWSLEY RD
FALCON RD
FALCON PK
Prim Sch
Med Cen
Muslim Comm Cen
Comm Cen
Prim Sch
YORK GDNS
ROAD
PENGE HO
179
Coll
Comm Cen
Lib
HOLDEN ST
Sch
EVERSLEIGH
KINGSLEY ST
GIDEON ROAD
HEATHWALL

A
B
C
1
2
3
4
ROYAL HOSPITAL CHELSEA
RANELAGH GARDENS
MUS
Chilianwalla Mem
NAT ARMY MUS
CHELSEA BRIDGE RD
LISTER HOSPITAL
Trans. Pol
Chimney
Pumping Sta
152
CHURCHILL GDNS
Sch
CHURCHILL GARDENS ROAD
GROSVENOR
SW1
EMBANKMENT
KENSINGTON & CHELSEA
WANDSWORTH
RIVER THAMES
CHELSEA BR
GROSVENOR BR
Battersea Wharf
FB
Jetty
Nine Elms Pier
REACH
Peace Pagoda
CARRIAGE DRIVE NORTH
Tenn Cts
HOWARD BUILDING
WARWICK BUILDING
Battersea Power Station (Disused)
Solid Waste Transfer Station
Tideway Ind Est
CRINGLE STREET
KIRTLING ST
A3205
THE PARADE
CHILDREN'S ZOO
Pav
Millennium Arena
CARRIAGE DRIVE EAST
Fountain Lake
BATTERSEA PARK
QUEENSTOWN ROAD
SOPW. WAY
Marco Polo Ho
NINE ELMS
Battersea Dogs & Cats Home
Gas Works
TOLL
Bandstand
AVENUE
PUMP HOUSE GALL
CENTRAL
Bowl Grn
SW11
REC GRDS
165
Boating Lake
SOUTH DRIVE
BATTERSEA PARK
PRI. OF WALES DR
BATTERSEA PARK ROAD
SLEAFORD ST
THESSALY
SAVONA EST
STEWART'S RD
ASCALON ST
Comm Room
Prim Sch
CORUN. RD
PATMORE
83
81
DRIVE
PRINCE OF WALES ROAD
LURLINE GDNS
MACDUFF RD
ALEXANDRA AV
A3216
Sch
LOCKINGTON RD
HAVELOCK TER
INGATE PL
PATMORE EST
QUEENSTOWN ROAD (BATTERSEA)
STRASBURG ROAD
Lib
WARRINER GDNS
CHARLOTTE DESPARD AV
FRANCIS CHICHESTER WY
BATTERSEA
TRAIN DEPOT
SW8
PARK
Sec Sch
CASTLEMAINE TWR
DAGNALL ST
BLONDEL ST
ASTLE ST
LONGHEDGE ST
ROWDITCH LA
BUS GARAGE
HEATHBROOK PARK
Tenn Cts
Clubho
PORTSLADE RD
PENSBURY PL
PENSBURY STREET
REFORM ST
CULVERT ROAD
Comm Cen
WEYBRIDGE PT
LANE
BROUGHTON ROAD
PRAIRIE ST
B224
SILVERTHORNE ROAD
DICKENS ST
ST. PHILIP SQ
THACKERAY RD
BEWICK ST
ST. PHILIP ST
TENNYSON ST
CULVERT PL
FB
Prim Sch
WYCLIFFE RD
CAROLINE PL
STANLEY GROVE
INGELOW RD
QUEENSTOWN ROAD
HEATH RD
ROBERTSON ST
Hall
ROAD
WESTBURY STREET
PO
WANDSWORTH ROAD
IVELEY ROAD
BRAYBURNE AV
NETHERFORD RD
LARKHALL
TURRET GRO
CUBITT TERRACE
EVERSLEIGH ROAD
HOLDEN ST
ASHBURY
Sch
MORRISON
DUNSTON RD
TYNEHAM RD
BIRLEY ST
KINGSLEY
SABINE
ELSLEY
0 500 yds
0 500 m
HEATHER CL
TESSA SAND
180
Fitness Cen

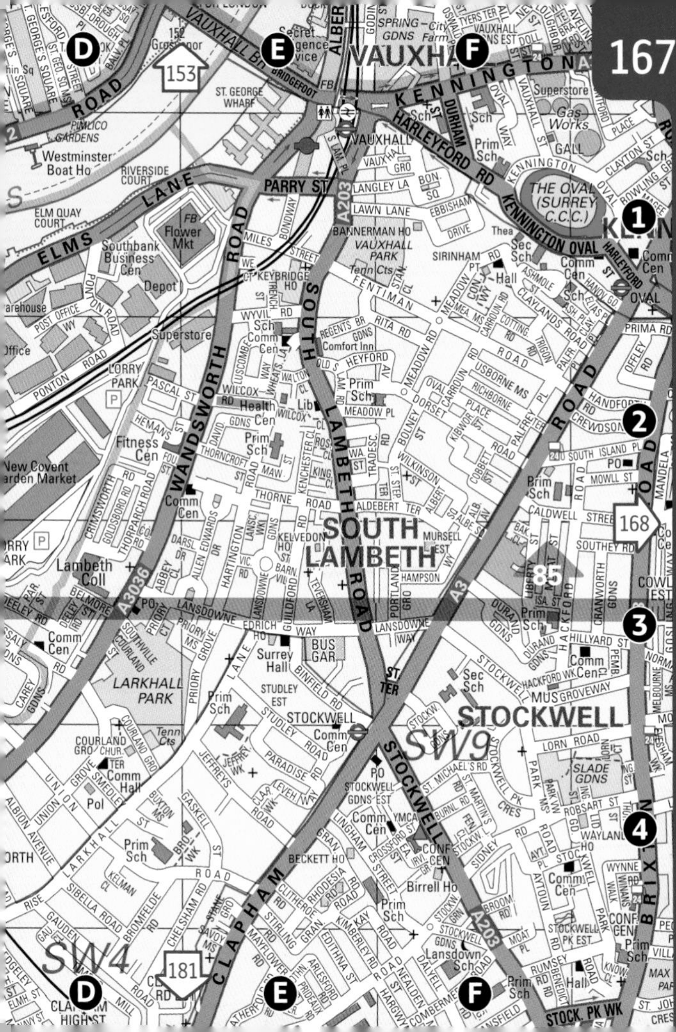
D
E
F
VAUXHALL
153
VAUXHALL BR
Secret Intelligence Service
ST. GEORGE WHARF
KENNINGTON
HARLEYFORD RD
Superstore
Gas Works
PIMLICO GARDENS
Westminster Boat Ho
RIVERSIDE COURT
PARRY ST
ELM QUAY COURT
LANE
ELMS
FB Flower Mkt
Southbank Business Cen
Depot
A203
LANGLEY LA
LAWN LANE
BANNERMAN HO
VAUXHALL PARK
Tenn Cts
THE OVAL (SURREY C.C.C.)
KENNINGTON OVAL
OVAL
1
FENTIMAN
SOUTH LAMBETH ROAD
WANDSWORTH ROAD
PONTON ROAD
POST OFFICE WY
Superstore
LORRY PARK
Comfort Inn
HEYFORD AV
Prim Sch
MEADOW PL
Health Cen
Lib
RITA RD
MEADOW RD
DORSET ROAD
USBORNE MS
RICHBORNE
CLAYLANDS ROAD
2
HANDFORTH RD
CREWDSON
SOUTH ISLAND PL
MOWLL ST
PO
CALDWELL STREET
168
SOUTHEY RD
Fitness Cen
New Covent Garden Market
Comm Cen
THORNE ROAD
ALDEBERT TER
SOUTH LAMBETH
KELVEDON HO
HAMPSON
A3
85
Lambeth Coll
A3036
LANSDOWNE
EDRICH WAY
LANSDOWNE WAY
3
HILLYARD ST
HACKFORD
Prim Sch
Surrey Hall
BUS GAR
LARKHALL PARK
STUDLEY EST
STOCKWELL
Comm Cen
Sec Sch
STOCKWELL
SW9
LORN ROAD
SLADE GDNS
GROVEWAY
STOCKWELL PK CRES
ROBSART ST
WAYLAND HO
4
Prim Sch
PARADISE RD
Comm Hall
Pol
LARKHALL
UNION GROVE
ALBION AVENUE
Prim Sch
STOCKWELL GDNS EST
Comm Cen
YMCA
CONF CEN
Birrell Ho
BECKETT HO
RHODESIA RD
KIMBERLEY RD
CLAPHAM ROAD
STOCKWELL PK EST
Prim Sch
Lansdown Sch
CONF CEN
Hall
BRIXTON ROAD
SW4
181
CLAPHAM HIGH ST
STOCK. PK WK

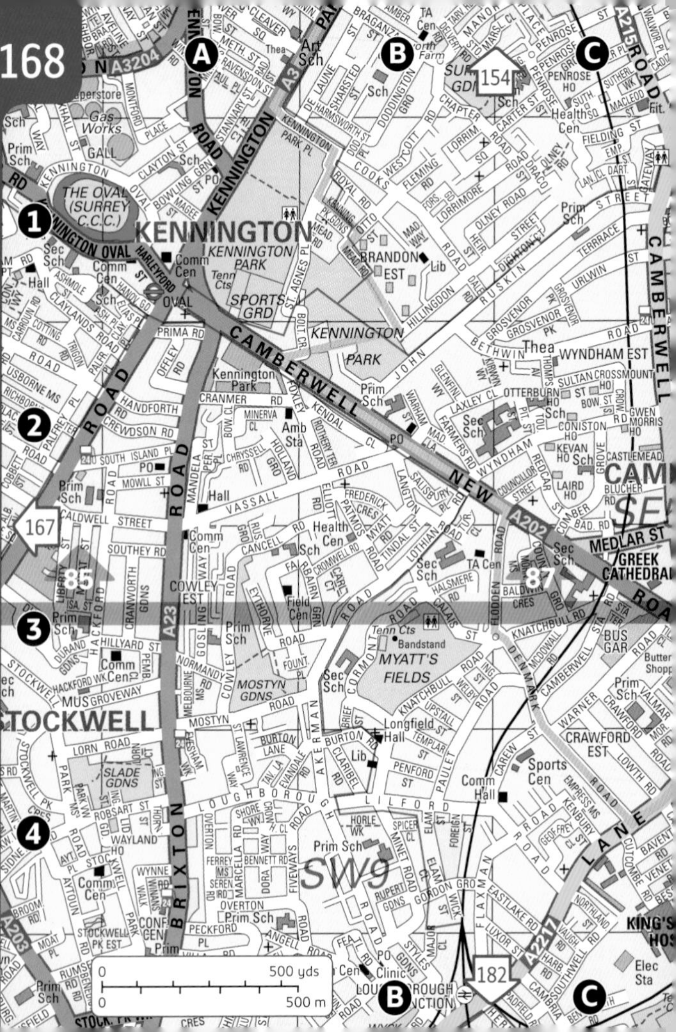
A
B
C
1
2
3
4
154
167
182
85
87
KENNINGTON
THE OVAL (SURREY C.C.C.)
KENNINGTON PARK
SPORTS GRD
KENNINGTON OVAL
OVAL
KENNINGTON ROAD
KENNINGTON PARK PL
CAMBERWELL NEW ROAD
A202
A23
A3
A3204
A203
A215
A2217
BRIXTON ROAD
STOCKWELL
SW9
MYATT'S FIELDS
MOSTYN GDNS
SLADE GDNS
BRANDON EST
COWLEY EST
WYNDHAM EST
CRAWFORD EST
STOCKWELL PK EST
LOUGHBOROUGH JUNCTION
GREEK CATHEDRAL
KING'S HOS
Gas Works
Sports Cen
Longfield Hall
Field Cen
Bandstand
VASSALL ROAD
LOUGHBOROUGH ROAD
LILFORD ROAD
DENMARK ROAD
CAMBERWELL ROAD
COLDHARBOUR LANE
MEDLAR ST
CALDWELL STREET
SOUTHEY RD
HANDFORTH RD
CREWDSON RD
CLAYLANDS ROAD
USBORNE MS
CLAYTON ST
HARLEYFORD ST
CRANMER RD
MINERVA CL
FOXLEY RD
KENDAL CL
JOHN RUSKIN ST
HILLINGDON ST
GROSVENOR PK
BETHWIN ROAD
OTTERBURN HO
WYNDHAM RD
CONISTON HO
KEVAN HO
LAIRD HO
CASTLEMEAD
BLUCHER RD
KNATCHBULL RD
FLODDEN ROAD
CALAIS ST
LOTHIAN RD
LANGTON RD
COWLEY ROAD
MOSTYN ROAD
CORMONT ROAD
LORN ROAD
STOCKWELL PARK RD
ROBSART ST
WAYLAND HO
OVERTON RD
MINET ROAD
CRAWFORD RD
WARNER RD
LOWTH RD
HOLLAND GRO
PATMOS RD
CANCELL RD
EYTHORNE RD
BURTON RD
AKERMAN RD
PENFORD ST
PAULET RD
ELAM ST
FLAXMAN RD
EASTLAKE RD
LUXOR ST
HORLE WK
SPICER CL
0 500 yds
0 500 m

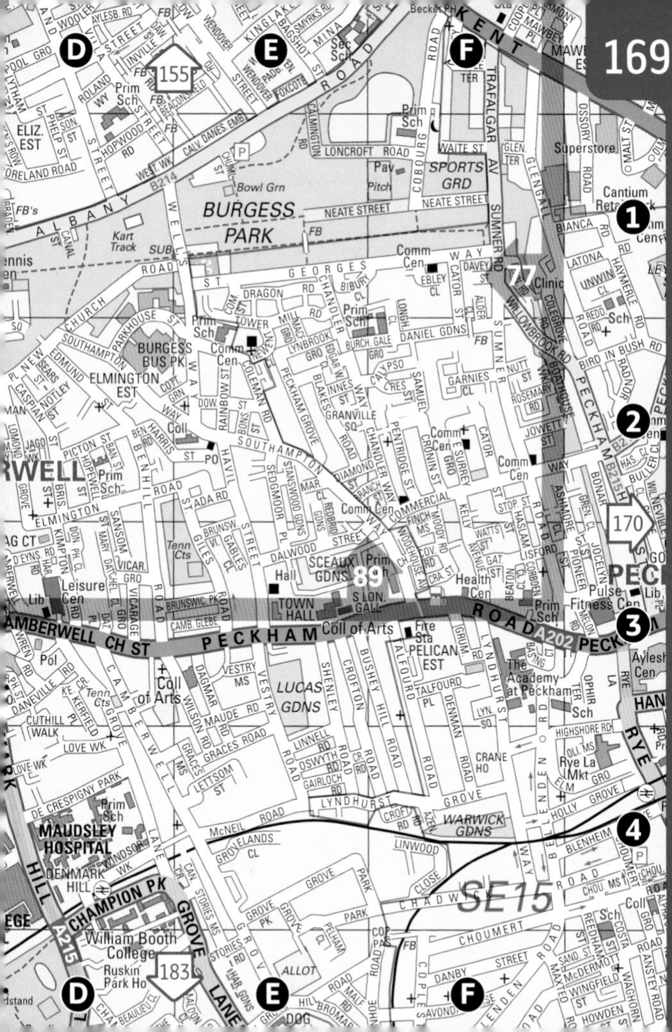

D
E
F
155
BURGESS PARK
SPORTS GRD
Bowl Grn
Kart Track
Pav
Pitch
ALBANY ROAD
B214
WELLS WAY
NEATE STREET
LONCROFT ROAD
CALMINGTON RD
WAITE ST
TRAFALGAR AV
COBOURG ROAD
KENT
GLENGALL
OSSORY ROAD
Superstore
Cantium Retail Park
1
2
3
4
BIANCA RD
LATONA RD
UNWIN CL
HAYMERLE RD
Sch
BIRD IN BUSH RD
RADNOR
77
Clinic
WILLOWBROOK RD
COLEGROVE RD
BOATHOUSE WK
SUMNER RD
SUMNER
GEORGES WAY
Comm Cen
EBLEY CL
CATOR ST
DAVEY ST
ALDER
CHURCH ST
DRAGON RD
CHANDLER
BIBURY CL
Prim Sch
TOWER MILL RD
LONGH. CL
DANIEL GDNS
FB
PARKHOUSE ST
BURGESS BUS PK
SOUTHAMPTON WAY
Prim Sch
Comm Cen
COLEMAN RD
LYNBROOK GRO
BURCH. GALE GRO
CALYPSO CRES
SAMUEL
GARNIES CL
NUTT ST
ROSEMARY RD
ELMINGTON EST
EDMUND
SEARS ST
NOTLEY ST
CASPIAN ST
Coll
PECKHAM GROVE
BLAKES RD
INNES ST
GRANVILLE SQ
CHANDLER WAY
PENTRIDGE ST
CRONIN ST
Comm Cen
E SURREY GRO
CATOR
JOWETT ST
Comm Cen
WAY
PICTON ST
JAGO WK
BEN. HARRIS RD
PO
RAINBOW ST
SOUTHAMPTON
STANSWOOD GDNS
SEDGMOOR PL
DIAMOND ST
KELLY AVENUE
COMMERCIAL
FINCH MS
MOODY RD
STOP. ST
HASLAM ST
ASHMORE
BONAR
PECKHAM
B215
170
CAMBERWELL
Prim Sch
ELMINGTON
BENHILL ROAD
HAVIL ST
ADA RD
MAR. CL
REDBRID GDNS
Comm Cen
WATTS ST
GAT. ST
LISFORD ST
PIONEER ST
JOCELYN
Tenn Cts
GILES
BRUNSW. VI.
GABLES CL
STREET
DALWOOD
SCEAUX GDNS
Prim Sch
89
WODEHOUSE AV
COV. RD
CRA. ST
Health Cen
BEATON CL
CORBDEN CL
Prim Sch
Pulse Fitness Cen
PECKHAM
Lib
Leisure Cen
Lib
VICARAGE GRO
VICAR.
SANSOM ST
MARY DATCHEL
DON. PH. CL
KIMPTON
D'EYNS. RD
Hall
TOWN HALL
S LON. GALL
BRUNSWIC. PK
CAMB. GLEBE
CAMBERWELL CH ST
PECKHAM
ROAD
A202
Coll of Arts
Fire Sta
PELICAN EST
IGRUM. RD
LYNDHURST
The Academy at Peckham
Sch
OPHIR TER
Aylesham Cen
RYE LA
HANOVER
Pol
WREN RD
DANEVILLE RD
KE. CR.
KERFIELD
Tenn Cts
CAMBERWELL GROVE
Coll of Arts
DAGMAR
WILSON RD
VESTRY MS
VESTRY
LUCAS GDNS
SHENLEY
CROFTON
BUSHEY HILL ROAD
TALFOURD
TALFOURD PL
DENMAN ROAD
LYN. SQ
CUTHILL WALK
LOVE WK
MAUDE RD
GRACES ROAD
GRACES MS
LETTSOM ST
LINNELL RD
OSWYTH RD
GAIRLOCH RD
CR. RD
CRANE HO
HIGHSHORE RD
OLI. MS
Rye La Mkt
ELM GRO
RYE
DE CRESPIGNY PARK
Prim Sch
MAUDSLEY HOSPITAL
WINDSOR WK
DENMARK HILL
CAMBERWELL
McNEIL ROAD
GROVELANDS CL
LYNDHURST GROVE
CROFT RD
AZENBY
WARWICK GDNS
BELLENDEN RD
HOLLY GROVE
BLENHEIM
LINWOOD CLOSE
GROVE PARK
CHAMPION PK
A215
GROVE
STORIES MS
GROVE PK
PELHAM CL
CHADWICK
SE15
CHOUMERT
Coll
CHOU. MS
William Booth College
Ruskin Park Ho
183
STORIES RD
GROVE
ALLOT
FB
COPLESTON
DANBY STREET
Sch
REEDHAM ST
COSTA ST
McDERMOTT
WINGFIELD ST
MAXTED RD
HOWDEN
ANSTEY ROAD
WAGHORN
BEAULIEU CL
MALF RD
DOG

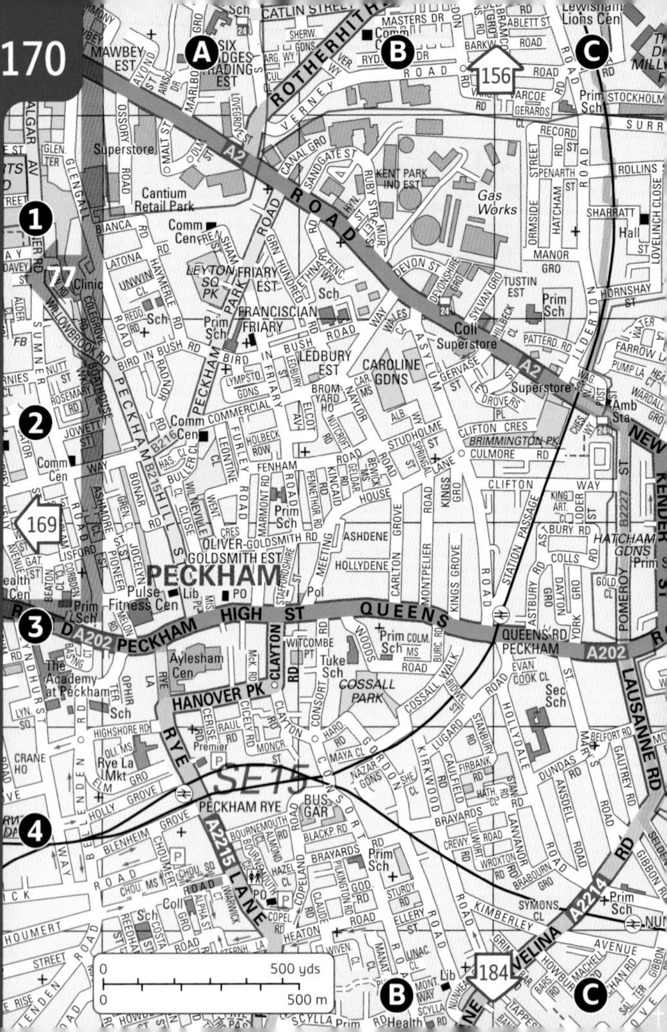
A
B
C
1
2
3
4
156
169
184
77
SIX BRIDGES TRADING EST
MAWBEY EST
CATLIN STREET
MASTERS DR
ABLETT ST
Lewisham Lions Cen
ROTHERHITHE NEW ROAD
VERNEY ROAD
A2
OLD KENT ROAD
Superstore
Cantium Retail Park
Comm Cen
KENT PARK IND EST
Gas Works
CANAL GRO
SANDGATE ST
RUBY STREET
ORMSIDE STREET
HATCHAM ROAD
STOCKHOLM
SURREY
RECORD ST
SPENARTH
ROLLINS ST
SHARRATT ST
Hall
LOVELINCH CLOSE
MANOR GRO
TUSTIN EST
HORNSHAY ST
Prim Sch
LEYTON SQ PK
FRIARY EST
FRANCISCIAN FRIARY
PECKHAM PARK ROAD
GRN HUNDRED RD
DEVON ST
DEVONSHIRE GRO
SYLVAN GRO
HILLBECK CL
Coll
PATTERD. RD
ILDERTON ROAD
FARROW LA
PUMP LA
WARDALL GRO
Amb Sta
NEW CROSS ROAD
BIANCA RD
LATONA RD
UNWIN CL
HAYMERLE RD
Clinic
WILLOWBROOK RD
COLEGROVE RD
BOATHOUSE WK
PECKHAM HILL ST
BIRD IN BUSH RD
RADNOR
LEDBURY EST
LYMPSTO. GDNS
BROMYARD HO
CAROLINE GDNS
ASYLUM ROAD
GERVASE ST
DROVERS PL
SUMNER RD
ROSEMARY RD
JOWETT ST
COMMERCIAL WAY
B216
B215
FURLEY ROAD
HOLBECK ROW
NUTCROFT RD
STUDHOLME ST
CLIFTON CRES
BRIMMINGTON PK
CULMORE RD
CLIFTON WAY
BONAR RD
ASHMORE
FENHAM RD
MARMONT RD
PENNETHORNE RD
KINCAID RD
HOUSE
CARLTON GROVE
MONTPELIER ROAD
KINGS GROVE
STATION PASSAGE
KING ART. CL
LODER ST
BURY RD
B2227
HATCHAM GDNS
POMEROY ST
OLIVER-GOLDSMITH EST
GOLDSMITH RD
ASHDENE
HOLLYDENE
MEETING
PECKHAM
Pulse Fitness Cen
Lib
PO
Pol
LISFORD ST
JOCELYN ST
PIONEER ST
BEATON CL
ASTBURY RD
DAYTON GRO
COLLS RD
GOLD. CL
Prim Sch
PECKHAM HIGH ST
QUEENS RD
A202
QUEENS RD PECKHAM
The Academy at Peckham
Aylesham Cen
CLAYTON RD
WITCOMBE PT
Tuke Sch
COSSALL PARK
COSSALL WALK
WOODS ROAD
EVAN COOK CL
Sec Sch
LAUSANNE RD
HANOVER PK
RYE LANE
HIGHSHORE RD
Rye La Mkt
Premier
SE15
CONSORT RD
GORDON RD
HOLLYDALE
KIRKWOOD RD
LUGARD RD
DUNDAS RD
ST MARY'S ROAD
GAUTREY RD
BELFORT RD
HOLLY GROVE
PECKHAM RYE
A2215
BUS GAR
BLENHEIM GROVE
CHOUMERT ROAD
BOURNEMOUTH RD
BLACKP. RD
BRAYARDS RD
A2214
EVELINA RD
KIMBERLEY AVENUE
SYMONS CL
Coll
Sch
HEATON RD
ELLERY ST
500 yds
0
500 m
Lib
Health
SCYLLA RD

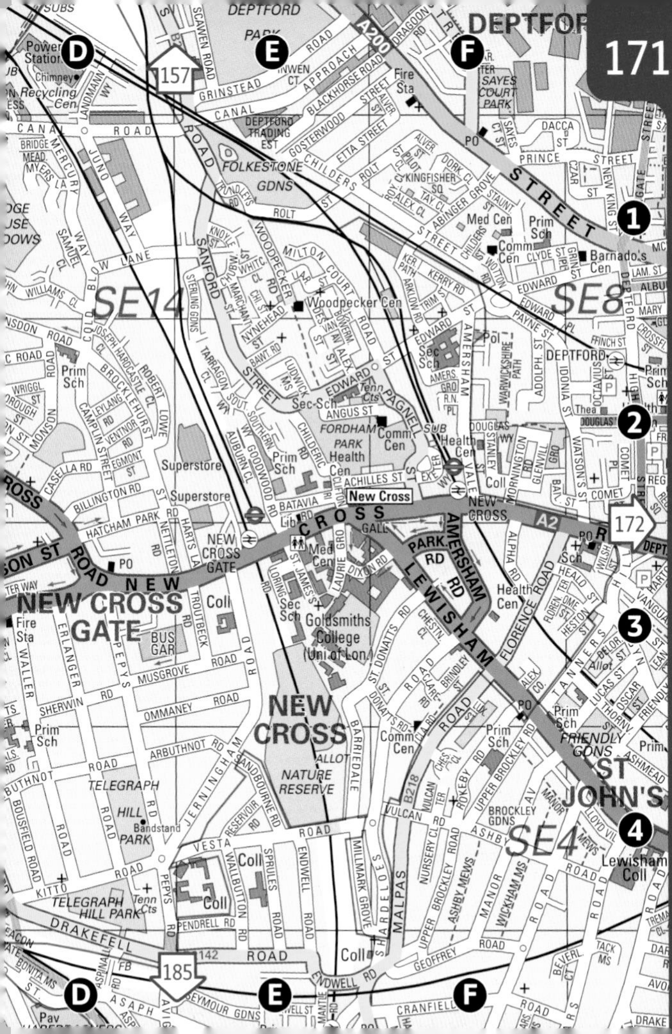
DEPTFORD PARK
DEPTFORD
Power Station
Chimney
Recycling Cen
157
GRINSTEAD ROAD
CANAL APPROACH
BLACKHORSE ROAD
A200
DRAGOON RD
Fire Sta
SAYES COURT PARK
CANAL ROAD
DEPTFORD TRADING EST
GOSTERWOOD STREET
ETTA STREET
DACCA ST
PRINCE STREET
NEW KING ST
FOLKESTONE GDNS
CHILDERS ST
KINGFISHER SQ
ABINGER GROVE
STREET
Med Cen
Prim Sch
Comm Cen
Barnado's Cen
CLYDE ST
ROLT ST
MERCURY WAY
JUNO WAY
SAMUEL CL
BLOW LANE
WOODPECKER RD
MILTON COURT ROAD
Woodpecker Cen
KERRY RD
ARKLOW RD
EDWARD ST
EDWARD PL
SE14
SE8
PAYNE ST
FINCH ST
DEPTFORD
Prim Sch
SANFORD ST
STERLING GDNS
NYNEHEAD ST
AMERSHAM VALE
Pol
WARWICKSHIRE PATH
ADOLPH ST
IDONIA ST
OCTAVIUS ST
Sec Sch
Tenn Cts
HIGH
Prim Sch
ROBERT LOWE CL
BROCKLEHURST
CAMPLIN STREET
MONSON ROAD
TARRAGON CL
PAGNELL ST
ANGUS ST
FORDHAM PARK
Comm Cen
Health Cen
DOUGLAS WY
STANLEY ST
MORNINGTON RD
GLENVILLE GRO
WATSON'S ST
COMET PL
Thea
Superstore
Superstore
Prim Sch
Health Cen
ACHILLES ST
New Cross
COMET ST
Coll
CASELLA RD
BILLINGTON RD
HATCHAM PARK RD
NETTLETON RD
HARTS LA
BATAVIA RD
Lib
NEW CROSS
A2
172
PO
NEW CROSS GATE
CROSS
PARK RD
AMERSHAM RD
LEWISHAM
Health Cen
FLORENCE ROAD
ALPHA RD
HEALD ST
ROAD NEW
NEW CROSS GATE
Fire Sta
Med Cen
LAURIE GRO
DIXON RD
Sec Sch
Goldsmiths College (Uni of Lon)
ST DONATTS RD
TANNERS HILL
LUCAS ST
OSCAR ST
BUS GAR
Coll
TROUTBECK RD
ERLANGER RD
PEPYS RD
MUSGROVE ROAD
SHERWIN RD
OMMANEY ROAD
WALLER RD
Prim Sch
NEW CROSS
ALLOT
NATURE RESERVE
BARRIEDALE
Comm Cen
Prim Sch
UPPER BROCKLEY RD
FRIENDLY GDNS
ST JOHN'S
ARBUTHNOT RD
TELEGRAPH HILL
Bandstand
PARK
JERNINGHAM ROAD
SANDBOURNE RD
RESERVOIR RD
VULCAN RD
B218
BROCKLEY GDNS
ASHBY RD
SE4
Lewisham Coll
BOUSFIELD ROAD
VESTA ROAD
Coll
WALLBUTTON RD
SPRULES ROAD
ENDWELL ROAD
MILLMARK GROVE
SHARDELOES RD
MALPAS RD
NURSERY CL
UPPER BROCKLEY ROAD
ASHBY MEWS
MANOR AV
WICKHAM MS
KITTO ROAD
TELEGRAPH HILL PARK
Tenn Cts
Coll
PENDRELL RD
DRAKEFELL ROAD
185
A2142
ROAD
Coll
ENDWELL RD
GEOFFREY ROAD
CRANFIELD ROAD
SEYMOUR GDNS
ASAPH
Pav
D
E
F
1
2
3
4

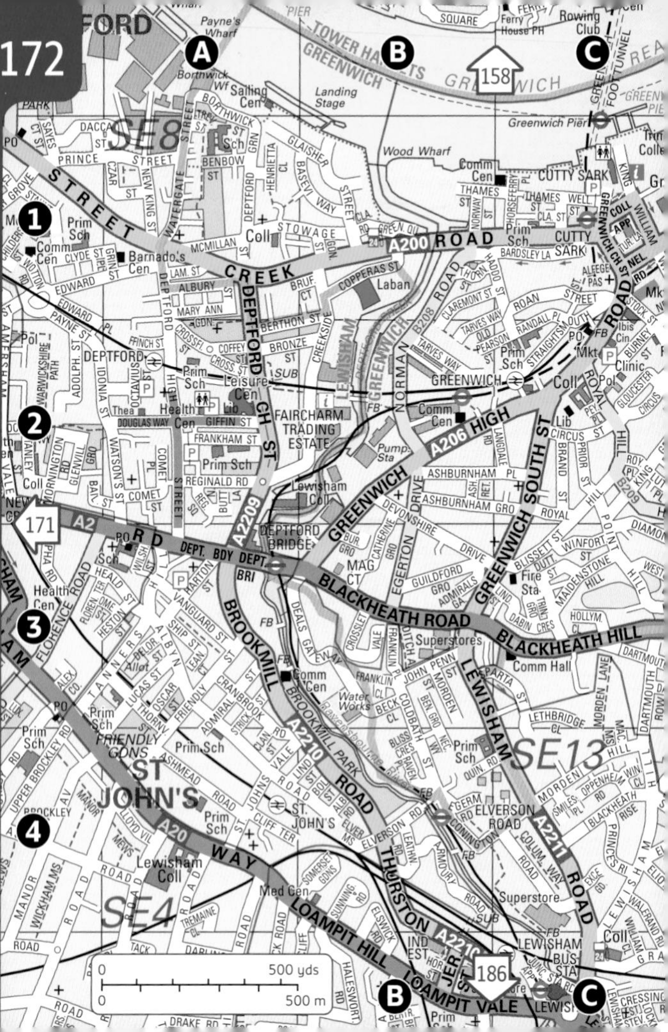
A
B
C
1
2
3
4
158
171
186
SE8
SE13
SE4
TOWER HAMLETS
GREENWICH
Payne's Wharf
Borthwick Wf
Sailing Cen
Landing Stage
Greenwich Pier
Wood Wharf
Ferry House PH
Rowing Club
GREENWICH FOOT TUNNEL
CUTTY SARK
THAMES ST
PRINCE STREET
CREEK ROAD
A200 ROAD
DEPTFORD CH ST
DEPTFORD HIGH STREET
WATERGATE STREET
NEW KING ST
BENBOW ST
GLAISHER ST
STOWAGE
MCMILLAN ST
Barnado's Cen
EDWARD ST
ALBURY ST
MARY ANN GDN
COPPERAS ST
Laban
CREEKSIDE
BERTHON ST
BRONZE ST
DEPTFORD
Leisure Cen
FAIRCHARM TRADING ESTATE
GREENWICH
A206 HIGH
NORMAN ROAD
B208
GREENWICH SOUTH ST
ROYAL HILL
CIRCUS ST
CROOMS HILL
DOUGLAS WAY
GIFFIN ST
FRANKHAM ST
REGINALD RD
COMET ST
Lewisham Coll
A2209
DEPTFORD BRIDGE
A2 RD
BLACKHEATH ROAD
BLACKHEATH HILL
DEVONSHIRE DRIVE
ASHBURNHAM PL
ASHBURNHAM GRO
EGERTON DRIVE
GUILDFORD GRO
Superstores
Comm Hall
BROOKMILL ROAD
A2210
BROOKMILL PARK
Ravensbourne River
Water Works
LEWISHAM ROAD
A2211
LETHBRIDGE CL
MORDEN HILL
ELVERSON ROAD
ST JOHN'S
FRIENDLY GDNS
ST JOHN'S VALE
A20 WAY
LOAMPIT HILL
LOAMPIT VALE
THURSTON
Med Cen
Lewisham Coll
LEWISHAM
BUS STA
Superstore
BROCKLEY
UPPER BROCKLEY RD
FLORENCE ROAD
TANNERS HILL
LUCAS ST
VANGUARD ST
CRANBROOK RD
Health Cen
Prim Sch
0 500 yds
0 500 m

D
E
F
159
187
1
2
3
4
GREENWICH
SE10
GREENWICH PARK
BLACKHEATH
SE3
EAST GREENWICH PLEASAUNCE
Power Sta
Trafalgar Rowing Cen
Prim Sch
Arches Leisure Cen
MAZE HILL
QUEEN'S HOUSE
NATIONAL MARITIME MUSEUM
ROYAL OBSERVATORY GREENWICH (Flamsteed House)
One Tree Hill
The Gardens
Bandstand
THE WILDERNESS (DEER PARK)
War Mem
Mem
Croom's Hill Gate
COV RES
Tenn Cts
RANGER'S HOUSE
Blackheath Gate
Bowl Grn
Health Cen
Sec Sch
High Sch
Comm Cen
Clarendon Hotel
Lib
PO
Coll
Sch
TRAFALGAR RD
A206
A2
B210
B212
SHOOTERS HILL ROAD
CHARLTON WAY
MAZE HILL
VANBRUGH HILL
VANBRUGH PARK
WESTCOMBE PARK ROAD
HUMBER ROAD
CROSS AVENUE
GREAT CROSS AV
BLACKHEATH AVENUE
BOWER AVENUE
LOVERS WALK
GENERAL WOLFE RD
CHESTERFIELD WK
PRINCE CHARLES RD
PRINCE OF WALES RD
ST. GERMAN'S PLACE
LONG POND ROAD
GOFFERS RD
HARE & BILLET ROAD
MOUNTS POND RD
TALBOT PL
DUKE HUMPHREY ROAD
TRANQUIL VALE
ROYAL PAR
MONTPELIER VALE
MONTP. ROW
PARAGON PL
SOUTH ROW
THE PARAGON
POND ROAD
FULTHORP RD
WEMYSS RD
BLACKHEATH GRO
BIRCHM. ROW
BLACKHEATH VILLAGE
BENNETT PK
CRESSWELL PK
ROCQUE LA
CORNER
BERNERSMEDE
BLACKHEATH PK
ELIOT PLACE
ELIOT VALE
HEATHFIELD GDNS
BAIZDON ROAD
HEATH LANE
ST. JOSEPH'S VALE
HURREN CLOSE
COLLINS ST
LAWN TERRACE
SELWYN CT
PAGODA GDNS
ABERDEEN TER
ORCHARD DRIVE
LANGTON WAY
ST. JOHN'S PARK
STRATHEDEN RD
HEATHWAY
MARY LAWRENSON PL
PARKSIDE
COMBE MS
FERNDALE CT
BEACONSFIELD ROAD
MYCENAE ROAD
HARDY ROAD
COLERAINE ROAD
FOYLE ROAD
ULUNDI ROAD
HIGHMORE RD
DINSDALE RD
PEACHUM RD
ANNANDALE RD
CALVERT RD
WOODLANDS
TUSKAR ST
THALIA CL
PARK VISTA
ROYAL HILL
BLACKHEATH

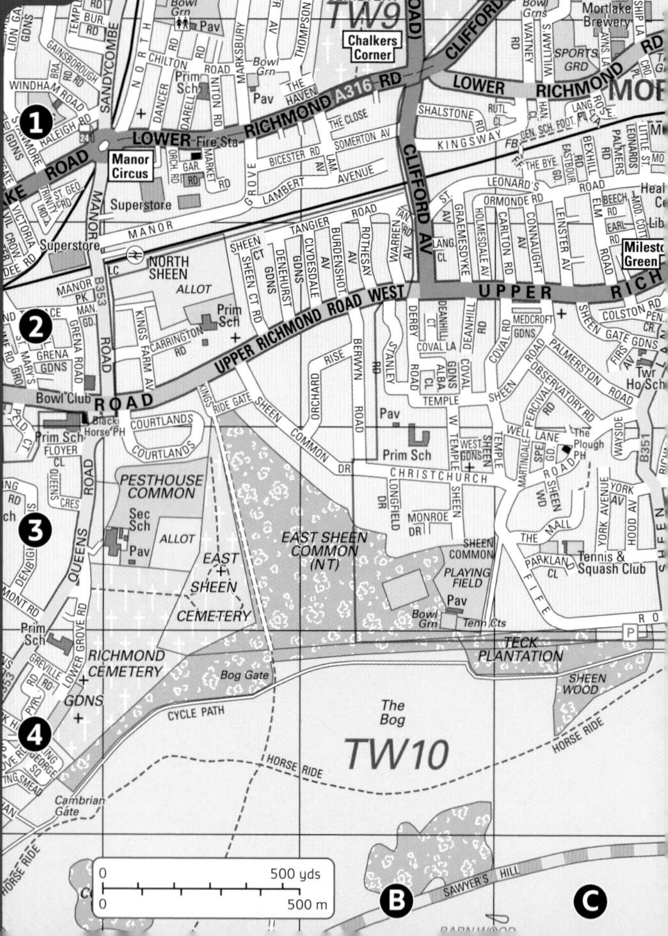
NORTH SHEEN
NORTH SHEEN CEMETERY
HAMMERSMITH CEMETERY
TW9
Chalkers Corner
160
A
B
C
1
2
3
4
ATWOOD
AVENUE
CARMEL WY
CHAUCER AV
THOMPSON AV
MARKSBURY AVENUE
NORTH RD
CHILTON ROAD
DANCER RD
DARELL RD
NITON RD
Bowl Grn
Pav
Prim Sch
THE HAVEN
LOWER RICHMOND RD
A316
Fire Sta
Manor Circus
ORCH. RD
GAR. RD
MARKET RD
GROVE
THE CLOSE
SOMERTON AV
BICESTER RD
LAM. AV
LAMBERT AVENUE
Superstore
MANOR ROAD
TANGIER ROAD
SHEEN CT
SHEEN CT RD
DENEHURST GDNS
CLYDESDALE GDNS
BURDENSHOT AV
ROTHESAY AV
WARREN AV
TAN. RD
CLIFFORD AV
CLIFFORD AVENUE
MORTLAKE ROAD
THAMES BK
The Ship PH
The Mortlake Brewery
SHIP LA
WATNEY RD
WILLIAM'S LA
SPORTS GRD
Bowl Grns
LOWER RICHMOND RD
SHALSTONE RD
RUTL. CL
KINGSWAY
LANG. PL
ROSE
FB
GEN. SCH. FOOT.
THE BYE
EASTBOUR. GD.
BEXHILL RD
PALMERS RD
LEONARDS RD
LITTLE ST.
LEONARD'S ROAD
ST. LEONARD'S AV
ORMONDE RD
GRAEMESDYKE AV
HOLMESDALE AV
CARLTON RD
CONNAUGHT AV
LEINSTER AV
ELM RD
BEECH RD
EARL RD
MOD. COTT.
Lib
Health Ce
Milestone Green
LANG. CL
UPPER RICHMOND ROAD WEST
UPPER RICHMOND
DERBY ROAD
DEANHILL CT
DEANHILL RD
MEDCROFT GDNS
COVAL RD
COVAL LA
COVAL GDNS
ALBA. CL
STANLEY RD
BERWYN ROAD
ORCHARD RISE
SHEEN GATE GDNS
COLSTON RD
PEN. CR.
FIRS AV
Twr Ho Sch
PALMERSTON ROAD
OBSERVATORY RD
PERCIVAL RD
SHEEN ROAD
TEMPLE SHEEN
WELL LANE
MARTINDALE
SPE. GD.
The Plough PH
WAYSIDE
B351
WEST TEMPLE SHEEN
WEST GDNS
Pav
Prim Sch
CHRISTCHURCH ROAD
LONGFIELD DR
MONROE DR
SHEEN WD
THE MALL
YORK AVENUE
YORK AV
HOOD AV
SHEEN COMMON
PLAYING FIELD
Pav
Bowl Grn
Tenn Cts
PARKLANDS CL
Tennis & Squash Club
FIFE RO
P
SHEEN COMMON DR
KINGS RIDE GATE
EAST SHEEN COMMON (NT)
TECK PLANTATION
SHEEN WOOD
The Bog
TW10
HORSE RIDE
Bog Gate
CYCLE PATH
Cambrian Gate
SAWYER'S HILL
LION GATE GDNS
GAINSBOROUGH RD
WINDHAM ROAD
BRA. RD
HALEIGH RD
SANDYCOMBE
TEMPLE RD
DUDLEY RD
GORD. RD
BUR. RD
B353
B353
LOWER
ROAD
TRINITY RD
ST. GEO. RD
VICTORIA
CROW.
Superstore
NORTH SHEEN
ALLOT
LC
Prim Sch
KINGS FARM AV
CARRINGTON RD
MANOR PK
MAN. GD.
ST. MARY'S GRO
GRENA GDNS
GRENA ROAD
Bowl Club
ROAD
Black Horse PH
COURTLANDS
COURTLANDS
Prim Sch
FLOYER CL
QUEENS CRES
QUEENS ROAD
PESTHOUSE COMMON
Sec Sch
ALLOT
Pav
DENBIGH
MONT RD
LOWER GROVE RD
Prim Sch
EAST SHEEN CEMETERY
RICHMOND CEMETERY
GREVILLE RD
PYRL. RD
GDNS
HORSE RIDE
0
500 yds
0
500 m

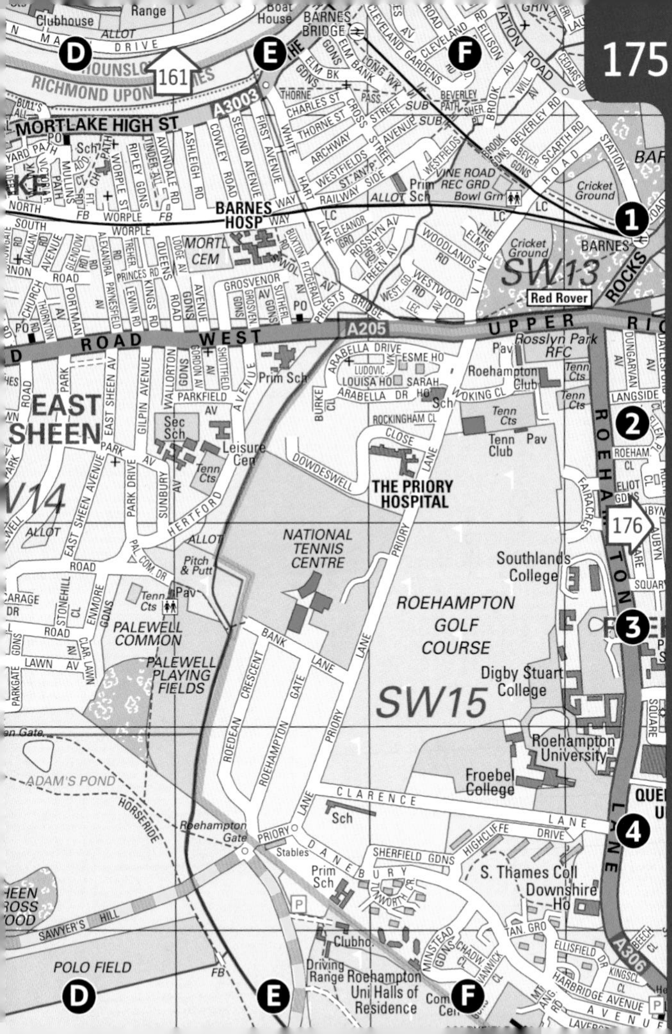
161
176
D
E
F
1
2
3
4
MORTLAKE HIGH ST
RICHMOND UPON THAMES
A3003
A205
A306
BARNES BRIDGE
BARNES
BARNES HOSP
MORTL CEM
SW13
SW14
SW15
EAST SHEEN
Red Rover
UPPER RICHMOND ROAD WEST
THE PRIORY HOSPITAL
NATIONAL TENNIS CENTRE
ROEHAMPTON GOLF COURSE
PALEWELL COMMON
PALEWELL PLAYING FIELDS
ADAM'S POND
POLO FIELD
Southlands College
Digby Stuart College
Roehampton University
Froebel College
S. Thames Coll
Downshire Ho
Rosslyn Park RFC
Roehampton Club
Roehampton Gate
Roehampton Uni Halls of Residence
Driving Range
Clubho.
SAWYER'S HILL
ROEHAMPTON LANE
PRIORY LANE
CLARENCE LANE
DANEBURY AVENUE
HARBRIDGE AVENUE
ROCKS LANE
STATION ROAD
VINE ROAD
Cricket Ground
Leisure Cen
Sec Sch
Prim Sch

BARNES
SW13
PUTNEY
162
175
Beverley Brook
RANELAGH AVENUE
LAUREL ROAD
MILL HILL
MILL HILL
BARNES COMMON
Cricket Ground
Cricket Ground
BARNES
Red Rover
ROCKS LANE
A306
STATION ROAD
BEVERLEY RD
SCARTH RD
PUTNEY CEM
LOWER RICHMOND RD
COMMON ROAD
COMMON
QUEENS RIDE
B306
COMMON SOUTH
EGLISTON MS
DRYBURGH ROAD
ERPINGHAM
LANDFORD RD
HOTHAM
Putney Leisure Cen
CLARENDON
UPPER RICHMOND ROAD (SOUTH CIRC)
Rosslyn Park RFC
Roehampton Club
Tenn Cts
Pav
DUNGARVAN AV
DAYLESFORD AV
PUTNEY PK AV
MARRICK CL
LANGSIDE AV
PUTNEY PARK LA
BALE PL
Putney Park Sch
Hall
ROEHAMPTON LANE
HUNTINGFIELD ROAD
DOVER HOUSE ROAD
Putney Park Sch
WOODBOROUGH RD
BRIAR WALK
MALBROOK ROAD
COLINETTE ROAD
DEALTRY RD
PARKFIELDS
HOWARDS LANE
CAMPION RD
COALECROFT RD
HOLROYD ROAD
ENMORE RD
Southlands College
AUBYN SQUARE
GIBBON WK
LYSONS WK
HUTTON MS
ELMSHAW RD
HAWKESBURY RD
WILLIAM GDNS
HAZLEWELL
Health Cen
ROEHAMPTON
Prim Sch
PARKSTEAD RD
SUNNYMEAD
GRANARD AV
LUTTRELL AVENUE
LARPENT AVENUE
CHARTFIELD AV
SW15
Digby Stuart College
Roehampton University
Froebel College
QUEEN MARY'S UNI HOSP
CRESTWAY
HIGHDOWN RD
WESTLEIGH AV
CORTIS ROAD
TILDESLEY RD
Clinic
ROEHAMPTON PLAYING FIELDS
PARKMEAD
PUTNEY HEATH
S. Thames Coll
Downshire Ho
WESTMEAD
PUTNEY HEATH
TELEGRAPH
CONVENT
0 500 yds
0 500 m

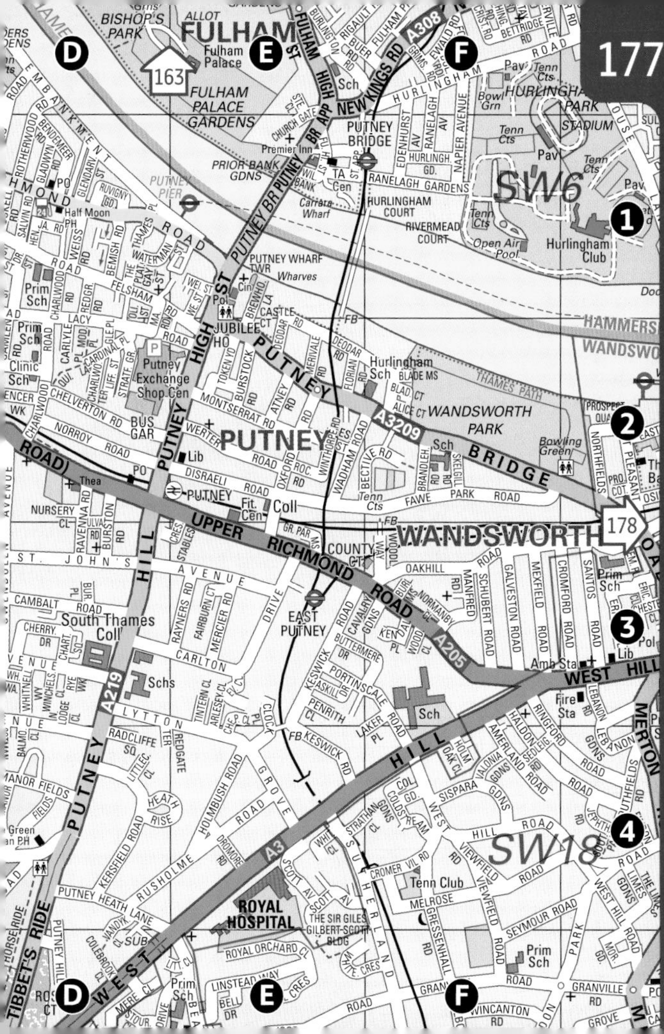
D
E
F
FULHAM
BISHOP'S PARK
Fulham Palace
163
FULHAM PALACE GARDENS
PUTNEY BRIDGE
HURLINGHAM PARK STADIUM
SW6
Hurlingham Club
Open Air Pool
PRIOR BANK GDNS
Premier Inn
PUTNEY PIER
Half Moon PH
Carrara Wharf
HURLINGHAM COURT
RIVERMEAD COURT
RANELAGH GARDENS
PUTNEY WHARF TWR
Wharves
NEW KINGS RD
A308
PUTNEY HIGH ST
PUTNEY BR APP
EMBANKMENT
LOWER RICHMOND ROAD
FELSHAM ROAD
JUBILEE HO
Putney Exchange Shop Cen
PUTNEY
PUTNEY BRIDGE ROAD
A3209
Hurlingham Sch
WANDSWORTH PARK
THAMES PATH
HAMMERSMITH
WANDSWORTH
Bowling Green
FAWE PARK ROAD
DISRAELI ROAD
Lib
BUS GAR
Thea
UPPER RICHMOND ROAD
A205
WANDSWORTH
178
COUNTY CT
EAST PUTNEY
OAKHILL ROAD
ST. JOHN'S AVENUE
South Thames Coll
CARLTON
A219
Schs
PUTNEY HILL
WEST HILL
A3
SW18
Tenn Club
ROYAL HOSPITAL
THE SIR GILES GILBERT-SCOTT BLDG
TIBBET'S RIDE
PUTNEY HEATH LANE
ROYAL ORCHARD CL
LINSTEAD WAY
Prim Sch
GRANVILLE ROAD
WINCANTON RD
MELROSE ROAD
SEYMOUR ROAD
SUTHERLAND GROVE
MERTON ROAD
Amb Sta
Fire Sta
1
2
3
4

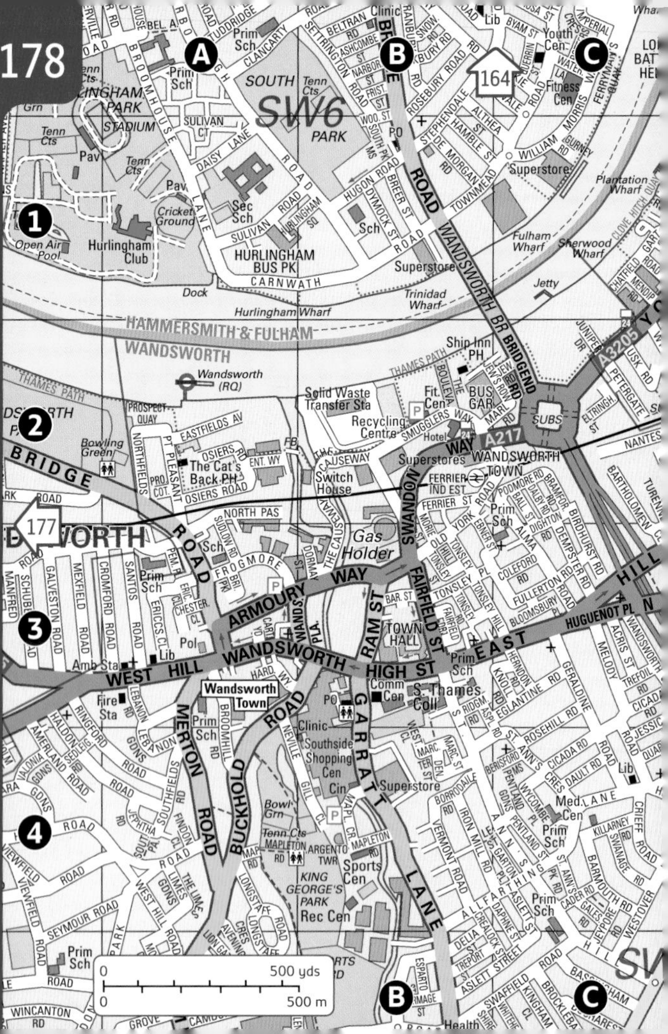
A
B
C
1
2
3
4
164
177
SW6
SOUTH PARK
Prim Sch
Tenn Cts
HURLINGHAM PARK
STADIUM
Pav
Cricket Ground
Open Air Pool
Hurlingham Club
Sec Sch
HURLINGHAM BUS PK
CARNWATH
Dock
Hurlingham Wharf
Superstore
Trinidad Wharf
Fulham Wharf
Sherwood Wharf
Plantation Wharf
Jetty
HAMMERSMITH & FULHAM
WANDSWORTH
THAMES PATH
Wandsworth (RQ)
Ship Inn PH
Solid Waste Transfer Sta
Recycling Centre
Fit. Cen
BUS GAR
SUBS
Hotel
Superstores
WANDSWORTH TOWN
FERRIER IND EST
A217
A3205
BRIDGE ROAD
Bowling Green
The Cat's Back PH
Switch House
Gas Holder
ARMOURY WAY
WANDSWORTH HIGH ST
WEST HILL
EAST HILL
TOWN HALL
Wandsworth Town
Comm Cen
S. Thames Coll
Clinic
Southside Shopping Cen
Cin
Superstore
Sports Cen
KING GEORGE'S PARK
Rec Cen
Bowl Grn
Tenn Cts
Amb Sta
Lib
Fire Sta
Pol
Med. Cen
WANDSWORTH BRIDGE ROAD
SWANDON WAY
FAIRFIELD ST
RAM ST
GARRATT LANE
MERTON ROAD
BUCKHOLD ROAD
HUGUENOT PL
ALMA RD
YORK ROAD
DAISY LANE
BROOMHOUSE LANE
HUGON ROAD
SULIVAN ROAD
ROSEBURY ROAD
TOWNMEAD
WILLIAM MORRIS
OSIERS ROAD
EASTFIELDS AV
NORTHFIELDS
PROSPECT QUAY
SMUGGLERS WAY
NANTES
FROGMORE
SANTOS ROAD
CROMFORD ROAD
MEXFIELD ROAD
GALVESTON ROAD
VIEWFIELD ROAD
SEYMOUR ROAD
WINCANTON RD
ASLETT STREET
SWAFFIELD ROAD
ST. ANN'S HILL
GERALDINE RD
ROSEHILL RD
CICADA RD
IRON MILL RD
VERMONT ROAD
0 500 yds
0 500 m

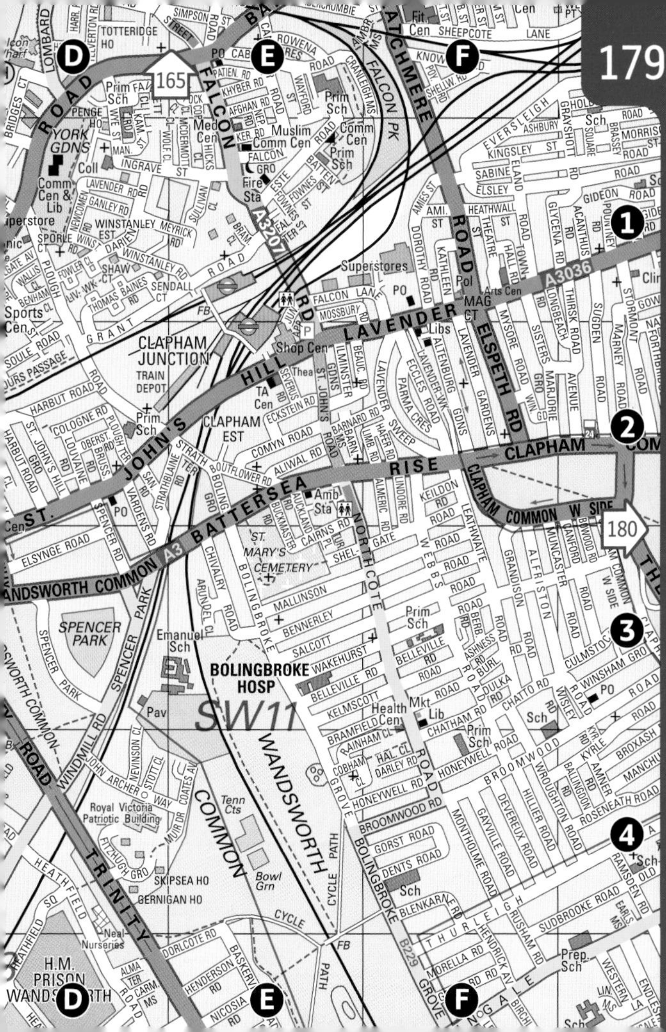
D
E
F
1
2
3
4
165
180
CLAPHAM JUNCTION
TRAIN DEPOT
LAVENDER HILL
ST. JOHN'S HILL
CLAPHAM COMMON W SIDE
BATTERSEA RISE
A3036
A3207
A3
B229
ELSPETH RD
FALCON RD
FALCON LANE
FALCON PK
NORTHCOTE ROAD
BOLINGBROKE GROVE
BOLINGBROKE HOSP
ST. MARY'S CEMETERY
SPENCER PARK
WANDSWORTH COMMON
TRINITY ROAD
SW11
Emanuel Sch
Royal Victoria Patriotic Building
H.M. PRISON WANDSWORTH
Superstores
Shop Cen
Sports Cen
Muslim Comm Cen
YORK GDNS
Comm Cen & Lib
CLAPHAM EST
WINSTANLEY EST
SHEEPCOTE LANE
GRANT ROAD
PLOUGH ROAD
SPENCER RD
HONEYWELL RD
BROOMWOOD RD
WROUGHTON ROAD
SUDBROOKE ROAD
THURLEIGH ROAD
NIGHTINGALE LANE
ST. JOHN'S RD
LAVENDER SWEEP
LAVENDER GARDENS
ALTENBURG GDNS
WEBBS ROAD
LEATHWAITE ROAD
CHATHAM RD
MALLINSON
BENNERLEY
SALCOTT
WAKEHURST
BELLEVILLE RD
KELMSCOTT
BRAMFIELD
GORST ROAD
DENTS ROAD
BLENKARNE RD
MORELLA RD
HENDRICK AV
RUSHAM RD
MONTHOLME ROAD
GAYVILLE ROAD
DEVEREUX ROAD
HILLIER ROAD
GRANDISON ROAD
ALFRISTON ROAD
MUNCASTER ROAD
CULMSTOCK
WINSHAM GRO
ROSENEATH ROAD
RAMSDEN RD
WANDSWORTH COMMON CYCLE PATH
Tenn Cts
Bowl Grn
SKIPSEA HO
GERNIGAN HO
Neal Nurseries
HEATHFIELD SQ.
DORLCOTE RD
HENDERSON RD
NICOSIA RD
BASKERVILLE
ALMA TER
Health Cen
Mkt
Lib
Prim Sch
Amb Sta
Fire Sta
PO
Pol
Arts Cen
MAG CT
Libs
Thea
TA Cen
ESTE RD
GIDEON ROAD
SABINE RD
KINGSLEY ST
EVERSLEIGH RD
ELSLEY
HEATHWALL ST
TOWNLEY RD
ELSYNGE ROAD
WANDSWORTH COMMON

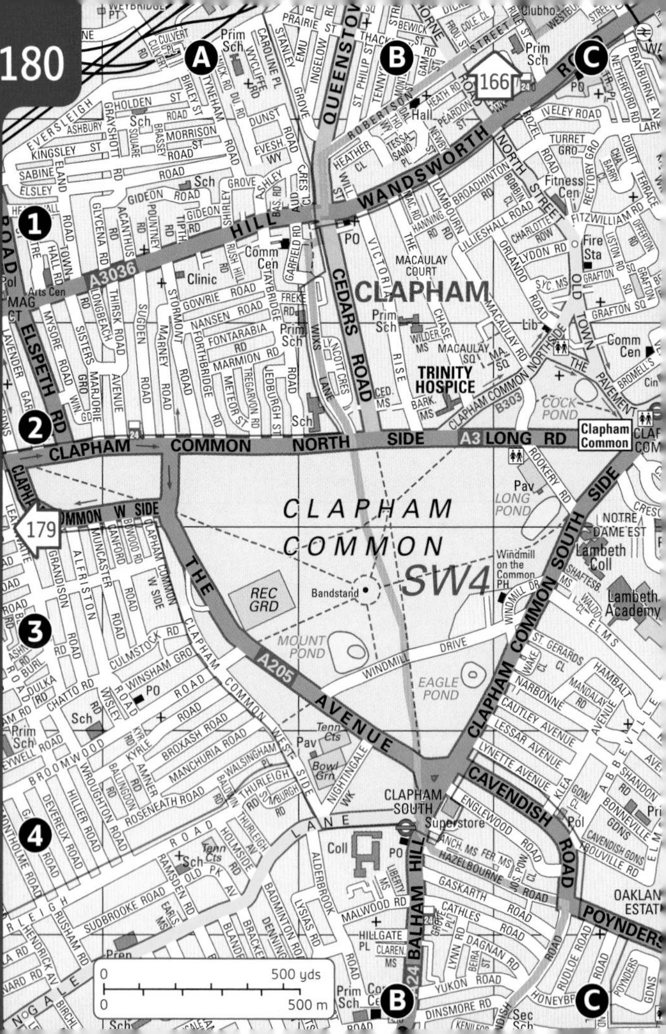
A
B
C
1
2
3
4
166
179
CLAPHAM
CLAPHAM COMMON
SW4
TRINITY HOSPICE
MACAULAY COURT
WANDSWORTH ROAD
WANDSWORTH HILL
A3036
QUEENSTOWN ROAD
CEDARS ROAD
VICTORIA RISE
NORTH STREET
OLD TOWN
THE PAVEMENT
CLAPHAM COMMON NORTH SIDE
A3 LONG RD
Clapham Common
CLAPHAM COMMON SOUTH SIDE
CLAPHAM COMMON W SIDE
CLAPHAM COMMON WEST SIDE
THE AVENUE
A205
WINDMILL DRIVE
CAVENDISH ROAD
POYNDERS
BALHAM HILL
CLAPHAM SOUTH
LANE
ELSPETH RD
LAVENDER GDNS
GIDEON ROAD
MORRISON ROAD
HOLDEN ST
ASHBURY
EVERSLEIGH
KINGSLEY ST
SABINE ROAD
ELSLEY
GOWRIE ROAD
NANSEN ROAD
FONTARABIA RD
MARMION RD
SISTERS AVENUE
MARJORIE GRO
THIRSK ROAD
SUGDEN ROAD
MARNEY ROAD
STORMONT ROAD
FORTHBRIDGE RD
JEDBURGH ST
WIXS LANE
LYNCOTT CRES
ROBERTSON ST
BROADHINTON RD
LILLIESHALL ROAD
FITZWILLIAM RD
GRAFTON SQ
IVELEY ROAD
TURRET GRO
CUBITT TERRACE
RECTORY GRO
Fitness Cen
Fire Sta
Lib
Comm Cen
Prim Sch
Sch
Clinic
Arts Cen
Pol
PO
Hall
COCK POND
LONG POND
MOUNT POND
EAGLE POND
REC GRD
Bandstand
Windmill on the Common PH
Pav
Tenn Cts
Bowl Grn
NOTRE DAME EST
Lambeth Coll
Lambeth Academy
ELMS
ST. GERARDS CL
NARBONNE
CAUTLEY AVENUE
LESSAR AVENUE
LYNETTE AVENUE
HAMBALT
MANDALAY RD
ABBEVILLE
SHANDON RD
BONNEVILLE GDNS
CAVENDISH GDNS
TROUVILLE RD
OAKLANDS ESTATE
ENGLEWOOD ROAD
HAZELBOURNE ROAD
GASKARTH ROAD
CATHLES ROAD
DAGNAN RD
YUKON ROAD
DINSMORE RD
RUDLOE ROAD
Superstore
Coll
LIBERTY MS
ALDERBROOK
MALWOOD RD
HILLGATE PL
CULMSTOCK RD
WINSHAM GRO
BROXASH ROAD
MANCHURIA ROAD
ROSENEATH ROAD
WALSINGHAM
NIGHTINGALE WK
THURLEIGH RD
HOLMSIDE RD
BROOMWOOD ROAD
WROUGHTON ROAD
HILLIER ROAD
DEVEREUX ROAD
SUDBROOKE ROAD
RAMSDEN RD
BADMINTON RD
GRANDISON ROAD
ALFRISTON ROAD
MUNCASTER ROAD
CHATTO RD
Sec Sch
0 500 yds
0 500 m

D
E
F
167
182
1
2
3
4
CLAPHAM
CLAPHAM HIGH STREET
CLAPHAM HIGH ST.
CLAPHAM NORTH
CLAPHAM RD EST
CLAPHAM PARK
CLAPHAM PARK EST
CLAPHAM PARK ROAD
LAMBETH HOSPITAL
SW9
SW2
BRIXTON
BRIXTON ACADEMY
BRIXTON HILL
BRIXTON WATER LANE
BRIXTON RD
H.M. PRISON BRIXTON
Brixton Windmill
ACRE LANE
FERNDALE ROAD
SANDMERE ROAD
BEDFORD ROAD
B221
A23
A203
A204
STOCK. PK WK
STOCKWELL PK EST.
Lansdown Sch
Landor Theatre
Fenwick Hall
Birrell Ho
ELLERSLIE SQ INDUSTRIAL EST
RUSH COMMON
TULSE HILL ESTATE
TOWN HALL
Superstore
Swim Pool
Sports Cen
Health Cen
Youth Cen
Comm Cen
TILSON HOUSE
WILLIAM BONNEY EST
ARLINGTON LODGE
BAYTREE ROAD
EFFRA RD
ST. MATT.
ST. MATTHEW'S ROAD
ELECTRIC AV
BRIGHTON TER
COLDHARBOUR
JEBB AVENUE
KING'S AVENUE
UPPER TULSE HILL
ENDYMION ROAD
JOSEPHINE AVENUE
ARODENE ROAD
BEECHDALE RD
FAIRMOUNT RD
DUMBARTON RD
KINGSWOOD ROAD
THORNBURY RD
ROSEBERY
LYHAM RD
BRANKSOME ROAD
STRATHLEVEN ROAD
SUDBOURNE ROAD
HAYTER
HORSFORD RD
LAMBERT ROAD
GLANVILLE RD
BONHAM ROAD
BARNESBURY HO
BELGRAVIA HO
BLOOMSBURY HO
CLARENCE AVENUE
CLARENCE CRESCENT
ALLOT
Prim Sch
Coll
Hall
Lib
PO
Clinic

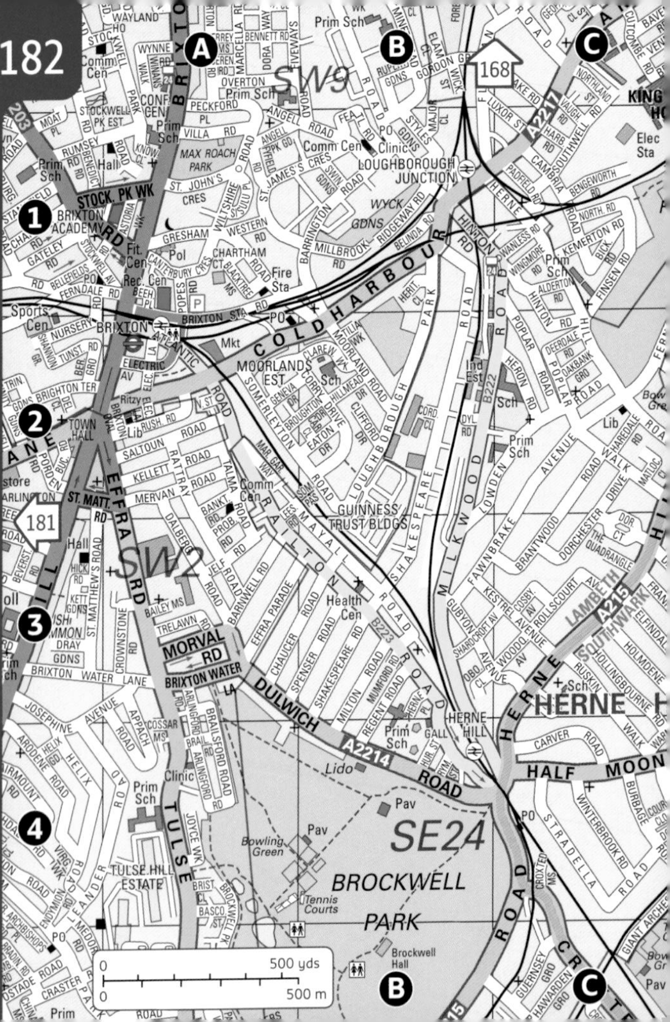
A
B
C
SW9
168
181
SW2
SE24
1
2
3
4
BRIXTON ACADEMY
STOCK. PK WK
STOCKWELL PK EST
MAX ROACH PARK
LOUGHBOROUGH JUNCTION
COLDHARBOUR
BRIXTON
BRIXTON STA RD
ATLANTIC
ELECTRIC AV
Mkt
MOORLANDS EST
TOWN HALL
EFFRA RD
RAILTON
MAYALL ROAD
SHAKESPEARE
MILKWOOD ROAD
LOUGHBOROUGH
GUINNESS TRUST BLDGS
HERNE HILL
HERNE
LAMBETH
SOUTHWARK
A215
A2217
A2214
B222
B223
DULWICH ROAD
HALF MOON
BRIXTON WATER LANE
MORVAL RD
TULSE HILL ESTATE
TULSE
BROCKWELL PARK
Brockwell Hall
Lido
Pav
Bowling Green
Tennis Courts
CROXTED ROAD
STRADELLA ROAD
WINTERBROOK RD
JOSEPHINE AVENUE
SHAKESPEARE RD
MILTON ROAD
REGENT ROAD
CHAUCER ROAD
SPENSER ROAD
EFFRA PARADE
BARNWELL RD
DALBERG
SALTOUN
KELLETT
MERVAN
RATTRAY ROAD
TALMA ROAD
SOMERLEYTON ROAD
HINTON RD
POPLAR ROAD
FAWNBRAKE AVENUE
BRANTWOOD
DORCHESTER DRIVE
KESTREL AVENUE
ROLLSCOURT AV
CARVER ROAD
500 yds
500 m
0

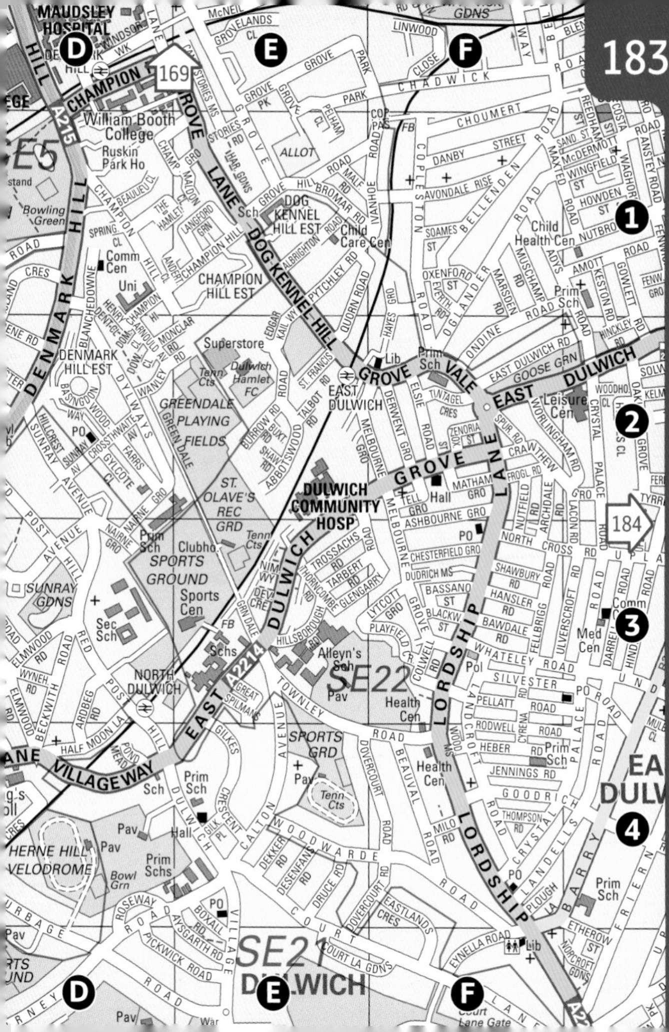
D
E
F
1
2
3
4
169
184
MAUDSLEY HOSPITAL
DENMARK HILL
CHAMPION
WINDSOR WK
McNEIL
GROVELANDS CL
LINWOOD CLOSE
GDNS
CHADWICK ROAD
CHOUMERT
GROVE PARK
GROVE PK
PELHAM CL
ALLOT
STORIES MS
STORIES RD
HAB. GDNS
COP. PAS
FB
William Booth College
Ruskin Park Ho
SE5
Bowling Green
DENMARK HILL
A215
CHAMPION HILL
CHAMPION CL
SPRING CL
Comm Cen
Uni
BEAUVEU CL
THE HAMLET
LANGFORD GRN
CHAMP.
MALDON CL
GROVE LANE
Sch
DOG KENNEL HILL EST
DOG KENNEL HILL
CHAMPION HILL
CHAMPION HILL EST
ALBRIGHTON ROAD
Child Care Cen
PYTCHLEY RD
QUORN ROAD
BROMAR RD
MALF. RD
IVANHOE ROAD
GROVE HILL ROAD
COPLESTON ROAD
DANBY STREET
AVONDALE RISE
BELLENDEN ROAD
SOAMES ST
OXENFORD ST
EVERTH. RD
OGLANDER ROAD
MARSDEN RD
MUSCHAMP ROAD
ADYS ROAD
Child Health Cen
NUTBROOK
HOWDEN ST
WINGFIELD ST
McDERMOTT
SAND. ST
MAXTED ROAD
REEDHAM ST
COSTA ST
WAGHORN
ANSTEY ROAD
AMOTT ROAD
KESTON RD
GOWLETT ROAD
Prim Sch
HINCKLEY RD
ONDINE ROAD
EAST DULWICH RD
GOOSE GRN
EAST DULWICH
Leisure Cen
WORLINGHAM RD
CRYSTAL PALACE ROAD
WOODHO. CL
OAK
SOLW
KELM
GROVE
DENMARK HILL EST
MONCLAR RD
HENRY DENT CL
DOMETT CL
ARNOULD AV
CHAMPION HI
DOWN CL
WANLEY RD
DYLWAYS
BASINGDON WAY
WOOD.
PO
SUNRAY AV
CROSSTHWAITE AV
FARRS
GYLCOTE CL
HILLCREST
SUNRAY AVENUE
BLANCHEDOWNE
Superstore
Tenn Cts
Dulwich Hamlet FC
GREENDALE PLAYING FIELDS
GREEN DALE
EDGAR KAIL WY
ST. FRANCIS RD
TALBOT RD
BURROW RD
BUXT. RD
SHAWB. RD
ABBOTSWOOD RD
EAST DULWICH
Lib
Prim Sch
GROVE VALE
HAYES GRO
MELBOURNE GRO
DERWENT GRO
ELSIE ROAD
TINTAGEL CRES
ZENORIA ST
FOXL ST
LORDSHIP LANE
SPUR RD
CRAWTHEW GRO
FROGL. RD
ST. OLAVE'S REC GRD
Tenn Cts
DULWICH COMMUNITY HOSP
GROVE
Hall
MATHAM GRO
TELL GRO
ASHBOURNE GRO
NUTFIELD RD
ARCHDALE RD
LACON RD
TYRR
POST AVENUE
HILL
NAIRNE GRO
Prim Sch
Clubho.
SPORTS GROUND
Sports Cen
SUNRAY GDNS
Sec Sch
DULWICH
TROSSACHS RD
TARBERT RD
GLENGARRY
THORNCOMBE RD
NIMR WY
DEVA CRES
PO
NORTH CROSS RD
CHESTERFIELD GRO
DUDRICH MS
BASSANO ST
SHAWBURY RD
HANSLER RD
BAWDALE RD
FELLBRIGG
ULVERSCROFT RD
UPLAND ROAD
Comm C
Med Cen
DARREL
HIND
LYTCOTT GRO
PLAYFIELD CR.
GROVE
BLACKW. ST
WHATELEY ROAD
FB
Schs
GRN DALE
A2214
HILLSBOROUGH RD
Alleyn's Sch
SE22
Pav
COLWELL RD
Pol
SILVESTER RD
PELLATT ROAD
ELMWOOD RD
WYNEH. RD
RED POST HILL
NORTH DULWICH
ARDBEG RD
BECKWITH ROAD
HALF MOON LA
VILLAGE WAY
POND MEAD
EAST DULWICH GROVE
GREAT SPILMANS
TOWNLEY ROAD
AVENUE
Health Cen
LANDCROFT
RODWELL ROAD
CYRENA RD
HEBER RD
Prim Sch
JENNINGS RD
GOODRICH ROAD
THOMPSON RD
Prim Sch
Sch
GILKES CRES
SPORTS GRD
Pav
Tenn Cts
DOVERCOURT ROAD
BEAUVAL ROAD
Health Cen
WOOD MS
EA DULW
HERNE HILL VELODROME
Pav
Bowl Grn
Prim Schs
Hall
GILK. PL
CALTON AVENUE
DEKKER RD
DESENFANS RD
DRUCE RD
WOODWARDE ROAD
MILO RD
LORDSHIP LANE
LANDELLS
PLOUGH LA
BARRY ROAD
CRYSTAL
PO
Prim Sch
FRIERN
BURBAGE ROAD
ROSEWAY
AYSGARTH RD
PICKWICK ROAD
BOXALL RD
PO
VILLAGE
COURT LANE
COURT LA GDNS
EASTLANDS CRES
DOVERCOURT RD
EYNELLA ROAD
Lib
ETHEROW ST
NORCROFT GDNS
SE21
DULWICH
Court Lane Gate
Pav
War
TURNEY ROAD
SPORTS GROUND
A2

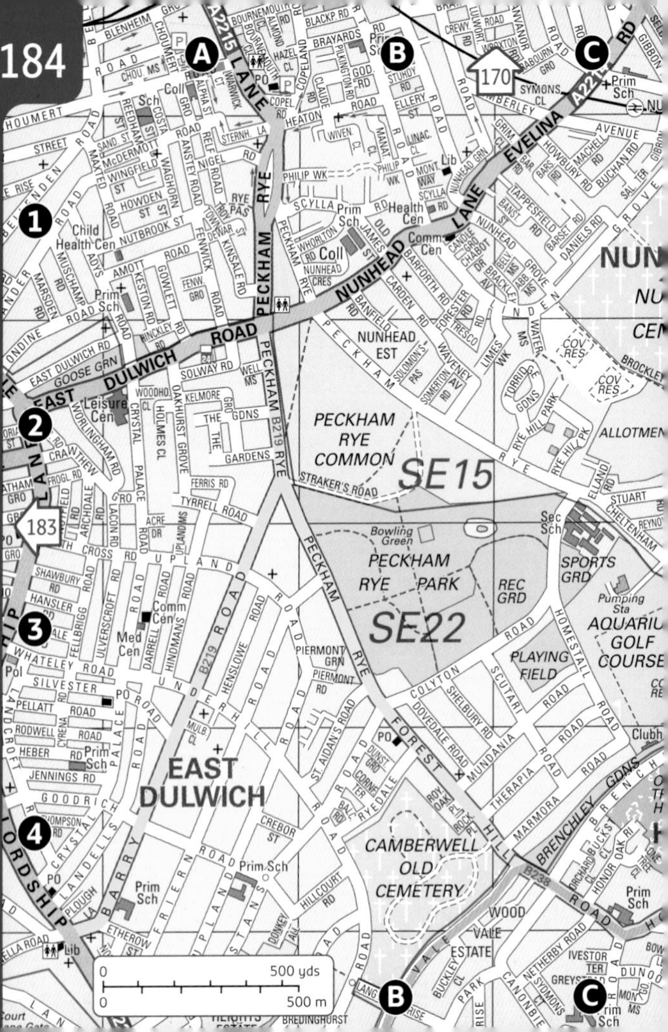
A
B
C
1
2
3
4
170
183
PECKHAM RYE COMMON
SE15
PECKHAM RYE PARK
SE22
Bowling Green
REC GRD
PLAYING FIELD
SPORTS GRD
Pumping Sta
AQUARIUS GOLF COURSE
ALLOTMENTS
NUNHEAD EST
CAMBERWELL OLD CEMETERY
EAST DULWICH
WOOD VALE ESTATE
EAST DULWICH ROAD
NUNHEAD LANE
EVELINA RD
PECKHAM RYE
B219
A2215
RYE LANE
LORDSHIP LANE
FOREST HILL ROAD
BRENCHLEY GDNS
B238
UPLAND ROAD
NORTH CROSS RD
CRYSTAL PALACE ROAD
BARRY ROAD
UNDERHILL ROAD
COLYTON ROAD
HOMESTALL ROAD
LINDEN GROVE
NUNHEAD GROVE
GOOSE GRN
Leisure Cen
Child Health Cen
Comm Cen
Med Cen
Health Cen
Lib
Prim Sch
Sec Sch
Coll
PO
Pol
0 500 yds
0 500 m

D
E
F
D
E
F
1
2
3
4
171
186
TELEGRAPH HILL PARK
DRAKEFELL ROAD
B2142
VESTA ROAD
KITTO ROAD
PENDRELL RD
WALLBUTTON RD
ENDWELL ROAD
MILLMARK GROVE
SHARDELOES RD
MALPAS RD
NURSERY CL
UPPER BROCKLEY ROAD
ASHBY RD
MANOR RD
WICKHAM MS
GEOFFREY ROAD
BEVERLEY CT
TACK MS
ENDWELL RD
MANTLE RD
FOXWELL ST
SEYMOUR GDNS
ASAPH ST
ASPINALL RD
ASPINALL ROAD
AVIGNON ROAD
CRANFIELD ROAD
HAREFIELD ROAD
GARS MS
HABERDASHERS ASKE'S PLAYING FIELD
Pav
LEWISHAM
SOUTHWARK
DUNDALK RD
FINLAND RD
Meadowgate Sch
REVELON RD
ARICA RD
MALL CL
MERET CL
NORBERT RD
BROCKILL CRES
DENE CL
ST. NORBERT GRN
BROCKLEY
Prim Sch
PO
COULGATE ST
FOXBERRY RD
FOXBERRY ROAD
HARCOURT RD
BROCKLEY ROAD
B218
WICKHAM GDNS
WICKHAM ROAD
GLENSDALE RD
BREAKSPEARS ROAD
TRESSILLIAN CRES
TRESSILLIAN ROAD
HILLY FIELDS CRES
SE4
HILLY FIELDS
Tennis Courts
Sec Sch
CHALSEY ROAD
MONTAGUE AVENUE
MEREDITH MS
ST. MARGARETS RD
ROUNDEL CL
ADELAIDE AVENUE
B236
IVY ROAD
KNELLER RD
Pol
ARABIN ROAD
BRAXFIELD ROAD
COMERFORD ROAD
WHITBREAD ROAD
DALRYMPLE RD
HOWSON ROAD
BEECROFT RD
Prim Sch
BROCKLEY CEMETERY
LADYWELL CEMETERY
War Memorial
IVYDALE ROAD
LIMESFORD ROAD
HARLESCOTT ROAD
LANBURY ROAD
INVERTON RD
Bredinghurst Sch
BELLWOOD RD
HAINFORD CL
PINCOTT PL
BILLINGFORD CL
FRENDSBURY RD
ALDERSFORD CL
ST. NORBERT ROAD
Prim Sch
CHELW WK
KENTWELL CL
NASH RD
ROCA RD
TURNHAM ROAD
Health Cen
Tenn Cts
Comm Cen
MERTTINS RD
BROCKLEY WAY
BROCKLEY
HOMELEIGH RD
FERNHOLME RD
ROSENTHORPE RD
HAWKSLADE RD
ATHENLAY RD
GARDENS
HONOR OAK SPORTS GRD
Crem
BROCKLEY MS
CROFTON PARK
Lib
MERRITT ROAD
DARFIELD RD
CROFTON PARK ROAD
MARNOCK ROAD
LINDAL RD
HUXBEAR ST
ABBOTSWELL RD
CHUDLEIGH RD
ELSIEMAUD ROAD
HENRYSON ROAD
AMYRUTH RD
GORDONBROCK RD
ARTHURDON ROAD
CHUDLEIGH
FOXBOROUGH GDNS
MANWOOD ROAD
HOLDENBY RD
HAZELDON RD
EDDYSTONE RD
BUCKTHORNE ROAD
Thea
CYPRESS GDNS
BARTRAM RD
HALL RD
BEARSTEAD RI
SEVENOAKS ROAD
HORSMAN RD
GLYNDE ST
EWHURST ROAD
Leisure
Sec Sch
CAMBERWELL NEW CEMETERY
SE23
ALLOT
HONOR OAK PARK
B238
COURTRAI ROAD
HOLMESLEY RD
KILGOUR RD
MACLEAN RD
PARBURY RD
TATNELL ROAD
RISELDINE ROAD
GUY'S U.M.D.S. ATHLETIC GRD
HONOR OAK PARK
Clubho.
Prim Schs
OTFORD CRES
LADY HTS
CROFTON PARK
SALEHURST ROAD
BEXHILL ROAD
RUSHFORD RD
BRIGHTLING RD
EWHURST RD
LADYWELL FIELDS
STILLNESS ROAD
STONDON PARK
BROCKLEY RISE
WALTERS WAY
BOVENEY ROAD
GRIERSON ROAD
BALLINA ST
LESSING ST
WYLEU ST
GABRIEL STREET
PO
CODRINGTON HILL
BROCKLEY
ACKROYD RD
AGNEW ROAD
Comm Cen
BLYTHE HILL FIELDS
RAVENSBOURNE
IONA CLOSE
GDNS

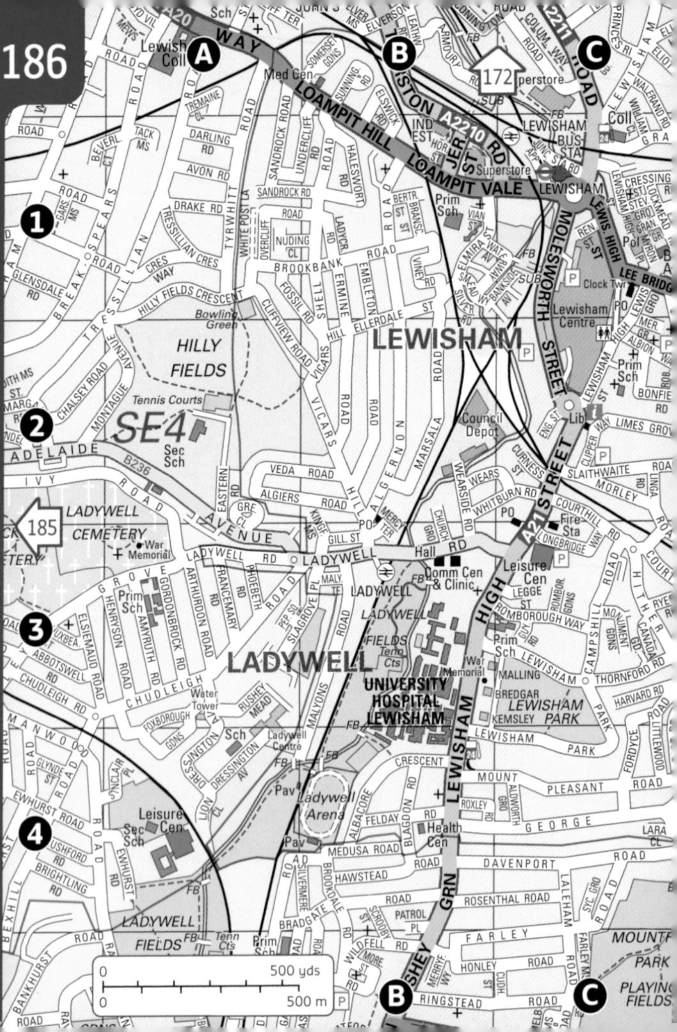
A
B
C
1
2
3
4
172
185
LEWISHAM
LADYWELL
SE4
HILLY FIELDS
LADYWELL CEMETERY
LADYWELL FIELDS
UNIVERSITY HOSPITAL LEWISHAM
LEWISHAM PARK
Ladywell Arena
LOAMPIT HILL
LOAMPIT VALE
LOAMPIT WAY
MOLESWORTH STREET
LEWISHAM HIGH STREET
LEWIS GRN
LEE BRIDGE
LEWISHAM BUS STA
Lewisham Centre
Clock Twr
Council Depot
Bowling Green
Tennis Courts
Sec Sch
Prim Sch
Comm Cen & Clinic
Leisure Cen
Fire Sta
War Memorial
Water Tower
Ladywell Centre
Health Cen
Lewisham Coll
Med Cen
HILLY FIELDS CRESCENT
TRESSILLIAN CRES
TRESSILLIAN ROAD
BROCKLEY ROAD
ADELAIDE AVENUE
IVY ROAD
LADYWELL RD
GROVE
ELSIEMAUD ROAD
CHUDLEIGH RD
MANWOOD ROAD
EWHURST ROAD
BEXHILL
BANKHURST ROAD
VICARS HILL
ALGERNON ROAD
MARSALA ROAD
ELMIRA ST
BROOKBANK ROAD
ELLERDALE ST
VEDA ROAD
ALGIERS ROAD
GILL ST
HALL RD
WEARSIDE RD
WHITBURN RD
SLAITHWAITE ROAD
MORLEY
LIMES GROVE
ROMBOROUGH WAY
CAMPSHILL ROAD
THORNFORD RD
HITHER GREEN
HARVARD RD
MOUNT PLEASANT ROAD
GEORGE LANE
DAVENPORT ROAD
ROSENTHAL ROAD
FARLEY ROAD
HONLEY ROAD
RINGSTEAD ROAD
RUSHEY GRN
MEDUSA ROAD
HAWSTEAD ROAD
BRADGATE ROAD
CRESCENT
MALYONS ROAD
DRESSINGTON AV
FOXBOROUGH GDNS
HENRYSON ROAD
ARTHURDON ROAD
FRANCEMARY ROAD
MOUNTSFIELD PARK
PLAYING FIELDS
0
500 yds
0
500 m

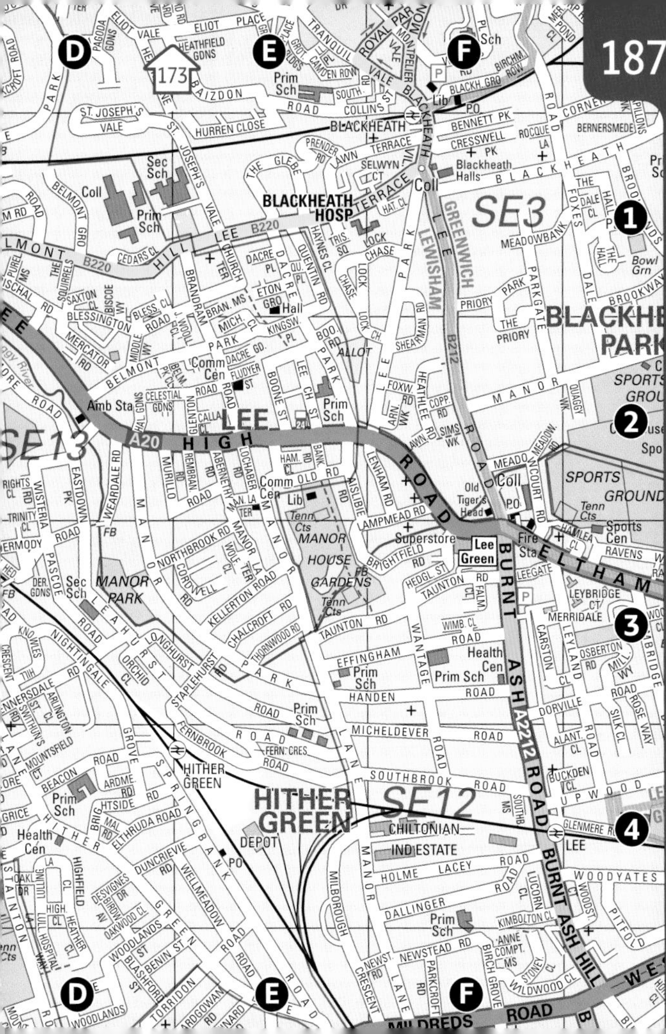
D
E
F
173
ELIOT PLACE
ELIOT VALE
HEATHFIELD GDNS
PAGODA GDNS
BAIZDON ROAD
ST. JOSEPH'S VALE
HURREN CLOSE
Prim Sch
SOUTH.
COLLINS ST
BLACKHEATH
TRANQUIL VALE
ROYAL PAR
MONTPELIER VALE
BLACKH. GRO
BIRCHM. ROW
Lib
P.O.
BENNETT PK
CRESSWELL PK
ROCQUE LA
CORNER
BERNERSMEDE
THE GLEBE
PRENDER RD
LAWN TERRACE
SELWYN CT
TERRACE
Coll
Blackheath Halls
BLACKHEATH
Sec Sch
Coll
Prim Sch
BLACKHEATH HOSP
HAT. CL
SE3
THE FOXES
DALE CL
MEADOWBANK
THE HALL
Bowl Grn
BELMONT GRO
BELMONT HILL
LEE B220
B220
CEDARS CL
THE SQUIRRELS
PUREL MS
DACRE PL
QU. PL
ETON GRO
Hall
TRIS. SQ
VOCK
CHASE
LOCK CHASE
LEE PARK
LEWISHAM
GREENWICH
LEE
BRANDRAM
CHURCH TER
QUENTIN RD
HAYNES CL
SAXTON CL
BISCOE WY
BLESS. CL
BLESSINGTON ROAD
MERCATOR RD
BRAN. MS
MICH. CL
KINGSW. PL
PRIORY PARK
PARKGATE
THE PRIORY
BLACKHEATH PARK
BROOKWAY
SPORTS GROUND
DACRE PARK
DACRE GD.
BOO. RD
ALLOT
SHEARMAN RD
B212
BELMONT PARK
Comm Cen
FLUDYER ST
CELESTIAL GDNS
ROAD
BOONE ST
LEE CH. ST
Prim Sch
FOXW. RD
HEATHLEE RD
COPP. RD
ARN. WK
SIMS WK
MANOR
QUAGGY WK
Amb Sta
LEE
LEE HIGH ROAD
A20
SE13
EASTDOWN PK
WEARDALE RD
MURILLO
REMBRAN. RD
ABERNETHY RD
LOCHABER RD
HAM. CL
BANK
OLD RD
Comm Cen
Lib
MAN. LA TER
AISLIBIE RD
LENHAM RD
LAMPMEAD RD
MEADOWCOURT RD
MEADOW CL
Old Tiger's Head
P.O.
Coll
SPORTS GROUND
Tenn Cts
Sports Cen
WISTERIA RD
TRINITY CL
KERMODY ROAD
FB
MANOR PARK
NORTHBROOK RD
CORDWELL RD
MANOR LA TER
WOLF. CL
Tenn Cts
MANOR HOUSE GARDENS
Superstore
BRIGHTFIELD RD
Lee Green
Fire Sta
HAMLEA CL
RAVENS
ELTHAM
PASCOE RD
DER. GDNS
Sec Sch
LEAHURST ROAD
KELLERTON ROAD
CHALCROFT RD
FB
HEDGL. ST
TAUNTON RD
FALM. CT
BURNT ASH ROAD
LEEGATE
P
LEYBRIDGE CT
MERRIDALE
NIGHTINGALE
KNOWLES
CRESCENT
LONGHURST RD
ORCHID CL
STAPLEHURST RD
THORNWOOD RD
TAUNTON RD
EFFINGHAM
Prim Sch
WIMB. CL
ROAD
WANTAGE
Health Cen
Prim Sch
A2212
CARSTON CL
LEYLAND RD
OSBERTON RD
MILL. WY
ROAD
ROSE WAY
ENNERSDALE RD
ST. SWITHUN'S
ARLINGTON CL
PARK ROAD
HANDEN ROAD
Prim Sch
DORVILLE
SILK CL
ALANT. CL
MOUNTSFIELD CT
LANE
GROVE
FERNBROOK ROAD
FERN. CRES
MICHELDEVER ROAD
ROAD
BUCKDEN CL
SPRINGBANK
HITHER GREEN
SOUTHBROOK ROAD
UPWOOD
BEACON
ARDME. RD
Prim Sch
HTSIDE
HITHER GREEN
SE12
SOUTHB. MS
GLENMERE
LEE
BRIG
MAL RD
ELTHRUDA ROAD
DEPOT
CHILTONIAN IND ESTATE
Health Cen
DUNCRIEVIE RD
PO
HOLME LACEY ROAD
WOODYATES
HIGHFIELD CL
WELLMEADOW
MILBOROUGH
LUCORN CL
WOODST.
DESVIGNES DR
OAKWOOD CL
HIGH. CL
HEATHER CL
DALLINGER ROAD
KIMBOLTON CL
BURNT ASH HILL
PITFOLD
WOODLANDS ST
BENIN ST
GREEN
Prim Sch
ANNE COMPT. MS
NEWST. RD
NEWSTEAD RD
PARKCROFT RD
BIRCH GROVE
STONEY CL
WILDWOOD CL
STAINTON
LULL. HOSPITAL WAY
BLASHFORD ST
TORRIDON
ARDGOWAN RD
CRESCENT
WOODLANDS
MILDREDS ROAD

West End theatres & cinemas

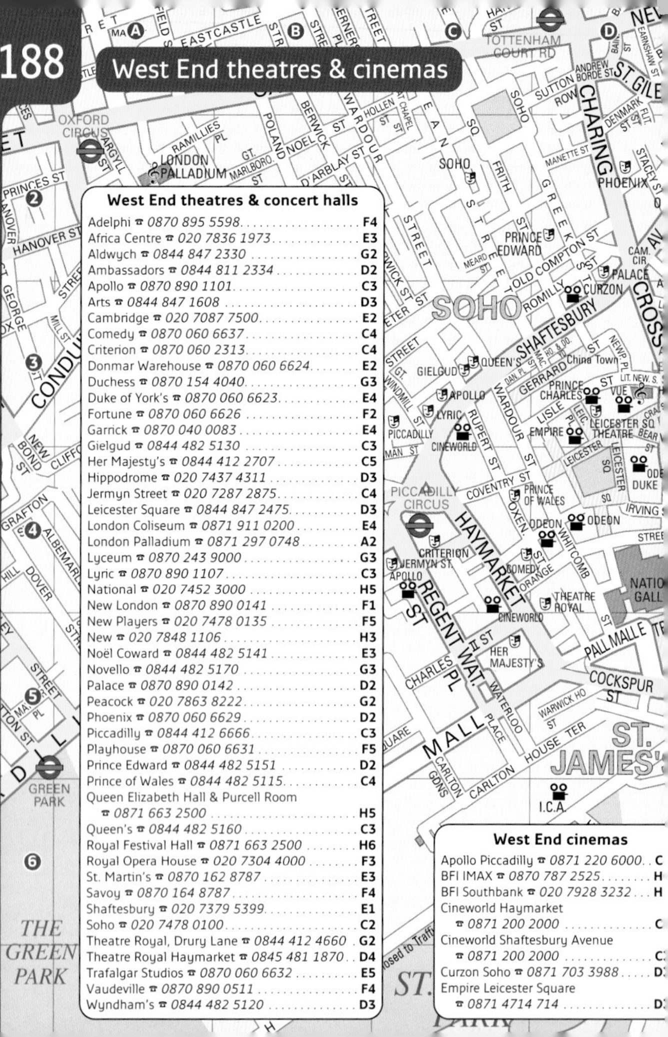

West End theatres & concert halls

Adelphi	☎ 0870 895 5598	F4
Africa Centre	☎ 020 7836 1973	E3
Aldwych	☎ 0844 847 2330	G2
Ambassadors	☎ 0844 811 2334	D2
Apollo	☎ 0870 890 1101	C3
Arts	☎ 0844 847 1608	D3
Cambridge	☎ 020 7087 7500	E2
Comedy	☎ 0870 060 6637	C4
Criterion	☎ 0870 060 2313	C4
Donmar Warehouse	☎ 0870 060 6624	E2
Duchess	☎ 0870 154 4040	G3
Duke of York's	☎ 0870 060 6623	E4
Fortune	☎ 0870 060 6626	F2
Garrick	☎ 0870 040 0083	E4
Gielgud	☎ 0844 482 5130	C3
Her Majesty's	☎ 0844 412 2707	C5
Hippodrome	☎ 020 7437 4311	D3
Jermyn Street	☎ 020 7287 2875	C4
Leicester Square	☎ 0844 847 2475	D3
London Coliseum	☎ 0871 911 0200	E4
London Palladium	☎ 0871 297 0748	A2
Lyceum	☎ 0870 243 9000	G3
Lyric	☎ 0870 890 1107	C3
National	☎ 020 7452 3000	H5
New London	☎ 0870 890 0141	F1
New Players	☎ 020 7478 0135	F5
New	☎ 020 7848 1106	H3
Noël Coward	☎ 0844 482 5141	E3
Novello	☎ 0844 482 5170	G3
Palace	☎ 0870 890 0142	D2
Peacock	☎ 020 7863 8222	G2
Phoenix	☎ 0870 060 6629	D2
Piccadilly	☎ 0844 412 6666	C3
Playhouse	☎ 0870 060 6631	F5
Prince Edward	☎ 0844 482 5151	D2
Prince of Wales	☎ 0844 482 5115	C4
Queen Elizabeth Hall & Purcell Room	☎ 0871 663 2500	H5
Queen's	☎ 0844 482 5160	C3
Royal Festival Hall	☎ 0871 663 2500	H6
Royal Opera House	☎ 020 7304 4000	F3
St. Martin's	☎ 0870 162 8787	E3
Savoy	☎ 0870 164 8787	F4
Shaftesbury	☎ 020 7379 5399	E1
Soho	☎ 020 7478 0100	C2
Theatre Royal, Drury Lane	☎ 0844 412 4660	G2
Theatre Royal Haymarket	☎ 0845 481 1870	D4
Trafalgar Studios	☎ 0870 060 6632	E5
Vaudeville	☎ 0870 890 0511	F4
Wyndham's	☎ 0844 482 5120	D3

West End cinemas

Apollo Piccadilly	☎ 0871 220 6000	C
BFI IMAX	☎ 0870 787 2525	H
BFI Southbank	☎ 020 7928 3232	H
Cineworld Haymarket	☎ 0871 200 2000	C
Cineworld Shaftesbury Avenue	☎ 0871 200 2000	C
Curzon Soho	☎ 0871 703 3988	D
Empire Leicester Square	☎ 0871 4714 714	D

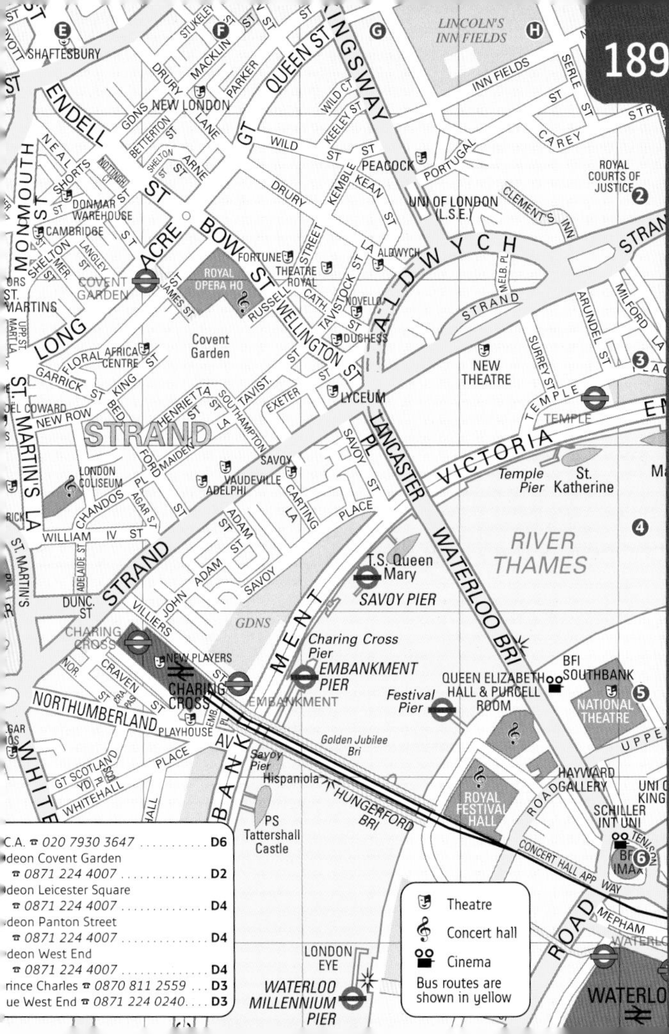

C.A. ☎ 020 7930 3647 .... D6
Odeon Covent Garden
☎ 0871 224 4007 .... D2
Odeon Leicester Square
☎ 0871 224 4007 .... D4
Odeon Panton Street
☎ 0871 224 4007 .... D4
Odeon West End
☎ 0871 224 4007 .... D4
Prince Charles ☎ 0870 811 2559 ... D3
Vue West End ☎ 0871 224 0240.... D3

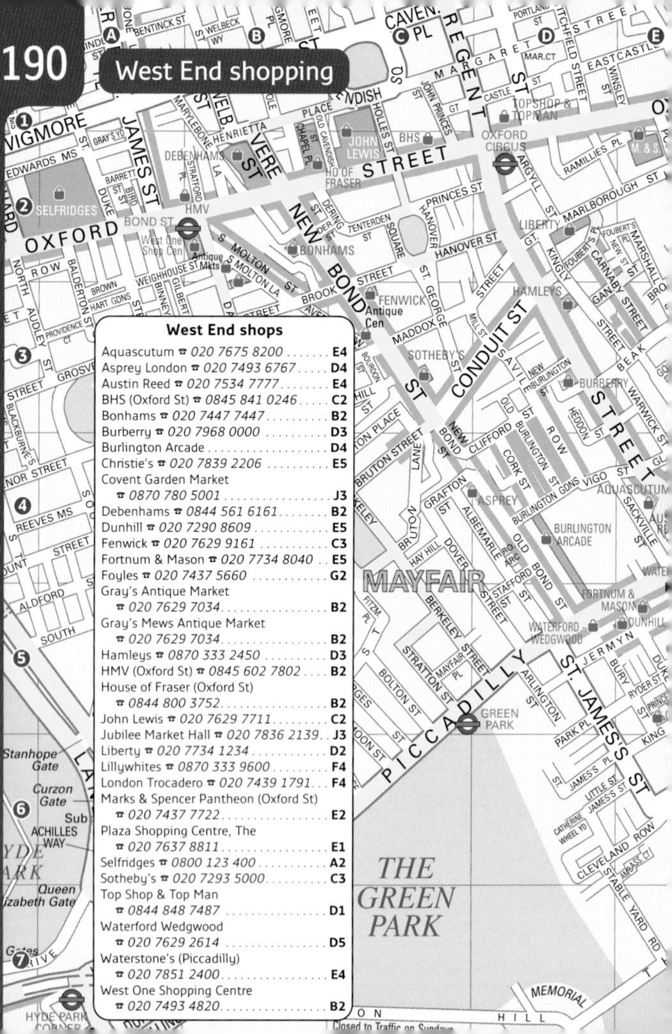

West End shops

Aquascutum ☎ 020 7675 8200	....	E4
Asprey London ☎ 020 7493 6767	.....	D4
Austin Reed ☎ 020 7534 7777	....	E4
BHS (Oxford St) ☎ 0845 841 0246	.....	C2
Bonhams ☎ 020 7447 7447	....	B2
Burberry ☎ 020 7968 0000	....	D3
Burlington Arcade	....	D4
Christie's ☎ 020 7839 2206	....	E5
Covent Garden Market ☎ 0870 780 5001	....	J3
Debenhams ☎ 0844 561 6161	....	B2
Dunhill ☎ 020 7290 8609	....	E5
Fenwick ☎ 020 7629 9161	....	C3
Fortnum & Mason ☎ 020 7734 8040	..	E5
Foyles ☎ 020 7437 5660	....	G2
Gray's Antique Market ☎ 020 7629 7034	....	B2
Gray's Mews Antique Market ☎ 020 7629 7034	....	B2
Hamleys ☎ 0870 333 2450	....	D3
HMV (Oxford St) ☎ 0845 602 7802	....	B2
House of Fraser (Oxford St) ☎ 0844 800 3752	....	B2
John Lewis ☎ 020 7629 7711	....	C2
Jubilee Market Hall ☎ 020 7836 2139	..	J3
Liberty ☎ 020 7734 1234	....	D2
Lillywhites ☎ 0870 333 9600	....	F4
London Trocadero ☎ 020 7439 1791	...	F4
Marks & Spencer Pantheon (Oxford St) ☎ 020 7437 7722	....	E2
Plaza Shopping Centre, The ☎ 020 7637 8811	....	E1
Selfridges ☎ 0800 123 400	....	A2
Sotheby's ☎ 020 7293 5000	....	C3
Top Shop & Top Man ☎ 0844 848 7487	....	D1
Waterford Wedgwood ☎ 020 7629 2614	....	D5
Waterstone's (Piccadilly) ☎ 020 7851 2400	....	E4
West One Shopping Centre ☎ 020 7493 4820	....	B2

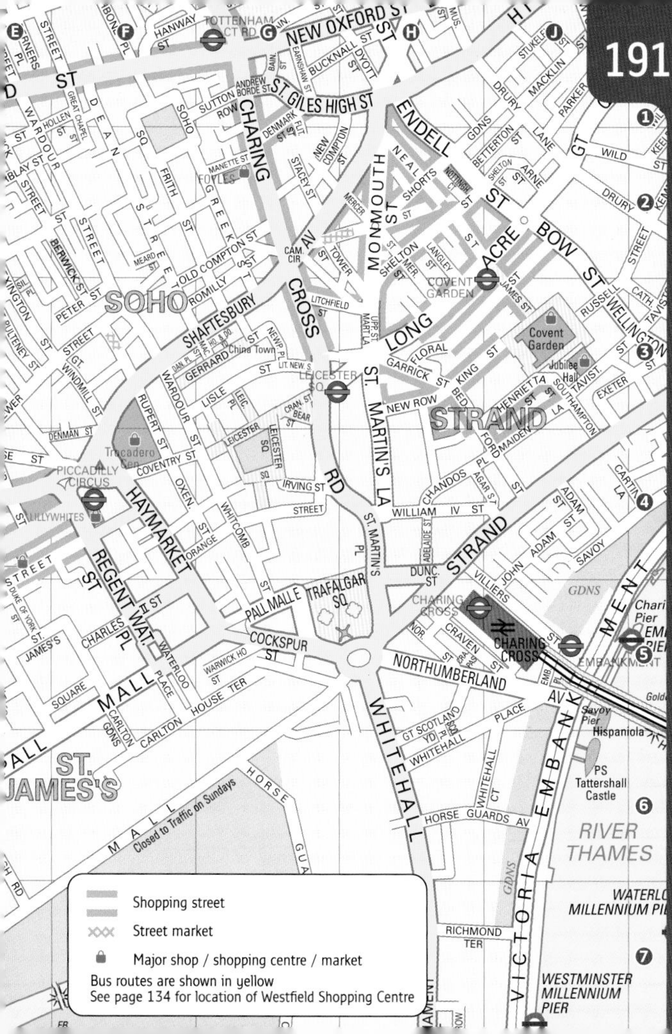

E
F
G
H
J
1
2
3
4
5
6
7
HANWAY ST
TOTTENHAM CT RD
NEW OXFORD ST
BUCKNALL ST
DYOTT ST
EARNSHAW ST
STUKELEY ST
MACKLIN ST
DRURY LANE
PARKER ST
ST. GILES HIGH ST
ANDREW BORDE ST
SUTTON ROW
CHARING CROSS RD
SOHO SQ
DENMARK ST
FLIT. ST
NEW COMPTON ST
ENDELL ST
BETTERTON ST
SHELTON ST
ARNE ST
WILD ST
DRURY LANE
WARDOUR ST
HOLLEN ST
GREAT CHAPEL ST
DEAN ST
FRITH ST
GREEK ST
MANETTE ST
FOYLES
STACEY ST
MERCER ST
MONMOUTH ST
NEAL ST
SHORTS GDNS
NOTTINGH. CT
BOW ST
BERWICK ST
MEARD ST
OLD COMPTON ST
CAM. CIR
TOWER ST
SHELTON ST
MER. ST
LANGLEY ST
COVENT GARDEN
ACRE
JAMES ST
RUSSELL ST
WELLINGTON ST
CATH. ST
SOHO
PETER ST
ROMILLY ST
SHAFTESBURY AV
LITCHFIELD ST
UPP. ST. MART. LA
LONG ACRE
Covent Garden
Jubilee Hall
TAVIST. ST
EXETER ST
FLORAL ST
GARRICK ST
KING ST
SOUTHAMPTON ST
HENRIETTA ST
China Town
GERRARD ST
WARDOUR ST
NEWPORT PL
LIT. NEW. S.
LEICESTER SQ
ST. MARTIN'S LA
NEW ROW
BEDFORD ST
STRAND
MAIDEN LA
WINDMILL ST
RUPERT ST
LISLE ST
LEIC. PL
CRAN. ST
BEAR ST
LEICESTER SQ
LEICESTER SQ
DENMAN ST
Trocadero Cen.
COVENTRY ST
PICCADILLY CIRCUS
HAYMARKET
OXEN. ST
IRVING ST
CHANDOS PL
AGAR ST
CARTING LA
ADAM ST
LILLYWHITES
WHITCOMB ST
ORANGE ST
WILLIAM IV ST
ADELAIDE ST
JOHN ADAM ST
SAVOY ST
REGENT ST
WAT. PL
PALL MALL E
TRAFALGAR SQ
DUNC. ST
STRAND
VILLIERS ST
GDNS
CHARING CROSS
NOR. AV
CRAVEN ST
CHARING CROSS
EMBANKMENT
DUKE OF YORK ST
ST. JAMES'S SQUARE
CHARLES II ST
WATERLOO PLACE
WARWICK HO ST
COCKSPUR ST
NORTHUMBERLAND AV
EMB. PL
Chari. Pier
Savoy Pier
Hispaniola
PS Tattershall Castle
MALL
CARLTON GDNS
CARLTON HOUSE TER
GT SCOTLAND YD
WHITEHALL
WHITEHALL PL
WHITEHALL CT
PLACE
ST. JAMES'S
HORSE GUARDS RD
THE MALL Closed to Traffic on Sundays
HORSE GUARDS AV
VICTORIA EMBANKMENT
RIVER THAMES
GDNS
WATERLOO MILLENNIUM PIER
RICHMOND TER
WESTMINSTER MILLENNIUM PIER
Shopping street
Street market
Major shop / shopping centre / market
Bus routes are shown in yellow
See page 134 for location of Westfield Shopping Centre

The London Congestion Charging Zone was introduced to reduce traffic congestion within Central London.

- The eastern section of the zone operates inside the 'Inner Ring Road' linking Marylebone Road, Euston Road, Pentonville Road, Tower Bridge, Elephant and Castle, Vauxhall Bridge and Park Lane. The western section of the zone is bounded by Harrow Road, the West Cross Route, the inner southbound arm of the Earls Court one way system, Chelsea Embankment, Vauxhall Bridge Road and Park Lane. The route around the zone and between the two sections is exempt from charge (see map below).

- The daily operating time is from 7am to 6pm, Monday to Friday, excluding public holidays and the period between Christmas and New Year's Day.

- Payment of the daily £8 congestion charge, either in advance or on the day of travel, allows the registered vehicle to enter, drive around and leave the congestion zone as many times as required on that one day.

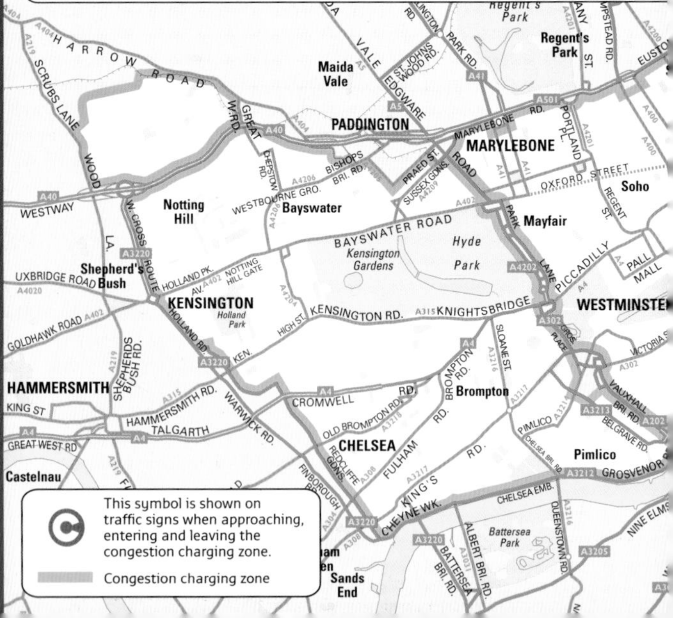

This symbol is shown on traffic signs when approaching, entering and leaving the congestion charging zone.

Congestion charging zone

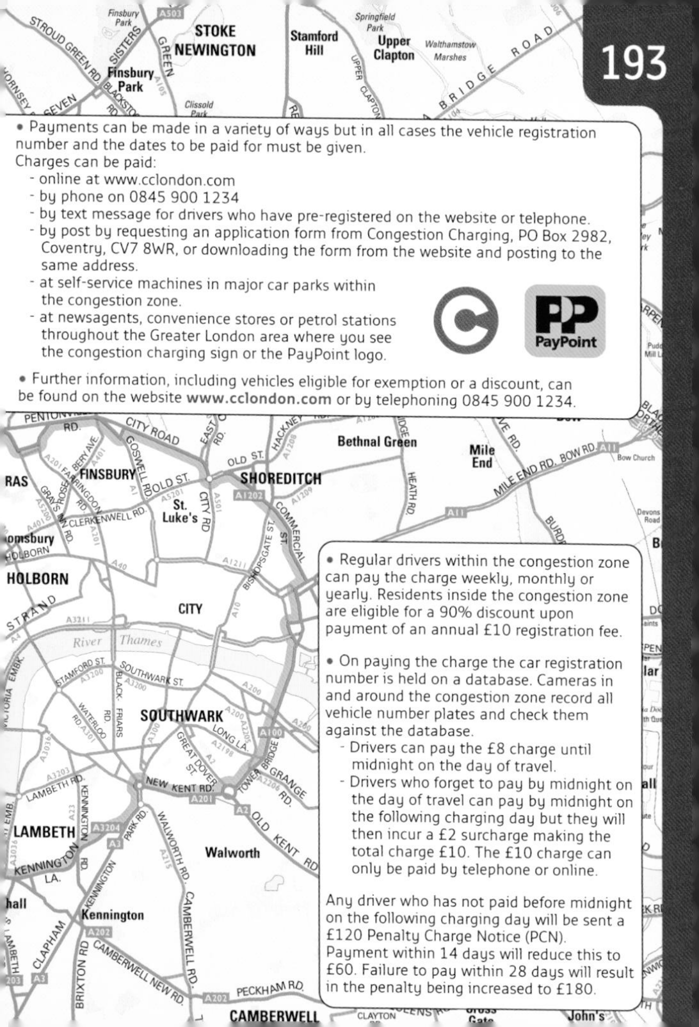

- Payments can be made in a variety of ways but in all cases the vehicle registration number and the dates to be paid for must be given.

Charges can be paid:
  - online at www.cclondon.com
  - by phone on 0845 900 1234
  - by text message for drivers who have pre-registered on the website or telephone.
  - by post by requesting an application form from Congestion Charging, PO Box 2982, Coventry, CV7 8WR, or downloading the form from the website and posting to the same address.
  - at self-service machines in major car parks within the congestion zone.
  - at newsagents, convenience stores or petrol stations throughout the Greater London area where you see the congestion charging sign or the PayPoint logo.

- Further information, including vehicles eligible for exemption or a discount, can be found on the website **www.cclondon.com** or by telephoning 0845 900 1234.

- Regular drivers within the congestion zone can pay the charge weekly, monthly or yearly. Residents inside the congestion zone are eligible for a 90% discount upon payment of an annual £10 registration fee.

- On paying the charge the car registration number is held on a database. Cameras in and around the congestion zone record all vehicle number plates and check them against the database.
  - Drivers can pay the £8 charge until midnight on the day of travel.
  - Drivers who forget to pay by midnight on the day of travel can pay by midnight on the following charging day but they will then incur a £2 surcharge making the total charge £10. The £10 charge can only be paid by telephone or online.

Any driver who has not paid before midnight on the following charging day will be sent a £120 Penalty Charge Notice (PCN). Payment within 14 days will reduce this to £60. Failure to pay within 28 days will result in the penalty being increased to £180.

Low Emission Zone

The **London Low Emission Zone (LEZ)** is a charging scheme administered by Transport for London (TfL) with the aim of reducing the pollution emissions of diesel-powered commercial vehicles in London.

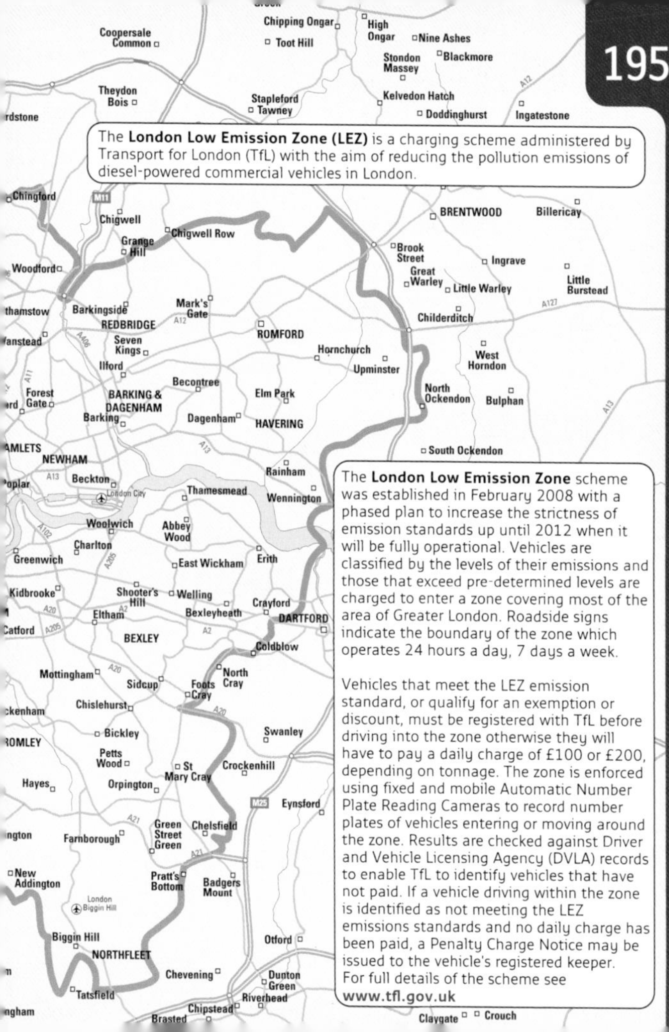

The **London Low Emission Zone** scheme was established in February 2008 with a phased plan to increase the strictness of emission standards up until 2012 when it will be fully operational. Vehicles are classified by the levels of their emissions and those that exceed pre-determined levels are charged to enter a zone covering most of the area of Greater London. Roadside signs indicate the boundary of the zone which operates 24 hours a day, 7 days a week.

Vehicles that meet the LEZ emission standard, or qualify for an exemption or discount, must be registered with TfL before driving into the zone otherwise they will have to pay a daily charge of £100 or £200, depending on tonnage. The zone is enforced using fixed and mobile Automatic Number Plate Reading Cameras to record number plates of vehicles entering or moving around the zone. Results are checked against Driver and Vehicle Licensing Agency (DVLA) records to enable TfL to identify vehicles that have not paid. If a vehicle driving within the zone is identified as not meeting the LEZ emissions standards and no daily charge has been paid, a Penalty Charge Notice may be issued to the vehicle's registered keeper. For full details of the scheme see **www.tfl.gov.uk**

How to use this index

This index combines entries for place names, street names and other features. All entries are followed by the page number and grid reference for the map page where the name will be found.

Place names are shown in capital letters e.g. ACTON.

Street names and residential addresses are shown in black type. When there is more than one street with exactly the same name then that name is shown only once in the index and it is followed by a list of postal districts to distinguish between streets in different areas. If there is not enough space to name a street on the map then the index shows the adjoining or nearest named street in italics e.g. Abady Ho, SW1 is off Page St.

Other features are shown by the following colours and symbols:-

- H Hospital
- Uni University
- Coll College
- ⇌ Railway station
- London Overground station
- London Underground station
- DLR Docklands Light Railway station
- Riv Pedestrian ferry landing stage
- Bus station
- ★ Place of interest (including parks, gardens, museums, galleries, theatres and other locations of tourist interest)
- Major shop / shopping centre / market
- Jct Road junction
- ● Industrial estate / commercial building

Some names are abbreviated in the index and lists of these abbreviations are given below.

General abbreviations

Acad	Academy
All	Alley
Allot	Allotments
Amb	Ambulance
Apts	Apartments
App	Approach
Arc	Arcade
Assoc	Association
Av	Avenue
Bdy	Broadway
Bk	Bank
Bldg	Building
Bldgs	Buildings
Boul	Boulevard
Bowl	Bowling
Br	Bridge
BUPA	British United Provident Association
C of E	Church of England
Cath	Cathedral
Cem	Cemetery
Cen	Central, Centre
Cft	Croft
Cfts	Crofts
Ch	Church
Chyd	Churchyard
Cin	Cinema
Circ	Circus
Cl	Close
Co	County
Coll	College
Comb	Combined
Comm	Community
Comp	Comprehensive
Conf	Conference
Cont	Continuing
Conv	Convent
Cor	Corner
Coron	Coroners
Cors	Corners
Cotts	Cottages
Cov	Covered
Crem	Crematorium
Cres	Crescent
Ct	Court
Cts	Courts

Ctyd	Courtyard
Dep	Depot
Dept	Department
Dev	Development
Dr	Drive
Dws	Dwellings
E	East
Ed	Education, Educational
Elec	Electricity
Embk	Embankment
Est	Estate
Ex	Exchange
Exhib	Exhibition
FB	Footbridge
FC	Football Club
Fld	Field
Flds	Fields
Fm	Farm
GM	Grant Maintained
Gall	Gallery
Gar	Garage
Gdn	Garden
Gdns	Gardens
Gen	General
Govt	Government
Gra	Grange
Grad	Graduate
Gram	Grammar
Grd	Ground
Grds	Grounds
Grn	Green
Grns	Greens
Gro	Grove
Gros	Groves
Gt	Great
HQ	Headquarters
Ho	House
Hos	Houses
Hosp	Hospital
Hts	Heights
Ind	Industrial
Indep	Independent
Inf	Infant(s)
Inst	Institute
Int	International
JM	Junior Mixed
JMI	Junior Mixed & Infant(s)
Jun	Junior
Junct	Junction
La	Lane
Las	Lanes
Lib	Library
Lit	Literary
Lo	Lodge
Lwr	Lower
Mag	Magistrates
Mans	Mansions
Med	Medical, Medicine
Mem	Memorial
Met	Metropolitan
Mid	Middle
Mkt	Market
Mkts	Markets
Ms	Mews
Mt	Mount
Mus	Museum
N	North
NHS	National Health Service
NT	National Trust
Nat	National
Nurs	Nursery
PH	Public House
PO	Post Office
PRU	Pupil Referral Unit
Par	Parade
Pas	Passage
Pav	Pavilion
Pk	Park
Pl	Place
Pol	Police
Poly	Polytechnic
Prec	Precinct
Prep	Preparatory
Prim	Primary
Prom	Promenade
Pt	Point
Quad	Quadrant
Rbt	Roundabout
RC	Roman Catholic
Rd	Road
Rds	Roads
Rec	Recreation
Rehab	Rehabilitation
Res	Reservoir, Residence
Ri	Rise
S	South
SM	Secondary Mixed
Sch	School
Schs	Schools
Sec	Secondary
Sen	Senior
Shop	Shopping
Spec	Special
Sq	Square
St	Street
St.	Saint
Sta	Station
Sts	Streets
Sub	Subway
Swim	Swimming
TA	Territorial Army
TH	Town Hall
Tech	Technical, Technology
Tenn	Tennis
Ter	Terrace
Thea	Theatre
Trd	Trading
Twr	Tower
Twrs	Towers
Uni	University
Upr	Upper
VA	Voluntary Aided
VC	Voluntary Controlled
Vet	Veterinary
Vil	Villa
Vil	Villas
Vw	View
W	West
Wd	Wood
Wds	Woods
Wf	Wharf
Wk	Walk
Wks	Works
Yd	Yard

Post town abbreviations

Brent.	Brentford
Rich.	Richmond
Wem.	Wembley

● 1 Canada Sq, E14 ......144 B4
Uni 200 Pentonville Rd, Hall of Res, N1 ....13 E3
★ 2 Willow Rd, NW3 .....109 E1
● 30 St. Mary Axe, EC3 *off St. Mary Axe* 41 D2
● 99 Bishopsgate, EC2 *off Bishopsgate* 40 C2

A

Abady Ho, SW1 *off Page St* **60** B4
Abberley Ms, SW4 *off Cedars Rd* **180** B1
Abbeville Ms, SW4 ....**181** D2
Abbeville Rd, SW4 ....**180** C4
● Abbey Business Cen, SW8 ....83 D4
Abbey Cl, E5 ....**114** A1
SW8 ....**84** B4
Abbeydale Rd, Wem. HA0 ..**118** A1
Abbeyfield Rd, SE16 ....**156** C3
Abbeyfields Cl, NW10 ......**118** A2
Abbey Gdns, NW8 ....**7** E3
SE16 *off Monnow Rd* **156** A3
SW1 *off Great Coll St* **60** C2
W6 ....**163** E1
Abbey La, E15 ....**130** C2
Abbey Orchard St, SW1 .....**60** B2
Abbey Rd, E15 ....**131** E2
NW6 ....**108** B4
NW8 ....**7** E1
NW10 ....**118** B2
Abbey Rd Est, NW8 ....**6** C1
Abbey St, SE1 ....**65** D2
Abbot Ct, SW8 *off Hartington Rd* **84** C3
Abbotsbury Cl, E15 ....**130** C2
W14 *off Abbotsbury Rd* ..**149** F1
Abbotsbury Ms, SE15 ......**184** C1
Abbotsbury Rd, W14 ......**149** E1
Abbots Gdns, W8 ....**54** C3
Abbotshade Rd, SE16 ......**143** D4
Abbots La, SE1 ....**53** D3
Abbots Manor Est, SW1 .....**70** C1
Abbot's Pl, NW6 ....**122** B1
Abbotstone Rd, SW15 ......**176** C1
Abbot St, E8 ....**113** F3
Abbots Wk, W8 ....**54** C3
Abbotswell Rd, SE4 ....**185** F3
Abbotswood Rd, SE22 .....**183** E2
Abbott Rd, E14 ....**144** C1
Abbotts Cl, N1 *off Alwyne Rd* **112** C3
Abbotts Pk Rd, E10 ....**102** C1
Abbotts Wf, E14 *off Stainsby Rd* **144** A2
Abchurch La, EC4 ....**40** B4
Abchurch Yd, EC4 ....**40** A4
Abdale Rd, W12 ....**134** B4
Aberavon Rd, E3 ....**129** E3
Abercorn Cl, NW8 ....**7** E3
Abercorn Pl, NW8 ....**7** E4
Abercorn Wk, NW8 ....**7** E4
Abercorn Way, SE1 ....**156** A4
Abercrombie St, SW11 .....**165** E4
Aberdale Ct, SE16 *off Poolmans St* **157** D1
Aberdare Gdns, NW6 ......**108** B4
Aberdeen La, N5 ....**112** B2
Aberdeen Pk, N5 ....**112** B2
Aberdeen Pk Ms, N5 ....**112** C1
Aberdeen Pl, NW8 ....**20** A3
Aberdeen Rd, N5 ....**112** C1
NW10 ....**105** F2
Aberdeen Sq, E14 *off Westferry Circ* **144** A4
Aberdeen Ter, SE3 ....**173** D4
Aberdour St, SE1 ....**64** C4
Aberfeldy St, E14 ....**144** C2
Abernethy Rd, SE13 ....**187** E2
Abersham Rd, E8 ....**113** F2
Ability Twrs, EC1 ....**15** E4
Abingdon Cl, NW1 *off Camden Ms* **111** D3
SE1 ....**77** F2
Abingdon Rd, W8 ....**54** A2
Abingdon St, SW1 ....**60** C2
Abingdon Vil, W8 ....**54** A3
Abinger Gro, SE8 ....**171** F1
Abinger Ms, W9 ....**18** A2
Abinger Rd, W4 ....**147** E2
Ablett St, SE16 ....**156** C4
Abney Gdns, N16 *off Stoke Newington High St* **99** F3
Aboyne Rd, NW10 ....**91** E4
Abyssinia Cl, SW11 *off Cairns Rd* **179** E2
Abyssinia Rd, SW11 *off Auckland Rd* **179** E2
● Acacia Business Cen, E11 *off Howard Rd* 103 E4
Acacia Cl, SE8 ....**157** E3
Acacia Gdns, NW8 ....**8** B2
Acacia Pl, NW8 ....**8** B2
Acacia Rd, E11 ....**103** E3
NW8 ....**8** B2
W3 ....**132** C3
Academy Gdns, W8 ....**42** A4
Acanthus Dr, SE1 ....**156** A4
Acanthus Rd, SW11 ....**180** A1
Accommodation Rd, NW11 ..**93** F1
Acfold Rd, SW6 ....**164** B3
Achilles Cl, SE1 ....**156** A4
Achilles Rd, NW6 ....**108** A2
Achilles St, SE14 ....**171** E2
Achilles Way, W1 ....**46** A3
Acklam Rd, W10 ....**135** F1
Ackmar Rd, SW6 ....**164** A3
Ackroyd Dr, E3 ....**143** F1
Acland Cres, SE5 ....**183** D1
Acland Rd, NW2 ....**106** B3
Acol Rd, NW6 ....**108** A4
Acorn Gdns, W3 ....**133** D1
Acorn Par, SE15 *off Carlton Gro* **170** B2
Acorn Wk, SE16 ....**143** E4
Acre Dr, SE22 ....**184** A2
Acre La, SW2 ....**181** E2
Acris St, SW18 ....**178** C3
ACTON, W3 ....**132** A4
Coll Acton & W London Coll, W3 *off Gunnersbury La* 132 B4
★ Acton Central 133 D4
Acton Ho, W3 ....**132** C2
Acton La, NW10 ....**119** E2
W3 ....**146** C1
W4 ....**147** D2
⇌ Acton Main Line 132 C2
Acton Ms, E8 ....**127** F1
● Acton Pk Est, W3 ......147 D1
Acton St, WC1 ....**25** E1
⊖ Acton Town 146 A1
Ada Ct, W9 ....**19** F1
Ada Gdns, E14 ....**145** D2
E15 ....**131** F1
Adair Rd, W10 ....**121** E4
Adair Twr, W10 *off Appleford Rd* **121** E4
Adam & Eve Ct, W1 ....**35** F2
Adam & Eve Ms, W8 ....**54** B2
Adam Ct, SW7 ....**55** F4
Adam Meere Ho, E1 *off Tarling St* **142** C2
Adams Cl, NW9 ....**90** B3
Adams Ct, EC2 ....**40** B2
Adams Gdns Est, SE16 *off St. Marychurch St* ...**156** C1
Adams Ho, N16 *off Stamford Hill* **99** F2
Adamson Rd, NW3 ....**109** D4
Adams Pl, N7 *off George's Rd* **111** F2
Adams Row, W1 ....**46** B1
Adam St, WC2 ....**49** D1
Adam Wk, SW6 ....**162** C2
Ada Pl, E2 ....**128** A1
Ada Rd, SE5 ....**88** C3
Ada St, E8 ....**128** B1
Adderley Gro, SW11 *off Culmstock Rd* **180** A3
Adderley St, E14 ....**144** C2
Addington Ct, SW14 ....**175** D1
Addington Rd, E3 ....**130** A3
E16 ....**131** E4
N4 ....**98** A1
Addington Sq, SE5 ....**87** F2
Addington St, SE1 ....**61** F1
Addison Av, W11 ....**135** E4
Addison Br Pl, W14 ....**149** F3
Addison Cres, W14 ....**149** E2
Addison Gdns, W14 ....**149** D2
Addison Gro, W4 ....**147** E2
Addison Pl, W11 ....**135** E4
Addison Rd, W14 ....**149** F2
Addle Hill, EC4 ....**39** D4
Addy Ho, SE16 *off Rotherhithe New Rd* **156** C3
Adelaide Av, SE4 ....**185** F2
Adelaide Cl, SW9 *off Broughton Dr* **182** A2
Adelaide Ct, E9 *off Kenworthy Rd* **115** E2
Adelaide Gro, W12 ....**134** A4
Adelaide Rd, E10 ....**102** B4
NW3 ....**109** D4
SW18 *off Putney Br Rd* **178** A3
Adelaide St, WC2 ....**48** C1
Adela St, W10 *off Kensal Rd* **121** E4
Adelina Gro, E1 ....**142** C1
Adeline Pl, WC1 ....**36** B1
Adelphi Ct, SE16 *off Poolmans St* **157** D1
Adelphi Ter, WC2 ....**49** D1
Adeney Cl, W6 ....**163** D1
Aden Gro, N16 ....**113** D1
Aden Ter, N16 ....**113** D1
Adie Rd, W6 ....**148** C2
Adisham Ho, E5 *off Pembury Rd* **114** B2
Adler St, E1 ....**142** A2
Adley St, E5 ....**115** E2
● Admiral Hyson Trd Est, SE16 *off Galleywall Rd* 156 B4
Admiral Pl, SE16 ....**143** E4
Admirals Gate, SE10 ....**172** B3
Admiral Sq, SW10 ....**79** F4

Admiral St, SE8 . . . . .172 A4
Admirals Wk, NW3 . . . . .94 C4
Admirals Way, E14 . . . . .158 A1
★ Admiralty Arch, SW1 . . . .48 B2
Admiralty Cl, SE8
off Reginald Sq 172 A2
Admiral Wk, W9 . . . . .18 B4
Adolphus Rd, N4 . . . . .98 B3
Adolphus St, SE8 . . . . .171 F2
Adpar St, W2 . . . . .20 A3
Adrian Av, NW2
off North Circular Rd 92 B2
Adrian Ms, SW10 . . . . .67 D4
Adriatic Bldg, E14
off Narrow St 143 E3
[Coll] ADT Coll, SW15
off West Hill 177 F3
Adventurers Ct, E14
off Newport Av 145 D3
Adys Rd, SE15 . . . . .183 F1
Affleck St, N1 . . . . .13 F3
Afghan Rd, SW11 . . . . .165 E4
★ Africa Cen, WC2 . . . . .36 C4
Agamemnon Rd, NW6 . . . . .107 F2
Agar Gro, NW1 . . . . .110 C4
Agar Gro Est, NW1 . . . . .111 D4
Agar Pl, NW1 . . . . .110 C4
Agar St, WC2 . . . . .48 C1
Agate Cl, NW10 . . . . .118 A3
Agate Rd, W6 . . . . .148 C2
Agatha Cl, E1
off Prusom St 142 C4
Agave Rd, NW2 . . . . .106 C1
Agdon St, EC1 . . . . .26 C2
Agincourt Rd, NW3 . . . . .109 F1
Agnes Rd, W3 . . . . .133 F4
Agnes St, E14 . . . . .143 F2
Agricola Ct, E3
off Parnell Rd 129 F1
Aileen Wk, E15 . . . . .117 F4
Ailsa St, E14 . . . . .144 C1
Ainger Ms, NW3
off Ainger Rd 109 F4
Ainger Rd, NW3 . . . . .109 F4
Ainsdale Dr, SE1 . . . . .156 A4
Ainsley St, E2 . . . . .128 B3
Ainsty Est, SE16 . . . . .157 D1
Ainsworth Cl, NW2 . . . . .92 A4
SE15
off Lyndhurst Gro 169 E4
Ainsworth Rd, E9 . . . . .114 C4
Ainsworth Way, NW8 . . . . . .122 C1
Aintree Est, SW6
off Dawes Rd 163 E2
Aintree St, SW6 . . . . .163 E2
Aird Ho, SE1
off Rockingham St 63 E3
Airdrie Cl, N1 . . . . .111 F4
Airedale Av, W4 . . . . .147 F3
Airedale Av S, W4
off Netheravon Rd S 147 F4
Airlie Gdns, W8 . . . . .42 A3
Air St, W1 . . . . .47 F1
Aisgill Av, W14 . . . . .149 F4
Aislibie Rd, SE12 . . . . .187 E2
Aiten Pl, W6
off Standish Rd 148 A3
Aitken Cl, E8
off Pownall Rd 128 A1
Aitman Dr, Brent. TW8
off Chiswick High Rd . . .146 A4
Ajax Rd, NW6 . . . . .108 A2
Akehurst St, SW15 . . . . .176 A4
Akenside Rd, NW3 . . . . .109 D2
Akerman Rd, SW9 . . . . .168 B4
Alamaro Lo, SE10
off Renaissance Wk 159 F2
Aland Ct, SE16
off Finland St 157 E2
Alan Hocken Way, E15 . . . . .131 E2
Alanthus Cl, SE12 . . . . .187 F4
Alaska Bldg, SE13
off Deals Gateway 172 B3
Alaska St, SE1 . . . . .50 A3
Albacore Cres, SE13 . . . . . . .186 B4
Alban Highwalk, EC2
off London Wall 39 F1
Albany, W1 . . . . .47 E1
Albany Cl, SW14 . . . . .174 B2
Albany Ct, E10 . . . . .102 A1
Albany Ctyd, W1 . . . . .47 F1
Albany Mans, SW11 . . . . .81 D3
Albany Ms, N1
off Barnsbury Pk 112 A4
SE5 . . . . .87 F1
Albany Rd, E10 . . . . .102 A1
SE5 . . . . .88 A1
SE17 . . . . .88 A1
Albany St, NW1 . . . . .10 C2
Alba Pl, W11
off Portobello Rd 135 F2
Albatross Way, SE16 . . . . . .157 D1
Albemarle St, W1 . . . . .47 D1
Albemarle Way, EC1 . . . . .26 C3
Alberta Est, SE17 . . . . .75 D2
Alberta St, SE17 . . . . .74 C2
Albert Av, SW8 . . . . .85 E3
Albert Barnes Ho, SE1 . . . . . .63 E3
Albert Bigg Pt, E15 . . . . .130 C1
Albert Br, SW3 . . . . .81 D1
SW11 . . . . .81 D1
Albert Br Rd, SW11 . . . . .81 D2
Albert Cl, E9
off Northiam St 128 B1
Albert Ct, SW7 . . . . .56 A1
Albert Embk, SE1 . . . . .73 D3
Albert Gdns, E1 . . . . .143 D2
Albert Gate, SW1 . . . . .45 F4
Albert Hall Mans, SW7 . . . . . .56 A1
Albert Mans, SW11 . . . . .81 E4
★ Albert Mem, SW7 . . . . . . .44 A4
Albert Ms, E14
off Narrow St 143 E3
N4 . . . . .97 F2
SE4 off Arabin Rd 185 E2
W8 . . . . .55 E2
Albert Pl, W8 . . . . .55 D1
Albert Rd, E10 . . . . .102 C3
N4 . . . . .97 F2
NW6 . . . . .121 F2
Albert Sq, E15 . . . . .117 E2
SW8 . . . . .85 E3
Albert St, NW1 . . . . .11 D1
Albert Ter, NW1 . . . . .124 A1
NW10 . . . . .119 D1
W6 off Beavor La 148 A4
Albert Ter Ms, NW1 . . . . .10 A1
Albert Way, SE15 . . . . .170 B2
Albion Av, SW8 . . . . .167 D4
Albion Cl, W2 . . . . .33 D4
Albion Dr, E8 . . . . .113 F4
Albion Est, SE16 . . . . .156 C1
Albion Gro, N16 . . . . .113 E1
Albion Ms, N1 . . . . .126 A1
NW6
off Kilburn High Rd 107 F4
W2 . . . . .33 D3
W6 off Galena Rd 148 B3
Albion Par, N16
off Albion Rd 113 D1
Albion Pl, EC1 . . . . .26 C4
W6 . . . . .148 B3
Albion Riverside Bldg, SW11 . .81 D2
Albion Rd, N16 . . . . .113 D1
Albion Sq, E8 . . . . .113 F4
Albion St, SE16 . . . . .156 C1
W2 . . . . .33 D3
Albion Ter, E8 . . . . .113 F4
Albion Wk, N1 . . . . .13 D3
Albion Way, EC1 . . . . .39 E1
SE13 . . . . .186 C2
Wembley HA9
off North End Rd 90 B4
Albion Yd, N1 . . . . .13 D3
Albon Ho, SW18
off Neville Gill Cl 178 B4
Albrighton Rd, SE22 . . . . . . .183 E1
Albury St, SE8 . . . . .172 A1
Albyn Rd, SE8 . . . . .172 A3
Alcester Cres, E5 . . . . .100 B3
Alconbury Rd, E5 . . . . .100 A3
Aldbourne Rd, W12 . . . . .133 F4
Aldbridge St, SE17 . . . . .77 D2
Aldburgh Ms, W1 . . . . .34 B2
Aldbury Av, Wem. HA9 . . . . .104 B4
Aldebert Ter, SW8 . . . . .85 D3
Aldeburgh Cl, E5
off Southwold Rd 100 B3
Alden Av, E15 . . . . .131 F3
Aldenham St, NW1 . . . . .11 F3
Aldensley Rd, W6 . . . . .148 B2
Alderbrook Rd, SW12 . . . . . .180 B4
Alderbury Rd, SW13 . . . . . . .162 A1
Alder Cl, SE15 . . . . .89 F1
Alder Gro, NW2 . . . . .92 B3
Alder Ho, NW3
off Maitland Pk Vil 109 F3
Aldermanbury, EC2 . . . . .39 F2
Aldermanbury Sq, EC2 . . . . . .39 F1
Alderman's Wk, EC2 . . . . .40 C1
Alder Ms, N19
off Bredgar Rd 96 C3
Alderney Ho, N1
off Arran Wk 112 C3
Alderney Ms, SE1 . . . . .64 A2
Alderney Rd, E1 . . . . .129 D4
Alderney St, SW1 . . . . .71 D2
Alder Rd, SW14 . . . . .175 D1
Aldersford Cl, SE4 . . . . .185 D3
Aldersgate St, EC1 . . . . .39 E2
Aldershot Rd, NW6 . . . . .121 F1
Alderson St, W10
off Kensal Rd 121 E4
Alderton Cl, NW10 . . . . .91 D4
Alderton Rd, SE24 . . . . .182 C1
Alderville Rd, SW6 . . . . .163 F4
Aldford St, W1 . . . . .46 A2
⊖ Aldgate 41 E3
⊖ Aldgate 41 E3
Aldgate, EC3 . . . . .41 E3
Aldgate Av, E1 . . . . .41 E2
🔒 Aldgate Barrs Shop Cen,
E1 . . . . .41 F2
⊖ Aldgate East 41 F2
Aldgate High St, EC3 . . . . . . .41 E3
Aldine Ct, W12
off Aldine St 134 C4
Aldine Pl, W12
off Uxbridge Rd 148 C1
Aldine St, W12 . . . . .148 C1
Aldred Rd, NW6 . . . . .108 A2
Aldridge Rd Vil, W11 . . . . . . .135 F1

Aldsworth Cl, W9 ....18 C3
Aldworth Gro, SE13 ....186 C4
Aldworth Rd, E15 ....117 E4
Aldwych, WC2 ....37 E4
Aldwych Underpass, WC2
off Kingsway 37 E3
Alexa Ct, W8 ....54 C4
Alexander Av, NW10 ....106 B4
★ Alexander Fleming
Laboratory Mus, W2 .....32 B2
Alexander Ms, W2 ....30 C2
Alexander Pl, SW7 ....56 C4
Alexander Rd, N19 ....97 E4
Alexander Sq, SW3 ....56 C4
Alexander St, W2 ....30 B2
Alexandra Av, SW11 ....82 A4
W4 ....161 D2
Alexandra Cl, SE8 ....171 F1
Alexandra Cotts, SE14 .....171 F3
Alexandra Ct, N16 ....113 E1
W9 ....19 F2
Alexandra Gdns, W4 ....161 E2
Alexandra Gro, N4 ....98 B2
Alexandra Pl, NW8 ....122 C1
Alexandra Rd, E10 ....102 C4
NW8 ....108 C4
SW14 ....175 D1
W4 ....147 D1
Alexandra St, SE14 ....171 E2
Alexis St, SE16 ....156 A3
Alfearn Rd, E5 ....114 C1
Alford Pl, N1 ....15 F3
Alfreda St, SW11 ....82 C4
Alfred Cl, W4 ....147 D3
Alfred Ms, W1 ....24 A4
Alfred Pl, WC1 ....24 A4
Alfred Rd, E15 ....117 F2
W2 ....18 B4
W3 ....132 C4
Alfred St, E3 ....129 F3
Alfriston Rd, SW11 ....179 F3
Algernon Rd, NW6 ....6 A1
SE13 ....186 B2
Algiers Rd, SE13 ....186 A2
Alice Ct, SW15 ....177 F2
Alice Gilliatt Ct, W14 ....163 F1
Alice La, E3 ....129 F1
Alice St, SE1 ....64 C3
Alice Walker Cl, SE24
off Shakespeare Rd 182 B2
Alie St, E1 ....41 F3
Alington Cres, NW9 ....90 C2
Aliwal Rd, SW11 ....179 E2
Alkerden Rd, W4 ....147 E4
Alkham Rd, N16 ....99 F3
Allan Way, W3 ....132 C1
Allard Gdns, SW4 ....181 D3
Allardyce St, SW4 ....181 F2
Allcroft Rd, NW5 ....110 A2
Allendale Cl, SE5
off Daneville Rd 169 D3
Allen Edwards Dr, SW8 ......84 C4
Allenford Ho, SW15
off Tunworth Cres 175 F4
Allen Rd, E3 ....129 F2
N16 ....113 E1
Allensbury Pl, NW1 ....111 D4
Allen St, W8 ....54 B2
Allerton Rd, N16 ....98 C3
Allerton Wk, N7
off Durham Rd 97 F3
Allestree Rd, SW6 ....163 E2
Allfarthing La, SW18 .....178 B4
Allgood St, E2 ....17 F3
Allhallows La, EC4 ....52 A1
★ All Hallows-on-the-Wall
C of E Ch, EC2 ....40 B1
● Alliance Ct, W3
off Alliance Rd 132 B1
Alliance Rd, W3 ....118 B4
Allied Ct, N1
off Enfield Rd 113 E4
Allied Way, W3
off Larden Rd 147 E1
Allingham Ms, N1 ....15 E2
Allingham St, N1 ....15 E2
Allington Rd, W10 ....121 E2
Allington St, SW1 ....59 E3
Allison Cl, SE10
off Dartmouth Hill 172 C3
Allison Rd, W3 ....132 C2
Allitsen Rd, NW8 ....8 C3
Allnutt Way, SW4 ....181 D3
Alloa Rd, SE8 ....157 D4
Allonby Ho, E14
off Aston St 143 E1
Allotment Way, NW2
off Midland Ter 93 D4
Alloway Rd, E3 ....129 E3
Allport Ms, E1
off Stepney Grn 128 C4
DLR All Saints 144 B3
All Saints Cl, SW8 ....84 C4
All Saints Dr, SE3 ....173 E4
All Saints Pas, SW18
off Wandsworth
High St 178 A3
All Saints Rd, W3 ....146 C2
W11 ....135 F1
All Saints St, N1 ....13 E2
All Saints Twr, E10 ....102 B1
Allsop Pl, NW1 ....21 F3
All Souls Av, NW10 ....120 B2
All Souls Pl, W1 ....35 D1
Almack Rd, E5 ....114 C1
Alma Gro, SE1 ....77 F1
Alma Pl, NW10
off Harrow Rd 120 B3
Alma Rd, SW18 ....178 C3
Alma Sq, NW8 ....7 F4
Alma St, E15 ....117 D3
NW5 ....110 B3
Alma Ter, W8
off Allen St 54 B3
Almeida St, N1 ....112 B4
Almeric Rd, SW11 ....179 F2
Almington St, N4 ....97 E2
Almond Cl, SE15 ....170 A4
Almond Rd, SE16 ....156 B3
Almorah Rd, N1 ....113 D4
Alperton St, W10 ....121 E4
Alphabet Sq, E3
off Hawgood St 144 A1
Alpha Cl, NW1 ....21 D2
Alpha Gro, E14 ....158 A1
Alpha Pl, NW6 ....6 B2
SW3 ....69 D4
Alpha Rd, SE14 ....171 F3
Alpha St, SE15 ....170 A4
Alpine Gro, E9 ....114 C4
Alpine Rd, E10 ....102 B3
SE16 ....156 C3
Alric Av, NW10 ....105 D4
Alroy Rd, N4 ....98 A1
Alsace Rd, SE17 ....76 C2
Alscot Rd, SE1 ....65 F4
Alscot Way, SE1 ....65 E4
Altenburg Gdns, SW11 .....179 F2
Althea St, SW6 ....164 B4
Althorpe Gro, SW11 ....80 B4
Althorpe Ms, SW11
off Battersea High St ...165 D3
Altima Ct, SE22
off East Dulwich Rd 184 A2
Alton Ho, E3
off Bromley High St 130 B3
Alton St, E14 ....144 B1
Alvanley Gdns, NW6 ......108 B2
Alverstone Rd, NW2 ......106 C4
Alverton St, SE8 ....157 F4
Alvey Est, SE17 ....76 C1
Alvey St, SE17 ....76 C2
Alvington Cres, E8 ......113 F2
Alwyn Av, W4 ....147 D4
Alwyne La, N1
off Alwyne Vil 112 B4
Alwyne Pl, N1 ....112 C3
Alwyne Rd, N1 ....112 C4
Alwyne Sq, N1 ....112 C3
Alwyne Vil, N1 ....112 B4
Alwyn Gdns, W3 ....132 B2
Alzette Ho, E2 ....129 D3
Amazon St, E1
off Hessel St 142 B2
Ambassador's Ct, SW1 ......47 F3
Ambassador Sq, E14
off Cahir St 158 B3
Ambergate St, SE17 ....75 D2
Amber Gro, NW2 ....93 D2
Amberley Rd, E10 ....102 A1
W9 ....18 B4
Amber St, E15
off Great Eastern Rd 117 D3
Amber Wf, E2 ....17 E1
Ambler Rd, N4 ....98 B4
Ambleside Cl, E9
off Churchill Wk 114 C2
E10 ....102 B1
Ambleside Pt, SE15
off Ilderton Rd 170 C2
Ambleside Rd, NW10 ......105 F4
Ambrosden Av, SW1 ....59 F3
Ambrose Av, NW11 ....93 E1
Ambrose Ms, SW11 ....165 E4
Ambrose St, SE16 ....156 B3
Ambrose Wk, E3
off Malmesbury Rd 130 A2
● AMC Business Cen,
NW10 ....118 B3
Amelia Cl, W3 ....132 B4
Amelia St, SE17 ....75 D2
Amen Cor, EC4 ....39 D3
Amen Ct, EC4 ....39 D2
America Sq, EC3 ....41 E4
America St, SE1 ....51 E3
Amerland Rd, SW18 ....177 F4
Amersham Gro, SE14 ......171 F2
Amersham Rd, SE14 ....171 F2
Amersham Vale, SE14 .....171 F2
Amery Gdns, NW10 ....120 B1
Amesbury Twr, SW8
off Westbury St 166 C4
Amethyst Rd, E15 ....117 D1
Amhurst Par, N16
off Amhurst Pk 99 F1
Amhurst Pk, N16 ....99 D1
Amhurst Pas, E8 ....114 A1
Amhurst Rd, E8 ....114 B2
N16 ....113 F1
Amhurst Ter, E8 ....114 A1
Amiel St, E1 ....128 C4
Amies St, SW11 ....179 F1

Amina Way, SE16
off Yalding Rd **156** A2
Amity Rd, E15 . . . . **131** F1
Amner Rd, SW11 . . . . **180** A4
Amor Rd, W6 . . . . **148** C2
Amott Rd, SE15 . . . . **184** A1
Amoy Pl, E14 . . . . **144** A2
Ampthill Sq Est, NW1 . . . . **11** F3
Ampton Pl, WC1 . . . . **25** E1
Ampton St, WC1 . . . . **25** E1
Amsterdam Rd, E14 . . . . **158** C2
Amundsen Ct, E14
off Napier Av **158** A4
Amwell Ct Est, N4 . . . . **98** C2
Amwell St, EC1 . . . . **14** A4
Amyruth Rd, SE4 . . . . **186** A3
Anatola Rd, N19
off Dartmouth Pk Hill **96** B3
Anchorage Pt, E14
off Cuba St **158** A1
Anchor Ho, SW18
off Smugglers Way **178** B2
Anchor Ms, N1
off Balls Pond Rd **113** E3
SW11
off Westbridge Rd **165** D3
SW12 . . . . **180** B4
Anchor Retail Pk, E1 . . . . **128** C4
Anchor St, SE16 . . . . **156** B3
Anchor Ter, E1
off Cephas Av **128** C4
Anchor Wf, E3
off Watts Gro **144** B1
Anchor Yd, EC1 . . . . **27** F2
Ancill Cl, W6 . . . . **163** E1
Ancona Rd, NW10 . . . . **120** A2
Andalus Rd, SW9 . . . . **181** E1
Anderson Cl, W3 . . . . **133** D2
Anderson Rd, E9 . . . . **115** D3
Andersons Sq, N1 . . . . **14** C1
Anderson St, SW3 . . . . **69** E2
Anderton Cl, SE5 . . . . **183** D1
Andover Est, N7 . . . . **97** F3
Andover Pl, NW6 . . . . **6** C2
Andover Rd, N7 . . . . **97** F3
Andre St, E8 . . . . **114** A2
Andrew Borde St, WC2 . . . . . . **36** B2
Andrewes Ho, EC2 . . . . **39** F1
Andrew Pl, SW8 . . . . **84** B4
Andrews Crosse, WC2 . . . . **38** A3
Andrew's Rd, E8 . . . . **128** B1
Andrew St, E14 . . . . **144** C2
Andrews Wk, SE17 . . . . **87** D1
Anerley St, SW11 . . . . **165** F4
Angel **14** B2
Angel All, E1 . . . . **41** F2
Angel Ct, EC2 . . . . **40** B2
SW1 . . . . **47** F3
Angel Gate, EC1 . . . . **15** D4
Angelis Apts, N1
off Graham St **15** D3
Angel La, E15 . . . . **117** D3
Angell Pk Gdns, SW9 . . . . . . **182** A1
Angell Rd, SW9 . . . . **182** A1
Angell Town Est, SW9
off Overton Rd **168** A4
Angel Ms, E1
off Cable St **142** B3
N1 . . . . **14** B3
Angel Pas, EC4 . . . . **52** A1
Angel Pl, SE1 . . . . **52** A4
Angel Southside, EC1 . . . . **14** B3
Angel Sq, EC1 . . . . **14** B3
Angel St, EC1 . . . . **39** E2
Angel Wk, W6 . . . . **148** C3
Angel Wf, N1
off Eagle Wf Rd **126** C2
Angerstein La, SE3 . . . . **173** F2
Angler's La, NW5 . . . . **110** B3
Anglesea Ter, W6
off Wellesley Av **148** B2
Anglia Ho, E14 . . . . **143** E2
Anglian Rd, E11 . . . . **103** D4
Anglo Rd, E3 . . . . **129** F2
Angrave Ct, E8 . . . . **127** F1
Angrave Pas, E8
off Haggerston Rd **127** F1
Angus St, SE14 . . . . **171** E2
Anhalt Rd, SW11 . . . . **81** D2
Anley Rd, W14 . . . . **149** D1
Annabel Cl, E14 . . . . **144** B2
Anna Cl, E8 . . . . **127** F1
Annandale Rd, SE10 . . . . **173** F1
W4 . . . . **147** E3
Anne Goodman Ho, E1
off Jubilee St **142** C2
Annesley Cl, NW10 . . . . **91** E4
Annesley Wk, N19
off Highgate Hill **96** C3
Annette Cres, N1
off Essex Rd **112** C4
Annette Rd, N7 . . . . **111** F1
Annie Besant Cl, E3 . . . . **129** F1
Anning St, EC2 . . . . **29** D2
Annis Rd, E9 . . . . **115** E3
Ann La, SW10 . . . . **80** A2
Ann Moss Way, SE16 . . . . . . **156** C2
Ann's Cl, SW1 . . . . **57** F1
Ann's Pl, E1 . . . . **41** E1
Ansdell Rd, SE15 . . . . **170** C4
Ansdell St, W8 . . . . **55** D2
Ansdell Ter, W8 . . . . **55** D2
Anselm Rd, SW6 . . . . **78** A1
Ansleigh Pl, W11 . . . . **135** D3
Anson Ho, E1
off Shandy St **129** E4
Anson Rd, N7 . . . . **110** C1
NW2 . . . . **107** D2
Anstey Rd, SE15 . . . . **184** A1
Anstice Cl, W4 . . . . **161** E2
Anthony St, E1
off Commercial Rd **142** B2
Antill Rd, E3 . . . . **129** E3
Antill Ter, E1 . . . . **143** D2
Antonine Hts, SE1 . . . . **64** C1
Anton Pl, Wem. HA9 . . . . **90** B4
Anton St, E8 . . . . **114** A2
Antony Ho, E5
off Pembury Pl **114** B2
Antrim Gro, NW3 . . . . **109** F3
Antrim Mans, NW3 . . . . **109** E3
Antrim Rd, NW3 . . . . **109** F3
Antrobus Rd, W4 . . . . **146** C3
Apex Ind Est, NW10
off Hythe Rd **119** F4
Apollo, E14
off Newton Pl **158** A3
Apollo Hammersmith,
W6 . . . . **148** C4
Apollo Pl, E11 . . . . **103** E4
SW10 . . . . **80** A2
Apollo Thea, W1 . . . . **36** A4
Apollo Victoria Thea,
SW1 . . . . **59** E3
Apothecary St, EC4 . . . . **38** C3
Appach Rd, SW2 . . . . **182** A3
Apple Blossom Ct, SW8
off Pascal St **84** B2
Appleby Ct, W3
off Newport Rd **146** C1
Appleby Rd, E8 . . . . **114** A4
E16 . . . . **145** F2
Appleby St, E2 . . . . **17** E2
Appleford Rd, W10 . . . . **121** E4
Applegarth Rd, W14 . . . . **149** D2
Apple Rd, E11 . . . . **103** E4
Apple Tree Yd, SW1 . . . . **47** F2
Applewood Cl, NW2 . . . . **92** B4
Appold St, EC2 . . . . **28** C4
Apprentice Way, E5
off Clarence Rd **114** B1
Approach, The, W3 . . . . **133** D2
Approach Cl, N16
off Cowper Rd **113** E1
Approach Rd, E2 . . . . **128** C2
April St, E8 . . . . **113** F1
Apsley Ho
(Wellington Mus), W1 . . . . **46** A4
Apsley Way, NW2 . . . . **92** A3
W1 . . . . **46** B4
Aquarius Business Pk,
NW2 . . . . **91** F2
Aquila St, NW8 . . . . **8** B2
Aquinas St, SE1 . . . . **50** B2
Arabella Dr, SW15 . . . . **175** E2
Arabin Rd, SE4 . . . . **185** E2
Aragon Twr, SE8 . . . . **157** F3
Aran Ms, N7
off Barnsbury Gro **112** A4
Arbery Rd, E3 . . . . **129** E3
Arbor Ct, N16 . . . . **99** D3
Arbour Sq, E1 . . . . **143** D2
Arbuthnot Rd, SE14 . . . . **171** D4
Arbutus St, E8 . . . . **127** E1
Arcade, The, EC2 . . . . **40** C1
Arcadia St, E14 . . . . **144** A2
Archangel St, SE16 . . . . **157** D1
Archbishops Pl, SW2 . . . . . . **181** F4
Archdale Rd, SE22 . . . . **183** F3
Archel Rd, W14 . . . . **163** F1
Archer Ho, N1
off Phillipp St **17** D1
SW11
off Vicarage Cres **165** D4
Archer Sq, SE14
off Knoyle St **171** E1
Archer St, W1 . . . . **36** A4
Archery Cl, W2 . . . . **33** D3
Archery Steps, W2
off St. Georges Flds **33** D4
Arches, SW9
off Ridgeway Rd **182** B1
Arches, The, SW6
off Munster Rd **163** F4
SW8 *off New Covent Gdn*
Mkt **84** B2
WC2 . . . . **49** D2
Archibald Ms, W1 . . . . **46** B1
Archibald Rd, N7 . . . . **111** D1
Archibald St, E3 . . . . **130** A3
Archie St, SE1 . . . . **65** D1
Architectural Assoc
Sch of Architecture, WC1 . **36** B1
Arch St, SE1 . . . . **63** E3
Archway **96** C3
Archway Business Cen, N19
off Wedmore St **97** D4
Archway Campus, The, N19
off Highgate Hill **96** C3
Archway Cl, N19
off Archway Rd **96** C3
W10 . . . . **135** D1

Archway Mall, N19 ....**96** C3
Archway Ms, SW15
off Putney Br Rd **177** E2
Archway Rd, N19 ....**96** C2
Archway St, SW13 ....**175** E1
Arcola St, E8 ....**113** F2
Arctic St, NW5
off Gillies St **110** B2
Ardbeg Rd, SE24 ....**183** D4
Arden Cres, E14 ....**158** A3
Arden Est, N1 ....**16** C3
Arden Ho, SW9
off Grantham Rd **167** E4
Ardilaun Rd, N5 ....**112** C1
Ardleigh Rd, N1 ....**113** D3
Ardley Cl, NW10 ....**91** E4
Ardmere Rd, SE13 ....**187** D4
Ardshiel Cl, SW15
off Bemish Rd **177** D1
Ardwick Rd, NW2 ....**108** A1
Arena Sq, Wem. HA9 ......**104** A1
Argall Av, E10 ....**101** D1
Argall Way, E10 ....**101** D2
Argenta Way, NW10 ......**104** B4
Argento Twr, SW18 ....**178** B4
Argon Ms, SW6 ....**78** B3
Argyle Pl, W6 ....**148** B3
Argyle Rd, E1 ....**129** D4
E15 ....**117** E1
Argyle Sq, WC1 ....**13** D4
Argyle St, WC1 ....**12** C4
Argyle Wk, WC1 ....**25** D1
Argyle Way, SE16 ....**156** A4
Argyll Cl, SW9
off Dalyell Rd **181** F1
Argyll Rd, W8 ....**54** A1
Argyll St, W1 ....**35** E3
Aria Ho, WC2 ....**37** D2
Arica Ho, SE16 ....**156** B2
Arica Rd, SE4 ....**185** E2
Ariel Rd, NW6 ....**108** A3
Ariel Way, W12 ....**134** C4
Aristotle Rd, SW4 ....**181** D1
Arizona Bldg, SE13
off Deals Gateway **172** B3
Arklow Ho, SE17 ....**76** A4
Arklow Rd, SE14 ....**171** F1
Arkwright Rd, NW3 ....**108** C2
Arlesey Cl, SW15 ....**177** E3
Arlesford Rd, SW9 ....**181** E1
Arlingford Rd, SW2 ....**182** A3
Arlington Av, N1 ....**15** F1
Arlington Bldg, E3
off Fairfield Rd **130** A2
Arlington Cl, SE13 ....**187** D3
Arlington Ct, W3
off Mill Hill Rd **132** B4
Arlington Gdns, W4 ....**146** C4
Arlington Lo, SW2 ....**181** F2
Arlington Pl, SE10
off Greenwich S St **172** C2
Arlington Rd, NW1 ....**11** D1
Arlington Sq, N1 ....**15** F1
Arlington St, SW1 ....**47** E2
Arlington Way, EC1 ....**14** B4
Armada Ct, SE8
off Watergate St **172** A1
Armadale Rd, SW6 ....**78** A2
Armagh Rd, E3 ....**129** F1
Arminger Rd, W12 ....**134** B4
Armitage Rd, NW11 ....**93** F2
SE10 ....**159** F4
Armour Cl, N7
off Roman Way **111** F3
Armoury Rd, SE8 ....**172** B4
Armoury Way, SW18 ......**178** A3
Armstrong Rd, NW10 ......**105** E4
SW7 ....**56** A3
W3 ....**133** F4
Arndale Wk, SW18
off Garratt La **178** B3
Arne Ho, SE11 ....**73** E2
Arne St, WC2 ....**37** D3
Arne Wk, SE3 ....**187** F2
Arneway St, SW1 ....**60** B3
Arnhem Pl, E14 ....**158** A2
Arnhem Way, SE22
off East Dulwich Gro **183** E3
Arnhem Wf, E14
off Arnhem Pl **158** A2
Arnold Circ, E2 ....**29** E1
Arnold Est, SE1 ....**65** F1
Arnold Rd, E3 ....**130** A3
Arnott Cl, W4 ....**147** D3
Arnould Av, SE5 ....**183** D2
Arnside St, SE17 ....**75** F4
Arodene Rd, SW2 ....**181** F4
Arran Wk, N1 ....**112** C4
Arrol Ho, SE1 ....**63** F3
Arrow Rd, E3 ....**130** B3
Arrowsmith Ho, SE11 ....**73** E2
⊖ Arsenal **98** A4
★ Arsenal FC, N5 ....**112** A1
Arta Ho, E1
off Devonport St **142** C2
Artesian Cl, NW10 ....**105** D4
Artesian Rd, W2 ....**30** A3
Artesian Wk, E11 ....**103** E4
Arthingworth St, E15 ......**131** E1
Arthur Ct, SW11
off Charlotte
Despard Av **166** A3
W2 ....**30** C2
Arthurdon Rd, SE4 ....**186** A3
Arthur Henderson Ho,
SW6 ....**163** F4
Arthur Horsley Wk, E7
off Magpie Cl **117** F2
Arthur Newton Ho, SW11
off Lavender Rd **179** D1
Arthur Rd, N7 ....**111** F1
Arthur St, EC4 ....**52** B1
Artichoke Hill, E1
off Pennington St **142** B3
Artichoke Pl, SE5 ....**88** A4
Artillery La, E1 ....**41** D1
W12 ....**134** A2
Artillery Mans, SW1 ....**60** A2
Artillery Pas, E1 ....**41** D1
Artillery Pl, SW1 ....**60** A3
Artillery Row, SW1 ....**60** A3
Artizan St, E1 ....**41** D2
Arundel Cl, E15 ....**117** E1
SW11 ....**179** E3
Arundel Gdns, W11 ....**135** F3
Arundel Gt Ct, WC2 ....**37** F4
Arundel Gro, N16 ....**113** E2
Arundel Pl, N1 ....**112** A3
Arundel Sq, N7 ....**112** A3
Arundel St, WC2 ....**37** F4
Arundel Ter, SW13 ....**162** B1
Arvon Rd, N5 ....**112** A2
Ascalon Ho, SW8
off Ascalon St **83** E3
Ascalon St, SW8 ....**83** E3
Ascham St, NW5 ....**110** C2
Ashanti Ms, E8
off Lower Clapton Rd ...**114** B2
Ashbourne Cl, W5 ....**132** A1
Ashbourne Ct, E5
off Daubeney Rd **115** E1
Ashbourne Gro, SE22 ......**183** F3
W4 ....**147** E4
Coll Ashbourne Indep
6th Form Coll, W8 ......**42** C4
Ashbridge Rd, E11 ....**103** E1
Ashbridge St, NW8 ....**20** C3
Ashbrook Rd, N19 ....**97** D2
Ashburn Gdns, SW7 ....**55** E4
Ashburnham Gro, SE10 ....**172** B2
Ashburnham Pl, SE10 ......**172** B2
Ashburnham Retreat, SE10 .**172** B2
Ashburnham Rd, NW10 ....**120** C3
SW10 ....**79** F3
Ashburnham Twr, SW10
off Blantyre St **80** A2
Ashburn Pl, SW7 ....**55** E4
Ashburton Triangle, N5
off Drayton Pk **112** A1
Ashbury Rd, SW11 ....**179** F1
Ashby Gro, N1 ....**112** C4
Ashby Ho, N1
off Essex Rd **112** C4
Ashby Ms, SE4 ....**171** F4
SW2 *off Prague Pl* **181** E3
Ashby Rd, SE4 ....**171** F4
Ashby St, EC1 ....**27** D1
Ashchurch Gro, W12 ....**148** A1
Ashchurch Pk Vil, W12 .....**148** A2
Ashchurch Ter, W12 ....**148** A2
Ashcombe Pk, NW2 ....**91** E4
Ashcombe St, SW6 ....**164** B4
Ashcroft Rd, E3 ....**129** E3
Ashcroft Sq, W6
off King St **148** C3
Ashdene, SE15 ....**170** B3
Ashdon Rd, NW10 ....**119** E1
Ashdown Cres, NW5
off Queen's Cres **110** A2
Ashdown Wk, E14 ....**158** A3
Ashenden, SE17 ....**63** E4
Ashenden Rd, E5 ....**115** D2
Ashentree Ct, EC4 ....**38** B3
Asher Way, E1 ....**142** A4
Ashfield Rd, W3 ....**133** F4
Ashfield St, E1 ....**142** B1
Ashfield Yd, E1
off Ashfield St **142** C1
Ashford Rd, NW2 ....**107** D1
Ashford St, N1 ....**16** C4
Ash Gro, E8 ....**128** B1
NW2 ....**107** D1
Ash Ho, SE1
off Longfield Est **77** F1
Ashington Ho, E1
off Barnsley St **128** B4
Ashington Rd, SW6 ....**163** F4
Ashland Pl, W1 ....**22** A4
Ashleigh Rd, SW14 ....**175** E1
Ashley Cres, SW11 ....**180** A1
Ashley Gdns, SW1 ....**59** F3
Ashley Pl, SW1 ....**59** E3
Ashley Rd, N19 ....**97** E2
Ashlin Rd, E15 ....**117** D1
Ashlone Rd, SW15 ....**176** C1
Ashmead Ho, E9
off Kingsmead Way **115** E2
Ashmead Rd, SE8 ....**172** A4
Ashmere Gro, SW2 ....**181** E2
Ashmill St, NW1 ....**20** C4
Ashmole Pl, SW8 ....**85** F1
Ashmole St, SW8 ....**85** F1

Ashmore Cl, SE15 . . . . **89** F3
Ashmore Rd, W9 . . . . **121** F4
Ashmount Rd, N19 . . . . **96** C1
Ashness Rd, SW11 . . . . **179** F3
Ash Rd, E15 . . . . **117** E2
Ashtead Rd, E5 . . . . **100** A1
Ashton Rd, E15 . . . . **117** D2
Ashton St, E14 . . . . **144** C3
Ashville Rd, E11 . . . . **103** D3
Ashwin St, E8 . . . . **113** F3
Ashworth Cl, SE5
off Love Wk **169** D4
Ashworth Rd, W9 . . . . **7** D4
Asker Ho, N7
off Tufnell Pk Rd **111** E1
Aske St, N1 . . . . **16** C4
Askew Cres, W12 . . . . **147** F1
Askew Rd, W12 . . . . **133** F4
Askham Ct, W12 . . . . **134** A4
Askham Rd, W12 . . . . **134** A4
Askill Dr, SW15 . . . . **177** E3
Asland Rd, E15 . . . . **131** E1
Asmara Rd, NW2 . . . . **107** E2
Asolando Dr, SE17 . . . . **75** F1
Aspect Ct, SW6
off Lensbury Av **164** C4
Aspen Cl, N19
off Hargrave Pk **96** C3
Aspen Gdns, W6 . . . . **148** B4
Aspen Ho, NW3
off Maitland Pk Vil **109** F3
Aspenlea Rd, W6 . . . . **163** D1
Aspen Way, E14 . . . . **144** A3
Aspern Gro, NW3 . . . . **109** E2
Aspinall Rd, SE4 . . . . **185** D1
Aspinden Rd, SE16 . . . . **156** B3
Aspley Rd, SW18 . . . . **178** B3
Assam St, E1
off White Ch La **142** A2
Assata Ms, N1
off St. Paul's Rd **112** B3
Assembly Pas, E1 . . . . **142** C1
Astbury Business Pk, SE15
off Station Pas **170** C3
Astbury Ho, SE11 . . . . **62** A3
Astbury Rd, SE15 . . . . **170** C3
Astell St, SW3 . . . . **69** D2
Aster Ct, E5 . . . . **100** C3
Aste St, E14 . . . . **158** C1
Asteys Row, N1
off River Pl **112** C4
Astle St, SW11 . . . . **166** A4
Astley Av, NW2 . . . . **106** C2
Astley Ho, SE1
off Rowcross St **77** F2
Aston Ct, N4
off Queens Dr **98** C3
Aston Ho, SW8
off Wandsworth Rd **167** D3
Aston St, E14 . . . . **143** E2
Aston Ter, SW12
off Cathles Rd **180** B4
Astoria Wk, SW9 . . . . **182** A1
Astrop Ms, W6 . . . . **148** C2
Astrop Ter, W6 . . . . **148** C2
Astwood Ms, SW7 . . . . **55** E4
Asylum Rd, SE15 . . . . **170** B2
Atalanta St, SW6 . . . . **163** D3
Athelstane Gro, E3 . . . . **129** F2
Athelstane Ms, N4
off Stroud Grn Rd **98** A2
Athelstan Gdns, NW6 . . . . . . **107** E4
Athelstan Ho, E9
off Kingsmead Way **115** F2
Athena Ct, SE1
off Long La **64** C1
Athenaeum Ct, N5 . . . . **112** C1
Athenlay Rd, SE15 . . . . **185** D3
Athens Gdns, W9 . . . . **18** A3
Atherden Rd, E5 . . . . **114** C1
Atherfold Rd, SW9 . . . . **181** E1
Atherstone Ct, W2 . . . . **19** D4
Atherstone Ms, SW7 . . . . **55** F4
Atherton Ms, E7 . . . . **117** F3
Atherton Rd, E7 . . . . **117** F2
SW13 . . . . **162** A2
Atherton St, SW11 . . . . **165** E4
Athlone Cl, E5
off Goulton Rd **114** B2
Athlone St, NW5 . . . . **110** A3
Atholl Ho, W9 . . . . **19** E1
Athol Sq, E14 . . . . **144** C2
Atkinson Ho, SW11
off Austin Rd **166** A3
Atlanta Bldg, SE13
off Deals Gateway **172** B3
Atlantic Rd, SW9 . . . . **182** A2
● Atlas Business Cen,
NW2 . . . . **92** B3
Atlas Ms, E8
off Dalston La **113** F3
N7 . . . . **111** F3
Atlas Rd, NW10 . . . . **119** E3
Wembley HA9 . . . . **104** C1
Atley Rd, E3 . . . . **130** A1
Atney Rd, SW15 . . . . **177** E2
Atterbury St, SW1 . . . . **72** B1
Attewood Av, NW10 . . . . **91** E4
Attneave St, WC1 . . . . **26** A1
Atwell Rd, SE15
off Rye La **170** A4
Atwood Av, Rich. TW9 . . . . . **160** A4
Atwood Rd, W6 . . . . **148** B3
Atwoods All, Rich. TW9
off Leyborne Pk **160** A3
Aubert Ct, N5 . . . . **112** B1
Aubert Pk, N5 . . . . **112** B1
Aubert Rd, N5 . . . . **112** B1
Aubrey Beardsley Ho, SW1
off Vauxhall Br Rd **71** F1
Aubrey Moore Pt, E15 . . . . . **130** C2
Aubrey Pl, NW8 . . . . **7** E3
Aubrey Rd, W8 . . . . **135** F4
Aubrey Wk, W8 . . . . **135** F4
Auburn Cl, SE14 . . . . **171** E2
Aubyn Sq, SW15 . . . . **176** A2
Auckland Rd, E10 . . . . **102** B4
SW11 . . . . **179** E2
Auckland St, SE11 . . . . **73** E3
Auden Pl, NW1 . . . . **124** A1
Audley Cl, SW11 . . . . **180** A1
Audley Sq, W1 . . . . **46** B2
Audrey St, E2 . . . . **128** A2
Augusta St, E14 . . . . **144** B2
Augustine Rd, W14 . . . . **149** D2
Augustus Cl, W12
off Goldhawk Rd **148** B1
Augustus Ct, SE1 . . . . **64** C4
Augustus Ho, NW1
off Augustus St **11** E4
Augustus St, NW1 . . . . **11** D3
Aulton Pl, SE11 . . . . **74** B3
Auriga Ms, N1 . . . . **113** D2
Auriol Rd, W14 . . . . **149** E3
Austen Ho, NW6 . . . . **6** A4
Austin Friars, EC2 . . . . **40** B2
Austin Friars Pas, EC2 . . . . . . **40** B2
Austin Friars Sq, EC2 . . . . **40** B2
Austin Rd, SW11 . . . . **166** A3
Austin St, E2 . . . . **29** E1
Australia Rd, W12 . . . . **134** B3
Austral St, SE11 . . . . **62** C4
Autumn St, E3 . . . . **130** A1
Avalon Rd, SW6 . . . . **78** C4
Avebury Ct, N1
off Avebury St **16** A1
Avebury Rd, E11
off Southwest Rd **103** D2
Avebury St, N1 . . . . **16** A1
Aveline St, SE11 . . . . **74** A3
Ave Maria La, EC4 . . . . **39** D3
Avenell Rd, N5 . . . . **98** B4
Avening Ter, SW18 . . . . **178** A4
Avenue, The, E11
(Leytonstone) **103** F3
NW6 . . . . **121** D1
NW10 *off Hillside* **119** D1
SE10 . . . . **173** D2
SW4 . . . . **180** A3
W4 . . . . **147** E2
Avenue Cl, NW8 . . . . **9** D1
Avenue Cres, W3 . . . . **146** B1
Avenue Gdns, SW14 . . . . **175** E1
W3 . . . . **146** B1
Avenue Rd, N6 . . . . **96** C1
NW3 . . . . **109** D4
NW8 . . . . **109** D4
NW10 . . . . **119** F2
W3 . . . . **146** B1
Avenue Rd Est, E11
off High Rd
Leytonstone **117** D1
Averill St, W6 . . . . **163** D1
Avery Fm Row, SW1 . . . . **70** C1
Avery Row, W1 . . . . **34** C4
Aviary Cl, E16 . . . . **145** F1
Avignon Rd, SE4 . . . . **185** D1
Avington Ct, SE1
off Old Kent Rd **77** D1
Avis Sq, E1 . . . . **143** D2
Avocet Cl, SE1
off Rolls Rd **156** A4
Avondale Av, NW2 . . . . **91** E4
Avondale Ct, E11 . . . . **103** E2
E16 *off Avondale Rd* **145** E1
Avondale Ho, SE1
off Avondale Sq **156** A4
Avondale Pk Gdns, W11 . . . . **135** E3
Avondale Pk Rd, W11 . . . . . . **135** E3
Avondale Ri, SE15 . . . . **183** F1
Avondale Rd, E16 . . . . **145** E1
E17 . . . . **102** A1
SW14 . . . . **175** D1
Avondale Sq, SE1 . . . . **156** A4
Avonley Rd, SE14 . . . . **170** C2
Avonmore Gdns, W14
off Avonmore Rd **149** F3
Avonmore Pl, W14
off Avonmore Rd **149** E3
Avonmore Rd, W14 . . . . **149** F3
Avonmouth St, SE1 . . . . **63** E2
Avon Pl, SE1 . . . . **63** F1
Avon Rd, SE4 . . . . **186** A1
Axis Ct, SE10
off Woodland Cres **173** E1
SE16 *off East La* **156** A1
Axminster Rd, N7 . . . . **97** E4
Aybrook St, W1 . . . . **34** A1
Aycliffe Rd, W12 . . . . **133** F4
Aylesbury Cl, E7
off Atherton Rd **117** F3
Aylesbury Est, SE17 . . . . **76** B3

Aylesbury Rd, SE17 **76** B3
Aylesbury St, EC1 **26** C3
NW10 **91** D4
Aylesford St, SW1 **72** A2
Aylesham Cen, SE15 **170** A3
Aylestone Av, NW6 **121** D1
Aylmer Rd, E11 **103** F2
W12 **147** E1
Aylton Est, SE16
off Renforth St **156** C1
Aylward St, E1 **142** C2
Aylwyn Est, SE1 **65** D2
Aynhoe Rd, W14 **149** D3
Aynscombe La, SW14 **174** C1
Aynscombe Path, SW14
off Thames Bk **160** C4
Ayr Ct, W3 **132** A1
Ayres St, SE1 **51** F4
Aysome Rd, N16 **99** E4
Ayrton Gould Ho, E2
off Smart St **129** D3
Ayrton Rd, SW7 **56** A2
Aysgarth Rd, SE21 **183** E4
Aytoun Pl, SW9 **167** F4
Aytoun Rd, SW9 **167** F4
Azania Ms, NW5 **110** B2
Azenby Rd, SE15 **169** F4
Azof St, SE10 **159** E3

B

Baalbec Rd, N5 **112** B2
Babington Ct, WC1
off Ormond Cl **25** D4
Babington Ri, Wem. HA9 **104** A3
Babmaes St, SW1 **48** A1
Bacchus Wk, N1 **16** C3
Baches St, N1 **28** B1
Back Ch La, E1 **142** A3
Back Hill, EC1 **26** A3
Backhouse Pl, SE17 **77** D1
Back La, NW3
off Heath St **108** C1
Bacon Gro, SE1 **65** E3
Bacons La, N6 **96** A2
Bacon St, E1 **29** F2
E2 **29** F2
Bacton, NW5 **110** A2
Bacton St, E2
off Roman Rd **128** C3
Baddow Wk, N1
off Popham Rd **126** C1
Baden Pl, SE1 **52** A4
Badminton Rd, SW12 **180** A4
Badric Ct, SW11
off Yelverton Rd **165** D4
Badsworth Rd, SE5 **87** E3
Baffin Way, E14
off Prestons Rd **144** C3
Bagley's La, SW6 **164** B3
Bagshot St, SE17 **77** D3
Baildon St, SE8 **171** F2
Bailey Ms, SW2 **182** A3
W4 *off Herbert Gdns* **160** B1
Bainbridge St, WC1 **36** B2
Baird Cl, E10
off Marconi Rd **102** A2
Baird St, EC1 **27** F2
Baizdon Rd, SE3 **173** E4
Baker Pas, NW10
off Baker Rd **119** E1
Baker Rd, NW10 **119** E1
Bakers Fld, N7 **111** D1
Bakers Hall Ct, EC3 **53** D1
Bakers Hill, E5 **100** C2
Baker's Ms, W1 **34** A2
Bakers Pas, NW3
off Heath St **108** C1
Baker's Rents, E2 **29** E1
Bakers Row, E15 **131** E2
Baker's Row, EC1 **26** A3
Baker Street **21** F4
Baker St, NW1 **21** F3
W1 **21** F4
Baker's Yd, EC1 **26** A3
Bakery Cl, SW9 **85** F4
Bakery Pl, SW11
off Altenburg Gdns **179** F2
Balaclava Rd, SE1 **77** F1
Balchier Rd, SE22 **184** B4
Balcombe St, NW1 **21** E3
Balcorne St, E9 **114** C4
Balderton St, W1 **34** B3
Baldock St, E3 **130** B2
Baldwin Cres, SE5 **87** E4
Baldwin Rd, SW11 **180** A4
Baldwin's Gdns, EC1 **26** A4
Baldwin St, EC1 **28** A1
Baldwin Ter, N1 **15** E2
Baldwyn Gdns, W3 **132** C3
Bale Rd, E1 **143** E1
Coll Bales Coll, W10
off Harrow Rd **121** D3
Balfern Gro, W4 **147** E4
Balfern St, SW11 **165** E3
Balfe St, N1 **13** D3
Balfour Ho, W10
off St. Charles Sq **135** D1
Balfour Ms, W1 **46** B2
Balfour Pl, SW15 **176** B2
W1 **46** B1
Balfour Rd, N5 **112** C1
W3 **132** C1
Balfour St, SE17 **64** A4
Balfron Twr, E14
off St. Leonards Rd **144** C2
Balham Hill, SW12 **180** B4
Balkan Wk, E1
off Tobacco Dock **142** B3
Balladier Wk, E14 **144** B1
Ballance Rd, E9 **115** D3
Ballantine St, SW18 **178** C2
Ballards Rd, NW2 **92** A3
Ballast Quay, SE10 **159** D4
Ballater Rd, SW2 **181** E2
Ball Ct, EC3
off Castle Ct **40** B3
Ballingdon Rd, SW11 **180** A4
Ballinger Pt, E3
off Bromley High St **130** B3
Balliol Rd, W10 **134** C2
Ballogie Av, NW10 **105** E1
Ballow Cl, SE5 **88** C3
Balls Pond Pl, N1
off Balls Pond Rd **113** D3
Balls Pond Rd, N1 **113** D3
Balmer Rd, E3 **129** F2
Balmes Rd, N1 **127** D1
Balmoral Apts, W2
off Praed St **32** C1
Balmoral Cl, SW15 **177** D4
Balmoral Gro, N7 **111** F3
Balmoral Ms, W12 **147** F2
Balmoral Rd, E10 **102** B3
NW2 **106** B3
Balmore Cl, E14 **144** C2
Balmore St, N19 **96** B3
Balmuir Gdns, SW15 **176** C2
Balnacraig Av, NW10 **105** E1
Balniel Gate, SW1 **72** B2
Baltic Ct, SE16
off Timber Pond Rd **157** D1
Baltic Pl, N1 **17** D1
Baltic Quay, SE16
off Sweden Gate **157** E3
Baltic St E, EC1 **27** E3
Baltic St W, EC1 **27** E3
Baltimore Ho, SW18
off Juniper Dr **178** C2
Balvaird Pl, SW1 **72** B3
Bamber Rd, SE15 **89** E4
Bamboo Ct, E5 **100** C3
Bamborough Gdns, W12 **148** C1
Banbury Ct, WC2 **36** C4
Banbury Rd, E9 **115** D4
Banbury St, SW11 **165** E4
Bancroft Ct, SW8 **84** C4
Bancroft Rd, E1 **128** C3
Banfield Rd, SE15 **184** B1
Bangalore St, SW15 **176** C1
Banim St, W6 **148** B2
Banister Ms, NW6 **108** B4
Banister Rd, W10 **121** D3
Bank **40** A3
DLR Bank **40** A3
Bank, The, N6
off Cholmeley Pk **96** B2
Bank End, SE1 **51** F2
Bank La, SW15 **175** E3
★ Bank of England, EC2 **40** A3
★ Bank of England Mus, EC2 **40** B3
Banks Ho, SE1 **63** E3
Bankside, SE1 **51** E1
Bankside Av, SE13 **186** B1
★ Bankside Gall, SE1 **51** D1
Bankside Lofts, SE1 **51** D2
Riv Bankside Pier **51** E1
Bank St, E14 **144** A4
Bankton Rd, SW2 **182** A2
Bankwell Rd, SE13 **187** E2
Bannerman Ho, SW8 **85** E1
Banner St, EC1 **27** F3
Banning St, SE10 **159** E4
Bannister Ho, E9
off Homerton High St **115** D2
★ Banqueting Ho, SW1 **48** C3
Banstead Ct, W12
off Hilary Rd **133** F3
Banstead St, SE15 **184** C1
Bantry St, SE5 **88** B3
Banyard Rd, SE16
off Southwark Pk Rd **156** B2
Baptist Gdns, NW5
off Queen's Cres **110** A3
Barandon Wk, W11 **135** D3
Barbara Brosnan Ct, NW8 **8** A3
Barbara Castle Cl, SW6 **163** F1
Barbauld Rd, N16 **99** E4
Barbers Rd, E15 **130** B2
BARBICAN, EC2 **39** E1
Barbican **27** D4
Barbican **27** D4
★ Barbican Arts & Conf Cen, EC2 **27** F4
Barb Ms, W6 **148** C2
Barbon Cl, WC1 **25** D4
Barchard St, SW18 **178** B3
Barchester St, E14 **144** B1
Barclay Cl, SW6 **78** A3
Barclay Rd, E11 **103** E2
SW6 **78** A3

ardolph Rd, N7 ..... 111 E1
ard Rd, W10 ..... 135 D3
ardsey Pl, E1
off Mile End Rd 142 C1
ardsey Wk, N1
off Clephane Rd 112 C3
ardsley La, SE10 ..... 172 C1
arfett St, W10 ..... 121 F4
arfield Rd, E11 ..... 103 F2
arfleur La, SE8 ..... 157 F3
arford St, N1 ..... 14 B1
arforth Rd, SE15 ..... 184 B1
arge Ho St, SE1 ..... 50 B2
arge La, E3
off Birdsfield La 129 F1
aring St, N1 ..... 16 A1
Barkantine Shop Par, The, E14
off The Quarterdeck 158 A1
arker Cl, Rich. TW9 ..... 160 B4
arker Dr, NW1 ..... 110 C4
arker Ms, SW4 ..... 180 B2
arker St, SW10 ..... 67 E4
arkham Ter, SE1 ..... 62 B2
arking Rd, E16 ..... 145 F1
ark Pl, W2 ..... 30 C4
arkston Gdns, SW5 ..... 66 C2
arkway Ct, N4
off Queens Dr 98 C3
arkworth Rd, SE16 ..... 156 B4
arlborough St, SE14 ..... 170 C2
arlby Gdns, W10 ..... 121 D4
arlby Rd, W10 ..... 135 D1
arleycorn Way, E14 ..... 143 F3
arley Mow Pas, EC1 ..... 39 D1
W4 ..... 147 D4
Barley Shotts Business Pk, W10
off Acklam Rd 135 F1
arlow Ho, SE16
off Rennie Est 156 B3
arlow Pl, W1 ..... 47 D1
arlow Rd, NW6 ..... 107 F3
W3 ..... 132 B4
arlow St, SE17 ..... 64 B4
armouth Rd, SW18 ..... 178 C4
arnabas Rd, E9 ..... 115 D2
arnaby Pl, SW7 ..... 68 A1
arnard Gro, E15
off Vicarage La 117 F4
arnard Ms, SW11 ..... 179 E2
arnardo Gdns, E1
off Devonport St 143 D2
arnardo St, E1
off Devonport St 143 D2
arnard Rd, SW11 ..... 179 E2
arnard's Inn, EC1 ..... 38 B2
arnby Sq, E15
off Barnby St 131 E1
arnby St, E15 ..... 131 E1
NW1 ..... 11 F3
arn Elms Pk, SW15 ..... 162 C4
BARNES, SW13 ..... 162 A4
Barnes 176 A1
Barnes Av, SW13 ..... 162 A2
Barnes Bridge 161 E4
Barnes Br, SW13 ..... 161 E4
W4 ..... 161 E4
Barnesbury Ho, SW4 ..... 181 D3
Barnes Common, SW13 ..... 176 A1
Barnes High St, SW13 ..... 161 F4
Barnes Hosp, SW14 ..... 175 E1
Barnes St, E14 ..... 143 E2
Barnes Ter, SE8 ..... 157 F4
Barnet Gro, E2 ..... 128 A3
Barnett St, E1
off Cannon St Rd 142 B2
Barn Fld, NW3
off Upper Pk Rd 109 F2
Barnfield Cl, N4
off Crouch Hill 97 E1
Barnfield Pl, E14 ..... 158 A3
Barnham St, SE1 ..... 53 D4
Barn Hill, Wem. HA9 ..... 90 B3
Barnhill Rd, Wem. HA9 ..... 90 C4
Barn Ri, Wem. HA9 ..... 90 A2
BARNSBURY, N1 ..... 111 F4
Barnsbury Est, N1 ..... 13 F1
Barnsbury Gro, N7 ..... 111 F4
Barnsbury Pk, N1 ..... 112 A4
Barnsbury Rd, N1 ..... 14 A2
Barnsbury Sq, N1 ..... 112 A4
Barnsbury St, N1 ..... 112 A4
Barnsbury Ter, N1 ..... 111 F4
Barnsdale Av, E14 ..... 158 A3
Barnsdale Rd, W9 ..... 121 F4
Barnsley St, E1 ..... 128 B4
Barnstaple La, SE13
off Lewisham High St 186 C2
Barnston Wk, N1
off Popham St 126 C1
Barn St, N16 ..... 99 E3
Barn Way, Wem. HA9 ..... 90 A2
Barnwell Rd, SW2 ..... 182 A3
Barnwood Cl, W9 ..... 18 C3
Baroness Rd, E2 ..... 17 F4
Barons Court 149 E4
Barons Ct Rd, W14 ..... 149 E4
Barons Keep, W14 ..... 149 E4
Baronsmead Rd, SW13 ..... 162 A3
Barons Pl, SE1 ..... 62 B1
Baron St, N1 ..... 14 A2
Baron Wk, E16 ..... 145 F1
Barque Ms, SE8
off Watergate St 172 A1
Barratt Ind Pk, E3 ..... 130 C4
Barretts Grn Rd, NW10 ..... 118 C2
Barretts Gro, N16 ..... 113 E2
Barrett St, W1 ..... 34 B3
Barriedale, SE14 ..... 171 E3
Barrie Est, W2 ..... 32 A4
Barrington Cl, NW5 ..... 110 A2
Barrington Ct, W3
off Cheltenham Pl 146 B1
Barrington Rd, SW9 ..... 182 B1
Barrowgate Rd, W4 ..... 146 C4
Barrow Hill Est, NW8 ..... 8 C3
Barrow Hill Rd, NW8 ..... 8 C3
Barrs Rd, NW10 ..... 105 D4
Barry Ho, SE16
off Rennie Est 156 B4
Barry Rd, NW10 ..... 104 C4
SE22 ..... 184 A4
Barset Rd, SE15 ..... 184 C1
Barter St, WC1 ..... 37 D1
Bartholomew Cl, EC1 ..... 39 E1
SW18 ..... 178 C2
Bartholomew Ct, E14
off Newport Av 145 D3
Bartholomew La, EC2 ..... 40 B3
Bartholomew Pl, EC1 ..... 39 E1
Bartholomew Rd, NW5 ..... 110 C3
Bartholomew Sq, E1
off Coventry Rd 128 B4
EC1 ..... 27 F2
Bartholomew St, SE1 ..... 64 A3
Bartholomew Vil, NW5 ..... 110 C3
Bartle Rd, W11 ..... 135 E2
Bartlett Cl, E14 ..... 144 A2
Bartlett Ct, EC4 ..... 38 B2
Bartletts Pas, EC4 ..... 38 B2
Barton Cl, E9
off Churchill Wk 114 C2
SE15
off Kirkwood Rd 184 B1
Barton Ho, SW6
off Wandsworth Br Rd 178 B1
E3 off Bow Rd 130 B3
N1 off Sable St 112 B4
Barton Rd, W14 ..... 149 E4
Barton St, SW1 ..... 60 C2
Bartonway, NW8 ..... 8 A1
Bartram Rd, SE4 ..... 185 E3
Barville Cl, SE4
off St. Norbert Rd 185 E2
Barwick Ho, W3 ..... 146 C1
Bascombe St, SW2 ..... 182 A4
Basevi Way, SE8 ..... 172 B1
Bashley Rd, NW10 ..... 119 D4
Basil St, SW3 ..... 57 E2
Basin App, E14
off Commercial Rd 143 E2
Basing Ct, SE15 ..... 169 F3
Basingdon Way, SE5 ..... 183 D2
Basinghall Av, EC2 ..... 40 A1
Basinghall St, EC2 ..... 40 A2
Basing Hill, NW11 ..... 93 F2
Basing Ho Yd, E2 ..... 17 D4
Basing Pl, E2 ..... 17 D4
Basing St, W11 ..... 135 F2
Basire St, N1 ..... 126 C1
Baskerville Gdns, NW10 ..... 105 E1
Baslow Wk, E5 ..... 115 D1
Basnett Rd, SW11 ..... 180 A1
Basque Ct, SE16
off Poolmans St 157 D1
Bassano St, SE22 ..... 183 F3
Bassein Pk Rd, W12 ..... 147 F1
Bassett Rd, W10 ..... 135 D2
Bassett St, NW5 ..... 110 A3
Bassishaw Highwalk, EC2
off Aldermanbury Sq 39 F1
Bastion Highwalk, EC2 ..... 39 E1
Bastion Ho, EC2
off London Wall 39 E1
Bastwick St, EC1 ..... 27 E2
Basuto Rd, SW6 ..... 164 A3
Batavia Ms, SE14
off Goodwood Rd 171 E2
Batavia Rd, SE14 ..... 171 E2
Batchelor St, N1 ..... 14 A2
Bateman Ho, SE17 ..... 86 C1
Bateman's Bldgs, W1 ..... 36 A3
Bateman's Row, EC2 ..... 29 D2
Bateman St, W1 ..... 36 A3
Bate St, E14
off Three Colt St 143 F3
Bath Cl, SE15
off Asylum Rd 170 B2
Bath Ct, EC1 ..... 26 A3
EC1 (St. Luke's Est)
off St. Luke's Est 28 A1
Bath Ho, SE1
off Bath Ter 63 F2
Bath Pl, EC2 ..... 28 C1
Bath Rd, W4 ..... 147 E3
Bath St, EC1 ..... 27 F1
Bath Ter, SE1 ..... 63 E3
Bathurst Gdns, NW10 ..... 120 B2
Bathurst Ms, W2 ..... 32 A4
Bathurst St, W2 ..... 32 A4

Batley Pl, N16 **99** F4
Batley Rd, N16 *off Stoke Newington High St* **99** F4
Batman Cl, W12 **134** B4
Batoum Gdns, W6 **148** C2
Batson Ho, E1 *off Fairclough St* **142** A2
Batson St, W12 **148** A1
Batten St, SW11 **179** E1
BATTERSEA, SW11 **81** F4
Battersea Br, SW3 **80** B2
SW11 **80** B2
Battersea Br Rd, SW11 **80** C3
● Battersea Business Cen, SW11 *off Lavender Hill* **180** A1
Battersea Ch Rd, SW11 **80** B4
★ Battersea Dogs Home, SW8 **83** D3
Battersea High St, SW11 **165** D3
★ Battersea Park, SW11 **81** F2
⇌ Battersea Park **82** C4
Battersea Pk Rd, SW8 **82** C4
SW11 **165** E4
Battersea Ri, SW11 **179** E3
Battersea Sq, SW11 *off Battersea High St* **165** D3
Battishill Gdns, N1 *off Waterloo Ter* **112** B4
Battishill St, N1 *off Waterloo Ter* **112** B4
Battlebridge Ct, N1 **13** D2
Battle Br La, SE1 **52** C3
Battle Br Rd, NW1 **12** C3
Battledean Rd, N5 **112** B2
Batty St, E1 **142** A2
Batwa Ho, SE16 *off Verney Rd* **156** B4
Bavaria Rd, N19 **97** E3
Bavent Rd, SE5 **168** C4
Bawdale Rd, SE22 **183** F3
Bawtree Rd, SE14 **171** E2
Baxendale St, E2 **128** A3
Baxter Ho, E3 *off Bromley High St* **130** B3
Baxter Rd, N1 **113** D3
NW10 **119** E4
Bayford Ms, E8 *off Bayford St* **114** B4
Bayford Rd, NW10 **121** D3
Bayford St, E8 **114** B4
Bayham Pl, NW1 **11** E2
Bayham Rd, W4 **147** D2
Bayham St, NW1 **11** E1
Bayley St, WC1 **36** A1
Baylis Rd, SE1 **62** A1
Baynes Ms, NW3 *off Belsize La* **109** D3
Baynes St, NW1 **110** C4
Bayonne Rd, W6 **163** E1
Bayston Rd, N16 **99** F4
BAYSWATER, W2 **31** D3
⊖ Bayswater **30** C4
Bayswater Rd, W2 **32** B4
Baythorne St, E3 **143** F1
Baytree Ms, SE17 **64** A4
Baytree Rd, SW2 **181** F2
Bazalgette Ct, W6 *off Great W Rd* **148** A4
Bazely St, E14 **144** C3
Beachcroft Rd, E11 **103** E4
Beachcroft Way, N19 **97** D2
Beachy Rd, E3 **116** A4
Beacon Gate, SE14 **185** D1
Beacon Hill, N7 **111** E2
Beacon Rd, SE13 **187** D4
Beaconsfield Cl, W4 **146** C4
Beaconsfield Rd, E10 **102** C3
E16 **131** F4
NW10 **105** F3
SE3 **173** F2
SE17 **76** B3
W4 **147** D2
Beaconsfield Ter Rd, W14 **149** E2
Beaconsfield Wk, SW6 **163** F3
Beacontree Rd, E11 **103** F1
Beadon Rd, W6 **148** C3
Beak St, W1 **35** F4
Beale Pl, E3 **129** F2
Beale Rd, E3 **129** F1
Beames Rd, NW10 **119** D1
Beaminster Ho, SW8 *off Dorset Rd* **85** E2
Beamish Ho, SE16 *off Rennie Est* **156** C3
Beanacre Cl, E9 **115** F3
Bear All, EC4 **38** C2
Beardsley Way, W3 **147** D1
Bear Gdns, SE1 **51** E2
Bear La, SE1 **51** D2
Bearstead Ri, SE4 **185** F3
Bear St, WC2 **36** B4
Beaton Cl, SE15 **89** F4
Beatrice Pl, W8 **54** C3
Beatrice Rd, N4 **98** A1
SE1 **156** A3
Beatson Wk, SE16 **143** D4
Beatty Rd, N16 **113** E1
Beatty St, NW1 **11** E2
Beauchamp Cl, W4 *off Beaumont Rd* **146** C2
Beauchamp Pl, SW3 **57** D2
Beauchamp Rd, SW11 **179** E2
Beauchamp St, EC1 **38** A1
Beauchamp Ter, SW15 *off Dryburgh Rd* **176** B1
Beauclerc Rd, W6 **148** B2
Beaufort Ct, SW6 **66** A4
Beaufort Gdns, SW3 **57** D2
Beaufort Ms, SW6 *off Lillie Rd* **163** F1
Beaufort St, SW3 **80** B1
Beaufoy Wk, SE11 **73** F1
Beaulieu Cl, SE5 **183** D1
Beaulieu Pl, W4 **146** C2
Beaumaris Twr, W3 **146** B1
Beaumont Av, W14 **149** F4
Beaumont Cres, W14 **149** F4
Beaumont Gdns, NW3 **94** A4
Beaumont Gro, E1 **129** D4
Beaumont Ms, W1 **22** B4
Beaumont Pl, W1 **23** F2
Beaumont Ri, N19 **97** D2
Beaumont Rd, E10 **102** B1
W4 **146** C2
Beaumont Sq, E1 **129** D4
Beaumont St, W1 **22** B4
Beaumont Wk, NW3 **109** F4
Beauval Rd, SE22 **183** F4
Beavor Gro, W6 *off Beavor La* **148** A4
Beavor La, W6 **148** A3
Beccles St, E14 **143** F3
Beck Cl, SE13 **172** B3
Beckers, The, N16 **114** A1
Becket St, SE1 **64** A2
Beckett Cl, NW10 **105** D3
Beckett Ho, SW9 **167** E4
Beckford Cl, W14 **149** F3
Beckford Pl, SE17 **75** F3
Beckham Ho, SE11 *off Marylee Way* **73** F1
Becklow Gdns, W12 *off Becklow Rd* **148** A1
Becklow Ms, W12 *off Becklow Rd* **147** F1
Becklow Rd, W12 **148** A1
Beck Rd, E8 **128** B1
Beckton Rd, E16 **145** F1
Beckway St, SE17 **76** B1
Beckwith Rd, SE24 **183** D4
Becquerel Ct, SE10 *off West Parkside* **159** F2
Bective Pl, SW15 *off Bective Rd* **177** F2
Bective Rd, SW15 **177** F2
Bedale St, SE1 **52** A3
Bedford Av, WC1 **36** B1
Bedfordbury, WC2 **36** C4
Bedford Cl, W4 **161** E1
Bedford Cor, W4 **147** E3
Bedford Ct, WC2 **48** C1
Bedford Gdns, W8 **42** A3
Bedford Ho, SW4 **181** E2
BEDFORD PARK, W4 **147** D2
Bedford Pk Cor, W4 *off Bath Rd* **147** E3
Bedford Pas, SW6 *off Dawes Rd* **163** E2
Bedford Pl, WC1 **24** C4
Bedford Rd, SW4 **181** E1
W4 **147** D2
Bedford Row, WC1 **25** F4
Bedford Sq, WC1 **36** B1
Bedford St, WC2 **36** C4
Bedford Ter, SW2 *off Lyham Rd* **181** E3
Bedford Way, WC1 **24** B3
Bedlam Ms, SE11 **62** A4
Bedser Cl, SE11 **73** F4
Beech Av, W3 **133** E4
Beech Cl, SE8 *off Clyde St* **171** F1
Beechcroft Av, NW11 **93** F1
Beechcroft Rd, SW14 **174** C1
Beechdale Rd, SW2 **181** F4
Beech Gdns, EC2 *off White Lyon Ct* **27** E4
Beech Ho, NW3 *off Maitland Pk Vil* **109** F3
Beechmore Rd, SW11 **165** F3
Beecholme Est, E5 **100** B4
Beech St, EC2 **27** E4
Beech Tree Cl, N1 **112** A4
Beech Way, NW10 **105** D4
Beechwood Av, Rich. TW9 **160** A3
Beechwood Gro, W3 **133** E3
Beechwood Rd, E8 **113** F3
Beechworth Cl, NW3 **94** A3
Beecroft La, SE4 *off Beecroft Rd* **185** E3
Beecroft Ms, SE4 *off Beecroft Rd* **185** E3
Beecroft Rd, SE4 **185** E3
Beehive Cl, E8 **113** F4
Beehive Pas, EC3 **40** C3
Beehive Pl, SW9 **182** A1
Beeston Cl, E8 *off Ferncliff Rd* **114** A2

Beeston Pl, SW1 **59** D3
Beethoven St, W10 **121** E3
Begonia Wk, W12
off Du Cane Rd **133** F2
Bekesbourne St, E14
off Ratcliffe La **143** E2
Belfast Rd, N16 **99** F3
Belfont Wk, N7 **111** E1
Belfort Rd, SE15 **170** C4
Belfry Cl, SE16
off Masters Dr **156** B4
Belgrade Rd, N16 **113** E1
Belgrave Cl, W3
off Avenue Rd **146** B1
Belgrave Ct, E14
off Westferry Circ **143** F3
Belgrave Gdns, NW8 **7** D1
Belgrave Ms N, SW1 **58** A1
Belgrave Ms S, SW1 **58** B2
Belgrave Ms W, SW1 **58** A2
Belgrave Pl, SW1 **58** B2
Belgrave Rd, E10 **102** C2
SW1 **71** E1
SW13 **161** F2
Belgrave Sq, SW1 **58** A2
Belgrave St, E1 **143** D2
Belgrave Yd, SW1 **58** C3
BELGRAVIA, SW1 **58** A3
Belgravia Ho, SW4 **181** D4
Belgrove St, WC1 **12** C4
Belham Wk, SE5 **88** B4
Belinda Rd, SW9 **182** B1
Belitha Vil, N1 **111** F4
Bellamy Cl, E14
off Manilla St **158** A1
W14 *off Aisgill Av* **149** F4
Bellefields Rd, SW9 **181** F1
Bellenden Rd, SE15 **169** F4
Coll Bellerbys Coll, SE8
off Stowage **172** A1
Belleville Rd, SW11 **179** F3
Bellevue Pl, E1 **128** C4
Bellevue Rd, SW13 **162** A4
Bellgate Ms, NW5
off York Ri **96** B4
Bellhaven, E15
off Millstone Cl **117** D3
Bellina Ms, NW5
off Fortess Rd **110** C1
● Bell Ind Est, W4
off Cunnington St **146** C3
Bell Inn Yd, EC3 **40** B3
Bell La, E1 **41** E1
Bellmaker Ct, E3
off St. Pauls Way **144** A1
Bellot Gdns, SE10
off Bellot St **159** E4
Bellot St, SE10 **159** E4
Bells All, SW6 **164** A4
Bells Gdn Est, SE15
off Buller Cl **170** A2
Bell St, NW1 **20** C4
Bell Wf La, EC4 **51** F1
Bellwood Rd, SE15 **185** D2
Bell Yd, WC2 **38** A2
Bell Yd Ms, SE1 **65** D1
Belmont Cl, SW4 **180** C1
Belmont Gro, SE13 **187** D1
W4 *off Belmont Ter* **147** D3
Belmont Hall Ct, SE13
off Belmont Gro **187** D1
Belmont Hill, SE13 **187** D1
Belmont Pk, SE13 **187** D2
Belmont Pk Cl, SE13 **187** D2
Belmont Rd, SW4 **180** C1
W4
off Chiswick High Rd **147** D3
Belmont St, NW1 **110** A4
Belmont Ter, W4 **147** D3
Belmore La, N7 **111** D2
Belmore St, SW8 **84** A4
Beloe Cl, SW15 **176** A1
Belper Ct, E5
off Pedro St **115** D1
Belsham St, E9 **114** C3
Belsize Av, NW3 **109** D3
Belsize Ct, NW3
off Belsize La **109** E2
Belsize Cres, NW3 **109** D2
Belsize Gro, NW3 **109** E3
Belsize La, NW3 **109** D3
Belsize Ms, NW3
off Belsize La **109** D3
BELSIZE PARK, NW3 **109** E3
⊖ Belsize Park **109** E2
Belsize Pk, NW3 **109** D3
Belsize Pk Gdns, NW3 **109** E3
Belsize Pk Ms, NW3
off Belsize La **109** D3
Belsize Pl, NW3
off Belsize La **109** D3
Belsize Rd, NW6 **122** B1
Belsize Sq, NW3 **109** D3
Belsize Ter, NW3 **109** D3
Belton Rd, E11 **117** E1
NW2 **106** A3
Belton Way, E3 **144** A1
Beltran Rd, SW6 **164** B4
Belvedere, The, SW10 **164** C3
Belvedere Bldgs, SE1 **63** D1
Belvedere Ct, N1
off De Beauvoir Cres **127** E1
Belvedere Ms, SE15 **184** C1
Belvedere Pl, SE1 **63** D1
SW2 **181** F2
Belvedere Rd, E10 **101** E2
SE1 **49** F4
Belvoir Ho, SW1
off Vauxhall Br Rd **59** F4
Bembridge Cl, NW6 **107** E4
Bemerton Est, N1 **111** E4
Bemerton St, N1 **125** F1
Bemish Rd, SW15 **177** D1
Benbow Rd, W6 **148** B2
Benbow St, SE8 **172** A1
Bendall Ms, NW1 **21** D4
Bendemeer Rd, SW15 **177** D1
Benedict Rd, SW9 **181** F1
Bengal Ct, EC3
off Birchin La **40** B3
Bengeworth Rd, SE5 **182** C1
Benham Cl, SW11 **179** D1
Benhams Pl, NW3
off Holly Wk **108** C1
Benhill Rd, SE5 **88** B3
Benington Ct, N4
off Brownswood Rd **98** C3
Benjamin Cl, E8 **128** A1
Benjamin St, EC1 **26** C4
Ben Jonson Ho, EC2
off The Barbican **27** F4
Ben Jonson Rd, E1 **143** E1
Benledi Rd, E14 **145** D2
Bennelong Cl, W12 **134** B3
Bennerley Rd, SW11 **179** E3
Bennet's Hill, EC4 **39** D4
Bennet St, SW1 **47** E2
Bennett Gro, SE13 **172** B3
Bennett Ho, SW1
off Page St **60** B4
Bennett Pk, SE3 **187** F1
Bennett Rd, N16 **113** E1
SW9 **168** A4
Bennett St, W4 **161** E1
Bennetts Yd, SW1 **60** B3
Benn St, E9 **115** E3
Ben Smith Way, SE16
off Jamaica Rd **156** A2
Benson Ct, SW8
off Hartington Rd **84** C4
Benson Quay, E1
off Garnet St **142** C3
Benthal Rd, N16 **100** A3
Bentham Ct, N1
off Rotherfield St **112** C4
Bentham Ho, SE1
off Falmouth Rd **64** A2
Bentham Rd, E9 **115** D3
Bentham Wk, NW10 **104** C2
Bentinck Cl, NW8
off Prince Albert Rd **9** D3
Bentinck Ms, W1 **34** B2
Bentinck St, W1 **34** B2
Bentley Ct, SE13
off Whitburn Rd **186** C2
Bentley Dr, NW2 **93** F4
Bentley Rd, N1
off Tottenham Rd **113** E3
Bentworth Rd, W12 **134** B2
Benville Ho, SW8 **85** F3
Benwell Rd, N7 **112** A1
Benwick Cl, SE16
off Aspinden Rd **156** B3
Benworth St, E3 **129** F3
Benyon Rd, N1
off Southgate Rd **127** D1
Benyon Wf, E8
off Kingsland Rd **127** E1
Berber Pl, E14
off Birchfield St **144** A3
Berber Rd, SW11 **179** F3
Berenger Twr, SW10 **80** A2
Berenger Wk, SW10
off Blantyre St **80** A2
Berens Rd, NW10 **121** D3
Beresford Rd, N5 **112** C2
Beresford Ter, N5 **112** C2
Berestede Rd, W6 **147** F4
Bere St, E1
off Cranford St **143** D3
Bergen Sq, SE16
off Norway Gate **157** E2
Berger Rd, E9 **115** D3
Berghem Ms, W14
off Blythe Rd **149** D2
Bergholt Cres, N16 **99** E1
Bergholt Ms, NW1
off Rossendale Way **110** C4
Berglen Ct, E14
off Branch Rd **143** E2
Bering Sq, E14
off Napier Av **158** A4
Berisford Ms, SW18 **178** B4
Berkeley Gdns, W8 **42** B3
Berkeley Ho, E3 **129** F4
Berkeley Ms, W1 **33** F2
Berkeley Rd, SW13 **162** A3
Berkeley Sq, W1 **47** D1
Berkeley St, W1 **47** D1
Berkeley Twr, E14 **143** F4
Berkeley Wk, N7
off Durham Rd **97** F3

Berkley Gro, NW1
off Berkley Rd **110** A4
Berkley Rd, NW1 . . . . **109** F4
Berkshire Rd, E9 . . . . **115** F3
Bermans Way, NW10 . . . . . . **105** E1
BERMONDSEY, SE1 . . . . **65** E3
Bermondsey 156 A2
Bermondsey Sq, SE1 . . . . **65** D2
Bermondsey St, SE1 . . . . **52** C3
Bermondsey Trd Est, SE16
off Rotherhithe New Rd .156 C4
Bermondsey Wall E, SE16 . . **156** A1
Bermondsey Wall W, SE16 . . **156** A1
Bernard Cassidy St, E16 . . . . **145** F1
Bernard Shaw Ho, NW10
off Knatchbull Rd **119** D1
Bernard St, WC1 . . . . **24** C3
Bernays Gro, SW9 . . . . **181** F2
Berners Ms, W1 . . . . **35** F1
Berners Pl, W1 . . . . **35** F2
Berners Rd, N1 . . . . **14** B2
Berners St, W1 . . . . **35** F1
Bernhardt Cres, NW8 . . . . **20** C2
Berridge Ms, NW6
off Hillfield Rd **108** A2
Berriman Rd, N7 . . . . **97** F4
Berryfield Rd, SE17 . . . . **75** D2
Berrymead Gdns, W3 . . . . . . **132** C4
Berrymede Rd, W4 . . . . **147** D2
Berry Pl, EC1 . . . . **27** D1
Berry St, EC1 . . . . **27** D2
Berthon St, SE8 . . . . **172** A2
Bertie Rd, NW10 . . . . **106** A3
Bertram St, N19 . . . . **96** B3
Bertrand St, SE13 . . . . **186** B1
Berwick St, W1 . . . . **36** A3
Berwyn Rd, Rich. TW10 . . . . **174** B2
Beryl Rd, W6 . . . . **149** D4
Besant Ct, N1
off Newington Grn Rd . . **113** D2
Besant Pl, SE22
off Hayes Gro **183** F2
Besant Rd, NW2 . . . . **107** E1
Besant Wk, N7
off Newington
Barrow Way **97** F3
Besant Way, NW10 . . . . **104** C2
Bessant Dr, Rich. TW9 . . . . . **160** B3
Bessborough Gdns, SW1 . . . . . **72** B2
Bessborough Pl, SW1 . . . . **72** A2
Bessborough St, SW1 . . . . **72** A2
Bessemer Rd, SE5 . . . . **168** C4
Bessingham Wk, SE4
off Aldersford Cl **185** D3
Besson St, SE14 . . . . **170** C3
Bessy St, E2
off Roman Rd **128** C3
Bestwood St, SE8 . . . . **157** D3
Beswick Ms, NW6
off Dresden Cl **108** B3
Beta Pl, SW4
off Santley St **181** F2
Bethell Av, E16 . . . . **131** F4
BETHNAL GREEN, E2 . . . . . . **128** A2
Bethnal Green 128 B4
Bethnal Green 128 C3
Bethnal Grn Est, E2
off Roman Rd **128** C3
Bethnal Grn Rd, E1 . . . . **29** E2
E2 . . . . **29** E2
Bethnal Grn Training Cen,
E1 *off Hanbury St* 142 A1
Bethune Rd, N16 . . . . **99** D1
NW10 . . . . **119** D4
Bethwin Rd, SE5 . . . . **87** D2
Betterton St, WC2 . . . . **36** C3
Bettons Pk, E15 . . . . **131** E1
Bettridge Rd, SW6 . . . . **163** F4
Betts St, E1
off The Highway **142** B3
Bevan St, N1 . . . . **15** F1
Bev Callender Cl, SW8
off Daley Thompson
Way **180** B1
Bevenden St, N1 . . . . **16** B4
Beveridge Rd, NW10 . . . . **105** E4
Beverley Cl, SW11
off Maysoule Rd **179** D2
SW13 . . . . **161** F4
Beverley Ct, SE4 . . . . **185** F1
Beverley Gdns, NW11 . . . . **93** E1
SW13 . . . . **175** F1
Beverley Path, SW13 . . . . . . **161** F4
Beverley Rd, SW13 . . . . **175** F1
W4 . . . . **147** F4
Beverly, NW8 . . . . **20** C1
Beversbrook Rd, N19 . . . . **97** D4
Beverstone Rd, SW2 . . . . **181** F3
Beverston Ms, W1 . . . . **33** E1
Bevin Cl, SE16
off Stave Yd Rd **143** E4
Bevin Ct, WC1 . . . . **13** F4
Bevington Path, SE1
off Tanner St **65** E1
Bevington Rd, W10 . . . . **135** E1
Bevington St, SE16 . . . . **156** A1
Bevin Way, WC1 . . . . **14** A4
Bevis Marks, EC3 . . . . **41** D2
Bewdley St, N1 . . . . **112** A4
Bewick Ms, SE15 . . . . **170** B2
Bewick St, SW8 . . . . **166** B4
Bewley St, E1
off Cable St **142** B3
Bexhill Rd, SW14 . . . . **174** C1
Bexhill Wk, E15
off Mitre Rd **131** E1
Bianca Rd, SE15 . . . . **169** F1
Bibury Cl, SE15 . . . . **89** D1
Bicester Rd, Rich. TW9 . . . . . **174** A1
Bickenhall St, W1 . . . . **21** F4
Bickerton Rd, N19 . . . . **96** C3
Bickley Rd, E10 . . . . **102** B1
Bicknell Rd, SE5 . . . . **182** C1
Bidborough St, WC1 . . . . **24** C1
Bidder St, E16 . . . . **145** E1
Biddestone Rd, N7 . . . . **111** F1
Biddulph Rd, W9 . . . . **18** C1
Bidwell St, SE15 . . . . **170** B3
Big Ben
(St. Stephens Twr), SW1 . . 61 D1
Biggerstaff Rd, E15 . . . . **130** C1
Biggerstaff St, N4 . . . . **98** A3
Biggs Row, SW15
off Felsham Rd **177** D1
Big Hill, E5 . . . . **100** B2
Bigland St, E1 . . . . **142** B2
Bill Faust Ho, E1
off Tarling St **142** C2
Billingford Cl, SE4 . . . . **185** D2
Billing Pl, SW10 . . . . **79** D2
Billing Rd, SW10 . . . . **79** D2
Billingsgate Mkt, E14 . . . 144 B4
Billing St, SW10 . . . . **79** D2
Billington Ms, W3
off High St **132** B4
Billington Rd, SE14 . . . . **171** D2
Billiter Sq, EC3 . . . . **41** D4
Billiter St, EC3 . . . . **41** D3
Billson St, E14 . . . . **158** C3
Bilton Twrs, W1
off Great
Cumberland Pl **33** F3
Bina Gdns, SW5 . . . . **67** E1
Binden Rd, W12 . . . . **147** F2
Binfield Rd, SW4 . . . . **167** E3
Bingfield St, N1 . . . . **125** E1
Bingham Ct, N1
off Halton Rd **112** B4
Bingham Pl, W1 . . . . **22** A4
Bingham St, N1 . . . . **113** D3
Binley Ho, SW15
off Highcliffe Dr **176** A4
Binne Ho, SE1
off Bath Ter **63** E3
Binney St, W1 . . . . **34** B4
Binns Rd, W4 . . . . **147** E4
Binns Ter, W4
off Binns Rd **147** E4
Bircham Path, SE4
off Aldersford Cl **185** D3
Birch Cl, E16 . . . . **145** E1
N19 . . . . **96** C3
SE15
off Bournemouth Rd . . . **170** A4
Birchdown Ho, E3
off Rainhill Way **130** B3
Birchen Cl, NW9 . . . . **91** D3
Birchen Gro, NW9 . . . . **91** D3
Birchfield St, E14 . . . . **144** A3
Birch Gro, E11 . . . . **103** E4
W3 . . . . **132** A4
Birchgrove Ho, Rich. TW9
off Strand Dr **160** B2
Birchington Ho, E5
off Pembury Rd **114** B2
Birchington Rd, NW6 . . . . . . **122** A1
Birchin La, EC3 . . . . **40** B3
Birchmere Row, SE3 . . . . **173** F4
Birchmore Wk, N5 . . . . **98** C4
Birchwood Dr, NW3 . . . . **94** B4
Birdcage Wk, SW1 . . . . **59** F1
Birdhurst Rd, SW18 . . . . **178** C2
Bird in Bush Rd, SE15 . . . . . . **170** A2
Bird in Hand Yd, NW3
off Hampstead
High St **108** C1
Birdsfield La, E3 . . . . **129** F1
Bird St, W1 . . . . **34** B3
Birdwood Av, SE13 . . . . **187** D4
Birkbeck Av, W3 . . . . **132** C3
Birkbeck Coll,
Main Bldg, WC1 . . . . 24 B3
Clore Management
Cen, WC1 . . . . 24 B3
Gordon Ho & Ingold
Laboratories, WC1 . . . . . . 24 A2
Gordon Sq, WC1 . . . . 24 B2
Russell Sq, WC1 . . . . 24 B4
Birkbeck Gro, W3 . . . . **147** D1
Birkbeck Ms, E8
off Sandringham Rd **113** F2
W3 . . . . **133** D4
Birkbeck Rd, E8 . . . . **113** F2
W3 . . . . **133** D4
Birkbeck St, E2 . . . . **128** B3
Birkdale Cl, SE16
off Masters Dr **156** B4
Birkenhead St, WC1 . . . . **13** D4
Birley St, SW11 . . . . **166** A4
Birnam Rd, N4 . . . . **97** F3
Birrell Ho, SW9 . . . . **167** F4
Birse Cres, NW10 . . . . **105** E1

scayne Av, E14
off Fairmont Av 145 D3
scay Rd, W6 ....149 D4
scoe Way, SE13 ....187 D1
sham Gdns, N6 ....96 A2
shop Kings Rd, W14 .....149 E3
shop's Av, SW6 ....163 D4
shops Av, The, N2 ....95 D1
shops Br, W2 ....31 F2
shops Br Rd, W2 ....31 D3
shop's Cl, N19 ....96 C4
shops Cl, W4 ....146 C4
shop's Ct, EC4 ....38 C2
WC2 ....38 A2
shopsgate, EC2 ....40 C3
shopsgate Arc, EC2 ....41 D1
shopsgate Chyd, EC2 ......40 C1
Bishopsgate Inst, EC2 ....41 D1
shops Ho, SW8
off South Lambeth Rd ...85 D3
shopsmead, SE5
off Camberwell Rd 87 F3
shop's Pk, SW6 ....163 D4
shop's Pk Rd, SW6 ....163 D4
shops Rd, SW6 ....163 F3
shop's Rd, SW11 ....81 D2
shops Sq, E1 ....29 D4
shops Ter, SE11 ....62 B4
shop St, N1 ....126 C1
shops Way, E2 ....128 B2
shopswood Rd, N6 ....95 F1
shop Wilfred Wd Cl, SE15
off Moncrieff St 170 A4
sson Rd, E15 ....130 C2
ttern St, SE1 ....63 E1
ackall St, EC2 ....28 C2
ackbird Hill, NW9 ....90 C3
ackbird Yd, E2 ....17 F4
ack Bull Yd, EC1
off Hatton Wall 26 A4
ackburne's Ms, W1 ....34 A4
ackburn Rd, NW6 ....108 B3
ackett St, SW15 ....177 D1
Blackfriars 39 D4
ackfriars Br, EC4 ....38 C4
SE1 ....38 C4
ackfriars Ct, EC4 ....38 C4
ack Friars La, EC4 ....38 C4
Blackfriars
Millennium Pier 38 B4
ackfriars Pas, EC4 ....38 C4
ackfriars Rd, SE1 ....62 C1
LACKHEATH, SE3 ....173 E3
Blackheath, SE3 ....173 D3
Blackheath 187 E1
ackheath Av, SE10 ......173 D2
Blackheath Business
Est, SE10
off Blackheath Hill 172 C3
Blackheath Conservatoire
of Music & The Arts, SE3
off Lee Rd 187 F1
ackheath Gro, SE3 ....173 F4
ackheath Hill, SE10 ......172 C3
Blackheath Hosp, The,
SE3 ....187 E1
LACKHEATH PARK, SE3 ...187 F2
lackheath Pk, SE3 ....187 F1
lackheath Ri, SE13 ....172 C4
lackheath Rd, SE10 ......172 B3
lackheath Vale, SE3 ......173 E4
lackheath Village, SE3 ....173 F4
ack Horse Ct, SE1 ....64 B2
lackhorse Rd, SE8 ....157 E4
Blacklands Ter, SW3 ....69 E1
Black Lion La, W6 ....148 A3
Black Lion Ms, W6
off Black Lion La 148 A3
Blackmore Dr, NW10 ......104 B4
Blackmore Twr, W3
off Stanley Rd 146 C2
Black Path, E10 ....101 D1
Blackpool Rd, SE15 ....170 B4
Black Prince Rd, SE1 ....73 E1
SE11 ....73 F1
Blacks Rd, W6
off Queen Caroline St ...148 C3
Blackstock Ms, N4
off Blackstock Rd 98 B3
Blackstock Rd, N4 ....98 B3
N5 ....98 B3
Blackstone Est, E8 ....114 A4
Blackstone Ho, SW1
off Churchill Gdns 71 E3
Blackstone Rd, NW2 ....106 C2
Black Swan Yd, SE1 ....52 C4
Blackthorn St, E3 ....130 A4
Blacktree Ms, SW9 ....182 A1
Blackwall 144 C3
Blackwall La, SE10 ....159 E4
Blackwall Pier, E14 ....145 E3
Blackwall Trd Est,
E14 ....145 D1
Blackwall Tunnel, E14 .....145 D4
Blackwall Tunnel App,
SE10 ....159 E1
Blackwall Tunnel
Northern App, E3 ......130 A2
E14 ....130 A2
Blackwall Way, E14 ....144 C3
Blackwater Cl, E7 ....117 F1
Blackwater St, SE22 ....183 F3
Blackwell Cl, E5 ....115 D1
Blackwood St, SE17 ....76 A2
Blade Ms, SW15 ....177 F2
Blades Ct, SW15 ....177 F2
Blagdon Rd, SE13 ....186 B4
Blagrove Rd, W10 ....135 E1
Blair Av, NW9 ....91 E1
Blair Cl, N1 ....112 C3
Blair Ho, SW9
off Stockwell Gdns 167 F4
Blair St, E14 ....144 C2
Blake Cl, W10 ....134 C1
Blake Gdns, SW6 ....78 C4
Blake Ms, Rich. TW9
off High Pk Rd 160 A3
Blakemore Gdns, SW13
off Lonsdale Rd 162 B1
Blakeney Cl, E8
off Ferncliff Rd 114 A2
NW1
off Rossendale Way 111 D4
Blake Rd, E16 ....131 F4
Blaker Rd, E15 ....130 C1
Blakes Rd, SE15 ....89 D2
Blake St, SE8
off Watergate St 172 A1
Blanchard Way, E8 ....114 A3
Blanch Cl, SE15
off Culmore Rd 170 C2
Blanchedowne, SE5 ....183 D2
Blanche St, E16 ....131 F4
Blandfield Rd, SW12 ......180 A4
Blandford Rd, W4 ....147 E2
Blandford Sq, NW1 ....21 D3
Blandford St, W1 ....33 F2
Blantyre St, SW10 ....80 A2
Blantyre Twr, SW10 ....80 A2
Blantyre Wk, SW10
off Blantyre St 80 A2
Blashford, NW3 ....109 F4
Blasker Wk, E14 ....158 A4
Blechynden St, W10
off Bramley Rd 135 D3
Bledlow Cl, NW8 ....20 B3
Bleeding Heart Yd, EC1 .....38 B1
Blemundsbury, WC1
off Dombey St 25 E4
Blenheim Ct, N19 ....97 E3
Blenheim Cres, W11 ....135 E2
Blenheim Gdns, NW2 ......106 C2
SW2 ....181 F4
Blenheim Gro, SE15 ....170 A4
Blenheim Pas, NW8 ....7 E2
Blenheim Rd, E15 ....117 E1
NW8 ....7 E2
W4 ....147 E2
Blenheim St, W1 ....34 C3
Blenheim Ter, NW8 ....7 E2
Blenkarne Rd, SW11 ....179 F4
Blessington Cl, SE13 ....187 D1
Blessington Rd, SE13 ......187 D1
Bletchley Ct, N1 ....16 A3
Bletchley St, N1 ....15 F3
Bletsoe Wk, N1 ....15 F2
Bliss Cres, SE13 ....172 B4
Blissett St, SE10 ....172 C3
Bliss Ms, W10
off Third Av 121 E3
Blithfield St, W8 ....54 C3
Bloemfontein Av, W12 .....134 B4
Bloemfontein Rd, W12 .....134 B3
Bloemfontein Way, W12
off Bloemfontein Rd 134 B4
Blomfield Ct, SW11
off Westbridge Rd 165 E3
Blomfield Ms, W2 ....31 E1
Blomfield Rd, W9 ....19 E4
Blomfield St, EC2 ....40 B1
Blomfield Vil, W2 ....31 D1
Blondel St, SW11 ....166 A4
Blondin St, E3 ....130 A2
Bloomburg St, SW1 ....71 F1
Bloomfield Ct, E10
off Brisbane Rd 102 B4
Bloomfield Pl, W1 ....35 D4
Bloomfield Ter, SW1 ....70 B2
Bloom Pk Rd, SW6 ....163 F2
BLOOMSBURY, WC1 ....36 B1
Bloomsbury Ct, WC1 ....37 D1
Bloomsbury Ho, SW4 ......181 D4
Bloomsbury Pl, SW18 ......178 C3
WC1 ....25 D4
Bloomsbury Sq, WC1 ....37 D1
Bloomsbury St, WC1 ....36 B1
Bloomsbury Way, WC1 ......36 C2
Blore Cl, SW8
off Thessaly Rd 167 D3
Blore Ct, W1 ....36 A3
Blossom St, E1 ....29 D4
Blount St, E14 ....143 E2
Bloxhall Rd, E10 ....101 F2
Blucher Rd, SE5 ....87 F3
Blue Anchor La, SE16 ......156 A3
Blue Anchor Yd, E1 ....142 A3
Blue Ball Yd, SW1 ....47 E3
Bluebell Cl, E9
off Moulins Rd 128 C1
Bluelion Pl, SE1 ....64 C2
Bluewater Ho, SW18
off Smugglers Way 178 B2

Blundell Cl, E8
off Amhurst Rd **114** A1
Blundell St, N7 **111** E4
Blurton Rd, E5 **114** C1
Blyth Cl, E14
off Manchester Rd **159** D3
Blythe Ms, W14
off Blythe Rd **149** D2
Blythe Rd, W14 **149** D2
Blythe St, E2 **128** B3
Blyth Rd, E17 **101** F1
Blyth's Wf, E14
off Narrow St **143** E3
Blythwood Rd, N4 **97** E1
Boades Ms, NW3
off New End **109** D1
Boadicea St, N1 **13** E1
Boardwalk Pl, E14 **144** C4
Boatemah Wk, SW9
off Peckford Pl **168** A4
Boathouse Wk, SE15 **89** F2
Boat Lifter Way, SE16
off Sweden Gate **157** E3
Bobbin Cl, SW4 **180** C1
Bob Marley Way, SE24
off Mayall Rd **182** A2
Bocking St, E8 **128** B1
Boddington Gdns, W3 **146** A1
Bodney Rd, E8 **114** B2
Bohemia Pl, E8 **114** B3
Bohn Rd, E1 **143** E1
Boileau Rd, SW13 **162** A2
Bolden St, SE8 **172** B4
Boleyn Rd, N16 **113** E2
Bolina Rd, SE16 **156** C4
Bolingbroke Gro, SW11 **179** E2
H Bolingbroke Hosp,
SW11 179 E3
Bolingbroke Rd, W14 **149** D2
Bolingbroke Wk, SW11 **80** B3
Bolliger Ct, NW10
off Park Royal Rd **118** C4
Bollo Br Rd, W3 **146** B2
Bollo La, W3 **146** B1
W4 **146** C3
Bolney Gate, SW7 **56** C1
Bolney St, SW8 **85** E3
Bolsover St, W1 **23** D3
Bolt Ct, EC4 **38** B3
Bolton Cres, SE5 **86** B1
Bolton Gdns, NW10 **121** D2
SW5 **66** C2
Bolton Gdns Ms,
SW10 **67** E2
Bolton Rd, E15 **117** F3
NW8 **7** D1
NW10 **119** E1
W4 **160** C2
Boltons, The, SW10 **67** E2
Boltons Pl, SW5 **67** E2
Bolton St, W1 **47** D2
Bolton Wk, N7
off Durham Rd **97** F3
Bombay St, SE16 **156** B3
Bomore Rd, W11 **135** D3
Bonar Rd, SE15 **170** A2
Bonchurch Rd, W10 **135** E1
Bond Ct, EC4 **40** A3
Bonding Yd Wk, SE16
off Finland St **157** E2
⊖ Bond Street 34 B3
Bond St, E15 **117** E2
W4 **147** E3
⊖ Bondway 73 D4
Bondway, SW8 **85** D1
Bonfield Rd, SE13 **186** C2
Bonham Rd, SW2 **181** F3
Bonheur Rd, W4 **147** D1
Bonhill St, EC2 **28** B3
Bonita Ms, SE4 **185** D1
Bonner Rd, E2 **128** C2
Bonner St, E2 **128** C2
Bonneville Gdns, SW4 **180** C4
Bonnington Ho, N1
off Killick St **13** E3
Bonnington Sq, SW8 **73** E4
Bonny St, NW1 **110** C4
Bonsor St, SE5 **88** C3
Booker Cl, E14
off Wallwood St **143** F1
Book Ms, WC2 **36** B3
Boones Rd, SE13 **187** E2
Boone St, SE13 **187** E2
Boord St, SE10 **159** E2
Boothby Rd, N19 **97** D3
Booth Cl, E9
off Victoria Pk Rd **128** B1
Booth La, EC4 **39** E4
Booth's Pl, W1 **35** F1
Boot St, N1 **28** C1
Boreas Wk, N1 **15** D3
Boreham Cl, E11
off Hainault Rd **102** C2
Borland Rd, SE15 **184** C2
Borneo St, SW15 **176** C1
⊖ Borough 63 F1
BOROUGH, THE, SE1 **63** E1
Borough High St, SE1 **63** E1
★ Borough Mkt, SE1 52 A3
Borough Rd, SE1 **62** C2
Borough Sq, SE1 **63** E1
Borrett Cl, SE17 **75** E3
Borrodaile Rd, SW18 **178** B4
Borthwick Ms, E15
off Borthwick Rd **117** E1
Borthwick Rd, E15 **117** E1
Borthwick St, SE8 **158** A4
Boscastle Rd, NW5 **96** B4
Boscobel Pl, SW1 **58** B4
Boscobel St, NW8 **20** B3
Boscombe Av, E10 **103** D1
Boscombe Cl, E5 **115** E2
Boscombe Rd, W12 **134** A4
Boss Ho, SE1 **53** E4
Boss St, SE1 **53** E4
Boston Gdns, W4 **161** E1
Boston Pl, NW1 **21** E3
Bosun Cl, E14
off Byng St **158** A1
Boswell Ct, WC1 **25** D4
Boswell St, WC1 **25** D4
Bosworth Rd, W10 **121** E4
Bothwell Cl, E16 **145** F1
Bothwell St, W6
off Delorme St **163** D1
Botolph All, EC3 **40** C4
Botolph La, EC3 **52** B1
Botts Ms, W2 **30** B3
Botts Pas, W2 **30** B3
Boulcott St, E1 **143** D2
Boulevard, The, SW6 **164** C3
SW18
off Smugglers Way **178** B2
Wembley HA9
off Engineers Way **104** A1
Boundary Av, E17 **101** F1
Boundary La, SE17 **87** F1
Boundary Pas, E2 **29** E2
Boundary Rd, E17 **101** F1
NW8 **7** D1
Boundary Row, SE1 **50** C4
Boundary St, E2 **29** E1
Bourbon La, W12 **135** D4
Bourchier St, W1 **36** A4
Bourdon Pl, W1 **35** D4
Bourdon St, W1 **35** D4
Bourke Cl, NW10 **105** E3
SW4 **181** E4
Bourlet Cl, W1 **35** E1
Bourne Est, EC1 **26** A4
Bournemouth Cl, SE15 **170** A4
Bournemouth Rd, SE15 **170** A4
Bourne Pl, W4 **147** D4
Bourne Rd, E7 **103** F4
Bourne St, SW1 **70** A1
Bourne Ter, W2 **18** C4
Bousfield Rd, SE14 **171** D4
Boutflower Rd, SW11 **179** E2
Boutique Hall, SE13
off Lewisham Cen 186 C2
Bouton Pl, N1
off Waterloo Ter **112** B4
Bouverie Ms, N16 **99** E3
Bouverie Pl, W2 **32** B2
Bouverie Rd, N16 **99** E3
Bouverie St, EC4 **38** B3
Bovingdon Av, Wem.
HA9 **104** A3
Bovingdon Cl, N19
off Brookside Rd **96** C3
Bovingdon Rd, SW6 **164** B3
BOW, E3 **129** F2
Bowater Cl, SW2 **181** E4
Bowater Rd, Wem. HA9 **90** B4
Bow Br Est, E3 **130** B3
DLR Bow Church 130 A3
Bow Chyd, EC4 **39** F3
Bow Common La, E3 **129** F4
Bowden St, SE11 **74** B3
Bowditch, SE8 **157** F4
Bowdon Rd, E17 **102** A1
Bowen St, E14 **144** B2
Bower Av, SE10 **173** E3
Bowerdean St, SW6 **164** B3
Bowerman Av, SE14 **171** E1
Bower St, E1 **143** D2
Bowes Rd, W3 **133** E3
Bowfell Rd, W6 **162** C1
Bowhill Cl, SW9 **86** B2
Bowland Rd, SW4 **181** D2
Bowland Yd, SW1 **57** F1
Bow La, EC4 **39** F3
Bowl Ct, EC2 **29** D3
Bowling Grn La, EC1 **26** B2
Bowling Grn Pl, SE1 **52** A4
Bowling Grn St, SE11 **74** A4
Bowling Grn Wk, N1 **16** C4
Bowman Av, E16 **145** F3
Bowmans Ms, E1
off Hooper St **142** A2
Bowman's Ms, N7
off Seven Sisters Rd **97** E4
Bowmans Pl, N7
off Holloway Rd **97** E4
Bowmore Wk, NW1
off St. Paul's Cres **111** D4
Bowness Cl, E8
off Beechwood Rd **113** F3
Bowood Rd, SW11 **180** A2
⊖ Bow Road 129 F3
Bow Rd, E3 **129** F3
Bowsprit Pt, E14 **158** A2

w St, E15 **117** E2
WC2 **37** D3
Bow Triangle Business Cen, E3 *off Eleanor St* **130** A4
wyer Pl, SE5 **87** F2
wyer St, SE5 **87** E2
xall Rd, SE21 **183** E4
xworth Gro, N1 *off Richmond Av* **125** F1
yce St, SE1 **49** F3
ydell Ct, NW8 *off St. John's Wd Pk* **109** D4
yd St, E1 **142** A2
yfield St, SE1 **63** D1
yle St, W1 **35** E4
yne Rd, SE13 **186** C1
yne Ter Ms, W11 **135** F4
yson Rd, SE17 **76** A4
yton Cl, E1 *off Stayner's Rd* **129** D4
abant Ct, EC3 **40** C4
abazon St, E14 **144** B2
abourn Gro, SE15 **170** C4
acer Ho, N1 *off Nuttall St* **17** D2
acewell Rd, W10 **134** C1
acey Ms, N4 *off Bracey St* **97** E3
acey St, N4 **97** E3
acken Av, SW12 **180** A4
ackenbury Gdns, W6 **148** B2
ackenbury Rd, W6 **148** B2
ackenfield Cl, E5 **100** B4
acken Gdns, SW13 **162** A4
ackley Av, SE15 **184** B1
ackley Rd, W4 **147** E4
ackley St, EC1 **27** E4
ackley Ter, W4 **147** E4
acklyn Cl, N1 **16** A2
acklyn Ct, N1 **16** A2
acklyn St, N1 **16** A2
acknell Gdns, NW3 **108** B1
acknell Gate, NW3 **108** B2
acknell Way, NW3 **108** B1
adbourne St, SW6 **164** A4
adbury Ms, N16 *off Bradbury St* **113** E2
adbury St, N16 **113** E2
addyll St, SE10 **159** E4
adenham Cl, SE17 **76** A4
aden St, W9 **18** C3
adfield Ho, SW8 *off Wandsworth Rd* **167** D4
adford Rd, W3 *off Warple Way* **147** E1
adgate Rd, SE6 **186** A4
ading Ter, W12 **148** B2
adiston Rd, W9 **121** F3
adley Cl, N1 **14** B2
N7 *off Sutterton St* **111** F3
adley Ho, E3 *off Bromley High St* **130** B2
adley Lynch Ct, E2 *off Morpeth St* **129** D3
admead, SW8 **83** D3
admore Pk Rd, W6 **148** B2
adstock Rd, E9 **115** D3
ad St, SE1 **50** B3
adwell St, E1 **129** D3
ady St, E1 **128** B4
aemar Av, NW10 **91** D4
aemar Cl, SE16 *off Masters Dr* **156** B4
aemar Rd, E13 **131** F4
Braemer Ho, W9 **19** E1
Braes St, N1 **112** B4
Braganza St, SE17 **74** C2
Braham St, E1 **41** F3
Braid Av, W3 **133** E2
Braid Ct, W4 *off Lawford Rd* **160** C2
Braidwood Pas, EC1 *off Cloth St* **27** E4
Braidwood St, SE1 **52** C3
Brailsford Rd, SW2 **182** A3
Braintree St, E2 **128** C3
Braithwaite Ho, EC1 **27** F2
Braithwaite Twr, W2 **20** A4
Bramah Grn, SW9 **86** B4
★ Bramah Mus, SE1 **51** F3
Bramall Cl, E15 *off Idmiston Rd* **117** F2
Bramall Ct, N7 *off Watkinson Rd* **111** F3
Bramber Rd, W14 **163** F1
Bramble Gdns, W12 **133** F3
Bramcote Gro, SE16 **156** C4
Bramcote Rd, SW15 **176** B2
Bramerton St, SW3 **68** C4
Bramfield Ct, N4 *off Queens Dr* **98** C3
Bramfield Rd, SW11 **179** E4
Bramford Rd, SW18 **178** C2
Bramham Gdns, SW5 **66** C2
Bramlands Cl, SW11 **179** E1
Bramley Cres, SW8 **84** B2
Bramley Ho, SW15 *off Tunworth Cres* **175** F4
W10 *off Bramley Rd* **135** D2
Bramley Rd, W10 **135** D3
Brampton Cl, E5 **100** B3
Brampton Gro, Wem. HA9 **90** A2
Bramshaw Rd, E9 **115** D3
Bramshill Gdns, NW5 **96** B4
Bramshill Rd, NW10 **119** F2
Bramston Rd, NW10 **120** A2
Bramwell Ho, SE1 *off Harper Rd* **63** F3
SW1 **71** E3
Bramwell Ms, N1 **125** F1
Branch Hill, NW3 **94** C4
Branch Pl, N1 **127** D1
Branch Rd, E14 **143** E3
Branch St, SE15 **89** D3
Brand Cl, N4 **98** B2
Brandlehow Rd, SW15 **177** F2
Brandon Est, SE17 **87** D1
Brandon Ms, EC2 *off The Barbican* **40** A1
Brandon Rd, N7 **111** E4
Brandon St, SE17 **75** E1
Brandram Ms, SE13 **187** E1
Brandram Rd, SE13 **187** E1
Brand St, SE10 **172** C2
Brangton Rd, SE11 **73** F3
Branksea St, SW6 **163** E2
Branksome Rd, SW2 **181** E3
Branscombe St, SE13 **186** B1
Bransdale Cl, NW6 *off West End La* **122** B1
Brantwood Rd, SE24 **182** C3
Brasenose Dr, SW13 **162** C1
Brassett Pt, E15 **131** E1
Brassey Rd, NW6 **107** F3
Brassey Sq, SW11 **180** A1
Brassie Av, W3 **133** E2
Brass Tally All, SE16 *off Middleton Dr* **157** D1
Bratley St, E1 *off Weaver St* **128** A4
Bravington Pl, W9 *off Bravington Rd* **121** F4
Bravington Rd, W9 **121** F2
Bravingtons Wk, N1 **13** D3
Brawne Ho, SE17 **87** D1
Braxfield Rd, SE4 **185** E2
Bray, NW3 **109** E4
Brayards Rd, SE15 **170** B4
Braybrook St, W12 **133** F1
Brayburne Av, SW4 **166** C4
Bray Cres, SE16 *off Marlow Way* **157** D1
Braydon Rd, N16 **99** F2
Bray Dr, E16 **145** F3
Brayfield Ter, N1 *off Lofting Rd* **112** A4
Brayford Sq, E1 *off Summercourt Rd* **142** C2
Bray Pl, SW3 **69** E1
Bread St, EC4 **39** F3
Breakspears Ms, SE4 *off Ashby Rd* **172** A4
Breakspears Rd, SE4 **185** F1
Bream's Bldgs, EC4 **38** A2
Bream St, E3 **116** A4
Breasley Cl, SW15 **176** B2
Brechin Pl, SW7 **67** F1
Brecknock Rd, N7 **110** C1
N19 **110** C1
Brecknock Rd Est, N19 **110** C1
Brecon Ms, N7 *off Brecknock Rd* **111** D2
Brecon Rd, W6 **163** E1
Bredgar, SE13 **186** C3
Bredgar Rd, N19 **96** C3
Breer St, SW6 **178** B1
Breezers Hill, E1 *off Pennington St* **142** A3
Bremner Rd, SW7 **55** F1
Brenchley Gdns, SE23 **184** C4
Brendon Av, NW10 **105** E1
Brendon St, W1 **33** D2
Coll Brent Adult Coll, NW10 *off Morland Gdns* **119** D1
Brent Cross **93** D1
Jct Brent Cross Interchange, The, NW2 **93** D1
Brent Cross Shop Cen, NW4 **92** C1
Brentfield, NW10 **104** B4
Brentfield Cl, NW10 **105** D3
Brentfield Gdns, NW2 *off Hendon Way* **93** D1
Brentfield Ho, NW10 *off Stonebridge Pk* **105** D4
Brentfield Rd, NW10 **105** D3
Brent Grn Wk, Wem. HA9 **90** C4
Brenthouse Rd, E9 **114** B4
Brenthurst Rd, NW10 **105** F2
Brent New Enterprise Cen, NW10 *off Cobbold Rd* **105** F3
Brenton St, E14 **143** E2
Brent Pk, NW10 **105** D2
Brent Pk Rd, NW4 **92** B1
NW9 **92** A2
Brent S Shop Pk, NW2 **92** C2
Brent Ter, NW2 **92** C3
Brent Vw Rd, NW9 **92** A1
Brent Way, Wem. HA9 **104** B3
Bressenden Pl, SW1 **59** D2
Breton Ho, EC2 *off The Barbican* **27** F4

Brett Cl, N16 **99** E3
Brett Cres, NW10 **105** D4
Brettell St, SE17 **76** B3
Brett Ho Cl, SW15
off Putney Heath La **177** D4
Brett Pas, E8
off Kenmure Rd **114** B2
Brett Rd, E8 **114** B2
Brewer's Grn, SW1 **60** A2
Brewers Hall Gdns, EC2 **39** F1
Brewer St, W1 **35** F4
★ Brewery, The, EC1 **27** F4
Brewery Rd, N7 **111** E4
Brewery Sq, EC1 **26** C2
SE1 **53** E3
Brewhouse La, E1 **142** B4
SW15 **177** E1
Brewhouse Wk, SE16 **143** E4
Brewhouse Yd, EC1 **27** D2
Brewster Gdns, W10 **134** C1
Brewster Ho, E14 **143** F3
Brewster Rd, E10 **102** B2
Briant Est, SE1 **62** A3
Briant Ho, SE1 **61** F3
Briant St, SE14 **171** D3
Briardale Gdns, NW3 **94** A4
Briar Rd, NW2 **106** C1
Briar Wk, SW15 **176** B2
W10 *off Droop St* **121** E4
Briarwood Rd, SW4 **181** D3
Briary Cl, NW3
off Fellows Rd **109** E4
Briary Ct, E16
off Turner St **145** F2
Brick Ct, EC4 **38** A3
Brick Fm Cl, Rich. TW9 **160** B3
Brickfield Cl, E9
off Brenthouse Rd **114** C3
Brick La, E1 **29** F2
E2 **29** F1
● Bricklayer's Arms Distribution Cen, SE1 **77** D1
Jct Bricklayer's Arms Rbt, SE1 **64** A4
Brick St, W1 **46** C3
Brideale Cl, SE15 **89** F1
Bride Ct, EC4 **38** C3
Bride La, EC4 **38** C3
Bridel Ms, N1 **14** C1
Brides Pl, N1
off De Beauvoir Rd **113** E4
Bride St, N7 **111** F3
Bridewain St, SE1 **65** E2
Bridewell Pl, E1
off Brewhouse La **142** B4
EC4 **38** C3
Bridford Ms, W1 **23** D4
Bridge, The, SW8 **82** C3
Bridge App, NW1 **110** A4
Bridge Av, W6 **148** C4
Bridge Cl, W10
off Kingsdown Cl **135** D2
Bridge Ct, E14
off Newport Av **145** D3
Bridgefoot, SE1 **72** C3
Bridge Gdns, N16 **113** D1
Bridge Ho, NW3
off Adelaide Rd **110** A4
SW8 *off St. George Wf* **72** C3
Bridge Ho Quay, E14
off Prestons Rd **144** C4
Bridge La, SW11 **165** E3
Bridgeman Rd, N1 **111** F4
Bridgeman St, NW8 **8** C3
Bridge Meadows, SE14 **171** D1
Bridgend Rd, SW18 **178** C2
Bridge Pk, SW18 **178** A3
Bridge Pl, SW1 **59** D4
Bridgepoint Pl, N6
off Hornsey La **96** C2
Bridgeport Pl, E1
off Kennet St **142** A4
Bridge Rd, E15 **117** D4
E17 **101** F1
NW10 **105** E3
Wembley HA9 **90** A4
Bridges Ct, SW11 **179** D1
Bridges Pl, SW6 **163** F3
Bridge St, SW1 **60** C1
W4 **147** D3
Bridge Ter, E15
off Bridge Rd **117** D4
SE13
off Mercator Rd **187** D2
Bridge Vw, W6 **148** C4
Bridgewater Rd, E15 **130** C1
Bridgewater Sq, EC2 **27** E4
Bridgewater St, EC2 **27** E4
Bridgeway St, NW1 **11** F3
Bridge Yd, SE1 **52** B2
Bridgman Rd, W4 **146** C2
Bridle La, W1 **35** F4
Bridport Pl, N1 **16** B2
Bridport Ter, SW8
off Wandsworth Rd **167** D3
Bridstow Pl, W2 **30** B2
Brief St, SE5 **168** B3
Brierley Rd, E11 **117** D1
Brierly Gdns, E2
off Royston St **128** C2
Brigade St, SE3
off Royal Par **173** F4
Briggeford Cl, E5 **100** A3
Brightfield Rd, SE12 **187** F3
Brightling Rd, SE4 **185** F4
Brightlingsea Pl, E14 **143** F3
Brighton Gro, SE14
off Harts La **171** E3
Brighton Rd, N16 **113** E1
Brighton Ter, SW9 **181** F2
Brightside Rd, SE13 **187** D4
Bright St, E14 **144** B2
Brig Ms, SE8
off Watergate St **172** A1
Brill Pl, NW1 **12** B3
Brimstone Ho, E15
off Victoria St **117** E4
Brindley St, SE14 **171** F3
Brinklow Ho, W2 **18** B4
Brinkworth Way, E9 **115** F3
Brinsley Ho, E1
off Tarling St **142** C2
Brinton Wk, SE1 **50** C3
Brion Pl, E14 **144** C1
Brisbane Rd, E10 **102** B3
Brisbane St, SE5 **88** A3
Briscoe Cl, E11 **103** F3
Briset St, EC1 **26** C4
Briset Way, N7 **97** F3
Bristol Gdns, W9 **19** D3
Bristol Ho, SE11
off Lambeth Wk **62** A3
Bristol Ms, W9 **19** D3
Bristowe Cl, SW2 **182** A4
★ Britain at War Experience, SE1 **52** C3
Britannia Bldg, N1
off Ebenezer St **16** A4
Britannia Cl, SW4
off Bowland Rd **181**
Britannia Rd, E14 **158**
SW6 **78**
Britannia Row, N1 **126**
Britannia St, WC1 **13**
Britannia Wk, N1 **16**
Britannia Way, NW10 **118**
SW6 **79**
★ British Dental Assoc Mus, W1 **34**
British Gro, W4 **147**
British Gro N, W4
off Middlesex Ct **147**
British Gro Pas, W4 **147**
British Gro S, W4
off British Gro Pas **147**
★ British Lib, NW1 **12**
★ British Med Assoc, WC1 **24**
★ British Mus, The, WC1 **36**
★ British Red Cross Mus & Archives, SW1 **28**
Coll British Sch of Osteopathy, SE1 **63**
British St, E3 **129**
Brittany Pt, SE11 **74**
Britten Cl, NW11 **94**
Britten St, SW3 **68**
Brittidge Rd, NW10
off Paulet Way **105**
Britton St, EC1 **26**
BRIXTON, SW2 **181**
⇌ Brixton **181**
⊖ Brixton **181**
★ Brixton Acad, The, SW9 **181**
Brixton Hill, SW2 **181**
Brixton Oval, SW2 **182**
Brixton Rd, SW9 **86**
Brixton Sta Rd, SW9 **182**
Brixton Village Mkt, SW9
off Coldharbour La **182**
Brixton Water La, SW2 **181**
Broadbent Cl, N6 **96**
Broadbent St, W1 **34**
Broad Common Est, N16
off Osbaldeston Rd **100**
Broad Ct, WC2 **37**
Broadfield Cl, NW2 **92**
Broadfield La, NW1 **111**
Broadfields Way, NW10 **105**
BROADGATE, EC2 **28**
Broadgate Circle, EC2 **28**
Broadhinton Rd, SW4 **180**
Broadhurst Cl, NW6
off Broadhurst Gdns **108**
Broadhurst Gdns, NW6 **108**
Broadlands Cl, N6 **96**
Broadlands Rd, N6 **95**
Broad La, EC2 **28**
Broadley St, NW8 **20**
Broadley Ter, NW1 **21**
Broadmayne, SE17 **75**
Broadoak Ct, SW9
off Gresham Rd **182**
Broad Sanctuary, SW1 **60**
Broadstone Pl, W1 **34**
Broad St Av, EC2 **40**
Broad St Pl, EC2 **40**
Broad Wk, NW1 **22**
W1 **46**
Broad Wk, The, W8 **43**
Broadwalk Ct, W8 **42**
Broad Wk La, NW11 **93**

roadwall, SE1 ... **50** B2
roadway, E15 ... **117** D4
SW1 ... **60** A2
roadway, The, SW13
off The Terrace ... **161** E4
roadway Mkt, E8 ... **128** B1
roadway Mkt Ms, E8
off Regents Row ... **128** A1
roadway Ms, E5 ... **99** F1
Broadway Shop Cen, W6
off Hammersmith Bdy ... 148 C3
roadway Wk, E14
off Alpha Gro ... **158** A2
roadwick St, W1 ... **35** F4
roadwood Ter, W8
off Pembroke Rd ... **149** F3
Broad Yd, EC1 ... **26** C3
Brocas Cl, NW3
off Fellows Rd ... **109** E4
rockbridge Ho, SW15
off Tangley Gro ... **175** F4
rockham St, SE1 ... **63** F2
Brockill Cres, SE4 ... **185** E2
Brocklehurst St, SE14 ... **171** D2
BROCKLEY, SE4 ... **185** E3
Brockley ... 185 E1
rockley Cross, SE4
off Endwell Rd ... **185** F1
Brockley Footpath, SE15 ... **184** C2
Brockley Gdns, SE4 ... **171** F4
Brockley Gro, SE4 ... **185** F3
Brockley Hall Rd, SE4 ... **185** E4
Brockley Ms, SE4 ... **185** E3
Brockley Ri, SE23 ... **185** E4
Brockley Rd, SE4 ... **185** F1
Brockley Way, SE4 ... **185** D3
Brock Pl, E3 ... **130** B4
Brock St, SE15
off Evelina Rd ... **184** C1
Brockway Cl, E11 ... **103** E2
Brockweir, E2
off Cyprus St ... **128** C2
★ Brockwell Park, SE24 ... 182 B4
Brockwell Pk Row, SW2 ... **182** A4
Brodia Rd, N16 ... **99** E4
Brodick Ho, E3
off Saxon Rd ... **129** F2
Brodie Ho, SE1
off Coopers Rd ... **77** F2
Brodie St, SE1 ... **77** F2
Brodlove La, E1 ... **143** D3
Broken Wf, EC4 ... **39** E4
Brokesley St, E3 ... **129** F4
Broke Wk, E8 ... **128** A1
Bromar Rd, SE5 ... **183** E1
Bromehead Rd, E1
off Commercial Rd ... **142** C2
Bromehead St, E1
off Commercial Rd ... **142** C2
Bromell's Rd, SW4 ... **180** C2
Bromfelde Rd, SW4 ... **181** D1
Bromfelde Wk, SW4 ... **167** D4
Bromfield St, N1 ... **14** B2
BROMLEY, E3 ... **130** B4
Bromley-by-Bow ... 130 B4
Bromley Hall Rd, E14 ... **144** C1
Bromley High St, E3 ... **130** B3
Bromley Pl, W1 ... **23** E4
Bromley St, E1 ... **143** D1
BROMPTON, SW3 ... **56** C3
Brompton Arc, SW3 ... **57** E1
★ Brompton Oratory, SW7 ... 56 C3
Brompton Pk Cres, SW6 ... **78** C1
Brompton Pl, SW3 ... **57** D2
Brompton Rd, SW1 ... **57** D2
SW3 ... **56** C4
SW7 ... **57** D2
Brompton Sq, SW3 ... **56** C2
Bromwich Av, N6 ... **96** A3
Bromyard Av, W3 ... **133** E4
Bromyard Ho, SE15 ... **170** B2
W3 ... **133** E4
BRONDESBURY, NW2 ... **107** E4
★ Brondesbury ... 107 F4
Brondesbury Ct, NW2 ... **106** C3
Brondesbury Ms, NW6
off Willesden La ... **108** A4
BRONDESBURY PARK, NW6 ... **106** C4
★ Brondesbury Park ... 121 D1
Brondesbury Pk, NW2 ... **106** B3
NW6 ... **107** D4
Brondesbury Rd, NW6 ... **121** F2
Brondesbury Vil, NW6 ... **121** F2
Bronsart Rd, SW6 ... **163** E2
Bronte Ho, NW6 ... **6** B4
Bronti Cl, SE17 ... **75** F3
Bronze St, SE8 ... **172** A2
Brook Av, Wem. HA9 ... **90** A4
Brookbank Rd, SE13 ... **186** A1
Brook Cl, W3 ... **132** A4
Brookdale Rd, SE6 ... **186** B4
Brook Dr, SE11 ... **62** B3
Brooke Ct, W10
off Kilburn La ... **121** E2
Brooke Rd, E5 ... **100** A4
N16 ... **99** F4
Brooke's Ct, EC1 ... **26** A4
Brookes Mkt, EC1 ... **26** B4
Brooke St, EC1 ... **38** A1
Brookfield, N6 ... **96** A4
Brookfield Pk, NW5 ... **96** B4
Brookfield Rd, E9 ... **115** E3
W4 ... **147** D1
Brook Gdns, SW13 ... **175** F1
Brook Gate, W1 ... **45** F1
Brook Grn, W6 ... **149** D3
Brooklands Pas, SW8 ... **84** A4
Brooklyn Pas, W12
off Lime Gro ... **148** C1
Brookmarsh Ind Est, SE10
off Norman Rd ... 172 B2
Brook Ms N, W2 ... **31** F4
Brookmill Rd, SE8 ... **172** A3
Brook Rd, NW2 ... **92** A3
Brooksbank St, E9 ... **114** C3
Brooksby Ms, N1
off Brooksby St ... **112** A4
Brooksby St, N1 ... **112** A4
Brooksby's Wk, E9 ... **115** D2
Brookside Rd, N19 ... **96** C3
Brooks La, W4 ... **160** A1
Brook's Ms, W1 ... **34** C4
Brooks Rd, W4 ... **146** A4
Brook St, W1 ... **34** B4
W2 ... **32** B4
Brooksville Av, NW6 ... **121** E1
Brookville Rd, SW6 ... **163** F2
Brookwood Av, SW13 ... **175** F1
Broome Ho, E5
off Pembury Rd ... **114** B2
Broome Way, SE5 ... **88** A3
Broomfield, E17 ... **101** F1
Broomfield St, E14 ... **144** A1
Broomgrove Rd, SW9 ... **167** F4
Broomhill Rd, SW18 ... **178** A3
Broomhouse La, SW6 ... **164** A4
Broomhouse Rd, SW6 ... **164** A4
Broomsleigh St, NW6 ... **107** F2
Broomwood Rd, SW11 ... **179** F4
Brougham Rd, E8 ... **128** A1
W3 ... **132** C2
Brougham St, SW11 ... **165** F4
Brough Cl, SW8 ... **85** D3
Broughton Dr, SW9 ... **182** A2
Broughton Rd, SW6 ... **164** B4
Broughton Rd App, SW6
off Wandsworth Br Rd ... **164** B4
Broughton St, SW8 ... **166** A4
Brouncker Rd, W3 ... **146** C1
Brownfield St, E14 ... **144** B2
Brown Hart Gdns, W1 ... **34** B4
Browning Cl, W9 ... **19** F3
Browning Ms, W1 ... **34** C1
Browning Rd, E11 ... **103** F1
Browning St, SE17 ... **75** F2
Brownlow Ms, WC1 ... **25** F3
Brownlow Rd, E8 ... **127** F1
NW10 ... **105** E4
Brownlow St, WC1 ... **37** F1
Brown's Bldgs, EC3 ... **41** D3
Browns La, NW5 ... **110** B2
Brown St, W1 ... **33** E2
Brownswood Rd, N4 ... **98** B4
Broxash Rd, SW11 ... **180** A4
Broxwood Way, NW8 ... **9** D1
Bruce Cl, W10
off Ladbroke Gro ... **135** E1
Bruce Rd, E3 ... **130** B3
NW10 ... **105** D4
Bruckner St, W10 ... **121** F3
Bruford Ct, SE8 ... **172** A1
Bruges Pl, NW1
off Randolph St ... **110** C4
★ Brunei Gall, WC1 ... 24 B4
★ Brunel Engine Ho, SE16 ... 156 C1
Brunel Est, W2 ... **30** A1
Brunel Ho, N16
off Stamford Hill ... **99** F2
Brunel Ms, W10
off Kilburn La ... **121** E3
Brunel Rd, SE16 ... **156** C1
W3 ... **133** E1
Brunel St, E16
off Victoria Dock Rd ... **145** F2
Brune St, E1 ... **41** E1
Brunlees Ho, SE1
off Bath Ter ... **63** E3
Bruno Pl, NW9 ... **90** C3
Brunswick Ct, EC1
off Tompion St ... **26** C1
SE1 ... **65** D1
SW1 *off Regency St* ... **72** B1
Brunswick Gdns, W8 ... **42** B3
Brunswick Ms, W1 ... **33** F2
Brunswick Pk, SE5 ... **88** B4
Brunswick Pl, N1 ... **28** B1
NW1 ... **22** B2
Brunswick Quay, SE16 ... **157** D2
Brunswick Rd, E10 ... **102** C2
E14
off Blackwall Tunnel Northern App ... **144** C2
Brunswick Shop Cen, WC1 ... 24 C2
Brunswick Sq, WC1 ... **25** D3
Brunswick Vil, SE5 ... **88** C4
Brunton Pl, E14 ... **143** E2
Brushfield St, E1 ... **29** D4
Brushwood Cl, E14
off Uamvar St ... **144** B1
Brussels Rd, SW11 ... **179** D2

Bruton La, W1 **47** D1
Bruton Pl, W1 **47** D1
Bruton St, W1 **47** D1
Bryan Av, NW10 **106** B4
Bryan Rd, SE16 **157** F1
Bryan's All, SW6
off Wandsworth Br Rd **164** B4
Bryanston Ms E, W1 **33** E1
Bryanston Ms W, W1 **33** E1
Bryanston Pl, W1 **33** E1
Bryanston Sq, W1 **33** E1
Bryanston St, W1 **33** E3
Bryant Ct, E2 **17** E2
W3 **133** D4
Bryant St, E15 **117** D4
Bryantwood Rd, N7 **112** A2
Brydale Ho, SE16
off Rotherhithe New Rd **157** D3
Brydges Pl, WC2 **48** C1
Brydges Rd, E15 **117** D2
Brydon Wk, N1
off Outram Pl **125** E1
Bryer Ct, EC2
off Bridgewater St **27** E4
Bryett Rd, N7 **97** E4
Brymay Cl, E3 **130** A2
Brynmaer Rd, SW11 **165** F3
Bryony Rd, W12 **134** A3
Coll BSix, Brooke Ho 6th Form Coll, E5
off Kenninghall Rd 100 B4
Buchanan Gdns, NW10 **120** B2
Buchan Rd, SE15 **184** C1
Buckden Cl, SE12 **187** F4
Buckfast St, E2 **128** A3
Buck Hill Wk, W2 **44** B1
Buckhold Rd, SW18 **178** A4
Buckhurst St, E1 **128** B4
Buckingham Arc, WC2 **49** D1
Buckingham Chambers, SW1
off Greencoat Pl **59** F4
Buckingham Gate, SW1 **59** E1
Buckingham Ms, N1
off Buckingham Rd **113** E3
NW10 **119** F2
SW1 **59** E2
★ Buckingham Palace, SW1 59 D1
Buckingham Palace Rd, SW1 **70** C1
Buckingham Pl, SW1 **59** E2
Buckingham Rd, E10 **102** B4
E15 **117** F2
N1 **113** E3
NW10 **119** F2
Buckingham St, WC2 **49** D1
Buckland Cres, NW3 **109** D4
Buckland Rd, E10 **102** C3
Buckland St, N1 **16** B3
Buckland Wk, W3 **132** C4
Bucklebury, NW1 **23** E2
Buckler Ct, N7
off Eden Gro **111** F2
Bucklers All, SW6 **163** F1
Bucklersbury, EC4 **40** A3
Bucklersbury Pas, EC4 **40** A3
Buckle St, E1 **41** F2
Buckley Rd, NW6 **107** F4
Buckley St, SE1 **50** A3
Buckmaster Cl, SW9
off Stockwell Pk Rd **182** A1
Buckmaster Rd, SW11 **179** E2
Bucknall St, WC2 **36** B2
Bucknell Cl, SW2 **181** F2
Buckner Rd, SW2 **181** F2
Buckstone Cl, SE23 **184** C4
Buck St, NW1 **110** B4
Buckters Rents, SE16 **143** E4
Buckthorne Rd, SE4 **185** E4
Buddings Circle, Wem. HA9 **90** C4
Budge Row, EC4 **40** A4
Budge's Wk, W2 **43** E2
Buer Rd, SW6 **163** E4
Bugsby's Way, SE10 **159** F3
Coll Building Crafts Coll, E15
off Kennard Rd 117 D4
Bulinga St, SW1 **72** B1
Bullace Row, SE5 **87** F4
Bullards Pl, E2 **129** D3
Bullen Ho, E1
off Collingwood St **128** B4
Bullen St, SW11 **165** E4
Buller Cl, SE15 **170** A2
Buller Rd, NW10
off Chamberlayne Rd **121** D3
Bullied Way, SW1 **71** D1
Bull Inn Ct, WC2 **49** D1
Bullivant St, E14 **144** C3
Bull Rd, E15 **131** F2
Bull's All, SW14 **161** D4
Bulls Gdns, SW3 **57** D4
Bull's Head Pas, EC3 **40** C3
Bull Yd, SE15
off Peckham High St **170** A3
Bulmer Ms, W11 **42** A2
Bulmer Pl, W11 **42** A2
Bulow Est, SW6
off Pearscroft Rd **164** B3
Bulstrode Pl, W1 **34** B1
Bulstrode St, W1 **34** B2
Bulwer Ct Rd, E11 **103** D2
Bulwer Rd, E11 **103** D1
Bulwer St, W12 **134** C4
Bunhill Row, EC1 **28** A2
Bunhouse Pl, SW1 **70** A2
Bunkers Hill, NW11 **94** C1
Bunning Way, N7 **111** E4
Bunsen St, E3
off Kenilworth Rd **129** E2
Bunyan Ct, EC2
off The Barbican **27** E4
Buonaparte Ms, SW1 **72** A2
Burbage Cl, SE1 **64** A3
Burbage Rd, SE21 **183** D4
SE24 **182** C4
Burcham St, E14 **144** B2
Burchell Rd, E10 **102** B2
SE15 **170** B3
Burcher Gale Gro, SE15 **89** D2
Burdenshott Av, Rich. TW10 **174** B2
Burder Cl, N1 **113** E3
Burder Rd, N1
off Balls Pond Rd **113** E3
Burdett Ms, NW3
off Belsize Cres **109** D3
W2 **30** C2
Burdett Rd, E3 **129** F4
E14 **129** F4
Burdett St, SE1 **62** A2
Burford Rd, E15 **117** D4
Burford Wk, SW6 **79** D3
Burford Wf Apts, E15
off Cam Rd **131** D1
Burges Gro, SW13 **162** B2
● Burgess Business Pk, SE5 88 B2
Burgess Hill, NW2 **108** A1
Burgess Rd, E15 **117** E1
Burgess St, E14 **144** A1
Burge St, SE1 **64** B3
★ Burgh Ho (Hampstead Mus), NW3
off New End Sq 109 D1
Burghley Rd, E11 **103** E2
NW5 **110** B2
Burghley Twr, W3 **133** F3
Burgh St, N1 **15** D2
Burgon St, EC4 **39** D3
Burgos Gro, SE10 **172** B3
Burgoyne Rd, SW9 **181** F1
Burke Cl, SW15 **175** E2
Burke Ho, SW11
off Maysoule Rd **179** D2
Burke St, E16 **145** F2
Burland Rd, SW11 **179** F3
Burleigh Ho, W10
off St. Charles Sq **135** D1
Burleigh Pl, SW15 **177** D3
Burleigh St, WC2 **37** E4
🔒 Burlington Arc, W1 47 E1
Burlington Av, Rich. TW9 **160** A3
Burlington Cl, W9 **121** F4
Burlington Gdns, W1 **47** E1
W3 **132** C4
W4 **146** C4
Burlington La, W4 **161** E2
Burlington Ms, SW15 **177** F3
W3 **132** C4
Burlington Pl, SW6
off Burlington Rd **163** E4
Burlington Rd, SW6 **163** E4
W4 **146** C4
Burma Rd, N16 **113** D1
Burnaby Cres, W4 **160** B1
Burnaby Gdns, W4 **160** C1
Burnaby St, SW10 **79** E3
Burne Jones Ho, W14 **149** F3
Burnell Wk, SE1 **77** F2
Burness Cl, N7
off Roman Way **111** F3
Burne St, NW1 **20** C4
Burnett Cl, E9 **114** C2
Burnett Ho, SE13
off Lewisham Hill **172** C4
Burney St, SE10 **172** C2
Burnfoot Av, SW6 **163** E3
Burnham, NW3 **109** E4
Burnham Cl, SE1 **77** F1
Burnham St, E2 **128** C3
Burnhill Cl, SE15
off Gervase St **170** B2
Burnley Rd, NW10 **106** A2
SW9 **167** F4
Burnsall St, SW3 **69** D2
Burnside Cl, SE16 **143** D4
Burns Rd, NW10 **119** F1
SW11 **165** F4
Burnt Ash Hill, SE12 **187** F4
Burnt Ash Rd, SE12 **187** F3
Burnthwaite Rd, SW6 **164** A2
Buross St, E1
off Commercial Rd **142** B2
Burrard Rd, NW6 **108** A2
Burr Cl, E1 **142** A4
Burrell St, SE1 **50** C2
Burrells Wf Sq, E14 **158** B4
Burrell Twrs, E10 **102** A1
Burrow Rd, SE22 **183** E2
Burrows Ms, SE1 **50** C4
Burrows Rd, NW10 **120** C3
Burslem St, E1 **142** A2

urstock Rd, SW15 ....177 E2
urston Rd, SW15 ....177 D3
urston Vil, SW15
off St. John's Av 177 D3
urtley Cl, N4 ....98 C2
urton Ct, SW3
off Franklin's Row 69 F2
urton Gro, SE17 ....76 A3
urton La, SW9 ....168 A4
urton Ms, SW1 ....70 B1
urton Pl, WC1 ....24 B1
urton Rd, NW6 ....107 F4
SW9 ....168 B4
urton St, WC1 ....24 B1
urwash Ho, SE1 ....64 B1
urwell Cl, E1
off Bigland St 142 B2
urwell Rd, E10 ....101 E2
urwell Wk, E3 ....130 A4
urwood Pl, W2 ....33 D2
ury Cl, SE16
off Rotherhithe St 143 D4
ury Ct, EC3 ....41 D2
ury Pl, WC1 ....36 C1
ury St, EC3 ....41 D3
SW1 ....47 F2
ury Wk, SW3 ....68 C1
usbridge Ho, E14
off Brabazon St 144 A1
usby Ms, NW5
off Busby Pl 111 D3
usby Pl, NW5 ....111 D3
usby St, E2 ....29 F2
ushbaby Cl, SE1 ....64 C3
ushberry Rd, E9 ....115 E3
ush Cotts, SW18
off Putney Br Rd 178 A3
ush Ct, W12
off Shepherds Bush Grn 149 D1
ushell St, E1
off Hermitage Wall 142 A4
ushey Hill Rd, SE5 ....169 E3
ush Gro, NW9 ....90 C1
Bush Ind Est, N19 ....96 C4
NW10 ....119 D4
ush La, EC4 ....40 A4
ush Rd, E8 ....128 B1
E11 ....103 F1
SE8 ....157 D3
ushwood, E11 ....103 F2
ushwood Dr, SE1 ....77 F1
ushwood Rd, Rich. TW9 ...160 A1
★ Business Design Cen, N1 .14 B1
utcher Row, E1 ....143 D3
E14 ....143 D3
ute Gdns, W6 ....149 D3
ute St, SW7 ....56 A4
ute Wk, N1
off Marquess Rd 113 D3
utler Pl, SW1 ....60 A2
utler Rd, NW10 ....105 F4
utlers & Colonial Wf, SE1 ...53 F4
utler St, E2
off Knottisford St 128 C3
utlers Wf, SE1 ....53 E3
utterfield Cl, SE16
off Wilson Gro 156 B1
Butterfly Wk Shop Cen, SE5 ....168 C3
uttermere Cl, E15 ....117 D1
SE1 ....77 E1
uttermere Dr, SW15 ......177 E3
uttermere Wk, E8 ....113 F3
Butterwick, W6 ....148 C3
Buttesland St, N1 ....16 B4
Buxhall Cres, E9 ....115 F3
Buxted Rd, E8 ....113 F4
SE22 ....183 E2
Buxton Ct, N1 ....15 F4
Buxton Gdns, W3 ....132 B3
Buxton Ho, SW11
off Maysoule Rd 179 D2
Buxton Ms, SW4 ....167 D4
Buxton Rd, E15 ....117 E2
N19 ....97 D2
NW2 ....106 B3
SW14 ....175 E1
Buxton St, E1 ....29 F3
Byam St, SW6 ....164 C4
Bye, The, W3 ....133 E2
Byeway, The, SW14 ....174 C1
Byfeld Gdns, SW13 ....162 A3
Byfield Cl, SE16 ....157 E1
Byford Cl, E15 ....117 E4
Bygrove St, E14 ....144 B2
Bylands Cl, SE16
off Rotherhithe St 143 D4
Byng Pl, WC1 ....24 A3
Byng St, E14 ....158 A1
Byron Cl, E8 ....128 A1
Byron Ct, W9 ....18 B2
Byron Ms, NW3 ....109 E2
W9 ....18 B2
Byron Rd, E10 ....102 B2
NW2 ....92 B3
Byron St, E14
off St. Leonards Rd 144 C2
Bythorn St, SW9 ....181 F1
Byward St, EC3 ....53 D1
Bywater Pl, SE16 ....143 E4
Bywater St, SW3 ....69 E2
Bywell Pl, W1 ....35 E1
Byworth Wk, N19
off Courtauld Rd 97 E2

C

Cabbell St, NW1 ....32 C1
Cable Pl, SE10
off Diamond Ter 172 C3
Cable St, E1 ....142 A3
Cabot Pl, E14 ....144 A4
Cabot Sq, E14 ....144 A4
Cabul Rd, SW11 ....165 E4
Cactus Cl, SE15
off Lyndhurst Gro 169 E4
Cactus Wk, W12
off Du Cane Rd 133 F2
Cadbury Way, SE16 ....65 F3
Caddington Rd, NW2 ....93 E4
Cadell Cl, E2 ....17 F3
Cade Rd, SE10 ....173 D3
Cader Rd, SW18 ....178 C4
Cadet Dr, SE1 ....77 F2
Cadet Pl, SE10 ....159 E4
Cadiz St, SE17 ....75 F3
Cadman Cl, SW9
off Langton Rd 86 C3
Cadmus Cl, SW4
off Aristotle Rd 181 D1
Cadogan Cl, E9
off Cadogan Ter 115 F4
Cadogan Gdns, SW3 ....57 F4
Cadogan Gate, SW1 ....57 F4
Cadogan La, SW1 ....58 A3
Riv Cadogan Pier 81 D1
Cadogan Pl, SW1 ....57 F2
Cadogan Sq, SW1 ....57 F3
Cadogan St, SW3 ....69 E1
Cadogan Ter, E9 ....115 F3
Caedmon Rd, N7 ....111 F1
Cahill St, EC1 ....27 F3
Cahir St, E14 ....158 B3
Caird St, W10 ....121 E3
Cairnfield Av, NW2 ....91 E4
Cairns Rd, SW11 ....179 E3
Caistor Pk Rd, E15 ......131 F1
Caithness Rd, W14 ....149 D3
Calabria Rd, N5 ....112 B3
Calais Gate, SE5 ....86 C4
Calais St, SE5 ....87 D4
Caldecot Rd, SE5 ....168 C4
Caldecott Way, E5 ....101 D4
Calderon Pl, W10
off St. Quintin Gdns 134 C1
Calderon Rd, E11 ....116 C1
Caldervale Rd, SW4 ......181 D3
Caldwell Gdns Est, SW9 ....86 A4
Caldwell St, SW9 ....85 F3
Caldy Wk, N1
off Clifton Rd 112 C3
Caleb St, SE1 ....51 E4
Caledonian Road 111 E3
Caledonian Rd, N1 ....13 D3
N7 ....111 F2
★ Caledonian Road & Barnsbury 111 F4
Caledonian Sq, NW1
off Canal Boul 111 D3
Caledonian Wf, E14 ......159 D3
Caledonia St, N1 ....13 D3
Cale St, SW3 ....68 C2
Caletock Way, SE10 ......159 F4
Calico Row, SW11
off Cinnamon Row 178 C1
Calidore Cl, SW2 ....181 F4
California Bldg, SE13
off Deals Gateway 172 B3
Callaby Ter, N1
off Wakeham St 113 D3
Callaghan Cl, SE13 ......187 E2
Callcott Rd, NW6 ....107 F4
Callcott St, W8 ....42 A2
Callendar Rd, SW7 ....56 A2
Callingham Cl, E14
off Wallwood St 143 F1
Callisons Pl, SE10
off Bellot St 159 E4
Callow St, SW3 ....67 F4
Calmington Rd, SE5 ....77 D3
Calshot St, N1 ....13 E2
Calthorpe St, WC1 ....25 F2
Calton Av, SE21 ....183 E3
Calverley Gro, N19 ....97 D2
Calvert Av, E2 ....29 D1
Calverton, SE5 ....76 B4
Calvert Rd, SE10 ....159 F4
Calvert's Bldgs, SE1 ......52 A3
Calvert St, NW1
off Chalcot Rd 124 A1
Calvin St, E1 ....29 E3
Calypso Cres, SE15 ....89 E2
Calypso Way, SE16 ....157 F2
Cambalt Rd, SW15 ....177 D3
CAMBERWELL, SE5 ....87 F3
Camberwell Business Cen, SE5 ....88 A3
Camberwell Ch St, SE5 ....169 D3
Uni Camberwell Coll of Arts, Peckham Rd, SE5 ....89 D4
Wilson Rd, SE5 ....169 E3

Camberwell Glebe, SE5 .....169 D3
Jct Camberwell Grn, SE5 ....87 F4
SE5 .....88 A4
Camberwell Gro, SE5 .....169 D3
Camberwell New Rd, SE5 ....86 A1
Camberwell Pas, SE5 .....87 F4
Camberwell Rd, SE5 .....87 F1
Camberwell Sta Rd, SE5 ....168 C3
Camborne Ms, W11
off St. Marks Rd 135 E2
Cambrian Rd, E10 .....102 A1
Cambria Rd, SE5 .....182 C1
Cambria St, SW6 .....79 D3
Cambridge Av, NW6 .....6 B2
Cambridge Circ, WC2 .....36 B3
Cambridge Cl, NW10
off Lawrence Way 90 C4
Cambridge Cotts, Rich.
TW9 .....160 A1
Cambridge Cres, E2 .....128 B2
Cambridge Gdns, NW6 .....6 B2
W10 .....135 E2
Cambridge Gate, NW1 .....23 D1
Cambridge Gate Ms, NW1 ...23 D1
Cambridge Gro, W6 .....148 B3
Cambridge Heath 128 B2
Cambridge Heath Rd, E1 ...128 B2
E2 .....128 B2
Cambridge Mans, SW11
off Cambridge Rd 165 F3
Cambridge Pl, W8 .....55 D1
Cambridge Rd, NW6 .....6 A4
SW11 .....165 F3
SW13 .....161 F4
Richmond TW9 .....160 A2
Cambridge Rd N, W4 .....146 B4
Cambridge Rd S, W4 .....146 B4
Coll Cambridge Sch of English,
The, WC2 .....37 D2
Cambridge Sq, W2 .....32 C2
Cambridge St, SW1 .....71 D1
Cambridge Ter, NW1 .....23 D1
Cambridge Ter Ms, NW1 .....23 D1
★ Camden Arts Cen, NW3 .108 B2
Camden Gdns, NW1
off Kentish Town Rd 110 B4
Camden High St, NW1 .....124 B1
Camdenhurst St, E14 .....143 E2
Camden La, N7
off Rowstock Gdns 111 D3
★ Camden Lock Mkt &
Waterbuses, NW1 .....110 B4
Camden Lock Pl, NW1
off Chalk Fm Rd 110 B4
Camden Ms, NW1 .....111 D3
Camden Pk Rd, NW1 .....111 D3
Camden Pas, N1 .....14 C2
Camden Road 110 C4
Camden Rd, N7 .....111 D2
NW1 .....124 C1
Camden Row, SE3 .....173 E4
Camden Sq, NW1 .....111 D3
SE15 .....89 E4
Camden St, NW1 .....110 B4
Camden Ter, NW1
off North Vil 111 D3
CAMDEN TOWN, NW1 .....11 E1
Camden Town 124 B1
Camden Wk, N1 .....14 C1
Camelford Wk, W11
off St. Marks Rd 135 E2
Camellia St, SW8 .....84 C3
Camelot Ho, NW1
off Camden Pk Rd 111 D3
Camelot St, SE15
off Bird in Bush Rd 170 B2
Camera Pl, SW10 .....80 A1
Cameron Ho, SE5
off Comber Gro 87 E3
Cameron Pl, E1
off Varden St 142 B2
Camerton Cl, E8
off Buttermere Wk 113 F3
Camilla Rd, SE16 .....156 B3
Camlet St, E2 .....29 E2
Camley St, NW1 .....12 B2
★ Camley St Natural Pk,
NW1 .....12 B2
Camomile St, EC3 .....40 C2
Campana Rd, SW6 .....78 A4
Campbell Gordon Way,
NW2 .....106 B1
Campbell Rd, E3 .....130 A3
E15
off Trevelyan Rd 117 F1
Campbell Wk, N1
off Outram Pl 125 E1
Campdale Rd, N7 .....97 D4
Campden Gro, W8 .....42 B4
Campden Hill, W8 .....42 A4
Campden Hill Ct, W8 .....42 B4
Campden Hill Gdns, W8 ...136 A4
Campden Hill Gate, W8 .....42 A4
Campden Hill Pl, W11
off Holland Pk Av 135 F4
Campden Hill Rd, W8 .....54 B1
Campden Hill Sq, W8 .....135 F4
Campden Hill Twrs, W11 ....42 A2
Campden Ho Cl, W8 .....42 A4
Campden St, W8 .....42 A3
Camperdown St, E1 .....41 F3
Campion Rd, SW15 .....176 C2
Campion Ter, NW2 .....93 D4
Camplin St, SE14 .....171 D2
Campshill Pl, SE13
off Campshill Rd 186 C3
Campshill Rd, SE13 .....186 C3
Cam Rd, E15 .....131 D1
Canada Cres, W3 .....132 C1
Canada Est, SE16 .....156 C2
Canada Gdns, SE13 .....186 C3
Canada Rd, W3 .....118 C4
Canada Sq, E14 .....144 B4
Canada St, SE16 .....157 D1
Canada Water 156 C1
Canada Way, W12 .....134 B3
Canal App, SE8 .....171 E1
Canal Boul, NW1 .....111 D3
Canal Bldg, N1
off Shepherdess Wk 15 F2
Canal Cl, E1 .....129 E4
W10 .....121 D4
Canal Gro, SE15 .....170 A1
Canal Path, E2 .....17 E1
Canal St, SE5 .....88 A1
Canal Wk, N1 .....127 D1
NW10
off West End Cl 104 C4
Canal Way, N1 .....15 F2
NW1 .....9 D4
NW8 .....20 C1
NW10 .....119 F4
W2 .....19 D4
W9
off Great Western Rd ...135 F1
W10 .....121 D4
Canal Way Wk, W10 .....121 D4
Canary Wharf 144 B4
DLR Canary Wharf 144 A4
Riv Canary Wharf Pier .....143 F
Canberra Pl, Rich. TW9
off Marksbury Av 174 A1
Cancell Rd, SW9 .....86 B4
Candahar Rd, SW11 .....165 E4
Candle Gro, SE15 .....184 B1
Candlemakers Apts, SW11
off York Rd 179 D1
Candle St, E1 .....143 E1
Candover St, W1 .....35 E1
Candy St, E3 .....129 F1
Caney Ms, NW2 .....93 D
Canfield Gdns, NW6 .....108 C4
Canfield Pl, NW6
off Canfield Gdns .....108 C
Canford Rd, SW11 .....180 A
Canham Rd, W3 .....147 E
Cann Hall Rd, E11 .....117 E
Canning Cross, SE5 .....169 E4
Canning Pas, W8 .....55 E
Canning Pl, W8 .....55 E
Canning Pl Ms, W8 .....55 E1
Canning Rd, E15 .....131 E
N5 .....98 B4
Canning Town .....145 E
DLR Canning Town .....145 E
Canning Town .....145 E
Jct Canning Town, E16 .....145 E1
Cannon Ct, EC1
off Brewhouse Yd .....27 D
Cannon Dr, E14 .....144 A
Cannon Hill, NW6 .....108 A
Cannon La, NW3 .....95 D4
Cannon Pl, NW3 .....95 D4
Cannon Street .....52 A
Cannon Street .....52 A
Cannon St, EC4 .....39 E
Cannon St Rd, E1 .....142 B
● Cannon Trd Est, Wem.
HA9 .....104 B
● Cannon Wf Business Cen,
SE8 .....157 E
● Cannon Workshops, E14
off Cannon Dr .....144 A
Canon All, EC4
off St. Paul's Chyd .....39 D
Canon Beck Rd, SE16 .....156 C1
CANONBURY, N1 .....112 C
★ Canonbury .....112 C
Canonbury Cres, N1 .....112 C4
Canonbury Gro, N1 .....112 C4
Canonbury La, N1 .....112 B4
Canonbury Pk N, N1 .....112 C
Canonbury Pk S, N1 .....112 C
Canonbury Pl, N1 .....112 B
Canonbury Rd, N1 .....112 B
Canonbury Sq, N1 .....112 B4
Canonbury St, N1 .....112 C4
Canonbury Vil, N1 .....112 B4
Canonbury Yd, N1
off New N Rd 126 C1
Canonbury Yd W, N1
off Compton Rd .....112 B
Canon Row, SW1 .....60 C
Canons Cl, N2 .....95 D
Canon St, N1 .....15 E
Canrobert St, E2 .....128 B
Cantelowes Rd, NW1 .....111 D
Canterbury Cres, SW9 .....182 A
Canterbury Ho, E3
off Bow Rd .....130 B
SE1 .....61 F
Canterbury Pl, SE17 .....75 D

Canterbury Rd, E10 .... 102 C1
NW6 .... 6 A3
Canterbury Ter, NW6 .... 6 A2
Cantium Retail Pk,
SE1 .... 170 A1
Canton St, E14 .... 144 A2
Cantrell Rd, E3 .... 129 F4
Canute Gdns, SE16 .... 157 D3
Canvey St, SE1 .... 51 D2
Capel Ct, EC2 .... 40 B3
Coll Capel Manor Coll,
Regent's Pk, NW1 .... 22 B1
Capener's Cl, SW1 .... 58 A1
Cape Yd, E1
off Asher Way 142 A4
H Capio Nightingale Hosp,
NW1 .... 21 D4
Coll Capital Coll, SE15
off Old Kent Rd 170 B2
Coll Capital Coll (CIFE)
London Sch of Insurance,
WC1 .... 25 E4
Capital Interchange Way,
Brent. TW8 .... 146 A4
Capland St, NW8 .... 20 B2
Caple Par, NW10
off Harley Rd 119 E2
Caple Rd, NW10 .... 119 F2
Capper St, WC1 .... 23 F3
Capstan Rd, SE8 .... 157 F3
Capstan Sq, E14 .... 158 C1
Capstan Way, SE16 .... 143 E4
Capulet Sq, E3
off Talwin St 130 B3
Capworth St, E10 .... 102 A2
Caradoc Cl, W2 .... 30 A2
Caradoc St, SE10 .... 159 E4
Caradon Cl, E11 .... 103 E2
Caravel Cl, E14
off Tiller Rd 158 A2
Caravel Ms, SE8
off Watergate St 172 A1
Carbis Rd, E14 .... 143 F2
Carburton St, W1 .... 23 D4
Cardale St, E14
off Plevna St 158 C2
Carden Rd, SE15 .... 184 B1
Cardigan Rd, E3 .... 129 F2
SW13 .... 162 A4
Cardigan St, SE11 .... 74 A2
Cardigan Wk, N1
off Ashby Gro 112 C4
Cardinal Bourne St, SE1 ..... 64 B3
Cardinal Cap All, SE1
off New Globe Wk 51 E1
Cardinal Hinsley Cl, NW10 .. 120 A2
Cardinal Pl, SW15 .... 177 D2
Cardinals Way, N19 .... 97 D2
Cardinal Wk, SW1
off Palace St 59 E2
Cardine Ms, SE15 .... 170 B2
Cardington St, NW1 .... 11 E4
Cardozo Rd, N7 .... 111 E2
Cardross St, W6 .... 148 B2
Cardwell Rd, N7 .... 111 E1
Carew Cl, N7 .... 97 F3
Carew St, SE5 .... 168 C4
Carey Gdns, SW8 .... 166 C3
Carey La, EC2 .... 39 E2
Carey Pl, SW1 .... 72 A1
Carey St, WC2 .... 37 F3
Carey Way, Wem. HA9 ..... 104 B1
Carfax Pl, SW4
off Holwood Pl 181 D2
Carfree Cl, N1
off Bewdley St 112 A4
Carisbrooke Gdns, SE15 ..... 89 F2
Carker's La, NW5 .... 110 B2
Carleton Rd, N7 .... 111 D2
Carlile Cl, E3 .... 129 F2
Carlingford Rd, NW3 ...... 109 D1
Carlisle Av, EC3 .... 41 D3
W3 .... 133 E2
Carlisle La, SE1 .... 61 F3
Carlisle Ms, NW8 .... 20 B4
Carlisle Pl, SW1 .... 59 E3
Carlisle Rd, E10 .... 102 A3
N4 .... 98 A1
NW6 .... 121 E1
Carlisle St, W1 .... 36 A3
Carlisle Wk, E8
off Cumberland Cl 113 F3
Carlos Pl, W1 .... 46 B1
Carlow St, NW1 .... 11 E2
Carlton Cl, NW3 .... 94 A3
Carlton Ct, SW9 .... 86 C4
Carlton Dr, SW15 .... 177 E3
Carlton Gdns, SW1 .... 48 A3
Carlton Gro, SE15 .... 170 B3
Carlton Hill, NW8 .... 7 E1
Carlton Ho Ter, SW1 .... 48 A3
Carlton Rd, E11 .... 103 F2
N4 .... 98 A1
SW14 .... 174 C1
W4 .... 147 D1
Carlton Sq, E1
off Argyle Rd 129 D4
Carlton St, SW1 .... 48 A1
Carlton Twr Pl, SW1 .... 57 F2
Carlton Vale, NW6 .... 6 B3
Carlton Vil, SW15
off St. John's Av 177 D3
Carlyle Ct, SW10
off Chelsea Harbour 79 F4
Carlyle Ms, E1
off Alderney Rd 129 D4
Carlyle Pl, SW15 .... 177 D2
Carlyle Rd, NW10 .... 119 D1
★ Carlyle's Ho, SW3 .... 80 C1
Carlyle Sq, SW3 .... 68 B3
Carly Ms, E2
off Barnet Gro 128 A3
Carmalt Gdns, SW15 ...... 176 C2
Carmarthen Pl, SE1 .... 52 C4
Carmel Ct, W8 .... 42 C4
Wembley HA9 .... 90 B3
Carmelite St, EC4 .... 38 B4
Carmel Way, Rich. TW9 .... 160 B4
Carmen St, E14 .... 144 B2
Carmichael Cl, SW11
off Darien Rd 179 D1
Carnaby St, W1 .... 35 E3
Carnarvon Rd, E15 .... 117 F3
Carnegie St, N1 .... 13 E1
Carnoustie Dr, N1 .... 111 F4
Carnwath Rd, SW6 .... 178 A1
Carolina Cl, E15 .... 117 E2
Caroline Cl, W2 .... 43 D1
Caroline Gdns, SE15 ...... 170 B2
Caroline Pl, SW11 .... 166 A4
W2 .... 31 D4
Caroline Pl Ms, W2 .... 43 D1
Caroline St, E1 .... 143 D2
Caroline Ter, SW1 .... 70 A1
Caroline Wk, W6 .... 163 E1
Carol St, NW1 .... 124 C1
Carpenters Ms, N7
off North Rd 111 E2
Carpenters Pl, SW4 .... 181 D2
Carpenters Rd, E15 .... 116 C4
Carpenter St, W1 .... 46 C1
Carrara Cl, SW9 .... 182 B2
Carrara Ms, E8 .... 114 A3
Carrara Wf, SW6 .... 177 E1
Carre Ms, SE5
off Calais St 168 B3
Carriage Dr E, SW11 .... 82 A2
Carriage Dr N, SW11 .... 82 B1
Carriage Dr S, SW11 .... 81 E4
Carriage Dr W, SW11 .... 81 E3
Carriage Pl, N16 .... 99 D4
Carrick Ms, SE8
off Watergate St 172 A1
Carrington Rd, Rich. TW10 .. 174 A2
Carrington St, W1 .... 46 C3
Carrol Cl, NW5 .... 110 B1
Carroll Cl, E15 .... 117 F2
Carronade Ct, N7
off Eden Gro 111 F2
Carron Cl, E14 .... 144 B2
Carroun Rd, SW8 .... 85 E2
Carr St, E14 .... 143 E1
Carslake Rd, SW15 .... 176 C4
Carson Ter, W11
off Princes Pl 135 E4
Carston Cl, SE12 .... 187 F3
Carteret St, SW1 .... 60 A1
Carteret Way, SE8 .... 157 E3
Carter Ho, SW11
off Petergate 178 C2
Carter La, EC4 .... 39 D3
Carter Pl, SE17 .... 75 F3
Carter St, SE17 .... 75 E4
Carters Yd, SW18 .... 178 A3
Carthew Rd, W6 .... 148 B2
Carthew Vil, W6 .... 148 B2
Carthusian St, EC1 .... 27 E4
Cartier Circle, E14 .... 144 B4
Carting La, WC2 .... 49 D1
Cartmel, NW1 .... 11 E4
Carton St, W1 .... 33 F2
Cartwright Gdns, WC1 ...... 24 C1
Cartwright St, E1 .... 41 F4
Cartwright Way, SW13 ..... 162 B2
Carver Cl, W4 .... 146 C2
Carver Rd, SE24 .... 182 C4
Cary Rd, E11 .... 117 E1
Carysfort Rd, N16 .... 99 D4
Casby Ho, SE16 .... 156 A2
Cascades Twr, E14 .... 143 F4
Casella Rd, SE14 .... 171 D2
Casey Cl, NW8 .... 20 C1
Casimir Rd, E5 .... 100 B4
Casino Av, SE24 .... 182 C3
Caspian St, SE5 .... 88 A2
Caspian Wf, E3
off Violet Rd 144 B1
Casselden Rd, NW10 ...... 105 D4
Cassidy Rd, SW6 .... 78 A3
Cassilis Rd, E14 .... 158 A1
Cassland Rd, E9 .... 114 C4
Casson St, E1 .... 142 A1
Castalia Sq, E14
off Roserton St 158 C1
Castellain Rd, W9 .... 19 E3
Castello Av, SW15 .... 176 C3
CASTELNAU, SW13 .... 162 A1
Castelnau, SW13 .... 162 B1
Castelnau Gdns, SW13
off Arundel Ter 162 B1
Castelnau Pl, SW13
off Castelnau 162 B1

Castelnau Row, SW13
off Lonsdale Rd **162** B1
Casterbridge, NW6 **122** B1
Casterton St, E8
off Wilton Way **114** B3
Castle Baynard St, EC4 **39** D4
Castlebrook Cl, SE11 **62** C4
Castle Cl, E9
off Swinnerton St **115** E2
W3 **146** B1
Castle Ct, EC3 **40** B3
SW15 **177** E1
Castlehaven Rd, NW1 **110** B4
Castle La, SW1 **59** F2
Castlemaine Twr, SW11 **165** F3
Castlemain St, E1 **142** B1
Castlemead, SE5 **87** F3
Castle Ms, NW1
off Castle Rd **110** B3
Castle Pl, NW1 **110** B3
W4 *off Windmill Rd* **147** E3
Castlereagh St, W1 **33** D2
Castle Rd, NW1 **110** B3
Castletown Rd, W14 **149** E4
Castleview Cl, N4 **98** C2
Castlewood Rd, N16 **100** A1
Castle Yd, N6
off North Rd **96** A1
SE1 **51** D2
Castor La, E14 **144** B3
Catalpa Ct, SE13
off Hither Grn La **187** D4
Caterham Rd, SE13 **186** C1
Catesby St, SE17 **76** B1
Cathall Rd, E11 **103** D4
Cathay St, SE16 **156** B1
Cathcart Hill, N19 **96** C4
Cathcart Rd, SW10 **67** D4
Cathcart St, NW5 **110** B3
Cathedral Piazza, SW1 **59** E3
Cathedral St, SE1 **52** A2
Cathedral Wk, SW1 **59** E2
Catherall Rd, N5 **98** C4
Catherine Griffiths Ct,
EC1 **26** B2
Catherine Gro, SE10 **172** B3
Catherine Ho, N1
off Phillipp St **17** D1
Catherine Pl, SW1 **59** E2
Catherine St, WC2 **37** E4
Catherine Wheel All, E1 **41** D1
Catherine Wheel Yd,
SW1 **47** E3
Catherwood Ct, N1
off Murray Gro **16** A3
Cathles Rd, SW12 **180** B4
Cathnor Rd, W12 **148** B1
Catlin St, SE16 **156** A4
Cato Rd, SW4 **181** D1
Cator St, SE15 **89** E1
Cato St, W1 **33** D1
Catton St, WC1 **37** E1
Caughley Ho, SE11
off Lambeth Wk **62** A3
Caulfield Rd, SE15 **170** B4
Causeway, The, SW18 **178** B2
Causton Rd, N6 **96** B1
Causton St, SW1 **72** B1
Cautley Av, SW4 **180** C3
Cavalry Gdns, SW15 **177** E3
Cavalry Sq, SW3 **69** F2
Cavaye Pl, SW10 **67** F3
Cavell St, E1 **142** B1
Cavendish Av, NW8 **8** B3
Cavendish Cl, NW6
off Cavendish Rd **107** F4
NW8 **8** B4
Coll Cavendish Coll, WC1 **24** A4
Cavendish Ct, EC3 **41** D2
Cavendish Dr, E11 **103** D2
Cavendish Gdns, SW4 **180** C4
Cavendish Ms N, W1 **23** D4
Cavendish Ms S, W1 **35** D1
Cavendish Par, SW4
off Clapham Common S Side **180** B4
Cavendish Pl, NW2 **107** D3
W1 **35** D2
Cavendish Rd, NW6 **107** E4
SW12 **180** B4
W4 **160** C3
Cavendish Sq, W1 **35** D2
Cavendish St, N1 **16** A3
Caversham Flats, SW3 **69** E4
Caversham Rd, NW5 **110** C3
Caversham St, SW3 **69** E4
Caverswall St, W12 **134** C2
Caxton Gro, E3 **130** A3
Caxton Rd, W12 **149** D1
Caxton St, SW1 **59** F2
Caxton St N, E16
off Victoria Dock Rd **145** F3
Cayenne Ct, SE1 **53** F3
Cayford Ho, NW3 **109** E2
Cayton Pl, EC1 **28** A1
Cayton St, EC1 **28** A1
Cazenove Rd, N16 **99** F3
Cecil Ct, WC2 **48** B1
★ Cecilia Coleman Gall, NW8 **8** B2
Cecilia Rd, E8 **114** A2
Cecil Rd, E11 **103** E4
NW10 **119** E1
W3 **132** C1
★ Cecil Sharp Ho, NW1 **124** A1
Cedar Cl, E3 **129** F1
Cedar Ct, N1
off Essex Rd **112** C4
Cedar Ms, SW15
off Cambalt Rd **177** D3
Cedarne Rd, SW6 **78** C3
Cedar Rd, NW2 **106** C1
Cedars, The, E15
off Portway **131** F1
Cedars Cl, SE13 **187** D1
Cedars Ms, SW4 **180** B2
Cedars Rd, E15 **117** E3
SW4 **180** B1
SW13 **161** F4
W4 **146** C4
Cedar Way, NW1 **111** D4
Cedra Ct, N16 **100** A2
Celandine Cl, E14 **144** A1
Celandine Dr, E8 **113** F4
Celandine Way, E15 **131** E3
Celbridge Ms, W2 **31** D2
Celestial Gdns, SE13 **187** D2
Celia Rd, N19 **110** C1
Celtic St, E14 **144** B1
Cemetery Rd, E7 **117** F1
Cenacle Cl, NW3 **94** A4
★ Cenotaph, The, SW1 **48** C4
Centaur St, SE1 **61** F2
Central Av, E11 **103** D3
SW11 **81** E3
● Central Business Cen, NW10
off Great Cen Way **105** E2
★ Central Criminal Ct (Old Bailey), EC4 **39** D2
Central Ho, E15
off High St **130** C2
H Central Middlesex Hosp, NW10 **118** C3
Uni Central St. Martins Coll of Art & Design, WC1 **37** E1
Back Hill Site, EC1 **26** B3
Byam Shaw Sch of Art, N19
off Elthorne Rd **97** D3
Catton St Site, WC1 **37** E1
Charing Cross Rd Site, WC2 **36** B3
Central Sch Footpath,
SW14 **174** C1
Coll Central Sch of Ballet, EC1 **26** B3
Uni Central Sch of Speech & Drama, NW3
off Eton Av **109** D4
Central St, EC1 **27** E1
Central Way, NW10 **118** C3
Centre Av, W3 **133** D4
W10 *off Harrow Rd* **120** C3
● Centrepoint, WC1 **36** B2
Centre Pt, SE1
off Avondale Sq **156** A4
Centre St, E2 **128** B2
Centric Cl, NW1
off Oval Rd **124** B1
Centurion Bldg, SW8 **82** C1
Centurion Cl, N7 **111** F4
Centurion La, E3
off Libra Rd **129** F2
Century Ms, E5
off Lower Clapton Rd **114** C1
Cephas Av, E1 **128** C4
Cephas St, E1 **128** C4
Cerise Rd, SE15 **170** A3
Cerney Ms, W2 **32** A4
Cervantes Ct, W2 **31** D3
Cester St, E2
off Whiston Rd **128** A1
Ceylon Rd, W14 **149** D2
Chabot Dr, SE15 **184** B1
Chadbourn St, E14 **144** B1
Chadwell St, EC1 **14** B4
Chadwick Ms, W4
off Thames Rd **160** B1
Chadwick Rd, E11 **103** E1
NW10 **119** F1
SE15 **169** F4
Chadwick St, SW1 **60** B3
Chagford St, NW1 **21** E3
Chailey St, E5 **100** C4
Chalbury Wk, N1 **13** F2
Chalcot Cres, NW1 **123** F1
Chalcot Gdns, NW3 **109** F3
Chalcot Rd, NW1 **110** A4
Chalcot Sq, NW1 **110** A4
Chalcroft Rd, SE13 **187** E3
Chaldon Rd, SW6 **163** E2
Chale Rd, SW2 **181** E4
Chalfont Av, Wem.
HA9 **104** B3
Jct Chalkers Cor, SW14 **174** B1
⊖ Chalk Farm **110** A4
Chalk Fm Rd, NW1 **110** A4
Chalk Hill Rd, W6
off Shortlands **149** D3
Chalkhill Rd, Wem. HA9 **90** B4
Chalklands, Wem. HA9 **90** C4

Challoner Cres, W14
off Challoner St **149** F4
Challoner St, W14 . . . . **149** F4
Chalmers Ho, SW11
off York Rd **178** C1
Chalmers Wk, SE17 . . . . **87** D1
Chaloner Ct, SE1 . . . . **52** A4
Chalsey Rd, SE4 . . . . **185** F2
Chalton St, NW1 . . . . **12** B4
Chamberlain Cotts, SE5
off Camberwell Gro **169** D3
Chamberlain St, NW1
off Regents Pk Rd **109** F4
Chamberlayne Rd, NW10 . . . **121** D3
Chambers La, NW10 . . . . **106** B4
Chambers Rd, N7 . . . . **111** E1
Chambers St, SE16 . . . . **156** A1
Chamber St, E1 . . . . **41** F4
Chambon Pl, W6
off Beavor La **148** A3
Chambord St, E2 . . . . **29** F1
Chamers Ct, W12
off Heathstan Rd **134** A2
Champion Gro, SE5 . . . . **183** D1
Champion Hill, SE5 . . . . **183** D1
Champion Hill Est, SE5 . . . . . **183** E1
Champion Pk, SE5 . . . . **169** D4
Champion Pk Est, SE5
off Denmark Hill **183** D1
Chancellor Pas, E14
off The South
Colonnade **144** A4
Chancellors Ct, WC1
off Orde Hall St **25** E4
Chancellors Rd, W6 . . . . **148** C4
Chancellors St, W6 . . . . **148** C4
Chancellors Wf, W6
off Crisp Rd **148** C4
Chancel St, SE1 . . . . **50** C2
⊖ Chancery Lane **38** A1
Chancery La, WC2 . . . . **38** A2
Chance St, E1 . . . . **29** E2
E2 . . . . **29** E2
Chandlers Ms, E14 . . . . **158** A1
Chandler St, E1
off Wapping La **142** B4
Chandler Way, SE15 . . . . **89** D1
Chandos Pl, WC2 . . . . **48** C1
Chandos Rd, E15 . . . . **117** D2
NW2 . . . . **106** C2
NW10 . . . . **119** E4
Chandos St, W1 . . . . **35** D1
Chandos Way, NW11 . . . . **94** B2
Change All, EC3 . . . . **40** B3
Channel Gate Rd, NW10
off Old Oak La **119** F3
Channel Ho, E14
off Aston St **143** E1
SE16 *off Canada St* **157** D1
Channel Islands Est, N1
off Clifton Rd **112** C3
● Channelsea Ho Business
Cen, E15
off Canning Rd **131** D2
Channelsea Rd, E15 . . . . **131** D1
Chantrey Rd, SW9 . . . . **181** F1
Chantry Cl, W9
off Elgin Av **121** F4
Chantry Cres, NW10 . . . . **105** F3
Chantry Sq, W8
off St. Mary's Pl **54** C3
Chantry St, N1 . . . . **15** D1
Chant Sq, E15 . . . . **117** D4
Chant St, E15 . . . . **117** D4
Chapel Cl, NW10 . . . . **105** F2
Chapel Ct, SE1 . . . . **52** A4
Chapel Gate Ms, SW4
off Bedford Rd **181** E1
Chapel Ho St, E14 . . . . **158** B4
Chapelier Ho, SW18
off Eastfields Av **178** A2
Chapel Mkt, N1 . . . . **14** A2
Chapel Pl, EC2 . . . . **28** C1
N1 . . . . **14** B2
W1 . . . . **34** C3
Chapel Side, W2 . . . . **30** C4
Chapel St, NW1 . . . . **32** C1
SW1 . . . . **58** B2
Chapel Way, N7
off Sussex Way **97** F4
Chapel Yd, SW18
off Wandsworth
High St **178** A3
Chaplin Cl, SE1 . . . . **50** B4
Chaplin Rd, E15 . . . . **131** E2
NW2 . . . . **106** A3
● Chapman Pk Ind Est,
NW10 . . . . **105** F3
Chapman Pl, N4 . . . . **98** B3
Chapman Rd, E9 . . . . **115** F3
Chapman St, E1 . . . . **142** B3
Chapone Pl, W1 . . . . **36** A3
Chapter Chambers, SW1
off Chapter St **72** A1
Chapter Cl, W4 . . . . **146** C2
Chapter Ho Ct, EC4 . . . . **39** E3
Chapter Rd, NW2 . . . . **106** A2
SE17 . . . . **75** D3
Chapter St, SW1 . . . . **72** A1
Chara Pl, W4 . . . . **161** D1
Charcot Ho, SW15
off Highcliffe Dr **175** F4
Chardin Rd, W4
off Elliott Rd **147** E3
Chardmore Rd, N16 . . . . **100** A2
Charecroft Way, W12 . . . . . . **149** D1
W14 . . . . **149** D1
Charfield Ct, W9 . . . . **18** C3
Chargeable La, E13 . . . . **131** F4
Chargeable St, E16 . . . . **131** F4
Chargrove Cl, SE16
off Marlow Way **157** D1
⇌ Charing Cross **48** C2
⊖ Charing Cross **48** C2
Charing Cross, SW1 . . . . **48** B2
H Charing Cross Hosp,
W6 . . . . **163** D1
Charing Cross Rd, WC2 . . . . . **36** B2
Chariot Cl, E3
off Garrison Rd **130** A1
Charlbert St, NW8 . . . . **8** C2
Charles Barry Cl, SW4 . . . . . **180** C1
Charles Burton Ct, E5
off Ashenden Rd **115** E2
Charles Coveney Rd, SE15 . . . **89** E4
Charles Dickens Ho, E2 . . . . . **128** B3
★ Charles Dickens Mus,
WC1 . . . . **25** F2
Charles Gardner Ct, N1 . . . . . . **16** B4
Charles Hocking Ho, W3
off Bollo Br Rd **146** C1
Charles La, NW8 . . . . **8** B3
Charles Mackenzie Ho, SE16
off Linsey St **156** A3
Charles Pl, NW1 . . . . **23** F1
Charles Rowan Ho, WC1 . . . . . **26** A1
Charles II Pl, SW3
off King's Rd **69** E3
Charles II St, SW1 . . . . **48** A2
Charles Sq, N1 . . . . **28** B1
Charles Sq Est, N1 . . . . **28** B1
Charles St, SW13 . . . . **161** E4
W1 . . . . **46** C2
Charleston St, SE17 . . . . **75** F1
Charles Townsend Ho, EC1 . . . **26** B2
Charlesworth Pl, SW13
off Eleanor Gro **175** F1
Charleville Rd, W14 . . . . **149** E4
Charlie Chaplin Wk, SE1
off Waterloo Br **49** F3
Charlotte Ct, W6
off Invermead Cl **148** A3
Charlotte Despard Av,
SW11 . . . . **166** A3
Charlotte Ms, W1 . . . . **23** F4
W10 . . . . **135** D2
W14 *off Munden St* **149** E3
Charlotte Pl, SW1 . . . . **71** E1
W1 . . . . **35** F1
Charlotte Rd, EC2 . . . . **28** C2
SW13 . . . . **161** F3
Charlotte Row, SW4 . . . . **180** C1
Charlotte St, W1 . . . . **23** F4
Charlotte Ter, N1 . . . . **13** F1
Charlow Cl, SW6
off Townmead Rd **164** C4
Charlton Kings Rd, NW5 . . . . **111** D2
Charlton Pl, N1 . . . . **14** C2
Charlton Rd, NW10 . . . . **119** E1
Charlton Way, SE3 . . . . **173** E3
Charlwood Ho, SW1
off Vauxhall Br Rd **72** A1
Richmond TW9
off Strand Dr **160** B2
Charlwood Pl, SW1 . . . . **71** F1
Charlwood Rd, SW15 . . . . . . **177** D1
Charlwood St, SW1 . . . . **71** F1
Charlwood Ter, SW15 . . . . . . **177** D2
Charman Ho, SW8
off Hemans St **84** C2
Charmouth Ho, SW8
off Dorset Rd **85** E2
Charnock Rd, E5 . . . . **100** B4
Charnwood Gdns, E14 . . . . . **158** A3
Charnwood St, E5 . . . . **100** A3
Charrington St, NW1 . . . . **12** A2
★ Charterhouse, EC1 . . . . . . **27** D4
Charterhouse Bldgs, EC1 . . . . **27** D3
Charterhouse Ms, EC1 . . . . . . **27** D4
Charterhouse Rd, E8 . . . . . . **114** A1
Charterhouse Sq, EC1 . . . . . . **27** D4
Charterhouse St, EC1 . . . . **38** B1
Charteris Rd, N4 . . . . **98** A2
NW6 . . . . **121** F1
Chartfield Av, SW15 . . . . **176** B3
Chartfield Sq, SW15 . . . . **177** D3
Chartham Ct, SW9 . . . . **182** A1
Chartley Av, NW2 . . . . **91** E4
Chart St, N1 . . . . **16** B4
Chase, The, SW4 . . . . **180** B1
Chaseley Dr, W4 . . . . **146** B4
Chaseley St, E14 . . . . **143** E2
Chase Rd, NW10 . . . . **119** D4
W3 . . . . **119** D4
Chaston Pl, NW5
off Grafton Ter **110** A2
Chater Ho, E2
off Roman Rd **129** D3
Chatfield Rd, SW11 . . . . **178** C1
Chatham Pl, E9 . . . . **114** C3
Chatham Rd, SW11 . . . . **179** F4
Chatham St, SE17 . . . . **64** A4

Chatsworth Ct, W8 ....54 A4
Chatsworth Est, E5
off Elderfield Rd 115 D1
Chatsworth Gdns, W3 ......132 B3
Chatsworth Rd, E5 ....100 C4
E15 ....117 F2
NW2 ....107 D3
W4 ....160 C1
Chatterton Ms, N4
off Chatterton Rd 98 B4
Chatterton Rd, N4 ....98 B4
Chatto Rd, SW11 ....179 F3
Chaucer Av, Rich. TW9 .....160 A4
Chaucer Ct, N16 ....113 D1
Chaucer Dr, SE1 ....77 F1
Chaucer Ho, SW1 ....71 E3
Chaucer Rd, SE24 ....182 A3
W3 ....132 C4
Cheam St, SE15
off Nunhead La 184 B1
Cheapside, EC2 ....39 F3
Chearsley, SE17
off Deacon Way 63 F4
Chedworth Cl, E16
off Hallsville Rd 145 F2
Cheesemans Ter, W14 .....149 F4
Chelmer Rd, E9 ....115 D2
Chelmsford Cl, W6 ....163 D1
Chelmsford Rd, E11 ....103 D2
Chelmsford Sq, NW10 ......120 C1
CHELSEA, SW3 ....68 A4
Chelsea & Westminster Hosp, SW10 ....79 F1
Chelsea Antique Mkt, SW3 ....68 B4
Chelsea Br, SW1 ....70 C4
SW8 ....70 C4
Chelsea Br Rd, SW1 ....70 A2
Chelsea Cloisters, SW3 ......69 D1
Chelsea Cl, NW10
off Winchelsea Rd 119 D1
Chelsea Coll of Art & Design, SW1 ....72 C2
Chelsea Cres, SW10
off Harbour Av 164 C3
Chelsea Embk, SW3 ....81 D1
Chelsea FC, SW6 ....78 C2
Chelsea Gdns, SW1
off Chelsea Br Rd 70 B3
Chelsea Harbour, SW10 ....164 C3
Chelsea Harbour Design Cen, SW10
off Harbour Av 79 F4
Chelsea Harbour Dr, SW10 ...79 F4
Chelsea Harbour Pier ...165 D3
Chelsea Manor Ct, SW3 ......69 D4
Chelsea Manor Gdns, SW3 ...69 D4
Chelsea Manor St, SW3 ......68 C3
Chelsea Pk Gdns, SW3 ......68 A4
Chelsea Physic Gdn, SW3 ....69 E4
Chelsea Reach Twr, SW10 ....80 A2
Chelsea Sq, SW3 ....68 B2
Chelsea Twrs, SW3 ....69 D3
Chelsea Village, SW6 ....79 D2
Chelsea Vista, SW6
off The Boulevard 164 C3
Chelsea Wf, SW10 ....80 A3
Chelsham Rd, SW4 ....181 D1
Cheltenham Pl, W3 ....132 B4
Cheltenham Rd, SE15 ......184 C2
Cheltenham Ter, SW3 ....69 F2
Chelverton Rd, SW15 ......177 D2
Chelwood Gdns, Rich. TW9 ..160 A4
Chelwood Gdns Pas, Rich. TW9
off Chelwood Gdns 160 A4
Chelwood Wk, SE4 ....185 E2
Cheneys Rd, E11 ....103 E4
Chenies Ms, WC1 ....24 A3
Chenies Pl, NW1 ....12 A2
Chenies St, WC1 ....24 A4
Cheniston Gdns, W8 ....54 C2
Chepstow Cl, SW15 ....177 E4
Chepstow Cres, W11 ....30 A4
Chepstow Pl, W2 ....30 B4
Chepstow Rd, W2 ....30 B2
Chepstow Vil, W11 ....135 F3
Chequer St, EC1 ....27 F3
Cherbury Ct, N1 ....16 B3
Cherbury St, N1 ....16 B3
Cheriton Ho, E5
off Pembury Rd 114 B2
Cherry Gdn St, SE16 ......156 B1
Cherrylands Cl, NW9 ....90 C3
Cherry Laurel Wk, SW2
off Beechdale Rd 181 F4
Cherry Tree Cl, E9
off Moulins Rd 128 C1
Cherry Tree Rd, E15
off Wingfield Rd 117 E2
Cherry Tree Wk, EC1 ....27 F3
Cherrywood Cl, E3 ....129 E3
Cherrywood Dr, SW15 .....177 D3
Cherrywood Lo, SE13
off Birdwood Av 187 D4
Chertsey Rd, E11 ....103 D3
Cherwell Ho, NW8
off Church St Est 20 B3
Cheryls Cl, SW6 ....79 D4
Chesham Cl, SW1 ....58 A3
Chesham Ms, SW1 ....58 A2
Chesham Pl, SW1 ....58 A3
Chesham St, NW10 ....91 D4
SW1 ....58 A3
Cheshire Cl, SE4 ....171 F4
Cheshire Ct, EC4 ....38 B3
Cheshire St, E2 ....29 F2
Chesholm Rd, N16 ....99 E4
Chesil Ct, E2 ....128 C2
Chesilton Rd, SW6 ....163 F3
Chesney St, SW11 ....166 A3
Chessington Mans, E10
off Albany Rd 102 A1
Chesson Rd, W14 ....163 F1
Chester Cl, SW1 ....58 B1
SW13 ....176 B1
Chester Cl N, NW1 ....11 D4
Chester Cl S, NW1 ....23 D1
Chester Cotts, SW1 ....70 A1
Chester Ct, NW1
off Albany St 23 D1
SE5 ....88 A3
Chester Cres, E8
off Ridley Rd 113 F2
Chesterfield Gdns, SE10
off Crooms Hill 173 D2
W1 ....46 C2
Chesterfield Gro, SE22 .....183 F3
Chesterfield Hill, W1 ....46 C1
Chesterfield Rd, W4 ....160 C1
Chesterfield St, W1 ....46 C2
Chesterfield Wk, SE10 .....173 D3
Chesterfield Way, SE15 ....170 C2
Chesterford Gdns, NW3 ....108 B1
Chester Gate, NW1 ....22 C1
Chester Ms, SW1 ....58 C2
Chester Pl, NW1 ....10 C4
Chester Rd, E16 ....131 E4
N19 ....96 B3
NW1 ....22 B1
Chester Row, SW1 ....70 A1
Chester Sq, SW1 ....58 C4
Chester Sq Ms, SW1 ....58 C3
Chester St, E2 ....128 A4
SW1 ....58 B2
Chester Ter, NW1 ....10 C4
Chesterton Cl, SW18 ....178 A3
Chesterton Ho, SW11
off Ingrave St 179 D1
Chesterton Rd, W10 ....135 D1
Chesterton Sq, W8
off Pembroke Rd 149 F3
Chester Way, SE11 ....74 B1
Chestnut All, SW6
off Lillie Rd 163 F1
Chestnut Av, SW14
off Thornton Rd 175 D1
Chestnut Cl, N16 ....99 D3
SE14 ....171 F3
Chestnut Ct, SW6
off North End Rd 163 F1
Chestnut Ho, NW3
off Maitland Pk Vil 109 F3
Chettle Cl, SE1 ....64 A2
Chetwynd Rd, NW5 ....110 B1
Cheval Pl, SW7 ....57 D2
Cheval St, E14 ....158 A2
Chevening Rd, NW6 ....121 D2
SE10 ....159 F4
Cheverton Rd, N19 ....97 D2
Chevet St, E9
off Kenworthy Rd 115 E2
Cheviot Gdns, NW2 ....93 D3
Cheviot Gate, NW2 ....93 E3
Cheyne Ct, SW3 ....69 E4
Cheyne Gdns, SW3 ....69 D4
Cheyne Ms, SW3 ....69 D4
Cheyne Pl, SW3 ....69 E4
Cheyne Row, SW3 ....80 C1
Cheyne Wk, SW3 ....81 D1
SW10 ....80 A2
Chichele Rd, NW2 ....107 D2
Chicheley St, SE1 ....49 F4
Chichester Ct, NW1
off Royal Coll St 110 C4
Chichester Rents, WC2 ......38 A2
Chichester Rd, E11 ....103 E4
NW6 ....6 A3
W2 ....19 D4
Chichester St, SW1 ....71 F3
Chichester Way, E14 ......159 D3
Chicksand St, E1 ....41 F1
Chiddingstone St, SW6 .....164 A4
Chigwell Hill, E1
off Pennington St 142 B3
Chilcot Cl, E14
off Grundy St 144 B2
Childeric Rd, SE14 ....171 E2
Childerley St, SW6
off Fulham Palace Rd ...163 E3
Childers St, SE8 ....171 E1
Child La, SE10 ....159 F2
CHILDS HILL, NW2 ....94 A3
Childs Hill Wk, NW2 ....93 F4
Child's Ms, SW5
off Child's Pl 66 C1
Child's Pl, SW5 ....66 B1
Child's St, SW5 ....66 B1
Child's Wk, SW5 ....66 B1
Chillington Dr, SW11 ......178 C2
Chillingworth Rd, N7 ......111 F2

Chiltern Gdns, NW2 ....93 D4
Chiltern Pl, E5 ....100 B3
Chiltern Rd, E3 ....130 A4
Chiltern St, W1 ....22 A4
Chilton Gro, SE8 ....157 D3
● Chiltonian Ind Est, SE12 ....187 F4
Chilton Rd, Rich. TW9 ......174 A1
Chilton St, E2 ....29 F2
Chilver St, SE10 ....159 F4
Chilworth Ms, W2 ....31 F3
Chilworth St, W2 ....31 F3
China Hall Ms, SE16
off Lower Rd 156 C2
★ Chinatown, W1
off Gerrard St 36 B4
Ching Ct, WC2 ....36 C3
Chipka St, E14 ....158 C1
Chipley St, SE14 ....171 E1
Chippendale Ho, SW1 ....71 D3
Chippendale St, E5 ....101 D4
Chippenham Av, Wem. HA9 ....104 B2
Chippenham Gdns, NW6 .....18 A1
Chippenham Ms, W9 ....18 A3
Chippenham Rd, W9 ....18 A3
Chipstead Gdns, NW2 ....92 B3
Chipstead St, SW6 ....164 A3
Chip St, SW4 ....181 D1
Chisenhale Rd, E3 ....129 E2
Chisledon Wk, E9
off Southmoor Way 115 F3
Chiswell St, EC1 ....27 F4
SE5 ....88 B2
CHISWICK, W4 ....161 D1
⇌ Chiswick 160 C2
Chiswick Br, SW14 ....160 C4
W4 ....160 C4
Chiswick Common Rd, W4 ....147 D3
Chiswick Grn Studios, W4
off Evershed Wk 146 C3
Chiswick High Rd, W4 ......147 D3
Brentford TW8 ....146 A4
★ Chiswick Ho, W4 ....161 E1
Chiswick Ho Grds, W4 ......161 D1
Chiswick La, W4 ....147 E4
Chiswick La S, W4 ....147 F4
Chiswick Mall, W4 ....161 F1
W6 ....161 F1
⊖ Chiswick Park 146 C3
● Chiswick Pk, W4 ....146 B3
Chiswick Pier, W4 ....161 F2
Chiswick Quay, W4 ....160 C3
Chiswick Rd, W4 ....146 C3
Jct Chiswick Rbt, W4 ......146 A4
Chiswick Sq, W4
off Hogarth Rbt 161 E1
Chiswick Staithe, W4 ......160 C3
Chiswick Ter, W4
off Acton La 146 C3
Chiswick Village, W4 ....146 B4
Chiswick Wf, W4 ....161 F1
Chitty St, W1 ....23 F4
Chivalry Rd, SW11 ....179 E3
Chobham Rd, E15 ....117 D2
Cholmeley Cres, N6 ....96 B1
Cholmeley Pk, N6 ....96 B2
Cholmley Gdns, NW6
off Fortune Grn Rd 108 A2
Cholmondeley Av, NW10 ....120 A2
Choppins Ct, E1
off Wapping La 142 B4
Chopwell Cl, E15
off Bryant St 117 E4
Choumert Gro, SE15 ....170 A4
Choumert Ms, SE15 ....170 A4
Choumert Rd, SE15 ....183 F1
Choumert Sq, SE15 ....170 A4
Chow Sq, E8
off Arcola St 113 F2
Chrisp St, E14 ....144 B1
Christchurch Av, NW6 ......107 E4
Christchurch Ct, NW6 ......107 E4
Christchurch Hill, NW3 ......95 D4
Christ Ch Pas, EC1 ....39 D2
Christchurch Pas, NW3 ......94 C4
Christchurch Rd, SW14 .....174 B3
Christchurch Sq, E9
off Victoria Pk Rd 128 C1
Christchurch St, SW3 ....69 E4
Christchurch Ter, SW3 ....69 E4
Christchurch Way, SE10 ....159 E3
Christian Ct, SE16 ....143 F4
Christian St, E1 ....142 A2
Christie Ct, N19
off Hornsey Rd 97 E3
Christie Ho, W12
off Du Cane Rd 134 B2
Christie Rd, E9 ....115 E3
Coll Christie's Ed, W1 ....23 D4
Christina Sq, N4 ....98 B2
Christina St, EC2 ....28 C2
Christopher Cl, SE16 ....157 D1
Christopher Pl, NW1 ....24 B1
Christopher's Ms, W11
off Penzance St 135 E4
Christopher St, EC2 ....28 B3
Coll Christ the King 6th Form Coll, SE13
off Belmont Hill 187 D1
Chryssell Rd, SW9 ....86 B3
Chubworthy St, SE14 ......171 E1
Chudleigh Rd, NW6 ....107 D4
SE4 ....185 F3
Chudleigh St, E1 ....143 D2
Chumleigh Gdns, SE5
off Chumleigh St 169 E1
Chumleigh St, SE5 ....76 C4
Church Av, NW1
off Kentish Town Rd 110 B3
SW14 ....175 D1
Church Cl, W8 ....42 C4
Church Cres, E9 ....115 D4
Church Dr, NW9 ....91 D2
CHURCH END, NW10 ......105 E3
Church Entry, EC4 ....39 D3
Churchfield Rd, W3 ....132 C4
Churchfields, SE10
off Roan St 172 C1
Church Garth, N19
off Pemberton Gdns 97 D3
Church Gate, SW6 ....177 E1
Church Grn, SW9
off Mostyn Rd 168 A3
Church Gro, SE13 ....186 B2
Churchill Gdns, SW1 ....71 E3
W3 ....132 A2
Churchill Gdns Rd, SW1 .....71 D3
★ Churchill Mus & Cabinet War Rooms, SW1 ....48 B4
Churchill Pl, E14 ....144 B4
Churchill Rd, NW2 ....106 B3
NW5 ....110 B1
Churchill Wk, E9 ....114 C2
Church La, E11 ....103 E2
NW9 ....90 C3
Church Manor Est, SW9 .....86 B3
Churchmead, SE5
off Camberwell Rd 87 F3
Churchmead Rd, NW10 ....106 A3
Church Pas, EC2
off Gresham St 39 F2
Church Path, N5 ....112 B2
NW10 ....105 E4
SW14 ....175 D1
W4 ....146 C2
Church Pl, SW1 ....47 F1
Church Rd, E10 ....102 B3
N1 ....112 C3
NW10 ....105 E3
SW13 ....161 F4
W3 ....146 C1
Church Row, NW3 ....108 C1
Church St, E15 ....131 E1
NW8 ....20 B4
W2 ....20 B4
W4 ....161 E1
Church St Est, NW8 ....20 B3
Church St N, E15 ....131 E1
Church St Pas, E15
off Church St 131 E1
Church Ter, SE13 ....187 E1
SW8 ....167 D4
Church Wk, N6 ....96 A4
N16 ....113 D2
NW2 ....93 F4
NW9 ....91 D3
SW13 ....162 A3
SW15 ....176 B3
Churchward Ho, W14
off Ivatt Pl 149 F4
Churchway, NW1 ....12 B4
Churchwell Path, E9 ....114 C2
Churchyard Row, SE11 ....63 D4
Church Yd Wk, W2 ....20 A4
Churton Pl, SW1 ....71 F1
Churton St, SW1 ....71 F1
Chusan Pl, E14
off Commercial Rd 143 F2
Cicada Rd, SW18 ....178 C3
Cicely Rd, SE15 ....170 A3
Cinderella Path, NW11
off North End Rd 94 B2
Cinnabar Wf, E1 ....142 A4
Cinnamon Cl, SE15 ....89 E2
Cinnamon Row, SW11 .....178 C1
Cinnamon St, E1 ....142 B4
Circle, The, NW2 ....91 E4
SE1 ....53 E4
Circus Lo, NW8 ....8 A4
Circus Ms, W1 ....21 E4
Circus Pl, EC2 ....40 B1
Circus Rd, NW8 ....8 A4
Coll Circus Space, N1 ....28 C1
Circus St, SE10 ....172 C2
Cirencester St, W2 ....18 C4
Citadel Pl, SE11 ....73 E2
Citizen Ho, N7
off Harvist Est 112 A1
Citizen Rd, N7 ....112 A1
Citron Ter, SE15
off Nunhead La 184 B1
Coll City & Guilds of London Art Sch, SE11 ....74 B3
Coll City & Islington Coll, Adult Learning Cen, N19 *off Junction Rd* 96 C3

Coll City & Islington Coll,
Cen for Applied Sciences,
EC1 . . . . . 14 C4
Cen for Business,
Arts & Tech, N7
off Camden Rd 111 E1
Cen for Health, Social &
Child Care, N7
off Holloway Rd 111 E1
Cen for Lifelong Learning,
N4 *off Blackstock Rd* 98 B3
Dalby Ho, EC4 . . . . . 14 C3
Coll City & Islington
6th Form Coll, EC1 . . . . . 14 C4
City Business Cen, SE16
off Lower Rd **156** C1
Coll City Business Coll, EC1 . . . 27 D1
Coll City Coll, The, N1 . . . . . 16 A4
● City Cross Business Pk,
SE10 *off Salutation Rd* . . 159 E3
● City Forum, EC1 . . . . . 15 E4
City Gdn Row, N1 . . . . . **15** D3
Coll City Learning Cen, NW10
off Tiverton Rd 121 D1
Coll City Lit, Keeley Ho, WC2 . . 37 E3
Stukeley St, WC2 . . . . . 37 D2
City Mill River Towpath, E15
off Blaker Rd **130** C1
★ City of Westminster
Archives Cen, SW1 . . . . . 60 B2
Coll City of Westminster Coll,
Cockpit Thea, NW8 . . . . . 20 C3
Cosway St Cen, NW1 . . . . . 21 D4
Maida Vale Cen, W9 . . . . . 18 C1
Paddington Grn Cen, W2 . . 20 A4
Queens Pk Cen, W9 . . . . . 18 A1
● City Pt, EC2 . . . . . 28 A4
City Rd, EC1 . . . . . **14** C3
⇌ City Thameslink 38 C3
City Twr, E14
off Limeharbour **158** B1
Uni City Uni, Cass Business Sch,
EC1 . . . . . 28 A3
Halls of Res & Saddlers
Sports Cen, EC1 . . . . . 27 E2
Northampton Sq Campus,
EC1 . . . . . 26 C1
Walmsley Bldg, EC1 . . . . . 26 C2
Walter Sickert Hall, N1 . . . . 15 E4
Uni City Uni - Inns of Ct
Sch of Law,
Atkin Bldg, WC1 . . . . . 25 F4
Gray's Inn Pl, WC1 . . . . . 37 F1
Princeton St, WC1 . . . . . 25 F4
Uni City Uni - St. Bartholomew
Sch of Nursing & Midwifery,
E1 *off Ashfield St* 142 B1
City Vw Apts, N1
off Essex Rd **112** C4
City Wk, SE1 . . . . . **64** C1
Clabon Ms, SW1 . . . . . **57** E3
Clack St, SE16 . . . . . **156** C1
Claire Pl, E14 . . . . . **158** A2
Clancarty Rd, SW6 . . . . . **164** A4
Clandon Cl, W3 . . . . . **146** B1
Clandon St, SE8 . . . . . **172** A4
Clanricarde Gdns, W2 . . . . . **42** B1
CLAPHAM, SW4 . . . . . **180** B1
★ Clapham Common, SW4 . 180 A2
⊖ Clapham Common 180 C2
Jct Clapham Common,
SW4 . . . . . **180** C2
Clapham Common N Side,
SW4 . . . . . **180** B2
Clapham Common S Side,
SW4 . . . . . **180** B3
Clapham Common W Side,
SW4 . . . . . **180** A2
Clapham Cres, SW4 . . . . . **181** D2
Clapham Est, SW11 . . . . . **179** E2
⇌ Clapham High Street . . . 181 D1
Clapham High St, SW4 . . . . . **181** D2
⇌ Clapham Junction 179 D2
⊖ Clapham Junction 179 D2
Clapham Manor St, SW4 . . . . **180** C1
⊖ Clapham North 181 E1
CLAPHAM PARK, SW4 . . . . . **181** D4
Clapham Pk Est, SW4 . . . . . **181** D4
Clapham Pk Rd, SW4 . . . . . **181** D2
Clapham Rd, SW9 . . . . . **85** F4
Clapham Rd Est, SW4 . . . . . **181** D1
⊖ Clapham South 180 B4
⇌ Clapton 100 B3
Clapton Common, E5 . . . . . **99** F1
CLAPTON PARK, E5 . . . . . **115** E1
Clapton Pk Est, E5
off Blackwell Cl **115** D1
Clapton Pas, E5 . . . . . **114** C2
Clapton Sq, E5 . . . . . **114** C2
Clapton Ter, E5
off Clapton Common . . . **100** A2
Clapton Way, E5 . . . . . **114** A1
Claredale St, E2 . . . . . **128** A2
Clare Gdns, W11
off Westbourne Pk Rd . . . **135** E2
Clare Ho, E3 . . . . . **129** F1
Clare La, N1 . . . . . **112** C4
Clare Lawn Av, SW14 . . . . . **175** D3
Clare Mkt, WC2 . . . . . **37** E3
Clare Ms, SW6 . . . . . **78** C3
Claremont Cl, N1 . . . . . **14** B3
Claremont Gro, W4
off Edensor Gdns **161** E2
Claremont Rd, E11
off Grove Grn Rd **103** D4
N6 . . . . . **96** C1
NW2 . . . . . **93** D4
W9 . . . . . **121** E2
Claremont Sq, N1 . . . . . **14** A3
Claremont St, SE10 . . . . . **172** B1
Claremont Way, NW2 . . . . . **92** C2
● Claremont Way Ind Est,
NW2 . . . . . 92 C2
Clarence Av, SW4 . . . . . **181** D4
Clarence Cres, SW4 . . . . . **181** D4
Clarence Gdns, NW1 . . . . . **23** D1
Clarence Gate Gdns, NW1
off Glentworth St **21** F3
★ Clarence Ho, SW1 . . . . . 47 F4
Clarence La, SW15 . . . . . **175** E4
Clarence Ms, E5 . . . . . **114** B2
SE16 . . . . . **143** D4
Clarence Pl, E5 . . . . . **114** B2
Clarence Rd, E5 . . . . . **114** B1
E16 . . . . . **131** E4
NW6 . . . . . **107** F4
SE8 . . . . . **172** B1
W4 . . . . . **146** A4
Clarence Ter, NW1 . . . . . **21** F2
Clarence Wk, SW4 . . . . . **167** E4
Clarence Way, NW1 . . . . . **110** B4
Clarence Way Est, NW1 . . . . **110** B4
Clarendon Cl, E9 . . . . . **114** C4
W2 . . . . . **32** C4
Clarendon Cross, W11
off Portland Rd **135** E3
Clarendon Dr, SW15 . . . . . **176** C2
Clarendon Gdns, W9 . . . . . **19** F3
Clarendon Gro, NW1 . . . . . **12** A4
Clarendon Ms, W2 . . . . . **32** C3
Clarendon Pl, W2 . . . . . **32** C4
Clarendon Ri, SE13 . . . . . **186** C1
Clarendon Rd, E11 . . . . . **103** D2
W11 . . . . . **135** E3
Clarendon St, SW1 . . . . . **71** D3
Clarendon Ter, W9 . . . . . **19** F2
Clarendon Wk, W11 . . . . . **135** E2
Clare Pt, NW2
off Claremont Rd **93** D2
Clare Rd, NW10 . . . . . **106** A4
SE14 . . . . . **171** F3
Clare St, E2 . . . . . **128** B2
Clareville Gro, SW7 . . . . . **67** F1
Clareville St, SW7 . . . . . **67** F1
Clarewood Wk, SW9 . . . . . **182** B2
Clarges Ms, W1 . . . . . **46** C2
Clarges St, W1 . . . . . **47** D2
Claribel Rd, SW9 . . . . . **168** B4
Clarissa St, E8 . . . . . **17** E1
Clarke Ct, W6
off Great W Rd **148** A4
Clarke Path, N16 . . . . . **100** A2
Clarke's Ms, W1 . . . . . **22** B4
Clark Lawrence Ct, SW11
off Winstanley Rd **179** D1
Clarkson Rd, E16 . . . . . **145** F2
Clarkson Row, NW1 . . . . . **11** E3
Clarkson St, E2 . . . . . **128** B3
Clarks Pl, EC2 . . . . . **40** C2
Clark St, E1 . . . . . **142** B1
Claude Rd, E10 . . . . . **102** C3
SE15 . . . . . **170** B4
Claude St, E14 . . . . . **158** A3
Claudia Jones Way, SW2 . . . **181** E4
Clavell St, SE10 . . . . . **172** C1
Clavering Av, SW13 . . . . . **162** B1
Claverton St, SW1 . . . . . **71** F3
Clave St, E1
off Cinnamon St **142** C4
Claxton Gro, W6 . . . . . **149** D4
Claxton Path, SE4
off Hainford Cl **185** D2
Claybank Gro, SE13
off Algernon Rd **186** B1
Claybrook Rd, W6 . . . . . **163** D1
Claydon, SE17
off Deacon Way **63** E4
Claylands Pl, SW8 . . . . . **86** A2
Claylands Rd, SW8 . . . . . **85** F1
Claypole Rd, E15 . . . . . **130** C2
Clay St, W1 . . . . . **33** F1
Clayton Cres, N1 . . . . . **13** D1
Clayton Dr, SE8
off Sapphire Rd **157** E4
Clayton Ms, SE10 . . . . . **173** D3
Clayton Rd, SE15 . . . . . **170** A3
Clayton St, SE11 . . . . . **74** A4
Clearbrook Way, E1
off West Arbour St **142** C2
Clearwater Ter, W11
off Lorne Gdns **149** D1
Clearwell Dr, W9 . . . . . **18** C3
Cleaver Sq, SE11 . . . . . **74** B2
Cleaver St, SE11 . . . . . **74** B2
● Cleeve Studios, E2
off Boundary St 29 E1
Cleeve Way, SW15
off Danebury Av **175** F4
Clegg St, E1
off Prusom St **142** B4
Clematis St, W12 . . . . . **133** F3
Clem Attlee Ct, SW6 . . . . . **163** F1

Clem Attlee Par, SW6
off North End Rd 163 F1
Clemence St, E14 ....143 F1
Clement Av, SW4 ....181 D2
Clement Cl, NW6 ....106 C4
W4 ....147 D2
Clementina Rd, E10 ......101 F2
Clement's Inn, WC2 ....37 F3
Clement's Inn Pas,
WC2 ....37 F3
Clements La, EC4 ....40 B4
Clements Rd, SE16 ....156 A2
Clennam St, SE1 ....51 F4
Clenston Ms, W1 ....33 E2
★ Cleopatra's Needle,
WC2 ....49 E2
Clephane Rd, N1 ....112 C3
Clere St, EC2 ....28 B2
CLERKENWELL, EC1 ....26 C3
Clerkenwell Cl, EC1 ....26 B2
Clerkenwell Grn, EC1 ....26 B3
Clerkenwell Rd, EC1 ....26 A3
Clermont Rd, E9 ....128 C1
Clevedon Cl, N16
off Smalley Cl 99 F4
Cleveland Av, W4 ....147 F3
Cleveland Gdns, NW2 ....93 D3
SW13 ....161 F4
W2 ....31 E3
Cleveland Gro, E1
off Cleveland Way 128 C4
Cleveland Ms, W1 ....23 E4
Cleveland Pl, SW1 ....47 F2
Cleveland Rd, N1 ....113 D4
SW13 ....161 F4
W4 off Antrobus Rd 146 C2
Cleveland Row, SW1 ....47 E3
Cleveland Sq, W2 ....31 E3
Cleveland St, W1 ....23 E3
Cleveland Ter, W2 ....31 F2
Cleveland Way, E1 ....128 C4
Cleveleys Rd, E5 ....100 B4
Cleverly Est, W12 ....134 A4
Cleve Rd, NW6 ....108 A4
Clichy Est, E1 ....142 C1
Clifden Ms, E5
off Clifden Rd 115 D1
Clifden Rd, E5 ....114 C2
Clifford Av, SW14 ....174 B1
Clifford Dr, SW9 ....182 B2
Clifford Gdns, NW10 ....120 C2
Clifford Haigh Ho, SW6
off Fulham Palace Rd ...163 D2
Clifford Rd, E16 ....131 F4
Clifford's Inn Pas, EC4 ....38 A3
Clifford St, W1 ....47 E1
Clifford Way, NW10 ....105 F1
Cliff Rd, NW1 ....111 D3
Cliff Ter, SE8 ....172 A4
Cliffview Rd, SE13 ....186 A1
Cliff Vil, NW1 ....111 D3
Cliff Wk, E16 ....145 F1
Clifton Av, W12 ....133 F4
Clifton Ct, N4
off Biggerstaff St 98 A3
NW8 ....20 A2
Clifton Cres, SE15 ....170 B2
Clifton Est, SE15
off Consort Rd 170 B3
Clifton Gdns, W4
off Dolman Rd 147 D3
W9 ....19 E3
Clifton Gro, E8 ....114 A3
Clifton Hill, NW8 ....7 E1
Clifton Pl, SE16
off Canon Beck Rd 156 C1
W2 ....32 B4
Clifton Ri, SE14 ....171 E2
Clifton Rd, E16 ....145 E1
N1 ....112 C3
NW10 ....120 A2
W9 ....19 F2
Clifton St, EC2 ....28 C4
Clifton Ter, N4 ....98 A3
Clifton Vil, W9 ....19 D4
Clifton Wk, W6
off Galena Rd 148 B3
Clifton Way, SE15 ....170 B2
Clinger Ct, N1 ....16 C1
★ Clink Prison Mus, SE1 ....52 A2
Clink St, SE1 ....51 F2
Clinton Rd, E3 ....129 E3
Clipper Cl, SE16
off Kinburn St 157 D1
Clipper Way, SE13 ....186 C2
Clipstone Ms, W1 ....23 E3
Clipstone St, W1 ....23 D4
Clissold Ct, N4 ....98 C3
Clissold Cres, N16 ....99 D4
Clissold Rd, N16 ....99 D4
Clitheroe Rd, SW9 ....167 E4
Clitterhouse Cres, NW2 ......92 C2
Clitterhouse Rd, NW2 ....92 C2
Clive Ct, W9 ....19 F2
Cliveden Pl, SW1 ....58 A4
Cloak La, EC4 ....39 F4
Clockhouse Pl, SW15 ......177 E3
★ Clockmakers Company
Collection, The
(Guildhall Lib), EC2 ......39 F2
Clock Twr Ms, N1 ....15 F1
Clock Vw Cres, N7 ....111 E3
Cloister Rd, NW2 ....93 F4
W3 ....132 C1
● Cloisters Business Cen, SW8
off Battersea Pk Rd 83 D3
Clonbrock Rd, N16 ....113 E1
Cloncurry St, SW6 ....163 D4
Clonmel Rd, SW6 ....163 F2
Clorane Gdns, NW3 ....94 A4
Close, The, SE3
off Heath La 173 D4
Richmond TW9 ....174 B1
Wembley
(Barnhill Rd) HA9 ....90 C4
Cloth Ct, EC1 ....39 D1
Cloth Fair, EC1 ....39 D1
Clothier St, E1 ....41 D2
Cloth St, EC1 ....27 E4
Cloudesley Pl, N1 ....14 A1
Cloudesley Rd, N1 ....126 A1
Cloudesley Sq, N1 ....14 A1
Cloudesley St, N1 ....14 B1
Clova Rd, E7 ....117 F3
Clove Cres, E14 ....145 D3
Clove Hitch Quay,
SW11 ....178 C1
Clovelly Rd, W4 ....146 C1
Clovelly Way, E1
off Jamaica St 142 C2
Clover Cl, E11
off Norman Rd 103 D3
Clover Ms, SW3 ....69 E4
Cloysters Grn, E1 ....142 A4
Club Row, E1 ....29 E2
E2 ....29 E2
Clunbury St, N1 ....16 B3
Cluny Est, SE1 ....64 C2
Cluny Ms, SW5 ....66 A1
Cluny Pl, SE1 ....64 C2
Cluse Ct, N1 ....15 E2
Clutton St, E14 ....144 B1
Clyde Pl, E10 ....102 B1
Clydesdale Gdns, Rich.
TW10 ....174 B2
Clydesdale Rd, W11 ....135 F2
Clyde St, SE8 ....171 F1
Clyston St, SW8 ....166 C4
Coach & Horses Yd, W1 .....35 D4
Coach Ho La, N5
off Highbury Hill 112 B1
Coach Ho Ms, SE14
off Waller Rd 171 D4
SE23 ....185 D4
Coach Ho Yd, SW18
off Ebner St 178 B2
Coachmaker Ms, SW4
off Fenwick Pl 181 E1
W4 off Berrymede Rd 147 D2
Coach Yd Ms, N19 ....97 E2
Coalecroft Rd, SW15 ....176 C2
Coalport Ho, SE11
off Walnut Tree Wk 62 A4
Coates Av, SW18 ....179 E4
Coate St, E2 ....128 A2
Cobbett St, SW8 ....85 F3
Cobble La, N1
off Edwards Ms 112 B4
Cobble Ms, N5 ....98 C4
N6
off Highgate W Hill 96 A2
● Cobbold Est, NW10 ....105 F3
Cobbold Ms, W12
off Cobbold Rd 147 F1
Cobbold Rd, E11 ....103 F4
NW10 ....105 F3
W12 ....147 E1
Cobb's Ct, EC4
off Pilgrim St 39 D3
Cobb St, E1 ....41 E1
Cobden Rd, E11 ....103 E4
Cobham Cl, SW11 ....179 E4
Cobham Ms, NW1
off Agar Gro 111 D4
Coborn Rd, E3 ....129 F3
Coborn St, E3 ....129 F3
Cobourg Rd, SE5 ....77 E4
Cobourg St, NW1 ....23 F1
Coburg Cl, SW1 ....59 F4
Cochrane Ms, NW8 ....8 B3
Cochrane St, NW8 ....8 B3
Cockayne Way, SE8 ....157 E4
Cockerell Rd, E17 ....101 E1
Cock Hill, E1 ....41 D1
Cock La, EC1 ....38 C1
Cockpit Steps, SW1 ....60 B1
Cockpit Yd, WC1 ....25 F4
Cockspur Ct, SW1 ....48 B2
Cockspur St, SW1 ....48 B2
● Coda Cen, The, SW6 ....163 E3
Code St, E1 ....29 F3
Codling Cl, E1
off Torrington Pl 142 A4
Codrington Ms, W11
off Blenheim Cres 135 E2
Cody Rd, E16 ....131 D4
● Cody Rd Business Cen,
E16 ....131 D4
Coffey St, SE8 ....172 A2
Coin St, SE1 ....50 A2
Coity Rd, NW5 ....110 A3
Coke St, E1 ....142 A2

Colas Ms, NW6
off Birchington Rd **122** A1
Colbeck Ms, SW7 ....**67** D1
Colberg Pl, N16 ....**99** E1
Colchester Rd, E10 ....**102** C1
Colchester St, E1 ....**41** F2
Coldbath Sq, EC1 ....**26** A2
Coldbath St, SE13 ....**172** B3
Cold Blow La, SE14 ....**171** D2
Cold Harbour, E14 ....**158** C1
Coldharbour La, SE5 ....**182** A2
SW9 ....**182** A2
● Coldharbour La Ind Est, SE5
off Coldharbour La **168** C4
Coldharbour Pl, SE5
off Denmark Hill **169** D4
Coldstream Gdns, SW18 ....**177** F4
Colebeck Ms, N1 ....**112** B3
Colebert Av, E1 ....**128** C4
Colebrooke Pl, N1 ....**15** D1
Colebrooke Row, N1 ....**14** C3
Colebrook Ho, E14
off Ellesmere St **144** B2
Coleby Path, SE5 ....**88** B3
Colechurch Ho, SE1
off Avondale Sq **156** A4
Coleford Rd, SW18 ....**178** C3
Colegrave Rd, E15 ....**117** D2
Colegrove Rd, SE15 ....**89** F1
Coleherne Ct, SW5 ....**67** D3
Coleherne Ms, SW10 ....**66** C3
Coleherne Rd, SW10 ....**66** C3
Colehill Gdns, SW6 ....**163** E3
Colehill La, SW6 ....**163** E3
Coleman Flds, N1 ....**126** C1
Coleman Rd, SE5 ....**88** C2
Coleman St, EC2 ....**40** A2
Colenso Rd, E5 ....**114** C1
Coleraine Rd, SE3 ....**173** F1
Coleridge Cl, SW8 ....**166** B4
Coleridge Gdns, NW6
off Fairhazel Gdns **108** C4
SW10 ....**79** D2
Coleridge Ho, SW1 ....**71** E3
Coleridge Rd, N4 ....**98** A3
Coleridge Sq, SW10 ....**79** E2
Coles Grn Ct, NW2 ....**92** A3
Coles Grn Rd, NW2 ....**92** A2
Coleshill Flats, SW1
off Pimlico Rd **70** B1
Colestown St, SW11 ....**165** E4
Cole St, SE1 ....**63** F1
Colet Gdns, W14 ....**149** D3
Coley St, WC1 ....**25** F3
Colinette Rd, SW15 ....**176** C2
Colin Rd, NW10 ....**106** A3
Colinsdale, N1 ....**14** C1
Collard Pl, NW1
off Harmood St **110** B4
College App, SE10 ....**172** C1
College Cl, E9
off Median Rd **114** C2
College Cres, NW3 ....**109** D3
College Cross, N1 ....**112** A4
College Gro, NW1 ....**12** A1
College Hill, EC4 ....**39** F4
College La, NW5 ....**110** B1
College Ms, SW1 ....**60** C2
SW18 *off St. Ann's Hill* ...**178** B3
★ College of Arms, EC4 ....**39** D4
Coll College of Law, The,
Bream's Bldgs, EC4 .....**38** A2
Moorgate Cen, EC1 ....**28** A3
Bloomsbury Cen, WC1 ....**24** A4
Coll College of N W London,
Kilburn Cen, NW6
off Priory Pk Rd **122** A1
Wembley Pk Cen, Wem. HA9
off North End Rd **90** A4
Willesden Cen, NW10
off Dudden Hill La **105** F2
College Pk Cl, SE13 ....**187** D2
College Pl, NW1 ....**11** F1
SW10 ....**79** E2
College Pt, E15 ....**117** F3
College Rd, NW10 ....**120** C2
College Row, E9 ....**115** D2
College St, EC4 ....**39** F4
College Ter, E3 ....**129** F3
College Yd, NW5
off College La **110** B1
Collent St, E9 ....**114** C3
Collett Ho, N16
off Stamford Hill **99** F2
Collett Rd, SE16 ....**156** A2
Collier St, N1 ....**13** E3
Collingbourne Rd, W12 .....**134** B4
Collingham Gdns, SW5 ......**67** D1
Collingham Pl, SW5 ....**66** C1
Collingham Rd, SW5 ....**55** D4
Collington St, SE10
off Hoskins St **159** D4
Collingwood St, E1 ....**128** B4
Collinson St, SE1 ....**63** E1
Collinson Wk, SE1 ....**63** E1
Collins Rd, N5 ....**112** C1
Collins Sq, SE3
off Tranquil Vale **173** F4
Collins St, SE3 ....**173** E4
Collin's Yd, N1 ....**14** C1
Collison Pl, N16 ....**99** E3
Colls Rd, SE15 ....**170** C3
Collyer Pl, SE15
off Peckham High St ...**170** A3
Colmar Cl, E1
off Alderney Rd **129** D4
Colmore Ms, SE15 ....**170** B3
Colnbrook St, SE1 ....**62** C3
Colne Rd, E5 ....**115** E1
Cologne Rd, SW11 ....**179** D2
Colombo St, SE1 ....**50** C3
Colomb St, SE10 ....**159** E4
Colonial Dr, W4 ....**146** C3
Colonnade, WC1 ....**24** C3
Colonnade Wk, SW1 ....**70** C1
Colony Ms, N1
off Mildmay Gro N **113** D2
Colorado Bldg, SE13
off Deals Gateway **172** B3
Colosseum Ter, NW1
off Albany St **23** D2
Colston Rd, SW14 ....**174** C2
Colthurst Cres, N4 ....**98** C3
Coltman St, E14 ....**143** E1
Columbas Dr, NW3 ....**95** D2
Columbia Pt, SE16
off Moodkee St **156** C2
Columbia Rd, E2 ....**17** E4
E13 ....**131** F4
Columbia Sq, SW14
off Upper Richmond Rd W **174** C2
Columbine Way,
SE13 ....**172** C4
Columbus Ct, SE16
off Rotherhithe St **142** C4
Columbus Ctyd, E14
off West India Av **144** A4
Colva Wk, N19
off Chester Rd **96** B3
Colvestone Cres, E8 ....**113** F2
Colville Est, N1 ....**16** C1
Colville Gdns, W11 ....**135** F2
Colville Hos, W11 ....**135** F2
Colville Ms, W11
off Lonsdale Rd **135** F2
Colville Pl, W1 ....**35** F1
Colville Rd, E11 ....**102** C4
W3 ....**146** B2
W11 ....**135** F2
Colville Sq, W11 ....**135** F2
Colville Ter, W11 ....**135** F2
Colwell Rd, SE22 ....**183** F3
Colwick Cl, N6 ....**97** D1
Colwith Rd, W6 ....**162** C1
Colworth Gro, SE17 ....**75** F1
Colwyn Ho, SE1
off Briant Est **62** A3
Colwyn Rd, NW2 ....**92** B4
Colyer Cl, N1 ....**13** F2
Colyton Rd, SE22 ....**184** B3
Combe, The, NW1 ....**23** D1
Combe Av, SE3 ....**173** F2
Combe Ms, SE3 ....**173** F2
Comber Cl, NW2 ....**92** B4
Comber Gro, SE5 ....**87** E4
Comber Ho, SE5
off Comber Gro **87** F3
Combermere Rd, SW9 ......**181** F1
Comberton Rd, E5 ....**100** B3
Comeragh Ms, W14 ....**149** E4
Comeragh Rd, W14 ....**149** E4
Comerford Rd, SE4 ....**185** E2
Comet Pl, SE8 ....**172** A2
Comet St, SE8 ....**172** A2
Comfort St, SE15 ....**88** C1
Commercial Rd, E1 ....**142** A2
E14 ....**142** C2
Commercial St, E1 ....**29** E3
Commercial Way, NW10 ...**118** B2
SE15 ....**89** E3
Commerell St, SE10 ....**159** E4
Commodity Quay, E1 ....**53** F1
Commodore Ho, SW18
off Juniper Dr **178** C2
Commodore St, E1 ....**129** E4
Common, The, E15 ....**117** E3
Commondale, SW15 ....**176** C1
Common Mile Cl, SW4 .....**181** D3
Common Rd, SW13 ....**176** A1
Commonwealth Av, W12 ...**134** B3
Coll Community Coll Hackney,
London Flds, E8
off Mare St **114** B4
Shoreditch Campus, N1 ...**17** D4
Coll Community Ed Lewisham,
Granville Pk Adult Learning
Cen, SE13 ....**186** C1
Mornington Cen, SE8
off Stanley St **171** F2
Community La, N7 ....**111** D2
Community Rd, E15 ....**117** D2
Compass Ho, SW18
off Smugglers Way **178** B2
Compayne Gdns, NW6 .....**108** B4
Compton Av, N1 ....**112** B3
N6 ....**95** E1
Compton Cl, E3 ....**144** A1
NW1 ....**23** D1
NW11 ....**93** D4
SE15
off Commercial Way **170** A2

ompton Cres, W4 ....**160** C1
ompton Ho, SW11
off Parkham St **80** C4
ompton Pas, EC1 ....**27** D2
ompton Pl, WC1 ....**24** C2
ompton Rd, N1 ....**112** B3
NW10 ....**121** D3
ompton St, EC1 ....**26** C2
ompton Ter, N1 ....**112** B3
omus Pl, SE17 ....**76** C1
omyn Rd, SW11 ....**179** E2
omyns Cl, E16 ....**145** F1
onant Ms, E1
off Back Ch La **142** A3
oncanon Rd, SW2 ....**181** F2
oncert Hall App, SE1 ....**49** F3
Concord Business Cen, W3
off Concord Rd **132** B1
oncorde Way, SE16 ......**157** D3
oncord Rd, W3 ....**118** B4
ondell Rd, SW8 ....**166** C3
onder St, E14
off Salmon La **143** E2
ondray Pl, SW11 ....**80** C3
onduit Av, SE10
off Crooms Hill **173** D2
onduit Ct, WC2 ....**36** C4
onduit Ms, W2 ....**32** A3
onduit Pas, W2 ....**32** A3
onduit Pl, W2 ....**32** A3
onduit St, W1 ....**35** D4
onduit Way, NW10 ....**104** C4
onewood St, N5 ....**98** B4
oney Way, SW8 ....**85** F1
ongreve St, SE17 ....**64** C4
oniger Rd, SW6 ....**164** A4
oningham Ms, W12 ......**134** A4
oningham Rd, W12 ......**148** B1
oningsby Rd, N4 ....**98** B1
onington Rd, SE13 ....**172** B4
oniston Cl, SW13
off Lonsdale Rd **161** F2
W4 ....**160** C3
onistone Way, N7 ....**111** E4
oniston Ho, SE5 ....**87** E2
oniston Wk, E9
off Clifden Rd **114** C2
onlan St, W10 ....**121** E4
onley Rd, NW10 ....**105** E3
onley St, SE10
off Pelton Rd **159** E4
onnaught Av, SW14 ......**174** C1
onnaught Cl, E10 ....**101** E3
W2 ....**32** C3
onnaught Ms, NW3
off Pond St **109** E2
onnaught Pl, W2 ....**33** E4
onnaught Rd, E11 ....**103** D2
N4 ....**98** A1
NW10 ....**119** E1
onnaught Sq, W2 ....**33** E3
onnaught St, W2 ....**32** C3
onnor Cl, E11 ....**103** E2
onnor Ct, SW11
off Alfreda St **166** B3
onnor St, E9
off Lauriston Rd **129** D1
onrad Ho, N16 ....**113** E2
onsort Rd, SE15 ....**170** B3
ons St, SE1 ....**50** B4
onstable Ho, E14
off Cassilis Rd **158** A1
NW3 *off Adelaide Rd* **109** F4
onstantine Rd, NW3 ......**109** E1
Constitution Hill, SW1 ....**46** C4
Content St, SE17 ....**75** F1
Convent Gdns, W11
off Kensington Pk Rd ...**135** F2
Conway Gro, W3 ....**133** D1
Conway Ms, W1 ....**23** E4
Conway Rd, NW2 ....**92** C3
Conway St, W1 ....**23** E3
Conybeare, NW3
off King Henry's Rd **109** E4
Conyer St, E3 ....**129** E2
Cook Ct, SE16
off Rotherhithe St **142** C4
Cookes Cl, E11 ....**103** F3
Cookham Cres, SE16
off Marlow Way **157** D1
Cooks Cl, E14
off Cabot Sq **144** A4
Cook's Rd, E15 ....**130** B2
Cooks Rd, SE17 ....**74** C4
Cool Oak La, NW9 ....**91** E1
Coomassie Rd, W9
off Bravington Rd **121** F4
Coombe Rd, NW10 ....**91** D4
W4 ....**147** E4
Coombs St, N1 ....**15** D3
Coomer Ms, SW6
off Coomer Pl **163** F1
Coomer Pl, SW6 ....**163** F1
Coomer Rd, SW6
off Coomer Pl **163** F1
Co-operative Ho, SE15
off Rye La **184** A1
Cooper Cl, SE1 ....**62** B1
Cooper Rd, NW10 ....**105** F2
Coopersale Rd, E9 ....**115** D2
Coopers Cl, E1 ....**128** C4
Coopers La, E10 ....**102** B2
NW1 ....**12** B2
Coopers Rd, SE1 ....**77** F3
Cooper's Row, EC3 ....**41** E4
Cooper St, E16
off Lawrence St **145** F1
Coopers Wk, E15
off Maryland St **117** E2
Coopers Yd, N1
off Upper St **112** B4
Copeland Dr, E14 ....**158** A3
Copeland Ho, SE11 ....**61** F3
Copeland Rd, SE15 ....**170** A4
Copenhagen Gdns, W4 ....**146** C1
Copenhagen Pl, E14 ....**143** F2
Copenhagen St, N1 ....**13** D1
Cope Pl, W8 ....**54** A3
Cope St, SE16 ....**157** D3
Copford Wk, N1
off Popham St **126** C1
Copleston Ms, SE15
off Copleston Rd **183** F1
Copleston Pas, SE15 ......**183** F1
Copleston Rd, SE15 ....**183** F1
Copley Cl, SE17 ....**87** D1
Copley St, E1 ....**143** D1
Coppelia Rd, SE3 ....**187** F2
Copperas St, SE8 ....**172** B1
Copperfield Rd, E3 ....**129** E4
Copperfield St, SE1 ....**51** D4
Copper Mead Cl, NW2 ....**92** C4
Copper Ms, W4 ....**146** C2
Copper Row, SE1 ....**53** E3
Coppice Dr, SW15 ....**176** B4
Coppock Cl, SW11 ....**165** E4
Coptain Ho, SW18
off Eastfields Av **178** A2
Copthall Av, EC2 ....**40** B2
Copthall Bldgs, EC2 ....**40** A2
Copthall Cl, EC2 ....**40** A2
Copthall Ct, EC2 ....**40** A2
Coptic St, WC1 ....**36** C1
Coral Row, SW11
off Gartons Way **178** C1
Coral St, SE1 ....**62** B1
★ Coram's Flds, WC1 ......**25** D3
Coram St, WC1 ....**24** C3
Corbden Cl, SE15 ....**89** F4
Corbet Ct, EC3 ....**40** B3
Corbet Pl, E1 ....**29** E4
Corbetts La, SE16
off Rotherhithe
New Rd **156** C3
Corbetts Pas, SE16
off Silwood St **156** C3
Corbicum, E11 ....**103** E1
Corbidge Ct, SE8
off Glaisher St **172** B1
Corbiere Ho, N1 ....**127** E1
Corbin Ho, E3
off Bromley High St **130** B3
Corbridge Cres, E2 ....**128** B2
Corbyn St, N4 ....**97** E2
Corby Rd, NW10 ....**119** D2
Corby Way, E3
off Knapp Rd **130** A4
Cordelia Cl, SE24 ....**182** B2
Cordelia St, E14 ....**144** B2
Cording St, E14
off Chrisp St **144** B1
Uni Cordwainers at London
Coll of Fashion, EC1 .....**27** E3
Cord Way, E14
off Mellish St **158** A2
Cordwell Rd, SE13 ....**187** E3
Corfe Ho, SW8
off Dorset Rd **85** E2
Corfe Twr, W3 ....**146** B1
Corfield St, E2 ....**128** B3
Coriander Av, E14 ....**145** D2
Corinne Rd, N19 ....**110** C1
Corker Wk, N7 ....**97** F3
Cork Sq, E1
off Smeaton St **142** B4
Cork St, W1 ....**47** E1
Cork St Ms, W1 ....**47** E1
Corlett St, NW1 ....**20** C4
Cormont Rd, SE5 ....**168** B3
Cormorant Rd, E7 ....**117** F2
Cornelia St, N7 ....**111** F3
Corner Ho St, WC2 ....**48** C2
Corney Reach Way, W4 ....**161** E2
Corney Rd, W4 ....**161** E1
Cornflower Ter, SE22 ......**184** B4
Cornhill, EC3 ....**40** B3
Cornish Ho, SE17 ....**86** C1
Cornmow Dr, NW10 ....**105** F2
Cornthwaite Rd, E5 ....**100** C4
Cornwall Av, E2 ....**128** C3
Cornwall Cres, W11 ....**135** E3
Cornwall Gdns, NW10 .....**106** B3
SW7 ....**55** D3
Cornwall Gdns Wk, SW7 .....**55** D3
Cornwall Gro, W4 ....**147** E4
Cornwallis Ct, SW8 ....**84** C4
Cornwallis Rd, N19 ....**97** E3
Cornwallis Sq, N19 ....**97** E3
Cornwall Ms S, SW7 ....**55** E3
Cornwall Ms W, SW7 ....**55** D3
Cornwall Rd, N4 ....**98** A1
SE1 ....**50** A2

Cornwall Sq, SE11 **74** B2
Cornwall St, E1
off Watney St **142** B3
Cornwall Ter, NW1 **21** F3
Cornwall Ter Ms, NW1 **21** F3
Corn Way, E11 **103** D4
Cornwood Dr, E1 **142** C2
Coronation Av, N16
off Victorian Rd **99** F4
Coronation Rd, NW10 **118** A4
★ Coronet, The, SE1 **63** D3
Coronet St, N1 **28** C1
Corporation Row, EC1 **26** B2
Corporation St, E15 **131** E2
N7 **111** E2
Corrance Rd, SW2 **181** E2
Corringham Ct, NW11
off Corringham Rd **94** A1
Corringham Rd, NW11 **94** A1
Wembley HA9 **90** A3
Corringway, NW11 **94** B1
W5 **118** A4
Corry Dr, SW9 **182** B2
Corsham St, N1 **28** B1
Corsica St, N5 **112** B3
Cortayne Rd, SW6 **163** F4
Cortis Rd, SW15 **176** B4
Cortis Ter, SW15 **176** B4
Corunna Rd, SW8 **83** F4
Corunna Ter, SW8 **83** E4
Corvette Sq, SE10
off Feathers Pl **173** D1
Coryton Path, W9
off Fernhead Rd **121** F4
Cosbycote Av, SE24 **182** C3
Cosmo Pl, WC1 **25** D4
Cosmur Cl, W12 **147** F2
Cossall Wk, SE15 **170** B3
Cossar Ms, SW2 **182** A4
Cosser St, SE1 **62** A2
Costa St, SE15 **170** A4
Coston Wk, SE4
off Hainford Cl **185** D2
Cosway St, NW1 **21** D4
Cotall St, E14 **144** A2
Cotesbach Rd, E5 **100** C4
Cotham St, SE17 **75** F1
Cotleigh Rd, NW6 **108** A4
Cotman Cl, SW15 **177** D4
Cotswold Ct, EC1 **27** E2
Cotswold Gdns, NW2 **93** D3
Cotswold Gate, NW2 **93** E2
Cotswold Ms, SW11
off Battersea High St **165** D3
Cottage Grn, SE5 **88** B2
Cottage Gro, SW9 **181** E1
Cottage Pl, SW3 **56** C2
Cottage Rd, N7 **111** F2
Cottage St, E14 **144** B3
Cottage Wk, N16
off Brooke Rd **99** F4
Cottesbrook St, SE14
off Nynehead St **171** E2
Cottesloe Ms, SE1 **62** B2
Cottesmore Gdns, W8 **55** D2
Cottingham Rd, SW8 **85** F1
Cottington St, SE11 **74** B2
Cottle Way, SE16
off St. Marychurch St **156** C1
Cotton Av, W3 **133** D2
Cotton Cl, E11 **103** E3
Cotton Row, SW11 **178** C1
Cottons Gdns, E2 **17** D4
Cottons La, SE1 **52** B2
Cotton St, E14 **144** C3
Cottrell Ct, SE10
off Greenroof Way **159** F3
Cottrill Gdns, E8
off Marcon Pl **114** B3
Coulgate St, SE4 **185** E1
Coulson St, SW3 **69** E2
Coulter Rd, W6 **148** B2
Councillor St, SE5 **87** E3
Counter Ct, SE1
off Borough High St **52** A3
Counter St, SE1 **52** C2
Countess Rd, NW5 **110** C2
County Gro, SE5 **87** E4
★ County Hall, SE1 **49** E4
County St, SE1 **63** F3
Courland Gro, SW8 **167** D3
Courland Gro Hall, SW8 **167** D4
Courland St, SW8 **167** D3
★ Courtauld Inst of Art, WC2 **37** E4
Courtauld Rd, N19 **97** D2
Courtenay Rd, E11 **103** F4
Courtenay Sq, SE11 **74** A3
Courtenay St, SE11 **74** A2
Courtfield Gdns, SW5 **55** D4
Courtfield Ms, SW5 **67** E1
Courtfield Rd, SW7 **67** D1
Court Gdns, N7 **112** A3
Courthill Rd, SE13 **186** C2
Courthope Rd, NW3 **109** F1
Courtlands, Rich. TW10 **174** A2
Courtlands Av, Rich. TW9 **160** B4
Court La, SE21 **183** E4
Courtmead Cl, SE24 **182** C4
Courtnell St, W2 **30** A2
Courtney Rd, N7
off Bryantwood Rd **112** A2
Courtrai Rd, SE23 **185** E4
Court St, E1
off Whitechapel Rd **142** B1
Court Way, W3 **132** C1
Courtyard, The, N1 **111** F4
Courtyard Ho, SW6
off Lensbury Av **164** C4
Cousin La, EC4 **52** A1
Coutts Cres, NW5 **96** A4
Coval Gdns, SW14 **174** B2
Coval La, SW14 **174** B2
Coval Pas, SW14
off Coval Rd **174** C2
Coval Rd, SW14 **174** B2
Covell Ct, SE8
off Reginald Sq **172** A2
★ Covent Garden, WC2 **37** D4
⊖ Covent Garden **36** C4
🔒 Covent Gdn Mkt, WC2 **37** D4
Coventry Cl, NW6 **6** B1
Coventry Rd, E1 **128** B4
E2 **128** B4
Coventry St, W1 **48** A1
Coverdale Rd, NW2 **107** D4
W12 **134** B4
Coverley Cl, E1 **142** A1
Cowcross St, EC1 **26** C4
Cowdenbeath Path, N1 **125** F1
Cowdry Rd, E9
off East Cross Route **115** F3
Cowley Est, SW9 **86** A4
Cowley Rd, SW9 **168** A3
SW14 **175** E1
W3 **133** F4
Cowley St, SW1 **60** C2
Cowling Cl, W11
off Wilsham St **135** E4
Cowper Rd, N16 **113** E2
W3 **133** D4
Cowpers Ct, EC3
off Birchin La **40** B3
Cowper St, EC2 **28** B2
Cowper Ter, W10
off St. Quintin Av **135** D1
Cowthorpe Rd, SW8 **84** B4
Coxson Way, SE1 **65** E1
Crabtree Cl, E2 **17** E3
Crabtree La, SW6 **163** D2
Craddock St, NW5
off Prince of Wales Rd **110** A3
Craigs Ct, SW1 **48** C2
Craik Ct, NW6
off Carlton Vale **121** F2
Crail Row, SE17 **76** B1
Cramer St, W1 **34** B1
Crammond Cl, W6 **163** E1
Crampton St, SE17 **75** E1
Cranberry La, E16 **131** E4
Cranbourn All, WC2
off Cranbourn St **36** B4
Cranbourne Pas, SE16
off Marigold St **156** B1
Cranbourne Rd, E15 **116** C1
Cranbourn St, WC2 **36** B4
Cranbrook Ho, E5
off Pembury Rd **114** B2
Cranbrook Rd, SE8 **172** A3
W4 **147** E4
Cranbrook St, E2
off Mace St **129** D2
Cranbury Rd, SW6 **164** B4
Crandale Ho, E5
off Pembury Rd **114** B2
Crane Av, W3 **132** C3
Crane Ct, EC4 **38** B3
Crane Gro, N7 **112** A3
Crane Ho, SE15
off Talfourd Pl **169** F3
Crane St, SE10 **159** D4
SE15 **89** E4
Cranfield Rd, SE4 **185** F1
Cranfield Row, SE1 **62** B2
Cranford Cotts, E1
off Cranford St **143** D3
Cranford St, E1 **143** D3
Cranhurst Rd, NW2 **106** C2
Cranleigh Ms, SW11 **165** E4
Cranleigh St, NW1 **11** F3
Cranley Gdns, SW7 **67** F2
Cranley Ms, SW7 **67** F2
Cranley Pl, SW7 **68** A1
Cranmer Ct, SW3 **69** D1
SW4 **181** D1
Cranmer Ho, SW11
off Surrey La **80** C4
Cranmer Rd, SW9 **86** B2
Cranston Est, N1 **16** B3
Cranswick Rd, SE16 **156** B4
Cranwell Cl, E3 **130** B4
Cranwich Rd, N16 **99** D1
Cranwood St, EC1 **28** A1
Cranworth Gdns, SW9 **168** A3
Craven Cl, N16 **100** A1
Craven Hill, W2 **31** F4
Craven Hill Gdns, W2 **31** E4
Craven Hill Ms, W2 **31** F4
Craven Ms, SW11
off Taybridge Rd **180** A1
Craven Pk, NW10 **119** E1

raven Pk Ms, NW10 ......**105** E4
raven Pk Rd, NW10 ......**119** E1
raven Pas, WC2 ....**48** C2
raven Rd, NW10 ....**119** D1
W2 ....**31** F4
raven St, WC2 ....**48** C2
raven Ter, W2 ....**31** F4
raven Wk, N16 ....**100** A1
rawford Est, SE5 ....**168** C4
rawford Ms, W1 ....**33** E1
rawford Pas, EC1 ....**26** A3
rawford Pl, W1 ....**33** D2
rawford Rd, SE5 ....**168** C3
rawford St, NW10
off Fawood Av **105** D4
W1 ....**33** E1
rawley Rd, E10 ....**102** B2
rawshay Ct, SW9 ....**86** B4
rawthew Gro, SE22 ....**183** F2
rayford Rd, N7 ....**111** D1
realock St, SW18 ....**178** B4
reasy Est, SE1 ....**64** C3
rebor St, SE22 ....**184** A4
rediton Hill, NW6 ....**108** B2
rediton Rd, NW10 ....**121** D1
redon Rd, SE16 ....**156** B4
reechurch La, EC3 ....**41** D3
reechurch Pl, EC3 ....**41** D3
reed Ct, EC4
off Ludgate Sq **39** D3
reed La, EC4 ....**39** D3
reek Rd, SE8 ....**172** A1
SE10 ....**172** A1
reekside, SE8 ....**172** B2
refeld Cl, W6 ....**163** D1
reighton Cl, W12 ....**134** A3
reighton Rd, NW6 ....**121** D2
remer St, E2 ....**17** E3
remorne Est, SW10 ....**80** A2
remorne Rd, SW10 ....**79** F3
rescent, EC3 ....**41** E4
rescent, The, NW2 ....**92** B4
SW13 ....**161** F4
W3 ....**133** E2
rescent Arc, SE10
off Creek Rd **172** C1
rescent Gro, SW4 ....**180** C2
rescent Ho, SE13
off Ravensbourne Pl **172** B4
rescent La, SW4 ....**181** D3
rescent Pl, SW3 ....**56** C4
rescent Rd, E10 ....**102** B3
N8 ....**97** D1
rescent Row, EC1 ....**27** E3
rescent Stables, SW15 ....**177** E3
rescent St, N1 ....**111** F4
rescent Way, SE4 ....**186** A1
resford Rd, SW6 ....**164** B3
resset Rd, E9 ....**114** C3
resset St, SW4 ....**181** D1
ressfield Cl, NW5 ....**110** A2
ressida Rd, N19 ....**96** C2
ressingham Rd, SE13 .....**186** C1
ressington Cl, N16 ....**113** E2
resswell Gdns, SW5 ....**67** E2
resswell Pk, SE3 ....**187** F1
resswell Pl, SW10 ....**67** E2
Cressy Ct, E1
off Cressy Pl **142** C1
W6 ....**148** B2
Cressy Ho, E1
off Hannibal Rd **142** C1
Cressy Pl, E1 ....**142** C1
Cressy Rd, NW3 ....**109** F2
Crestfield St, WC1 ....**13** D4
Crest Rd, NW2 ....**91** F3
Crestway, SW15 ....**176** B4
Creswick Rd, W3 ....**132** B3
Creswick Wk, E3
off Addington Rd **130** A3
Creukhorne Rd, NW10 .....**105** E4
Crewdson Rd, SW9 ....**86** A3
Crewe Pl, NW10 ....**119** F3
Crews St, E14 ....**158** A3
Crewys Rd, NW2 ....**93** F3
SE15 ....**170** B4
Crichton St, SW8
off Westbury St **166** C4
Cricketers Ct, SE11 ....**74** C1
Cricketers Ms, SW18
off East Hill **178** B3
Cricketfield Rd, E5 ....**114** B1
CRICKLEWOOD, NW2 ....**93** D4
⇌ Cricklewood **107** D1
Cricklewood Bdy, NW2 ......**92** C4
Cricklewood La, NW2 ......**107** D1
Cridland St, E15
off Church St **131** F1
Crieff Rd, SW18 ....**178** C4
Crimscott St, SE1 ....**65** D3
Crimsworth Rd, SW8 ....**84** B4
Crinan St, N1 ....**13** D2
Cringle St, SW8 ....**83** E2
Cripplegate St, EC2 ....**27** E4
Crispian Cl, NW10 ....**105** E1
Crispin Pl, E1 ....**29** E4
Crispin St, E1 ....**41** E1
Crisp Rd, W6 ....**148** C4
Cristowe Rd, SW6 ....**163** F4
Criterion Ms, N19 ....**97** D3
SE24
off Shakespeare Rd **182** B3
Croft, The, NW10 ....**119** F2
Croftdown Rd, NW5 ....**96** A4
Crofters Ct, SE8
off Croft St **157** E3
Crofters Way, NW1 ....**125** D1
Crofton Av, W4 ....**161** D2
Croftongate Way, SE4 .....**185** E3
⇌ Crofton Park **185** F3
Crofton Pk Rd, SE4 ....**185** F4
Crofton Rd, SE5 ....**169** E3
Crofton Ter, E5
off Studley Cl **115** E2
Crofts St, E1 ....**142** A3
Croft St, SE8 ....**157** E3
Croftway, NW3 ....**108** A1
Crogsland Rd, NW1 ....**110** A4
Cromartie Rd, N19 ....**97** D1
Crome Rd, NW10 ....**105** E3
Cromer Rd, E10 ....**103** D1
Cromer St, WC1 ....**25** D1
Cromer Ter, E8
off Ferncliff Rd **114** A2
Cromer Vil Rd, SW18 ......**177** F4
Cromford Path, E5
off Overbury St **115** D1
Cromford Rd, SW18 ....**178** A3
Crompton St, W2 ....**20** A3
Cromwell Av, N6 ....**96** B2
W6 ....**148** B4
Cromwell Cl, W3
off High St **132** C4
Cromwell Cres, SW5 ....**54** A4
Cromwell Gdns, SW7 ....**56** B3
Cromwell Gro, W6 ....**148** C2
Cromwell Highwalk, EC2
off Silk St **27** F4
H Cromwell Hosp, The,
SW5 ....**54** C4
● Cromwell Ind Est, E10 ..**101** E2
Cromwell Ms, SW7 ....**56** B4
Cromwell Pl, N6 ....**96** B2
SW7 ....**56** B4
SW14 ....**174** C1
W3 *off Grove Pl* **132** C4
Cromwell Rd, SW5 ....**54** B4
SW7 ....**56** A4
SW9 ....**86** C4
Cromwell Twr, EC2 ....**27** F4
Crondace Rd, SW6 ....**164** A3
Crondall Ct, N1 ....**16** C3
Crondall St, N1 ....**16** B3
Cronin St, SE15 ....**89** E3
Crooked Billet Yd, E2 ....**17** D4
Crooke Rd, SE8 ....**157** E4
Crookham Rd, SW6 ....**163** F3
Crooms Hill, SE10 ....**173** D2
Crooms Hill Gro, SE10 .....**172** C2
Cropley Ct, N1 ....**16** A2
Cropley St, N1 ....**16** A2
Cropthorne Ct, W9 ....**19** F1
Crosby Ct, SE1 ....**52** A4
Crosby Row, SE1 ....**64** A1
Crosby Sq, EC3 ....**40** C3
Crosby Wk, E8
off Beechwood Rd **113** F3
Crosland Pl, SW11
off Taybridge Rd **180** A1
Cross Av, SE10 ....**173** D1
Cross Cl, SE15
off Gordon Rd **170** B4
Crossfield Rd, NW3 ....**109** D4
Crossfield St, SE8 ....**172** A2
Crossford St, SW9 ....**167** F4
DLR Crossharbour **158** B2
Cross Keys Cl, W1 ....**34** B1
Cross Keys Sq, EC1 ....**39** E1
Cross La, EC3 ....**52** C1
Crosslet St, SE17 ....**64** B4
Crosslet Vale, SE10 ....**172** B3
Crossley St, N7 ....**112** A3
Crossmount Ho, SE5 ....**87** E2
Cross Rd, SE5 ....**169** E4
Cross St, N1 ....**126** B1
SW13 ....**161** E4
Crossthwaite Av, SE5 ......**183** D2
Crosstrees Ho, E14
off Cassilis Rd **158** A2
Crosswall, EC3 ....**41** E4
Crossway, N16 ....**113** E2
Cross Way, NW10 ....**106** A4
Crossways, The, Wem.
HA9 ....**90** A3
Coll Crossways Acad, SE4
off Sprules Rd **171** E4
Croston St, E8 ....**128** A1
Crouch End Hill, N8 ....**97** D1
⊖ Crouch Hill **97** F1
Crouch Hill, N4 ....**97** E1
N8 ....**97** E1
Crouch Rd, NW10 ....**105** D4
Crowder St, E1 ....**142** B3
Crowfoot Cl, E9
off Lee Conservancy Rd **115** F2
Crowhurst Cl, SW9 ....**168** A4
Crowland Ter, N1 ....**113** D4
Crowline Wk, N1
off Clephane Rd **112** C3
Crown Cl, E3 ....**130** A1
NW6 ....**108** B3

● Crown Cl Business Cen, E3
off Crown Cl **130** A1
Crown Ct, EC2 .... **39** F3
WC2 .... **37** D3
Crowndale Rd, NW1 .... **11** E2
Crownfield Rd, E15 .... **117** D2
Crowngate Ho, E3
off Hereford Rd **129** F2
Crownhill Rd, NW10 .... **119** F1
Crown Ms, W6 .... **148** A3
Crown Office Row, EC4 .... **38** A4
Crown Pas, SW1 .... **47** F3
Crown Pl, EC2 .... **28** C4
NW5
off Kentish Town Rd **110** B3
SE16 *off Varcoe Rd* **156** B4
Crown Reach, SW1 .... **72** B3
Crownstone Rd, SW2 .... **182** A3
Crown St, SE5 .... **87** F2
W3 .... **132** B4
Crown Wks, E2
off Temple St **128** B2
Crows Rd, E15 .... **131** D3
Crowther Cl, SW6
off Coomer Pl **163** F1
Crowthorne Rd, W10 .... **135** D2
Croxley Rd, W9 .... **121** F3
Croxted Ms, SE24 .... **182** C4
Croxteth Ho, SW8
off Wandsworth Rd **167** D4
Croydon Rd, E13 .... **131** F4
Crozier Ter, E9 .... **115** D2
Crucifix La, SE1 .... **52** C4
Cruden Ho, SE17 .... **86** C1
Cruden St, N1 .... **15** D1
Cruikshank Rd, E15 .... **117** E1
Cruikshank St, WC1 .... **14** A4
Crusoe Ms, N16 .... **99** D3
Crutched Friars, EC3 .... **41** D4
Crystal Palace Rd, SE22 .... **184** A2
Crystal Wf, N1 .... **15** D3
Cuba St, E14 .... **158** A1
Cubitt Bldg, SW1 .... **70** C3
Cubitt Steps, E14
off Cabot Sq **144** A4
Cubitt St, WC1 .... **25** F1
Cubitts Yd, WC2 .... **37** D4
Cubitt Ter, SW4 .... **180** C1
CUBITT TOWN, E14 .... **158** C2
Cuddington, SE17 .... **63** E4
Cudworth St, E1 .... **128** B4
Cuff Pt, E2 .... **17** E4
Culford Gdns, SW3 .... **69** F1
Culford Gro, N1 .... **113** E3
Culford Ms, N1
off Culford Rd **113** E3
Culford Rd, N1 .... **113** E4
Cullen Way, NW10 .... **118** C4
Culling Rd, SE16
off Lower Rd **156** C2
Cullingworth Rd, NW10 .... **106** A2
Culloden Cl, SE16 .... **156** A4
Culloden St, E14 .... **144** C2
Cullum St, EC3 .... **40** C4
Culmore Rd, SE15 .... **170** B2
Culmstock Rd, SW11 .... **180** A3
Culross St, W1 .... **46** A1
Culvert Pl, SW11 .... **166** A4
Culvert Rd, SW11 .... **165** F4
Culworth St, NW8 .... **8** C3
Cumberland Av, NW10 .... **118** B3
● Cumberland Business Pk, NW10 .... **118** A3
Cumberland Cl, E8 .... **113** F3
Cumberland Cres, W14 .... **149** E3
Cumberland Gdns, WC1 .... **13** F4
Cumberland Gate, W1 .... **33** E4
Cumberland Mkt, NW1 .... **11** D4
Cumberland Mkt Est, NW1 .... **11** D4
Cumberland Ms, SE11 .... **74** B3
Cumberland Mills Sq, E14
off Saunders Ness Rd **159** D4
● Cumberland Pk, NW10 .... **120** A3
W3 .... **132** C3
Cumberland Pl, NW1 .... **10** C4
Cumberland Rd, SW13 .... **161** F3
W3 .... **132** C3
Richmond TW9 .... **160** A2
Cumberland St, SW1 .... **71** D2
Cumberland Ter, NW1 .... **10** C3
Cumberland Ter Ms, NW1 .... **10** C3
Cumberland Vil, W3
off Cumberland Rd **132** C3
Cumbrian Gdns, NW2 .... **93** D3
★ Cuming Mus, SE17
off Walworth Rd **75** E1
Cumming St, N1 .... **13** E3
Cunard Pl, EC3 .... **41** D3
Cunard Rd, NW10 .... **119** D3
Cunard Wk, SE16 .... **157** E3
Cundy St, SW1 .... **70** B1
Cundy St Est, SW1 .... **70** B1
Cunningham Ct, E10
off Oliver Rd **102** B4
Cunningham Pl, NW8 .... **20** A2
Cunnington St, W4 .... **146** C2
Cupar Rd, SW11 .... **82** B4
Cureton St, SW1 .... **72** B1
Curlew St, SE1 .... **53** E4
Curness St, SE13 .... **186** C2
Curnock Est, NW1 .... **11** E1
Curricle St, W3 .... **133** E4
Cursitor St, EC4 .... **38** A2
Curtain Pl, EC2 .... **29** D2
Curtain Rd, EC2 .... **28** C3
Curtis Dr, W3 .... **133** D2
Curtis St, SE1 .... **65** E4
Curtis Way, SE1 .... **65** E4
Curve, The, W12 .... **134** A3
Curwen Rd, W12 .... **148** A1
Curzon Cres, NW10 .... **105** F4
Curzon Gate, W1 .... **46** A3
Curzon Sq, W1 .... **46** B3
Curzon St, W1 .... **46** B3
Custom Ho Reach, SE16 .... **157** F1
Custom Ho Wk, EC3 .... **52** C1
Cut, The, SE1 .... **50** B4
Cutcombe Rd, SE5 .... **168** C4
Cuthbert St, W2 .... **20** A4
Cuthill Wk, SE5 .... **169** D3
Cutlers Gdns, E1 .... **41** D2
Cutlers Gdns Arc, EC2
off Devonshire Sq **41** D2
Cutlers Sq, E14
off Britannia Rd **158** A3
Cutlers Ter, N1
off Balls Pond Rd **113** E3
Cutler St, E1 .... **41** D2
★ Cutty Sark, SE10 .... **172** C1
DLR Cutty Sark for Maritime Greenwich **172** C1
Cutty Sark Gdns, SE10
off King William Wk **172** C1
Cyclops Ms, E14 .... **158** A3
Cygnet Cl, NW10 .... **105** D2
Cygnet St, E1 .... **29** F2
● Cygnus Business Cen, NW10 .... **105** F3
Cynthia St, N1 .... **13** F3
Cyntra Pl, E8 .... **114** B4
Cypress Cl, E5 .... **100** A3
Cypress Gdns, SE4 .... **185** E3
Cypress Pl, W1 .... **23** F3
Cyprus Pl, E2 .... **128** C2
Cyprus St, E2 .... **128** C2
Cyrena Rd, SE22 .... **183** F4
Cyril Mans, SW11 .... **165** F3
Cyrus St, EC1 .... **27** D2
Czar St, SE8 .... **172** A1

D

Dabin Cres, SE10 .... **172** C3
Dacca St, SE8 .... **171** F1
Dace Rd, E3 .... **116** A4
Dacre Gdns, SE13 .... **187** E2
Dacre Pk, SE13 .... **187** E1
Dacre Pl, SE13 .... **187** E1
Dacre Rd, E11 .... **103** F2
Dacre St, SW1 .... **60** A2
Daffodil St, W12 .... **133** F3
Dagenham Rd, E10 .... **101** F2
Dagmar Gdns, NW10 .... **121** D2
Dagmar Pas, N1
off Cross St **126** B1
Dagmar Rd, N4 .... **98** A1
SE5 .... **169** E3
Dagmar Ter, N1 .... **126** B1
Dagnall St, SW11 .... **165** F4
Daintry Way, E9
off Osborne Rd **115** F3
Dairy Cl, NW10 .... **120** A1
Dairy Fm Pl, SE15
off Queens Rd **170** C3
Dairyman Cl, NW2
off Claremont Rd **93** E4
Dairy Ms, SW9 .... **181** E1
Daisy Dobbins Wk, N19
off Hillrise Rd **97** E1
Daisy La, SW6 .... **178** A1
Daisy Rd, E16
off Cranberry La **131** E4
Dakin Pl, E1
off White Horse Rd **143** E1
Dakota Bldg, SE13
off Deals Gateway **172** A3
Dalberg Rd, SW2 .... **182** A2
Dalby Rd, SW18 .... **178** C2
Dalby St, NW5 .... **110** B3
Daleham Gdns, NW3 .... **109** D2
Daleham Ms, NW3 .... **109** D3
Dalehead, NW1 .... **11** E3
Dale Rd, NW5
off Grafton Rd **110** A2
SE17 .... **87** D1
Dale Row, W11
off St. Marks Rd **135** E2
Dale St, W4 .... **147** E4
Daley St, E9 .... **115** D3
Daley Thompson Way, SW8 .... **166** B4
Dalgarno Gdns, W10 .... **134** C1
Dalgarno Way, W10 .... **120** C4
Dalgleish St, E14 .... **143** E2
Daling Way, E3 .... **129** E1
Dallas Rd, NW4 .... **92** A1
Dallinger Rd, SE12 .... **187** F4
Dalling Rd, W6 .... **148** B2
Dallington Sq, EC1
off Dallington St **27** D2
Dallington St, EC1 .... **27** D2
Dalmeny Av, N7 .... **111** D1

almeny Rd, N7 .... 97 D4
almeyer Rd, NW10 .... 105 F3
alrymple Rd, SE4 .... 185 E2
ALSTON, E8 .... 114 A4
Dalston Junction 113 F3
Dalston Kingsland 113 E3
alston La, E8 .... 113 F3
alwood St, SE5 .... 88 C4
alyell Rd, SW9 .... 181 F1
amask Cres, E16
off Cranberry La 131 E4
amer Ter, SW10 .... 79 F3
ame St, N1 .... 15 E2
amien St, E1 .... 142 B2
anbury St, N1 .... 15 D2
anby St, SE15 .... 183 F1
ancer Rd, SW6 .... 163 F3
Richmond TW9 .... 174 A1
andridge Cl, SE10 .... 159 F4
anebury Av, SW15 .... 175 E4
anecroft Rd, SE24 .... 182 C3
anehurst St, SW6 .... 163 E3
anemere St, SW15 .... 176 C1
ane Pl, E3
off Roman Rd 129 F2
anes Ct, Wem. HA9
off North End Rd 90 B4
anesdale Rd, E9 .... 115 E3
anesfield, SE5 .... 76 C4
ane St, WC1 .... 37 E1
aneville Rd, SE5 .... 169 D3
aniel Bolt Cl, E14
off Uamvar St 144 B1
aniel Gdns, SE15 .... 89 E2
aniels Rd, SE15 .... 184 C1
an Leno Wk, SW6 .... 78 C3
an Mason Dr, W4 .... 161 D4
ansey Pl, W1 .... 36 A4
ante Pl, SE11 .... 63 D4
ante Rd, SE11 .... 62 C4
anube St, SW3 .... 69 D2
anvers St, SW3 .... 80 B1
aphne St, SW18 .... 178 C4
aplyn St, E1
off Hanbury St 142 A1
D'Arblay St, W1 .... 35 F3
arcy Ho, E8
off Warburton Rd 128 B1
arell Rd, Rich. TW9 ...... 174 A1
arenth Rd, N16 .... 99 F1
arfield Rd, SE4 .... 185 F3
arfield Way, W10 .... 135 D2
arfur St, SW15 .... 177 D1
arien Rd, SW11 .... 179 D1
ark Ho Wk, EC3
off Grant's Quay Wf 52 B1
arlan Rd, SW6 .... 163 F2
arley Rd, SW11 .... 179 F4
arling Rd, SE4 .... 186 A1
arling Row, E1 .... 128 B4
arnaway Pl, E14
off Abbott Rd 144 C2
arnley Ho, E14 .... 143 E2
arnley Rd, E9 .... 114 B3
arnley Ter, W11
off St. James's Gdns 135 D4
arrell Rd, SE22 .... 184 A3
arren Cl, N4 .... 97 F1
arsley Dr, SW8 .... 84 B4
artford Ho, SE1
off Longfield Est 77 F1
artford St, SE17 .... 75 F4
artmoor Wk, E14
off Charnwood Gdns 158 A3
Dartmouth Cl, W11 .... 135 F2
Dartmouth Gro, SE10 ...... 172 C3
Dartmouth Hill, SE10 ...... 172 C3
DARTMOUTH PARK, NW5 ... 96 B4
Dartmouth Pk Av, NW5 ..... 96 B4
Dartmouth Pk Hill, N19 ..... 96 B2
NW5 .... 96 B2
Dartmouth Pk Rd, NW5 .... 110 B1
Dartmouth Pl, W4 .... 161 E1
Dartmouth Rd, NW2 .... 107 D3
Dartmouth Row, SE10 ..... 172 C4
Dartmouth St, SW1 .... 60 A1
Dartmouth Ter, SE10 ...... 173 D3
Dartrey Twr, SW10
off Blantyre St 80 A2
Dartrey Wk, SW10
off Blantyre St 80 A2
Dart St, W10 .... 121 E3
Darville Rd, N16 .... 99 F4
Darwen Pl, E2
off Wharf Pl 128 B1
Darwin Ct, SE17 .... 76 B1
Darwin St, SE17 .... 64 B4
Datchelor Pl, SE5 .... 169 D3
Datchworth Ct, N4
off Queens Dr 98 C4
Date St, SE17 .... 76 A3
Daubeney Rd, E5 .... 115 E1
Daubeney Twr, SE8 .... 157 F4
Dault Rd, SW18 .... 178 C4
Davenant Rd, N19 .... 97 D3
Davenant St, E1 .... 142 A1
Davenport Ho, SE11
off Walnut Tree Wk 62 A4
Davenport Rd, SE6 .... 186 B4
Daventry St, NW1 .... 20 C4
Davern Cl, SE10 .... 159 F3
Davey Cl, N7 .... 111 F3
Davey Rd, E9 .... 116 A4
Davey St, SE15 .... 89 F1
Davidge St, SE1 .... 62 C1
David Lee Pt, E15 .... 131 E1
David Ms, W1 .... 21 F4
Davidson Gdns, SW8 .... 84 C3
David St, E15 .... 117 D3
Coll Davies Laing &
Dick Indep Coll, W1 ..... 34 B2
Davies La, E11 .... 103 E3
Davies Ms, W1 .... 34 C4
Davies St, W1 .... 34 C4
Da Vinci Lo, SE10
off Renaissance Wk 159 F2
Davis Rd, W3 .... 133 F4
Davisville Rd, W12 .... 148 A1
Dawes Ho, SE17 .... 76 A1
Dawes Rd, SW6 .... 163 E2
Dawes St, SE17 .... 76 B2
Dawlish Rd, E10 .... 102 C3
NW2 .... 107 D3
Dawn Cres, E15
off Bridge Rd 131 D1
Dawpool Rd, NW2 .... 91 F3
Dawson Pl, W2 .... 30 A4
Dawson Rd, NW2 .... 106 C2
Dawson St, E2 .... 17 F3
Daylesford Av, SW15 ...... 176 A2
Dayton Gro, SE15 .... 170 C3
Deacon Ms, N1 .... 113 D4
Deacon Rd, NW2 .... 106 A2
Deacon Way, SE17 .... 63 E4
Deal Porters Way, SE16 .... 156 C2
Deals Gateway, SE13 ...... 172 A3
Deal St, E1 .... 142 A1
Dealtry Rd, SW15 .... 176 C2
Deal Wk, SW9 .... 86 A3
Dean Bradley St, SW1 .... 60 C3
Dean Cl, E9
off Churchill Wk 114 C2
SE16
off Surrey Water Rd 143 D4
Dean Ct, SW8
off Thorncroft St 84 C3
Deancross St, E1 .... 142 C2
Deanery Ms, W1 .... 46 B2
Deanery Rd, E15 .... 117 E3
Deanery St, W1 .... 46 B2
Dean Farrar St, SW1 .... 60 A2
Deanhill Ct, SW14 .... 174 B2
Deanhill Rd, SW14 .... 174 B2
Dean Ho, E1
off Tarling St 142 C2
N16
off Stamford Hill 99 F2
Dean La, EC4
off New Fetter La 38 B2
Dean Rd, NW2 .... 106 C3
Dean Ryle St, SW1 .... 60 C4
Deans Bldgs, SE17 .... 76 A1
Deans Cl, W4 .... 160 B1
Deans Ct, EC4 .... 39 D3
Deanscroft Av, NW9 .... 90 C3
Deans La, W4
off Deans Cl 160 B1
Deans Ms, W1 .... 35 D2
Dean Stanley St, SW1 .... 60 C3
Dean St, W1 .... 36 A2
Dean's Yd, SW1 .... 60 B2
Dean Trench St, SW1 .... 60 C3
Deason St, E15
off High St 130 C1
De Barowe Ms, N5
off Leigh Rd 112 B1
De Beauvoir, N1
off Tottenham Rd 113 E3
De Beauvoir Cres, N1 ...... 127 E1
De Beauvoir Est, N1 .... 127 D1
De Beauvoir Rd, N1 .... 127 E1
De Beauvoir Sq, N1 .... 113 E4
DE BEAUVOIR TOWN, N1 ... 127 D1
Debnams Rd, SE16
off Rotherhithe
New Rd 156 C3
Decima St, SE1 .... 64 C2
Deck Cl, SE16
off Thame Rd 157 D1
De Crespigny Pk, SE5 ...... 169 D4
Deeley Rd, SW8 .... 84 A4
Deepdene Rd, SE5 .... 183 D2
Deerdale Rd, SE24 .... 182 C2
Deerhurst Rd, NW2 .... 107 D3
Dee St, E14 .... 144 C2
Defoe Av, Rich. TW9 .... 160 A2
Defoe Cl, SE16
off Vaughan St 157 F1
Defoe Ho, EC2
off The Barbican 27 E4
Defoe Pl, EC2
off The Barbican 27 F4
Defoe Rd, N16 .... 99 E3
De Gama Pl, E14
off Maritime Quay 158 A4
Dehar Cres, NW9 .... 92 A1
Dekker Rd, SE21 .... 183 E4
Delafield Ho, E1
off Christian St 142 A2
Delaford Rd, SE16 .... 156 B4
Delaford St, SW6 .... 163 E2
Delamere St, W2 .... 19 E4

Delamere Ter, W2 ... **19** D4
Delancey Pas, NW1 ... **11** D1
Delancey St, NW1 ... **10** C1
De Laune St, SE17 ... **74** C3
Delaware Rd, W9 ... **18** C2
Delawyk Cres, SE24 ... **182** C4
Delft Way, SE22
off East Dulwich Gro ... **183** E3
Delhi St, N1 ... **13** D1
Delius Gro, E15 ... **131** D2
Della Path, E5 ... **100** B4
Dell Cl, E15 ... **131** D1
Dellow St, E1 ... **142** B3
Dell's Ms, SW1 ... **71** F1
Delmare Cl, SW9 ... **181** F2
Deloraine St, SE8 ... **172** A3
Delorme St, W6 ... **163** D1
Delta Ct, NW2 ... **92** A3
Delta Ho, N1
off Nile St ... **16** A4
Delta St, E2
off Wellington Row ... **128** A3
Delverton Rd, SE17 ... **75** D3
Delvino Rd, SW6 ... **164** A3
Demeta Cl, Wem. HA9 ... **90** C4
De Morgan Rd, SW6 ... **178** B1
Dempster Rd, SW18 ... **178** C3
Denbigh Cl, W11 ... **135** F3
Denbigh Ms, SW1 ... **71** E1
Denbigh Pl, SW1 ... **71** E2
Denbigh Rd, W11 ... **135** F3
Denbigh St, SW1 ... **71** E1
Denbigh Ter, W11 ... **135** F3
Dene Cl, SE4 ... **185** E1
Denehurst Gdns, W3 ... **132** B4
Richmond TW10 ... **174** A2
Denford St, SE10
off Woolwich Rd ... **159** F4
Dengie Wk, N1
off Basire St ... **126** C1
Denholme Rd, W9 ... **121** F3
Denis Way, SW4
off Gauden Rd ... **181** D1
Denman Pl, W1
off Great Windmill St ... **48** A1
Denman Rd, SE15 ... **169** F3
Denman St, W1 ... **48** A1
Denmark Gro, N1 ... **14** A2
⇌ Denmark Hill ... 169 D4
Denmark Hill, SE5 ... **169** D3
Denmark Hill Est, SE5 ... **183** D2
Denmark Pl, E3
off Kitcat Ter ... **130** A3
WC2 ... **36** B2
Denmark Rd, NW6 ... **121** F2
SE5 ... **168** C3
Denmark St, E11
off High Rd Leytonstone ... **103** E4
WC2 ... **36** B3
Denmead Ho, SW15
off Highcliffe Dr ... **175** F4
Denne Ter, E8 ... **17** F1
Dennetts Gro, SE14
off Dennetts Rd ... **171** D4
Dennetts Rd, SE14 ... **170** C3
Denning Cl, NW8 ... **7** F4
Denning Ms, SW12 ... **180** A4
Denning Pt, E1 ... **41** E2
Denning Rd, NW3 ... **109** D1
Dennington Cl, E5
off Detmold Rd ... **100** B3
Dennington Pk Rd, NW6 ... **108** A3
Dennison Pt, E15 ... **116** C4
Denny Cres, SE11 ... **74** B1
Denny St, SE11 ... **74** B2
Densham Rd, E15 ... **131** E1
Denton, NW1
off Malden Cres ... **110** A3
Denton St, SW18 ... **178** B4
Denton Way, E5 ... **101** D4
Dents Rd, SW11 ... **179** F4
Denver Rd, N16 ... **99** E1
Denyer St, SW3 ... **69** D1
Denzil Rd, NW10 ... **105** F2
Deodar Rd, SW15 ... **177** E2
★ Department for Environment, Food & Rural Affairs (Defra), SW1 ... 48 C3
★ Department for Transport (DfT), SW1 ... 60 B4
★ Department of Health, SW1 ... 48 C4
Depot App, NW2 ... **107** D1
Depot Rd, W12 ... **134** C3
DEPTFORD, SE8 ... **157** F4
⇌ Deptford ... 171 F2
DLR Deptford Bridge ... 172 A3
Deptford Br, SE8 ... **172** A3
Deptford Bdy, SE8 ... **172** A3
Deptford Ch St, SE8 ... **172** A1
Deptford Ferry Rd, E14 ... **158** A3
Deptford Grn, SE8 ... **172** A1
Deptford High St, SE8 ... **172** A1
Deptford Strand, SE8 ... **157** F3
● Deptford Trd Est, SE8 ... 171 E1
Deptford Wf, SE8 ... **157** F3
De Quincey Ho, SW1
off Lupus St ... **71** E3
Derby Ct, E5
off Overbury St ... **115** D1
Derby Gate, SW1 ... **48** C4
Derby Ho, SE11
off Walnut Tree Wk ... **62** A4
Derby Rd, E9 ... **129** D1
SW14 ... **174** B2
Derbyshire St, E2 ... **128** A3
Derby St, W1 ... **46** B3
Dereham Pl, EC2 ... **29** D1
Derek Av, Wem. HA9 ... **104** B4
Derek Walcott Cl, SE24
off Shakespeare Rd ... **182** B2
Dericote St, E8 ... **128** A1
Dering St, W1 ... **34** C3
Dermody Gdns, SE13 ... **187** D3
Dermody Rd, SE13 ... **187** D3
Derry St, W8 ... **54** C1
Dersingham Rd, NW2 ... **93** E4
Derwent Gro, SE22 ... **183** F2
Derwent St, SE10 ... **159** E4
Derwentwater Rd, W3 ... **132** C4
Desborough Cl, W2 ... **19** D4
Desborough Ho, W14
off North End Rd ... **163** F1
Desborough St, W2 ... **18** C4
Desenfans Rd, SE21 ... **183** E4
Desford Ms, E16
off Desford Rd ... **131** E4
Desford Rd, E16 ... **131** E4
★ Design Mus, SE1 ... 53 F3
Desmond St, SE14 ... **171** E1
Despard Rd, N19 ... **96** C2
Desvignes Dr, SE13 ... **187** D4
Detmold Rd, E5 ... **100** C3
Devas St, E3 ... **130** B4
Devenay Rd, E15 ... **117** F4
Deventer Cres, SE22 ... **183** E3
De Vere Gdns, W8 ... **55** E1
Deverell St, SE1 ... **64** A3
De Vere Ms, W8 ... **55** E2
Devereux Ct, WC2 ... **38** A3
Devereux La, SW13 ... **162** B2
Devereux Rd, SW11 ... **179** F4
Devizes St, N1 ... **16** B1
Devonhurst Pl, W4
off Heathfield Ter ... **147** D4
Devonia Rd, N1 ... **15** D2
Devon Mans, SE1
off Tooley St ... **53** E4
Devonport Ms, W12
off Devonport Rd ... **134** B4
Devonport Rd, W12 ... **148** B1
Devonport St, E1 ... **142** C2
Devons Est, E3 ... **130** B3
Devonshire Cl, E15 ... **117** E1
W1 ... **22** C4
Devonshire Dr, SE10 ... **172** B2
Devonshire Gdns, W4 ... **160** C2
Devonshire Gro, SE15 ... **170** B1
Devonshire Ho, SE1
off Bath Ter ... **63** E2
Devonshire Ms, SW10
off Park Wk ... **68** A4
W4 ... **147** E4
Devonshire Ms N, W1 ... **22** C4
Devonshire Ms S, W1 ... **22** C4
Devonshire Ms W, W1 ... **22** C3
Devonshire Pas, W4 ... **147** E4
Devonshire Pl, NW2 ... **94** A4
W1 ... **22** B3
W8 ... **54** C3
Devonshire Pl Ms, W1 ... **22** B3
Devonshire Rd, W4 ... **147** E4
Devonshire Row, EC2 ... **41** D1
Devonshire Row Ms, W1 ... **23** D3
Devonshire Sq, EC2 ... **41** D2
Devonshire St, W1 ... **22** B4
W4 ... **147** E4
Devonshire Ter, W2 ... **31** F3
DLR Devons Road ... 130 B4
Devons Rd, E3 ... **144** A1
Devon St, SE15 ... **170** B1
De Walden St, W1 ... **34** B1
Dewar St, SE15 ... **184** A1
Dewberry St, E14 ... **144** C1
Dewey La, SW2
off Tulse Hill ... **182** A4
Dewey Rd, N1 ... **14** A2
Dewhurst Rd, W14 ... **149** D2
Dewsbury Ct, W4
off Chiswick Rd ... **146** C3
Dewsbury Rd, NW10 ... **106** A2
Dewsbury Ter, NW1
off Camden High St ... **124** B1
D'Eynsford Rd, SE5 ... **88** A4
Dhonan Ho, SE1
off Longfield Est ... **65** F4
Diadem Ct, W1 ... **36** A3
Dial Wk, The, W8 ... **43** D4
Diamond St, NW10 ... **105** D4
SE15 ... **89** D3
Diamond Ter, SE10 ... **172** C3
Diamond Way, SE8
off Crossfield St ... **172** A2
Diana Cl, SE8
off Staunton St ... **171** F1
Diana Ho, SW13 ... **161** F3
★ Diana Princess of Wales Mem, W2 ... 44 C4
Dibden St, N1 ... **126** B1
Dibdin Ho, W9 ... **6** C2
Dicey Av, NW2 ... **106** C2

ickens Est, SE1 ... 155 F1
SE16 ... 155 F1
ickens Ho, NW6 ... 6 A4
ickens Ms, EC1 ... 26 C4
ickenson Rd, N8 ... 97 E1
ickens Sq, SE1 ... 63 F2
ickens St, SW8 ... 166 B4
ickinson Ct, EC1
off Brewhouse Yd ... 27 D3
ieppe Cl, W14 ... 149 F4
igby Cres, N4 ... 98 C3
igby Rd, E9 ... 115 D3
igby St, E2 ... 128 C3
iggon St, E1
off Stepney Way ... 143 D1
ighton Ct, SE5 ... 87 E1
ighton Rd, SW18 ... 178 C3
ignum St, N1 ... 14 A2
igswell St, N7
off Holloway Rd ... 112 A3
ilke St, SW3 ... 69 F4
ilston Gro, SE16
off Abbeyfield Rd ... 156 C3
imes Pl, W6
off King St ... 148 B3
imsdale Dr, NW9 ... 90 C2
imson Cres, E3 ... 130 A4
ingle Gdns, E14 ... 144 A3
ingley Pl, EC1 ... 27 F1
ingley Rd, EC1 ... 27 E1
inmont St, E2
off Coate St ... 128 B2
insdale Rd, SE3 ... 173 F1
irleton Rd, E15 ... 131 F1
isbrowe Rd, W6 ... 163 E1
● Discovery Business Pk, SE16
off St. James's Rd ... 156 A2
iscovery Dock Apts E, E14 ... 158 B1
iscovery Dock Apts W, E14 ... 158 B1
iscovery Wk, E1 ... 142 B4
isney Pl, SE1 ... 51 F4
isney St, SE1 ... 51 F4
israeli Cl, W4
off Acton La ... 147 D2
israeli Gdns, SW15
off Fawe Pk Rd ... 177 F2
israeli Rd, NW10 ... 118 C2
SW15 ... 177 E2
iss St, E2 ... 17 E4
istaff La, EC4 ... 39 E4
istillery La, W6
off Fulham Palace Rd ... 148 C4
istillery Rd, W6 ... 148 C4
istin St, SE11 ... 74 A1
itch All, SE10 ... 172 B3
itchburn St, E14 ... 144 C3
ivis Way, SW15
off Dover Pk Dr ... 176 B4
ixon Clark Ct, N1
off Canonbury Rd ... 112 B3
ixon Ho, W10 ... 135 D2
ixon Rd, SE14 ... 171 E3
ixon's All, SE16 ... 156 B1
ixon Way, NW10
off Church Rd ... 105 E4
obree Av, NW10 ... 106 B4
obson Cl, NW6 ... 109 D4
oby Ct, EC4 ... 39 F4
ockers Tanner Rd, E14 ... 158 A2
ockhead, SE1 ... 65 F1
Dock Hill Av, SE16 ... 157 D1
Dockley Rd, SE16 ... 156 A2
● Dockley Rd Ind Est, SE16
off Rouel Rd ... 156 A2
Dock Rd, E16 ... 145 F3
Dock St, E1 ... 142 A3
★ Doctor Johnson's Ho, EC4 ... 38 B3
Docwra's Bldgs, N1 ... 113 E3
Dodd Ho, SE16
off Rennie Est ... 156 B3
Doddington Gro, SE17 ... 74 C4
Doddington Pl, SE17 ... 74 C4
Dodson St, SE1 ... 62 B1
Dod St, E14 ... 143 F2
Dog Kennel Hill, SE22 ... 183 E1
Dog Kennel Hill Est, SE22 ... 183 E1
Dog La, NW10 ... 105 E1
Dolben St, SE1 ... 50 C3
Dolby Rd, SW6 ... 163 F4
Dolland St, SE11 ... 73 F3
DOLLIS HILL, NW2 ... 92 B4
⊖ Dollis Hill ... 106 A2
Dollis Hill Av, NW2 ... 92 B4
Dollis Hill La, NW2 ... 92 B4
Dolman Rd, W4 ... 147 D3
Dolman St, SW4 ... 181 F2
Dolphin Cl, SE16
off Kinburn St ... 157 D1
Dolphin Ho, SW18
off Smugglers Way ... 178 B2
Dolphin La, E14 ... 144 B3
Dolphin Sq, SW1 ... 71 F3
W4 ... 161 E2
Dolphin Twr, SE8
off Abinger Gro ... 171 F1
Dombey St, WC1 ... 25 E4
Domett Cl, SE5 ... 183 D2
Domfe Pl, E5
off Rushmore Rd ... 114 C1
Domingo St, EC1 ... 27 E2
Dominion St, EC2 ... 28 B4
★ Dominion Thea, W1 ... 36 B2
Donaldson Rd, NW6 ... 121 F1
Donato Dr, SE15 ... 88 C1
Donegal St, N1 ... 13 F3
Doneraile St, SW6 ... 163 D4
Dongola Rd, E1 ... 143 E1
Donkin Ho, SE16
off Rennie Est ... 156 B3
Donne Ct, SE24 ... 182 C4
Donne Pl, SW3 ... 57 D4
Donnington Ct, NW10 ... 106 B4
Donnington Rd, NW10 ... 106 B4
Donovan Ct, SW10
off Drayton Gdns ... 68 A3
Don Phelan Cl, SE5 ... 88 B4
Doon St, SE1 ... 50 A3
Dorando Cl, W12 ... 134 B3
Doran Wk, E15 ... 116 C4
Dora St, E14 ... 143 F2
Dora Way, SW9 ... 168 A4
Dorchester Ct, SE24 ... 182 C3
Dorchester Dr, SE24 ... 182 C3
Dorchester Gro, W4 ... 147 E4
Dorchester Ho, Rich. TW9
off Strand Dr ... 160 B2
Dordrecht Rd, W3 ... 133 E4
Doreen Av, NW9 ... 91 D2
Doria Rd, SW6 ... 163 F4
Doric Way, NW1 ... 12 A4
Dorking Cl, SE8 ... 171 F1
Dorman Wk, NW10 ... 104 C2
Dorman Way, NW8 ... 123 D1
● Dorma Trd Pk, E10 ... 101 D2
Dormay St, SW18 ... 178 B3
Dormer Cl, E15 ... 117 F3
Dorncliffe Rd, SW6 ... 163 E4
Dorney, NW3 ... 109 E4
Dornfell St, NW6 ... 107 F2
Dorothy Rd, SW11 ... 179 F1
Dorrell Pl, SW9
off Brixton Rd ... 182 A2
Dorrington Pt, E3
off Bromley High St ... 130 B3
Dorrington St, EC1 ... 26 A4
Dorrit St, SE1 ... 51 F4
Dors Cl, NW9 ... 91 D2
Dorset Bldgs, EC4 ... 38 C3
Dorset Cl, NW1 ... 21 E4
Dorset Est, E2 ... 17 F4
Dorset Ms, SW1 ... 58 C2
Dorset Pl, E15 ... 117 D3
Dorset Ri, EC4 ... 38 C3
Dorset Rd, SW8 ... 85 D2
Dorset Sq, NW1 ... 21 E3
Dorset St, W1 ... 33 F1
Dorton Cl, SE15 ... 89 D3
Dorville Cres, W6 ... 148 B2
Dorville Rd, SE12 ... 187 F3
Doughty Ms, WC1 ... 25 E3
Doughty St, WC1 ... 25 E2
Douglas Ms, NW2 ... 93 E4
Douglas Path, E14
off Manchester Rd ... 158 C4
Douglas Rd, N1 ... 112 C4
NW6 ... 121 F1
Douglas St, SW1 ... 72 A1
Douglas Way, SE8 ... 171 F2
Doulton Ho, SE11
off Lambeth Wk ... 61 F3
Doulton Ms, NW6
off Dresden Cl ... 108 B3
Douro Pl, W8 ... 55 D2
Douro St, E3 ... 130 A2
Douthwaite Sq, E1
off Torrington Pl ... 142 A4
Dovecote Gdns, SW14
off Avondale Rd ... 175 D1
Dovecote Ho, SE16
off Canada St ... 157 D1
Dove Ct, EC2 ... 40 A3
Dovedale Rd, SE22 ... 184 B3
Dovehouse St, SW3 ... 68 C2
Dove Ms, SW5 ... 67 E1
Dover Cl, NW2
off Brent Ter ... 93 D3
Dovercourt Est, N1 ... 113 D3
Dovercourt Rd, SE22 ... 183 E4
Doverfield Rd, SW2 ... 181 E4
Dover Flats, SE1 ... 77 D1
Dover Ho Rd, SW15 ... 176 A2
Dove Rd, N1 ... 113 D3
Dove Row, E2 ... 128 A1
Dover Pk Dr, SW15 ... 176 B4
Dover St, W1 ... 47 D1
Dover Yd, W1 ... 47 D2
Doves Yd, N1 ... 14 B1
Dovet Ct, SW8 ... 85 E4
Doveton St, E1
off Malcolm Rd ... 128 C4
Dove Wk, SW1 ... 70 A2
Dowdeswell Cl, SW15 ... 175 E2
Dowdney Cl, NW5 ... 110 C2
Dowgate Hill, EC4 ... 40 A4
Dowland St, W10 ... 121 E2
Dowlas Est, SE5 ... 88 C2

Dowlas St, SE5 **88** C2
Downbury Ms, SW18
off Merton Rd **178** A4
Downers Cotts, SW4
off Old Town **180** C2
Downfield Cl, W9 **18** C3
Downham Rd, N1 **113** D4
Downing St, SW1 **48** C4
Down Pl, W6 **148** B3
Downsbury Ms, SW18
off Merton Rd **178** A3
Downsell Rd, E15 **116** C1
Downshire Hill, NW3 **109** D1
Downside Cres, NW3 **109** E2
Downs La, E5
off Downs Rd **114** B1
Downs Pk Rd, E5 **114** A2
E8 **113** F2
Downs Rd, E5 **114** A1
Down St, W1 **46** C3
Down St Ms, W1 **46** C3
Downtown Rd, SE16 **157** E1
Dowrey St, N1
off Richmond Av **126** A1
Dowson Cl, SE5 **183** D2
Doyce St, SE1 **51** E4
Doyle Gdns, NW10 **120** A1
D'Oyley St, SW1 **58** A4
Doynton St, N19 **96** B3
Draco Gate, SW15
off Erpingham Rd **176** C1
Draco St, SE17 **75** E4
Dragon Rd, SE15 **88** C1
Dragoon Rd, SE8 **157** F4
Dragor Rd, NW10 **118** C4
Drake Cl, SE16
off Middleton Dr **157** D1
Drake Ct, W12 **148** C1
Drakefell Rd, SE4 **171** D4
SE14 **171** D4
Drake Ho, SW8
off St. George Wf **72** C3
Drakeley Ct, N5 **112** B1
Drake Rd, SE4 **186** A1
Drakes Ctyd, NW6 **107** F4
Drake St, WC1 **37** E1
Draper Ho, SE1 **63** D4
Draper Pl, N1
off Dagmar Ter **126** B1
Drapers' Ct, SW11 **82** B4
Drapers Rd, E15 **117** D1
Drappers Way, SE16
off St. James's Rd **156** A3
Drawdock Rd, SE10 **145** D4
Draycott Av, SW3 **57** D4
Draycott Cl, NW2 **93** D4
SE5 **88** A3
Draycott Ms, SW6
off New Kings Rd **163** F4
Draycott Pl, SW3 **69** E1
Draycott Ter, SW3 **57** F4
Drayford Cl, W9 **121** F4
Dray Gdns, SW2 **181** F3
Draymans Ms, SE15
off Chadwick Rd **169** F4
Drayson Ms, W8 **54** B1
Drayton Gdns, SW10 **67** F2
⇌ Drayton Park 112 A2
Drayton Pk, N5 **112** A2
Drayton Pk Ms, N5
off Drayton Pk **112** A2
Drayton Rd, E11 **103** D2
NW10 **119** F1
Dresden Cl, NW6 **108** B3
Dresden Ho, SE11
off Lambeth Wk **61** F4
Dresden Rd, N19 **96** C2
Dressington Av, SE4 **186** A4
Driffield Rd, E3 **129** E2
Drive, The, NW10
off Longstone Av **119** F1
NW11 **93** E1
SW6 *off Fulham Rd* **163** E4
W3 **132** C2
Wembley HA9 **90** C3
Dromore Rd, SW15 **177** E4
Droop St, W10 **121** E4
Drovers Pl, SE15 **170** B2
Drovers Way, N7 **111** E3
Druce Rd, SE21 **183** E4
Druid St, SE1 **53** D4
Drummond Cres, NW1 **12** A4
Drummond Gate, SW1 **72** B2
Drummond Rd, SE16 **156** B2
Drummond St, NW1 **23** E2
Drum St, E1 **41** F2
Drury La, WC2 **37** D3
Drury Way, NW10 **105** D2
● Drury Way Ind Est, NW10 104 C2
Dryad St, SW15 **177** D1
Dryburgh Rd, SW15 **176** B1
Dryden Cl, SW4 **181** D3
Dryden Ct, SE11 **74** B1
Dryden St, WC2 **37** D3
Dryfield Cl, NW10 **104** C3
Dryfield Wk, SE8
off New King St **172** A1
Drysdale Pl, N1 **17** D4
Drysdale St, N1 **29** D1
Dublin Av, E8 **128** A1
Ducal St, E2 **29** F1
Du Cane Rd, W12 **133** F2
Duchess Ms, W1 **35** D1
Duchess of Bedford's Wk, W8 **54** A1
Duchess St, W1 **35** D1
Duchy Pl, SE1 **50** B2
Duchy St, SE1 **50** B2
Ducie St, SW4 **181** F2
Duckett St, E1 **129** D4
Duck La, W1 **36** A3
Du Cros Rd, W3
off The Vale **133** E4
Dudden Hill La, NW10 **105** F1
Dudley Ho, W2
off North Wf Rd **32** A1
Dudley Ms, SW2
off Bascombe St **182** A4
Dudley Rd, NW6 **121** E2
Dudley St, W2 **32** A1
Dudlington Rd, E5 **100** C3
Dudmaston Ms, SW3 **68** B2
Dudrich Ms, SE22 **183** F3
Duffell Ho, SE11 **73** F2
Dufferin Av, EC1 **28** A3
Dufferin St, EC1 **27** F3
Duff St, E14 **144** B2
Dufour's Pl, W1 **35** F3
Dugard Way, SE11 **62** C4
Dugolly Av, Wem. HA9 **90** B4
Duke Humphrey Rd, SE3 **173** E3
Duke of Wellington Pl, SW1 **46** B4
Duke of York Sq, SW3 **69** F1
Duke of York St, SW1 **47** F2
Duke Rd, W4 **147** D4
Dukes Av, W4 **147** D4
Dukes Gate, W4
off Acton La **146** C3
Dukes Head Yd, N6
off Highgate High St **96** B2
Duke Shore Pl, E14
off Narrow St **143** F3
Duke Shore Wf, E14
off Narrow St **143** F3
Dukes La, W8 **42** B4
Duke's Meadows, W4 **161** D3
Duke's Ms, W1 **34** B2
Dukes Pl, EC3 **41** D3
Dukes Rd, W3 **132** A1
Duke's Rd, WC1 **24** B1
Duke St, SW1 **47** F2
W1 **34** B2
Duke St Hill, SE1 **52** B2
Duke's Yd, W1 **34** B4
Dulas St, N4 **97** F2
Dulford St, W11 **135** E3
Dulka Rd, SW11 **179** F3
H Dulwich Comm Hosp, SE22 183 E2
Dulwich Lawn Cl, SE22
off Colwell Rd **183** F3
Dulwich Ri Gdns, SE22
off Lordship La **183** F3
Dulwich Rd, SE24 **182** A3
Dulwich Village, SE21 **183** E4
Dumbarton Rd, SW2 **181** E4
Dumont Rd, N16 **99** E4
Dumpton Pl, NW1
off Gloucester Av **110** A4
Dunboyne Rd, NW3 **109** F2
Dunbridge Ho, SW15
off Highcliffe Dr **175** F4
Dunbridge St, E2 **128** A4
Duncan Gro, W3 **133** E2
Duncannon St, WC2 **48** C1
Duncan Rd, E8 **128** B1
Duncan St, N1 **14** C2
Duncan Ter, N1 **14** C3
Dunch St, E1
off Watney St **142** B2
Duncombe Rd, N19 **97** D2
Duncrievie Rd, SE13 **187** D4
Dundalk Rd, SE4 **185** E1
Dundas Rd, SE15 **170** C4
Dundee Ho, W9 **7** E4
Dundee St, E1 **142** B4
Dundee Wf, E14
off Three Colt St **143** F3
Dundonald Rd, NW10 **121** D1
Dunedin Rd, E10 **102** B4
Dunelm St, E1 **143** D2
Dunford Rd, N7 **111** F1
Dungarvan Av, SW15 **176** A2
Dunlace Rd, E5 **114** C1
Dunloe St, E2 **17** E3
Dunlop Pl, SE16 **65** F3
Dunmore Pt, E2 **29** E1
Dunmore Rd, NW6 **121** E1
Dunmow Rd, E15 **117** D1
Dunmow Wk, N1
off Popham St **126** C1
Dunnage Cres, SE16
off Plough Way **157** E3
Dunns Pas, WC1 **37** D2
Dunn St, E8 **113** F2
Dunollie Pl, NW5
off Dunollie Rd **110** C2
Dunollie Rd, NW5 **110** C2
Dunraven Rd, W12 **134** A4
Dunraven St, W1 **33** F4

Dunsany Rd, W14 ....149 D2
Dunsford Way, SW15 ......176 B4
Dunsmure Rd, N16 ....99 E2
Dunstable Ms, W1 ....22 B4
Dunstan Ho, E1
off Stepney Grn 142 C1
Dunstan Rd, NW11 ....93 F2
Dunstans Gro, SE22 ....184 B4
Dunster Ct, EC3 ....40 C4
Dunster Dr, NW9 ....90 C2
Dunster Gdns, NW6 ....107 F4
Dunsterville Way, SE1 ....64 B1
Dunston Rd, E8 ....17 E1
SW11 ....166 A4
Dunston St, E8 ....127 F1
Dunton Rd, E10 ....102 B1
SE1 ....77 E2
Dunworth Ms, W11
off Portobello Rd 135 F2
Duplex Ride, SW1 ....57 F1
Durand Gdns, SW9 ....85 F4
Durands Wk, SE16 ....157 F1
Durand Way, NW10 ....104 C4
Durant St, E2 ....128 A2
Durban Rd, E15 ....131 E3
Durfey Pl, SE5 ....88 B2
Durham Ho St, WC2 ....49 D1
Durham Pl, SW3 ....69 E3
Durham Rd, E16 ....131 E4
N7 ....97 F3
Durham Row, E1 ....143 E1
Durham St, SE11 ....73 E3
Durham Ter, W2 ....30 C2
Durham Yd, E2
off Teesdale St 128 B3
Durley Rd, N16 ....99 E1
Durlston Rd, E5 ....100 A3
Durnford St, SE10
off Greenwich Ch St 172 C1
Durrell Rd, SW6 ....163 F3
Durrington Rd, E5 ....115 E1
Durrington Twr, SW8
off Westbury St 166 C4
Durward St, E1 ....142 B1
Durweston Ms, W1 ....21 F4
Durweston St, W1 ....21 F4
Dutch Yd, SW18
off Wandsworth High St 178 A3
Dutton St, SE10 ....172 C3
Dwight Ct, SW6
off Burlington Rd 163 E4
Dye Ho La, E3 ....130 A1
Dyer's Bldgs, EC1 ....38 A1
Dyers Hall Rd, E11 ....103 E2
Dyers La, SW15 ....176 B2
Dylan Rd, SE24 ....182 B2
Dylways, SE5 ....183 D2
Dymock St, SW6 ....178 B1
Dyne Rd, NW6 ....107 F4
Dynevor Rd, N16 ....99 E4
Dynham Rd, NW6 ....108 A4
Dyott St, WC1 ....36 C2
Dysart St, EC2 ....28 B3
Dyson Rd, E15 ....117 F3

E

Eade Rd, N4 ....98 C1
Eagle Cl, SE16
off Varcoe Rd 156 C4
Eagle Ct, EC1 ....26 C4
Eagle Hts, SW11
off Bramlands Cl 179 E1
Eagle Ho Ms, SW4
off Narbonne Av 180 C3
Eagle Lo, NW11 ....93 F1
Eagle Ms, N1
off Tottenham Rd 113 E3
Eagle Pl, SW1 ....47 F1
SW7 ....67 F2
Eagle St, WC1 ....37 E1
Eagle Wf Rd, N1 ....15 F2
Eagling Cl, E3
off Rounton Rd 130 A3
Coll Ealing City Learning Cen, W3
off Gunnersbury La 146 A1
Eamont St, NW8 ....8 C2
Eardley Cres, SW5 ....66 B3
Earldom Rd, SW15 ....176 C2
Earlham Gro, E7 ....117 F2
Earlham St, WC2 ....36 B3
Earl Rd, SW14 ....174 C2
EARLS COURT, SW5 ....149 F4
Earls Court 66 B1
Earls Court Exhib Cen, SW5 ....66 A2
Earls Ct Gdns, SW5 ....66 C1
Earls Ct Rd, SW5 ....54 B4
W8 ....54 B4
Earls Ct Sq, SW5 ....66 C2
Earlsferry Way, N1 ....111 F4
Earls Ho, Rich. TW9
off Strand Dr 160 B2
Earlsmead Rd, NW10 ......120 C2
Earls Ter, W8 ....149 F2
Earlsthorpe Ms, SW12 .....180 A4
Earlstoke St, EC1 ....14 C4
Earlston Gro, E9 ....128 B1
Earl St, EC2 ....28 C4
Earls Wk, W8 ....54 A3
Earlswood St, SE10 ....159 E4
Early Ms, NW1
off Arlington Rd 124 B1
Earnshaw St, WC2 ....36 B2
Earsby St, W14 ....149 E3
Easley's Ms, W1 ....34 B2
East 10 Enterprise Pk, E10
off Argall Way 101 E2
EAST ACTON, W3 ....133 D4
East Acton 133 F2
East Acton La, W3 ....133 E3
East Arbour St, E1 ....143 D2
East Bk, N16 ....99 E1
Eastbourne Av, W3 ....133 D2
Eastbourne Gdns, SW14 ....174 C1
Eastbourne Ms, W2 ....31 F2
Eastbourne Rd, E15 ....131 E1
W4 ....160 C1
Eastbourne Ter, W2 ....31 F2
Eastbury Gro, W4 ....147 E4
Eastbury Ter, E1 ....129 D4
Eastcastle St, W1 ....35 E2
Eastcheap, EC3 ....40 B4
East Churchfield Rd, W3 ....133 D4
East Cl, W5 ....118 A4
Eastcote St, SW9 ....167 F4
East Cross Route, E3 ....115 F4
E9 ....115 F4
Eastdown Pk, SE13 ....187 D2
EAST DULWICH, SE22 ......184 A4
East Dulwich 183 E2
East Dulwich Gro, SE22 ....183 E4
East Dulwich Rd, SE15 .....183 F2
SE22 ....183 F2
Eastern Rd, SE4 ....186 A2
East Ferry Rd, E14 ....158 B2
Eastfields Av, SW18 ....178 A2
Eastfields Rd, W3 ....132 C1
Eastfield St, E14 ....143 E1
Eastgate Business Pk, E10 ....101 E2
East Harding St, EC4 ....38 B2
East Heath Rd, NW3 ....95 D4
East Hill, SW18 ....178 B3
Wembley HA9 ....90 A3
DLR East India 145 D3
East India Dock Rd, E14 ....144 A2
Eastlake Ho, NW8
off Frampton St 20 B3
Eastlake Rd, SE5 ....168 B4
Eastlands Cres, SE21 ......183 F4
East La, SE16 ....156 A1
Eastlea Ms, E16
off Desford Rd 131 E4
Eastleigh Cl, NW2 ....91 E4
H Eastman Dental Hosp, WC1 ....25 E1
Eastman Rd, W3 ....133 D4
East Mt St, E1 ....142 B1
Eastney St, SE10 ....159 D4
Easton St, WC1 ....26 A1
East Parkside, SE10 ....159 E1
East Pas, EC1 ....27 D4
East Pier, E1
off Wapping High St 142 B4
East Pt, SE1
off Avondale Sq 156 A4
East Poultry Av, EC1 ....38 C1
East Putney 177 E3
East Rd, N1 ....28 A1
SW3 ....70 A3
East Row, W10 ....121 E4
EAST SHEEN, SW14 ....175 D2
East Sheen Av, SW14 ......175 D2
Eastside Ms, E3 ....130 A2
East Smithfield, E1 ....53 F1
East St, SE17 ....75 F2
East Surrey Gro, SE15 ....89 E3
East Tenter St, E1 ....41 F3
East Vale, W3
off The Vale 133 F4
Eastway, E9 ....115 F3
Eastwood Cl, N7
off Eden Gro 112 A2
Eaton Cl, SW1 ....70 A1
Eaton Dr, SW9 ....182 B2
Eaton Gate, SW1 ....58 A4
Eaton Ho, E14
off Westferry Circ 143 F3
Eaton La, SW1 ....59 D3
Eaton Ms N, SW1 ....58 A4
Eaton Ms S, SW1 ....58 B4
Eaton Ms W, SW1 ....58 B4
Eaton Pl, SW1 ....58 A3
Eaton Row, SW1 ....58 C2
Eaton Sq, SW1 ....58 C2
Eaton Ter, SW1 ....58 A4
Eaton Ter Ms, SW1 ....58 A4
Ebbett Ct, W3
off Victoria Rd 133 D1
Ebbisham Dr, SW8 ....73 E4
Ebbsfleet Rd, NW2 ....107 E2
Ebenezer Ho, SE11 ....74 B1
Ebenezer St, N1 ....16 A4
Ebley Cl, SE15 ....89 E1
Ebner St, SW18 ....178 B3
Ebor St, E1 ....29 E2
Eburne Rd, N7 ....97 E4
Ebury Br, SW1 ....70 C2
Ebury Br Est, SW1 ....70 C2

Ebury Br Rd, SW1 .... **70** B3
Ebury Ms, SW1 .... **58** B4
Ebury Ms E, SW1 .... **58** C4
Ebury Sq, SW1 .... **70** B1
Ebury St, SW1 .... **58** C4
Ecclesbourne Rd, N1 .... **112** C4
Eccles Rd, SW11 .... **179** F2
Eccleston Br, SW1 .... **59** D4
Eccleston Ms, SW1 .... **58** B3
Eccleston Pl, SW1 .... **58** C4
Eccleston Sq, SW1 .... **71** D1
Eccleston Sq Ms, SW1 .... **71** E1
Eccleston St, SW1 .... **58** C3
Eckford St, N1 .... **14** A2
Eckstein Rd, SW11 .... **179** E2
Edbrooke Rd, W9 .... **18** A2
Eddiscombe Rd, SW6 .... **163** F4
Eddystone Rd, SE4 .... **185** E3
Eddystone Twr, SE8 .... **157** E3
Edenbridge Cl, SE16
off Masters Dr **156** B4
Edenbridge Rd, E9 .... **115** D4
Eden Cl, NW3 .... **94** A3
W8 .... **54** B2
Eden Gro, N7 .... **111** F2
NW10
off St. Andrews Rd **106** B3
Edenham Way, W10
off Elkstone Rd **135** F1
Eden Ho, SE16
off Canada St **157** D1
Edenhurst Av, SW6 .... **177** F1
Edensor Gdns, W4 .... **161** E2
Edensor Rd, W4 .... **161** E2
Edenvale St, SW6 .... **164** B4
Eden Way, E3
off Old Ford Rd **129** F1
Edgar Kail Way, SE22 .... **183** E2
Edgarley Ter, SW6 .... **163** E3
Edgar Rd, E3 .... **130** B3
Edgar Wallace Cl, SE15 .... **89** D2
● Edge Business Cen,
NW2 .... **92** B3
Edgecote Cl, W3
off Cheltenham Pl **132** C4
Edgeley La, SW4
off Edgeley Rd **181** D1
Edgeley Rd, SW4 .... **181** D1
Edgel St, SW18
off Ferrier St **178** B2
Edge St, W8 .... **42** B2
Edgson Ho, SW1
off Ebury Br Rd **70** C2
⊖ Edgware Road **32** C1
Edgware Rd, NW2 .... **92** B2
W2 .... **33** D2
Edgware Rd Sub, W2
off Edgware Rd **32** C1
Edinburgh Cl, E2
off Russia La **128** C2
Edinburgh Gate, SW1 .... **45** E4
Edinburgh Ho, W9 .... **7** D4
Edison Ct, SE10
off Greenroof Way **159** F2
Edis St, NW1 .... **124** A1
Edith Cavell Cl, N19
off Hillrise Rd **97** E1
Edith Gro, SW10 .... **79** E1
Edithna St, SW9 .... **181** E1
Edith Rd, E15
off Chandos Rd **117** D2
W14 .... **149** E3
Edith Row, SW6 .... **79** D4
Edith St, E2 .... **128** A2
Edith Summerskill Ho, SW6
off Clem Attlee Ct **163** F2
Edith Ter, SW10 .... **79** E2
Edith Vil, SW15
off Bective Rd **177** E2
W14 .... **149** F3
Edith Yd, SW10 .... **79** F2
Edmeston Cl, E9 .... **115** E3
Edmund Halley Way, SE10 .... **159** E1
Edmund St, SE5 .... **88** A2
Edna St, SW11 .... **165** E3
Edrich Ho, SW4 .... **167** E3
Edric Ho, SW1
off Page St **60** B4
Edric Rd, SE14 .... **171** D2
Edward Cl, NW2 .... **107** D1
Edwardes Pl, W8
off Edwardes Sq **149** F2
Edwardes Sq, W8 .... **54** A2
Edward Ms, NW1 .... **11** D3
Edward Pl, SE8 .... **171** F1
Edwards Cotts, N1
off Compton Av **112** B3
Edwards La, N16 .... **99** D3
Edwards Ms, N1 .... **112** A4
W1 .... **34** A3
Edward Sq, N1 .... **13** E1
SE16
off Rotherhithe St **143** E4
Edward St, SE8 .... **171** F1
SE14 .... **171** E2
Edward's Way, SE4
off Adelaide Av **186** A3
Edward Temme Av, E15 .... **117** F4
Edwin Hall Pl, SE13
off Hither Grn La **187** D4
Edwin's Mead, E9
off Lindisfarne Way **115** E1
Edwin St, E1 .... **128** C4
Edwyn Ho, SW18
off Neville Gill Cl **178** B4
Eel Brook Cl, SW6 .... **78** C4
Eel Brook Studios, SW6 .... **78** B3
Effie Pl, SW6 .... **78** B3
Effie Rd, SW6 .... **78** B3
Effingham Rd, SE12 .... **187** E3
Effra Par, SW2 .... **182** A3
Effra Rd, SW2 .... **182** A2
Egbert St, NW1 .... **124** A1
Egbury Ho, SW15
off Tangley Gro **175** F4
Egeremont Rd, SE13 .... **172** B4
Egerton Cres, SW3 .... **57** D4
Egerton Dr, SE10 .... **172** B3
Egerton Gdns, NW10 .... **120** C1
SW3 .... **56** C3
Egerton Gdns Ms, SW3 .... **57** D3
Egerton Pl, SW3 .... **57** D3
Egerton Rd, N16 .... **99** F1
Egerton Ter, SW3 .... **57** D3
Eglantine Rd, SW18 .... **178** C3
Eglington Ct, SE17 .... **75** E4
Egliston Ms, SW15 .... **176** C1
Egliston Rd, SW15 .... **176** C1
Eglon Ms, NW1
off Berkley Rd **109** F4
Egmont St, SE14 .... **171** D2
Egremont Ho, SE13
off Conington Rd **172** B4
Eider Cl, E7 .... **117** F2
Elaine Gro, NW5 .... **110** A2
Elam Cl, SE5 .... **168** B4
Elam St, SE5 .... **168** B4
Eland Rd, SW11 .... **179** F1
Elba Pl, SE17 .... **63** F4
Elbe St, SW6 .... **164** C4
Elcho St, SW11 .... **80** C3
Elcot Av, SE15 .... **170** B2
Elderfield Rd, E5 .... **114** C1
Elderflower Way, E15 .... **117** E4
Elder St, E1 .... **29** E4
Elder Wk, N1
off Essex Rd **126** B1
SE13
off Bankside Av **186** C1
Eldon Gro, NW3 .... **109** D2
Eldon Rd, W8 .... **55** D3
Eldon St, EC2 .... **40** B1
Eldon Way, NW10 .... **118** B2
Eleanor Cl, SE16 .... **157** D1
Eleanor Gro, SW13 .... **175** E1
Eleanor Rd, E8 .... **114** B3
E15 .... **117** F3
Eleanor St, E3 .... **130** A3
● Electra Business Pk,
E16 .... **145** D1
Electric Av, SW9 .... **182** A2
Electric La, SW9 .... **182** A2
Elektron Ho, E14
off Blackwall Way **145** D3
⇌ Elephant & Castle **63** E4
⊖ Elephant & Castle **63** E4
Elephant & Castle, SE1 .... **63** D3
🔒 Elephant & Castle
Shop Cen, SE1
off Elephant & Castle **63** E4
Elephant La, SE16 .... **156** C1
Elephant Rd, SE17 .... **63** E4
Elfindale Rd, SE24 .... **182** C3
Elfort Rd, N5 .... **112** A1
Elf Row, E1 .... **142** C3
Elgar Av, NW10 .... **105** D3
Elgar Cl, SE8
off Comet St **172** A2
Elgar St, SE16 .... **157** E2
Elgin Av, W9 .... **18** C1
W12 .... **148** A1
Elgin Cl, W12 .... **148** B1
Elgin Cres, W11 .... **135** F2
Elgin Ms, W11
off Ladbroke Gro **135** E2
Elgin Ms N, W9 .... **7** D4
Elgin Ms S, W9 .... **7** D4
Elgood Cl, W11
off Avondale Pk Rd **135** E3
Elham Ho, E5
off Pembury Rd **114** B2
Elia Ms, N1 .... **14** C3
Elias Pl, SW8 .... **86** A1
Elia St, N1 .... **14** C3
Elim Est, SE1 .... **64** C2
Elim St, SE1 .... **64** B2
Elim Way, E13 .... **131** F3
Eliot Cotts, SE3
off Eliot Pl **173** E4
Eliot Gdns, SW15 .... **176** A2
Eliot Hill, SE13 .... **172** C4
Eliot Ms, NW8 .... **7** F3
Eliot Pk, SE13 .... **186** C1
Eliot Pl, SE3 .... **173** E4
Eliot Vale, SE3 .... **173** D4
Elizabeth Av, N1 .... **112** C4
Elizabeth Br, SW1 .... **70** C1
Elizabeth Cl, E14
off Grundy St **144** B2
W9 .... **19** F2
Elizabeth Ct, SW1 .... **60** B3
Elizabeth Est, SE17 .... **76** A4

Elizabeth Fry Rd, E8
off Lamb La **114** B4
Elizabeth Gdns, W3 **133** F4
Elizabeth Ms, NW3 **109** E3
Elizabeth Sq, SE16
off Rotherhithe St **143** E3
Elizabeth St, SW1 **58** B4
Elkington Pt, SE11 **74** A1
Elkstone Rd, W10 **135** F1
Ellaline Rd, W6 **163** D1
Ella Ms, NW3
off Cressy Rd **109** F2
Elland Rd, SE15 **184** C2
Ella Rd, N8 **97** E1
Ellenborough Pl,
SW15 **176** A2
Ellen St, E1 **142** A2
Ellen Wilkinson Ho, E2
off Usk St **129** D3
Ellerby St, SW6 **163** D3
Ellerdale Cl, NW3
off Ellerdale Rd **108** C1
Ellerdale Rd, NW3 **108** C2
Ellerdale St, SE13 **186** B2
Ellerslie Gdns, NW10 **120** A1
Ellerslie Rd, W12 **134** B4
Ellerslie Sq Ind Est,
SW2 181 E3
Ellerton, NW6
off Mill La **107** F2
Ellerton Rd, SW13 **162** A3
Ellery St, SE15 **170** B4
Ellesmere Rd, E3 **129** E2
NW10 **106** A2
W4 **161** D1
Ellesmere St, E14 **144** B2
Ellingfort Rd, E8 **114** B4
Ellingham Rd, E15 **117** D1
W12 **148** A1
Ellington Ho, SE1 **63** F2
Ellington St, N7 **112** A3
Elliot Cl, E15 **117** E4
Elliott Rd, SW9 **86** C3
W4 **147** E3
Elliott's Pl, N1 **15** D1
Elliott Sq, NW3 **109** E4
Elliotts Row, SE11 **62** C4
Ellis Cl, NW10
off High Rd **106** B3
Ellison Ho, SE13
off Lewisham Rd **172** C4
Ellison Rd, SW13 **161** F4
Ellis St, SW1 **57** F4
Ellsworth St, E2 **128** B3
Ellwood Ct, W9 **18** C3
Elm Bk Gdns, SW13 **161** E4
Elmbridge Wk, E8
off Wilman Gro **114** A4
Elm Cl, N19 **96** C3
Elm Ct, EC4 **38** A4
Elmcroft Av, NW11 **93** F1
Elmcroft Cres, NW11 **93** E1
Elmcroft St, E5 **114** C1
Elmfield Way, W9 **18** A4
Elm Friars Wk, NW1 **111** D4
Elm Grn, W3 **133** E2
Elmgreen Cl, E15
off Church St N **131** E1
Elm Gro, NW2 **107** D1
SE15 **169** F4
Elm Gro Rd, SW13 **162** A4
Elmhurst Mans, SW4
off Edgeley Rd **181** D1
Elmhurst St, SW4 **181** D1
Elmhurst Vil, SE15
off Cheltenham Rd **184** C2
Elmington Est, SE5 **88** B2
Elmington Rd, SE5 **88** A4
Elmira St, SE13 **186** B1
Elmore Rd, E11 **102** C4
Elmore St, N1 **112** C4
Elm Pk, SW2 **181** F4
Elm Pk Gdns, SW10 **68** A3
Elm Pk La, SW3 **68** A3
Elm Pk Mans, SW10 **67** F4
Elm Pk Rd, E10 **101** E2
SW3 **68** A4
Elm Pl, SW7 **68** A2
Elm Quay Ct, SW8 **72** A4
Elm Rd, E7 **117** F3
E11 **103** D3
SW14 **174** C1
Elm Row, NW3 **94** C4
Elms, The, SW13 **175** F1
Elms Cres, SW4 **180** C4
Elmshaw Rd, SW15 **176** A3
Elmside Rd, Wem. HA9 **90** A4
Elmslie Pt, E3 **143** F1
Elms Ms, W2 **32** A4
Elms Rd, SW4 **180** C3
Elmstone Rd, SW6 **78** A4
Elm St, WC1 **25** F3
Elm Ter, NW2 **94** A4
Elm Tree Cl, NW8 **8** A4
Elm Tree Rd, NW8 **8** A4
Elm Wk, NW3 **94** A3
Elm Way, NW10 **105** E1
Elmwood Ct, SW11 **82** C4
Elmwood Rd, SE24 **183** D3
W4 **160** C1
Elnathan Ms, W9 **19** D3
Elphinstone St, N5 **112** B1
Elrington Rd, E8 **114** A3
Elsa St, E1 **143** E1
Elsdale St, E9 **114** C3
Elsden Ms, E2
off Old Ford Rd **128** C2
Elsham Rd, E11 **103** E4
W14 **149** E1
Elsham Ter, W14 **149** E1
Elsiemaud Rd, SE4 **185** F3
Elsie Rd, SE22 **183** F2
Elsinore Gdns, NW2 **93** E4
Elsinore Way, Rich. TW9
off Lower Richmond Rd **174** B1
Elsley Rd, SW11 **179** F1
Elspeth Rd, SW11 **179** F2
Elsted St, SE17 **76** B1
Elswick Rd, SE13 **172** B4
Elswick St, SW6 **164** C4
Elsworthy Ri, NW3 **109** E4
Elsworthy Rd, NW3 **123** E1
Elsworthy Ter, NW3 **109** E4
Elsynge Rd, SW18 **179** D3
Eltham Rd, SE12 **187** F3
Elthiron Rd, SW6 **164** A3
Elthorne Rd, N19 **97** D3
NW9 **91** D1
Elthruda Rd, SE13 **187** D4
Elton Ho, E3 **129** F1
Elton Pl, N16 **113** E2
Eltringham St, SW18 **178** C2
Eluna Apts, E1
off Wapping La **142** B3
Elvaston Ms, SW7 **55** F2
Elvaston Pl, SW7 **55** E3
Elveden Pl, NW10 **118** A2
Elveden Rd, NW10 **118** A2
Elver Gdns, E2
off St. Peter's Cl **128** A2
Elverson Ms, SE8 **172** B4
DLR Elverson Road 172 B4
Elverson Rd, SE8 **172** B4
Elverton St, SW1 **60** A4
Elvis Rd, NW2 **106** C3
Elwin St, E2 **128** A3
Elwood St, N5 **98** B4
Ely Ct, EC1 **38** B1
Ely Pl, EC1 **38** B1
Elysium Bldg, The, SE8
off Trundleys Rd **157** D4
Elysium Pl, SW6
off Fulham Pk Gdns **163** F4
Elysium St, SW6
off Fulham Pk Gdns **163** F4
Elystan Pl, SW3 **69** D2
Elystan St, SW3 **68** C1
Elystan Wk, N1 **14** A1
Emanuel Av, W3 **132** C2
Embankment 49 D2
Embankment, SW15 **163** D4
Embankment Gdns, SW3 **69** F4
RIV Embankment Pier 49 E2
Embankment Pl, WC2 **49** D2
Emba St, SE16 **156** A1
Emberton, SE5 **76** C4
Emberton Ct, EC1
off Tompion St **26** C1
Embleton Rd, SE13 **186** B1
Emden St, SW6 **79** D4
Emerald Rd, NW10 **119** D1
Emerald St, WC1 **25** E4
Emerson St, SE1 **51** E2
Emery Hill St, SW1 **59** F3
Emery St, SE1 **62** B2
Emlyn Gdns, W12 **147** E1
Emlyn Rd, W12 **147** E1
Emma Rd, E13 **131** F2
Emma St, E2 **128** B2
Emmott Cl, E1 **129** E4
Emperor's Gate, SW7 **55** D3
Empire Ct, Wem. HA9 **90** B4
Empire Sq, N7 **97** E4
SE1 **64** A1
Empire Sq E, SE1
off Empire Sq **64** A1
Empire Sq S, SE1
off Empire Sq **64** A1
Empire Sq W, SE1
off Empire Sq **64** A1
Empire Wf Rd, E14 **159** D3
Empress App, SW6 **66** A3
Empress Approach Terminus 66 A4
Empress Ms, SE5 **168** C4
Empress Pl, SW6 **66** A3
Empress St, SE17 **75** F4
Empson St, E3 **130** B4
Emu Rd, SW8 **166** B4
Enbrook St, W10 **121** E3
Endell St, WC2 **36** C2
Enderby St, SE10 **159** E4
Endsleigh Gdns, WC1 **24** A2
Endsleigh Pl, WC1 **24** B2
Endsleigh St, WC1 **24** A2
Endwell Rd, SE4 **171** E4
Endymion Rd, N4 **98** A1
SW2 **181** F4
Energen Cl, NW10 **105** E3
Enfield Rd, N1 **113** E4
W3 **146** B1

Enford St, W1 **21** E4
Engate St, SE13 **186** C2
Engineers Way, Wem.
HA9 **104** A1
Englands La, NW3 **109** F3
Englefield Rd, N1 **113** D3
Englewood Rd, SW12 **180** B4
English Grds, SE1 **52** C3
English St, E3 **129** F4
Enid St, SE16 **65** F2
Enmore Gdns, SW14 **175** D3
Enmore Rd, SW15 **176** C2
Ennerdale Ho, E3 **129** F4
Ennersdale Rd, SE13 **187** D3
Ennismore Av, W4 **147** F3
Ennismore Gdns, SW7 **56** C1
Ennismore Gdns Ms, SW7 **56** C2
Ennismore Ms, SW7 **56** C2
Ennismore St, SW7 **56** C2
Ennis Rd, N4 **98** A2
Ensign Ho, SW8
off St. George Wf **72** C4
Ensign St, E1 **142** A3
Ensor Ms, SW7 **68** A2
Enterprise Ho, E9
off Tudor Gro **114** C4
Enterprise Ind Est, SE16
off Bolina Rd 156 C4
Enterprise Way, NW10 **120** A3
SW18 **178** A2
Enterprize Way, SE8 **157** F3
Entertainment Av, SE10
off Millennium Way **145** E4
Epirus Ms, SW6 **78** A2
Epirus Rd, SW6 **163** F2
Epping Cl, E14 **158** A3
Epping Pl, N1
off Liverpool Rd **112** A3
Epple Rd, SW6 **163** F3
Epworth St, EC2 **28** B3
Equana Apts, SE8
off Evelyn St **157** E4
Equity Sq, E2 **29** F1
Erasmus St, SW1 **72** B1
Erconwald St, W12 **133** F2
Eresby Pl, NW6 **108** A4
Erica St, W12 **134** A3
Ericcson Cl, SW18 **178** A3
Eric Fletcher Ct, N1
off Essex Rd **112** C4
Eric Rd, NW10 **105** F3
Ericson Ho, N16
off Stamford Hill **99** E2
Eric St, E3 **129** F4
Eridge Rd, W4 **147** D2
Erin Ct, NW2 **106** C3
Erlanger Rd, SE14 **171** D3
Ermine Ms, E2 **17** E1
Ermine Rd, SE13 **186** B1
Ernest Gdns, W4 **160** B1
Ernest St, E1 **129** D4
Ernshaw Pl, SW15
off Carlton Dr **177** E3
Eros, W1 48 A1
Erpingham Rd, SW15 **176** C1
Errington Rd, W9 **121** F4
Errol St, EC1 **27** F3
Erskine Ms, NW3
off Erskine Rd **109** F4
Erskine Rd, NW3 **109** F4
ESCP-EAP European
Sch of Management,
NW3
off Finchley Rd 108 A1
Eskdale, NW1 **11** E3
Esmar Cres, NW9 **92** A1
Esme Ho, SW15 **175** F2
Esmeralda Rd, SE1 **156** A3
Esmond Gdns, W4
off South Par **147** D3
Esmond Rd, NW6 **121** F1
W4 **147** D3
Esmond St, SW15 **177** E2
Essendine Rd, W9 **18** B2
Essex Ct, EC4 **38** A3
SW13 **161** F4
Essex Ho, E14
off Giraud St **144** B2
Essex Pk Ms, W3 **133** E4
Essex Pl, W4 **146** C3
Essex Pl Sq, W4
off Chiswick High Rd **147** D3
Essex Road 112 C4
Essex Rd, N1 **126** B1
NW10 **105** E4
W3 **132** C3
W4 *off Belmont Ter* **147** D3
Essex Rd S, E11 **103** D1
Essex St, WC2 **38** A4
Essex Vil, W8 **54** A1
Essex Wf, E5 **100** C3
Essian St, E1 **143** E1
Estate Way, E10 **101** F2
Estcourt Rd, SW6 **163** F2
Estelle Rd, NW3 **109** F1
Esterbrooke St, SW1 **72** A1
Este Rd, SW11 **179** E1
Esther Rd, E11 **103** E1
Estorick Collection of
Modern Italian Art, N1 112 B3
Etchingham Rd, E15 **116** C1
Eternit Wk, SW6 **162** C3
Ethelburga St, SW11 **81** D4
Ethelburga Twr, SW11 **81** D4
Ethelden Rd, W12 **134** B4
Ethelred Est, SE11 **73** F1
Ethel St, SE17 **75** E1
Etheridge Rd, NW4 **92** C1
Etherow St, SE22 **184** A4
Ethnard Rd, SE15 **170** B1
Etloe Rd, E10 **102** A3
Eton Av, NW3 **109** D4
Eton Coll Rd, NW3 **109** F3
Eton Ct, NW3
off Eton Av **109** D4
Eton Garages, NW3
off Lambolle Pl **109** E3
Eton Gro, SE13 **187** E1
Eton Hall, NW3
off Eton Coll Rd **109** F3
Eton Pl, NW3
off Haverstock Hill **110** A4
Eton Ri, NW3
off Eton Coll Rd **109** F3
Eton Rd, NW3 **109** F4
Eton Vil, NW3 **109** F3
Etta St, SE8 **171** E1
Ettrick St, E14 **144** C2
Eugenia Rd, SE16 **156** C3
Eurocentres, Lee Grn, SE3
off Meadowcourt Rd 187 F2
London Cen, SW1 71 D1
Euro Cl, NW10 **106** A3
Europa Pl, EC1 **27** E1
Eustace Bldg, SW8 **82** C1
Eustace Rd, SW6 **78** A2
Euston 11 F4
Euston 11 F4
Euston 11 F4
Euston 24 A1
Euston Cen, NW1
off Triton Sq **23** E2
Euston Gro, NW1 **24** A1
Euston Rd, N1 **12** C4
NW1 **23** D3
Euston Square 23 F2
Euston Sq, NW1 **24** A1
Euston Sta Colonnade,
NW1 **24** A1
Euston St, NW1 **23** F2
Euston Twr, NW1 23 E2
Evan Cook Cl, SE15 **170** C3
Evandale Rd, SW9 **168** A4
Evangelist Rd, NW5 **110** B1
Evans Business Cen,
NW2 92 A4
Evans Cl, E8
off Buttermere Wk **113** F3
Evelina Children's Hosp,
SE1 61 E2
Evelina Rd, SE15 **184** C1
Eveline Lowe Est,
SE16 **156** A2
Evelyn Ct, N1 **16** A3
Evelyn Fox Ct, W10 **134** C1
Evelyn Gdns, SW7 **68** A3
Evelyn Rd, W4 **147** D2
Evelyn St, SE8 **157** E4
Evelyn Wk, N1 **16** A3
Evelyn Yd, W1 **36** A2
Evenwood Cl, SW15 **177** E3
Everatt Cl, SW18
off Amerland Rd **177** F4
Everdon Rd, SW13 **162** A1
Everest Pl, E14 **144** C1
Evergreen Sq, E8 **113** F4
Everilda St, N1 **13** F1
Evering Rd, E5 **99** F4
N16 **99** F4
Everington St, W6 **163** D1
Everitt Rd, NW10 **119** D3
Everleigh St, N4 **97** F2
Eve Rd, E11 **117** E1
E15 **131** E2
Evershed Wk, W4 **146** C2
Eversholt St, NW1 **11** F2
Evershot Rd, N4 **97** F2
Eversleigh Rd, SW11 **179** F1
Eversley Av, Wem. HA9 **90** A3
Everthorpe Rd, SE15 **183** F1
Everton Bldgs, NW1 **23** E1
Evesham Rd, E15 **131** F1
Evesham St, W11 **135** D3
Evesham Wk, SE5
off Love Wk **169** D4
SW9 **168** A4
Evesham Way, SW11 **180** A1
Ewald Rd, SW6 **163** F4
Ewart Pl, E3
off Roman Rd **129** F2
Ewe Cl, N7 **111** E3
Ewer St, SE1 **51** E3
Ewhurst Cl, E1 **142** C1
Ewhurst Rd, SE4 **185** F4
Excel Ct, WC2 **48** B1
Excelsior Gdns, SE13 **172** C4
Exchange, The, E1
off Commercial St **29** E3
Exchange Arc, EC2 **29** D4
Exchange Ct, WC2 **49** D1
Exchange Pl, EC2 **28** C4
Exchange Sq, EC2 **28** C4

xeter Ho, SW15
off Putney Heath 176 C4
xeter Ms, NW6
off West Hampstead
Ms 108 B3
SW6 ....78 A2
xeter Rd, NW2 ....107 E2
xeter St, WC2 ....37 D4
xeter Way, SE14 ....171 F2
xhibition Cl, W12 ....134 C3
xhibition Rd, SW7 ....56 B1
xmoor St, W10 ....121 D4
xmouth Mkt, EC1 ....26 A2
xmouth Ms, NW1 ....23 F1
xmouth Pl, E8 ....114 B4
xmouth St, E1
off Commercial Rd 142 C2
xning Rd, E16 ....131 F4
xon St, SE17 ....76 C1
xton Rd, NW10 ....104 C4
xton St, SE1 ....50 A3
yhurst Cl, NW2 ....92 A3
ynham Rd, W12 ....134 C2
yot Gdns, W6 ....147 F4
yot Grn, W4 ....147 F4
yre Ct, NW8 ....8 A2
yre St Hill, EC1 ....26 A3
ythorne Rd, SW9 ....86 B4
zra St, E2 ....17 F4

:

abian Rd, SW6 ....163 F2
airacres, SW15 ....176 A2
airbairn Grn, SW9 ....86 B4
airbank Est, N1 ....16 B3
airbridge Rd, N19 ....97 D3
airburn Ct, SW15 ....177 E3
airburn Ho, N16
off Stamford Hill 99 E2
W14 off Ivatt Pl 149 F4
airby Ho, SE1 ....65 F4
● Faircharm Trd Est,
SE8 ....172 A2
airchild Cl, SW11
off Wye St 165 D4
airchild Pl, EC2 ....29 D3
airchild St, EC2 ....29 D3
airclough St, E1 ....142 A2
airdale Gdns, SW15 ......176 B2
airfax Ms, SW15 ....176 C2
airfax Pl, NW6 ....108 C4
W14 ....149 E2
airfax Rd, NW6 ....108 C4
W4 ....147 E2
airfield Ct, NW10 ....120 A1
airfield Dr, SW18 ....178 B3
airfield Rd, E3 ....130 A2
airfield St, SW18 ....178 B3
airfoot Rd, E3 ....130 A4
airford Ho, SE11 ....74 B1
airhazel Gdns, NW6 ......108 B3
airholme Rd, W14 ....149 E4
airholt Cl, N16 ....99 E2
airholt Rd, N16 ....99 D2
airholt St, SW7 ....57 D2
airland Rd, E15 ....117 F3
airlawn Av, W4 ....146 C3
airlawn Gro, W4 ....146 C3
airlead Ho, E14
off Cassilis Rd 158 A2
airlie Ct, E3
off Stroudley Wk 130 B3
airlight Av, NW10 ....119 E2

Fairlop Rd, E11 ....103 D1
Fairmead Ho, E9
off Kingsmead Way 115 E1
Fairmead Rd, N19 ....97 D4
Fairmont Av, E14 ....145 D4
Fairmount Rd, SW2 ....181 F4
Fairstead Wk, N1
off Popham Rd 126 C1
Fair St, SE1 ....53 D4
Fairway, The, W3 ....133 E2
Fairway Cl, NW11 ....94 C1
● Fairways Business Pk, E10
off Lammas Rd 101 E3
Fakruddin St, E1 ....128 A4
Falconberg Ct, W1 ....36 B2
Falconberg Ms, W1 ....36 A2
Falcon Cl, W4
off Sutton La S 160 C1
Falcon Ct, EC4 ....38 A3
Falconer Wk, N7
off Newington Barrow
Way 97 F3
Falcon Gro, SW11 ....179 E1
Falcon La, SW11 ....179 E1
● Falcon Pk Ind Est,
NW10 ....105 E2
Falcon Rd, SW11 ....165 E4
Falcon Ter, SW11 ....179 E1
Falcon Way, E14 ....158 B3
Falcon Wf, SW11 ....165 D4
Falkirk Ho, W9 ....7 D4
Falkirk St, N1 ....17 D3
Falkland Pl, NW5
off Falkland Rd 110 C2
Falkland Rd, NW5 ....110 C2
Fallow Ct, SE16
off Argyle Way 156 A4
Fallowfield, N4
off Six Acres Est 97 F3
Falmouth Cl, SE12 ....187 F3
Falmouth Ho, SE11
off Seaton Cl 74 B2
Falmouth Rd, SE1 ....63 F2
Falmouth St, E15 ....117 D2
Fane St, W14
off North End Rd 163 F1
★ Fan Mus, SE10 ....172 C2
Fann St, EC1 ....27 E3
EC2 ....27 E3
Fanshaw St, N1 ....16 C4
Fanthorpe St, SW15 ......176 C1
Faraday Cl, N7
off Bride St 111 F3
Faraday Lo, SE10
off Renaissance Wk 159 F2
★ Faraday Mus, W1 ....47 E1
Faraday Rd, E15 ....117 F3
W3 ....132 C3
W10 ....135 E1
Fareham St, W1 ....36 A2
Faringford Rd, E15 ....117 E4
Farleigh Pl, N16 ....113 F1
Farleigh Rd, N16 ....113 F1
Farlow Rd, SW15 ....177 D1
Farm Av, NW2 ....93 E4
Farm Cl, SW6 ....78 B2
Farmer Rd, E10 ....102 B2
Farmers Rd, SE5 ....87 D2
Farmer St, W8 ....42 A2
Farmilo Rd, E17 ....101 F1
Farm La, SW6 ....78 B1
● Farm La Trd Cen, SW6 ...78 A1
Farm Pl, W8 ....42 A2
Farm Rd, NW10 ....119 D1

Farm St, W1 ....46 C1
Farnborough Cl, Wem.
HA9 ....90 B3
Farncombe St, SE16 ....156 A1
Farnell Ms, SW5 ....66 C2
Farnell Pl, W3 ....132 B3
Farnham Pl, SE1 ....51 D3
Farnham Royal, SE11 ....73 F3
Farnsworth Ct, SE10
off West Parkside 159 F2
Faroe Rd, W14 ....149 D2
Farrance St, E14 ....143 F2
Farrell Ho, E1 ....142 C2
Farriers Ms, SE15
off Machell Rd 184 C1
Farrier St, NW1 ....110 B4
Farrier Wk, SW10 ....67 E4
⇌ Farringdon 26 B4
⊖ Farringdon 26 B4
Farringdon Ho, Rich. TW9
off Strand Dr 160 B2
Farringdon La, EC1 ....26 B3
Farringdon Rd, EC1 ....26 A2
Farringdon St, EC4 ....38 C2
Farrins Rents, SE16 ....143 E4
Farrow La, SE14 ....170 C2
Farrow Pl, SE16
off Ropemaker Rd 157 E2
Farthingale Wk, E15 ......117 D4
Farthing All, SE1
off Wolseley St 156 A1
Farthing Flds, E1
off Raine St 142 B4
Fashion St, E1 ....41 E1
Fassett Rd, E8 ....114 A3
Fassett Sq, E8 ....114 A3
Fauconberg Rd, W4 ......160 C1
Faulkner's All, EC1 ....26 C4
Faulkner St, SE14 ....170 C3
Faunce St, SE17 ....74 C4
Favart Rd, SW6 ....78 B4
Fawcett Cl, SW11 ....165 D4
Fawcett Est, E5 ....100 A2
Fawcett Rd, NW10 ....119 F1
Fawcett St, SW10 ....67 E4
Fawe Pk Rd, SW15 ....177 F2
Fawe St, E14 ....144 B1
Fawkham Ho, SE1
off Longfield Est 77 F1
Fawley Rd, NW6 ....108 B2
Fawnbrake Av, SE24 ......182 B3
Fawood Av, NW10 ....105 D4
Feathers Pl, SE10 ....173 D1
Featherstone St, EC1 ....28 A2
Featley Rd, SW9 ....182 B1
Feeny Cl, NW10 ....105 F1
Felbridge Ho, SE22
off Pytchley Rd 183 E1
Felday Rd, SE13 ....186 B4
Felden St, SW6 ....163 F3
Feldman Cl, N16 ....100 A2
Felgate Ms, W6 ....148 B3
Felix Pl, SW2
off Talma Rd 182 A3
Felixstowe Rd, NW10 .....120 B3
Fellbrigg Rd, SE22 ....183 F3
Fellbrigg St, E1
off Headlam St 128 B4
Fellmongers Path, SE1 ......65 D1
Fellows Ct, E2 ....17 E3
Fellows Rd, NW3 ....109 D4
Felmersham Cl, SW4 ......181 D2
Felsberg Rd, SW2 ....181 E4
Felsham Rd, SW15 ....177 D1

Felstead Gdns, E14
off Ferry St 158 C4
Felstead St, E9 .....115 F3
Felton St, N1 .....16 B1
Fenchurch Av, EC3 .....40 C3
Fenchurch Bldgs, EC3 .....41 D3
Fenchurch Pl, EC3 .....41 D4
Fenchurch Street 41 D4
Fenchurch St, EC3 .....40 C4
Fen Ct, EC3 .....40 C3
Fendall St, SE1 .....65 D3
Fendt Cl, E16
off Bowman Av 145 F3
Fenelon Pl, W14 .....149 F3
Fenham Rd, SE15 .....170 A2
Fen La, SW13 .....162 B3
Fennel Cl, E16
off Cranberry La 131 E4
Fenner Cl, SE16
off Layard Rd 156 B3
Fenner Sq, SW11
off Thomas Baines Rd 179 D1
Fenning St, SE1 .....52 C4
Fenn St, E9 .....114 C2
Fen St, E16
off Huntingdon St 145 F3
Fentiman Rd, SW8 .....85 D1
Fenton Cl, E8
off Laurel St 113 F3
SW9 .....167 F4
★ Fenton Ho, NW3 .....94 C4
Fenwick Gro, SE15 .....184 A1
Fenwick Pl, SW9 .....181 E1
Fenwick Rd, SE15 .....184 A1
Ferdinand Pl, NW1
off Ferdinand St 110 A4
Ferdinand St, NW1 .....110 A3
Ferguson Cl, E14 .....158 A3
Ferguson Dr, W3 .....133 D2
Fergus Rd, N5
off Calabria Rd 112 B2
Fermoy Rd, W9 .....121 F4
Fernbank Ms, SW12 .....180 B4
Fernbrook Cres, SE13 .....187 E4
Fernbrook Rd, SE13 .....187 E4
Ferncliff Rd, E8 .....114 A2
Fern Cl, N1 .....16 C2
Ferncroft Av, NW3 .....94 A4
Ferndale Ct, SE3 .....173 F2
Ferndale Rd, E11 .....103 E3
SW4 .....181 E2
SW9 .....181 F1
Ferndene Rd, SE24 .....182 C2
Fernhead Rd, W9 .....121 F4
Fernholme Rd, SE15 .....185 D3
Fernhurst Rd, SW6 .....163 E3
Fernleigh Cl, W9 .....121 F3
Fernsbury St, WC1 .....26 A1
Fernshaw Rd, SW10 .....79 E1
Fernside, NW11 .....94 A3
Ferns Rd, E15 .....117 F3
Fern St, E3 .....130 A4
Ferntower Rd, N5 .....113 D2
Fern Wk, SE16
off Argyle Way 156 A4
Ferrey Ms, SW9 .....168 A4
Ferriby Cl, N1
off Bewdley St 112 A4
● Ferrier Ind Est,
SW18 .....178 B2
Ferrier St, SW18 .....178 B2
Ferris Rd, SE22 .....184 A2
Ferron Rd, E5 .....100 B4
Ferrybridge Ho, SE11 .....61 F3
Ferry Ho, E5
off Harrington Hill 100 C2
Ferry La, SW13 .....161 F1
Ferryman's Quay, SW6 .....164 C4
Ferry Rd, SW13 .....162 A2
Ferry St, E14 .....158 C4
Festing Rd, SW15 .....177 D1
Riv Festival Pier 49 E2
Fetter La, EC4 .....38 B3
Ffinch St, SE8 .....172 A2
Field Cl, NW2 .....92 A3
Field Ct, WC1 .....37 F1
Fieldgate St, E1 .....142 A1
Fielding Ho, NW6 .....6 B4
Fielding Ms, SW13
off Castelnau 162 B1
Fielding Rd, W4 .....147 D2
W14 .....149 D2
Fielding St, SE17 .....75 E4
Field Rd, E7 .....117 F1
W6 .....149 E4
Fields Est, E8 .....114 A4
Field St, WC1 .....13 E4
Field Way, NW10 .....104 C4
Fieldway Cres, N5 .....112 A2
Fife Rd, SW14 .....174 C3
Fife Ter, N1 .....13 F2
Fifth Av, W10 .....121 E3
Fifth Way, Wem. HA9 .....104 B1
Fig Tree Cl, NW10
off Craven Pk 119 E1
Filey Av, N16 .....100 A2
Filigree Ct, SE16
off Silver Wk 143 F4
Fillebrook Rd, E11 .....103 D2
Filmer Rd, SW6 .....163 E3
Finborough Rd, SW10 .....66 C4
Finch Cl, NW10 .....105 D2
Finch La, EC3 .....40 B3
Finchley Pl, NW8 .....8 A2
Finchley Road 108 C3
Finchley Rd, NW2 .....94 A4
NW3 .....108 C3
NW8 .....8 A1
Finchley Road &
Frognal 108 C2
Finch Ms, SE15 .....89 E4
Findhorn St, E14 .....144 C2
Findon Cl, SW18 .....178 A4
Findon Rd, W12 .....148 A1
Fingal St, SE10 .....159 F4
Finland Quay, SE16
off Finland St 157 E2
Finland Rd, SE4 .....185 E1
Finland St, SE16 .....157 E2
Finlay St, SW6 .....163 D3
Finnis St, E2 .....128 B3
FINSBURY, EC1 .....14 B4
Finsbury Av, EC2 .....40 B1
Finsbury Av Sq, EC2 .....40 B1
Finsbury Circ, EC2 .....40 B1
Finsbury Est, EC1 .....26 B1
Finsbury Mkt, EC2 .....28 C3
FINSBURY PARK, N4 .....98 A2
★ Finsbury Park, N4 .....98 B1
Finsbury Park 98 A3
Finsbury Park 98 A3
Finsbury Park 98 A3
Finsbury Pk Rd, N4 .....98 B3
Finsbury Pavement, EC2 .....28 B4
Finsbury Sq, EC2 .....28 B4
Finsbury St, EC2 .....28 A4
● Finsbury Twr, EC1 .....28 A3
Finsen Rd, SE5 .....182 C1
Finstock Rd, W10 .....135 D2
Firbank Rd, SE15 .....170 B4
Firecrest Dr, NW3 .....94 B4
Fir Gro Rd, SW9
off Marcella Rd 168 A4
Firs Av, SW14 .....174 C2
Firsby Rd, N16 .....99 F2
First Av, SW14 .....175 E1
W3 .....133 F4
W10 .....121 F4
First Dr, NW10 .....104 C4
First St, SW3 .....57 D4
First Way, Wem. HA9 .....104 B1
Firth Gdns, SW6 .....163 E3
Fir Trees Cl, SE16 .....143 E4
Fisher Cl, E9
off Brooksby's Wk 115 D2
Fisher Ho, N1 .....14 A1
Fishermans Dr, SE16 .....157 D1
Fisherman's Wk, E14 .....144 A4
Fishers Ct, SE14
off Besson St 171 D3
Fishers La, W4 .....147 D3
Fisher St, WC1 .....37 D1
Fisherton St, NW8 .....20 A3
Fish St Hill, EC3 .....40 B4
Fitzalan St, SE11 .....62 A4
Fitzgeorge Av, W14 .....149 E3
Fitzgerald Av, SW14 .....175 E1
Fitzgerald Ho, E14 .....144 B2
SW9
off Stockwell Pk Rd 168 A4
Fitzgerald Rd, SW14 .....175 D1
Fitzhardinge St, W1 .....34 A2
Fitzhugh Gro, SW18 .....179 D4
Fitzjames Av, W14 .....149 E3
Fitzjohn's Av, NW3 .....109 D2
Fitzmaurice Ho, SE16
off Rennie Est 156 B3
Fitzmaurice Pl, W1 .....47 D2
Fitzneal St, W12 .....133 F2
Fitzroy Cl, N6 .....95 F2
Fitzroy Ct, W1 .....23 F3
Fitzroy Cres, W4 .....161 D2
Fitzroy Ms, W1 .....23 E3
Fitzroy Pk, N6 .....95 F2
Fitzroy Rd, NW1 .....124 A1
Fitzroy Sq, W1 .....23 E3
Fitzroy St, W1 .....23 E3
Fitzroy Yd, NW1
off Fitzroy Rd 124 A1
Fitzsimmons Ct, NW10
off Knatchbull Rd 119 D1
Fitzwarren Gdns, N19 .....96 C2
Fitzwilliam Rd, SW4 .....180 C1
Five Bell All, E14
off Three Colt St 143 F3
Fives Ct, SE11 .....62 C4
Fiveways Rd, SW9 .....168 A4
Flagstaff Ho, SW8
off St. George Wf 72 C4
Flamborough St, E14 .....143 E2
Flamborough Wk, E14
off Flamborough St 143 E2
Flamsted Av, Wem. HA9 .....104 A3
Flanchford Rd, W12 .....147 F2
Flanders Rd, W4 .....147 E3
Flanders Way, E9 .....115 D3
Flank St, E1
off Dock St 142 A3
Flannery Ct, SE16
off Drummond Rd 156 B2
Flask Cotts, NW3
off New End Sq 109 D1

lask Wk, NW3 ....109 D1
lat Iron Sq, SE1
off Union St 51 F3
lavell Ms, SE10 ....159 E4
laxman Ct, W1 ....36 A3
laxman Rd, SE5 ....168 B4
laxman Ter, WC1 ....24 B1
leece Wk, N7
off Manger Rd 111 E3
leet Pl, EC4
off Limeburner La 38 C2
leet Rd, NW3 ....109 E2
leet Sq, WC1 ....25 F1
leet St, EC4 ....38 A3
leet St Hill, E1
off Weaver St 128 A4
leetwood Gro, W3
off East Acton La 133 E3
leetwood Rd, NW10 ....106 A2
leetwood St, N16
off Stoke Newington Ch St 99 E3
leming Cl, W9 ....18 A3
leming Ct, W2 ....20 A4
leming Rd, SE17 ....75 D4
lempton Rd, E10 ....101 E1
letcher La, E10 ....102 C1
letcher Path, SE8
off New Butt La 172 A2
letcher Rd, W4 ....146 C2
letcher St, E1
off Cable St 142 A3
letching Rd, E5 ....100 C4
leur de Lis St, E1 ....29 D3
lint Cl, E15 ....117 F4
linton St, SE17 ....77 D2
lint St, SE17 ....76 B1
litcroft St, WC2 ....36 B2
lockton St, SE16
off George Row 156 A1
lodden Rd, SE5 ....168 C3
lood St, SW3 ....69 D3
lood Wk, SW3 ....69 D4
lora Cl, E14 ....144 B2
lora Gdns, W6 ....148 B3
lora Ho, E3
off Garrison Rd 130 A1
loral Pl, N1
off Northampton Gro 113 D2
loral St, WC2 ....36 C4
lorence Cantwell Wk, N19
off Hillrise Rd 97 E1
lorence Ct, W9
off Maida Vale 19 F1
lorence Gdns, W4 ....160 C1
lorence Nightingale Ho, N1
off Nightingale Rd 112 C3
★ Florence Nightingale Mus, SE1 ....61 E1
lorence Rd, E13 ....131 F2
N4 ....98 A2
SE14 ....171 F3
W4 ....147 D2
lorence St, E16 ....131 F4
N1 ....112 B4
lorence Ter, SE14 ....171 F3
lorfield Pas, E8
off Reading La 114 B3
lorfield Rd, E8
off Reading La 114 B3
lorian Rd, SW15 ....177 E2
lorida St, E2 ....128 A3
lorin Ct, EC1 ....27 E4
SE1 off Tanner St 65 E1
Floris Pl, SW4
off Fitzwilliam Rd 180 C1
Floss St, SW15 ....162 C4
Flower & Dean Wk, E1 ....41 F1
Flowers Cl, NW2 ....92 A4
Flowers Ms, N19
off Archway Rd 96 C3
Flower Wk, The, SW7 ....55 E1
Fludyer St, SE13 ....187 E2
Foley Ho, E1
off Tarling St 142 C2
Foley St, W1 ....35 E1
Folgate St, E1 ....29 D4
Foliot Ho, N1
off Priory Grn Est 13 E2
Foliot St, W12 ....133 F2
Follett St, E14 ....144 C2
Folly Ms, W11
off Portobello Rd 135 F2
Folly Wall, E14 ....158 C1
Fontarabia Rd, SW11 ....180 A2
Fontenelle, SE5 ....88 C4
Fonthill Ms, N4 ....97 F3
Fonthill Rd, N4 ....97 F2
Footpath, The, SW15 ....176 A3
Forbes Cl, NW2 ....92 A4
Forbes St, E1
off Ellen St 142 A2
Forburg Rd, N16 ....100 A2
Ford Cl, E3
off Roman Rd 129 E2
Fordham St, E1 ....142 A2
Fordingley Rd, W9 ....121 F3
Ford Rd, E3 ....129 E1
Ford Sq, E1 ....142 B1
Ford St, E3 ....129 E1
E16 ....145 F2
Fordwych Rd, NW2 ....107 E1
Fordyce Rd, SE13 ....186 C4
★ Foreign & Commonwealth Office, SW1 ....48 B4
Foreign St, SE5 ....168 B4
Foreshore, SE8 ....157 F3
● Forest Business Pk, E10 ....101 D1
Forest Cl, NW6 ....107 E4
Forest Dr E, E11 ....103 D1
Forest Dr W, E11 ....102 C1
Forester Rd, SE15 ....184 B2
Forest Gro, E8 ....113 F3
Forest Hill Rd, SE22 ....184 B3
SE23 ....184 B3
Forest La, E7 ....117 E2
E15 ....117 E2
Fore St, EC2 ....39 F1
Fore St Av, EC2 ....40 A1
Forest Rd, E8 ....113 F3
E11 ....103 D1
Richmond TW9 ....160 A2
Forest Vw, E11 ....103 F1
Forest Way, N19
off Hargrave Pk 96 C3
Forfar Rd, SW11 ....82 B4
Forge Pl, NW1
off Malden Cres 110 A3
Forman Pl, N16
off Farleigh Rd 113 F1
Formosa St, W9 ....19 E3
Formunt Cl, E16
off Vincent St 145 F1
Forset St, W1 ....33 D2
Forston St, N1 ....16 A2
Forsyth Gdns, SE17 ....75 D4
Forsyth Ho, SW1
off Tachbrook St 71 F2
Fortescue Av, E8
off Mentmore Ter 114 B4
Fortess Gro, NW5
off Fortess Rd 110 C2
Fortess Rd, NW5 ....110 B2
Fortess Wk, NW5
off Fortess Rd 110 B2
Fortess Yd, NW5
off Fortess Rd 110 B1
Forthbridge Rd, SW11 ....180 A2
Fortnam Rd, N19 ....97 D3
★ Fortnum & Mason, W1 ....47 E2
Fort Rd, SE1 ....77 F1
Fortrose Cl, E14 ....145 D2
Fort St, E1 ....41 D1
Fortuna Cl, N7
off Jupiter Way 111 F3
Fortune Gate Rd, NW10 ....119 E1
Fortune Grn Rd, NW6 ....108 A1
Fortune Pl, SE1 ....77 F3
Fortune St, EC1 ....27 F3
Fortune Way, NW10 ....120 A3
Forty Footpath, SW14 ....174 C1
Forty La, Wem. HA9 ....90 B3
Forum Cl, E3
off Garrison Rd 130 A1
★ Forum Club, NW5 ....110 B2
Forum Magnum Sq, SE1 ....49 E4
Fosbury Ms, W2 ....43 D1
Foscote Ms, W9 ....18 B3
Foskett Rd, SW6 ....163 F4
Fossil Rd, SE13 ....186 A1
Foster La, EC2 ....39 E2
Foster Rd, W3 ....133 E3
W4 ....147 D4
Foubert's Pl, W1 ....35 E3
Foulden Rd, N16 ....113 F1
Foulden Ter, N16
off Foulden Rd 113 F1
Foulis Ter, SW7 ....68 B2
Founders Ct, EC2 ....40 A2
★ Foundling Mus, WC1 ....25 D2
Foundry Cl, SE16 ....143 E4
Foundry Ms, NW1 ....23 F2
Foundry Pl, E1
off Redman's Rd 142 C1
Fountain Cl, E5
off Lower Clapton Rd 100 B4
Fountain Ct, EC4 ....38 A4
Fountain Grn Sq, SE16
off Bermondsey Wall E 156 A1
Fountain Ho, SW6
off The Boulevard 164 C4
SW8
off St. George Wf 73 D3
Fountain Ms, N5
off Highbury Gra 112 C1
NW3 ....109 F3
Fountain Pl, SW9 ....168 A3
Fountain Sq, SW1 ....58 C4
Fountayne Rd, N16 ....100 A3
Fount St, SW8 ....84 B3
Fournier St, E1 ....29 E4
Four Seasons Cl, E3 ....130 A2
Fourth Av, W10 ....121 E4
Fourth Way, Wem. HA9 ....104 C1
Fowey Cl, E1
off Kennet St 142 B4
Fowler Cl, SW11 ....179 D1
Fowler Rd, N1
off Halton Rd 112 B4
Fownes St, SW11 ....179 E1

Fox & Knot St, EC1 **27** D4
Foxberry Rd, SE4 **185** E1
Foxborough Gdns, SE4 **186** A4
Fox Cl, E1 **128** C4
Foxcote, SE5 **77** D3
Foxglove St, W12 **133** F3
Foxham Rd, N19 **97** D4
Foxholt Gdns, NW10 **104** C4
Fox Ho, SW11
off Maysoule Rd **179** D2
Foxley Cl, E8
off Ferncliff Rd **114** A2
Foxley Ho, E3
off Bromley High St **130** B3
Foxley Rd, SW9 **86** B2
Foxley Sq, SW9 **86** C4
Foxmore St, SW11 **165** F3
Fox Rd, E16 **145** F1
Foxwell Ms, SE4
off Foxwell St **185** E1
Foxwell St, SE4 **185** E1
Foxwood Rd, SE3 **187** F2
Foyle Rd, SE3 **173** F1
Framfield Rd, N5 **112** B2
Framlingham Cl, E5
off Detmold Rd **100** C3
Frampton Pk Est, E9 **114** C4
Frampton Pk Rd, E9 **114** C3
Frampton St, NW8 **20** A3
Francemary Rd, SE4 **186** A3
Coll Frances King Sch of English,
South Kensington, SW7 **55** F4
Victoria, SW1 **59** D2
Francis Bentley Ms, SW4
off Old Town **180** C1
Francis Chichester Way,
SW11 **166** A3
Francis Cl, E14
off Saunders Ness Rd **159** D3
Francis Pl, N6
off Holmesdale Rd **96** B1
Francis Rd, E10 **102** C2
Francis St, E15 **117** E2
SW1 **59** E4
Francis Ter, N19 **96** C4
Francis Ter Ms, N19
off Francis Ter **96** C4
Francis Wk, N1
off Bingfield St **125** F1
Franconia Rd, SW4 **180** C3
Frankfurt Rd, SE24 **182** C3
Frankham St, SE8 **172** A2
Frankland Cl, SE16 **156** B2
Frankland Rd, SW7 **56** A3
Franklin Cl, SE13 **172** B3
Franklin Ho, NW9 **91** F1
Franklin Pl, SE13 **172** B3
Franklin Sq, W14
off Marchbank Rd **149** F4
Franklin's Row, SW3 **69** F2
Franklin St, E3 **130** B3
Franklyn Rd, NW10 **105** F4
Fraser Ct, W12
off Heathstan Rd **134** A2
Fraser St, W4 **147** E4
Frazier St, SE1 **62** A1
Frean St, SE16 **156** A2
Freda Corbett Cl, SE15
off Radnor Rd **170** A2
Frederica St, N7
off Caledonian Rd **111** F4
Frederick Cl, W2 **33** D4
Frederick Ct, NW2 **93** E4
Frederick Cres, SW9 **86** C3
Frederick Rd, SE17 **75** D4
Frederick's Pl, EC2 **40** A3
Frederick Sq, SE16
off Rotherhithe St **143** E3
Frederick's Row, EC1 **14** C4
Frederick St, WC1 **25** E1
Frederick Ter, E8
off Arbutus St **127** F1
Frederic Ms, SW1 **57** F1
Fred White Wk, N7
off Market Rd **111** E3
Fred Wigg Twr, E11 **103** F3
Freedom St, SW11 **165** F4
Freegrove Rd, N7 **111** E2
Freeling St, N1
off Caledonian Rd **111** F4
Freeman Ct, N7
off Tollington Way **97** E4
Freemantle St, SE17 **76** C2
★ Freemason's Hall
(United Grand Lodge
of England), WC2 **37** D2
Free Trade Wf, E1
off The Highway **143** D3
★ Freightliners Fm, N7 **111** F3
Freke Rd, SW11 **180** A1
Fremont St, E9 **128** C1
French Ordinary Ct,
EC3 **41** D4
French Pl, E1 **29** D2
Frendsbury Rd, SE4 **185** E2
Frensham St, SE15 **170** A1
Frere St, SW11 **165** E4
Freshfield Av, E8 **113** F4
Freshfield Cl, SE13
off Mercator Rd **187** D2
Freston Rd, W10 **135** D3
W11 **135** D3
★ Freud Mus, NW3 **108** C3
Friars Cl, SE1 **50** C3
Friars Gdns, W3
off St. Dunstans Av **133** D2
Friars Mead, E14 **158** C2
Friars Pl La, W3 **133** D3
Friar St, EC4 **39** D3
Friars Way, W3 **133** D2
Friary Ct, SW1 **47** F3
Friary Est, SE15 **170** A1
Friary Pk Est, W3
off Friary Rd **133** D2
Friary Rd, SE15 **170** A2
W3 **133** D2
Friday St, EC4 **39** E3
Frideswide Pl, NW5
off Islip St **110** C2
Friendly Pl, SE13
off Lewisham Rd **172** B3
Friendly St, SE8 **172** A3
Friendly St Ms, SE8
off Friendly St **172** A4
Friendship Way, E15
off Carpenters Rd **130** C1
Friend St, EC1 **14** C4
Friern Rd, SE22 **184** A4
Frigate Ms, SE8
off Watergate St **172** A1
Frimley Way, E1 **129** D4
Frinstead Ho, W10 **135** D3
Friston St, SW6 **164** B4
Frith Rd, E11 **116** C1
Frith St, W1 **36** A3
Frithville Gdns, W12 **134** C4
Frobisher Cres, EC2
off The Barbican **27** F4
Frobisher Pas, E14
*off The North
Colonnade* **144** A4
Frobisher Pl, SE15
off St. Mary's Rd **170** C3
Frobisher St, SE10 **173** E1
Frogley Rd, SE22 **183** F2
Frogmore, SW18 **178** A3
● Frogmore Ind Est, N5
off Kelvin Rd **112** C1
NW10 **118** C3
Frognal, NW3 **108** C2
Frognal Cl, NW3 **108** C2
Frognal Ct, NW3 **108** C3
Frognal Gdns, NW3 **108** C1
Frognal La, NW3 **108** B2
Frognal Par, NW3
off Frognal Ct **108** C3
Frognal Ri, NW3 **108** C1
Frognal Way, NW3 **108** C1
Frome St, N1 **15** E2
Frostic Wk, E1 **41** F1
Froude St, SW8 **166** B4
Fruiterers Pas, EC4
off Southwark Br **51** F1
Frying Pan All, E1 **41** E1
Fry Rd, NW10 **119** F1
Fulbourne St, E1
off Durward St **142** B1
Fulbrook Ms, N19
off Junction Rd **110** C1
Fulbrook Rd, N19
off Junction Rd **110** C1
Fulford St, SE16 **156** B1
FULHAM, SW6 **163** E4
Fulham Broadway **78** B2
Fulham Bdy, SW6 **78** B2
Fulham Bdy Retail Cen,
SW6 *off Fulham Bdy* **78** B2
Fulham Ct, SW6 **78** A4
★ Fulham FC, SW6 **163** D3
Fulham High St, SW6 **163** E4
★ Fulham Palace, SW6 **163** E4
Fulham Palace Rd, SW6 **163** D2
W6 **148** C4
Fulham Pk Gdns, SW6 **163** F4
Fulham Pk Rd, SW6 **163** F4
Fulham Rd, SW3 **68** A3
SW6 **79** D2
SW10 **68** A3
Fuller Cl, E2
off St. Matthew's Row **128** A4
★ Fuller's Griffin Brewery,
W4 **161** F1
Fullerton Rd, SW18 **178** C3
Fullwoods Ms, N1 **16** B4
Fulmead St, SW6 **164** B3
Fulthorp Rd, SE3 **173** F4
Fulton Ms, W2 **31** E4
Fulton Rd, Wem. HA9 **90** A4
Fulwood Pl, WC1 **37** F1
Furber St, W6 **148** B2
Furley Rd, SE15 **170** A2
Furlong Rd, N7 **112** A3
Furness Rd, NW10 **120** A2
SW6 **164** B4
Furnival St, EC4 **38** A2
Furrow La, E9 **114** C2
Furze St, E3 **144** A1
Fyefoot La, EC4
off Queen Victoria St **39** E4
Fyfield, N4
off Six Acres Est **98** A3
Fyfield Rd, SW9 **182** A1

ynes St, SW1 . . . .**60** A4

G

ables, The, Wem. HA9 . . . . .**90** A4
ables Cl, SE5 . . . .**88** C4
abrielle Ct, NW3 . . . .**109** D3
abriel Ms, NW2 . . . .**93** F3
abriel's Wf, SE1 . . . .**50** A2
age Rd, E16
off Malmesbury Rd **145** E1
age St, WC1 . . . .**25** D4
ainford St, N1
off Richmond Av **126** A1
ainsborough Ct, W12
off Lime Gro **148** C1
ainsborough Gdns, NW3 . . .**95** D4
NW11 . . . .**93** F1
ainsborough Ho, E14
off Cassilis Rd **158** A1
ainsborough Rd, E11 . . . . .**103** E1
E15 . . . .**131** E3
W4 . . . .**147** F3
ainsborough St, E9
off Trowbridge Rd **115** F3
ainsborough Studios, N1 . . .**16** A1
ainsford St, SE1 . . . .**53** E4
airloch Rd, SE5 . . . .**169** E4
aisford St, NW5 . . . .**110** C3
aitskell Ct, SW11 . . . .**165** D4
aitskell Way, SE1
off Weller St **51** E4
alata Rd, SW13 . . . .**162** A2
alatea Sq, SE15
off Scylla Rd **184** B1
alaxy, E14
off Crews St **158** A3
albraith St, E14 . . . .**158** C2
alena Rd, W6 . . . .**148** B3
alen Pl, WC1 . . . .**37** D1
alesbury Rd, SW18 . . . .**178** C4
ales Gdns, E2 . . . .**128** B3
ale St, E3 . . . .**144** A1
alleon Cl, SE16
off Kinburn St **157** D1
alleon Ho, SW8
off St. George Wf **72** C4
alleywall Rd, SE16 . . . .**156** B3
allia Rd, N5 . . . .**112** B2
alloway Rd, W12 . . . .**134** A4
alsworthy Av, E14 . . . .**143** E1
alsworthy Rd, NW2 . . . . . .**107** E1
alsworthy Ter, N16 . . . .**99** E4
alton St, W10 . . . .**121** E4
alveston Rd, SW15 . . . .**177** F3
alway Cl, SE16
off Masters Dr **156** B4
alway Ho, EC1 . . . .**27** F1
alway St, EC1 . . . .**27** F1
ambetta St, SW8 . . . .**166** B4
ambia St, SE1 . . . .**51** D3
ambier Ho, EC1 . . . .**15** F4
amlen Rd, SW15 . . . .**177** D2
andolfi St, SE15 . . . .**88** C1
anley Ct, SW11
off Newcomen Rd **179** D1
anley Rd, SW11 . . . .**179** D1
anton St, W1 . . . .**35** E4
arage Rd, W3 . . . .**132** A2
arand Ct, N7
off Eden Gro **111** F2
arbutt Pl, W1 . . . .**22** B4
arden Ct, EC4 . . . .**38** A4
arden Ms, W2 . . . .**42** B1

Garden Pl, E8
off Haggerston Rd **127** F1
Garden Rd, NW8 . . . .**7** F4
Richmond TW9 . . . .**174** A1
Garden Row, SE1 . . . .**62** C3
Gardens, The, E5 . . . .**99** F1
SE22 . . . .**184** A2
Garden St, E1 . . . .**143** D1
Garden Ter, SW1 . . . .**72** A2
Garden Wk, EC2 . . . .**28** C1
Garden Way, NW10 . . . .**104** C3
Gardiner Av, NW2 . . . .**106** C2
Gardner Ct, EC1
off Brewery Sq **26** C2
N5 *off Kelvin Rd* **112** C1
Gardners La, EC4 . . . .**39** E4
Gardnor Rd, NW3
off Flask Wk **109** D1
Gard St, EC1 . . . .**15** D4
Garfield Ms, SW11
off Garfield Rd **180** B1
Garfield Rd, E13 . . . .**131** F4
SW11 . . . .**180** A1
Garford St, E14 . . . .**144** A3
Garland Ct, SE17
off Wansey St **75** F1
Garland Ho, N16 . . . .**99** D4
Garlick Hill, EC4 . . . .**39** F4
Garlinge Rd, NW2 . . . .**107** F3
Garnault Ms, EC1 . . . .**26** B1
Garnault Pl, EC1 . . . .**26** B1
Garner St, E2
off Coate St **128** A2
Garnet Rd, NW10 . . . .**105** E3
Garnet St, E1 . . . .**142** C3
Garnett Rd, NW3 . . . .**109** F2
Garnham Cl, N16
off Garnham St **99** F3
Garnham St, N16 . . . .**99** F3
Garnies Cl, SE15 . . . .**89** E2
Garrard Wk, NW10
off Garnet Rd **105** E3
Garratt Ho, N16
off Stamford Hill **99** E2
Garratt La, SW18 . . . .**178** B3
Garrett Cl, W3
off Jenner Av **133** D1
Garrett St, EC1 . . . .**27** F2
Garrick Cl, SW18 . . . .**178** C2
Garrick Rd, Rich. TW9 . . . . .**160** A4
Garrick St, WC2 . . . .**36** C4
Garrison Rd, E3 . . . .**130** A1
Garsington Ms, SE4 . . . .**185** F1
Garter Way, SE16
off Poolmans St **157** D1
Garth Cl, W4 . . . .**147** D4
Garth Ct, W4 . . . .**147** D4
Garth Ho, NW2
off Granville Rd **93** F3
Garth Rd, NW2 . . . .**93** F3
W4 . . . .**161** D1
Garton Pl, SW18 . . . .**178** C4
Gartons Way, SW11 . . . .**178** C1
Garway Rd, W2 . . . .**30** C3
Gascoigne Pl, E2 . . . .**29** E1
Gascony Av, NW6 . . . .**108** A4
Gascoyne Rd, E9 . . . .**115** D4
Gaselee St, E14 . . . .**144** C3
Gaskarth Rd, SW12 . . . .**180** B4
Gaskell St, SW4 . . . .**167** E4
Gaskin St, N1 . . . .**126** B1
Gaspar Cl, SW5 . . . .**55** D4
Gaspar Ms, SW5 . . . .**55** D4
Gastein Rd, W6 . . . .**163** D1

★ Gasworks Gall, SE11 . . . . .**73** F4
Gataker St, SE16 . . . .**156** B2
Gatcombe Ho, SE22
off Pytchley Rd **183** E1
Gatcombe Rd, N19 . . . .**97** D4
Gateforth St, NW8 . . . .**20** C3
Gate Ho Sq, SE1 . . . .**51** F2
Gateley Rd, SW9 . . . .**181** F1
Gate Ms, SW7 . . . .**57** D1
Gatesborough St, EC2 . . . . . .**28** C2
Gate St, WC2 . . . .**37** E2
Gateway, SE17 . . . .**75** F4
● Gateway Ind Est, NW10 . . . .**119** F3
Gateway Ms, E8
off Shacklewell La **113** F2
Gateway Rd, E10 . . . .**102** B4
Gateways, The, SW3 . . . .**69** D1
Gathorne St, E2
off Mace St **129** D2
Gatliff Cl, SW1
off Ebury Br Rd **70** C3
Gatliff Rd, SW1 . . . .**70** B3
Gatonby St, SE15 . . . .**89** F4
Gauden Cl, SW4 . . . .**181** D1
Gauden Rd, SW4 . . . .**167** D4
Gaumont Ter, W12
off Lime Gro **148** C1
Gaunt St, SE1 . . . .**63** D2
Gautrey Rd, SE15 . . . .**170** C4
Gavel St, SE17 . . . .**64** B4
Gaverick Ms, E14
off Westferry Rd **158** A3
Gaviller Pl, E5
off Clarence Rd **114** B1
Gawber St, E2 . . . .**128** C3
Gawsworth Cl, E15
off Ash Rd **117** E2
Gawthorne Ct, E3
off Mostyn Gro **130** A2
Gay Cl, NW2 . . . .**106** B2
Gaydon Ho, W2 . . . .**19** D4
Gayfere St, SW1 . . . .**60** C3
Gayford Rd, W12 . . . .**147** F1
Gayhurst, SE17 . . . .**76** B4
Gayhurst Rd, E8 . . . .**114** A4
Gay Rd, E15 . . . .**131** D2
Gay St, SW15 . . . .**177** D1
Gayton Cres, NW3 . . . .**109** D1
Gayton Ho, E3 . . . .**130** A4
Gayton Rd, NW3 . . . .**109** D1
Gayville Rd, SW11 . . . .**179** F4
Gaywood Est, SE1 . . . .**62** C3
Gaywood St, SE1 . . . .**63** D3
Gaza St, SE17 . . . .**74** C3
Gazelle Ho, E15
off Manbey Pk Rd **117** E3
Geary Rd, NW10 . . . .**106** A2
Geary St, N7 . . . .**111** F2
Gedling Ho, SE22
off Quorn Rd **183** F1
Gedling Pl, SE1 . . . .**65** F2
Geere Rd, E15 . . . .**131** F1
Gees Ct, W1 . . . .**34** B3
Gee St, EC1 . . . .**27** E2
Geffrye Ct, N1 . . . .**17** D3
Geffrye Est, N1 . . . .**17** D3
★ Geffrye Mus, E2 . . . .**17** D3
Geffrye St, E2 . . . .**17** E2
Geldart Rd, SE15 . . . .**170** B2
Geldeston Rd, E5 . . . .**100** A3
Gellatly Rd, SE14 . . . .**170** C4
Gemini Ho, E3
off Garrison Rd **130** A1

● Gemini Project, SE14
off Landmann Way 157 D4
General Wolfe Rd, SE10 .... 173 D3
Geneva Dr, SW9 .... 182 A2
Genoa Av, SW15 .... 176 C3
Gentian Row, SE13
off Sparta St 172 C3
Geoffrey Cl, SE5 .... 168 C4
Geoffrey Rd, SE4 .... 185 F1
George Beard Rd, SE8 .... 157 F3
George Belt Ho, E2
off Smart St 129 D3
George Ct, WC2 .... 49 D1
George Downing Est, N16 .... 99 F3
George Eliot Ho, SW1
off Vauxhall Br Rd 71 F1
George Elliston Ho, SE1
off Old Kent Rd 156 A4
★ George Inn, SE1 .... 52 A3
George Inn Yd, SE1 .... 52 A3
George La, SE13 .... 186 C4
George Loveless Ho, E2 .... 17 F4
George Lowe Ct, W2 .... 18 C4
George Mathers Rd, SE11 .... 62 C4
George Ms, NW1 .... 23 E1
SW9 off Brixton Rd 168 A4
George Row, SE16 .... 156 A1
George's Rd, N7 .... 111 F2
Georges Sq, SW6
off North End Rd 163 F1
George St, E16 .... 145 F2
W1 .... 33 F2
Georgette Pl, SE10
off King George St 172 C2
George Yd, EC3 .... 40 B3
W1 .... 34 B4
Georgiana St, NW1 .... 124 C1
Georgian Ct, Wem. HA9 .... 104 A3
Georgina Gdns, E2 .... 17 F4
Geraldine Rd, SW18 .... 178 C3
W4 .... 160 A1
Geraldine St, SE11 .... 62 C3
Gerald Ms, SW1 .... 58 B4
Gerald Rd, E16 .... 131 F4
SW1 .... 58 B4
Gerard Ct, NW2 .... 107 D2
Gerard Pl, E9
off Groombridge Rd 115 D4
Gerard Rd, SW13 .... 161 F3
Gerards Cl, SE16 .... 156 C4
Germander Way, E15 .... 131 E3
Gernigan Ho, SW18 .... 179 D4
Gernon Rd, E3 .... 129 E2
Geron Way, NW2 .... 92 B2
Gerrard Ho, SE14
off Briant St 171 D2
Gerrard Pl, W1 .... 36 B4
Gerrard Rd, N1 .... 15 D2
Gerrard St, W1 .... 36 A4
Gerridge St, SE1 .... 62 B1
Gerry Raffles Sq, E15
off Great Eastern Rd 117 D3
Gertrude St, SW10 .... 79 F1
Gervase Cl, Wem. HA9 .... 90 C4
Gervase St, SE15 .... 170 B2
Ghent Way, E8
off Tyssen St 113 F3
Gibbins Rd, E15 .... 116 C4
Gibbon Rd, SE15 .... 170 C4
W3 .... 133 E3
Gibbons Rents, SE1
off Magdalen St 52 C3
Gibbons Rd, NW10 .... 105 D3
Gibbon Wk, SW15 .... 176 A2
Gibbs Grn, W14 .... 149 F4
Gibraltar Wk, E2 .... 29 F1
Gibson Cl, E1
off Colebert Av 128 C4
Gibson Gdns, N16 .... 99 F3
Gibson Rd, SE11 .... 73 F1
Gibson Sq, N1 .... 126 A1
Gibson St, SE10 .... 159 E4
Gideon Rd, SW11 .... 180 A1
Giesbach Rd, N19 .... 96 C3
Giffin St, SE8 .... 172 A2
Gifford Rd, NW10 .... 105 E4
Gifford St, N1 .... 111 E4
Gift La, E15 .... 131 E1
Gilbert Ho, EC2
off The Barbican 27 F4
SE8 off McMillan St 172 A1
SW1 .... 71 D3
Gilbert Pl, WC1 .... 36 C1
Gilbert Rd, SE11 .... 74 B1
Gilbert St, E15 .... 117 E1
W1 .... 34 B3
Gilbeys Yd, NW1 .... 110 A4
Gilda Cres, N16 .... 100 A2
Gildea St, W1 .... 35 D1
Gilden Cres, NW5 .... 110 A2
Gilkes Cres, SE21 .... 183 E4
Gilkes Pl, SE21 .... 183 E4
Gillender St, E3 .... 130 C4
E14 .... 130 C4
Gillespie Rd, N5 .... 98 A4
Gillett Pl, N16
off Gillett St 113 E2
Gillett Sq, N16
off Gillett St 113 E2
Gillett St, N16 .... 113 E2
Gillfoot, NW1 .... 11 E3
Gillian St, SE13 .... 186 B3
Gillies St, NW5 .... 110 A2
Gilling Ct, NW3 .... 109 E3
Gillingham Rd, NW2 .... 93 E4
Gillingham Row, SW1 .... 59 E4
Gillingham St, SW1 .... 59 D4
Gillison Wk, SE16
off Tranton Rd 156 A2
Gillman Dr, E15 .... 131 F1
Gill St, E14 .... 143 F2
Gilmore Rd, SE13 .... 187 D2
Gilpin Av, SW14 .... 175 D2
Gilpin Cl, W2 .... 20 A4
Gilpin Rd, E5 .... 115 E1
Gilstead Rd, SW6 .... 164 B4
Gilston Rd, SW10 .... 67 F3
Giltspur St, EC1 .... 39 D2
Ginsburg Yd, NW3
off Heath St 108 C1
Gipsy La, SW15 .... 176 A1
Giraud St, E14 .... 144 B2
Girdlers Rd, W14 .... 149 D3
Girdlestone Wk, N19 .... 96 C3
Gironde Rd, SW6 .... 163 F2
Girton Vil, W10 .... 135 D2
Gissing Wk, N1
off Lofting Rd 112 A4
Given Wilson Wk, E13 .... 131 F2
Giverny Ho, SE16
off Canada St 157 D1
Gladiator St, SE23 .... 185 E4
Glading Ter, N16 .... 99 F4
Gladsmuir Rd, N19 .... 96 C2
Gladstone Ct, SW1
off Regency St 72 B1
SW8
off Havelock Ter 83 D4
Gladstone Ms, NW6
off Cavendish Rd 107 F4
Gladstone Par, NW2
off Edgware Rd 92 B2
Gladstone Pk Gdns, NW2 .... 92 B4
Gladstone Pl, E3
off Roman Rd 129 F2
Gladstone Rd, W4
off Acton La 147 D2
Gladstone St, SE1 .... 62 C2
Gladwyn Rd, SW15 .... 177 D1
Gladys Rd, NW6 .... 108 A4
Glaisher St, SE8 .... 172 A1
Glamis Pl, E1 .... 142 C3
Glamis Rd, E1 .... 142 C3
Glanville Rd, SW2 .... 181 E3
Glaserton Rd, N16 .... 99 E1
Glasgow Ho, W9 .... 7 D3
Glasgow Ter, SW1 .... 71 E3
Glasier Ct, E15
off Glenavon Rd 117 E4
Glaskin Ms, E9
off Danesdale Rd 115 E3
Glasshill St, SE1 .... 51 D4
Glasshouse Flds, E1 .... 143 D3
Glasshouse St, W1 .... 47 F1
Glasshouse Wk, SE11 .... 73 D2
Glasshouse Yd, EC1 .... 27 E3
Glass St, E2
off Coventry Rd 128 B4
Glastonbury Ho, SW1 .... 70 C2
Glastonbury Pl, E1
off Sutton St 142 C2
Glastonbury St, NW6 .... 107 F2
Glaucus St, E3 .... 144 B1
Glazbury Rd, W14 .... 149 E3
Glebe, The, SE3 .... 187 E1
Glebe Cl, W4 .... 147 E4
Glebe Pl, SW3 .... 68 C4
Glebe Rd, E8
off Middleton Rd 113 F4
NW10 .... 105 F3
SW13 .... 162 A4
Glebe St, W4 .... 147 E4
Glebe Ter, W4
off Glebe St 147 E4
Gledhow Gdns, SW5 .... 67 E1
Gledstanes Rd, W14 .... 149 E4
Glegg Pl, SW15 .... 177 D2
Glenaffric Av, E14 .... 159 D3
Glenarm Rd, E5 .... 114 C2
Glenavon Rd, E15 .... 117 E4
Glenbrook Rd, NW6 .... 108 A2
Glendall St, SW9 .... 181 F2
Glendarvon St, SW15 .... 177 D1
Glendower Gdns, SW14
off Glendower Rd 175 D1
Glendower Pl, SW7 .... 56 A4
Glendower Rd, SW14 .... 175 D1
Glendun Rd, W3 .... 133 E3
Gleneagles Cl, SE16
off Ryder Dr 156 B4
Glenelg Rd, SW2 .... 181 E3
Glenfinlas Way, SE5 .... 87 D2
Glenforth St, SE10 .... 159 F4
Glengall Causeway, E14 .... 158 A2
Glengall Gro, E14 .... 158 B2
Glengall Rd, NW6 .... 121 F1
SE15 .... 77 F4
Glengall Ter, SE15 .... 77 F4
Glengarnock Av, E14 .... 158 C3
Glengarry Rd, SE22 .... 183 E3
Glenhurst Av, NW5 .... 110 A1
Glenilla Rd, NW3 .... 109 E3

enister Rd, SE10 159 F4
enkerry Ho, E14
off Burcham St 144 C2
enloch Rd, NW3 109 E3
enmore Rd, NW3 109 E3
enrosa St, SW6 164 C4
enroy St, W12 134 C2
ensdale Rd, SE4 185 F1
en Ter, E14
off Manchester Rd 158 C1
entham Gdns, SW13 162 B1
entham Rd, SW13 162 A1
enthorne Ms, W6
off Glenthorne Rd 148 B3
enthorne Rd, W6 148 C3
enton Rd, SE13 187 E2
entworth St, NW1 21 F3
enville Gro, SE8 171 F2
enwood Av, NW9 91 E2
enwood Gro, NW9 90 C2
enworth Av, E14 159 D3
ddon Dr, E5 114 A1
ddon Rd, W14 149 E3
obal App, E3
off Hancock Rd 130 B2
obe Pond Rd, SE16 143 E4
obe Rd, E1 128 C3
E2 128 C3
E15 117 F2
obe Rope Wk, E14 158 C3
obe St, SE1 63 F2
obe Ter, E2
off Globe Rd 128 C3
obe Town, E2
off Mace St 129 D2
obe Wf, SE16
off Rotherhithe St 143 D3
obe Yd, W1 34 C3
oucester Arc, SW7 55 E4
oucester Av, NW1 110 A4
oucester Circ, SE10 172 C2
oucester Cl, NW10 105 D4
oucester Ct, Rich. TW9 160 A2
oucester Cres, NW1 124 B1
oucester Dr, N4 98 B3
oucester Gdns, NW11 93 F1
W2 31 D2
oucester Gate, NW1 10 C2
oucester Gate Ms, NW1 10 C2
oucester Ho, NW6 6 B3
oucester Ms, E10
off Gloucester Rd 102 A1
W2 31 F3
oucester Ms W, W2 31 E3
Gloucester Pk, SW7 55 E4
oucester Pl, NW1 21 E2
W1 21 F4
oucester Pl Ms, W1 33 F1
Gloucester Road 55 F4
oucester Rd, E10 102 A1
SW7 55 E2
W3 146 C1
Richmond TW9 160 A2
oucester Sq, E2
off Whiston Rd 128 A1
W2 32 B3
oucester St, SW1 71 E3
oucester Ter, W2 31 E2
oucester Wk, W8 42 B4
oucester Way, EC1 26 B1
cena Rd, SW11 179 F1
nde Ms, SW3 57 D3
nde St, SE4 185 F4
nfield Rd, NW10 105 E4

Glyn Rd, E5 101 D4
Glyn St, SE11 73 E3
Goaters All, SW6 163 F2
Godalming Rd, E14 144 B1
Godbold Rd, E15 131 E3
Goddard Pl, N19 96 C4
Godfrey Ho, EC1 28 A1
Godfrey St, E15 130 C2
SW3 69 D2
Goding St, SE11 73 D3
Godley Cl, SE14
off Kender St 170 C3
Godliman St, EC4 39 E3
Godman Rd, SE15 170 B4
Godolphin Pl, W3 133 D3
Godolphin Rd, W12 148 B1
Godson St, N1 14 A2
Godson Yd, NW6
off Kilburn Pk Rd 18 A1
Godwin Cl, N1 15 F2
Godwin Ct, NW1 11 F2
Godwin Ho, NW6
off Tollgate Gdns 6 C2
Goethe Institut, SW7 56 B2
Goffers Rd, SE3 173 D3
Golborne Gdns, W10
off Golborne Rd 121 F4
Golborne Ms, W10
off Portobello Rd 135 E1
Golborne Rd, W10 135 E1
Golden Cross Ms, W11
off Basing St 135 F2
★ Golden Hinde, SE1 52 A2
Golden Jubilee Br, SE1 49 E3
WC2 49 D2
Golden La, EC1 27 E3
Golden La Est, EC1 27 E3
Golden Sq, W1 35 F4
Golden Yd, NW3
off Heath St 108 C1
Golders Gdns, NW11 93 E1
GOLDERS GREEN, NW11 94 A1
Golders Green 94 A1
Golders Green 94 A2
Golders Grn Cres, NW11 93 F1
Golders Pk Cl, NW11 94 A2
Golders Way, NW11 93 F1
Goldhawk Ms, W12
off Devonport Rd 148 B1
Goldhawk Road 148 B1
Goldhawk Rd, W6 147 F3
W12 148 A2
Goldhurst Ter, NW6 108 B4
Golding St, E1 142 A2
Golding Ter, SW11
off Longhedge St 166 A4
Goldington Cres, NW1 12 A2
Goldington St, NW1 12 A2
Goldman Cl, E2 128 A4
Goldney Rd, W9 18 A3
Goldsboro Rd, SW8 84 B4
Goldsmith Av, W3 133 D3
Goldsmith Cl, W3 133 D4
Goldsmith Rd, E10 102 A2
SE15 170 A3
W3 133 D4
Goldsmiths Coll, SE14
off Lewisham Way 171 E3
★ Goldsmiths' Hall, EC2 39 E2
Goldsmith's Pl, NW6 6 C1
Goldsmith's Row, E2 128 A2
Goldsmith's Sq, E2 128 A2
Goldsmith St, EC2 39 F2
Goldsworthy Gdns, SE16 156 C3

Goldwell Ho, SE22
off Quorn Rd 183 E1
Goldwin Cl, SE14 170 C3
Gomm Rd, SE16 156 C2
Gondar Gdns, NW6 107 F2
Gonson St, SE8 172 B1
Gonville St, SW6
off Putney Br App 177 E1
Gooch Ho, E5 100 B4
Goodall Rd, E11 102 C4
Goodge Pl, W1 35 F1
Goodge Street 23 F4
Goodge St, W1 35 F1
Goodhall St, NW10 119 E3
Goodhart Pl, E14 143 E3
Goodinge Cl, N7 111 E3
Goodman Rd, E10 102 C1
Goodmans Ct, E1 41 E4
Goodman's Stile, E1 142 A2
Goodman's Yd, E1 41 E4
Goodrich Rd, SE22 183 F4
Goodson Rd, NW10 105 E4
Goods Way, NW1 12 C2
Goodway Gdns, E14 145 D2
Goodwin Cl, SE16 65 F3
Goodwin Rd, W12 148 A1
Goodwins Ct, WC2 36 C4
Goodwin St, N4
off Fonthill Rd 98 A3
Goodwood Rd, SE14 171 E2
Gophir La, EC4 40 A4
Gopsall St, N1 16 B1
Gordon Av, SW14 175 E2
Gordonbrock Rd, SE4 186 A3
Gordon Cl, N19 96 C3
Gordon Gro, SE5 168 B4
Gordon Hosp, SW1 72 A1
Gordon Ho, E1
off Glamis Rd 142 C3
Gordon Ho Rd, NW5 110 A1
Gordon Pl, W8 42 B4
Gordon Rd, E15 116 C1
SE15 170 B4
W4 160 B1
Gordon Sq, WC1 24 B3
Gordon St, WC1 24 A2
Gorefield Pl, NW6 6 A2
Gore Rd, E9 128 C1
Gore St, SW7 55 F2
Gorham Pl, W11
off Mary Pl 135 E3
Goring St, EC3 41 D2
Gorleston St, W14 149 E3
Gorst Rd, NW10 118 C4
SW11 179 F4
Gorsuch Pl, E2 17 E4
Gorsuch St, E2 17 E4
Gosfield St, W1 23 E4
Goslett Yd, WC2 36 B3
Gosling Way, SW9 168 A3
GOSPEL OAK, NW5 110 A1
Gospel Oak 110 A1
Gosset St, E2 17 F4
Gosterwood St, SE8 171 E1
Goswell Rd, EC1 27 E3
Gottfried Ms, NW5
off Fortess Rd 110 C1
Gough Rd, E15 117 F1
Gough Sq, EC4 38 B2
Gough St, WC1 25 F2
Gough Wk, E14
off Saracen St 144 A2
Goulden Ho App,
SW11 165 E4

Gould Ter, E8
off Kenmure Rd **114** B2
Goulston St, E1 **41** E2
Goulton Rd, E5 **114** B1
Govan St, E2
off Whiston Rd **128** A1
Govier Cl, E15 **117** E4
Gowan Av, SW6 **163** E3
Gowan Rd, NW10 **106** B3
Gower Cl, SW4 **180** C4
Gower Ct, WC1 **24** A2
Gower Ms, WC1 **36** A1
Gower Pl, WC1 **23** F2
Gower St, WC1 **23** F2
Gower's Wk, E1 **142** A2
Gowlett Rd, SE15 **184** A1
Gowrie Rd, SW11 **180** A1
Gracechurch St, EC3 **40** B4
Grace Jones Cl, E8
off Parkholme Rd **114** A3
Grace Pl, E3
off St. Leonards St **130** B3
Grace's All, E1 **142** A3
Graces Ms, SE5 **169** E4
Graces Rd, SE5 **169** E4
Grace St, E3 **130** B3
Graduate Pl, SE1
off Long La **64** C2
Graemesdyke Av, SW14 **174** B1
Grafton Cres, NW1 **110** B3
Grafton Ho, E3 **130** A3
Grafton Ms, W1 **23** E3
Grafton Pl, NW1 **24** A1
Grafton Rd, NW5 **110** A2
W3 **132** C3
Graftons, The, NW2
off Hermitage La **94** A4
Grafton Sq, SW4 **180** C1
Grafton St, W1 **47** D1
Grafton Ter, NW5 **109** F2
Grafton Way, W1 **23** E3
WC1 **23** E3
Grafton Yd, NW5
off Prince of Wales Rd **110** B3
Graham Rd, E8 **113** F3
W4 **147** D2
Graham St, N1 **15** D3
Graham Ter, SW1 **70** A1
Gramer Cl, E11
off Norman Rd **103** D3
Grampian Gdns, NW2 **93** E2
Granard Av, SW15 **176** B3
Granary Ct, E15
off Millstone Cl **117** D3
Granary Rd, E1 **128** B4
Granary Sq, N1
off Liverpool Rd **112** A3
Granary St, NW1 **12** A1
Granby Pl, SE1 **62** A1
Granby St, E2 **29** F2
Granby Ter, NW1 **11** E3
Grand Av, EC1 **27** D4
Wembley HA9 **104** A2
Grand Av E, Wem. HA9 **104** B2
Grandison Rd, SW11 **179** F3
Grand Junct Wf, N1 **15** E3
Grand Par Ms, SW15 **177** E3
Grand Union Cl, W9
off Woodfield Rd **135** F1
Grand Union Cres, E8 **114** A4
● Grand Union Ind Est, NW10 **118** B2
Grand Union Wk, NW1 **110** B4
Grand Wk, E1
off Solebay St **129** E4
Granfield St, SW11 **165** D3
Grange, The, SE1 **65** E2
W14 *off Lisgar Ter* **149** F3
Wembley HA0 **104** A4
Grange Ct, WC2 **37** F3
Grangecourt Rd, N16 **99** E2
Grange Gdns, NW3 **94** B4
Grange Gro, N1 **112** B3
Grange Pk Rd, E10 **102** B2
Grange Pl, NW6 **108** A4
Grange Rd, E10 **102** A2
E13 **131** F3
NW10 **106** B3
SE1 **65** D2
SW13 **162** A3
W4 **146** B4
Grange St, N1 **16** B1
Grange Wk, SE1 **65** D2
Grange Wk Ms, SE1 **65** D3
Grangeway, NW6
off Messina Av **108** A4
Grange Yd, SE1 **65** E3
Granite Apts, E15
off Windmill La **117** D3
Granleigh Rd, E11 **103** E3
Gransden Av, E8 **114** B4
Gransden Rd, W12
off Wendell Rd **147** F1
Grantbridge St, N1 **15** D2
Grantham Pl, W1 **46** C3
Grantham Rd, SW9 **167** E4
W4 **161** E2
Grantley St, E1 **129** D3
Grant Rd, SW11 **179** D2
Grant's Quay Wf, EC3 **52** B1
Grant St, N1 **14** A2
Grantully Rd, W9 **18** C1
Granville Ct, N1 **127** D1
Granville Gro, SE13 **186** C1
● Granville Ind Est, NW2 **93** F3
Granville Pk, SE13 **186** C1
Granville Pl, SW6 **78** C3
W1 **34** A3
Granville Pt, NW2 **93** F3
Granville Rd, NW2 **93** F3
NW6 **6** A3
Granville Sq, SE15 **89** D2
WC1 **25** F1
Granville St, WC1 **25** F1
Grape St, WC2 **36** C2
Graphite Sq, SE11 **73** E2
Grasgarth Cl, W3 **132** C3
Grasmere Av, W3 **132** C3
Grasmere Pt, SE15
off Ilderton Rd **170** C2
Gratton Rd, W14 **149** E2
Gratton Ter, NW2 **93** D4
Gravel La, E1 **41** E2
Gravesend Rd, W12 **134** A3
Grayling Cl, E16
off Cranberry La **131** E4
Grayling Rd, N16 **99** D3
Grayling Sq, E2 **128** A3
Grayshott Rd, SW11 **166** A4
★ Gray's Inn, WC1 **25** F4
Gray's Inn Pl, WC1 **37** F1
Gray's Inn Rd, WC1 **25** E1
Gray's Inn Sq, WC1 **26** A4
Grayson Ho, EC1 **27** F1
Gray St, SE1 **62** B1
Gray's Yd, W1 **34** B3
Grazebrook Rd, N16 **99** D3
Great Acre Ct, SW4
off Clapham Pk Rd **181** D
Great Arthur Ho, EC1 **27** E
Great Bell All, EC2 **40** A
Great Castle St, W1 **35** D
Great Cen St, NW1 **21** E
Great Cen Way, NW10 **105** E
Wembley HA9 **104** C
Great Chapel St, W1 **36** A
Great Chart St, SW11 **179** D
Great Chertsey Rd, W4 **160** C
Great Ch La, W6 **149** D
Great Coll St, SW1 **60** C
Great Cross Av, SE10 **173** E
Great Cumberland Ms, W1 **33** E
Great Cumberland Pl, W1 **33** E
Great Dover St, SE1 **63** F
● Great Eastern Enterprise Cen, E14 **158** B
Great Eastern Rd, E15 **117** D
Great Eastern St, EC2 **28** C
Great Eastern Wk, EC2 **41** D
Greatfield Cl, N19
off Warrender Rd **110** C
SE4 **186** A
Great George St, SW1 **60** B
Great Guildford St, SE1 **51** E
Great Hall, SW11
off Battersea Pk Rd **82** B
Great James St, WC1 **25** E
Great Marlborough St, W1 **35** E
Great Maze Pond, SE1 **52** B
Great Newport St, WC2
off Charing Cross Rd **36** B
Great New St, EC4 **38** B
Greatorex St, E1 **142** A
Great Ormond St, WC1 **25** D
H Great Ormond St Hosp for Children, The, WC1 **25** D
Great Percy St, WC1 **13** F
Great Peter St, SW1 **60** A
⊖ Great Portland Street **23** D
Great Portland St, W1 **23** D
Great Pulteney St, W1 **35** F
Great Queen St, WC2 **37** D
Great Russell St, WC1 **36** B
Great St. Helens, EC3 **40** C
Great St. Thomas Apostle, EC4 **39** F
Great Scotland Yd, SW1 **48** C
Great Smith St, SW1 **60** B
Great Spilmans, SE22 **183** E
Great Suffolk St, SE1 **51** D
Great Sutton St, EC1 **27** D
Great Swan All, EC2 **40** A
Great Titchfield St, W1 **35** E
Great Twr St, EC3 **40** C
Great Trade Cen, NW10
off Hythe Rd **120** A
Great Trinity La, EC4 **39** F
Great Turnstile, WC1 **37** F
Great Western Rd, W2 **30** A
W9 **135** F
W11 **30** A
Great W Rd, W4 **146** B
W6 **147** F
Brentford TW8 **146** B
Great Winchester St, EC2 **40** B
Great Windmill St, W1 **36** A
Great Yd, SE1 **53** D
Greaves Twr, SW10 **79** F
Grebe Cl, E7
off Cormorant Rd **117** F
Greek Ct, W1 **36** B

★ Greek Orthodox Cath
of the Divine Wisdom
(St. Sophia), W2 .... 30 B4
reek St, W1 .... **36** B3
reek Yd, WC2 .... **36** C4
reen, The, E15 .... **117** E3
SW14 .... **174** C1
W3 .... **133** E2
reenacre Sq, SE16
off Fishermans Dr **157** D1
reen Arbour Ct, EC1 .... **38** C2
reenaway Gdns, NW3 .... **108** B1
reen Bk, E1 .... **142** B4
reenberry St, NW8 .... **8** C3
reen Cl, NW11 .... **94** C1
reencoat Pl, SW1 .... **59** F4
reencoat Row, SW1 .... **59** F3
reencrest Pl, NW2
off Dollis Hill La **92** A4
reencroft Gdns, NW6 ..... **108** B4
reen Dale, SE5 .... **183** D2
SE22 .... **183** E3
reen Dale Cl, SE22
off Green Dale **183** E3
reen Dragon Ct, SE1 .... **52** A2
reen Dragon Yd, E1
off Old Montague St **142** A1
reenend Rd, W4 .... **147** E1
reenfell Mans, SE8
off Glaisher St **172** B1
reenfield Gdns, NW2 .... **93** E3
reenfield Rd, E1 .... **142** A1
reenham Cl, SE1 .... **62** A1
● Greenheath Business Cen,
E2 *off Three Colts La* ... 128 B4
reenhill, NW3
off Prince Arthur Rd **109** D1
Wembley HA9 .... **90** B3
reenhill Pk, NW10 .... **119** E1
reenhill Rd, NW10 .... **119** E1
reenhill's Rents, EC1 .... **26** C4
reenhills Ter, N1
off Baxter Rd **113** D3
reenhill Way, Wem. HA9 ... **90** B3
reen Hundred Rd, SE15 ... **170** A1
reenland Ms, SE8
off Trundleys Rd **157** D4
Greenland Pier 157 F2
reenland Pl, NW1
off Greenland Rd **124** B1
reenland Quay, SE16 ..... **157** D3
reenland Rd, NW1 .... **124** C1
reenland St, NW1
off Camden High St **124** B1
reen Las, N4 .... **98** C2
N16 .... **98** C4
reenlink Wk, Rich. TW9 ... **160** B3
Green Man Rbt, E11 .... **103** F1
reenman St, N1 .... **112** C4
reenock Rd, W3 .... **146** B2
Green Park 47 E3
★ Green Park, The, SW1 .... 47 D3
reen Pl, SE10
off Millennium Way **159** E1
reen Pt, E15 .... **117** E3
reenroof Way, SE10 ...... **159** F2
reen's Ct, W1 .... **36** A4
reenside Rd, W12 .... **148** A2
reenstead Gdns, SW15 .... **176** A3
reen St, W1 .... **33** F4
reen Ter, EC1 .... **26** B1
reenview Cl, W3 .... **133** E4
reen Wk, SE1 .... **64** C3
reenway Cl, N4 .... **98** C3

Greenwell St, W1 .... **23** D3
GREENWICH, SE10 .... **173** D1
Greenwich 172 B2
Greenwich 172 B2
● Greenwich Cen Business
Pk, SE10
off Norman Rd 172 B2
Greenwich Ch St, SE10 ..... **172** C1
Greenwich Foot Tunnel,
E14 .... **158** C4
SE10 .... **158** C4
Greenwich High Rd, SE10 ... **172** B3
Greenwich Ho, SE13
off Hither Grn La **187** D4
Greenwich Mkt, SE10
off King William Wk 172 C1
★ Greenwich Pk, SE10 .... 173 D2
Greenwich Pk St, SE10 ..... **159** D4
Greenwich Pier 172 C1
Greenwich Quay, SE8 ...... **172** B1
Greenwich Sch
of Management, SE10
off Royal Hill 172 C2
Greenwich S St, SE10 ...... **172** B3
Greenwich Vw Pl, E14 ..... **158** B2
Greenwood Ct, SW1 .... **71** E2
Greenwood Pl, NW5
off Highgate Rd **110** B2
Greenwood Rd, E8 .... **114** A3
Greenwood Ter, NW10 ..... **119** D1
Greet St, SE1 .... **50** B3
Gregory Pl, W8 .... **42** C4
Greig Ter, SE17 .... **75** D4
Grenade St, E14 .... **143** F3
Grenard Cl, SE15 .... **170** A2
Grendon Gdns, Wem.
HA9 .... **90** A3
Grendon Ho, N1
off Priory Grn Est **13** E3
Grendon St, NW8 .... **20** C2
Grenfell Ho, SE5
off Comber Gro **87** E3
Grenfell Rd, W11 .... **135** D3
Grenfell Twr, W11 .... **135** D3
Grenfell Wk, W11 .... **135** D3
Grenville Ms, N19 .... **97** E2
Grenville Pl, SW7 .... **55** E3
Grenville Rd, N19 .... **97** E2
Grenville St, WC1 .... **25** D3
Gresham Gdns, NW11 ...... **93** E2
Gresham Pl, N19 .... **97** D3
Gresham Rd, NW10 .... **105** D2
SW9 .... **182** A1
Gresham St, EC2 .... **39** E2
Gresley Rd, N19 .... **96** C2
Gressenhall Rd, SW18 ..... **177** F4
Gresse St, W1 .... **36** A1
Greswell St, SW6 .... **163** D3
Greville Ct, E5
off Napoleon Rd **100** B4
Greville Hall, NW6 .... **6** C2
Greville Ms, NW6 .... **6** C1
Greville Pl, NW6 .... **7** D2
Greville Rd, NW6 .... **6** C2
Greville St, EC1 .... **38** B1
Greycoat Gdns, SW1
off Greycoat St **60** A3
Greycoat Pl, SW1 .... **60** A3
Greycoat St, SW1 .... **60** A3
Grey Eagle St, E1 .... **29** E4
Greyfriars Pas, EC1 .... **39** D2
Greyhound Rd, NW10 ..... **120** B3
W6 .... **163** D1
W14 .... **163** E1

Greyladies Gdns, SE10
off Wat Tyler Rd **172** C3
Greystoke Pl, EC4 .... **38** A2
Greystone Path, E11
off Grove Rd **103** F1
Griffin Cl, NW10 .... **106** B2
Griggs Pl, SE1 .... **65** D3
Grimsby St, E2 .... **29** F3
Grimsel Path, SE5 .... **87** D2
Grimshaw Cl, N6 .... **96** A1
Grimston Rd, SW6 .... **163** F4
Grimthorpe Ho, EC1 .... **26** C2
Grimwade Cl, SE15 .... **184** C1
Grindal St, SE1 .... **62** A1
Grinling Pl, SE8 .... **172** A1
Grinstead Rd, SE8 .... **157** E4
Grittleton Av, Wem. HA9 ... **104** B3
Grittleton Rd, W9 .... **18** A2
Grocer's Hall Ct, EC2 ...... **40** A3
Groombridge Rd, E9 ...... **115** D4
Groom Pl, SW1 .... **58** B2
Grosse Way, SW15 .... **176** B4
Grosvenor Av, N5 .... **112** C2
SW14 .... **175** E1
Grosvenor Cotts, SW1 ...... **58** A4
Grosvenor Ct, NW6 .... **121** D1
Grosvenor Cres, SW1 ...... **58** B1
Grosvenor Cres Ms, SW1 .... **58** A1
Grosvenor Est, SW1 .... **60** B4
Grosvenor Gdns, NW2 ..... **106** C2
SW1 .... **58** C2
SW14 .... **175** E1
Grosvenor Gdns Ms E, SW1 ... **59** D2
Grosvenor Gdns Ms N,
SW1 .... **58** C3
Grosvenor Gdns Ms S, SW1 ... **59** D3
Grosvenor Gate, W1 .... **45** F1
Grosvenor Hill, W1 .... **34** C4
Grosvenor Pk, SE5 .... **87** E1
Grosvenor Pl, SW1 .... **58** B1
Grosvenor Rd, E10 .... **102** C2
SW1 .... **70** C4
W4 .... **146** B4
Grosvenor Sq, W1 .... **34** B4
Grosvenor St, W1 .... **34** C4
Grosvenor Ter, SE5 .... **87** D2
Grosvenor Way, E5 .... **100** C3
Grosvenor Wf Rd, E14 ..... **159** D3
Grote's Bldgs, SE3 .... **173** E4
Grote's Pl, SE3 .... **173** E4
Grotto Pas, W1 .... **22** B4
Grove, The, E15 .... **117** E3
N4 .... **97** F1
N6 .... **96** A2
NW11 .... **93** E1
Grove Cotts, SW3 .... **69** D4
Grove Cres Rd, E15 .... **117** D3
Grovedale Rd, N19 .... **97** D3
Grove Dws, E1
off Adelina Gro **142** C1
Grove End, NW5
off Chetwynd Rd **110** B1
Grove End Gdns, NW8
off Grove End Rd **8** A3
Grove End Rd, NW8 .... **8** A3
Grove Gdns, NW8 .... **21** D1
Grove Grn Rd, E11 .... **102** C4
Grove Hall Ct, NW8 .... **7** F4
Grove Hill Rd, SE5 .... **183** E1
Groveland Ct, EC4 .... **39** F3
Grovelands Cl, SE5 .... **169** E4
Grove La, SE5 .... **169** D3
Grove La Ter, SE5
off Grove La **183** E1

Grove Ms, W6 ....148 C2
W11
off Portobello Rd 135 F2
GROVE PARK, W4 ....160 B2
Grove Pk, SE5 ....169 E4
Grove Pk Br, W4 ....160 C2
Grove Pk Gdns, W4 ....160 B1
Grove Pk Ms, W4 ....160 C2
Grove Pk Rd, W4 ....160 B2
Grove Pk Ter, W4 ....160 B1
Grove Pas, E2 ....128 B2
Grove Pl, NW3
off Christchurch Hill 95 D4
SW12 ....180 B4
W3 ....132 C4
Grove Rd, E3 ....129 D1
E11 ....103 F1
NW2 ....106 C3
SW13 ....161 F4
W3 ....132 C4
Groveside Cl, W3 ....132 A2
Grove St, SE8 ....157 F3
Grove Ter, NW5 ....96 B4
Grove Ter Ms, NW5
off Grove Ter 96 B4
Grove Vale, SE22 ....183 E2
Grove Vil, E14 ....144 B3
Groveway, SW9 ....167 F3
Grove Way, Wem. HA9 ....104 B2
Grovewood, Rich. TW9
off Sandycombe Rd 160 A3
Grummant Rd, SE15 ....89 E4
Grundy St, E14 ....144 B2
★ Guards Mus, SW1 ....59 F1
Gubyon Av, SE24 ....182 B3
Guerin Sq, E3 ....129 F3
Guernsey Ho, N1
off Clifton Rd 112 C3
Guernsey Rd, E11 ....103 D2
Guildford Gro, SE10 ....172 B3
Guildford Rd, SW8 ....85 D4
★ Guildhall, The, EC2 ....40 A2
★ Guildhall Art Gall
(Guildhall Lib), EC2 ....39 F2
Guildhall Bldgs, EC2 ....40 A2
Coll Guildhall Sch of Music
& Drama, EC2 ....27 F4
Hall of Res, EC1 ....28 A4
Guildhall Yd, EC2 ....39 F2
Guildhouse St, SW1 ....59 E4
Guilford Pl, WC1 ....25 E3
Guilford St, WC1 ....25 D3
Guinness Cl, E9 ....115 E4
Guinness Ct, E1 ....41 F3
Guinness Sq, SE1 ....64 C4
Guinness Trust Bldgs,
SE11 ....74 C2
SW3 ....69 E1
SW9 ....182 B2
SE1 *off Snowsfields* 52 C4
W6
off Fulham Palace Rd 148 C4
Guinness Trust Est, N16 ....99 E2
Guion Rd, SW6 ....163 F4
Gulland Wk, N1
off Nightingale Rd 112 C3
Gulliver St, SE16 ....157 F2
Gulston Wk, SW3 ....69 F1
Gunmakers La, E3 ....129 E1
GUNNERSBURY, W4 ....146 B3
Gunnersbury 146 B4
Gunnersbury 146 B4
Gunnersbury Av, W3 ....146 A2
W4 ....146 A2
Gunnersbury Cl, W4
off Grange Rd 146 B4
Gunnersbury Ct, W3 ....146 B1
Gunnersbury Cres, W3 ....146 A1
Gunnersbury Gdns, W3 ....146 A1
Gunnersbury La, W3 ....146 A2
Gunnersbury Ms, W4
off Chiswick High Rd 146 B4
★ Gunnersbury Park Mus,
W3 ....146 A2
Gunpowder Sq, EC4 ....38 B2
Gunstor Rd, N16 ....113 E1
Gun St, E1 ....41 E1
Gunter Gro, SW10 ....79 E1
Gunterstone Rd, W14 ....149 E3
Gunthorpe St, E1 ....41 F1
Gunton Rd, E5 ....100 B4
Gunwhale Cl, SE16 ....143 D4
Gurney Cl, E15
off Gurney Rd 117 E2
Gurney Rd, E15 ....117 E2
SW6 ....178 C1
Guthrie St, SW3 ....68 C2
Gutter La, EC2 ....39 F2
Guyscliff Rd, SE13 ....186 C3
H Guy's Hosp, SE1 ....52 B4
Guy St, SE1 ....52 B4
Gwalior Rd, SW15
off Felsham Rd 177 D1
Gwendolen Av, SW15 ....177 D3
Gwendolen Cl, SW15 ....176 C3
Gwendwr Rd, W14 ....149 E4
Gwen Morris Ho, SE5 ....87 F3
Gwyn Cl, SW6 ....79 E3
Gwynne Cl, W4
off Pumping Sta Rd 161 F1
Gwynne Pl, WC1 ....25 F1
Gwynne Rd, SW11 ....165 D4
Gylcote Cl, SE5 ....183 D2
Jct Gypsy Cor, W3 ....132 C1

H

Haarlem Rd, W14 ....149 D2
Haberdasher Est, N1
off Haberdasher St 16 B4
Haberdasher Pl, N1 ....16 B4
Haberdasher St, N1 ....16 B4
Habitat Cl, SE15
off Gordon Rd 170 B4
Hackford Rd, SW9 ....86 A3
Hackford Wk, SW9 ....167 F3
HACKNEY, E8 ....114 B3
Hackney Central 114 B3
★ Hackney City Fm,
E2 ....128 A2
Hackney Downs 114 B2
Hackney Gro, E8
off Reading La 114 B3
★ Hackney Marsh, E9 ....101 E4
★ Hackney Mus, E8 ....114 B3
Hackney Rd, E2 ....29 E1
HACKNEY WICK, E9 ....116 A2
Hackney Wick 116 A3
Hackworth Ho, N16
off Stamford Hill 99 E2
Hackworth Pt, E3
off Rainhill Way 130 B3
Hacon Sq, E8
off Richmond Rd 114 B4
Haddo Ho, SE10
off Haddo St 172 B1
Haddonfield, SE8 ....157 D3
Haddo St, SE10 ....172 B1
Haden Ct, N4
off Lennox Rd ....98 A
Hadleigh Cl, E1
off Mantus Rd ....128 C
Hadleigh St, E2 ....128 C
Hadley Gdns, W4 ....147 D
Hadley St, NW1 ....110 B
Hadrian Cl, E3
off Garrison Rd ....130 A
Hadrian Est, E2 ....128 A
Hadrian Ms, N7
off Roman Way ....111 F
Hadrian St, SE10 ....159 E
Hadyn Pk Rd, W12 ....148 A
Hafer Rd, SW11 ....179 F
HAGGERSTON, E2 ....17 F
Haggerston ....127 F
Haggerston Rd, E8 ....113 F
Haggerston Studios, E8
off Kingsland Rd 127 F1
Hague St, E2
off Derbyshire St 128 A3
Hainault Rd, E11 ....102 C
Haines Cl, N1 ....113 E
Hainford Cl, SE4 ....185 D
Haining Cl, W4
off Wellesley Rd ....146 A
Hainton Cl, E1 ....142 B
Halberd Ms, E5 ....100 B3
Halcomb St, N1 ....16 C1
Halcrow St, E1
off Newark St 142 B1
Haldane Rd, SW6 ....163 F
Haldon Rd, SW18 ....177 F3
Hale Gdns, W3 ....132 A
Hales Prior, N1
off Calshot St ....13 E
Hales St, SE8
off Deptford High St ....172 A
Hale St, E14 ....144 B3
Halesworth Cl, E5
off Theydon Rd 100 C3
Halesworth Rd, SE13 ....186 B1
Half Moon Ct, EC1 ....39 E
Half Moon Cres, N1 ....13 F
Half Moon La, SE24 ....182 C
Half Moon Pas, E1 ....41 F3
Half Moon St, W1 ....47 D
Halford Rd, SW6 ....78 B1
Haliday Wk, N1
off Balls Pond Rd 113 D3
Halidon Cl, E9
off Urswick Rd ....114 C
Halkin Arc, SW1 ....58 A
Halkin Ms, SW1 ....58 A
Halkin Pl, SW1 ....58 A
Halkin St, SW1 ....58 B1
Hallam Ms, W1 ....23 D
Hallam Rd, SW13 ....176 B1
Hallam St, W1 ....23 D3
Halley Gdns, SE13 ....187 D
Halley St, E14 ....143 E1
Hallfield Est, W2 ....31 E
Hall Gate, NW8 ....7 F4
Halliday Ho, E1
off Christian St ....142 A
Halliford St, N1 ....112 C4
Hallings Wf Studios, E15
off Channelsea Rd 131 D1
Halliwell Rd, SW2 ....181 F4
● Hallmark Trd Cen, Wem.
HA9 ....104 C1
Hall Oak Wk, NW6
off Barlow Rd 107 F3

Hall Pl, W2 .... 20 A3
Hall Rd, E15 .... 117 D1
NW8 .... 19 F1
Hall St, EC1 .... 15 D4
Hallsville Rd, E16 .... 145 F2
Hall Twr, W2 .... 20 B4
Halpin Pl, SE17 .... 76 B1
Halsbury Rd, W12 .... 134 B4
Halsey Ms, SW3 .... 57 E4
Halsey St, SW3 .... 57 E4
Halsmere Rd, SE5 .... 87 D4
Halstead Ct, N1 .... 16 A3
Halston Cl, SW11 .... 179 F4
Halstow Rd, NW10 .... 121 D3
Halton Cross St, N1 .... 126 B1
Halton Pl, N1
off Dibden St 126 C1
Halton Rd, N1 .... 112 B4
Hambalt Rd, SW4 .... 180 C3
Hamble St, SW6 .... 178 B1
Hambley Ho, SE16
off Manor Est 156 B3
Hamelin St, E14
off St. Leonards Rd 144 C2
Hamfrith Rd, E15 .... 117 F3
Hamilton Cl, NW8 .... 20 A1
SE16
off Somerford Way 157 E1
Hamilton Ct, W9 .... 7 E4
Hamilton Gdns, NW8 .... 7 F4
Hamilton Ho, SW8
off St. George Wf 72 C4
Hamilton La, N5
off Hamilton Pk 112 B1
Hamilton Ms, W1 .... 46 C4
Hamilton Pk, N5 .... 112 B1
Hamilton Pk W, N5 .... 112 B1
Hamilton Pl, N19 .... 97 D4
W1 .... 46 B3
Hamilton Rd, E15 .... 131 E3
NW10 .... 106 A2
NW11 .... 93 D1
W4 .... 147 E1
Coll Hamilton Rd Cen, E15
off Hamilton Rd 131 E3
Hamilton Sq, SE1 .... 52 B4
Hamilton St, SE8
off Deptford High St 172 A1
Hamilton Ter, NW8 .... 7 F4
Hamlet, The, SE5 .... 183 D1
Hamlet Cl, SE13 .... 187 E2
Hamlet Gdns, W6 .... 148 A3
Hamlet Sq, NW2 .... 93 E4
Hamlets Way, E3 .... 129 F4
Hamlet Way, SE1 .... 52 B4
★ Hamleys, W1 .... 35 E4
Hammelton Grn, SW9 .... 86 C4
HAMMERSMITH, W6 .... 148 C4
⊖ Hammersmith 148 C3
⊖ Hammersmith 148 C3
Coll Hammersmith & W London Coll, W14 *off Gliddon Rd* 149 E4
Hammersmith Br, SW13 .... 162 B1
W6 .... 162 B1
Hammersmith Br Rd, W6 .... 148 C4
Jct Hammersmith Bdy, W6 .... 148 C3
W6 .... 148 C3
Hammersmith Flyover, W6 .... 148 C4
Hammersmith Gro, W6 .... 148 C2
H Hammersmith Hosp, W12 .... 134 B2
Hammersmith Rd, W6 .... 149 D3
W14 .... 149 D3
Hammersmith Ter, W6 .... 148 A4
Hammett St, EC3 .... 41 E4
Hammond Ho, SE14
off Lubbock St 170 C2
Hammond St, NW5 .... 110 C3
Hamond Sq, N1 .... 16 C2
Ham Pk Rd, E7 .... 117 F4
E15 .... 117 F4
Hampden Cl, NW1 .... 12 B3
Hampden Gurney St, W1 .... 33 E3
Hampden Rd, N19
off Holloway Rd 97 D3
Hampshire Hog La, W6
off King St 148 B3
Hampshire St, NW5
off Torriano Av 111 D3
Hampson Way, SW8 .... 85 E4
HAMPSTEAD, NW3 .... 109 D1
⊖ Hampstead 108 C1
Hampstead Grn, NW3 .... 109 E2
Hampstead Gro, NW3 .... 94 C4
★ Hampstead Heath, NW3 .... 95 D3
⊖ Hampstead Heath 109 E1
Hampstead High St, NW3 .... 108 C1
Hampstead Hill Gdns, NW3 .... 109 D1
Hampstead La, N6 .... 95 D1
NW3 .... 95 D1
Hampstead Rd, NW1 .... 11 E2
Hampstead Sq, NW3 .... 94 C4
Hampstead Wk, E3
off Waterside Cl 129 F1
Hampstead Way, NW11 .... 94 C2
Hampton Cl, NW6 .... 18 A1
Hampton Ct, N1
off Upper St 112 B3
Hampton Ho, SW8
off Ascalon St 83 E3
Hampton Ms, NW10
off Minerva Rd 119 D3
Hampton Rd, E11 .... 103 D2
Hampton St, SE1 .... 75 D1
SE17 .... 75 D1
Ham Yd, W1 .... 36 A4
Hana Ms, E5
off Goulton Rd 114 C1
Hanbury Dr, E11
off High Rd Leytonstone 103 F1
Hanbury Ms, N1 .... 15 F1
Hanbury Rd, W3 .... 146 B1
Hanbury St, E1 .... 29 E4
Hancock Rd, E3 .... 130 C3
Handa Wk, N1
off Clephane Rd 112 C3
Hand Ct, WC1 .... 37 F1
Handel Pl, NW10 .... 105 D3
Handel St, WC1 .... 24 C2
Handen Rd, SE12 .... 187 E3
Handforth Rd, SW9 .... 86 A2
Handley Gro, NW2 .... 93 D4
Handley Rd, E9 .... 114 C4
Hanger Grn, W5 .... 118 A4
Hanger Vw Way, W3 .... 132 A2
Hanging Sword All, EC4 .... 38 B3
Hankey Pl, SE1 .... 64 B1
Hanley Gdns, N4 .... 97 E2
Hanley Rd, N4 .... 97 E2
Hanmer Wk, N7
off Newington Barrow Way 97 F4
Hannah Cl, NW10 .... 104 C1
Hannah Mary Way, SE1
off Simms Rd 156 A3
Hannay La, N8 .... 97 D1
Hannell Rd, SW6 .... 163 E2
Hannibal Rd, E1 .... 142 C1
Hannington Rd, SW4 .... 180 B1
Hanover Cl, Rich. TW9 .... 160 A2
Hanover Ct, W12
off Uxbridge Rd 134 A4
Hanover Gdns, SE11 .... 86 A1
Hanover Gate, NW1 .... 21 D1
Hanover Gate Mans, NW1 .... 21 D2
Hanover Pk, SE15 .... 170 A3
Hanover Pl, E3
off Brokesley St 129 F3
WC2 .... 37 D3
Hanover Rd, NW10 .... 106 C4
Hanover Sq, W1 .... 35 D3
Hanover Steps, W2
off St. Georges Flds 33 D3
Hanover St, W1 .... 35 D3
Hanover Ter, NW1 .... 21 D1
Hanover Ter Ms, NW1 .... 21 D1
● Hanover W Ind Est, NW10 .... 119 D2
Hanover Yd, N1 .... 15 D2
Hansard Ms, W14
off Holland Rd 149 D1
Hanscomb Ms, SW4
off Bromell's Rd 180 C2
Hans Cres, SW1 .... 57 E2
Hansler Rd, SE22 .... 183 F3
Hanson Cl, SW14 .... 174 C1
Hanson St, W1 .... 23 E4
Hans Pl, SW1 .... 57 F2
Hans Rd, SW3 .... 57 E2
Hans St, SW1 .... 57 F3
Hanway Pl, W1 .... 36 A2
Hanway St, W1 .... 36 A2
Harads Pl, E1
off Ensign St 142 A3
Harben Rd, NW6 .... 108 C4
Harberson Rd, E15 .... 131 F1
Harberton Rd, N19 .... 96 C2
Harbet Rd, W2 .... 32 B1
Harbinger Rd, E14 .... 158 B3
Harbledown Rd, SW6 .... 78 A4
Harbord Cl, SE5
off De Crespigny Pk 169 D4
Harbord St, SW6 .... 163 D3
Harbour Av, SW10 .... 79 F4
Harbour Ex Sq, E14 .... 158 B1
Harbour Reach, SW6
off The Boulevard 164 C3
Harbour Rd, SE5 .... 182 C1
Harbour Yd, SW10
off Harbour Av 164 C3
Harbut Rd, SW11 .... 179 D2
Harcombe Rd, N16 .... 99 E4
Harcourt Rd, E15 .... 131 F2
SE4 .... 185 E2
Harcourt St, W1 .... 33 D1
Harcourt Ter, SW10 .... 67 D3
Harders Rd, SE15 .... 170 B4
Hardess St, SE24
off Herne Hill Rd 182 C1
Hardie Cl, NW10 .... 105 D2
Harding Cl, SE17 .... 75 E4
Hardinge Rd, NW10 .... 120 B1
Hardinge St, E1 .... 142 C2

Hardwicke Ho, E3 *off Bromley High St* **130** B3
Hardwicke Ms, WC1 **25** F1
Hardwicke Rd, W4 **146** C3
Hardwick St, EC1 **26** B1
Hardwicks Way, SW18 **178** A3
Hardwidge St, SE1 **52** C4
Hardy Cl, SE16 *off Middleton Dr* **157** D1
Hardy Rd, SE3 **173** F2
Hare & Billet Rd, SE3 **173** D3
Hare Ct, EC4 **38** A3
Harecourt Rd, N1 **112** C3
Haredale Rd, SE24 **182** C2
Harefield Ms, SE4 **185** F1
Harefield Rd, SE4 **185** F1
Hare Marsh, E2 *off Cheshire St* **128** A4
Hare Pl, EC4 **38** B3
Hare Row, E2 **128** B2
Hare Wk, N1 **17** D3
Harewood Av, NW1 **21** D3
Harewood Pl, W1 **35** D3
Harewood Row, NW1 **21** D4
Harfield Gdns, SE5 **183** E1
Harford Ms, N19 **97** D4
Harford St, E1 **129** E4
Hargrave Pk, N19 **96** C3
Hargrave Pl, N7 *off Brecknock Rd* **111** D2
Hargrave Rd, N19 **96** C3
Hargwyne St, SW9 **181** F1
Harkness Ho, E1 *off Christian St* **142** A2
Harlech Twr, W3 **146** B1
Harlescott Rd, SE15 **185** D2
HARLESDEN, NW10 **119** E2
⊖ Harlesden **119** D2
⊖ Harlesden **119** D2
Harlesden Gdns, NW10 **119** F1
Harlesden La, NW10 **120** A1
Harlesden Rd, NW10 **120** A1
Harleston Cl, E5 *off Theydon Rd* **100** C3
Harleyford Rd, SE11 **73** E4
Harleyford St, SE11 **86** A1
Harley Gdns, SW10 **67** F3
Harley Gro, E3 **129** F3
Harley Pl, W1 **34** C1
Harley Rd, NW3 **109** D4
NW10 **119** E2
Harley St, W1 **34** C1
H Harley St Clinic, The, W1 **22** C4
Harling Ct, SW11 *off Burns Rd* **165** F4
Harman Cl, NW2 **93** E4
SE1 *off Avondale Sq* **156** A4
Harman Dr, NW2 **93** E4
Harmony Pl, SE1 **77** F2
Harmood Gro, NW1 *off Clarence Way* **110** B4
Harmood Pl, NW1 *off Harmood St* **110** B4
Harmood St, NW1 **110** B4
Harmsworth Ms, SE11 **62** C3
Harmsworth St, SE17 **74** C3
Harold Est, SE1 **65** D3
Harold Laski Ho, EC1 **26** C1
Harold Pl, SE11 *off Kennington La* **74** A3
Harold Rd, E11 **103** E2
NW10 **119** D3
Harp All, EC4 **38** C2
● Harp Business Cen, NW2 **91** F3
Harpenmead Pt, NW2 **93** F3
Harper Rd, SE1 **63** E2
Harp Island Cl, NW10 **91** D3
Harp La, EC3 **52** C1
Harpley Sq, E1 **128** C3
Harpsden St, SW11 *off Battersea Pk Rd* **166** A3
Harpur Ms, WC1 **25** E4
Harpur St, WC1 **25** E4
Harrap St, E14 **144** C3
Harriet Cl, E8 **128** A1
Harriet St, SW1 **57** F1
Harriet Wk, SW1 **57** F1
Harrington Cl, NW10 **91** D4
Harrington Ct, W10 *off Dart St* **121** F3
Harrington Gdns, SW7 **67** D1
Harrington Hill, E5 **100** B2
Harrington Ho, NW1 **11** E4
Harrington Rd, E11 **103** E2
SW7 **56** A4
Harrington Sq, NW1 **11** E3
Harrington St, NW1 **11** E4
Harriott Cl, SE10 **159** F3
Harrison St, WC1 **25** D1
Harris St, E17 **101** F1
SE5 **88** B3
★ Harrods, SW1 **57** E2
Harroway Rd, SW11 **165** D4
Harrowby St, W1 **33** D2
Harrowgate Rd, E9 **115** E3
Harrow Grn, E11 **103** E4
Harrow La, E14 **144** C3
Harrow Pl, E1 **41** D2
Harrow Rd, E11 **103** E4
NW10 **120** B3
W2 **30** C1
W9 **18** A3
W10 **121** D4
Wembley HA9 **104** A2
Hartfield Ter, E3 **130** A2
Hart Gro, W5 **132** A4
Hartham Cl, N7 **111** E2
Hartham Rd, N7 **111** E2
Hartington Ct, W4 **160** B2
Hartington Rd, SW8 **84** C3
W4 **160** B2
Hartismere Rd, SW6 **163** F2
Hartlake Rd, E9 **115** D3
Hartland Rd, E15 **117** F4
NW1 **110** B4
NW6 **121** F2
Hartley Ho, SE1 *off Longfield Est* **65** F4
Hartley Rd, E11 **103** F2
Hartley St, E2 **128** C3
Hartnoll St, N7 *off Eden Gro* **111** F2
Harton St, SE8 **172** A3
Hartopp Pt, SW6 *off Pellant Rd* **163** E2
Hartshorn All, EC3 **41** D3
Harts La, SE14 **171** E2
Hart St, EC3 **41** D4
Hartswood Gdns, W12 **147** F2
Hartswood Rd, W12 **147** F1
Hartsworth Cl, E13 **131** F2
Hartwell St, E8 *off Dalston La* **113** F3
Harvard Hill, W4 **160** B1
Harvard La, W4 **146** C4
Harvard Rd, SE13 **186** C3
W4 **146** B4
Harvey Gdns, E11 **103** F2
Harvey Rd, E11 **103** F2
SE5 **88** A4
Harvey St, N1 **16** B1
Harvington Wk, E8 *off Wilman Gro* **114** A4
Harvist Est, N7 **111** F1
Harvist Rd, NW6 **121** D3
Harwood Rd, SW6 **78** B3
Harwood Ter, SW6 **78** C4
Hascombe Ter, SE5 *off Love Wk* **169** D4
Haselrigge Rd, SW4 **181** D2
Hasker St, SW3 **57** D4
Haslam Cl, N1 **112** A4
Haslam St, SE15 **89** F3
Haslemere Rd, N8 **97** D1
Hassard St, E2 **17** F3
Hassett Rd, E9 **115** D3
Hassop Rd, NW2 **107** D1
Hastings Cl, SE15 **170** A2
Hastings St, WC1 **24** C1
Hat & Mitre Ct, EC1 **27** D3
● Hatcham Ms Business Cen, SE14 *off Hatcham Pk Rd* **171** D3
Hatcham Pk Ms, SE14 *off Hatcham Pk Rd* **171** D3
Hatcham Pk Rd, SE14 **171** D3
Hatcham Rd, SE15 **170** C1
Hatchard Rd, N19 **97** D3
Hatchers Ms, SE1 **65** D1
Hatcliffe Cl, SE3 **187** F1
Hatcliffe St, SE10 **159** F4
Hatfield Cl, SE14 *off Reaston St* **171** D2
Hatfield Rd, E15 **117** E2
W4 **147** D1
Hatfields, SE1 **50** B2
Hatherley Gro, W2 **30** C2
Hatherley St, SW1 **71** F1
Hathersage Ct, N1 *off Newington Grn* **113** D2
Hathorne Cl, SE15 **170** B4
Hathway St, SE15 *off Gibbon Rd* **170** C4
Hathway Ter, SE14 *off Gibbon Rd* **171** D4
Hatley Rd, N4 **97** F3
Hatteraick St, SE16 *off Brunel Rd* **156** C1
Hatton Gdn, EC1 **26** B4
Hatton Ho, E1 *off Cable St* **142** A3
Hatton Pl, EC1 **26** B3
Hatton Row, NW8 **20** B3
Hatton St, NW8 **20** B3
Hatton Wall, EC1 **26** A4
Haul Rd, NW1 **12** C2
Haunch of Venison Yd, W1 **34** C3
Hauteville Ct Gdns, W6 *off Stamford Brook Av* **147** F2
Havannah St, E14 **158** A1
Havelock Cl, W12 *off India Way* **134** B3
Havelock St, N1 **125** E1
Havelock Ter, SW8 **83** D3
Haven, The, Rich. TW9 **174** A1
Haven Ms, N1 *off Liverpool Rd* **112** A4
Haven St, NW1 *off Castlehaven Rd* **110** B4

avenwood, Wem. HA9 **90** B4
averfield Gdns, Rich.
TW9 **160** A2
averfield Rd, E3 **129** E3
avering St, E1
off Devonport St **143** D2
aversham Pl, N6 **95** F3
averstock Hill, NW3 **109** E2
averstock Pl, N1
off Haverstock St **15** D4
averstock Rd, NW5 **110** A2
averstock St, N1 **15** D3
avil St, SE5 **88** C3
awarden Hill, NW2 **92** A4
awbridge Rd, E11 **103** D2
awes St, N1 **112** B4
awgood St, E3 **144** A1
awke Pl, SE16
off Middleton Dr **157** D1
awkesbury Rd, SW15 **176** B3
awke Twr, SE14
off Nynehead St **171** E1
awkins Rd, NW10 **105** E4
awkridge, NW5
off Warden Rd **110** A3
awkshead, NW1 **11** E4
awkshead Rd,
NW10 **105** F4
W4 **147** E1
awkslade Rd, SE15 **185** D3
awksley Rd, N16 **99** E4
awks Ms, SE10
off Luton Pl **172** C2
awksmoor Ms, E1
off Cable St **142** B3
awksmoor St, W6 **163** D1
awkstone Est, SE16 **156** C3
awkstone Rd, SE16 **156** C3
awkwell Wk, N1
off Basire St **126** C1
awkwood Mt, E5 **100** B2
awley Cres, NW1 **110** B4
awley Ms, NW1
off Hawley St **110** B4
awley Rd, NW1 **110** B4
awley St, NW1 **110** B4
awstead Rd, SE6 **186** B4
awthorn Av, E3 **129** F1
awthorne Cl, N1 **113** E3
awthorne Gro, NW9 **90** C1
awthorn Rd, NW10 **106** A4
awthorn Wk, W10
off Fifth Av **121** E4
awtrey Rd, NW3 **109** E4
ay Cl, E15 **117** E4
aycroft Gdns, NW10 **120** A1
aycroft Rd, SW2 **181** E3
ay Currie St, E14 **144** B2
aydens Pl, W11
off Portobello Rd **135** F2
aydns Ms, W3 **132** C2
aydon St, EC3 **41** E4
aydon Wk, E1 **41** F3
aydon Way, SW11 **179** D2
ayes Gro, SE22 **183** F2
ayes Pl, NW1 **21** D3
ayfield Pas, E1
off Stepney Grn **128** C4
ayfield Yd, E1
off Mile End Rd **128** C4
ay Hill, W1 **47** D1
ayles St, SE11 **62** C4
ayling Cl, N16
off Boleyn Rd **113** E2
Hayman St, N1
off Hawes St **112** B4
Haymarket, SW1 **48** A1
Haymarket Arc, SW1 **48** A1
Haymerle Rd, SE15 **170** A1
Hay Ms, NW3
off Haverstock Hill **109** F3
Haynes Cl, SE3 **187** E1
Hayne St, EC1 **27** D4
Hay's Galleria, SE1 52 C2
Hay's La, SE1 **52** C3
Hay's Ms, W1 **46** C1
Hay St, E2 **128** A1
Hayter Rd, SW2 **181** E3
Hayton Cl, E8
off Buttermere Wk **113** F3
Hayward Gall, SE1 49 F2
Hayward Gdns, SW15 **176** C4
Hayward's Pl, EC1 **26** C3
Hazelbourne Rd, SW12 **180** B4
Hazel Cl, N19 **96** C3
SE15 **170** A4
Hazeldean Rd, NW10 **105** D4
Hazeldon Rd, SE4 **185** E3
Hazel Ho, NW3
off Maitland Pk Rd **109** F3
Hazellville Rd, N19 **97** D1
Hazelmere Rd, NW6 **122** A1
Hazel Rd, E15
off Burgess Rd **117** E2
NW10 **120** C3
Hazel Way, SE1 **65** E4
Hazelwood Ct, NW10
off Neasden La N **91** E4
Hazlebury Rd, SW6 **164** B4
Hazledene Rd, W4 **160** C1
Hazlewell Rd, SW15 **176** B3
Hazlewood Cl, E5 **101** E4
Hazlewood Cres, W10 **121** E4
Hazlewood Twr, W10
off Golborne Rd **121** F4
Hazlitt Ms, W14
off Hazlitt Rd **149** E2
Hazlitt Rd, W14 **149** E2
Headfort Pl, SW1 **58** B1
Headlam Rd, SW4 **181** D4
Headlam St, E1 **128** B4
Head's Ms, W11 **30** A3
Head St, E1 **143** D2
Heald St, SE14 **171** F3
Healey St, NW1 **110** B3
Heanor Ct, E5
off Pedro St **115** D1
Hearne Rd, W4 **160** A1
Hearn's Bldgs, SE17 **76** B1
Hearnshaw St, E14 **143** E1
Hearn St, EC2 **29** D3
Heart Hosp, The, W1 34 B1
Heath Brow, NW3
off North End Way **94** C4
Heath Cl, NW11 **94** B1
Heathcock Ct, WC2
off Exchange Ct **49** D1
Heathcote Pt, E9
off Wick Rd **115** D3
Heathcote St, WC1 **25** E2
Heathcroft, NW11 **94** B2
Heath Dr, NW3 **108** B1
Heather Cl, N7 **97** F4
SE13 **187** D4
SW8 **180** B1
Heatherley's Sch
of Fine Art, SW10 79 F3
Heather Pk Dr, Wem. HA0 **104** A4
Heather Rd, NW2 **91** F3
Heather Wk, W10
off Droop St **121** E4
Heathfield Ct, SE14 **170** C2
Heathfield Gdns, SE3 **173** E4
SW18 **179** D4
W4 **146** C4
Heathfield Pk, NW2 **106** C3
Heathfield Rd, SW18 **178** C4
W3 **146** B1
Heathfield St, W11
off Portland Rd **135** E3
Heathfield Ter, W4 **146** C4
Heathgate Pl, NW3
off Agincourt Rd **109** F2
Heath Hurst Rd, NW3 **109** E1
Heathland Rd, N16 **99** E2
Heath La, SE3 **173** D4
Heathlee Rd, SE3 **187** F2
Heathmans Rd, SW6 **163** F3
Heath Pas, NW3 **94** B3
Heath Ri, SW15 **177** D4
Heath Rd, SW8 **166** B4
Heath Side, NW3 **109** D1
Heathside, NW11 **94** A2
Heathstan Rd, W12 **134** A2
Heath St, NW3 **94** C4
Heathville Rd, N19 **97** E1
Heathwall St, SW11 **179** F1
Heathway, SE3 **173** F2
Heaton Rd, SE15 **184** A1
Heaven Tree Cl, N1 **112** C2
Heaver Rd, SW11
off Wye St **179** D1
Hebden Ct, E2 **17** E1
Heber Rd, NW2 **107** D2
SE22 **183** F4
Hebron Rd, W6 **148** B2
Heckfield Pl, SW6 **78** A3
Heckford St, E1
off The Highway **143** D3
Heddington Gro, N7 **111** F2
Heddon St, W1 **35** E4
Hedgers Gro, E9 **115** E3
Hedger St, SE11 **62** C4
Hedgley Ms, SE12
off Hedgley St **187** F3
Hedgley St, SE12 **187** F3
Hedingham Cl, N1
off Popham Rd **112** C4
Hedley Row, N5
off Poets Rd **113** D2
Heidegger Cres, SW13
off Wyatt Dr **162** B2
Heiron St, SE17 **87** D1
Helby Rd, SW4 **181** D4
Helena Pl, E9
off Fremont St **128** C1
Helena Rd, E13 **131** F2
NW10 **106** B2
Helena Sq, SE16
off Rotherhithe St **143** E3
Helenslea Av, NW11 **93** F2
Helen's Pl, E2
off Roman Rd **128** C3
Heligan Ho, SE16
off Canada St **157** D1
Heliport Ind Est, SW11 164 C4
Helix Gdns, SW2 **181** F4
Helix Rd, SW2 **181** F4
Hellings St, E1
off Wapping High St **142** A4
Helmet Row, EC1 **27** F2
Helmsley Pl, E8 **114** B4

Helperby Rd, NW10 ....**105** E4
Helsinki Sq, SE16 ....**157** E2
Hemans Est, SW8 ....**84** B3
Hemans St, SW8 ....**84** B2
Hemberton Rd, SW9 ....**181** E1
Hemingford Rd, N1 ....**13** F1
Hemingway Cl, NW5 ......**110** A1
Hemlock Rd, W12 ....**133** F3
Hemming St, E1 ....**128** A4
Hemp Wk, SE17 ....**64** B4
Hemstal Rd, NW6 ....**108** A4
Hemsworth Ct, N1 ....**16** C1
Hemsworth St, N1 ....**16** C2
Hemus Pl, SW3 ....**69** D3
Hen & Chicken Ct, EC4 ......**38** A3
Henchman St, W12 ....**133** F2
Henderson Cl, NW10 ......**104** C3
Henderson Dr, NW8 ....**20** A2
Hendon Way, NW2 ....**93** F4
Hendre Rd, SE1 ....**77** D1
Hendrick Av, SW12 ....**179** F4
Heneage La, EC3 ....**41** D3
Heneage St, E1 ....**29** F4
Henfield Cl, N19 ....**96** C2
Henley Cl, SE16
off St. Marychurch St ...**156** C1
Henley Dr, SE1 ....**65** F4
Henley Prior, N1
off Collier St **13** E3
Henley Rd, NW10 ....**120** C1
Henley St, SW11 ....**166** A4
Henniker Ms, SW3 ....**68** A4
Henniker Pt, E15 ....**117** D2
Henniker Rd, E15 ....**117** D2
Henning St, SW11 ....**165** E3
Henrietta Cl, SE8 ....**172** A1
Henrietta Ms, WC1 ....**25** D2
Henrietta Pl, W1 ....**34** C3
Henrietta St, E15 ....**116** C2
WC2 ....**37** D4
Henriques St, E1 ....**142** A2
Henry Dent Cl, SE5 ....**183** D1
Henry Dickens Ct, W11 .....**135** D4
Henry Jackson Rd,
SW15 ....**177** D1
Henry Rd, N4 ....**98** C2
Henryson Rd, SE4 ....**186** A3
Henry Wise Ho, SW1
off Vauxhall Br Rd **71** F1
Henshall Pt, E3
off Bromley High St **130** B3
Henshall St, N1 ....**113** D3
Henshaw St, SE17 ....**64** A4
Hensley Pt, E9
off Wick Rd **115** D3
Henslowe Rd, SE22 ....**184** A3
Henson Av, NW2 ....**106** C2
Henstridge Pl, NW8 ....**8** C2
Henty Cl, SW11 ....**81** D3
Henty Wk, SW15 ....**176** B3
Hepburn Ms, SW11
off Webbs Rd **179** F3
Hepplestone Cl, SW15 .....**176** B4
Hepscott Rd, E9 ....**116** A4
Hepworth Ct, SW1 ....**70** B3
Hepworth Wk, NW3
off Haverstock Hill **109** E2
Herald's Pl, SE11 ....**62** C4
Herald St, E2
off Three Colts La **128** B4
Herbal Hill, EC1 ....**26** B3
Herbert Cres, SW1 ....**57** F2
Herbert Gdns, NW10 ......**120** B2
W4 ....**160** B1
Herbert Ms, SW2
off Bascombe St **182** A4
Herbert Morrison Ho, SW6
off Clem Attlee Ct **163** F1
Herbert Rd, E17 ....**101** F1
Herbert St, NW5 ....**110** A3
Herbrand St, WC1 ....**24** C2
Hercules Pl, N7 ....**97** E4
Hercules Rd, SE1 ....**61** F3
Hercules St, N7 ....**97** E4
Hereford Gdns, SE13
off Longhurst Rd **187** E3
Hereford Ho, NW6 ....**6** B3
Hereford Ms, W2 ....**30** B3
Hereford Pl, SE14
off Royal Naval Pl **171** F2
Hereford Retreat, SE15
off Bird in Bush Rd **170** A2
Hereford Rd, E3 ....**129** F2
W2 ....**30** B2
W3 ....**132** B3
Hereford Sq, SW7 ....**67** F1
Hereford St, E2 ....**128** A4
Heritage Cl, SW9 ....**182** B1
Hermes Cl, W9 ....**18** A3
Hermes St, N1 ....**14** A3
Hermitage, The, SE13
off Lewisham Hill **172** C4
SW13 ....**161** F3
Hermitage Ct, NW2
off Hermitage La **94** A4
Hermitage Gdns, NW2 ......**94** A4
Hermitage La, NW2 ....**94** A4
Hermitage Rd, N4 ....**98** B1
N15 ....**98** B1
Hermitage Row, E8 ....**114** A2
Hermitage St, W2 ....**32** A1
Hermitage Wall, E1 ....**142** A4
Hermitage Waterside, E1
off Thomas More St **142** A4
Hermit Pl, NW6 ....**6** C1
Hermit Rd, E16 ....**145** F1
Hermit St, EC1 ....**14** C4
Herndon Rd, SW18 ....**178** C3
Herne Cl, NW10
off North Circular Rd ...**105** D2
HERNE HILL, SE24 ....**182** C3
⇌ Herne Hill **182** B4
Herne Hill, SE24 ....**182** C4
Herne Hill Ho, SE24
off Railton Rd **182** B4
Herne Hill Rd, SE24 ....**182** C1
Herne Pl, SE24 ....**182** B3
Heron Cl, NW10 ....**105** E3
Heron Ct, E5
off Big Hill **100** B2
Heron Dr, N4 ....**98** C3
Heron Pl, SE16 ....**143** E4
Heron Quay, E14 ....**144** A4
DLR Heron Quays **144** A4
Heron Rd, SE24 ....**182** C2
● Heron Trd Est, W3
off Alliance Rd **118** B4
Herrick Rd, N5 ....**98** C4
Herrick St, SW1 ....**60** B4
Herries St, W10 ....**121** E2
Hersant Cl, NW10 ....**120** A1
Herschell Ms, SE5
off Bicknell Rd **182** C1
Hertford Av, SW14 ....**175** D3
Hertford Rd, N1 ....**127** E1
Hertford St, W1 ....**46** C2
Hertslet Rd, N7 ....**97** F4
Hertsmere Rd, E14 ....**144** A3
Hesewall Cl, SW4
off Brayburne Av **166** C4
Hesketh Pl, W11 ....**135** E3
Hesper Ms, SW5 ....**66** C2
Hesperus Cres, E14 ....**158** B3
Hessel St, E1 ....**142** B2
Hestercombe Av, SW6 .....**163** E4
Hester Rd, SW11 ....**80** C3
Hester Ter, Rich. TW9
off Chilton Rd **174** A1
Hestia Ho, SE1
off Royal Oak Yd **64** C1
Heston St, SE14 ....**171** F3
Hetherington Rd, SW4 .....**181** E2
Hetley Rd, W12 ....**134** B4
Hevelius Cl, SE10 ....**159** F4
Hewer St, W10 ....**135** D1
Hewett St, EC2 ....**29** D3
Hewison St, E3 ....**129** F2
Hewlett Rd, E3 ....**129** E2
Hexagon, The, N6 ....**95** F2
Hexton Ct, N4
off Brownswood Rd **98** C3
Heybridge Way, E10 ....**101** E1
Heyford Av, SW8 ....**85** D2
Heyford Ter, SW8
off Heyford Av **85** D2
Heygate St, SE17 ....**75** E1
Heylyn Sq, E3
off Malmesbury Rd **129** F3
Heysham La, NW3 ....**94** B4
Uni Heythrop Coll, W8 ....**54** C2
Heyworth Rd, E5 ....**114** B1
E15 ....**117** F2
Hibbert Rd, E17 ....**101** F1
Hibbert St, SW11 ....**178** C1
Hichisson Rd, SE15 ....**184** C3
Hicken Rd, SW2 ....**181** F3
Hickin St, E14
off Plevna St **158** C2
Hickmore Wk, SW4 ....**180** C1
Hicks Cl, SW11 ....**179** E1
Hicks St, SE8 ....**157** E4
Hide Pl, SW1 ....**72** A1
Hides St, N7
off Sheringham Rd **111** F3
Hide Twr, SW1 ....**72** A1
High Br, SE10 ....**159** D4
High Br Wf, SE10 ....**159** D4
HIGHBURY, N5 ....**112** B2
Highbury & Islington ...**112** B3
Highbury & Islington ...**112** B3
Highbury Cor, N5 ....**112** A3
Highbury Cres, N5 ....**112** A2
Highbury Est, N5 ....**112** C2
Highbury Gra, N5 ....**112** B1
Highbury Gro, N5 ....**112** B3
Highbury Hill, N5 ....**98** A4
Highbury New Pk, N5 ......**112** C2
Highbury Pk, N5 ....**98** B4
Highbury Pl, N5 ....**112** B3
Highbury Quad, N5 ....**98** B4
Highbury Sta Rd, N1 ....**112** A3
Highbury Ter, N5 ....**112** B2
Highbury Ter Ms, N5 ......**112** B2
Highcliffe Dr, SW15 ....**175** F4
Highcroft Av, Wem. HA0 ....**104** A4
Highcroft Rd, N19 ....**97** E1
Highdown Rd, SW15 ....**176** B4
Highfield Av, NW11 ....**93** D1
Highfield Cl, SE13 ....**187** D4
Highfield Ms, NW6
off Compayne Gdns **108** B4
Highfield Rd, W3 ....**132** B1

Highfields Gro, N6 . . . . **95** F2
HIGHGATE, N6 . . . . **96** A3
Highgate Acute Mental Health Cen, N19 . . . . **96** B3
★ Highgate Cem, N6 . . . . . . **96** A2
Highgate Cl, N6 . . . . **96** A1
Highgate High St, N6 . . . . **96** A2
Highgate Hill, N6 . . . . **96** B2
N19 . . . . **96** B2
Highgate Rd, NW5 . . . . **110** B1
Highgate W Hill, N6 . . . . **96** A3
High Hill, E5
off Mount Pleasant La **100** B2
High Hill Ferry, E5
off Big Hill **100** B2
High Holborn, WC1 . . . . **37** D2
Highlands Av, W3 . . . . **132** C3
Highlands Cl, N4
off Mount Vw Rd **97** E1
Highlever Rd, W10 . . . . **134** C1
Highmore Rd, SE3 . . . . **173** E2
High Pk Av, Rich. TW9 . . . . . **160** A3
High Pk Rd, Rich. TW9 . . . . . **160** A3
High Pt, N6 . . . . **96** A1
High Rd, NW10
(Willesden) **106** B3
High Rd Leyton, E10 . . . . . . **102** B2
E15 . . . . **102** C4
High Rd Leytonstone, E11 . . **117** E1
E15 . . . . **117** E1
Highshore Rd, SE15 . . . . **169** F4
High St, E15 . . . . **130** C2
NW10 (Harlesden) **119** F2
W3 . . . . **132** B4
⊖ High Street Kensington . . **54** C1
High Timber St, EC4 . . . . **39** E4
Highway, The, E1 . . . . **142** B3
E14 . . . . **142** B3
Highwood Rd, N19 . . . . **97** E4
Hilary Cl, SW6 . . . . **78** C2
Hilary Rd, W12 . . . . **133** F2
Hilda Lockert Wk, SW9
off Fiveways Rd **168** B4
Hilda Rd, E16 . . . . **131** E4
Hilda Ter, SW9
off St. Lawrence Way . . . **168** A4
Hildyard Rd, SW6 . . . . **66** B4
Hiley Rd, NW10 . . . . **120** C3
Hilgrove Rd, NW6 . . . . **108** C4
Hillbeck Cl, SE15 . . . . **170** C2
Hill Cl, NW2 . . . . **92** B4
Hillcourt Est, N16 . . . . **99** D2
Hillcourt Rd, SE22 . . . . **184** B4
Hillcrest, N6 . . . . **96** A1
SE24 . . . . **183** D2
Hillcrest Gdns, NW2 . . . . **92** A4
Hillcrest Rd, W3 . . . . **132** A4
Hill Dr, NW9 . . . . **90** C2
Hilldrop Cres, N7 . . . . **111** D2
Hilldrop Est, N7 . . . . **111** D2
Hilldrop La, N7 . . . . **111** D2
Hilldrop Rd, N7 . . . . **111** D2
Hillersdon Av, SW13 . . . . **162** A4
Hillery Cl, SE17 . . . . **76** B1
Hill Fm Rd, W10 . . . . **134** C1
Hillfield Ct, NW3 . . . . **109** E2
Hillfield Rd, NW6 . . . . **107** F2
Hillgate Pl, W8 . . . . **42** A2
Hillgate St, W8 . . . . **42** A2
Hill Ho, E5 . . . . **100** B2
Hilliards Ct, E1
off Wapping High St **142** C4
Hillier Rd, SW11 . . . . **179** F4
Hillingdon St, SE17 . . . . **87** D1
Hillman Dr, W10 . . . . **120** C4
Hillman St, E8 . . . . **114** B3
Hillmarton Rd, N7 . . . . **111** E2
Hillmead Dr, SW9 . . . . **182** B2
Hillrise Rd, N19 . . . . **97** E1
Hill Rd, NW8 . . . . **7** F3
Hillsboro Rd, SE22 . . . . **183** E3
Hillside, NW10 . . . . **118** C1
Hillside Cl, NW8 . . . . **7** D2
Hillside Rd, N15 . . . . **99** E1
Hillsleigh Rd, W8 . . . . **135** F4
Hills Pl, W1 . . . . **35** E3
Hillstowe St, E5 . . . . **100** C3
Hill St, W1 . . . . **46** B2
Hilltop Av, NW10 . . . . **104** C4
Hilltop Rd, NW6 . . . . **108** A4
Hillway, N6 . . . . **96** A3
NW9 . . . . **91** E2
Hillyard St, SW9 . . . . **168** A3
Hillyfield Cl, E9
off Mabley St **115** E2
Hilly Flds Cres, SE4 . . . . **186** A1
Hilsea St, E5 . . . . **114** C1
Riv Hilton Docklands Nelson Dock Pier **143** F4
Hilversum Cres, SE22
off East Dulwich Gro **183** E3
Hinckley Rd, SE15 . . . . **184** A2
Hind Ct, EC4 . . . . **38** B3
Hinde Ms, W1
off Marylebone La **34** B2
Hinde St, W1 . . . . **34** B2
Hind Gro, E14 . . . . **144** A2
Hindhead Cl, N16 . . . . **99** E2
Hind Ho, N7
off Harvist Est **112** A1
Hindle Ho, E8
off Arcola St **113** F2
Hindmans Rd, SE22 . . . . **184** A3
Hindmarsh Cl, E1
off Cable St **142** A3
Hindon Ct, SW1 . . . . **59** E4
Hindrey Rd, E5 . . . . **114** B2
Hinton Rd, SE24 . . . . **182** B1
Hippodrome Ms, W11
off Portland Rd **135** E3
Hippodrome Pl, W11 . . . . . . **135** E3
Hirst Ct, SW1 . . . . **70** C3
Hitcham Rd, E17 . . . . **101** F1
Hitchin Sq, E3 . . . . **129** E2
Hithe Gro, SE16
off Lower Rd **156** C2
HITHER GREEN, SE13 . . . . **187** E4
⇌ Hither Green **187** E4
Hither Grn La, SE13 . . . . **186** C3
★ H.M.S. Belfast, SE1 . . . . . . **53** D2
★ H.M.S. President, EC4 . . . . **50** B1
★ H.M. Treasury, SW1 . . . . . **48** C4
Hobart Pl, SW1 . . . . **58** C2
Hobbes Wk, SW15 . . . . **176** B3
Hobbs Pl Est, N1 . . . . **16** C1
Hobday St, E14 . . . . **144** B1
Hobsons Pl, E1
off Hanbury St **142** A1
Hobury St, SW10 . . . . **79** F1
Hocker St, E2 . . . . **29** E1
Hockett Cl, SE8
off Grove St **157** F3
Hocroft Av, NW2 . . . . **93** F4
Hocroft Rd, NW2 . . . . **107** F1
Hocroft Wk, NW2 . . . . **93** F4
Hodes Row, NW3
off Estelle Rd **110** A1
Hodford Rd, NW11 . . . . **93** F3
Hodister Cl, SE5 . . . . **87** F3
Hodnet Gro, SE16 . . . . **157** D3
Hoffman Sq, N1
off Chart St **16** B4
Hofland Rd, W14 . . . . **149** D2
Hogan Ms, W2 . . . . **20** A4
Hogan Way, E5 . . . . **100** A3
● Hogarth Business Pk, W4 . . . . **161** E1
Hogarth Ct, EC3 . . . . **41** D4
Hogarth La, W4 . . . . **161** E1
Hogarth Pl, SW5 . . . . **66** C1
Hogarth Rd, SW5 . . . . **66** C1
Jct Hogarth Rbt, W4 . . . . . . **161** F1
Hogarth Rbt Flyover, W4
off Burlington La **161** E1
★ Hogarth's Ho, W4
off Hogarth La **161** E1
Hogshead Pas, E1
off Tobacco Dock **142** B3
Holbeck Row, SE15 . . . . **170** A2
Holbein Ms, SW1 . . . . **70** A2
Holbein Pl, SW1 . . . . **70** A1
Holberton Gdns, NW10 . . . . . **120** B3
HOLBORN, WC2 . . . . **37** E2
⊖ Holborn **37** D2
Holborn, EC1 . . . . **38** A1
Holborn Circ, EC1 . . . . **38** B1
Holborn Pl, WC1 . . . . **37** E1
Holborn Viaduct, EC1 . . . . **38** B1
Holbrook Cl, N19
off Dartmouth Pk Hill **96** B2
Holbrooke Ct, N7 . . . . **111** E1
Holbrook Rd, E15 . . . . **131** F2
Holcombe St, W6 . . . . **148** B4
Holcroft Rd, E9 . . . . **114** C4
Holden Av, NW9 . . . . **90** C2
Holdenby Rd, SE4 . . . . **185** E3
Holden Pt, E15
off Waddington Rd **117** D3
Holden St, SW11 . . . . **166** A4
Holford Ho, SE16
off Manor Est **156** B3
Holford Ms, WC1 . . . . **14** A3
Holford Pl, WC1 . . . . **13** F4
Holford Rd, NW3 . . . . **94** C4
Holford St, WC1 . . . . **14** A4
Holford Yd, WC1 . . . . **13** F3
Holgate Av, SW11 . . . . **179** D1
Holland Gdns, W14 . . . . **149** E2
Holland Gro, SW9 . . . . **86** B3
★ Holland Pk, W8 . . . . **149** F1
⊖ Holland Park **135** E4
Holland Pk, W11 . . . . **149** E1
Holland Pk Av, W11 . . . . **149** E1
Holland Pk Gdns, W14 . . . . . . **135** E4
Holland Pk Ms, W11 . . . . **135** E4
Holland Pk Rd, W14 . . . . **149** F2
Jct Holland Pk Rbt, W11 . . . **149** D1
Holland Pas, N1
off Basire St **126** C1
Holland Pl, W8 . . . . **42** C4
Holland Ri Ho, SW9 . . . . **85** F3
Holland Rd, E15 . . . . **131** E3
NW10 . . . . **120** A1
W14 . . . . **149** D1
Holland St, SE1 . . . . **51** D2
W8 . . . . **54** B1
Holland Town Est, SW9
off Mandela St **86** B3
Holland Vil Rd, W14 . . . . **149** E1

Holland Wk, N19
off Duncombe Rd **97** D2
W8 . . . . **149** F1
Hollar Rd, N16
off Stoke Newington
High St **99** F4
Hollen St, W1 . . . . **36** A2
Holles St, W1 . . . . **35** D2
Holley Rd, W3 . . . . **147** E1
Holliday Sq, SW11
off Fowler Cl **179** D1
Hollingbourne Rd, SE24 . . . . **182** C3
Hollins Ho, N7
off Tufnell Pk Rd **111** E1
HOLLOWAY, N7 . . . . **111** D2
⊖ Holloway Road **111** F2
Holloway Rd, E11 . . . . **103** E4
N7 . . . . **111** F1
N19 . . . . **97** D3
Hollyberry La, NW3
off Holly Wk **108** C1
Hollybush Gdns, E2 . . . . **128** B3
Holly Bush Hill, NW3 . . . . . . **108** C1
Hollybush Pl, E2
off Bethnal Grn Rd **128** B3
Holly Bush Steps, NW3
off Heath St **108** C1
Holly Bush Vale, NW3
off Heath St **108** C1
Holly Ct, SE10
off West Parkside **159** F2
Hollycroft Av, NW3 . . . . **94** A4
Hollydale Rd, SE15 . . . . **170** C3
Hollydene, SE15 . . . . **170** B3
Hollydown Way, E11 . . . . . . **103** D4
Holly Gro, NW9 . . . . **90** C1
SE15 . . . . **169** F4
Holly Hedge Ter, SE13 . . . . . **187** D3
Holly Hill, NW3 . . . . **108** C1
Holly Lo Gdns, N6 . . . . **96** A3
Holly Ms, SW10 . . . . **67** F3
Holly Mt, NW3
off Holly Bush Hill **108** C1
Hollymount Cl, SE10 . . . . . . **172** C3
Holly Pk, N4 . . . . **97** F1
Holly Pk Est, N4
off Blythwood Rd **97** E1
Holly Pl, NW3
off Holly Wk **108** C1
Holly Rd, E11
off Green Man Rbt **103** F1
W4 *off Dolman Rd* **147** D3
Holly St, E8 . . . . **113** F3
Holly Ter, N6
off Highgate W Hill **96** A2
Holly Village, N6
off Swains La **96** B3
Holly Wk, NW3 . . . . **108** C1
Hollywood Ms, SW10 . . . . **67** E4
Hollywood Rd, SW10 . . . . **67** E3
Holman Ho, E2
off Roman Rd **129** D3
Holman Rd, SW11 . . . . **165** D4
Holmbury Vw, E5 . . . . **100** B2
Holmbush Rd, SW15 . . . . **177** E4
Holmcote Gdns, N5 . . . . **112** C2
Holmdale Rd, NW6 . . . . **108** A2
Holmdale Ter, N15 . . . . **99** E1
Holmdene Av, SE24 . . . . **182** C3
Holmead Rd, SW6 . . . . **79** D3
Holmefield Ct, NW3 . . . . **109** E3
Holme Lacey Rd, SE12 . . . . . **187** F4
Holmes Cl, SE22 . . . . **184** A2
Holmesdale Av, SW14 . . . . . **174** B1
Holmesdale Rd, N6 . . . . **96** B1
Holmesley Rd, SE23 . . . . **185** E4
Holmes Pl, SW10 . . . . **67** F4
Holmes Rd, NW5 . . . . **110** B2
Holmes Ter, SE1 . . . . **50** A4
Holmleigh Rd, N16 . . . . **99** E2
Holmleigh Rd Est, N16
off Holmleigh Rd **99** E2
Holm Oak Cl, SW15 . . . . **177** F4
Holm Oak Ms, SW4 . . . . **181** E3
Holmside Rd, SW12 . . . . **180** A4
Holms St, E2 . . . . **128** A2
Holness Rd, E15 . . . . **117** F3
Holroyd Rd, SW15 . . . . **176** C2
Holst Ho, W12
off Du Cane Rd **134** B2
Holsworthy Sq, WC1 . . . . **25** F3
Holton St, E1 . . . . **129** D4
Holwood Pl, SW4 . . . . **181** D2
Holyhead Cl, E3
off Campbell Rd **130** A3
Holyoake Ct, SE16
off Bryan Rd **157** F1
Holyoak Rd, SE11 . . . . **62** C4
Holyport Rd, SW6 . . . . **162** C2
Holyrood St, SE1 . . . . **52** C3
Holywell Cl, SE16
off Masters Dr **156** B4
Holywell La, EC2 . . . . **29** D2
Holywell Row, EC2 . . . . **28** C3
Homefield Cl, NW10 . . . . **104** C3
Homefield Rd, W4 . . . . **147** F3
Homefield St, N1 . . . . **16** C3
Homeleigh Rd, SE15 . . . . **185** D3
★ Home Office, SW1 . . . . **60** B3
Homer Dr, E14 . . . . **158** A3
Home Rd, SW11 . . . . **165** E4
Homer Rd, E9 . . . . **115** E3
Homer Row, W1 . . . . **33** D1
Homer St, W1 . . . . **33** D1
HOMERTON, E9 . . . . **115** E2
⊖ Homerton **115** D3
Homerton Gro, E9 . . . . **115** D2
Homerton High St, E9 . . . . . **114** C2
Homerton Rd, E9 . . . . **115** E2
Homerton Row, E9 . . . . **114** C2
Homerton Ter, E9
off Morning La **114** C3
H Homerton Uni Hosp,
E9 . . . . **115** D2
Homestall Rd, SE22 . . . . **184** C3
Homestead Pk, NW2 . . . . **91** F4
Homestead Rd, SW6 . . . . **163** F2
Honduras St, EC1 . . . . **27** E2
Honeybourne Rd, NW6 . . . . . **108** B2
Honey La, EC2 . . . . **39** F3
Honeyman Cl, NW6 . . . . **107** D4
Honeywell Rd, SW11 . . . . . . **179** F4
Honeywood Rd, NW10 . . . . . **119** F2
Honiton Gdns, SE15
off Gibbon Rd **170** C4
Honiton Rd, NW6 . . . . **121** F2
HONOR OAK, SE23 . . . . **184** C4
HONOR OAK PARK, SE4 . . . . **185** E4
⇌ Honor Oak Park **185** D4
Honor Oak Pk, SE23 . . . . **184** C4
Honor Oak Ri, SE23 . . . . **184** C4
Hood Av, SW14 . . . . **174** C3
Hood Ct, EC4 . . . . **38** B3
Hooks Cl, SE15
off Woods Rd **170** B3
Hooper's Ct, SW3 . . . . **57** E1
Hoopers Ms, W3 . . . . **132** C4
Hooper St, E1 . . . . **142** A2
Hoopers Yd, NW6
off Kimberley Rd **121** F1
Hoop La, NW11 . . . . **93** F1
Hope Cl, N1
off Wallace Rd **112** C3
Hopefield Av, NW6 . . . . **121** E2
Hope Gdns, W3
off Park Rd N **146** B1
Hope St, SW11 . . . . **179** D1
Hopetown St, E1 . . . . **41** F1
Hopewell St, SE5 . . . . **88** B3
Hopewell Yd, SE5 . . . . **88** B3
Hope Wf, SE16
off St. Marychurch St . . . **156** C1
Hop Gdns, WC2 . . . . **48** C1
Hopgood St, W12
off Macfarlane Rd **134** C4
Hopkins Ms, E15 . . . . **131** F1
Hopkinsons Pl, NW1
off Fitzroy Rd **124** A1
Hopkins Rd, E10 . . . . **102** B1
Hopkins St, W1 . . . . **35** F3
Hopping La, N1
off St. Mary's Gro **112** B3
Hop St, SE10 . . . . **159** F3
Hopton's Gdns, SE1 . . . . **51** D2
Hopton St, SE1 . . . . **51** D2
Hopwood Rd, SE17 . . . . **76** B4
Hopwood Wk, E8
off Wilman Gro **114** A4
Horace Bldg, SW8
off Queenstown Rd **82** C2
Horatio Ct, SE16
off Rotherhithe St **142** C4
Horatio Pl, E14
off Cold Harbour **158** C1
Horatio St, E2 . . . . **17** F3
Horbury Cres, W11 . . . . **42** A1
Horbury Ms, W11
off Ladbroke Rd **135** F3
Horder Rd, SW6 . . . . **163** E3
Horle Wk, SE5 . . . . **168** B4
Hormead Rd, W9 . . . . **121** F4
Hornbeam Cl, SE11 . . . . **62** A4
Hornbeam Ho, NW3
off Maitland Pk Vil **109** F3
Hornbeam Sq, E3
off Hawthorn Av **129** F1
Hornblower Cl, SE16
off Greenland Quay **157** E3
Hornby Cl, NW3 . . . . **109** D4
Horne Way, SW15 . . . . **162** C4
Horn La, W3 . . . . **132** C3
Hornsey La, N6 . . . . **96** B2
Hornsey La Est, N19 . . . . **97** D1
Hornsey La Gdns, N6 . . . . **96** C1
Hornsey Ri, N19 . . . . **97** D1
Hornsey Ri Gdns, N19 . . . . . . **97** D1
Hornsey Rd, N7 . . . . **97** F3
N19 . . . . **97** E2
Hornsey St, N7 . . . . **111** F2
Hornshay St, SE15 . . . . **170** C1
Hornton Pl, W8 . . . . **54** B1
Hornton St, W8 . . . . **42** B4
Horse & Dolphin Yd, W1 . . . . . **36** B4
Horseferry Pl, SE10 . . . . **172** C1
Horseferry Rd, E14 . . . . **143** E3
SW1 . . . . **60** A3
Horse Guards Av, SW1 . . . . . . **48** C3
★ Horse Guards Par, SW1 . . **48** B3
Horse Guards Rd, SW1 . . . . . . **48** B3
Horsell Rd, N5 . . . . **112** A2
Horselydown La, SE1 . . . . **53** E4
Horsemongers Ms, SE1 . . . . . . **63** F1

Horse Ride, SW1 . . . . .48 A3
Horseshoe Cl, E14 . . . . .158 C4
NW2 . . . . .92 B3
Horse Shoe Ct, EC1
off Brewhouse Yd 27 D2
Horseshoe Ms, SW2
off Acre La 181 E2
Horse Yd, N1
off Essex Rd 126 B1
Horsford Rd, SW2 . . . . .181 F3
Horsleydown Old Stairs, SE1 . .53 E3
Horsley St, SE17 . . . . .76 A4
Horsmonden Rd, SE4 . . . . . .185 F3
Hortensia Rd, SW10 . . . . .79 E1
Horticultural Pl, W4 . . . . . . .147 D4
Horton Av, NW2 . . . . .107 E1
Horton Ho, SW8 . . . . .85 E2
Horton Rd, E8 . . . . .114 B3
Horton St, SE13 . . . . .186 B1
Hosier La, EC1 . . . . .38 C1
Hoskins St, SE10 . . . . .159 D4
Hospital of St. John & St. Elizabeth, NW8 . . . . .8 A3
Hospital Rd, E9
off Homerton Row 115 D2
Hotham Rd, SW15 . . . . .176 C1
Hotham St, E15 . . . . .131 E1
Hothfield Pl, SE16
off Lower Rd 156 C2
Hotspur St, SE11 . . . . .74 A2
Houghton Cl, E8
off Buttermere Wk 113 F3
Houghton Sq, SW9
off Clapham Rd 167 E4
Houghton St, WC2 . . . . .37 F3
Houndsditch, EC3 . . . . .41 D2
Houseman Way, SE5 . . . . . . .88 B3
Houses of Parliament, SW1 . . . . .61 D1
Hoveden Rd, NW2 . . . . .107 E2
Howard Bldg, SW8 . . . . .82 C1
Howard Cl, NW2 . . . . .107 E1
W3 . . . . .132 B2
Howard Ms, N5
off Hamilton Pk 112 B1
Howard Rd, E11 . . . . .103 E4
N16 . . . . .113 D1
NW2 . . . . .107 D1
Howards La, SW15 . . . . .176 B3
Howbury Rd, SE15 . . . . .184 C1
Howden St, SE15 . . . . .184 A1
Howell Wk, SE1 . . . . .75 D1
Howgate Rd, SW14 . . . . .175 D1
Howick Pl, SW1 . . . . .59 F3
Howie St, SW11 . . . . .80 C3
Howitt Cl, N16
off Allen Rd 113 E1
NW3 *off Howitt Rd* 109 E3
Howitt Rd, NW3 . . . . .109 E3
Howland Est, SE16 . . . . .156 C2
Howland Ms E, W1 . . . . .23 F4
Howland St, W1 . . . . .23 E4
Howland Way, SE16 . . . . . . .157 E1
Howletts Rd, SE24 . . . . .182 C4
Howley Pl, W2 . . . . .19 F4
Howsman Rd, SW13 . . . . . . .162 A1
Howson Rd, SE4 . . . . .185 E2
Hows St, E2 . . . . .17 E2
HOXTON, N1 . . . . .16 C3
Hoxton 17 D3
Hoxton Mkt, N1 . . . . .28 C1
Hoxton Sq, N1 . . . . .28 C1
Hoxton St, N1 . . . . .29 D1
Hoylake Rd, W3 . . . . .133 E2
Hoyland Cl, SE15
off Commercial Way 170 B2
Hoy St, E16 . . . . .145 F2
H.Q.S. Wellington, Master Mariners' Hall, WC2 . . . . .38 A4
Hubbard St, E15 . . . . .131 E1
Hubert Gro, SW9 . . . . .181 E1
Huddart St, E3 . . . . .143 F1
Huddleston Cl, E2 . . . . .128 C2
Huddlestone Rd, E7 . . . . . . .117 F1
NW2 . . . . .106 B3
Huddleston Rd, N7 . . . . .111 D1
Hudson Cl, W12
off Canada Way 134 B3
Hudson Ct, E14
off Maritime Quay 158 A4
Hudson's Pl, SW1 . . . . .59 D4
Hudson Way, NW2
off Gratton Ter 93 D4
Huggin Ct, EC4 . . . . .39 F4
Huggin Hill, EC4 . . . . .39 F4
Hughan Rd, E15 . . . . .117 D2
Hugh Dalton Av, SW6 . . . . . .163 F1
Hughendon Ter, E15
off Westdown Rd 116 C1
Hughes Ter, SW9
off Styles Gdns 182 B1
Hugh Gaitskell Cl, SW6 . . . . .163 F1
Hugh Ms, SW1 . . . . .71 D1
Hugh St, SW1 . . . . .71 D1
Hugon Rd, SW6 . . . . .178 B1
Hugo Rd, N19 . . . . .110 C1
Huguenot Pl, E1 . . . . .29 F4
SW18 . . . . .178 C3
Huguenot Sq, SE15
off Scylla Rd 184 B1
Hullbridge Ms, N1
off Sherborne St 127 D1
Hull Cl, SE16 . . . . .157 D1
Hull St, EC1 . . . . .27 E1
Hulme Pl, SE1 . . . . .63 F1
Humber Dr, W10 . . . . .121 D4
Humber Rd, NW2 . . . . .92 B3
SE3 . . . . .173 F1
Humberton Cl, E9
off Marsh Hill 115 E2
Humbolt Rd, W6 . . . . .163 E1
Humphrey St, SE1 . . . . .77 E2
Hungerford Br, SE1 . . . . .49 D2
WC2 . . . . .49 D2
Hungerford La, WC2 . . . . .48 C2
Hungerford Rd, N7 . . . . .111 D2
Hungerford St, E1
off Commercial Rd 142 B2
Hunsdon Rd, SE14 . . . . .171 D1
Hunslett St, E2
off Royston St 128 C2
Hunt Cl, W11 . . . . .135 D4
Hunter Cl, SE1 . . . . .64 B3
Hunter St, WC1 . . . . .25 D2
Huntingdon Gdns, W4 . . . . .160 C2
Huntingdon St, E16 . . . . . . .145 F2
N1 . . . . .111 F4
Huntingfield Rd, SW15 . . . . .176 A2
Huntley St, WC1 . . . . .23 F3
Hunton St, E1 . . . . .128 A4
Hunt's Ct, WC2 . . . . .48 B1
Hunts La, E15 . . . . .130 C2
Huntsman St, SE17 . . . . .76 B1
Huntsworth Ms, NW1 . . . . . . .21 E3
Hurdwick Pl, NW1
off Harrington Sq 11 E2
Hurley Cres, SE16
off Marlow Way 157 D1
Hurley Ho, SE11 . . . . .74 B1
Hurlingham Business Pk, SW6 . . . . .178 A1
Hurlingham Club, SW6 . . . . .177 F1
Hurlingham Ct, SW6 . . . . . . .177 F1
Hurlingham Gdns, SW6 . . . .177 F1
Hurlingham Park, SW6 . . . . .163 F4
Hurlingham Retail Pk, SW6 *off Carnwath Rd* . . .178 B1
Hurlingham Rd, SW6 . . . . . .163 F4
Hurlingham Sq, SW6 . . . . . . .178 A1
Hurlock St, N5 . . . . .98 B4
Huron Uni USA in London, WC1 . . . . .24 C4
Hurren Cl, SE3 . . . . .187 E1
Hurry Cl, E15 . . . . .117 E4
Hurstbourne Ho, SW15
off Tangley Gro 175 F4
Hurstdene Gdns, N15 . . . . . . .99 E1
Hurst St, SE24 . . . . .182 B4
Hurstway Wk, W11 . . . . .135 D3
Huson Cl, NW3 . . . . .109 E4
Hutchings St, E14 . . . . .158 A1
Hutchins Cl, E15
off Gibbins Rd 116 C4
Hutton Ms, SW15 . . . . .176 B3
Hutton St, EC4 . . . . .38 B3
Huxbear St, SE4 . . . . .185 F3
Huxley Rd, E10 . . . . .102 C3
Huxley St, W10 . . . . .121 E3
Hyde La, SW11 . . . . .80 C4
Hyde Park, W2 . . . . .44 C2
Hyde Pk, SW7 . . . . .44 C2
W1 .44 C2
Hyde Park Corner 46 A4
Hyde Pk Cor, W1 . . . . .46 B4
Hyde Pk Cres, W2 . . . . .32 C3
Hyde Pk Gdns, W2 . . . . .32 B4
Hyde Pk Gdns Ms, W2 . . . . . .32 B4
Hyde Pk Gate, SW7 . . . . .55 F1
Hyde Pk Gate Ms, SW7 . . . . . .55 F1
Hyde Pk Pl, W2 . . . . .33 D4
Hyde Pk Sq, W2 . . . . .32 C3
Hyde Pk Sq Ms, W2 . . . . .32 C3
Hyde Pk St, W2 . . . . .32 C3
Hyderabad Way, E15 . . . . . .117 E4
Hyde Rd, N1 . . . . .16 B1
Hydes Pl, N1
off Compton Av 112 B4
Hyde St, SE8
off Deptford High St 172 A1
Hyde Vale, SE10 . . . . .172 C2
Hyndman St, SE15 . . . . .170 B1
Hyperion Ho, E3
off Arbery Rd 129 E2
Hyson Rd, SE16
off Galleywall Rd 156 B3
Hythe Rd, NW10 . . . . .120 A4
Hythe Rd Ind Est, NW10 . . . . .120 A3

I

Ibbotson Av, E16 . . . . .145 F2
Ibbott St, E1
off Mantus Rd 128 C4
Ibex Ho, E15
off Forest La 117 E3
Ibis La, W4 . . . . .160 C3
Iceland Rd, E3 . . . . .130 A1
Iceland Wf, SE16
off Plough Way 157 E3

Iceni Ct, E3
off Roman Rd **129** F1
Ice Wf, N1 **13** D2
Ice Wf Marina, N1
off New Wf Rd **13** D2
Ickburgh Est, E5 **100** B3
Ickburgh Rd, E5 **100** B4
Idaho Bldg, SE13
off Deals Gateway **172** B3
Ida St, E14 **144** C2
Idmiston Rd, E15 **117** F2
Idol La, EC3 **52** C1
Idonia St, SE8 **171** F2
Iffley Rd, W6 **148** B2
Ifield Rd, SW10 **67** D4
Ifor Evans Pl, E1
off Mile End Rd **129** D4
Ilbert St, W10 **121** D3
Ilchester Gdns, W2 **30** C4
Ilchester Pl, W14 **149** F2
Ilderton Rd, SE15 **170** C2
SE16 **156** B4
Ilex Ho, N4 **97** F1
Ilex Rd, NW10 **105** F3
Iliffe St, SE17 **75** D2
Iliffe Yd, SE17 **75** D2
Ilkeston Ct, E5
off Overbury St **115** D1
Ilminster Gdns, SW11 **179** E2
Imber St, N1 **16** A1
Imperial Av, N16 **99** F4
Imperial Cl, NW2 **106** B2
Uni Imperial Coll London,
Charing Cross Campus, W6
off St. Dunstans Rd **149** D4
Hammersmith Campus,
W12 *off Du Cane Rd* **134** A2
St. Mary's Campus, W2 **32** B2
South Kensington Campus,
SW7 **56** A2
Imperial Coll Rd, SW7 **56** A3
Imperial Ct, NW8 **9** D2
Imperial Cres, SW6 **164** C4
Imperial Rd, SW6 **79** D4
Imperial Sq, SW6 **79** D4
Imperial St, E3 **130** C3
★ Imperial War Mus, SE1 **62** B3
Imperial Wf, SW6 **164** C4
Imre Cl, W12
off Ellerslie Rd **134** B4
Coll Inchbald Sch of Design,
Garden Design Faculty,
SW1 **71** D1
Interior Design Faculty,
SW1 **58** A4
Independent Pl, E8
off Downs Pk Rd **113** F2
Independents Rd, SE3
off Blackheath Village **187** F1
Indescon Ct, E14 **158** A1
Indiana Bldg, SE13
off Deals Gateway **172** A3
India Pl, WC2 **37** E4
India St, EC3 **41** E3
India Way, W12 **134** B3
Indigo Ms, E14
off Ashton St **144** C3
N16 **99** D4
Industry Ter, SW9
off Canterbury Cres **182** A1
Inforum Ms, SE15
off Commercial Way **170** A2
Ingate Pl, SW8 **166** B3
Ingelow Rd, SW8 **166** B4
Ingersoll Rd, W12 **134** B4
Ingestre Ct, W1
off Ingestre Pl **35** F4
Ingestre Pl, W1 **35** F3
Ingestre Rd, NW5 **110** B1
Ingham Rd, NW6 **108** A1
Inglebert St, EC1 **14** A4
Ingleborough St, SW9 **168** A4
Ingleby Rd, N7
off Bryett Rd **97** E4
Ingle Ms, EC1 **14** A4
Inglesham Wk, E9 **115** F3
Ingleside Gro, SE3 **173** F1
Inglethorpe St, SW6 **163** D3
Ingleton St, SW9 **168** A4
Inglewood Cl, E14 **158** A3
Inglewood Rd, NW6 **108** A2
Inglis St, SE5 **168** B3
Ingram Av, NW11 **94** C1
Ingram Cl, SE11 **61** F4
Ingram Ho, E3
off Daling Way **129** E2
Ingrave St, SW11 **179** D1
Ingress St, W4
off Devonshire Rd **147** E4
Inigo Pl, WC2 **36** C4
Inkerman Rd, NW5 **110** B3
Inkerman Ter, W8
off Allen St **54** B3
Inkster Ho, SW11
off Ingrave St **179** E1
Inman Rd, NW10 **119** E1
Inner Circle, NW1 **22** A1
Inner Temple La, EC4 **38** A3
Innes Gdns, SW15 **176** B4
Innes St, SE15 **89** D2
Inskip Cl, E10 **102** B3
Insley Ho, E3
off Bow Rd **130** B3
★ Institute of Contemporary
Arts (I.C.A.), SW1 **48** B3
Uni Institute of Ed, WC1 **24** B3
Institute Pl, E8 **114** B2
Integer Gdns, E11 **103** D1
● Interchange E Ind Est, E5
off Grosvenor Way **100** C3
Inver Cl, E5
off Theydon Rd **100** C3
Inver Ct, W2 **31** D3
W6 *off Invermead Cl* **148** A2
Inverforth Cl, NW3
off North End Way **94** C3
Invermead Cl, W6 **148** A3
Inverness Gdns, W8 **42** C3
Inverness Ms, W2 **31** D4
Inverness Pl, W2 **31** D4
Inverness St, NW1 **124** B1
Inverness Ter, W2 **31** D4
Inverton Rd, SE15 **185** D2
Invicta Cl, E3
off Hawgood St **144** A1
Invicta Plaza, SE1 **50** C2
Inville Rd, SE17 **76** B3
Inwen Ct, SE8 **157** E4
Inwood Ho, SE22
off Pytchley Rd **183** E1
Inworth St, SW11 **165** E4
Inworth Wk, N1
off Popham St **126** C1
Ionian Bldg, E14
off Narrow St **143** E3
Ion Sq, E2
off Hackney Rd **128** A2
Ireland Yd, EC4 **39** D3
Irene Rd, SW6 **164** A3
Ireton St, E3
off Tidworth Rd **130** A4
Iron Br Cl, NW10 **105** E2
Iron Mill Pl, SW18
off Garratt La **178** B4
Iron Mill Rd, SW18 **178** B4
Ironmonger La, EC2 **40** A3
Ironmonger Pas, EC1 **27** F2
Ironmonger Row, EC1 **27** F1
Ironmongers Pl, E14
off Spindrift Av **158** A3
Ironside Cl, SE16
off Kinburn St **157** D1
Iron Wks, E3 **130** A1
Irvine Cl, E14
off Uamvar St **144** C1
Irving Gro, SW9 **167** F4
Irving Ms, N1
off Alwyne Rd **112** C3
Irving Rd, W14 **149** D2
Irving St, WC2 **48** B1
Irwell Est, SE16
off Neptune St **156** C1
Irwin Gdns, NW10 **120** B1
Isaac Way, SE1 **51** F4
Isabella Ms, N1
off Balls Pond Rd **113** E3
Isabella Rd, E9 **114** C2
Isabella St, SE1 **50** C3
Isabel St, SW9 **85** F4
Isambard Ms, E14 **158** C2
Isambard Pl, SE16
off Rotherhithe St **142** C4
Isel Way, SE22
off East Dulwich Gro **183** E3
Isis Cl, SW15 **176** C2
Coll Islamic Coll for Advanced
Studies, NW10
off High Rd **106** B3
DLR Island Gardens **158** C3
Island Ho, E3 **130** C3
Island Rd, SE16 **157** D3
Island Row, E14 **143** F2
Islay Wk, N1
off Douglas Rd **112** C3
Isledon Rd, N7 **98** A4
ISLINGTON, N1 **14** A1
Coll Islington City Learning
Cen, N5
off Highbury New Pk **112** C2
Islington Grn, N1 **14** C1
Islington High St, N1 **14** B3
Islington Pk Ms, N1
off Islington Pk St **112** B4
Islington Pk St, N1 **112** A4
Islip St, NW5 **110** C2
★ Ismaili Cen, SW7 **56** B4
Issigonis Ho, W3
off Cowley Rd **133** F4
Ivanhoe Rd, SE5 **183** F1
Ivatt Pl, W14 **149** F4
Iveagh Av, NW10 **118** A2
Iveagh Cl, E9 **129** D1
NW10 **118** A2
Iveagh Ter, NW10
off Iveagh Av **118** A2
Ive Fm Cl, E10 **102** A3
Ive Fm La, E10 **102** A3
Iveley Rd, SW4 **166** C4
Iverna Ct, W8 **54** B2
Iverna Gdns, W8 **54** B2
Iverson Rd, NW6 **107** F3
Ives Rd, E16 **145** E1

es St, SW3 ....57 D4
imey St, E2 ....128 A3
or Pl, NW1 ....21 E3
or St, NW1 ....110 C4
ory Sq, SW11
off Gartons Way 178 C1
ybridge Ho, SE22
off Pytchley Rd 183 E1
ybridge La, WC2 ....49 D1
ychurch La, SE17 ....77 E2
y Cotts, E14
off Grove Vil 144 B3
y Ct, SE16
off Argyle Way 156 A4
y Cres, W4 ....146 C3
ydale Rd, SE15 ....185 D1
y Rd, NW2 ....106 C1
SE4 ....185 F2
y St, N1 ....16 C2
worth Pl, SW3 ....68 C2

acaranda Gro, E8 ....113 F4
ack Clow Rd, E15 ....131 E2
ackman Ms, NW2 ....91 E4
ackman St, E8 ....128 B1
ackson Cl, E9 ....114 C4
ackson Rd, N7 ....111 F1
acksons La, N6 ....96 A1
ack Walker Ct, N5 ....112 B1
acob St, SE1 ....53 F4
acob's Well Ms, W1 ....34 B2
ade Cl, NW2 ....93 D1
ago Wk, SE5 ....88 A3
amaica Rd, SE1 ....65 F1
SE16 ....155 F1
amaica St, E1 ....142 C2
ames Av, NW2 ....106 C2
ames Collins Cl, W9
off Fermoy Rd 121 F4
ames Ct, N1
off Morton Rd 112 C4
ames Dudson Ct, NW10 ...104 C4
ames Hammett Ho, E2 .....17 F3
ames Joyce Wk, SE24
off Shakespeare Rd 182 B2
ames La, E10 ....103 D1
ameson Cl, W3
off Acton La 146 C1
ameson Ct, E2 ....128 C2
ameson Ho, SE11
off Glasshouse Wk 73 E2
ameson St, W8 ....42 B2
ames Riley Pt, E15
off Carpenters Rd 130 C1
ames's Cotts, Rich. TW9 ...160 A2
ames St, W1 ....34 B2
WC2 ....37 D4
ames Ter, SW14
off Mullins Path 175 D1
amestown Rd, NW1 ....124 B1
amestown Way, E14 ....145 D3
ames Voller Way, E1
off Tarling St 142 C2
amuna Cl, E14 ....143 E1
ane St, E1
off Commercial Rd 142 B2
anet St, E14 ....158 A2
aneway Pl, SE16
off Janeway St 156 B1
aneway St, SE16 ....156 A1
ansen Wk, SW11
off Hope St 179 D2

Janson Cl, E15
off Janson Rd 117 E2
NW10 ....91 D4
Janson Rd, E15 ....117 E2
Japan Cres, N4 ....97 F2
Jardine Rd, E1 ....143 D3
Jarman Ho, E1
off Jubilee St 142 C1
Jarrow Rd, SE16 ....156 C3
Jarrow Way, E9 ....115 E1
Jarvis Rd, SE22
off Melbourne Gro 183 E2
Jasmine Sq, E3
off Birdsfield La 129 F1
Jason Ct, W1
off Marylebone La 34 B2
Jasper Wk, N1 ....16 A4
Jay Ms, SW7 ....55 F1
Jebb Av, SW2 ....181 E4
Jebb St, E3 ....130 A2
Jedburgh St, SW11 ....180 A2
Jeddo Rd, W12 ....147 F1
Jeeva Mans, N16
off Shacklewell La 113 F1
Jeffreys Pl, NW1
off Jeffreys St 110 C4
Jeffreys Rd, SW4 ....167 E4
Jeffreys St, NW1 ....110 B4
Jeffreys Wk, SW4 ....167 E4
Jeffries Ho, NW10 ....118 C1
Coll Jeff Wooller Coll, WC1 ...25 D4
Jeger Av, E2 ....17 E1
Jelf Rd, SW2 ....182 A3
Jellicoe Ho, SW8
off St. George Wf 72 C4
Jenkinson Ho, E2
off Usk St 129 D3
Jenner Av, W3 ....133 D1
Jenner Pl, SW13 ....162 B1
Jenner Rd, N16 ....99 F3
Jennings Rd, SE22 ....183 F4
Jenny Hammond Cl, E11
off Newcomen Rd 103 F4
Jephson St, SE5
off Grove La 169 D3
Jephtha Rd, SW18 ....178 A4
Jepson Ho, SW6
off Pearscroft Rd 164 B3
Jerdan Pl, SW6 ....78 B2
Jeremiah St, E14 ....144 B2
Jermyn St, SW1 ....47 E2
Jerningham Rd, SE14 .....171 E4
Jerome Cres, NW8 ....20 C2
Jerome St, E1 ....29 E4
Jerome Twr, W3 ....146 B1
Jerrard St, N1 ....17 D3
SE13 ....186 B1
Jersey Ho, N1
off Clifton Rd 112 C3
Jersey Rd, E11 ....103 D2
Jersey St, E2
off Bethnal Grn Rd 128 B3
Jerusalem Pas, EC1 ....26 C3
Jervis Ct, W1 ....35 D3
Jervis Rd, SW6
off Lillie Rd 163 F1
Jessam Av, E5 ....100 B2
Jessel Ho, SW1
off Page St 60 B4
Jesse Rd, E10 ....102 C2
Jessica Rd, SW18 ....178 C4
Jessie Blythe La, N19 .....97 E1
Jessop Ct, N1
off Graham St 15 D3

Jessop Rd, SE24
off Milkwood Rd 182 B2
Jessop Sq, E14
off Heron Quay 144 A4
Jethou Ho, N1
off Nightingale Rd 112 C3
★ Jewel Twr
(Houses of Parliament),
SW1 ....60 C2
★ Jewish Mus, NW1 ....10 C1
Jewry St, EC3 ....41 E3
Jew's Row, SW18 ....178 B2
Jeymer Av, NW2 ....106 B2
Jim Griffiths Ho, SW6
off Clem Attlee Ct 163 F1
Jim Veal Dr, N7 ....111 E3
Joan St, SE1 ....50 C3
Jocelyn St, SE15 ....170 A3
Jockey's Flds, WC1 ....25 F4
Jodane St, SE8 ....157 F3
Jodrell Rd, E3 ....129 F1
Johanna St, SE1 ....62 A1
John Adam St, WC2 ....49 D2
John Aird Ct, W2 ....19 F4
John Archer Way, SW18 ....179 D4
John Ashby Cl, SW2 ......181 E4
John Barnes Wk, E15 .....117 F3
John Campbell Rd, N16 ....113 E2
John Carpenter St, EC4 ....38 C4
John Drinkwater Cl, E11
off Browning Rd 103 F1
John Fearon Wk, W10
off Dart St 121 E3
John Felton Rd, SE16 .....156 A1
John Fisher St, E1 ......142 A3
John Harrison Ho, E1
off Philpot St 142 B2
John Harrison Way, SE10 ...159 F2
John Horner Ms, N1 ....15 E2
H John Howard Cen, E9 ...115 D2
John Islip St, SW1 ....72 C1
John Kennedy Ho, SE16
off Rotherhithe Old Rd ..157 D3
John Maurice Cl, SE17 .....64 A4
John McKenna Wk, SE16
off Tranton Rd 156 A2
John Parker Sq, SW11
off Thomas Baines Rd ..179 D1
John Penn St, SE13 ......172 B3
John Princes St, W1 ......35 D2
John Rennie Wk, E1
off Wine Cl 142 C4
John Roll Way, SE16 .....156 A2
John Ruskin St, SE5 ....86 C2
John Silkin La, SE8 .....157 D4
John's Ms, WC1 ....25 F3
John Smith Av, SW6 ......163 F2
John Smith Ms, E14
off Newport Av 145 D3
Johnson Cl, E8 ....128 A1
Johnson Ho, E2
off Roberta St 128 A3
Johnson Rd, NW10 ....119 D1
Johnson's Ct, EC4
off Fleet St 38 B3
Johnson's Pl, SW1 ....71 E3
Johnson St, E1
off Cable St 142 C3
Johnsons Way, NW10 .....118 B4
John Spencer Sq, N1 .....112 B3
John's Pl, E1
off Damien St 142 B2
Johnston Cl, SW9
off Hackford Rd 167 F3

Johnston Ct, E10
off Oliver Rd **102** B4
Johnston Ter, NW2
off Kara Way **93** D4
John St, E15 **131** F1
WC1 **25** F3
John Trundle Ct, EC2
off The Barbican **27** E4
John Walsh Twr, E11 **103** F3
John Williams Cl, SE14 **171** D1
John Woolley Cl, SE13 **187** E2
Joiner's Arms Yd, SE5
off Denmark Hill **169** D3
Joiners Pl, N5
off Leconfield Rd **113** D1
Joiner St, SE1 **52** B3
Joiners Yd, N1
off Caledonia St **13** D3
Jolles Ho, E3
off Bromley High St **130** B3
Jonathan Ct, W4
off Windmill Rd **147** E3
Jonathan St, SE11 **73** E2
Jones Ho, N16
off Stamford Hill **99** E2
Jones St, W1 **46** C1
Jordan Ct, SW15
off Charlwood Rd **177** D2
Joseph Av, W3 **133** D2
Joseph Conrad Ho, SW1
off Tachbrook St **71** F1
Joseph Hardcastle Cl, SE14 **171** D2
Josephine Av, SW2 **181** F3
Joseph Powell Cl, SW12 **180** C4
Joseph Ray Rd, E11 **103** E3
Joseph St, E3 **129** F4
Joseph Trotter Cl, EC1
off Myddelton St **26** B1
Joshua St, E14
off St. Leonards Rd **144** C2
Joslings Cl, W12 **134** B3
Joubert St, SW11 **165** F4
Jowett St, SE15 **89** F3
Joyce Wk, SW2 **182** A4
Jubilee Cl, NW10 **119** E2
Jubilee Cres, E14 **158** C2
★ Jubilee Gdns, SE1 **49** E3
🔒 Jubilee Mkt Hall, WC2 **37** D4
Jubilee Pl, SW3 **69** D2
Jubilee St, E1 **142** C2
Jubilee Trust, SE10
off Egerton Dr **172** B2
Judd St, WC1 **24** C1
Jude St, E16 **145** F2
Juer St, SW11 **81** D3
Julian Av, W3 **132** B3
Julian Pl, E14 **158** B4
Julia St, NW5
off Oak Village **110** A1
Juliette Rd, E13 **131** F2
Julius Nyerere Cl, N1 **13** E1
Junction App, SE13 **186** C1
SW11 **179** E1
Junction Av, W10
off Harrow Rd **120** C3
Junction Ms, W2 **32** C2
Junction Pl, W2 **32** B2
Junction Rd, N19 **110** C1
🔒 Junction Shop Cen, The, SW11
off St. John's Hill **179** E2
🔒 Junction, Wembley Retail Pk, The, Wem. HA9 **104** B1
Juniper Cres, NW1 **110** A4
Juniper Dr, SW18 **178** C2
Juniper St, E1 **142** C3
Juno Ho, E3
off Garrison Rd **130** A1
Juno Way, SE14 **171** D1
Jupiter Way, N7 **111** F3
Jupp Rd, E15 **117** D4
Jupp Rd W, E15 **130** C1
Justice Wk, SW3 **80** C1
Justines Pl, E2
off Palmers Rd **129** D3
Jutland Cl, N19 **97** E2
Juxon St, SE11 **61** F4

K

Kambala Rd, SW11 **165** D4
Kapuvar Cl, SE15
off Alpha St **170** A4
Kara Way, NW2 **107** D1
Karen Ct, SE4
off Wickham Rd **185** F1
Karen Ter, E11
off Montague Rd **103** F3
Kassala Rd, SW11 **165** F3
Katherine Cl, SE16
off Rotherhithe St **143** D4
Katherine Sq, W11
off Wilsham St **135** E4
Kathleen Av, W3 **132** C1
Kathleen Rd, SW11 **179** F1
Kay Rd, SW9 **167** E4
Kay St, E2 **128** A2
Kay Way, SE10
off Greenwich High Rd **172** B2
Kean St, WC2 **37** E3
Keats Cl, NW3
off Keats Gro **109** E1
SE1 **77** E1
Keats Gro, NW3 **109** D1
★ Keats Ho, NW3 **109** E1
Keats Ho, SW1 **71** F4
Keats Pl, EC2 **40** A1
Keble Pl, SW13
off Somerville Av **162** B1
Kedelston Ct, E5
off Redwald Rd **115** E1
Kedleston Wk, E2
off Middleton St **128** B3
Keel Cl, SE16 **143** D4
Keel Ct, E14
off Newport Av **145** D3
Keeley St, WC2 **37** E3
Keeling Ho, E2
off Claredale St **128** B2
Keens Yd, N1
off St. Paul's Rd **112** B3
Keetons Rd, SE16 **156** B2
Keighley Cl, N7 **111** E1
Keildon Rd, SW11 **179** F2
Keir Hardie Est, E5
off Springfield **100** B2
Keir Hardie Ho, W6
off Lochaline St **162** C1
Keith Connor Cl, SW8
off Daley Thompson Way **180** B1
Keith Gro, W12 **148** A1
Kelceda Cl, NW2 **92** A3
Kelday Hts, E1
off Watney St **142** B2
Kelfield Gdns, W10 **134** C2
Kelfield Ms, W10
off Kelfield Gdns **135** D2
Kellerton Rd, SE13 **187** E3
Kellett Rd, SW2 **182** A2
Kell St, SE1 **63** D2
Kelly Av, SE15 **89** E3
Kelly Cl, NW10 **91** D4
Kelly Ms, W9
off Woodfield Rd **135** F1
Kelly St, NW1 **110** B3
Kelman Cl, SW4 **167** D4
Kelmore Gro, SE22 **184** A2
Kelmscott Gdns, W12 **148** A2
Kelmscott Rd, SW11 **179** E3
Kelross Pas, N5
off Kelross Rd **112** C1
Kelross Rd, N5 **112** B1
Kelsall Ms, Rich. TW9 **160** B3
Kelsey St, E2 **128** A4
Kelshall Ct, N4
off Brownswood Rd **98** C3
Kelson Ho, E14 **158** C2
Kelso Pl, W8 **55** D2
Kelvedon Ho, SW8 **85** D4
Kelvedon Rd, SW6 **163** F2
Kelvington Rd, SE15 **185** D3
Kelvin Rd, N5 **112** B1
Kember St, N1
off Carnoustie Dr **111** F4
Kemble St, WC2 **37** E3
Kemerton Rd, SE5 **182** C1
Kemeys St, E9 **115** E2
Kemp Ct, SW8 **84** C3
Kempe Rd, NW6 **121** D2
Kemp Ho, W1
off Berwick St **36** A4
Kempis Way, SE22
off East Dulwich Gro **183** E3
Kemplay Rd, NW3 **109** D1
Kemp's Ct, W1 **35** F3
Kemps Dr, E14
off Morant St **144** A3
Kempsford Gdns, SW5 **66** B3
Kempsford Rd, SE11 **74** B1
Kemps Gdns, SE13
off Thornford Rd **186** C3
Kempson Rd, SW6 **78** B4
Kempthorne Rd, SE8 **157** E3
Kempton Ct, E1
off Durward St **142** B1
Kemsley, SE13 **186** C3
Kenbury Gdns, SE5
off Kenbury St **168** C4
Kenbury St, SE5 **168** C4
Kenchester Cl, SW8 **85** D3
Kendal Av, W3 **118** A4
Kendal Cl, SW9 **86** C2
Kendal Ho, N1 **13** F2
Kendall Pl, W1 **34** A1
Kendal Pl, SW15 **177** F3
Kendal Rd, NW10 **106** A1
Kendal Steps, W2
off St. Georges Flds **33** D3
Kendal St, W2 **33** D3
Kender St, SE14 **170** C2
Kendoa Rd, SW4 **181** D2
Kendrick Ms, SW7 **56** A4
Kendrick Pl, SW7 **68** A1
Kenilworth Ct, SW15
off Lower Richmond Rd **177** E1
Kenilworth Rd, E3 **129** E2
NW6 **121** F1
Kenley Wk, W11 **135** E3

enmere Gdns, Wem. HA0 **118** A1
enmont Gdns, NW10 **120** B3
enmore Cl, Rich. TW9
off Kent Rd **160** A2
enmure Rd, E8 **114** B2
enmure Yd, E8
off Kenmure Rd **114** B2
ennard Rd, E15 **117** D4
ennard St, SW11 **166** A3
ennedy Ho, SE11
off Vauxhall Wk **73** E2
ennedy Wk, SE17
off Flint St **76** B1
ennet Cl, SW11
off Maysoule Rd **179** D2
enneth Cres, NW2 **106** B2
ennet Ho, NW8 **20** B4
ennet Rd, W9 **121** F4
ennet St, E1 **142** A4
ennet Wf La, EC4 **39** F4
enninghall Rd, E5 **100** A4
enning St, SE16
off Railway Av **156** C1
ennings Way, SE11 **74** B2
enning Ter, N1 **127** E1
ENNINGTON, SE11 **86** A1
Kennington **74** C2
ennington Grn, SE11 **74** A3
ennington La, SE11 **74** B2
ennington Oval, SE11 **73** F4
Kennington Pk, SW9 **86** B2
ennington Pk Est, SE11 **86** A1
ennington Pk Gdns, SE11 **74** C4
ennington Pk Pl, SE11 **74** B3
ennington Pk Rd, SE11 **74** B4
ennington Rd, SE1 **62** A2
SE11 **62** A3
enrick Pl, W1 **22** A4
ENSAL GREEN, NW10 **120** C3
Kensal Green **120** C3
Kensal Green **120** C3
★ Kensal Green Cem,
W10 **120** C3
ENSAL RISE, NW6 **121** D2
Kensal Rise **120** C2
ensal Rd, W10 **121** E4
ENSAL TOWN, W10 **121** D4
ensal Wf, W10
off Ladbroke Gro **121** D4
ENSINGTON, W8 **149** F1
Kensington & Chelsea Coll,
Hortensia Cen, SW10 **79** E2
Marlborough Cen, SW3 **69** D1
Wornington Cen, W10
off Wornington Rd **135** E1
ensington Ch Ct, W8 **54** C1
ensington Ch St, W8 **42** B2
ensington Ch Wk, W8 **42** C4
Kensington Coll of Business,
WC2 **37** E2
ensington Ct, W8 **55** D1
ensington Ct Gdns, W8
off Kensington Ct Pl **55** D2
ensington Ct Ms, W8 **55** D1
ensington Ct Pl, W8 **55** D2
★ Kensington Gdns, W2 **43** F3
ensington Gdns Sq, W2 **30** C3
ensington Gate, W8 **55** E2
ensington Gore, SW7 **56** A1
ensington Grn, W8 **54** C3
ensington Hall Gdns, W14
off Beaumont Av **149** F4
ensington High St, W8 **54** A2
W14 **149** E3
Kensington Mall, W8 **42** B2
Kensington (Olympia) **149** E2
Kensington (Olympia) **149** E2
★ Kensington Palace, W8 **43** D3
Kensington Palace Gdns,
W8 **42** C2
Kensington Pk Gdns, W11 **135** F3
Kensington Pk Ms, W11
off Kensington Pk Rd **135** F2
Kensington Pk Rd, W11 **135** F3
Kensington Pl, W8 **42** A3
Kensington Rd, SW7 **56** B1
W8 **55** D1
Kensington Sq, W8 **54** C1
Kensington Village, W14
off Avonmore Rd **149** F3
Kentish Bldgs, SE1 **52** A3
KENTISH TOWN, NW5 **110** C3
Kentish Town **110** C2
Kentish Town **110** C2
Kentish Town Rd, NW1 **110** B4
NW5 **110** B4
Kentish Town West **110** A3
Kenton Ct, W14
off Kensington High St **149** F2
Kenton Rd, E9 **115** D3
Kenton St, WC1 **24** C2
● Kent Pk Ind Est, SE15 **170** B1
Kent Pas, NW1 **21** E2
Kent Rd, W4 **146** C2
Richmond TW9 **160** A2
Kent St, E2 **17** F2
Kent Ter, NW1 **21** D1
Kentwell Cl, SE4 **185** E2
Kentwode Grn, SW13 **162** A2
Kent Yd, SW7 **57** D1
Ken Way, Wem. HA9 **90** C3
Kenway Rd, SW5 **66** C1
Kenwood Av, SE14
off Briant St **171** D3
Kenwood Cl, NW3 **95** D2
★ Kenwood Ho, NW3 **95** E2
Kenworthy Rd, E9 **115** E2
Kenwyn Dr, NW2 **91** E4
Kenwyn Rd, SW4 **181** D2
Kenyon St, SW6 **163** D3
Keogh Rd, E15 **117** E3
Kepler Rd, SW4 **181** E2
Keppel Row, SE1 **51** E3
Keppel St, WC1 **24** B4
Kerbela St, E2
off Cheshire St **128** A4
Kerbey St, E14 **144** B2
Kerfield Cres, SE5 **169** D3
Kerfield Pl, SE5 **169** D3
Kerridge Ct, N1 **113** E3
Kerrison Rd, E15 **131** D1
SW11 **179** E1
Kerry Ho, E1
off Sidney St **142** C2
Kerry Path, SE14 **171** F1
Kerry Rd, SE14 **171** F1
Kersfield Rd, SW15 **177** D4
Kershaw Cl, SW18 **178** C4
Kersley Ms, SW11 **165** F4
Kersley Rd, N16 **99** E4
Kersley St, SW11 **165** F4
Kerwick Cl, N7
off Sutterton St **111** F4
Keslake Rd, NW6 **121** D2
Keston Rd, SE15 **184** A1
Kestrel Av, SE24 **182** B3
Kestrel Cl, NW10 **105** D2
Kestrel Ho, EC1 **15** E4
SW8
off St. George Wf **72** C4
Kestrel Pl, SE14
off Milton Ct Rd **171** E1
Keswick Bdy, SW15
off Upper Richmond Rd **177** F3
Keswick Rd, SW15 **177** E3
Kett Gdns, SW2 **181** F3
Kettlebaston Rd, E10 **101** F2
Kevan Ho, SE5 **87** E3
KEW, Rich. TW9 **160** A1
Kew Br Ct, W4 **146** A4
Kew Grn, Rich. TW9 **160** A2
Kew Meadows Path, Rich.
TW9 **160** B4
Kew Retail Pk, Rich.
TW9 **160** B3
Kew Rd, Rich. TW9 **160** A1
Key Cl, E1 **128** B4
Keyes Rd, NW2 **107** D2
Keyham Ho, W2 **30** A1
Keyse Rd, SE1 **65** E3
Keystone Cres, N1 **13** D3
Keyworth Cl, E5 **115** E1
Keyworth Pl, SE1 **63** D2
Keyworth St, SE1 **63** D2
Kezia Ms, SE8
off Trundleys Rd **157** E4
Kezia St, SE8
off Trundleys Rd **157** E4
Khyber Rd, SW11 **165** E4
Kibworth St, SW8 **85** E3
Kidderpore Av, NW3 **108** A1
Kidderpore Gdns, NW3 **108** A1
Kiffen St, EC2 **28** B2
KILBURN, NW6 **6** A2
Kilburn **107** F3
Kilburn Br, NW6 **6** B1
Kilburn Gate, NW6 **6** C2
Kilburn High Road **6** B1
Kilburn High Rd, NW6 **107** F4
Kilburn La, W9 **121** D3
W10 **121** D3
Kilburn Park **6** A2
Kilburn Pk Rd, NW6 **18** A1
Kilburn Pl, NW6 **6** B1
Kilburn Priory, NW6 **6** C1
Kilburn Sq, NW6 **122** A1
Kilburn Vale, NW6 **6** C1
Kilby Ct, SE10
off Child La **159** F2
Kildare Gdns, W2 **30** B2
Kildare Ter, W2 **30** B2
Kildare Wk, E14
off Farrance St **144** A2
Kildoran Rd, SW2 **181** E3
Kilgour Rd, SE23 **185** E4
Kilkie St, SW6 **164** C4
Killarney Rd, SW18 **178** C4
Killick St, N1 **13** E2
Killip Cl, E16 **145** F2
Killowen Rd, E9 **115** D3
Killyon Rd, SW8 **166** C4
Killyon Ter, SW8 **166** C4
Kilmaine Rd, SW6 **163** E2
Kilmarsh Rd, W6 **148** C3
Kilmington Rd, SW13 **162** A1
Kilner St, E14 **144** A1
Kiln Pl, NW5 **110** A2
Kilravock St, W10 **121** E3
Kimbell Gdns, SW6 **163** E3
Kimberley Av, SE15 **170** B4

Kimberley Rd, E11 **103** D3
E16 **131** F4
NW6 **121** E1
SW9 **167** E4
Kimbolton Cl, SE12 **187** F4
Kimbolton Row, SW3 **68** C1
Kimpton Rd, SE5 **88** A4
Kinburn St, SE16 **157** D1
Kincaid Rd, SE15 **170** B2
Kincardine Gdns, W9 **18** A3
Kinder St, E1
off Cannon St Rd **142** B2
Kinefold Ho, N7
off York Way **111** E3
King & Queen St, SE17 **75** F1
King & Queen Wf, SE16
off Rotherhithe St **143** D4
King Arthur Cl, SE15 **170** C2
King Charles St, SW1 **48** B4
King Charles Ter, E1
off Sovereign Cl **142** B3
King David La, E1 **142** C3
Kingdom St, W2 **31** E1
Kingdon Rd, NW6 **108** A3
King Edward Ms, SW13 **162** A3
King Edward Rd, E10 **102** C2
King Edward VII's Hosp for Officers, W1 **22** B4
King Edward's Gdns, W3 **132** A4
King Edward's Pl, W3 **132** A4
King Edwards Rd, E9 **128** B1
King Edward St, EC1 **39** E2
King Edward III Ms, SE16
off Paradise St **156** B1
King Edward Wk, SE1 **62** B2
Kingfield St, E14 **158** C3
Kingfisher Ho, SW18
off Juniper Dr **178** C1
Kingfisher Ms, SE13 **186** B2
Kingfisher Sq, SE8 **171** F1
Kingfisher Way, NW10 **105** D2
King Frederik IX Twr, SE16 **157** F2
King George St, SE10 **172** C2
Kingham Cl, W11 **149** E1
King Henry's Reach, W6 **162** C1
King Henry's Rd, NW3 **109** E4
King Henry St, N16 **113** E2
King Henry's Wk, N1 **113** E3
King Henry Ter, E1
off Sovereign Cl **142** B3
Kinghorn St, EC1 **39** E1
King James Ct, SE1 **63** D1
King James St, SE1 **63** D1
King John Ct, EC2 **29** D2
King John St, E1 **143** D1
Kinglake Est, SE17 **77** D2
Kinglake St, SE17 **76** C3
Kingly Ct, W1 **35** F4
Kingly St, W1 **35** E3
Kings Arms Ct, E1
off Old Montague St **142** A1
Kings Arms Yd, EC2 **40** A2
King's Av, SW4 **181** D4
Kings Bench St, SE1 **51** D4
Kings Bench Wk, EC4 **38** B3
Kingsbridge Ct, E14
off Dockers Tanner Rd **158** A2
Kingsbridge Rd, W10 **134** C2
Kingsbury Rd, N1 **113** E3
Kingsbury Ter, N1 **113** E3
Kings Cl, E10 **102** B1
King's Coll - Denmark Hill Campus, SE5
off Champion Hill **183** D1
King's Coll - Guy's Campus, SE1 **64** A2
King's Coll - Half Moon La, SE24 **183** D4
King's Coll - Hampstead Campus, NW3
off Kidderpore Av **108** A1
King's Coll - Maughan Lib & Information Services Cen, WC2 **38** A2
King's Coll - Strand Campus, WC2 **37** F4
King's Coll - Waterloo Campus, SE1 **50** A3
King's Coll Hosp, SE5 **169** D4
Kings Coll Rd, NW3 **109** E4
Kingscote Rd, W4 **147** D2
Kingscote St, EC4 **38** C4
Kings Ct, W6
off Hamlet Gdns **148** A3
Wembley HA9 **90** B3
Kings Ct S, SW3
off Chelsea Manor Gdns **69** D3
Kings Cres, N4 **98** C4
Kings Cres Est, N4 **98** C3
Kingscroft Rd, NW2 **107** F3
KING'S CROSS, N1 **125** D1
King's Cross **12** C3
King's Cross Br, N1 **13** D4
King's Cross Rd, WC1 **13** F4
King's Cross St. Pancras **12** C3
Kingsdale Gdns, W11 **135** D4
Kingsdown Av, W3 **133** E3
Kingsdown Cl, SE16
off Masters Dr **156** B4
W10 **135** D2
Kingsdown Rd, E11 **103** E4
N19 **97** E3
Kings Dr, Wem. HA9 **90** B3
Kings Fm Av, Rich. TW10 **174** A2
Kingsford St, NW5 **109** F2
Kings Gdns, NW6
off West End La **108** A4
Kingsgate, Wem. HA9 **90** C4
Kingsgate Est, N1
off Tottenham Rd **113** E3
Kingsgate Pl, NW6 **108** A4
Kingsgate Rd, NW6 **108** A4
Kings Gro, SE15 **170** B2
Kings Hall Ms, SE13
off Lewisham Rd **186** C1
Kings Head Yd, SE1 **52** A3
Kingshill, SE17 **75** F1
Kingshold Est, E9
off Victoria Pk Rd **128** C1
Kingshold Rd, E9 **114** C4
King's Ho, SW8 **85** D2
King's Keep, SW15
off Westleigh Av **177** D3
KINGSLAND, N1 **113** E3
Kingsland, NW8 **9** D1
Kingsland Basin, N1
off Kingsland Rd **127** E1
Kingsland Grn, E8 **113** E3
Kingsland High St, E8 **113** F2
Kingsland Pas, E8
off Kingsland Grn **113** E3
Kingsland Rd, E2 **17** D4
E8 **127** E2
Kingsland Shop Cen, E8 **113** F3
Kingslawn Cl, SW15 **176** B3
Kingsley Flats, SE1 **64** C4
Kingsley Ms, E1
off Wapping La **142** B3
W8 **55** D3
Kingsley Pl, N6 **96** A1
Kingsley Rd, NW6 **121** F1
Kingsley St, SW11 **179** F1
Kings Mall, W6 **148** C3
Kingsmead Av, NW9 **91** D1
Kingsmead Est, E9 **115** E2
Kingsmead Ho, E9
off Kingsmead Way **115** E1
Kingsmead Way, E9 **115** E1
Kingsmere Cl, SW15
off Felsham Rd **177** D1
Kingsmere Pk, NW9 **90** B2
Kingsmere Pl, N16 **99** D2
Kings Ms, SW4
off King's Av **181** E3
King's Ms, WC1 **25** F3
Kingsmill Ter, NW8 **8** B2
King's Pas, E11 **103** E1
Kings Pl, N1 **13** D2
Kings Pl, SE1 **63** E1
W4 **146** C4
King Sq, EC1 **27** E1
King's Quay, SW10 **79** F4
King's Reach Twr, SE1 **50** B2
Kings Ride Gate, Rich. TW10 **174** A2
Kings Rd, E11 **103** E1
NW10 **106** B4
King's Rd, SW3 **69** D2
SW6 **79** D3
SW10 **79** D3
Kings Rd, SW14 **175** D1
King's Scholars' Pas, SW1 **59** E3
King Stairs Cl, SE16
off Elephant La **156** C1
King's Ter, NW1 **11** E1
Kingstown St, NW1 **124** A1
King St, EC2 **39** F3
SW1 **47** F3
W3 **132** B4
W6 **148** A3
WC2 **36** C4
Kings Wk Shop Mall, SW3
off King's Rd **69** E2
Kingswater Pl, SW11
off Battersea Ch Rd **80** C3
Kingsway, SW14 **174** B1
WC2 **37** E2
Kingsway Pl, EC1 **26** B2
Kingsway Shop Cen, NW3
off Hampstead High St **108** C1
Kingswear Rd, NW5 **96** B4
Kings Wf, E8
off Kingsland Rd **127** E1
Kingswood Av, NW6 **121** E1
Kingswood Cl, SW8 **85** D3
Kingswood Ct, SE13
off Hither Grn La **187** D4
Kingswood Pl, SE13 **187** E2
Kingswood Rd, E11 **103** E1
SW2 **181** E4
W4 **146** C2
Wembley HA9 **90** A4
Kingswood Ter, W4
off Kingswood Rd **146** C2
King's Yd, SW15
off Stanbridge Rd **176** C1
Kingthorpe Rd, NW10 **105** D4
Kingthorpe Ter, NW10 **105** D3
Kingweston Cl, NW2 **93** E4

King William La, SE10
off Trafalgar Rd 159 E4
King William St, EC4 ....52 B1
King William Wk, SE10 .....172 C1
Coll Kingwood City
Learning Cen, The,
SW6 off Kingwood Rd ...163 E3
Kingwood Rd, SW6 ....163 D3
Kinloch Dr, NW9 ....91 E1
Kinloch St, N7 ....97 F4
Kinnaird Av, W4 ....160 C2
Kinnaird Ho, N6 ....97 D1
Kinnear Rd, W12 ....147 F1
Kinnerton Pl N, SW1 ....57 F1
Kinnerton Pl S, SW1 ....57 F1
Kinnerton St, SW1 ....58 A1
Kinnerton Yd, SW1 ....57 F1
Kinnoul Rd, W6 ....163 E1
Kinsale Rd, SE15 ....184 A1
Kintore Way, SE1 ....65 E4
Kipling Est, SE1 ....64 B1
Kipling St, SE1 ....64 B1
Kipling Twr, W3 ....146 C2
Kirby Est, SE16 ....156 B2
Kirby Gro, SE1 ....52 C4
Kirby St, EC1 ....26 B4
Kirkdale Rd, E11 ....103 E2
Kirkland Wk, E8 ....113 F3
Kirkman Pl, W1 ....36 A1
Kirkmichael Rd, E14
off Dee St 144 C2
Kirkstead Ct, E5
off Mandeville St 115 E1
Kirk St, WC1 ....25 E3
Kirkwall Pl, E2 ....128 C3
Kirkwood Rd, SE15 ....170 B4
Kirtley Ho, N16
off Stamford Hill 99 E2
Kirtling St, SW8 ....83 E2
Kirton Cl, W4 ....147 D3
Kirton Gdns, E2 ....29 F1
Kirwyn Way, SE5 ....87 D2
Kitcat Ter, E3 ....130 A3
Kitchen Ct, E10
off Brisbane Rd 102 B3
Kite Pl, E2
off Nelson Gdns 128 A3
Kite Yd, SW11
off Cambridge Rd 165 F3
Kitson Rd, SE5 ....87 F2
SW13 ....162 A3
Kitto Rd, SE14 ....171 D4
Kiver Rd, N19 ....97 D3
Klea Av, SW4 ....180 C4
Kleine Wf, N1 ....17 D1
Knapp Cl, NW10 ....105 E3
Knapp Rd, E3 ....130 A4
Knaresborough Pl, SW5 .....54 C4
Knatchbull Rd, NW10 ......119 D1
SE5 ....168 C3
Knebworth Rd, N16 ....113 E1
Kneller Rd, SE4 ....185 E2
Knighten St, E1 ....142 B4
Knighthead Pt, E14 ....158 A2
Knightland Rd, E5 ....100 B3
Knightrider Ct, EC4
off Knightrider St 39 E4
Knightrider St, EC4 ....39 E4
⊖ Knightsbridge 57 E1
Knightsbridge, SW1 ....57 F1
SW7 ....57 D1
Knightsbridge Apts, The, SW7
off Knightsbridge 57 E1
Knightsbridge Grn, SW1 .....57 E1
Knights Cl, E9
off Churchill Wk 114 C2
Knights Wk, SE11 ....74 C1
Knivet Rd, SW6 ....78 A1
Knoll Rd, SW18 ....178 C3
Knottisford St, E2 ....128 C3
Knowle Cl, SW9 ....182 A1
Knowles Hill Cres, SE13 ....187 D3
Knowles Ho, SW18
off Neville Gill Cl 178 B4
Knowles Wk, SW4 ....180 C1
Knowsley Rd, SW11 ....165 F4
Knox Rd, E7 ....117 F3
Knox St, W1 ....21 E4
Knoyle St, SE14 ....171 E1
Kossuth St, SE10 ....159 E4
Kotree Way, SE1
off Beatrice Rd 156 A3
Kramer Ms, SW5 ....66 B3
Kreedman Wk, E8 ....114 A2
Kylemore Rd, NW6 ....108 A4
Kynance Ms, SW7 ....55 E3
Kynance Pl, SW7 ....55 E3
Kynaston Av, N16
off Dynevor Rd 99 F4
Kynaston Rd, N16 ....99 E4
Kyrle Rd, SW11 ....180 A3
Kyverdale Rd, N16 ....99 F3

L

Laburnum Cl, SE15
off Clifton Way 170 C2
Wembley HA0 ....104 A4
Laburnum Ct, E2 ....17 E1
Laburnum Gro, NW9 ....90 C1
Laburnum St, E2 ....17 E1
Lacey Ms, E3 ....130 A2
Lackington St, EC2 ....28 B4
Lacon Rd, SE22 ....184 A2
Lacy Rd, SW15 ....177 D2
Ladbroke Cres, W11
off Ladbroke Gro 135 E2
Ladbroke Gdns, W11 ......135 F3
⊖ Ladbroke Grove 135 E2
Ladbroke Gro, W10 ....121 D4
W11 ....135 E2
Ladbroke Ms, W11
off Ladbroke Rd 135 E4
Ladbroke Rd, W11 ....135 F4
Ladbroke Sq, W11 ....135 F3
Ladbroke Ter, W11 ....135 F3
Ladbroke Wk, W11 ....135 F4
Ladycroft Rd, SE13 ....186 B1
Lady Dock Path, SE16
off Salter Rd 157 E1
Lady Margaret Rd, N19 ....110 C1
NW5 ....110 C2
Ladysmith Rd, E16 ....131 F3
Lady Somerset Rd,
NW5 ....110 B1
LADYWELL, SE13 ....186 A3
⇌ Ladywell 186 B3
Ladywell Cl, SE4
off Adelaide Av 186 A2
Ladywell Hts, SE4 ....185 F4
Ladywell Rd, SE13 ....186 A3
Ladywell St, E15
off Plaistow Gro 131 F1
Lafone St, SE1 ....53 E4
Lagado Ms, SE16 ....143 D4
Laing Ho, SE5
off Comber Gro 87 E3
Laird Ho, SE5 ....87 E3
Lairs Cl, N7
off Manger Rd 111 E3
Lakanal, SE5
off Sceaux Gdns 89 D4
Lake Rd, E10 ....102 B1
Laker Pl, SW15 ....177 E4
Lakeside Ct, N4 ....98 B3
Lakeside Rd, W14 ....149 D2
Lakeview Est, E3
off Old Ford Rd 129 D2
Lakis Cl, NW3
off Flask Wk 108 C1
Laleham Rd, SE6 ....186 C4
Lalor St, SW6 ....163 E4
Lambert Av, Rich. TW9 .....174 B1
Lambert Jones Ms, EC2
off The Barbican 27 E4
Lambert Rd, SW2 ....181 E3
Lambert St, N1 ....112 A4
LAMBETH, SE1 ....61 E2
Lambeth Br, SE1 ....61 D4
SW1 ....61 D4
Coll Lambeth Coll, Brixton Cen,
SW2 off Brixton Hill 181 F3
Clapham Cen, SW4
off Clapham Common
S Side 180 C3
Vauxhall Cen, SW8 ....84 B4
Lambeth High St, SE1 ....73 E1
Lambeth Hill, EC4 ....39 E4
H Lambeth Hosp, SW9 ....181 E1
⊖ Lambeth North 62 A1
★ Lambeth Palace, SE1 ....61 E3
Lambeth Palace Rd, SE1 .....61 E3
Lambeth Pier, SE1 ....61 D3
Lambeth Rd, SE1 ....61 F3
SE11 ....61 F3
Lambeth Twrs, SE11 ....62 A3
Lambeth Wk, SE1 ....61 F4
SE11 ....61 F4
Lambfold Ho, N7
off York Way 111 E3
Lamb La, E8 ....114 B4
Lamble St, NW5 ....110 A2
Lambolle Pl, NW3 ....109 E3
Lambolle Rd, NW3 ....109 E3
Lambourne Gro, SE16 ......157 D3
Lambourne Rd, E11 ....102 C1
Lambourn Rd, SW4 ....180 B1
Lambrook Ter, SW6 ....163 E3
Lamb's Bldgs, EC1 ....28 A3
Lambs Conduit Pas,
WC1 ....25 E4
Lamb's Conduit St, WC1 .....25 E3
Lambs Ms, N1 ....14 C1
Lamb's Pas, EC1 ....28 A4
Lamb St, E1 ....29 E4
Lambton Ms, N19
off Lambton Rd 97 E2
Lambton Pl, W11
off Westbourne Gro 135 F2
Lambton Rd, N19 ....97 E2
Lamb Wk, SE1 ....64 C1
Lamerton St, SE8 ....172 A1
Lamington St, W6 ....148 B3
Lamlash St, SE11 ....62 C4
Lammas Rd, E9 ....115 D4
E10 ....101 E3
Lamont Rd, SW10 ....79 F1
Lamont Rd Pas, SW10
off Lamont Rd 80 A1
Lampard Gro, N16 ....99 F2
Lampern Sq, E2
off Nelson Gdns 128 A3

Lampeter Sq, W6
off Humbolt Rd **163** E1
Lamplighter Cl, E1
off Cleveland Way **128** C4
Lampmead Rd, SE12 .... **187** E3
Lamp Office Ct, WC1 .... **25** E3
Lanark Ms, W9 .... **19** E1
Lanark Pl, W9 .... **19** F2
Lanark Rd, W9 .... **19** E1
Lanark Sq, E14 .... **158** B2
Lanbury Rd, SE15 .... **185** D2
Lancashire Ct, W1 .... **35** D4
Lancaster Cl, N1
off Hertford Rd **113** E4
Lancaster Ct, SW6 .... **78** A3
W2 .... **43** F1
Lancaster Dr, E14
off Prestons Rd **144** C4
NW3 .... **109** E3
Lancaster Gate 32 A4
Lancaster Gate, W2 .... **43** F1
Lancaster Gro, NW3 .... **109** D3
Lancaster Ho, SW1 .... 47 E4
Lancaster Ms, SW18
off East Hill **178** B3
W2 .... **31** F4
Lancaster Pl, WC2 .... **37** E4
Lancaster Rd, E11 .... **103** E3
N4 .... **98** A1
NW10 .... **105** F2
W11 .... **135** E2
Lancaster St, SE1 .... **63** D1
Lancaster Ter, W2 .... **32** A4
Lancaster Wk, W2 .... **44** A4
Lancaster W, W11
off Grenfell Rd **135** D3
Lancefield St, W10 .... **121** F3
Lancell St, N16 .... **99** E4
Lancelot Pl, SW7 .... **57** E1
Lancer Sq, W8 .... **42** C4
Lanchester Way,
SE14 .... **170** C3
Lancing St, NW1 .... **24** A1
Lancresse Ct, N1 .... **127** E1
Landcroft Rd, SE22 .... **183** F4
Landells Rd, SE22 .... **183** F4
Landford Rd, SW15 .... **176** C1
Landmann Ho, SE16 .... **156** B3
Landmann Way,
SE14 .... **171** D1
Landmark Hts, E5 .... **115** E1
Landon Pl, SW1 .... **57** E2
Landons Cl, E14 .... **144** C4
Landon Wk, E14
off Cottage St **144** B3
Landor Rd, SW9 .... **181** E1
Landor Wk, W12 .... **148** A1
Landridge Rd, SW6 .... **163** F4
Landseer Rd, N19 .... **97** E4
Lane, The, NW8 .... **7** E2
Lane Cl, NW2 .... **92** B4
Lanesborough Pl, SW1 .... **46** B4
Laneway, SW15 .... **176** B3
Lanfranc Rd, E3 .... **129** E2
Lanfrey Pl, W14
off North End Rd **149** F4
Langbourne Av, N6 .... **96** A3
Langbourne Pl, E14 .... **158** B4
Langdale, NW1 .... **11** E4
Langdale Cl, SE17 .... **75** E4
SW14 .... **174** B2
Langdale Rd, SE10 .... **172** C2
Langdale St, E1
off Burslem St **142** B2
Langdon Ct, EC1
off City Rd **15** D3
NW10 .... **119** E1
Langdon Dr, NW9 .... **90** C2
DLR Langdon Park 144 B1
Langdon Pk Rd, N6 .... **96** C1
Langdon Pl, SW14 .... **174** C1
Langdon Way, SE1
off Simms Rd **156** A3
Langford Cl, E8 .... **114** A2
NW8 .... **7** F2
W3 .... **146** B1
Langford Ct, NW8 .... **7** E3
Langford Grn, SE5 .... **183** E1
Langford Ms, N1
off Liverpool Rd **112** A4
Langford Pl, NW8 .... **7** F3
Langford Rd, SW6 .... **164** B4
Langham Pl, W1 .... **35** D1
W4 .... **161** E1
Langham St, W1 .... **35** D1
Langland Gdns, NW3 .... **108** B2
Langler Rd, NW10 .... **120** C2
Langley Ct, WC2 .... **36** C4
Langley Dr, W3 .... **132** B4
Langley La, SW8 .... **73** D4
Langley St, WC2 .... **36** C3
Langside Av, SW15 .... **176** A2
Langston Hughes Cl, SE24
off Shakespeare Rd **182** B2
Lang St, E1 .... **128** C4
Langthorn Ct, EC2 .... **40** A2
Langthorne Rd, E11 .... **103** D4
Langthorne St, SW6 .... **163** D2
Langton Cl, WC1 .... **25** F1
Langton Rd, NW2 .... **92** C4
SW9 .... **87** D3
Langton St, SW10 .... **79** F1
Langton Way, SE3 .... **173** F3
Langtry Pl, SW6 .... **66** B4
Langtry Rd, NW8 .... **6** C1
Langtry Wk, NW8
off Alexandra Pl **122** C1
Lanhill Rd, W9 .... **18** A2
Lanier Rd, SE13 .... **186** C4
Lannoy Pt, SW6
off Pellant Rd **163** E2
Lanrick Rd, E14 .... **145** D2
Lansbury Cl, NW10 .... **104** C2
Lansbury Est, E14 .... **144** B2
Lansbury Gdns, E14 .... **145** D2
Lanscombe Wk, SW8 .... **84** C4
Coll Lansdowne Coll, W2 .... 42 C1
Lansdowne Cres, W11 .... **135** E3
Lansdowne Dr, E8 .... **114** A3
Lansdowne Gdns, SW8 .... **84** C4
Lansdowne Grn, SW8 .... **84** B3
Lansdowne Gro, NW10 .... **105** E1
Lansdowne Ms, W11
off Lansdowne Rd **135** F4
Lansdowne Pl, SE1 .... **64** B2
Lansdowne Ri, W11 .... **135** E3
Lansdowne Rd, E11 .... **103** F3
W11 .... **135** E3
Lansdowne Row, W1 .... **47** D2
Lansdowne Ter, WC1 .... **25** D3
Lansdowne Wk, W11 .... **135** E4
Lansdowne Way, SW8 .... **84** B4
Lanson Bldg, SW8 .... **82** C2
Lantern Cl, SW15 .... **176** A2
Lanterns Ct, E14 .... **158** A1
Lant St, SE1 .... **51** E4
Lanvanor Rd, SE15 .... **170** C4
Lapford Cl, W9 .... **121** F4
Lapis Cl, NW10 .... **118** A3
Lapwing Twr, SE8
off Abinger Gro **171** F1
Lara Cl, SE13 .... **186** C4
Larch Av, W3 .... **133** E4
Larch Cl, N19
off Bredgar Rd **96** C3
SE8 off Clyde St **171** F1
Larch Dr, W4
off Gunnersbury Av **146** A4
Larches Av, SW14 .... **175** D2
Larch Rd, E10 .... **102** A3
NW2 .... **106** C1
Larcom St, SE17 .... **75** F1
Larden Rd, W3 .... **133** E4
Larissa St, SE17 .... **76** B2
Larkhall La, SW4 .... **167** D4
Larkhall Ri, SW4 .... **180** C1
Lark Row, E2 .... **128** C1
Larnach Rd, W6 .... **163** D1
Larner Ct, W12
off Heathstan Rd **134** A2
Larpent Av, SW15 .... **176** C3
Lascelles Cl, E11 .... **103** D3
Lassell St, SE10 .... **159** D4
Lasseter Pl, SE3
off Vanbrugh Hill **173** F1
Latchmere Pas, SW11
off Cabul Rd **165** E4
Latchmere Rd, SW11 .... **165** F4
Latchmere St, SW11 .... **165** F4
Latham Ho, E1 .... **143** D2
Latimer, SE17 .... **76** C3
Latimer Ind Est, W10
off Latimer Rd 134 C2
Latimer Pl, W10 .... **134** C2
Latimer Road 135 D3
Latimer Rd, W10 .... **134** C2
Latitude Apts, N16 .... **99** E2
Latona Rd, SE15 .... **170** A1
Lattimer Pl, W4 .... **161** E1
Latymer Ct, W6 .... **149** D3
Lauderdale Pl, EC2
off The Barbican **27** E4
Lauderdale Rd, W9 .... **18** C1
Lauderdale Twr, EC2 .... **27** E4
Laud St, SE11 .... **73** E2
Laugan Wk, SE17
off East St **75** F2
Launcelot St, SE1 .... **62** A1
Launceston Pl, W8 .... **55** E2
Launch St, E14 .... **158** C2
Launders Gate, W3 .... **146** B1
Laundress La, N16 .... **100** A4
Laundry La, N1
off Greenman St **126** C1
Laundry Rd, W6 .... **163** E1
Laura Pl, E5 .... **114** C1
Laurel Apts, SE17
off Townsend St **64** C4
Laurel Bk Gdns, SW6
off New Kings Rd **163** F4
Laurel Cl, N19
off Hargrave Pk **96** C3
Laurel Rd, SW13 .... **162** A4
Laurel St, E8 .... **113** F3
Laurence Ms, W12
off Askew Rd **148** A1
Laurence Pountney Hill, EC4 .... **40** A4
Laurence Pountney La, EC4 .... **40** A4
Laurie Gro, SE14 .... **171** E3
Laurier Rd, NW5 .... **96** B4
Lauriston Rd, E9 .... **129** D1
Lausanne Rd, SE15 .... **170** C3

Lavell St, N16 . . . . .113 D1
Lavender Av, NW9 . . . . .90 C2
Lavender Cl, SW3 . . . . .80 B1
Lavender Gdns, SW11 . . . . . .179 F2
Lavender Gro, E8 . . . . .113 F4
Lavender Hill, SW11 . . . . . . .179 E2
Lavender Rd, SE16 . . . . .143 E4
SW11 . . . . .179 D1
Lavender St, E15
off Manbey Gro 117 E3
Lavender Sweep, SW11 . . . . .179 F2
Lavender Ter, SW11
off Falcon Rd 179 E1
Lavender Wk, SW11 . . . . . . .179 F2
Lavers Rd, N16 . . . . .99 E4
Laverton Ms, SW5 . . . . .67 D1
Laverton Pl, SW5 . . . . .67 D1
Lavina Gro, N1 . . . . .13 E2
Lavington Cl, E9 . . . . .115 F3
Lavington St, SE1 . . . . .51 D3
Lawford Rd, N1 . . . . .113 E4
NW5 . . . . .110 C3
W4 . . . . .160 C2
Lawless St, E14 . . . . .144 B3
Lawley St, E5 . . . . .114 C1
Lawn Ho Cl, E14 . . . . .158 C1
Lawn La, SW8 . . . . .73 D4
Lawn Rd, NW3 . . . . .109 F2
Lawns, The, SE3
off Lee Ter 187 F1
Lawnside, SE3 . . . . .187 F2
Lawn Ter, SE3 . . . . .187 E1
Lawrence Av, NW10 . . . . . . .119 D1
Lawrence Bldgs, N16 . . . . . . .99 F4
Lawrence Cl, E3 . . . . .130 A2
W12
off Australia Rd 134 B3
Lawrence La, EC2 . . . . .39 F3
Lawrence Pl, N1
off Outram Pl 125 E1
Lawrence St, E16 . . . . .145 F1
SW3 . . . . .80 C1
Lawrence Way, NW10 . . . . . .90 C4
Lawson Est, SE1 . . . . .64 A3
Law St, SE1 . . . . .64 B2
Lawton Rd, E3 . . . . .129 E3
E10 . . . . .102 C2
Laxcon Cl, NW10 . . . . .104 C2
Laxley Cl, SE5 . . . . .87 D2
Laxton Pl, NW1 . . . . .23 D2
Layard Rd, SE16 . . . . .156 B3
Layard Sq, SE16 . . . . .156 B3
Laycock St, N1 . . . . .112 A3
Layer Gdns, W3 . . . . .132 A3
Layfield Cl, NW4 . . . . .92 B1
Layfield Cres, NW4 . . . . .92 B1
Layfield Rd, NW4 . . . . .92 B1
Laystall St, EC1 . . . . .26 A3
Layton Pl, Rich. (Kew) TW9
off Station Av 160 A3
Laytons Bldgs, SE1 . . . . .51 F4
Lazar Wk, N7
off Briset Way 97 F3
Lazenby Ct, WC2 . . . . .36 C4
Leabank Sq, E9 . . . . .116 A3
LEA BRIDGE, E5 . . . . .101 D4
Lea Br Rd, E5 . . . . .100 C4
E10 . . . . .101 E2
Leadenhall Mkt, EC3 . . . . . .40 C3
Leadenhall Pl, EC3 . . . . .40 C3
Leadenhall St, EC3 . . . . .40 C3
Leadenham Ct, E3
off Spanby Rd 130 A4
Leadings, The, Wem. HA9 . . . .90 C4
Leagrave St, E5 . . . . .100 C4
Lea Hall Gdns, E10
off Lea Hall Rd 102 A2
Lea Hall Rd, E10 . . . . .102 A2
Leahurst Rd, SE13 . . . . .187 D3
Jct Lea Interchange, E9 . . . .116 A2
Leake St, SE1 . . . . .49 F4
Leamington Pk, W3 . . . . . . .133 D1
Leamington Rd Vil, W11 . . . .135 F1
Leamore St, W6 . . . . .148 B3
Leamouth Rd, E14 . . . . .145 D2
Leander Ct, SE8 . . . . .172 A3
Leander Rd, SW2 . . . . .181 F4
Lea Pk Trd Estates, E10
off Warley Cl 101 F2
Leaside Rd, E5 . . . . .100 C2
Leasowes Rd, E10 . . . . .102 A2
Lea Sq, E3
off Legion Ter 129 F1
Leatherdale St, E1
off Portelet Rd 129 D3
Leather Gdns, E15
off Abbey Rd 131 E1
Leatherhead Cl, N16 . . . . .99 F2
Leather La, EC1 . . . . .38 B1
Leather Mkt, The, SE1 . . . . . . .64 C1
Leathermarket Ct, SE1 . . . . . .64 C1
Leathermarket St, SE1 . . . . . .64 C1
Leather Rd, SE16 . . . . .157 D3
Leathwaite Rd, SW11 . . . . . .179 F2
Leathwell Rd, SE8 . . . . .172 B4
Lea Valley Business Pk, E10
off Lammas Rd 101 E3
Lea Valley Wk, E3 . . . . .130 C4
E5 . . . . .101 E4
E9 . . . . .101 E4
E10 . . . . .101 E4
E14 . . . . .144 B1
E15 . . . . .130 C3
Lea Vw Ho, E5
off Springfield 100 B2
Leaway, E10 . . . . .101 D2
Lebanon Gdns, SW18 . . . . . .178 A4
Lebanon Rd, SW18 . . . . .178 A3
Lechmere Rd, NW2 . . . . .106 B3
Lecky St, SW7 . . . . .68 A2
Leconfield Av, SW13 . . . . . . .175 F1
Leconfield Rd, N5 . . . . .113 D1
Ledbury Est, SE15 . . . . .170 B2
Ledbury Ho, SE22
off Pytchley Rd 183 E1
Ledbury Ms N, W11 . . . . .30 A4
Ledbury Ms W, W11 . . . . .30 A4
Ledbury Rd, W11 . . . . .135 F2
Ledbury St, SE15 . . . . .170 A2
LEE, SE12 . . . . .187 E2
Lee Br, SE13 . . . . .186 C1
Lee Ch St, SE13 . . . . .187 E2
Lee Conservancy Rd, E9 . . . .115 F2
Leeds Pl, N4 . . . . .97 F2
Leefern Rd, W12 . . . . .148 A1
Leegate, SE12 . . . . .187 F3
Jct Lee Grn, SE12
off Lee High Rd 187 F3
Lee High Rd, SE12 . . . . .187 D1
SE13 . . . . .187 D1
Leeke St, WC1 . . . . .13 E4
Leeland Way, NW10 . . . . . . .105 E1
Lee Pk, SE3 . . . . .187 F2
Leerdam Dr, E14 . . . . .158 C2
Lee Rd, SE3 . . . . .187 F1
Leeside Ct, SE16
off Rotherhithe St 143 D4
Leeson Rd, SE24 . . . . .182 A2
Lees Pl, W1 . . . . .34 A4
Lee St, E8 . . . . .127 F1
Lee Ter, SE3 . . . . .187 E1
SE13 . . . . .187 E1
Lee Valley Pathway, E9 . . . .101 F4
E10 . . . . .100 C1
E17 . . . . .100 C1
Leeway, SE8 . . . . .157 F4
Leewood Cl, SE12
off Upwood Rd 187 F4
Lefevre Wk, E3
off Parnell Rd 130 A2
Lefroy Rd, W12 . . . . .147 F1
Legard Rd, N5 . . . . .112 B1
Leggatt Rd, E15 . . . . .130 C2
Legge St, SE13 . . . . .186 C3
Leghorn Rd, NW10 . . . . .119 F2
Legion Cl, N1 . . . . .112 A3
Legion Ter, E3 . . . . .129 F1
Leicester Ct, WC2 . . . . .36 B4
Leicester Pl, WC2 . . . . .36 B4
Leicester Square 36 B4
Leicester Sq, WC2 . . . . .48 B1
Leicester St, WC2 . . . . .36 B4
Leigh Ct, SE4
off Lewisham Way 172 A4
Leigh Gdns, NW10 . . . . .120 C2
Leigh Hunt St, SE1 . . . . .51 E4
Leigh Pl, EC1 . . . . .26 A4
Leigh Rd, E10 . . . . .102 C1
N5 . . . . .112 B1
Leigh St, WC1 . . . . .24 C2
Leighton Cres, NW5 . . . . . . .110 C2
Leighton Gdns, NW10 . . . . .120 B2
Leighton Gro, NW5 . . . . .110 C2
★ Leighton Ho Mus,
W14 . . . . .149 F2
Leighton Pl, NW5 . . . . .110 C2
Leighton Rd, NW5 . . . . .111 D2
Leinster Av, SW14 . . . . .174 C1
Leinster Gdns, W2 . . . . .31 E3
Leinster Ms, W2 . . . . .31 E4
Leinster Pl, W2 . . . . .31 E3
Leinster Sq, W2 . . . . .30 B4
Leinster Ter, W2 . . . . .31 E4
Leith Cl, NW9 . . . . .91 D2
Leith Yd, NW6
off Quex Rd 122 A1
Lelitia Cl, E8
off Pownall Rd 128 A1
Leman St, E1 . . . . .41 F3
Lemmon Rd, SE10 . . . . .173 E1
Lemna Rd, E11 . . . . .103 E1
Lemsford Ct, N4
off Brownswood Rd 98 C3
Lemuel St, SW18 . . . . .178 B4
Lena Gdns, W6 . . . . .148 C2
Lenanton Steps, E14
off Manilla St 158 A1
Lendal Ter, SW4 . . . . .181 D1
Len Freeman Pl, SW6
off John Smith Av 163 F2
Lenham Rd, SE12 . . . . .187 F2
Lennon Rd, NW2 . . . . .106 C2
Lennox Gdns, NW10 . . . . . . .105 F1
SW1 . . . . .57 E3
Lennox Gdns Ms, SW1 . . . . . .57 E3
Lennox Rd, N4 . . . . .97 F3
Lensbury Av, SW6 . . . . .164 C4
Lenthall Ho, SW1 . . . . .71 F3
Lenthall Rd, E8 . . . . .113 F4
Lenthorp Rd, SE10 . . . . .159 F3
Lenton Ter, N4
off Fonthill Rd 98 A3

Leonard Pl, N16
off Allen Rd **113** E1
Leonard St, EC2 **28** B2
Leontine Cl, SE15 **170** A2
Leopards Ct, EC1 **26** A4
Leopold Ms, E9
off Fremont St **128** C1
Leopold Rd, NW10 **105** E4
Leopold St, E3 **143** F1
Leo St, SE15 **170** B2
Leo Yd, EC1 **27** D3
Leppoc Rd, SW4 **181** D3
Leroy St, SE1 **64** C4
Lerry Cl, W14
off Thaxton Rd **163** F1
Leslie Rd, E11 **116** C1
Lessar Av, SW4 **180** C3
Lester Av, E15 **131** E3
Leswin Pl, N16 **99** F4
Leswin Rd, N16 **99** F4
Letchford Gdns, NW10 **120** A3
Letchford Ms, NW10
off Letchford Gdns **120** A3
Lethbridge Cl, SE13 **172** C3
Letterstone Rd, SW6
off Varna Rd **163** F2
Lettice St, SW6 **163** F3
Lett Rd, E15 **117** D4
Lettsom St, SE5 **169** E4
Levehurst Way, SW4 **167** E4
Leven Rd, E14 **144** C1
Leverett St, SW3 **57** D4
Lever St, EC1 **27** D1
Leverton Pl, NW5
off Leverton St **110** C2
Leverton St, NW5 **110** C2
Levison Way, N19
off Grovedale Rd **97** D3
Leweston Pl, N16 **99** F1
Lewey Ho, E3 **129** F4
Lewin Rd, SW14 **175** D1
Lewis Cres, NW10 **104** C2
Lewis Gro, SE13 **186** C1
LEWISHAM, SE13 **186** B2
Lewisham 186 C1
DLR Lewisham 186 C1
Lewisham 186 C1
Lewisham Cen, SE13 186 C1
Coll Lewisham Coll, Deptford Campus, SE8
off Deptford Ch St 172 A3
Lewisham Way Campus, SE4
off Breakspears Rd 172 A4
Lewisham High St, SE13 **186** C1
Lewisham Hill, SE13 **172** C4
Lewisham Pk, SE13 **186** B4
Lewisham Rd, SE13 **172** B3
Lewisham St, SW1 **60** B1
Lewisham Way, SE4 **171** F3
SE14 **171** F3
Lewis Pl, E8 **114** A2
Lewis St, NW1 **110** B3
Lexden Rd, W3 **132** B3
Lexham Gdns, W8 **54** C4
Lexham Gdns Ms, W8 **55** D3
Lexham Ms, W8 **54** B4
Lexham Wk, W8 **55** D3
Lexington Apts, EC1 **28** A2
Lexington Bldg, E3
off Fairfield Rd **130** A2
Lexington St, W1 **35** F3
Leyborne Pk, Rich. TW9 **160** A3
Leybourne Rd, E11 **103** F2
NW1 **110** B4
Leybourne St, NW1
off Hawley St **110** B4
Leyden St, E1 **41** E1
Leydon Cl, SE16
off Lagado Ms **143** D4
Leylang Rd, SE14 **171** D2
Leysfield Rd, W12 **148** A1
Leyspring Rd, E11 **103** F2
Leythe Rd, W3 **146** C1
LEYTON, E11 **102** B2
Leyton 102 C4
Leyton Business Cen, E10 102 A3
Leyton Gra, E10 **102** A3
Leyton Gra Est, E10
off Leyton Gra **102** A3
Leyton Ind Village, E10 101 D1
Leyton Midland Road 102 C2
★ Leyton Orient FC, E10 102 B4
Leyton Pk Rd, E10 **102** C4
Leyton Rd, E15 **117** D2
LEYTONSTONE, E11 **103** D1
Leytonstone 103 E2
Leytonstone High Road 103 E3
Leytonstone Rd, E15 **117** E2
Leywick St, E15 **131** E2
Liardet St, SE14 **171** E1
Liberia Rd, N5 **112** B3
★ Liberty, W1 35 E3
Liberty Ms, SW12 **180** B4
Liberty St, SW9 **167** F3
Libra Rd, E3 **129** F1
Library Pl, E1
off Cable St **142** B3
Library St, SE1 **62** C1
Lichfield Rd, E3 **129** E3
NW2 **107** E1
Lickey Ho, W14
off North End Rd **163** F1
Lidcote Gdns, SW9 **168** A4
Liddell Gdns, NW10 **120** C2
Liddell Rd, NW6 **108** A3
Liddington Rd, E15 **131** F1
Liden Cl, E17 **101** F1
Lidfield Rd, N16 **113** D1
Lidgate Rd, SE15 **89** E3
Lidlington Pl, NW1 **11** E3
Lidyard Rd, N19 **96** C2
Coll Lifelong Learning, The Shadwell Cen, E1
off The Highway 143 D3
Liffords Pl, SW13 **161** F4
Lifford St, SW15 **177** D2
Lighter Cl, SE16 **157** E3
Lighterman Ms, E1 **143** D2
Lightermans Rd, E14 **158** A1
Ligonier St, E2 **29** E2
Lilac Pl, SE11 **73** E1
Lilac St, W12 **134** A3
Lilburne Wk, NW10 **104** C3
Lilestone St, NW8 **20** C2
Lilford Rd, SE5 **168** B4
Lilian Cl, N16 **99** E4
Lilley Cl, E1
off Hermitage Wall **142** A4
Lillian Av, W3 **146** A1
Lillian Rd, SW13 **162** A1
Lillie Rd, SW6 **163** E2
Lillieshall Rd, SW4 **180** B1
Lillie Yd, SW6 **66** A4
Lillingston Ho, N7
off Harvist Est **112** A1
Lillington Gdns Est, SW1 **71** F1
Lily Cl, W14 **149** E3
Lily Pl, EC1 **26** B4
Lilyville Rd, SW6 **163** F3
Limburg Rd, SW11 **179** F2
Limeburner La, EC4 **38** C3
Lime Cl, E1 **142** A4
Lime Gro, W12 **148** C1
Limeharbour, E14 **158** B2
LIMEHOUSE, E14 **143** E3
Limehouse 143 E2
DLR Limehouse 143 E2
Limehouse Causeway, E14 **143** F3
Limehouse Link, E14 **143** E3
Limerston St, SW10 **67** F4
Limes, The, SW18 **178** A4
W2 **42** B1
Limes Av, NW11 **93** E1
SW13 **161** F4
Limes Fld Rd, SW14
off First Av **175** E1
Limesford Rd, SE15 **185** D2
Limes Gdns, SW18 **178** A4
Limes Gro, SE13 **186** C2
Lime St, EC3 **40** C4
Lime St Pas, EC3 **40** C3
Limes Wk, SE15 **184** B2
Lime Wk, E15
off Church St N **131** E1
Linacre Cl, SE15 **184** B1
Linacre Ct, W6 **149** D4
Linacre Rd, NW2 **106** B3
Linale Ho, N1
off Murray Gro **16** A3
Linberry Wk, SE8 **157** F3
Lincoln Ct, N16 **99** D1
Lincoln Ms, NW6
off Willesden La **121** F1
★ Lincoln's Inn, WC2 37 F2
Lincoln's Inn Flds, WC2 **37** E2
Lincoln St, E11 **103** E3
SW3 **69** E1
Lindal Rd, SE4 **185** F3
Linden Av, NW10 **121** D2
Linden Ct, W12 **134** C4
Linden Gdns, W2 **42** B1
W4 **147** D4
Linden Gro, SE15 **184** B1
Linden Mans, N6
off Hornsey La **96** B2
Linden Ms, N1 **113** D2
W2 **42** B1
Linden Pas, W4
off Linden Gdns **147** D4
Lindens, The, W4 **160** C3
Linden Wk, N19
off Hargrave Pk **96** C3
Lindfield Gdns, NW3 **108** B2
Lindfield St, E14 **144** A2
Lindisfarne Way, E9 **115** E1
Lindley Est, SE15
off Bird in Bush Rd **170** A2
Lindley Pl, Rich. (Kew) TW9 **160** A3
Lindley Rd, E10 **102** B3
Lindley St, E1 **142** C1
Lindore Rd, SW11 **179** F2
Lindo St, SE15
off Selden Rd **170** C4
Lindrop St, SW6 **164** C4
Lindsay Ct, SW11
off Battersea High St **165** D3
Lindsay Sq, SW1 **72** B2
Lindsell St, SE10 **172** C3
Lindsey Ms, N1 **112** C4

Lindsey St, EC1 **27** D4
Lind St, SE8 **172** B4
Linford St, SW8 **83** E4
Lingards Rd, SE13 **186** C2
Lingham St, SW9 **167** E4
Lingwood Rd, E5 **100** A1
Linhope St, NW1 **21** E2
Link, The, W3 **132** B2
Links Rd, NW2 **91** F3
W3 **132** A2
Link St, E9 **114** C3
Links Yd, E1
off Spelman St **142** A1
Linkway, N4 **98** C1
Linkwood Wk, NW1
off Maiden La **111** D4
★ Linley Sambourne Ho,
W8 54 B1
Linnell Rd, SE5 **169** E4
Linom Rd, SW4 **181** E2
Linscott Rd, E5 **114** C1
Linsey St, SE16 **156** A3
Linstead St, NW6 **108** A4
Lintaine Cl, W6
off Moylan Rd **163** E1
Linthorpe Rd, N16 **99** E1
Linton St, N1 **15** F1
Linver Rd, SW6 **164** A4
Linwood Cl, SE5 **169** F4
Lion Cl, SE4 **186** A4
Lionel Ms, W10
off Telford Rd **135** E1
Lion Mills, E2
off Hackney Rd **128** A2
Lion Plaza, EC2
off Lothbury **40** A2
Lion Yd, SW4
off Tremadoc Rd **181** D2
Lipton Rd, E1
off Bower St **143** D2
Lisburne Rd, NW3 **109** F1
Lisford St, SE15 **89** F4
Lisgar Ter, W14 **149** F3
Lisle St, WC2 **36** B4
Lismore Circ, NW5 **109** F2
Lismore Wk, N1
off Clephane Rd **112** C3
Lissenden Gdns, NW5 **110** A1
Lisson Grn Est, NW8 **20** C1
LISSON GROVE, NW8 **20** B2
Lisson Gro, NW1 **20** C2
NW8 **20** B1
Lisson St, NW1 **20** C4
Lister Cl, W3 **133** D1
H Lister Hosp, The, SW1 70 C3
Lister Rd, E11 **103** E2
Liston Rd, SW4 **180** C1
Listowel Cl, SW9 **86** B2
Listria Pk, N16 **99** E3
Litchfield Av, E15 **117** E3
Litchfield Gdns, NW10 **106** A3
Litchfield St, WC2 **36** B4
Lithos Rd, NW3 **108** B3
Little Albany St, NW1 **23** D2
Little Argyll St, W1 **35** E3
Little Boltons, The, SW5 **67** D2
SW10 **67** D2
Little Britain, EC1 **39** E2
Littlebury Rd, SW4 **181** D1
Little Chester St, SW1 **58** B2
Little Cloisters, SW1
off College Ms **60** C2
Little Coll La, EC4
off College St **40** A4
Little Coll St, SW1 **60** C2
Littlecombe Cl, SW15 **177** D4
Little Cottage Pl, SE10
off Tarves Way **172** B2
Little Dean's Yd, SW1 **60** C2
Little Dorrit Ct, SE1 **51** F4
Little Edward St, NW1 **11** D4
Little Essex St, WC2 **38** A4
Littlefield Cl, N19
off Tufnell Pk Rd **110** C1
Little George St, SW1 **60** C1
Little Grn St, NW5
off College La **110** B1
Little London Ct, SE1
off Mill St **65** F1
Little Marlborough St, W1
off Foubert's Pl **35** E3
Little Newport St, WC2 **36** B4
Little New St, EC4 **38** B2
Little Portland St, W1 **35** E2
Little Russell St, WC1 **36** C1
Little St. James's St, SW1 **47** E3
Little St. Leonards, SW14 **174** C1
Little Sanctuary, SW1 **60** B1
Little Smith St, SW1 **60** B2
Little Somerset St, E1 **41** E3
Little Titchfield St, W1 **35** E1
Littleton Ho, SW1
off Lupus St **71** E3
Little Trinity La, EC4 **39** F4
Little Turnstile, WC1 **37** E2
★ Little Venice (Waterbuses),
W2 19 E4
Littlewood, SE13 **186** C3
Livermere Rd, E8 **127** F1
Liverpool Gro, SE17 **75** F3
Liverpool Rd, E16 **145** E1
N1 **126** A2
N7 **112** A2
⇌ Liverpool Street 40 C1
⊖ Liverpool Street 40 C1
Liverpool St, EC2 **40** C1
Livesey Pl, SE15
off Peckham Pk Rd **170** A1
Livingstone Pl, E14
off Ferry St **158** C4
Livingstone Rd, E15 **130** C1
SW11
off Winstanley Rd **179** D1
Livingstone Wk, SW11 **179** D1
Livonia St, W1 **35** F3
Lizard St, EC1 **27** F1
Llanelly Rd, NW2 **93** F3
Llanvanor Rd, NW2 **93** F3
Llewellyn St, SE16
off Chambers St **156** A1
Lloyd Baker St, WC1 **25** F1
Lloyd's Av, EC3 **41** D3
★ Lloyd's of London, EC3 40 C3
Lloyds Pl, SE3 **173** E4
Lloyd Sq, WC1 **14** A4
Lloyd's Row, EC1 **26** B1
Lloyd St, WC1 **14** A4
Lloyd Vil, SE4 **172** A4
Loampit Hill, SE13 **172** A4
Jct Loampit Vale, SE13
off Lewisham High St **186** C1
SE13 **186** B1
Loanda Cl, E8
off Clarissa St **127** F1
Loats Rd, SW2 **181** E4
Locarno Rd, W3 **132** C4
Lochaber Rd, SE13 **187** E2
Lochaline St, W6 **162** C1
Lochnagar St, E14 **144** C1
Lock Bldg, The, E15
off High St **130** C2
Lock Chase, SE3 **187** E1
Locke Ho, N16
off Stamford Hill **99** E2
Lockesfield Pl, E14 **158** B4
Lockgate Cl, E9
off Lee Conservancy Rd **115** F2
Lockhart Cl, N7 **111** F3
Lockhart St, E3 **129** F4
Lockhurst St, E5 **115** D1
Lockington Rd, SW8 **83** D4
Lockmead Rd, SE13 **186** C1
Lock Ms, NW1
off Northpoint Sq **111** D3
Locksley Est, E14 **143** F2
Locksley St, E14 **143** F1
Locksons Cl, E14
off Broomfield St **144** B1
Lockton St, W10 **135** D3
Lockwood Ho, SE11
off Kennington Oval **86** A1
Lockwood Sq, SE16 **156** B2
Lockyer Est, SE1 **52** B4
Lockyer St, SE1 **64** B1
Locton Grn, E3
off Ruston St **129** F1
Loddiges Rd, E9 **114** C4
Loder St, SE15 **170** C3
Lodge Av, SW14 **175** E1
Lodge Rd, NW8 **20** B1
Lodore St, E14 **144** C2
Loftie St, SE16 **156** A1
Lofting Rd, N1 **111** F4
Loftus Rd, W12 **134** B4
Logan Ms, W8 **54** A4
Logan Pl, W8 **54** A4
Lohmann Ho, SE11
off Kennington Oval **74** A4
Lolesworth Cl, E1 **41** E1
Lollard St, SE11 **61** F4
Loman St, SE1 **51** D4
Lomas Dr, E8 **113** F4
Lomas St, E1 **142** A1
Lombard Ct, EC3 **40** B4
W3 *off Crown St* **132** B4
Lombard La, EC4 **38** B3
Lombard Rd, SW11 **165** D4
Lombard St, EC3 **40** B3
Lombardy Pl, W2 **42** C1
Lomond Gro, SE5 **88** A2
Loncroft Rd, SE5 **77** D4
Londesborough Rd, N16 **113** E1
Londinium Twr, E1
off Mansell St **41** F4
★ London 2012 Olympic
Park Site, E15 116 B2
Coll London Acad of Music
& Dramatic Art, W14
off Talgarth Rd **149** D4
★ London Aquarium, SE1 49 E4
★ London Brass Rubbing Cen
(St. Martin-in-the-Fields Ch),
WC2 48 C1
⇌ London Bridge 52 C3
⊖ London Bridge 52 C3
London Br, EC4 **52** B2
SE1 **52** B2
Riv London Bridge City Pier 52 C2
H London Br Hosp, SE1 52 B2
London Br St, SE1 **52** A3
Coll London Business Sch,
NW1 21 E2

★ London Canal Mus, The, N1 *off New Wf Rd* 13 D2
London Cen Mkts, EC1 . . .26 C4
★ London Cen Mosque, NW8 . . . . .9 D4
H London Chest Hosp, E2 . . . . .128 C2
Coll London City Coll, SE1 . . . .50 A3
H London Clinic, The, W1 . . .22 B3
★ London Coliseum, WC2 . .48 C1
Coll London Coll of Beauty Therapy, W1 . . . . .35 E3
Uni London Coll of Communication, SE1 . . . .63 D3
Uni London Coll of Fashion, Barrett St, W1 . . . . .34 B3
Curtain Rd, EC2 . . . . .29 D2
John Princes St, W1 . . . . . .35 D2
Lime Gro, W12 . . . . .148 C1
Mare St, E8 . . . . .114 B4
★ London Dungeon, SE1 . . .52 B3
Coll London Electronics Coll, SW5 . . . . .66 C2
★ London Eye, SE1 . . . . .49 E4
London Fields 114 B4
London Flds, E8 . . . . .114 B4
London Flds E Side, E8 . . . . .114 B4
London Flds W Side, E8 . . . .114 A4
★ London Fire Brigade Mus, SE1 . . . . .51 E4
London Fruit Ex, E1 *off Brushfield St* 41 E1
H London Indep Hosp, E1 . . . . .143 D1
London La, E8 . . . . .114 B4
★ London Met Archives, EC1 . . . . .26 B2
Uni London Met Uni - London City Campus, Calcutta Ho, E1 .41 F2
Central Ho, E1 *off Whitechapel High St* .142 A2
Commercial Rd, E1 . . . . . .142 A2
Goulston St, E1 . . . . .41 E2
Jewry St, EC3 . . . . .41 E3
Moorgate, EC2 . . . . .40 B1
Students Union, E1 . . . . . . .41 F2
Tower Hill, EC3 . . . . .41 E4
Whitechapel High St, E1 . . .41 F2
Uni London Met Uni - London N Campus, Carleton Gra Hall of Res, N7 *off Carleton Rd* 111 D1
Dept of Architecture, N7 *off Holloway Rd* 112 A3
Eden Gro, N7 . . . . .111 F2
Harglenis, N7 *off Hornsey Rd* 112 A2
James Leicester Hall of Res, N7 *off Market Rd* 111 E3
Ladbroke Ho, N5 *off Highbury Gro* 112 B2
Learning Cen, N7 *off Holloway Rd* 111 F1
Science Cen, N7 *off Hornsey Rd* 112 A1
Stapleton Ho, N7 *off Holloway Rd* 111 F2
The Arc Hall of Res, N7 *off Holloway Rd* 111 E1
Tower Bldg, N7 *off Holloway Rd* 112 A2
Tufnell Pk Hall of Res, N7 *off Huddleston Rd* 96 C4
London Ms, W2 . . . . .32 B3
★ London Palladium, W1 . . .35 E3
★ London Peace Pagoda, SW11 . . . . .81 F2
London Rd, SE1 . . . . .62 C2
Uni London Sch of Economics & Political Science, WC2 . . . . .37 F3
Uni London Sch of Hygiene & Tropical Medicine, WC1 . . . . .24 B4
London Silver Vaults, WC2 . . . . .38 A1
Uni London S Bk Uni, SE1 . . . .63 D2
Caxton Ho, SE1 . . . . .62 C2
London Stile, W4 *off Wellesley Rd* 146 A4
★ London Stone, EC4 . . . . . .40 A4
London St, EC3 . . . . .41 D4
W2 . . . . .32 A3
Coll London Studio Cen, N1 . . . . .13 D2
★ London Television Cen, SE1 . . . . .50 A2
London Ter, E2 *off Hackney Rd* 128 A2
★ London Transport Mus, WC2 . . . . .37 D4
London Trocadero, The, W1 . . . . .48 A1
London Wall, EC2 . . . . .39 F1
London Wall Bldgs, EC2 . . . . .40 B1
★ London Zoo, NW1 . . . . . . .10 A2
Long Acre, WC2 . . . . .36 C4
Longbeach Rd, SW11 . . . . . .179 F1
Longberrys, NW2 . . . . .93 F4
Longbridge Way, SE13 . . . . .186 C3
Long Dr, W3 . . . . .133 E2
Longfellow Way, SE1 . . . . . . .77 F1
Longfield Dr, SW14 . . . . .174 B3
Longfield Est, SE1 . . . . .77 F1
Longford Ct, E5 *off Pedro St* 115 D1
Longford Ho, E1 *off Jubilee St* 142 C2
Longford St, NW1 . . . . .23 D2
Longhedge St, SW11 . . . . . .166 A4
Longhope Cl, SE15 . . . . .89 E1
Longhurst Rd, SE13 . . . . . . .187 D3
Longland Ct, SE1 *off Rolls Rd* 156 A4
Longlands Ct, W11 *off Portobello Rd* 135 F3
Long La, EC1 . . . . .27 D4
SE1 . . . . .64 A1
Longleat Ho, SW1 *off Rampayne St* 72 A2
Longlents Ho, NW10 . . . . . .119 D1
Longley Ct, SW8 . . . . .84 C4
Longley St, SE1 . . . . .156 A3
Longley Way, NW2 . . . . .92 C4
Long Meadow, NW5 *off Torriano Av* 111 D2
Longmoore St, SW1 . . . . .71 E1
Longnor Rd, E1 . . . . .129 D3
Long Pond Rd, SE3 . . . . .173 E3
Longridge Ho, SE1 . . . . .63 F3
Longridge Rd, SW5 . . . . .66 A1
Long Rd, SW4 . . . . .180 B2
Long's Ct, WC2 . . . . .36 A4
Longshore, SE8 . . . . .157 F3
Longstaff Cres, SW18 . . . . . .178 A4
Longstaff Rd, SW18 . . . . . . .178 A4
Longstone Av, NW10 . . . . . .105 F4
Longstone Ct, SE1 . . . . .63 F1
Long St, E2 . . . . .17 E4
Longthorpe Ct, W6 *off Invermead Cl* 148 A2
Longton Ho, SE11 *off Lambeth Wk* 61 F4
Longville Rd, SE11 . . . . .62 C4
Long Wk, SE1 . . . . .65 D2
SW13 . . . . .161 E4
Longwood Dr, SW15 . . . . . . .176 A4
Long Yd, WC1 . . . . .25 E3
Lonsdale Ms, W11 *off Lonsdale Rd* 135 F2
Lonsdale Pl, N1 *off Barnsbury St* 112 A4
Lonsdale Rd, E11 . . . . .103 F1
NW6 . . . . .121 F2
SW13 . . . . .162 A1
W4 . . . . .147 F3
W11 . . . . .135 F2
Lonsdale Sq, N1 . . . . .112 A4
Loraine Rd, N7 . . . . .111 F1
W4 . . . . .160 B1
Lord Amory Way, E14 . . . . .158 C1
Lorden Wk, E2 . . . . .128 A3
Lord Hills Br, W2 . . . . .31 D1
Lord Hills Rd, W2 . . . . .19 D4
Lord Holland La, SW9 *off Mostyn Rd* 168 A4
Lord Napier Pl, W6 *off Oil Mill La* 148 A4
Lord N St, SW1 . . . . .60 C3
Lord Roberts Ms, SW6 . . . . . . .78 C3
★ Lord's (Marylebone CC & Mus, Middlesex CCC), NW8 . . . . .8 B4
Lordship Gro, N16 . . . . .99 D3
Lordship La, SE22 . . . . .183 F4
Lordship Pk, N16 . . . . .98 C3
Lordship Pk Ms, N16 . . . . .98 C3
Lordship Pl, SW3 . . . . .80 C1
Lordship Rd, N16 . . . . .99 D3
Lordship Ter, N16 . . . . .99 D3
Lord's Vw, NW8 . . . . .20 B1
Lorenzo St, WC1 . . . . .13 E4
Loring Rd, SE14 . . . . .171 E3
Loris Rd, W6 . . . . .148 C2
Lorn Ct, SW9 . . . . .168 A4
Lorne Cl, NW8 . . . . .21 D1
Lorne Gdns, W11 . . . . .149 D1
Lorne Rd, N4 . . . . .97 F2
Lorn Rd, SW9 . . . . .167 F4
Lorrimore Rd, SE17 . . . . .75 D4
Lorrimore Sq, SE17 . . . . .75 D4
Lothair Rd S, N4 . . . . .98 A1
Lothair St, SW11 *off Grant Rd* 179 E1
Lothbury, EC2 . . . . .40 A2
Lothian Rd, SW9 . . . . .87 D4
Lothrop St, W10 . . . . .121 E3
Lots Rd, SW10 . . . . .79 E3
Loudoun Rd, NW8 . . . . .7 F2
Loughborough Est, SW9 *off Loughborough Rd* . . .168 B4
Loughborough Junction .182 B1
Loughborough Pk, SW9 . . . .182 B2
Loughborough Rd, SW9 . . . .168 A4
Loughborough St, SE11 . . . . .73 F2
Lough Rd, N7 . . . . .111 F3
Louisa Cl, E9 *off Wetherell Rd* 129 D1
Louisa Gdns, E1 *off Louisa St* 129 D4
Louisa Ho, SW15 . . . . .175 E2
Louisa St, E1 . . . . .129 D4

ouise Aumonier Wk, N19
off Hillrise Rd **97** E1
ouise Bennett Cl, SE24
off Shakespeare Rd **182** B2
ouise Rd, E15 **117** E3
ouvaine Rd, SW11 **179** D2
ovat Cl, NW2 **91** F4
ovat La, EC3 **52** C1
ovegrove St, SE1 **156** A4
ovegrove Wk, E14 **144** C4
ove La, EC2 **39** F2
ovelinch Cl, SE15 **170** C1
ovell Ho, E8 **128** A1
ovell Pl, SE16
off Ropemaker Rd **157** E2
overidge Ms, NW6
off Loveridge Rd **107** F3
overidge Rd, NW6 **107** F3
overs Wk, SE10 **173** E1
over's Wk, W1 **46** A2
ovett's Pl, SW18
off Old York Rd **178** B2
ovett Way, NW10 **104** C2
ove Wk, SE5 **169** D4
owden Rd, SE24 **182** B2
owell St, E14 **143** E2
ower Addison Gdns,
W14 **149** E1
ower Belgrave St, SW1 **58** C3
OWER CLAPTON, E5 **115** D1
ower Clapton Rd, E5 **114** B2
ower Clarendon Wk, W11
off Lancaster Rd **135** E2
ower Common S, SW15 **176** B1
ower Grosvenor Pl, SW1 **58** C2
OWER HOLLOWAY, N7 **111** F2
ower James St, W1 **35** F4
ower John St, W1 **35** F4
ower Lea Crossing, E14 **145** E3
E16 **145** E3
ower Mall, W6 **148** B4
ower Marsh, SE1 **62** A1
ower Merton Ri, NW3 **109** E4
● Lower Pl Business Cen,
NW10 *off Steele Rd* **118** C2
ower Richmond Rd,
SW14 **174** B1
SW15 **176** C1
Richmond TW9 **174** A1
ower Rd, SE1 **50** A4
SE8 **156** C2
SE16 **156** C2
ower Robert St, WC2
off John Adam St **49** D1
ower Sloane St, SW1 **70** A1
ower Talbot Wk, W11
off Talbot Wk **135** E2
ower Ter, NW3 **94** C4
ower Thames St, EC3 **52** B1
owestoft Cl, E5
off Theydon Rd **100** C3
owfield Rd, NW6 **108** A4
W3 **132** C2
owman Rd, N7 **111** F1
owndes Cl, SW1 **58** B3
owndes Ct, W1 **35** E3
owndes Pl, SW1 **58** A3
owndes Sq, SW1 **57** F1
owndes St, SW1 **57** F2
owood St, E1
off Dellow St **142** B3
owry Ho, E14
off Cassilis Rd **158** A1
owther Gdns, SW7 **56** A2
Lowther Rd, N7
off Liverpool Rd **112** A2
SW13 **161** F3
Lowth Rd, SE5 **168** C4
Loxham St, WC1 **25** D1
Coll L.S.O. St. Luke's, EC1 **27** F2
Lubbock St, SE14 **170** C2
Lucan Pl, SW3 **68** C1
Lucas Cl, NW10
off Pound La **106** A4
Lucas Ct, SW11
off Strasburg Rd **166** A3
Lucas St, SE8 **172** A3
Lucerne Ms, W8 **42** B2
Lucerne Rd, N5 **112** B1
Lucey Rd, SE16 **156** A2
Lucey Way, SE16 **156** A2
Lucorn Cl, SE12 **187** F4
Lucy Cres, W3 **132** C1
Ludgate Bdy, EC4 **38** C3
Ludgate Circ, EC4 **38** C3
Ludgate Hill, EC4 **38** C3
Ludgate Sq, EC4 **39** D3
Ludlow St, EC1 **27** E2
Ludovick Wk, SW15 **175** E2
Ludwick Ms, SE14 **171** E2
Lugard Rd, SE15 **170** B4
Luke Ho, E1 **142** B2
Luke St, EC2 **28** C2
Lukin St, E1 **142** C2
Lullingstone La, SE13 **187** D4
Lulot Gdns, N19 **96** B3
Lulworth, NW1
off Agar Pl **111** D4
SE17 **76** A2
Lulworth Ho, SW8 **85** E2
Lulworth Rd, SE15 **170** B4
Lumley Ct, WC2 **49** D1
Lumley Flats, SW1
off Holbein Pl **70** A2
Lumley St, W1 **34** B3
Luna Ho, SE16
off Bermondsey Wall W **156** A1
Lund Pt, E15
off Carpenters Rd **130** C1
Lundy Wk, N1
off Clifton Rd **112** C3
Lupino Ct, SE11 **73** F1
Lupin Pt, SE1 **65** F1
Lupton St, NW5 **110** C1
Lupus St, SW1 **71** F3
Luralda Gdns, E14
off Saunders Ness Rd **158** C4
Lurgan Av, W6 **163** D1
Lurline Gdns, SW11 **82** B4
Luscombe Way, SW8 **84** C2
Lushington Rd, NW10 **120** B2
Lushington Ter, E8
off Wayland Av **114** A2
Luton Pl, SE10 **172** C2
Luton St, NW8 **20** B3
Lutton Ter, NW3 **108** C1
Luttrell Av, SW15 **176** B3
Lutyens Ho, SW1
off Churchill Gdns **71** E3
Luxborough St, W1 **22** A4
Luxborough Twr, W1
off Luxborough St **22** A4
Luxembourg Ms, E15
off Leytonstone Rd **117** E2
Luxemburg Gdns, W6 **149** D3
Luxford St, SE16 **157** D3
Luxmore St, SE4 **171** F3
Luxor St, SE5 **168** B4
Lyall Ms, SW1 **58** A3
Lyall Ms W, SW1 **58** A3
Lyall St, SW1 **58** A3
Lyal Rd, E3 **129** E2
Lycée, The, SE11 **74** B3
Lycett Pl, W12
off Becklow Rd **148** A1
Lydford Cl, N16
off Pellerin Rd **113** E2
Lydford Rd, NW2 **107** D3
W9 **121** F4
Lydon Rd, SW4 **180** C1
Lygon Ho, SW6
off Fulham Palace Rd **163** E3
Lygon Pl, SW1 **58** C3
Lyham Cl, SW2 **181** E4
Lyham Rd, SW2 **181** E3
Lyme Gro, E9
off St. Thomas's Sq **114** C4
Lyme St, NW1 **110** C4
Lyme Ter, NW1
off Royal Coll St **110** C4
Lymington Rd, NW6 **108** B3
Lympstone Gdns, SE15 **170** A2
Lynbrook Gro, SE15 **89** D2
Lynch Cl, SE3
off Paragon Pl **173** F4
Lynch Wk, SE8
off Prince St **171** F1
Lyncott Cres, SW4 **180** B2
Lyncroft Gdns, NW6 **108** A2
Lyndale, NW2 **107** F1
Lyndale Av, NW2 **93** F4
Lyndale Cl, SE3 **173** F1
Lyndhurst Cl, NW10 **91** D4
Lyndhurst Dr, E10 **102** C1
Lyndhurst Gdns, NW3 **109** D2
Lyndhurst Gro, SE15 **169** E4
Lyndhurst Rd, NW3 **109** D2
Lyndhurst Sq, SE15 **169** F3
Lyndhurst Ter, NW3 **109** D2
Lyndhurst Way, SE15 **89** F4
Lyneham Wk, E5
off Boscombe Cl **115** E2
Lynette Av, SW4 **180** B4
Lyn Ms, E3
off Tredegar Sq **129** F3
N16 **113** E1
Lynmouth Rd, N16 **99** F2
Lynn Ms, E11
off Lynn Rd **103** E3
Lynn Rd, E11 **103** E3
Lynton Cl, NW10 **105** E2
Lynton Est, SE1
off Lynton Rd **156** A3
Lynton Rd, NW6 **121** F1
SE1 **77** F1
W3 **132** A3
Lynton Ter, W3 **132** B2
Lyons Pl, NW8 **20** A2
Lyon St, N1
off Caledonian Rd **111** F4
Lyons Wk, W14 **149** E3
★ Lyric Hammersmith,
W6 **148** C3
Lyric Rd, SW13 **161** F3
Lyric Sq, W6
off King St **148** C3
Lysander Gro, N19 **97** D2
Lysander Ho, E2
off Temple St **128** B2
Lysander Ms, N19 **96** C2
Lysias Rd, SW12 **180** A4
Lysia St, SW6 **163** D2

Lysons Wk, SW15 . . . . .176 A3
Lytcott Gro, SE22 . . . . .183 F3
Lyte St, E2
off Bishops Way 128 C2
Lytham St, SE17 . . . . .76 A3
Lyttelton Cl, NW3 . . . . .109 E4
Lyttelton Rd, E10 . . . . .102 B4
Lytton Gro, SW15 . . . . .177 D3
Lytton Rd, E11 . . . . .103 E1

M

Mabledon Pl, WC1 . . . . .24 B1
Mablethorpe Rd, SW6 . . . . . .163 E2
Mabley St, E9 . . . . .115 E3
MacArthur Cl, Wem. HA9 . . .104 B3
Macaulay Ct, SW4 . . . . .180 B1
Macaulay Rd, SW4 . . . . .180 B1
Macaulay Sq, SW4 . . . . .180 C2
McAuley Cl, SE1 . . . . .62 A2
Macauley Ms, SE13 . . . . . . .172 C4
Macbeth St, W6 . . . . .148 B4
McCabe Ct, E16
off Barking Rd 145 F1
McCall Cl, SW4
off Jeffreys Rd 167 E4
McCall Ho, N7
off Tufnell Pk Rd 97 E4
Macclesfield Br, NW1 . . . . .9 D2
Macclesfield Rd, EC1 . . . . .15 E4
Macclesfield St, W1 . . . . .36 B4
McCoid Way, SE1 . . . . .63 E1
McCrone Ms, NW3
off Belsize La 109 D3
McCullum Rd, E3 . . . . .129 F1
McDermott Cl, SW11 . . . . . .179 E1
McDermott Rd, SE15 . . . . . .184 A1
Macdonald Rd, N19 . . . . .96 C3
McDowall Cl, E16 . . . . .145 F1
McDowall Rd, SE5 . . . . .168 C3
Macduff Rd, SW11 . . . . .82 B4
Mace Cl, E1
off Kennet St 142 B4
Mace St, E2 . . . . .129 D2
McEwen Way, E15 . . . . .131 D1
Macey Ho, SW11
off Surrey La 165 E3
Macfarland Gro, SE15 . . . . . . .89 D2
Macfarlane Rd, W12 . . . . . . .134 C4
Macfarren Pl, NW1 . . . . .22 B3
McGrath Rd, E15 . . . . .117 F2
McGregor Rd, W11 . . . . .135 F2
Machell Rd, SE15 . . . . .184 C1
Mackay Rd, SW4 . . . . .180 B1
Mackennal St, NW8 . . . . .9 D3
Mackenzie Cl, W12
off Australia Rd 134 B3
Mackenzie Rd, N7 . . . . .111 F3
Mackenzie Wk, E14 . . . . .144 A4
McKerrell Rd, SE15 . . . . . . .170 A3
Mackeson Rd, NW3 . . . . . . .109 F1
Mackintosh La, E9
off Homerton High St . . .115 D2
Macklin St, WC2 . . . . .37 D2
Mackrow Wk, E14
off Robin Hood La 144 C3
Macks Rd, SE16 . . . . .156 A3
Mackworth St, NW1 . . . . .11 E4
Maclaren Ms, SW15 . . . . . . .176 C2
Maclean Rd, SE23 . . . . .185 E4
McLeod's Ms, SW7 . . . . .55 D3
Macleod St, SE17 . . . . .75 F3
Maclise Rd, W14 . . . . .149 E2
McMillan St, SE8 . . . . .172 A1
McMillan Student Village,
SE8 *off Creek Rd* 172 A1
McNeil Rd, SE5 . . . . .169 E4
McNicol Dr, NW10 . . . . .118 C2
Maconochies Rd, E14 . . . . . .158 B4
Macquarie Way, E14 . . . . . .158 B3
Macroom Rd, W9 . . . . .121 F3
Mac's Pl, EC4 . . . . .38 B2
★ Madame Tussauds,
NW1 . . . . .22 A3
Maddams St, E3 . . . . .130 B4
Maddock Way, SE17 . . . . .87 D1
Maddox St, W1 . . . . .35 D4
Madeira Rd, E11 . . . . .103 D2
Madinah Rd, E8 . . . . .114 A3
Madison Bldg, SE10
off Blackheath Rd 172 B3
Madras Pl, N7 . . . . .112 A3
Madrid Rd, SW13 . . . . .162 A3
Madrigal La, SE5 . . . . .87 D3
Madron St, SE17 . . . . .77 D2
Mafeking Rd, E16 . . . . .131 F4
Magdala Av, N19 . . . . .96 B3
Magdalene Cl, SE15
off Pilkington Rd 170 B4
Magdalen Ms, NW3
off Frognal 108 C3
Magdalen Pas, E1 . . . . .41 F4
Magdalen St, SE1 . . . . .52 C3
Magee St, SE11 . . . . .74 A4
Magellan Pl, E14
off Maritime Quay 158 A3
Maggie Blakes Causeway,
SE1 *off Shad Thames* 53 E3
Magnin Cl, E8
off Wilde Cl 128 A1
Magnolia Cl, E10 . . . . .102 A3
Magnolia Pl, SW4 . . . . .181 D3
Magnolia Rd, W4 . . . . .160 B1
Magpie All, EC4 . . . . .38 B3
Magpie Cl, E7 . . . . .117 F2
Magpie Pl, SE14
off Milton Ct Rd 171 E1
Magri Wk, E1
off Ashfield St 142 C1
Maguire St, SE1 . . . . .53 F4
● Mahatma Gandhi Ind Est,
SE24 *off Milkwood Rd* . .182 B2
Mahogany Cl, SE16 . . . . . . .143 E4
Maida Av, W2 . . . . .19 F4
MAIDA HILL, W9 . . . . .18 A2
MAIDA VALE, W9 . . . . .19 D2
⊖ Maida Vale 7 D4
Maida Vale, W9 . . . . .19 E1
Maiden La, NW1 . . . . .111 D4
SE1 . . . . .51 F2
WC2 . . . . .49 D1
Maiden Pl, NW5 . . . . .96 C4
Maiden Rd, E15 . . . . .117 E4
Maidenstone Hill, SE10 . . . .172 C3
Maidstone Bldgs Ms, SE1 . . . .51 F3
Maidstone Ho, E14
off Carmen St 144 B2
Maismore St, SE15
off Peckham Pk Rd 170 A1
Maitland Cl Est, SE10
off Greenwich High Rd . .172 B2
Maitland Pk Est, NW3 . . . . . .109 F3
Maitland Pk Rd, NW3 . . . . . .109 F3
Maitland Pk Vil, NW3 . . . . . .109 F3
Maitland Pl, E5
off Lower Clapton Rd . . .114 C1
Maitland Rd, E15 . . . . .117 F3
Major Cl, SW9 . . . . .182 B1
Major Rd, E15 . . . . .116 C2
SE16 *off Jamaica Rd* 156 A2
Makepeace Av, N6 . . . . .96 A3
Makins St, SW3 . . . . .69 D1
Malabar St, E14 . . . . .158 A1
Malam Ct, SE11 . . . . .74 A1
Malam Gdns, E14
off Wades Pl 144 B3
Malbrook Rd, SW15 . . . . . . .176 B2
Malcolm Pl, E2 . . . . .128 C4
Malcolm Rd, E1 . . . . .128 C4
Malden Cres, NW1 . . . . .110 A3
Malden Pl, NW5
off Grafton Ter 110 A2
Malden Rd, NW5 . . . . .110 A2
Maldon Cl, E15
off Maryland St 117 D2
N1 . . . . .126 C1
SE5 . . . . .183 E1
Maldon Rd, W3 . . . . .132 C3
Malet Pl, WC1 . . . . .24 A3
Malet St, WC1 . . . . .24 A3
Malfort Rd, SE5 . . . . .183 E1
Mall, The, SW1 . . . . .47 F4
SW14 . . . . .174 C3
Mallams Ms, SW9
off St. James's Cres 182 B1
Mallard Cl, E9
off Berkshire Rd 115 F3
NW6 .6 B1
Mallard Pt, E3
off Rainhill Way 130 B3
Mallard Way, NW9 . . . . .90 C1
Mall Chambers, W8
off Kensington Mall 42 B2
Mallet Rd, SE13 . . . . .187 D4
★ Mall Galleries, SW1 . . . . . .48 B2
Malling, SE13 . . . . .186 C3
Mallinson Rd, SW11 . . . . . . .179 E3
Mallord St, SW3 . . . . .68 B4
Mallory Cl, E14
off Uamvar St 144 B1
SE4 . . . . .185 E2
Mallory St, NW8 . . . . .21 D2
Mallow St, EC1 . . . . .28 A2
Mall Rd, W6 . . . . .148 B4
Malmesbury, E2
off Cyprus St 128 C2
Malmesbury Rd, E3 . . . . . . .129 F3
E16 . . . . .145 E1
Malmesbury Ter,
E16 . . . . .145 F1
Malmsmead Ho, E9
off Kingsmead Way 115 E2
Malpas Rd, E8 . . . . .114 B3
SE4 . . . . .171 F4
Malta Rd, E10 . . . . .102 A2
Malta St, EC1 . . . . .27 D2
Maltby St, SE1 . . . . .65 E1
Malthouse Dr, W4 . . . . .161 E1
Malthouse Pas, SW13
off The Terrace 161 E4
Malting Ho, E14 . . . . .143 F3
Maltings Cl, E3 . . . . .130 C3
SW13
off Cleveland Gdns 161 E4
Maltings Pl, SE1 . . . . .65 D1
SW6 . . . . .164 B3
Malton Ms, W10
off Cambridge Gdns 135 E2
Malton Rd, W10
off St. Marks Rd 135 E2
Maltravers St, WC2 . . . . .37 F4
Malt St, SE1 . . . . .170 A1

Malva Cl, SW18
off St. Ann's Hill 178 B3
Malvern Cl, W10 ....135 F1
Malvern Ct, SE14
off Avonley Rd 170 C2
SW7 ....68 B1
Malvern Gdns, NW2 ....93 E3
NW6
off Carlton Vale 121 F2
Malvern Ms, NW6 ....18 A1
Malvern Pl, NW6 ....121 F3
Malvern Rd, E8 ....114 A4
E11 ....103 E3
NW6 ....6 A4
Malvern Ter, N1 ....126 A1
Malwood Rd, SW12 ....180 B4
Malyons Rd, SE13 ....186 B3
Malyons Ter, SE13 ....186 B3
Managers St, E14
off Prestons Rd 144 C4
Manaton Cl, SE15 ....184 B1
Manbey Gro, E15 ....117 E3
Manbey Pk Rd, E15 ....117 E3
Manbey Rd, E15 ....117 E3
Manbey St, E15 ....117 E3
Manbre Rd, W6 ....162 C1
Manchester Dr, W10 ....121 E4
Manchester Gro, E14 ......158 C4
Manchester Ms, W1 ....34 A1
Manchester Rd, E14 ....158 C4
Manchester Sq, W1 ....34 A2
Manchester St, W1 ....34 A1
Manchuria Rd, SW11 ......180 A4
Manciple St, SE1 ....64 A1
Mandalay Rd, SW4 ....180 C3
Mandarin St, E14
off Salter St 144 A3
Mandela Cl, NW10 ....104 C4
Mandela St, NW1 ....124 C1
SW9 ....86 A3
Mandela Way, SE1 ....65 D4
Mandel Ho, SW18
off Eastfields Av 178 A2
Coll Mander Portman Woodward 6th Form Tutorial Coll, SW7 ....68 A1
Mandeville Cl, SE3
off Vanbrugh Pk 173 F2
Mandeville Ho, SE1 ....77 F2
Mandeville Ms, SW4
off Clapham Pk Rd 181 E2
Mandeville Pl, W1 ....34 B2
Mandeville St, E5 ....101 E4
Mandrake Way,
E15 ....117 E4
Mandrell Rd, SW2 ....181 E3
Manette St, W1 ....36 B3
Manfred Rd, SW15 ....177 F3
Manger Rd, N7 ....111 E3
Manhattan Bldg, E3
off Fairfield Rd 130 A2
Manilla St, E14 ....158 A1
Manitoba Ct, SE16
off Renforth St 156 C1
Manley Ct, N16 ....99 F4
Manley St, NW1 ....124 A1
Manneby Prior, N1
off Cumming St 13 F3
Manningford Cl, EC1 ....14 C4
Manningtree St, E1
off White Ch La 142 A2
Manor Av, SE4 ....171 F4
Jct Manor Circ, Rich. TW9 ....174 A1
Manor Ct, E10
off Grange Pk Rd 102 B2
SW6 off Bagley's La 164 B3
Manor Est, SE16 ....156 B3
Manorfield Cl, N19
off Junction Rd 110 C1
Manor Flds, SW15 ....177 D4
Manor Gdns, N7 ....97 E4
W3 ....146 A3
W4
off Devonshire Rd 147 E4
Manor Gro, SE15 ....170 C1
Richmond TW9 ....174 A2
Manorhall Gdns, E10 ......102 A2
⊖ Manor House 98 B1
Manor Ho Dr, NW6 ....107 D4
Manor La, SE12 ....187 E4
SE13 ....187 E2
Manor La Ter, SE13 ....187 E2
Manor Ms, NW6 ....6 B2
SE4 ....171 F4
Manor Par, NW10
off Station Rd 119 F2
Manor Pk, SE13 ....187 D2
Manor Pk Par, SE13
off Lee High Rd 187 D2
Manor Pk Rd, NW10 ....119 F1
Manor Pl, SE17 ....75 D3
Manor Rd, E10 ....102 A1
E15 ....131 E3
E16 ....131 E3
N16 ....99 D3
Manor Way, SE3 ....187 F2
Manresa Rd, SW3 ....68 C3
Mansell Rd, W3 ....147 D1
Mansell St, E1 ....53 F1
Manse Rd, N16 ....99 F4
Mansfield Ms, W1 ....34 C1
Mansfield Pl, NW3
off New End 108 C1
Mansfield Rd, NW3 ....109 F2
W3 ....118 B4
Mansfield St, W1 ....34 C1
Mansford St, E2 ....128 A2
Mansion Cl, SW9 ....86 B4
Mansion Gdns, NW3 ....94 B4
★ Mansion Ho, EC4 ....40 A3
⊖ Mansion House 39 F4
Mansion Ho Pl, EC4 ....40 A3
Mansion Ho St, EC4 ....40 A3
Mansions, The, SW5
off Earls Ct Rd 66 C2
Manson Ms, SW7 ....67 F1
Manson Pl, SW7 ....68 A1
Manstone Rd, NW2 ....107 E2
Mantle Rd, SE4 ....185 E1
Mantle Way, E15
off Romford Rd 117 E4
Mantua St, SW11 ....179 D1
Mantus Cl, E1
off Mantus Rd 128 C4
Mantus Rd, E1 ....128 C4
Manwood Rd, SE4 ....185 F3
Mapesbury Rd, NW2 ....107 E4
Mapeshill Pl, NW2 ....106 C3
Mape St, E2 ....128 B4
Maple Av, W3 ....133 E4
Maple Cl, SW4 ....181 D4
Mapledene Est, E8
off Mapledene Rd 114 A4
Mapledene Rd, E8 ....113 F4
Maple Gro, NW9 ....90 C1
Maple Ho, NW3
off Maitland Pk Vil 109 F3
Maple Leaf Sq, SE16
off Fishermans Dr 157 D1
Maple Ms, NW6 ....6 C2
Maple Pl, W1 ....23 F3
Maples Pl, E1
off Raven Row 142 B1
Maple St, E2 ....128 A2
W1 ....23 E4
Mapleton Cres, SW18 ......178 B4
Mapleton Rd, SW18 ....178 B4
Maple Wk, W10
off Sixth Av 121 E4
Maplin St, E3 ....129 F3
Marathon Ho, NW1 ....21 E4
Marban Rd, W9 ....121 F3
★ Marble Arch, W1 ....33 F4
⊖ Marble Arch 33 F4
Marble Arch Apts, W1
off Harrowby St 33 D2
Marble Cl, W3 ....132 B4
Marble Dr, NW2 ....93 D2
Marble Quay, E1 ....142 A4
Marcella Rd, SW9 ....168 A4
Marchant Rd, E11 ....103 D3
Marchant St, SE14 ....171 E1
Marchbank Rd, W14 ....163 F1
Marchmont St, WC1 ....24 C2
Marchwood Cl, SE5 ....89 D3
Marcia Rd, SE1 ....77 D1
Marcilly Rd, SW18 ....179 D3
Marconi Rd, E10 ....102 A2
Marcon Pl, E8 ....114 B3
Marco Rd, W6 ....148 C2
Marcus Ct, E15 ....131 E1
Marcus Garvey Ms, SE22
off St. Aidan's Rd 184 B3
Marcus Garvey Way, SE24 ..182 A2
Marcus St, E15 ....131 F1
SW18 ....178 B4
Marcus Ter, SW18 ....178 B4
Marden Ho, E8 ....114 B2
Marden Sq, SE16 ....156 B2
Mardyke Ho, SE17
off Crosslet St 64 B4
Maresfield Gdns, NW3 .....108 C2
Mare St, E8 ....128 B1
Margaret Bldgs, N16
off Margaret Rd 99 F2
Margaret Ct, W1 ....35 E2
Margaret Ingram Cl, SW6
off John Smith Av 163 F2
Margaret Rd, N16 ....99 F2
Margaret St, W1 ....35 D2
Margaretta Ter, SW3 ....68 C4
Margate Rd, SW2 ....181 E3
Margery Fry Ct, N7 ....97 E4
Margery St, WC1 ....26 A1
Margravine Gdns, W6 ......149 D4
Margravine Rd, W6 ....149 D4
Maria Cl, SE1
off Beatrice Rd 156 A3
Marian Pl, E2 ....128 B2
Marian Sq, E2
off Pritchard's Rd 128 A2
Marian St, E2
off Hackney Rd 128 B2
Marian Way, NW10 ....105 F4
Maria Ter, E1 ....143 D1
Marie Curie, SE5
off Sceaux Gdns 89 D4
Marie Lloyd Gdns, N19 .....97 E1
Marie Lloyd Ho, N1 ....16 A3
Marie Lloyd Wk, E8
off Forest Rd 114 A3

Marigold All, SE1 ..... 50 C1
Marigold St, SE16 ..... 156 B1
Marinefield Rd, SW6 ..... 164 B4
Mariners Ms, E14 ..... 159 D3
Marine St, SE16
off Enid St 156 A2
Marine Twr, SE8
off Abinger Gro 171 F1
Marischal Rd, SE13 ..... 187 D1
Maritime Quay, E14 ..... 158 A4
Maritime St, E3 ..... 129 F4
Marjorie Gro, SW11 ..... 179 F2
Marjorie Ms, E1
off Arbour Sq 143 D2
Market App, W12
off Lime Gro 148 C1
Market Ct, W1 ..... 35 E2
Market Dr, W4 ..... 161 E2
Market Est, N7 ..... 111 E3
Market La, W12
off Goldhawk Rd 148 C1
Market Ms, W1 ..... 46 C3
Market Pl, SE16
off Southwark Pk Rd 156 A3
W1 ..... 35 E2
W3 ..... 132 C4
Market Rd, N7 ..... 111 E3
Richmond TW9 ..... 174 A1
Market Row, SW9
off Atlantic Rd 182 A2
Market Sq, E14
off Chrisp St 144 B2
Market St, E1 ..... 29 E4
Market Way, E14
off Kerbey St 144 B2
Market Yd Ms, SE1 ..... 64 C2
Markham Pl, SW3 ..... 69 E2
Markham Sq, SW3 ..... 69 E2
Markham St, SW3 ..... 69 D2
Markland Ho, W10 ..... 134 C3
Mark La, EC3 ..... 53 D1
Markmanor Av, E17 ..... 101 E1
Marksbury Av, Rich.
TW9 ..... 174 A1
Mark Sq, EC2 ..... 28 C2
Mark St, E15 ..... 117 E4
EC2 ..... 28 C2
Marlborough, SW3 ..... 57 D4
Marlborough Av, E8 ..... 128 A1
Marlborough Cl, SE17 ..... 75 D1
Marlborough Ct, W1 ..... 35 E3
W8 ..... 54 A4
Marlborough Cres, W4 ..... 147 D2
Marlborough Gate Ho, W2 ..... 32 A4
Marlborough Gro, SE1 ..... 156 A4
Marlborough Hill, NW8 ..... 7 F1
Marlborough Ho, SW1 ..... 47 F3
Marlborough Ms, SW2
off Acre La 181 F2
Marlborough Pl, NW8 ..... 7 E3
Marlborough Prim Sch,
SW3 ..... 69 D1
Marlborough Rd, E15
off Borthwick Rd 117 E1
N19 ..... 97 D3
SW1 ..... 47 F3
W4 ..... 146 C4
Marlborough St, SW3 ..... 68 C1
Marlborough Yd, N19 ..... 97 D3
Marley St, SE16 ..... 157 D3
Marley Wk, NW2
off Lennon Rd 106 C2
Marloes Rd, W8 ..... 54 C3
Marlow Ct, NW6 ..... 107 D4
Marlowe Path, SE8
off Glaisher St 172 B1
Marlowes, The, NW8 ..... 8 A1
Marlow Way, SE16 ..... 157 D1
Marl Rd, SW18 ..... 178 B2
Marlton St, SE10
off Woolwich Rd 159 F4
Marmion Ms, SW11
off Taybridge Rd 180 A1
Marmion Rd, SW11 ..... 180 A2
Marmont Rd, SE15 ..... 170 A3
Marmora Rd, SE22 ..... 184 C4
Marne St, W10 ..... 121 E3
Marney Rd, SW11 ..... 180 A2
Marnham Av, NW2 ..... 107 E1
Marnock Rd, SE4 ..... 185 E3
Maroon St, E14 ..... 143 E1
Marquess Est, N1 ..... 112 C3
Marquess Rd, N1 ..... 113 D3
Marquis Rd, N4 ..... 97 F2
NW1 ..... 111 D3
Marrick Cl, SW15 ..... 176 A2
Marriott Rd, E15 ..... 131 E1
N4 ..... 97 F2
Marryat Sq, SW6 ..... 163 E3
Marsala Rd, SE13 ..... 186 B2
Marsden Rd, SE15 ..... 183 F1
Marsden St, NW5 ..... 110 A3
Marshall, W2
off Hermitage St 32 A1
Marshall Cl, SW18
off Allfarthing La 178 C4
Marshall Rd, E10 ..... 102 B4
Marshalls Pl, SE16 ..... 65 F3
Marshall St, NW10 ..... 105 D4
W1 ..... 35 F3
Marshalsea Rd, SE1 ..... 51 F4
Marsham St, SW1 ..... 60 B3
Marshfield St, E14 ..... 158 C2
Marshgate La, E15 ..... 130 C2
Marsh Hill, E9 ..... 115 E2
Marsh La, E10 ..... 102 A3
Marsh St, E14
off Harbinger Rd 158 B3
Marsh Wall, E14 ..... 144 A4
Marsland Cl, SE17 ..... 75 D3
Marston, SE17
off Deacon Way 63 F4
Marston Cl, NW6 ..... 108 C4
Marsworth Ho, E2
off Whiston Rd 128 A1
Martaban Rd, N16 ..... 99 E3
Martara Ms, SE17 ..... 75 E3
Martello St, E8 ..... 114 B4
Martello Ter, E8 ..... 114 B4
Martel Pl, E8
off Dalston La 113 F3
Martha Ct, E2 ..... 128 B2
Martha Rd, E15 ..... 117 E3
Martha's Bldgs,
EC1 ..... 28 A2
Martha St, E1 ..... 142 B2
Martindale, SW14 ..... 174 C3
Martineau Ms, N5
off Martineau Rd 112 B1
Martineau Rd, N5 ..... 112 B1
Martineau St, E1 ..... 142 C3
Martin Ho, SE1 ..... 63 F3
Martin La, EC4 ..... 40 B4
Martlett Ct, WC2 ..... 37 D3
Marton Rd, N16 ..... 99 E3
Martys Yd, NW3
off Hampstead High St 109 D1
Marville Rd, SW6 ..... 163 F2
Marvin St, E8
off Sylvester Rd 114 B3
Mary Ann Gdns, SE8 ..... 172 A1
Mary Datchelor Cl, SE5 ..... 88 B4
Mary Grn, NW8 ..... 7 D1
Maryland 117 E3
Maryland Ind Est, E15
off Maryland Rd 117 D2
Maryland Pk, E15 ..... 117 E2
Maryland Pt, E15
off The Grove 117 E3
Maryland Rd, E15 ..... 117 D2
Maryland Sq, E15 ..... 117 E2
Marylands Rd, W9 ..... 18 B3
Maryland St, E15 ..... 117 D2
Maryland Wk, N1
off Popham St 126 C1
Mary Lawrenson Pl, SE3 ..... 173 F2
MARYLEBONE, NW1 ..... 33 E2
Marylebone 21 E3
Marylebone 21 E3
Marylebone Flyover, NW1 ..... 32 B1
W2 ..... 32 B1
Marylebone High St, W1 ..... 22 B4
Marylebone La, W1 ..... 34 C3
Marylebone Ms, W1 ..... 34 C1
Marylebone Pas, W1 ..... 35 F2
Marylebone Rd, NW1 ..... 21 D4
Marylebone St, W1 ..... 34 B1
Marylee Way, SE11 ..... 73 F2
Mary Macarthur Ho, E2
off Warley St 129 D3
W6 *off Field Rd* 163 E1
Maryon Ms, NW3
off South End Rd 109 E1
Mary Pl, W11 ..... 135 E3
Mary Seacole Cl, E8
off Clarissa St 127 F1
Mary Seacole Ho, W6
off Invermead Cl 148 A2
Mary St, E16
off Barking Rd 145 F1
N1 ..... 15 F1
Mary Ter, NW1 ..... 11 D1
Mary Ward Adult Ed
Cen, The, WC1 ..... 25 D4
Masbro Rd, W14 ..... 149 D2
Mascotte Rd, SW15 ..... 177 D2
Mascotts Cl, NW2 ..... 92 B4
Mashie Rd, W3 ..... 133 E2
Maskelyne Cl, SW11 ..... 81 D4
Mason Cl, SE16
off Stevenson Cres 156 A4
Masons Arms Ms, W1 ..... 35 D3
Masons Av, EC2 ..... 40 A2
Masons Grn La, W3 ..... 132 A1
Masons Pl, EC1 ..... 15 D4
Mason St, SE17 ..... 76 B1
Masons Yd, EC1 ..... 15 D4
Mason's Yd, SW1 ..... 47 F2
Massie Rd, E8
off Graham Rd 114 A3
Massinger St, SE17 ..... 76 C1
Massingham St, E1 ..... 129 D4
Masterman Ho, SE5 ..... 87 F2
Masters Dr, SE16 ..... 156 B4
Masters St, E1 ..... 143 D1
Masthouse Terrace 158 A4
Mast Ho Ter, E14 ..... 158 A3
Mast Leisure Pk,
SE16 ..... 157 D2
Mastmaker Rd, E14 ..... 158 A1
Matcham Rd, E11 ..... 103 E4
Matham Gro, SE22 ..... 183 F2

atheson Rd, W14 **149** F3
athews Pk Av, E15 **117** F3
atilda Gdns, E3 **130** A2
atilda St, N1 **13** F1
atlock Cl, SE24 **182** C2
atlock Ct, SE5
off Denmark Hill Est **183** D2
atlock St, E14 **143** E2
atrimony Pl, SW8 **166** C4
atson Ho, SE16
off Slippers Pl **156** B2
atthew Cl, W10 **121** D4
atthew Parker St, SW1 **60** B1
atthews St, SW11 **165** F4
atthews Yd, WC2 **36** C3
atthias Rd, N16 **113** D2
attingley Way, SE15 **89** E2
aud Chadburn Pl, SW4
off Balham Hill **180** B4
aude Rd, SE5 **169** E3
aud Gdns, E13 **131** F1
audlin's Grn, E1
off Marble Quay **142** A4
aud Rd, E10 **102** C4
E13 **131** F2
H Maudsley Hosp, SE5 **169** D4
aud St, E16 **145** F1
aud Wilkes Cl, NW5 **110** C2
auleverer Rd, SW2 **181** E3
aundeby Wk, NW10
off Neasden La **105** E3
aunsel St, SW1 **60** A4
aurer Ct, SE10
off John Harrison Way **159** F2
aurice St, W12 **134** B2
auritius Rd, SE10 **159** E3
aury Rd, N16 **100** A3
averton Rd, E3 **130** A1
awbey Est, SE1 **155** F4
awbey Ho, SE1
off Old Kent Rd **77** F3
awbey Pl, SE1 **77** F3
awbey Rd, SE1 **77** F3
awbey St, SW8 **84** C3
awson La, W4
off Great W Rd **161** F1
axilla Gdns, W10
off Cambridge Gdns **135** D2
axilla Wk, W10
off Kingsdown Cl **135** D2
axted Rd, SE15 **183** F1
axwell Rd, SW6 **78** C3
aya Cl, SE15 **170** B4
ayall Rd, SE24 **182** B3
aybury Gdns,
NW10 **106** B3
aybury Ms, N6 **96** C1
aydew Ho, SE16 **156** C3
AYFAIR, W1 **46** C1
ayfair Ms, NW1
off Regents Pk Rd **109** F4
ayfair Pl, W1 **47** D2
ayfield Av, W4 **147** E3
ayfield Cl, E8
off Forest Rd **113** F3
SW4 **181** D3
ayfield Rd, E8 **113** F4
E13 **131** F4
W3 **132** B3
W12 **147** E1
ayfields, Wem. HA9 **90** A3
ayfields Cl, Wem. HA9 **90** A3
ayflower Cl, SE16
off Greenland Quay **157** D3
Mayflower Ct, SE16
off St. Marychurch St **156** C1
Mayflower Rd, SW9 **181** E1
Mayflower St, SE16 **156** C1
Maygood St, N1 **13** F2
Maygrove Rd, NW6 **107** F3
Maynard Cl, SW6 **79** D3
Maynards Quay, E1
off Garnet St **142** C3
Mayola Rd, E5 **114** C1
Mayo Rd, NW10 **105** E3
May's Bldgs Ms, SE10
off Crooms Hill **172** C2
Mays Ct, WC2 **48** C1
Maysoule Rd, SW11 **179** D2
May St, W14
off North End Rd **149** F4
Mayton St, N7 **97** F4
Mayville Est, N16
off King Henry St **113** E2
Mayville Rd, E11 **103** E3
⇌ Maze Hill **173** E1
Maze Hill, SE3 **173** E1
SE10 **173** E1
Mazenod Av, NW6 **108** A4
Maze Rd, Rich. TW9 **160** A2
Mead Cl, NW1
off Belmont St **110** A4
Meadcroft Rd, SE11 **86** C1
Meade Cl, W4 **160** A1
Meadowbank, NW3 **109** F4
SE3 **187** F1
Meadowbank Cl, SW6 **162** C2
Meadowbank Rd, NW9 **91** D1
Meadow Cl, E9 **115** F2
Meadowcourt Rd, SE3 **187** F2
Meadow Garth, NW10 **104** C4
Meadow Ms, SW8 **85** E1
Meadow Pl, SW8 **85** D2
W4 *off Edensor Rd* **161** E2
Meadow Rd, SW8 **85** E2
Meadow Row, SE1 **63** E3
Meadows Cl, E10 **102** A3
Mead Pl, E9 **114** C3
Mead Plat, NW10 **104** C3
Mead Row, SE1 **62** A2
Meadway, The, SE3
off Heath La **173** D4
Meakin Est, SE1 **64** C2
Meard St, W1 **36** A3
Meath Cres, E2 **129** D3
Meath Rd, E15 **131** F2
Meath St, SW11 **82** C4
Mecklenburgh Pl, WC1 **25** E2
Mecklenburgh Sq, WC1 **25** E2
Mecklenburgh St, WC1 **25** E2
Medburn St, NW1 **12** A2
Medcroft Gdns, SW14 **174** C2
Medhurst Cl, E3
off Arbery Rd **129** E2
Median Rd, E5 **114** C2
★ Medici Galleries, W1 **47** D1
Medina Gro, N7 **98** A4
Medina Rd, N7 **98** A4
Medland Ho, E14
off Branch Rd **143** E3
Medlar St, SE5 **87** F4
Medley Rd, NW6 **108** A3
Medusa Rd, SE6 **186** B4
Medway Bldgs, E3
off Medway Rd **129** E2
Medway Ms, E3
off Medway Rd **129** E2
Medway Rd, E3 **129** E2
Medway St, SW1 **60** B3
Medwin St, SW4 **181** F2
Meecham Ct, SW11
off Shuttleworth Rd **165** D4
Meeson Rd, E15 **131** F1
Meeson St, E5 **115** E1
Meeting Fld Path, E9
off Chatham Pl **114** C3
Meeting Ho All, E1
off Watts St **142** B4
Meeting Ho La, SE15 **170** B3
Mehetabel Rd, E9 **114** C3
Melba Way, SE13
off Morden St **172** B3
Melbourne Ct, E5
off Daubeney Rd **115** E1
Melbourne Gro, SE22 **183** E2
Melbourne Ms, SW9 **168** A3
Melbourne Pl, WC2 **37** F4
Melbourne Rd, E10 **102** B1
Melbourne Sq, SW9
off Melbourne Ms **168** A3
Melbourne Ter, SW6
off Moore Pk Rd **78** C3
Melbray Ms, SW6
off Hurlingham Rd **163** F4
Melbreak Ho, SE22
off Pytchley Rd **183** E1
Melbury Ct, W8 **149** F2
Melbury Dr, SE5 **88** C3
Melbury Rd, W14 **149** F2
Melchester Ho, N19
off Wedmore St **97** D4
Melcombe Ho, SW8
off Dorset Rd **85** E3
Melcombe Pl, NW1 **21** E4
Melcombe St, NW1 **21** F3
Meldon Cl, SW6
off Bagley's La **164** B3
Melford Rd, E11 **103** E3
Melgund Rd, N5 **112** A2
Melina Pl, NW8 **20** A1
Melina Rd, W12 **148** B1
Melior Pl, SE1 **52** C4
Melior St, SE1 **52** B4
Mellish St, E14 **158** A2
Melliss Av, Rich. TW9 **160** B3
Mellitus St, W12 **133** F2
Mell St, SE10
off Trafalgar Rd **159** E4
Melody La, N5 **112** B2
Melody Rd, SW18 **178** C3
Melon Pl, W8 **42** C4
Melon Rd, E11 **103** E4
SE15 **170** A3
Melrose Av, NW2 **106** B2
Melrose Gdns, W6 **148** C2
Melrose Rd, SW13 **161** F4
SW18 **177** F4
W3 *off Stanley Rd* **146** C2
Melrose Ter, W6 **148** C1
Melton Ct, SW7 **68** B1
Melton St, NW1 **23** F1
Melville Ct, W12
off Goldhawk Rd **148** B2
Melville Pl, N1
off Essex Rd **112** C4
Melville Rd, NW10 **105** D4
SW13 **162** A3
Melville Vil Rd, W3
off High St **133** D4
Melyn Cl, N7
off Anson Rd **110** C1
Memel Ct, EC1 **27** E3

Memel St, EC1 **27** E3
Memorial Av, E15 **131** E3
Menai Pl, E3
off Blondin St **130** A2
Mendip Dr, NW2 **93** D3
Mendip Hos, E2
off Globe Rd **128** C3
Mendip Rd, SW11 **178** C1
Mendora Rd, SW6 **163** E2
Menelik Rd, NW2 **107** E1
★ Menier Chocolate Factory, SE1 *off Southwark St* **51** F3
Menotti St, E2
off Dunbridge St **128** A4
Mentmore Ter, E8 **114** B4
Meon Rd, W3 **146** C1
Mepham St, SE1 **49** F3
Merbury Cl, SE13 **186** C3
Mercator Pl, E14
off Napier Av **158** B4
Mercator Rd, SE13 **187** D2
Merceron Hos, E2
off Globe Rd **128** C3
Merceron St, E1 **128** B4
Mercers Cl, SE10 **159** F3
Mercers Ms, N19 **97** D4
Mercers Pl, W6 **148** C3
Mercers Rd, N19 **97** D4
Mercer St, WC2 **36** C3
Merchants Ho, SE10
off Hoskins St **159** D4
Merchants Row, SE10
off Hoskins St **159** D4
Merchant St, E3 **129** F3
Mercia Gro, SE13 **186** C2
Mercier Rd, SW15 **177** E3
Mercury Ho, E3
off Garrison Rd **130** A1
Mercury Way, SE14 **171** D1
Mercy Ter, SE13 **186** B2
Meredith Av, NW2 **106** C2
Meredith Ms, SE4 **185** F2
Meredith St, EC1 **26** C1
Meredyth Rd, SW13 **162** A4
Meretone Cl, SE4 **185** E2
Mereton Mans, SE8
off Brookmill Rd **172** A3
Meridian Ct, SE16
off East La **156** A1
Meridian Gate, E14 **158** C1
Meridian Pl, E14 **158** B1
Meridian Sq, E15 **117** D4
Merivale Rd, SW15 **177** E2
Merley Ct, NW9 **90** C2
Merlin St, WC1 **26** A1
Mermaid Ct, SE1 **52** A4
SE16 **143** F4
Mermaid Twr, SE8
off Abinger Gro **171** F1
Merredene St, SW2 **181** F4
Merriam Av, E9 **115** F3
Merrick Sq, SE1 **63** F2
Merrington Rd, SW6 **66** B4
Merritt Rd, SE4 **185** F3
Merrow St, SE17 **76** A4
Merrow Wk, SE17 **76** B2
Merryfield, SE3 **173** F4
Merthyr Ter, SW13 **162** B1
Merton Av, W4 **147** F3
Merton La, N6 **95** F3
Merton Ri, NW3 **109** E4
Merton Rd, SW18 **178** A3
Merttins Rd, SE15 **185** D3
Meru Cl, NW5 **110** A2
Mervan Rd, SW2 **182** A2
Messaline Av, W3 **132** C2
Messina Av, NW6 **108** A4
Metcalfe Ct, SE10
off John Harrison Way **159** F2
Meteor St, SW11 **180** A2
Methley St, SE11 **74** B3
★ Methodist Cen Hall, SW1 **60** B1
Methwold Rd, W10 **135** D1
Metro Cen Hts, SE1 **63** E3
Metropolitan Cl, E14
off Broomfield St **144** A1
Mews, The, N1
off St. Paul St **126** C1
Mews Deck, E1
off Sovereign Cl **142** B3
Mews St, E1 **142** A4
Mexfield Rd, SW15 **177** F3
Meymott St, SE1 **50** C3
Meynell Cres, E9 **115** D4
Meynell Gdns, E9 **115** D4
Meynell Rd, E9 **115** D4
Meyrick Rd, NW10 **106** A3
SW11 **179** D1
★ MI5 (Security Service) Thames Ho, SW1 **60** C4
Miah Ter, E1
off Wapping High St **142** A4
Micawber St, N1 **15** F4
Michael Cliffe Ho, EC1 **26** B1
Michael Faraday Ho, SE17 **76** B3
Michael Rd, E11 **103** E2
SW6 **79** D4
Michaels Cl, SE13 **187** E2
Michael Stewart Ho, SW6
off Clem Attlee Ct **163** F1
Micheldever Rd, SE12 **187** E4
Michigan Bldg, E14
off Blackwall Way **144** C3
Micklethwaite Rd, SW6 **78** B1
Middle Dartrey Wk, SW10
off Blantyre St **80** A2
Middle Fld, NW8 **123** D1
Middle Row, W10 **121** E4
Middlesex Ct, W4 **147** F4
Middlesex Pas, EC1 **39** D1
Middlesex St, E1 **41** D1
Middlesex Wf, E5 **100** C3
Middle St, EC1 **27** E4
Middle Temple, EC4 **38** A4
Middle Temple La, EC4 **38** A3
Middleton Dr, SE16 **157** D1
Middleton Gro, N7 **111** E2
Middleton Ms, N7
off Middleton Gro **111** E2
Middleton Pl, W1 **35** E1
Middleton Rd, E8 **113** F4
NW11 **94** A1
Middleton St, E2 **128** B3
Middleton Way, SE13 **187** D2
Middle Yd, SE1 **52** B2
Midford Pl, W1 **23** F3
Midholm, Wem. HA9 **90** A2
Midhope St, WC1 **25** D1
Midhurst Way, E5 **114** A1
Midland Cres, NW3
off Finchley Rd **108** C3
Midland Pl, E14
off Ferry St **158** C4
Midland Rd, E10 **102** C1
NW1 **12** B3
Midland Ter, NW2 **93** D4
NW10 **119** E4
Midlothian Rd, E3
off Burdett Rd **129** F4
Midship Cl, SE16
off Surrey Water Rd **143** D4
Midship Pt, E14 **158** A1
Midstrath Rd, NW10 **105** E1
Midwood Cl, NW2 **92** B4
Milborne Gro, SW10 **67** F3
Milborne St, E9 **114** C3
Milborough Cres, SE12 **187** E4
Milcote St, SE1 **62** C1
Mildenhall Rd, E5 **114** C1
Mildmay Av, N1 **113** D3
Mildmay Gro N, N1 **113** D2
Mildmay Gro S, N1 **113** D2
Mildmay Pk, N1 **113** D2
Mildmay Pl, N16 **113** E2
Mildmay Rd, N1 **113** E2
Mildmay St, N1 **113** D3
MILE END, E1 **129** D3
⊖ Mile End **129** E3
H Mile End Hosp, E1 **129** D4
Mile End Pl, E1 **129** D4
Mile End Rd, E1 **142** C1
E3 **142** C1
Miles Pl, NW1 **20** B4
Miles St, SW8 **84** C1
Jct Milestone Grn, SW14 **174** C2
Milfoil St, W12 **134** A3
Milford La, WC2 **37** F4
Milk St, EC2 **39** F3
Milkwell Yd, SE5
off Denmark Hill **169** D3
Milkwood Rd, SE24 **182** B3
Milk Yd, E1 **142** C3
Millais Rd, E11 **116** C1
Millard Cl, N16
off Boleyn Rd **113** E2
Millard Rd, SE8 **157** F4
Millbank, SW1 **60** C3
Millbank Ct, SW1 **60** C4
Riv Millbank Millennium Pier **73** D1
● Millbank Twr, SW1 **72** C1
Millbrook Pl, NW1
off Hampstead Rd **11** E2
Millbrook Rd, SW9 **182** B1
Mill Ct, E10 **102** C4
Millender Wk, SE16 **156** C3
Millennium Br, EC4 **39** E4
SE1 **39** E4
● Millennium Business Cen, NW2 **92** B3
Millennium Dr, E14 **159** D3
Millennium Harbour, E14 **157** F1
Millennium Pl, E2 **128** B2
Millennium Sq, SE1 **53** E4
Millennium Way, SE10 **159** E1
Miller's Av, E8 **113** F2
Millers Ct, W4
off Chiswick Mall **147** F4
Millers Meadow Cl, SE3
off Meadowcourt Rd **187** F3
Miller's Ter, E8 **113** F2
Miller St, NW1 **11** E2
Millers Way, W6 **148** C1
Miller Wk, SE1 **50** B3
Millfield, N4
off Six Acres Est **98** A3
Millfield La, N6 **95** F3
Millfield Pl, N6 **96** A3
Millfields Est, E5 **101** D4
Millfields Rd, E5 **114** C1
Millgrove St, SW11 **166** A4
Millharbour, E14 **158** B2

Mill Hill, SW13 . . . . **176** A1
Mill Hill Gro, W3 . . . . **132** B4
Mill Hill Rd, SW13 . . . . **162** A4
W3 . . . . **146** B1
Millicent Rd, E10 . . . . **101** F2
Milligan St, E14 . . . . **143** F3
Milliners Ho, SW18
off Eastfields Av **178** A2
Mill La, NW6 . . . . **107** F2
Millman Ms, WC1 . . . . **25** E3
Millman Pl, WC1
off Millman St **25** E3
Millman St, WC1 . . . . **25** E3
Millmark Gro, SE14 . . . . **171** E4
Mill Pl, E14
off Commercial Rd **143** E2
Mill Pond Cl, SW8 . . . . **84** B3
Millpond Est, SE16
off West La **156** B1
Mill Row, N1 . . . . **17** D1
Mills Ct, EC2 . . . . **29** D1
Mills Gro, E14
off Dewberry St **144** C1
Millshott Cl, SW6 . . . . **162** C2
Mills Row, W4 . . . . **147** D3
Millstone Cl, E15 . . . . **117** D3
Millstream Rd, SE1 . . . . **65** E1
Mill St, SE1 . . . . **65** F1
W1 . . . . **35** D4
Mills Yd, SW6
off Hugon Rd **178** B1
MILLWALL, E14 . . . . **158** B2
Millwall Dock Rd, E14 . . . . . . **158** A2
★ Millwall FC, SE16 . . . . . . **156** C4
Millwood St, W10
off St. Charles Sq **135** E1
Mill Yd, E1
off Cable St **142** A3
Milman Rd, NW6 . . . . **121** E2
Milman's St, SW10 . . . . **80** A1
Milner Pl, N1 . . . . **126** A1
Milner Rd, E15 . . . . **131** E3
Milner Sq, N1 . . . . **112** B4
Milner St, SW3 . . . . **57** E4
Milnthorpe Rd, W4 . . . . **161** D1
Milo Gdns, SE22
off Milo Rd **183** F4
Milo Rd, SE22 . . . . **183** F4
Milroy Wk, SE1 . . . . **50** C2
Milson Rd, W14 . . . . **149** E2
Milstead Ho, E5
off Pembury Rd **114** B2
Milton Av, N6 . . . . **96** C1
NW10 . . . . **118** C1
Milton Cl, SE1 . . . . **77** E1
Milton Ct, EC2 . . . . **28** A4
Milton Ct Rd, SE14 . . . . **171** E1
Milton Gdn Est, N16
off Milton Gro **113** E1
Milton Gro, N16 . . . . **113** D1
Milton Pk, N6 . . . . **96** C1
Milton Pl, N7
off George's Rd **112** A2
Milton Rd, N6 . . . . **96** C1
SE24 . . . . **182** B3
SW14 . . . . **175** D1
W3 . . . . **133** D4
Milton St, EC2 . . . . **28** A4
Milverton Rd, NW6 . . . . **106** C4
Milverton St, SE11 . . . . **74** B3
Milward St, E1
off Stepney Way **142** B1
Mimosa St, SW6 . . . . **163** F3
Mina Rd, SE17 . . . . **77** D3
Mincing La, EC3 . . . . **40** C4
Minera Ms, SW1 . . . . **58** B4
Minerva Cl, SW9 . . . . **86** B3
Minerva Rd, NW10 . . . . **118** C4
Minerva St, E2 . . . . **128** B2
Minet Av, NW10 . . . . **119** E2
Minet Gdns, NW10 . . . . **119** E2
Minet Rd, SW9 . . . . **168** B4
Minford Gdns, W14 . . . . **149** D1
Mingard Wk, N7
off Hornsey Rd **97** F4
Ming St, E14 . . . . **144** A3
★ Ministry of Defence,
SW1 . . . . **48** C4
★ Ministry of Justice,
SW1 . . . . **59** F2
Miniver Pl, EC4
off Garlick Hill **39** F4
Minnow St, SE17 . . . . **77** D1
Minnow Wk, SE17
off Minnow St **77** D1
Minories, EC3 . . . . **41** E4
Minshull St, SW8
off Wandsworth Rd **167** D3
Minson Rd, E9 . . . . **129** D1
● Minster Ct, EC3 . . . . **40** C4
Minster Pavement, EC3
off Mincing La **40** C4
Minster Rd, NW2 . . . . **107** E2
Mintern St, N1 . . . . **16** B2
Minton Ho, SE11
off Walnut Tree Wk **62** A4
Minton Ms, NW6
off Dresden Cl **108** B3
Mint St, SE1 . . . . **51** E4
Mirabel Rd, SW6 . . . . **163** F2
Miranda Cl, E1
off Sidney St **142** C1
Miranda Rd, N19 . . . . **96** C2
Mission Pl, SE15 . . . . **170** A3
Mistral, SE5
off Sceaux Gdns **89** D4
Mitali Pas, E1
off Back Ch La **142** A2
Mitchellbrook Way,
NW10 . . . . **105** D3
Mitchell St, EC1 . . . . **27** E2
Mitchell Way, NW10 . . . . **104** C3
Mitchison Rd, N1 . . . . **113** D3
Mitford Rd, N19 . . . . **97** E3
Mitre, The, E14
off Three Colt St **143** F3
● Mitre Br Ind Est,
W10 . . . . **120** B4
Mitre Ct, EC2 . . . . **39** F2
Mitre Rd, E15 . . . . **131** E2
SE1 . . . . **50** B4
Mitre Sq, EC3 . . . . **41** D3
Mitre St, EC3 . . . . **41** D3
Mitre Way, W10 . . . . **120** B4
Mitre Wf, NW10 . . . . **120** B4
Moat Pl, SW9 . . . . **181** F1
W3 . . . . **132** B2
Modbury Gdns, NW5
off Queen's Cres **110** A3
Modder Pl, SW15 . . . . **177** D2
Model Cotts, SW14 . . . . **174** C1
Modling Ho, E2 . . . . **128** C2
Moelwyn Hughes Ct, N7
off Hilldrop Cres **111** D2
Moffat Ho, SE5
off Comber Gro **87** E3
Mohmmad Khan Rd, E11
off Harvey Rd **103** F2
Molasses Row, SW11
off Cinnamon Row **178** C1
Molesford Rd, SW6 . . . . **164** A3
Molesworth St, SE13 . . . . . . **186** C1
Molyneux St, W1 . . . . **33** D1
Mona Rd, SE15 . . . . **170** C4
Mona St, E16 . . . . **145** F1
Monck St, SW1 . . . . **60** B3
Monclar Rd, SE5 . . . . **183** D2
Moncorvo Cl, SW7 . . . . **56** C1
Moncrieff Pl, SE15
off Rye La **170** A4
Moncrieff St, SE15 . . . . **170** A4
Monier Rd, E3 . . . . **116** A4
Monks Dr, W3 . . . . **132** A1
Monks Pk, Wem. HA9 . . . . . **104** C3
Monks Pk Gdns, Wem.
HA9 . . . . **104** B3
Monkton Ho, E5
off Pembury Rd **114** B2
Monkton St, SE11 . . . . **62** B4
Monkwell Sq, EC2 . . . . **39** F1
Monmouth Cl, W4 . . . . **147** D2
Monmouth Ho, NW5
off Raglan St **110** B3
Monmouth Pl, W2 . . . . **30** B3
Monmouth Rd, W2 . . . . **30** B3
Monmouth St, WC2 . . . . **36** C3
Monnery Rd, N19 . . . . **96** C4
Monnow Rd, SE1 . . . . **156** A3
Monroe Dr, SW14 . . . . **174** B3
Monro Way, E5 . . . . **114** A1
Monsal Ct, E5
off Redwald Rd **115** E1
Monsell Ct, N4
off Monsell Rd **98** B4
Monsell Rd, N4 . . . . **98** B4
Monson Rd, NW10 . . . . **120** A2
SE14 . . . . **171** D2
Montague Av, SE4 . . . . **185** F2
Montague Cl, SE1 . . . . **52** A2
Montague Gdns, W3 . . . . **132** A3
Montague Pl, WC1 . . . . **24** B4
Montague Rd, E8 . . . . **114** A2
E11 . . . . **103** F3
Montague Sq, SE15
off Clifton Way **170** C2
Montague St, EC1 . . . . **39** E1
WC1 . . . . **24** C4
Montagu Mans, W1 . . . . **21** F4
Montagu Ms N, W1 . . . . **33** F1
Montagu Ms S, W1 . . . . **33** F2
Montagu Ms W, W1 . . . . **33** F2
Montagu Pl, W1 . . . . **33** E1
Montagu Row, W1 . . . . **33** F1
Montagu Sq, W1 . . . . **33** F1
Montagu St, W1 . . . . **33** F2
Montaigne Cl, SW1 . . . . **72** B1
Montana Bldg, SE13
off Deals Gateway **172** B3
Montclare St, E2 . . . . **29** E1
Monteagle Way, E5 . . . . **100** A4
SE15 . . . . **184** B1
Montefiore St, SW8 . . . . **166** B4
Montego Cl, SE24
off Railton Rd **182** A2
Montem St, N4
off Thorpedale Rd **97** F2
Montevetro, SW11 . . . . **80** A4
Montford Pl, SE11 . . . . **74** A3
Montgomery Ct, W2
off Harrow Rd **32** A1
W4
off St. Thomas' Rd **160** C1

Montgomery Rd, W4 . . . . . . 146 C3
Montgomery St, E14 . . . . . . 144 B4
Montholme Rd, SW11 . . . . . . 179 F4
Monthope Rd, E1
off Casson St 142 A1
Montolieu Gdns, SW15 . . . . . 176 B3
Montpelier Gro, NW5 . . . . . . 110 C2
Montpelier Ms, SW7 . . . . 57 D2
Montpelier Pl, E1 . . . . 142 C2
SW7 . . . . 57 D2
Montpelier Ri, NW11 . . . . 93 E1
Montpelier Rd, SE15 . . . . 170 B3
Montpelier Row, SE3 . . . . 173 F4
Montpelier Sq, SW7 . . . . 57 D1
Montpelier St, SW7 . . . . 57 D1
Montpelier Ter, SW7 . . . . 57 D1
Montpelier Vale, SE3 . . . . . . 173 F4
Montpelier Wk, SW7 . . . . 57 D2
Montpelier Way, NW11 . . . . . . 93 E1
Montreal Pl, WC2 . . . . 37 E4
Montrose Av, NW6 . . . . 121 E2
Montrose Ct, SW7 . . . . 56 B1
Montrose Pl, SW1 . . . . 58 B1
Montserrat Rd, SW15 . . . . . . 177 E2
Monument 40 B4
Monument, The, EC3 . . . . 40 B4
Monument Gdns, SE13 . . . . . 186 C3
Monument St, EC3 . . . . 52 B1
Monza St, E1 . . . . 142 C3
Moodkee St, SE16 . . . . 156 C2
Moody Rd, SE15 . . . . 89 E3
Moody St, E1 . . . . 129 D3
Moon St, N1 . . . . 126 B1
Moore Cl, SW14 . . . . 174 C1
Moore Ho, E14
off Cassilis Rd 158 A1
Moore Pk Rd, SW6 . . . . 78 C3
Moore St, SW3 . . . . 57 E4
Moorey Cl, E15
off Stephen's Rd 131 F1
Moorfields, EC2 . . . . 40 A1
Moorfields Eye Hosp,
EC1 . . . . 28 A1
Moorfields Highwalk, EC2 . . . . 40 A1
Moorgate 40 A1
Moorgate 40 A1
Moorgate, EC2 . . . . 40 A2
Moorgate Pl, EC2 . . . . 40 A2
Moorhouse Rd, W2 . . . . 30 A2
Moorland Rd, SW9 . . . . 182 B2
Moorlands Est, SW9 . . . . 182 A2
Moor La, EC2 . . . . 40 A1
Moor Pl, EC2 . . . . 40 A1
Moor St, W1 . . . . 36 B3
Morant St, E14 . . . . 144 A3
Mora Rd, NW2 . . . . 106 C1
Mora St, EC1 . . . . 27 F1
Morat St, SW9 . . . . 85 F4
Moravian Pl, SW10 . . . . 80 B1
Moravian St, E2 . . . . 128 C2
Moray Ms, N7 . . . . 97 F3
Moray Rd, N4 . . . . 97 F3
Mordaunt Rd, NW10 . . . . 119 D1
Mordaunt St, SW9 . . . . 181 F1
Morden Hill, SE13 . . . . 172 C4
Morden La, SE13 . . . . 172 C3
Morden St, SE13 . . . . 172 B3
Morden Wf Rd, SE10 . . . . 159 E2
Morecambe Cl, E1 . . . . 143 D1
Morecambe St, SE17 . . . . 75 F1
More Cl, E16 . . . . 145 F2
W14 . . . . 149 E3
Moreland St, EC1 . . . . 15 D4
More London Pl, SE1 . . . . 52 C3
More London Riverside,
SE1 . . . . 53 D3
Moresby Rd, E5 . . . . 100 B2
Moresby Wk, SW8 . . . . 166 B4
Moreton Cl, E5 . . . . 100 C3
SW1 . . . . 71 F2
Moreton Ho, SE16
off Slippers Pl 156 B2
Moreton Pl, SW1 . . . . 71 F2
Moreton St, SW1 . . . . 71 F2
Moreton Ter, SW1 . . . . 71 F2
Moreton Ter Ms N, SW1 . . . . . . 71 F2
Moreton Ter Ms S, SW1 . . . . . . 71 F2
Moreton Twr, W3 . . . . 132 B4
Morgan Ct, SW11
off Battersea High St . . . 165 D3
Morgan Ho, SW1
off Vauxhall Br Rd 71 F1
Morgan Rd, N7 . . . . 112 A2
W10 . . . . 135 F1
Morgans La, SE1 . . . . 52 C3
Morgan St, E3 . . . . 129 E3
E16 . . . . 145 F1
Moriatry Cl, N7 . . . . 111 E1
Morie St, SW18 . . . . 178 B2
Morieux Rd, E10 . . . . 101 F2
Morland Cl, NW11 . . . . 94 B2
Morland Est, E8
off Richmond Rd 114 A4
Morland Gdns, NW10 . . . . . . 105 D4
Morland Ms, N1
off Lofting Rd 112 A4
Coll Morley Coll, SE1 . . . . 62 B2
Morley Rd, E10 . . . . 102 C2
E15 . . . . 131 F2
SE13 . . . . 186 C2
Morley St, SE1 . . . . 62 B2
Morna Rd, SE5 . . . . 168 C4
Morning La, E9 . . . . 114 C3
Mornington Av, W14 . . . . 149 F3
Mornington Crescent 11 E2
Mornington Cres, NW1 . . . . . . 11 E2
Mornington Gro, E3 . . . . 130 A3
Mornington Ms, SE5 . . . . 87 E4
Mornington Pl, NW1 . . . . 11 D2
Mornington Rd, E11 . . . . 103 F2
SE8 . . . . 171 F2
Mornington St, NW1 . . . . 11 D2
Mornington Ter, NW1 . . . . 11 D1
Morocco St, SE1 . . . . 64 C1
Morpeth Gro, E9 . . . . 129 D1
Morpeth Rd, E9 . . . . 128 C1
Morpeth St, E2 . . . . 129 D3
Morpeth Ter, SW1 . . . . 59 E3
Morrells Yd, SE11 . . . . 74 B2
Morris Ho, W3
off Swainson Rd 147 F1
Morrison Rd, SW9
off Marcella Rd 168 A4
Morrison St, SW11 . . . . 180 A1
Morris Pl, N4 . . . . 98 A3
Morris Rd, E14 . . . . 144 B1
E15 . . . . 117 E1
Morris St, E1 . . . . 142 B2
Morshead Rd, W9 . . . . 18 B1
Morten Cl, SW4 . . . . 181 D4
Mortham St, E15 . . . . 131 D1
Mortimer Cl, NW2 . . . . 93 F4
Mortimer Cres, NW6 . . . . 6 C1
Mortimer Est, NW6 . . . . 6 C1
Mortimer Ho, W11
off St. Anns Rd 135 D4
Mortimer Mkt, WC1 . . . . 23 F3
Mortimer Pl, NW6 . . . . 6 C1
Mortimer Rd, N1 . . . . 113 E4
NW10 . . . . 120 C3
Mortimer Sq, W11
off St. Anns Rd 135 D3
Mortimer St, W1 . . . . 35 E2
Mortimer Ter, NW5
off Gordon Ho Rd 110 B1
MORTLAKE, SW14 . . . . 174 C1
Mortlake 174 C1
Mortlake High St, SW14 . . . . 175 D1
Mortlake Rd, Rich. TW9 . . . . 160 A2
Mortlake Sta Pas, SW14
off Sheen La 174 C1
Mortlake Ter, Rich. TW9
off Kew Rd 160 A2
Mortlock Cl, SE15
off Cossall Wk 170 B4
Morton Cl, E1
off Deancross St 142 C2
Morton Ms, SW5 . . . . 66 C1
Morton Pl, SE1 . . . . 62 A3
Morton Rd, E15 . . . . 117 F4
N1 . . . . 112 C4
Morval Rd, SW2 . . . . 182 A3
Morville Ho, SW18
off Fitzhugh Gro 179 D4
Morville St, E3 . . . . 130 A2
Morwell St, WC1 . . . . 36 B1
Moscow Pl, W2 . . . . 30 C4
Moscow Rd, W2 . . . . 30 C4
Moseley Row, SE10 . . . . 159 F3
Mossbury Rd, SW11 . . . . 179 E1
Moss Cl, E1
off Old Montague St 142 A1
Mossford St, E3 . . . . 129 F4
Mossington Gdns, SE16
off Abbeyfield Rd 156 C3
Mossop St, SW3 . . . . 57 D4
Mostyn Gdns, NW10 . . . . 121 D3
Mostyn Gro, E3 . . . . 129 F2
Mostyn Rd, SW9 . . . . 168 A3
Motcomb St, SW1 . . . . 57 F2
Mothers' Sq, E5 . . . . 114 B1
Motley Av, EC2 . . . . 28 C2
Motley St, SW8
off St. Rule St 166 C4
Moulins Rd, E9 . . . . 128 C1
Moulsford Ho, N7 . . . . 111 D2
Mount, The, E5 . . . . 100 B3
NW3 *off Heath St* 108 C1
W3 . . . . 132 B4
Wembley HA9 . . . . 90 B3
Mountague Pl, E14 . . . . 144 C3
Mountain Ho, SE11 . . . . 73 E2
Mountbatten Ct, SE16
off Rotherhithe St 142 C4
Mount Ct, SW15
off Weimar St 177 E1
Mount Dr, Wem. HA9 . . . . 90 C3
Mountford Mans, SW11
off Battersea Pk Rd 166 A3
Mountfort Cres, N1
off Barnsbury Sq 112 A4
Mountfort Ter, N1
off Barnsbury Sq 112 A4
Mountgrove Rd, N5 . . . . 98 B4
Mountjoy Ho, EC2
off The Barbican 39 F1
Mount Mills, EC1 . . . . 27 D1
Mount Pl, W3
off High St 132 B4
Mount Pleasant, WC1 . . . . 25 F3
Mount Pleasant Cres, N4 . . . . 97 F1
Mount Pleasant Hill, E5 . . . . 100 B3

Mount Pleasant La, E5 . . . . . **100** B3
Mount Pleasant Rd,
NW10 . . . . **106** C4
SE13 . . . . **186** B4
Mount Pleasant Vil,
N4 . . . . **97** F1
Mount Rd, NW2 . . . . **92** B4
Mount Row, W1 . . . . **46** C1
Mountsfield Ct, SE13 . . . . . **187** D4
Mounts Pond Rd, SE3 . . . . . **173** D4
Mount Sq, The, NW3
off Heath St **94** C4
Mount St, W1 . . . . **46** B1
Mount St Ms, W1 . . . . **46** C1
Mount Ter, E1
off New Rd **142** B1
Mount Vernon, NW3 . . . . . . **108** C1
Mountview Cl, NW11 . . . . . . **94** B2
Mount Vw Rd, N4 . . . . **97** E1
★ Movieum of London,
The, SE1 . . . . **49** E4
Mowatt Cl, N19 . . . . **97** D2
Mowbray Rd, NW6 . . . . **107** E4
Mowlem St, E2 . . . . **128** B2
Mowll St, SW9 . . . . **86** A3
Moxon Cl, E13
off Whitelegg Rd **131** F2
Moxon St, W1 . . . . **34** A1
Moye Cl, E2
off Dove Row **128** A2
Moyers Rd, E10 . . . . **102** C1
Moylan Rd, W6 . . . . **163** E1
Moyne Pl, NW10 . . . . **118** A2
Mozart St, W10 . . . . **121** F3
Mozart Ter, SW1 . . . . **70** B1
DLR Mudchute **158** B3
Mudlarks Boul, SE10
off John Harrison Way . . **159** F2
Muirdown Av, SW14 . . . . . . **174** C2
Muir Dr, SW18 . . . . **179** E4
Muirfield, W3 . . . . **133** E2
Muirfield Cl, SE16
off Ryder Dr **156** B4
Muirfield Cres, E14
off Millharbour **158** B2
Muir Rd, E5 . . . . **100** A4
● Mulberry Business Cen,
SE16 *off Quebec Way* . . **157** D1
Mulberry Cl, NW3
off Hampstead High St . . **109** D1
SE22 . . . . **184** A3
SW3 *off Beaufort St* **80** B1
Mulberry Ct, EC1
off Tompion St **27** D1
Mulberry Ms, SE14
off Lewisham Way **171** F3
Mulberry Pl, W6
off Chiswick Mall **148** A4
Mulberry Rd, E8 . . . . **113** F4
Coll Mulberry Sch for Girls -
St. George's, E1
off Cable St **142** B3
Mulberry St, E1
off Adler St **142** A2
Mulberry Tree Ms, W4
off Clovelly Rd **146** C1
Mulberry Wk, SW3 . . . . **68** B4
Mulgrave Rd, NW10 . . . . **105** F1
SW6 . . . . **163** F1
Mulkern Rd, N19 . . . . **97** D2
Muller Rd, SW4 . . . . **181** D4
Mullet Gdns, E2
off St. Peter's Cl **128** A2
Mullins Path, SW14 . . . . **175** D1
Mull Wk, N1
off Clephane Rd **112** C3
Mulready St, NW8 . . . . **20** C3
Multi-way, W3
off Valetta Rd **147** E1
Mulvaney Way, SE1 . . . . **64** B1
Mumford Mills, SE10
off Greenwich High Rd . . **172** B3
Mumford Rd, SE24 . . . . **182** B3
Muncaster Rd, SW11 . . . . . . **179** F3
Mundania Rd, SE22 . . . . **184** B4
Munden Ho, E3
off Bromley High St **130** B3
Munden St, W14 . . . . **149** E3
Mundford Rd, E5 . . . . **100** C3
Mund St, W14 . . . . **149** F4
Mundy St, N1 . . . . **16** C4
Munkenbeck, W2
off Hermitage St **32** A1
Munro Ms, W10 . . . . **135** E1
Munro Ter, SW10 . . . . **80** A1
Munster Ms, SW6
off Lillie Rd **163** E2
Munster Rd, SW6 . . . . **163** F3
Munster Sq, NW1 . . . . **23** D1
Munton Rd, SE17 . . . . **63** F4
Murchison Rd, E10 . . . . **102** C3
Murdock Cl, E16
off Rogers Rd **145** F2
Murdock St, SE15 . . . . **170** B1
Muriel St, N1 . . . . **13** F2
Murillo Rd, SE13 . . . . **187** D2
Murphy St, SE1 . . . . **62** A1
Murray Gro, N1 . . . . **15** F3
Murray Ms, NW1 . . . . **111** D4
Murray St, NW1 . . . . **111** D4
Murray Ter, NW3
off Flask Wk **109** D1
Mursell Est, SW8 . . . . **85** E4
Musard Rd, W6 . . . . **163** E1
W14 . . . . **163** E1
Musbury St, E1 . . . . **142** C2
Muscal, W6 . . . . **163** E1
Muscatel Pl, SE5 . . . . **89** D3
Muschamp Rd,
SE15 . . . . **183** F1
Muscovy St, EC3 . . . . **53** D1
★ Museum in Docklands,
E14 *off Hertsmere Rd* . . . **144** A3
Museum La, SW7 . . . . **56** B3
★ Museum of Childhood
at Bethnal Grn, E2 . . . . . **128** B3
★ Museum of Gdn History,
SE1 . . . . **61** E3
★ Museum of Instruments
(Royal Coll of Music),
SW7 . . . . **56** A2
★ Museum of London,
EC2 . . . . **39** E1
Museum Pas, E2
off Victoria Pk Sq **128** C3
Museum St, WC1 . . . . **36** C1
Museum Way, W3 . . . . **146** A1
Musgrave Cres, SW6 . . . . **78** B3
Musgrove Rd, SE14 . . . . **171** D3
Musjid Rd, SW11
off Kambala Rd **165** D4
Muston Rd, E5 . . . . **100** B3
Mustow Pl, SW6
off Munster Rd **163** F4
Mutrix Rd, NW6 . . . . **122** A1
Mutton Pl, NW1
off Harmood St **110** B3
Myatt Rd, SW9 . . . . **86** C4
Myatts Flds S, SW9
off St. Lawrence Way . . . **168** A4
Myatts N, SW9
off Fairbairn Grn **86** B4
Myddelton Pas, EC1 . . . . **14** B4
Myddelton Sq, EC1 . . . . **14** B4
Myddelton St, EC1 . . . . **26** B1
Myddleton Av, N4 . . . . **98** C3
Myers La, SE14 . . . . **171** D1
Mylius Cl, SE14
off Kender St **170** C3
Mylne Cl, W6 . . . . **148** A4
Mylne St, EC1 . . . . **14** A3
Myrdle St, E1 . . . . **142** A1
Myron Pl, SE13 . . . . **186** C1
Myrtleberry Cl, E8
off Beechwood Rd **113** F3
Myrtle Rd, W3 . . . . **132** C4
Myrtle Wk, N1 . . . . **16** C3
Mysore Rd, SW11 . . . . **179** F1

N

N1 Shop Cen, N1 . . . . **14** B2
Jct Nags Head, N7 . . . . **111** F1
Nags Head Cen, N7 . . . . **111** F1
Nag's Head Ct, EC1 . . . . **27** E3
Nairne Gro, SE24 . . . . **183** D3
Nairn St, E14 . . . . **144** C1
Nankin St, E14 . . . . **144** A2
Nansen Rd, SW11 . . . . **180** A2
Nant Ct, NW2
off Granville Rd **93** F3
Nantes Cl, SW18 . . . . **178** C2
Nantes Pas, E1 . . . . **29** E4
Nant Rd, NW2 . . . . **93** F3
Nant St, E2
off Cambridge Heath
Rd **128** B3
Naoroji St, WC1 . . . . **26** A1
Napier Av, E14 . . . . **158** A4
SW6 . . . . **177** F1
Napier Cl, SE8
off Amersham Vale **171** F2
W14 *off Napier Rd* **149** F2
Napier Ct, SW6
off Ranelagh Gdns **177** F1
Napier Gro, N1 . . . . **15** F3
Napier Pl, W14 . . . . **149** F2
Napier Rd, E11 . . . . **117** E1
E15 . . . . **131** E2
NW10 . . . . **120** B3
W14 . . . . **149** F2
Napier Ter, N1 . . . . **112** B4
Napoleon Rd, E5 . . . . **100** B4
Narbonne Av, SW4 . . . . **180** C3
Narborough St, SW6 . . . . **164** B4
Narcissus Rd, NW6 . . . . **108** A2
Narford Rd, E5 . . . . **100** A4
Narrow St, E14 . . . . **143** E3
Nascot St, W12 . . . . **134** C2
Naseby Cl, NW6 . . . . **108** C4
Nash Ho, SW1 . . . . **71** D3
Nash Rd, SE4 . . . . **185** D2
Nash St, NW1 . . . . **23** D1
Nasmyth St, W6 . . . . **148** B2
Nassau Rd, SW13 . . . . **161** F3
Nassau St, W1 . . . . **35** E1
Nassington Rd, NW3 . . . . . . **109** E1
Nathaniel Cl, E1 . . . . **41** F1
★ National Archives, The,
Rich. TW9 . . . . **160** B2
★ National Army Mus,
SW3 . . . . **69** F4

★ National Gall, WC2 ......48 B1
National Hosp for Neurology & Neurosurgery, The, WC1 ....25 D3
★ National Maritime Mus, SE10 ....173 D1
★ National Portrait Gall, WC2 ....48 B1
Coll National Sch of Govt, SW1 ....71 E1
National Ter, SE16
off Bermondsey Wall E ..**156** B1
★ National Thea, SE1 ......49 F2
★ Natural History Mus, SW7 ....56 A3
Naval Row, E14 ....**144** C3
Navarino Gro, E8 ....**114** A3
Navarino Rd, E8 ....**114** A3
Navarre St, E2 ....**29** E2
Navenby Wk, E3
off Burwell Wk **130** A4
Navy St, SW4 ....**181** D1
Naxos Bldg, E14
off Hutchings St **158** A1
Nayim Pl, E8
off Amhurst Rd **114** B2
Naylor Rd, SE15 ....**170** B2
Nazareth Gdns, SE15 ......**170** B4
Nazrul St, E2 ....**17** E4
● NCR Business Cen, NW10
off Great Cen Way 105 E2
Nealden St, SW9 ....**181** F1
Neal St, WC2 ....**36** C3
Neal's Yd, WC2 ....**36** C3
NEASDEN, NW2 ....**91** E4
⊖ Neasden 105 E2
Neasden Cl, NW10 ....**105** E2
Jct Neasden Junct, NW10
off North Circular Rd ...**105** E1
Neasden La, NW10 ....**105** E1
Neasden La N, NW10 ....**91** D4
Neate St, SE5 ....**77** E4
Neathouse Pl, SW1 ....**59** E4
Nebraska Bldg, SE13
off Deals Gateway **172** B3
Nebraska St, SE1 ....**64** A1
Neckinger, SE16 ....**65** F2
Neckinger Est, SE16 ....**65** F2
Neckinger St, SE1 ....**65** F1
Nectarine Way, SE13 ......**172** B4
Needham Rd, W11 ....**30** A3
Needham Ter, NW2
off Kara Way **93** D4
Needleman St, SE16 ......**157** D1
Neeld Cres, Wem. HA9 .....**104** A2
Neeld Par, Wem. HA9
off Harrow Rd **104** A2
Nella Rd, W6 ....**163** D1
Nelldale Rd, SE16 ....**156** C3
Nelson Cl, NW6 ....**6** A4
Nelson Ct, SE16
off Brunel Rd **142** C4
Nelson Gdns, E2 ....**128** A3
Nelson Pas, EC1 ....**27** F1
Nelson Pl, N1 ....**15** D3
Nelson Rd, SE10 ....**172** C1
★ Nelson's Column, WC2 ...48 C2
Nelson Sq, SE1 ....**50** C4
Nelson's Row, SW4 ....**181** D2
Nelson St, E1 ....**142** B2
E16
off Huntingdon St **145** F2
Nelsons Yd, NW1 ....**11** E2
Nelson Ter, N1 ....**15** D3
Nelson Wk, SE16
off Salter Rd **143** E4
Nemoure Rd, W3 ....**132** C3
Nepaul Rd, SW11 ....**165** E4
Nepean St, SW15 ....**176** A4
Neptune Ho, E3
off Garrison Rd **130** A1
Neptune St, SE16 ....**156** C2
Nesbitt Cl, SE3
off Hurren Cl **187** E1
Nesham St, E1 ....**142** A4
Ness St, SE16
off Spa Rd **156** A2
Netheravon Rd, W4 ....**147** F3
Netheravon Rd S, W4 ......**147** F4
Netherford Rd, SW4 ......**166** C4
Netherhall Gdns, NW3 .....**108** C3
Netherhall Way, NW3
off Netherhall Gdns **108** C2
Netherleigh Cl, N6 ....**96** B2
Netherton Gro, SW10 ......**79** F1
Netherwood Pl, W14
off Netherwood Rd **149** D2
Netherwood Rd, W14 ......**149** D2
Netherwood St, NW6 ......**107** F4
Netley St, NW1 ....**23** E1
Nettleden Av, Wem. HA9 ...**104** A3
Nettleton Rd, SE14 ....**171** D3
Nevada Bldg, SE10
off Blackheath Rd **172** B3
Nevada St, SE10 ....**172** C1
Nevern Pl, SW5 ....**66** B1
Nevern Rd, SW5 ....**66** A1
Nevern Sq, SW5 ....**66** B1
Neville Cl, E11 ....**103** F4
NW1 ....**12** B3
NW6 ....**121** F2
SE15 ....**170** A2
W3 *off Acton La* **146** C1
Neville Gill Cl, SW18 ......**178** A4
Neville Rd, NW6 ....**121** F2
Nevilles Ct, NW2 ....**92** A4
Neville St, SW7 ....**68** A2
Neville Ter, SW7 ....**68** A2
Nevill Rd, N16 ....**113** E1
Nevinson Cl, SW18 ....**179** D4
Newall Ct, W12
off Heathstan Rd **134** A2
Newall Ho, SE1 ....**63** F2
Newark Cres, NW10 ......**119** D3
Newark St, E1 ....**142** B1
New Atlas Wf, E14
off Arnhem Pl **158** A2
New Bond St, W1 ....**34** C3
New Br St, EC4 ....**38** C3
New Broad St, EC2 ....**40** C1
Newburgh Rd, W3 ....**132** C4
Newburgh St, W1 ....**35** E3
New Burlington Ms, W1 .....**35** E4
New Burlington Pl, W1 ......**35** E4
New Burlington St, W1 ......**35** E4
Newburn St, SE11 ....**73** F3
Newbury Ms, NW5
off Malden Rd **110** A3
Newbury St, EC1 ....**39** E1
New Butt La, SE8 ....**172** A2
New Butt La N, SE8
off Reginald Rd **172** A2
Newby Pl, E14 ....**144** C3
Newby St, SW8 ....**180** B1
New Caledonian Wf, SE16 ..**157** F2
Newcastle Cl, EC4 ....**38** C2
Newcastle Pl, W2 ....**32** B1
Newcastle Row, EC1 ....**26** B2
New Cavendish St, W1 ......**23** D4
New Change, EC4 ....**39** E3
New Charles St, EC1 ....**15** D4
New Ch Rd, SE5 ....**87** F2
New Clock Twr Pl, N7 ......**111** E3
New Coll Ct, NW3
off Finchley Rd **108** C3
New Coll Ms, N1
off Islington Pk St **112** A4
New Coll Par, NW3
off Finchley Rd **109** D3
Newcombe St, W8 ....**42** B2
Newcomen Rd, E11 ....**103** F4
SW11 ....**179** D1
Newcomen St, SE1 ....**52** A4
New Compton St, WC2 ......**36** B3
New Concordia Wf, SE1 .....**53** F4
New Ct, EC4 ....**38** A4
Newcourt St, NW8 ....**8** C3
New Covent Gdn Flower Mkt, SW8 ....84 B1
New Covent Gdn Mkt, SW8 ....84 A3
New Crane Pl, E1
off Garnet St **142** C4
NEW CROSS, SE14 ....**171** E3
⇌ New Cross 171 F2
⊖ New Cross 171 F2
Jct New Cross, SE14 ......**171** E2
NEW CROSS GATE, SE14 ...**171** D3
⇌ New Cross Gate 171 E3
⊖ New Cross Gate 171 E3
New Cross Rd, SE14 ....**170** C2
Newell St, E14 ....**143** F2
New End, NW3 ....**108** C1
New End Sq, NW3 ....**109** D1
Newent Cl, SE15 ....**88** C2
New Fetter La, EC4 ....**38** B2
Newfield Ri, NW2 ....**92** B4
Newgate St, EC1 ....**39** D2
New Globe Wk, SE1 ....**51** E2
New Goulston St, E1 ....**41** E2
Coll Newham Coll of Further Ed, SE1 ....53 D4
Stratford Campus, E15
off Welfare Rd 117 E4
Coll Newham 6th Form Coll, Stratford Site, E15
off High St 117 D4
Newhams Row, SE1 ....**65** D1
Newham Way, E16 ....**145** F1
Newhaven La, E16 ....**131** F4
Newick Rd, E5 ....**100** B4
NEWINGTON, SE1 ....**63** E4
Newington Barrow Way, N7 ....**97** F4
Newington Butts, SE1 ......**75** D1
SE11 ....**75** D1
Newington Causeway, SE1 ...**63** D3
Newington Grn, N1 ....**113** D2
N16 ....**113** D2
Newington Grn Rd, N1 .....**113** D3
New Inn Bdy, EC2 ....**29** D2
New Inn Pas, WC2 ....**37** F3
New Inn Sq, EC2 ....**29** D2
New Inn St, EC2 ....**29** D2
New Inn Yd, EC2 ....**29** D2
New James Ct, SE15
off Nunhead La **184** B1
New Jersey Ter, SE15
off Nunhead La **184** B1
New Kent Rd, SE1 ....**63** E3
New Kings Rd, SW6 ....**163** F4
New King St, SE8 ....**172** A1

ewland Ct, EC1
off St. Luke's Est . . . **28** A2
Wembley HA9 . . . **90** A3
ewlands Quay, E1 . . . **142** C3
ewlands Ter, SW8
off Queenstown Rd . . . **166** B4
ew London St, EC3 . . . **41** D4
ewman Pas, W1 . . . **35** F1
ewman's Ct, EC3 . . . **40** B3
ewman's Row, WC2 . . . **37** F1
ewman St, W1 . . . **35** F1
ewman Yd, W1 . . . **35** F2
ew Mt St, E15 . . . **117** D4
ewnes Path, SW15
off Putney Pk La . . . **176** B2
ewnham Ter, SE1 . . . **62** A2
ew N Pl, EC2 . . . **28** C3
ew N Rd, N1 . . . **16** B3
ew N St, WC1 . . . **25** E4
ewnton Cl, N4 . . . **99** D1
ew Orleans Wk, N19 . . . **97** D1
ew Oxford St, WC1 . . . **36** B2
ew Pl Sq, SE16 . . . **156** B2
ew Plaistow Rd, E15 . . . **131** E1
ewport Av, E14 . . . **145** D3
ewport Ct, WC2 . . . **36** B4
ewport Pl, WC2 . . . **36** B4
ewport Rd, E10 . . . **102** C3
SW13 . . . **162** A3
W3 . . . **146** C1
ewport St, SE11 . . . **73** E1
ew Priory Ct, NW6
off Mazenod Av . . . **108** A4
ew Providence Wf, E14 . . . **145** D4
ew Quebec St, W1 . . . **33** F3
ew Ride, SW7 . . . **45** E4
ew River Ct, N5 . . . **113** D1
ew River Head, EC1 . . . **14** B4
ew River Wk, N1 . . . **112** C3
ew River Way, N4 . . . **99** D1
ew Rd, E1 . . . **142** B1
ew Row, WC2 . . . **36** C4
★ New Scotland Yd, SW1 . . . **60** A2
New Spitalfields Mkt,
E10 . . . **102** A4
ew Spring Gdns Wk,
SE11 . . . **73** D3
ew Sq, WC2 . . . **37** F2
ew St, EC2 . . . **41** D1
ew St Sq, EC4 . . . **38** B2
ewton Av, W3 . . . **146** C1
ewton Gro, W4 . . . **147** E3
ewton Lo, SE10
off West Parkside . . . **159** F2
ewton Pl, E14 . . . **158** A3
ewton Rd, E15 . . . **117** D2
NW2 . . . **92** C4
W2 . . . **30** B3
ewton St, WC2 . . . **37** D2
ewtons Yd, SW18
off Wandsworth High St . **178** A3
ewtown St, SW11 . . . **82** C4
ew Turnstile, WC1 . . . **37** E1
ew Union Cl, E14 . . . **158** C2
ew Union St, EC2 . . . **40** A1
ew Wf Rd, N1 . . . **13** D2
ew Zealand Way, W12 . . . **134** B3
exus Ct, E11
off Kirkdale Rd . . . **103** E1
iagara Cl, N1
off Cropley St . . . **15** F2
Nice Business Pk, SE15
off Sylvan Gro . . . **170** B1
icholas Ct, N7 . . . **111** F2
Nicholas La, EC4 . . . **40** B4
Nicholas Ms, W4
off Short Rd . . . **161** E1
Nicholas Pas, EC4 . . . **40** B4
Nicholas Rd, E1 . . . **128** C4
W11 . . . **135** D3
Nicholay Rd, N19 . . . **97** D3
Nichollsfield Wk, N7
off Hillmarton Rd . . . **111** F2
Nicholl St, E2 . . . **128** A1
Nichols Cl, N4
off Osborne Rd . . . **98** A2
Nichols Ct, E2 . . . **17** E3
Nicholson St, SE1 . . . **50** C3
Nickols Wk, SW18
off Jew's Row . . . **178** B2
Nicoll Rd, NW10 . . . **119** E1
Nigel Playfair Av, W6
off King St . . . **148** B3
Nigel Rd, SE15 . . . **184** A1
Nightingale Cl, W4 . . . **160** C1
Nightingale Est, E5 . . . **100** A4
Nightingale Gro, SE13 . . . **187** D3
Nightingale Ho, E1
off Thomas More St . . . **142** A4
W12 *off Du Cane Rd* . . . **134** C2
Nightingale La, N6 . . . **95** E2
Nightingale Ms, E3
off Chisenhale Rd . . . **129** E2
SE11 . . . **62** B4
Nightingale Pl, SW10 . . . **67** F4
Nightingale Rd, E5 . . . **100** B4
N1 . . . **112** C3
NW10 . . . **119** F2
Nightingale Wk, SW4 . . . **180** B4
Nile Cl, N16 . . . **99** F4
Nile St, N1 . . . **15** F4
Nile Ter, SE15 . . . **77** E3
Nimegen Way, SE22 . . . **183** E3
Nimrod Pas, N1
off Tottenham Rd . . . **113** E3
Nina Mackay Cl, E15
off Arthingworth St . . . **131** E1
NINE ELMS, SW8 . . . **83** F2
Nine Elms La, SW8 . . . **83** F1
Nisbet Ho, E9
off Homerton High St . . . **115** D2
Niton Rd, Rich. TW9 . . . **174** A1
Niton St, SW6 . . . **163** D2
Noble St, EC2 . . . **39** E2
Noel Coward Ho, SW1
off Vauxhall Br Rd . . . **71** F1
Noel Rd, N1 . . . **14** C2
W3 . . . **132** B2
Noel St, W1 . . . **35** F3
Noko, W10 . . . **121** D3
Nolan Way, E5 . . . **114** A1
Norbiton Rd, E14 . . . **143** F2
Norbroke St, W12 . . . **133** F3
Norburn St, W10
off Chesterton Rd . . . **135** E1
Norcombe Ho, N19
off Wedmore St . . . **97** D4
Norcott Rd, N16 . . . **100** A3
Norfolk Cres, W2 . . . **33** D2
Norfolk Ho, SE3 . . . **173** E1
SW1 *off Regency St* . . . **60** B4
Norfolk Ms, W10
off Blagrove Rd . . . **135** F1
Norfolk Pl, W2 . . . **32** B2
Norfolk Rd, NW8 . . . **8** B1
NW10 . . . **105** E4
Norfolk Row, SE1 . . . **61** E4
Norfolk Sq, W2 . . . **32** B3
Norfolk Sq Ms, W2 . . . **32** B3
Norfolk Ter, W6
off Field Rd . . . **149** E4
Norland Ho, W11 . . . **135** D4
Norland Pl, W11 . . . **135** E4
Norland Rd, W11 . . . **135** D4
Norland Sq, W11 . . . **135** E4
Norlington Rd, E10 . . . **102** C2
E11 . . . **102** C2
Normanby Cl, SW15 . . . **177** F3
Normanby Rd, NW10 . . . **105** F1
Normand Gdns, W14
off Greyhound Rd . . . **163** E1
Normand Ms, W14
off Normand Rd . . . **163** F1
Normand Rd, W14 . . . **163** F1
Normandy Rd, SW9 . . . **168** A3
Norman Gro, E3 . . . **129** E2
Norman Rd, E11 . . . **103** D3
SE10 . . . **172** B2
Normans Cl, NW10 . . . **105** D3
Normans Mead, NW10 . . . **105** D3
Norman St, EC1 . . . **27** E1
Norman Way, W3 . . . **132** B1
Norris St, SW1 . . . **48** A1
Norroy Rd, SW15 . . . **177** D2
NORTH ACTON, W3 . . . **119** D4
⊖ North Acton . . . **119** D4
North Acton Rd, NW10 . . . **119** D3
Northampton Gro, N1 . . . **113** D2
Northampton Pk, N1 . . . **112** C3
Northampton Rd, EC1 . . . **26** B2
Northampton Row, EC1 . . . **26** B1
Northampton Sq, EC1 . . . **26** C1
Northampton St, N1 . . . **112** C4
North Audley St, W1 . . . **34** A3
North Av, Rich. TW9
off Sandycombe Rd . . . **160** A3
North Bk, NW8 . . . **20** B1
North Birkbeck Rd, E11 . . . **103** D4
Northbourne Ho, E5
off Pembury Rd . . . **114** B2
Northbourne Rd, SW4 . . . **181** D2
North Branch Av, W10
off Harrow Rd . . . **120** C3
Northbrook Rd, SE13 . . . **187** D3
Northburgh St, EC1 . . . **27** D2
North Carriage Dr, W2 . . . **32** C4
Northchurch, SE17 . . . **76** B2
Northchurch Rd, N1 . . . **113** D4
Northchurch Ter, N1 . . . **113** E4
North Circular Rd,
NW2 (A406) . . . **91** E4
NW10 (A406) . . . **104** B4
North Colonnade, The, E14 . **144** A4
Northcote Ms, SW11
off Northcote Rd . . . **179** E2
Northcote Rd, NW10 . . . **105** E4
SW11 . . . **179** E2
North Cres, E16 . . . **131** D4
WC1 . . . **24** A4
North Cross Rd, SE22 . . . **183** F3
Northdown St, N1 . . . **13** D2
⇌ North Dulwich . . . **183** D3
North End, NW3 . . . **94** C3
North End Av, NW3 . . . **94** C3
North End Cres, W14 . . . **149** F3
North End Ho, W14 . . . **149** E3
North End Par, W14
off North End Rd . . . **149** E3
North End Rd, NW11 . . . **94** A2
SW6 . . . **163** F1
W14 . . . **149** E3
Wembley HA9 . . . **90** A4

North End Way, NW3 . . . . **94** C3
North Eyot Gdns, W6 . . . . . . **148** A4
Northey St, E14 . . . . **143** E3
Northfield Rd, N16 . . . . **99** E1
Northfields, SW18 . . . . **178** A2
Northfields Ind Est, Wem. HA0 . . . . **118** A1
Northfields Rd, W3 . . . . **132** B1
North Flockton St, SE16
off Chambers St **156** A1
North Gdn, E14
off Westferry Circ **143** F4
North Gate, NW8 . . . . **8** C3
Northgate Ct, SW9
off Canterbury Cres **182** A1
North Gower St, NW1 . . . . **23** F1
North Greenwich **159** E1
North Greenwich **159** E1
North Gro, N6 . . . . **96** A1
Northiam St, E9 . . . . **128** B1
Northington St, WC1 . . . . **25** E3
NORTH KENSINGTON, W10 . **134** C2
Northlands St, SE5 . . . . **168** C4
North Lo Cl, SW15 . . . . **177** D3
North Ms, WC1 . . . . **25** F3
Northolme Rd, N5 . . . . **112** C1
North Pas, SW18 . . . . **178** A2
Northpoint Ho, N1
off Essex Rd **113** D3
Northpoint Sq, NW1 . . . . **111** D3
North Pole Rd, W10 . . . . **134** C1
Northport St, N1 . . . . **16** B1
North Ride, W2 . . . . **44** C1
North Ri, W2
off St. Georges Flds **33** D3
North Rd, N6 . . . . **96** A1
N7 . . . . **111** E3
Richmond TW9 . . . . **174** A1
North Row, W1 . . . . **33** F4
North Several, SE3 . . . . **173** D4
NORTH SHEEN, Rich. TW9 . . **160** A4
North Sheen **174** A2
North Side Wandsworth Common, SW18 . . . . **178** C3
North St, SW4 . . . . **180** C1
North Tenter St, E1 . . . . **41** F3
North Ter, SW3 . . . . **56** C3
Northumberland All, EC3 . . . . **41** D3
Northumberland Av, WC2 . . . . **48** C2
Northumberland Pl, W2 . . . . . **30** A2
Northumberland Rd, E17 . . . **102** A1
Northumberland St, WC2 . . . . **48** C2
Northumbria St, E14 . . . . . . **144** A2
North Verbena Gdns, W6
off St. Peter's Sq **148** A4
Northview, N7 . . . . **97** E4
Northview Cres, NW10 . . . . . **105** F1
North Vil, NW1 . . . . **111** D3
North Wk, W2 . . . . **43** E1
Northway Rd, SE5 . . . . **182** C1
Northways Par, NW3
off Finchley Rd **109** D4
North Western Commercial Cen, NW1
off Broadfield La **111** E4
Northwest Pl, N1 . . . . **14** B2
North Wf Rd, W2 . . . . **32** A1
Northwick Cl, NW8 . . . . **20** A2
Northwick Ter, NW8 . . . . **20** A2
Northwold Est, E5 . . . . **100** A3
Northwold Rd, E5 . . . . **99** F3
N16 . . . . **99** F3
Northwood Hall, N6 . . . . **96** C1
Northwood Rd, N6 . . . . **96** B1
North Worple Way, SW14 . . . . **175** D1
Norton Folgate, E1 . . . . **29** D4
Norton Rd, E10 . . . . **101** F2
Norway Gate, SE16 . . . . **157** E2
Norway Pl, E14
off Commercial Rd **143** F2
Norway St, SE10 . . . . **172** B1
Norwich Ho, E14
off Cordelia St **144** B2
Norwich St, EC4 . . . . **38** A2
Norwood Cl, NW2 . . . . **93** E4
Notley St, SE5 . . . . **88** A2
Notre Dame Est, SW4 . . . . . . **180** C2
Notting Barn Rd, W10 . . . . . **121** D4
Nottingdale Sq, W11
off Wilsham St **135** E4
Nottingham Ct, WC2 . . . . **36** C3
Nottingham Pl, W1 . . . . **22** A3
Nottingham St, W1 . . . . **22** A4
Nottingham Ter, NW1 . . . . . . **22** A3
NOTTING HILL, W11 . . . . . . **135** E3
Notting Hill Gate **42** A1
Notting Hill Gate, W11 . . . . . . **42** A2
Nova, E14 *off Newton Pl* . . . **158** A3
Novello St, SW6 . . . . **164** A3
Nowell Rd, SW13 . . . . **162** A1
Nuding Cl, SE13 . . . . **186** A1
Nugent Rd, N19 . . . . **97** E2
Nugent Ter, NW8 . . . . **7** F3
Nun Ct, EC2 . . . . **40** A2
NUNHEAD, SE15 . . . . **184** C1
Nunhead **170** C4
Nunhead Cres, SE15 . . . . . . **184** B1
Nunhead Est, SE15 . . . . **184** B2
Nunhead Grn, SE15 . . . . **184** B1
Nunhead Gro, SE15 . . . . **184** B1
Nunhead La, SE15 . . . . **184** B1
Nunhead Pas, SE15
off Peckham Rye **184** A1
Nursery Cl, SE4 . . . . **171** F4
SW15 . . . . **177** D2
Nursery La, E2 . . . . **17** E1
W10 . . . . **134** C1
Nursery Rd, E9
off Morning La **114** C3
SW9 . . . . **181** F2
Nursery Row, SE17 . . . . **76** A1
Nutbourne St, W10 . . . . **121** E3
Nutbrook St, SE15 . . . . **184** A1
Nutcroft Rd, SE15 . . . . **170** B2
Nutfield Rd, E15 . . . . **116** C1
NW2 . . . . **92** A3
SE22 . . . . **183** F3
Nutford Pl, W1 . . . . **33** D2
Nutley Ter, NW3 . . . . **108** C3
Nutmeg Cl, E16
off Cranberry La **131** E4
Nutmeg La, E14 . . . . **145** D2
Nuttall St, N1 . . . . **17** D2
Nutt St, SE15 . . . . **89** F2
Nye Bevan Est, E5 . . . . **101** D4
Nylands Av, Rich. TW9 . . . . . **160** A3
Nynehead St, SE14 . . . . **171** E2
Nyton Cl, N19
off Courtauld Rd **97** E2

O

O2, The, SE10 . . . . **145** E4
O2 Shop Cen, NW3
off Finchley Rd **108** C3
Oakbank Gro, SE24 . . . . **182** C2
Oakbury Rd, SW6 . . . . **164** B4
Oak Cres, E16 . . . . **145** E1
Oakcroft Rd, SE13 . . . . **173** D4
Oakdale Rd, E11 . . . . **103** D3
SE15 . . . . **184** C1
Oakdene, SE15
off Carlton Gro **170** B3
Oakden St, SE11 . . . . **62** B4
Oake Ct, SW15
off Portinscale Rd **177** E3
Oakeshott Av, N6 . . . . **96** A3
Oakey La, SE1 . . . . **62** A2
Oakfield Ct, N8 . . . . **97** E1
NW2 *off Hendon Way* **93** D1
Oakfield St, SW10 . . . . **67** E4
Oakford Rd, NW5 . . . . **110** C1
Oak Gro, NW2 . . . . **107** E1
Oakhill Av, NW3 . . . . **108** B1
Oak Hill Pk, NW3 . . . . **108** B1
Oak Hill Pk Ms, NW3 . . . . . . **108** C1
Oakhill Pl, SW15
off Oakhill Rd **178** A3
Oakhill Rd, SW15 . . . . **177** F3
Oak Hill Way, NW3 . . . . **108** C1
Oak Ho, NW3
off Maitland Pk Vil **109** F3
Oakhurst Gro, SE22 . . . . **184** A2
Oakington Manor Dr, Wem. HA9 . . . . **104** A2
Oakington Rd, W9 . . . . **18** B2
Oakland Rd, E15 . . . . **117** D1
Oaklands Ct, W12
off Uxbridge Rd **134** B4
Oaklands Est, SW4 . . . . **180** C4
Oaklands Gro, W12 . . . . **134** A4
Oaklands Ms, NW2
off Oaklands Rd **107** D1
Oaklands Pl, SW4
off St. Alphonsus Rd **180** C2
Oaklands Rd, NW2 . . . . **107** D1
SW14 . . . . **175** D1
Oak La, E14 . . . . **143** F3
Oakleigh Ct, N1 . . . . **16** A3
Oakley Av, W5 . . . . **132** A3
Oakley Cres, EC1 . . . . **15** D3
Oakley Dr, SE13 . . . . **187** D4
Oakley Gdns, SW3 . . . . **69** D4
Oakley Pl, SE1 . . . . **77** E3
Oakley Rd, N1 . . . . **113** D4
Oakley Sq, NW1 . . . . **11** F3
Oakley St, SW3 . . . . **68** C4
Oakley Wk, W6 . . . . **163** D1
Oakley Yd, E2 . . . . **29** F2
Oak Pk Ms, N16 . . . . **99** F4
Oak Pl, SW18
off East Hill **178** B3
Oaks Shop Cen, W3
off High St **132** C4
Oak Tree Rd, NW8 . . . . **20** B1
Oak Village, NW5 . . . . **110** A1
Oak Way, W3 . . . . **133** E4
Oakwood Ct, W14 . . . . **149** F2
Oakwood La, W14 . . . . **149** F2
Oakworth Rd, W10 . . . . **134** C1
Oat La, EC2 . . . . **39** E2
Oban Ho, E14
off Oban St **145** D2
Oban St, E14 . . . . **145** D2
Oberstein Rd, SW11 . . . . **179** D2
Oborne Cl, SE24 . . . . **182** B3
O'Brien Ho, E2
off Smart St **129** D3
Observatory Gdns, W8 . . . . . . **42** A4
Observatory Ms, E14
off Storers Quay **159** D3

Observatory Rd, SW14 **174** C2
Occupation Rd, SE17 **75** E2
Ocean Est, E1 **129** D4
Ocean St, E1 **143** D1
Ocean Wf, E14 **157** F1
Ockendon Ms, N1
off Ockendon Rd **113** D3
Ockendon Rd, N1 **113** D3
Octagon Arc, EC2 **40** C1
Octavia Ms, W9
off Bravington Rd **121** F4
Octavia St, SW11 **165** E3
Octavius St, SE8 **172** A2
Odell Wk, SE13
off Bankside Av **186** B1
Odessa Rd, E7 **103** F4
NW10 **120** A2
Odessa St, SE16 **157** F1
Odger St, SW11 **165** F4
Odhams Wk, WC2 **37** D3
Offa's Mead, E9 **115** E1
Offenbach Ho, E2 **129** D2
Offerton Rd, SW4 **180** C1
Offley Rd, SW9 **86** A2
Offord Rd, N1 **111** F4
Offord St, N1 **111** F4
Oglander Rd, SE15 **183** F2
Ogle St, W1 **23** E4
Ohio Bldg, SE13
off Deals Gateway **172** B3
Ohio Rd, E13 **131** F4
Oil Mill La, W6 **148** A4
Okehampton Rd, NW10 **120** C1
Olaf St, W11 **135** D3
★ Old Admiralty Bldg
(M.o.D.), SW1 **48** B3
Old Bailey, EC4 **39** D3
Old Barge Ho All, SE1
off Upper Grd **50** B2
Old Barrack Yd, SW1 **46** A4
Old Barrowfield, E15
off Stephen's Rd **131** F1
Old Bellgate Pl, E14 **158** A2
Old Bethnal Grn Rd, E2 **128** A3
★ Old Billingsgate Mkt,
EC3 **52** C1
Old Billingsgate Wk, EC3
off Lower Thames St **52** C1
Old Bond St, W1 **47** E1
Old Brewers Yd, WC2 **36** C3
Old Brewery Ms, NW3
off Hampstead High St **109** D1
Old Broad St, EC2 **40** B3
Old Brompton Rd, SW5 **66** B3
SW7 **66** B3
Old Bldgs, WC2 **38** A2
Old Burlington St, W1 **35** E4
Oldbury Pl, W1 **22** B4
Old Canal Ms, SE15 **77** F3
Old Castle St, E1 **41** E1
Old Cavendish St, W1 **34** C2
Old Change Ct, EC4
off Carter La **39** E3
Old Chelsea Ms, SW3 **80** B1
Old Ch La, NW9 **90** C3
Old Ch Rd, E1 **143** D2
Old Ch St, SW3 **68** B3
Old Compton St, W1 **36** A4
Old Ct Pl, W8 **42** C4
★ Old Curiosity Shop,
WC2 **37** E2
Old Dairy Ms, SW4
off Tintern St **181** E2
Old Dock Cl, Rich. TW9 **160** A1
Oldfield Gro, SE16 **157** D3
Oldfield Ms, N6 **96** C1
Oldfield Rd, N16 **99** E4
NW10 **105** F4
W3 *off Valetta Rd* **147** F1
Old Fish St Hill, EC4 **39** E4
Old Fleet La, EC4 **38** C2
OLD FORD, E3 **115** F4
Old Ford Rd, E2 **128** C2
E3 **129** E2
Old Forge Ms, W12
off Goodwin Rd **148** B1
Old Forge Rd, N19 **97** D3
Old Gloucester St, WC1 **25** D4
Oldham Ter, W3 **132** C4
Oldhill St, N16 **100** A2
Old Jamaica Rd, SE16 **156** A2
Old James St, SE15 **184** B1
Old Jewry, EC2 **40** A3
Old Kent Rd, SE1 **64** B3
SE15 **155** E3
Old Manor Yd, SW5 **66** B2
Old Mkt Sq, E2 **17** E4
Old Marylebone Rd, NW1 **33** D1
Old Mitre Ct, EC4 **38** B3
Old Montague St, E1 **142** A1
Old Nichol St, E2 **29** E2
Old N St, WC1 **25** E4
OLD OAK COMMON,
NW10 **133** F1
Old Oak Common La,
NW10 **133** E1
W3 **133** E1
Old Oak La, NW10 **119** E3
Old Oak Rd, W3 **133** F3
★ Old Operating Thea Mus
& Herb Garret, SE1 **52** B3
Old Orchard, The, NW3
off Nassington Rd **109** F1
Old Palace Yd, SW1 **60** C2
Old Paradise St, SE11 **61** E4
Old Pk Av, SW12 **180** A4
Old Pk La, W1 **46** B3
Old Pearson St, SE10 **172** B2
Old Pye St, SW1 **60** A2
Old Quebec St, W1 **33** F3
Old Queen St, SW1 **60** B1
Old Rd, SE13 **187** E2
Old Royal Free Pl, N1
off Old Royal Free Sq **14** B1
Old Royal Free Sq, N1 **14** B1
Old Sch Cl, SE10 **159** E2
Old Sch Sq, E14
off Pelling St **144** A2
Old Seacoal La, EC4 **38** C2
Old S Lambeth Rd, SW8 **85** D2
Old Spitalfields Mkt, E1 **29** E4
Old Sq, WC2 **37** F2
Old Sta Way, SW4
off Voltaire Rd **181** D1
Old Street **28** A1
Old Street **28** A1
Old St, EC1 **27** E2
Old Thea Ct, SE1
off Porter St **51** F2
Old Town, SW4 **180** C1
Old Woolwich Rd, SE10 **173** D1
Old York Rd, SW18 **178** B3
O'Leary Sq, E1 **142** C1
Olga St, E3 **129** E2
Oliphant St, W10 **121** D3
● Oliver Business Pk, NW10
off Oliver Rd **118** C2
Oliver Cl, W4 **160** B1
Oliver-Goldsmith Est,
SE15 **170** A3
Oliver Ms, SE15 **170** A4
Olive Rd, NW2 **106** C1
Oliver Rd, E10 **102** B3
NW10 **118** C2
Olivers Yd, EC1 **28** B2
Olivette St, SW15 **177** D1
Ollerton Grn, E3 **129** F1
Ollgar Cl, W12 **133** F4
Olliffe St, E14 **158** C2
Olmar St, SE1 **170** A1
Olney Rd, SE17 **75** E4
★ Olympia, W14 **149** E2
Olympia Ms, W2 **43** D1
Olympia Way, W14 **149** E2
Olympic Sq, Wem. HA9 **90** A4
Olympic Way, Wem. HA9 **104** A1
Olympus Sq, E5
off Nolan Way **100** A4
Oman Av, NW2 **106** C1
O'Meara St, SE1 **51** F3
Omega Bldg, SW18
off Smugglers Way **178** B2
Omega Cl, E14
off Tiller Rd **158** B2
Omega Pl, N1 **13** D3
Omega St, SE14 **172** A3
● Omega Wks, E3 **116** A4
Ommaney Rd, SE14 **171** D3
Ondine Rd, SE15 **183** F2
Onega Gate, SE16 **157** E2
One Tree Cl, SE23 **184** C4
Ongar Rd, SW6 **66** A4
Onra Rd, E17 **102** A1
Onslow Cl, W10
off Dowland St **121** F3
Onslow Cres, SW7 **68** B1
Onslow Gdns, SW7 **68** A1
Onslow Ms E, SW7 **68** A1
Onslow Ms W, SW7 **68** A1
Onslow Sq, SW7 **56** B4
Onslow St, EC1 **26** B3
Ontario St, SE1 **63** D3
Ontario Twr, E14 **145** D3
Ontario Way, E14 **144** A3
Onyx Ms, E15
off Vicarage La **117** E3
Opal Ms, NW6
off Priory Pk Rd **122** A1
Opal St, SE11 **74** C1
Uni Open Uni in London, The,
NW1 *off Hawley Cres* **110** B4
Ophelia Gdns, NW2
off Hamlet Sq **93** E4
Ophir Ter, SE15 **170** A3
Oppenheim Rd, SE13 **172** C4
Oppidans Ms, NW3
off Meadowbank **109** F4
Oppidans Rd, NW3 **109** F4
Orange Ct, E1
off Hermitage Wall **142** A4
Orange Gro, E11 **103** D4
Orange Pl, SE16
off Lower Rd **156** C2
Orange Sq, SW1 **70** B1
Orange St, WC2 **48** A1
Orange Yd, W1 **36** B3
Oransay Rd, N1 **112** C3
Oransay Wk, N1
off Oransay Rd **112** C3
Oratory La, SW3 **68** B2
Orbain Rd, SW6 **163** E2
Orbel St, SW11 **165** E3

Orb St, SE17 **76** A1
Orchard, The, SE3 **173** D4
W4 **147** D3
Orchard Cl, N1 **112** C4
NW2 **92** A4
SE23 **184** C4
W10 **135** E1
Orchard Dr, SE3 **173** D4
Orchard Hill, SE13
off Coldbath St **172** B4
Orchard Mead Ho, NW11 **93** F3
Orchard Ms, N1
off Southgate Gro **113** D4
N6 *off Orchard Rd* **96** B1
Orchard Pl, E5 **114** B2
E14 **145** E3
Orchard Ri, Rich. TW10 **174** B2
Orchard Rd, N6 **96** B1
SE3 **173** E4
Richmond TW9 **174** A1
Orchardson Ho, NW8
off Orchardson St **20** B2
Orchardson St, NW8 **20** A3
Orchard Sq, W14
off Sun Rd **149** F4
Orchard St, W1 **34** A3
Orchid Cl, SE13 **187** D3
Orchid St, W12 **134** A3
Orde Hall St, WC1 **25** E3
Ordell Rd, E3 **129** F2
Ordnance Cres, SE10 **159** D1
Ordnance Hill, NW8 **8** B1
Ordnance Ms, NW8 **8** B2
Ordnance Rd, E16 **145** F1
Oregano Dr, E14 **145** D2
Oregon Bldg, SE13
off Deals Gateway **172** B3
Orestes Ms, NW6
off Aldred Rd **108** A2
Oriel Ct, NW3
off Heath St **108** C1
Oriel Dr, SW13 **162** B1
Oriel Pl, NW3
off Heath St **108** C1
Oriel Rd, E9 **115** D3
Oriental St, E14
off Morant St **144** A3
● Orient Ind Pk, E10 102 A3
Orient St, SE11 **62** C4
Orient Way, E5 **101** D4
E10 **101** E3
● Orion Business Cen, SE14 157 D4
Orion Ho, E1
off Coventry Rd **128** B4
Orion Pt, E14
off Crews St **158** A3
Orkney St, SW11 **166** A4
Orlando Rd, SW4 **180** C1
Orleston Ms, N7 **112** A3
Orleston Rd, N7 **112** A3
Orlop St, SE10 **159** E4
Orme Ct, W2 **42** C1
Orme Ct Ms, W2 **43** D1
Orme La, W2 **42** C1
Orme Sq, W2 **42** C1
Ormiston Gro, W12 **134** B4
Ormond Cl, WC1 **25** D4
Ormonde Gate, SW3 **69** F3
Ormonde Pl, SW1 **70** A1
Ormonde Rd, SW14 **174** B1
Ormonde Ter, NW8 **9** E1
Ormond Ms, WC1 **25** D3
Ormond Rd, N19 **97** E2
Ormond Yd, SW1 **47** F2
Ormsby Pl, N16 **99** F4
Ormsby St, E2 **17** E2
Ormside St, SE15 **170** C1
Ornan Rd, NW3 **109** E2
Orpen Wk, N16 **99** E4
Orpheus St, SE5 **169** D3
Orsett St, SE11 **73** F2
Orsett Ter, W2 **31** D2
Orsman Rd, N1 **16** C1
Orton St, E1
off Hermitage Wall **142** A4
Orville Rd, SW11 **165** D4
Orwell Ct, N5 **112** C1
Osbaldeston Rd, N16 **100** A3
Osbert St, SW1 **72** A1
Osborn Cl, E8 **128** A1
Osborne Gro, N4 **98** A2
Osborne Rd, E9 **115** F3
E10 **102** B4
N4 **97** F2
NW2 **106** B3
W3 **146** B2
Osborn St, E1 **41** F1
Osborn Ter, SE3
off Lee Rd **187** F2
Oscar Faber Pl, N1
off St. Peter's Way **113** E4
Oscar St, SE8 **172** A3
Oseney Cres, NW5 **110** C3
Osier La, SE10 **159** F2
Osier Ms, W4 **161** F1
Osiers Rd, SW18 **178** A2
Osier St, E1 **128** C4
Osier Way, E10 **102** B4
Oslo Ct, NW8 **8** C3
Oslo Sq, SE16 **157** E2
Osman Rd, W6
off Batoum Gdns **148** C2
Osmington Ho, SW8 **85** E3
Osmund St, W12
off Braybrook St **133** F1
Osnaburgh St, NW1 **23** D3
NW1 (north section) **23** D1
Osnaburgh Ter, NW1 **23** D2
Osprey Hts, SW11
off Bramlands Cl **179** E1
Ospringe Rd, NW5 **110** C1
Osram Ct, W6
off Lena Gdns **148** C2
Osric Path, N1 **16** C3
Ossian Ms, N4 **97** F1
Ossian Rd, N4 **97** F1
Ossington Bldgs, W1 **22** A4
Ossington Cl, W2 **42** B1
Ossington St, W2 **42** B1
Ossory Rd, SE1 **156** A4
Ossulston St, NW1 **12** A3
Osten Ms, SW7 **55** D3
Osterley Ho, E14
off Giraud St **144** B2
Osterley Rd, N16 **113** E1
Oswald Bldg, SW8 **82** C1
Oswald's Mead, E9
off Lindisfarne Way **115** E1
Oswald St, E5 **101** D4
Oswald Ter, NW2
off Temple Rd **92** C4
Oswell Ho, E1 **142** B4
Oswin St, SE11 **63** D4
Oswyth Rd, SE5 **169** E4
Otford Cres, SE4 **185** F4
Othello Cl, SE11 **74** C2
Otis St, E3 **130** C3
Otley Ter, E5 **101** D3
Ottaway St, E5 **100** A4
Otterburn Ho, SE5 **87** E2
Otter Cl, E15 **130** C1
Otto St, SE17 **86** C1
Oulton Cl, E5
off Mundford Rd **100** C3
Outer Circle, NW1 **22** A3
Outgate Rd, NW10 **105** F4
Outram Pl, N1 **125** E1
Outwich St, EC3 **41** D2
⊖ Oval 86 A1
★ Oval, The (Surrey CCC), SE11 73 F4
Oval, The, E2 **128** B2
Oval Pl, SW8 **85** E2
Oval Rd, NW1 **124** B1
Oval Way, SE11 **73** F3
Ovanna Ms, N1
off Buckingham Rd **113** E3
Overbury St, E5 **115** D1
Overcliff Rd, SE13 **186** A1
Overlea Rd, E5 **100** A1
Oversley Ho, W2 **18** A4
Overstone Rd, W6 **148** C2
Overton Cl, NW10 **104** C3
Overton Rd, E10 **101** E2
SW9 **168** A4
Ovex Cl, E14 **158** C1
Ovington Gdns, SW3 **57** D3
Ovington Ms, SW3 **57** D3
Ovington Sq, SW3 **57** D3
Ovington St, SW3 **57** D3
Owens Ms, E11
off Short Rd **103** E3
Owen's Row, EC1 **14** C4
Owen St, EC1 **14** C3
Owen Way, NW10 **104** C3
Owgan Cl, SE5 **88** B3
Oxberry Av, SW6 **163** E4
Oxendon St, SW1 **48** A1
Oxenford St, SE15 **183** F1
Oxenholme, NW1 **11** F3
Oxestalls Rd, SE8 **157** E4
⊖ Oxford Circus 35 E3
Oxford Circ Av, W1 **35** E3
Oxford Ct, EC4 **40** A4
W3 **132** A2
Oxford Dr, SE1 **52** C3
Oxford Gdns, W4 **146** A4
W10 **135** E2
Oxford Gate, W6 **149** D3
Oxford Pl, NW10
off Press Rd **91** D4
Oxford Rd, E15 **117** D3
N4 **98** A2
NW6 **6** B3
SW15 **177** E2
Oxford Rd N, W4 **146** B4
Oxford Rd S, W4 **146** A4
Oxford Sq, W2 **33** D3
Oxford St, W1 **35** F2
● Oxgate Cen Ind Est, The, NW2 92 B2
Oxgate Gdns, NW2 **92** B4
Oxgate La, NW2 **92** B3
Oxley Cl, SE1 **77** F2
Oxleys Rd, NW2 **92** B4
Oxonian St, SE22 **183** F2
Oxo Twr Wf, SE1 **50** B1
Oystergate Wk, EC4
off Swan La **52** A1
Oyster Row, E1
off Lukin St **142** C2
Oyster Wf, SW11 **165** D4

P

Pablo Neruda Cl, SE24
off Shakespeare Rd **182** B2
Pace Pl, E1
off Bigland St **142** B2
Pacific Ms, SW9
off Saltoun Rd **182** A2
Pacific Wf, SE16
off Rotherhithe St **143** D4
Packington Rd, W3 **146** C2
Packington Sq, N1 **15** E1
Packington St, N1 **126** B1
Padbury, SE17 **76** C3
Padbury Ct, E2 **29** F1
Paddenswick Rd, W6 **148** A2
PADDINGTON, W2 **31** E1
Paddington 32 A2
Paddington 32 A2
Paddington Grn, W2 **20** B4
Paddington St, W1 **22** A4
Paddock Rd, NW2 **92** A4
Paddocks, The, Wem. HA9 **90** B3
Padfield Rd, SE5 **182** C1
Pagden St, SW8 **83** D4
Pageant Cres, SE16
off Rotherhithe St **143** E4
Pageantmaster Ct, EC4 **38** C3
Page Av, Wem. HA9 **90** C4
Page St, SW1 **60** B4
Pages Wk, SE1 **64** C4
Pages Yd, W4
off Church St **161** E1
Paget Rd, N16 **99** D2
Paget St, EC1 **14** C4
Pagnell St, SE14 **171** F2
Pagoda Gdns, SE3 **173** D4
Painsthorpe Rd, N16
off Oldfield Rd **99** E4
Painters Ms, SE16
off Macks Rd **156** A3
Pakeman St, N7 **97** F4
Pakenham St, WC1 **25** F1
Palace Av, W8 **43** D3
Palace Cl, E9 **115** F3
Palace Ct, NW3 **108** B2
W2 **30** C4
Palace Gdns Ms, W8 **42** B2
Palace Gdns Ter, W8 **42** B2
Palace Gate, W8 **55** E1
Palace Grn, W8 **43** D4
Palace Ms, SW1 **70** B1
SW6
off Hartismere Rd **163** F2
Palace of Industry, Wem.
HA9 off Fulton Rd 104 A1
Palace Pl, SW1 **59** E2
Palace St, SW1 **59** E2
Palamos Rd, E10 **102** A2
Palatine Av, N16 **113** E1
Palatine Rd, N16 **113** E1
Palemead Cl, SW6 **162** C3
Palermo Rd, NW10 **120** A2
Palewell Common Dr,
SW14 **175** D3
Palewell Pk, SW14 **175** D3
Palfrey Pl, SW8 **85** F2
Palgrave Gdns, NW1 **21** D2
Palgrave Ho, NW3 **109** F2
Palgrave Rd, W12 **147** F2
Palissy St, E2 **29** E1
Palladio Ct, SW18
off Mapleton Rd **178** B4
Palliser Rd, W14 **149** E4
Pall Mall, SW1 **47** F3
Pall Mall E, SW1 **48** B2
Palm Cl, E10 **102** B4
Palmer Ho, SE14
off Lubbock St **171** D2
Palmer Pl, N7 **112** A2
Palmers Pas, SW14
off Palmers Rd **174** C1
Palmers Rd, E2 **129** D2
SW14 **174** C1
Palmerston Ho, SW11
off Strasburg Rd **166** A3
W8 **42** A3
Palmerston Rd, NW6 **108** A4
SW14 **174** C2
W3 **146** C2
Palmerston Way, SW8 **83** D3
Palmer St, SW1 **60** A1
Pamela Wk, E8
off Marlborough Av **128** A1
Pancras La, EC4 **39** F3
Pancras Rd, NW1 **12** A2
Pancras Way, E3 **130** A2
Pandian Way, NW1
off Busby Pl **111** D3
Pandora Rd, NW6 **108** A3
Pangbourne Av, W10 **134** C1
Pangbourne Ho, N7 **111** E2
Pankhurst Cl, SE14
off Briant St **171** D2
Panmure Cl, N5 **112** B1
Panoramic, The, NW3
off Pond St **109** E2
Pansy Gdns, W12 **134** A3
Panther Dr, NW10 **105** D2
Panton St, SW1 **48** A1
Panyer All, EC4 **39** E3
Papworth Gdns, N7
off Chillingworth Rd **111** F2
Parade, The, SW11 **81** F2
Paradise Pas, N7 **112** A2
Paradise Rd, SW4 **167** E4
Paradise Row, E2
off Bethnal Grn Rd **128** B3
Paradise St, SE16 **156** B1
Paradise Wk, SW3 **69** E4
Paragon, The, SE3 **173** F4
Paragon Ms, SE1 **64** B4
Paragon Pl, SE3 **173** F4
Paragon Rd, E9 **114** C3
Parbury Rd, SE23 **185** E4
Pardoe Rd, E10 **102** B1
Pardoner St, SE1 **64** B2
Pardon St, EC1 **27** D2
Parfett St, E1 **142** A1
Parfitt Cl, NW3
off North End **94** C3
Parfrey St, W6 **162** C1
Paris Gdn, SE1 **50** C2
Park, The, NW11 **94** B2
Park Av, E15 **117** E3
NW2 **106** B3
NW11 **94** B2
SW14 **175** D2
Park Av N, NW10 **106** B2
Park Cen Bldg, E3
off Fairfield Rd **130** A2
Park Cl, E9 **128** C1
NW2 **92** B4
SW1 **57** E1
W4 **147** D4
W14 **149** F2
Park Ct, SW11 **82** C4
Park Cres, W1 **22** C3
Park Cres Ms E, W1 **23** D3
Park Cres Ms W, W1 **22** C4
Park Dr, NW11 **94** B2
SW14 **175** D2
W3 **146** A2
Park E Bldg, E3
off Fairfield Rd **130** A2
Park End, NW3
off South Hill Pk **109** E1
Parker Ms, WC2 **37** D2
Parke Rd, SW13 **162** A3
Parkers Row, SE1 **65** F1
Parker St, WC2 **37** D2
Parkfield Av, SW14 **175** E2
Parkfield Rd, NW10 **106** A4
SE14 **171** F3
Parkfields, SW15 **176** C2
Parkfields Av, NW9 **91** D2
Parkfield St, N1 **14** B2
Parkgate, SE3 **187** F1
Parkgate Gdns, SW14 **175** D3
Parkgate Ms, N6 **96** C1
Parkgate Rd, SW11 **80** C3
Park Gro Rd, E11 **103** E3
Parkham St, SW11 **165** E3
Park Hill, SW4 **181** D3
Parkhill Rd, NW3 **109** F2
Parkhill Wk, NW3 **109** F2
Parkholme Rd, E8 **113** F3
Parkhouse St, SE5 **88** B2
Parkhurst Ho, W12
off Du Cane Rd **134** C2
Parkhurst Rd, N7 **111** E1
Parkinson Ho, SW1
off Tachbrook St **72** A2
Parklands, N6 **96** B1
Parklands Cl, SW14 **174** C3
Parkland Wk, N4 **97** F1
N6 **97** D1
Park La, E15
off High St **131** D1
W1 **46** B3
Park Mans, SW1
off Knightsbridge **57** E1
SW8 **73** D4
Parkmead, SW15 **176** B4
Park Ms, SE10
off Calvert Rd **159** F4
Park Par, NW10 **119** F2
Park Piazza, SE13
off Highfield Cl **187** D4
Park Pl, E14 **144** A4
N1 **127** D1
SW1 **47** E3
W3 **146** A3
Park Pl Vil, W2 **19** F4
Park Rd, E10 **102** A2
NW1 **8** C4
NW4 **92** A1
NW8 **8** C4
NW9 **91** D1
NW10 **119** E1
W4 **160** C2
Park Rd E, W3 **146** B1
Park Rd N, W3 **146** B1
W4 **147** D4
Park Row, SE10 **173** D1
PARK ROYAL, NW10 **118** A3
Park Royal 118 A4
Park Royal Cen for
Mental Health, NW10 118 C2
Park Royal Metro Cen,
NW10 118 B4

Park Royal Rd, NW10 . . . . . . **118** C3
W3 . . . . **118** C3
Parkside, NW2 . . . . **92** A4
SE3 . . . . **173** F2
● Parkside Business Est, SE8 *off Rolt St* **171** E1
Parkside Cres, N7 . . . . **98** A4
Parkside Est, E9 *off Rutland Rd* **129** D1
Parkside Rd, SW11 . . . . **166** A3
Parkside Wk, SE10 . . . . **159** E4
Park S, SW11 *off Austin Rd* **166** A3
Park Sq E, NW1 . . . . **22** C2
Park Sq Ms, NW1 . . . . **22** C3
Park Sq W, NW1 . . . . **22** C2
Parkstead Rd, SW15 . . . . **176** A3
Park Steps, W2 *off St. Georges Flds* **33** D4
Parkstone Rd, SE15 *off Rye La* **170** A4
Park St, SE1 . . . . **51** E2
W1 . . . . **34** A4
Park Twrs, W1 *off Brick St* **46** C3
Park Vw, W3 . . . . **132** C1
Wembley HA9 . . . . **104** B2
Parkview Ct, SW18 *off Broomhill Rd* **178** A4
Park Vw Est, E2 . . . . **128** C2
N5 . . . . **112** C1
Park Vw Ho, SE24 *off Hurst St* **182** B4
Park Vw Ms, SW9 . . . . **167** F4
Park Vw Rd, NW10 . . . . **105** F1
Park Village E, NW1 . . . . **10** C1
Park Village W, NW1 . . . . **10** C2
Parkville Rd, SW6 . . . . **163** F2
Park Vista, SE10 . . . . **173** D1
Park Wk, N6 *off North Rd* **96** A1
SE10 *off Crooms Hill* **173** D2
SW10 . . . . **67** F4
Parkway, NW1 . . . . **10** C1
Parkway Cres, E15 . . . . **116** C2
Park W, W2 . . . . **33** D3
Park W Bldg, E3 *off Fairfield Rd* **130** A2
Park W Pl, W2 . . . . **33** D2
Parliament Ct, E1 . . . . **41** D1
Parliament Hill, NW3 . . . . . . **109** E1
Parliament Ms, SW14 *off Thames Bk* **160** C4
Parliament Sq, SW1 . . . . **60** C1
Parliament St, SW1 . . . . **60** C1
Parliament Vw Apts, SE1 . . . . **61** E4
Parma Cres, SW11 . . . . **179** F2
● Parmiter Ind Cen, E2 *off Parmiter St* **128** B2
Parmiter St, E2 . . . . **128** B2
Parmoor Ct, EC1 . . . . **27** E2
Parnell Cl, W12 . . . . **148** B2
Parnell Rd, E3 . . . . **129** F1
Parnham St, E14 *off Blount St* **143** E2
Parolles Rd, N19 . . . . **96** C2
Parr Ct, N1 . . . . **16** A2
Parr Pl, W4 *off Chiswick High Rd* . . . **147** F3
Parr St, N1 . . . . **16** A2
Parry Rd, W10 . . . . **121** E3
Parry St, SW8 . . . . **72** C4
Parsifal Rd, NW6 . . . . **108** A2
Parsonage St, E14 . . . . **158** C3
PARSONS GREEN, SW6 . . . . . **78** A4
⊖ Parsons Green **163** F3
Parsons Grn, SW6 . . . . **164** A3
Parsons Grn La, SW6 . . . . **78** A4
Parson's Ho, W2 . . . . **20** A3
Parthenia Rd, SW6 . . . . **164** A3
Partington Cl, N19 . . . . **97** D2
Parvin St, SW8 . . . . **84** A4
Pascal St, SW8 . . . . **84** B2
Pascoe Rd, SE13 . . . . **187** D3
Pasley Cl, SE17 . . . . **75** E3
Passfield Dr, E14 *off Uamvar St* **144** B1
Passing All, EC1 . . . . **27** D3
Passmore St, SW1 . . . . **70** A1
★ Passport Office, SW1 . . . . **59** D4
Paston Cl, E5 *off Caldecott Way* **101** D4
Pastor St, SE11 . . . . **63** D4
Pastures Path, E11 *off Lister Rd* **103** E2
Patcham Ter, SW8 . . . . **83** D4
Paternoster La, EC4 *off Warwick La* **39** D3
Paternoster Row, EC4 . . . . **39** E3
Paternoster Sq, EC4 . . . . **39** D3
Paterson Ct, EC1 *off St. Luke's Est* **28** A1
Pater St, W8 . . . . **54** A3
Patience Rd, SW11 . . . . **165** E4
Patio Cl, SW4 . . . . **181** D4
Patmore Est, SW8 . . . . **83** E4
Patmore St, SW8 . . . . **83** F4
Patmos Rd, SW9 . . . . **86** C3
Paton Cl, E3 . . . . **130** A3
Paton St, EC1 . . . . **27** E1
Patrick Connolly Gdns, E3 *off Talwin St* **130** B3
Patriot Sq, E2 . . . . **128** B2
Patrol Pl, SE6 . . . . **186** B4
Patshull Pl, NW5 *off Patshull Rd* **110** C3
Patshull Rd, NW5 . . . . **110** C3
Patterdale Rd, SE15 . . . . **170** C2
Pattina Wk, SE16 . . . . **143** F4
Pattison Rd, NW2 . . . . **94** A4
Paul Cl, E15 . . . . **117** E4
Paulet Rd, SE5 . . . . **168** B4
Paulet Way, NW10 . . . . **105** E4
Pauline Ho, E1 . . . . **142** A1
Paul Julius Cl, E14 . . . . **145** D3
Paul St, E15 . . . . **131** D1
EC2 . . . . **28** B3
Paul's Wk, EC4 . . . . **39** D4
Paultons Sq, SW3 . . . . **68** B4
Paultons St, SW3 . . . . **80** B1
Pauntley St, N19 . . . . **96** C2
Paveley Dr, SW11 . . . . **80** C3
Paveley Ho, N1 *off Priory Grn Est* **13** E3
Paveley St, NW8 . . . . **21** D2
Pavement, The, SW4 . . . . . . **180** C2
Pavilion Ho, SE16 *off Canada St* **157** D1
Pavilion Par, W12 *off Wood La* **134** C2
Pavilion Rd, SW1 . . . . **57** F3
Pavilion St, SW1 . . . . **57** F3
Pavilion Ter, W12 *off Wood La* **134** C2
Pavillion Ms, N4 . . . . **97** F3
Paxton Rd, W4 . . . . **161** E1
Paxton Ter, SW1 . . . . **71** D4
Paynell Ct, SE3 *off Lawn Ter* **187** E1
Payne Rd, E3 . . . . **130** B2
Paynesfield Av, SW14 . . . . . . **175** D1
Payne St, SE8 . . . . **171** F1
Paynes Wk, W6 . . . . **163** E1
Peabody Av, SW1 . . . . **70** C2
Peabody Cl, SE10 *off Devonshire Dr* **172** B3
SW1 . . . . **71** D4
Peabody Dws, WC1 . . . . **24** C2
Peabody Est, EC1 (St. Luke's) **27** F3
N1 (Islington) *off Greenman St* **126** C1
SE1 . . . . **50** B3
SE17 . . . . **76** A1
SW1 . . . . **59** E4
SW3 . . . . **69** D4
SW6 . . . . **66** A4
W6 *off The Square* **148** C4
W10 . . . . **134** C1
EC1 (Clerkenwell) *off Farringdon La* **26** B3
Peabody Sq, SE1 . . . . **62** C1
Peabody Twr, EC1 *off Golden La* **27** F3
Peabody Trust, SE1 . . . . **51** E3
Peabody Trust Camberwell Grn Est, SE5 . . . . **88** A4
Peabody Trust Old Pye St Est, SW1 *off Old Pye St* **60** A3
Peabody Yd, N1 *off Greenman St* **126** C1
Peace Gro, Wem. HA9 . . . . **90** B4
Peach Gro, E11 . . . . **103** D4
Peach Rd, W10 . . . . **121** D3
Peachum Rd, SE3 . . . . **173** F1
Peachwalk Ms, E3 *off Grove Rd* **129** D2
Peacock St, SE17 . . . . **75** D1
Peacock Yd, SE17 . . . . **75** D1
Pear Cl, SE14 *off Southerngate Way* . . **171** E2
Pearcroft Rd, E11 . . . . **103** D3
Peardon St, SW8 . . . . **180** B1
Pearl Cl, NW2 . . . . **93** D1
Pearl St, E1 *off Penang St* **142** B4
Pearman St, SE1 . . . . **62** B2
Pear Pl, SE1 . . . . **50** A4
Pear Rd, E11 . . . . **103** D4
Pearscroft Ct, SW6 . . . . **164** B3
Pearscroft Rd, SW6 . . . . **164** B3
Pearse St, SE15 . . . . **89** D1
Pearson Cl, SE5 . . . . **87** F4
Pearson Ms, SW4 . . . . **181** D1
Pearsons Av, SE14 *off Tanners Hill* **172** A3
Pearson St, E2 . . . . **17** D2
Pear Tree Cl, E2 . . . . **17** E1
Pear Tree Ct, EC1 . . . . **26** B3
Peartree La, E1 *off Glamis Rd* **142** C3
Pear Tree St, EC1 . . . . **27** D2
Peary Pl, E2 *off Kirkwall Pl* **128** C3
Pebble Way, W3 . . . . **132** B4
Peckett Sq, N5 *off Highbury Gra* **112** B1
Peckford Pl, SW9 . . . . **168** A4
PECKHAM, SE15 . . . . **170** A3
Peckham Gro, SE15 . . . . **89** D2
Peckham High St, SE15 . . . . **170** A3

Peckham Hill St, SE15 .....**170** A2
Peckham Pk Rd, SE15 ......**170** A2
Peckham Rd, SE5 ....**169** E3
SE15 ....**169** E3
⇄ Peckham Rye 170 A4
Peckham Rye, SE15 ....**184** A1
SE22 ....**184** A2
Pecks Yd, E1 ....**29** E4
Peckwater St, NW5 ....**110** C2
Pedlars Wk, N7 ....**111** E3
Pedley St, E1 ....**29** F3
Pedro St, E5 ....**101** D4
Pedworth Gdns, SE16
off Rotherhithe New Rd .**156** C3
Peel Gro, E2 ....**128** C2
Peel Pas, W8 ....**42** A3
Peel Prec, NW6 ....**6** A3
Peel St, W8 ....**42** A3
Peerless St, EC1 ....**28** A1
Pegasus Cl, N16
off Green Las **113** D1
Pegasus Ct, W3
off Horn La **132** C2
Pegasus Pl, SE11 ....**74** A4
SW6 *off Ackmar Rd* **164** A3
Pekin Cl, E14
off Pekin St **144** A2
Pekin St, E14 ....**144** A2
Peldon Wk, N1
off Britannia Row **126** B1
Pelham Cl, SE5 ....**169** E4
Pelham Cres, SW7 ....**68** C1
Pelham Ho, W14
off Mornington Av **149** F3
Pelham Pl, SW7 ....**68** C1
Pelham St, SW7 ....**56** B4
Pelican Est, SE15 ....**169** F3
Pelican Ho, SE5
off Peckham Rd **169** F3
Pelican Pas, E1
off Cambridge Heath Rd **128** C4
Pelier St, SE17 ....**75** F4
Pellant Rd, SW6 ....**163** E2
Pellatt Rd, SE22 ....**183** F3
Pellerin Rd, N16 ....**113** E2
Pelling St, E14 ....**144** A2
Pelter St, E2 ....**17** E4
Pelton Rd, SE10 ....**159** E4
Pember Rd, NW10 ....**121** D3
Pemberton Gdns, N19 ......**96** C4
Pemberton Pl, E8
off Mare St **114** B4
Pemberton Row, EC4 ....**38** B2
Pemberton Ter, N19 ....**96** C4
Pembridge Cres, W11 ....**30** A4
Pembridge Gdns, W2 ....**42** A1
Coll Pembridge Hall, W2 .....42 B1
Pembridge Ms, W11 ....**30** A4
Pembridge Pl, SW15 ....**178** A3
W2 ....**30** B4
Pembridge Rd, W11 ....**42** A1
Pembridge Sq, W2 ....**42** A1
Pembridge Vil, W2 ....**30** A4
W11 ....**30** A4
Pembroke Av, N1 ....**125** E1
Pembroke Cl, SW1 ....**58** B1
Pembroke Cotts, W8
off Pembroke Sq **54** A3
Pembroke Gdns, W8 ....**149** F3
Pembroke Gdns Cl, W8 ....**150** A2
Pembroke Ms, E3
off Morgan St **129** E3
W8 ....**54** A3
Pembroke Pl, W8 ....**54** A3
Pembroke Rd, W8 ....**54** A4
Pembroke Sq, W8 ....**54** A3
Pembroke St, N1 ....**111** E4
Pembroke Studios, W8 .....**149** F2
Pembroke Vil, W8 ....**54** A4
Pembroke Wk, W8 ....**54** A4
Pembry Cl, SW9 ....**168** A3
Pembury Cl, E5
off Shellness Rd **114** B2
Pembury Pl, E5 ....**114** B2
Pembury Rd, E5 ....**114** B2
Pemell Cl, E1
off Colebert Av **128** C4
Penally Pl, N1
off Shepperton Rd **127** D1
Penang St, E1 ....**142** B4
Penarth St, SE15 ....**170** C1
Pencombe Ms, W11
off Denbigh Rd **135** F3
Pencraig Way, SE15 ....**170** B1
Penda's Mead, E9 ....**115** E1
Penderyn Way, N7 ....**111** D1
Pendolino Way, NW10 .....**104** A4
Pendrell Rd, SE4 ....**171** E4
Pendulum Ms, E8
off Birkbeck Rd **113** F2
Penfields Ho, N7
off York Way **111** E3
Penfold Pl, NW1 ....**20** B4
Penfold St, NW1 ....**20** B3
NW8 ....**20** B3
Penford St, SE5 ....**168** B4
Penge Ho, SW11
off Wye St **179** D1
Penhurst Pl, SE1 ....**61** F3
Peninsula Apts, W2
off Praed St **32** C1
Peninsula Hts, SE1 ....**73** D2
Peninsula Sq, SE10
off Millennium Way **159** E1
Pennack Rd, SE15 ....**89** F1
Pennant Ms, W8 ....**54** C4
Pennard Mans, W12
off Goldhawk Rd **148** C1
Pennard Rd, W12 ....**148** C1
Pennethorne Cl, E9
off Victoria Pk Rd **128** C1
Pennethorne Ho, SW11
off Wye St **179** D1
Pennethorne Rd, SE15 .....**170** B2
Pennine Dr, NW2 ....**93** E3
Pennine La, NW2 ....**93** E3
Pennington St, E1 ....**142** A3
Penn Rd, N7 ....**111** E2
Penn St, N1 ....**16** B1
Pennyfields, E14 ....**144** A3
Pennymoor Wk, W9
off Riverton Cl **121** F3
Penny Rd, NW10 ....**118** B3
Penpoll Rd, E8 ....**114** B3
Penrhyn Cres, SW14 ....**174** C2
Penrith Cl, SW15 ....**177** E3
Penrose Gro, SE17 ....**75** E3
Penrose Ho, SE17 ....**75** E3
Penrose St, SE17 ....**75** E3
Penryn St, NW1 ....**12** A2
Penry St, SE1 ....**77** D1
Pensbury Pl, SW8 ....**166** C4
Pensbury St, SW8 ....**166** C4
Pensford Av, Rich. TW9 ....**160** A4
Penshurst Rd, E9 ....**115** D4
Pentland Cl, NW11 ....**93** E3
Pentland Gdns, SW18 ......**178** C4
Pentland Rd, NW6 ....**6** A4
Pentland St, SW18 ....**178** C4
Pentlow St, SW15 ....**176** C1
Penton Gro, N1 ....**14** A3
Penton Pl, SE17 ....**75** D2
Penton Ri, WC1 ....**13** F4
Penton St, N1 ....**14** A2
PENTONVILLE, N1 ....**14** A3
Pentonville Rd, N1 ....**13** E3
Pentridge St, SE15 ....**89** E2
Penwood Ho, SW15
off Tunworth Cres **175** F4
Penywern Rd, SW5 ....**66** B2
Penzance Pl, W11 ....**135** E4
Penzance St, W11 ....**135** E4
Peony Gdns, W12 ....**134** A3
Pepler Ms, SE5 ....**77** E4
Peploe Rd, NW6 ....**121** D2
Peppermead Sq, SE13 ......**186** A3
Peppermint Pl, E11
off Birch Gro **103** E4
Pepper St, E14 ....**158** B2
SE1 ....**51** E4
Peppie Cl, N16 ....**99** E3
Pepys Rd, SE14 ....**171** D3
Pepys St, EC3 ....**41** D4
Perceval Av, NW3 ....**109** E2
Perch St, E8 ....**113** F1
★ Percival David Foundation of Chinese Art, WC1
off Gordon Sq 24 B3
Percival Rd, SW14 ....**174** C2
Percival St, EC1 ....**26** C2
Percy Circ, WC1 ....**13** F4
Percy Ms, W1 ....**36** A1
Percy Pas, W1 ....**35** F1
Percy Rd, E11 ....**103** E1
E16 ....**145** E1
W12 ....**148** A1
Percy St, W1 ....**36** A1
Percy Yd, WC1 ....**13** F4
Peregrine Cl, NW10 ....**105** D2
Peregrine Ho, EC1 ....**15** D4
Perham Rd, W14 ....**149** E4
Perkin's Rents, SW1 ....**60** A2
Perkins Sq, SE1 ....**51** F2
Perks Cl, SE3
off Hurren Cl **187** E1
Perren St, NW5
off Ryland Rd **110** B3
Perrers Rd, W6 ....**148** B3
Perrins Ct, NW3
off Hampstead High St ..**108** C1
Perrins La, NW3 ....**108** C1
Perrin's Wk, NW3 ....**108** C1
Perry Av, W3 ....**133** D2
Perry Ct, E14
off Maritime Quay **158** A4
Perrymead St, SW6 ....**164** A3
Perryn Rd, SE16
off Drummond Rd **156** B2
W3 ....**133** D3
Perrys Pl, W1 ....**36** A2
Perrywood Ho, E5
off Pembury Rd **114** B2
Perseverance Pl, SW9 ....**86** B3
Perth Av, NW9 ....**91** D1
Perth Rd, E10 ....**101** E2
N4 ....**98** A2
Peter Av, NW10 ....**106** B4
Peterboat Cl, SE10
off Tunnel Av **159** E3
Peterborough Ms, SW6 .....**164** A4
Peterborough Rd, SW6 .....**164** A4

Peterborough Vil, SW6 ...... **78** C4
Peterchurch Ho, SE15
off Commercial Way **170** B1
Petergate, SW11 .... **178** C2
Peter Heathfield Ho, E15
off High St **131** D1
Peterhouse Gdns, SW6
off Bagley's La **164** B3
● Peterley Business Cen,
E2 *off Hackney Rd* 128 B2
★ Peter Pan Statue, W2 .... 44 A2
Petersfield Rd, W3 .... **146** C1
Petersham La, SW7 .... **55** E2
Petersham Ms, SW7 .... **55** E3
Petersham Pl, SW7 .... **55** E2
Peters Hill, EC4 .... **39** E4
Peter's La, EC1 .... **27** D4
Peter St, W1 .... **35** F4
Petherton Rd, N5 .... **112** C2
Petiver Cl, E9
off Frampton Pk Rd **114** C4
Petley Rd, W6 .... **162** C1
Peto Pl, NW1 .... **23** D2
Peto St N, E16
off Victoria Dock Rd **145** F3
Petrie Cl, NW2 .... **107** E3
★ Petrie Mus of Egyptian
Archaeology, WC1
off Malet Pl 24 A3
Petros Gdns, NW3
off Lithos Rd **108** C2
🔒 Petticoat La, E1 .... 41 D1
Petticoat Sq, E1 .... **41** E2
Petticoat Twr, E1 .... **41** E2
Pettiward Cl, SW15 .... **176** C2
Petty France, SW1 .... **59** F2
Petty Wales, EC3 .... **53** D1
Petworth Ho, SE22
off Pytchley Rd **183** E1
Petworth St, SW11 .... **81** D4
Petyt Pl, SW3 .... **80** C1
Petyward, SW3 .... **69** D1
Pevensey Rd, E7 .... **117** F1
Peyton Pl, SE10 .... **172** C2
Phelp St, SE17 .... **76** A4
Phene St, SW3 .... **69** D4
Philbeach Gdns,
SW5 .... **150** A4
Phil Brown Pl, SW8
off Daley Thompson
Way **180** B1
Philchurch Pl, E1
off Ellen St **142** A2
Philip Wk, SE15 .... **184** A1
Phillimore Gdns, NW10 .... **120** C1
W8 .... **54** A1
Phillimore Gdns Cl,
W8 .... **54** A2
Phillimore Pl, W8 .... **54** A1
Phillimore Wk, W8 .... **54** A2
Phillipp St, N1 .... **16** C1
Philpot La, EC3 .... **40** C4
Philpot Sq, SW6
off Peterborough Rd **178** B1
Philpot St, E1 .... **142** B2
Phipp's Ms, SW1 .... **59** D3
Phipp St, EC2 .... **28** C2
Phoebeth Rd, SE4 .... **186** A3
Phoenix Cl, E8
off Stean St **127** F1
W12 .... **134** B3
Phoenix Pl, WC1 .... **25** F2
Phoenix Rd, NW1 .... **12** A4
Phoenix St, WC2 .... **36** B3
Phoenix Way, SW18
off North Side
Wandsworth Common .. **178** C3
Phoenix Wf, SE10 .... **159** F1
Phoenix Wf Rd, SE1 .... **65** F1
Phoenix Yd, WC1 .... **25** F1
★ Photographers' Gall,
WC2 .... 36 B4
★ Physical Energy Statue,
W2 .... 43 F3
Physic Pl, SW3 .... **69** E4
Piccadilly, W1 .... **47** D3
Piccadilly Arc, SW1 .... **47** E2
⊖ Piccadilly Circus 47 F1
Piccadilly Circ, W1 .... **48** A1
Piccadilly Ct, N7
off Caledonian Rd **111** F3
Piccadilly Pl, W1 .... **47** F1
Pickard St, EC1 .... **15** D4
Pickering Cl, E9
off Cassland Rd **115** D4
Pickering Ms, W2 .... **31** D2
Pickering Pl, SW1 .... **47** F3
Pickering St, N1
off Essex Rd **126** B1
Pickfords Wf, N1 .... **15** E3
Pickwick St, SE1 .... **63** E1
Pickworth Cl, SW8 .... **85** D3
Picton Pl, W1 .... **34** B3
Picton St, SE5 .... **88** A3
Pied Bull Yd, N1
off Theberton St **126** B1
Pier Head, E1
off Wapping High St **142** B4
Piermont Grn, SE22 .... **184** B3
Piermont Rd, SE22 .... **184** B3
Pierrepoint Arc, N1 .... **14** C2
Pierrepoint Rd, W3 .... **132** B3
Pierrepoint Row, N1 .... **14** C2
Pier St, E14 .... **158** C3
Pier Ter, SW18
off Jew's Row **178** B2
Pigott St, E14 .... **144** A2
Pilgrimage St, SE1 .... **64** A1
Pilgrim's La, NW3 .... **109** D1
Pilgrims Ms, E14
off Newport Av **145** D3
Pilgrims Pl, NW3
off Hampstead High St .. **109** D1
Pilgrim St, EC4 .... **38** C3
Pilgrims Way, N19 .... **97** D2
Pilgrim's Way, Wem. HA9 .... **90** B2
Pilkington Rd, SE15 .... **170** B4
Pilot Busway, SE10 .... **159** E1
Pilot Cl, SE8 .... **171** F1
Pilton Pl, SE17 .... **75** F2
PIMLICO, SW1 .... **71** E2
⊖ Pimlico 72 A2
Pimlico Rd, SW1 .... **70** A2
Pimlico Wk, N1 .... **16** C4
Pinchin St, E1 .... **142** A3
Pincott Pl, SE4 .... **185** D2
Pindar St, EC2 .... **28** C4
Pindock Ms, W9 .... **19** D3
Pineapple Ct, SW1 .... **59** E2
Pine Av, E15 .... **117** D2
Pine Cl, E10 .... **102** A3
N19 .... **96** C3
Pinedene, SE15
off Meeting Ho La **170** B3
Pinefield Cl, E14 .... **144** A3
Pine Gro, N4 .... **97** E3
Pinelands Cl, SE3
off St. John's Pk **173** F2
Pinemartin Cl, NW2 .... **92** C4
Pine Ms, NW10
off Clifford Gdns **121** D2
Pine Rd, NW2 .... **106** C1
Pine St, EC1 .... **26** A2
Pine Tree Way, SE13
off Elmira St **186** B1
Pinter Ho, SW9
off Grantham Rd **167** E4
Pioneer Cl, E14
off Broomfield St **144** B1
Pioneer St, SE15 .... **170** A3
Pioneer Way, W12
off Du Cane Rd **134** B2
Piper Cl, N7 .... **111** F3
Pippin Cl, NW2 .... **92** B4
Pirie Cl, SE5
off Denmark Hill **183** D1
Pitchford St, E15 .... **117** D4
Pitfield Est, N1 .... **16** B4
Pitfield St, N1 .... **28** C1
Pitfield Way, NW10 .... **104** C3
Pitman Ho, SE8
off Tanners Hill **172** A3
Pitman St, SE5 .... **87** E2
Pitmaston Ho, SE13
off Lewisham Rd **172** C4
Pitmaston Rd, SE13
off Morden Hill **172** C4
Pitsea Pl, E1
off Pitsea St **143** D2
Pitsea St, E1 .... **143** D2
Pitt Ho, SW11
off Maysoule Rd **179** D2
Pitt's Head Ms, W1 .... **46** B3
Pitt St, W8 .... **42** B4
Pixley St, E14 .... **143** F2
PLAISTOW, E13 .... **131** F3
⊖ Plaistow 131 F2
Plaistow Gro, E15 .... **131** F1
Plaistow Rd, E13 .... **131** F1
E15 .... **131** F1
Plantain Gdns, E11
off Hollydown Way **103** D4
Plantain Pl, SE1 .... **52** A4
Plantation Cl, SW4
off King's Av **181** E3
Plantation La, EC3
off Rood La **40** C4
Plantation Wf, SW11 ...... **178** C1
Platina St, EC2 .... **28** B2
Plato Rd, SW2 .... **181** E2
Platt, The, SW15 .... **177** D1
Platt's La, NW3 .... **108** A1
Platt St, NW1 .... **12** A2
Plaxton Ct, E11
off Woodhouse Rd **103** F4
Playfair St, W6
off Winslow Rd **148** C4
Playfield Cres, SE22 ...... **183** F3
Playford Rd, N4 .... **97** F3
Playhouse Ct, SE1
off Southwark Br Rd **51** E4
Playhouse Yd, EC4 .... **38** C3
Plaza Par, NW6
off Kilburn High Rd **6** C2
🔒 Plaza Shop Cen, The,
W1 .... 35 F2
Pleasance, The, SW15 ..... **176** B2
Pleasance Rd, SW15 ...... **176** B3
Pleasant Pl, N1 .... **112** B4
Pleasant Row, NW1 .... **11** D1
Plender St, NW1 .... **11** E1
Pleshey Rd, N7 .... **111** D1

Plevna St, E14 . . . . .158 C2
Pleydell Av, W6 . . . . .147 F3
Pleydell Ct, EC4 . . . . .38 B3
Pleydell Est, EC1
off Radnor St 27 F1
Pleydell St, EC4 . . . . .38 B3
Plimley Pl, W12
off Sterne St 149 D1
Plimsoll Cl, E14
off Grundy St 144 B2
Plimsoll Rd, N4 . . . . .98 A4
Plough Ct, EC3 . . . . .40 B4
Plough La, SE22 . . . . .183 F4
Ploughmans Cl, NW1
off Crofters Way 125 D1
Plough Ms, SW11
off Plough Ter 179 D2
Plough Pl, EC4 . . . . .38 B2
Plough Rd, SW11 . . . . .179 D1
Plough St, E1
off Leman St 141 F2
Plough Ter, SW11 . . . . .179 D2
Plough Way, SE16 . . . . .157 D3
Plough Yd, EC2 . . . . .29 D3
Plover Way, SE16 . . . . .157 E2
Plowden Bldgs, EC4
off Middle Temple La 38 A4
Plumbers Row, E1 . . . . .142 A1
Plumbridge St, SE10
off Blackheath Hill 172 C3
Plumtree Ct, EC4 . . . . .38 B2
Plymouth Wf, E14 . . . . .159 D3
Plympton Av, NW6 . . . . .107 F4
Plympton Pl, NW8 . . . . .20 C3
Plympton Rd, NW6 . . . . .107 F4
Plympton St, NW8 . . . . .20 C3
Pocock St, SE1 . . . . .50 C4
Podium, The, E2
off Roman Rd 128 C3
Podmore Rd, SW18 . . . . .178 C2
Poets Rd, N5 . . . . .113 D2
Point Cl, SE10
off Point Hill 172 C3
Pointers Cl, E14 . . . . .158 B4
Point Hill, SE10 . . . . .172 C2
Point of Thomas Path, E1
off Glamis Rd 142 C3
Point Pl, Wem. HA9 . . . . . . .104 B4
Point Pleasant, SW18 . . . . . .178 A2
Point W, SW7 . . . . .55 D4
Poland Ho, E15 . . . . .131 D1
Poland St, W1 . . . . .35 F3
Polesworth Ho, W2 . . . . .18 B4
★ Polish Inst & Sikorski Mus,
SW7 *off Princes Gate* 56 B1
Pollard Cl, N7 . . . . .111 F2
Pollard Row, E2 . . . . .128 A3
Pollard St, E2 . . . . .128 A3
Pollen St, W1 . . . . .35 D3
Pollitt Dr, NW8 . . . . .20 A2
★ Pollock's Toy Mus, W1 . . .23 F4
Polperro Ms, SE11 . . . . .62 B4
Polygon, The, SW4
off Old Town 180 C2
Polygon Rd, NW1 . . . . .12 A3
Pomell Way, E1 . . . . .41 F2
Pomeroy St, SE14 . . . . .170 C3
Pomfret Rd, SE5
off Flaxman Rd 182 B1
Pomoja La, N19 . . . . .97 D3
Pond Cl, SE3 . . . . .173 F4
Ponder St, N7 . . . . .111 F4
Pond Fm Est, E5
off Millfields Rd 100 C4
Pond Mead, SE21 . . . . .183 D4
Pond Pl, SW3 . . . . .68 C1
Pond Rd, E15 . . . . .131 E2
SE3 . . . . .173 F4
Pond Sq, N6
off South Gro 96 A2
Pond St, NW3 . . . . .109 E2
Ponler St, E1 . . . . .142 B2
Ponsard Rd, NW10 . . . . .120 B3
Ponsford St, E9 . . . . .114 C3
Ponsonby Pl, SW1 . . . . .72 B2
Ponsonby Ter, SW1 . . . . .72 B2
Ponton Rd, SW8 . . . . .84 B1
Pont St, SW1 . . . . .57 E3
Pont St Ms, SW1 . . . . .57 E3
Pontypool Pl, SE1 . . . . .50 C4
Poole Ho, SE11
off Lambeth Wk 61 F3
Poole Rd, E9 . . . . .115 D3
Pooles Bldgs, EC1 . . . . .26 A3
Pooles La, SW10 . . . . .79 E3
Pooles Pk, N4 . . . . .98 A3
Poole St, N1 . . . . .16 A1
Pooley Dr, SW14
off Sheen La 174 C1
Poolmans St, SE16 . . . . .157 D1
Poonah St, E1
off Hardinge St 142 C2
Pope Ho, SE16
off Manor Est 156 B3
Pope's Head All, EC3
off Cornhill 40 B3
Popes Rd, SW9 . . . . .182 A1
Pope St, SE1 . . . . .65 D1
Popham Gdns, Rich. TW9
off Lower Richmond Rd .174 A1
Popham Rd, N1 . . . . .15 E1
Popham St, N1 . . . . .126 B1
● Popin Business Cen, Wem.
HA9 . . . . .104 B2
POPLAR, E14 . . . . .144 B3
DLR Poplar 144 B3
Poplar Bath St, E14
off Lawless St 144 B3
● Poplar Business Pk,
E14 . . . . .144 C3
Poplar Cl, E9
off Lee Conservancy Rd 115 F2
Poplar Gro, W6 . . . . .148 C1
Wembley HA9 . . . . .90 C4
Poplar High St, E14 . . . . . . .144 A3
Poplar Pl, W2 . . . . .30 C4
Poplar Rd, SE24 . . . . .182 C2
Poplars Av, NW10 . . . . .106 C3
Poplar Wk, SE24 . . . . .182 C2
Poppins Ct, EC4 . . . . .38 C3
Porchester Cl, SE5 . . . . .182 C2
Porchester Gdns, W2 . . . . . . .30 C4
Porchester Gdns Ms, W2 . . . . .31 D3
Porchester Gate, W2
off Bayswater Rd 43 E1
Porchester Ms, W2 . . . . .31 D2
Porchester Pl, W2 . . . . .33 D3
Porchester Rd, W2 . . . . .30 C2
Porchester Sq, W2 . . . . .31 D2
Porchester Sq Ms, W2 . . . . . .31 D2
Porchester Ter, W2 . . . . .31 E3
Porchester Ter N, W2 . . . . . . .31 D2
Porden Rd, SW2 . . . . .181 F2
Porlock St, SE1 . . . . .52 A4
Portal Way, W3 . . . . .133 D1
Portbury Cl, SE15
off Clayton Rd 170 A3
★ Portcullis Ho, SW1
off Bridge St 61 D1
Portelet Ct, N1
off De Beauvoir Est 127 E1
Portelet Rd, E1 . . . . .129 D3
Porten Rd, W14 . . . . .149 E2
Porter Sq, N19 . . . . .97 E2
Porter St, SE1 . . . . .51 F2
W1 .21 F4
Porters Wk, E1
off Tobacco Dock 142 B3
Porteus Rd, W2 . . . . .31 F1
Portgate Cl, W9 . . . . .121 F4
Portia Way, E3 . . . . .129 F4
Coll Portico City Learning Cen,
E5 *off Linscott Rd* 114 C1
Portinscale Rd,
SW15 . . . . .177 E3
Portland Av, N16 . . . . .99 F1
Portland Ct, SE1
off Falmouth Rd 64 A2
Portland Gro, SW8 . . . . .85 E4
H Portland Hosp for Women
& Children, The, W1 . . . . .23 D3
Portland Ms, W1 . . . . .35 F3
Portland Pl, W1 . . . . .22 C3
Portland Ri, N4 . . . . .98 B2
Portland Ri Est, N4 . . . . .98 B2
Portland Rd, W11 . . . . .135 E3
Portland Sq, E1
off Reardon St 142 B4
Portland St, SE17 . . . . .76 A2
Portland Wk, SE17 . . . . .76 B4
Portman Av, SW14 . . . . .175 D1
Portman Cl, W1 . . . . .33 F2
Portman Gate, NW1 . . . . .21 D3
Portman Ms S, W1 . . . . .34 A3
Portman Pl, E2 . . . . .128 C3
Portman Sq, W1 . . . . .33 F2
Portman St, W1 . . . . .34 A3
Portnall Rd, W9 . . . . .121 F2
Portobello Ct, W11
off Westbourne Gro 135 F2
Portobello Ms, W11 . . . . .42 A1
Portobello Rd, W10 . . . . . . .135 F2
W11 . . . . .135 F2
Portpool La, EC1 . . . . .26 A4
Portree St, E14 . . . . .145 D2
Portsea Ms, W2 . . . . .33 D3
Portsea Pl, W2 . . . . .33 D3
Portslade Rd, SW8 . . . . .166 C4
Portsmouth St, WC2 . . . . .37 E3
Portsoken St, E1 . . . . .41 E4
Portugal St, WC2 . . . . .37 E3
Portway, E15 . . . . .131 F1
Post Office Ct, EC3 . . . . .40 B3
Post Office Way, SW8 . . . . . . .84 A2
Potier St, SE1 . . . . .64 B3
Potters Cl, SE15 . . . . .89 D2
Potters Flds, SE1 . . . . .53 D3
Potters Rd, SW6 . . . . .164 C4
Pottery La, W11
off Penzance Pl 135 E4
Pottery St, SE16 . . . . .156 B1
Pott St, E2 . . . . .128 B3
Poulton Cl, E8
off Marcon Pl 114 B2
Poulton Ct, W3
off Victoria Rd 133 D1
Poultry, EC2 . . . . .40 A3
Pound La, NW10 . . . . .106 A3
Pountney Rd, SW11 . . . . . . .180 A1
Powell Rd, E5 . . . . .100 B4
Powell's Wk, W4 . . . . .161 E1

Powergate Business Pk, NW10 . . . . 119 D3
Power Rd, W4 . . . . 146 A3
Powerscroft Rd, E5 . . . . 114 C1
Powis Gdns, NW11 . . . . 93 F1
W11 . . . . 135 F2
Powis Ms, W11
off Westbourne Pk Rd . . . 135 F2
Powis Pl, WC1 . . . . 25 D3
Powis Rd, E3 . . . . 130 B3
Powis Sq, W11 . . . . 135 F2
Powis Ter, W11 . . . . 135 F2
Powlett Pl, NW1
off Harmood St 110 B3
Pownall Rd, E8 . . . . 17 F1
Poynders Ct, SW4
off Poynders Rd 180 C4
Poynders Rd, SW4 . . . . 180 C4
Poynings Rd, N19 . . . . 96 C4
Poynter Ho, W11 . . . . 135 D4
Poyntz Rd, SW11 . . . . 165 F4
Poyser St, E2 . . . . 128 B2
Praed Ms, W2 . . . . 32 B2
Praed St, W2 . . . . 32 C1
Prague Pl, SW2 . . . . 181 E3
Prah Rd, N4 . . . . 98 A3
Prairie St, SW8 . . . . 166 A4
Pratt Ms, NW1 . . . . 11 E1
Pratt St, NW1 . . . . 11 E1
Pratt Wk, SE11 . . . . 61 F4
Prayle Gro, NW2 . . . . 93 D2
Prebend Gdns, W4 . . . . 147 F2
W6 . . . . 147 F2
Prebend St, N1 . . . . 15 E1
Premier Cor, W9
off Kilburn La 121 F2
Premiere Pl, E14
off Garford St 144 A3
Premier Pk, NW10 . . . . 118 B1
Premier Pk Rd, NW10 . . . . . . 118 B2
Prendergast Rd, SE3 . . . . 187 E1
Prescot St, E1 . . . . 41 F4
Prescott Ho, SE17 . . . . 87 D1
Prescott Pl, SW4 . . . . 181 D1
President Dr, E1
off Waterman Way 142 B4
President St, EC1 . . . . 15 E4
Press Ct, SE1
off Marlborough Gro 156 A4
Press Rd, NW10 . . . . 91 D4
Prestage Way, E14 . . . . 144 C3
Prested Rd, SW11
off St. John's Hill 179 E2
Preston Cl, SE1 . . . . 64 C4
Preston Gdns, NW10
off Church Rd 105 E3
Preston Pl, NW2 . . . . 106 A3
Prestons Rd, E14 . . . . 158 C1
Prestwood St, N1 . . . . 15 F3
Pretoria Rd, E11 . . . . 103 D2
E16 . . . . 131 F3
Price's Ct, SW11 . . . . 179 D1
Prices Ms, N1 . . . . 125 F1
Price's St, SE1 . . . . 51 D3
Prichard Ct, N7
off Piper Cl 111 F2
Prideaux Pl, W3 . . . . 133 D3
WC1 . . . . 13 F4
Prideaux Rd, SW9 . . . . 181 E1
Priest Ct, EC2 . . . . 39 E2
Priestley Cl, N16 . . . . 99 F1
Priestley Way, NW2 . . . . 92 A2
Priestman Pt, E3
off Rainhill Way 130 B3
Priests Br, SW14 . . . . 175 E2
SW15 . . . . 175 E2
Prima Rd, SW9 . . . . 86 A2
Primrose Cl, E3 . . . . 130 A2
Primrose Gdns, NW3 . . . . . . 109 E3
PRIMROSE HILL, NW8 . . . . . . 123 F1
Primrose Hill, EC4 . . . . 38 B3
Primrose Hill Ct, NW3 . . . . . . 109 F4
Primrose Hill Rd, NW3 . . . . . 109 E4
Primrose Hill Studios, NW1
off Fitzroy Rd 124 A1
Primrose Ms, NW1
off Sharpleshall St 109 F4
Primrose Rd, E10 . . . . 102 B2
Primrose Sq, E9 . . . . 114 C4
Primrose St, EC2 . . . . 28 C4
Primrose Wk, SE14
off Alexandra St 171 E2
Primula St, W12 . . . . 134 A2
Prince Albert Rd, NW1 . . . . 9 D3
NW8 . . . . 9 D3
Prince Arthur Ms, NW3
off Perrins La 108 C1
Prince Arthur Rd, NW3 . . . . . 108 C2
Prince Charles Dr, NW4 . . . . . . 92 C1
Prince Charles Rd, SE3 . . . . . 173 F3
Prince Consort Rd, SW7 . . . . . 55 F2
Princedale Rd, W11 . . . . 135 E4
Prince Edward Rd, E9 . . . . . . 115 F3
Prince George Rd, N16 . . . . . 113 E1
Prince Henry's Room, EC4 . . . . 38 A3
Princelet St, E1 . . . . 29 F4
Prince of Orange La, SE10
off Greenwich High Rd . . 172 C2
Prince of Wales Dr, SW8 . . . . . 83 D3
SW11 . . . . 165 F3
Prince of Wales Gate, SW7 . . . . 44 C4
Prince of Wales Pas, NW1 . . . . 23 E1
Prince of Wales Rd, NW5 . . . 110 A3
SE3 . . . . 173 F3
Prince of Wales Ter, W4 . . . . 147 E4
W8 . . . . 55 D1
Prince Regent Ms, NW1 . . . . . 23 E1
Prince's Arc, SW1 . . . . 47 F2
Princes Av, W3 . . . . 146 A2
Princes Cl, N4 . . . . 98 B2
SW4 *off Old Town* 180 C1
Princes Ct, SE16 . . . . 157 F2
SW3 *off Brompton Rd* 57 E2
Princes Ct Business Cen, E1 . . . . 142 B3
Prince's Foundation, The, EC2 . . . . 28 C2
Princes Gdns, SW7 . . . . 56 B2
W3 . . . . 132 A1
Princes Gate, SW7 . . . . 56 C1
Princes Gate Ct, SW7 . . . . 56 B1
Princes Gate Ms, SW7 . . . . 56 B2
Princes Ms, W2 . . . . 30 C4
Princes Pl, SW1 . . . . 47 F2
W11 . . . . 135 E4
Princes Ri, SE13 . . . . 172 C4
Princes Riverside Rd, SE16 . . 143 D4
Princes Rd, SW14 . . . . 175 D1
Princess Cres, N4 . . . . 98 B3
Princess Grace Hosp, The, W1 . . . . 22 A3
Princess Louise Cl, W2 . . . . . . 20 B4
Princess May Rd, N16 . . . . . 113 E1
Princess Ms, NW3
off Belsize Cres 109 D3
Princes Sq, W2 . . . . 30 C4
Princess Rd, NW1 . . . . 124 A1
NW6 . . . . 6 A3
Princess St, SE1 . . . . 63 D3
Princes St, EC2 . . . . 40 A2
W1 . . . . 35 D3
Prince St, SE8 . . . . 171 F1
Princes Yd, W11
off Princedale Rd 135 E4
Princethorpe Ho, W2 . . . . 18 B4
Princeton Ct, SW15
off Felsham Rd 177 D1
Princeton St, WC1 . . . . 25 E4
Principal Sq, E9
off Chelmer Rd 115 D2
Printers Inn Ct, EC4 . . . . 38 A2
Printers Ms, E3 . . . . 129 E1
Printer St, EC4 . . . . 38 B2
Printing Ho Yd, E2 . . . . 17 D4
Print Village, SE15
off Chadwick Rd 169 F4
Prior Bolton St, N1 . . . . 112 B3
Prioress Ho, E3
off Bromley High St 130 B3
Prioress St, SE1 . . . . 64 B3
Prior St, SE10 . . . . 172 C2
Priory, The, SE3 . . . . 187 F2
Priory Av, W4 . . . . 147 E3
Priory Ct, EC4
off Carter La 39 D3
SW8 . . . . 167 D3
Priory Gdns, SW13 . . . . 175 F1
W4 . . . . 147 E3
Priory Grn Est, N1 . . . . 13 E2
Priory Gro, SW8 . . . . 167 E3
Priory Hts, N1 . . . . 13 E2
Priory Hosp, The, SW15 . . . . 175 F2
Priory La, SW15 . . . . 175 E4
Richmond TW9 . . . . 160 A2
Priory Ms, SW8 . . . . 167 D3
Priory Pk, SE3 . . . . 187 F1
Priory Pk Rd, NW6 . . . . 121 F1
Priory Rd, NW6 . . . . 122 B1
W4 . . . . 147 D2
Richmond TW9 . . . . 160 A1
Priory St, E3 . . . . 130 B3
Priory Ter, NW6 . . . . 122 B1
Priory Wk, SW10 . . . . 67 F3
Pritchard's Rd, E2 . . . . 128 A1
Priter Rd, SE16 . . . . 156 A2
Probert Rd, SW2 . . . . 182 A3
Probyn Ho, SW1
off Page St 60 B4
Procter Ho, SE1
off Avondale Sq 156 A4
Procter St, WC1 . . . . 37 E1
Promenade, The, W4 . . . . . . 161 E3
Promenade App Rd, W4 . . . . 161 E2
Prospect Cotts, SW18 . . . . . . 178 A2
Prospect Pl, E1 . . . . 142 C4
N7 *off Parkhurst Rd* 111 E1
NW2 *off Ridge Rd* 93 F4
NW3 *off Holly Wk* 108 C1
W4
off Chiswick High Rd . . . 147 D4
Prospect Quay, SW18 . . . . . . 178 A2
Prospect Rd, NW2 . . . . 93 F4
Prospect St, SE16
off Jamaica Rd 156 B1
Prospero Rd, N19 . . . . 96 C2
Protea Cl, E16
off Hermit Rd 131 F4
Prothero Rd, SW6 . . . . 163 E2
Prout Gro, NW10 . . . . 105 E1

Prout Rd, E5 . . . . .100 B4
Provence St, N1 . . . . .15 E2
Providence Cl, E9
off Wetherell Rd 129 D1
Providence Ct, W1 . . . . .34 B4
Providence Pl, N1
off Upper St 126 B1
Providence Row, N1
off Pentonville Rd 13 E3
Providence Row Cl, E2
off Ainsley St 128 B3
Providence Sq, SE1
off Jacob St 156 A1
Providence Yd, E2
off Ezra St 128 A3
Provost Est, N1 . . . . .16 A4
Provost Rd, NW3 . . . . .109 F4
Provost St, N1 . . . . .28 A1
Prowse Pl, NW1
off Bonny St 110 C4
Prudent Pas, EC2 . . . . .39 F2
Prusom St, E1 . . . . .142 B4
Pryors, The, NW3 . . . . .95 D4
P.S. Tattershall Castle, SW1 . . . . .49 D3
Pudding La, EC3 . . . . .52 B1
Pudding Mill Lane 130 B1
Pudding Mill La, E15 . . . . . . .130 B1
Puddle Dock, EC4 . . . . .39 D4
Pulham Ho, SW8
off Dorset Rd 85 E3
Pullman Gdns, SW15 . . . . . .176 C4
Pulross Rd, SW9 . . . . .181 F1
Pulse Apts, NW6
off Lymington Rd 108 B2
Pulteney Cl, E3 . . . . .129 F1
Pulteney Ter, N1 . . . . .13 F1
Pulton Pl, SW6 . . . . .78 A3
Puma Ct, E1 . . . . .29 E4
Pump Ct, EC4 . . . . .38 A3
Pump Ho Cl, SE16
off Renforth St 156 C1
Pumphouse Ed Mus, Rotherhithe, SE16 . . . . .143 E4
Pump Ho Ms, E1
off Hooper St 142 A3
Pumping Sta Rd, W4 . . . . . .161 E2
Pump La, SE14 . . . . .170 C2
Pundersons Gdns, E2 . . . . . .128 B3
Purbeck Dr, NW2 . . . . .93 E3
Purbeck Ho, SW8
off Bolney St 85 E3
Purbrook Est, SE1 . . . . .65 D1
Purbrook St, SE1 . . . . .65 D2
Purcell Cres, SW6 . . . . .163 E2
Purcell St, N1 . . . . .16 C2
Purchese St, NW1 . . . . .12 B2
Purdy St, E3 . . . . .130 B4
Purelake Ms, SE13 . . . . .187 D1
Purley Av, NW2 . . . . .93 E4
Purley Pl, N1
off Islington Pk St 112 B4
Purser's Cross Rd, SW6 . . . . .163 F3
Purves Rd, NW10 . . . . .120 C2
Puteaux Ho, E2 . . . . .129 D2
PUTNEY, SW15 . . . . .177 E2
Putney 177 E2
Putney Bridge 177 E1
Putney Br, SW6 . . . . .177 E1
SW15 . . . . .177 E1
Putney Br App, SW6 . . . . . . .177 E1
Putney Br Rd, SW15 . . . . . . .177 E2
SW18 . . . . .177 E2
Putney Common, SW15 . . . .176 C1
Putney Ex Shop Cen, SW15 . . . . .177 D2
PUTNEY HEATH, SW15 . . . . .176 C4
Putney Heath, SW15 . . . . . .176 C4
Putney Heath La, SW15 . . . .177 D4
Putney High St, SW15 . . . . .177 D2
Putney Hill, SW15 . . . . .177 D4
Putney Pk Av, SW15 . . . . . . .176 A2
Putney Pk La, SW15 . . . . . . .176 B2
Putney Pier 177 D1
Putney Sch of Art & Design, SW15 off Oxford Rd 177 E2
Putney Wf Twr, SW15 . . . . . .177 E1
Pylon Trd Est, E16 . . . . .131 D4
Pynfolds, SE16
off Paradise St 156 B1
Pyrland Rd, N5 . . . . .113 D2
Pyrmont Rd, W4 . . . . .160 A1
Pytchley Rd, SE22 . . . . .183 E1

Q

Quadrangle, The, SE24 . . . . .182 C3
SW10 . . . . .79 F4
W2 . . . . .32 C2
Quadrangle Cl, SE1 . . . . .64 C4
Quadrangle Ho, E15
off Romford Rd 117 E3
Quadrant Arc, W1 . . . . .47 F1
Quadrant Gro, NW5 . . . . . . .109 F2
Quainton St, NW10 . . . . .91 D4
Quaker Ct, E1 . . . . .29 E3
EC1 . . . . .28 A2
Quaker St, E1 . . . . .29 E3
Quality Ct, WC2 . . . . .38 A2
Quantock Gdns, NW2 . . . . . . .93 D3
Quantock Ms, SE15
off Choumert Gro 170 A4
Quarrendon St, SW6 . . . . . . .164 A4
Quarry Rd, SW18 . . . . .178 C4
Quarterdeck, The, E14 . . . . .158 A1
Quarter Mile La, E10 . . . . . . .116 B1
Quebec Ms, W1 . . . . .33 F3
Quebec Way, SE16 . . . . .157 D1
Queen Anne Ms, W1 . . . . .35 D1
Queen Anne Rd, E9 . . . . . . .115 D3
Queen Anne's Gdns, W4 . . . .147 E2
Queen Anne's Gate, SW1 . . . .60 A1
Queen Anne's Gro, W4 . . . . .147 E2
Queen Annes Sq, SE1
off Monnow Rd 156 A3
Queen Anne St, W1 . . . . .34 C2
Queen Anne's Wk, WC1
off Queen Sq 25 D3
Queen Anne Ter, E1
off Sovereign Cl 142 B3
Queen Caroline Est, W6 . . . .148 C4
Queen Caroline St, W6 . . . . .148 C3
Queen Charlotte's & Chelsea Hosp, W12 . . . . .134 A2
Queen Elizabeth Hall & Purcell Room, SE1 . . . . .49 E2
Queen Elizabeths Cl, N16 . . . .99 D3
Queen Elizabeth's Coll, SE10
off Greenwich High Rd . .172 C2
Queen Elizabeth II Conf Cen, SW1 . . . . .60 B1
Queen Elizabeth St, SE1 . . . . .53 D4
Queen Elizabeths Wk, N16 . . .99 D3
Queen Elizabeth Wk, SW13 . . . . .162 B3
Queenhithe, EC4 . . . . .39 F4
Queen Margaret's Gro, N1 . .113 E2
Queen Mary, Mile End Campus, E1
off Mile End Rd 129 E4
Queen Mary - Barts & The London Sch of Med & Dentistry, EC1 . . . . .27 D3
Royal London Hosp, E1
off Turner St 142 B1
Queen Marys Bldgs, SW1
off Stillington St 59 F4
Queen Mary's Gdns, NW1 . . . . .22 A1
Queen Mary's Hosp, NW3 . . . . .94 C4
Queen Mary's Hosp (Roehampton), SW15 . . .176 A4
Queen of Denmark Ct, SE16 . . . . .157 F2
Queensberry Ms W, SW7 . . . .56 A4
Queensberry Pl, SW7 . . . . . . .56 A4
Queensberry Way, SW7 . . . . .56 A4
Queensborough Ms, W2 . . . . .31 E4
Queensborough Pas, W2 . . . .31 E4
Queensborough Studios, W2 .31 E4
Queensborough Ter, W2 . . . . .31 D4
Queensbridge Rd, E2 . . . . . .127 F1
E8 . . . . .113 F4
Queensbury Rd, NW9 . . . . . . .91 D1
Queensbury St, N1 . . . . .112 C4
Queen's Circ, SW8 . . . . .82 C3
SW11 . . . . .82 C3
Queens Club (Tennis Cen), W14 . . . . .149 E4
Queens Club Gdns, W14 . . . .163 E1
Queen's Cres, NW5 . . . . .110 A3
Queensdale Cres, W11 . . . . .135 D4
Queensdale Pl, W11 . . . . . . .135 E4
Queensdale Rd, W11 . . . . . . .135 D4
Queensdale Wk, W11 . . . . . .135 E4
Queensdown Rd, E5 . . . . . . .114 B1
Queens Dr, E10 . . . . .102 A1
N4 .98 B3
Queens Elm Par, SW3
off Old Ch St 68 B2
Queen's Elm Sq, SW3 . . . . . . .68 B3
Queen's Gall, The, SW1 . . . . .59 D1
Queens Gdns, W2 . . . . .31 E4
Queen's Gate, SW7 . . . . .55 F1
Queen's Gate Gdns, SW7 . . . .55 F3
Queens Gate Gdns, SW15 . . .176 B2
Queensgate Ho, E3
off Hereford Rd 129 F2
Queen's Gate Ms, SW7 . . . . . .55 F1
Queensgate Pl, NW6 . . . . . .108 A4
Queen's Gate Pl, SW7 . . . . . . .55 F3
Queen's Gate Pl Ms, SW7 . . . .55 F3
Queen's Gate Ter, SW7 . . . . . .55 E2
Queen's Gro, NW8 . . . . .8 A1
Queen's Gro Ms, NW8 . . . . .8 A1
Queen's Head Pas, EC4 . . . . . .39 E2
Queen's Head St, N1 . . . . .15 D1
Queens Head Yd, SE1 . . . . . . .52 A3
Queen's Ho, The, SE10 . . . . .173 D1
Queen's Ice & Bowl, W2 . . . . .43 D1
Queensland Rd, N7 . . . . .112 A1
Queensmead, NW8 . . . . .123 D1
Queens Ms, W2 . . . . .31 D4
Queensmill Rd, SW6 . . . . . . .163 D2
Queen's Park 121 E2
Queen's Park 121 E2

Queens Pk Ct, W10 . . . . .121 D3
★ Queens Park Rangers FC, W12 . . . . .134 B4
Queen Sq, WC1 . . . . .25 D3
Queen Sq Pl, WC1 . . . . .25 D3
Queens Ride, SW13 . . . . . . .176 A1
SW15 . . . . .176 A1
Queens Rd, E11 . . . . .103 D1
SE14 . . . . .170 B3
SE15 . . . . .170 B3
SW14 . . . . .175 D1
⇌ Queens Road Peckham .170 C3
Queen's Row, SE17 . . . . .76 A4
Queen's Ter, NW8 . . . . .8 A2
★ Queen's Twr, SW7 . . . . . .56 A2
Queenstown Ms, SW8
off Queenstown Rd 166 B3
Queenstown Rd, SW8 . . . . . . .82 C1
⇌ Queenstown Road (Battersea) 83 D4
Queen St, EC4 . . . . .39 F4
W1 . . . . .46 C2
Queen St Pl, EC4 . . . . .51 F1
Queens Wk, NW9 . . . . .90 C3
Queen's Wk, SW1 . . . . .47 E3
Queen's Wk, The, SE1 . . . . . . .49 E3
⊖ Queensway 43 D1
Queensway, W2 . . . . .31 D3
Queens Yd, WC1 . . . . .23 F3
★ Queen Victoria Mem, SW1 . . . . .47 E4
Queen Victoria St, EC4 . . . . . .39 D4
Queen Victoria Ter, E1
off Sovereign Cl 142 B3
Quemerford Rd, N7 . . . . . . .111 F2
Quentin Pl, SE13 . . . . .187 E1
Quentin Rd, SE13 . . . . .187 E1
Querrin St, SW6 . . . . .164 C4
Quex Ms, NW6
off Quex Rd 122 A1
Quex Rd, NW6 . . . . .122 A1
Quick Rd, W4 . . . . .147 E4
Quick St, N1 . . . . .15 D3
Quick St Ms, N1 . . . . .14 C3
Quickswood, NW3
off King Henry's Rd 109 E4
Quill La, SW15 . . . . .177 D2
Quill St, N4 . . . . .98 A4
Quilp St, SE1 . . . . .51 E4
Quilter St, E2 . . . . .128 A3
Quilting Ct, SE16
off Poolmans St 157 D1
Quince Rd, SE13 . . . . .172 B4
Quixley St, E14 . . . . .145 D3
Quorn Rd, SE22 . . . . .183 E2

R

Rabbit Row, W8 . . . . .42 B2
Raby St, E14
off Salmon La 143 E2
Racton Rd, SW6 . . . . .78 A1
Radbourne Cl, E5 . . . . .115 D1
Radcliffe Av, NW10 . . . . .120 A2
Radcliffe Path, SW8
off Robertson St 166 B4
Radcliffe Rd, SE1 . . . . .65 D2
Radcliffe Sq, SW15 . . . . .177 D4
Radcot St, SE11 . . . . .74 B3
Raddington Rd, W10 . . . . . .135 E1
Radford Rd, SE13 . . . . .186 C4
Radipole Rd, SW6 . . . . .163 F3
Radland Rd, E16 . . . . .145 F2
Radlett Cl, E7 . . . . .117 F3
Radlett Pl, NW8 . . . . .123 E1
Radley Ct, SE16
off Marlow Way 157 D1
Radley Ms, W8 . . . . .54 B3
Radley Sq, E5
off Dudlington Rd 100 C3
Radlix Rd, E10 . . . . .102 A2
Radnor Ms, W2 . . . . .32 B3
Radnor Pl, W2 . . . . .32 C3
Radnor Rd, NW6 . . . . .121 E1
SE15 . . . . .170 A2
Radnor St, EC1 . . . . .27 F1
Radnor Ter, W14 . . . . .149 F3
Radnor Wk, E14
off Copeland Dr 158 A3
SW3 . . . . .69 D3
Radnor Way, NW10 . . . . . . .118 B4
Radstock St, SW11 . . . . .80 C3
Raeburn St, SW2 . . . . .181 E2
Raft Rd, SW18
off North Pas 178 A2
★ Ragged Sch Mus, E3
off Copperfield Rd 143 E1
Raglan St, NW5 . . . . .110 B3
Ragley Cl, W3
off Church Rd 146 C1
Rahere Ho, EC1 . . . . .15 E4
Railey Ms, NW5 . . . . .110 C2
Railton Rd, SE24 . . . . .182 A2
Railway App, SE1 . . . . .52 B2
Railway Arches, W12
off Shepherds Bush Mkt .148 C1
Railway Av, SE16 . . . . .156 C1
Railway Ms, E3
off Wellington Way 130 A3
W10
off Ladbroke Gro 135 E2
Railway Ri, SE22
off Grove Vale 183 E2
Railway Side, SW13 . . . . . . .175 E1
Railway St, N1 . . . . .13 D3
Railway Ter, SE13
off Ladywell Rd 186 B3
Rainborough Cl, NW10 . . . . .104 C3
Rainbow Av, E14 . . . . .158 B4
Rainbow Quay, SE16 . . . . . .157 E2
Rainbow St, SE5 . . . . .88 C3
Raines Ct, N16
off Northwold Rd 99 F3
Raine St, E1 . . . . .142 B4
Rainham Cl, SW11 . . . . .179 E4
Rainham Rd, NW10 . . . . . . .120 C3
Rainhill Way, E3 . . . . .130 A3
Rainsborough Av, SE8 . . . . .157 E3
Rainsford Rd, NW10 . . . . . . .118 B3
Rainsford St, W2 . . . . .32 C2
Rainville Rd, W6 . . . . .162 C1
Raleana Rd, E14 . . . . .144 C4
Raleigh Gdns, SW2
off Brixton Hill 181 F4
Raleigh Ms, N1
off Queen's Head St 15 D1
Raleigh St, N1 . . . . .15 D1
Ralph Ct, W2 . . . . .31 D2
Ralston St, SW3 . . . . .69 E3
Ramilles Cl, SW2 . . . . .181 E4
Ramillies Pl, W1 . . . . .35 E3
Ramillies Rd, W4 . . . . .147 D3
Ramillies St, W1 . . . . .35 E3
Rampart St, E1
off Commercial Rd 142 B2
Rampayne St, SW1 . . . . .72 A2
Ram Pl, E9
off Chatham Pl 114 C3
Ramsay Ms, SW3 . . . . .68 C4
Ramsay Rd, E7 . . . . .117 E1
W3 . . . . .146 C2
Ramsden Rd, SW12 . . . . . . .180 A4
Ramsey Ho, SW11
off Maysoule Rd 179 D2
Ramsey St, E2 . . . . .128 A4
Ramsey Wk, N1 . . . . .113 D3
Ramsfort Ho, SE16
off Manor Est 156 B3
Ramsgate St, E8
off Dalston La 113 F3
Ram St, SW18 . . . . .178 B3
Randall Av, NW2 . . . . .91 F4
Randall Cl, SW11 . . . . .80 C4
Randall Pl, SE10 . . . . .172 C2
Randall Rd, SE11 . . . . .73 E2
Randall Row, SE11 . . . . .73 E1
Randell's Rd, N1 . . . . .125 E1
Randolph Av, W9 . . . . .19 F2
Randolph Cres, W9 . . . . .19 E3
Randolph Gdns, NW6 . . . . .6 C3
Randolph Ms, W9 . . . . .19 F3
Randolph Rd, W9 . . . . .19 E3
Randolph St, NW1 . . . . .110 C4
Ranelagh Av, SW6 . . . . .177 F1
SW13 . . . . .162 A4
Ranelagh Br, W2
off Gloucester Ter 31 D1
★ Ranelagh Gdns, SW3 . . . .70 A3
Ranelagh Gdns, SW6 . . . . . .177 F1
W4 . . . . .160 C2
W6 . . . . .147 F2
Ranelagh Gdns Mans, SW6
off Ranelagh Gdns 177 E1
Ranelagh Gro, SW1 . . . . .70 B2
Ranelagh Rd, E11 . . . . .117 E1
E15 . . . . .131 E1
NW10 . . . . .119 F2
SW1 . . . . .71 F3
Rangers Sq, SE10 . . . . .173 D3
Rangoon St, EC3 . . . . .41 E3
Rankine Ho, SE1
off Bath Ter 63 E3
Rannoch Rd, W6 . . . . .162 C1
Rannock Av, NW9 . . . . .91 E1
● Ransome's Dock Business Cen, SW11 . . . . .81 D3
Ranston St, NW1 . . . . .20 C4
Ranulf Rd, NW2 . . . . .107 F1
Ranwell Cl, E3
off Beale Rd 129 F1
Ranwell St, E3 . . . . .129 F1
Raphael St, SW7 . . . . .57 E1
Rashleigh St, SW8
off Peardon St 166 B4
Ratcliffe Cross St, E1 . . . . .143 D2
Ratcliffe La, E14 . . . . .143 E2
Ratcliffe Orchard, E1
off Cranford St 143 D3
Coll Rathbone Ed Cen, The, E16
off Barking Rd 145 F1
🔒 Rathbone Mkt, E16
off Barking Rd 145 F1
Rathbone Pl, W1 . . . . .36 A2
Rathbone St, E16 . . . . .145 F1
W1 .35 F1
Rathgar Rd, SW9
off Coldharbour La 182 B1
Rathmell Dr, SW4 . . . . .181 D4
Rattray Rd, SW2 . . . . .182 A2
Raul Rd, SE15 . . . . .170 A4
Raveley St, NW5 . . . . .110 C1

Raven Ct, E5
off *Stellman Cl* **100** A4
Ravenet St, SW11
off *Strasburg Rd* **166** B3
Ravenna Rd, SW15 **177** D3
Raven Row, E1 **142** B1
Ravensbourne Pl, SE13 **172** B4
Ravenscourt Av, W6 **148** A3
Ravenscourt Gdns, W6 **148** A3
Ravenscourt Park **148** A3
Ravenscourt Pk, W6 **148** A2
Ravenscourt Pl, W6 **148** B3
Ravenscourt Rd, W6 **148** B3
Ravenscourt Sq, W6 **148** A2
Ravenscroft Av, NW11 **93** F1
Ravenscroft Pt, E9
off *Kenton Rd* **115** D3
Ravenscroft Rd, W4 **146** C3
Ravenscroft St, E2 **17** F3
Ravensdale Rd, N16 **99** F1
Ravensdon St, SE11 **74** B3
Ravenshaw St, NW6 **107** F2
Ravensmede Way, W4 **147** F3
Ravenstone, SE17 **77** D3
Ravensworth Rd, NW10 **120** B3
Ravey St, EC2 **28** C2
Rav Pinter Cl, N16 **99** E1
Rawlings Cres, Wem. HA9 **90** B4
Rawlings St, SW3 **57** E4
Rawlinson Ho, SE13
off *Mercator Rd* **187** D2
Rawreth Wk, N1
off *Basire St* **126** C1
Rawson Ct, SW11
off *Strasburg Rd* **166** B3
Rawson St, SW11
off *Alfreda St* **166** B3
Rawstorne Pl, EC1 **14** C4
Rawstorne St, EC1 **14** C4
Raydon St, N19 **96** B3
Raymond Bldgs, WC1 **25** F4
Raymouth Rd, SE16 **156** B3
Rayners Rd, SW15 **177** E3
Rayner Twrs, E10 **102** A1
Raynham, W2 **32** C3
Raynham Rd, W6 **148** B3
Raynor Pl, N1
off *Elizabeth Av* **126** C1
Ray St, EC1 **26** B3
Ray St Br, EC1 **26** B3
Ray Wk, N7
off *Andover Rd* **97** F3
Reachview Cl, NW1
off *Baynes St* **110** C4
Reading La, E8 **114** B3
Reapers Cl, NW1
off *Crofters Way* **125** D1
Reardon Path, E1 **142** B4
Reardon St, E1 **142** B4
Reaston St, SE14 **170** C2
Reckitt Rd, W4 **147** E4
Record St, SE15 **170** C1
Rector St, N1 **15** E1
Rectory Gdns, SW4
off *Fitzwilliam Rd* **180** C1
Rectory Gro, SW4 **180** C1
Rectory Road **100** A4
Rectory Rd, N16 **99** F4
SW13 **162** A4
W3 **132** B4
Rectory Sq, E1 **143** D1
Reculver Rd, SE16 **157** D4
Red Anchor Cl, SW3 **80** C1
Redan Pl, W2 **30** C3
Redan St, W14 **149** D2
Redan Ter, SE5
off *Flaxman Rd* **168** C4
Redbridge Gdns, SE5 **89** D3
Redburn St, SW3 **69** E4
Redcar St, SE5 **87** E3
Redcastle Cl, E1 **142** C3
Redchurch St, E2 **29** E2
Redcliffe Cl, SW5
off *Old Brompton Rd* **66** C3
Redcliffe Ct, E5
off *Napoleon Rd* **100** B4
Redcliffe Gdns, SW5 **67** D3
SW10 **67** D3
W4 **160** B2
Redcliffe Ms, SW10 **67** D3
Redcliffe Pl, SW10 **79** E1
Redcliffe Rd, SW10 **67** E3
Redcliffe Sq, SW10 **67** D3
Redcliffe St, SW10 **67** D4
Redcross Way, SE1 **51** F4
Reddington Ho, N1 **13** F2
Reddins Rd, SE15 **170** A1
Rede Pl, W2 **30** B3
Redesdale St, SW3 **69** D4
Redfern Rd, NW10 **105** E4
Redfield La, SW5 **54** B4
Redfield Ms, SW5 **54** B4
Redford Wk, N1
off *Britannia Row* **126** B1
Redgate Ter, SW15 **177** E4
Redgrave Rd, SW15 **177** D1
Redhill St, NW1 **11** D4
Red Ho Sq, N1
off *Ashby Gro* **112** C4
Redington Gdns, NW3 **108** B1
Redington Rd, NW3 **108** B1
Red Lion Cl, SE17 **75** F4
Red Lion Ct, EC4 **38** B2
Red Lion Row, SE17 **75** F4
Red Lion Sq, SW18
off *Wandsworth High St* **178** A3
WC1 **37** E1
Red Lion St, WC1 **25** E4
Red Lion Yd, W1 **46** B2
Redman's Rd, E1 **142** C1
Redmead La, E1
off *Wapping High St* **142** A4
Redmore Rd, W6 **148** B3
Red Path, E9 **115** F3
Red Pl, W1 **34** A4
Red Post Hill, SE21 **183** D3
SE24 **183** D2
Redriffe Rd, E13 **131** F1
Redriff Est, SE16 **157** E2
Redriff Rd, SE16 **157** D3
Jct Red Rover, SW15 **175** F1
Redruth Rd, E9 **129** D1
Red Sq, N16 **99** D4
Redstart Cl, SE14
off *Southerngate Way* **171** E2
Redvers St, N1 **17** D4
Redwald Rd, E5 **115** D1
Redwing Ms, SE5
off *Vaughan Rd* **168** C4
Redwood Cl, E3 **130** A2
SE16 **143** E4
Redwood Ct, NW6
off *The Avenue* **107** E4
Redwood Ms, SW4
off *Hannington Rd* **180** B1
Reece Ms, SW7 **56** A4
Reedham St, SE15 **170** A4
Reedholm Vil, N16 **113** D1
Reed Pl, SW4 **181** D2
Reeds Pl, NW1
off *Royal Coll St* **110** C4
Reedworth St, SE11 **74** B1
Rees St, N1 **15** F1
Reeves Av, NW9 **91** D1
Reeves Ms, W1 **46** A1
Reeves Rd, E3 **130** B4
Reform St, SW11 **165** F4
Regal Cl, E1
off *Old Montague St* **142** A1
Regal Ho, SW6
off *Lensbury Av* **164** C4
Regal La, NW1 **10** B1
Regal Pl, E3
off *Coborn St* **129** F3
SW6 **79** D3
Regal Row, SE15
off *Astbury Rd* **170** C3
Regan Way, N1 **16** C3
Regency Ho, SW6
off *The Boulevard* **164** C3
Regency Ms, NW10 **106** A3
SW9 **87** D3
Regency Pl, SW1 **60** B4
Regency St, NW10 **119** E4
SW1 **60** A4
Regency Ter, SW7
off *Fulham Rd* **68** A2
Regeneration Rd, SE16 **157** D3
Regent Pl, W1 **35** F4
Regent Rd, SE24 **182** B4
Regents Br Gdns, SW8 **85** D2
Coll Regent's Coll, NW1 **22** A2
Regents Ms, NW8 **7** F2
REGENT'S PARK, NW1 **10** B3
Regent's Park **22** C3
★ Regent's Park, The, NW1 **9** F3
Regent's Pk Est, NW1 **23** D1
Regents Pk Rd, NW1 **123** F1
Regents Pk Ter, NW1
off *Oval Rd* **124** B1
Regent Sq, E3 **130** B3
WC1 **25** D1
Regents Row, E8 **128** A1
Regent St, NW10
off *Wellington Rd* **121** D3
SW1 **48** A1
W1 **35** D2
W4 **146** A4
Regents Wf, N1 **13** E2
Reginald Rd, SE8 **172** A2
Reginald Sq, SE8 **172** A2
Regina Pt, SE16
off *Renforth St* **156** C2
Regina Rd, N4 **97** F2
Regis Pl, SW2 **181** F2
Regis Rd, NW5 **110** B2
Regnart Bldgs, NW1 **23** F2
Reighton Rd, E5 **100** A4
Reizel Cl, N16 **99** F2
Relay Rd, W12 **134** C4
Relf Rd, SE15 **184** A1
Reliance Sq, EC2 **29** D2
Relton Ms, SW7 **57** D2
Rembrandt Cl, E14 **159** D2
SW1 **70** A1
Rembrandt Rd, SE13 **187** E2
Remington St, N1 **15** D3
Remnant St, WC2 **37** E2
Remus Rd, E3
off *Monier Rd* **116** A4
Renaissance Wk, SE10 **159** F2
Rendlesham Rd, E5 **114** A1

Renforth St, SE16 . . . . **156** C1
Renfrew Rd, SE11 . . . . **62** C4
Rennell St, SE13 . . . . **186** C1
Rennie Ct, SE1
off Upper Grd **50** C2
Rennie Est, SE16 . . . . **156** B3
Rennie Ho, SE1
off Bath Ter **63** E3
Rennie St, SE1 . . . . **50** C2
Rephidim St, SE1 . . . . **64** C3
Reporton Rd, SW6 . . . . **163** E3
Repton St, E14 . . . . **143** E2
Reservoir Rd, SE4 . . . . **171** E4
Resolution Way, SE8
off Deptford High St **172** A2
Restell Cl, SE3 . . . . **173** E1
Reston Pl, SW7 . . . . **55** E1
Restoration Sq, SW11
off Battersea High St . . . **165** D3
Retcar Cl, N19
off Dartmouth Pk Hill **96** B3
Retcar Pl, N19 . . . . **96** B3
Retford St, N1 . . . . **17** D3
Retreat, The, SW14
off South Worple Way . . **175** E1
Retreat Pl, E9 . . . . **114** C3
Reunion Row, E1
off Tobacco Dock **142** B3
Reuters Plaza, E14
off The South Colonnade **144** B4
Reveley Sq, SE16
off Howland Way **157** E1
Revelon Rd, SE4 . . . . **185** E2
Reverdy Rd, SE1 . . . . **156** A3
Review Rd, NW2 . . . . **91** F3
Rewell St, SW6 . . . . **79** E3
Rex Pl, W1 . . . . **46** B1
Reynard Cl, SE4
off Foxwell St **185** E1
Reynard Pl, SE14
off Milton Ct Rd **171** E1
Reynolds Cl, NW11 . . . . **94** B1
Reynolds Ct, E11
off Cobbold Rd **103** F4
Reynolds Rd, SE15 . . . . **184** C3
W4 . . . . **146** C2
Rheidol Ms, N1 . . . . **15** E2
Rheidol Ter, N1 . . . . **15** D2
Rhoda St, E2 . . . . **29** F2
Rhodesia Rd, E11 . . . . **103** D3
SW9 . . . . **167** E4
Rhodes St, N7
off Mackenzie Rd **111** F2
Rhodeswell Rd, E14 . . . . . . **143** E1
Rhondda Gro, E3 . . . . **129** E3
Rhyl St, NW5 . . . . **110** A3
Ribbon Dance Ms, SE5
off Camberwell Gro **169** D3
Ricardo St, E14 . . . . **144** B2
Richard Foster Cl, E17 . . . . **101** F1
Richard Robert Res, The, E15 *off Broadway* **117** D3
Richardson Cl, E8
off Clarissa St **127** F1
Richardson Rd, E15 . . . . **131** E2
Richardson's Ms, W1 . . . . **23** E3
Richards Pl, SW3 . . . . **57** D4
Richard St, E1
off Commercial Rd **142** B2
Richbell Pl, WC1 . . . . **25** E4
Richborne Ter, SW8 . . . . **85** F2
Richborough Ho, E5
off Pembury Rd **114** B2
Richborough Rd, NW2 . . . . . **107** D1
Richbourne Ct, W1
off Harrowby St **33** D2
Richford Gate, W6
off Richford St **148** C2
Richford Rd, E15 . . . . **131** F1
Richford St, W6 . . . . **148** C1
● Rich Ind Est, SE1 . . . . **65** D3
Rich La, SW5 . . . . **66** C3
★ Rich Mix Cen, The, E1
off Bethnal Grn Rd **29** F2
Richmond Av, N1 . . . . **125** F1
NW10 . . . . **106** C3
Richmond Bldgs, W1 . . . . **36** A3
Richmond Cres, N1 . . . . **125** F1
Richmond Gro, N1 . . . . **112** B4
Richmond Ho, NW1
off Park Village E **11** D3
Richmond Ms, W1 . . . . **36** A3
Richmond Pk Rd, SW14 . . . . **174** C3
Richmond Rd, E8 . . . . **113** F4
E11 . . . . **103** D3
Richmond Ter, SW1 . . . . **48** C4
Uni Richmond Uni - The American Int Uni In London, Kensington Campus, W8 . . . . **55** D2
Richmond Way, W12 . . . . . . **149** D1
W14 . . . . **149** D2
Rich St, E14 . . . . **143** F3
Rickett St, SW6 . . . . **66** B4
Rickman St, E1
off Mantus Rd **128** C3
Rick Roberts Way, E15 . . . . **130** C1
Rickthorne Rd, N19 . . . . **97** E3
Ridgdale St, E3 . . . . **130** B2
Ridge Hill, NW11 . . . . **93** E2
Ridge Rd, NW2 . . . . **93** F4
Ridgeway, The, NW11 . . . . . . **93** F2
W3 . . . . **146** A1
Ridgeway Gdns, N6 . . . . **96** C1
Ridgeway Rd, SW9 . . . . **182** B1
Ridgewell Cl, N1
off Basire St **126** C1
Ridgmount Gdns, WC1 . . . . . . **24** A3
Ridgmount Pl, WC1 . . . . **24** A4
Ridgmount Rd, SW18 . . . . . . **178** B3
Ridgmount St, WC1 . . . . **24** A4
Riding Ho St, W1 . . . . **35** E1
Ridings Cl, N6 . . . . **96** C1
Ridley Rd, E8 . . . . **113** F2
NW10 . . . . **120** A2
Riffel Rd, NW2 . . . . **106** C2
Rifle Ct, SE11 . . . . **74** B4
Rifle Pl, W11
off St. Anns Rd **135** D4
Rifle St, E14 . . . . **144** B1
Riga Ms, E1
off Commercial Rd **142** A2
Rigault Rd, SW6 . . . . **163** E4
Rigden St, E14 . . . . **144** B2
Rigeley Rd, NW10 . . . . **120** A3
Rigg App, E10 . . . . **101** D2
Rigge Pl, SW4 . . . . **181** D2
Riley Rd, SE1 . . . . **65** D2
Riley St, SW10 . . . . **80** A2
Ring, The, W2 . . . . **32** C4
Ringcroft St, N7 . . . . **112** A2
Ringford Rd, SW18 . . . . **177** F3
Ringmer Av, SW6 . . . . **163** E3
Ringmer Gdns, N19 . . . . **97** E3
Ringmer Ho, SE22
off Pytchley Rd **183** E1
Ring Rd, W12 . . . . **134** C3
Ringwood Gdns, E14
off Inglewood Cl **158** A3
Ripley Gdns, SW14 . . . . **175** D1
★ Ripley's Believe It or Not!, W1 . . . . **48** A1
Ripplevale Gro, N1 . . . . **111** F4
Risborough, SE17
off Deacon Way **63** E4
Risborough St, SE1 . . . . **51** D4
Risdon St, SE16 . . . . **156** C1
Rise, The, NW10 . . . . **105** D1
Riseholme Ho, SE22
off Albrighton Rd **183** E1
Riseldine Rd, SE23 . . . . **185** E4
Risinghill St, N1 . . . . **13** F2
Rising Sun Ct, EC1 . . . . **39** D1
Rita Rd, SW8 . . . . **85** D1
Ritchie St, N1 . . . . **14** B2
Ritson Rd, E8 . . . . **114** A3
Rivaz Pl, E9 . . . . **114** C3
River Barge Cl, E14
off Stewart St **158** C1
River Ct, SE1 . . . . **50** C1
Rivercourt Rd, W6 . . . . **148** B3
Riverdale, SE13
off Lewisham High St . . . **186** C1
Rivermead Ct, SW6 . . . . **177** F1
Rivermead Ho, E9
off Kingsmead Way **115** E2
Rivermill, SW1 . . . . **72** B3
River Pl, N1 . . . . **112** C4
Riversdale Rd, N5 . . . . **98** B4
Rivers Ho, Brent. TW8
off Chiswick High Rd . . . **146** A4
Riverside, NW4 . . . . **92** B1
Riverside Cl, E5 . . . . **100** C2
Riverside Ct, SW8 . . . . **72** B4
Riverside Dr, W4 . . . . **161** E2
Riverside Gdns, W6 . . . . **148** B4
Riverside Mans, E1
off Milk Yd **142** C3
Riverside Rd, E15 . . . . **130** C2
Riverside Twr, SW6 . . . . **164** C4
Riverside Wk, E14
off Ferry St **158** C4
River St, EC1 . . . . **14** A4
River Ter, W6
off Crisp Rd **148** C4
Riverton Cl, W9 . . . . **121** F3
Riverview Gdns, SW13 . . . . . **162** B1
Riverview Gro, W4 . . . . **160** B1
River Vw Hts, SE16
off Bermondsey Wall W . **156** A1
Riverview Rd, W4 . . . . **160** B2
River Way, SE10 . . . . **159** F2
Rivet Ho, SE1 . . . . **77** F2
Rivington Ct, NW10 . . . . **120** A1
Rivington Pl, EC2 . . . . **29** D1
Rivington St, EC2 . . . . **28** C1
Rivington Wk, E8
off Wilde Cl **128** A1
Rixon St, N7 . . . . **98** A4
Roach Rd, E3 . . . . **116** A4
Roads Pl, N19 . . . . **97** E3
Roan St, SE10 . . . . **172** C1
Robert Adam St, W1 . . . . **34** A2
Roberta St, E2 . . . . **128** A3
Robert Burns Ms, SE24
off Mayall Rd **182** B3
Robert Cl, W9 . . . . **19** F3
Robert Dashwood Way, SE17 . . . . **75** E1
Robert Keen Cl, SE15
off Cicely Rd **170** A3

Robert Lowe Cl, SE14 **171** D2
Robert Owen Ho, SW6 **163** D3
Roberts Cl, SE16 **157** D1
Roberts Ms, SW1 **58** A3
Robertson Rd, E15 **130** C1
Robertson St, SW8 **180** B1
Robert's Pl, EC1 **26** B2
Robert Sq, SE13 **186** C2
Robert St, NW1 **23** D1
WC2 **49** D1
Robert Sutton Ho, E1
off Tarling St **142** C2
Robeson St, E3
off Ackroyd Dr **143** F1
Robin Ct, SE16 **156** A3
Robin Gro, N6 **96** A3
Robin Hood Gdns, E14
off Woolmore St **144** C3
Robin Hood La, E14 **144** C3
Robin Ho, NW8
off Newcourt St **8** C3
Robinia Cres, E10 **102** B3
Robinscroft Ms, SE10
off Sparta St **172** B3
Robinson Cl, E11 **103** E4
Robinson Ho, W10
off Bramley Rd **135** D2
Robinson Rd, E2 **128** C2
Robinson St, SW3 **69** E4
Robinswood Ms, N5 **112** B2
Robsart St, SW9 **167** F4
Robson Av, NW10 **120** A1
Rocastle Rd, SE4 **185** E3
Rochdale Rd, E17 **102** A1
Rochdale Way, SE8
off Octavius St **172** A2
Rochelle Cl, SW11 **179** D2
Rochelle St, E2 **29** E1
Rochemont Wk, E8 **17** F1
Rochester Ms, NW1 **110** C4
Rochester Pl, NW1 **110** C3
Rochester Rd, NW1 **110** C3
Rochester Row, SW1 **59** F4
Rochester Sq, NW1 **110** C4
Rochester St, SW1 **60** A3
Rochester Ter, NW1 **110** C3
Rochester Wk, SE1 **52** A2
Rochford St, NW5 **109** F2
Rochford Wk, E8
off Wilman Gro **114** A4
Rock Av, SW14
off South Worple Way **175** D1
Rockells Pl, SE22 **184** B4
Rock Gro Way, SE16
off Blue Anchor La **156** B3
Rockhall Rd, NW2 **107** D1
Rockhall Way, NW2
off Midland Ter **93** D4
Rockingham Cl, SW15 **175** F2
Rockingham Est, SE1 **63** E3
Rockingham St, SE1 **63** E3
Rockland Rd, SW15 **177** E2
Rockley Rd, W14 **149** D1
Rocks La, SW13 **162** A3
Rock St, N4 **98** A3
Rockwood Pl, W12 **148** C1
Rocliffe St, N1 **15** D3
Rocque La, SE3 **187** F1
Rodborough Rd,
NW11 **94** A2
Roden Ct, N6 **97** D1
Rodenhurst Rd, SW4 **180** C4
Roden St, N7 **97** F4
Roderick Rd, NW3 **109** F1
Roding Ms, E1
off Kennet St **142** A4
Roding Rd, E5 **115** D1
Rodmarton St, W1 **33** F1
Rodmere St, SE10
off Trafalgar Rd **159** E4
Rodney Ct, W9 **19** F2
Rodney Pl, SE17 **63** F4
Rodney Rd, SE17 **63** F4
Rodney St, N1 **13** F2
Rodwell Rd, SE22 **183** F4
Roedean Cres, SW15 **175** E4
ROEHAMPTON, SW15 **176** A3
Roehampton Cl, SW15 **176** A2
Roehampton Gate, SW15 **175** E4
Roehampton La, SW15 **176** A2
Uni Roehampton Uni -
Digby Stuart Coll, SW15
off Roehampton La **176** A3
Coll Roehampton Uni -
Downshire Ho, SW15
off Roehampton La **176** A4
Uni Roehampton Uni -
Froebel Coll, SW15
off Roehampton La **175** F4
Uni Roehampton Uni -
Southlands Coll, SW15
off Roehampton La **176** A3
Roffey St, E14 **158** C1
Rogate Ho, E5
off Muir Rd **100** B4
Roger Dowley Ct, E2 **128** C2
Rogers Est, E2
off Globe Rd **128** C3
Rogers Ho, SW1
off Page St **60** B4
Rogers Rd, E16 **145** F2
Roger St, WC1 **25** F3
Rokeby Rd, SE4 **171** F4
Rokeby St, E15 **131** E1
Roland Gdns, SW7 **67** F2
Roland Ms, E1
off Stepney Grn **143** D1
Roland Way, SE17 **76** B3
SW7 **67** F2
Rollins St, SE15 **170** C1
Rollit St, N7
off Hornsey Rd **112** A2
Rolls Bldgs, EC4 **38** A2
Rollscourt Av, SE24 **182** C3
Rolls Pas, EC4 **38** A2
Rolls Rd, SE1 **77** F2
Rolt St, SE8 **171** E1
Roman Cl, W3
off Avenue Gdns **146** B1
Roman Rd, E2 **128** C3
E3 **129** E2
NW2 **92** C4
W4 **147** E3
Roman Way, N7 **111** F3
SE15
off Clifton Way **170** C2
● Roman Way Ind Est, N1
off Offord St **111** F4
Romborough Gdns, SE13 **186** C3
Romborough Way, SE13 **186** C3
Romero Cl, SW9
off Stockwell Rd **181** F1
Romford Rd, E15 **117** E4
Romford St, E1 **142** A1
Romilly Rd, N4 **98** B3
Romilly St, W1 **36** A4
Romney Cl, NW11 **94** C2
SE14 *off Kender St* **170** C2
Romney Ms, W1 **22** A4
Romney Rd, SE10 **172** C1
Romney Row, NW2
off Brent Ter **93** D3
Romney St, SW1 **60** B3
Ronald Av, E15 **131** E3
Ronalds Rd, N5 **112** A2
Ronald St, E1
off Devonport St **142** C2
Rona Rd, NW3 **110** A1
Rona Wk, N1
off Ramsey Wk **113** D3
Rondu Rd, NW2 **107** E2
Rood La, EC3 **40** C4
Rook Cl, Wem. HA9 **90** B4
Rookery Rd, SW4 **180** C2
Rooke Way, SE10 **159** F4
Rookwood Rd, N16 **99** F1
★ Roosevelt Mem, W1 **34** B4
Rootes Dr, W10 **121** D4
Ropemaker Rd, SE16 **157** E2
Ropemakers Flds, E14
off Narrow St **143** F3
Ropemaker St, EC2 **28** A4
Roper La, SE1 **53** D4
Ropers Orchard, SW3 **80** B1
Ropery St, E3 **129** F4
Rope St, SE16 **157** E3
Ropewalk Gdns, E1
off Commercial Rd **142** A2
Ropewalk Ms, E8
off Middleton Rd **114** A4
Ropley St, E2 **128** A2
Rosa Alba Ms, N5
off Kelross Rd **112** C1
Rosaline Rd, SW6 **163** E2
Rosary Gdns, SW7 **67** E1
Rosaville Rd, SW6 **163** F2
Roscoe St, EC1 **27** F3
Rose All, EC2
off New St **41** D1
SE1 **51** F2
Rose & Crown Ct, EC2 **39** E2
Rose & Crown Yd, SW1 **47** F2
Rosebank Gdns, E3 **129** F2
Rosebank Wk, NW1
off Maiden La **111** D4
Rosebank Way, W3 **133** D2
Roseberry Pl, E8 **113** F3
Roseberry St, SE16 **156** B3
Rosebery Av, EC1 **26** A3
Rosebery Ct, EC1
off Rosebery Av **26** A2
Rosebery Ms, SW2
off Rosebery Rd **181** E4
Rosebery Rd, SW2 **181** E4
Rosebery Sq, EC1 **26** A3
Rosebury Rd, SW6 **164** B4
Rose Ct, E1 **41** E1
Rosecroft Av, NW3 **94** A4
Rosecroft Gdns, NW2 **92** A4
Rosedale Ct, N5 **112** B1
Rosedale Ter, W6
off Dalling Rd **148** B2
Rosedene, NW6 **121** D1
Rosedene Ter, E10 **102** B3
Rosedew Rd, W6 **163** D1
Rosefield Gdns, E14 **144** A3
Roseford Ct, W12 **149** D1
Rosegate Ho, E3
off Hereford Rd **129** F2
Rosehart Ms, W11 **30** A3
Rosehill Rd, SW18 **178** C4
Rose Joan Ms, NW6 **108** A1

Roseleigh Av, N5 **112** B1
Rosemary Dr, E14 **145** D2
Rosemary Gdns, SW14
off Rosemary La **174** C1
Rosemary La, SW14 **174** C1
Rosemary Rd, SE15 **89** F2
Rosemary St, N1
off Shepperton Rd **127** D1
Rosemead, NW9 **91** F1
Rosemont Rd, NW3 **108** C3
W3 **132** B3
Rosemoor St, SW3 **69** E1
Rosenau Cres, SW11 **165** E3
Rosenau Rd, SW11 **81** D4
Roseneath Rd, SW11 **180** A4
Rosenthal Rd, SE6 **186** B4
Rosenthorpe Rd, SE15 **185** D3
Roserton St, E14 **158** C1
Rose Sq, SW3 **68** B2
Rose St, EC4 **39** D2
WC2 **36** C4
Rosetta Cl, SW8 **85** D3
Roseway, SE21 **183** D4
Rosewood Gdns, SE13
off Morden Hill **172** C4
Rosewood Sq, W12
off Primula St **134** A2
Rosher Cl, E15 **117** D4
Rosina St, E9 **115** D2
Roskell Rd, SW15 **177** D1
Roslin Rd, W3 **146** B2
● Roslin Sq, W3 **146** B2
Rosmead Rd, W11 **135** E3
Rosoman Pl, EC1 **26** B2
Rosoman St, EC1 **26** B1
Ross Ct, E5
off Napoleon Rd **114** B1
Rossdale Dr, NW9 **90** C2
Rossdale Rd, SW15 **176** C2
Rosse Gdns, SE13
off Desvignes Dr **187** D4
Rossendale St, E5 **100** B3
Rossendale Way, NW1 **110** C4
Rossetti Ms, NW8 **8** B1
Rossetti Rd, SE16 **156** B4
Rossington St, E5 **100** A3
Rosslyn Av, SW13 **175** E1
Rosslyn Hill, NW3 **109** D1
Rosslyn Ms, NW3
off Rosslyn Hill **109** D1
Rosslyn Pk Ms, NW3
off Lyndhurst Rd **109** D2
Rossmore Ct, NW1 **21** E2
Rossmore Rd, NW1 **21** D3
Rostrevor Ms, SW6 **163** F3
Rostrevor Rd, SW6 **163** F3
Rotary St, SE1 **62** C2
Rothbury Rd, E9 **115** F4
Rotherfield St, N1 **112** C4
Rotherham Wk, SE1 **50** C3
ROTHERHITHE, SE16 **157** D2
⊖ Rotherhithe **156** C1
Rotherhithe New Rd, SE16 **156** A4
Rotherhithe Old Rd, SE16 **157** D3
Rotherhithe St, SE16 **156** C1
Rotherhithe Tunnel, E1 **142** C4
Rotherhithe Tunnel App,
E14 **143** E3
SE16 **156** C1
Rotherwick Rd, NW11 **94** A1
Rotherwood Rd, SW15 **177** D1
Rothery St, N1
off Gaskin St **126** B1
Rothery Ter, SW9 **86** C3
Rothesay Av, Rich. TW10 **174** B2
Rothsay St, SE1 **64** C2
Rothsay Wk, E14
off Charnwood Gdns **158** A3
Rothschild Rd, W4 **146** C3
Roth Wk, N7
off Durham Rd **98** A3
Rothwell St, NW1 **123** F1
Rotten Row, SW1 **46** A4
SW7 **44** C4
Rotterdam Dr, E14 **158** C2
Rouel Rd, SE16 **156** A2
Roundel Cl, SE4 **185** F2
Roundwood Pk, NW10 **106** A4
Roundwood Rd, NW10 **105** F3
Rounton Rd, E3 **130** A4
Roupell St, SE1 **50** B3
Rousden St, NW1 **110** C4
Rover Ho, N1
off Phillipp St **17** D1
Rowallan Rd, SW6 **163** E2
Rowan Ho, NW3
off Maitland Pk Rd **109** F3
Rowan Rd, W6 **149** D3
Rowan Ter, W6
off Bute Gdns **149** D3
Rowan Wk, N19
off Bredgar Rd **96** C3
W10 *off Sixth Av* **121** E4
Rowberry Cl, SW6 **162** C2
Rowcross St, SE1 **77** E2
Rowditch La, SW11 **166** A4
Rowdon Av, NW10 **106** B4
Rowe La, E9 **114** C2
Rowena Cres, SW11 **165** E4
Rowhill Rd, E5 **114** B1
Rowington Cl, W2 **18** C4
Rowland Ct, E16 **131** F4
Rowland Hill St, NW3 **109** E2
Rowley Gdns, N4 **98** C1
● Rowley Ind Pk, W3 **146** B2
Rowley Way, NW8 **122** B1
Rowntree Cl, NW6
off Iverson Rd **108** A3
Rowse Cl, E15 **130** C1
Rowstock Gdns, N7 **111** D2
Roxby Pl, SW6 **66** B4
Roxley Rd, SE13 **186** B4
Roxwell Rd, W12 **148** A1
● Roxwell Trd Pk, E10 **101** D1
★ Royal Acad of Arts, W1 **47** E1
Coll Royal Acad of Dance,
SW11 *off Battersea Sq* **165** D3
★ Royal Acad of Dramatic Art
(R.A.D.A.), WC1 **24** B4
Uni Royal Acad of Music,
NW1 **22** B3
★ Royal Albert Hall, SW7 **56** A1
Royal Arc, W1 **47** E1
Royal Av, SW3 **69** E2
Coll Royal Ballet Sch, The,
Upr Sch, WC2 **37** D3
H Royal Brompton Hosp,
SW3 **68** C2
Annexe, SW3 **68** B2
Royal Cl, N16 **99** E2
SE8 **171** F1
Coll Royal Coll of
Anaesthetists, The,
WC1 **37** E1
Uni Royal Coll of Art, SW7 **55** F1
Sculpture Sch, SW11 **80** C3
Coll Royal Coll of Defence Studies,
SW1 **58** B2
Coll Royal Coll of Music,
SW7 **56** A2
Coll Royal Coll of Nursing,
W1 **34** C2
Coll Royal Coll of Obstetricians
& Gynaecologists, NW1 **21** E2
Coll Royal Coll of Physicians,
NW1 **23** D2
★ Royal Coll of Surgeons
of England, WC2 **37** F2
Royal Coll St, NW1 **110** C4
Royal Ct, EC3
off Royal Ex Bldgs **40** B3
SE16 **157** F2
★ Royal Courts of Justice,
WC2 **37** F3
Royal Cres, W11 **135** D4
Royal Cres Ms, W11
off Queensdale Rd **135** D4
★ Royal Dress Collection
(Kensington Palace),
W8 **43** D3
Royale Leisure Pk, W3 **118** A4
★ Royal Exchange, EC3 **40** B3
Royal Ex Av, EC3 **40** B3
Royal Ex Bldgs, EC3 **40** B3
★ Royal Festival Hall,
SE1 **49** F3
Uni Royal Free & Uni Coll Med Sch,
Royal Free Campus, NW3
off Rowland Hill St **109** E2
H Royal Free Hosp, The,
NW3 **109** E2
★ Royal Geographical Society,
SW7 **56** A1
Royal Hill, SE10 **172** C2
★ Royal Horticultural Society
(Lawrence Hall), SW1 **60** A3
★ Royal Horticultural Society
(Lindley Hall), SW1 **60** A4
★ Royal Hosp Chelsea & Mus,
SW3 **70** A3
H Royal Hosp for Neuro-Disability,
SW15 **177** E4
Royal Hosp Rd, SW3 **69** E4
H Royal London Homoeopathic
Hosp, WC1 **25** D4
H Royal London Hosp, The,
St. Clements, E3 **129** F3
Whitechapel, E1 **142** B1
Whitechapel - Dentistry Cen,
E1 **142** B1
H Royal Marsden Hosp, The,
SW3 **68** B2
★ Royal Mews, The, SW1 **59** D2
Royal Mint Ct, EC3 **53** F1
Royal Mint Pl, E1 **41** F4
Royal Mint St, E1 **41** F4
H Royal Nat Orthopaedic Hosp,
W1 **23** D3
H Royal National Throat,
Nose & Ear Hosp, WC1 **13** E4
Royal Naval Pl, SE14 **171** F2
⊖ Royal Oak **31** D1
Royal Oak Ct, N1 **16** C4
Royal Oak Pl, SE22 **184** B4
Royal Oak Rd, E8 **114** B3
Royal Oak Yd, SE1 **64** C1
★ Royal Observatory Greenwich
(Flamsteed Ho),
SE10 **173** D2
Royal Opera Arc, SW1 **48** A2
★ Royal Opera Ho,
WC2 **37** D4

Royal Par, SE3 ....**173** E4
SW6 *off Dawes Rd* **163** E2
Richmond TW9
off Station App **160** A3
Royal Par Ms, SE3
off Royal Par **173** F4
Royal Pl, SE10 ....**172** C2
Royal Rd, SE17 ....**74** C4
Royal St, SE1 ....**61** F2
Royalty Ms, W1 ....**36** A3
Uni Royal Vet Coll -
Camden Campus,
Beaumont Animal's Hosp,
NW1 ....11 F1
Royal Coll St, NW1 ....12 A1
● Royal Victoria Patriotic Bldg,
SW18 ....179 D4
Royal Victor Pl, E3 ....**129** D2
Roydon Cl, SW11
off Reform St **165** F4
Roydon St, SW11 ....**82** C4
Royle Bldg, N1 ....**15** E2
Roy Sq, E14
off Narrow St **143** E3
Royston Ct, SE24 ....**182** C4
Royston St, E2 ....**128** C2
Rozel Ct, N1 ....**127** E1
Rozel Rd, SW4 ....**166** C4
Rubens Pl, SW4
off Dolman St **181** F2
Ruby St, NW10 ....**104** C4
SE15 ....**170** B1
Ruby Triangle, SE15
off Sandgate St **170** B1
Ruckholt Cl, E10 ....**102** B4
Ruckholt Rd, E10 ....**116** A1
Rucklidge Av, NW10 ....**119** F2
Rudall Cres, NW3
off Willoughby Rd **109** D1
Ruddington Cl, E5 ....**115** E1
Rudgwick Ter, NW8 ....**9** D1
Rudolf Pl, SW8 ....**85** D1
Rudolph Rd, E13 ....**131** F2
NW6 ....**6** B3
Rudstone Ho, E3
off Bromley High St **130** B3
Rufford St, N1 ....**125** E1
Rufford Twr, W3 ....**132** B4
Rufus St, N1 ....**28** C1
Rugby Rd, W4 ....**147** E1
Rugby St, WC1 ....**25** E3
Rugg St, E14 ....**144** A3
Rumbold Rd, SW6 ....**79** D3
Rum Cl, E1 ....**142** C3
Rumford Ho, SE1
off Bath Ter **63** E2
Rumsey Ms, N4 ....**98** B4
Rumsey Rd, SW9 ....**181** F1
Runbury Circle, NW9 ....**91** D3
Runcorn Pl, W11 ....**135** E3
Rundell Twr, SW8 ....**85** E4
Runnymede Ho, E9
off Kingsmead Way **115** E1
Rupack St, SE16
off St. Marychurch St ...**156** C1
Rupert Ct, W1 ....**36** A4
Rupert Gdns, SW9 ....**168** B4
Rupert Rd, N19
off Holloway Rd **97** D3
NW6 ....**121** F2
W4 ....**147** E2
Rupert St, W1 ....**36** A4
Rusbridge Cl, E8
off Amhurst Rd **114** A2
Ruscoe Rd, E16 ....**145** F2
Rusham Rd, SW12 ....**179** F4
Rushcroft Rd, SW2 ....**182** A2
Rushey Mead, SE4 ....**186** A3
Rushford Rd, SE4 ....**185** F4
Rush Hill Ms, SW11
off Rush Hill Rd **180** A1
Rush Hill Rd, SW11 ....**180** A1
Rushmead, E2
off Florida St **128** B3
Rushmore Cres, E5
off Rushmore Rd **115** D1
Rushmore Rd, E5 ....**114** C1
Rusholme Rd, SW15 ....**177** D4
Rushton St, N1 ....**16** B2
Rushworth St, SE1 ....**51** D4
Ruskin Av, Rich. TW9 ......**160** A2
Ruskin Pk Ho, SE5 ....**183** D1
Ruskin Wk, SE24 ....**182** C3
Rusper Cl, NW2 ....**92** C4
Russell Cl, NW10 ....**104** C4
W4 ....**161** F1
Russell Ct, SW1 ....**47** F3
Russell Gdns, W14 ....**149** E2
Russell Gdns Ms, W14 .....**149** E2
Russell Gro, SW9 ....**86** B3
Russell Kerr Cl, W4 ....**160** C2
Russell Lo, SE1
off Spurgeon St **64** A2
Russell Pl, NW3
off Aspern Gro **109** E2
SE16 *off Onega Gate* **157** E2
Russell Rd, W14 ....**149** E2
⊖ Russell Square 24 C3
Russell Sq, WC1 ....**24** C3
Russell St, WC2 ....**37** D4
Russell's Wf Flats, W10
off Harrow Rd **121** F4
Russet Cres, N7
off Stock Orchard Cres ..**111** F2
Russia Dock Rd, SE16 ......**143** E4
Russia La, E2 ....**128** C2
Russia Row, EC2 ....**39** F3
Russia Wk, SE16 ....**157** E1
Rusthall Av, W4 ....**147** D3
Ruston Ms, W11
off St. Marks Rd **135** E2
Ruston St, E3 ....**129** F1
Rust Sq, SE5 ....**88** A2
Rutherford St, SW1 ....**60** A4
Rutherford Way, Wem.
HA9 ....**104** A1
Ruthven St, E9
off Lauriston Rd **129** D1
Rutland Cl, SW14 ....**174** B1
Rutland Ct, SW7
off Rutland Gdns **57** D1
Rutland Gdns, SW7 ....**57** D1
Rutland Gdns Ms, SW7 ......**57** D1
Rutland Gate, SW7 ....**57** D1
Rutland Gate Ms, SW7 ......**56** C1
Rutland Gro, W6 ....**148** B4
Rutland Ms, NW8 ....**7** D1
Rutland Ms E, SW7 ....**56** C2
Rutland Ms S, SW7 ....**56** C2
Rutland Ms W, SW7
off Ennismore St **56** C2
Rutland Pk, NW2 ....**106** C3
Rutland Pk Gdns, NW2
off Rutland Pk **106** C3
Rutland Pk Mans, NW2
off Rutland Pk **106** C3
Rutland Pl, EC1 ....**27** E3
Rutland Rd, E9 ....**128** C1
Rutland St, SW7 ....**57** D2
Rutley Cl, SE17 ....**74** C4
Rutts Ter, SE14 ....**171** D3
Ruvigny Gdns, SW15 ......**177** D1
Ryculff Sq, SE3 ....**173** F4
Ryder Ct, SW1 ....**47** F2
Ryder Dr, SE16 ....**156** B4
Ryder Ms, E9
off Homerton High St ...**114** C2
Ryders Ter, NW8 ....**7** E2
Ryder St, SW1 ....**47** F2
Ryder Yd, SW1 ....**47** F2
Rydon St, N1
off St. Paul St **126** C1
Rydston Cl, N7
off Sutterton St **111** F4
Ryecroft Rd, SE13 ....**186** C3
Ryecroft St, SW6 ....**164** B3
Ryedale, SE22 ....**184** B4
Ryegates, SE15
off Caulfield Rd **170** B4
Rye Hill Pk, SE15 ....**184** C2
Rye La, SE15 ....**170** A3
Rye Pas, SE15 ....**184** A1
Rye Rd, SE15 ....**185** D2
Rye Wk, SW15 ....**177** D3
Rylandes Rd, NW2 ....**92** A4
Ryland Rd, NW5 ....**110** B3
Rylett Cres, W12 ....**147** F2
Rylett Rd, W12 ....**147** F1
Rylston Rd, SW6 ....**163** F1
Rymer St, SE24 ....**182** B4
Rysbrack St, SW3 ....**57** E2

S

★ Saatchi Gall, The, SW3 ...69 F1
Sabbarton St, E16
off Silvertown Way **145** F2
Sabella Ct, E3
off Mostyn Gro **129** F2
Sabine Rd, SW11 ....**179** F1
Sable St, N1 ....**112** B4
Sach Rd, E5 ....**100** B3
Sackville St, W1 ....**47** F1
Saddlers Ms, SW8
off Portland Gro **85** D4
Saddle Yd, W1 ....**46** C2
Sadler Ho, E3
off Bromley High St **130** B3
Sadlers Gate Ms, SW15
off Commondale **176** C1
★ Sadler's Wells Thea,
EC1 ....14 C4
Coll SAE Inst, N7
off North Rd 111 E2
Saffron Av, E14 ....**145** D3
Saffron Hill, EC1 ....**26** B3
Saffron St, EC1 ....**26** B4
Sage Ms, SE22
off Lordship La **183** F3
Sage St, E1
off Cable St **142** C3
Sage Way, WC1 ....**25** E1
Sailacre Ho, SE10
off Calvert Rd **159** F4
Sail Ct, E14
off Newport Av **145** D3
Sailmakers Ct, SW6
off William Morris Way ..**178** C1
Sail St, SE11 ....**61** F4
St. Agnes Cl, E9
off Gore Rd **128** C1
St. Agnes Pl, SE11 ....**86** C1

St. Agnes Well, EC1
off Old St **28** B2
St. Aidan's Rd, SE22 **184** B4
St. Alban's Av, W4 **147** D3
St. Albans Cl, NW11 **94** A2
St. Albans Ct, EC2 **39** F2
St. Albans Gro, W8 **55** D2
St. Albans La, NW11 **94** A2
St. Alban's Pl, N1 **14** C1
St. Albans Rd, NW5 **96** A4
NW10 **119** E1
St. Albans St, SW1 **48** A1
St. Albans Ter, W6
off Margravine Rd **163** E1
St. Alban's Vil, NW5
off Highgate Rd **96** A4
St. Alfege Pas, SE10 **172** C1
St. Alphage Gdns, EC2 **39** F1
St. Alphage Highwalk,
EC2 **40** A1
St. Alphonsus Rd, SW4 **180** C2
St. Andrews Cl, NW2 **92** B4
SE16 *off Ryder Dr* **156** B4
St. Andrew's Gro, N16 **99** D2
St. Andrew's Hill, EC4 **39** D4
St. Andrew's Ms, N16 **99** E2
St. Andrews Pl, NW1 **23** D2
St. Andrews Rd, NW9 **91** D2
NW10 **106** B3
W3 **133** E3
W14 **163** E1
St. Andrews Sq, W11
off Bartle Rd **135** E2
St. Andrew St, EC4 **38** B1
St. Andrews Way, E3 **130** B4
St. Anne's Cl, N6 **96** A4
St. Anne's Ct, W1 **36** A3
St. Annes Pas, E14
off Newell St **143** F2
St. Annes Rd, E11 **103** D3
St. Anne's Row, E14
off Commercial Rd **143** F2
St. Anne St, E14
off Commercial Rd **143** F2
St. Ann's Cres, SW18 **178** C4
St. Ann's Gdns, NW5
off Queen's Cres **110** A3
St. Ann's Hill, SW18 **178** B3
St. Ann's La, SW1 **60** B2
St. Ann's Pk Rd, SW18 **178** C4
St. Ann's Pas, SW13 **175** E1
St. Ann's Rd, SW13 **161** F4
St. Anns Rd, W11 **135** D3
St. Ann's St, SW1 **60** B2
St. Ann's Ter, NW8 **8** B2
St. Anns Vil, W11 **135** D4
St. Anselm's Pl, W1 **34** C3
St. Anthonys Cl, E1 **142** A4
St. Asaph Rd, SE4 **185** D1
St. Aubins Ct, N1
off De Beauvoir Est **127** D1
St. Augustines Ct, SE1
off Lynton Rd **156** B4
St. Augustine's Path, N5
off Highbury New Pk **112** C1
St. Augustines Rd, NW1 **111** D4
St. Austell Rd, SE13 **172** C4
St. Barnabas Cl, SE22
off East Dulwich Gro **183** E3
St. Barnabas St, SW1 **70** B2
St. Barnabas Ter, E9 **115** D2
St. Barnabas Vil, SW8 **85** D4
H St. Bartholomew's Hosp,
EC1 **39** D1
★ St. Bartholomew-the-Great Ch,
EC1 **39** D1
St. Benet's Pl, EC3 **40** B4
St. Botolph Row, EC3 **41** E3
St. Botolph St, EC3 **41** E3
St. Brelades Ct, N1
off Balmes Rd **127** D1
St. Brides Av, EC4 **38** C3
★ St. Bride's Ch, EC4 **38** C3
St. Bride's Pas, EC4
off Salisbury Ct **38** C3
St. Bride St, EC4 **38** C2
St. Catherines Dr, SE14
off Kitto Rd **171** D4
St. Catherine's Ms, SW3 **57** E4
St. Chad's Pl, WC1 **13** D4
St. Chad's St, WC1 **13** D4
Coll St. Charles Catholic
6th Form Coll, W10
off St. Charles Sq **135** D1
H St. Charles Hosp, W10 **135** D1
St. Charles Pl, W10
off Chesterton Rd **135** E1
St. Charles Sq, W10 **135** E1
St. Christopher's Pl, W1 **34** B2
St. Clare St, EC3 **41** E3
★ St. Clement Danes Ch,
WC2 **37** F3
St. Clements Ct, EC4
off Clements La **40** B4
N7 *off Arundel Sq* **111** F3
St. Clement's La, WC2 **37** F3
St. Clements St, N7 **112** A3
St. Clements Yd, SE22
off Archdale Rd **183** F3
St. Crispins Cl, NW3 **109** E1
St. Cross St, EC1 **26** B4
St. Cuthberts Rd, NW2 **107** F3
St. Davids Cl, SE16
off Masters Dr **156** B4
Wembley HA9 **90** C4
St. Davids Ms, E3
off Morgan St **129** E3
St. Davids Pl, NW4 **92** B1
St. Davids Sq, E14 **158** B4
St. Dionis Rd, SW6 **163** F4
St. Donatts Rd, SE14 **171** F3
St. Dunstan's All, EC3 **40** C4
St. Dunstans Av, W3 **133** D3
St. Dunstan's Ct, EC4
off Fleet St **38** B3
St. Dunstans Gdns, W3 **133** D3
St. Dunstan's Hill, EC3 **52** C1
St. Dunstan's La, EC3 **52** C1
St. Dunstans Rd, W6 **149** D4
St. Edmunds Cl, NW8 **9** E1
St. Edmunds Sq, SW13 **162** C1
St. Edmunds Ter, NW8 **9** D2
St. Elmo Rd, W12 **133** F4
St. Elmos Rd, SE16 **157** E1
St. Ermin's Hill, SW1 **60** A2
St. Ervans Rd, W10 **135** E1
St. Francis Pl, SW12
off Malwood Rd **180** B4
St. Francis Rd, SE22 **183** E2
Coll St. Francis Xavier
6th Form Coll, SW12
off Malwood Rd **180** B4
St. Frideswides Ms, E14
off Lodore St **144** C2
St. Gabriel's Cl, E14
off Morris Rd **144** B1
St. Gabriels Rd, NW2 **107** D2
St. Georges Av, N7 **111** D1
St. Georges Circ, SE1 **62** C2
St. George's Cl, SW8 **83** F4
St. Georges Ct, EC4 **38** C2
SW7 **55** E2
St. George's Dr, SW1 **71** D1
St. Georges Flds, W2 **33** D3
St. Georges La, EC3
off Pudding La **40** B4
St. Georges Ms, NW1
off Regents Pk Rd **109** F4
SE1 **62** B2
SE8 *off Grove St* **157** F3
St. Georges Rd, E10 **102** C4
SE1 **62** B2
W4 **147** E1
St. Georges Sq, E14
off Narrow St **143** E3
SE8 **157** F3
St. George's Sq, SW1 **72** A2
St. George's Sq Ms, SW1 **72** A3
St. Georges Ter, NW1
off Regents Pk Rd **109** F4
St. George St, W1 **35** D3
St. Georges Way, SE15 **88** C1
St. George Wf, SW8 **72** C3
St. Gerards Cl, SW4 **180** C3
Coll St. Giles Coll, London Cen,
WC1 **25** D4
St. Giles Ct, WC2
off St. Giles High St **36** C2
St. Giles High St, WC2 **36** B2
St. Giles Pas, WC2 **36** B3
St. Giles Rd, SE5 **88** C3
St. Gilles Ho, E2 **129** D2
St. Helena Rd, SE16 **157** D3
St. Helena St, WC1 **26** A1
St. Helens Gdns, W10 **135** D2
St. Helens Pl, E10 **101** E1
EC3 **40** C2
St. Hildas Cl, NW6 **107** D4
St. Hilda's Rd, SW13 **162** B1
St. James Cl, NW8
off St. James's Ter **9** E1
St. James Gate, NW1
off St. Paul's Cres **111** D4
St. James Gro, SW11
off Reform St **165** F4
St. James Ms, E14 **158** C2
St. James Rd, E15 **117** F2
ST. JAMES'S, SW1 **48** A3
St. James's, SE14 **171** E3
Coll St. James's & Lucie Clayton
Coll, SW5 **67** E1
St. James's Av, E2 **128** C2
St. James's Ct, SW1 **59** F2
St. James's Cres, SW9 **182** A1
St. James's Gdns, W11 **135** E4
St. James's Mkt, SW1 **48** A1
★ St. James's Palace,
SW1 **47** F4
★ St. James's Park,
SW1 **48** A4
⊖ St. James's Park **60** A2
St. James's Pas, EC3 **41** D3
St. James's Pl, SW1 **47** E3
St. James's Rd, SE1 **156** A4
SE16 **156** A2
St. James's Sq, SW1 **47** F2
St. James's St, SW1 **47** E2
St. James's Ter, NW8 **9** E2
St. James's Ter Ms, NW8 **9** E1
St. James St, W6 **148** C4
St. James's Wk, EC1 **26** C2
ST. JOHN'S, SE8 **172** A4

St. John's 172 A4
St. John's Av, NW10 ....119 F1
SW15 ....177 D3
St. John's Ch Rd, E9 ....114 C2
St. John's Cl, SW6 ....78 A2
St. John's Cres, SW9 ....182 A1
St. John's Est, N1 ....16 B3
SE1 ....65 E1
St. John's Gdns, W11 ....135 F3
St. John's Gate & Mus of the Order of St. John, EC1 ....26 C3
St. Johns Gro, N19 ....96 C3
SW13 off Terrace Gdns 161 F4
St. John's Hill, SW11 ....179 D2
St. John's Hill Gro, SW11 ....179 D2
St. John's La, EC1 ....26 C3
St. John's Ms, W11 ....30 A3
St. John's Pk, SE3 ....173 F2
St. John's Path, EC1 ....26 C3
St. John's Pl, EC1 ....26 C3
St. John's Rd, SW11 ....179 E2
St. John's Sq, EC1 ....26 C3
St. Johns Ter, W10 off Harrow Rd 121 D4
St. John St, EC1 ....27 D3
St. Johns Vale, SE8 ....172 A4
St. Johns Vil, N19 ....97 D3
St. John's Vil, W8 ....55 D3
St. Johns Way, N19 ....97 D2
ST. JOHN'S WOOD, NW8 ....8 A4
St. John's Wood 8 A2
St. John's Wd Ct, NW8 ....20 B1
St. John's Wd High St, NW8 ....8 B3
St. John's Wd Pk, NW8 ....8 B1
St. John's Wd Rd, NW8 ....20 A2
St. John's Wd Ter, NW8 ....8 C2
St. Josephs Cl, W10 off Bevington Rd 135 E1
St. Josephs St, SW8 ....83 D4
St. Joseph's Vale, SE3 ....173 D4
St. Jude's Rd, E2 ....128 B2
St. Jude St, N16 ....113 E2
St. Julian's Rd, NW6 ....107 F4
St. Katharine Docks, E1 ....53 F1
St. Katharine's Pier 53 E2
St. Katharines Prec, NW1 ....10 C2
St. Katharine's Way, E1 ....53 F2
St. Katherine's Row, EC3 off Fenchurch St 41 D3
St. Katherine's Wk, W11 off Freston Rd 135 D3
St. Kilda's Rd, N16 ....99 D2
St. Laurence Cl, NW6 ....121 D1
St. Lawrence Jewry Ch, EC2 ....39 F2
St. Lawrence St, E14 ....144 C4
St. Lawrence Ter, W10 ....135 E1
St. Lawrence Way, SW9 ....168 A3
St. Leonards Ct, N1 ....16 B4
St. Leonards Rd, E14 ....144 B1
NW10 ....119 D4
St. Leonard's Rd, SW14 ....174 B1
St. Leonards Sq, NW5 ....110 A3
St. Leonards St, E3 ....130 B3
St. Leonard's Ter, SW3 ....69 E3
St. Loo Av, SW3 ....69 D4
St. Lucia Dr, E15 ....131 F1
ST. LUKE'S, EC1 ....27 F2
St. Luke's Av, SW4 ....181 D2
St. Luke's Cl, EC1 ....27 F2
St. Luke's Est, EC1 ....28 A1
St. Luke's Hosp for the Clergy, W1 ....23 E3
St. Lukes Ms, W11 off Basing St 135 F2
St. Lukes Rd, W11 ....135 F1
St. Lukes Sq, E16 ....145 F2
St. Luke's St, SW3 ....68 C2
St. Luke's Yd, W9 ....121 F2
St. Margarets Cl, EC2 off Lothbury 40 A2
St. Margaret's Ct, SE1 ....51 F3
St. Margaret's Cres, SW15 ....176 B3
St. Margaret's Gro, E11 ....103 F4
St. Margarets La, W8 ....54 C3
St. Margarets Pas, SE13 off Church Ter 187 E1
St. Margaret's Rd, NW10 ....120 C3
St. Margarets Rd, SE4 ....185 F2
St. Margarets Sq, SE4 off Adelaide Av 185 F2
St. Margaret's St, SW1 ....60 C1
St. Marks Cl, SE10 off Ashburnham Gro 172 C2
SW6 off Ackmar Rd 164 A3
W11 off St. Marks Rd 135 E2
St. Marks Cres, NW1 ....124 A1
St. Mark's Gate, E9 off Cadogan Ter 115 F4
St. Mark's Gro, SW10 ....79 D1
St. Marks Pl, W11 ....135 E2
St. Marks Ri, E8 ....113 F2
St. Marks Rd, W10 ....135 D2
W11 ....135 E2
St. Marks Sq, NW1 ....124 A1
St. Mark St, E1 ....41 F3
St. Martin-in-the-Fields Ch, WC2 ....48 C1
St. Martins Cl, NW1 ....124 C1
St. Martin's Coll, E3 off English St 129 F4
St. Martin's Ct, WC2 off St. Martin's La 36 C4
St. Martin's La, WC2 ....36 C4
St. Martin's-le-Grand, EC1 ....39 E2
St. Martin's Ms, WC2 ....48 C1
St. Martin's Pl, WC2 ....48 C1
St. Martin's Rd, SW9 ....167 F4
St. Martin's St, WC2 ....48 B1
St. Mary Abbots Pl, W8 ....149 F2
St. Mary Abbots Ter, W14 ....149 F2
St. Mary at Hill, EC3 ....52 C1
St. Mary at Hill Ch, EC3 ....52 C1
St. Mary Axe, EC3 ....40 C3
St. Marychurch St, SE16 ....156 C1
St. Mary Graces Ct, E1 ....41 F4
St. Marylebone Cl, NW10 off Craven Pk 119 E1
St. Mary-le-Bow Ch, EC2 ....39 F3
St. Mary Newington Cl, SE17 off Surrey Sq 77 D2
St. Marys Est, SE16 off St. Marychurch St 156 C1
St. Mary's Gdns, SE11 ....62 B4
St. Mary's Gate, W8 ....54 C3
St. Mary's Gro, N1 ....112 B3
SW13 ....176 B1
W4 ....160 B1
St. Mary's Hosp, W2 ....32 B2
St. Marys Mans, W2 ....20 A4
St. Mary's Ms, NW6 off Priory Rd 108 B4
St. Marys Path, N1 ....126 B1
St. Mary's Pl, W8 ....54 C3
St. Marys Rd, E10 ....102 C4
St. Mary's Rd, NW10 ....119 E1
St. Marys Rd, NW11 ....93 E1
St. Mary's Rd, SE15 ....170 C3
St. Marys Sq, W2 ....20 A4
St. Marys Ter, W2 ....20 A4
St. Mary's Twr, EC1 off Fortune St 27 F3
St. Mary's Wk, SE11 ....62 B4
St. Matthew's Rd, SW2 ....181 F2
St. Matthew's Row, E2 ....128 A3
St. Matthew St, SW1 ....60 A3
St. Maur Rd, SW6 ....163 F3
St. Michael's All, EC3 ....40 B3
St. Michael's Av, Wem. HA9 ....104 A3
St. Michaels Gdns, W10 off St. Lawrence Ter 135 E1
St. Michael's Ms, SW1 ....70 A1
St. Michaels Rd, NW2 ....106 C1
St. Michael's Rd, SW9 ....167 F4
St. Michaels St, W2 ....32 B2
St. Mildred's Ct, EC2 off Poultry 40 A3
St. Nicholas St, SE8 off Lucas St 172 A3
St. Norbert Grn, SE4 ....185 E2
St. Norbert Rd, SE4 ....185 E2
St. Olaf's Rd, SW6 ....163 E2
St. Olaves Ct, EC2 ....40 A3
St. Olave's Est, SE1 ....53 D4
St. Olaves Gdns, SE11 ....62 A4
St. Olav's Sq, SE16 ....156 C1
St. Oswald's Pl, SE11 ....73 E3
St. Oswulf St, SW1 ....72 B1
ST. PANCRAS, WC1 ....24 C1
St. Pancras Commercial Cen, NW1 off Pratt St 124 C1
St. Pancras Hosp, NW1 ....12 A1
St. Pancras International 12 C3
St. Pancras International 12 C3
St. Pancras Way, NW1 ....110 C4
St. Paul's 39 E2
St. Paul's All, EC4 off St. Paul's Chyd 39 D3
St. Paul's Av, NW2 ....106 B3
SE16 ....143 D4
St. Paul's Cath, EC4 ....39 E3
St. Paul's Chyd, EC4 ....39 D3
St. Paul's Ct, W14 off Colet Gdns 149 D3
St. Pauls Ctyd, SE8 off Deptford High St 172 A1
St. Paul's Cres, NW1 ....111 D4
St. Pauls Dr, E15 ....117 D2
St. Paul's Ms, NW1 ....111 D4
St. Paul's Pl, N1 ....113 D3
St. Paul's Rd, N1 ....112 B3
St. Paul's Shrubbery, N1 ....113 D3
St. Paul's Ter, SE17 ....75 D4
St. Paul St, N1 ....15 E1
St. Pauls Way, E3 ....143 F1
E14 ....143 F1
St. Paul's Way Comm Sch, E3 off Shelmerdine Cl 144 A1
St. Peter's All, EC3 ....40 B3
St. Peter's Av, E2 off St. Peter's Cl 128 A2
St. Petersburgh Ms, W2 ....30 C4
St. Petersburgh Pl, W2 ....30 C4
St. Peter's Cl, E2 ....128 A2

St. Peters Ct, SE3
off Eltham Rd **187** F3
SE4 *off Wickham Rd* **171** F4
St. Peter's Gro, W6 . . . . **148** A3
St. Peter's Pl, W9 . . . . **18** C3
St. Peter's Rd, W6 . . . . **148** A4
St. Peter's Sq, E2
off St. Peter's Cl **128** A2
W6 . . . . **148** A4
St. Peters St, N1 . . . . **15** D1
St. Peter's St Ms, N1 . . . . **15** D2
St. Peters Ter, SW6 . . . . **163** E2
St. Peter's Vil, W6 . . . . **147** F3
St. Peter's Way, N1 . . . . **113** E4
St. Philip Sq, SW8 . . . . **166** B4
St. Philip's Rd, E8 . . . . **114** A3
St. Philip St, SW8 . . . . **166** B4
St. Philip's Way, N1
off Linton St **126** C1
St. Quentin Ho, SW18
off Fitzhugh Gro **179** D4
St. Quintin Av, W10 . . . . **134** C1
St. Quintin Gdns, W10 . . . . . **134** C1
St. Raphael's Way,
NW10 . . . . **104** C2
St. Rule St, SW8 . . . . **166** C4
St. Saviour's Est, SE1 . . . . **65** E2
St. Saviour's Rd, SW2 . . . . . . **181** F3
St. Silas Pl, NW5 . . . . **110** A3
St. Silas St Est, NW5 . . . . **110** A3
St. Simon's Av, SW15 . . . . . . **176** C3
St. Stephens Av, W12 . . . . . . **148** B1
St. Stephens Cl, NW8 . . . . **9** D1
St. Stephens Cres, W2 . . . . **30** B2
St. Stephens Gdn Est, W2 . . . . **30** A2
St. Stephens Gdns, SW15
off Manfred Rd **177** F3
W2 . . . . **30** B1
St. Stephens Gro, SE13 . . . . . **186** C1
St. Stephens Ms, W2 . . . . **30** B1
St. Stephen's Rd, E3 . . . . **129** F2
St. Stephens Row, EC4 . . . . . . **40** A3
St. Stephens Ter, SW8 . . . . **85** E3
St. Stephen's Wk, SW7 . . . . . . **55** E4
St. Swithin's La, EC4 . . . . **40** A4
St. Swithun's Rd, SE13 . . . . . **187** D3
H St. Thomas' Hosp, SE1 . . . **61** E2
Coll St. Thomas' Med Sch
& the Nightingale Sch,
SE1 . . . . **61** E3
St. Thomas' Rd, W4 . . . . **160** C1
St. Thomas's Gdns, NW5
off Queen's Cres **110** A3
St. Thomas's Pl, E9 . . . . **114** C4
St. Thomas's Rd, N4 . . . . **98** A3
NW10 . . . . **119** E1
St. Thomas's Sq, E9 . . . . **114** B4
St. Thomas St, SE1 . . . . **52** A3
St. Thomas's Way, SW6 . . . . **163** F2
St. Vincent St, W1 . . . . **34** B1
Salamanca Pl, SE1 . . . . **73** E1
Salamanca St, SE1 . . . . **73** D1
Salcombe Rd, E17 . . . . **101** F1
N16 . . . . **113** E2
Salcott Rd, SW11 . . . . **179** E3
Salehurst Rd, SE4 . . . . **185** F4
Salem Rd, W2 . . . . **31** D4
Sale Pl, W2 . . . . **32** C1
Sale St, E2
off Hereford St **128** A4
Salisbury Cl, SE17 . . . . **64** A4
Salisbury Ct, EC4 . . . . **38** C3
Salisbury Ho, E14
off Hobday St **144** B2
Salisbury Ms, SW6
off Dawes Rd **163** F2
Salisbury Pl, SW9 . . . . **87** D3
W1 . . . . **21** E4
Salisbury Rd, E10 . . . . **102** C3
Salisbury Sq, EC4 . . . . **38** B3
Salisbury St, NW8 . . . . **20** B3
W3 . . . . **146** C1
Salisbury Ter, SE15 . . . . **184** C1
Salisbury Wk, N19 . . . . **96** C3
Salmen Rd, E13 . . . . **131** F2
Salmon La, E14 . . . . **143** E2
Salmon St, E14
off Salmon La **143** F2
NW9 . . . . **90** B2
Saltcoats Rd, W4 . . . . **147** E1
Saltcroft Cl, Wem.
HA9 . . . . **90** B2
Salter Rd, SE16 . . . . **143** D4
Salters Hall Ct, EC4 . . . . **40** A4
Salters Rd, W10 . . . . **121** D4
Salter St, E14 . . . . **144** A3
NW10 . . . . **120** A3
Salter St Alleyway, NW10
off Hythe Rd **120** A4
Salterton Rd, N7 . . . . **97** E4
Saltoun Rd, SW2 . . . . **182** A2
Saltram Cres, W9 . . . . **121** F3
Saltwell St, E14 . . . . **144** A3
Saltwood Gro, SE17 . . . . **76** A3
Salusbury Rd, NW6 . . . . **121** E1
Salutation Rd, SE10 . . . . **159** E3
Salvin Rd, SW15 . . . . **177** D1
Salway Pl, E15
off Broadway **117** E3
Salway Rd, E15
off Great Eastern Rd **117** D3
Samantha Cl, E17 . . . . **101** F1
Sambrook Ho, SE11 . . . . **74** A1
Samels Ct, W6
off South Black Lion La . **148** A4
Samford Ho, N1 . . . . **14** A1
Samford St, NW8 . . . . **20** B3
Sampson St, E1 . . . . **142** A4
Samuel Cl, E8
off Pownall Rd **127** F1
SE14 . . . . **171** D1
Samuel Lewis Trust Dws, N1
off Liverpool Rd **112** A3
SW3 . . . . **68** C1
SW6 . . . . **78** B2
W14 *off Lisgar Ter* **149** F3
Samuel Lewis Trust Est, SE5
off Warner Rd **168** C3
Samuels Cl, W6 . . . . **148** A4
Samuel St, SE15 . . . . **89** E2
Sancroft Cl, NW2 . . . . **92** B4
Sancroft St, SE11 . . . . **73** F2
Sanctuary, The, SW1 . . . . **60** B1
Sanctuary Ms, E8
off Queensbridge Rd **113** F3
Sanctuary St, SE1 . . . . **63** F1
Sandall Ho, E3
off Daling Way **129** E2
Sandall Rd, NW5 . . . . **110** C3
Sandal St, E15 . . . . **131** E1
Sandalwood Cl, E1
off Solebay St **129** E4
Sandbourne Rd, SE4 . . . . **171** E4
Sandbrook Rd, N16 . . . . **99** E4
Sandell St, SE1 . . . . **50** A4
Sanderson Cl, NW5 . . . . **110** B1
Sanderstead Av, NW2 . . . . **93** E3
Sanderstead Rd, E10 . . . . . . **101** E2
Sanders Way, N19
off Sussex Way **97** D2
Sandford Ct, N16 . . . . **99** E2
Sandford St, SW6 . . . . **79** D3
Sandgate Ho, E5
off Downs Pk Rd **114** B1
Sandgate St, SE15 . . . . **170** B1
Sandhills, The, SW10
off Limerston St **67** F4
Sandifer Dr, NW2 . . . . **93** D4
Sandilands Rd, SW6 . . . . **164** B3
Sandison St, SE15 . . . . **183** F1
Sandland St, WC1 . . . . **37** F1
Sandlings Cl, SE15
off Pilkington Rd **170** B4
Sandmere Rd, SW4 . . . . **181** E2
Sandpiper Cl, SE16 . . . . **157** F1
Sandridge St, N19 . . . . **96** C3
Sandringham Ct, W9 . . . . **19** F1
Sandringham Flats, WC2
off Charing Cross Rd **36** B4
Sandringham Rd, E8 . . . . **113** F2
NW2 . . . . **106** B3
NW11 . . . . **93** E1
Sandrock Rd, SE13 . . . . **186** A1
SANDS END, SW6 . . . . **164** C3
Sand's End La, SW6 . . . . **79** D4
Sandstone Pl, N19 . . . . **96** B3
Sandwell Cres, NW6 . . . . **108** A3
Sandwich St, WC1 . . . . **24** C1
Sandycombe Rd, Rich.
TW9 . . . . **174** A1
Sandy Rd, NW3 . . . . **94** B4
Sandy's Row, E1 . . . . **41** D1
Sanford La, N16
off Lawrence Bldgs **99** F3
Sanford St, SE14 . . . . **171** E1
Sanford Ter, N16 . . . . **99** F4
Sanford Wk, N16
off Sanford Ter **99** F3
SE14
off Cold Blow La **171** E1
Sangora Rd, SW11 . . . . **179** D2
San Ho, E9
off Bradstock Rd **115** D3
Sansom Rd, E11 . . . . **103** E3
Sansom St, SE5 . . . . **88** B3
Sans Wk, EC1 . . . . **26** B2
Santley St, SW4 . . . . **181** F2
Santos Rd, SW18 . . . . **178** A3
● Sapcote Trd Cen,
NW10 . . . . **105** F2
Saperton Wk, SE11 . . . . **61** F4
Sapperton Ct, EC1 . . . . **27** E2
Sapphire Rd, NW10 . . . . **104** C4
SE8 . . . . **157** E3
Saracen's Head Yd, EC3 . . . . . **41** D3
Saracen St, E14 . . . . **144** A2
Sarah Ho, SW15 . . . . **175** F2
Saratoga Rd, E5 . . . . **114** C1
Sardinia St, WC2 . . . . **37** E3
Sark Ho, N1
off Clifton Rd **112** C3
Sarnesfield Ho, SE15
off Pencraig Way **170** B1
Sarre Rd, NW2 . . . . **107** F2
Sartor Rd, SE15 . . . . **185** D2
Sarum Ter, E3
off Bow Common La **129** F4
Satchwell Rd, E2 . . . . **128** A3
Sattar Ms, N16
off Clissold Rd **99** D4
Saturn Ho, E3
off Garrison Rd **130** A1

Sauls Grn, E11
off Napier Rd **103** E4
Saunders Cl, E14
off Limehouse Causeway **143** F3
Saunders Ness Rd, E14 ....**158** C4
Saunders St, SE11 ....**74** A1
Savage Gdns, EC3 ....**41** D4
Savannah Cl, SE15 ....**89** E3
Savernake Rd, NW3 ....**109** F1
Savile Row, W1 ....**35** E4
Saville Rd, W4 ....**147** D2
Savona Est, SW8 ....**83** E3
Savona St, SW8 ....**83** E3
Savoy Bldgs, WC2 ....**49** E1
Jct Savoy Circ, W3 ....**133** F3
Savoy Cl, E15
off Arthingworth St **131** E1
Savoy Ct, WC2 ....**49** D1
Savoy Hill, WC2 ....**49** E1
Savoy Ms, SW9 ....**181** E1
Riv Savoy Pier 49 E1
Savoy Pl, WC2 ....**49** D1
Savoy Row, WC2 ....**37** E4
Savoy Steps, WC2
off Savoy Row **49** E1
Savoy St, WC2 ....**37** E4
Savoy Way, WC2 ....**49** E1
Sawley Rd, W12 ....**134** A4
Sawmill Yd, E3 ....**129** E1
Sawyer St, SE1 ....**51** E4
Saxon Cl, E17 ....**102** A1
Saxon Dr, W3 ....**132** B2
Saxon Rd, E3 ....**129** F2
Wembley HA9 ....**90** C4
Saxton Cl, SE13 ....**187** D1
Sayes Ct, SE8
off Sayes Ct St **171** F1
Sayes Ct St, SE8 ....**171** F1
Scala St, W1 ....**23** F4
Scampston Ms, W10 ....**135** D2
Scandrett St, E1 ....**142** B4
Scarab Cl, E16 ....**145** F3
Scarba Wk, N1
off Marquess Rd **113** D3
Scarborough Rd, E11 .....**103** D2
N4 ....**98** A1
Scarborough St, E1 ......**41** F3
Scarsdale Pl, W8 ....**54** C2
Scarsdale Vil, W8 ....**54** B3
Scarth Rd, SW13 ....**175** F1
Scawen Rd, SE8 ....**157** E4
Scawfell St, E2 ....**17** F3
Sceaux Gdns, SE5 ....**89** D4
Sceptre Rd, E2 ....**128** C3
Uni Schiller Int Uni, SE1 .....50 A3
Scholars Pl, N16 ....**99** E4
Scholefield Rd, N19 .....**97** D2
Schomberg Ho, SW1
off Page St **60** B4
Schonfeld Sq, N16 ....**99** D3
Schoolbank Rd, SE10 .....**159** F3
Schoolbell Ms, E3
off Arbery Rd **129** E2
Schoolhouse La, E1 ......**143** D3
Coll School of Economic Science, W1 ....34 B2
Uni School of Oriental & African Studies,
Russell Sq Campus, WC1 .24 B3
Vernon Sq Campus, WC1 ..13 F4
Uni School of Pharmacy, WC1 ....25 D2
School Rd, NW10 ....**119** D4
School Sq, SE10
off Greenroof Way **159** F2
Schooner Cl, E14 ....**159** D2
SE16 *off Kinburn St* **157** D1
Schubert Rd, SW15 ....**177** F3
★ Science Mus, SW7 ....56 B3
Sclater St, E1 ....**29** E2
Scoble Pl, N16 ....**113** F1
Scoresby St, SE1 ....**50** C3
Scotland Pl, SW1 ....**48** C2
Scotswood St, EC1 ....**26** B2
Scott Av, SW15 ....**177** E4
Scott Ct, SW8
off Silverthorne Rd **166** B4
W3
off Petersfield Rd **147** D1
Scott Ellis Gdns, NW8 ....**20** A1
Scott Lidgett Cres, SE16 ....**156** A1
Scott Russell Pl, E14
off Westferry Rd **158** B4
Scotts Rd, E10 ....**102** C2
W12 ....**148** B1
Scott St, E1 ....**128** B4
Scoulding Rd, E16 ....**145** F2
Scouler St, E14
off Quixley St **145** D3
Scout App, NW10 ....**105** E1
Scout La, SW4
off Old Town **180** C1
Scovell Cres, SE1 ....**63** E1
Scovell Rd, SE1 ....**63** E1
Scriven St, E8 ....**127** F1
Scrooby St, SE6 ....**186** B4
Scrubs La, NW10 ....**120** A3
W10 ....**120** A3
Scrutton St, EC2 ....**28** C3
Scutari Rd, SE22 ....**184** C3
Scylla Rd, SE15 ....**184** B1
Seabright St, E2
off Bethnal Grn Rd **128** B3
Seacole Cl, W3 ....**133** D1
Seacon Twr, E14 ....**157** F1
Seaford St, WC1 ....**25** D1
Seaforth Cres, N5 ....**112** C2
Seaforth Pl, SW1
off Buckingham Gate **59** F2
Seagrave Cl, E1
off Wellesley St **143** D1
Seagrave Rd, SW6 ....**66** B4
Seal St, E8 ....**113** F1
Searle Pl, N4 ....**97** F2
Searles Cl, SW11 ....**81** D3
Searles Rd, SE1 ....**64** B4
Sears St, SE5 ....**88** A2
Seaton Cl, SE11 ....**74** B2
Seaton Pt, E5 ....**114** A1
Sebastian St, EC1 ....**27** D1
Sebbon St, N1 ....**112** B4
Sebright Pas, E2
off Hackney Rd **128** A2
Secker St, SE1 ....**50** A3
Second Av, SW14 ....**175** E1
W3 ....**133** F4
W10 ....**121** E4
Second Way, Wem. HA9 ....**104** B1
Sedan Way, SE17 ....**76** C2
Sedding St, SW1 ....**58** A4
Seddon Highwalk, EC2
off The Barbican **27** E4
Seddon Ho, EC2
off The Barbican **27** E4
Seddon St, WC1 ....**25** F1
Sedgeford Rd, W12 ....**133** F4
Sedgmoor Pl, SE5 ....**89** D3
Sedgwick Rd, E10 ....**102** C3
Sedgwick St, E9 ....**115** D2
Sedleigh Rd, SW18 ....**177** F4
Sedlescombe Rd, SW6 .....**163** F1
Sedley Pl, W1 ....**34** C3
Seelig Av, NW9 ....**92** A1
Seething La, EC3 ....**53** D1
Sefton St, SW15 ....**162** C4
Sekforde St, EC1 ....**26** C3
Selbie Av, NW10 ....**105** F2
Selborne Rd, SE5
off Denmark Hill **169** D4
Selby Rd, E11 ....**103** E4
Selby Sq, W10 ....**121** E3
Selby St, E1 ....**128** A4
Selden Rd, SE15 ....**170** C4
Selden Wk, N7
off Durham Rd **97** F3
Seldon Ho, SW8 ....**83** E3
★ Selfridges, W1 ....34 A3
Sellons Av, NW10 ....**119** F1
Selsdon Rd, NW2 ....**91** F3
Selsdon Way, E14 ....**158** B2
Selsea Pl, N16
off Crossway **113** E2
Selsey St, E14 ....**144** A1
Selway Ho, SW8
off South Lambeth Rd ...**85** D4
Selwood Pl, SW7 ....**68** A2
Selwood Ter, SW7 ....**68** A2
Selworthy Ho, SW11 ......**80** B4
Selwyn Ct, SE3 ....**187** E1
Selwyn Rd, E3 ....**129** F2
NW10 ....**105** D4
Semley Pl, SW1 ....**70** B1
Senate St, SE15 ....**170** C4
Sendall Ct, SW11 ....**179** D1
Senior St, W2 ....**18** C4
Senrab St, E1 ....**143** D2
Sentinel Pt, SW8
off St. George Wf **72** C4
Serbin Cl, E10 ....**102** C1
Serenaders Rd, SW9 ......**168** A4
Serjeants Inn, EC4 ......**38** B3
Serle St, WC2 ....**37** F2
Sermon La, EC4 ....**39** E3
★ Serpentine, The, W2 .....44 C3
★ Serpentine Gall, W2 .....44 B3
Serpentine Rd, W2 ....**45** E3
Setchell Rd, SE1 ....**65** E4
Setchell Way, SE1 ....**65** E4
Seth St, SE16
off Swan Rd **156** C1
Settlers Ct, E14
off Newport Av **145** D3
Settles St, E1 ....**142** A1
Settrington Rd, SW6 .....**164** B4
Sevenoaks Rd, SE4 ....**185** E4
Seven Sisters Rd, N4 ....**97** F4
N7 ....**97** F4
N15 ....**98** C1
Seven Stars Cor, W12
off Goldhawk Rd **148** A2
Seven Stars Yd, E1 ......**29** F4
Severnake Cl, E14 ....**158** A3
Severn Av, W10
off Selby Sq **121** E3
Severn Way, NW10 ....**105** F2
Severus Rd, SW11 ....**179** E2
Seville Ms, N1 ....**113** E4
Seville St, SW1 ....**57** F1
Sevington St, W9 ....**18** C3
Sewardstone Rd, E2 ......**128** C2
Seward St, EC1 ....**27** D2

Sewdley St, E5 . . . . **101** D4
Sextant Av, E14 . . . . **159** D3
Sexton Ct, E14
off Newport Av **145** D3
Seymour Gdns, SE4 . . . . **185** E1
Seymour Ms, W1 . . . . **34** A2
Seymour Pl, W1 . . . . **33** E1
Seymour Rd, E10 . . . . **101** F2
W4 . . . . **146** C3
Seymour St, W1 . . . . **33** E3
W2 . . . . **33** E3
Seymour Wk, SW10 . . . . **67** E4
Seyssel St, E14 . . . . **158** C3
Shaa Rd, W3 . . . . **133** D3
Shackleton Ct, W12 . . . . **148** B1
E14
off Maritime Quay **158** A4
SHACKLEWELL, N16 . . . . **113** F1
Shacklewell Grn, E8 . . . . **113** F1
Shacklewell La, E8 . . . . **113** F2
N16 . . . . **113** F2
Shacklewell Rd, N16 . . . . . . **113** F1
Shacklewell Row, E8 . . . . . . **113** F1
Shacklewell St, E2 . . . . **29** F2
Shad Thames, SE1 . . . . **53** E3
SHADWELL, E1 . . . . **142** C3
Shadwell **142** C3
Shadwell **142** C3
Shadwell Gdns Est, E1
off Martha St **142** C3
Shadwell Pierhead, E1
off Glamis Rd **142** C3
Shadwell Pl, E1
off Sutton St **142** C3
Shaftesbury Av, W1 . . . . **36** A4
WC2 . . . . **36** A4
Shaftesbury Ct, N1 . . . . **16** A3
SE1 *off Alderney Ms* **64** A2
Shaftesbury Gdns, NW10 . . . **119** E4
Shaftesbury Ms, SW4 . . . . . . **180** C3
W8 . . . . **54** B3
Shaftesbury Pl, W14
off Warwick Rd **149** F3
Shaftesbury Rd, E10 . . . . **102** A2
N19 . . . . **97** E2
Shaftesbury St, N1 . . . . **15** F3
Shafto Ms, SW1 . . . . **57** E3
Shafton Rd, E9 . . . . **129** D1
Shakespeare Av, NW10 . . . . **119** D1
Shakespeare Rd, NW10 . . . . **119** D1
SE24 . . . . **182** B3
W3 . . . . **132** C4
★ Shakespeare's Globe Thea,
SE1 . . . . **51** E1
Shakespeare Twr, EC2 . . . . **27** F4
Shakspeare Ms, N16
off Shakspeare Wk **113** E1
Shakspeare Wk, N16 . . . . . . **113** E1
Shalbourne Sq, E9 . . . . **115** F2
Shalcomb St, SW10 . . . . **79** F1
Shalden Ho, SW15
off Tunworth Cres **175** F4
Shalfleet Dr, W10 . . . . **135** D3
Shalimar Gdns, W3 . . . . **132** C3
Shalimar Rd, W3 . . . . **132** C3
Shalstone Rd, SW14 . . . . **174** B1
Shamrock St, SW4 . . . . **181** D1
Shandon Rd, SW4 . . . . **180** C4
Shand St, SE1 . . . . **52** C4
Shandy St, E1 . . . . **143** D1
Shannon Cl, NW2 . . . . **93** D4
Shannon Gro, SW9 . . . . **181** F2
Shannon Pl, NW8 . . . . **9** D2
Shardcroft Av, SE24 . . . . **182** B3
Shardeloes Rd, SE4 . . . . **185** F1
SE14 . . . . **185** F1
Sharnbrook Ho, W14 . . . . **66** A4
Sharon Gdns, E9 . . . . **128** C1
Sharon Rd, W4 . . . . **147** D4
Sharpleshall St, NW1 . . . . . . **109** F4
Sharratt St, SE15 . . . . **170** C1
Sharsted St, SE17 . . . . **74** C3
Shavers Pl, SW1 . . . . **48** A1
Shawbury Rd, SE22 . . . . **183** F3
Shaw Ct, SW11 . . . . **179** D1
Shaw Cres, E14 . . . . **143** E1
Shawfield St, SW3 . . . . **69** D3
Shaw Rd, SE22 . . . . **183** E2
Shearling Way, N7 . . . . **111** E3
Shearman Rd, SE3 . . . . **187** F2
Shearsmith Ho, E1
off Cable St **142** A3
Sheba Pl, E1 . . . . **29** F3
Sheen Common, SW14 . . . . . **174** B3
Sheen Common Dr, Rich.
TW10 . . . . **174** A2
Sheen Ct, Rich. TW10 . . . . . . **174** A2
Sheen Ct Rd, Rich. TW10 . . . **174** A2
Sheen Gate Gdns, SW14 . . . . **174** C2
Sheen Gate Mans Pas, SW14
off East Sheen Av **175** D2
Sheen Gro, N1
off Richmond Av **126** A1
Sheen La, SW14 . . . . **174** C1
Sheen Wd, SW14 . . . . **174** C3
Sheepcote La, SW11 . . . . **165** F4
Sheep La, E8 . . . . **128** B1
Sheffield Sq, E3
off Malmesbury Rd **129** F3
Sheffield St, WC2 . . . . **37** E3
Sheffield Ter, W8 . . . . **42** A3
Shelburne Rd, N7 . . . . **111** F1
Shelbury Rd, SE22 . . . . **184** B3
Sheldon Av, N6 . . . . **95** E1
Sheldon Ct, SW8
off Thorncroft St **84** C3
Sheldon Pl, E2 . . . . **128** A2
Sheldon Rd, NW2 . . . . **107** D1
Sheldon Sq, W2 . . . . **31** F1
Sheldrake Pl, W8 . . . . **42** A4
Shelduck Cl, E15 . . . . **117** F2
Shelford Pl, N16 . . . . **99** D4
Shelgate Rd, SW11 . . . . **179** E3
★ Shell Cen, SE1 . . . . **49** F3
Shelley Cl, SE15 . . . . **170** B4
Shelley Ct, N4 . . . . **97** F2
Shelley Ho, SW1 . . . . **71** F4
Shelley Rd, NW10 . . . . **119** D1
Shellgrove Est, N16 . . . . **113** E2
Shellness Rd, E5 . . . . **114** B2
Shell Rd, SE13 . . . . **186** B1
Shellwood Rd, SW11 . . . . **165** F4
Shelmerdine Cl, E3 . . . . **144** A1
Shelton St, WC2 . . . . **36** C3
Shenfield St, N1 . . . . **17** D3
Shenley Rd, SE5 . . . . **169** E3
Shepherdess Pl, N1 . . . . **15** F4
Shepherdess Wk, N1 . . . . **15** F2
Shepherd Mkt, W1 . . . . **46** C2
SHEPHERD'S BUSH, W12 . . . **134** C4
Shepherd's Bush **149** D1
Shepherd's Bush **149** D1
Shepherds Bush Grn, W12 . . **148** C1
Shepherd's Bush
Market **134** C4
Shepherds Bush Mkt, W12 . . **148** C1
Shepherds Bush Pl, W12 . . . . **149** D1
Shepherds Bush Rd, W6 . . . . **148** C3
Shepherds Cl, W1
off Lees Pl **34** A4
Shepherds Ct, W12
off Shepherds Bush Grn . **149** D1
Shepherds Ho, N7
off York Way **111** E3
Shepherds La, E9 . . . . **115** D2
Shepherd's Pl, W1 . . . . **34** A4
Shepherd St, W1 . . . . **46** C3
Shepherds Wk, NW2 . . . . **92** A3
NW3 . . . . **109** D2
Sheppard Dr, SE16 . . . . **156** B4
Sheppard St, E16 . . . . **131** F4
Shepperton Rd, N1 . . . . **126** C1
Sheppey Wk, N1
off Ashby Gro **112** C4
Shepton Hos, E2
off Globe Rd **128** C3
Sherard Ct, N7
off Manor Gdns **97** E4
Sheraton St, W1 . . . . **36** A3
Sherborne Ho, SW8
off Bolney St **85** E3
Sherborne La, EC4 . . . . **40** A4
Sherborne St, N1 . . . . **127** D1
Sherbrooke Rd, SW6 . . . . **163** F2
Sherfield Gdns, SW15 . . . . . . **175** F4
Sheridan Hts, E1
off Watney St **142** B2
Sheridan Pl, SW13 . . . . **161** F4
Sheridan Rd, E7 . . . . **103** F4
Sheringham Rd, N7 . . . . **111** F3
★ Sherlock Holmes Mus,
NW1 . . . . **21** F3
Sherlock Ms, W1 . . . . **22** A4
Sherrick Grn Rd, NW10 . . . . . **106** B2
Sherriff Rd, NW6 . . . . **108** A3
Sherrin Rd, E10 . . . . **116** A1
Sherwin Rd, SE14 . . . . **171** D3
Sherwood Cl, SW13
off Lower Common S . . . **176** B1
Sherwood Gdns, E14 . . . . **158** A3
SE16 . . . . **156** A4
Sherwood St, W1 . . . . **35** F4
Shetland Rd, E3 . . . . **129** F2
Shillibeer Pl, W1 . . . . **21** D4
Shillingford St, N1
off Hawes St **112** B4
Shinfield St, W12 . . . . **134** C2
Ship All, W4
off Thames Rd **160** A1
Ship & Mermaid Row, SE1 . . . **52** B4
Ship La, SW14 . . . . **160** C4
Ship St, SE8 . . . . **172** A3
Ship Tavern Pas, EC3 . . . . **40** C4
Shipton St, E2 . . . . **17** F4
Shipwright Rd, SE16 . . . . **157** E1
Shipwright Yd, SE1 . . . . **52** C3
Ship Yd, E14
off Napier Av **158** B4
Shirbutt St, E14 . . . . **144** B3
Shirland Ms, W9 . . . . **121** F3
Shirland Rd, W9 . . . . **18** A1
Shirley Gro, SW11 . . . . **180** A1
Shirley Rd, E15 . . . . **117** E4
W4 . . . . **147** D1
Shirley St, E16 . . . . **145** F2
Shirlock Rd, NW3 . . . . **109** F1
Shobroke Cl, NW2 . . . . **92** C4
Shoe La, EC4 . . . . **38** B2
Shooters Hill Rd, SE3 . . . . . . **173** F3
SE10 . . . . **173** D3
Shoot Up Hill, NW2 . . . . **107** E2
SHOREDITCH, E1 . . . . **29** E3

⊖ Shoreditch High Street . . .29 D3
horeditch High St, E1 . . . . . .29 D3
horeditch Ho, N1 . . . . .28 B1
horeham Cl, SW18
off Ram St 178 B3
hore Pl, E9 . . . . .114 C4
hore Rd, E9 . . . . .114 C4
hore Way, SW9 . . . . .168 A4
horncliffe Rd, SE1 . . . . .77 E2
horrolds Rd, SW6 . . . . .163 F2
horter St, E1 . . . . .41 E4
hortlands, W6 . . . . .149 D3
hortlands Rd, E10 . . . . .102 B1
hort Rd, E11 . . . . .103 E3
W4 . . . . .161 E1
horts Gdns, WC2 . . . . .36 C3
hort St, SE1 . . . . .50 B4
hort Wall, E15 . . . . .130 C3
hottendane Rd, SW6 . . . . . . .78 A4
hottfield Av, SW14 . . . . . . .175 E2
houlder of Mutton All, E14
off Narrow St 143 E3
houldham St, W1 . . . . .33 D1
hrewsbury Av, SW14 . . . . . .174 C2
hrewsbury Ct, EC1
off Whitecross St 27 F3
hrewsbury Cres, NW10 . . . .119 D1
hrewsbury Ms, W2 . . . . .30 A1
hrewsbury Rd, NW10
off Shakespeare Rd 119 D1
W2 . . . . .30 A2
hrewsbury St, W10 . . . . . . .120 C4
hropshire Pl, WC1 . . . . .23 F3
hroton St, NW1 . . . . .20 C4
hrubbery Cl, N1 . . . . .15 F1
hrubland Rd, E8 . . . . .128 A1
E10 . . . . .102 A1
huna Wk, N1
off St. Paul's Rd 113 D3
hurland Gdns, SE15 . . . . . . .89 F2
huters Sq, W14
off Sun Rd 149 F4
huttle St, E1
off Buxton St 128 A4
huttleworth Rd, SW11 . . . .165 E4
ibella Rd, SW4 . . . . .167 D4
icilian Av, WC1 . . . . .37 D1
idbury St, SW6 . . . . .163 E3
iddons La, NW1 . . . . .21 F3
idford Ho, SE1
off Briant Est 61 F3
idford Pl, SE1 . . . . .61 F3
idings, The, E11 . . . . .102 C2
idings Ms, N7 . . . . .98 A4
idmouth Par, NW2
off Sidmouth Rd 106 C4
idmouth Rd, E10 . . . . .102 C4
NW2 . . . . .106 C4
idmouth St, WC1 . . . . .25 D1
idney Gro, EC1 . . . . .14 C3
idney Rd, SW9 . . . . .167 F4
idney Sq, E1 . . . . .142 C2
idney St, E1 . . . . .142 B1
idney Webb Ho, SE1 . . . . . . .64 B2
idworth St, E8 . . . . .114 B4
igdon Pas, E8
off Sigdon Rd 114 A2
igdon Rd, E8 . . . . .114 A2
ignmakers Yd, NW1 . . . . . . .11 D1
ilbury St, N1 . . . . .16 A4
ilchester Rd, W10 . . . . . . .135 D2
ilesia Bldgs, E8
off London La 114 B4
ilex St, SE1 . . . . .63 D1
Silkin Ms, SE15
off Fenham Rd 170 A2
Silk Mills Pas, SE13
off Egeremont Rd 172 B4
Silk Mills Path, SE13
off Lewisham Rd 186 C1
Silk Mills Sq, E9 . . . . .115 F3
Silk St, EC2 . . . . .27 F4
Silsoe Ho, NW1
off Park Village E 11 D3
Silverbirch Wk, NW3
off Queen's Cres 110 A3
Silver Cl, SE14
off Southerngate Way . .171 E2
Silver Cres, W4 . . . . .146 B3
Silverdale, NW1 . . . . .11 E4
Silvermere Rd, SE6 . . . . . . .186 B4
Silver Pl, W1 . . . . .35 F4
Silver Rd, SE13 . . . . .186 B1
W12 . . . . .135 D3
Silverthorne Rd, SW8 . . . . .166 B4
Silverton Rd, W6 . . . . .163 D1
Silvertown Way, E16 . . . . . .145 F2
Silver Wk, SE16 . . . . .143 F4
Silvester Rd, SE22 . . . . .183 F3
Silvester St, SE1 . . . . .63 F1
Silvocea Way, E14 . . . . .145 D2
Silwood Est, SE16
off Concorde Way 157 D3
Silwood St, SE16 . . . . .156 C3
Simla Ho, SE1 . . . . .64 B1
Simms Rd, SE1 . . . . .156 A3
Simon Cl, W11
off Portobello Rd 135 F3
Simonds Rd, E10 . . . . .102 A3
Simons Wk, E15
off Waddington Rd 117 D2
Simpson Dr, W3 . . . . .133 D2
Simpsons Rd, E14 . . . . .144 B3
Simpson St, SW11 . . . . .165 E4
Simrose Ct, SW18
off Wandsworth High St .178 A3
Sims Wk, SE3 . . . . .187 F2
Sinclair Gdns, W14 . . . . . . .149 D1
Sinclair Pl, SE4 . . . . .186 A4
Sinclair Rd, W14 . . . . .149 D1
Singer St, EC2 . . . . .28 B1
Sir Alexander Cl, W3 . . . . . .133 F4
Sir Alexander Rd, W3 . . . . .133 F4
Sirdar Rd, W11 . . . . .135 D3
Sir Giles Gilbert Scott Bldg,
The, SW15 . . . . .177 E4
Sirinham Pt, SW8 . . . . .85 E1
Sir James Black Ho, SE5
off Coldharbour La 169 D4
Sir John Kirk Cl, SE5 . . . . . . .87 E2
Sir John Lyon Ho, EC4
off Gardners La 39 E4
★ Sir John Soane's Mus, WC2
off Lincoln's Inn Flds 37 E2
Sir Thomas More Est, SW3 . . .80 B1
Sise La, EC4 . . . . .40 A3
Sispara Gdns, SW18 . . . . . . .177 F4
Sister Mabel's Way, SE15
off Radnor Rd 170 A2
Sisters Av, SW11 . . . . .179 F2
Sisulu Pl, SW9 . . . . .182 A1
Sivill Ho, E2 . . . . .17 F4
Six Acres Est, N4 . . . . .98 A3
● Six Bridges Trd Est,
SE1 . . . . .156 A4
Sixth Av, W10 . . . . .121 E3
Skardu Rd, NW2 . . . . .107 E2
Skelgill Rd, SW15 . . . . .177 F2
Skelley Rd, E15 . . . . .117 F4
Skelton Cl, E8
off Buttermere Wk 113 F3
Skeltons La, E10 . . . . .102 B1
Skelwith Rd, W6 . . . . .162 C1
Skenfrith Ho, SE15
off Commercial Way 170 B1
Sketchley Gdns, SE16 . . . . .157 D4
Skiers St, E15 . . . . .131 E1
Skinner Ct, E2
off Parmiter St 128 B2
Skinner Pl, SW1 . . . . .70 A1
★ Skinners' Hall, EC4
off Dowgate Hill 40 A4
Skinners La, EC4 . . . . .39 F4
Skinner St, EC1 . . . . .26 B1
Skipsea Ho, SW18 . . . . .179 D4
Skipworth Rd, E9 . . . . .128 C1
Skomer Wk, N1
off Ashby Gro 112 C4
Skylines Village, E14 . . . . . .158 C1
Slade Twr, E10 . . . . .102 A3
Slade Wk, SE17 . . . . .87 D1
Slagrove Pl, SE13 . . . . .186 A3
Slaidburn St, SW10 . . . . .79 F1
Slaithwaite Rd, SE13 . . . . .186 C2
Slaney Pl, N7
off Hornsey Rd 112 A2
Sleaford Ho, E3 . . . . .130 A4
Sleaford St, SW8 . . . . .83 E2
Slievemore Cl, SW4
off Voltaire Rd 181 D1
Slingsby Pl, WC2 . . . . .36 C4
Slippers Pl, SE16 . . . . .156 B2
Slippers Pl Est, SE16
off Slippers Pl 156 B2
Sloane Av, SW3 . . . . .69 D1
Sloane Ct E, SW3 . . . . .70 A2
Sloane Ct W, SW3 . . . . .70 A2
Sloane Gdns, SW1 . . . . .70 A1
⊖ Sloane Square 70 A1
Sloane Sq, SW1 . . . . .70 A1
Sloane St, SW1 . . . . .57 F2
Sloane Ter, SW1 . . . . .57 F4
Sly St, E1
off Cannon St Rd 142 B2
Smallbrook Ms, W2 . . . . .32 A3
Smalley Cl, N16 . . . . .99 F4
Smalley Rd Est, N16
off Smalley Cl 99 F3
Smardale Rd, SW18
off Alma Rd 178 C3
Smart's Pl, WC2 . . . . .37 D2
Smart St, E2 . . . . .129 D3
Smead Way, SE13 . . . . .186 B1
Smeaton Ct, SE1 . . . . .63 E3
Smeaton St, E1 . . . . .142 B4
Smedley St, SW4 . . . . .167 D4
SW8 . . . . .167 D4
Smeed Rd, E3 . . . . .116 A4
Smiles Pl, SE13 . . . . .172 C4
Smith Cl, SE16 . . . . .143 D4
Smithfield St, EC1 . . . . .38 C1
Smith's Ct, W1 . . . . .35 F4
Smith Sq, SW1 . . . . .60 C3
Smith St, SW3 . . . . .69 E2
Smith Ter, SW3 . . . . .69 E3
Smithy St, E1 . . . . .142 C1
Smokehouse Yd, EC1 . . . . . . .27 D4
Smugglers Way, SW18 . . . . .178 B2
Smyrks Rd, SE17 . . . . .77 D3
Smyrna Rd, NW6 . . . . .108 A4
Smythe St, E14 . . . . .144 B3
Snarsgate St, W10 . . . . .134 C1

Sneath Av, NW11 .... **93** F1
Sneyd Rd, NW2 .... **106** C1
Snowberry Cl, E15 .... **117** D1
Snowbury Rd, SW6 .... **164** B4
Snowden St, EC2 .... **28** C3
Snow Hill, EC1 .... **38** C1
Snow Hill Ct, EC1 .... **39** D2
Snowman Ho, NW6 .... **122** B1
Snowsfields, SE1 .... **52** B4
Soames St, SE15 .... **183** F1
SOHO, W1 .... **36** A4
Soho Sq, W1 .... **36** A2
Soho St, W1 .... **36** A2
Sojourner Truth Cl, E8
off Richmond Rd **114** B3
Solander Gdns, E1
off Dellow St **142** B3
Soldene Ct, N7
off Piper Cl **111** F3
Solebay St, E1 .... **129** E4
Solent Rd, NW6 .... **108** A2
Soley Ms, WC1 .... **14** A4
Solna Av, SW15 .... **176** C3
Solomon's Pas, SE15 .... **184** B2
Solon New Rd, SW4 .... **181** E2
Solon Rd, SW2 .... **181** E2
Solway Cl, E8
off Buttermere Wk **113** F3
Solway Rd, SE22 .... **184** A2
Somali Rd, NW2 .... **107** F1
Somerfield Rd, N4 .... **98** B3
Somerfield St, SE16 .... **157** D4
Somerford Gro, N16 .... **113** F1
Somerford Gro Est, N16
off Somerford Gro **113** F1
Somerford St, E1 .... **128** B4
Somerford Way, SE16 .... **157** E1
Somerleyton Pas, SW9 .... **182** B2
Somerleyton Rd, SW9 .... **182** A2
Somers Cl, NW1 .... **12** A2
Somers Cres, W2 .... **32** C3
Somerset Est, SW11 .... **80** B4
Somerset Gdns, N6 .... **96** A1
SE13 .... **172** B4
★ Somerset Ho, WC2 .... 37 E4
Somerset Rd, W4 .... **147** D2
Somerset Sq, W14 .... **149** E1
Somers Ms, W2 .... **32** C3
Somers Rd, SW2 .... **181** F4
SOMERS TOWN, NW1 .... **12** B4
Somerton Av, Rich. TW9 .... **174** B1
Somerton Rd, NW2 .... **93** E4
SE15 .... **184** B2
Somerville Av, SW13 .... **162** B1
Somerville Cl, SW9
off Stockwell Pk Cres **167** F4
Sonderburg Rd, N7 .... **97** F3
Sondes St, SE17 .... **76** A4
Sonia Gdns, NW10 .... **105** F1
Sophia Cl, N7
off Mackenzie Rd **111** F3
Sophia Rd, E10 .... **102** B2
Sophia Sq, SE16
off Rotherhithe St **143** E3
Sopwith Way, SW8 .... **82** C2
Sorrel La, E14 .... **145** D2
Sorrell Cl, SE14
off Southerngate Way **171** E2
SW9 *off Tavern La* **168** A4
Sotheby Rd, N5 .... **98** B4
Sotheran Cl, E8 .... **128** A1
Sotheron Rd, SW6 .... **79** D3
Soudan Rd, SW11 .... **165** F3
Souldern Rd, W14 .... **149** D2
South Access Rd, E17 .... **101** E1
SOUTH ACTON, W3 .... **146** A2
⊖ South Acton 146 C2
South Acton Est, W3 .... **146** B1
South Africa Rd, W12 .... **134** B4
Southall Pl, SE1 .... **64** A1
Southampton Bldgs, WC2 .... **38** A2
Southampton Pl, WC1 .... **37** D1
Southampton Rd, NW5 .... **109** F2
Southampton Row, WC1 .... **25** D4
Southampton St, WC2 .... **37** D4
Southampton Way, SE5 .... **88** B2
Southam St, W10 .... **121** E4
South Audley St, W1 .... **46** B1
South Av, Rich. TW9
off Sandycombe Rd **160** A4
● Southbank Business Cen, SW8 .... 84 B1
⇌ South Bermondsey 156 C4
South Birkbeck Rd, E11 .... **103** D4
South Black Lion La, W6 .... **148** A4
South Bolton Gdns, SW5 .... **67** D2
Southborough Rd, E9 .... **128** C1
Southbrook Ms, SE12 .... **187** F4
Southbrook Rd, SE12 .... **187** F4
Coll South Camden City Learning Cen, NW1 .... 12 A2
South Carriage Dr, SW1 .... **45** E4
SW7 .... **56** B1
South Circular Rd,
SW4 (A205) **180** A3
SW11 (A3) **179** E3
SW14 (A205) **175** E2
SW15 (A205) **176** C2
SW18 (A3) **179** E3
W4 (A205) **146** A4
Brentford (A205) TW8 .... **146** A4
Richmond (A205) TW9 .... **160** B4
South City Ct, SE15 .... **89** D2
South Colonnade, The, E14 .... **144** A4
Southcombe St, W14 .... **149** E3
Southcote Rd, N19 .... **110** C1
Southcott Ms, NW8 .... **8** C3
South Cres, E16 .... **131** D4
WC1 .... **36** A1
Coll South E London Coll, SE4
off Shardeloes Rd 185 E1
South Eaton Pl, SW1 .... **58** B4
South Edwardes Sq, W8 .... **149** F2
South End, W8 .... **55** D2
South End Cl, NW3 .... **109** E1
South End Grn, NW3
off South End Rd **109** E1
South End Rd, NW3 .... **109** E1
South End Row, W8 .... **55** D2
Southerngate Way, SE14 .... **171** E2
Southern Gro, E3 .... **129** F3
Southern Row, W10 .... **121** E4
Southern St, N1 .... **13** E2
Southern Way, SE10 .... **159** F3
Southerton Rd, W6 .... **148** C2
Southey Rd, SW9 .... **86** A4
Southfield Rd, W4 .... **147** E2
Southfields Ms, SW18
off Southfields Rd **178** A4
Southfields Pas, SW18 .... **178** A4
Southfields Rd, SW18 .... **178** A4
Southgate Gro, N1 .... **113** D4
Southgate Rd, N1 .... **127** D1
South Gro, N6 .... **96** A2
South Gro Ho, N6 .... **96** A2
SOUTH HACKNEY, E9 .... **114** C4
SOUTH HAMPSTEAD, NW6 .... **108** B4
⊖ South Hampstead 108 C4
South Hill Pk, NW3 .... **109** E1
South Hill Pk Gdns, NW3 .... **109** E1
Southill St, E14
off Chrisp St **144** B2
South Island Pl, SW9 .... **85** F3
SOUTH KENSINGTON, SW7 .... **67** E1
⊖ South Kensington 56 B4
South Kensington Sta Arc, SW7
off Pelham St **56** B4
SOUTH LAMBETH, SW8 .... **85** D4
South Lambeth Est, SW8
off Dorset Rd **85** E3
South Lambeth Pl, SW8 .... **73** D4
South Lambeth Rd, SW8 .... **85** D1
South Lo, NW8 .... **8** A4
SW7
off Knightsbridge **57** D1
★ South London Art Gall, SE5 .... 89 D4
South Molton La, W1 .... **34** C3
South Molton St, W1 .... **34** C3
Southmoor Way, E9 .... **115** F3
Southolm St, SW11 .... **166** B3
South Par, SW3 .... **68** B2
W4 .... **147** D3
South Pk, SW6 .... **164** A4
South Pk Ms, SW6 .... **178** B1
South Pl, EC2 .... **28** B4
South Pl Ms, EC2 .... **40** B1
DLR South Quay 158 B1
● South Quay Plaza, E14 .... 158 B1
South Quay Sq, E14
off Marsh Wall **158** B1
South Row, SE3 .... **173** F4
South Sea St, SE16 .... **157** F2
South Side, W6 .... **147** F2
🔒 Southside Shop Cen, SW18 .... 178 B4
South Sq, WC1 .... **38** A1
South St, W1 .... **46** B2
South Tenter St, E1 .... **41** F4
South Ter, SW7 .... **56** C4
Coll South Thames Coll,
Putney Cen, SW15
off Putney Hill 177 D3
Roehampton Cen, SW15
off Roehampton La 176 A4
Wandsworth Cen, SW18
off Wandsworth High St 178 B3
Southvale Rd, SE3 .... **173** E4
Southview Av, NW10 .... **105** F2
South Vil, NW1 .... **111** D3
Southville, SW8 .... **84** B4
SOUTHWARK, SE1 .... **51** D3
⊖ Southwark 50 C3
Coll Southwark Adult Ed,
Nunhead Cen, SE15
off Whorlton Rd 184 B1
Thomas Calton Cen, SE15
off Alpha St 170 A4
Southwark Br, EC4 .... **51** F2
SE1 .... **51** F2
Southwark Br Rd, SE1 .... **63** D2
★ Southwark Cath, SE1 .... 52 A2
Coll Southwark Coll,
Bermondsey Cen, SE16
off Keetons Rd 156 B2
Camberwell Cen, SE5 .... 88 C3
Grange Cen, SE1 .... 65 D3
Waterloo Cen, SE1 .... 50 C4
Southwark Pk, SE16 .... **156** C3
Southwark Pk Est, SE16 .... **156** B3
Southwark Pk Rd, SE16 .... **65** F4
Southwark St, SE1 .... **51** D2

Southwater Cl, E14 ....143 F2
South Way, Wem. HA9 .....104 A2
Southway Cl, W12 ....148 B1
Southwell Gdns, SW7 ....55 E4
Southwell Gro Rd, E11 .....103 E3
Southwell Rd, SE5 ....182 C1
Southwest Rd, E11 ....103 D2
South Wf Rd, W2 ....32 A2
Southwick Ms, W2 ....32 B2
Southwick Pl, W2 ....32 C3
Southwick St, W2 ....32 C2
Southwold Rd, E5 ....100 B3
Southwood Av, N6 ....96 B1
Southwood La, N6 ....96 A1
Southwood Lawn Rd, N6 ....96 A1
Southwood Pk, N6 ....96 A1
Southwood Smith St, N1 .....14 C1
South Worple Av, SW14 ....175 E1
South Worple Way, SW14 ...175 D1
Sovereign Cl, E1 ....142 B3
Sovereign Cres, SE16
  off Rotherhithe St 143 E4
Sovereign Ms, E2 ....17 E2
Sovereign Pk, NW10 ....118 B4
Spafield St, EC1 ....26 A2
Spa Grn Est, EC1 ....14 B4
Spanby Rd, E3 ....130 A4
Spaniards Cl, NW11 ....95 D2
Spaniards End, NW3 ....94 C2
Spaniards Rd, NW3 ....94 C3
Spanish Pl, W1 ....34 B2
Spanish Rd, SW18 ....178 C3
Sparke Ter, E16
  off Clarkson Rd 145 F2
Sparkford Ho, SW11 ....80 B4
Sparks Cl, W3 ....133 D2
Spa Rd, SE16 ....65 E3
Sparsholt Rd, N19 ....97 E2
Sparta St, SE10 ....172 B3
★ Speaker's Cor, W2 ....33 F4
Spear Ms, SW5 ....66 B1
Spears Rd, N19 ....97 E2
Spectrum Pl, SE17 ....76 A4
Spedan Cl, NW3 ....94 B4
Speechly Ms, E8
  off Alvington Cres 113 F2
Speed Highwalk, EC2
  off Silk St 27 F4
Speed Ho, EC2 ....28 A4
Speedwell St, SE8
  off Comet St 172 A2
Speedy Pl, WC1 ....24 C1
Speldhurst Rd, E9 ....115 D4
  W4 ....147 D2
Spellbrook Wk, N1
  off Basire St 126 C1
Spelman St, E1 ....142 A1
Spence Cl, SE16
  off Vaughan St 157 F1
Spencer Gdns, SW14 ....174 C3
★ Spencer Ho, SW1 ....47 E3
Spencer Ms, SW8
  off Lansdowne Way 167 F3
  W6 *off Greyhound Rd* 163 E1
Spencer Pk, SW18 ....179 D3
Spencer Pas, E2
  off Pritchard's Rd 128 B2
Spencer Pl, N1
  off Canonbury La 112 B4
Spencer Ri, NW5 ....110 B1
Spencer Rd, SW18 ....179 D2
  W3 ....132 C4
  W4 ....160 C2
Spencer St, EC1 ....26 C1
Spencer Wk, NW3 ....109 D1
  SW15 ....177 D2
Spencer Way, E1
  off Watney St 142 B2
Spencer Yd, SE3
  off Blackheath Village ..173 F4
Spenser Gro, N16 ....113 E1
Spenser Rd, SE24 ....182 A3
Spenser St, SW1 ....59 F2
Spensley Wk, N16 ....99 D4
Spert St, E14 ....143 E3
Spey St, E14 ....144 C1
Spezia Rd, NW10 ....120 A2
Sphere, The, E16
  off Hallsville Rd 145 F2
Spice Quay Hts, SE1 ....53 F3
Spicer Cl, SW9 ....168 B4
Spindrift Av, E14 ....158 B3
Spire Ho, W2 ....31 F4
Spirit Quay, E1
  off Smeaton St 142 A4
★ Spitalfields City Fm,
  E1 ....128 A4
Spital Sq, E1 ....29 D4
Spital St, E1 ....128 A4
Spital Yd, E1 ....29 D4
Spode Ho, SE11
  off Lambeth Wk 62 A3
Spode Wk, NW6
  off Dresden Cl 108 B2
Spooners Ms, W3
  off Churchfield Rd 133 D4
Sporle Ct, SW11 ....179 D1
Sportsman Ms, E2
  off Whiston Rd 128 A1
Sprimont Pl, SW3 ....69 E2
Springall St, SE15 ....170 B2
Springbank Rd, SE13 ......187 D4
Springbank Wk, NW1
  off St. Paul's Cres 111 D4
Springdale Ms, N16 ....113 D1
Springdale Rd, N16 ....113 D1
Springfield, E5 ....100 B2
Springfield Gdns, E5 ....100 B2
Springfield La, NW6 ....6 C1
Springfield Rd, E15 ....131 E3
  NW8 ....7 E1
Springfield Wk, NW6 ....6 C1
Spring Gdns, N5
  off Grosvenor Av 112 C2
  SW1 ....48 B2
Spring Gro, W4 ....146 A4
Spring Hill, E5 ....100 A1
Springhill Cl, SE5 ....183 D1
Spring La, E5 ....100 B2
Spring Ms, W1 ....21 F4
Spring Pk Dr, N4 ....98 C2
Spring Pas, SW15
  off Embankment 177 D1
Spring Path, NW3 ....109 D2
Spring Pl, NW5 ....110 B2
Springrice Rd, SE13 ....186 C4
Spring St, W2 ....32 A3
Spring Tide Cl, SE15
  off Staffordshire St 170 A3
Springvale Est, W14
  off Blythe Rd 149 E2
Springvale Ter, W14 ....149 D2
Spring Wk, E1
  off Old Montague St 142 A1
Springwell Av, NW10 ......119 F1
Springwood Cl, E3 ....130 A2
Sprules Rd, SE4 ....171 E4
Spurgeon St, SE1 ....64 A3
Spurling Rd, SE22 ....183 F2
Spur Rd, SE1 ....50 A4
  SW1 ....59 E1
Spurstowe Rd, E8
  off Marcon Pl 114 B2
Spurstowe Ter, E8 ....114 B2
Square, The, E10 ....102 C4
  W6 ....148 C4
Square Rigger Row, SW11
  off York Pl 178 C1
Squire Gdns, NW8 ....20 A1
Squires Mt, NW3
  off East Heath Rd 95 D4
Squirrels, The, SE13 ....187 D1
Squirries St, E2 ....128 A3
Stable Ms, NW5
  off Grafton Rd 110 B3
Stables Way, SE11 ....74 A2
Stable Wk, N1
  off Wharfdale Rd 125 E2
Stable Way, W10
  off Latimer Rd 134 C2
Stable Yd, SW1 ....47 E4
  SW9
  off Broomgrove Rd 167 F4
  SW15
  off Danemere St 176 C1
Stable Yd Rd, SW1 ....47 E3
Stacey St, N7 ....98 A4
  WC2 ....36 B3
Stackhouse St, SW3 ....57 E2
Stacy Path, SE5 ....88 C3
● Stadium Business Cen,
  Wem. HA9 ....90 B4
🔒 Stadium Retail Pk, Wem.
  HA9 ....90 A4
Stadium Rd, NW2 ....92 B1
Stadium Rd E, NW2 ....92 C1
Stadium St, SW10 ....79 F3
Staffa Rd, E10 ....101 E2
Stafford Cl, NW6 ....18 A1
Stafford Ct, SW8
  off Allen Edwards Dr 84 C3
  W8 ....54 A2
Stafford Cripps Ho, E2
  off Globe Rd 128 C3
  SW6
  off Clem Attlee Ct 163 F1
Stafford Pl, SW1 ....59 E2
Stafford Rd, E3 ....129 F2
  NW6 ....6 A4
Staffordshire St, SE15 .....170 A3
Stafford St, W1 ....47 E2
Stafford Ter, W8 ....54 A2
Staff St, EC1 ....28 B1
Stagshaw Ho, SE22
  off Pytchley Rd 183 E1
Stainer St, SE1 ....52 B3
Staining La, EC2 ....39 F2
Stainsbury St, E2
  off Royston St 128 C2
Stainsby Rd, E14 ....144 A2
Stainton Rd, SE6 ....187 D4
Stalbridge St, NW1 ....21 D4
Stalham St, SE16 ....156 B2
⊖ Stamford Brook 147 F3
Stamford Brook Av, W6 ....147 F2
Stamford Brook Gdns, W6
  off Stamford Brook Rd ..147 F2
Stamford Brook Rd, W6 ....147 F2
Stamford Cotts, SW10 ......79 D2
Stamford Ct, W6 ....148 A3
Stamford Gro E, N16 ......100 A2
Stamford Gro W, N16 ......100 A2

STAMFORD HILL, N16 **99** E2
⇄ Stamford Hill **99** E1
Stamford Hill, N16 **99** F3
Stamford Hill Est, N16 **99** F2
Stamford Rd, N1 **113** E4
Stamford St, SE1 **50** A3
Stamp Pl, E2 **17** E4
Stanard Cl, N16 **99** E1
Stanborough Pas, E8
off Kingsland Rd **113** F3
Stanbridge Rd, SW15 **176** C1
Stanbury Rd, SE15 **170** B3
Standard Pl, EC2 **29** D1
Standard Rd, NW10 **118** C4
Standish Rd, W6 **148** A3
Stane Gro, SW9 **167** E4
Stanfield Ho, NW8
off Frampton St **20** B2
Stanfield Rd, E3 **129** E2
Stanford Ct, SW6
off Bagley's La **164** B3
Stanford Ms, E8
off Dalston La **114** A2
Stanford Pl, SE17 **76** C1
Stanford Rd, W8 **55** D2
Stanford St, SW1 **72** A1
Stangate, SE1 **61** E2
Stanhope Cl, SE16
off Middleton Dr **157** D1
Stanhope Gdns, SW7 **55** F4
Stanhope Gate, W1 **46** B2
Stanhope Ms E, SW7 **55** F4
Stanhope Ms S, SW7 **67** F1
Stanhope Ms W, SW7 **55** F4
Stanhope Par, NW1
off Stanhope St **11** E4
Stanhope Pl, W2 **33** E3
Stanhope Row, W1 **46** C3
Stanhope St, NW1 **23** E1
Stanhope Ter, W2 **32** B4
Stanier Cl, W14
off Aisgill Av **149** F4
Stanlake Ms, W12 **134** C4
Stanlake Rd, W12 **134** B4
Stanlake Vil, W12 **134** B4
Stanley Cl, SW8 **85** E1
Stanley Cres, W11 **135** F3
Stanley Gdns, NW2 **106** C2
W3 **133** E4
W11 **135** F3
Stanley Gdns Ms, W11
off Kensington Pk Rd **135** F3
Stanley Gro, SW8 **166** A4
Stanley Rd, E15 **131** D1
SW14 **174** B2
W3 **146** C2
Stanley St, SE8 **171** F2
Stanley Ter, N19 **97** E3
Stanliff Ho, E14
off Lightermans Rd **158** A2
Stanmer St, SW11 **165** E3
Stanmore Rd, E11 **103** F2
Stanmore St, N1
off Caledonian Rd **125** F1
Stannard Ms, E8 **114** A3
Stannard Rd, E8 **114** A3
Stannary St, SE11 **74** B4
Stansbury Sq, W10
off Beethoven St **121** E3
Stansfield Ho, SE1 **77** F1
Stansfield Rd, SW9 **181** F1
Stanswood Gdns, SE5 **89** D3
Stanton Ho, SE16
off Rotherhithe St **157** F1
Stanton Rd, SW13 **161** F4
Stanway Ct, N1 **17** D3
Stanway Gdns, W3 **132** A4
Stanway St, N1 **17** D2
Stanwick Rd, W14 **149** F3
Stanworth St, SE1 **65** E1
Staplehurst Rd, SE13 **187** E3
Staple Inn, WC1 **38** A1
Staple Inn Bldgs, WC1 **38** A1
Staples Cl, SE16 **143** E4
Jct Staples Cor, NW2 **92** B2
● Staples Cor Retail Pk, NW2
off Geron Way **92** B3
Staple St, SE1 **64** B1
Stapleton Hall Rd, N4 **97** F1
Star All, EC3 **41** D4
Starboard Way, E14 **158** A2
Starcross St, NW1 **23** F1
Starfield Rd, W12 **148** A1
Star La, E16 **131** E4
Star Pl, E1 **53** F1
Star Rd, W14 **163** F1
Star St, E16 **145** F1
W2 **32** B2
Star Wf, NW1
off St. Pancras Way **124** C1
Star Yd, WC2 **38** A2
Staten Bldg, E3
off Fairfield Rd **130** A2
Statham Ct, N7 **97** E4
Statham Gro, N16
off Green Las **113** D1
Station App, N16
(Stoke Newington)
off Stamford Hill **99** F3
NW10 *off Station Rd* **119** F3
SE1 **49** F3
SW6 **177** E1
Richmond TW9 **160** A3
Station App Rd, W4 **160** C2
Station Av, SW9
off Coldharbour La **182** B1
Richmond (Kew) TW9 **160** A3
Station Ct, SW6 **164** C3
Stationers Hall Ct, EC4
off Ludgate Hill **39** D3
Station Gdns, W4 **160** C2
Station Par, NW2 **106** C3
W3 **132** A2
Richmond TW9 **160** A3
Station Pas, SE15 **170** C3
Station Path, E8
off Amhurst Rd **114** B3
Station Pl, N4
off Seven Sisters Rd **98** A3
Station Rd, N19 **96** C4
NW10 **119** F2
SE13 **186** C1
SW13 **176** A1
Station St, E15 **117** D4
Station Ter, NW10 **121** D2
SE5 **87** F4
Staunton St, SE8 **171** F1
★ Stave Hill Ecological Pk,
SE16 **157** E1
Staveley Cl, E9
off Churchill Wk **114** C2
N7 **111** E1
SE15 *off Asylum Rd* **170** B3
Staveley Gdns, W4 **161** D3
Staveley Rd, W4 **161** D2
Staverton Rd, NW2 **106** C4
Stave Yd Rd, SE16 **143** E4
Stavordale Rd, N5 **112** B1
Stayner's Rd, E1 **129** D4
Stead St, SE17 **76** A1
Stean St, E8 **127** F1
Stebbing Ho, W11 **135** D4
Stebondale St, E14 **158** C4
Stedham Pl, WC1 **36** C2
Steedman St, SE17 **75** E1
Steele Rd, E11 **117** E1
NW10 **118** C2
W4 **146** C2
Steeles Ms N, NW3
off Steeles Rd **109** F3
Steeles Ms S, NW3
off Steeles Rd **109** F3
Steeles Rd, NW3 **109** F3
Steel's La, E1
off Devonport St **142** C2
Steelyard Pas, EC4 **52** A1
Steen Way, SE22
off East Dulwich Gro **183** E3
Steeple Cl, SW6 **163** E4
Steeple Ct, E1
off Coventry Rd **128** B4
Steeple Wk, N1
off Basire St **126** C1
Steers Way, SE16 **157** E1
Stellman Cl, E5 **100** A4
Stephan Cl, E8 **128** A1
Stephendale Rd, SW6 **164** B4
Stephen Ms, W1 **36** A1
Stephen Pl, SW4
off Rectory Gro **180** C1
Stephenson Cl, E3
off Rainhill Way **130** B3
Stephenson Ho, SE1
off Bath Ter **63** E2
Stephenson St, E16 **131** E4
NW10 **119** E3
Stephenson Way, NW1 **23** F2
Stephen's Rd, E15 **131** E1
Stephen St, W1 **36** A1
STEPNEY, E1 **142** C1
Stepney Causeway, E1 **143** D2
⊖ Stepney Green **129** D4
Stepney Grn, E1 **142** C1
Stepney High St, E1 **143** D1
Stepney Way, E1 **142** B1
Sterling Cl, NW10 **106** A4
Sterling Gdns, SE14 **171** E1
Sterling St, SW7 **57** D2
Sterndale Rd, W14 **149** D2
Sterne St, W12 **149** D1
Sternhall La, SE15 **184** A1
Sterry St, SE1 **64** A1
Steve Biko Rd, N7 **98** A4
Stevedore St, E1
off Waterman Way **142** B4
Stevenage Rd, SW6 **163** D2
Stevens Av, E9 **114** C3
Stevenson Cres, SE16 **156** A4
Stevens St, SE1 **65** D2
Steventon Rd, W12 **133** F3
Steward St, E1 **41** D1
Stewart Rd, E15 **116** C1
Stewart's Gro, SW3 **68** B2
Stewart's Rd, SW8 **83** E3
Stewart St, E14 **158** C1
Stew La, EC4 **39** E4
Steyne Rd, W3 **132** C4
Stile Hall Gdns, W4 **146** A4
Stile Hall Par, W4
off Chiswick High Rd **146** A4
Stillingfleet Rd, SW13 **162** A1
Stillington St, SW1 **59** F4

tillness Rd, SE23 .... **185** E4
tirling Rd, SW9 .... **167** E4
W3 .... **146** B2
★ Stock Exchange, EC4 .... 39 D2
tockholm Ho, E1 .... **142** A3
tockholm Rd, SE16 .... **156** C4
tockholm Way, E1 .... **142** A4
tockhurst Cl, SW15 .... **162** C4
tockleigh Hall, NW8
off Prince Albert Rd **9** E2
tock Orchard Cres, N7 .... **111** F2
tock Orchard St, N7 .... **111** F2
tocks Pl, E14
off Grenade St **143** F3
tockton Ho, E2
off Ellsworth St **128** B3
TOCKWELL, SW9 .... **167** F3
⊖ Stockwell 167 E3
tockwell Av, SW9 .... **181** F1
tockwell Gdns, SW9 .... **167** F4
tockwell Gdns Est, SW9 .... **167** E4
tockwell Grn, SW9 .... **167** F4
tockwell La, SW9 .... **167** F4
tockwell Ms, SW9
off Stockwell Rd **167** F4
tockwell Pk Cres, SW9 .... **167** F4
tockwell Pk Est, SW9 .... **181** F1
tockwell Pk Rd, SW9 .... **167** F3
tockwell Pk Wk, SW9 .... **181** F1
tockwell Rd, SW9 .... **167** F4
tockwell St, SE10 .... **172** C1
tockwell Ter, SW9 .... **167** F3
tokenchurch St, SW6 .... **164** B3
TOKE NEWINGTON, N16 .... **99** E3
⇌ Stoke Newington 99 F3
toke Newington Ch St, N16 .... **99** D4
toke Newington Common,
N16 .... **99** F4
toke Newington High St,
N16 .... **99** F4
toke Newington Rd, N16 .... **113** F2
toke Pl, NW10 .... **119** F3
tokesley St, W12 .... **133** F2
toll Cl, NW2 .... **92** C4
TONEBRIDGE, NW10 .... **118** B1
tonebridge Common, E8
off Mayfield Rd **113** F4
⊖ Stonebridge Park 104 A4
⊖ Stonebridge Park 104 A4
tonebridge Pk, NW10 .... **105** D4
Stonebridge Shop Cen, NW10
off Shakespeare Rd 119 D1
tonebridge Way, Wem.
HA9 .... **104** B3
tone Bldgs, WC2 .... **37** F1
tone Cl, SW4
off Larkhall Ri **180** C1
tonecutter St, EC4 .... **38** C2
tonefield, N4 .... **97** F3
tonefield St, N1 .... **126** A1
tone Hall Gdns, W8 .... **54** C3
tone Hall Pl, W8 .... **54** C3
tonehill Cl, SW14 .... **175** D3
tonehill Rd, SW14 .... **174** C3
W4 .... **146** A4
tone Ho Ct, EC3 .... **40** C2
toneleigh Ms, E3
off Stanfield Rd **129** E2
toneleigh Pl, W11 .... **135** D3
toneleigh St, W11 .... **135** D3
toneleigh Ter, N19 .... **96** B3
tonells Rd, SW11
off Chatham Rd **179** F3
tonenest St, N4 .... **97** F2
Stones End St, SE1 .... **63** E1
Stoneyard La, E14
off Poplar High St **144** B3
Stoney La, E1 .... **41** D2
Stoney St, SE1 .... **52** A2
Stonhouse St, SW4 .... **181** D1
Stonor Rd, W14 .... **149** F3
Stopes St, SE15 .... **89** F3
Stopford Rd, SE17 .... **75** D3
Storers Quay, E14 .... **159** D3
Store St, E15 .... **117** D2
WC1 .... **36** A1
Storey Ct, NW8
off St. John's Wd Rd **20** A1
Storey's Gate, SW1 .... **60** B1
Stories Ms, SE5 .... **169** E4
Stories Rd, SE5 .... **183** E1
Stork Rd, E7 .... **117** F3
Storks Rd, SE16 .... **156** A2
Stormont Rd, N6 .... **95** F1
SW11 .... **180** A1
Story St, N1
off Carnoustie Dr **111** F4
Stothard Pl, E1
off Spital Yd **29** D4
Stothard St, E1
off Colebert Av **128** C4
Stott Cl, SW18 .... **179** D4
Stoughton Cl, SE11 .... **73** F1
Stourcliffe St, W1 .... **33** E3
Stourhead Ho, SW1
off Tachbrook St **72** A2
Stour Rd, E3 .... **116** A4
Stowage, SE8 .... **172** A1
Stowe Rd, W12 .... **148** B1
Stracey Rd, NW10 .... **119** D1
Stradbroke Rd, N5 .... **112** C1
Stradella Rd, SE24 .... **182** C4
Strafford Rd, W3 .... **146** C1
Strafford St, E14 .... **158** A1
Strahan Rd, E3 .... **129** E3
Straightsmouth, SE10 .... **172** C2
Straker's Rd, SE15 .... **184** B2
STRAND, WC2 .... **36** C4
Strand, WC2 .... **48** C1
Strand Dr, Rich. TW9 .... **160** B2
Strand La, WC2 .... **37** F4
Strand on the Grn, W4 .... **160** A1
Strand Sch App, W4
off Thames Rd **160** A1
Strangways Ter, W14
off Holland Pk Rd **149** F2
Stranraer Way, N1 .... **111** E4
Strasburg Rd, SW11 .... **166** B3
STRATFORD, E15 .... **116** C3
Stratford 117 D4
Stratford Av, W8 .... **54** B3
Stratford Cen, The, E15 .... 117 D4
Stratford Gro, SW15 .... **177** D2
Stratford Hub, E15 .... **130** B2
⇌ Stratford International 116 C3
Stratford Office Village, The,
E15 *off Romford Rd* **117** E4
Stratford Pl, W1 .... **34** C3
⊖ Stratford Regional 116 C3
⊖ Stratford Regional 116 C3
DLR Stratford Regional 116 C3
Stratford Rd, E13 .... **131** F1
W8 .... **54** B4
Stratford Vil, NW1 .... **110** C4
Strathan Cl, SW18 .... **177** E4
Strathblaine Rd, SW11 .... **179** D2
Strathearn Pl, W2 .... **32** B4
Strathleven Rd, SW2 .... **181** E3
Strathmore Gdns, W8 .... **42** B2
Strathnairn St, SE1 .... **156** A3
Strathray Gdns, NW3 .... **109** E3
Strath Ter, SW11 .... **179** E2
Strattondale St, E14 .... **158** C2
Stratton St, W1 .... **47** D2
Strauss Rd, W4 .... **147** D1
Streakes Fld Rd, NW2 .... **92** A3
Streatham St, WC1 .... **36** B2
Streatley Pl, NW3
off New End **108** C1
Streatley Rd, NW6 .... **107** F4
Streimer Rd, E15 .... **130** C2
Strelley Way, W3 .... **133** E3
Stretton Mans, SE8
off Glaisher St **172** A1
Strickland St, SE8 .... **172** A4
Stride Rd, E13 .... **131** F2
Strode Rd, NW10 .... **106** A3
SW6 .... **163** D2
Stronsa Rd, W12 .... **147** F1
Stroud Grn Rd, N4 .... **97** F2
Stroudley Wk, E3 .... **130** B3
Strouts Pl, E2 .... **17** E4
Strutton Grd, SW1 .... **60** A2
Strype St, E1 .... **41** E1
Stuart Av, NW9 .... **92** A1
Stuart Rd, NW6 .... **18** A1
SE15 .... **184** C2
W3 .... **132** C4
Stuart Twr, W9 .... **19** F1
Stubbs Dr, SE16 .... **156** B4
Stucley Pl, NW1
off Hawley Cres **110** B4
Studdridge St, SW6 .... **164** A4
Studd St, N1 .... **126** B1
Studholme Ct, NW3 .... **108** A1
Studholme St, SE15 .... **170** B2
Studio Pl, SW1 .... **57** F1
Studland, SE17 .... **76** A2
Studland Ho, E14
off Aston St **143** E2
Studland St, W6 .... **148** B3
Studley Cl, E5 .... **115** E2
Studley Ct, E14
off Jamestown Way **145** D3
Studley Est, SW4 .... **167** E3
Studley Rd, SW4 .... **167** E3
Stukeley St, WC1 .... **37** D2
WC2 .... **37** D2
Sturdy Rd, SE15 .... **170** B4
Sturgeon Rd, SE17 .... **75** E3
Sturgess Av, NW4 .... **92** B1
Sturge St, SE1 .... **51** E4
Sturmer Way, N7 .... **111** F2
Sturry St, E14 .... **144** B2
Sturt St, N1 .... **15** F3
Stutfield St, E1 .... **142** A2
Styles Gdns, SW9 .... **182** B1
Stylus Ho, E1
off Devonport St **142** C2
Sudbourne Rd, SW2 .... **181** E3
Sudbrooke Rd, SW12 .... **179** F4
Sudbury Ct, SW8
off Allen Edwards Dr **84** C4
Sudbury Ho, SW18
*off Wandsworth
High St* **178** B3
Sudeley St, N1 .... **15** D3
Sudlow Rd, SW18 .... **178** A2
Sudrey St, SE1 .... **63** E1
Suffolk Ct, E10 .... **102** A1
Suffolk La, EC4 .... **40** A4
Suffolk Pl, SW1 .... **48** B2

Suffolk Rd, E13 **131** F3
NW10 **105** E4
SW13 **161** F2
Suffolk St, SW1 **48** B2
Sugar Bakers Ct, EC3
off Creechurch La **41** D3
Sugar Ho La, E15 **130** C2
Sugar Loaf Wk, E2
off Victoria Pk Sq **128** C3
Sugar Quay Wk, EC3 **53** D1
Sugden Rd, SW11 **180** A1
Sulgrave Gdns, W6
off Sulgrave Rd **148** C1
Sulgrave Rd, W6 **148** C1
Sulivan Ct, SW6 **178** A1
Sulivan Enterprise Cen, SW6 *off Sulivan Rd* **178** A1
Sulivan Rd, SW6 **178** A1
Sulkin Ho, E2
off Knottisford St **129** D3
Sullivan Cl, SW11 **179** E1
Sullivan Ho, SW1
off Churchill Gdns **71** D3
Sullivan Rd, SE11 **62** B4
Sultan St, SE5 **87** E2
Sumatra Rd, NW6 **108** A2
Sumburgh Rd, SW12 **180** A4
Summercourt Rd, E1 **142** C2
Summerfield Av, NW6 **121** E2
Summerhouse Rd, N16 **99** E3
Summerlands Av, W3 **132** C3
Summers Cl, Wem. HA9 **90** B2
Summerskill Cl, SE15
off Philip Wk **184** B1
Summers St, EC1 **26** A3
Summit Ct, NW2 **107** E2
Summit Est, N16 **100** A1
Sumner Av, SE15 **89** F4
Sumner Ct, SW8
off Darsley Dr **84** C4
Sumner Pl, SW7 **68** B1
Sumner Pl Ms, SW7 **68** B1
Sumner Rd, SE15 **89** F1
Sumner St, SE1 **51** D2
Sumpter Cl, NW3 **108** C3
Sunbeam Cres, W10 **120** C4
Sunbeam Rd, NW10 **118** C4
Sunbury Av, SW14 **175** D2
Sunbury La, SW11 **80** B4
Sunbury Workshops, E2
off Swanfield St **29** E1
Sun Ct, EC3 **40** B3
Sunderland Ter, W2 **30** C2
Sundew Av, W12 **134** A3
Sundew Cl, W12 **134** A3
Sundra Wk, E1
off Beaumont Gro **129** D4
Sunlight Sq, E2 **128** B3
Sunningdale Av, W3 **133** E3
Sunningdale Cl, SE16
off Ryder Dr **156** B4
Sunningdale Gdns, W8 **54** B3
Sunninghill Ct, W3
off Bollo Br Rd **146** C1
Sunninghill Rd, SE13 **172** B4
Sunny Cres, NW10 **104** C4
Sunnyhill Cl, E5 **115** E1
Sunnymead Rd, NW9 **91** D1
SW15 **176** B3
Sunnyside, NW2 **93** F4
Sunnyside Rd, E10 **102** A2
N19 **97** D1
Sun Pas, SE16
off Frean St **156** A2
Sunray Av, SE24 **183** D2
Sun Rd, W14 **149** F4
Sunset Rd, SE5 **182** C2
Sun St, EC2 **40** C1
Sun Wk, E1 *off Mews St* **142** A4
Sunwell Cl, SE15
off Cossall Wk **170** B4
Surma Cl, E1 **128** B4
Surrendale Pl, W9 **18** B3
Surrey Canal Rd, SE14 **170** C1
SE15 **170** C1
Surrey Cres, W4 **146** A4
★ Surrey Docks Fm, SE16 **157** F1
Surrey Gro, SE17 **76** C3
Surrey La, SW11 **165** E3
Surrey La Est, SW11 **80** C4
Surrey Quays **157** D2
Surrey Quays Rd, SE16 **156** C2
Surrey Quays Shop Cen, SE16 **157** D2
Surrey Rd, SE15 **185** D3
Surrey Row, SE1 **50** C4
Surrey Sq, SE17 **76** C2
Surrey St, WC2 **37** F4
Surrey Ter, SE17 **77** D1
Surrey Water Rd, SE16 **143** D4
Surr St, N7 **111** E2
Susan Constant Ct, E14
off Newport Av **145** D3
Susannah St, E14 **144** B2
Sussex Cl, N19 **97** E3
Sussex Gdns, W2 **32** A4
Sussex Ms E, W2 **32** B3
Sussex Ms W, W2 **32** B4
Sussex Pl, NW1 **21** E1
W2 **32** B3
W6 **148** C4
Sussex Sq, W2 **32** B4
Sussex St, SW1 **71** D3
Sussex Way, N7 **97** E3
N19 **97** E2
Sutherland Av, W9 **19** E1
Sutherland Gdns, SW14 **175** E1
Sutherland Gro, SW18 **177** E4
Sutherland Pl, W2 **30** A2
Sutherland Rd, W4 **161** E1
Sutherland Row, SW1 **71** D2
Sutherland Sq, SE17 **75** E3
Sutherland St, SW1 **70** C2
Sutherland Wk, SE17 **75** F3
Sutterton St, N7 **111** F3
Sutton Ct, W4 **160** C1
Sutton Ct Rd, W4 **160** C2
Sutton Est, SW3 **69** D2
W10 **134** C1
Sutton Est, The, N1 **112** B4
★ Sutton Ho, E9 **114** C2
Sutton La, EC1 **27** D3
Sutton La N, W4 **146** C4
Sutton La S, W4 **160** C1
Sutton Pl, E9 **114** C2
Sutton Rd, E13 **131** F4
Sutton Row, W1 **36** B2
Sutton Sq, E9
off Urswick Rd **114** C2
Sutton St, E1 **142** C2
Sutton's Way, EC1 **27** F3
Sutton Wk, SE1 **49** F3
Sutton Way, W10 **134** C1
Swains La, N6 **96** A4
Swainson Rd, W3 **147** F1
Swain St, NW8 **20** C2
Swallow Cl, SE14 **170** C3
Swallow Dr, NW10
off Kingfisher Way **105** D3
Swallowfield, NW1
off Munster Sq **23** D1
Swallow Ho, NW8
off Allitsen Rd **8** C2
Swallow Pas, W1
off Swallow Pl **35** D3
Swallow Pl, W1 **35** D3
Swallow St, W1 **47** F1
Swanage Ho, SW8 **85** E3
Swanage Rd, SW18 **178** C4
Swanbourne, SE17 **75** E1
Swan Ct, SW3 **69** D3
Swandon Way, SW18 **178** B3
Swanfield St, E2 **29** E1
Swan La, EC4 **52** A1
Swan Mead, SE1 **64** C3
Swan Ms, SW6
off Purser's Cross Rd **78** A4
Swan Pas, E1
off Cartwright St **53** F1
Swan Path, E10
off Jesse Rd **102** C2
Swan Pl, SW13 **161** F4
Swan Rd, SE16 **156** C1
Swanscombe Ho, W11
off St. Anns Rd **135** D4
Swanscombe Rd, W4 **147** E4
W11 **135** D4
Swan St, SE1 **63** F2
Swan Wk, SW3 **69** E4
Swan Yd, N1
off Highbury Sta Rd **112** B3
Swaton Rd, E3 **130** A4
Swaythling Ho, SW15
off Tunworth Cres **175** F4
Swedenborg Gdns, E1 **142** A3
Sweden Gate, SE16 **157** E2
Sweeney Cres, SE1 **65** F1
Swift St, SW6 **163** F3
Swinbrook Rd, W10 **135** E1
Swinburne Ct, SE5
off Basingdon Way **183** D2
Swinburne Rd, SW15 **176** A2
Swindon St, W12 **134** B4
Swinford Gdns, SW9 **182** B1
Swinnerton St, E9 **115** E2
Swinton Cl, Wem. HA9 **90** B2
Swinton Pl, WC1 **13** E4
Swinton St, WC1 **13** E4
Swiss Cottage **109** D4
Swiss Ct, W1 **48** B1
Swiss Ter, NW6 **109** D4
Switch Ho, E14
off Blackwall Way **145** D3
Sybil Phoenix Cl, SE8 **157** D4
Sybourn St, E17 **101** F1
Sycamore Av, E3 **129** F1
Sycamore Cl, E16
off Clarence Rd **131** E4
W3 *off Bromyard Av* **133** E4
Sycamore Gdns, W6 **148** B1
Sycamore Gro, NW9 **90** C1
SE6 **186** C4
Sycamore Ho, NW3
off Maitland Pk Vil **109** F3
Sycamore Ms, SW4 **180** C1
Sycamore St, EC1 **27** E3
Sycamore Wk, W10
off Fifth Av **121** E4
Sydner Ms, N16 **113** F1
Sydner Rd, N16 **113** F1
Sydney Cl, SW3 **68** B1

Sydney Ms, SW3 .68 B1
Sydney Pl, SW7 .68 B1
Sydney St, SW3 .68 C2
Sylvan Gro, NW2 .107 D1
SE15 .170 B2
Sylvester Path, E8
off Sylvester Rd .114 B3
Sylvester Rd, E8 .114 B3
E17 .101 F1
Sylvia Ct, Wem. HA9
off Harrow Rd .104 B4
Sylvia Gdns, Wem. HA9 .104 B4
Symes Ms, NW1 .11 E2
Symington Ho, SE1 .64 A3
Symington Ms, E9
off Coopersale Rd .115 D2
Symister Ms, N1 .28 C1
Symons Cl, SE15 .170 C4
Symons St, SW3 .69 F1
Symphony Ms, W10
off Third Av .121 E3
Uni Syracuse Uni - London Program, WC1 .25 D4

T

Tabard Cen, SE1
off Prioress St .64 B3
Tabard Gdns Est, SE1 .64 B1
Tabard St, SE1 .64 A1
Tabernacle St, EC2 .28 B3
Tableer Av, SW4 .180 C3
Tabley Rd, N7 .111 E1
Tabor Rd, W6 .148 B2
Tachbrook Est, SW1 .72 B3
Tachbrook Ms, SW1 .59 E4
Tachbrook St, SW1 .71 F1
Tack Ms, SE4 .186 A1
Tadema Ho, NW8 .20 B3
Tadema Rd, SW10 .79 F2
Tadmor St, W12 .135 D4
Tadworth Rd, NW2 .92 A3
Taeping St, E14 .158 B3
Taft Way, E3
off Franklin St .130 B3
Tailworth St, E1
off Chicksand St .142 A1
Tait Ct, SW8
off Darsley Dr .84 B4
Tait St, E1 .142 B2
Takhar Ms, SW11
off Cabul Rd .165 E4
Talacre Rd, NW5 .110 A3
Talbot Ct, EC3 .40 B4
Talbot Ho, E14
off Giraud St .144 B2
N7 *off Harvist Est* .98 A4
Talbot Pl, SE3 .173 E4
Talbot Rd, SE22 .183 E2
W2 .30 B2
W11 .135 F2
Talbot Sq, W2 .32 B3
Talbot Wk, NW10
off Garnet Rd .105 E3
W11 .135 E2
Talbot Yd, SE1 .52 A3
Talfourd Pl, SE15 .169 F3
Talfourd Rd, SE15 .169 F3
Talgarth Rd, W6 .149 E4
W14 .149 E4
Tallack Rd, E10 .101 F2
Tallis St, EC4 .38 B4
Tallis Vw, NW10 .105 D3
Talma Rd, SW2 .182 A2
Talwin St, E3 .130 B3
Tamar Cl, E3
off Legion Ter .129 F1
Tamarind Yd, E1
off Asher Way .142 A4
Tamarisk Sq, W12 .133 F3
Tamworth St, SW6 .66 A4
Tanfield Av, NW2 .105 F1
Tangier Rd, Rich.
TW10 .174 B1
Tangley Gro, SW15 .175 F4
Tankerton St, WC1 .25 D1
Tankridge Rd, NW2 .92 B3
Tanners Hill, SE8 .171 F3
Tanners Ms, SE8
off Tanners Hill .171 F3
Tanner St, SE1 .65 D1
Tanners Yd, E2
off Treadway St .128 B2
Tannington Ter, N5 .98 A4
Tansley Cl, N7
off Hilldrop La .111 D2
Tanswell Est, SE1 .62 A1
Tanswell St, SE1 .62 A1
Tant Av, E16 .145 F2
Tanza Rd, NW3 .109 F1
Taplow, NW3 .109 D4
SE17 .76 B2
Taplow St, N1 .15 F3
Tappesfield Rd, SE15 .184 C1
Tapp St, E1 .128 B4
Taransay Wk, N1
off Essex Rd .113 D3
Tarbert Rd, SE22 .183 E3
Tarbert Wk, E1
off Juniper St .142 C3
Tariff Cres, SE8 .157 F3
Tarling Rd, E16 .145 F2
Tarling St, E1 .142 B2
Tarling St Est, E1 .142 C2
Tarn St, SE1 .63 E3
Tarragon Cl, SE14 .171 E2
Tarrant Pl, W1 .33 E1
Tarver Rd, SE17 .75 D3
Tarves Way, SE10 .172 B2
Tasker Rd, NW3 .109 F2
Tasman Ct, E14
off Westferry Rd .158 B3
Tasman Rd, SW9 .181 E1
Tasso Rd, W6 .163 E1
Tatam Rd, NW10 .104 C4
Tatchbury Ho, SW15
off Tunworth Cres .175 F4
★ Tate Britain, SW1 .72 C1
★ Tate Modern, SE1 .51 D2
Tatham Pl, NW8 .8 B2
Tatnell Rd, SE23 .185 E4
Tatton Cres, N16 .99 F1
Tatum St, SE17 .76 B1
Tauheed Cl, N4 .98 C3
Taunton Ms, NW1 .21 E3
Taunton Pl, NW1 .21 E2
Taunton Rd, SE12 .187 E3
Taverners Cl, W11
off Addison Av .135 E4
Taverner Sq, N5
off Highbury Gra .112 C1
Tavern La, SW9 .168 A4
Tavistock Cl, N16
off Crossway .113 E2
Tavistock Ct, WC2
off Tavistock St .37 D4
Tavistock Cres, W11 .135 F1
Tavistock Pl, WC1 .24 B2
Tavistock Rd, E7 .117 F1
E15 .117 F3
NW10 .119 F2
W11 .135 F2
Tavistock Sq, WC1 .24 B2
Tavistock St, WC2 .37 D4
Tavistock Ter, N19 .97 D4
Tavistock Twr, SE16
off Finland St .157 E2
Taviton St, WC1 .24 A2
Tavy Cl, SE11 .74 B2
Tawny Way, SE16 .157 D3
Taybridge Rd, SW11 .180 A1
Tayburn Cl, E14 .144 C2
Taylor Av, Rich. TW9 .160 B4
Taylor Cl, SE8 .171 F1
Taylors Grn, W3 .133 E2
Tayport Cl, N1 .111 E4
Teak Cl, SE16 .143 E4
Tealby Ct, N7
off Watkinson Rd .111 F3
Teale St, E2 .128 A2
Teal St, SE10 .159 F2
Teasel Way, E15 .131 E3
Tedworth Gdns, SW3 .69 E3
Tedworth Sq, SW3 .69 E3
Tee, The, W3 .133 E2
Teesdale Cl, E2 .128 A2
Teesdale St, E2 .128 B2
Teesdale Yd, E2
off Teesdale St .128 B2
Teignmouth Cl, SW4 .181 D2
Teignmouth Rd, NW2 .107 D2
★ Telecom Twr, W1 .23 E4
Telegraph Hill, NW3 .94 B4
Telegraph Pl, E14 .158 B3
Telegraph St, EC2 .40 A2
Telephone Pl, SW6
off Lillie Rd .163 F1
Telfer Cl, W3
off Church Rd .146 C1
Telford Cl, E17 .101 E1
Telford Ho, SE1 .63 E3
Telford Rd, W10 .135 E1
Telfords Yd, E1
off The Highway .142 A3
Telford Ter, SW1 .71 E4
Telford Way, W3 .133 E1
Tell Gro, SE22 .183 F2
Temair Ho, SE10
off Tarves Way .172 B2
Temeraire St, SE16
off Albion St .156 C1
Templar Ct, NW8
off St. John's Wd Rd .20 A1
Templar Ho, NW2
off Shoot Up Hill .107 F3
Templar St, SE5 .168 B4
⊖ Temple .37 F4
★ Temple, The, EC4 .38 A4
Temple Av, EC4 .38 B4
★ Temple Bar, EC4 .39 D3
★ Temple Bar Mem, EC4 .38 A3
Temple Cl, E11 .103 E1
Templecombe Rd, E9 .128 C1
Temple Ct, E1
off Rectory Sq .143 D1
SW8
off Thorncroft St .84 C3
Temple Dws, E2
off Temple St .128 B2
Templehof Av, NW2 .92 C1
Temple La, EC4 .38 B3
Templemead Cl, W3 .133 E2

Templemead Ho, E9
off Kingsmead Way **115** E1
Temple Mill La, E15 ....**116** B1
★ Temple of Mithras, EC4
off Queen Victoria St **40** A3
Temple Pl, WC2 ....**37** F4
Temple Rd, NW2 ....**106** C1
W4 ....**146** C2
Temple Sheen, SW14 ......**174** C3
Temple Sheen Rd, SW14 ....**174** B2
Temple St, E2 ....**128** B2
Templeton Cl, N16
off Boleyn Rd **113** E2
Templeton Pl, SW5 ....**66** B1
Temple W Ms, SE11 ....**62** C3
Templewood Av, NW3 ....**94** B4
Templewood Gdns, NW3 .....**94** B4
Templewood Pt, NW2 ....**93** F3
Temple Yd, E2
off Temple St **128** B2
Tench St, E1 ....**142** B4
Tenda Rd, SE16
off Roseberry St **156** B3
Tenison Ct, W1 ....**35** E4
Tenison Way, SE1 ....**50** A3
Tenniel Cl, W2 ....**31** E3
Tennis St, SE1 ....**52** A4
Tennyson Rd, E10 ....**102** B3
E15 ....**117** E4
NW6 ....**121** F1
Tennyson St, SW8 ....**166** B4
Tenterden St, W1 ....**35** D3
Tenter Grd, E1 ....**41** E1
Tenter Pas, E1 ....**41** F3
Tent St, E1 ....**128** B4
Tequila Wf, E14
off Commercial Rd **143** E2
Terborch Way, SE22
off East Dulwich Gro **183** E3
Teredo St, SE16 ....**157** D2
Terling Cl, E11 ....**103** F4
Terling Wk, N1
off Britannia Row **126** C1
Terminus Pl, SW1 ....**59** D3
Terrace, The, NW6 ....**122** A1
SW13 ....**161** E4
Terrace Apts, N5
off Drayton Pk **112** A2
Terrace Gdns, SW13 ....**161** F4
Terrace Rd, E9 ....**114** C4
Terretts Pl, N1
off Upper St **112** B4
Terrick St, W12 ....**134** B2
Tessa Sanderson Pl, SW8 ...**180** B1
Testerton Wk, W11 ....**135** D3
Tetbury Pl, N1 ....**14** C1
Tetcott Rd, SW10 ....**79** E2
Teversham La, SW8 ....**85** D4
Teviot St, E14 ....**144** C1
Thackeray Rd, SW8 ....**166** B4
Thackeray St, W8 ....**55** D1
Thalia Cl, SE10 ....**173** D1
Thame Rd, SE16 ....**157** D1
Thames Av, SW10 ....**79** F4
Thames Bk, SW14 ....**160** C4
Thames Circle, E14
off Westferry Rd **158** A3
Thames Cres, W4
off Corney Rd **161** E2
Thames Link, SE16
off Salter Rd **143** D4
Thames Pl, SW15 ....**177** D1
Thames Pt, SW6
off The Boulevard **164** C4
Thames Quay, SW10
off Harbour Av **164** C3
Thames Rd, W4 ....**160** A1
Thames St, SE10 ....**172** B1
Thames Tunnel Mills, SE16
off Rotherhithe St **156** C1
Thames Village, W4 ....**160** C3
Thames Wf, E16 ....**145** F4
Thanet St, WC1 ....**24** C1
Thane Vil, N7 ....**97** F4
Thane Wks, N7 ....**97** F4
Thant Cl, E10 ....**102** B4
Thavies Inn, EC1 ....**38** B2
Thaxted Ct, N1 ....**16** A3
Thaxton Rd, W14 ....**163** F1
Thayer St, W1 ....**34** B1
★ Theatre Royal, WC2 .....**37** D3
Theatre Sq, E15
off Great Eastern Rd **117** D3
Theatre St, SW11 ....**179** F1
Theberton St, N1 ....**126** A1
Theed St, SE1 ....**50** A3
Theobald Rd, E17 ....**101** F1
Theobalds Ct, N4
off Queens Dr **98** C4
Theobald's Rd, WC1 ....**25** E4
Theobald St, SE1 ....**64** A3
Theodore Rd, SE13 ....**186** C4
Therapia Rd, SE22 ....**184** C4
Theresa Rd, W6 ....**148** A3
Therfield Ct, N4
off Brownswood Rd **98** C3
Thermopylae Gate, E14 ....**158** B3
Theseus Wk, N1 ....**15** D3
Thessaly Ho, SW8 ....**83** E3
Thessaly Rd, SW8 ....**83** E3
Thetis Ter, Rich. TW9
off Kew Grn **160** A1
Theydon Rd, E5 ....**100** C3
Theydon St, E17 ....**101** F1
Third Av, W3 ....**133** F4
W10 ....**121** E3
Third Way, Wem. HA9 .....**104** B1
Thirleby Rd, SW1 ....**59** F3
Thirsk Rd, SW11 ....**180** A1
Thistle Gro, SW10 ....**67** F2
Thistlewaite Rd, E5 ....**100** B4
Thistlewood Cl, N7 ....**97** F3
Thistley Ct, SE8
off Glaisher St **172** B1
Thomas Baines Rd, SW11 ..**179** D1
Thomas Darby Ct, W11 ....**135** E2
Thomas Doyle St, SE1 ......**62** C2
Thomas Hollywood Ho, E2
off Approach Rd **128** C2
Thomas More Ho, EC2
off The Barbican **39** E1
Thomas More St, E1 ....**142** A3
Thomas N Ter, E16
off Barking Rd **145** F1
Thomas Pl, W8 ....**54** C3
Thomas Rd, E14 ....**143** F2
● Thomas Rd Ind Est, E14
off Thomas Rd **144** A1
Thompson Av, Rich. TW9 ...**174** A1
Thompson Rd, SE22 ....**183** F4
Thompsons Av, SE5 ....**87** E2
Thorburn Sq, SE1 ....**156** A3
Thoresby St, N1 ....**15** F4
Thornbury Cl, N16
off Boleyn Rd **113** E2
Thornbury Rd, SW2 ....**181** E4
Thornbury Sq, N6 ....**96** C2
Thornby Rd, E5 ....**100** C4
Thorncliffe Rd, SW2 ....**181** E4
Thorncombe Rd, SE22 .....**183** E3
Thorncroft St, SW8 ....**84** C3
Thorndike Cl, SW10 ....**79** E2
Thorndike Ho, SW1
off Vauxhall Br Rd **72** A2
Thorndike Rd, N1 ....**112** C3
Thorndike St, SW1 ....**72** A1
Thorne Cl, E11 ....**117** E1
Thorne Pas, SW13 ....**161** E4
Thorne Rd, SW8 ....**84** C3
Thorne St, E16 ....**145** F2
SW13 ....**175** E1
Thorney Cres, SW11 ....**80** B3
Thorney Hedge Rd, W4 .....**146** B3
Thorney St, SW1 ....**60** C4
Thornfield Rd, W12 ....**148** B1
Thornford Rd, SE13 ....**186** C3
Thorngate Rd, W9 ....**18** B2
Thornham Gro, E15 ....**117** D2
Thornham St, SE10 ....**172** B1
Thornhaugh Ms, WC1 ....**24** B3
Thornhaugh St, WC1 ....**24** B4
Thornhill Br Wf, N1 ....**13** E1
Thornhill Cres, N1 ....**111** F4
Thornhill Gdns, E10 ....**102** B3
Thornhill Gro, N1
off Lofting Rd **111** F4
Thornhill Rd, E10 ....**102** B3
N1 ....**112** A4
Thornhill Sq, N1 ....**111** F4
Thornley Pl, SE10
off Caradoc St **159** E4
Thorn Ter, SE15
off Nunhead Gro **184** C1
Thornton Av, W4 ....**147** E3
Thornton Ho, SE17 ....**76** B1
Thornton Pl, W1 ....**21** F4
Thornton Rd, E11 ....**103** D3
SW14 ....**175** D1
Thornton St, SW9 ....**168** A4
Thornville St, SE8 ....**172** A3
Thornwood Gdns, W8 ....**42** A4
Thornwood Rd, SE13 ......**187** E3
Thorogood Gdns, E15 ......**117** E2
Thorparch Rd, SW8 ....**84** B4
Thorpebank Rd, W12 ......**134** A4
Thorpe Cl, W10
off Cambridge Gdns **135** E2
Thorpedale Rd, N4 ....**97** E2
Thorpe Rd, E7 ....**117** F1
Thorverton Rd, NW2 ....**93** E4
Thoydon Rd, E3 ....**129** E2
Thrale St, SE1 ....**51** F3
Thrasher Cl, E8
off Dunston Rd **127** F1
Thrawl St, E1 ....**41** F1
Threadneedle St, EC2 ....**40** B3
Three Barrels Wk, EC4 ....**51** F1
Three Colts Cor, E2
off Pedley St **128** A4
Three Colts La, E2 ....**128** B4
Three Colt St, E14 ....**143** F3
Three Cranes Wk, EC4
off Bell Wf La **51** F1
Three Cups Yd, WC1 ....**37** F1
Three Kings Yd, W1 ....**34** C4
Three Mill La, E3 ....**130** C3
Three Oak La, SE1 ....**53** E4
Three Quays Wk, EC3 ....**53** D1
Threshers Pl, W11 ....**135** E3
Throgmorton Av, EC2 ....**40** B2
Throgmorton St, EC2 ....**40** B2
Thrush St, SE17 ....**75** E2

Thurland Ho, SE16
off Manor Est 156 B3
Thurland Rd, SE16 ....156 A2
Thurleigh Av, SW12 ....180 A4
Thurleigh Rd, SW12 ....180 A4
Thurloe Cl, SW7 ....56 C4
Thurloe Pl, SW7 ....56 B4
Thurloe Pl Ms, SW7 ....56 B4
Thurloe Sq, SW7 ....56 C4
Thurloe St, SW7 ....56 B4
Thurlow Rd, NW3 ....109 D2
Thurlow St, SE17 ....76 B2
Thurlow Ter, NW5 ....110 A2
Thurso Ho, NW6 ....6 C3
Thurston Rd, SE13 ....172 B4
● Thurston Rd Ind Est, SE13
off Jerrard St 186 B1
Thurtle Rd, E2 ....17 F1
Tibbatts Rd, E3 ....130 B4
Tibbenham Wk, E13 ....131 F2
Tibberton Sq, N1
off Popham Rd 112 C4
Tiber Cl, E3
off Garrison Rd 130 A1
Tiber Gdns, N1 ....13 D1
Tidal Basin Rd, E16 ....145 F3
Tideswell Rd, SW15 ....176 C3
● Tideway Ind Est, SW8 ....83 F1
Tideway Wk, SW8 ....83 E1
Tidey St, E3 ....144 A1
Tidworth Ho, SE22
off Albrighton Rd 183 E1
Tidworth Rd, E3 ....130 A4
Tiger Way, E5 ....114 B1
Tilbury Cl, SE15 ....89 F2
Tilbury Rd, E10 ....102 C1
Tildesley Rd, SW15 ....176 C4
Tile Kiln La, N6 ....96 C2
Tile Yd, E14
off Commercial Rd 143 F2
Tileyard Rd, N7 ....111 E4
Tilia Rd, E5
off Clarence Rd 114 B1
Tilia Wk, SW9 ....182 B2
Tiller Rd, E14 ....158 A2
Tillett Cl, NW10 ....104 C3
Tillett Sq, SE16
off Howland Way 157 E1
Tillett Way, E2
off Gosset St 128 A3
Tilling Rd, NW2 ....92 C2
Tillings Cl, SE5 ....168 C3
Tillman St, E1
off Bigland St 142 B2
Tilloch St, N1
off Carnoustie Dr 111 F4
Tillotson Ct, SW8
off Wandsworth Rd 84 C3
Tilney Ct, EC1 ....27 F2
Tilney Gdns, N1 ....113 D3
Tilney St, W1 ....46 B2
Tilson Cl, SE5 ....88 C2
Tilston Cl, E11
off Matcham Rd 103 F4
Tilton St, SW6 ....163 E1
Tiltwood, The, W3 ....132 C3
Timberland Cl, SE15
off Peckham Hill St 170 A2
Timberland Rd, E1
off Hainton Cl 142 B2
Timber Mill Way, SW4 .....181 D1
Timber Pond Rd, SE16 .....157 D1
Timber St, EC1 ....27 E2
Timber Wf, E2 ....17 E1
Timbrell Pl, SE16
off Silver Wk 143 F4
Time Sq, E8 ....113 F2
Times Sq, E1
off Hooper St 142 A2
Timothy Cl, SW4
off Elms Rd 180 C3
Tindal St, SW9 ....86 C4
Tinderbox All, SW14 ....175 D1
Tinniswood Cl, N5
off Drayton Pk 112 A2
Tinsley Rd, E1 ....142 C1
Tintagel Cres, SE22 ....183 F2
Tintagel Gdns, SE22
off Oxonian St 183 F2
Tintern Cl, SW15 ....177 E3
Tintern St, SW4 ....181 E2
Tinworth St, SE11 ....73 D2
Tipthorpe Rd, SW11 ....180 A1
Tisbury Ct, W1
off Rupert St 36 A4
Tisdall Pl, SE17 ....76 B1
Tissington Ct, SE16
off Rotherhithe New Rd .157 D3
Titchborne Row, W2 ....33 D3
Titchfield Rd, NW8 ....9 D1
Tite St, SW3 ....69 E3
Titmuss St, W12
off Goldhawk Rd 148 C1
Tiverton Rd, NW10 ....121 D1
Tiverton St, SE1 ....63 E3
Tivoli Ct, SE16 ....157 F1
Tobacco Dock, E1 ....142 B3
Tobacco Quay, E1
off Wapping La 142 B3
Tobago St, E14
off Manilla St 158 A1
Tobin Cl, NW3 ....109 E4
Toby La, E1 ....129 E4
Todds Wk, N7
off Andover Rd 97 F3
Tokenhouse Yd, EC2 ....40 A2
Token Yd, SW15 ....177 E2
TOKYNGTON, Wem. HA9 ...104 B3
Tokyngton Av, Wem. HA9 ..104 A3
Toland Sq, SW15 ....176 A3
Tolhurst Dr, W10
off Beethoven St 121 E3
Tollbridge Cl, W10
off Kensal Rd 121 E4
Tollet St, E1 ....129 D4
Tollgate Gdns, NW6 ....6 C2
Tollgate Ho, NW6 ....6 B2
Tollhouse Way, N19 ....96 C3
Tollington Pk, N4 ....97 F3
Tollington Pl, N4 ....97 F3
Tollington Rd, N7 ....111 F1
Tollington Way, N7 ....97 E4
Tolmers Sq, NW1 ....23 F2
Tolpaide Ho, SE11 ....74 A1
Tolpuddle St, N1 ....14 A2
Tolsford Rd, E5 ....114 B2
Tom Gros Cl, E15
off Maryland St 117 D2
Tom Hood Cl, E15
off Maryland St 117 D2
Tomlins Gro, E3 ....130 A3
Tomlinson Cl, E2 ....29 F1
W4 ....146 B4
Tomlins Ter, E14
off Rhodeswell Rd 143 F1
Tomlins Wk, N7
off Briset Way 97 F3
Tom Nolan Cl, E15 ....131 E2
Tompion Ho, EC1
off Percival St 27 D2
Tompion St, EC1 ....26 C1
Tom Smith Cl, SE10
off Maze Hill 173 E1
Tom Thumbs Arch, E3
off Malmesbury Rd 130 A2
Tom Williams Ho, SW6
off Clem Attlee Ct 163 F1
Tonbridge St, WC1 ....12 C4
Tonbridge Wk, WC1
off Bidborough St 12 C4
Tonsley Hill, SW18 ....178 B3
Tonsley Pl, SW18 ....178 B3
Tonsley Rd, SW18 ....178 B3
Tonsley St, SW18 ....178 B3
Tony Cannell Ms, E3
off Maplin St 129 F3
Took's Ct, EC4 ....38 A2
Tooley St, SE1 ....52 B2
Topaz Ct, E11
off High Rd
Leytonstone 103 E2
Topaz Ho, E15
off Romford Rd 117 F3
Topaz Wk, NW2
off Marble Dr 93 D1
Topham St, EC1 ....26 A2
Topmast Pt, E14 ....158 A1
Topp Wk, NW2 ....92 C3
Torbay Rd, NW6 ....107 F4
Torbay St, NW1
off Hawley Rd 110 B4
Tor Gdns, W8 ....42 A4
Tornay Ho, N1
off Priory Grn Est 13 E2
Torquay St, W2 ....30 C1
Torrens Rd, E15 ....117 F3
SW2 ....181 F3
Torrens Sq, E15 ....117 E3
Torrens St, EC1 ....14 B3
Torres Sq, E14
off Maritime Quay 158 A4
Torrey Dr, SW9
off Overton Rd 168 A4
Torriano Av, NW5 ....111 D2
Torriano Cotts, NW5
off Torriano Av 111 D2
Torriano Ms, NW5 ....110 C2
Torridge Gdns, SE15 ......184 C2
Torridon Ho, NW6 ....6 C3
Torrington Pl, E1 ....142 A4
WC1 ....23 F4
Torrington Sq, WC1 ....24 B3
Torwood Rd, SW15 ....176 A3
Tothill Ho, SW1
off Page St 60 B4
Tothill St, SW1 ....60 A1
Tottan Ter, E1 ....143 D2
⊖ Tottenham Court Road ...36 A2
Tottenham Ct Rd, W1 ....23 F3
Tottenham Ms, W1 ....23 F4
Tottenham Rd, N1 ....113 E3
Tottenham St, W1 ....35 F1
Totteridge Ho, SW11 ......165 D4
Toucan Cl, NW10 ....118 A3
Toulmin St, SE1 ....63 E1
Toulon St, SE5 ....87 E2
Tournay Rd, SW6 ....163 F2
Tours Pas, SW11 ....179 D2
Toussaint Wk, SE16
off John Roll Way 156 A2
Tovy Ho, SE1
off Avondale Sq 156 A4

Towcester Rd, E3 **130** B4
● Tower 42, EC2 **40** C2
Tower Br, E1 **53** E3
SE1 **53** E3
Tower Br App, E1 **53** E2
★ Tower Br Exhib, SE1 **53** E3
Tower Br Piazza, SE1 **53** E3
Tower Br Rd, SE1 **64** C3
Tower Br Wf, E1 **142** A4
Tower Bldgs, E1
off Brewhouse La **142** B4
Tower Cl, NW3
off Lyndhurst Rd **109** D2
Tower Ct, WC2 **36** C3
DLR Tower Gateway **41** F4
Coll Tower Hamlets Coll,
Arbour Sq Cen, E1
off Arbour Sq **143** D2
Bethnal Grn Cen, E2
off Bethnal Grn Rd **128** A3
East India Dock Rd, E14 **144** B2
Poplar Cen, E14
off Poplar High St **144** B3
Tower Hamlets Rd, E7 **117** F1
⊖ Tower Hill **41** D4
Tower Hill, EC3 **53** E1
Tower Hill Ter, EC3
off Byward St **53** D1
★ Tower Millennium Pier,
EC3 **53** D2
Tower Mill Rd, SE15 **88** C1
★ Tower of London, EC3 **53** E1
● Tower Pl E, EC3 **53** D1
● Tower Pl W, EC3 **53** D1
Tower Rd, NW10 **106** A4
Tower Royal, EC4 **39** F4
● Towers Business Pk, Wem.
HA9 *off Carey Way* **104** C1
Tower St, WC2 **36** B3
Tower Ter, SE4
off Foxberry Rd **185** E2
Towing Path Wk, N1 **12** C2
Town Ct Path, N4 **98** C2
Town Hall App, N16
off Milton Gro **113** D1
Town Hall Av, W4 **147** D4
Town Hall Rd, SW11 **179** F1
Townley Ct, E15 **117** F3
Townley Rd, SE22 **183** E3
Townley St, SE17 **76** A2
● Townmead Business Cen,
SW6
off William Morris Way **178** C1
Townmead Rd, SW6 **164** C4
Richmond TW9 **160** B4
● Townsend Ind Est,
NW10 **118** C2
Townsend La, NW9 **91** D1
Townsend St, SE17 **76** B1
Townsend Yd, N6 **96** B2
Townshend Est, NW8 **8** C2
Townshend Rd, NW8 **8** C1
Towpath Wk, E9 **115** F2
Toynbee St, E1 **41** E1
Tracey Av, NW2 **106** C2
Tradescant Rd, SW8 **85** D3
Trading Est Rd, NW10 **118** C4
Trafalgar Av, SE15 **77** F3
Trafalgar Cl, SE16
off Greenland Quay **157** E3
Trafalgar Ct, E1
off Glamis Rd **142** C3
Trafalgar Gdns, E1 **143** D1
W8 **54** C2
Trafalgar Gro, SE10 **173** D1
Trafalgar Ms, E9 **115** F3
Trafalgar Rd, SE10 **173** D1
Trafalgar Sq, SW1 **48** B2
WC2 **48** B2
Trafalgar St, SE17 **76** A2
Trafalgar Way, E14 **144** C4
Trahorn Cl, E1 **128** B4
Tralee Ct, SE16
off Masters Dr **156** B4
Tram Cl, SE24
off Hinton Rd **182** B1
Tramway Av, E15 **117** E4
Tranby Pl, E9
off Homerton High St **115** D2
Tranley Ms, NW3
off Fleet Rd **109** E2
Tranquil Pas, SE3
off Tranquil Vale **173** F4
Tranquil Vale, SE3 **173** E4
Transept St, NW1 **32** C1
Transom Cl, SE16
off Plough Way **157** E3
Transom Sq, E14 **158** B3
Tranton Rd, SE16 **156** A2
Trappes Ho, SE16
off Manor Est **156** B3
Travers Rd, N7 **98** A4
Treadgold St, W11 **135** D3
Treadway St, E2 **128** B2
Treaty St, N1 **13** E1
Trebeck St, W1 **46** C2
Trebovir Rd, SW5 **66** B2
Treby St, E3 **129** F4
Trecastle Way, N7
off Carleton Rd **111** D1
Tredegar Ms, E3
off Tredegar Ter **129** F3
Tredegar Rd, E3 **129** F2
Tredegar Sq, E3 **129** F3
Tredegar Ter, E3 **129** F3
Trederwen Rd, E8 **128** A1
Treen Av, SW13 **175** F1
Trefil Wk, N7 **111** E1
Trefoil Rd, SW18 **178** C3
Tregarvon Rd, SW11 **180** A2
Trego Rd, E9 **116** A4
Tregothnan Rd, SW9 **181** E1
Tregunter Rd, SW10 **67** E4
Treherne Ct, SW9 **86** B4
Trehern Rd, SW14 **175** D1
Trehurst St, E5 **115** E2
Trelawney Est, E9 **114** C3
Trelawn Rd, E10 **102** C4
SW2 **182** A3
Trellick Twr, W10 **121** F4
Trellis Sq, E3
off Malmesbury Rd **129** F3
Tremadoc Rd, SW4 **181** D2
Tremaine Cl, SE4 **172** A4
Tremlett Gro, N19 **96** C4
Tremlett Ms, N19 **96** C4
Trenchard St, SE10 **159** D4
Trenchold St, SW8 **84** C1
Trenmar Gdns, NW10 **120** B3
Trentham Ct, W3
off Victoria Rd **133** D1
Trent Rd, SW2 **181** F3
Tresco Rd, SE15 **184** B2
Tresham Cres, NW8 **20** C2
Tresham Wk, E9
off Churchill Wk **114** C2
Tressell Cl, N1
off Sebbon St **112** B4
Tressillian Cres, SE4 **186** A1
Tressillian Rd, SE4 **185** F2
Trevanion Rd, W14 **149** E4
Trevelyan Gdns, NW10 **120** C1
Trevelyan Ho, E2
off Morpeth St **129** D3
Trevelyan Rd, E15 **117** E1
Treveris St, SE1 **50** C3
Treverton St, W10 **121** D4
Trevithick Ho, SE16 **156** B3
Trevithick St, SE8 **158** A4
Trevor Pl, SW7 **57** D1
Trevor Sq, SW7 **57** E1
Trevor St, SW7 **57** D1
Trevor Wk, SW7
off Trevor Sq **57** E1
Triangle, The, EC1 **27** D2
● Triangle Business Cen,
NW10
off Enterprise Way **120** A3
Triangle Est, SE11 **74** A3
Triangle Pl, SW4 **181** D2
Triangle Rd, E8 **128** B1
Trident St, SE16 **157** D3
Trig La, EC4 **39** E4
Trigon Rd, SW8 **85** F2
Trim St, SE14 **171** F1
Trinder Gdns, N19 **97** E2
Trinder Rd, N19 **97** E2
Tring Av, Wem. HA9 **104** A3
Trinidad St, E14 **143** F3
Trinity Buoy Wf, E14 **145** F3
Trinity Ch Pas, SW13 **162** B1
Trinity Ch Rd, SW13 **162** B1
Trinity Ch Sq, SE1 **63** F2
Trinity Cl, E8 **113** F3
E11 **103** E3
NW3
off Willoughby Rd **109** D1
SE13 **187** D2
SW4
off The Pavement **180** C2
Coll Trinity Coll of Music, SE10
off King William Wk **172** C1
Trinity Ct, N1
off Downham Rd **113** E4
NW2 *off Anson Rd* **106** C2
Trinity Gdns, E16
off Cliff Wk **145** F1
SW9 **181** F2
Trinity Gro, SE10 **172** C3
★ Trinity Ho, EC3 **41** D4
Trinity Ho, SE1
off Bath Ter **63** F2
Trinity Ms, W10
off Cambridge Gdns **135** D2
Trinity Pl, EC3 **53** E1
Trinity Rd, SW18 **179** D3
Trinity Sq, EC3 **53** D1
Trinity St, SE1 **63** F1
Trinity Wk, NW3 **108** C3
Trinity Way, W3 **133** E3
Trio Pl, SE1 **63** F1
Tristan Sq, SE3 **187** E1
● Triton Sq, NW1 **23** E2
Trocette Mansion, SE1
off Bermondsey St **65** D2
Troon Cl, SE16
off Masters Dr **156** B4
Troon St, E1
off White Horse Rd **143** E2
Trossachs Rd, SE22 **183** E3
Trothy Rd, SE1
off Monnow Rd **156** A3

rott St, SW11 **165** E3
routbeck Rd, SE14 **171** E3
rouville Rd, SW4 **180** C4
rowbridge Est, E9
off Osborne Rd **115** F3
rowbridge Rd, E9 **115** F3
roy Ct, W8 **54** A2
roy Town, SE15 **184** A1
ruman's Rd, N16 **113** E2
rumpington Rd, E7 **117** F1
rump St, EC2 **39** F3
rundle St, SE1 **51** E4
rundleys Rd, SE8 **157** D4
rundleys Ter, SE8 **157** D3
ruro St, NW5 **110** A3
russley Rd, W6 **148** C2
ryon Cres, E9 **128** C1
ryon St, SW3 **69** E2
ubbs Rd, NW10 **119** F2
udor Cl, N6 **96** C1
NW3 **109** E2
NW9 **90** C3
SW2 **181** F4
udor Ct, E17 **101** E1
udor Ct N, Wem. HA9 **104** A2
udor Ct S, Wem. HA9 **104** A2
● Tudor Est, NW10 **118** B2
udor Gdns, NW9 **90** C3
SW13 *off Treen Av* **175** E1
W3 **132** A2
udor Gro, E9 **114** C4
udor Rd, E9 **128** B1
udor St, EC4 **38** B4
udor Way, W3 **146** A1
UFNELL PARK, N7 **111** D1
⊖ Tufnell Park **110** C1
ufnell Pk Rd, N7 **110** C1
N19 **110** C1
ufton St, SW1 **60** B2
uilerie St, E2 **128** A2
ulse Hill, SW2 **182** A4
ulse Hill Est, SW2 **182** A4
unis Rd, W12 **134** B4
unley Grn, E14
off Burdett Rd **143** F1
unley Rd, NW10 **119** E1
unnel Av, SE10 **159** D1
● Tunnel Av Trd Est,
SE10 **159** D1
unnel Rd, SE16
off St. Marychurch St **156** C1
unstall Rd, SW9 **181** F2
unworth Cres, SW15 **175** F4
un Yd, SW8
off Peardon St **166** B4
upelo Rd, E10 **102** B3
urenne Cl, SW18 **178** C2
urin St, E2 **128** A3
urk's Head Yd, EC1 **26** C4
urks Row, SW3 **69** F2
urle Rd, N4 **97** F2
urlewray Cl, N4 **97** F2
urley Cl, E15 **131** E1
urnagain La, EC4 **38** C2
urnberry Cl, SE16
off Ryder Dr **156** B4
urnberry Quay, E14
off Pepper St **158** B2
urnchapel Ms, SW4
off Cedars Rd **180** B1
urner Cl, SW9 **87** D4
urner Ho, E14
off Cassilis Rd **158** A1
urner Pl, SW11 **179** E3
Turners Rd, E3 **143** F1
Turner St, E1 **142** B1
E16 **145** F2
Turners Wd, NW11 **94** C2
Turneville Rd, W14 **163** F1
⊖ Turnham Green **147** E3
Turnham Grn Ter, W4 **147** E3
Turnham Grn Ter Ms, W4 **147** E3
Turnham Rd, SE4 **185** E3
Turnmill St, EC1 **26** B3
Turnpike Cl, SE8
off Amersham Vale **171** F2
Turnpike Ho, EC1 **27** D1
Turnpin La, SE10 **172** C1
Turpentine La, SW1 **71** D2
Turpin Ho, SW11 **82** C4
Turpin Way, N19 **97** D3
Turquand St, SE17 **75** F1
Turret Gro, SW4 **180** C1
Turville St, E2 **29** E2
Tuscan Ho, E2 **128** C3
Tuskar St, SE10 **159** E4
Tustin Est, SE15 **170** C1
Tweed Ho, E14 **130** C4
Tweezer's All, WC2 **38** A4
● Twelvetrees Business Pk, E3
off Twelvetrees Cres **131** D4
Twelvetrees Cres, E3 **130** C4
Twickenham Rd, E11 **103** D3
Twig Folly Cl, E2
off Roman Rd **129** D2
Twine Ct, E1 **142** C3
Twine Ter, E3
off Ropery St **129** F4
Twisden Rd, NW5 **110** B1
Twybridge Way, NW10 **104** C4
Twycross Ms, SE10
off Blackwall La **159** E3
Twyford Av, W3 **132** A3
Twyford Cres, W3 **132** A4
Twyford Pl, WC2 **37** E2
Twyford St, N1 **125** F1
Tyas Rd, E16 **131** F4
Tyburn Way, W1 **33** F4
Tyers Est, SE1 **52** C4
Tyers Gate, SE1 **52** C4
Tyers St, SE11 **73** E2
Tyers Ter, SE11 **73** E3
Tyler Cl, E2 **17** E2
Tyler's Ct, W1 **36** A3
Tyler St, SE10 **159** E4
Tyndale Ct, E14 **158** B4
Tyndale La, N1
off Upper St **112** B4
Tyndale Ter, N1
off Canonbury La **112** B4
Tyndall Rd, E10 **102** C3
Tyneham Cl, SW11
off Shirley Gro **180** A1
Tyneham Rd, SW11 **166** A4
Tynemouth St, SW6 **164** C4
Tyne St, E1
off Old Castle St **41** F2
Tynsdale Rd, NW10 **105** E4
Type St, E2 **129** D2
Tyrawley Rd, SW6 **78** C4
Tyrrell Rd, SE22 **184** A2
Tyrrel Way, NW9 **91** F1
Tyrwhitt Rd, SE4 **186** A1
Tysoe St, EC1 **26** A1
Tyssen Pas, E8 **113** F3
Tyssen Rd, N16 **99** F4
Tyssen St, E8 **113** F3
N1 **17** D2
Tytherton Rd, N19 **97** D4

U

Uamvar St, E14 **144** B1
Udall St, SW1 **71** F1
Uffington Rd, NW10 **120** A1
Ufford St, SE1 **50** B4
Ufton Gro, N1 **113** D4
Ufton Rd, N1 **113** D4
Uhura Sq, N16 **99** E4
Ullin St, E14
off St. Leonards Rd **144** C1
Ullswater Rd, SW13 **162** A2
Ulster Pl, NW1 **22** C3
Ulster Ter, NW1 **22** C3
Ulundi Rd, SE3 **173** E1
Ulva Rd, SW15 **177** D3
Ulverscroft Rd, SE22 **183** F3
Ulysses Rd, NW6 **107** F2
Umberston St, E1
off Hessel St **142** B2
Umbria St, SW15 **176** A4
Undercliff Rd, SE13 **186** A1
Underhill Pas, NW1
off Camden High St **124** B1
Underhill Rd, SE22 **184** B4
Underhill St, NW1 **11** D1
Undershaft, EC3 **40** C3
Underwood Rd, E1 **128** A4
Underwood Row, N1 **15** F4
Underwood St, N1 **15** F4
Undine Rd, E14 **158** B3
Unicorn Pas, SE1
off Tooley St **53** D3
Union Cl, E11 **117** D1
Union Cotts, E15
off Welfare Rd **117** E4
Union Ct, EC2 **40** C2
Union Dr, E1
off Canal Cl **129** E4
Union Gro, SW8 **167** D4
Union Jack Club, SE1 **50** A4
Union Pk, SE10 **159** F4
Union Rd, SW4 **167** D4
SW8 **167** D4
Union Sq, N1 **15** E1
Union St, E15 **130** C1
SE1 **51** D3
Union Wk, E2 **17** D4
Union Wf, N1 **15** E3
Unity Cl, NW10 **106** A3
Unity Ct, SE1
off Mawbey Pl **77** F2
Unity Wf, SE1 **53** F4
H University Coll Hosp,
NW1 **23** F2
Elizabeth Garrett Anderson
Wing, NW1 **23** F2
Hosp for Tropical Diseases,
WC1 **23** F3
Obstetric Hosp, WC1 **23** F3
Private Wing, WC1 **23** F3
Uni University Coll London,
WC1 **24** A2
Arthur Stanley Ho, W1 **23** F4
Dorville & Doran Ho, W1 **35** E1
Eastman Dental Inst, WC1 **25** E1
Inst of Ophthalmology,
EC1 **28** A1
Ludwig Inst for Cancer
Research, W1 **23** F4
Prankerd Ho, NW1 **23** F2
Ramsay Hall, W1 **23** E3

University Coll London,
Slade Research Cen, WC1 . 24 B3
The Inst of Neurology,
WC1 . . . . 25 D3
The Warburg Inst, WC1 . . . 24 B3
Windeyer Bldg, W1 . . . . 23 F4
Wolfson Ho, NW1 . . . . 23 F1
Wolfson Inst for Biomedical
Research, WC1 . . . . 23 F3
University Hosp Lewisham,
SE13 . . . . 186 B3
University of E London -
Stratford Campus, Arthur
Edwards Bldg, E15
off The Green 117 E3
Cen for Clinical Ed, E15
off Water La 117 E3
Duncan Ho, E15
off High St 131 D1
Sch of Ed, E15
off Cedars Rd 117 E3
Student Services Cen, E15
off Ferns Rd 117 E3
Uni Ho, E15
off Romford Rd 117 E3
University of Gloucestershire,
Urban Learning Foundation,
E14
off East India Dock Rd . . 144 A3
University of Greenwich -
Maritime Greenwich Campus,
Cooper Bldg, SE10
off King William Wk 173 D1
Old Royal Naval Coll, SE10
off Park Row 173 D1
University of London,
Canterbury Hall, WC1 . . . . 24 C1
Commonwealth Hall, WC1 . 24 C1
Hughes Parry Hall, WC1 . . . 24 C1
International Hall, WC1 . . . 25 D3
Senate Ho, WC1 . . . . 24 B4
Stewart Ho, WC1 . . . . 24 B4
Union, WC1 . . . . 24 A3
University of the Arts, W1 . 34 C3
University of Westminster -
Cavendish Campus, W1 . . 23 E4
University of Westminster -
Marylebone Campus,
NW1 . . . . 22 A4
University of Westminster -
Regent Campus, W1 . . . . . 35 D2
Great Portland St, W1 . . . . . 23 D4
Little Titchfield St, W1 . . . . 35 E1
Riding Ho St, W1 . . . . 35 E1
University St, WC1 . . . . 23 F3
Unwin Cl, SE15 . . . . 170 A1
Unwin Rd, SW7 . . . . 56 B2
Upbrook Ms, W2 . . . . 31 F3
Upcerne Rd, SW10 . . . . 79 F3
Upham Pk Rd, W4 . . . . 147 E3
Upland Ms, SE22 . . . . 184 A3
Upland Rd, E13
off Sutton Rd 131 F4
SE22 . . . . 184 A3
Uplands Cl, SW14
off Monroe Dr 174 B3
Upnor Way, SE17 . . . . 77 D2
Upper Addison Gdns, W14 . . 149 E1
Upper Bk St, E14 . . . . 144 B4
Upper Bardsey Wk, N1
off Clephane Rd 112 C3
Upper Belgrave St, SW1 . . . . 58 B2
Upper Berenger Wk, SW10
off Blantyre St 80 A2
Upper Berkeley St, W1 . . . . . . 33 E3
Upper Blantyre Wk, SW10
off Blantyre St 80 A2
Upper Brockley Rd, SE4 . . . . 171 F4
Upper Brook St, W1 . . . . 46 A1
Upper Caldy Wk, N1
off Clifton Rd 112 C3
Upper Camelford Wk, W11
off St. Marks Rd 135 E2
Upper Cheyne Row, SW3 . . . . 80 C1
UPPER CLAPTON, E5 . . . . . . 100 B2
Upper Clapton Rd, E5 . . . . . . 100 B2
Upper Clarendon Wk, W11
off Clarendon Wk 135 E2
Upper Dartrey Wk, SW10
off Blantyre St 80 A2
Upper Dengie Wk, N1
off Popham Rd 126 C1
Upper Grosvenor St, W1 . . . . . 46 A1
Upper Grd, SE1 . . . . 50 A2
Upper Gulland Wk, N1
off Nightingale Rd 112 C3
Upper Hampstead Wk, NW3
off New End 108 C1
Upper Handa Wk, N1
off Clephane Rd 112 C3
Upper Hawkwell Wk, N1
off Popham Rd 126 C1
UPPER HOLLOWAY, N19 . . . . . 96 C4
Upper Holloway 97 D3
Upper James St, W1 . . . . 35 F4
Upper John St, W1 . . . . 35 F4
Upper Lismore Wk, N1
off Clephane Rd 112 C3
Upper Mall, W6 . . . . 148 A4
Upper Marsh, SE1 . . . . 61 F2
Upper Montagu St, W1 . . . . . . 21 E4
Upper N St, E14 . . . . 144 A1
Upper Pk Rd, NW3 . . . . 109 F2
Upper Phillimore Gdns, W8 . . . 54 A1
Upper Ramsey Wk, N1
off Ramsey Wk 113 D3
Upper Rawreth Wk, N1
off Popham Rd 126 C1
Upper Richmond Rd,
SW15 . . . . 177 E2
Upper Richmond Rd W,
SW14 . . . . 174 B2
Richmond TW10 . . . . 174 A2
Upper St. Martin's La, WC2 . . . 36 C4
Upper St, N1 . . . . 14 B2
Upper Tachbrook St, SW1 . . . . 59 E4
Upper Talbot Wk, W11
off Talbot Wk 135 E2
Upper Ter, NW3 . . . . 94 C4
Upper Thames St, EC4 . . . . . . 39 D4
Upper Tollington Pk, N4 . . . . . 98 A2
Upper Whistler Wk, SW10
off Blantyre St 79 F2
Upper Wimpole St, W1 . . . . . . 22 C4
Upper Woburn Pl, WC1 . . . . . . 24 B1
Upstall St, SE5 . . . . 168 B3
Upton Cl, NW2 . . . . 93 E4
Upwood Rd, SE12 . . . . 187 F4
Urban Ms, N4 . . . . 98 B1
Urdang Acad, The, EC1 . . 26 B1
Urlwin St, SE5 . . . . 87 E1
Urlwin Wk, SW9
off Mostyn Rd 168 A3
Ursula Ms, N4 . . . . 98 B2
Ursula St, SW11 . . . . 165 E3
Urswick Rd, E9 . . . . 114 C2
Usborne Ms, SW8 . . . . 85 E2
Usher Rd, E3 . . . . 129 F2
Usk Rd, SW11 . . . . 178 C2
Usk St, E2 . . . . 129 D3
Utah Bldg, SE13
off Deals Gateway 172 B3
Utopia Village, NW1
off Chalcot Rd 124 A1
Uverdale Rd, SW10 . . . . 79 F3
Uxbridge Rd, W12 . . . . 134 A4
Uxbridge St, W8 . . . . 42 A2

V

Vale, The, NW11 . . . . 93 D4
SW3 . . . . 68 A4
W3 . . . . 133 D4
Vale Cl, W9 . . . . 19 E1
Vale Ct, W3
off The Vale 133 F4
W9 . . . . 19 E1
Vale End, SE22
off Grove Vale 183 E2
Vale Gro, N4 . . . . 98 C1
W3 *off The Vale* 133 D4
Vale La, W3 . . . . 132 A1
Valentia Pl, SW9
off Brixton Sta Rd 182 A2
Valentine Ho, E3
off Garrison Rd 129 F1
Valentine Pl, SE1 . . . . 50 C4
Valentine Rd, E9 . . . . 115 D3
Valentine Row, SE1 . . . . 62 C1
Vale of Health, NW3 . . . . 95 D4
Valerian Way, E15 . . . . 131 E3
Vale Ri, NW11 . . . . 93 F2
Vale Rd, N4 . . . . 98 C1
Vale Row, N5
off Gillespie Rd 98 B4
Vale Royal, N7 . . . . 111 E4
Valetta Rd, W3 . . . . 147 E1
Valette St, E9 . . . . 114 B3
Vallance Rd, E1 . . . . 128 A4
E2 . . . . 128 A3
Valliere Rd, NW10 . . . . 120 B3
Valmar Rd, SE5 . . . . 168 C3
Valmar Trd Est, SE5
off Valmar Rd 168 C3
Val McKenzie Av, N7
off Parkside Cres 98 A4
Valonia Gdns, SW18 . . . . 177 F4
Vanbrugh Flds, SE3 . . . . 173 F2
Vanbrugh Hill, SE3 . . . . 159 F4
SE10 . . . . 159 F4
Vanbrugh Pk, SE3 . . . . 173 F2
Vanbrugh Pk Rd, SE3 . . . . . . 173 F2
Vanbrugh Pk Rd W, SE3 . . . . 173 F2
Vanbrugh Rd, W4 . . . . 147 D2
Vanbrugh Ter, SE3 . . . . 173 F3
Vandon Pas, SW1 . . . . 59 F2
Vandon St, SW1 . . . . 59 F2
Vandy St, EC2 . . . . 28 C3
Vane Cl, NW3 . . . . 109 D1
Vane St, SW1 . . . . 59 F4
Vanguard Ho, E8
off Martello St 114 B4
Vanguard St, SE8 . . . . 172 A3
Vanneck Sq, SW15 . . . . 176 A3
Vanner Pt, E9
off Wick Rd 115 D3
Vansittart Rd, E7 . . . . 117 F1
Vansittart St, SE14 . . . . 171 E2
Vanston Pl, SW6 . . . . 78 A2
Vantage Ms, E14
off Prestons Rd 144 C4
Vantage Pl, W8 . . . . 54 B3

Varcoe Rd, SE16 **156** B4
Vardens Rd, SW11 **179** D2
Varden St, E1 **142** B2
Vardon Cl, W3 **133** D2
Varna Rd, SW6 **163** E2
Varndell St, NW1 **11** E4
Varnishers Yd, N1 **13** D3
Varsity Row, SW14 **160** C4
Vassall Rd, SW9 **86** A3
Vauban Est, SE16 **65** F3
Vauban St, SE16 **65** F3
Vaughan Av, W6 **147** F3
Vaughan Rd, E15 **117** F3
SE5 **168** C4
Vaughan St, SE16 **157** F1
Vaughan Way, E1 **142** A3
Vaughan Williams Cl, SE8
off Watson's St **172** A2
VAUXHALL, SE11 **73** D3
⇌ Vauxhall **73** D4
⊖ Vauxhall **73** D4
Vauxhall Br, SE1 **72** C3
SW1 **72** C3
Vauxhall Br Rd, SW1 **59** F4
Vauxhall Gdns Est, SE11 **73** E3
Vauxhall Gro, SW8 **73** E4
Vauxhall St, SE11 **73** F2
Vauxhall Wk, SE11 **73** E2
Vawdrey Cl, E1 **128** C4
Veda Rd, SE13 **186** A2
Velde Way, SE22
off East Dulwich Gro **183** E3
Velletri Ho, E2 **129** D2
Venables St, NW8 **20** B3
Vencourt Pl, W6 **148** A4
Venetian Rd, SE5 **168** C4
Venice Wk, W2 **19** F4
Venn St, SW4 **180** C2
Ventnor Rd, SE14 **171** D2
Venue St, E14 **144** C1
Venus Ho, E3
off Garrison Rd **130** A1
E14 *off Crews St* **158** A3
Vera Rd, SW6 **163** E3
Verbena Cl, E16
off Pretoria Rd **131** F4
Verbena Gdns, W6 **148** A4
Verdi Cres, W10
off Herries St **121** E2
Verdun Rd, SW13 **162** A1
Vereker Rd, W14 **149** E4
Vere St, W1 **34** C3
Verity Cl, W11 **135** E2
Vermeer Gdns, SE15
off Elland Rd **184** C2
Vermont Rd, SW18 **178** B4
Verney Rd, SE16 **170** A1
Verney St, NW10 **91** D4
Verney Way, SE16 **156** B4
Vernon Ms, W14
off Vernon St **149** E3
Vernon Pl, WC1 **37** D1
Vernon Ri, WC1 **13** F4
Vernon Rd, E3 **129** F2
E11 **103** E2
E15 **117** E4
SW14 **175** D1
Vernon Sq, WC1 **13** F4
Vernon St, W14 **149** E3
Vernon Yd, W11
off Portobello Rd **135** F3
Verona Ct, W4
off Chiswick La **147** E4
Verulam Bldgs, WC1 **25** F4
Verulam Ct, NW9 **92** A1
Verulam Ho, W6
off Hammersmith Gro **148** C1
Verulam St, WC1 **26** A4
Vesage Ct, EC1 **38** B1
Vesey Path, E14
off East India Dock Rd **144** B2
Vespan Rd, W12 **148** A1
Vesta Ct, SE1
off Morocco St **64** C1
Vesta Ho, E3
off Garrison Rd **130** A1
Vesta Rd, SE4 **171** E4
Vestry Ms, SE5 **169** E3
Vestry Rd, SE5 **169** E3
Vestry St, N1 **16** A4
Viaduct Pl, E2
off Viaduct St **128** B3
Viaduct St, E2 **128** B3
Vian St, SE13 **186** B1
Vibart Wk, N1
off Outram Pl **125** E1
Vicarage Ct, W8
off Vicarage Gate **42** C4
Vicarage Cres, SW11 **165** D3
Vicarage Dr, SW14 **175** D3
Vicarage Gdns, SW14
off Vicarage Rd **174** C3
W8 **42** B3
Vicarage Gate, W8 **42** C4
Vicarage Gro, SE5 **88** B4
Vicarage La, E15 **117** E4
Vicarage Path, N8 **97** E1
Vicarage Rd, E10 **102** B2
E15 **117** F4
SW14 **174** C3
Vicarage Wk, SW11
off Battersea Ch Rd **165** D3
Vicarage Way, NW10 **91** D4
Vicars Cl, E9
off Northiam St **128** C1
Vicars Hill, SE13 **186** B2
Vicars Rd, NW5 **110** A2
Viceroy Ct, NW8 **9** D2
Viceroy Rd, SW8 **84** C4
Vickery's Wf, E14
off Stainsby Rd **144** A2
⇌ Victoria **59** D4
⊖ Victoria **59** D4
⬬ Victoria **59** D3
★ Victoria & Albert Mus, SW7 **56** B3
Victoria Arc, SW1
off Terminus Pl **59** D3
Victoria Av, EC2 **41** D1
Wembley HA9 **104** B3
Victoria Cl, SE22
off Underhill Rd **184** A3
⬬ Victoria Coach Sta **70** C1
Victoria Ct, Wem. HA9 **104** A3
Victoria Dock Rd, E16 **145** F2
Victoria Embk, EC4 **49** E1
SW1 **49** D4
WC2 **49** E1
★ Victoria Embankment Gdns, WC2 **49** D1
Victoria Gdns, W11 **42** A2
Victoria Gro, W8 **55** E2
Victoria Gro Ms, W2 **42** B1
Victoria Ho, SW8
off South Lambeth Rd **85** D2
● Victoria Ind Est, NW10 **119** E3
W3 **133** D1
Victoria Mans, SW8
off South Lambeth Rd **85** D2
Victoria Ms, E8
off Dalston La **114** A3
NW6 **122** A1
SW4 *off Victoria Ri* **180** B2
Victoria Mills Studios, E15
off Burford Rd **131** D1
Victorian Gro, N16 **99** E4
Victorian Hts, SW8
off Thackeray Rd **166** B4
Victorian Rd, N16 **99** E4
★ Victoria Park, E9 **115** E4
● Victoria Pk Ind Cen, E9
off Rothbury Rd **116** A4
Victoria Pk Rd, E9 **128** C1
Victoria Pk Sq, E2 **128** C3
Victoria Pas, NW8 **20** A2
🔒 Victoria Pl, SW1 **59** D4
Victoria Ri, SW4 **180** B1
Victoria Rd, E11 **117** E1
N4 **97** F1
NW6 **121** F1
NW10 **133** D1
SW14 **175** D1
W3 **133** D1
W8 **55** E3
Victoria Sq, SW1 **59** D2
Victoria St, E15 **117** E4
SW1 **59** E3
Victoria Ter, N4 **98** A2
NW10 *off Old Oak La* **119** E4
Victoria Wf, E14 **143** E3
Victoria Yd, E1
off Fairclough St **142** A2
Victor Rd, NW10 **120** B3
Victory Pl, E14
off Northey St **143** E3
SE17 **64** A4
Victory Wk, SE8
off Ship St **172** A3
Victory Way, SE16 **157** E1
View Cl, N6 **95** F1
Viewfield Rd, SW18 **177** F4
View Rd, N6 **95** F1
Vigo St, W1 **47** E1
Viking Cl, E3
off Selwyn Rd **129** F2
Viking Ct, SW6 **66** B4
Viking Pl, E10 **101** F2
Village Cl, NW3
off Belsize La **109** D2
Village Ms, NW9 **91** D3
Village Way, NW10 **105** D1
SE21 **183** D4
Villa Rd, SW9 **182** A1
Villa St, SE17 **76** B3
Villiers Cl, E10 **102** A3
Villiers Rd, NW2 **106** A3
Villiers St, WC2 **48** C1
Vince Ct, N1
off Charles Sq **28** B1
Vincent Cl, SE16 **157** E1
Vincent Gdns, NW2 **91** F4
Vincent Ms, E3
off Fairfield Rd **130** A2
Vincent Rd, W3 **146** C2
Vincent Sq, SW1 **59** F4
Vincent St, E16 **145** F1
SW1 **60** A4
Vincent Ter, N1 **14** C2
Vince St, EC1 **28** B1
Vine Cl, E5
off Rendlesham Rd **114** A1

Vine Ct, E1
off Whitechapel Rd **142** A1
Vinegar St, E1
off Reardon St **142** B4
Vinegar Yd, SE1 . . . . **52** C4
Vine Hill, EC1 . . . . **26** A3
Vine La, SE1 . . . . **53** D3
Vine Rd, E15 . . . . **117** F4
SW13 . . . . **175** F1
Vine Sq, W14 . . . . **149** F4
Vine St, EC3 . . . . **41** E4
W1 . . . . **47** F1
Vine St Br, EC1 . . . . **26** B3
Vine Yd, SE1 . . . . **51** F4
Vineyard Path, SW14 . . . . . . **175** D1
Vineyard Wk, EC1 . . . . **26** A2
Viney Rd, SE13 . . . . **186** B1
Vining St, SW9 . . . . **182** A2
★ Vinopolis, SE1 . . . . **51** F2
Vintners Ct, EC4 . . . . **39** F4
Vintners Pl, EC4
off Vintners Ct **39** F4
Viola Sq, W12 . . . . **133** F3
Violet Cl, E16 . . . . **131** E4
SE8 *off Dorking Cl* **171** F1
Violet Hill, NW8 . . . . **7** E3
Violet Rd, E3 . . . . **130** B4
Violet St, E2
off Three Colts La **128** B4
Virgil Pl, W1 . . . . **33** E1
Virgil St, SE1 . . . . **61** F2
Virginia Rd, E2 . . . . **29** E1
Virginia St, E1 . . . . **142** A3
Virginia Wk, SW2 . . . . **181** F4
Viridian Apts, SW8 . . . . **83** E3
Visage Apts, NW3
off Winchester Rd **109** D4
Viscount St, EC1 . . . . **27** E3
Vitae, W6
off Goldhawk Rd **148** A2
Vivian Av, Wem. HA9 . . . . . . **104** A2
Vivian Comma Cl, N4 . . . . **98** B4
Vivian Ct, W9 . . . . **6** C2
Vivian Gdns, Wem. HA9 . . . . **104** A2
Vivian Rd, E3 . . . . **129** E2
Vivian Sq, SE15
off Scylla Rd **184** B1
Vogans Mill, SE1 . . . . **53** F4
Voltaire Rd, SW4 . . . . **181** D1
Volt Av, NW10 . . . . **119** D3
Vorley Rd, N19 . . . . **96** C3
Voss St, E2 . . . . **128** A3
● Voyager Business Est,
SE16 *off Spa Rd* **156** A2
Vulcan Rd, SE4 . . . . **171** F4
Vulcan Sq, E14
off Britannia Rd **158** A3
Vulcan Ter, SE4 . . . . **171** F4
Vulcan Way, N7 . . . . **111** F3
Vyner Rd, W3 . . . . **133** D3
Vyner St, E2 . . . . **128** B1

W

Wadding St, SE17 . . . . **76** A1
Waddington Rd, E15 . . . . . . **117** D2
Waddington St, E15 . . . . . . **117** D3
Wadeson St, E2 . . . . **128** B2
Wades Pl, E14 . . . . **144** B3
Wadham Gdns, NW3 . . . . . . **123** E1
Wadham Rd, SW15 . . . . **177** E2
Wadhurst Rd, SW8 . . . . **83** E4
W4 . . . . **147** D2
Wadley Rd, E11 . . . . **103** E1
Wager St, E3 . . . . **129** F4
Waghorn St, SE15 . . . . **184** A1
Wagner St, SE15 . . . . **170** C2
Waite St, SE15 . . . . **77** E4
Waithman St, EC4 . . . . **38** C3
Wakefield Ms, WC1 . . . . **25** D1
Wakefield St, WC1 . . . . **25** D2
Wakeford Cl, SW4 . . . . **180** C3
Wakeham St, N1 . . . . **113** D3
Wakehurst Rd, SW11 . . . . . . **179** E3
Wakeling St, E14 . . . . **143** E2
Wakelin Rd, E15 . . . . **131** E2
Wakeman Rd, NW10 . . . . . . **120** C3
Wakley St, EC1 . . . . **14** C4
Walberswick St, SW8 . . . . **85** D3
Walbrook, EC4 . . . . **40** A4
Walbrook Wf, EC4
off Bell Wf La **51** F1
Walburgh St, E1
off Bigland St **142** B2
Walcorde Av, SE17 . . . . **75** F1
Walcot Ho, SE22
off Albrighton Rd **183** E1
Walcot Sq, SE11 . . . . **62** B4
Walcott St, SW1 . . . . **59** F4
Waldeck Rd, SW14
off Lower Richmond Rd . **174** C1
W4 . . . . **160** A1
Waldeck Ter, SW14
off Lower Richmond Rd . **174** C1
Waldemar Av, SW6 . . . . **163** E3
Walden Ct, SW8
off Wandsworth Rd **84** B4
Walden St, E1 . . . . **142** B2
Waldo Cl, SW4 . . . . **180** C3
Waldo Rd, NW10 . . . . **120** A3
Waldron Ms, SW3 . . . . **68** B4
Walerand Rd, SE13 . . . . **172** C4
Waleran Flats, SE1 . . . . **64** C4
Wales Cl, SE15 . . . . **170** B2
Wales Fm Rd, W3 . . . . **133** D1
Waley St, E1 . . . . **143** D1
Walford Rd, N16 . . . . **113** E1
WALHAM GREEN, SW6 . . . . . . **78** C3
Walham Grn Ct, SW6 . . . . **78** C3
Walham Gro, SW6 . . . . **78** A2
Walham Yd, SW6 . . . . **78** A2
Walker Ms, SW2
off Effra Rd **182** A3
Walkers Ct, E8
off Wilton Way **114** A3
W1 . . . . **36** A4
Walkers Pl, SW15
off Felsham Rd **177** E2
Walkynscroft, SE15
off Firbank Rd **170** B4
★ Wallace Collection, W1 . . . **34** A2
Wallace Rd, N1 . . . . **112** C3
Wallace Way, N19
off Giesbach Rd **97** D3
Wallbutton Rd, SE4 . . . . **171** E4
Wallcote Av, NW2 . . . . **93** D2
Waller Rd, SE14 . . . . **171** D3
Waller Way, SE10
off Greenwich High Rd . . **172** B2
Wallflower St, W12 . . . . **133** F3
Wallgrave Rd, SW5 . . . . **54** C4
Wallingford Av, W10 . . . . **135** D1
Wallis All, SE1 . . . . **51** F4
Wallis Cl, SW11 . . . . **179** D1
Wallis Rd, E9 . . . . **115** F3
Wallorton Gdns, SW14 . . . . . **175** D2
Wallside, EC2 . . . . **39** F1
Wall St, N1 . . . . **113** D3
Wallwood Rd, E11 . . . . **103** D2
Wallwood St, E14 . . . . **143** F1
Walmer Pl, W1 . . . . **21** E4
Walmer Rd, W10
off Latimer Rd **134** C2
W11 . . . . **135** E3
Walmer St, W1 . . . . **21** E4
Walm La, NW2 . . . . **107** D2
Walney Wk, N1
off St. Paul's Rd **112** C3
Walnut Cl, SE8
off Clyde St **171** F1
Walnut Gdns, E15 . . . . **117** D2
Walnut Rd, E10 . . . . **102** A3
Walnut Tree Cl, SW13 . . . . . **161** F3
Walnut Tree Rd, SE10 . . . . . **159** E4
Walnut Tree Wk, SE11 . . . . . . **62** A4
Walpole Gdns, W4 . . . . **146** C4
Walpole Ms, NW8 . . . . **8** A1
Walpole St, SW3 . . . . **69** E2
Walsham Cl, N16
off Clarke Path **100** A2
Walsham Rd, SE14 . . . . **171** D4
Walsingham Pl, SW4
off Clapham Common W Side **179** F2
SW11 . . . . **180** A4
Walsingham Rd, E5 . . . . **100** A4
Walters Cl, SE17 . . . . **75** F1
Walters Ho, SE17 . . . . **86** C1
Walter St, E2 . . . . **129** D3
Walters Way, SE23 . . . . **185** D4
Walter Ter, E1 . . . . **143** D2
Walterton Rd, W9 . . . . **121** F4
Walton Av, Wem. HA9 . . . . **90** B4
Walton Cl, E5
off Orient Way **101** D4
NW2 . . . . **92** B3
SW8 . . . . **85** D2
Walton Dr, NW10 . . . . **105** D3
Walton Gdns, W3 . . . . **132** B1
Walton Pl, SW3 . . . . **57** E2
Walton St, SW3 . . . . **57** D4
Walton Way, W3 . . . . **132** B1
Walt Whitman Cl, SE24
off Shakespeare Rd **182** B2
WALWORTH, SE17 . . . . **75** E2
★ Walworth Garden Fm - Horticultural Training Cen, SE17 . . . . **75** D3
Walworth Pl, SE17 . . . . **75** F3
Walworth Rd, SE1 . . . . **63** E4
SE17 . . . . **63** E4
Wandon Rd, SW6 . . . . **79** D3
WANDSWORTH, SW18 . . . . . **177** F3
Wandsworth Br, SW6 . . . . . . **178** B1
SW18 . . . . **178** B1
Wandsworth Br Rd, SW6 . . . . . **78** C4
Wandsworth Common, SW12 . . . . **179** E4
Wandsworth Common W Side, SW18 . . . . **178** C3
Wandsworth High St, SW18 . . . . **178** A3
Wandsworth Plain, SW18 . . . **178** B3
RIV Wandsworth Riverside Quarter Pier **178** A2
⇌ Wandsworth Road **166** C4
Wandsworth Rd, SW8 . . . . **72** C4
⇌ Wandsworth Town **178** B2
Jct Wandsworth Town, SW18 . . . . **178** A3
Wanless Rd, SE24 . . . . **182** C1
Wanley Rd, SE5 . . . . **183** D2

Wansbeck Rd, E3 ....115 F4
E9 ....115 F4
Wansdown Pl, SW6 ....78 C2
Wansey St, SE17 ....75 F1
Wantage Rd, SE12 ....187 F3
WAPPING, E1 ....142 A4
Wapping 142 C4
Wapping Dock St, E1
off Cinnamon St 142 B4
Wapping High St, E1 ....142 A4
Wapping La, E1 ....142 B3
Wapping Wall, E1 ....142 C4
Warbeck Rd, W12 ....134 B4
Warburton Cl, N1
off Culford Rd 113 E3
Warburton Ho, E8
off Warburton Rd 128 B1
Warburton Rd, E8 ....128 B1
Warburton St, E8
off Warburton Rd 128 B1
Wardalls Gro, SE14 ....170 C2
Warden Rd, NW5 ....110 A3
Wardens Gro, SE1 ....51 E3
Wardle St, E9 ....115 D2
Wardo Av, SW6 ....163 E3
Wardour Ms, W1 ....35 F3
Wardour St, W1 ....36 A4
Ward Pt, SE11 ....74 A1
Ward Rd, E15 ....131 D1
N19 ....96 C4
Wardrobe Pl, EC4
off St. Andrew's Hill 39 D3
Wardrobe Ter, EC4 ....39 D3
Wareham Ho, SW8 ....85 E2
Warfield Rd, NW10 ....121 D3
Warfield Yd, NW10
off Warfield Rd 121 D3
Warham St, SE5 ....87 D2
Warley Cl, E10 ....101 F2
Warley St, E2 ....129 D3
Warlock Rd, W9 ....18 A2
Warlters Cl, N7
off Warlters Rd 111 E1
Warlters Rd, N7 ....111 E1
Warltersville Rd, N19 ....97 E1
Warmington Cl, E5
off Denton Way 101 D4
Warmington Rd, SE24 .....182 C4
Warndon St, SE16 ....157 D3
Warneford St, E9 ....128 B1
Warner Cl, E15 ....117 E2
NW9 ....91 F1
Warner Ho, SE13
off Conington Rd 172 B4
Warner Pl, E2 ....128 A2
Warner Rd, SE5 ....168 C3
Warner St, EC1 ....26 A3
Warner Ter, E14
off Broomfield St 144 A1
Warner Yd, EC1 ....26 A3
Warnford Ho, SW15
off Tunworth Cres 175 E4
Warple Ms, W3
off Warple Way 147 E1
Warple Way, W3 ....133 E4
Warren Av, E10 ....102 C4
Richmond TW10 ....174 B2
Warrender Rd, N19 ....96 C4
Warren Gdns, E15
off Ashton Rd 117 D2
Warren Ho, E3
off Bromley High St 130 B3
W14 ....149 F3
Warren Ms, W1 ....23 E3
Warren Rd, E10 ....102 C4
NW2 ....91 F3
Warren Street 23 F2
Warren St, W1 ....23 D3
Warriner Gdns, SW11 ......165 F3
Warrington Cres, W9 ....19 E3
Warrington Gdns, W9 ....19 E3
Warton Rd, E15 ....130 C1
Warwick Avenue 19 E3
Warwick Av, W2 ....19 E3
W9 ....19 E3
Warwick Bldg, SW8 ....82 C2
Warwick Chambers, W8
off Pater St 54 A2
Warwick Ct, SE15 ....170 A4
WC1 ....37 F1
Warwick Cres, W2 ....19 E4
Warwick Dr, SW15 ....176 B1
Warwick Est, W2 ....30 C1
Warwick Gdns, W14 ....149 F2
Warwick Gro, E5 ....100 B2
Warwick Ho St, SW1 ....48 B2
Warwick La, EC4 ....39 D3
Warwick Pas, EC4 ....39 D2
Warwick Pl, W9 ....19 E4
Warwick Pl N, SW1 ....71 E1
Warwick Rd, E15 ....117 F3
SW5 ....149 F3
W14 ....149 F3
Warwick Row, SW1 ....59 D2
Warwickshire Path, SE8 ....171 F2
Warwick Sq, EC4 ....39 D2
SW1 ....71 E2
Warwick Sq Ms, SW1 ....71 E1
Warwick St, W1 ....35 F4
Warwick Way, SW1 ....71 E1
Warwick Yd, EC1 ....27 F3
Washington Bldg, SE13
off Deals Gateway 172 B3
Washington Cl, E3 ....130 B3
Washington Rd, SW13 .....162 A2
Watchfield Ct, W4 ....146 C4
Watcombe Cotts, Rich.
TW9 ....160 A1
Watercress Pl, N1
off Hertford Rd 113 E4
Waterden Rd, E15
off Eastway 116 A2
Waterford Rd, SW6 ....79 D4
Waterford Way, NW10 .....106 B2
Water Gdns, The, W2 ....33 D2
Water Gdns Sq, SE16
off Canada St 157 D1
Watergate, EC4 ....38 C4
Watergate St, SE8 ....172 A1
Watergate Wk, WC2 ....49 D2
Waterhouse Cl, NW3
off Lyndhurst Rd 109 D2
W6 *off Great Ch La* 149 D4
Waterhouse Sq, EC1 ....38 A1
Wateridge Cl, E14
off Westferry Rd 158 A2
Water La, E15 ....117 E3
EC3 ....52 C1
NW1
off Kentish Town Rd 110 B4
SE14 ....170 C2
Waterloo 50 A4
Waterloo 50 A4
Waterloo Br, SE1 ....49 E1
WC2 ....49 E1
Waterloo Cl, E9
off Churchill Wk 114 C2
Waterloo East 50 A3
Waterloo Est, E2 ....128 C2
Waterloo Gdns, E2 ....128 C2
N1 *off Barnsbury St* 112 A4
Riv Waterloo Millennium
Pier 49 D4
Waterloo Pas, NW6 ....107 F4
Waterloo Pl, SW1 ....48 A2
Richmond (Kew) TW9
off Kew Grn 160 A1
Waterloo Rd, E7
off Wellington Rd 117 F2
E10 ....102 A1
NW2 ....92 A2
SE1 ....50 A4
Waterloo Ter, N1 ....112 B4
Waterlow Ct, NW11
off Heath Cl 94 B1
Waterlow Rd, N19 ....96 C2
Waterman St, SW15 ....177 D1
Waterman's Wk, EC4
off Allhallows La 52 A1
Watermans Wk, SE16 .....157 E2
Waterman Way, E1 ....142 B4
Watermead Ho, E9
off Kingsmead Way 115 E2
Watermeadow La, SW6 ....164 C4
Water Ms, SE15 ....184 C2
Watermint Quay, N16 .....100 A1
Waterside Cl, E3 ....129 F1
SE16
off Bevington St 156 A1
Waterside Ct, SE13
off Weardale Rd 187 D2
Waterside Path, SW18
off Smugglers Way 178 B2
Waterside Pl, NW1
off Princess Rd 124 A1
Waterside Pt, SW11 ....81 D2
Waterside Twr, SW6 ......164 C3
Waterson St, E2 ....17 D4
Waters Pl, SW15
off Danemere St 162 C4
Water St, WC2 ....37 F4
Water Twr Pl, N1 ....14 B1
Waterview Ho, E14 ....143 E1
Waterway Av, SE13 ....186 B1
Waterworks La, E5 ....101 D3
Waterworks Rd, SW2 .....181 E4
Watford Cl, SW11 ....81 D4
Watkin Rd, Wem. HA9 ......90 B4
Watkinson Rd, N7 ....111 F3
Watling Ct, EC4 ....39 F3
Watling Gdns, NW2 ....107 E3
Watling St, EC4 ....39 E3
SE15 ....89 D1
Watney Cotts, SW14
off Lower Richmond Rd .174 C1
Watney Mkt, E1
off Commercial Rd 142 B2
Watney Rd, SW14 ....174 C1
Watney St, E1 ....142 B2
Watson Cl, N16
off Matthias Rd 113 D2
Watsons Ms, W1 ....33 D1
Watson's St, SE8 ....172 A2
Wattisfield Rd, E5 ....100 C4
Watts Gro, E3 ....144 B1
Watts St, E1 ....142 B4
SE15 ....89 F4
Watts Way, SW7 ....56 B2
Wat Tyler Rd, SE3 ....172 C4
SE10 ....172 C4
Wavel Ms, NW6
off Acol Rd 108 B4

Wavendon Av, W4 ....147 D4
Waveney Av, SE15 ....184 B2
Waveney Cl, E1
off Kennet St 142 A4
Waverley Pl, N4 ....98 B2
NW8 ....8 A2
Waverley Wk, W2 ....18 B4
Waverton Ho, E3 ....129 F1
Waverton St, W1 ....46 B2
Waxham, NW3 ....109 F2
Waxlow Rd, NW10 ....118 C2
Wayford St, SW11 ....165 E4
Wayland Av, E8 ....114 A2
Wayland Ho, SW9 ....168 A4
Waylett Ho, SE11 ....74 A3
Wayman Ct, E8 ....114 B3
Waynflete Sq, W10 ....135 D3
Wayside, NW11 ....93 E2
SW14 ....174 C3
Wayside Ct, Wem.
HA9 ....90 A4
Weald Cl, SE16
off Stevenson Cres 156 B4
Weald Sq, E5 ....100 A3
Weardale Rd, SE13 ....187 D2
Wear Pl, E2 ....128 B3
Wearside Rd, SE13 ....186 B2
Weatherbury Ho, N19
off Wedmore St 97 D4
Weatherley Cl, E3 ....143 F1
Weavers La, SE1 ....53 D3
Weavers Ter, SW6 ....78 B1
Weaver St, E1 ....128 A4
Weavers Way, NW1 ....125 D1
Webb Cl, W10 ....120 C4
Webber Row, SE1 ....62 B1
Webber St, SE1 ....50 B4
Webb Est, E5 ....100 A1
Webb Ho, SW8 ....84 B3
Webb Pl, NW10 ....119 F3
Webb Rd, SE3 ....173 F1
Webbs Rd, SW11 ....179 F3
Webb St, SE1 ....64 C3
Webheath Est, NW6 ....107 F4
Webster Rd, E11 ....102 C4
SE16 ....156 A2
Wedderburn Rd, NW3 ....109 D2
Wedgwood Ho, SE11 ....62 A3
Wedgwood Ms, W1 ....36 B3
Wedgwood Wk, NW6
off Dresden Cl 108 B2
Wedlake St, W10
off Kensal Rd 121 E4
Wedmore Gdns, N19 ....97 D3
Wedmore Ms, N19 ....97 D4
Wedmore St, N19 ....97 D4
Weech Rd, NW6 ....108 A1
Weedington Rd, NW5 ....110 A2
Weekley Sq, SW11
off Thomas Baines Rd 179 D1
Weighhouse St, W1 ....34 B3
Weimar St, SW15 ....177 E1
Weir's Pas, NW1 ....12 B4
Weiss Rd, SW15 ....177 D1
Welbeck St, W1 ....34 C2
Welbeck Way, W1 ....34 C2
Welby St, SE5 ....168 B3
Welfare Rd, E15 ....117 E4
Welford Cl, E5
off Denton Way 101 D4
Welland Ms, E1
off Kennet St 142 A4
Welland St, SE10 ....172 C1
Wellclose Sq, E1 ....142 A3
Wellclose St, E1
off The Highway 142 A3
Coll Wellcome Trust, NW1 ....24 A2
Well Ct, EC4 ....39 F3
Weller St, SE1 ....51 E4
Wellesley Av, W6 ....148 B2
Wellesley Ct, W9 ....7 E4
Wellesley Pl, NW1 ....24 A1
Wellesley Rd, NW5 ....110 A2
W4 ....146 A4
Wellesley St, E1 ....143 D1
Wellesley Ter, N1 ....15 F4
Wellfit St, SE24
off Hinton Rd 182 B1
Wellgarth Rd, NW11 ....94 B2
★ Wellington Arch, W1 ....46 B4
Wellington Bldgs, SW1 ....70 B3
Wellington Cl, SE14
off Rutts Ter 171 D3
W11 ....30 A3
Wellington Ct, NW8 ....8 A3
Wellington Gro, SE10
off Crooms Hill 173 D2
H Wellington Hosp, NW8 ....8 B3
Wellington Ms, SE22 ....184 A2
● Wellington Pk Est, NW2 ....92 A3
Wellington Pl, NW8 ....8 B4
Wellington Rd, E7 ....117 F1
E10 ....101 E2
NW8 ....8 A2
NW10 ....121 D3
Wellington Row, E2 ....17 F4
Wellington Sq, N1
off Pembroke Av 125 F1
SW3 ....69 E2
Wellington St, WC2 ....37 D4
Wellington Ter, E1 ....142 B4
W2
off Notting Hill Gate 42 C1
Wellington Way, E3 ....130 A3
Well La, SW14 ....174 C3
Wellmeadow Rd, SE13 ....187 E4
Well Pas, NW3 ....95 D4
Well Rd, NW3 ....95 D4
Wells Dr, NW9 ....91 D2
Wells Ho Rd, NW10 ....133 E1
Wellside Gdns, SW14
off Well La 174 C3
Wells Ms, W1 ....35 F1
Wellspring Cres, Wem. HA9 ....90 B4
Wells Ri, NW8 ....9 E1
Wells Rd, W12 ....148 C1
Wells Sq, WC1 ....25 E1
Wells St, W1 ....35 E1
Wells Ter, N4 ....98 A3
Well St, E9 ....114 B4
E15 ....117 E3
Wells Way, SE5 ....76 B4
SW7 ....56 A2
Wells Yd S, N7
off George's Rd 112 A2
Well Wk, NW3 ....109 D1
Welmar Ms, SW4 ....181 D2
Welsford St, SE1 ....156 A4
Welshpool Ho, E8
off Benjamin Cl 128 A1
Welshpool St, E8
off Broadway Mkt 128 B1
Welstead Way, W4 ....147 F3
Weltje Rd, W6 ....148 A4
Welwyn St, E2
off Globe Rd 128 C3
★ Wembley Arena, Wem.
HA9 ....104 A1
⊖ Wembley Park 90 A4
● Wembley Pk Business Cen,
Wem. HA9 ....90 B4
Wembley Pt, Wem. HA9 ....104 B4
★ Wembley Stadium, Wem.
HA9 ....104 A1
⇌ Wembley Stadium 104 A2
Wembley Way, Wem. HA9 ....104 B3
Wembury Ms, N6
off Wembury Rd 96 B1
Wembury Rd, N6 ....96 B1
Wemyss Rd, SE3 ....173 F4
Wendell Rd, W12 ....147 F1
Wendle Ct, SW8 ....84 C1
Wendle Sq, SW11 ....81 D4
Wendling, NW5 ....109 F2
Wendon St, E3 ....129 F1
Wendover, SE17 ....76 C2
Wendover Ct, W3 ....118 B4
Wendover Rd, NW10 ....119 F2
Wenham Ho, SW8
off Ascalon St 83 E3
Wenlock Ct, N1 ....16 B3
Wenlock Rd, N1 ....15 E2
Wenlock St, N1 ....15 F3
Wennington Rd, E3 ....129 D2
Wentworth Cres, SE15 ....170 A2
Wentworth Ms, E3
off Eric St 129 F4
W3 ....133 E2
Wentworth St, E1 ....41 E2
Werrington St, NW1 ....11 F3
Werter Rd, SW15 ....177 E2
Wesleyan Pl, NW5
off Gordon Ho Rd 110 B1
Wesley Av, NW10 ....119 D3
Wesley Cl, N7 ....97 F3
SE17 ....75 D1
Wesley Rd, E10 ....102 C1
NW10 ....118 C1
★ Wesley's Ho, EC1 ....28 A3
Wesley Sq, W11
off Bartle Rd 135 E2
Wesley St, W1 ....34 B1
Wessex Gdns, NW11 ....93 E2
Wessex Ho, SE1 ....77 F2
Wessex St, E2 ....128 C3
Wessex Way, NW11 ....93 E1
Wessonmead, SE5
off Camberwell Rd 87 F3
🔒 West 12 Shop Cen,
W12 ....149 D1
Westacott Cl, N19 ....97 D2
WEST ACTON, W3 ....132 A2
⊖ West Acton 132 A2
West Arbour St, E1 ....143 D2
West Bk, N16 ....99 E1
Westbere Rd, NW2 ....107 E1
Westbourne Av, W3 ....133 D2
Westbourne Br, W2 ....31 E1
Westbourne Cres, W2 ....32 A4
Westbourne Cres Ms, W2 ....32 A4
Westbourne Gdns, W2 ....30 C2
WESTBOURNE GREEN, W2 ....30 A1
Westbourne Gro, W2 ....30 B3
W11 ....136 A2
Westbourne Gro Ms, W11 ....30 A3
Westbourne Gro Ter, W2 ....30 C2
⊖ Westbourne Park 135 F1
Westbourne Pk Ms, W2 ....30 C2
Westbourne Pk Pas, W2 ....30 B1
Westbourne Pk Rd, W2 ....30 B1
W11 ....135 E2
Westbourne Pk Vil, W2 ....30 B1

Westbourne Rd, N7 . . . . **112** A3
Westbourne St, W2 . . . . **32** A4
Westbourne Ter, W2 . . . . **31** F2
Westbourne Ter Ms, W2 . . . . . **31** E2
Westbourne Ter Rd, W2 . . . . . **31** E1
West Br Cl, W12 *off Percy Rd* **134** A4
Westbridge Rd, SW11 . . . . . . **165** D3
WEST BROMPTON, SW10 . . . . **66** C4
West Brompton **66** B3
West Brompton **66** B3
Westbury Par, SW12 *off Balham Hill* **180** B4
Westbury St, SW8 . . . . **166** C4
West Carriage Dr, W2 . . . . **44** B3
West Cen St, WC1 . . . . **36** C2
West Cen Av, W10 *off Harrow Rd* **120** B3
Westcliffe Apts, W2 . . . . **32** B1
Westcombe Ct, SE3 *off Westcombe Pk Rd* . . . **173** F2
Westcombe Pk Rd, SE3 . . . . . **173** E1
West Cotts, NW6 . . . . **108** A2
Westcott Ho, E14 *off East India Dock Rd* . . **144** A3
Westcott Rd, SE17 . . . . **74** C4
Westcroft Cl, NW2 . . . . **107** E1
Westcroft Sq, W6 . . . . **148** A3
Westcroft Way, NW2 . . . . . . **107** E1
West Cromwell Rd, SW5 . . . . . **66** A1
W14 . . . . **149** F3
West Cross Route, W10 . . . . **135** D3
W11 . . . . **135** D3
Westdean Cl, SW18 . . . . **178** B3
Westdown Rd, E15 . . . . **116** C1
West Eaton Pl, SW1 . . . . **58** A4
West Eaton Pl Ms, SW1 . . . . . . **58** A4
West Ella Rd, NW10 . . . . **105** E4
West End Cl, NW10 . . . . **104** C4
West End La, NW6 . . . . **6** B1
Westerley Ware, Rich. TW9 *off Kew Grn* **160** A1
Western Av, W3 . . . . **133** D1
Western Av Business Pk, W3 *off Mansfield Rd* **118** B4
Western Eye Hosp, NW1 . . . . **21** E4
Western Gdns, W5 . . . . **132** A3
Western Ms, W9 *off Great Western Rd* . . . **121** F4
Western Pl, SE16 *off Canon Beck Rd* **156** C1
Western Rd, NW10 . . . . **118** C4
SW9 . . . . **182** A1
Western Ter, W6 *off Chiswick Mall* **148** A4
Western Trd Est, NW10 . **118** C4
Westferry **144** A3
Westferry Circ, E14 . . . . **143** F4
Westferry Rd, E14 . . . . **144** A4
Westfield Cl, SW10 . . . . **79** E3
Westfield London, W12 . **134** C4
Westfields, SW13 . . . . **175** F1
Westfields Av, SW13 . . . . **175** E1
Westfields Rd, W3 . . . . **132** B1
Westfield Way, E1 . . . . **129** E3
West Gdn Pl, W2 . . . . **33** D3
West Gdns, E1 . . . . **142** B3
Westgate Ct, SW9 *off Canterbury Cres* **182** A1
Westgate St, E8 . . . . **128** B1
Westgate Ter, SW10 . . . . **67** D3
West Gro, SE10 . . . . **172** C3
Westgrove La, SE10 . . . . **172** C3
West Halkin St, SW1 . . . . **58** A2
West Hall Rd, Rich. TW9 . . . . **160** B3
WEST HAM, E15 . . . . **117** F4
West Ham **131** E3
West Ham **131** E3
West Ham La, E15 . . . . **117** E4
West Ham Pk, E7 . . . . **117** F4
WEST HAMPSTEAD, NW6 . . . **108** B2
West Hampstead **108** A3
West Hampstead **108** A3
West Hampstead Ms, NW6 . . **108** B3
West Hampstead (Thameslink) **108** A3
West Harding St, EC4 . . . . **38** B2
Westhay Gdns, SW14 . . . . . . **174** B3
West Heath Av, NW11 . . . . . . **94** A2
West Heath Cl, NW3 . . . . **94** A4
West Heath Dr, NW11 . . . . . . **94** A2
West Heath Gdns, NW3 . . . . . **94** A3
West Heath Rd, NW3 . . . . **94** A3
WEST HENDON, NW9 . . . . **91** E1
West Hill, SW18 . . . . **178** A3
West Hill Ct, N6 . . . . **96** A4
West Hill Pk, N6 . . . . **95** F3
West Hill Rd, SW18 . . . . **178** A4
Westhorpe Rd, SW15 . . . . . . **176** C1
West India Av, E14 . . . . **144** A4
West India Dock Rd, E14 . . . **143** F2
West India Quay **144** B4
West Kensington **149** F4
West Kensington Ct, W14 *off Edith Vil* **149** F4
WEST KILBURN, W9 . . . . **121** F3
Westland Pl, N1 . . . . **16** A4
Westlands Ter, SW12 *off Gaskarth Rd* **180** C4
West La, SE16 . . . . **156** B1
Westleigh Av, SW15 . . . . **176** B3
West Lo Av, W3 . . . . **132** A4
West London Coll, W1 . . . **34** B3
West Mall, W8 . . . . **42** B2
Westmead, SW15 . . . . **176** B4
West Ms, SW1 . . . . **71** D1
WESTMINSTER, SW1 . . . . **59** E2
Westminster **61** D1
Westminster Abbey, SW1 . . . . **60** C2
Westminster Abbey Mus, SW1 . . . . **60** C2
Westminster Adult Ed Service, Amberley Rd Cen, W9 . . . **18** C3
Ebury Br Cen, SW1 . . . . **70** C2
Frith St Cen, W1 . . . . **36** B3
Westminster Br, SE1 . . . . **61** D1
SW1 . . . . **61** D1
Westminster Br Rd, SE1 . . . . . **61** F1
Westminster Business Sq, SE11 *off Durham St* **73** E3
Westminster Cath, SW1 . . **59** E3
Westminster City Hall, SW1 . . . . **59** F2
Westminster Gdns, SW1 . . . . . **60** C4
Westminster Kingsway Coll, Castle La Cen, SW1 . . . . . . **59** F2
Kentish Town Cen, NW5 *off Holmes Rd* **110** B3
Kings Cross Cen, WC1 . . . . . **25** E1
Peter St Cen, W1 . . . . **36** A4
Regent's Pk Cen, NW1 . . . . **23** E2
Vincent Sq Cen, SW1 . . . . . **60** A4
Westminster Millennium Pier **49** D4
Westminster Palace Gdns, SW1 *off Artillery Row* **60** A3
Westmoreland Pl, SW1 . . . . . . **71** D3
Westmoreland Rd, SE17 . . . . . **75** F4
SW13 . . . . **161** F3
Westmoreland St, W1 . . . . **34** B1
Westmoreland Ter, SW1 . . . . . **71** D3
Westmoreland Wk, SE17 . . . . **76** B4
Weston Ct, N4 *off Queens Dr* **98** C4
West One Shop Cen, W1 . . **34** B3
Weston Ri, WC1 . . . . **13** F3
Weston Rd, W4 . . . . **146** C2
Weston St, SE1 . . . . **64** B1
Weston Wk, E8 *off Mare St* **114** B4
Westover Hill, NW3 . . . . **94** A3
Westover Rd, SW18 . . . . **178** C4
West Pk Av, Rich. TW9 . . . . . **160** A3
West Pk Rd, Rich. TW9 . . . . . **160** A3
West Parkside, SE10 . . . . **159** E1
West Pier, E1 *off Wapping High St* **142** B4
West Pt, SE1 *off Avondale Sq* **156** A4
Westpoint Trd Est, W3 . . **132** B1
Westport St, E1 . . . . **143** D2
West Poultry Av, EC1 . . . . **38** C1
West Quarters, W12 . . . . **134** A2
West Rd, E15 . . . . **131** F1
SW3 . . . . **69** F3
SW4 . . . . **181** D3
Westrow, SW15 . . . . **176** C3
West Row, W10 . . . . **121** E4
West Smithfield, EC1 . . . . **38** C1
West Sq, SE11 . . . . **62** C3
West St, E2 . . . . **128** B2
E11 . . . . **103** E4
WC2 . . . . **36** B3
West Temple Sheen, SW14 . . **174** B2
West Tenter St, E1 . . . . **41** F3
Westvale Ms, W3 . . . . **133** E4
Westview Cl, NW10 . . . . **105** F2
W10 . . . . **134** C2
Westville Rd, W12 . . . . **148** A1
West Warwick Pl, SW1 . . . . . . **71** E1
West Way, NW10 . . . . **91** D4
Westway, W2 . . . . **18** A4
W9 . . . . **18** A4
W10 . . . . **135** E2
W12 . . . . **134** A3
Westwick Gdns, W14 . . . . . . **149** D1
Westwood Gdns, SW13 . . . . . **175** F1
Westwood Pk Trd Est, W3 . . . . **132** A1
Westwood Rd, SW13 . . . . . . **175** F1
Wetherby Gdns, SW5 . . . . **67** E1
Wetherby Ms, SW5 . . . . **66** C2
Wetherby Pl, SW7 . . . . **67** E1
Wetherden St, E17 . . . . **101** F1
Wetherell Rd, E9 . . . . **129** D1
Wetland Cen, The, SW13 . . . . **162** B2
Weybridge Ct, SE16 *off Argyle Way* **156** A4
Weybridge Pt, SW11 . . . . **166** A4
Weyhill Rd, E1 *off Commercial Rd* **142** A2
Weymouth Ho, SW8 . . . . **85** E3
Weymouth Ms, W1 . . . . **22** C4
Weymouth St, W1 . . . . **34** B1
Weymouth Ter, E2 . . . . **17** F2
Whadcote St, N4 . . . . **98** A3
Whaddon Ho, SE22 *off Albrighton Rd* **183** E1
Whalebone Ct, EC2 . . . . **40** A2

Whalebone La, E15
off West Ham La **117** E4
Whales Yd, E15
off West Ham La **117** E4
Wharfdale Ct, E5
off Pedro St **115** D1
Wharfdale Rd, N1 ....**13** D2
Wharfedale St, SW10 ....**66** C3
Wharf La, E14
off Commercial Rd **143** F2
Wharf Pl, E2 ....**128** A1
Wharf Rd, N1 ....**15** E2
N1 (King's Cross) **12** C2
Wharfside Rd, E16 ....**145** E1
Wharf St, E16 ....**145** E1
Wharton Cl, NW10 ....**105** E3
Wharton Cotts, WC1
off Wharton St **25** F1
Wharton St, WC1 ....**25** F1
Whateley Rd, SE22 ....**183** F3
Wheatland Ho, SE22
off Albrighton Rd **183** E1
Wheatley St, W1 ....**34** B1
Wheat Sheaf Cl, E14 ....**158** B3
Wheatsheaf La, SW6 ....**162** C2
SW8 ....**85** D2
Wheatsheaf Ter, SW6 ......**163** F2
Wheatstone Rd, W10 ......**135** E1
Wheeler Gdns, N1
off Outram Pl **125** E1
Wheelwright St, N7 ....**111** F4
Wheler St, E1 ....**29** E3
Whellock Rd, W4 ....**147** E2
Whetstone Pk, WC2 ....**37** E2
Whewell Rd, N19 ....**97** E3
Whichcote St, SE1 ....**50** A3
Whidborne Cl, SE8
off Cliff Ter **172** A4
Whidborne St, WC1 ....**25** D1
Whiskin St, EC1 ....**26** C1
Whistler Ms, SE15 ....**89** F3
Whistlers Av, SW11 ....**80** B3
Whistler St, N5 ....**112** B1
Whistler Twr, SW10 ....**79** F2
Whistler Wk, SW10
off Blantyre St **79** F2
Whiston Rd, E2 ....**17** E2
Whitacre Ms, SE11 ....**74** B3
Whitbread Rd, SE4 ....**185** E2
Whitburn Rd, SE13 ....**186** B2
Whitby Av, NW10 ....**118** B3
Whitby Ct, N7
off Camden Rd **111** E1
Whitby St, E1 ....**29** E2
Whitcher Cl, SE14 ....**171** E1
Whitcher Pl, NW1
off Rochester Rd **110** C4
Whitchurch Rd, W11 ....**135** D3
Whitcomb Ct, WC2
off Whitcomb St **48** B1
Whitcomb St, WC2 ....**48** B1
Whitcome Ms, Rich. TW9 ...**160** B3
Whiteadder Way, E14 ......**158** B3
Whitear Wk, E15 ....**117** D3
Whitebeam Cl, SW9 ....**85** F3
Whitebeam Ho, NW3
off Maitland Pk Rd **109** F3
White Bear Pl, NW3
off New End Sq **109** D1
WHITECHAPEL, E1 ....**142** A2
⊖ Whitechapel **142** B1
★ Whitechapel Art Gall,
E1 ....**41** F2
Whitechapel High St, E1 .....**41** F2
Whitechapel Rd, E1 ....**142** A2
White Ch La, E1 ....**142** A2
White Ch Pas, E1
off White Ch La **142** A2
⊖ White City **134** C3
⊖ White City **134** C4
White City Cl, W12 ....**134** C3
White City Est, W12 ....**134** B3
White City Rd, W12 ....**134** B3
White Conduit St, N1 ....**14** B2
Whitecross Pl, EC2 ....**28** B4
Whitecross St, EC1 ....**27** F2
★ White Cube, N1
off Hoxton Sq **28** C1
★ White Cube, SW1 ....**47** F2
Whitefield Av, NW2 ....**92** C1
Whitefield Cl, SW15 ....**177** E4
Whitefriars St, EC4 ....**38** B3
Whitehall, SW1 ....**48** C2
Whitehall Ct, SW1 ....**48** C3
Whitehall Gdns, SW1 ....**48** C3
W3 ....**132** A4
W4 ....**160** B1
Whitehall Pk, N19 ....**96** C2
Whitehall Pk Rd, W4 ....**160** B1
Whitehall Pl, SW1 ....**48** C3
White Hart Ct, EC2 ....**40** C1
White Hart La, NW10
off Church Rd **105** F3
SW13 ....**175** E1
White Hart St, EC4 ....**39** D2
SE11 ....**74** B2
White Hart Yd, SE1 ....**52** A3
Whitehaven St, NW8 ....**20** C3
Whitehead's Gro, SW3 ......**69** D2
White Horse All, EC1 ....**26** C4
White Horse La, E1 ....**129** D4
White Horse Ms, SE1 ....**62** B2
White Horse Rd, E1 ....**143** E2
White Horse St, W1 ....**46** C3
White Horse Yd, EC2 ....**40** A2
Whitehouse Apts, SE1
off Belvedere Rd **49** F3
White Kennett St, E1 ....**41** D2
Whitelands Ho, SW3 ....**69** E2
Whitelegg Rd, E13 ....**131** F2
🔒 Whiteleys Shop Cen, W2 .**30** C3
White Lion Ct, EC3 ....**40** C3
White Lion Hill, EC4 ....**39** D4
White Lion St, N1 ....**14** A3
White Lyon Ct, EC2 ....**27** E4
White Post La, E9 ....**115** F4
SE13 ....**186** A1
White Post St, SE15 ....**170** C2
White Rd, E15 ....**117** E4
Whites Grds, SE1 ....**65** D1
Whites Grds Est, SE1
off Whites Grds **53** D4
White's Row, E1 ....**41** E1
White's Sq, SW4
off Nelson's Row **181** D2
Whitestone La, NW3 ....**94** C4
Whitestone Wk, NW3
off North End Way **94** C4
White Swan Ms, W4
off Bennett St **161** E1
Whitethorn St, E3 ....**130** A4
White Twr Way, E1 ....**143** E1
Whitfield Pl, W1 ....**23** E3
Whitfield Rd, SE3 ....**173** D3
Whitfield St, W1 ....**36** A1
Whitgift Ho, SW11
off Randall Cl **80** C4
Whitgift St, SE11 ....**61** E4
Whitley Ho, SW1 ....**71** F3
Whitman Rd, E3
off Mile End Rd **129** E4
Whitmore Est, N1 ....**17** D1
Whitmore Gdns, NW10 .....**120** C2
Whitmore Rd, N1 ....**16** C1
Whitnell Way, SW15 ....**177** D3
Whitney Ho, SE22
off Albrighton Rd **183** E1
Whitney Rd, E10 ....**102** B1
Whitstable Ho, W10 ....**135** D2
Whittaker St, SW1 ....**70** A1
Whittaker Way, SE1
off Lynton Rd **156** A3
Whittingstall Rd, SW6 .....**163** F3
Whittington Av, EC3 ....**40** C3
H Whittington Hosp, N19 ..**96** C3
Whittlesey St, SE1 ....**50** A3
Whitton Wk, E3 ....**130** A2
Whitworth Ho, SE1 ....**63** F3
Whitworth St, SE10 ....**159** E4
Whorlton Rd, SE15 ....**184** B1
Whychcote Pt, NW2
off Claremont Rd **92** C1
Wickersley Rd, SW11 ......**166** A4
Wicker St, E1
off Burslem St **142** B2
Wickford St, E1 ....**128** C4
Wickham Cl, E1 ....**142** C1
Wickham Gdns, SE4 ....**185** F1
Wickham Ms, SE4 ....**171** F4
Wickham Rd, SE4 ....**185** F2
Wickham St, SE11 ....**73** E2
Wick La, E3 ....**130** A2
Wickliffe Gdns, Wem. HA9 ...**90** B3
Wicklow St, WC1 ....**13** E4
Wick Rd, E9 ....**115** D3
Wicksteed Ho, SE1 ....**63** F3
Wickway Ct, SE15 ....**89** E1
Wickwood St, SE5 ....**168** B4
Widdenham Rd, N7 ....**111** F1
Widdin St, E15 ....**117** D4
Widegate St, E1 ....**41** D1
Widley Rd, W9 ....**18** B1
Wigan Ho, E5 ....**100** B2
Wigginton Av, Wem. HA9 ...**104** B3
Wigmore Pl, W1 ....**34** C2
Wigmore St, W1 ....**34** A3
Wigton Pl, SE11 ....**74** B3
Wilberforce Ms, SW4
off Stonhouse St **181** D2
Wilberforce Rd, N4 ....**98** B3
Wilberforce Wk, E15
off Albert Sq **117** E2
Wilbraham Pl, SW1 ....**57** F4
Wilby Ms, W11 ....**135** F4
Wilcox Cl, SW8 ....**85** D2
Wilcox Pl, SW1 ....**59** F3
Wilcox Rd, SW8 ....**84** C2
Wild Ct, WC2 ....**37** E2
Wilde Cl, E8 ....**128** A1
Wilderness Ms, SW4 ......**180** B2
Wilderton Rd, N16 ....**99** E1
Wild Goose Dr, SE14 ......**170** C3
Wild's Rents, SE1 ....**64** C2
Wild St, WC2 ....**37** D3
Wildwood Gro, NW3
off North End Way **94** C2
Wildwood Ri, NW11 ....**94** C2
Wildwood Rd, NW11 ....**94** C1
Wildwood Ter, NW3 ....**94** C2
Wilfred St, SW1 ....**59** E2
Wilfred Turney Est, W6
off Hammersmith Gro ..**148** C1

Wilfrid Gdns, W3 . . . . .132 C1
Wilkes St, E1 . . . . .29 F4
Wilkins Ho, SW1
off Churchill Gdns 71 E4
Wilkinson St, SW8 . . . . .85 E3
Wilkinson Way, W4 . . . . .147 D1
Wilkin St, NW5 . . . . .110 B3
Wilkin St Ms, NW5
off Wilkin St 110 B3
Wilks Pl, N1 . . . . .17 D3
Willan Wall, E16
off Victoria Dock Rd 145 F3
Willard St, SW8 . . . . .180 B1
Willcott Rd, W3 . . . . .132 B4
Willen Fld Rd, NW10 . . . . . . .118 C2
WILLESDEN, NW10 . . . . .105 F3
WILLESDEN GREEN, NW10 . .106 B4
Willesden Green 106 C3
Willesden Junction 119 F3
Willesden Junction 119 F3
Willesden La, NW2 . . . . .107 D3
NW6 . . . . .107 D3
Willes Rd, NW5 . . . . .110 B3
William Bonney Est, SW4 . . .181 D2
Coll William Booth Coll, SE5
off Champion Hill 169 D4
William Cl, SE13 . . . . .172 C4
SW6 off Pellant Rd 163 E2
William Dunbar Ho, NW6 . . .121 F2
William Ellis Way, SE16
off St. James's Rd 156 A2
William IV St, WC2 . . . . .48 C1
William Gdns, SW15 . . . . . . .176 B3
William Guy Gdns, E3
off Talwin St 130 B3
William Henry Wk, SW8 . . . . .84 A1
William Margrie Cl, SE15
off Moncrieff St 170 A4
William Ms, SW1 . . . . .57 F1
Coll William Morris 6th Form, W6
off St. Dunstans Rd 149 D4
William Morris Way, SW6 . . .178 C1
William Pl, E3
off Roman Rd 129 F2
William Rd, NW1 . . . . .23 E1
William Rushbrooke Ho, SE16
off Eveline Lowe Est 156 A3
William Saville Ho, NW6 . . . .121 F2
Williams Bldgs, E2 . . . . .128 C4
William's La, SW14 . . . . .174 C1
Williamson Cl, SE10
off Lenthorp Rd 159 F3
Williamson St, N7 . . . . .111 E1
William Sq, SE16
off Rotherhithe St 143 E3
William St, SW1 . . . . .57 F1
Willingham Cl, NW5 . . . . . . .110 C2
Willingham Ter, NW5 . . . . . .110 C2
Willington Ct, E5
off Mandeville St 101 E4
Willington Rd, SW9 . . . . .181 E1
Willis Rd, E15 . . . . .131 F1
Willis St, E14 . . . . .144 B2
Willoughby Ho, EC2
off The Barbican 40 A1
Willoughby Ms, SW4
off Wixs La 180 B2
Willoughby Pas, E14 . . . . . .144 A4
Willoughby Rd, NW3 . . . . . .109 D1
Willoughbys, The, SW14
off Upper Richmond Rd W 175 E1
Willoughby St, WC1 . . . . .36 C1
Willow Av, SW13 . . . . .161 F4
Willow Bk, SW6 . . . . .177 E1
Willow Br Rd, N1 . . . . .112 C3
Willowbrook Est, SE15
off Shurland Gdns 89 F2
Willowbrook Rd, SE15 . . . . . . .89 F1
Willow Cotts, Rich. TW9
off Kew Grn 160 A1
Willow Ct, EC2 . . . . .28 C2
Willowdene, N6
off View Rd 95 F1
Willow Fm La, SW15
off Queens Ride 176 B1
Willow Ho, NW3
off Maitland Pk Vil 109 F3
Willow Pl, SW1 . . . . .59 F4
Willow Rd, NW3 . . . . .109 D1
Willow St, EC2 . . . . .28 C2
Willow Tree Cl, E3
off Birdsfield La 129 F1
Willow Vale, W12 . . . . .134 A4
Willow Wk, SE1 . . . . .65 D4
Willow Way, W11
off Freston Rd 135 D3
Wilman Gro, E8 . . . . .114 A4
Wilmcote Ho, W2 . . . . .18 B4
Wilmer Gdns, N1 . . . . .16 C1
Wilmer Ho, E3
off Daling Way 129 E2
Wilmer Lea Cl, E15 . . . . .116 C4
Wilmer Pl, N16 . . . . .99 F3
Wilmington Av, W4 . . . . .161 D2
Wilmington Sq, WC1 . . . . .26 A1
Wilmington St, WC1 . . . . .26 A1
Wilmot Cl, SE15 . . . . .170 A2
Wilmot Pl, NW1 . . . . .110 C4
Wilmot Rd, E10 . . . . .102 B3
Wilmot St, E2 . . . . .128 B4
Wilsham St, W11 . . . . .135 D4
Wilshaw St, SE14 . . . . .172 A3
Wilson Gro, SE16 . . . . .156 B1
Wilson Rd, SE5 . . . . .169 E3
Wilsons Pl, E14
off Salmon La 143 F2
Wilsons Rd, W6 . . . . .149 D4
Wilson St, EC2 . . . . .28 B4
Wilton Av, W4 . . . . .147 E4
Wilton Cres, SW1 . . . . .58 A1
Wilton Est, E8
off Greenwood Rd 114 A3
Wilton Ho, SE22
off Albrighton Rd 183 E1
Wilton Ms, SW1 . . . . .58 B2
Wilton Pl, SW1 . . . . .58 A1
Wilton Rd, SW1 . . . . .59 D3
Wilton Row, SW1 . . . . .58 A1
Wilton Sq, N1 . . . . .127 D1
Wilton St, SW1 . . . . .58 C2
Wilton Ter, SW1 . . . . .58 A2
Wilton Vil, N1 . . . . .16 A1
Wilton Way, E8 . . . . .114 A3
Wiltshire Cl, SW3 . . . . .57 E4
Wiltshire Rd, SW9 . . . . .182 A1
Wiltshire Row, N1 . . . . .16 A1
Wimbolt St, E2 . . . . .128 A3
Wimborne Cl, SE12 . . . . .187 F3
Wimborne Ho, SW8 . . . . .85 F3
Wimbourne Ct, N1 . . . . .16 A2
Wimbourne St, N1 . . . . .16 A2
Wimpole Ms, W1 . . . . .22 C4
Wimpole St, W1 . . . . .34 C2
Winans Wk, SW9 . . . . .168 A4
Winchelsea Cl, SW15 . . . . . .177 D3
Winchelsea Rd, NW10 . . . . .119 D1
Winchendon Rd, SW6 . . . . . .163 F2
Winchester Av, NW6 . . . . . . .121 E1
Winchester Cl, SE17 . . . . .75 D1
Winchester Ms, NW3
off Winchester Rd 109 D4
Winchester Pl, E8
off Kingsland High St . . .113 F2
N6 .96 B2
Winchester Rd, N6 . . . . .96 B2
NW3 . . . . .109 D4
Winchester Sq, SE1 . . . . .52 A2
Winchester St, SW1 . . . . .71 D2
W3 . . . . .132 C4
Winchester Wk, SE1 . . . . .52 A2
Winchfield Ho, SW15
off Highcliffe Dr 175 F4
Wincott St, SE11 . . . . .62 B4
Windermere Av, NW6 . . . . . .121 E1
Windermere Ct, SW13 . . . . . .161 F1
Windermere Pt, SE15
off Ilderton Rd 170 C2
Windermere Rd, N19
off Holloway Rd 96 C3
Winders Rd, SW11 . . . . .165 E4
Windlass Pl, SE8 . . . . .157 E3
Windmill All, W4
off Windmill Rd 147 E3
Windmill Cl, SE1
off Beatrice Rd 156 A3
SE13 . . . . .172 C4
Windmill Ct, NW2 . . . . .107 E3
Windmill Dr, NW2 . . . . .93 E4
SW4 . . . . .180 B3
Windmill Hill, NW3 . . . . .94 C4
Windmill Ho, E14
off Westferry Rd 158 A3
Windmill La, E15 . . . . .117 D3
Windmill Ms, W4 . . . . .147 E3
Windmill Pas, W4 . . . . .147 E3
Windmill Rd, SW18 . . . . .179 D4
W4 . . . . .147 E3
Windmill Row, SE11 . . . . .74 A3
Windmill St, W1 . . . . .36 A1
Windmill Wk, SE1 . . . . .50 B3
Windrose Cl, SE16 . . . . .157 D1
Windrush Cl, SW11
off Maysoule Rd 179 D2
W4 . . . . .160 C3
Windrush Rd, NW10 . . . . . . .119 D1
Windrush Sq, SW2
off Rushcroft Rd 182 A2
Windsock Cl, SE16 . . . . .157 F3
Windsor Cres, Wem. HA9 . . . . .90 B4
Windsor Gdns, W9 . . . . .18 A4
Windsor Ho, N1 . . . . .15 E2
Windsor Pl, SW1 . . . . .59 F3
Windsor Rd, E10 . . . . .102 B3
N7 .97 E4
NW2 . . . . .106 B3
Windsor St, N1 . . . . .126 B1
Windsor Ter, N1 . . . . .15 F4
Windsor Wk, SE5 . . . . .169 D4
Windsor Way, W14 . . . . .149 D3
Windsor Wf, E9 . . . . .115 F2
Windspoint Dr, SE15
off Ethnard Rd 170 B1
Windus Rd, N16 . . . . .99 F2
Windus Wk, N16 . . . . .99 F2
Wine Cl, E1 . . . . .142 C3
Wine Office Ct, EC4 . . . . .38 B2
Winford Ho, E3 . . . . .115 F4
Winforton St, SE10 . . . . .172 C3
Wingate Rd, W6 . . . . .148 B2

Wingfield Ct, E14
off Newport Av 145 D3
Wingfield Ho, NW6
off Tollgate Gdns 6 C2
Wingfield Ms, SE15
off Wingfield St 184 A1
Wingfield Rd, E15 ....117 E2
Wingfield St, SE15 ....184 A1
Wingford Rd, SW2 ....181 E4
Wingmore Rd, SE24 ....182 C1
Wingrave Rd, W6 ....162 C1
Winifred Gro, SW11 ....179 F2
Winkley St, E2 ....128 B2
Winnett St, W1 ....36 A4
Winnington Rd, N2 ....95 D1
Winscombe St, N19 ....96 B3
Winsham Gro, SW11 ....180 A3
Winslade Rd, SW2 ....181 E3
Winsland Ms, W2 ....32 A2
Winsland St, W2 ....32 A2
Winsley St, W1 ....35 E2
Winslow, SE17 ....76 C3
Winslow Cl, NW10
off Neasden La N 91 E4
Winslow Rd, W6 ....162 C1
Winstanley Est, SW11 ....179 D1
Winstanley Rd, SW11 ....179 D1
Winston Av, NW9 ....91 E1
Winston Rd, N16 ....113 D1
Winston Wk, W4
off Beaconsfield Rd 147 D2
Winterbrook Rd, SE24 ....182 C4
Winter Gdn Ho, WC2
off Macklin St 37 D2
Winterton Ho, E1 ....142 C2
Winterton Pl, SW10 ....67 F4
Winterwell Rd, SW2 ....181 E3
Winthorpe Rd, SW15 ....177 E2
Winthrop St, E1 ....142 B1
Wiseman Rd, E10 ....102 A3
Wise Rd, E15 ....131 D1
Wisley Rd, SW11 ....180 A3
Wisteria Apts, E9
off Chatham Pl 114 C3
Wisteria Rd, SE13 ....187 D2
Witanhurst La, N6 ....96 A2
Witan St, E2 ....128 B3
Witcombe Pt, SE15 ....170 A3
Witherington Rd, N5 ....112 A2
Witley Rd, N19 ....96 C3
Wivenhoe Cl, SE15 ....184 B1
Wixs La, SW4 ....180 B2
Woburn Ct, SE16
off Masters Dr 156 B4
Woburn Pl, WC1 ....24 B2
Woburn Sq, WC1 ....24 B3
Woburn Wk, WC1 ....24 B1
Wodeham Gdns, E1 ....142 A1
Wodehouse Av, SE5 ....89 E4
Woking Cl, SW15 ....175 F2
Wolfe Cres, SE16 ....157 D1
Wolffe Gdns, E15 ....117 F3
Wolffram Cl, SE13 ....187 E3
Wolftencroft Cl, SW11 ....179 D1
Wollaston Cl, SE1 ....63 E4
Wolseley Gdns, W4 ....160 B1
Wolseley Rd, W4 ....146 C3
Wolseley St, SE1 ....65 F1
Wolsey Ms, NW5 ....110 C3
Wolsey Rd, N1 ....113 D2
Wolsey St, E1
off Sidney St 142 C1
Wolverley St, E2
off Bethnal Grn Rd 128 B3
Wolverton, SE17 ....76 B2
Wolverton Gdns, W6 ....149 D3
Wontner Cl, N1
off Greenman St 112 C4
Woodall Cl, E14
off Lawless St 144 B3
Woodberry Down, N4 ....98 C1
Woodberry Down Est, N4 ....98 C1
Woodberry Gro, N4 ....98 C1
Woodbine Ter, E9
off Chatham Pl 114 C3
Woodborough Rd, SW15 ....176 B2
Woodbridge Cl, N7 ....97 F3
NW2 ....92 A4
Woodbridge St, EC1 ....26 C2
Woodchester Sq, W2 ....18 C4
Woodchurch Rd, NW6 ....108 A4
Wood Cl, E2 ....128 A4
NW9 ....91 D1
Wood Ct, W12
off Heathstan Rd 134 A2
Woodcroft Ms, SE8
off Croft St 157 E3
Woodfall Rd, N4 ....98 A2
Woodfall St, SW3 ....69 E3
Woodfarrs, SE5 ....183 D2
Wood Fld, NW3
off Parkhill Rd 109 F2
Woodfield Gdns, W9
off Woodfield Rd 135 F1
Woodfield Pl, W9 ....121 F4
Woodfield Rd, W9 ....135 F1
Woodford Ct, W12
off Shepherds Bush Grn .149 D1
Woodger Rd, W12
off Goldhawk Rd 148 C1
Woodgrange Av, W5 ....132 A4
Woodhall, NW1 ....23 E1
Woodhall Ho, SW18
off Fitzhugh Gro 179 D4
Woodheyes Rd, NW10 ....105 D2
Woodhouse Cl, SE22 ....184 A2
Woodhouse Rd, E11 ....103 F4
Woodhurst Rd, W3 ....132 C3
Woodland Cres, SE10 ....173 E1
SE16 ....157 D1
Woodland Gro, SE10 ....159 E4
Woodland Hts, SE3
off Vanbrugh Hill 173 F1
Woodlands Av, W3 ....132 B4
Woodlands Pk Rd, SE10 ....173 E1
Woodlands Rd, E11 ....103 E3
SW13 ....175 F1
Woodland St, E8
off Dalston La 113 F3
Woodlands Way, SW15 ....177 F3
Woodland Wk, NW3 ....109 E2
SE10
off Woodland Gro 159 E4
⊖ Wood Lane 134 C3
Wood La, NW9 ....91 E1
W12 ....134 C2
Woodlawn Cl, SW15 ....177 F3
Woodlawn Rd, SW6 ....163 D2
Woodlea Rd, N16 ....99 E4
Woodman Ms, Rich. TW9 ....160 B3
Woodmans Gro, NW10 ....105 F2
Woodmans Ms, W12 ....134 B1
Woodmere Cl, SW11
off Lavender Hill 180 A1
Woodmill Rd, E5 ....100 C3
Woodpecker Ms, SE13
off Mercator Rd 187 D2
Woodpecker Rd, SE14 ....171 E1
Woodquest Av, SE24 ....182 C3
Woodriffe Rd, E11 ....103 D1
Wood Rd, NW10 ....104 C4
Woodrush Cl, SE14
off Southerngate Way ..171 E2
Wood's Bldgs, E1
off Whitechapel Rd 142 B1
Woodseer St, E1 ....29 F4
Woodsford, SE17 ....76 A3
Woodsford Sq, W14 ....149 E1
Woodside Ms, SE22 ....183 F4
Woods Ms, W1 ....33 F4
Woodsome Rd, NW5 ....96 A4
Woods Pl, SE1 ....65 D3
Woods Rd, SE15 ....170 B3
Woodstock Av, NW11 ....93 E1
Woodstock Gro, W12 ....149 D1
Woodstock Ms, W1 ....34 B1
Woodstock Rd, N4 ....98 A2
NW11 ....93 F1
W4 ....147 E2
Woodstock St, W1 ....34 C3
Woodstock Ter, E14 ....144 B3
Wood St, EC2 ....39 F3
W4 ....147 E4
Woodthorpe Rd, SW15 ....176 B2
Wood Vale Est, SE23 ....184 C4
Woodvale Way, NW11 ....93 D4
Woodview Cl, N4 ....98 B1
Woodville Gdns, NW11 ....93 D1
Woodville Rd, E11 ....103 F2
N16 ....113 E2
NW6 ....121 F2
NW11 ....93 D1
Woodwarde Rd, SE22 ....183 E4
Woodwell St, SW18
off Huguenot Pl 178 C3
Wood Wf, SE10 ....172 B1
Wood Wf Apts, SE10
off Horseferry Pl 172 C1
Woodyard Cl, NW5
off Gillies St 110 A2
Wooler St, SE17 ....76 A3
Woolf Ms, WC1 ....24 B2
Woolmead Av, NW9 ....92 A1
Woolmore St, E14 ....144 C3
Woolneigh St, SW6 ....178 B1
Woolridge Way, E9
off Loddiges Rd 114 C4
Woolstaplers Way, SE16 ....156 A3
Woolwich Rd, SE10 ....159 F4
Wooster Gdns, E14 ....145 D2
Wooster Pl, SE1 ....64 B4
Wootton St, SE1 ....50 B4
Worcester Cl, NW2
off Newfield Ri 92 B4
Worcester Dr, W4 ....147 E1
Worcester Gdns, SW11
off Grandison Rd 179 F3
Worcester Ho, SE11
off Kennington Rd 62 A3
Worcester Ms, NW6
off Dresden Cl 108 B3
Wordsworth Pl, NW5
off Southampton Rd 109 F2
Wordsworth Rd, N16 ....113 E1
SE1 ....77 E1
Worfield St, SW11 ....81 D3
Worgan St, SE11 ....73 E2
SE16 ....157 D2
Coll Working Men's Coll, The,
NW1 ....11 F2
Worland Rd, E15 ....117 E4
World's End Pas, SW10 ....80 A2

World's End Pl, SW10
off King's Rd **79** F2
Worlidge St, W6 .... **148** C4
Worlingham Rd, SE22 ...... **183** F2
Wormholt Rd, W12 .... **134** A3
Wormwood St, EC2 .... **40** C2
Wornington Rd, W10 ...... **135** E1
Woronzow Rd, NW8 .... **8** B1
Worple St, SW14 .... **175** D1
Worship St, EC2 .... **28** B3
Worsley Gro, E5 .... **114** A1
Worsley Rd, E11 .... **117** E1
Worsopp Dr, SW4 .... **180** C3
Worth Gro, SE17 .... **76** A3
Worthing Cl, E15
off Mitre Rd **131** E1
Wotton Rd, NW2 .... **106** C1
SE8 .... **171** F1
Wouldham Rd, E16 .... **145** F2
Wragby Rd, E11 .... **103** E4
Wray Cres, N4 .... **97** E3
Wren Av, NW2 .... **106** C2
Wren Cl, E16
off Ibbotson Av **145** F2
Wren Landing, E14
off Cabot Sq **144** A4
Wren Ms, SE13
off Lee High Rd **187** E2
Wren Rd, SE5 .... **169** D3
Wren St, WC1 .... **25** F2
Wrentham Av, NW10 ...... **121** D2
Wrestlers Ct, EC3
off Camomile St **40** C2
Wrexham Rd, E3 .... **130** A2
Wrigglesworth St, SE14 .... **171** D2
Wright Rd, N1
off Burder Cl **113** E3
Wrights Cl, SE13 .... **187** D2
Wrights Grn, SW4
off Nelson's Row **181** D2
Wrights La, W8 .... **54** C2
Wrights Pl, NW10
off Mitchell Way **104** C3
Wrights Rd, E3 .... **129** F2
Wrights Wk, SW14 .... **175** D1
Wrotham Rd, NW1
off Agar Pl **110** C4
Wrottesley Rd, NW10 ...... **120** A2
Wroughton Rd, SW11 ...... **179** F4
Wroxton Rd, SE15 .... **170** B4
Wulfstan St, W12 .... **133** F2
Wyatt Cl, SE16 .... **157** F1
Wyatt Dr, SW13 .... **162** C2
Wyatt Rd, N5 .... **98** C4
Wybert St, NW1 .... **23** D2
Wyborne Way, NW10 ...... **104** C4
Wycherley Cl, SE3 .... **173** F2
Wychwood End, N6 .... **96** C1
Wyclif Ct, EC1
off Wyclif St **26** C1
Wycliffe Rd, SW11 .... **166** A4
Wyclif St, EC1 .... **26** C1
Wycombe Gdns, NW11 ...... **94** A3
Wycombe Pl, SW18 .... **178** C4
Wycombe Rd, Wem. HA0 ... **118** A1
Wycombe Sq, W8 .... **42** A3
Wye St, SW11 .... **165** D4
Wyfold Rd, SW6 .... **163** E2
Wyke Rd, E3 .... **116** A4
Wyldes Cl, NW11 .... **94** C2
Wyld Way, Wem. HA9 ..... **104** B3
Wyllen Cl, E1 .... **128** C4
Wymering Rd, W9 .... **18** B1
Wymond St, SW15 .... **176** C1
Wynan Rd, E14 .... **158** B4
Wyndham Cres, N19 .... **96** C4
Wyndham Est, SE5 .... **87** E2
Wyndham Ms, W1 .... **33** E1
Wyndham Pl, W1 .... **33** E1
Wyndham Rd, SE5 .... **87** D3
Wyndham St, W1 .... **21** E4
Wyndham Yd, W1 .... **33** E1
Wyneham Rd, SE24 .... **183** D3
Wynford Rd, N1 .... **13** E2
Wynne Rd, SW9 .... **168** A4
Wynnstay Gdns, W8 .... **54** B2
Wynter St, SW11 .... **178** C2
Wynton Pl, W3 .... **132** B2
Wynyard Ter, SE11 .... **73** F2
Wynyatt St, EC1 .... **26** C1
Wythburn Pl, W1 .... **33** E3
Wyvil Est, SW8 .... **84** C2
Wyvil Rd, SW8 .... **84** C1
Wyvis St, E14 .... **144** B1

Y

Yabsley St, E14 .... **144** C4
Yalding Rd, SE16 .... **156** A2
Yardley St, WC1 .... **26** A1
Yarmouth Pl, W1 .... **46** C3
Yarnfield Sq, SE15
off Clayton Rd **170** A3
Yates Ct, NW2 .... **107** D3
Yates Ho, E2
off Roberta St **128** A3
Yeate St, N1 .... **113** D4
Yeats Cl, NW10 .... **105** E3
Yeldham Rd, W6 .... **149** D4
Yelverton Rd, SW11 ...... **165** D4
Yeoman's Row, SW3 .... **57** D3
Yeoman St, SE8 .... **157** E3
Yeomans Yd, E1 .... **41** F4
Yeo St, E3 .... **144** B1
Yerbury Rd, N19 .... **97** D4
Yewfield Rd, NW10 .... **105** F4
Yew Gro, NW2 .... **107** D1
Yew Tree Cl, SE13
off Bankside Av **186** C1
Yew Tree Rd, W12 .... **133** F3
Yoakley Rd, N16 .... **99** E3
Yoke Cl, N7 *off Ewe Cl* **111** E3
Yonge Pk, N4 .... **98** A4
York Av, SW14 .... **174** C3
York Br, NW1 .... **22** A2
York Bldgs, WC2 .... **49** D1
York Gate, NW1 .... **22** A3
York Gro, SE15 .... **170** C3
● York Ho, Wem. HA9 .... **104** A1
York Ho Pl, W8 .... **42** C4
York Ms, NW5
off Kentish Town Rd **110** B2
York Pl, SW11 .... **179** D1
WC2 .... **49** D1
York Ri, NW5 .... **96** B4
York Rd, E10 .... **102** C4
SE1 .... **49** F4
SW11 .... **178** C2
SW18 .... **178** C2
W3 .... **132** C2
Yorkshire Cl, N16 .... **99** E4
Yorkshire Grey Pl, NW3
off Heath St **108** C1
Yorkshire Grey Yd, WC1 ..... **37** E1
Yorkshire Rd, E14 .... **143** E2
York Sq, E14 .... **143** E2
York St, W1 .... **21** F4
York Ter E, NW1 .... **22** B3
York Ter W, NW1 .... **22** A3
Yorkton St, E2 .... **128** A2
York Way, N1 .... **125** E1
N7 .... **13** D1
York Way Ct, N1 .... **13** D1
York Way Est, N7
off York Way **111** E3
Young's Bldgs, EC1 .... **27** F2
Youngs Ct, SW11
off Charlotte Despard Av **166** A3
Young St, W8 .... **54** C1

Z

Zampa Rd, SE16 .... **156** C4
Zander Ct, E2
off St. Peter's Cl **128** A2
Zealand Rd, E3 .... **129** E2
Zenoria St, SE22 .... **183** F2
Zetland St, E14 .... **144** B1
Zion Ho, E1
off Jubilee St **142** C2
Zoar St, SE1 .... **51** E2
Zoffany St, N19 .... **97** D3
★ ZSL London Zoo, NW1 ... **10** A2

London Underground map

Reg. user No. 08/1077/LS

MAYOR OF LONDON

Website
tfl.gov.uk

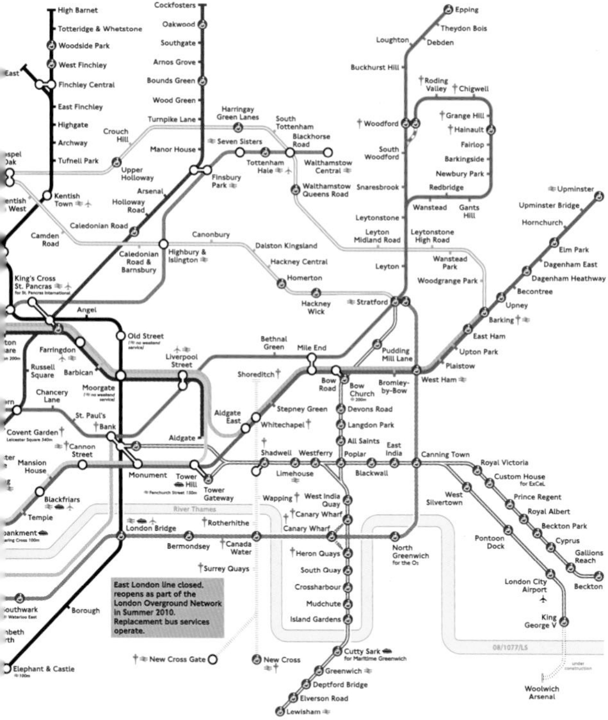

- Interchange stations
- Step-free access from the platform to the street
- Connections with National Rail
- Connections with riverboat services
- Connection with Tramlink
- Location of Airport
- Interchange with National Rail services to airport
- Check before you travel. See poster journey planners.

Improvement works may affect your journey, particularly at weekends. Check before you travel; look for publicity at stations, visit tfl.gov.uk/check or call 020 7222 1234

TfL FA(a) 09.07

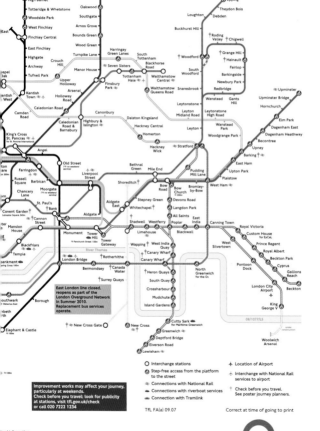

Correct at time of going to print

London information

Visit London is the official visitor organisation for London. For information about places to visit, places to eat, accommodation and entertainment go to their website www.visitlondon.com or phone the Visit London tourist information helpline on 0870 156 6366.

Transport for London (TfL) provides travel information at www.tfl.gov.uk or phone the London Travel Information helpline on 44 (0) 20 7222 1234.
The website has all the latest timetables for rail, tram, bus and river services with live travel news and information on tickets, fares and journey planning.

The London Cycling Campaign provides information on all aspects of cycling within London on their website www.lcc.org.uk

The Royal Parks is responsible for maintaining many of London's major green spaces, including Hyde Park, Kensington Gardens, St James's Park, The Green Park and The Regent's Park. Information on accessibility and events held within the parks is available at www.royalparks.org.uk

The Greater London Authority (GLA) is the strategic governing body for London, consisting of a directly elected executive Mayor of London and an elected 25 member London Assembly. www.london.gov.uk is the official website for the Mayor of London, the London Assembly and the Greater London Authority.

2012 Olympics www.london2012.com has all the latest news on London's preparations for the 2012 Olympics with information on sporting venues and images of the development of the Olympic Park site.